Handbook of Language and Communication:
Diversity and Change
HAL 9

Handbooks of Applied Linguistics
Communication Competence
Language and Communication Problems
Practical Solutions

Editors
Karlfried Knapp and Gerd Antos

Volume 9

Mouton de Gruyter · Berlin · New York

Handbook of Language and Communication: Diversity and Change

Edited by
Marlis Hellinger and Anne Pauwels

Mouton de Gruyter · Berlin · New York

Mouton de Gruyter (formerly Mouton, The Hague)
is a Division of Walter de Gruyter GmbH & Co. KG, Berlin.

∞ Printed on acid-free paper which falls within the guidelines
of the ANSI to ensure permanence and durability.

Library of Congress Cataloging-in-Publication Data

Handbook of language and communication − diversity and change /
edited by Marlis Hellinger, Anne Pauwels.
  p. cm. − (Handbooks of applied linguistics ; 9)
  Includes bibliographical references and index.
  ISBN 978-3-11-021423-9 (pbk. : alk. paper)
  1. Sociolinguistics. 2. Language and languages − Variation.
  3. Linguistic minorities. 4. Language planning. 5. Linguistic
  change. I. Hellinger, Marlis. II. Pauwels, Anne.
  P40.H3424 2009
  306.43′2−dc22
                                                    2009030974

Bibliographic information published by the Deutsche Nationalbibliothek

The Deutsche Nationalbibliothek lists this publication in the Deutsche Nationalbibliografie;
detailed bibliographic data are available in the Internet at http://dnb.d-nb.de.

ISBN 978-3-11-021423-9

© Copyright 2009 by Walter de Gruyter GmbH & Co. KG, D-10785 Berlin.
All rights reserved, including those of translation into foreign languages. No part of this book
may be reproduced in any form or by any means, electronic or mechanical, including photo-
copy, recording, or any information storage and retrieval system, without permission in writing
from the publisher.
Cover design: Martin Zech, Bremen.
Cover photo: Dawn M. Turner/morgueFile.
Typesetting: Dörlemann Satz GmbH & Co. KG, Lemförde.
Printing and binding: AZ Druck und Datentechnik GmbH, Kempten (Allgäu).
Printed in Germany.

Introduction to the handbook series
Linguistics for problem solving

Karlfried Knapp and Gerd Antos

1. **Science and application at the turn of the millennium**

The distinction between "pure" and "applied" sciences is an old one. According to Meinel (2000), it was introduced by the Swedish chemist Wallerius in 1751, as part of the dispute of that time between the scholastic disciplines and the then emerging epistemic sciences. However, although the concept of "Applied Science" gained currency rapidly since that time, it has remained problematic.

Until recently, the distinction between "pure" and "applied" mirrored the distinction between "theory and "practice". The latter ran all the way through Western history of science since its beginnings in antique times. At first, it was only philosophy that was regarded as a scholarly and, hence, theoretical discipline. Later it was followed by other leading disciplines, as e.g., the sciences. However, as academic disciplines, all of them remained theoretical. In fact, the process of achieving independence of theory was essential for the academic disciplines to become independent from political, religious or other contingencies and to establish themselves at universities and academies. This also implied a process of emancipation from practical concerns – an at times painful development which manifested (and occasionally still manifests) itself in the discrediting of and disdain for practice and practitioners. To some, already the very meaning of the notion "applied" carries a negative connotation, as is suggested by the contrast between the widely used synonym for "theoretical", i.e. "pure" (as used, e.g. in the distinction between "Pure" and "Applied Mathematics") and its natural antonym "impure". On a different level, a lower academic status sometimes is attributed to applied disciplines because of their alleged lack of originality – they are perceived as simply and one-directionally applying insights gained in basic research and watering them down by neglecting the limiting conditions under which these insights were achieved.

Today, however, the academic system is confronted with a new understanding of science. In politics, in society and, above all, in economy a new concept of science has gained acceptance which questions traditional views. In recent philosophy of science, this is labelled as "science under the pressure to succeed" – i.e. as science whose theoretical structure and criteria of evaluation are increasingly conditioned by the pressure of application (Carrier, Stöltzner, and Wette 2004):

> Whenever the public is interested in a particular subject, e.g. when a new disease develops that cannot be cured by conventional medication, the public requests science to provide new insights in this area as quickly as possible. In doing so, the public is less interested in whether these new insights fit seamlessly into an existing theoretical framework, but rather whether they make new methods of treatment and curing possible. (Institut für Wirtschafts- und Technikforschung 2004, our translation).

With most of the practical problems like these, sciences cannot rely on knowledge that is already available, simply because such knowledge does not yet exist. Very often, the problems at hand do not fit neatly into the theoretical framework of one particular "pure science", and there is competition among disciplines with respect to which one provides the best theoretical and methodological resources for potential solutions. And more often than not the problems can be tackled only by adopting an interdisciplinary approach.

As a result, the traditional "Cascade Model", where insights were applied top-down from basic research to practice, no longer works in many cases. Instead, a kind of "application oriented basic research" is needed, where disciplines – conditioned by the pressure of application – take up a certain still diffuse practical issue, define it as a problem against the background of their respective theoretical and methodological paradigms, study this problem and finally develop various application oriented suggestions for solutions. In this sense, applied science, on the one hand, has to be conceived of as a scientific strategy for problem solving – a strategy that starts from mundane practical problems and ultimately aims at solving them. On the other hand, despite the dominance of application that applied sciences are subjected to, as sciences they can do nothing but develop such solutions in a theoretically reflected and methodologically well founded manner. The latter, of course, may lead to the well-known fact that even applied sciences often tend to concentrate on "application oriented basic research" only and thus appear to lose sight of the original practical problem. But despite such shifts in focus: Both the boundaries between disciplines and between pure and applied research are getting more and more blurred.

Today, after the turn of the millennium, it is obvious that sciences are requested to provide more and something different than just theory, basic research or pure knowledge. Rather, sciences are increasingly being regarded as partners in a more comprehensive social and economic context of problem solving and are evaluated against expectations to be practically relevant. This also implies that sciences are expected to be critical, reflecting their impact on society. This new "applied" type of science is confronted with the question: Which role can the sciences play in solving individual, interpersonal, social, intercultural, political or technical problems? This question is typical of a conception of science that was especially developed and propagated by the influential philosopher Sir Karl Popper – a conception that also this handbook series is based on.

2. "Applied Linguistics": Concepts and controversies

The concept of "Applied Linguistics" is not as old as the notion of "Applied Science", but it has also been problematical in its relation to theoretical linguistics since its beginning. There seems to be a widespread consensus that the notion "Applied Linguistics" emerged in 1948 with the first issue of the journal *Language Learning* which used this compound in its subtitle *A Quarterly Journal of Applied Linguistics*. This history of its origin certainly explains why even today "Applied Linguistics" still tends to be predominantly associated with foreign language teaching and learning in the Anglophone literature in particular, as can bee seen e.g. from Johnson and Johnson (1998), whose *Encyclopedic Dictionary of Applied Linguistics* is explicitly subtitled *A Handbook for Language Teaching*. However, this theory of origin is historically wrong. As is pointed out by Back (1970), the concept of applying linguistics can be traced back to the early 19th century in Europe, and the very notion "Applied Linguistics" was used in the early 20th already.

2.1. Theoretically Applied vs. Practically Applied Linguistics

As with the relation between "Pure" and "Applied" sciences pointed out above, also with "Applied Linguistics" the first question to be asked is what makes it different from "Pure" or "Theoretical Linguistics". It is not surprising, then, that the terminologist Back takes this difference as the point of departure for his discussion of what constitutes "Applied Linguistics". In the light of recent controversies about this concept it is no doubt useful to remind us of his terminological distinctions.

Back (1970) distinguishes between "Theoretical Linguistics" – which aims at achieving knowledge for its own sake, without considering any other value –, "Practice" – i.e. any kind of activity that serves to achieve any purpose in life in the widest sense, apart from the striving for knowledge for its own sake – and "Applied Linguistics", as a being based on "Theoretical Linguistics" on the one hand and as aiming at usability in "Practice" on the other. In addition, he makes a difference between "Theoretical Applied Linguistics" and "Practical Applied Linguistics", which is of particular interest here. The former is defined as the use of insights and methods of "Theoretical Linguistics" for gaining knowledge in another, non-linguistic discipline, such as ethnology, sociology, law or literary studies, the latter as the application of insights from linguistics in a practical field related to language, such as language teaching, translation, and the like. For Back, the contribution of applied linguistics is to be seen in the planning of practical action. Language teaching, for example, is practical action done by practitioners, and what applied linguistics can contribute to this is, e.g., to provide contrastive descriptions of the languages involved as a foundation for teaching methods. These contrastive descriptions in turn have to be based on the descriptive methods developed in theoretical linguistics.

However, in the light of the recent epistemological developments outlined above, it may be useful to reinterpret Back's notion of "Theoretically Applied Linguistics". As he himself points out, dealing with practical problems can have repercussions on the development of the theoretical field. Often new approaches, new theoretical concepts and new methods are a prerequisite for dealing with a particular type of practical problems, which may lead to an – at least in the beginning – "application oriented basic research" in applied linguistics itself, which with some justification could also be labelled "theoretically applied", as many such problems require the transgression of disciplinary boundaries. It is not rare that a domain of "Theoretically Applied Linguistics" or "application oriented basic research" takes on a life of its own, and that also something which is labelled as "Applied Linguistics" might in fact be rather remote from the mundane practical problems that originally initiated the respective subject area. But as long as a relation to the original practical problem can be established, it may be justified to count a particular field or discussion as belonging to applied linguistics, even if only "theoretically applied".

2.2.   Applied linguistics as a response to structuralism and generativism

As mentioned before, in the Anglophone world in particular the view still appears to be widespread that the primary concerns of the subject area of applied linguistics should be restricted to second language acquisition and language instruction in the first place (see, e.g., Davies 1999 or Schmitt and Celce-Murcia 2002). However, in other parts of the world, and above all in Europe, there has been a development away from aspects of language learning to a wider focus on more general issues of language and communication.

This broadening of scope was in part a reaction to the narrowing down the focus in linguistics that resulted from self-imposed methodological constraints which, as Ehlich (1999) points out, began with Saussurean structuralism and culminated in generative linguistics. For almost three decades since the late 1950s, these developments made "language" in a comprehensive sense, as related to the everyday experience of its users, vanish in favour of an idealised and basically artificial entity. This led in "Core" or theoretical linguistics to a neglect of almost all everyday problems with language and communication encountered by individuals and societies and made it necessary for those interested in socially accountable research into language and communication to draw on a wider range of disciplines, thus giving rise to a flourishing of interdisciplinary areas that have come to be referred to as hyphenated variants of linguistics, such as sociolinguistics, ethnolinguistics, psycholinguistics, conversation analysis, pragmatics, and so on (Davies and Elder 2004).

That these hyphenated variants of linguistics can be said to have originated from dealing with problems may lead to the impression that they fall completely into the scope of applied linguistics. This the more so as their original thematic focus is in line with a frequently quoted definition of applied linguistics as "the theoretical and empirical investigation of real world problems in which language is a central issue" (Brumfit 1997: 93). However, in the recent past much of the work done in these fields has itself been rather "theoretically applied" in the sense introduced above and ultimately even become mainstream in linguistics. Also, in view of the current epistemological developments that see all sciences under the pressure of application, one might even wonder if there is anything distinctive about applied linguistics at all.

Indeed it would be difficult if not impossible to delimit applied linguistics with respect to the practical problems studied and the disciplinary approaches used: Real-world problems with language (to which, for greater clarity, should be added: "with communication") are unlimited in principle. Also, many problems of this kind are unique and require quite different approaches. Some might be tackled successfully by applying already available linguistic theories and methods. Others might require for their solution the development of new methods and even new theories. Following a frequently used distinction first proposed by Widdowson (1980), one might label these approaches as "Linguistics Applied" or "Applied Linguistics". In addition, language is a trans-disciplinary subject par excellence, with the result that problems do not come labelled and may require for their solution the cooperation of various disciplines.

2.3. Conceptualisations and communities

The questions of what should be its reference discipline and which themes, areas of research and sub-disciplines it should deal with, have been discussed constantly and were also the subject of an intensive debate (e.g. Seidlhofer 2003). In the recent past, a number of edited volumes on applied linguistics have appeared which in their respective introductory chapters attempt at giving a definition of "Applied Linguistics". As can be seen from the existence of the Association Internationale de Linguistique Appliquée (AILA) and its numerous national affiliates, from the number of congresses held or books and journals published with the label "Applied Linguistics", applied linguistics appears to be a well-established and flourishing enterprise. Therefore, the collective need felt by authors and editors to introduce their publication with a definition of the subject area it is supposed to be about is astonishing at first sight. Quite obviously, what Ehlich (2006) has termed "the struggle for the object of inquiry" appears to be characteristic of linguistics – both of linguistics at large and applied linguistics. Its seems then, that the meaning and scope of "Applied Linguistics" cannot be taken for granted, and this is why a wide variety of controversial conceptualisations exist.

For example, in addition to the dichotomy mentioned above with respect to whether approaches to applied linguistics should in their theoretical foundations and methods be autonomous from theoretical linguistics or not, and apart from other controversies, there are diverging views on whether applied linguistics is an independent academic discipline (e.g. Kaplan and Grabe 2000) or not (e.g. Davies and Elder 2004), whether its scope should be mainly restricted to language teaching related topics (e.g. Schmitt and Celce-Murcia 2002) or not (e.g. Knapp 2006), or whether applied linguistics is a field of interdisciplinary synthesis where theories with their own integrity develop in close interaction with language users and professionals (e.g. Rampton 1997/2003) or whether this view should be rejected, as a true interdisciplinary approach is ultimately impossible (e.g. Widdowson 2005).

In contrast to such controversies Candlin and Sarangi (2004) point out that applied linguistics should be defined in the first place by the actions of those who practically *do* applied linguistics:

> […] we see no especial purpose in reopening what has become a somewhat sterile debate on what applied linguistics is, or whether it is a distinctive and coherent discipline. […] we see applied linguistics as a many centered and interdisciplinary endeavour whose coherence is achieved in purposeful, mediated action by its practitioners. […]
> What we want to ask of applied linguistics is less what it is and more what it does, or rather what its practitioners do. (Candlin/Sarangi 2004:1–2)

Against this background, they see applied linguistics as less characterised by its thematic scope – which indeed is hard to delimit – but rather by the two aspects of "relevance" and "reflexivity". Relevance refers to the purpose applied linguistic activities have for the targeted audience and to the degree that these activities in their collaborative practices meet the background and needs of those addressed – which, as matter of comprehensibility, also includes taking their conceptual and language level into account. Reflexivity means the contextualisation of the intellectual principles and practices, which is at the core of what characterises a professional community, and which is achieved by asking leading questions like "What kinds of purposes underlie what is done?", "Who is involved in their determination?", "By whom, and in what ways, is their achievement appraised?", "Who owns the outcomes?".

We agree with these authors that applied linguistics in dealing with real world problems is determined by disciplinary givens – such as e.g. theories, methods or standards of linguistics or any other discipline – but that it is determined at least as much by the social and situational givens of the practices of life. These do not only include the concrete practical problems themselves but also the theoretical and methodological standards of cooperating experts from other disciplines, as well as the conceptual and practical standards of the practitioners who are confronted with the practical problems in the first place. Thus, as Sarangi and van Leeuwen (2003) point out, applied linguists have to become part of the respective "community of practice".

If, however, applied linguists have to regard themselves as part of a community of practice, it is obvious that it is the entire community which determines what the respective subject matter is that the applied linguist deals with and how. In particular, it is the respective community of practice which determines which problems of the practitioners have to be considered. The consequence of this is that applied linguistics can be understood from very comprehensive to very specific, depending on what kind of problems are considered relevant by the respective community. Of course, following this participative understanding of applied linguistics also has consequences for the Handbooks of Applied Linguistics both with respect to the subjects covered and the way they are theoretically and practically treated.

3. Applied linguistics for problem solving

Against this background, it seems reasonable not to define applied linguistics as an autonomous discipline or even only to delimit it by specifying a set of subjects it is supposed to study and typical disciplinary approaches it should use. Rather, in line with the collaborative and participatory perspective of the communities of practice applied linguists are involved in, this handbook series is based on the assumption that applied linguistics is a specific, problem-oriented way of "doing linguistics" related to the real-life world. In other words: applied linguistics is conceived of here as "linguistics for problem solving".

To outline what we think is distinctive about this area of inquiry: Entirely in line with Popper's conception of science, we take it that applied linguistics starts from the assumption of an imperfect world in the areas of language and communication. This means, firstly, that linguistic and communicative competence in individuals, like other forms of human knowledge, is fragmentary and defective – if it exists at all. To express it more pointedly: Human linguistic and communicative behaviour is not "perfect". And on a different level, this imperfection also applies to the use and status of language and communication in and among groups or societies.

Secondly, we take it that applied linguists are convinced that the imperfection both of individual linguistic and communicative behaviour and language based relations between groups and societies can be clarified, understood and to some extent resolved by their intervention, e.g. by means of education, training or consultancy.

Thirdly, we take it that applied linguistics proceeds by a specific mode of inquiry in that it mediates between the way language and communication is expertly studied in the linguistic disciplines and the way it is directly experienced in different domains of use. This implies that applied linguists are able to demonstrate that their findings – be they of a "Linguistics Applied" or "Applied Linguistics" nature – are not just "application oriented basic research" but can be made relevant to the real-life world.

Fourthly, we take it that applied linguistics is socially accountable. To the extent that the imperfections initiating applied linguistic activity involve both social actors and social structures, we take it that applied linguistics has to be critical and reflexive with respect to the results of its suggestions and solutions.

These assumptions yield the following questions which at the same time define objectives for applied linguistics:
1. Which linguistic problems are typical of which areas of language competence and language use?
2. How can linguistics define and describe these problems?
3. How can linguistics suggest, develop, or achieve solutions of these problems?
4. Which solutions result in which improvements in speakers' linguistic and communicative abilities or in the use and status of languages in and between groups?
5. What are additional effects of the linguistic intervention?

4. Objectives of this handbook series

These questions also determine the objectives of this book series. However, in view of the present boom in handbooks of linguistics and applied linguistics, one should ask what is specific about this series of nine thematically different volumes.

To begin with, it is important to emphasise what it is not aiming at:
– The handbook series does not want to take a snapshot view or even a "hit list" of fashionable topics, theories, debates or fields of study.
– Nor does it aim at a comprehensive coverage of linguistics because some selectivity with regard to the subject areas is both inevitable in a book series of this kind and part of its specific profile.

Instead, the book series will try
– to show that applied linguistics can offer a comprehensive, trustworthy and scientifically well-founded understanding of a wide range of problems,
– to show that applied linguistics can provide or develop instruments for solving new, still unpredictable problems,

– to show that applied linguistics is not confined to a restricted number of topics such as, e.g. foreign language learning, but that it successfully deals with a wide range of both everyday problems and areas of linguistics,
– to provide a state-of-the-art description of applied linguistics against the background of the ability of this area of academic inquiry to provide descriptions, analyses, explanations and, if possible, solutions of everyday problems. On the one hand, this criterion is the link to trans-disciplinary co-operation. On the other, it is crucial in assessing to what extent linguistics can in fact be made relevant.

In short, it is by no means the intention of this series to duplicate the present state of knowledge about linguistics as represented in other publications with the supposed aim of providing a comprehensive survey. Rather, the intention is to present the knowledge available in applied linguistics today firstly from an explicitly problem solving perspective and secondly, in a non-technical, easily comprehensible way. Also it is intended with this publication to build bridges to neighbouring disciplines and to critically discuss which impact the solutions discussed do in fact have on practice. This is particularly necessary in areas like language teaching and learning – where for years there has been a tendency to fashionable solutions without sufficient consideration of their actual impact on the reality in schools.

5. Criteria for the selection of topics

Based on the arguments outlined above, the handbook series has the following structure: Findings and applications of linguistics will be presented in concentric circles, as it were, starting out from the communication competence of the individual, proceeding via aspects of interpersonal and inter-group communication to technical communication and, ultimately, to the more general level of society. Thus, the topics of the nine volumes are as follows:

1. Handbook of Individual Communication Competence
2. Handbook of Interpersonal Communication
3. Handbook of Communication in Organisations and Professions
4. Handbook of Communication in the Public Sphere
5. Handbook of Multilingualism and Multilingual Communication
6. Handbook of Foreign Language Communication and Learning
7. Handbook of Intercultural Communication
8. Handbook of Technical Communication
9. Handbook of Language and Communication: Diversity and Change

This thematic structure can be said to follow the sequence of experience with problems related to language and communication a human passes through in the course of his or her personal biographical development. This is why the topic areas of applied linguistics are structured here in ever-increasing concentric circles: in line with biographical development, the first circle starts with the communicative competence of the individual and also includes interpersonal communication as belonging to a person's private sphere. The second circle proceeds to the everyday environment and includes the professional and public sphere. The third circle extends to the experience of foreign languages and cultures, which at least in officially monolingual societies, is not made by everybody and if so, only later in life. Technical communication as the fourth circle is even more exclusive and restricted to a more special professional clientele. The final volume extends this process to focus on more general, supra-individual national and international issues.

For almost all of these topics, there already exist introductions, handbooks or other types of survey literature. However, what makes the present volumes unique is their explicit claim to focus on topics in language and communication as areas of everyday problems and their emphasis on pointing out the relevance of applied linguistics in dealing with them.

Bibliography

Back, Otto
    1970   Was bedeutet und was bezeichnet der Begriff 'angewandte Sprachwissenschaft'? *Die Sprache* 16: 21–53.
Brumfit, Christopher
    1997   How applied linguistics is the same as any other science. *International Journal of Applied Linguistics* 7(1): 86–94.
Candlin, Chris N. and Srikant Sarangi
    2004   Making applied linguistics matter. *Journal of Applied Linguistics* 1(1): 1–8.
Carrier, Michael, Martin Stöltzner, and Jeanette Wette
    2004   *Theorienstruktur und Beurteilungsmaßstäbe unter den Bedingungen der Anwendungsdominanz.* Universität Bielefeld: Institut für Wissenschafts- und Technikforschung [http://www.uni-bielefeld.de/iwt/projekte/wissen/anwendungsdominanz.html, accessed Jan 5, 2007].
Davies, Alan
    1999   *Introduction to Applied Linguistics. From Practice to Theory.* Edinburgh: Edinburgh University Press.
Davies, Alan and Catherine Elder
    2004   General introduction – Applied linguistics: Subject to discipline? In: Alan Davies and Catherine Elder (eds.), *The Handbook of Applied Linguistics*, 1–16. Malden etc.: Blackwell.
Ehlich, Konrad
    1999   Vom Nutzen der „Funktionalen Pragmatik" für die angewandte Linguistik. In: Michael Becker-Mrotzek und Christine Doppler (eds.), *Medium Sprache im Beruf. Eine Aufgabe für die Linguistik*, 23–36. Tübingen: Narr.

Ehlich, Konrad
　2006　　Mehrsprachigkeit für Europa – öffentliches Schweigen, linguistische Distanzen. In: Sergio Cigada, Jean-Francois de Pietro, Daniel Elmiger, and Markus Nussbaumer (eds.), *Öffentliche Sprachdebatten – linguistische Positionen. Bulletin Suisse de Linguistique Appliquée/VALS-ASLA-Bulletin* 83/1: 11–28.
Grabe, William
　2002　　Applied linguistics: An emerging discipline for the twenty-first century. In: Robert B. Kaplan (ed.), *The Oxford Handbook of Applied Linguistics*, 3–12. Oxford: Oxford University Press.
Johnson, Keith and Helen Johnson (eds.)
　1998　　*Encyclopedic Dictionary of Applied Linguistics. A Handbook for Language Teaching.* Oxford: Blackwell.
Kaplan, Robert B. and William Grabe
　2000　　Applied linguistics and the Annual Review of Applied Linguistics. In: W. Grabe (ed.), *Applied Linguistics as an Emerging Discipline. Annual Review of Applied Linguistics* 20: 3–17.
Knapp, Karlfried
　2006　　Vorwort. In: Karlfried Knapp, Gerd Antos, Michael Becker-Mrotzek, Arnulf Deppermann, Susanne Göpferich, Joachim Gabowski, Michael Klemm und Claudia Villiger (eds.), *Angewandte Linguistik. Ein Lehrbuch.* 2nd ed., xix–xxiii. Tübingen: Francke – UTB.
Meinel, Christoph
　2000　　Reine und angewandte Wissenschaft. In: *Das Magazin.* Ed. Wissenschaftszentrum Nordrhein-Westfalen 11(1): 10–11.
Rampton, Ben
　1997 [2003]　Retuning in applied linguistics. *International Journal of Applied Linguistics* 7 (1): 3–25, quoted from Seidlhofer (2003), 273–295.
Sarangi, Srikant and Theo van Leeuwen
　2003　　Applied linguistics and communities of practice: Gaining communality or losing disciplinary autonomy? In: Srikant Sarangi and Theo van Leeuwen (eds.), *Applied Linguistics and Communities of Practice*, 1–8. London: Continuum.
Schmitt, Norbert and Marianne Celce-Murcia
　2002　　An overview of applied linguistics. In: Norbert Schmitt (ed.), *An Introduction to Applied Linguistics.* London: Arnold.
Seidlhofer, Barbara (ed.)
　2003　　*Controversies in Applied Linguistics.* Oxford: Oxford University Press.
Widdowson, Henry
　1984 [1980]　Model and fictions. In: Henry Widdowson (1984) *Explorations in Applied Linguistics 2*, 21–27. Oxford: Oxford University Press.
Widdowson, Henry
　2005　　Applied linguistics, interdisciplinarity, and disparate realities. In: Paul Bruthiaux, Dwight Atkinson, William G. Egginton, William Grabe, and Vaidehi Ramanathan (eds.), *Directions in Applied Linguistics. Essays in Honor of Robert B. Kaplan*, 12–25. Clevedon: Multilingual Matters.

Acknowledgements

In putting together this volume the editors were assisted by a number of people. Our most sincere thanks go to Helena McKenzie who provided invaluable editorial assistance to us throughout the various stages of the project. Special thanks also go to Dr. Friederike Braun who created the subject index for the volume. Britta Schneider, M.A., assisted us with the language index, while Dr. Heiko Motschenbacher took care of the the final stages of both indices. In addition, we would like to express our appreciation to Barbara Karlson and Wolfgang Konwitschny at Mouton de Gruyter for their quick responses to our many queries. Finally, of course, sincere thanks go to our authors for their willingness to contribute and for ensuring that this volume was delivered by the deadline.

Frankfurt am Main,   Marlis Hellinger
April 2007   Anne Pauwels

Contents

Introduction to the handbook series v
Karlfried Knapp and *Gerd Antos*

Acknowledgements xvii

Language and communication: Diversity and change – An introduction
Anne Pauwels and *Marlis Hellinger* 1

I. Language minorities and inequality

1. Regional and immigrant minority languages in Europe
   Guus Extra and *Durk Gorter* 15

2. Immigrant language minorities in the United States
   Terrence G. Wiley 53

3. Immigrant minorities: Australia
   Antonia Rubino 87

4. Linguistic diversity: Africa
   Jan Blommaert 123

5. Linguistic diversity: Asia
   Vanithamani Saravanan 151

6. Language contact, culture and ecology
   Alwin Fill 177

II. Language planning and language change

7. Models and approaches in language policy and planning
   Thomas Ricento 211

8. Back from the brink: The revival of endangered languages
   John Edwards 241

9. Economics and language policy
   François Grin 271

10. Language and colonialism
    Bettina Migge and *Isabelle Léglise* 299

11. Linguistic imperialism? English as a global language
    Andy Kirkpatrick 333

12. Language planning and language rights
    Tove Skutnabb-Kangas 365

III. Language variation and change in institutional contexts

13. Language and education
    Markus Bieswanger 401
14. Forensic linguistics
    John Gibbons 429
15. Language and religion
    Susanne Mühleisen 459
16. Language, war and peace
    William C. Gay 493
17. Language and science
    Augusto Carli and *Emilia Calaresu* 523
18. Multilingualism on the Internet
    Brenda Danet and *Susan C. Herring* 553

IV. The discourse of linguistic diversity and language change

19. Attitudes to language and communication
    Cindy Gallois and *Bernadette Watson* and *Madeleine Brabant* ... 595
20. Language, racism, and ethnicity
    Thomas Paul Bonfiglio 619
21. Language and sexism
    Marlis Hellinger and *Anne Pauwels* 651
22. Linguistic diversity and language standardization
    Suzanne Romaine 685
23. Borrowing as language conflict
    Manfred Görlach 715
24. Political correctness and freedom of speech
    Mary Talbot 751

Biographical notes 765
Language index 771
Subject index 777

Language and communication: Diversity and change – An introduction

Anne Pauwels and Marlis Hellinger

Volume IX of the Handbook Series focuses on language-related problems and issues arising in the context of linguistic diversity and change and how applied linguistic perspectives and approaches may contribute to solving or managing some of these problems. The contributions in this volume also bear witness to the diversity in the conceptualisation of applied linguistics as outlined in the General Introduction by the Series Editors. This volume is perhaps more diverse in its topic coverage than many of the other volumes in the Handbook Series. Consequently there is some similarity and overlap with themes and topics covered in other volumes, especially Vol. IV (Communication in the Public Sphere), Vol. V (Multilingual Communication) and Vol. VII (Intercultural Communication). However, the approach here is explicitly on problem identification, explanation and management: What unites the contributions in this volume is the theme of planning, management and policies of language issues.

We have organised the volume in four sections each focussing on different approaches to and/or perspectives of applied linguistic work on diversity and change:

Part I **Language minorities and inequality** approaches the theme of linguistic diversity from a regional or geographic perspective describing and discussing multilingual communities across the globe. Our primary aim for this section of the volume is to present the many facets of applied linguistic work on different types of multilingual situations found in diverse regions of the world.

The emphasis in these contributions is on the management of multilingualism by both state/government agencies and community organisations. Although we have attempted to cover as many regions of the world as possible it was not feasible within the confines and orientation of this volume to be either comprehensive or exhaustive. Consequently some large regions such as Central and South America have not been covered. The regions that are covered in this volume vary substantially in complexity – political, social and linguistic – resulting in contributors having to make different decisions about depth or breadth of coverage. In the case of the chapter on Europe, Guus Extra and Durk Gorter decided to combine a pan-European perspective (i.e. at the level of the European Union) with country-specific approaches to the management of linguistic minorities distinguishing between those indigenous to Europe and those resulting from migration to Europe.

The chapters on Australia (Antonia Rubino) and the United States (Terrence G. Wiley), each being single countries, do not face the same challenges with regard to regional coverage but their authors do grapple with the types of minorities to be discussed. Given their areas of expertise their focus is primarily on the linguistic minorities resulting from many centuries of immigration rather than on indigenous (Aboriginal) minorities. Wiley's contribution provides a historical perspective on how the languages of immigrant minorities have been treated in the United States whereas Rubino's chapter concentrates more on the management of multilingualism in contemporary Australia.

Given the phenomenal linguistic complexity and diversity of Africa (there are more than 2000 languages spoken in Africa) Jan Blommaert's contribution approaches the management of African multilingualisms from a macro-perspective by focussing on three major issues: (1) the management of linguistic rights and linguistic minorities, (2) language in education and (3) literacy. He discusses these by drawing upon examples from various political and other entities in Africa.

Vanitha Saravanan tackles the gigantic task of describing and discussing multilingualisms of Asia by focusing almost entirely on the management of multilingualism in the educational domain and by selecting three case studies in Asia – Singapore, Malaysia and Hong Kong – to pinpoint the major challenges. Although very brief insights into China and India are incorporated in the chapter, Saravanan refers readers to more elaborate discussions of specific communities and countries in Asia.

Applied linguistic approaches to the management of linguistic diversity or multilingualism cover a large number of issues ranging from the mapping of linguistic groups (linguistic demography), the status and/or protection of minority languages in and through legislature, the formulation and existence of policies affecting the status and use of different types of languages in a polity, the modernisation and standardisation processes to elevate languages to a different status, to ethnic community strategies and efforts to maintain their languages, the availability of different types of languages in education, as well as access of and provision for linguistic minorities to the learning of the *majority* or dominant language. The contributors to this first part address most of these issues in the context of their specific region, although understandably their emphasis may vary in line with local and regional needs, conditions and developments.

A common focus of attention, however, is on *education* and its central role in the management of linguistic diversity almost anywhere in the world. This is not surprising given the fact that "education was and is one of the key institutional instruments by means of which the state or powerful civil society actors could impose language regimes on the population, and such regimes could either be democratic or elitist" (Blommaert, this vol.). For Europe, Extra and Gorter note that education is the arena in which the *status* and *type* of minority languages probably affect their treatment most severely. Those minority languages which are considered indigenous to Europe are covered in the *European Charter for Regional and Minority Languages* and their speakers have a number of rights not extended to those minorities speaking non-indigenous European languages (immigrant languages). The former have the right (across Europe) to receive some education through the medium of their language whereas the latter are at the mercy of an array of other agencies (e.g., national and local governments, individual schools and school principals) in terms of their language being available in mainstream education. The authors discuss a comparative study on the status of immigrant languages in primary or secondary schools in six EU cities confirming the vastly different treatment of these languages in the schooling systems and highlighting the consequences of such treatment in terms of language maintenance and the acquisition of skills in the *majority* or dominant language.

Two English-dominant countries with large immigrant populations – the United States and Australia – may face similar questions in the maintenance of minority languages but have taken different routes in terms of their presence and treatment in education. Rubino shows how in Australia both federal and state education systems have endorsed the learning of languages (including minority languages also known as *community languages*) as a key learning area for all children in either primary or secondary school. The learning of community languages is not seen as the exclusive domain of linguistic minorities, hence the orientation is less on linguistic rights or on maintenance of a specific language but more on enrichment. Although this is not without its problems (both practical and political) it nevertheless expresses some commitment to multilingualism in Australia.

According to Wiley (this vol.) "the dogma of English monolingualism" still rules language policies and provisions in the United States. Immigrant minorities have limited if any access to the learning of their languages in education. Assimilation, including linguistic assimilation, continues to be the prevailing ideology to deal with immigrant minorities. Even during periods of greater tolerance of linguistic diversity leading to the introduction of bilingual education programmes for linguistic minorities the emphasis was still on the importance of English. The primary function of these bilingual programmes was to facilitate the child's transition to English-medium education rather than lead to maintenance and, consequently, bilingualism. More recent developments such as the English-only movement further stress the importance of English for all citizens of the United States. It seems that the learning of community/minority languages in the United States is largely left to the communities themselves.

Saravanan's three case studies of Asian countries as well as Blommaert's chapter on Africa particularly highlight the role of education in managing language diversity in postcolonial societies. Although there are some similarities between the challenges facing the three former British colonies/territories in Asia and those found in former British colonies in Africa, the difference in scale is so vast that comparisons are not terribly insightful. For these Asian societies the main challenge is to strike a balance between English and the Asian language(s) in education. This involves assigning a new role to English in education, i.e. English is no longer seen as the language of (former) colonial masters but as the necessary or desirable gateway to globalisation. It also involves strengthening or consolidating the Asian language(s) in education. In the case of African postcolonial societies, Blommaert sees the problems as much more basic: In many parts of Africa the education system has been wiped out due to prolonged tribal and other wars as well as many natural catastrophes. In such a context the issue of which language(s) to choose for education becomes secondary to the issue of providing education. Nevertheless Blommaert does elaborate on the problems surrounding choice of language.

The final chapter in this section deals with the broader issue of the applied linguistic approaches to the study of "Language contact, culture and ecology", distinguishing between societal and individual forms of language contact. Alwin Fill also outlines what he sees as the important contributions applied linguists can make in the maintenance of linguistic diversity in today's world. He is upfront about his support for linguistic diversity and aligns himself with those (applied) linguists who advocate the maintenance of linguistic diversity from an ecology perspective. Fill agrees with Mühlhäusler in that "linguistic diversity should not be seen as a problem but as an essential resource" (Fill, this vol.). This chapter provides an apt reflection on many of the issues raised in the previous chapters as well as serving as a precursor to issues being dealt with in the subsequent parts of the volume.

In Part II **Language planning and language change** the emphasis is squarely on applied linguistic approaches and contributions to language planning, language management and language policy. Many scholars would agree with Thomas Ricento's observation that "LPP [Language Planning and Policy – editors' insert] is an exemplary applied linguistics endeavor", thus deserving central attention in a Handbook of Applied Linguistics. Although the entire volume can be said to deal with various ways in which language and communication issues are being *managed*, in this second part the focus is on presenting shared as well as divergent interpretations of language planning and policy approaches and models within the field of applied linguistics. Of course, our emphasis on applied linguistic approaches does not diminish or deny the recognition that language policy and planning are ultimately multidisciplinary enterprises which need to draw upon other (inter)disciplinary knowledge associated with, for example, political science, economics, cultural and historical studies as well as other branches of linguistics. This *interdisciplinarity* is fully recognised by all contributors to this section whose contributions indeed draw upon insights from other disciplines. It is particularly explicit in the contribution by François Grin which brings to the fore an economic perspective on language matters including language management.

Ricento's contribution provides a suitable introduction to this section: He presents a critical historical overview of the developments in language planning and language policy. He examines in particular how models of language planning and language policy have addressed the challenges posed by multilingualism in the world's states and societies. Ricento distinguishes historical-structural approaches in LPP research from those linked to postmodern theories of power. In the former language policies are viewed as "instruments of social control imposed by dominant powers at the macro-social level" (Ricento, this vol.), whereas the latter are concerned with *language governmentality* focussing on the operation of power at the micro-level in respect to diverse practices including language. Many of these approaches and models are then exemplified and/or elaborated in the other papers in this section.

Another major concern for language planning and language policy is how to deal with languages which are on the brink of extinction and with community desires to *revive* languages. These issues are taken up in John Edwards' chapter which contains a critical assessment of the field known as *linguistic ecology* (see also Fill's chapter in Part I). In fact, Edwards claims that the focus of most modern writing on linguistic ecology has narrowed concentrating "upon an environmentalism that makes a specific case for the maintenance of diversity". His main criticism of this narrowed focus is that it underestimates how difficult the enterprise of language maintenance and/or revival really is claiming "that past efforts have often foundered on the shoals of romantic but unrealistic enthusiasm, and that approaching the topic from a position of initial aesthetic and moral commitment […] is neither in the best traditions of disinterested scholarship nor likely to realise longterm success" (Edwards, this vol.). Edwards thus not only addresses the issue of what constitutes language maintenance or language revival and how to go about maintaining an endangered language or a language at risk of obsolescence but he also tackles the difficult question of whether or not endangered languages should be revived and what the potential advocacy role of applied linguists and other language professionals might be in this revival process.

The main focus of Grin's contribution is on how insights from economics can assist language planning endeavours at the macro-level. He notes that "[e]conomics is increasingly often called upon to help analyse macro-level language issues, and to assist in the selection, design and evaluation of language policies" (Grin, this vol.). He defines this field as follows: "[T]he economics of language refers to the paradigm of theoretical economics and uses the concepts and tools of economics in the study of relationships featuring linguistic variables; it focuses principally, but not exclusively, on those relationships in which economics variables also play a part" (Grin 1996: 6, reference in Grin, this vol.).

Another major area of language planning and policy concerns the linguistic consequences of colonialism as well as postcolonialism. Two chapters in this section deal specifically with language and colonialism although from different angles. Bettina Migge and Isabelle Léglise take a comprehensive look at the relationships between language and colonialism covering language policies and practices associated with French and English colonial practices, the development of Creoles and the expansion of Anglophone and Francophone Creole communities. Major emphasis is given to language educational questions and problems associated with these communities: Which language(s) should be used in the school setting and for which functions, what is the most appropriate pedagogy to foster bilingualism, diglossia or the valorisation of the home language?

Andy Kirkpatrick's chapter also deals with colonialism in that he acknowledges that colonial expansion by Great Britain has been a major factor in the spread of English around the world. In this context he undertakes a critical appraisal of various applied linguistic positions concerning the consequences and effects of the global spread of English on other languages and speech communities, on the question of linguistic ownership as well as on questions of linguistic identity for users and speakers of English. In true applied linguistic fashion he examines the consequences of adopting any of these different stances for the teaching of English to speakers of other languages in a variety of different communities, using the framework of the Kachruvian "circles" model – with *inner circle*, *outer circle* and *expanding circle* – to distinguish communities of learners and users of English.

One of the language planning approaches mentioned in Ricento's chapter is that of *Linguistic Human Rights*. The notion of language rights and the distinction between language rights and linguistic human rights in relation to language planning/language policy are discussed and elaborated in the contribution by Tove Skutnabb-Kangas. She draws upon Rubio-Marín's distinction between *expressive language rights* which "aim at ensuring a person's capacity to enjoy a secure linguistic environment in her/his mother tongue and a linguistic group's fair chance of cultural self-reproduction" and *instrumental language rights* which "aim at ensuring that language is not an obstacle to the effective enjoyment of rights with a linguistic dimension, to the meaningful participation in public institutions and democratic process, and to the enjoyment of social and economic opportunities that require linguistic skills" (Skutnabb-Kangas, this vol.). The main focus of the chapter is the identification of those language rights which constitute linguistic human rights. Unlike Rubio-Marín, Skutnabb-Kangas considers both aspects of expressive and instrumental rights to qualify as linguistic human rights. For her, linguistic human rights are "those (and only those) language rights which, firstly, are necessary to satisfy people's basic needs (including the need to live a dignified life), and which, secondly, therefore are so basic, so fundamental that no state (or individual or group) is supposed to violate them. Some basic rights prohibit discrimination on the basis of language (*negative rights*); others ensure equal treatment to languages, individuals or language groups (*positive rights*)" (Skutnabb-Kangas, this vol.). The chapter also examines the state of Linguistic Human Rights in the crucial domain of education, thus leading into the issues discussed in detail in the next section.

In Part III **Language variation and change in institutional contexts** we shift our attention to another well-known area of applied linguistic research and scholarship, that of language use in institutional contexts. The study of language and/in institutions has been approached from various angles and paradigms: Some studies focus primarily on the linguistic and communicative features characteristic of specific types of institutional language, for example legal language, scientific communication, medical discourse, the language of aviation, etc. This type of approach to institutional language is often labelled as LSP or *Language for Special/Specific Purpose(s)*. Applied linguistic contributions to LSP have included descriptions of various types of institutional language as well as 'methods' for teaching and ways of learning such uses of language.

Other approaches in the area of institutional communication concentrate on the relationships between language, power, and ideology in institutionalised contexts. Studies in this mould investigate how language practices shape if not define an institution, how ideologies influence institutional discourse in explicit and implicit ways, or how access to institutional language is influenced and sometimes regulated by socioeconomic, cultural and other non-linguistic factors. *Critical discourse analysis* has become a prominent though not the sole "tool" to study institutional and other forms of public discourse. Particularly influential in the critical study of public and institutional discourses has been the work of Norman Fairclough, Ruth Wodak and Teun Van Dijk and their associated colleagues (for more discussion see Vol. IV in this Handbook Series). Some contributors to this volume (e.g. Gibbons, Gay, Danet and Herring) draw upon these scholars' insights in their chapters on language and the law, the language of war and peace, and communication on the internet. The institutional discourses chosen for inclusion in this volume relate to education (Markus Bieswanger), the law and legislature (John Gibbons), religion (Susanne Mühleisen), the state with specific attention to the institutional discourses of war and peace (William C. Gay) and to science (Augusto Carli and Emilia Calaresu). It also includes a contribution by Brenda Danet and Susan C. Herring on language and the internet, which can be considered a relatively new institution as well as "medium" of communication.

Language and education is a "mammoth" in the field of applied linguistics. Many would assert that education was the main trigger for the development of applied linguistics as the early applications of linguistic knowledge and theories focused almost entirely on education, specifically the teaching and learning of "foreign" languages. Bieswanger's contribution provides a thorough sketch of the development of the language and education focus in applied linguistics. This development is not only a matter of the widening of the issues covered under this rubric, for example, first and second language learning, bilingual education, language testing, educational language policy and literacy, but also involves an expansion of methodological approaches to and philosophical (ideological) perspectives on language in education. Bieswanger discusses these expansions exemplifying five central/key topics in the study of language and education: (a) the "traditional" field of second and foreign language learning, (b) the issue of the place and recognition of different language varieties in education, (c) the issue of multilingualism and education, (d) the role of education in (maintaining) linguistic diversity and (e) literacy.

In his contribution on language and the law Gibbons covers the main issues in which applied linguists have been interested and active: These include the description of various forms of legal language and how these are different from everyday language, the complexities and challenges of legal interpreting and translation as well as courtroom interactions (within a common law framework). These issues also exemplify the roles of applied linguists in this area of study: that of expert (witness) in linguistic description and analysis, of critical assessor and "exposer" of linguistic power and manipulation, and that of advocate for change.

The relationship between language and religion is also multi-faceted as Mühleisen demonstrates in her contribution: Besides the long-standing mythological relationship between language and religious beliefs in which language and especially naming are portrayed as a gift from the deity, there is also the role of religion in language spread with links to both westernisation and colonisation, and the role of religion in language codification and standardisation. Furthermore, the centuries-old practice of bible translation has had a significant influence on the emergence of descriptive linguistics and translation theory. With regard to the role of language and the state Gay's focus is on the construction of official discourses surrounding war, conflicts and peace with specific attention to linguistic processes used to 'naturalise' dominant discourses and to suppress alternative discourses. His contribution stresses the role of critical applied linguistics, not only in exposing these naturalisation processes but also in finding ways of challenging dominant discourses and creating new modes of speaking about peace and conflict.

Carli and Calaresu approach the discussion of another form of specialist language – scientific communication – from a mainly descriptive perspective. They define *scientific communication* as "that set of discourses whose aim is the transmission of knowledge and research results, performed by communication procedures which vary depending on who acts as sender (the scientist him/herself, the scientific journalist, the educator, etc.) and who is the addressee (a fellow scientist, a student, the lay public, etc.)" (Carli and Calaresu, this vol.). They discuss the different types of scientific communication based on the target audience, e.g. for specialists within the same field (the *intra-specialist* level), for specialists in other fields (the *inter-specialist* level), for learners (the *pedagogical* level) and the lay community (the *popular* level). The authors also touch upon sociolinguistic issues relating to the expansion of English as the scientific *lingua franca* and the consequences for scientific genres and registers in other languages. They see applied linguistics as playing a major role in identifying, developing and propagating a *meta*-awareness of the complex issues involved.

In their contribution on language, culture and the internet, Danet and Herring decided to focus on the growing multilingual character of the internet and on macro and micro-linguistic issues of linguistic diversity on the internet. Covering such aspects as web pages, instant messaging, email and chat they find that the internet is subject to similar linguistic trends and forces found in other modes of communication: the dominance of English at macro- and micro-levels, the growing resistance to this English dominance by non-English language internet communities and the use of the internet to strengthen if not revitalise other languages.

Part IV **The discourse of linguistic diversity and language change** analyses the ways in which language diversity and language change have become issues of public debates which are informed by various ideological orientations, values and attitudes. Of particular interest in this section is the identification of the historical and ideological roots of central issues such as ethnolinguistic prejudice, the construct of "pure" languages, or androcentric language practices.

Attitudes are a key concept in the analysis of linguistic diversity and language change. Cynthia Gallois, Bernadette Watson and Madeleine Brabant, in their chapter on attitudes to language and communication, review the field's history which starts in the 1950s with a strong grounding in social psychology. Controversial issues are the stability or dynamism of attitudes, attitude formation and maintenance, and the relation between attitudes and behaviour. These issues are discussed in various theoretical frameworks, e.g. social identity theory, communication accommodation theory, and the willingness to communicate approach. A major insight of the chapter is that attitudes are discursively negotiated in communicative contexts rather than given as stable features. Thus, applied linguistics contributes to the analysis of conversational dynamics, as for example in intercultural communication, where prejudice and identity are important factors in shaping attitudes and subsequent communicative behaviour. Solutions to problems created by ethnic and linguistic diversity require the cooperation between applied linguistics and social psychology of language.

In a related chapter on language, racism, and ethnicity, Thomas Paul Bonfiglio demonstrates how myths of language are integrated into discourses of nation-building. Myths of race and genetic ownership of language, as well as constructs of the native speaker contribute to the construction of an "other" as a biological contaminant and are thus portrayed as a threat to the matrix of nation, ethnicity and language. The most powerful image in the generation of ethnolinguistic prejudice is that of the Tower of Babel: Some 140 representations are known between 1550 and the early 17th century. The image constructs the traumatic birth of Europe, with the vernacular at the heart of nation-building. Bonfiglio traces the metaphor of language as an organic entity as it spread from renaissance Italy to Northern Europe, and shows how in various countries the respective vernaculars were constructed as pure, original and perfect: In one example from 17th century Sweden which describes the languages of Paradise, God speaks Swedish, Adam and Eve Danish, and the serpent French. Applied linguistics is able to analyse discourses in which (national, native) language, as a metonym for race or nativity, serves as a surrogate arena for ethnic conflict and ethnolinguistic discrimination.

In their chapter on language and sexism, Marlis Hellinger and Anne Pauwels discuss the major theoretical developments in the field since the 1970s, from more essentialist models to postmodern frameworks. Their focus is on linguistic sexism as one important area of language and gender. Categories of gender as well as asymmetrical representations of women and men, with particular emphasis on androcentric "generics", are analysed and illustrated by examples taken from a variety of languages. The major contribution of applied linguistics is in the area of language reform and language planning, more specifically in proposing, implementing and evaluating non-sexist/gender-inclusive usage in domains such as legal language, educational textbooks, reference works, and advertising. The discourse about non-sexist reform measures in the academy and in the media is interpreted as symbolic of an ongoing struggle over the equal participation of women in public domains.

Suzanne Romaine, in her chapter on linguistic diversity and language standardisation, presents a detailed picture of the ideological underpinnings of "standard languages", which are the result of deliberate language planning. Standardisation is often linked to processes of political unification and aims to remove linguistic variation which is seen as problematic and divisive. Code selection, elaboration and implementation are discussed for a large number of cases which particularly focus on linguistic diversity as a result of colonisation and imperialism. Thus, debates over different orthographies, e.g. in Creole-speaking societies, symbolise the struggles over inclusion and exclusion, and over the ways in which autonomy and distance from the old colonial/imperial power can be achieved. At the same time, spelling reforms which are one measure of language activism, may reproduce the dominant language ideology (of an idealised standard or "pure" language) and thus reproduce structures of discrimination.

Manfred Görlach addresses language diversity and change as it results from language contact. Borrowing is placed in the context of language mixing, multilingualism, merging and pidginisation, processes which are constrained by sociocultural factors, requirements of certain text-types, purist traditions or speakers' attitudes. Focussing on lexical borrowing, Görlach discusses the influences on English from Celtic, Scandinavian, French, Latin and Greek, but also from indigenous languages on the New Englishes in the context of colonisation and migration. The impact of English on other languages, in particular on European languages, is reflected in discourses about the forms and functions of anglicisms, which center around the necessity of borrowing, the integration of anglicisms (in pronunciation, spelling, inflection, etc.), the "purity" of the receptor language, and ultimately around cultural, ethnic and national identity. From an applied linguistic perspective, borrowing features significantly in language planning (e.g., in dealing with institutional and legal measures against, and often populist objections to anglicisms), in the development of reference books (e.g., usage dictionaries, style manuals and guidebooks), and in translation and interpreting.

Finally, in the chapter on political correctness and freedom of speech, Mary Talbot discusses political correctness (PC) as one strategy used in discourses about linguistic and ethnic diversity. PC signals resistance to change, and is frequently directed against feminist and anti-racist interventions, the wider context being issues of equity, inclusivity and ethics. Originally a term created by the new political left in the USA in the 1970s, the term has subsequently been used by the political right within various political and ideological contexts in the USA, UK, Australia, Germany and France. Talbot analyses the ideological and racial underpinnings of PC usages, in particular as these are linked to the argument of freedom of speech. The role of applied linguistics is to draw attention to these issues and to theorise them. By using Critical Discourse Analysis, applied linguistics is able to show how certain stylistic choices or reform measures (as they are found in codes of practice and style guides) may be politicised by political agents, the media and other culture industries. Thus, PC discourse is identified as one form of cultural politics.

In summary, the contributions to this volume in the Handbook of Applied Linguistics Series confirm that applied linguistics covers a plethora of approaches to and diverse perspectives on language issues and problems. The contributions also give voice to differing perceptions and interpretations of the role of applied linguists in dealing with issues of language diversity and communication problems: Whereas some applied linguists see their role limited to undertaking expert linguistic analysis of a language issue or problem, others expand the role to including not only expert analysis but also involvement in the identification of the problem and proposing solutions. Perhaps the most expansive interpretation of the applied linguist's role is one that not only covers all of the above aspects but also includes an active engagement (advocacy) with a specific community to address a problem and guide the implementation of a preferred solution. Of course, these variations in the perceived role of the expert-scholar are not unique to the field of applied linguistics. However, the centrality of communication (skills) in today's world has heightened the need to address a range of critical language issues (e.g., minimal or lack of skills in literacy, lack of access to the language of the institutions of power and advancement) thus putting more pressure on defining the role of applied linguists in providing solutions to these problems. The contributions to this volume also demonstrate that linguistic diversity and change are continuing features of the world's linguistic landscape: Although the nature and the extent of linguistic diversity change with time the cycle of change does seem to lead to new forms of linguistic diversity. This observation poses further questions as to the role of applied linguistics and applied linguists in managing future changes in this diversity. We do not believe that we have the answers to these questions but that the contributions selected for this volume provide some suggestions and clues on how the current and future generation of applied linguists could tackle the challenging issue of linguistic diversity and change.

I. Language minorities and inequality

1. Regional and immigrant minority languages in Europe

Guus Extra and Durk Gorter

1. Introduction

The theme of this chapter will be addressed from four different angles, i.e., in terms of phenomenological, demographic, sociolinguistic, and educational perspectives. Both multidisciplinary and crossnational perspectives will be offered on two major domains in which language transmission occurs, i.e., the domestic domain and the public domain. The home and the school are typical of these domains. At home, language transmission occurs between parents and children, at school this occurs between teachers and pupils. Viewed from the perspectives of majority language *versus* minority language speakers, language transmission becomes a very different issue. In the case of majority language speakers, transmission at home and at school are commonly taken for granted: At home, parents speak this language usually with their children, and at school, this language is usually the only or major subject and medium of instruction. In the case of minority language speakers, there is usually a mismatch between the language of the home and that of the school. Whether parents in such a context continue to transmit their language to their children is strongly dependent on the degree to which these parents, or the minority group, conceive of this language as a core value of cultural identity.

2. Phenomenological perspectives

This section deals with the semantics of our field of concern and with a number of central notions in this field. In Section 2.1, the European spectrum of references to languages is addressed. In Section 2.2, we discuss the relationship between language and identity. In Section 2.3, our focus is on two common notions in the European discourse on immigrant minority groups, i.e., the notions of *foreigners* and *integration*.

2.1. Europe's linguistic diversity: Regional minority and immigrant minority languages

Europe's identity is to a great extent determined by cultural and linguistic diversity. Figure 1 and Table 1 serve to illustrate this diversity in terms of nation-states and corresponding official state languages, respectively. In Figure 1, we present a map of European nation-states based on their national self-references as derived from the official EU website.

Figure 1. Map of European nation-states (source: *www.europa.eu.int/abc/index_en.htm*)

In this Section we focus on non-official state languages in European Union (henceforward EU) countries. Prototypical of these non-official state languages are regional and immigrant minority languages, in an earlier study referred to as the "other" languages of Europe (Extra and Gorter 2001). In Table 1 we give an overview of the present 29 EU (candidate) nation-states with their estimated populations (ranked in decreasing order of millions) and official state languages.

Table 1. Overview of 29 EU (candidate) nation-states with estimated populations and official state languages (EU figures for 2005)

No.	Nation-states	Population (in millions)	Official state language(s)
1	Germany	82.5	German
2	France	60.6	French
3	United Kingdom	60.0	English
4	Italy	58.5	Italian
5	Spain	43.0	Spanish
6	Poland	38.2	Polish
7	The Netherlands	16.3	Dutch
8	Greece	11.1	Greek
9	Portugal	10.5	Portuguese
10	Belgium	10.4	Dutch, French, German
11	Czechia	10.2	Czech
12	Hungary	10.1	Magyar (Hungarian)
13	Sweden	9.0	Swedish
14	Austria	8.2	German
15	Denmark	5.4	Danish
16	Slovakia	5.4	Slovakian
17	Finland	5.2	Finnish
18	Ireland	4.1	Irish, English
19	Lithuania	3.4	Lithuanian
20	Latvia	2.3	Latvian
21	Slovenia	2.0	Slovenian
22	Estonia	1.3	Estonian
23	Cyprus	0.7	Greek, Turkish
24	Luxembourg	0.5	Luxemburgish, French, German
25	Malta	0.4	Maltese, English
	Candidate nation-states	Population (in millions)	Official state language
26	Turkey	71.6	Turkish
27	Romania	21.7	Romanian
28	Bulgaria	7.8	Bulgarian
29	Croatia	4.4	Croatian

As Table 1 makes clear, there are large differences in population size amongst EU nation-states. German, French, English, Italian, Spanish, and Polish belong to the six most widely spoken official state languages in the present EU, whereas Turkish would come second to German in an enlarged EU. Table 1 also shows the close connection between nation-state references and official state language references. In 26 out of 29 cases, distinct languages are the clearest feature distinguishing one nation-state from its neighbours (Barbour 2000), the only exceptions (and for different reasons) being Belgium, Austria, and Cyprus. This match between nation-state references and official state language references obscures the very existence of different types of minority languages that are actually spoken across European nation-states. Many of these languages are indigenous minority languages with a regional base, many other languages stem from abroad without such a base. We will refer to these languages as regional minority (RM henceforth) languages and immigrant minority (IM) languages, respectively.

A number of things need to be kept in mind: Within and across EU nation-states, many RM and IM languages have larger numbers of speakers than many of the official state languages in Table 1. Moreover, RM and IM languages in one EU nation-state may be official state languages in another nation-state. Examples of the former result from language border crossing in adjacent nation-states, such as Finnish in Sweden or Swedish in Finland. Examples of the latter result from processes of migration and minorization, in particular from Southern to Northern Europe, such as Portuguese, Spanish, Italian or Greek. It should also be kept in mind that many, if not most, IM languages in particular European nation-states originate from countries outside Europe. In particular the context of migration and minorization makes our proposed distinction between RM and IM languages ambiguous. We see, however, no better alternative.

2.2. Language and identity

The construction and/or consolidation of nation-states has enforced the belief that an official state language should correspond to each nation-state, and that this language should be regarded as a core value of national identity. The equation of language and national identity, however, is based on a denial of the co-existence of majority and minority languages within the borders of any nation-state and has its roots in the German Romanticism at the end of the 18th and the early 19th century (see Fishman 1973: 39–85, 1989: 105–175, 270–287; and Edwards 1985: 23–27 for historical overviews). The equation of German and Germany was a reaction to the rationalism of the Enlightenment and was also based on anti-French sentiments. The concept of nationalism emerged at the end of the 18th century; the concept of nationality only a century later. Romantic philosophers like Johann Gottfried Herder and Wilhelm von Humboldt laid the foundation for the emergence of a linguistic nationalism in Germany on the basis of which the German language and nation were conceived of as superior to the French ones. The French, however, were no less reluctant to express their conviction that the reverse was true. Although every nation-state is characterized by heterogeneity, including linguistic heterogeneity, nationalistic movements have always invoked this classical European discourse in their equalization of language and nation.

The USA has not remained immune to this type of nationalism either. The English-only movement, *US English*, was founded in 1983 out of a fear of the growing number of Hispanics on American soil (Fishman 1988; May 2001: 202–224; see also Wiley, this vol.). This organization resisted bilingual Spanish-English education from the beginning because such an approach would lead to "identity confusion". Similarly, attempts have been made to give the assignment of English as the official language of the USA a constitutional basis. This was done on the presupposition that the recognition of other languages (in particular Spanish) would undermine the foundations of the nation-state. This nationalism has its roots in a white, protestant, English-speaking elite (Edwards 1994: 177–178).

The relationship between language and identity is not a static but a dynamic phenomenon. During the last decades of the 20th century, this relationship underwent strong transnational changes. Within the European context, these changes occurred in three different arenas (see Oakes 2001):
- in the national arenas of the EU nation-states: the traditional identity of these nation-states has been challenged by major demographic changes (in particular in urban areas) as a consequence of migration and minorization;
- in the European arena: the concept of a European identity has emerged as a consequence of increasing cooperation and integration at the European level;
- in the global arena: our world has become smaller and more interactive as a consequence of the increasing availability of information and communication technology.

Major changes in each of these three arenas have led to the development of concepts such as a transnational citizenship and transnational multiple identities. Inhabitants of Europe no longer identify exclusively with singular nation-states, but give increasing evidence of multiple affiliations. At the EU level, the notion of a European identity was formally expressed for the first time in the *Declaration on European Identity* of December 1973 in Copenhagen. Numerous institutions and documents have propagated and promoted this idea ever since. The most concrete and tangible expressions of this idea to date have been the introduction of a European currency in 2002 and the proposals for a European constitution in 2004. In discussing the concept of a European identity, Oakes (2001: 127–131) emphasizes that the recognition of the concept of multiple transnational identities is a prerequisite rather than an obstacle for the acceptance of a European identity. The recognition of multiple transnational identities not only occurs among the traditional inhabitants of European nation-states but also among newcomers and IM groups in Europe. At the same time we see a strengthening of regional identities in many regions in Europe, in particular those where a RM language is in use.

Multiple transnational identities and affiliations will require new competencies of European citizens in the 21st century. These include the ability to deal with increasing cultural diversity and heterogeneity (Van Londen and De Ruijter 1999). Multilingualism can be considered a core competence for such ability. In this context, processes of both convergence and divergence occur. In the European and global arena, English has increasingly assumed the role of *lingua franca* for international communication (Oakes 2001: 131–136, 149–154). The rise of English has occurred at the cost of all other official state languages of Europe, including French. At the same time, a growing number of newcomers to the national arenas of the EU nation-states need competence in the languages of their source and target countries.

RM and IM languages have much in common, much more than is usually thought. On their sociolinguistic, educational, and political agendas, we find issues such as their actual spread, their domestic and public vitality, the processes and determinants of language maintenance *versus* language shift towards majority languages, the relationship between language, ethnicity, and identity, and the status of minority languages in schools, in particular in the compulsory stages of primary and secondary education. The origin of most RM languages as *minority* languages lies in the 19th century, when, during the processes of state-formation in Europe, they found themselves excluded from the state level, in particular from general education. RM languages did not become official languages of the nation-states that were then established. Centralizing tendencies and the ideology of *one language – one state* have threatened the continued existence of RM languages. The greatest threat to RM languages, however, is lack of intergenerational transmission. When parents stop speaking the ancestral language with their children, it becomes almost impossible to reverse the ensuing language shift. Education can also be a major factor in the maintenance and promotion of a minority language. For most RM languages, some kind of educational provisions have been established in an attempt at reversing ongoing language shift. Only in the last few decades have some of these RM languages become relatively well protected in legal terms, as well as by affirmative educational policies and programmes, both at the level of various nation-states and at the level of the EU.

There have always been speakers of IM languages in Europe, but these languages have only recently emerged as community languages spoken on a wide scale in urban Europe, due to intensified processes of migration and minorization. Turkish and Arabic are good examples of so-called "non-European" languages that are spoken and learned by millions of inhabitants of the EU nation-states. Although IM languages are often conceived of and transmitted as core values by IM language groups, they are much less protected than RM languages by affirmative action and legal measures, e.g. in education. In fact, the learning and certainly the teaching of IM languages are often seen by mainstream language speakers and by policy makers as obstacles to integration. At the European level, guidelines and directives regarding IM languages are scant and outdated. Despite the possibilities and challenges of comparing the status of RM and IM languages, amazingly few connections have been made in the sociolinguistic, educational, and political domains (Extra and Gorter 2001).

As yet, we lack a common referential framework for the languages under discussion. As RM and IM languages are spoken by different language communities, it may seem logical to refer to them as community languages. However, the designation "community languages" would lead to confusion at the surface level because this concept is already in use to refer to the official languages of the EU. In that sense the designation "community languages" is occupied territory. From an inventory of the different terms in use, we learn that there are no standardized designations for these languages across nation-states. Table 2 gives a non-exhaustive overview of the nomenclature. The concept of "lesser used languages" has been adopted at the EU level; the *European Bureau for Lesser Used Languages* (EBLUL), established in Brussels and Dublin, speaks and acts on behalf of "the autochthonous regional and minority languages of the EU". Table 2 shows that the utilized terminology varies not only across different nation-states, but also across different types of education.

Table 2. Nomenclature of the field (source: Extra and Yağmur 2004: 19)

Reference to the people
– national/historical/regional/indigenous minorities *versus* non-national/non-historical/non-territorial/non-indigenous minorities
– non-national residents
– foreigners, étrangers, Ausländer
– (im)migrants
– newcomers, new Xmen (e.g., new Dutchmen)
– co-citizens (instead of citizens)
– ethnic/cultural/ethnocultural minorities
– linguistic minorities
– allochthones (e.g., in the Netherlands), allophones (e.g., in Canada)
– non-English-speaking (NES) residents (in particular in the USA)
– *anderstaligen* (Dutch: those who speak other languages)
– coloured/black people, visible minorities (the latter in particular in Canada)
Reference to their languages
– community languages (in Europe *versus* Australia)
– ancestral/heritage languages (common concept in Canada)
– national/historical/regional/indigenous minority languages *versus* non-territorial/non-regional/non-indigenous/non-European minority languages
– autochthonous *versus* allochthonous minority languages
– lesser used/less widely used/less widely taught languages (in EBLUL context)
– stateless/diaspora languages (in particular used for Romani)
– languages other than English (LOTE: common concept in Australia)

Reference to the teaching of these languages
– instruction in own language (and culture) – mother tongue teaching (MTT) – home language instruction (HLI) – community language teaching (CLT) – regional minority language instruction *versus* immigrant minority language instruction – enseignement des langues et cultures d'origine (ELCO: in French/Spanish primary schools) – enseignement des langues vivantes (ELV: in French/Spanish secondary schools) – muttersprachlicher Unterricht (MSU: in German primary schools) – muttersprachlicher Ergänzungsunterricht (in German primary/secondary schools) – herkunftssprachlicher Unterricht (in German primary/secondary schools)

2.3. The European discourse on immigrant minorities and integration

In the European public discourse on IM groups, two major characteristics emerge: IM groups are often referred to as *foreigners* (*étrangers*, *Ausländer*) and as being in need of *integration*. First of all, it is common practice to refer to IM groups in terms of *non-national* residents and to their languages in terms of *non-territorial, non-regional, non-indigenous,* or *non-European* languages (see Table 2). The call for integration is in sharp contrast with the language of exclusion. This conceptual exclusion rather than inclusion in the European public discourse derives from a restrictive interpretation of the notions of citizenship and nationality. From a historical point of view, such notions are commonly shaped by a constitutional *ius sanguinis* (law of the blood), in terms of which nationality derives from parental origins, in contrast to *ius soli* (law of the soil), in terms of which nationality derives from the country of birth. When European emigrants left their continent in the past and colonized countries abroad, they legitimized their claim to citizenship by spelling out *ius soli* in the constitutions of these countries of settlement. Good examples of this strategy can be found in English-dominant immigration countries like the USA, Canada, Australia, and South Africa. In establishing the constitutions of these (sub)continents, no consultation took place with the native inhabitants, such as Indians, Inuit, Aboriginals, and Zulus, respectively. At home, however, Europeans predominantly upheld *ius sanguinis* in their constitutions and/or perceptions of nationality and citizenship, in spite of the growing numbers of newcomers who strive for an equal status as citizens.

A second major characteristic of the European public discourse on IM groups is the focus on *integration*. This notion is both popular and vague, and it may actually refer to a whole spectrum of underlying concepts that vary over space and time. The extremes of the spectrum range from assimilation to multiculturalism. The concept of assimilation is based on the premise that cultural differences between IM groups and established majority groups should and will disappear over time in a society which is proclaimed to be culturally homogeneous. On the other side of the spectrum, the concept of multiculturalism is based on the premise that such differences are an asset to a pluralist society, which actually promotes cultural diversity in terms of new resources and opportunities. While the concept of assimilation focuses on unilateral tasks of *newcomers*, the concept of multiculturalism focuses on multilateral tasks for all inhabitants in changing societies. In practice, established majority groups often make strong demands on IM groups for integration in terms of assimilation and are commonly very reluctant to promote or even accept the notion of cultural diversity as a determining characteristic of an increasingly multicultural environment.

It is interesting to compare the underlying assumptions of "integration" in the European public discourse on IM groups at the national level with assumptions at the level of transnational cooperation and legislation. In the latter context, European politicians are eager to stress the importance of a proper balance between the loss and the maintenance of "national" norms and values. A prime concern in the public debate on such norms and values is cultural and linguistic diversity, mainly in terms of the official state languages of the EU. These languages are often referred to as core values of cultural identity. Paradoxically, in the same public discourse, IM languages and cultures are commonly conceived as sources of problems and deficits and as obstacles to integration, while official state languages and cultures in an expanding EU are regarded as sources of enrichment and as prerequisites for integration. This discussion on public discourse is relevant for applied linguistic studies of ideologies and rethorics in any multicultural context.

3. Demographic perspectives

Collecting reliable information about the number and spread of RM and IM population groups in EU countries is no easy enterprise. What is, however, more interesting than numbers or estimates of the size of particular groups, are the *criteria* for such numbers or estimates. Throughout the EU it is common practice to present data on RM groups on the basis of (home) language and/or ethnicity and to present data on IM groups on the basis of nationality and/or country of birth. However, *convergence* between these criteria for the two groups emerges over time, due to the increasing period of migration and minorization of IM groups in EU countries. Due to their prolonged/permanent stay, there is strong erosion in the utility of nationality or birth-country statistics. In this section, our focus is on RM and IM languages across Europe, respectively.

3.1. Regional minority languages across Europe

We will present an approximation of the distribution of different RM language groups in the EU, although we are faced with much diversity in the quality of the data. In some nation-states, there are fairly accurate figures because a language question has been included in the census several times; in other cases, we only have rough estimates by insiders to the language group (usually language activists who want to boost the figures) or by outsiders (e.g., state officials who quite often want to downplay the number of speakers). Figure 2 serves to illustrate our overview visually and is derived from the Mercator Education website (see also Section 5.1).

We will use a simple typology and distinguish between five categories of RM languages within the EU (O'Riagáin 2001; Gorter 1996). For each type of language we will give some examples and estimates. Figures for numbers of speakers are almost always problematic. In only a few cases they are based upon recent census or survey outcomes. Many other figures are, due to the lack of other data, derived from informed estimates by experts (these are sometimes referred to as "disputed numbers"). Also, some languages would perhaps not be included according to certain criteria; others might be split up further (e.g., for some outsiders, Frisian in the Netherlands and North Frisian and Saterfrisian in Germany are considered as one language, although speakers of different varieties cannot understand each other and would disagree). Again other varieties would be taken together as one group (e.g, outsiders would not distinguish between Catalan in Valencia and Catalonia, whereas this distinction is an important political issue in the region). Similarly, Limburgian is usually perceived as a dialect of Dutch, but in 1998 it was recognized by the government of the Netherlands as a regional language in terms of the *European Charter for Regional or Minority Languages*; in Belgium, where the same variety is spoken, the government has so far not followed this step. More extensive figures of RM languages in (mainly Western) Europe can be found in Breathnach (1998), Euromosaic (1996), Instituto della Enciclopedia Italiana (1986), Siguan (1990), and Tjeerdsma (1998), as well as in the Ethnologue (2001).

The first category concerns unique RM languages, spoken in only one EU member-state. Some examples of language communities in this category are Breton (300,000) and Corsican (160,000) in France; North Frisian (8,000), Saterfrisian (2,000) and Sorbian (60,000) in Germany; Friulian (550,000), Ladin (35,000) and Sardinian (1,000,000) in Italy; Frisian (450,000) in the Netherlands; Kashubian (200,000) in Poland; Ruthenian (25,000) in Slovakia; Galician (2,300,000) and Asturian (450,000) in Spain; Scottish Gaelic (59,000), Scots (1,500,000), Welsh (575,000) and Cornish (200) in the United Kingdom.

The second category concerns those RM languages that are spoken in more than one EU member-state. In this category we include among others the fol-

Figure 2. Overview of RM languages across European nation-states
(source: Mercator Education, Fryske Akademy, Leeuwarden)

lowing languages: Basque in Spain (Basque Autonomous Community 515,000, Navarre 50,000) and in France (Iparralde 70,000); Catalan in Spain (Catalonia 4 million, Balearic Islands 428,000, Valencia 1.9 million, Aragon 48,000), in

France (102,000) and in Italy (20,000); Occitan in Spain (4000), in France (3,500,000) and in Italy (50,000); Sami in Sweden (18,000) and in Finland (3000, spread over the dialects North, Inari and Solt); Low-Saxon in the Netherlands (1.8 million) and Low-German (8 million) in Germany.

The third category concerns RM languages which are a minority language in one state, but the official mainstream language in another, neighbouring state (the latter not necessarily being a member-state of the EU). There are quite a few of them and the linguistic relationship between the dominated and dominant language differs from case to case. Some of these languages might perhaps also be considered as examples of category 1. Multiple cases are for instance Albanian in Italy (100,000) and Greece (80,000); Croatian in Italy (2,000) and Austria (25,000); German in Belgium (69,000), Czech Republic (50,000), Denmark (20,000), France (975,000), Italy (280,000) and Poland (500,000); Polish in Germany (200,000), Czech Republic (50,000), Lithuania (200,000) and Latvia (57,000). Other examples are Berber (25,000) and Portuguese (3,600) in Spain; Dutch (80,000) in France; Danish (50,000) in Germany; Greek (11,000) in Italy.

The fourth category consists of two languages with a special status; they are official state languages but not official working languages of the EU. These are Luxemburgish (359,000), also spoken in France (35,000), and Irish (1.6 million speakers have some ability, 340,000 use it on a daily basis), also spoken in the United Kingdom (in Northern Ireland by 165,000 speakers who have some knowledge, of whom perhaps 25,000 use it regularly). Recently a request has been tabled for the official and working status of Irish in the EU. Maltese has obtained such a status when Malta entered the EU in 2004, although the status of Maltese is similar to that of Luxemburgish and Irish.

The fifth category consists finally of non-territorial minority languages, which exist in smaller or larger numbers in almost all EU nation-states; the most prominent ones are Romani and Yiddish.

Our typology refers mainly to the geographic dimension of state boundaries and partially to legal status. In that sense the typology has its inherent difficulties. The distinctions may be gradual or some language groups may not fit in nicely (e.g., Slovenian, Croatian or Czech). Of course, other typologies are possible (e.g., Edwards 1991: 215; Euromosaic 1996). Our aim is to present a typology here for the purpose of making the diversity of contexts visible (see also Gorter et al. 1990).

Demographic size has some importance for the sociolinguistic status of RM languages. Included in the latter are factors such as use in the family, legal status, institutional support by government, provisions in the media and in cultural life, development of a written standard, economic prosperity of the community, attitudes to language(s), and level of organized activities. The demographic and sociolinguistic status are related strongly with the educational status of these languages. Educational provisions in turn influence the numerical development and social status of RM languages.

3.2. Immigrant minority languages across Europe

Comparative information on population figures in EU nation-states can be obtained from the Statistical Office of the EU in Luxembourg (*EuroStat*). An overall decrease of the indigenous population has been observed in all EU countries over the last decade; at the same time, there has been an increase in the IM figures. Although free movement of migrants between EU nation-states is legally permitted, most IM groups in EU countries originate from non-EU countries. For various reasons, reliable demographic information on IM groups in EU countries is difficult to obtain. For some groups or countries, no updated information is available or no such data have ever been collected at all. Moreover, official statistics only reflect IM groups with legal resident status. Another source of disparity is the different data collection systems being used, ranging from nation-wide census data to more or less representative surveys. Most importantly, however, the most widely used criteria for IM status – nationality and/or country of birth – have become less valid over time because of an increasing trend toward naturalization and births within the countries of residence. In addition, most residents from former colonies already have the nationality of their country of immigration.

In most EU countries, only population data on nationality and/or birth country (of person and parents) are available. To illustrate the significance of such figures, Table 3 gives comparative statistics of population groups in the Netherlands, based on the birth-country criterion (of person and/or mother and/or father) *versus* the nationality criterion, as derived from the Dutch Central Bureau of Statistics (2000):

Table 3. Population of the Netherlands based on the combined birth-country criterion (BC-PMF) *versus* the nationality criterion on January 1, 1999 (*Antilleans are Dutch nationals) (source: CBS 2000)

Groups	BC-PMF	Nationality	Absolute difference
Dutch	13,061,000	15,097,000	2,036,000
Turks	300,000	102,000	198,000
Moroccans	252,000	128,600	123,400
Surinamese	297,000	10,500	286,500
Antilleans	99,000	*	99,000
Italians	33,000	17,600	15,400
(former) Yugoslavs	63,000	22,300	40,700
Spaniards	30,000	16,800	13,200

Groups	BC-PMF	Nationality	Absolute difference
Somalians	27,000	8,900	18,100
Chinese	28,000	7,500	20,500
Indonesians	407,000	8,400	398,600
Other groups	1,163,000	339,800	823,200
Total	15,760,000	15,760,000	–

Table 3 shows strong criterion effects of birth country *versus* nationality. All IM groups are underrepresented in nationality-based statistics. However, the combined birth-country criterion of person/mother/father does not solve the identification problem either. The use of this criterion leads to non-identification in at least the following cases:
- an increasing group of third and later generations (cf. Moluccan/Indonesian and Chinese communities in the Netherlands);
- different ethnolinguistic groups from the same country of origin (cf. Turks *versus* Kurds from Turkey or Berbers *versus* Arabs from Morocco);
- the same ethnocultural group from different countries of origin (cf. Chinese from China *versus* Vietnam);
- ethnocultural groups without territorial status (cf. Roma people).

From the data presented in Table 3, it is clear that collecting reliable information about the actual number and spread of IM population groups in EU countries is no easy enterprise. In 1982, the *Australian Institute of Multicultural Affairs* recognized the above-mentioned identification problems for inhabitants of Australia and proposed including questions in their censuses on birth country (of person and parents), ethnic origin (based on self-categorization in terms of which ethnic group a person considers him/herself to belong to), and home language use. As yet, little experience has been gained in EU countries with periodical censuses, or, if such censuses have been held, with questions on ethnicity or (home) language use. Although census data exist on RM languages (e.g., on Welsh in Great Britain), no such data exist on IM languages. In Table 4, the four criteria mentioned are discussed in terms of their major (dis)advantages.

Table 4. Criteria for the definition and identification of population groups in a multicultural society (P/F/M = person/father/mother) (source: Extra and Gorter 2001: 9)

Criterion	Advantages	Disadvantages
Nationality (NAT) (P/F/M)	– objective – relatively easy to establish	– (intergenerational) erosion through naturalization or double NAT – NAT not always indicative of ethnicity/identity – some (e.g., ex-colonial) groups have NAT of immigration country
Birth country (BC) (P/F/M)	– objective – relatively easy to establish	– intergenerational erosion through births in immigration country – BC not always indicative of ethnicity/identity – invariable/deterministic: does not take account of dynamics in society (in contrast to all other criteria)
Self-categorization (SC)	– touches the heart of the matter – emancipatory: SC takes account of person's own conception of ethnicity/identity	– subjective by definition: also determined by the language/ethnicity of interviewer and by the spirit of times – multiple SC possible – historically charged, especially by World War II experiences
Home language (HL)	– HL is most significant criterion of ethnicity in communication processes – HL data are prerequisite for government policy in areas such as public information or education	– complex criterion: who speaks what language to whom and when? – language is not always a core value of ethnicity/identity – useless in one-person households

First of all, Table 4 reveals that there is no simple road to solve the identification problem. Moreover, inspection of the criteria for multicultural population groups is as important as the actual figures themselves. Taken from a European perspective, there is a top-down development over time in the utility and utilization of different types of criteria, inevitably going from nationality and birth-country criteria in present statistics to self-categorization and home language in the future. The latter two criteria are generally conceived as complementary criteria. Self-categorization and home language references need not coincide, as languages may be conceived to variable degrees as core values of ethnocultural identity in contexts of migration and minorization. Both types of criteria have been suggested and used outside Europe in various countries with a longer immigration history, and, for this reason, with a longstanding history of collecting census data on multicultural population groups (Kertzer and Arel 2002). This holds in particular for non-European immigration countries in which English is the dominant language, like Australia, Canada, South Africa, and the USA. To identify the multicultural composition of their populations, these four countries employ a variety of questions in their periodical censuses. In Table 5, an overview of this array of questions is provided; for each country, the given census is taken as the norm.

Table 5: Overview of census questions in four multicultural countries (source: Extra and Yağmur 2004: 67)

Questions in the census	Australia 2001	Canada 2001	SA 2001	USA 2000	Coverage
1 Nationality of respondent	+	+	+	+	4
2 Birth country of respondent	+	+	+	+	4
3 Birth country of parents	+	+	–	–	2
4 Ethnicity	–	+	–	+	2
5 Ancestry	+	+	–	+	3
6 Race	–	+	+	+	3
7 Mother tongue	–	+	–	–	1
8 Language used at home	+	+	+	+	4
9 Language used at work	–	+	–	–	1
10 Proficiency in English	+	+	–	+	3
11 Religion	+	+	+	–	3
Total of dimensions	7	11	5	7	30

Both the type and number of questions are different per country. Canada has a prime position with the highest number of questions. Only three questions have been asked in all countries, whereas two questions have been asked in only one country. Four different questions have been asked about language. The operationalization of questions also shows interesting differences, both between and within countries over time (see also Clyne 1991).

Questions about ethnicity, ancestry and/or race have proven to be problematic in all of the countries under consideration. In some countries, ancestry and ethnicity have been conceived as equivalent. As far as ethnicity and ancestry have been distinguished in census questions, the former concept related most commonly to present self-categorization of the respondent and the latter to former generations. In what ways respondents themselves interpret both concepts, however, remains a problem that cannot be solved easily. While, according to Table 5, "ethnicity" has been mentioned in recent censuses of only two countries, four language-related questions have been asked in one to four countries. Only in Canada has the concept of "mother tongue" been included. It has been defined for respondents as *the language first learnt at home in childhood and still understood*, while two other questions related to the language *most often* used at home/work. Table 5 shows the added value of language-related census questions for the definition and identification of multicultural populations, in particular the added value of the question on home language use compared to questions on the more opaque concepts of mother tongue and ethnicity. Although the language-related census questions in the four countries under consideration differ in their precise formulation and commentary, the outcomes of these questions are generally conceived as cornerstones for educational policies with respect to the teaching of English as a first or second language and the teaching of languages other than English. A comparison of such questions seems highly relevant for other applied linguistic studies.

The presented overview shows that large-scale home language surveys are both feasible and meaningful, and that the interpretation of the resulting database is made easier by transparent and multiple questions on home language use. These conclusions become even more pertinent in the context of gathering data on multicultural *school* populations. European experiences in this domain have been gathered in particular in Great Britain and Sweden. In both countries, extensive municipal home language statistics have been collected through local educational authorities by asking school children questions about their oral and written skills in languages other than the mainstream language, and about their participation in and need for education in these languages.

An important similarity in the questions about home language use in these surveys is that the outcomes are based on reported rather than observed facts. Answers to questions on home language use may be coloured by the language of the questions themselves (which may or may not be the primary language of the respondent), by the ethnicity of the interviewer (which may or may not be the same as the ethnicity of the respondent), by the (perceived) goals of the sampling (which may or may not be defined by central state or local authorities), and by the spirit of the times (which may or may not be in favour of multiculturalism). These problems become even more evident in a school-related context in which pupils are respondents. Apart from the problems mentioned, the answers may be coloured by peer-group pressure and they may lead to interpretation problems in attempts to identify and classify languages. For a discussion of these and other possible effects, we refer to Nicholas (1988) and Alladina (1993). The problems referred to are inherent characteristics of large-scale data gathering through questionnaires about language-related behaviour and can only be compensated by small-scale data gathering through observing actual language behaviour. Such small-scale ethnographic research is not an alternative to large-scale language surveys, but a potentially valuable complement. For a discussion of (cor)relations between reported and measured bilingualism of IM children in the Netherlands, we refer to Broeder and Extra (1998).

Given the decreasing significance of nationality and birth-country criteria in the European context, the combined criteria of self-categorization (ethnicity) and home language use are potentially promising alternatives for obtaining basic information on the increasingly multicultural composition of European nation-states. As a result, convergence will emerge between the utilized criteria for the definition and identification of IM and RM groups in such societies. The added value of home language statistics is that they offer valuable insights into the distribution and vitality of home languages across different population groups and thus raise the awareness of multilingualism. Studies of language awareness in applied linguistics could profit form these insights.

4. Sociolinguistic perspectives

In this section, our focus is on the status of RM and IM languages in the major intergenerational domain of language transmission, i.e. the home.

4.1. Regional minority languages at home

There are many publications on the status and use of RM languages, both in Europe and abroad (e.g., Gorter et al. 1990). Baetens Beardsmore (1993) focuses on RM languages in Western Europe, whereas Synak and Wicherkiewicz (1997), Bratt-Paulston and Peckham (1998), and Hogan-Brun and Wolf (2003) deal with RM languages in Central and Eastern Europe. In a number of European countries a periodical census will include one or a few questions on language and ethnicity, but in other countries no such questions will be asked. An additional tool for obtaining data are sociolinguistic surveys. There are a handful of RM language communities where such surveys are carried out with regular intervals (ELSN 1996).

In Ireland there is a tradition of both a census that contains questions on language abilities and language use (NISRA 2004) and regular sociolinguistic surveys (O'Riagáin and O'Gliasáin 1994). The Irish case has thus been well documented. In language policy studies, Irish is regularly presented as the classic case of the failure of language management (Spolsky 2004; on language revival see also Edwards, this vol.). In Wales there is also a tradition of census data. A question on speaking Welsh has been included in the census since 1891, when 54% of the population reported to be able to speak Welsh. Since then the proportion of people speaking Welsh has declined, and in 2001 about 21% reported the ability to speak Welsh. In 2001, 39% of children aged 10–15 reported to be able to speak Welsh compared with 25% of 16–19 year olds (Office of National Statistics 2005). Other surveys give slightly more optimistic outcomes. Language use surveys moreover give deeper insight into the relation between language competence and actual use and the relevance of this relationship for language planning (Williams and Morris 2000).

In Spain the census has questions on the official languages of the Autonomous Communities in the Basque Country, Catalunya and Galicia. Moreover, in the Basque Country the regional government has carried out large-scale surveys in 1990, 1995 and 2000, which also cover Navarre and Iparralde (the Basque part in France). According to the most recent general survey (Euskararen Jarraipena III 2003), the percentage of Basque-Spanish or Basque-French bilinguals for the whole of the Basque Country (in Spain and France) is 22%, and 14.5% are "passive bilingual". With a few exceptions, the rest of the population is monolingual in either Spanish or French. The number of bilinguals in the Basque Autonomous Community is increasing and it is now 29% of the population. The Basque Government actively encourages the use of Basque as language of instruction. At present, 83% of kindergarten/primary school children and 65% of secondary school children have Basque as language of instruction (Cenoz 2001). Apart from promoting the use of Basque in education, the Basque Government has created specific institutions to teach and promote the use of Basque in other sectors such as government services, the media or private companies. This policy has had some effect in restoring the status of Basque and reversing language shift. In spite of the support given by the Basque Government, Basque is still a language at risk and according to the 2001 survey, only 11.9% of the population use Basque more than Spanish and 6.8% of the population consider that they use Basque as much as Spanish (Euskararen Jarraipena III 2003).

The Netherlands has not had a census since 1971 and never had a question on language. In the province of Friesland surveys have been carried out at regular intervals in 1967, 1980 and 1994 (Gorter 1994). The most recent figures show that approximately 94% of the population can understand Frisian, 74% can speak Frisian, 65% can read it and 17% can write it (Gorter and Jonkman 1995). Over a time span of more than 25 years a slow decline is observed in speaking proficiency and some increase in writing abilities. There is, however, an increased language shift among younger generations towards Dutch as their first language. The use of Frisian shows an uneven pattern over differing social domains. In the domains of the family, work and the village community Frisian demonstrates a relatively strong position, where a small majority of the population still uses Frisian. In the more formal domains of education, media, public administration and law, Dutch dominates (Gorter 2001).

The Euromosaic (1996) project has provided a general overview of 48 language communities in the EU. In about half of those cases data were also collected through small-scale sociolinguistic surveys. The European Language Survey Network has developed a core module of 28 questions that can be used as a standard for questionnaires in any RM language community in Europe in order to obtain a basic overview of the language situation (ELSN 1996; Gorter 1997).

4.2. Immigrant minority languages at home

Given the overwhelming focus on mainstream language acquisition by IM groups, there is much less evidence on the status and use of IM languages across Europe as a result of processes of immigration and minorization. In contrast to RM languages, IM languages have no established status in terms of period and area of residence. Obviously, typological differences between IM languages across EU nation-states do exist, e.g., in terms of the status of IM languages as EU or non-EU languages, or as languages of former colonies.

Tosi (1984) offers an early case study on Italian as an IM language in England. Most studies of IM languages in Europe have focused on a spectrum of IM languages at the level of one particular multilingual city (Kroon 1990; Baker and Eversley 2000), one particular nation-state (LMP 1985; Alladina and Edwards 1991; Extra and Verhoeven 1993a; Extra and De Ruiter 2001; Caubet, Chaker, and Sibille 2002; Extra et al. 2002), or on one particular IM language at the state or European level (Tilmatine 1997 and Obdeijn and De Ruiter 1998 on Arabic in Europe, or Jørgensen 2003 on Turkish in Europe). A number of studies have taken both a crossnational and a crosslinguistic perspective on the status and use of IM languages in Europe (e.g., Husén and Opper 1983; Jaspaert and Kroon 1991; Extra and Verhoeven 1993b, 1998; Extra and Gorter 2001). Churchill (1986) has offered an early crossnational perspective on the education of IM children in the OECD countries, whereas Reid and Reich (1992) have carried out a crossnational evaluative study of 15 pilot projects on the education of IM children supported by the European Commission.

Here, we present the major outcomes of the *Multilingual Cities Project* (MCP), carried out as a multiple case study in six major multicultural cities in different EU nation-states. For a full report of the project we refer to Extra and Yağmur (2004). In the participating cities, ranging from Northern to Southern

Europe, Germanic and/or Romance languages have a dominant status in public life. Table 6 gives an overview of the resulting database (only in The Hague were data also collected at secondary schools). The total crossnational sample consists of more than 160,000 pupils.

Table 6. Overview of the MCP database (*Dutch-medium schools only; **Réseau d'Education Prioritaire only) (source: Extra and Yağmur 2004: 115)

City	Total of schools	Total of schools in the survey	Total of pupils in schools	Total of pupils in the survey	Age range of pupils
Brussels	117 *	110 *	11,500	10,300	6–12
Göteborg	170	122	36,100	21,300	6–12
Hamburg	231 public 17 catholic	218 public 14 catholic	54,900	46,000	6–11
Lyon	173 **	42 **	60,000	11,650	6–11
Madrid	708 public 411 catholic	133 public 21 catholic	202,000 99,000	30,000	5–12
The Hague	142 primary 30 secondary	109 primary 26 secondary	41,170 19,000	27,900 13,700	4–12 12–17

On the basis of the home language profiles of all major language groups, a crosslinguistic and pseudolongitudinal comparison was made of the reported multiple dimensions of language proficiency, language choice, language dominance, and language preference. For comparative analyses, these four dimensions have been operationalized as follows:
- language proficiency: the extent to which the home language under consideration is *understood*;
- language choice: the extent to which this language is commonly spoken at home *with the mother*;
- language dominance: the extent to which this home language is spoken *best*;
- language preference: the extent to which this home language is *preferably* spoken.

The operationalization of the first and second dimensions (language proficiency and language choice) was aimed at a maximal scope for tracing language vitality. Language understanding is generally the least demanding of the four language skills involved, and the mother acts generally as the major gatekeeper for intergenerational language transmission (Clyne 2003). The final aim was the construction of a language vitality index (henceforth LVI), based on the outcomes of the four dimensions presented above. These four dimensions are compared as proportional scores in terms of the mean proportion of pupils per language group that indicated a positive response to the relevant questions. The LVI is, in turn, the mean value of these four proportional scores. This LVI is by definition an arbitrary index, in the sense that the *chosen* dimensions with the *chosen* operationalizations are *equally* weighted.

The outcomes of the local surveys were aggregated in one crossnational home language survey (HLS) database. Two criteria were used to select 20 languages for crossnational analyses: Each language should be represented by at least three cities, and each city should be represented in the crossnational HLS database by at least 30 pupils in the age range of 6–11 years. Our focus on this age range was motivated by comparability considerations: This range is represented in the local HLS databases of all participating cities (see Table 6). Romani/Sinte was included in the crossnational analyses because of its special status in our list of 20 languages as a language without territorial status. Two languages have an exceptional status: English "invaded" the local HLS's as a language of international prestige, and Romani/Sinte is solidly represented in Hamburg and Göteborg only.

In the crossnational and crosslinguistic analyses, three age groups and three generations are distinguished. The age groups consist of children aged 6/7, 8/9, and 10/11 years old. The three generations have been operationalized as follows: G1: pupil + father + mother born abroad; G2: pupil born in country of residence, father *and/or* mother born abroad; G3: pupil + father + mother born in country of residence. On the basis of this categorization, intergenerational shift can be globally estimated. In Table 7 we present the language vitality indices (LVI) of the combined age groups (6–11 years) per language group in decreasing order.

Table 7. LVI of combined age groups (6–11 years) per language group in decreasing order (derived from Extra and Yağmur 2004: 375)

No.	Language group	LVI	No.	Language group	LVI
1	Romani/Sinte	70	11	Polish	56
2	Turkish	68	12	Somali	55
3	Urdu	68	13	Portuguese	54
4	Armenian	63	14	Berber	52
5	Russian	60	15	Kurdish	51
6	Serbian/Croatian/Bosnian	59	16	Spanish	48
7	Albanian	59	17	French	44
8	Vietnamese	58	18	Italian	39
9	Chinese	58	19	English	36
10	Arabic	58	20	German	33

Romani/Sinte was found to have the highest language vitality across age groups, and English and German had the lowest. The bottom position of English was explained by the fact that this language has a higher status as *lingua franca* than as language at home. The top position of Romani/Sinte was also observed in earlier and similar research amongst children in the Netherlands, and confirmed by various other studies of this particular language community. One reason why language vitality is a core value for the Roma across Europe is the absence of source country references as alternative markers of identity – in contrast to almost all other language groups under consideration.

There are strong differences between language groups in the distribution of pupils across different generations. In most language groups, second-generation pupils are best represented and third-generation pupils least. In conformity with expectations, the obtained data finally show a stronger decrease of language vitality across generations than across age groups. The strongest intergenerational shift between first- and third-generation pupils emerges for Polish, whereas the strongest intergenerational maintenance of language vitality occurs for Romani/Sinte and Turkish.

The local language surveys have delivered a wealth of hidden evidence on the distribution and vitality of IM languages at home across European cities and nation-states. Apart from Madrid, late-comer amongst our focal cities in respect of immigration, the proportion of primary school children in whose homes other languages were used next to or instead of the mainstream language ranged per city between one third and more than a half. The total number of traced other languages ranged per city between 50 and 90; the common pattern was that few languages were often referred to by the children and that many languages were referred to only a few times. The findings show that making use of more than one language is a way of life for an increasing number of children across Europe. Mainstream and non-mainstream languages should not be conceived of in terms of competition. Rather, the data show that these languages are used as alternatives, dependent on such factors as type of context or interlocutor. The data also make clear that the use of other languages at home does not occur at the cost of competence in the mainstream language. Many children who addressed their parents in another language reported to be dominant in the mainstream language.

Amongst the major 20 languages in the participating cities, 10 languages are of European origin and 10 are not. These findings show that the traditional concept of language diversity in Europe should be reconsidered and extended. The outcomes of the local language surveys also demonstrate the high status of English amongst primary school children across Europe. Its intrusion in the children's homes is apparent from the position of English in the top five of non-national languages referred to by the children in all participating cities. This outcome cannot be explained as an effect of migration and minorization only.

The children's reference to English also derives from the status of English as the international language of power and prestige. English has become the dominant *lingua franca* for cross-national communication across Europe. Moreover, children have access to English through a variety of media, and English is commonly taught in particular grades at primary schools. In addition, children in all participating cities expressed a desire to learn a variety of languages that are not taught at school.

The outcomes of the local language surveys also show that children who took part in instruction in particular languages at school reported higher levels of literacy in these languages than children who did not take part in such instruction. Both the reported reading proficiency and the reported writing proficiency profited strongly from language instruction. The differences between participants and non-participants in language instruction were significant for both forms of literacy skills and for all the 20 language groups. In this domain in particular, the added value of language instruction for language maintenance and development is clear.

5. Educational perspectives

In this section we discuss the status of RM and IM languages in European education, respectively. Our focus is on primary and/or secondary schools as part of compulsory education in EU countries (on education, see also Bieswanger, this vol.).

5.1. Regional minority languages in education

In the *European Framework Convention on National Minorities* and in the *European Charter for Regional or Minority Languages* we find a sort of European standard. The groups covered by these two treaties are RM languages. The Framework Convention outlines some aims in a very general sense. In that way it forces a standard on the states that become signatories. As far as education is concerned, there is first of all the encouragement "to foster knowledge of the culture, language and history of the national minorities, also among the majority" (Article 12) as well as "the recognition of the right to learn the minority language" (Article 14). This means that all citizens have to be informed, through the school curriculum, about minorities, and also that members of a RM group have a right to receive at least some minimal RM language teaching.

In March 1998, the Council of Europe's *European Charter for Regional or Minority Languages* came into operation. The Charter functions as an international instrument for the comparison of legal measures and facilities of member-states in this policy domain (Craith 2003), and is aimed at the protection and the promotion of "the historical regional or minority languages of Europe". The concepts of "regional" and "minority" languages are not specified in the Charter and IM languages are explicitly excluded from the Charter. States are free in their choice of which RM languages to include. Also, the degree of protection is not prescribed; thus, a state can choose tight or loose policies. The result is a rich variety of different provisions accepted by the various states.

The European Charter is much more elaborate on the use of language in education than the European Framework Convention. The Charter offers the adhering states the opportunity of choice between different alternatives. Even if one has decided upon the goals of education, what languages are actually used within the curriculum can vary from situation to situation. The complexity can be summarized as a typology with four categories: (1) no RM language teaching at all; (2) the RM language as subject, the mainstream language as medium of instruction; (3) both the RM language and the mainstream language as medium of instruction; and (4) the RM language as medium of instruction and the mainstream language as subject. The fifth logical possibility, no teaching of the mainstream language, does not occur.

The number of RM languages in Europe for which there is no teaching at all, is decreasing, although in many cases there is only a very small amount of teaching available, confined to pre-primary education only (e.g., Saterfrisian in Germany). What happens most frequently is the pattern denoted in category 2, with the RM language as subject. Categories 3 and 4 contain fewer language groups, and especially category 4, whenever it occurs (Basque Country, Wales), is limited to a particular level of the educational system or to particular types of schools (immersion education).

Of greatest importance are, of course, the final outcomes of RM language teaching. Does such teaching lead to increased RM language maintenance or has it actually encouraged the transition to the mainstream language? Very few evaluation studies have been carried out throughout Europe. Here is still a task waiting for applied linguists. In the case of transitional education, where only a small amount of attention is given to the RM language (e.g., one lesson per week only at primary level), this may actually work as a stimulus for language shift to the mainstream language. In such cases, the RM language is often defined as a "learning deficit" which has to be remedied through education. In the case of stronger provisions for RM language teaching, learning the RM language is conceived as enrichment and the language is defined as worthy of maintenance and promotion. The outcome of such education is a contribution to cultural pluralism, and in principle, pupils do become bilingual and biliteral. Examples of such well-established RM languages are Catalan, Basque, Welsh, and Swedish (in Finland).

5.2. Immigrant minority languages in education

Across Europe, large contrasts occur in the status of IM languages at school, depending on particular nation-states, or even particular federal states within nation-states (as in Germany), and depending on particular IM languages, being official state languages in other European (Union) countries or not. Most commonly, IM languages are not part of mainstream education. In Great Britain, for example, IM languages are not part of the so-called "national" curriculum, and they are dealt with in various types of so-called "complementary" education at out-of-school hours (e.g., Martin et al. 2004).

Here, we present the major outcomes of a comparative study on the teaching of the languages of IM groups in the six EU cities and countries of the MCP, referred to in Section 4.2. Being aware of crossnational differences in denotation, we use the concept *community language teaching* (henceforth CLT) when referring to this type of education (see also Table 2). Our rationale for the CLT concept rather than the concepts *mother tongue teaching* or *home language instruction* is the inclusion of a broad spectrum of potential target groups. From a historical point of view, most of the countries in the MCP show a similar chronological development in their argumentation in favour of CLT. CLT was generally introduced into primary education with a view to family remigration. This objective was also clearly expressed in *Directive 77/486* of the European Community, on 25 July 1977. The Directive focused on the education of the children of "migrant workers" with the aim "principally to facilitate their possible reintegration into the Member State of origin". As is clear from this formulation, the Directive excluded all IM children originating from non-EU countries, although these children formed and form the large part of IM children in European primary schools. At that time, Sweden was not a EU member-state, and CLT policies for IM children in Sweden were not directed towards remigration but modelled according to bilingual education policies for the large minority of Finnish-speaking children in Sweden.

In the 1970s, the above argumentation for CLT was increasingly abandoned. Demographic developments showed no substantial signs of families remigrating to their source countries; instead, a process of family reunion and minorization came about in the target countries. This development resulted in a conceptual shift, and CLT became primarily aimed at combatting disadvantages. CLT had to bridge the gap between the home and the school environment, and to encourage school achievement in "regular" subjects. Because such an approach tended to underestimate the importance of other dimensions, a number of countries began to emphasize the intrinsic importance of CLT from cultural, legal, or economic perspectives:
- from a cultural perspective, CLT can contribute to maintaining and advancing a pluriform society;

- from a legal perspective, CLT can meet the internationally recognized right to language development and language maintenance, in correspondence with the fact that many IM groups consider their own language as a core value of their cultural identity;
- from an economic perspective, CLT can lead to an important pool of profitable knowledge in societies which are increasingly internationally oriented.

Table 8. Status of Community Language Teaching (CLT) in European primary and secondary education, according to 9 parameters in 6 countries (Sw/G/N/B/F/Sp = Sweden/Germany/Netherlands until 2004/Belgium/France/Spain) (source: Extra and Yağmur 2004: 385)

CLT parameters	Primary education	Secondary education
1 Target groups	IM children in a broad vs. narrow definition in terms of - the spectrum of languages taught (Sp < N B F < G Sw) - language use and language proficiency (G N B Sp < Sw F)	- *de iure:* mostly IM pupils; sometimes all pupils (in particular N) - *de facto:* IM pupils in a broad vs. narrow sense (see left) (limited participation, in particular B Sp)
2 Arguments	mostly in terms of a struggle against deficits, rarely in terms of multicultural policy (N B *vs.* other countries)	mostly in terms of multicultural policy, rarely in terms of deficits (all countries)
3 Objectives	rarely specified in terms of (meta)linguistic and (inter)cultural skills (Sw G Sp *vs.* N B F)	specified in terms of oral and written skills to be reached at interim and final stages (all countries)
4 Evaluation	mostly informal/subjective through teacher, rarely formal/objective through measurement and school report figures (Sw G F *vs.* B N Sp)	formal/objective assessment plus school report figures (Sw G N *vs.* B F Sp)
5 Minimal enrolment	specified at the level of classes, schools, or municipalities (Sw vs. G B F *vs.* N Sp)	specified at the level of classes, schools, or municipalities (Sw N *vs.* other countries)
6 Curricular status	- voluntary and optional - within vs. outside regular school hours (G N Sp *vs.* S B F) - 1–5 hours per week	- voluntary and optional - within regular school hours - one/more lessons per week (all countries)

CLT parameters	Primary education	Secondary education
7 Funding	– by national, regional or local educational authorities – by consulates/embassies of countries of origin (Sw N vs. B Sp, mixed G F)	– by national, regional or local educational authorities – by consulates/embassies of countries of origin (Sw N F vs. B Sp, mixed G)
8 Teaching materials	– from countries of residence – from countries of origin (Sw G N vs. B F Sp)	– from countries of residence – from countries of origin (Sw G N F vs. B Sp)
9 Teacher qualifications	– from countries of residence – from countries of origin (Sw G N vs. B F Sp)	– from countries of residence – from countries of origin (Sw G N F vs. B Sp)

In Table 8 we give a crossnational summary of the outcomes of our comparative study of nine parameters of CLT in primary and secondary education. A comparison of all nine parameters makes clear that CLT has gained a higher status in secondary schools than in primary schools. In primary education, CLT is generally not part of the "regular" or "national" curriculum, and, consequently, it tends to become a negotiable entity in a complex and often opaque interplay by a variety of factors. Another remarkable fact is that, in some countries (in particular France, Belgium, Spain, and some German federal states), CLT is funded by the consulates or embassies of the countries of origin. In these cases, the state government does not interfere in the organization of CLT, or in the requirements for, and the selection and employment of teachers. A paradoxical consequence of this phenomenon is that the earmarking of CLT budgets is often safeguarded by the above-mentioned consulates or embassies. National, regional, or local governments often fail to earmark budgets, so that funds meant for CLT may be appropriated for other educational purposes. It should be mentioned that CLT for primary school children in the Netherlands has been completely abolished in the school year 2004/2005, resulting in Dutch-only education in multicultural and multilingual primary schools (Extra and Yağmur 2006).

The higher status of CLT in secondary education is largely due to the fact that instruction in one or more languages other than the official state language is a traditional and regular component of the (optional) school curriculum, whereas primary education is highly determined by a monolingual *habitus* (Gogolin 1994). *Within* secondary education, however, CLT must compete with "foreign" languages that have a higher status or a longer tradition.

CLT may be part of a largely centralized or decentralized educational policy. In the Netherlands, national responsibilities and educational funds are gradually being transferred to the municipal level, and even to individual schools. In France, government policy is strongly centrally controlled. Germany has devolved governmental responsibilities chiefly to its federal states, with all their mutual differences. Sweden grants far-reaching autonomy to municipal councils in dealing with educational tasks and funding. In general, comparative cross-national references to experiences with CLT in the various EU member-states are rare, or they focus on particular language groups. With a view to the demographic development of European nation-states into multicultural societies, and the similarities in CLT issues, more comparative applied linguistic research would be highly desirable.

5.3. Dealing with multilingualism at school: An inclusive approach

In Europe, language policy has largely been considered a domain which should be developed within the boundaries of each EU nation-state (on language policy, see also Ricento, this vol.). Proposals for an overarching EU language policy were laboriously achieved and are non-committal in character (Coulmas 1991). The most important declarations, recommendations, or directives on language policy, each of which carries a different charge in the EU jargon, concern the recognition of the status of official EU languages; "indigenous" or RM languages; "non-territorial" or IM languages (in the order mentioned).

Bilingual education in majority languages and RM languages has been an area of interest and research for a long time (Baker 2001). More recently, local and global perspectives are taken into consideration that go beyond bilingualism for RM groups and focus on multilingualism and multilingual education. Apart from majority and RM languages, the focus is commonly on the learning and teaching of English as a third language, and in this way on promoting trilingualism from an early age on (Cenoz and Genesee 1998; Cenoz and Jessner 2000; Beetsma 2002; Hoffmann and Ytsma 2004).

It is remarkable that the teaching of RM languages is generally advocated for reasons of cultural diversity as a matter of course, whereas this is rarely a major argument in favour of teaching IM languages. The 1977 guideline of the Council of European Communities on education for "migrant" children (*Directive 77/486*, dated 25 July 1977) is now completely outdated. It needs to be put in a new and increasingly multicultural context and it needs to be extended to pupils originating from non-EU countries. Allocating special rights to one group of minorities and denying the same rights to other groups is hard to relate to the principle of equal human rights for everyone. Besides, most of the so-called "migrants" in EU countries have taken up the citizenship of the countries in which they live, and in many cases they belong to second or third generation groups. Against this background, there is a growing need for overarching human rights for every individual, irrespective of his/her ethnic, cultural, religious, or language background. For a similar inclusive approach to IM and RM language rights we refer to Grin (1995).

There is a great need for educational policies in Europe that take new realities of multilingualism into account. Processes of internationalization and globalization have brought European nation-states to the world, but they have also brought the world to European nation-states. This bipolar pattern of change has led to both convergence and divergence of multilingualism across Europe. On the one hand, English is on the rise as the *lingua franca* for international communication across the borders of European nation-states at the cost of all other state languages of Europe, including French. In spite of many objections against the hegemony of English (Phillipson 2003), this process of convergence will be enhanced by the extension of the EU in an eastward direction. Within the borders of European nation-states, however, there is an increasing divergence of home languages due to large-scale processes of global migration and intergenerational minorization.

The call for differentiation of the monolingual *habitus* of primary schools across Europe originates not only *bottom-up* from IM parents or organizations, but also *top-down* from supra-national institutions which emphasize the increasing need for European citizens with a transnational and multicultural affinity and identity. Multilingual competencies are considered prerequisites for such an affinity and identity. Both the European Commission and the Council of Europe have published many policy documents in which language diversity is cherished as a key element of the multicultural identity of Europe – now and in the future. This language diversity is considered to be a prerequisite rather than an obstacle for a united European space in which all citizens are equal (not the same) and enjoy equal rights (Council of Europe 2000). The maintenance of language diversity and the promotion of language learning and multilingualism are seen as essential elements for the improvement of communication and for the reduction of intercultural misunderstanding.

The European Commission (1995) opted in a so-called *Whitebook* for trilingualism as a policy goal for all European citizens. Apart from the "mother tongue", each citizen should learn at least two "community languages". In fact, the concept of "mother tongue" referred to the official languages of particular nation-states and ignored the fact that mother tongue and official state language do not coincide for many inhabitants of Europe. At the same time, the concept of "community languages" referred to the official languages of two other EU member-states. In later European Commission documents, reference was made to one foreign language with high international prestige (English was deliberately not referred to) and one so-called "neighbouring language". The latter concept related always to neighbouring countries, never to next-door neighbours. Also UNESCO adopted the term "multilingual education" in 1999 (General Conference Resolution 12) for reference to the use of at least three languages, i.e., the mother tongue, a regional or national language, and an international language in education.

In a follow-up to the European Year of Languages, the heads of state and government of all EU member-states gathered in March 2002 in Barcelona and called upon the European Commission to take further action to promote multilingualism across Europe, in particular by the learning and teaching of at least two foreign languages from a very young age (Nikolov and Curtain 2000). The resulting Action Plan 2004–2006, published by the European Commission (2003), may lead to an inclusive approach in which IM languages are no longer denied access to Europe's celebration of language diversity. In particular, the plea for the learning of three languages by all EU citizens, the plea for an early start to such learning experiences, and the plea for offering a wide range of languages to choose from, open the door to such an inclusive approach. Although this may sound paradoxical, such an approach can also be advanced by accepting the role of English as *lingua franca* for intercultural communication across Europe. Against this background, the following principles are proposed for the enhancement of multilingualism at the primary school level:

1. In the primary school curriculum, three languages are introduced for all children:
   - the official standard language of the particular nation-state (or in some cases a region) as a major school subject and the major language of communication for the teaching of other school subjects;
   - English as *lingua franca* for international communication;
   - an additional third language chosen from a variable and varied set of priority languages at the national, regional, and/or local level of the multicultural society.

2. The teaching of all these languages is part of the regular school curriculum and subject to educational inspection.

3. Regular primary school reports contain information on the children's proficiency in each of these languages.

4. National working programmes are established for the priority languages referred to under 1 in order to develop curricula, teaching methods, and teacher training programmes.

5. Part of these priority languages may be taught at specialized language schools.

This set of principles is aimed at reconciling *bottom-up* and *top-down* pleas in Europe for multilingualism, and is inspired by large-scale and enduring experiences with the learning and teaching of English (as L1 or L2) and one *Language Other Than English* (LOTE) for all children in Victoria State, Australia (see Extra and Yağmur 2004: 99–105). When each of the above-mentioned languages should be introduced in the curriculum and whether or when they should be subject and/or medium of instruction, has to be spelled out according to particular national, regional, or local demands. Derived from an overarching conceptual framework, priority languages could be specified in terms of both RM and IM languages for the development of curricula, teaching methods, and teacher training programmes. Moreover, the increasing internationalization of pupil populations in European schools requires that a language policy be introduced for *all* school children in which the traditional dichotomy between foreign language instruction for indigenous majority pupils and home language instruction for IM pupils is put aside. Given the experiences abroad (e.g., the Victorian School of Languages in Melbourne, Australia), language schools can become expert centres where a variety of languages are taught, if the demand for them is low and/or spread over many schools. In line with the proposed principles for primary schooling, similar ideas could be worked out for secondary schools where learning more than one language is already an established practice. The above-mentioned principles would recognize multilingualism in an increasingly multicultural environment as an asset for all children and for society at large. The EU, the Council of Europe, and UNESCO could function as leading transnational agencies in promoting such concepts. The UNESCO *Universal Declaration of Cultural Diversity* (last update 2002) is highly in line with the views expressed here, in particular in its plea to encourage linguistic diversity, to respect the mother tongue at all levels of education, and to foster the learning of several languages from the youngest age.

Recently, a feasibility study concerning the creation of a European Agency for linguistic diversity and language learning was carried out by Yellow Window (2005) and offered to the European Commission. If accepted, the report would open the door for an inclusive approach towards languages respecting the diversity of all the languages used in the EU, whether "official" state languages, regional or immigrant languages, other lesser-used languages or sign languages. It would thus raise awareness about the broad spectrum of languages in the EU, and encourage the learning of languages in general. As regards support for policy-making, the Agency would focus on providing "status" information, serving as an input for policy makers and thus complementing the work done by the Council of Europe. It remains to be seen how the discussed factors will contribute in shaping the future of multilingual Europe.

References

Alladina, Safder
   1993   South Asian languages in Britain. In: Guus Extra and Ludo Verhoeven (eds.), *Immigrant Languages in Europe*, 55–65. Clevedon: Multilingual Matters.

Alladina, Safder and Viv Edwards (eds.)
   1991   *Multilingualism in the British Isles.* Vol. 1: The older mother tongues and Europe; Vol. 2: Africa, the Middle East and Asia. London: Longman.

Baetens Beardsmore, Hugo
   1993   *European Models of Bilingual Education.* Clevedon: Multilingual Matters.

Baker, Colin
   2001   *Foundations of Bilingual Education and Bilingualism.* Clevedon: Multilingual Matters.

Baker, Philip and John Eversley (eds.)
   2000   *Multilingual Capital. The Languages of London's School Children and their Relevance to Economic, Social and Educational Policies.* London: Battlebridge Publications.

Barbour, Stephen
   2000   Nationalism, language, Europe. In: Stephen Barbour and Cathie Carmichael (eds.), *Language and Nationalism in Europe*, 1–17. Oxford: Oxford University Press.

Beetsma, Danny (ed.)
   2002   *Trilingual Primary Education in Europe.* Ljouwert: Fryske Akademie.

Bratt Paulston, Christina and Donald Peckham (eds.)
   1998   *Linguistic Minorities in Central and Eastern Europe.* Clevedon: Multilingual Matters.

Breathnach, Diarmaid (ed.)
   1998   *Mini Guide to Lesser Used Languages of the European Union.* Dublin: EBLUL.

Broeder, Peter and Guus Extra
   1998   *Language, Ethnicity and Education: Case Studies on Immigrant Minority Groups and Immigrant Minority Languages.* Clevedon: Multilingual Matters.

Caubet, Dominique, Salem Chaker and Jean Sibille (eds.)
   2002   *Codification des langues de France.* Paris: l'Harmattan.

CBS
   2000   *Allochtonen in Nederland.* Voorburg/Heerlen: CBS.

Cenoz, Jasone
   2001   Basque in Spain and France. In: Guus Extra and Durk Gorter (eds.), *The Other Languages of Europe*, 45–57. Clevedon: Multilingual Matters.

Cenoz, Jasone and Fred Genesee (eds.)
   1998   *Beyond Bilingualism. Multilingualism and Multilingual Education.* Clevedon: Multilingual Matters.

Cenoz, Jasone and Ulrike Jessner (eds.)
   2000   *English in Europe. The Acquisition of a Third Language.* Clevedon: Multilingual Matters.

Churchill, Stacy
   1986   *The Education of Linguistic and Cultural Minorities in the OECD Countries.* Clevedon: Multilingual Matters.

Clyne, Michael
   1991   *Community Languages: The Australian Experience.* Cambridge: Cambridge University Press.

Clyne, Michael
   2003   *Dynamics of Language Contact.* Cambridge: Cambridge University Press.

Coulmas, Florian
   1991   *A Language Policy for the European Community. Prospects and Quandaries.* Berlin: Mouton de Gruyter.

Council of Europe
   2000   *Linguistic Diversity for Democratic Citizenship in Europe. Towards a Framework for Language Education Policies. Proceedings Innsbruck (Austria) May 1999.* Strasbourg: Council of Europe.

Craith, Mairead Nic
   2003   Facilitating or generating linguistic diversity. The European charter for regional or minority languages. In: Gabrielle Hogan-Brun and Stefan Wolff (eds.), *Minority Languages in Europe. Frameworks, Status, Prospects,* 56–72. Hampshire: Palgrave Macmillan.

Directive 77/486
   1977   *Directive 77/486 of the Council of the European Communities on the Schooling of Children of Migrant Workers.* Brussels: CEC.

Edwards, John
   1985   *Language, Society and Identity.* Oxford: Basil Blackwell.

Edwards, John
   1991   Socio-educational issues concerning indigenous minority languages: Terminology, geography and status. In: Jantse Sikma and Durk Gorter (eds.), *European Lesser Used Languages in Primary Education,* 207–226. Leeuwarden: Mercator Education/Fryske Akademy.

Edwards, John
   1994   *Multilingualism.* London: Routledge.

ELSN
   1996   *European Language Survey Network. A Comparative Analysis of Four Language Surveys (Ireland, Friesland, Wales and the Basque Country).* Dublin: ITE.

Ethnologue
   2001   *Ethnologue: Languages of the World, 14th edition.* [www.ethnologue.org]

Euromosaic
   1996   *The Production and Reproduction of the Minority Language Groups of the EU.* Luxembourg: Office for Official Publications of the European Communities. [www.uoc.edu/euromosaic]

European Commission
   1995   *Whitebook. Teaching and Learning: Towards a Cognitive Society.* Brussels: COM.

European Commission
   2003   *Promoting Language Learning and Linguistic Diversity. An Action Plan 2004–2006.* Brussels: COM. <www.europa.eu.int/comm/education/policies/lang/languages/actionplan_en.html>

Euskararen Jarraipena III. La Continuidad del Euskera III. La Continuité de la Langue Basque II
    2003   Vitoria-Gasteiz: Eusko Jaurlaritza.
Extra, Guus, Rian Aarts, Tim van der Avoird, Peter Broeder and Kutlay Yağmur
    2002   *De andere talen van Nederland: Thuis en op school.* Bussum: Coutinho.
Extra, Guus and Durk Gorter (eds.)
    2001   *The Other Languages of Europe. Demographic, Sociolinguistic and Educational Perspectives.* Clevedon: Multilingual Matters.
Extra, Guus and Jan Jaap de Ruiter (eds.)
    2001   *Babylon aan de Noordzee. Nieuwe talen in Nederland.* Amsterdam: Bulaaq.
Extra, Guus and Ludo Verhoeven (eds.)
    1993a   *Community Languages in the Netherlands.* Amsterdam: Swets & Zeitlinger.
Extra, Guus and Ludo Verhoeven (eds.)
    1993b   *Immigrant Languages in Europe.* Clevedon: Multilingual Matters.
Extra, Guus and Ludo Verhoeven (eds.)
    1998   *Bilingualism and Migration.* Berlin: Mouton de Gruyter.
Extra Guus and Kutlay Yağmur (eds.)
    2004   *Urban Multilingualism in Europe. Immigrant Minority Languages at Home and School.* Clevedon: Multilingual Matters.
Extra, Guus and Kutlay Yağmur
    2006   Immigrant minority languages at home and at school. *European Education* 38/2: 50–63.
Fishman, Joshua
    1973   *Language and Nationalism. Two Integrative Essays.* Rowley Mass.: Newbury House.
Fishman, Joshua
    1988   'English only': Its ghosts, myths, and dangers. *International Journal of the Sociology of Language* 74: 125–140.
Fishman, Joshua
    1989   *Language and Ethnicity in Minority Sociolinguistic Perspective.* Clevedon: Multilingual Matters.
Gogolin, Ingrid
    1994   *Der monolinguale Habitus der multilingualen Schule.* Münster: Waxmann.
Gorter, Durk
    1994   A new sociolinguistic survey of the Frisian language situation. *Dutch Crossing. A Journal of Low Countries Studies* 18: 18–31.
Gorter, Durk
    1996   *Het Fries als kleine Europese taal.* Amsterdam/Leeuwarden: Fryske Akademy.
Gorter, Durk
    1997   Social surveys of minority language communities. In: Brunon Synak and Tomasz Wicherkiewicz (eds.), *Language Minorities and Minority Languages in the Changing Europe*, 59–76. Gdansk: University of Gdansk.
Gorter, Durk
    2001   A Frisian update of reversing language shift. In: Joshua Fishman (ed.), *Can Threatened Languages Be Saved? Reversing Language Shift: A 21st Century Perspective*, 215–233. Clevedon: Multilingual Matters.

Gorter, Durk, Jarich F. Hoekstra, Lammert G. Jansma and Jehannes Ytsma (eds.)
    1990   *Fourth International Conference on Minority Languages.* Vol. 1: General papers; Vol. 2: Western and Eastern European papers. Clevedon: Multilingual Matters.

Gorter, Durk and Reize J. Jonkman
    1995   *Taal yn Fryslân op 'e nij besjoen.* Leeuwarden: Fryske Akademy.

Grin, François
    1995   Combining immigrant and autochthonous language rights: A territorial approach to multilingualism. In: Tove Skutnabb-Kangas and Robert Phillipson (eds.), *Linguistic Human Rights. Overcoming Linguistic Discrimination,* 31–48. Berlin: Mouton de Gruyter.

Hoffmann, Charlotte and Jehannes Ytsma (eds.)
    2004   *Trilingualism in Family, School, and Community.* Clevedon: Multilingual Matters.

Hogan-Brun, Gabrielle and Stefan Wolff (eds.)
    2003   *Minority Languages in Europe. Frameworks, Status, Prospects.* Hampshire: Palgrave Macmillan.

Husén, Torsten and Susan Opper (eds.)
    1983   *Multicultural and Multilingual Education in Immigrant Countries.* Oxford: Pergamon Press.

Instituto della Enciclopedia Italiana
    1986   *Linguistic Minorities in Countries Belonging to the European Community.* Luxembourg: Office for Official Publications of the European Communities.

Jaspaert, Koen and Sjaak Kroon (eds.)
    1991   *Ethnic Minority Languages and Education.* Amsterdam: Lisse, Swets & Zeitlinger.

Jørgensen, Jens Normann (ed.)
    2003   *Turkish Speakers in North Western Europe.* Clevedon: Multilingual Matters.

Kertzer, David and Dominique Arel
    2002   *Census and Identity. The Politics of Race, Ethnicity, and Language in National Censuses.* Cambridge: Cambridge University Press.

Kroon, Sjaak
    1990   *Opportunities and Constraints of Community Language Teaching.* Münster: Waxmann.

LMP (Linguistic Minorities Project)
    1985   *The Other Languages of England.* London: Routledge & Kegan.

Martin, Peter, Aangela Creese, Arvind Bhaff and Nirmala Bhojani
    2004   *Complementary Schools and their Communities in Leicester. Final Report.* School of Education, University of Leicester.

May, Stephen
    2001   *Language and Minority Rights. Ethnicity, Nationalism and the Politics of Language.* London: Longman.

Nicholas, Joe
    1988   British language diversity surveys (1977–1987). A critical examination. *Language and Education* 2: 15–33.

Nikolov, Marianne and Helena Curtain (eds.)
    2000   *An Early Start. Young Learners and Modern Languages in Europe and Beyond.* Strasbourg: Council of Europe.

NISRA (Northern Ireland Statistics and Research Agency)
 2004 *Northern Ireland Census 2001 Theme Tables: 4. Irish Language.* Belfast: Nisra. [www.nisra.gov.uk]
Oakes, Leigh
 2001 *Language and National Identity. Comparing France and Sweden.* Amsterdam: John Benjamins.
Obdeijn, Herman and Jan Jaap de Ruiter (eds.)
 1998 *Le Maroc au coeur de l'Europe. L'enseignement de la langue et culture d'origine (ELCO) aux élèves marocains dans cinq pays européens.* Tilburg: Tilburg University Press.
Office of National Statistics
 2005 *Focus on Wales: Its People.* [www.statistics.gov.uk]
Ó'Riagáin, Dónall
 2001 All languages – great and small: A look at the linguistic future of Europe with particular reference to lesser used languages. In: Snezana Trifunovska (ed.), *Minority Rights in Europe – European Minorities and Languages*, 31–42. The Hague: Asser Press.
Ó'Riagáin, Pádraig and Míchaél Ó'Gliasáin
 1994 *National Survey on Languages 1993 Preliminary Report.* Dublin: Institiúid Teangeolaíochta Éireann.
Phillipson, Robert
 2003 *English-only Europe? Challenging Language Policy.* London: Routledge.
Reid, Euan and Hans Reich
 1992 *Breaking the Boundaries. Migrant Workers' Children in the EC.* Clevedon: Multilingual Matters.
Siguan, Miquel
 1990 *Linguistic Minorities in the European Economic Community: Spain, Portugal, Greece (Summary of the Report).* Luxembourg: Office for Official Publications of the European Communities.
Spolsky, Bernard
 2004 *Language Policy.* Cambridge: Cambridge University Press.
Synak, Brunon and Tomasz Wicherkiewicz (eds.)
 1997 *Language Minorities and Minority Languages in the Changing Europe.* Gdansk: University of Gdansk.
Tilmatine, Mohamed (ed.)
 1997 *Enseignement des langues d'origine et immigration nord-africaine en Europe: langue maternelle ou langue d'état?* Paris: INALCO/CEDREA-CRB.
Tjeerdsma, Rommert S.
 1998 *Mercator Guide to Organizations.* Leeuwarden: Mercator Education/ Fryske Akademy.
Tosi, Arturi
 1984 *Immigration and Bilingual Education. A Case Study of Movement of Population, Language Change and Education within the EEC.* Oxford: Pergamon Press.
Van Londen, Selma and Arie de Ruijter
 1999 Ethnicity and identity. In: Marie-Claire Foblets and Ching Lin Pang (eds.), *Culture, Ethnicity and Migration*, 69–79. Leuven/Leusden: Acco.

Williams, Glyn and Delyth Morris
   2000   *Language Planning and Language Use – Welsh in a Global Age.* Cardiff: University of Wales Press.

Yellow Window MC
   2005   *A Feasibility Study Concerning the Creation of a European Agency for Linguistic Diversity and Language Learning.* Antwerp.
            [*http://europa.eu.int/comm/education/policies/lang/key/studies_en.html*].

2. Immigrant language minorities in the United States

Terrence G. Wiley

1. Introduction: The historical and contemporary ideological context

This chapter provides a brief overview of the history and current status of immigrant language diversity in the United States. Immigrant language diversity is a controversial topic in the contemporary United States. It was likewise a century ago during the heyday of Americanization (Wiley 1998), when "the notion of assimilation became the master concept in both social theory and public discourse to designate the expected path to be followed by foreign groups in America" (Portes and Rumbaut 2001: 44). The ideology of English monolingualism carries an expectation for assimilation or shift into the English language, as well as the expectation of loss of mother tongues. As a master concept, it influences not only the kinds of educational language policies that are implemented for immigrants and other language minorities, but also frames questions that are asked in national surveys and thus limits the types of language data that are collected (Wiley 2005a: ch. 4). As a hegemonic social ideology, English monolingualism and the expectation for linguistic assimilation enables the dominant English-speaking majority "to gain consent for existing power relationships from those in subordinate positions" (Tollefson 1991: 11). Thus, it is an ideology that challenges immigrant language minority parents who wish for their children to maintain their home and community languages, even as they strive to learn English.

The contemporary ideology of English monolingualism, as manifested in the English-Only movement, had antecedents even in the British colonial period. Oral English monolingualism coupled with compulsory English illiteracy was compelled on enslaved Africans, and appears to represent the first minority language policy in British controlled North America (Weinberg 1995). Antipathy to German-speakers was evident in the disdain that Benjamin Franklin had in the 1750s, although this is a position from which he later retreated. During the early Nationalist period Noah Webster strove to create a distinctly American language and riled against regional dialects, which he sought to eliminate (Lepore 2002). Prior to the U.S. Civil War, Nativists endeavored to restrict immigration. In the 1880s, Native American children were taken from their parents and put in English-Only boarding schools and Chinese were excluded from entering the United States. Meanwhile millions of Europeans came to the U.S. during this period, and Americanizers of the early 1900s succeeded in making

English mandatory for naturalization and citizenship. It was not until the World War I era, however, that Americanizers succeeded in creating social and educational language policies to compel white European immigrants rapidly to acquire English in order to prove their loyalty as being "American" (Ricento 2003). Following nearly half a century of racially-based immigration quotas, in the 1960s these were lifted, and tens of millions of immigrants from around the globe have since taken up residence in the U.S. Nevertheless, during the past several decades, neo-Nativist sentiment has re-emerged (Tatalovich 1995), with official English-Only and anti-immigrant activism among the major social policy issues in the U.S. (Wiley 2004).

The dogma of English monolingualism has been very consistent in its tenets over time (Wiley 2000). The major beliefs of the ideology of English monolingualism embraced a series of expectations or prescriptions for language minority immigrants. These expectations are not new, and they parallel comparable monolingual ideologies in other countries, where immigration has also been an important source of language diversity (Kloss 1971). The basic tenets are that immigrants should surrender their native languages as a kind of recompense for the rite of passage into the receiving society because they will be more prosperous in their new country than they were in their countries of origin. While historically it is true that some European immigrant groups of the late 1800s and early 1900s did improve their economic condition, there is evidence that for many Latin American immigrants (Portes and Rumbaut 2001) and some Asian immigrants this is no longer the case (Weinberg 1997). Another common belief is that language and cultural maintenance by immigrants results in a self-imposed isolation from the "mainstream" American society and culture, which retards the mobility of these groups (Kloss 1971). This view distorts the historical experience of many immigrants who have been shunned and/or overtly discriminated against (Weinberg 1997). Probably the most pervasive belief is that immigrant language minorities represent a divisive force for maintaining national unity. Therefore, the receiving society must require linguistic assimilation and a surrender of language minority claims to their heritage languages and cultures. This clichéd theme has been recently revived within a post-9/11 context of national security by Harvard professor Samuel Huntington (2004), in his controversial book, *Who Are We: The Challenges to America's National Identity*. Against this ideologically charged background, nearly 50 million Americans, with many recent immigrants among them, speak languages in addition to English.

2. Incorporation of ethnolinguistically diverse peoples through immigration and territorial expansion

Immigration has long been the major source of language diversity in the United States. Since the suspension of racially-selective immigration quotas in 1965, the ethnolinguistic diversity of the United States has increased rapidly to levels not seen since the early decades of the 1900s. Despite the obvious importance of immigration in adding to the language diversity of the United States, it is necessary to note that immigration is not the sole source of that diversity. Although the primary focus of this chapter is on immigrant language diversity, some historical background regarding ethnolinguistic diversity, and how various peoples have come to be incorporated into the United States, is useful – given that immigration has interacted with other forms of incorporation. In addition, there has been considerable social and economic diversity among the immigrants who have come into the United States. There is also considerable variation in not only the ethnolinguistic background of immigrants, but also in how they have been incorporated into the national polity (Portes and Rumbaut 2001; Weiss 1982). There has also been variation in how different individuals of the same national origin groups have been incorporated at different times during U.S. history.

The area that now constitutes the United States resulted initially from the wresting of land from indigenous inhabitants and territorial expansion through annexation and conquest. British colonization along the Atlantic seaboard of the seventeenth century was followed by colonial competition between France and England during the "French and Indian Wars" (1754–1763), which was the North American extension of the European Seven Years War (1756–1763). Following the founding of the republic at the end of the eighteenth century, the United States rapidly expanded its territorial control largely through the annexation and conquest of formerly French and Spanish colonies, as well as the northern half of Mexico and Russian-controlled territory in Alaska during the nineteenth century (see Fig. 1). Into these newly acquired lands came steady streams of "settlers", many of whom were immigrants. The construct of "settler" implies that the areas into which they go are empty or untamed (Blaut 1993). Of course the newly appropriated lands were already populated by speakers of indigenous and old colonial languages from whose perspective the influx of newcomers was seen as an intrusion or outright invasion. The expansion of the U.S. into the Pacific and Caribbean from the late nineteenth to the mid twentieth century led to further linguistic diversification through the incorporation of speakers of indigenous languages, as in the case of the annexation of Hawaii, other Pacific islands, and Puerto Rico (see Fig. 2).

From an historical perspective, classifying languages in the U.S. context is also problematic. Consider Spanish, the second largest language spoken in the U.S. Historically, Spanish is an old colonial language (Molesky 1988) of the former Spanish Empire and/or what became Mexico in the early nineteenth century, and which ultimately became part of the continental U.S. These areas include Florida, Texas, California, Arizona, New Mexico, Utah, Nevada, Colorado, and part of Wyoming (see Fig. 1). Spanish was also the national language of those parts of Mexico that were conquered and annexed into the U.S. For many of those peoples who found themselves conquered or annexed, Spanish was an indigenous language insofar as it had become the native tongue of groups earlier conquered by the Spanish. Subsequently, Spanish has also been the language of immigrants largely from Mexico, Central and South America, to a lesser extent Spain, and even the Philippines. In the past four decades, Spanish has also been the language of a special class of immigrants, namely refugees, who have come in large numbers from Cuba and in smaller numbers from Central American countries. Spanish is also the dominant language of the nearly 3 million Puerto Ricans in the American-controlled Commonwealth of Puerto Rico and the language of secondary migrants from Puerto Rico who reside on the U.S. mainland. Thus, although immigration provides a necessary focus to understanding the linguistic diversity of the United States and its territories, an immigrant paradigm is insufficient to fully explain that diversity. Moreover, even within an immigrant paradigm it is imperative to distinguish among various types of immigrants.

With respect to language specifically, it is apparent that the imposition of restrictive English-Only policies have had a negative impact across immigrant

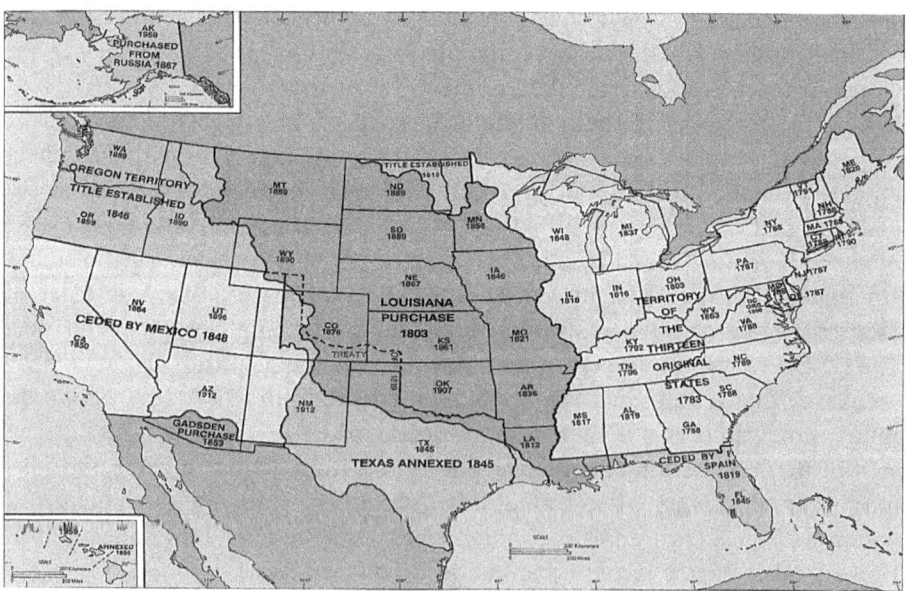

Figure 1. Territorial Expansion of the United States by Late Nineteenth Century
Perry-Castañeda Library, Map Collection, University of Texas, Austin.
http://www.lib.utexas.edu/maps/united_states/territory.jpg

groups based on: (1) the attitudes of the majority toward specific minority groups (Leibowitz 1971, 1974; Portes and Rumbaut 2001; see also Gallois, Watson, and Brabant, this vol.); (2) the extent to which English language and literacy requirements have been used as discriminatory gate-keeping mechanisms; (3) the extent to which immigrant and language minority groups have accepted the prescribed path (Gibson and Ogbu 1991); and (4) assuming that language minority groups do accept the prescribed path, the extent to which they are allowed an equal opportunity to learn (Weinberg 1995, 1997).

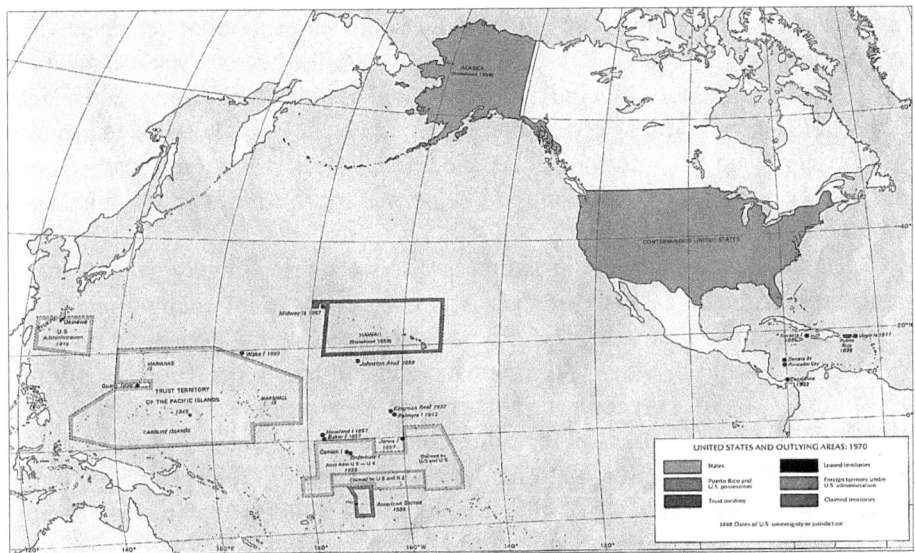

Figure 2. Territorial Expansion of the United States by Mid – Twentieth Century
Perry-Castañeda Library, Map Collection, University of Texas, Austin.
http://www.lib.utexas.edu/maps/united_states/us_terr_1970.jpg

2.1. Structural versus behavioral incorporation

Immigrants differ from those forcibly concurred or annexed. Gibson and Ogbu (1991) have distinguished among several types of immigrants based on their initial mode of incorporation: voluntary, involuntary, and autonomous immigrants. During the colonial and early republican periods, most immigrants fell into the first two categories, with most Europeans coming voluntarily and most enslaved Africans arriving as a result of abduction. The notion of "autonomous" immigrants has received less attention, but the Amish of Pennsylvania, who established their own communities and have maintained German, are probably the best example.

To voluntary, involuntary, and autonomous immigrants, "refugees" can be added as a special category. Among refugees, additional distinctions can be made based on former social class/ethnolinguistic standing within the source countries of origin. In recent decades, for example, Cuban refugees have been coming to the U.S. During the 1950s, prior to the Cuban Revolution, some 63,000 refugees fled the Batista regime. Following Castro's victory in 1959, the first "wave" fleeing the revolution began coming to the U.S., primarily to south Florida. The initial group was better educated and materially better off than subsequent groups (Otheguy, García, and Roca 2000). The same was true in the case of Vietnamese refugees (Chung 2000; Ferry 2004). The first wave who arrived in 1975 was largely composed of the educated middle class and those who had worked with the American military and South Vietnamese government. The second and third waves (1975–1983) were comprised of the traditional merchant classes, particularly ethnic Chinese Vietnamese, who became ideological targets of the Vietnamese government after the war (Ferry 2004). Subsequent immigrants, who have not been classified as refugees, nevertheless are reconnecting with former refugees and are being incorporated into communities established by refugees.

Over the past century, assimilation has been the proclaimed goal of Americanization with the caveat that there has been considerable debate regarding which racial and ethnic groups could be assimilated, and which could not. The rhetoric regarding the benefits of linguistic and cultural assimilation has offered a seemingly singular prescription: Learn English and adopt the American way and you will improve your lot, regardless of your race and ethnolinguistic background. Weiss (1982), in a historical analysis of the European immigrant migration to the U.S. between 1840 and 1940, made a distinction between *behavioral* assimilation and *structural* assimilation. Structural assimilation results in one being able to participate in, and benefit from, the educational, economic, and political institutions of the dominant society. Behavioral assimilation means that one speaks and acts like the dominant group, but does not necessarily benefit or fully participate economically, politically, or educationally. In other words, it represents a kind of domestication without equality. Thus, the prescription for assimilation can be measured by its results. Rarely are alternatives to assimilation considered in the "mainstream" discourse regarding immigration and language diversity. Bi/multilingualism and bi/multiculturalism are noteworthy more for their absence as alternatives than for serious considerations as options for either immigrants or those of the dominant culture.

3. Contemporary and historical language diversity in the U.S.

If one follows only the popular media discourse regarding language diversity in the United States, one would get the impression that the country is being "flooded" by non-English-speaking, predominantly Latino, immigrants who are less willing to learn English than those of generations past (Santa Ana 2002). According to the 2000 U.S. Census, about 18% of the U.S. population, aged five or older, can speak languages other than English. About 98% of those who speak languages other than English also speak English. Only about 5% of those who speak other languages indicate that they do not speak English "well" or "not at all" (Wiley 2005a: 16). The 28 million Spanish-speakers in the U.S. account for nearly three-fifths of those who speak languages other than English (Table 1). Although long characterized as a monolingual nation (Simon 1988), the U.S. ranks fifth among Spanish-speaking nations. Asian and Pacific languages have been rapidly increasing since 1965, with nearly seven million speakers, which accounts for nearly 15% of languages other than English (Table 1). Chinese, which includes Mandarin and Cantonese, as well as other so-called dialects, has grown to over two million speakers; Tagalog, the major indigenous language of the Philippines, now has over 1.2 million speakers in the U.S.; Vietnamese has over one million; and Korean nearly 900,000 (Tables 2 and 3). European languages remain plentiful with over ten million speakers, or about 21% of languages other than English (Table 1), but Italian, Hungarian, Yiddish, German, Polish, Greek, and French, all major immigrant languages of a century ago, are now declining (Table 3). Russian, however, following a rapid increase in immigration after the demise of the former Soviet Union, was the fastest growing language during the 1990s, increasing 191% from about one-quarter million in 1990 to over 700,000 in 2000 (Table 3).

Table 1. Languages spoken in the United States in 2000 by those age 5 and over

Languages spoken	Number
Total all speakers	262,375,152
Speak only English	215,423,557
Speak other language	46,951,595
Spanish or Spanish Creole	28,101,052
Other Indo-European languages	10,017,989
Asian and Pacific Island languages	6,960,065
Other languages	1,872,489
Native North American languages	381,480
African languages	418,505
Other unspecified languages	1,072,504

Source: U.S. Census 2000, Summary File 3, Table PCT10.
Internet release February 25, 2003.

Table 2. Top 30 languages in the United States in 2000

Language	Number	Historical status – mode of incorporation
1. English	215,423,557	Old Colonial – National* – Immigrant
2. Spanish / Spanish Creole	28,101,052	Old Colonial – Indigenous – Immigrant – Refugee
3. Chinese	2,022,143	Immigrant – Refugee
4. French, including Patois, Cajun	1,643,838	Old Colonial – Immigrant
5. German	1,383,442	Immigrant
6. Tagalog	1,224,241	Immigrant
7. Vietnamese	1,009,627	Immigrant-Refugee
8. Italian	1,008,370	Immigrant
9. Korean	894,063	Immigrant
10. Russian	706,242	Old Colonial – Immigrant
11. Polish	667,414	Immigrant
12. Arabic	614,582	Immigrant
13. Portuguese / Portuguese Creole	564,630	Immigrant
14. Japanese	477,997	Immigrant
15. French Creole	453,368	Immigrant – Refugee
16. Greek	365,436	Immigrant
17. Hindi	317,057	Immigrant
18. Persian	312,085	Immigrant
19. Urdu	262,900	Immigrant
20. Gujarathi	235,988	Immigrant
21. Serbo-Croatian	233,865	Immigrant – Refugee
22. Armenian	202,708	Immigrant – Refugee
23. Hebrew	195,374	Immigrant – Refugee
24. Mon-Khmer, Cambodian	181,889	Immigrant – Refugee
25. Yiddish	178,945	Immigrant – Refugee
26. Navajo	178,014	Indigenous
27. Miao, Hmong	168,063	Immigrant – Refugee
28. Laotian	149,303	Immigrant Refugee
29. Thai	120,464	Immigrant
30. Hungarian	117,973	Immigrant – Refugee

U.S. Census 2000, Summary File 3, Table PCT10. Internet release February 25, 2003.
*Although English is not the official language, it functions as the national language.

Table 3. Major languages of the U.S. Foreign born population 1910, 1940, 1970

Language	White only*		All races**
	1910	1940	1970
German	3,962,624	2,648,080	1,788,286
English	3,363,792	2,506,420	1,743,284
Yiddish***	2,759,032	1,589,040	1,201,535
Italian	2,267,009	2,475,880	3,301,184
Russian	1,690,703	1,671,540	921,330
French	1,365,110	1,561,100	1,025,994
Swedish	1,272,150	778,200	283,991
Dutch	1,051,767	924,440	438,116
Slovak	943,781	801,680	419,912
Danish	683,218	423,200	131,408
Spanish	528,842	359,520	410,580
Hungarian	382,048	389,240	325,074
Portuguese	258,131	428,360	1,696,240
Polish	228,738	159,640	70,703
Norwegian	183,844	122,180	58,218
Bulgarian	166,474	171,580	82,561
Lithuanian	140,963	122,660	95,188
Flemish	126,045	102,700	127,834
Basque	119,948	97,080	38,290
Albanian	118,379	165,220	193,745
Slovene	105,669	70,600	83,064
Romanian	72,649	83,780	140,299
Ukrainian	57,926	356,940	149,277
Greek	42,277	43,120	26,055
Czech	25,131	35,540	96,635

* For 1910 and 1940 data are for the white population only.
** The term "races" was used by the U.S. Census during this period as if ethnolinguistic labels and race were equivalent.
*** For 1910–1940, Hebrew included with Yiddish.
Source: Adapted from U.S. Census Bureau, Population Division. Authors Campbell Gibson and Emily Lennon. Maintained by: Information and Research Services Internet Staff (Population Division). Last Revised: January 18, 2001 at 10:02:40 AM. Retrieved 5/15/05 http://www.census.gov/population/www/documentation/twps0029/tab06.html

A commonly held notion is that the current ethnolinguistic diversity of the country represents a deviation from the past. During the British Colonial Period to 1776, English achieved dominant status over European languages in the British American colonies; nevertheless, a number of European immigrant languages were also spoken. Despite popular contemporary myths to the contrary, there has always been considerable language diversity in the United States. At the time of the first U.S. Census in 1790, there was no specific language background question, but national origin data was collected and can be taken as a rough proxy for language background. Based on that first census, approximately 49% of the population was English, 12% Scottish and/or Scotch Irish, and 3% Irish. Nearly one-fifth of the population was of African origin, with those of German origin comprising 7%, followed by Dutch 3%, French 2%, Spanish and Swedish with 1% each, and all others combined at 4% (Pitt 1976: 104). Germans were established about a century prior to the founding of the United States in 1683 (Toth 1990; Wiley 1998) and it was common for German communities to provide instruction in German until the World War I era. What has changed in recent decades is the composition of immigrant language diversity in the United States. The rapid increase in Spanish and Asian languages in particular is largely a function of a shift away from racially-based immigration quotas in the 1960s, and, in the case of Spanish, a considerable amount of migration of undocumented people from Mexico and Central America, which continues to be a controversial issue in the United States.

United States continental territorial expansion was rapidly achieved between 1789 and 1867. During this period many language minority peoples were conquered or annexed into the United States, and large numbers of European immigrants took up residence in the new territories. Germans and Scandinavians in particular established themselves in the Midwest. For European immigrants, this was a period of relative language tolerance, given that the federal government did not designate English as the official language. From 1820–1860, 95% of immigration to the U.S. was from northern and western Europe (Molesky 1988).

Between 1867 and the end of the Spanish American War, the United States added territories in Alaska, the Pacific, including Hawaii, and the Caribbean, including Puerto Rico. On the U.S. mainland, between 1860 and 1900, there was a shift in immigration patterns, with 68% of immigrants coming from northern and western Europe, 22% from southern and eastern Europe, 7% from North America, and 3% coming from Asia and elsewhere. There was anti-Asian discrimination, particularly in the western states, resulting in Chinese exclusion in 1882, followed by restrictions against the Japanese in 1906 (Weinberg 1997). During the late 1800s, German grew in numerical importance and by World War I, it was the nation's second largest language, roughly analogous to the position that Spanish holds today. In 1910, about 13% of the U.S. population was either first or second generation German-origin (Conzen 1980). Despite two World

Wars fanning anti-German sentiment, German remained the number two second language in the U.S. until it was displaced by Spanish, according to the 1970 census. As Table 4 indicates, there was considerable language diversity during most of the twentieth century.

Table 4. Increase/Decrease among major languages other than English 1990–2000

Selected languages other than English	2000	1990	Change	% Change
Russian	706,242	242,700	463,542	191%
French Creole (Haitian) *	453,368	187,700	265,668	142%
Vietnamese	1,009,627	507,100	502,527	99%
Miao and Hmong *	168,063	91,600	76,463	83%
Arabic	614,582	355,100	259,482	73%
Spanish or Spanish Creole	28,101,052	17,339,200	10,761,852	62%
Persian (Farsi)	312,085	201,900	110,185	55%
Chinese (Mandarin and others)*	2,022,143	1,319,500	702,643	53%
Korean	894,063	626,500	267,563	43%
Mon-Khmer, Cambodian	181,889	127,400	54,489	43%
Tagalog (Filipino)*	1,224,241	898,700	325,541	36%
Armenian	202,708	149,700	53,008	35%
Hebrew	195,374	144,300	51,074	35%
Portuguese and Portuguese Creole	564,630	429,900	134,730	31%
Thai and Laotian*	269,767	206,300	63,467	31%
Asian Indian Languages **	815,450	644,400	171,050	27%
Navajo	178,014	148,500	29,514	20%
Japanese	477,997	427,700	50,297	12%
French (includes Patois, Cajun)	1,643,838	1,702,200	−58,362	−3%
Greek	365,436	388,300	−22,864	−6%
Polish	667,414	723,500	−56,086	−8%
German	1,383,442	1,547,100	−163,658	−11%
Yiddish	178,945	213,100	−34,155	−16%
Hungarian	117,973	147,900	−29,927	−20%
Italian	1,008,370	1,308,600	−300,230	−23%

Adapted from Wiley 2005a, p. 12. Note, from 1990 Census of Population as reported in Numbers and Needs, September 1993, and from U.S. Census 2000, Summary File 3, Table PCT10, Internet release February 25, 2003.
* 1990 and 2000 comparison labels are not exactly parallel.
** 2000 U.S. Census totals for Gujarathi, Hindi, and Urdu only; 1990 was not delineated.

From 1910–1920, Southern and Eastern European immigration with 44% of the total, surpassed Western European immigration, which accounted for 41% of the total, while Asian and Latin American immigration each had 4% of the total (Molesky 1988). Filipino and Mexican workers began to replace other excluded populations. Racially-biased national quotas for immigration restriction were imposed in the 1920s, and persisted until the 1960s, as a result of the Civil Rights Movement and the struggle against racial segregation. As late as 1961, most Asian countries had quotas limiting entrants to only 100 per year (Molesky 1988).

During the early decades of the twentieth century, anti-immigrant activity and the Americanization Movement (roughly 1915–1924) had a direct effect on language education, and accelerated language shift. Amidst World War I, anti-German sentiment and xenophobia resulted in restrictions on foreign language in schools, churches, and the public sphere in many parts of the United States. English was designated as the official language of schooling in 34 states by 1922 (Leibowitz 1971; Wiley 1998). In many states it was unlawful to teach foreign languages until the sixth or eighth grade. In 1923 the Supreme Court (*Meyer v. Nebraska*) ruled against a Nebraska English-Only law that prohibited the teaching of any foreign language in schools. The *Meyer* decision, however, also confirmed the right of states to require that instruction be mediated in English. Nevertheless, the agenda of Americanization and anti-Germanism associated with wide-spread xenophobia, resulted in the rapid assimilation of millions of recent immigrants between 1914 and 1925 (McClymer 1982). Its means became coercive and led to the widespread persecution of speakers of German and other languages (Wiley 1998; see also Leibowitz 1971; Tatalovich 1995; and Toth 1990). Similarly, in Hawaii and California there were attempts to restrict native language instruction, even in private schools. Japanese and Chinese, in particular were targeted, but the Supreme Court upheld the right to private foreign language instruction in *Farrington v. Tokushige*, in 1927 (Leibowitz 1971; Wiley 2002).

4. Desegregation, federal bilingual education, and the resurgence of restrictionism

Following the Second World War, activism for desegregation became one of the major social issues. During the mid to late 1960s, bilingual education can be seen as an extension of the Civil Rights Movement. Transitional bilingual education was intended to remedy the problem of unequal educational opportunity. Provisions for bilingual ballots were likewise efforts to correct past attempts to block political access. By the 1970 census, a major shift reflecting the end of racially-based quotas was apparent, with rapid increases in Latin American and Asian immigration becoming evident (Table 4). During the 1960s and 1970s, there was likewise a reduction in restrictive requirements and there was some accommodation for the use of other languages, particularly in education, voting and other legal contexts. The *Lau* v. *Nichols* Supreme Court Decision in 1974 acknowledged that schools had to provide some affirmative means for teaching English and making the curriculum comprehensive. The 1970s, however, saw only limited implementation of transitional bilingual education as well as a mixed reaction from the dominant majority to policies of linguistic accommodation. In the late 1970s pundits began protesting federal bilingual education policies as hindering what was widely perceived to be the traditional path to "Americanization" through the American melting pot of assimilation. A prominent editor, Noel Epstein of the *Washington Post*, wrote an influential book entitled *Language, Ethnicity, and the Schools: Policy Alternatives for Bilingual Education,* which attacked bilingual education as an "affirmative ethnicity" program (see Crawford 1992a, 1995).

With the coming of the Reagan Administration in the 1980s, federal support for Bilingual Education began to wane despite increased immigration among Southeast Asian refugees, particularly Vietnamese, Vietnamese Chinese, Cambodians, Lao, and Lao Hmong, in addition to the rapidly increasing Spanish-speaking immigrant population. Claiming that English was under threat, activists on the political right, led by Senator S. I. Hayakawa, introduced a constitutional amendment to designate English as the official language of the United States. Two major organizations were formed to promote official English, U.S. English, and later, English First. U.S. English rapidly became well-funded, and solicited endorsements from high profile celebrities. Through the 1980s and 1990s, it failed in designating English as the official language at the national level, but achieved considerable success at the state level where Official English measures were approved in 21 states during the 1980s and 1990s (Crawford 1995). Designating English as the official language by itself poses no direct threat to language minorities if it is undertaken for symbolic purposes, but often the attempt to make English the official language has been coupled with restrictions on foreign languages. In 1986, California passed an official English ballot proposition, which was largely symbolic. Two years later, Arizona passed one, which the Supreme Court struck down as being too restrictive. Nevertheless, English-Only advocates continue seeking to implement more restrictive policies in Arizona and other states (Crawford 1992a, 1992b; Wiley 1998, 1999, 2000, 2004.)

There has been widespread criticism of English-Only policies from leaders of ethnic and immigrant groups, immigrant rights groups, as well as from professional language teaching organizations (Crawford 1992a, 1995; Wiley 2004). Baker and Jones (1998: 291) summarize six common criticisms of the English-Only movement, namely, it (1) ignores the civil rights traditions of the U.S.; (2) fails to support the integration of language minority children; (3) neglects the needs of American businesses to communicate with foreign markets; (4) restricts the ability of the government to accommodate or reach all citizens; (5) attempts to disenfranchise minority citizens; (6) encourages divisiveness and antagonism toward those whose first language is not English.

Allegations of racism have been made against the English-Only movement since its inauguration. Crawford (1995: 2) has concluded that given its widespread popular support, it must be seen as a "mainstream phenomenon", despite its reactionary fringes. Donahue (1995: 115) has concluded that U.S. English in particular has "showed a suspicious thrust toward disinformation [...] with [...] arguments that speaking Spanish causes racial tensions and low economic achievement". The concern of official English proponents for the so-called "Spanish threat" is apparent, despite the fact that there is no empirical evidence that there is any threat to English, according to Veltman (2000), who argues that language shift to English among Spanish-speakers is at an all time high. Nevertheless, it is no coincidence that the concerns over "protecting English" correlate with immigration more broadly, particularly record immigration among Spanish-speakers and speakers of Asian languages (Wiley 2004).

5. Language tolerance or intolerance toward immigrants and language minorities

From the standpoint of equity and language rights the important question is: To what extent have language minority immigrants enjoyed the same access, treatment, and social benefits as those among the majority, or to what extent has their status as immigrant language minorities resulted in forms of social, economic, or political discrimination? In the United States, the task of analyzing this question is complicated by the problem of disentangling the relationship between language and race.

For the period up to the mid 1970s, the work of Kloss (1998) and Leibowitz (1969, 1971, 1974) remain historically foundational in the absence of comprehensive subsequent work. Kloss' (1998) work, despite some limitations, continues to be the most extensive historical analysis regarding formal language policies and language rights in the United States. Kloss saw the history of language policies in the U.S. to be largely one of tolerance, with the xenophobia of the World War I era as largely a deviation from the history of tolerance. Kloss, however, limited his examination to what he called *nationality laws* and deliberately avoided analysis of what he termed *racial laws* (see Wiley 2002; Macías and Wiley 1998 for a critique). Leibowitz (1969, 1971, 1974), however, took the perspective that language policies are one strategy among other forms of discriminatory measures whose underlying purpose is to restrict educational, economic, and political access based on race or ethnicity. In other words, language restrictions are surrogates for racial and ethnic discrimination. Leibowitz (1969) saw an explicit connection between English language literacy requirements for political access through voting and similar requirements in immigration as direct attempts to discriminate on the basis of race and ethnicity. Leibowitz' (1971, 1974) analyses of attempts to impose English, without accommodation of mother tongues, on Native Americans from the 1880s to the 1930s, and on Mexican and Asian immigrants during the early to mid twentieth century, further document the use of language discrimination as surrogates for racial/ethnic diversity. The immediate effect of restrictionism usually results in either accelerating language shift, but it can also result in resistance to acculturation, particularly when there are no effective opportunities for social mobility (Portes and Rumbaut 2001). Thus, even when the immediate goal of rapid linguistic assimilation into English is achieved, it may result in the subordination of those who speak "non-standard" or code-mixed varieties of English such as "Pidgin", Hawaii English Creole, or "Spanglish". Those speaking so-called accented English have frequently been the targets of discrimination, particularly in employment (see Lippi-Green 1994, 1997).

Weinberg (1995, 1997), who focused on racial and ethnic discrimination in schooling, reached conclusions similar to those of Leibowitz. Weinberg (1997) in particular took aim at the so-called "model minority" stereotype that holds that Asian immigrants have been more successful because they acquired English and conformed to behavioral expectations of the dominant society. He notes that there was considerable discrimination against Asian immigrants prior to 1965, which resulted in blocked educational opportunities and lower educational achievement for some groups. The success of some Asian immigrants since 1965, as in the case of immigrants from India, for example, who outperform all other groups in educational attainment in the U.S., can in part be explained by the selective immigration of those who had social class advantages in their source countries and have been able to capitalize on those advantages after coming to the United States. Their achievements contrast markedly with Lao Hmong and Cambodian refugees, for example, who had faced oppression conditions prior to immigration, and who have faced some discrimination and inadequate accommodation since their arrival.

Haas (1992), in a case history analysis of social and educational practices in the state of Hawaii, documented a number of institutional practices and policies toward immigrants and minorities that are implicitly discriminatory. He concludes that these types of policies have received less attention than more explicit formal policies at the state or federal levels, but they result in differential treatment and lower educational attainment. Haas calls these practices *institutional racism* because they are *systematically* advantaging some groups and disadvantaging others. He analyzes a number of historical and contemporary institutional practices related to language that affect immigrant language minorities and speakers of "non-standard" varieties of English, such as Hawaiian English Creole. Haas notes that in 1924 an oral English test was used to assess children living in the Hawaiian Islands to determine school placement. Those deemed "nonstandard" English-speaking were tracked into separate schools from those with "mainland" (i.e. standard) accents. "This accent-biased form of assessment resulted in [m]any of the brightest immigrant children [being sent] to nonstandard schools, whereas less intelligent native-English speaking students went to standard schools, so both standard and nonstandard schools enrolled students heterogeneous in abilities according to other indicators of aptitude" (Haas 1992: 191). Thus, language tests resulted in the segregation of immigrant and minority children on the basis of their race. Haas notes that this institutional practice was eliminated only after many children of color acquired "mainland sounding accents". Despite the abolishment of this discriminatory policy in the early 1960s, other institutional policies and practices persist. Haas identifies some forty-four specific examples of contemporary discriminatory institutional practices, of which the following specifically related to language: insufficient use of immigrant/minority languages to communicate with parents; unequal grade distributions by race/ethnicity/language background among immigrants and language minorities; under-identification of students in need of language assistance; under-serving students needing language assistance; inappropriate staff composition to provide language accommodation to students who are attempting to learn English; and discriminatory requirements for language certification for immigrant and minority teachers (see Haas 1992: 191–214 for elaboration).

In a review of federal educational policy, Wiley and Wright (2004) have noted that, previous to 1968, the U.S. government had not implemented any policies for immigrants and other language minorities in need of language accommodation and English language instruction. Following the passage of the 1964 Civil Rights Act (Title VI), and President Johnson's War on Poverty, educators and policy began to focus on the needs of the rapidly growing immigrant and language minority populations (Crawford 2000). U.S. Census data from 1960 revealed large inequities in the number of years of schooling completed by whites (14 years) and Mexican Americans (4.7 years) (Kloss 1998; Leibowitz 1971). Against this backdrop Senator Ralph Yarborough (Democrat, Texas) introduced a bill to provide federal support for bilingual education programs, which became law in 1968. There was, however, lack of consensus about the intents and goals of the Bilingual Education Act and Title VII. In particular, there was concern regarding "the question of what beneficial effects instruction in the native language would have" (Leibowitz 1971: 34). There was also some dispute regarding whether Title VII was intended to be an anti-discrimination or anti-poverty program and the extent to which federally funded Title VII programs were supposed to facilitate students in becoming proficient bilinguals, or merely transition them to English mediated instruction as rapidly as possible

(Crawford 2000). By 1974, some 220 bilingual programs were serving 340,000 students through the assistance of federal Title VII funding. About 85 % of the funding went to programs serving Spanish-speaking students (Kloss 1998). Although these were all called "bilingual education" programs, there was considerable disparity regarding the extent to which native languages were actually used across these programs (Leibowitz 1980).

The Bilingual Education Act was reauthorized in 1984 and 1988, during the Reagan administration. At that time, the purpose of Title VII was constrained to focus on English acquisition and school achievement rather than maintenance of the home language. A portion of funding was allowed to go to Special Alternative Instructional Programs (SAIPs) which opened the door to English immersion as an alternative to transitional bilingual education.

The very last reauthorization of Title VII occurred under the Clinton administration in 1994, under the Improving America's Schools Act. It restored some attention to developmental maintenance bilingual programs. By 1999, thirty states had statutes allowing instruction in the native language, with nine requiring it. Seven other states had statutes prohibiting bilingual instruction, which were not enforced. Anti-bilingual education activists had succeeded in passing restrictive English-Only education in the states of California, Massachusetts, and Arizona. The federally supported Title VII Bilingual Education Program was allowed to lapse under the Bush administration in 2001 (see Wiley and Wright 2004 for elaboration).

Under the Bush administration, federal policy for immigrants and language minority students has changed significantly. With the passage of Bush's No Child Left Behind Act (NCLB), the term "bilingual" completely disappeared from federal educational law. The Bilingual Education Act (Title VII) was subsumed under Title III, "Language Instruction for Limited English Proficient and Immigrant Students". The Office for Bilingual Education and Minority Language Affairs (OBEMLA) became the "Office of English Language Acquisition, Language Enhancement, and Academic Achievement for Limited English Proficient Students" (OELA), and the National Clearinghouse for Bilingual Education (NCBE) was morphed into the "National Clearinghouse for English Language Acquisition and Language Instruction Educational Programs" (NCELA). The official discourse surrounding this shift was lofty. The official purpose of Title III is "to ensure that children who are limited English proficient, including immigrant children and youth, attain English proficiency" (Title III, Sec. 3102; see Wiley and Wright 2004). Under Title III, Federal funding for "limited English proficient students almost doubled, the funding is distributed more sparsely, resulting in a net reduction per entitled student" (Crawford 2002). The new Title III regulations allow funding for transitional bilingual education programs but not maintenance bilingual programs. Although some provision is made for dual immersion programs, which are growing in popularity even among Anglos, these programs only serve a fraction of students in need of services. Ironically, immigrant and language minority students who are classified as "limited English proficient" do not have the right to develop bilingualism in school, unless enough majority English-speaking students are interested in becoming bilingual through a dual-immersion program. Also, the demand for dual immersion is generally focused on Spanish, with just a small number of programs that also provide instruction in French, Chinese, and Japanese. This means that students who speak less commonly taught languages (e.g., Farsi, Khmer, Korean, Lao, Urdu, Vietnamese, etc.) have little hope for a dual immersion programs in their languages (Wiley and Wright 2004). In reflecting on the termination of the Bilingual Education Act, González (2002: 3) concluded:

> Title III is a hollow version of the hopeful legislative step taken in 1968 with the enactment of Title VII. We should be careful to distinguish between the best practices that are supported by research, and those that are fundable through this highly compromised version of the law. Title III is a highly negotiated piece of legislation. It no longer has a core of principles on which to build substantive programs with a real chance for success. Above all, we should resist the idea of having the federal government define what constitutes high quality programs [for ELLs]. That can only come from practitioners and researchers in the field; it cannot be negotiated in the back offices of Congressmen and Senators.

An additional area of conflict has been the intersection of restrictive educational language policies at the state level with those at the federal level. During the late 1990s – concurrent with but not directly related to – the Official English movement, Californian businessman Ron Unz drew national attention by introducing a voter-approved initiative, California's Proposition 227, which sought severely to limit access to bilingual education. This echoed restrictive educational policies of the World War I era, when most states passed restrictive Official English-Only policies (Kloss 1998; Tatalovich 1995; Wiley 1998, 1999). Unz succeeded in California in 1998, and followed in 2000 with even more restrictive propositions in Arizona and Massachusetts, which also passed with strong popular support. However, a similar effort subsequently failed in Colorado. The success of Unz's propositions at the polls was partly a result of how they were framed in popular discourse. He vilified bilingual education, shifting attention away from mainstream education. Only a minority of children eligible for bilingual education were enrolled in it. Thus, mainstream education was more responsible for poor performance of language minority students. Unz relied on noble sounding slogans, like "English for the children", but as implemented, the quality of the so-called structured English immersion programs is suspect, and many language minority children are unable to perform in English mediated tests required under NCLB (Wright 2005a, 2005b). By mid 2005, under pressure from some states and critics of NCLB, the federal Department of Education was under increasing pressure to back away from its stringent requirement that all children, including language minorities, be tested in English, given the dismal performance of children who lacked sufficient English to comprehend the test (see Wiley and Wright 2004; and Wright 2005a, 2005b for additional information regarding NCLB, testing requirements, and the intersection of state and federal requirements).

With respect to educational opportunities under federal jurisdiction and that of some states, where restrictive policies prevail, one conclusion is clear: Unless immigrant and language minority communities are able to provide and support their own programs, there is little opportunity for formal instruction in many less commonly taught languages.

6.   Language, social control, and status ascription

As was stated earlier, how immigrants are received or incorporated is one of the major determinants regarding their success in the new society (Portes and Rumbaut 2001). Of particular importance, are (1) the age on arrival and other individual characteristics including "education, occupational skills, wealth, knowledge of English; (2) the social environment that receives them, including the policies of the host government, the attitudes of the native population, and the presence or size of a co-ethnic community; and their family structure" (Portes and Rumbaut 2001: 46).

Portes and Rumbaut, in a major study of second generation immigrants and refugees in San Diego California and Miami Florida, note the continuing influence of the century-old theme of Americanization and assimilation as the prescribed path for immigrant groups. Again,

> [...] the notion of assimilation became the master concept in both social theory and public discourse to designate the expected path to be followed by foreign groups in America. The concept conveys a factual prediction about the final outcome of the encounters between the foreign minorities and the native majority and, simultaneously, as assessment of a socially desired goal.
> (Portes and Rumbaut 2001: 44–45)

The results of assimilation, however, based on its own predictions of success for conformity, are mixed. Portes and Rumbaut found that "segmented" or partial assimilation is common for members of many groups. Thus, assimilation as prescription for structural incorporation in Weiss' (1982) terms, is failing for many because segmented assimilation does not result in structural incorporation.

Portes and Rumbaut conclude there are groups in contemporary U.S. society, who, like many European immigrants of the past will exercise some degree of personal choice regarding their ethnolinguistic identities. For some the choice for ethnolinguistic affiliation will be a source of strength.

There are still others whose ethnicity will be neither a matter of choice nor a source of progress but a mark of subordination [...] The prospect that members of today's society will join those at the bottom of society – a new rainbow underclass – has more than a purely academic interest, for it can affect the life chances of millions of Americans and the quality of life where they concentrate.
(Portes and Rumbaut 2001: 45)

7. Language shift and community language maintenance efforts

7.1. From Spanish to English

According to Veltman, based on analyses of national census data (1983, 2000), there has been a three generational shift to English dominance. His emphasis, however, is on tracking language shift rather than bilingualism, which is the goal of most advocates of community language education in the United States. Among immigrant language minorities the usual pattern has been that the first generation acquires some English but maintains language dominance in the native tongue. The second generation typically becomes bilingual with stronger literacy skills in English given the lack of opportunity for bilingual education and dual immersion programs, and given that English is the medium of instruction. The third generation has generally become English speaking with little or no capability in the language of the grandparents. While this conclusion is generally accepted, there is some evidence from more regionalized studies of Spanish (e.g., Hunnicutt and Castro 2005) that the prevalence of Spanish is great and that language shift is from Spanish monolingualism to Spanish-English bilingualism. The widespread prevalence of bilingualism among Latino sub-groups, such as the Mexican, Cuban, and Puerto Rican origin populations in the United States was documented in a major study undertaken in the early 1990s, the Latino National Political Survey, which found that less than one percent of the Mexican origin population in the U.S. spoke only Spanish (see Valdés 2000 for elaboration). For the Cuban and Puerto Rican origin populations the rates were higher at about five and seven percent respectively. Thus, these findings refute the allegations of English-Only activists who represent Latinos in the U.S. "as a group" as "refusing to learn English" (Valdés 2000: 115–116). Nevertheless, they do not support the view that Spanish is being washed out. According to the same study, only 7.4% of the Mexican origin population spoke only English, compared to 2.8% for the Puerto Rican origin and 2.2% of the Cuban origin populations (Valdés 2000: 116). The Latino National Political Survey also found that the majority of Latinos live in bilingual households. English tends to be used more in Mexican origin households than in those of Puerto Rican or Cuban origin.

In surveys of language minority parental preferences for which languages their children should learn, parents from all groups indicate that they want their children to learn English. Some anti-bilingual education activists tend to misrepresent this fact as evidence that immigrants are against bilingual education. When language preference surveys allow parents the option to choose both English and a heritage language, immigrant parents consistently chose both (see Wiley 2005a: ch. 2).

Studies of language behavior between parents and children in the home, however, indicate that parental preferences do not necessarily translate into language practices. Among Puerto Rican immigrants, Zentella (2000: 144) observed four major patterns of interaction between parents and children:

1. Parents speak only Spanish to each other and the children respond to them in Spanish but speak English and Spanish to each other.
2. The parents speak Spanish to each other and the children; one of them sometimes speaks English as a second language [...] The children respond in both languages, preferring Spanish for their parents and English [to] each other.
3. The parents speak English to each other. One parent speaks English to the children, but the other speaks only Spanish to them. The children respond in English and speak it to each other.
4. The parents code switch frequently among themselves and to the children, who are too young to speak yet.

Unless parents consciously impose a language acquisition "policy" of the home, children often dictate the patterns of language use.

Studies of regional and sub-group differences are important and reveal patterns of language use and shift that are not as evident in national data analyses (e.g. Veltman 2000). Comparing different immigrant groups in the same locale, Portes and Rumbaut (2001: 123) found differential rates of bilingualism among second generation immigrants living in San Diego California and Miami Florida: ranging from a high of 61.6% for Cuban-origin youth attending private schools, compared with 44% attending public schools, compared to 39% for Mexican-origin students, 6.1% for Vietnamese-origin students, and less than 1% for Lao-origin students. They also found that bilingualism is high among students able to attend private schools, which indicates that bilingualism and social mobility are not at odds.

There are also regional cultural differences in which some level of bilingualism carries more status in one area than another. Otheguy, García, and Roca (2000: 177–178), for example, note the importance of "transculturation" in explaining Spanish language retention in Miami-Dade County Florida, where

> [...] young second- and third-generation Cuban Americans are only partially bilingual, having better receptive than productive bilingual skills, and often lacking in literacy in Spanish. The transcultural and bilingual context of Miami-Dade may be enough to maintain this partial bilingual competence even though full bilingual maintenance and especially biliteracy cannot be supported intergenerationally.

Moreover, if the standard for language retention of the mother tongue is literacy, many first generation immigrants would fail to meet the criteria of so-called "full proficiency" upon entry, given limited educational opportunities in some source countries. We should not be surprised then, to see only partial bilingualism among the second generation. The fact that there is substantial partial bilingualism is significant.

Regarding the retention of Spanish among the Mexican-origin population in the U.S., Valdés (2000: 119) notes:

> In sum, the language situation of Mexican American communities is more or less encouraging depending on one's views about language. Those who worry about Mexican Americans' being left out of the American dream will find it comforting to discover that Mexican Americans *are* learning English and that it is rapidly displacing Spanish. On the other hand, supporters of Spanish language maintenance can also take comfort in the fact that Spanish is still alive although – in the eyes of many – it is not well.

Increasingly, there has been a debate over code-mixed varieties of Spanish and English popularly called "Spanglish" (Stavans 2003). Many young speakers of Spanish do not speak the language well in the eyes of their teachers. "Like teachers of English, such teachers of Spanish find it difficult to accept the contact variety of Spanish" (Valdés 2000: 119) that students bring to school. In some respects, the debate over Spanglish parallels the debate of Ebonics, or African American Vernacular English (Ramírez et al. 2005), which is largely over the status of non-standard varieties of language. The primary difference, however, is that Spanglish involves code-mixing, borrowing, and coining/neologisms in contact situations, whereas Ebonics is generally understood within the context of social dialects (see Lippi-Green 1994, 1997).

Based on their countries of origin and locations of settlement, immigrants often come in contact with not only English speakers, but also speakers of other languages. Among immigrant Spanish-speaking groups, there is also considerable variation among the varieties of Spanish being spoken. Differences in "accent" and vocabulary mark speakers within immigrant communities who may be perceived as not belonging in the community. Zentella (2000: 148) notes that the "pronunciation of Latin American Spanish differs from Spain's Castilian dialect primarily in intonation and in a few consonants that changed centuries ago". Moreover, differences among various immigrant varieties of Spanish "sometimes become the focus of ignorant declarations about the superiority of one dialect over another, e.g., claims that Puerto Rican Spanish [...] is not real

Spanish". Teachers who are trained in a prestige variety, such as Castilian, can discourage heritage speakers of other varieties based on marked features, which become stigmatized. This problem is not limited to heritage language learners of Spanish, but has been noted in Chinese language instruction between instructors who speak the prestige Beijing variety of Mandarin and speakers with Taiwanese "accents" (Wiley in press). Similar problems are common among other language groups.

7.2. The utility of heritage and community language maintenance efforts

There is a long history of community and heritage language education in the United States and its prior colonial history, although they have not always been taught under these labels. "Heritage language" in recent years has increasingly been used in reference to both immigrant languages and indigenous languages. For some, it has a positive connotation, suggesting connections to ancestral languages. Baker and Jones (1998: 509), however, caution that the connection with past traditions "may fail to give the impression of a modern international language that is of value in a technological society". Thus, for many, "community language" is preferred because it deals "with people and their immediate reality. Above all, it allows them to become meaningfully involved in shaping their own futures through the school and other agencies in their community" (Corson 1999: 10). Community and heritage language education may be seen as part of a larger tradition, what Kloss (1998) called the "American bilingual tradition", which he understood to be a minority tradition amidst the more powerful tradition of English monolingualism. Historically, the momentum for the preservation and support for community languages has fallen on immigrant and language minority communities themselves (Kloss 1998; Toth 1990). Facing the domination of English in the broader society, it is not surprising that language acquisition into English has been accompanied by language loss.

The decision to maintain or promote community and heritage languages is connected to notions of identity and group self-interest and determination. Historically, in the United States, the notion of self-determination for immigrant groups has never had strong support. Among immigrant communities, there has been considerable variation in the desire and capacity for community-language education. For over two centuries, a succession of German immigrants was successful in maintaining their language for community and religious purposes across generations (Toth 1990). However, with the coming of World War I, these efforts rapidly eroded in the face of discrimination and language restrictionism (Wiley 1998). Italians came to the U.S. by the millions in the early 1900s, but many spoke regional dialects and lacked extensive formal education in the prestige variety. However, some 60% of Southern Italians retained their language between 1908 and 1923 because they returned home, as did 66% of

Hungarians and Romanians (Wyman 1993: 11). Emigration from the United States is a little studied phenomenon, but it is apparent that for many Mexican immigrants, the label of trans-national may be more appropriate than immigrant, given the number of back and forth border crossings that many make for economic and family reasons.

In the past few decades, some Southeast Asian refugees, particularly Cambodians, have been less successful in promoting language maintenance. Portes and Rumbaut (2001: 123) found only a 3.4% rate of bilingualism among second generation Cambodians. It is important to note that many of these students had little educational opportunity prior to immigrating to the U.S. (Weinberg 1997). Many of the families had been shattered as a result of the Cambodian Holocaust of the 1970s. Many children arrived in the U.S. with one or no parents. After arrival, economic marginalization and discrimination in local communities overshadowed concerns for community language maintenance. In the city of Long Beach California, which has the largest Cambodian populations outside of Southeast Asia, one of the few Khmer bilingual public school programs was dismantled with the passage of Proposition 227 in 1998 (Wright 1999).

By contrast, some immigrant communities have been resilient in promoting their languages. Koreans, with nearly 900,000 speakers, experience many of the challenges of other groups, but have an extensive network of community and church supported schools. They have their own professional teacher training association and professional conferences, a professional journal, and receive considerable support from the South Korean government in the form of educational language materials.

Cho (2000), in a survey of second generation Koreans, found both personal and professional reasons for maintaining the language:

> In addition to the HL [heritage language] being a tool needed to communicate and socialize with one's family and with others, HL development provided a personal gain, eventually contributing positively to the betterment of the society.
> In addition to wanting to communicate with family, friends, and community, and a desire to hold on to one's Korean heritage, a number of the respondents mentioned the career benefits of being bilingual as a reason for their desire to acquire the HL. Those interested in working with the Korean community especially believed that Korean proficiency would help them in their work, as well as give them more legitimacy. [...] Having developed one's HL was also shown to provide advantages for individuals when interacting with the community, such as knowing the Korean language provided, for some, the freedom to express their feelings and thoughts to HL speakers at any given moment; and knowing their HL allowed them to serve the community. For some, their ability helped them in translating and interpreting for others who were not fluent in English.
> (Cho 2000: 344)

The Hawaiian language was nearly eliminated as a result of the political and economic dominance of English in Hawaii. Yamauchi, Ceppi, and Lau-Smith (2000) note the benefits of a Hawaiian language medium program and its positive impact on language revival efforts and the identities of educators as members of the Hawaiian community. Heritage language speakers are sometimes ridiculed for their lack of proficiency in prestige/literate-standardized varieties of language. Shibata (2000) offers similar findings based on a case study in community-based efforts to establish Saturday Japanese schools.

Chinese has grown dramatically since the suspension of racially-based immigration quotas in the 1960s, and with over two million speakers is the third largest language group in the United States. Chinese communities, like Korean immigrant communities, are also active in promoting Mandarin and to a lesser extent, Cantonese. Other Chinese "dialects" are not generally taught in the U.S., although in some source countries, most notably Taiwan, there are some recent efforts to maintain minority Chinese language varieties, such as Taiwanese or Min. The level of community organization varies based on the original homeland of Chinese immigrants; for example, whether it is the People's Republic of China (PRC), Taiwan (Republic of China, ROC), Hong Kong, or Singapore. There are also many Chinese immigrants who, as part of the large Chinese Diaspora, come to the U.S. from other areas in the world. The majority of Chinese schools teach Mandarin, which is the national language of both the PRC and the ROC. However, even though both types of schools teach Mandarin, they vary in the scripts chosen for instruction, with PRC majority immigrants opting for the simplified characters taught on the mainland and Taiwanese immigrant majority schools choosing the more complicated traditional characters (Li 2005; Wiley in press). If the level of Chinese immigration persists, particularly with the rise of the PRC economy – which is projected to be the world's second largest by 2020, and largest by 2050 (National Intelligence Council, December 2004) – the importance of Mandarin as both a community and heritage language can be expected to rise unless there is a major political rift between the U.S. and the PRC that could result in stigmatization of that immigrant group and its language.

8. Contributions by applied linguists

Language policy as a field of applied linguistics deals with issues that have direct impact on language communities. Several applied linguists in the U.S. (Labov 1982; Rickford 1997; Wolfram 1998; see also Wiley 1996) have addressed issues of the professional role that applied linguists and language educators need to consider when engaging with, and formulating policies for language minority groups. Labov's (1982: 165) formulation of the question remains pertinent: "How can we reconcile the objectivity we need for scientific research with the social commitment we need to apply our knowledge in the social world?" He offers four principles to guide professional involvement (cf. Labov 1982: 172–187):

Error Correction:

> A scientist who becomes aware of a widespread idea or social practice with important consequences that is invalidated by his own data is obligated to bring this error to the attention of the widest possible audience. (172)

Debt Incurred:

> An investigator who has obtained linguistic data from members of a speech community has an obligation to use the knowledge based on that data for the benefit of the community, when it has need of it. (173; see also Rickford 1998; Wolfram 1998)

Linguistic Democracy:

> Linguists support the use of a standard dialect [or language] in so far as it is an instrument of wider communication for the general population, but oppose its use as a barrier to social mobility. (186)

Linguistic Autonomy:

> The choice of what language or dialect is to be used in a given domain of a speech community is reserved to members of that community. (186)

These principles allow applied linguists, particularly those working in language policy and immigrant language education, to consider their roles not only in terms of academic and disciplinary perspectives but in terms of social engagement with the communities that form the basis of their research.

9. Conclusion

Given that there are now nearly 50 million speakers of languages other than English in the United States, there is a need for a language policy based on the current and historical reality of multilingualism in this country. There is particular need to acknowledge that the United States is also one of the largest Spanish-speaking nations in the world. This fact has not been lost on Spanish-language media. Spanish-language television station Univision, for example, now boasts the fifth largest viewer market in the United States. Ironically, despite the presence of nearly 30 million speakers, Spanish in the United States is still being taught as if it were a foreign language in most public school and university programs.

What might a policy based on current and historical reality include? Spolsky (2002) has suggested a set of recommendations that are helpful in this connection: (1) policies that ensure there is no linguistic discrimination (cf. Labov 1982); (2) adequate programs for teaching English to all; (3) respect for both plurilingual capacity and for diverse individual languages; (4) programs that enhance heritage languages and community languages; (5) multi-branched language-capacity programs that assure heritage programs connect with advanced language training programs and overseas-experience approaches that lead to knowledge of, and respect for, other languages and cultures (see also Spolsky 2001).

Immigrant language policies need some provisions for "protective rights" from linguistic discrimination as well as "rights of access" to instruction in English (cf. Wiley 2002). These can only be promoted in a policy climate that values linguistic tolerance as well as linguistic diversity. In this respect, there is substantial room for progress in the United States. Spolsky's last consideration for promotion of language diversity requires the need for community-based and family input and support for the promotion of their own languages in collaboration with applied linguistics. Hornberger (1997) has referred to such efforts as bottom-up planning (see also Wiley 2005b). Such planning requires engagement with immigrant communities in assessing aspirations, needs, and logistics. This may require framing issues in non-academic terms in ways that lend voice to those in the community.

Within universities, there is often little advocacy for less commonly taught languages, with the exception of some government sponsored programs designed to increase intelligence capacity. There is a need for closer collaboration between universities and local communities in promoting the teaching of community-based languages, particularly those that are less commonly taught. There is much that can be learned from successful local community-based language maintenance efforts.

There is also a need to consider the long term impact of narrowly focused regional economic relationships, such as the North American Free Trade Agreement (NAFTA), which places emphasis on the free exchange of goods, but neither on the free exchange of linguistic and cultural knowledge, nor on free movement of people within the region. Given regional and global interdependence, the hour is growing late for the majority of Americans who speak only English to reflect on the implications of their linguistic deficiencies in a multilingual world and acknowledge the resources of the multilingual population in their midst.

References

Baker, Colin and Sylvia Prys Jones
   1998   *Encyclopedia of Bilingual Education and Bilingualism.* Clevedon: Multilingual Matters.

Blaut, James M.
   1993   *The Colonizer's Model of the World: Geographical Diffusionism and Eurocentric History.* New York: Guildford Press.

Cho, Grace
   2000   The role of heritage language in social interactions and relationships: Reflections from a language minority group. *Bilingual Research Journal* 24(4): 333–348.

Chung, Hoang Chung
   2000   English language learners of Vietnamese background. In: Sandra Lee McKay and Sau-Ling C. Wong (eds.), *New Immigrants in the United States*, 216–231. Cambridge: Cambridge University Press.

Conzen, Kathleen Neils
   1980   Germans. In: Stephan Thernstrom, Ann Orlov and Oscar Handlin (eds.), *Harvard Encyclopedia of American Ethnic Groups*, 404–425. Cambridge: Belknap Press of Harvard University Press.

Corson, David
   1999   Community-based education for indigenous cultures. In: Stephen May (ed.), *Indigenous Community-based Education*, 8–19. Clevedon: Multilingual Matters.

Crawford, James
   1992a   *Hold Your Tongue: Bilingualism and the Politics of "English Only".* Reading, MA: Addison-Wesley.

Crawford, James
   1992b   *Language Loyalties: A Source Book on the Official English Controversy.* Chicago, IL: University of Chicago Press.

Crawford, James
   1995   *Bilingual Education: History, Politics, Theory, and Practice.* 3rd ed. Los Angeles, CA: Bilingual Education Services.

Crawford, James
   2000   *At War with Diversity: US Language Policy in an Age of Anxiety.* Clevedon: Multilingual Matters.

Crawford, James
   2002   *Obituary: The Bilingual Education Act, 1968–2002.* Tempe, AZ: Language Policy Research Unit, Education Policy Studies Laboratory, Arizona State University. Retrieved April 25, 2005, from http://www.asu.edu/educ/epsl/LPRU/features/article2.htm

Donahue, Thomas S.
   1995   American language policy and compensatory opinion. In: James Tollefson (ed.), *Power and Inequality in Language Education*, 112–141. Cambridge: Cambridge University Press.

Ferry, Joseph
   2004   *Vietnamese Immigration. The Changing Face of North America: Immigration Since 1965.* Broomall, PA: Mason Crest Publishers.

Gibson, Margaret A. and John Ogbu (eds.)
   1991   *Minority Status and Schooling: A Comparative Study of Immigrant and Involuntary Minorities.* New York: Garlund.

González, Josué M.
   2002   *Bilingual Education and the Federal Role, if Any. Policy Brief.* Tempe, AZ: Language Policy Research Unit, Educational Policy Studies Laboratory, Arizona State University. Retrieved April 25, 2005, from http://www.asu.edu/educ/epsl/LPRU/features/article1.htm.

Haas, Michael
   1992   *Institutional Racism: The Case of Hawai'i.* Westport, CT: Praeger.

Hornberger, Nancy
   1997   Language planning from the bottom up. In: Nancy Hornberger (ed.), *Indigenous Literacies in the Americas: Language Planning from the Bottom up,* 357–366. Berlin and New York: Mouton de Gruyter.

Hunnicutt, Kay H. and Mario Castro
   2005   How census 2000 data suggest hostility toward Mexican-origin Arizonians. *Bilingual Research Journal* 29(1): 109–125.

Huntington, Samuel
   2004   *Who Are We: The Challenges to America's National Identity.* New York: Simon and Schuster.

Kloss, Heinz
   1971   Language rights of immigrant groups. *International Migration Review* 5: 250–268.

Kloss, Heinz
   1998   *The American Bilingual Tradition.* Revised Edition. Washington, DC: Center for Applied Linguistics.

Labov, William
   1982   Objectivity and commitment in linguistic science: The case of Black English trial in Ann Arbor. *Language in Society* 11: 165–201.

Leibowitz, Arnold H.
   1969   English literacy: Legal sanction for discrimination. *Notre Dame Lawyer* 25(1): 7–66.

Leibowitz, Arnold H.
   1971   Educational policy and political acceptance: The Imposition of English as the Language of Instruction in American Schools. Eric No. ED 047 321.

Leibowitz, Arnold H.
   1974   Language as a means of social control. Paper presented at the 8th World Congress of Sociology, University of Toronto, Canada, August 1974.

Leibowitz, Arnold H.
   1980   *The Bilingual Education Act: A Legislative Analysis.* Rosslyn, VA: National Clearinghouse on Bilingual Education.

Lepore, Jill
   2002   *A is for American: Letters and Other Characters in the Newly United States.* New York: Alfred Knopf.

Li, Mengying
   2005   The role of parents in Chinese heritage-language schools. *Bilingual Research Journal* 29(1): 199–207.

Lippi-Green, Rosina
   1994   Accent, standard language ideology, and discriminatory pretext in courts. *Language in Society* 23: 163–198.
Lippi-Green, Rosina
   1997   *English with an Accent: Language, Ideology, and Discrimination in the United States*. New York: Routledge.
Macías, Reynaldo F. and Terrence G. Wiley
   1998   Introduction. In: Heinz Kloss, *The American Bilingual Tradition*, vii–xiv. Washington, DC: Center for Applied Linguistics.
McClymer, John F.
   1982   The Americanization movement and the education of the foreign-born adult, 1914–1925. In: Bernard J. Weiss (ed.), *Education and the European Immigrant: 1840–1940*, 96–116. Urbana: University of Illinois Press.
Molesky, James
   1988   Understanding the American linguistic Mosaic: A historical overview of language maintenance and shift. In: Sandra Lee McKay and Sau-ling C. Wong (eds.), *Language Diversity: Problem or Resource?*, 29–68. Cambridge, MA: Newbury House.
National Intelligence Council
   2004   *Mapping the Global Future*. Report of the National Intelligence Council's 2020 Project, based on consultation with nongovernmental experts around the world. Washington, DC. Author NIC 2004–13.
Otheguy, Richardo, Ofelia García and Ana Roca
   2000   Speaking in Cuban: The language of Cuban Americans. In: Sandra Lee McKay and Sau-ling C. Wong (eds.), *New Immigrants in the United States*, 168–188. Cambridge: Cambridge University Press.
Pitt, Leonard
   1976   *We Americans, Vol 1: Colonial Times to 1877*. Glenview, IL: Scott, Foresman and Company.
Portes, Alejandro and Rubén G. Rumbaut
   2001   *Legacies: The Story of the Immigrant Second Generation*. Berkeley, CA: University of California Press.
Ramírez, J. David, Terrence G. Wiley, Gerda de Klerk, G. Enid Lee and Wayne E. Wright (eds.)
   2005   *Ebonics in the Urban Education Debate*. 2nd ed. Clevedon: Multilingual Matters.
Ricento, Thomas
   2003   The discursive construction of Americanism. *Discourse and Society* 14(5): 611–637.
Rickford, John
   1997   Unequal partnerships: Sociolinguistics and the African American speech community. *Language in Society* 26: 161–197.
Santa Ana, Otto
   2002   *Brown Tide Rising: Metaphors of Latinos in Contemporary American Public Discourse*. Austin, TX: University of Texas Press.
Simon, Paul
   1988   *The Tongue-Tied American: Confronting the Foreign Language Crisis*. Reissue edition. New York: Crossroad Publishing Company.

Shibata, Setsue
  2000   Opening a Japanese Saturday school in a small town in the United States: Community collaboration to teach Japanese as a heritage language. *Bilingual Research Journal* 24(4): 465–474.
Spolsky, Bernard
  2001   Heritage languages and national security: An ecological view. In: Steven Baker (ed.), *Language Policy: Lessons from Global Models*, 103–114. Monterey, CA: Monterey Institute of International Studies.
Spolsky, Bernard
  2002   Principles for drafting a policy statement paper. 2nd National Heritage Language Conference, "Building on our National Resources". Washington, DC, October 18–20, 2002.
Stavans, Ilan
  2003   *Spanglish: The Making of a New American Language*. New York: Harper Collins.
Tatalovich, Raymond
  1995   *Nativism Reborn? The Official English Language Movement and the American States*. Lexington, KY: University Press of Kentucky.
Tollefson, James
  1991   *Planning Language, Planning Inequality*. New York: Longman.
Toth, Carolyn R.
  1990   *German-English Bilingual Schools in America: The Cincinnati Tradition in Historical Context*. New York: Lang.
Valdés, Guadalupe
  2000   Bilingualism and language use among Mexican Americans. In: Sandra Lee McKay and Sau-ling C. Wong (eds.), *New Immigrants in the United States*, 99–136. Cambridge: Cambridge University Press.
Veltman, Calvin
  1983   *Language Shift in the United States*. Berlin: Mouton.
Veltman, Calvin
  2000   The American linguistic mosaic: Understanding language shift in the United States. In: Sandra Lee McKay and Sau-ling C. Wong (eds.), *New Immigrants in the United States*, 58–98. Cambridge: Cambridge University Press.
Weinberg, Meyer
  1995   *A Chance to Learn: A History of Race and Education in the United States*. 2nd ed. Long Beach, CA: California State University Press.
Weinberg, Meyer
  1997   *Asian-American Education: Historical Background and Current Realities*. Mahwah, NJ: Lawrence Erlbaum.
Weiss, Bernard J. (ed.)
  1982   *American Education and the European Immigrant, 1840–1940*. Urbana, IL: University of Illinois Press.
Wiley, Terrence G
  1996   Language planning and language policy. In: Sandra Lee McKay and Sau-ling C. Wong (eds.), *Sociolinguistics and Language Teaching*, 103–147. Cambridge: Cambridge University Press.

Wiley, Terrence G.
　1998　　The imposition of World War I era English-Only policies and the fate of German in North America. In: Thomas Ricento and Barbara Burnaby (eds.), *Language and Politics in the United States and Canada*, 211–241. Mahwah, NJ: Lawrence Erlbaum.

Wiley, Terrence G.
　1999　　What happens after English is declared the official language of the United States? Lessons from case histories. In: Douglas Kibbee (ed.), *Language Legislation and Linguistic Rights*, 179–195. Amsterdam: John Benjamins.

Wiley, Terrence G.
　2000　　Continuity and change in the function of language ideologies in the United States. In: Thomas Ricento (ed.), *Ideology, Politics, and Language Policies: Focus on English*, 67–85. Mahwah, NJ: Lawrence Erlbaum.

Wiley, Terrence G.
　2002　　Accessing language rights in education: A brief history of the U.S. context. In: James Tollefson (ed.), *Language Policies in Education: Critical Readings*, 39–64. Mahwah, NJ: Lawrence Erlbaum.

Wiley, Terrence G.
　2004　　Language planning, language policy and the English-Only Movement. In: Edward Finegan and John R. Rickford (eds.), *Language in the USA: Themes for the Twenty-First Century*, 319–338. Cambridge: Cambridge University Press.

Wiley, Terrence G.
　2005a　　*Literacy and Language Diversity in the United States*. 2nd ed. Washington, DC: Center for Applied Linguistics.

Wiley, Terrence G.
　2005b　　Discontinuities in heritage and community language education: Challenges for educational language policies. *The International Journal of Bilingual Education and Bilingualism* 8(2/3): 222–229.

Wiley, Terrence G.
　in press　　Dialect speakers as heritage language learners: A Chinese case study. In: Donna Brinton and Olga Kagan (eds.), *Heritage Language: A New Field Emerging*. Mahwah, NJ: Lawrence Erlbaum.

Wiley, Terrence G. and Wayne E. Wright
　2004　　Against the undertow: Language-minority education and politics in the age of accountability. *Educational Policy* 18(1): 142–168.

Wolfram, Walt
　1998　　Scrutinizing linguistic gratuity: A view from the field. *Journal of Sociolinguistics* 2: 271–279.

Wright, Wayne E.
　1999　　The education of Cambodian American Students in the Long Beach Unified School District: A language and educational policy analysis. MA Thesis, California State University, Long Beach.

Wright, Wayne E.
　2005a　　*Evolution of Federal Policy and Implications of No Child Left Behind For Language Minority Students*. Policy Brief. Tempe, AZ: Language Policy Research Unit, Educational Policy Studies Laboratory, Arizona State Uni-

versity. Retrieved May 11, 2005 from http://www.asu.edu/educ/epsl/EPRU/documents/EPSL-0501–101-LPRU.pdf

Wright, Wayne E.
    2005b   English language learners left behind in Arizona: The nullification of accommodations in the intersection of federal and state policies. *Bilingual Research Journal* 29(1): 1–29.

Wyman, Mark
    1993   *Round Trip to Europe: The Immigrants Return Home, 1880–1930.* Ithaca, NY: Cornell University Press.

Yamauchi, Lois A., Andrea K. Ceppi and Jo-Anne Lau-Smith
    2000   Teaching in a Hawaiian context: Educator perspectives on the Hawaiian language immersion program. *Bilingual Research Journal* 24(4): 385–403.

Zentella, Ana Celia
    2000   Puerto Ricans in the United States: Confronting the repercussions of colonialism. In: Sandra Lee McKay and Sau-Ling C. Wong (eds.), *New Immigrants in the United States*, 137–164. Cambridge: Cambridge University Press.

3. Immigrant minorities: Australia

Antonia Rubino

1. Introduction

Talking about "the diverse cultural backgrounds of their friends as a reflection of Australia's racial tolerance", a newly arrived migrant says to a newspaper: "It seems normal here to mix with people from all parts of the world. Our friends are from everywhere – white Australians, also Chinese, Turkish people, Lebanese; you don't really even notice it after a while." (*Sydney Morning Herald* 22/1/05). On the other hand, this is how Ali, who identifies himself as "an Australian with Lebanese background" describes his experience as an Australian: "I have come to realise I am an Australian but I am not treated like an Australian. I do not act like an Australian. I am more Lebanese. I am treated like a Lebanese so I will stick to what I am treated like." (Collins et al. 2000: 165). While these differences may be explained by resorting to a range of factors in these individual experiences (perhaps socio-economic status, levels of education, countries of origin), they aptly illustrate the two facets of Australia as a country of immigration: on the positive side, the relatively easy process of settlement and the peaceful co-existence of the hundreds of ethnic groups (see Price 2001: 81–82) which today constitute well over 20% of its population; on the negative side, the fact that after more than forty years of immigration, the Anglo-Celtic majority group still represents the core or the mainstream of Australian society while immigrant minorities – and much worse so the Indigenous population – remain in the main at its margins.

This chapter deals with the languages that immigrant minorities have brought to Australia and shows that, like their speakers, they are treated with the same ambivalence: Although Australia has been celebrating its cultural and linguistic diversity since the 1970s, overall it remains a strongly Anglocentric country, where the dominance of English is unchallenged. As major achievements of its multilingualism, Australia can boast excellent work in the official recognition of the languages of its minorities (as well as of its Indigenous population). For example, Australia has been recognised as "the first of the major English-speaking countries to formulate an explicit language policy" (Romaine 1991: 8). The *National Policy on Languages* (Lo Bianco 1987) acknowledges the multilingual nature of the country, emphasises the value of immigrant languages both for the ethnic groups and for the country at large, and recommends that such languages be maintained and developed through schools, as well as be taught to the community at large. Since the mid 1970s, the term *Community*

Languages has been used to refer to immigrant languages, in recognition of the fact that they are used by immigrants and their Australian-born children and grandchildren – as well as by other people (Clyne 1991: 3).

Nonetheless, there are still a number of areas where the contribution of applied linguists is still very much in need. First and foremost, although it falls outside the scope of this chapter, a matter of pressing urgency is the survival and revitalisation of the Indigenous languages, which are rapidly being lost on the continent. In fact, it should be remembered that Australia was a multilingual country well before the White occupation and that between 200 to 300 different languages were originally spoken (Walsh 1997). The most dire consequence of the contact with English has been language death, which has reduced Indigenous languages by over 50%, with a current estimate of 55,000 speakers and 14% of the Indigenous population declaring to speak an Indigenous language in the 1996 Census (McConvell and Thieberger 2001). In the past four decades much research has gone into recording and describing Indigenous languages (e.g., Dixon 2002), as well as into highlighting the endangered state of existing languages (e.g., Schmidt 1985; Walsh and Yallop 1993; Henderson and Nash 1997) and the severe problems faced by their speakers, such as language loss across generations and cross-cultural miscommunication, particularly in courts (e.g., Eades 1995). Throughout the 1980s and 1990s Indigenous languages enjoyed public recognition at the national level and studies have pointed to the positive effects of initiatives such as bilingual education (e.g., Hartman and Henderson 1994; but see also Hoogenraad 2001), to the reevaluation of Aboriginal English (e.g., Harkins 1994) and to cases of language revival (e.g., Amery 2000). A major point to notice is the increasing involvement in these initiatives of the Indigenous communities and of Indigenous experts, such as teachers and linguists. A recent comprehensive report (McConvell and Thieberger 2001) points to some encouraging signs of language revitalisation, as an increasing number of people under 30 are identifying as Indigenous speakers. However, overall the picture remains bleak, due to lack of adequate support – both political and financial – and the weakening of successful initiatives (e.g., the removal of bilingual programs in the Northern Territory, see McConvell and Thieberger 2001).

With regard to the languages of the immigrant minorities, of major concern is their overall vulnerable position, as demonstrated by the following issues. Firstly, immigrant minorities tend to abandon their languages relatively quickly, not only in the transition from the first generation (i.e. overseas born people) to the second (i.e. Australia born people with one or both overseas born parents) but also within the first generation. This is what is commonly referred to as *language shift*, a process whereby an individual, a group of speakers and/or a whole speech community gradually changes its dominant use from one language (in our case the immigrant language) to another (in our case the majority language,

English) in most spheres of life. Conversely, *language maintenance* indicates the continuous use of the immigrant language in some spheres of life, in spite of the pressure exercised by the majority language (see Pauwels 2004). Secondly, bilingual and/or multilingual skills are not fully recognised as valuable assets in the Australian society, particularly in the work environment. Thirdly, the maintenance and development of immigrant languages can be a fairly arduous task even for the committed individual. For example, in spite of the increased presence of languages at school, opportunities for advanced language studies are often limited, and bilingual education is still an exception. Fourthly, the broader Australian society shows a limited interest in languages and/or language study, as demonstrated by the fact that the study of a second language throughout the secondary school curriculum is still optional in most states.

The issues outlined above have all been areas of research in Australian applied linguistics in the past forty years. In particular, the process of language shift in the immigrant communities has been – and continues to be – a main focus of study, and has been investigated from a number of different perspectives, as will be seen below. It is important also to note that these issues have been concerns that the immigrant communities themselves have identified as particularly relevant for their lives in Australia, and for which they have struggled since the 1970s. Often they have had to address these concerns on their own, through the establishment of community based initiatives. For example, immigrant groups firstly set up their own after-hours and/or Saturday schools and bilingual schools, and multilingual libraries; immigrants worked on a voluntary basis as interpreters and translators before a public service was set up; and were at the forefront in the struggles to have a public television and radio that would broadcast in different languages (Ozolins 1993: 118–121, 123–127). Even though some of the responsibility of language maintenance today has been taken over by the Australian government, it is a fact that "much language maintenance is still financed by [immigrant] groups, families and individuals, who are in so doing offering an essential service to the nation" (Kipp, Clyne, and Pauwels 1995: 134).

2. Australia today – immigrant minorities

Australia is a country with a population of almost 19 million people. According to the 2001 Census data, over 4 million were born overseas, representing 21.9% of the entire population. The largest overseas born groups include people from the United Kingdom, New Zealand and Italy. Table 1 presents the top 10 countries of birth, with percentages calculated on the total Australian population.

Table 1. Top 10 countries of birth, 2001 Census (adapted from Australian Government/ Department of Foreign Affairs and Trade)

Birthplace	Number of immigrants	% of total overseas born
United Kingdom	1,036,437	5.5
New Zealand	355,684	1.9
Italy	218,754	1.2
Vietnam	154,831	0.8
China	142,717	0.8
Greece	116,531	0.6
Germany	108,238	0.6
Philippines	103,989	0.6
India	95,456	0.5
Netherlands	83,249	0.4
Top 10 Total	2,415,886	12.9
Total overseas born	4,106,187	21.9
Total Australian population	18,769,791	100.0

The immigrant minorities that make up Australia have become a substantial part of the Australian population particularly since the post World War II period, when the Australian government decided to increase significantly the population of the country (then 7.5 million people) in order to sustain its rapidly expanding economy and strengthen the country's defence capability. Up until the post World War II period Australia remained a fairly homogenous country that, due to openly racist policies, was characterised by an almost exclusive reliance on migrants from Britain. By contrast, what characterises the post World War II policy is that for the first time Australia considered "planned *non-British* immigration" (Ozolins 1993: 5). This set in motion a process that irrevocably changed the composition of the Australian population transforming the country from a nation of British based migration to a more culturally diverse nation of immigrants (for a comprehensive treatment of these issues see Collins 1991 and Jupp 2001, 2002, among others).

Of particular relevance to our discussion on immigrant languages are the policies adopted by the Australian governments since mass migration started. In the immediate post war years, the prevailing policy was Assimilation, whereby immigrants were expected to leave behind their languages and cultures and quickly assimilate into the broader Australian society. In the 1960s and early 1970s the policy of Integration identified the immigrant minorities of non English background as disadvantaged sections of the population but tried to address the issues by treating immigrants as a *problem* that needed to be solved. A breakthrough came in the early 1970s and particularly with the election of the progressive Whitlam government in 1972, when Australia embraced officially a policy of Multiculturalism (also adopted by the Liberal Party), as a pluralistic country where the different languages and cultures brought by immigrants had a legitimate space in all sectors of society. Consequently, among other measures, the teaching of *languages other than English*, or LOTEs, was expanded in schools, services were set up in different languages (e.g., interpreter services) and multilingual radio and television broadcasting funded by the government was established. In spite of the criticism that Multiculturalism has attracted (see e.g. Ozolins 1993: 164), considerable efforts were made to cater for the cultural and linguistic needs of immigrant communities. Throughout the 1990s the policy of Multiculturalism was still maintained and promoted. However, the changed economic circumstances of the country – an economic crisis and a major policy shift from an economy based on the export of raw materials to a service economy, with tourism as one of its main sources – as well as a major emphasis on the economic rationalist doctrine, led to languages being seen as a commodity, with negative effects on language policies (see Section 2). In present-day Australia, the current Liberal Coalition government of John Howard (in power since 1996), although it has never officially abandoned the policy of Multiculturalism, has done very little to promote and enforce it. Its conservative social and cultural agenda has led to the *mainstreaming* of social and cultural services, and LOTEs have suffered from this new trend.

Today in Australia there are 142 LOTEs, which are spoken at home by 16% of the Australian population (Clyne and Kipp 2002: 29). This information is based on data from the Australian Census, which since 1976 has included a question on language use, generally formulated in terms of home use (e.g., "Does a person speak a language other than English at home?" in the 2001 Census). Table 2 shows the twenty most spoken home languages according to the 2001 Census.

Table 2. Top 20 immigrant languages in Australia in the 2001 Census (from Clyne and Kipp 2002: 31)

Language	Number of speakers
Italian	353,606
Greek	263,718
Cantonese	225,307
Arabic	209,371
Vietnamese	174,236
Mandarin	139,288

Language	Number of speakers
Spanish	93,595
Tagalog	78,879
German	76,444
Macedonian	71,994
Croatian	69,850
Polish	59,056
Turkish	50,692
Serbian	49,202
Hindi	47,817
Maltese	41,392
Netherlandic	40,187
French	39,643
Korean	39,528
Indonesian	38,724

As shown in Table 2, the most spoken languages at home are either the languages of the longest established communities, that is Italian and Greek, or those of the communities of the largest current inflows, that is Arabic, Vietnamese, Cantonese and Mandarin. While Table 2 presents only a synoptic view of the national language situation, comparisons with the data from previous censuses can yield a measure of the language shift that these groups are undergoing both across the years and the generations, as well as highlight the different rates of language shift displayed by the various communities.

In the following sections, I shall first outline the field of study of Australia's immigrant languages over the past 40 years (Section 3), then the main research paradigms that have been applied (Section 4). In the next sections I shall focus on current developments in Australian research (Section 5) and on the contributions of applied linguistics to the field of immigrant languages (Section 6). Throughout the chapter the terms LOTEs, immigrant languages, minority languages and Community Languages are used interchangeably. Issues that are closely related to the topic of LOTEs but are dealt with in other chapters (e.g., the acquisition and use of English by immigrants, language policy) are either excluded or treated very briefly.

3. Australia's immigrant languages: History and major issues

The study of immigrant languages is acknowledged as one of the founding areas of Australian applied linguistics in the late 1960s (McNamara 2001). Throughout the past four decades the field has become increasingly more diversified and more complex, and still represents a significant section in the wider scene of applied linguistics in Australia.

As noted by Bettoni (1991a: 75), in Australia the serious study of LOTEs followed international trends where the rights and social conditions of minority groups became major areas of research, particularly in countries of high immigration (e.g., the United States). Also in Australia, research at first focused on what is one of the most conspicuous aspects in a situation of language contact, that is, the structural changes that minority languages undergo under the pressure of the majority language. Drawing on studies conducted in other parts of the world (e.g., by Weinreich 1953; Haugen 1953, 1956), research started with the seminal work carried out by Clyne (1967, 1972) on the Anglicisation of the speech of German migrants. Soon his work was followed by studies on a number of other languages (e.g., Greek, Italian, Russian, see Clyne 1991: 158) that investigated the changes in their lexicon, phonology and grammar occurring as a result of contact with English. These changes were subsumed under the label of *transference*, i.e. "the process of bringing over any items, features or rules from one language to another, and for the results of this process" (Clyne 1991: 160). In this area Australian work has been particularly fertile and has given a significant contribution to international research in a number of ways.

From the 1970s, when the new policies of Integration and Multiculturalism gave more visibility to immigrant minorities, studies of their languages flourished in the field of language maintenance and shift, following the work by Fishman and colleagues (1964, 1966) in the United States. The main concern was to study the collocation of LOTEs in the host country and to investigate their transmission from the first to the second generation by identifying the different variables that work in favour of language maintenance or against it. Hence, from 1976 onwards, the information derived from the language question used in the Census has been crosstabulated with socio-demographic data. These quantitative analyses represent an excellent basis for the study of the overall language ecology of the country and the identification of the main socio-demographic variables associated with language shift. Another quantitative paradigm that has been very productive in Australia since the 1980s is the so called sociology of language approach, which specifically investigates "who speaks what language to whom, when and where" (Fishman 1965). The analysis of patterns of language use in the different contextualised spheres of life or *domains* (Fishman 1964) has been particularly fruitful in that it has allowed the identification of situations where LOTEs are used or where they are instead making way to

English. This approach is often extended through a combination of quantitative and qualitative methodologies (e.g., Kouzmin 1988; Doucet 1991); recently it has been used for the in-depth study of language maintenance across different groups using the same language but coming from different birth places ("pluricentric languages", Clyne and Kipp 1999). Furthermore, a number of studies has explored the use of LOTEs in light of the social network approach (see Section 4.6), as it is considered a framework that can explain different linguistic practices in multilingual contexts and has been applied in research on intergenerational patterns of language shift in other countries.

Since the early 1980s, the field of language maintenance and shift in Australia has benefited greatly from another approach within the sociological perspective, that is, the humanistic approach of the *core values* adopted by Smolicz and his research associates (e.g., 1981, 1985). According to this paradigm, each immigrant group has particular cultural values that are considered *core* in that they are fundamental to its existence as a group. As language is a core value to some groups but less so to others, this would explain why some groups abandon their languages more easily and rapidly than others. In Australia the core value theory has been applied to a wide range of different minorities and, in spite of some limitations (see Section 4.3), it can provide a further explanation for the different linguistic outcomes of immigrant groups which otherwise share several similarities, such as the Greeks and the Italians.

Studies on the factors associated with language maintenance have been conducted also in the socio-psychological perspective, focusing in particular on the areas of language attitudes and the ethnolinguistic vitality of immigrant communities. The attitudes that speakers hold towards the language varieties that they use have long been recognised as a crucial variable in the process of language maintenance among immigrant minorities (e.g., Kloss 1966), with negative attitudes being acknowledged as a powerful factor in hindering language maintenance. Following North American and British research (e.g., Lambert 1967; Giles 1977), Australian studies have explored language attitudes within one group as well as across different groups (e.g., Callan and Gallois 1982 on Greeks and Italians) using a range of different methodologies (see Section 4.5). Language maintenance has also been studied in light of the ethnolinguistic vitality theory (e.g., Giles, Rosenthal, and Young 1985), particularly using the construct of the *Subjective Ethnolinguistic Vitality* (SEV), which stresses speakers' perceptions of the vitality of their own language as a relevant factor in language maintenance. According to this theory, speakers and/or communities with perceptions of high ethnolinguistic vitality are more likely to maintain their languages than those with perceptions of low ethnolinguistic vitality (on attitudes, see also Gallois, Watson, and Brabant, this vol.).

Two other main areas of research related to LOTEs have been the fields of language policy and language education. With the new policies of Integration and of Multiculturalism in the 1970s, linguists, teachers and educators started to pay attention to immigrant children's education and their underachievement at school. Areas of concern were the lack of provision of English teaching, the teaching of Community Languages and bilingual education, thus supporting migrant communities' efforts for language maintenance and highlighting the benefits of bilingualism (see e.g., Kalantzis, Cope, and Slade 1989). Throughout the 1980s a number of states (e.g., Victoria and South Australia) formulated language policies recommending the inclusion of LOTEs as part of the primary school curriculum. The work carried out throughout the 1970s and the 1980s culminated in the formulation of the *National Policy on Languages* (NLP, Lo Bianco 1987). While emphasising the primacy of English for all, it supported the maintenance and development of both Indigenous and immigrant languages, the provision of services in other languages and the importance of LOTEs not just for immigrant communities but for the whole country, in terms of cultural enrichment and economic advancement. The establishment of the *National Languages Institute of Australia* (NLIA) in 1989 (later to become the *National Languages and Literacy Institute of Australia*, NLLIA) also assured greater scope to the NLP, through the setting up of research centres and the development of major research projects focusing on languages and language education (see Ozolins 1991, 1993). Throughout the 1990s, in line with the new economic rationalist doctrine, the new *Australian Language and Literacy Policy* (ALLP, Dawkins 1991) shifted the emphasis from the study of languages for social reasons to the study for economic and instrumental reasons. The ALLP identified fourteen languages as priority languages at the national level, and four of these – Chinese (Mandarin), Indonesian, Japanese and Korean – were subsequently given special status (Council of Australian Governments 1994). While this policy has contributed to opening up new areas of debate (e.g., how to best teach Asian languages), overall it has not enhanced the position of LOTEs, in that it has (i) created a degree of division, as support for some languages has often been carried out at the expenses of other less preferred languages, even of large immigrant groups (two points in case are Arabic and Spanish, cf. Clyne and Kipp 1999: 24); (ii) weakened the role of non priority languages in some schools; and (iii) emphasised literacy in English but neglected biliteracy (Clyne 1997b: 130–131).

With regard to the bilingual upbringing and education of the younger generations, Australian research has not been as extensive as other areas outlined above. This is also related to the fact that bilingual education – where the LOTE is used as the medium of instruction – is still quite rare, as mentioned above, with less than 1 % of children receiving it in spite of the fact that at least 15 % of them speak a LOTE at home when they start school (Gibbons 1997: 210). In fact, research has repeatedly identified the school as the domain which promotes and accelerates language shift (e.g., Bettoni 1990). Although school programs with the specific aim of language maintenance are quite widespread throughout Australia, the limited number of hours that is generally allocated to them together with other organisational issues (e.g., pupils of very different language abilities being taught together) do not allow them to work effectively towards the development of the linguistic skills that immigrant children bring to school. Language maintenance and development often take place more effectively in the after-hours schools run by immigrant organisations, particularly in the case of the smaller LOTEs, and in the few bilingual schools/programs existing in the country, a number of which are also community based. Research has focused on the bilingual skills of immigrant children in ordinary schools (e.g., Clyne and Kipp 1997) as well as in bilingual programs (e.g., Fernandez 1992), using a combination of quantitative and qualitative methodologies. Few studies have also investigated the development of bilingualism in naturalistic situations according to the principle of *one person, one language* and adopting qualitative methodologies (e.g., Saunders 1982, 1988; Döpke 1992).

4. The study of LOTEs in Australia: A multifaceted approach

4.1. Structural changes in LOTEs

The investigation of changes occurring in the structures of immigrant languages is still a very fertile area of research in Australia, also as a result of the availability of data from typologically different languages. Studies conducted in this approach generally make use of detailed linguistic analyses of data elicited through semistructured interviews among relatively small samples of individuals.

In this area Australian research has been innovative in a number of ways. First, it has expanded the process of transference to include linguistic levels (e.g., syntactic, semantic, prosodic, graphemic, pragmatic, tonemic; Clyne 2003: 76–79) which had not been considered in research in other countries. Second, it has identified previously unnoticed phenomena accompanying transference, most notably the process of *triggering*, whereby a transfer can lead "the speaker's mind into the language which is the source of the transfer" (Clyne 1967: 84), thus causing more transfers or a switch to another language. Third, it has studied the linguistic process of transference in a fairly broad perspective that goes well beyond purely structural considerations. For example, from the very beginning transfers have been analysed also from the perspective of the listener, not just of the speaker, and considered in a discourse perspective in terms of their acceptability and communicability (Clyne 1972: ch. 5). Furthermore, the process of transference has been investigated in systematic correspondence with speakers' demographic and sociological variables, thus stressing the link between social and linguistic change (e.g., Clyne 1972; Bettoni 1981; Tamis 1991). Two variables that are found to impact upon patterns of transference in the use of the LOTE are generation and age of migration of the speaker, with the first generation displaying a higher incidence of lexical and semantic transfers from English, and the second generation displaying more transfers at the phonetic, morphosyntactic and pragmatic levels (Bettoni 1981; Tamis 1991). In other words, this area of research has always considered language contact as "an interaction between language systems, social and communicative factors and psycholinguistic processing" (Clyne 2003: 104).

Studies conducted across a number of languages demonstrate that (i) there are general trends common to most languages in the way structural changes take place under the impact of the majority language; and (ii) changes are also related to typological distance between languages. Clyne's work (1991: ch. 4; 2003: ch. 4) includes detailed reviews of a range of Australian studies that have dealt with structural and typological aspects of immigrant languages. While the reader is referred to both chapters, some of the major findings emerging from these studies are summarised below.

Analyses of transference patterns have confirmed that the lexicon is the area most affected by English, with different languages undergoing similar processes. Transference is particularly frequent when immigrants need to express concepts that are specific to the Australian context and that they have come to know in Australia, particularly with reference to the school and work domains and the Australian landscape. Common lexical transfers from English across different LOTEs are for example *bush*, *fence*, *farm* and *boss*. Furthermore, immigrants tend to create new words by combining English lexical morphemes with grammatical morphemes from their own languages: e.g., *flataki* 'little flat' from the English *flat* and the Greek diminutive suffix *-aki* (Tamis 1991: 256); *weldare* from the English *to weld* and the Italian verb ending *-are* (Bettoni 1981: 57); *farmerieren* 'to farm' from the English *farm* and the German verb ending *-ieren* (Clyne 1991: 163). While nouns and discourse markers are the items most commonly transferred, the study of the grammatical integration of lexical transfers into the LOTE has shown that verbs are the most highly integrated class of transfers across several languages. Furthermore, different languages tend to follow similar rules in grammatical integration, for example in assigning gender to English nouns.

Studies conducted across a range of languages have thus identified a number of regularities in the contact between English and LOTEs. However, they also conclude that the process of structural changes does not result in the creation of new stable language varieties but in a process of *convergence* (Clyne 2003: 79), whereby languages become more similar to each other, partly through the process of transference. Of special importance in this process is the notion of *markedness*, whereby more marked – i.e. less frequent and less basic (Clyne 2003:

98) – features of the immigrant language tend to be lost in favour of less marked features, under the influence of English (for example, the marked auxiliary "to be" gives way to the unmarked "to have" in Italian, French, German and Dutch; see Clyne 1991: 176–186; Clyne 2003: 117–142).

Australian research conducted within the structural paradigm has generally distinguished clearly between transferring a linguistic element from one language to another as part of the process of alternating between languages, and switching between languages, or *crossing over* to the other language (Clyne 2003: 76). Code switching between English and the LOTE is quite common, and can be motivated by linguistic reasons (e.g., lack of language competence), by sociolinguistic reasons, such as changes in the context of situation (e.g., a different interlocutor), or by discourse reasons (e.g., to introduce a quotation; to swear). Among the second generation dominant in English, code switching into the LOTE can be used as identity marker, for example in talking to other people from the same ethnic background (Tsokalidou 1994; Winter and Pauwels 2000; Rubino 2006) and with a symbolic, rather than a communicative function (as in the second generation children in Rubino 2000; see also Pauwels 1988a: 12).

The term *transversion* has recently been used (Clyne 2003: 75) in order to avoid the pitfalls of the polysemic term code switching. Expanding on previous studies about triggering as a process that facilitates transversion, recent work carried out on a wider range of languages, including tonal languages (e.g., Vietnamese and Mandarin), has found that such facilitation occurs not only at the lexical but also at the syntactic and especially tonal levels (e.g., Ho-Dac 2003: ch. 4). Interesting insights have also emerged from some pioneering work conducted among trilingual migrants (e.g., Italian, Spanish and English, see Clyne and Cassia 1999), which shows that trilingual speakers tend to mark clearer boundaries between the languages than bilinguals, possibly as a result of their higher metalinguistic awareness (Clyne 2003: 239).

Australian research has also dealt with the issue of language attrition, which refers to the decreased proficiency in a first or second language as a result of lack of contact with that language over time (Schmid and de Bot 2004). Australian studies have focused on attrition in LOTEs among the first and the second generation (e.g., Bettoni 1990, 1991b; de Bot and Clyne 1994; Yagmur 1997; Caruso 2004), and only to a lower extent on attrition in English as a second language among older immigrants (e.g., Clyne 1977). Special attention has been paid to the lexicon, as the language level where attrition first manifests itself. For example, in a longitudinal study among Dutch immigrants, de Bot and Clyne (1994) found that attrition had affected the specificity of meaning of certain Dutch lexical items, so that some terms had been overgeneralised under the influence of English. Attempts have also been made to demonstrate an overall vocabulary reduction in the attrited language (e.g., Yagmur 1997: 78), although it appears that lexical skills can remain unchanged over time (de Bot and Clyne

1994). With regard to the second language, there seems to be a relation between attrition and the level reached in the second language, with a threshold level indicating whether attrition will take place (Clyne 2003: 184).

Research into attrition has recently attracted a certain amount of criticism, both within Australia and outside, as the term attrition appears to be applied too broadly. For example, it has been noted that contact phenomena, e.g., temporary transference of features from one language to another, are often taken as instances of attrition, whereas this latter process should refer only to the loss of language skills (Clyne 2003: 208). Furthermore, the limitations of the methodologies used have been noted, in that the majority of studies make use of cross-sectional data, or rely on comparisons between first vs second generations or between immigrants vs people in the country of origin, whereas longitudinal studies would be more appropriate; also, data from different discourse types should be compared and contrasted (see Clyne 2003: 5–6; Schmid and de Bot 2004: 216–228).

4.2. The analysis of Census data

The extensive and detailed analyses of Census data carried out by Clyne (e.g., 1982, 1991) and associates (e.g., Kipp, Clyne, and Pauwels 1995; Clyne and Kipp 1997, 2002; Kipp and Clyne 2003) provide a macro picture of the process of language shift at the national level. Five sets of data which include language use have been analysed (from the 1976, 1986, 1991, 1996 and 2001 Censuses), where language shift is calculated by taking into account the proportion of speakers born in a particular country who have declared to speak "English only" at home. This has provided precious information about the extent of language shift within each immigrant group as well as across groups and across Censuses. Furthermore, the cross-tabulation of the language data with socio-demographic variables has yielded important insights into the dynamics of language shift, in spite of the limitations of survey data, particularly regarding self-assessed language use (see Pauwels 2004: 722).

Factors affecting language shift have been identified as operating either at the individual or at the speech community levels, although the overlap between the two is acknowledged (Kipp, Clyne, and Pauwels 1995: 116). At the individual level, Census data have pointed to generation, age and gender as the major socio-demographic factors affecting language maintenance in the Australian context. In fact higher rates of language maintenance occur among (i) the first rather than the second generation; (ii) older people in the first generation (see, however, Clyne 2003: 79–80 for variation among different groups); and (iii) women more than men (but see Clyne 2003: 79 for a different trend with regard to some Asian groups). Marriage patterns also seem to have an effect, with children of endogamous marriages (i.e. both parents born in the same overseas country) displaying higher language maintenance than children of exogamous marriages. To exemplify some of these factors, Table 3 shows the impact of the variable generation among different immigrant groups, across different Censuses:

Table 3. Language shift to English according to generation (based on Clyne and Kipp 2002; Kipp and Clyne 2003)

Birthplace	1991		1996		2001[2]
	First generation (%)	Second generation (%)[1]	First generation (%)	Second generation (%)	First generation (%)
Netherlands	57	95	61.9	95	62.6
Germany	42.4	88.7	48.2	89.7	54
Poland	17.2	74.4	19.6	75.7	22.3
Italy	11.2	49.8	14.7	57.9	15.9
Hong Kong	8.4	40	9.0	35.7	10.3
Greece	4.4	21.8	6.4	28	7.1

[1] The percentages for the second generation include the children of both endogamous and exogamous marriages.
[2] Language shift in the second generation cannot be calculated because the question on the parents' birthplace was removed in the 2001 Census.

As shown in Table 3, in every group language shift increases considerably from the first to the second generation. Furthermore, it also increases within each generation from one Census to the other, although to different extents (with the exception of the second generation of Hong Kong born, possibly as a result of intensive contacts with the homeland; Clyne and Kipp 1997: 463). Table 3 also shows remarkable differences across immigrant groups in the rates of shift within the same generation as well as across generations, with Greece born people and their children displaying the highest rates of language maintenance and Netherlands born people and their children the lowest. In fact, Census data point to a sort of scale among all immigrant groups in Australia, with some groups adopting English as their home language much more quickly than others. Table 3 highlights pairs of immigrant minorities characterised by high (Netherlands, Germany), intermediate (Poland and Italy) or low (Hong Kong and Greece) rates of shift (Kipp and Clyne 2003: 33). Possible reasons to explain such wide discrepancies have been offered by different models (see below), but there is general agreement on the fact that it is the interaction of different sets of factors that explains the process of language maintenance in the life of an individual or in an immigrant minority (see Clyne 2003: 69).

With regard to the group level, relevant factors identified by Census data are the numerical size of the immigrant group in conjunction with its settlement patterns, as a high concentration of speakers also provides more opportunities for using the language. Thus, higher rates of language maintenance occur (i) in those states where a group is numerically strongest but also there is less dispersion; (ii) in the urban rather than the rural setting, as 88% of LOTE speakers live in the capital cities; and (iii) in the local areas with high concentrations of speakers (Kipp and Clyne 2003). For example, the high concentration of Macedonians in urban centres is considered a factor contributing to the low language shift of the group (Clyne and Kipp 1997: 462), like the concentration of Vietnamese, Turkish or Khmer speakers in particular areas of some capital cities (Kipp and Clyne 2003: 39).

The analysis of the 2001 Census data has highlighted some considerable changes that are currently taking place in the language demography of Australia, as a result of the ageing of the post World War II communities and new migration patterns. Thus, languages such as Dutch, German, Hungarian, Italian and Greek, whose majority of speakers are in the higher age brackets, display accelerated rates of shift; on the contrary, there is an increase in the number of speakers of languages such as Mandarin, Arabic and Vietnamese, of more recently formed communities and/or new migration waves, mainly from Asia and the Middle East. Although Census data underrate the languages spoken in the longer established communities, where the older members of the second and third generation would use the language outside their own home (e.g., in their parents' home), it is a fact that the overall situation of the linguistic diversity of Australia is shifting away from the European languages of the post war period (Clyne and Kipp 2002).

Other socio-demographic factors that can have an impact on language maintenance are length of residence, education and socio-economic status. It appears that in the Australian context these factors are ambivalent, as anticipated by Kloss (1966), in the sense that they can be favourable to language maintenance in one group but unfavourable in another, because of other intervening factors.

With regard to length of residence, it has been observed that shift to English can occur also among recently arrived migrants, for example as a result of marital status (single) and settlement patterns (Kipp, Clyne, and Pauwels 1995: 118). Thus, like other factors, length of residence needs to be viewed in interaction with other variables. The policies and the attitudes of the host country are of particular relevance (Pauwels 1988a: 12; Clyne 1991: 75), as comparisons between different vintages and/or generations of migrants show that those who lived through the assimilationist period have shifted to English more quickly than those who lived during the policy of Multiculturalism (Bennett 1997 for the Dutch; Kipp and Clyne 2003: 35 for the Germans; Rubino 2003 for the Italians; Hatoss 2004 for the Hungarians) or show different attitudes towards the issue of language maintenance (Pham 1998 for the Vietnamese; Clyne and Kipp 1999: 319 for the Spanish speakers; Borland 2006 for the Maltese). Note, however, that the evaluation of the impact of different language policies on the language behaviour of an immigrant minority remains a debated issue, in that oppression of a group can also lead to greater efforts in language maintenance (see Kloss 1966). For example, in comparing the Turkish community in Australia and in Western Europe, Yagmur (2004) has found that the more positive Australian language policy does not seem to have promoted more language maintenance.

With regard to the ambivalence of education, it appears for example that among first generation Italo-Australians low levels of education can act as a catalyst for language maintenance while high levels tend to promote shift (Bettoni and Rubino 1996: 124). Likewise, high socio-economic status can correlate with both high rates of shift, as in the case of the Germans and the Dutch, and with much lower rates, as in the case of a group with similar socio-economic status like the Poles (Clyne 1991: 89, quoting Evans and Kelley 1988).

4.3. The role of socio-cultural factors

In research dealing with the investigation of factors that impact upon language maintenance, the role of socio-cultural variables has long been acknowledged (see Kloss 1966). Australian research has given ample scope to the study of cultural factors, in particular through the work by Smolicz and associates.

According to Smolicz (1981), a first element that can explain the different rates of language shift of the various minorities is the cultural distance between the core values of the majority and of the minority groups. An immigrant group can display low "ethnic tenacity", in the sense that they don't consider it very important to keep their cultures distinct from the majority group, hence the higher rate of language shift as a way to assimilate. Cultural distance can certainly contribute to explain language shift in the Australian context. In fact, very low rates of shift are displayed by speakers who are culturally very distant from the Anglo-Celtic majority group, such as those from predominantly Islamic or Eastern Orthodox cultures (Greek, Lebanese, Macedonian, Turkish) or from Asian cultures (e.g., Hindus; cf. Kipp and Clyne 2003: 39), while the highest rates of shift occur among speakers from northern, central and western Europe (see Table 3). Among the cultural variables an important role is played by religion as an element defining higher or lower distance from the majority group. This is confirmed for example in the study of pluricentric languages, where language maintenance is reported to be higher among Muslim Arabic speakers in both Egypt and Lebanon than among Arabic speakers who are Copts or Maronite. In the specific case of Muslims, an element favouring language maintenance appears to be the incentive to develop literacy skills in Arabic for religious reasons (Clyne and Kipp 1999: 330).

Cultural values have been explored widely also through the core value theory, which has been tested empirically on a number of immigrant groups (e.g.,

Poles, Greeks, Latvians, Chinese), working in the main with second generation participants and using a combination of qualitative data collected via the memoir approach, where participants are asked to write about their cultural experiences, and questionnaire data. The role of language is considered of central importance to the value system of some immigrant groups, and of peripheral importance to the system of others, which would explain their higher rate of shift. For example, for the Italians, the family rather than the language seems to be a core value (but see Smolicz, Secombe, and Hudson 2001: 164, where the role of dialect is acknowledged as integral to the southern Italian family), thus differing from other groups, such as the Greeks, the Polish or the Chinese, where language seems to play a much more crucial role (Smolicz 1981: 76). Furthermore, for some minorities, such as the Greeks, it may be a matter of three core values – language, family and religion – reinforcing each other (Smolicz, Secombe, and Hudson 2001: 168).

Although the core value theory provides an insightful perspective into the dynamics of language shift, it has received some criticism in that, for example, it cannot explain all the variations of shift occurring in the Australian context, nor the possible discrepancy between language use and language attitudes (see Clyne 1991: 91–105; Clyne and Pauwels 1997: 39; Clyne 2003: 64–66). Furthermore, it does not account for the fact that in some instances there is not a total coincidence between an immigrant group and a LOTE, as in the case of pluricentric languages; nor does it allow for multiple group membership (see however Smolicz, Secombe, and Hudson 2001: 167). The theory also presents a static view of the values held by a minority, without allowing for change over time or across generations (Kipp, Clyne, and Pauwels 1995: 129; see however Smolicz, Secombe, and Hudson 2001: 169).

4.4. Patterns of language use

Complementing the findings from the home based Census data, the domain approach is another paradigm that is used widely in Australian studies. This quantitative survey-based approach – the data are generally collected via questionnaire – explores patterns of language use in a wide range of social spheres, selected from those most relevant to the immigrant community. Although it generally deals with much smaller samples than the Census data and suffers from some of the same limitations (i.e. it is based on self-reported language use), it has yielded important information about the articulation of language maintenance across the various communities. The domain that is most investigated is the family, for the fundamental role that it plays in language maintenance, and the variable that is most explored is the interlocutor, for its major impact on language choice. Other variables taken into account – though to a much lower extent – are the topic of the conversation and the place where it takes place. Patterns of language use are then cross-tabulated with socio-demographic information about the subjects.

Studies conducted among a wide range of immigrant minorities, both larger (e.g., Greek: Tamis 1991; Dutch and German: Pauwels 1986, Clyne 1991, Clyne and Pauwels 1997; Italian: Bettoni and Rubino 1996; Chinese: Wu 1995, Clyne and Kipp 1999; Vietnamese: Ninnes 1996; Arabic and Spanish: Clyne and Kipp 1999), and smaller (e.g., Swedish: Garner 1988; Russian: Garner 1988 and Kouzmin 1988) have confirmed the important role of the family for language maintenance. However, they have also pointed out that it is necessary (i) to distinguish between the language behaviour of the parents vs the children, as the children among themselves use English rather than the LOTE; and (ii) to take into account the role of the extended family, as the use of LOTEs is highest with older relatives belonging to the first generation, such as the grandparents. Hence, the nuclear family is not necessarily the stronghold of language maintenance, as it has been postulated in a number of studies (e.g., Fishman 1964: 430), and the generation of the speaker vs the generation of the interlocutor appear to be the variables that exercise the greatest impact in selecting the language with various family members.

Other domains that have received some attention – although to a lower degree – are friendship, transaction, clubs/associations, church, work, media and education. With regard to friendship, it has been noted that the frequentation of friends from the same immigrant community has an effect on language maintenance. Several studies (e.g., Pauwels 1988b: 92 for the Dutch; Pütz 1991: 485 for the Germans; Bettoni and Rubino 1996: 130 for the Italians) have emphasised that this is much more so in the case of the first generation, as the second generation tends to use English, rather than the LOTE, with same-age friends from the same background. However, this finding has been challenged in recent studies conducted across different groups and using a combination of quantitative and qualitative methodologies. Working with German, Greek and Vietnamese second generation participants, Winter and Pauwels (2005, 2006) found that the use of the immigrant language can feature quite prominently in friendship contexts, more so in some groups and subgroups than in others: In their sample, it is particularly noticeable among German and Vietnamese women and among Greek men. Transactions also play an important role in language maintenance, as cafés, restaurants or shops run by immigrants as well as clubs and associations become gathering points where the use of LOTEs is prevailing. This has been shown to be the case for example among the Chinese and the Italians (Wu 1995: 115; Bettoni and Rubino 1996: 93). However, as in the case of friendship, transactions also appear to favour language maintenance more among the first than the second generation (Bettoni and Rubino 1996: 128; Clyne and Kipp 1999: 315 for the Spanish speakers).

The church is another domain that can be fundamental to language maintenance, particularly in the case of minorities following religious creeds that are different from the majority group (see above regarding the role of religion). For example, the church is one of those domains where Russian is used (Garner 1988: 45; Kouzmin 1988: 61). On the other hand, in the case of groups such as the Italians the impact of the church on language maintenance is much lower as many attend Catholic services and functions conducted in English. The work domain appears to be one where English tends to prevail compared with the LOTE (Clyne 1991: 139; see however the high use of Greek at work among the subjects studied by Tamis 1991: 249), due to the fact that English often becomes the *official* language even in workplaces characterised by high numbers of workers from a single ethnic background. Hence the use of LOTEs in the workplace is generally more common in informal interactions with co-workers (Clyne 1991: 140; Bettoni and Rubino 1996: 106).

Some of these survey-based studies have also investigated the impact of the media on language maintenance. While reading the ethnic press and listening to radio programs in the LOTE appear more widespread among the first generation (e.g., Bettoni and Rubino 1996: 46; Clyne and Kipp 1999: 296), television programs and videos in particular are quite popular across both generations, but in some minorities more so among the younger groups (e.g., among Arabic or Chinese speaking immigrants, Clyne and Kipp 1999: 215, 296). However, television programs and videos are not so easily available in all LOTEs and the usage is low among children (Lotherington and Ebert 1997). With regard to the new technology, from the little data available it seems that the use of the Internet is limited to the younger groups, and that in spite of its potential for language maintenance it is used mostly in English rather than in the LOTE (Clyne and Kipp 1999: 315).

An extremely important domain for language maintenance is the school, as entry to school has been identified as having a negative impact on language maintenance, except in the case of bilingual schooling. The teaching of LOTEs in Australia has advanced remarkably in the past three decades: In several states language study is compulsory for a varying number of years; languages are taught in primary schools, and even at some preschools; the typology of courses has diversified; and the range of languages offered has expanded considerably. For example, currently 43 languages can be taken at the end of high school examination (Clyne, Fernandez, and Grey 2004: 6). However, both at the national and state levels there is wide variation in opportunities for learning the various LOTEs, with some languages being offered in many more schools (e.g., French) than others (e.g., Arabic). Furthermore, the languages commonly taught at school do not necessarily reflect the demography of the country. Table 4 compares the ranking of the 10 most taught languages in Australia with their ranking in terms of number and age of home speakers according to the 2001 Census data.

Table 4. The top 10 Community Languages in Australian schools (from Clyne, Fernandez, and Grey 2004)

Ranking/Language	Number of students	Ranking in top 20 languages spoken at home nationally	Ranking in top 20 0–14 age group of home speakers nationally
1. Japanese	402,882	*	17
2. Italian	394,770	1	5
3. Indonesian	310,363	20	13
4. French	247,001	18	20
5. German	158,076	9	15
6. Chinese (Mandarin)	111,464	6	6
7. Arabic	31,844	4	1
8. Greek	28,188	2	4
9. Spanish	24,807	7	7
10. Vietnamese	22,428	5	2

*not in top 20

As shown in Table 4, three of the most widely studied languages, Japanese, French and Indonesian, are not among the top 10 most spoken languages at home. On the other hand, languages such as Arabic and Spanish display much lower numbers of students, despite being amongst the most spoken home languages and having large numbers of home speakers still of school age. Overall, as mentioned above, the impact of schools on language maintenance has been quite limited, with some exceptions (see e.g. the good results in Arabic reported by Clyne and Kipp 1999: 326).

Although better results may emerge from bilingual education, the number of bilingual programs, particularly of the immersion type (see Clyne et al. 1995: 10), is still quite limited both at primary and especially secondary level (Gibbons 1997). The majority of such programs is in the public schools of Victoria and some of them have been analysed and discussed extensively (e.g., Fernandez 1992; Clyne et al. 1995, 1997; Lotherington 2001). It must be noted that these programs are not specifically directed at LOTE speakers as they are generally attended by all the pupils of a particular school, in line with the principle of the NLP to offer all Australian children the opportunity to develop a second language. In actual fact, in many of these programs LOTE speakers represent only a small percentage. Furthermore, the impact of these programs on language maintenance is difficult to assess, given the very diverse levels of language competence displayed by LOTE pupils (Clyne et al. 1995: 162). Among the positive effects that can be acknowledged for all LOTE speakers are the provision of the additional language input that they receive, the development of literacy skills in the LOTE, the fostering of positive attitudes towards their own language and background, and an overall effect toward supporting the language maintenance effort of the pupils' families.

Since the 1980s there has been a resurgence in the establishment of independent bilingual schools. Islamic schools in particular are growing fast throughout Australia, attracting mainly Arabic speaking students but also students from other Muslim countries (Hall 1996). These schools appear to promote high usage of the Arabic language as a fundamental element of the curriculum as well as a means of interaction among the students. More research is certainly needed in this area given the growing popularity of these schools. On the other hand, studies carried out in a Greek Orthodox school (Bradshaw and Truckenbrodt 2002; Bradshaw 2006) point to some contradictory findings in terms of language maintenance, in that a strong commitment to the language appears to be weakened by ways of teaching it that are inappropriate in the Australian school context.

As well as in the investigation of language use in relation to particular social spheres, the domain approach has also been useful in the study of the linguistic factors that most impact on language maintenance in the Australian context, particularly the premigration situations of diglossia that characterise some minority groups. More specifically, these studies have highlighted (i) the different distribution of the standard language vs the dialect in the various domains (whereas Census data yield information only about the standard language); (ii) the impact of diglossia on language maintenance across different communities; and (iii) the stronger position of the standard language. For example, Bettoni and Rubino (1996: 140) report that in the majority of domains explored the intergenerational shift impacts upon dialect more than upon Italian, in spite of the fact that the reported use of the latter is overall more limited. In her domain based study of language maintenance among Swabians (i.e. speakers of a German dialect) and Limburgers (i.e. speakers of a Dutch dialect), Pauwels (1986) found that the better language maintenance among Limburgers can be explained by their reluctance to use the standard language, Dutch, with other non Limburgers, whereas Swabians more easily accommodate to speaking German to other German speakers. The study of pluricentric languages has also highlighted debates within the communities as to the best language and/or language variety to teach at school, in the case of Spanish and Arabic (Clyne and Kipp 1999: 132). A major linguistic factor that has emerged from the research is literacy, as premigration literacy among the first generation and the development of literacy skills among the younger generations are elements that facilitate language maintenance (Clyne and Kipp 1999: 313). Furthermore, the presence of a language in an educational institution increases its chances of maintenance, as in the case of Mandarin over Cantonese (Wu 1995: 108). Also premigration experience with language maintenance and situations of multilingualism (e.g., people coming from the multilingual context of Egypt; Clyne and Kipp 1999: 38) seems to have a facilitating role for language maintenance.

4.5. The socio-psychological perspective

Research conducted in the socio-psychological perspective has confirmed the impact of linguistic factors on language maintenance. Studies on language attitudes have identified overall puristic attitudes held by migrants towards the varieties that are spoken in the communities. For example, on the basis of judgments elicited through test sentences, Pauwels (1991) found that the Dutch hold negative attitudes towards contact phenomena, particularly when associated with the speech of the second generation. Likewise, using the matched guise test among Italo-Australians, Bettoni and Gibbons (1988) identified negative attitudes towards mixed varieties, particularly when the mixing involves transfers from English on a dialect. Thus, this study confirms the role of diglossia as a factor accelerating the shift towards English, in so far as dialect speakers display negative attitudes towards their own speech. A study of attitudes elicited through focus group discussions across different immigrant groups uncovered feelings of shame and strategies of avoidance among second generation late LOTE learners, as a result of their perceptions of insufficient proficiency in the LOTE (Clyne and Kipp 1999: 251). On the other hand, the attitudes held by the majority group towards the immigrant minority have been confirmed to act as an ambivalent factor (see Kloss 1966) with regard to language maintenance: While discrimination against Arabs and Muslims results in the promotion of their language and culture, in the case of the Chinese it encourages stronger efforts to integrate quickly into the mainstream, often causing the loss of the LOTE (Clyne and Kipp 1999: 325).

Socio-psychological research has also focused on the effect of speakers' perceptions on language maintenance. Studies on the subjective perceptions of ethnolinguistic vitality have been conducted into a number of LOTEs, using the Subjective Vitality Questionnaire (SVQ) developed by Bourhis, Giles, and Rosenthal (1981), but their findings are sometimes contradictory. For example, comparing the perceptions of Greek-Australians vs Anglo-Australians, Giles, Rosenthal, and Young (1985) report that overall the Anglo raters tend to accentuate the differences between the two groups (e.g., in terms of social status) and the Greek raters to moderate them. The discrepancy is particularly evident with specific regard to the language items of the questionnaire, with Greek-Australian subjects giving higher ratings to the vitality of the Greek language in Australia in terms of status of the language and its presence in the media. Although this finding can contribute to explain the high rates of language maintenance displayed by the Greeks, in Gibbons and Ashcroft (1995) Greek-Australian and Italo-Australian school students, in spite of the more rapid shift to English among the latter, hold similar perceptions of language vitality. On the contrary, Yagmur (2004) reports low ethnolinguistic vitality among Turkish immigrants in Sydney in spite of their high rates of language maintenance. Some studies even suggest that subjective ethnolinguistic vitality can have little relationship with language use, which can be better predicted by other variables such as ethnolinguistic identification (Hogg and Rigoli 1996). Also, it has been noted that the relationship between ethnolinguistic vitality and language maintenance can vary in different contexts: For example, Turkish migrants in Germany and in Australia display similar rates of language maintenance, in spite of the lower level of subjective ethnolinguistic vitality among the latter (Yagmur 2004).

An interesting development in this area of study is represented by Gibbons and Ramirez (2004a, 2004b), who investigate the maintenance of Spanish among a group of teenagers in Sydney. Using language tests to assess the participants' language ability – rather than relying on self ratings – and taking into account both attitudes and beliefs, Gibbons and Ramirez demonstrate that positive beliefs about bilingualism, as well as the determination to resist the pressure of the host language, correlate with high proficiency levels in both languages, English and Spanish.

4.6.   The social network approach

A small body of research into the LOTEs has adopted the social network approach to analyse patterns of language use in the Australian context. According to this paradigm, speakers' language use is influenced by their interpersonal relations, more specifically by the type of social network in which they move. Strong network ties are considered a "norm maintenance mechanism", while weak ties are taken as a factor facilitating language change (see Milroy 1987). Although this approach was originally adopted to investigate linguistic variation in urban dialectological studies (English variation in Belfast, Milroy 1987), it has also been used in bilingual contexts, most notably by Gal (1979) and Li Wei (1994).

In Australia, this approach has been used to study language maintenance across different immigrant minorities, as in Pauwels' (1995) and Winter and Pauwels' (2005, 2006) work on the role of gender in language maintenance among Germans, Greeks and Vietnamese, and within one single group, as in Cavallaro's (1997) investigation of language dynamics among the second and third generation Italians. It must be noted that some of these studies have adopted the network approach fairly broadly, following its main tenet (i.e. the belief in the impact of the network on language behaviour) and/or aspects of its fieldwork methodology (i.e. participant observation and the role of the fieldworker as "a friend of a friend", as in Milroy's study), but not necessarily its quantitative approach to the data analysis.

Overall the findings seem to confirm the validity of this approach. For example, according to Pauwels (1997: 281), differences in networks do contribute to explain different language use patterns and practices in the three groups as well as in the different generations within the groups. The higher use of the LOTE among the Greek and Vietnamese first generation compared with the German can be explained in light of the fact that the former operate in more dense and multiplex networks of people from the same background. Likewise, type of network can also be a reason for the higher use of LOTEs among the first generation compared with the second.

However, these studies have also exposed the limitations of this approach. For example, Pauwels (1997: 282) notes that differences in network cannot account for gender differences, as her data show a low use of the LOTE among Vietnamese men with dense and multiplex networks in contrast with a high use among young Vietnamese women with dense but less ethnocentric networks. More recent analyses (Winter and Pauwels 2006) have shown that in the domain of friendship, it is not just the presence of bilinguals in one's network that can account for language maintenance and/or use of LOTEs, but other crucial and more subtle elements. While "performances of masculinities" can explain why German and Vietnamese second generation men use the LOTE less than Greek men, "identities [...] constructed as prestigious and possibly liberating" explain instead why second generation Greek women prefer to use English in their friendship dyads. It appears therefore that the construct of network needs to be refined to increase its explanatory power (see also the notion of "community of practice" in Pauwels 1997: 283).

5. New developments in research on LOTEs

As can be drawn from the discussion above, research on LOTEs in Australia has demonstrated both breadth of interests and the adoption of a wide range of paradigms and methodological tools. Currently there are encouraging signs of research in areas which up to now have been less explored or that are dealing with new emerging issues. Some of these are outlined below.

Firstly, Australian scholars are steadily expanding the range of immigrant languages that are being investigated. While research has been very prolific regarding a small number of LOTEs (e.g., German, Dutch, Italian) for a combination of different factors (see Bettoni 1991a: 76–77), increasingly studies are now focusing on the less investigated languages. For example, the more recently formed minorities are receiving greater attention, both the larger ones, such as the Vietnamese (Ninnes 1996; Pauwels 1997; Pham 1998; Ho-Dac 2003), and the smaller ones, such as the Cambodian (Smolicz and Secombe 2003). Furthermore, studies are continuing on the smaller communities, such as the Danes (Søndergaard and Norrby 2006), and on the languages of long established communities that are considered of *lesser status,* for example the Turks (Yagmur 1997, 2004) and the Maltese (Borland 2005, 2006).

Secondly, research is now being undertaken on the third generation, given their growing impact particularly among the post war immigrant communities. Studies have explored such issues as the transmission of LOTE from the second to the third generation, for example analysing (i) the use of immigrant languages in a range of contexts and the emerging "ethnolect" (Clyne 2003: 154–155) used by second generation parents to their children (e.g. Cavallaro 1997 for the Italians); (ii) the variables that favour language maintenance among the third generation, such as the combined effect of language study at school, proximity of grandparents and visits to the country of origin, among others (Clyne et al. 1997: 51, 85, for German and Italian); and (iii) the grammatical changes in the use of the LOTE by the third generation (Clyne 1997a for German; Clyne et al. 1997: 48–51, 83–84 for German and Italian). Research on the younger generations could benefit from more studies investigating such issues as the mixed language varieties that often develop among migrant adolescents (see Hinnenkamp 2003), and the way they symbolically use them as markers of their bicultural identity in interacting among themselves as well as with out-group speakers. Furthermore, it would be important to analyse possible phenomena of "crossing" (Rampton 1995) where immigrant youths make use of linguistic features of LOTEs from other groups, as found in other countries of migration.

Thirdly, with globalisation has come a greater fluidity in the transnational movement of people. Hence some research paradigms that have been developed to investigate language issues in more permanent immigration contexts need to be reassessed in light of the increased permeability of the once more insulated LOTE speech communities. For example, dispersal of communities might no longer result in being a major factor in language shift given the increased contacts with the countries of origin and the increased opportunities for communication.

Fourthly, research on patterns of language use is now usefully adopting a combination of quantitative and qualitative methodologies, exploring in depth a greater range of domains (e.g., friendship; see Winter and Pauwels 2006) and taking into account the impact on language maintenance of newly formed domains, such as the virtual domain of the Internet (e.g. Clyne and Kipp 1999). Future research could continue the study of less explored domains and include in their samples not only the second but also the third generation. For example, it would be interesting to evaluate the role that domains such as transactions can play in language maintenance among the younger generations.

Finally, with regard to the educational sector, while research has been conducted in a wide range of contexts of LOTE teaching, more studies are needed particularly in the independent schools established by some communities which operate by clustering students of the same background. This would assess the outcomes of different educational models, and perhaps question the more integrated approach adopted by most schools in the public and also in the private sectors, where LOTE speakers are not allocated to different classes (see Clyne et al. 1995: 162 for issues raised in this regard).

6. The contribution of applied linguistics

As demonstrated from the previous sections, applied linguists in Australia have given a remarkable contribution to the area of immigrant languages both at the theoretical and practical levels, and have participated in the formulation of possible solutions to the concerns raised in relation to the presence of LOTEs in Australia.

At the theoretical level, Australian research has contributed to defining and refining paradigms in a number of areas, most notably (i) the descriptions of the speech repertoires of immigrant communities; (ii) models of language maintenance and shift; and (iii) the analysis of language contact phenomena. As a result, international research has also gained from Australian work a better understanding of the language dynamics that take place in the contact between majority and minority languages in contexts of migration.

At the practical level, possibly the most significant contribution has been the advocacy work undertaken by applied linguists to claim a legitimate place for immigrant languages in Australian society. The deep political engagement of much of the research, committed to the maintenance and development of immigrant languages has been noted elsewhere (Pauwels 1988c; Bettoni 1991a) but deserves to be reiterated.

More specifically, the findings from research into the maintenance and use of LOTEs and their contact with English have contributed to re-evaluate multilingualism and dispel prejudices about such phenomena as transference and code switching, too often viewed as *deviant* language behaviour. Furthermore, they have highlighted elements that play a crucial role in supporting efforts directed at language maintenance, such as the development of literacy; the importance not only of the family but also of other domains for LOTE use; the visibility of LOTEs in the broader society (e.g., through the media) and particularly in education to raise their status; and the role of bilingual education.

Of major importance has been the intense and continuous lobbying with the governments to achieve policies directed towards the recognition and the better utilisation of LOTEs in all sectors of the broad Australian society, for example in the workplace (Kipp, Clyne, and Pauwels 1995). This advocacy work has been particularly crucial in the area of education, in order to push federal and state authorities to formulate education policies that recognise the place of LOTEs in the curriculum and support initiatives to promote language maintenance. Furthermore, the involvement of applied linguists has been substantial in setting up, implementing and evaluating language programs in schools, especially at primary level, and bilingual programs in particular.

Another aspect that cannot be overlooked is the continuous support offered by scholars to immigrant communities in their efforts towards language maintenance and/or language revitalisation, for example by disseminating research findings, encouraging and offering advice about bilingualism in the family and presenting models of bilingual upbringing (e.g., the one parent one language approach) that can be feasible within second and third generation families. Particularly active in this area has been the *Language and Society Centre* at Monash University in Melbourne (see Clyne 2001).

Finally, it must be mentioned that a great deal of the work done around immigrant languages has been directed not just narrowly at their maintenance and development among their speakers but also more broadly at the promotion of learning a second language for everybody, as articulated by the *National Language Policy*. Hence, the contribution of immigrant minorities to the country has been twofold: (i) it has maintained and enhanced Australia's original multilingualism; and (ii) it has been a catalyst for the enrichment of the cultural and linguistic experiences of all Australians.

There is no doubt that applied linguistics in Australia is in a good position to continue flourishing and helping the immigrant minorities with the linguistic concerns and challenges that they face in the new century. For the older communities, it is a case of maintaining or developing bilingualism among the third generation while the first is ageing. For the younger communities, it is a case of learning from the experiences of the communities before them how to best ensure bilingual outcomes among the second generation. For all, it is a question of keeping up the struggle to ensure that present and future Australian governments fully understand the value of multilingualism in Australia and act so that it doesn't dissipate too easily and too quickly.

References

Amery, Rob
   2000   *Warrabarna Kaurna! Reclaiming an Australian Language.* Lisse: Swets & Zeitlinger B.V.
Australian Government/Department of Foreign Affairs and Trade
   2005   *A Diverse People.* http://www.dfat.gov.au/aib/society.html (retrieved January 28, 2005)

Bennett, Jane
 1997 Attitudes of the second generation to Dutch language maintenance and ethnic identity in Australia. In: Jetske Klatter-Folmer and Sjaak Kroon (eds.), *Dutch Overseas*, 51–68. Tilburg: Tilburg University Press.
Bettoni, Camilla
 1981 *Italian in North Queensland. Changes in the Speech of First and Second Generation Bilinguals*. Townsville: James Cook University.
Bettoni, Camilla
 1990 Italian language attrition in Sydney: The role of dialect. In: Michael A. K. Halliday, John Gibbons and Howard Nicholas (eds.), *Learning, Keeping and Using Language. Selected Papers from the 8th World Congress of Applied Linguistics*, 75–89, Sydney, 16–21 August 1987, Volume 2. Amsterdam: Benjamins.
Bettoni, Camilla
 1991a Other community languages. In: Michael Clyne (ed.), *Linguistics in Australia. Trends in Research*, 75–90. Canberra: Academy of the Social Sciences in Australia.
Bettoni, Camilla
 1991b Language shift and morphological attrition among second generation Italo-Australians. *Rivista di Linguistica* 3(2): 369–387.
Bettoni, Camilla and John Gibbons
 1988 Linguistic purism and language shift: A guise-voice study of the Italian community in Sydney. In: Anne Pauwels (ed.), *The Future of Ethnic Languages in Australia. International Journal of the Sociology of Language* 72: 15–35. Berlin: Mouton de Gruyter.
Bettoni, Camilla and Antonia Rubino
 1996 *Emigrazione e comportamento linguistico. Un'indagine sul trilinguismo dei siciliani e dei veneti in Australia*. Galatina: Congedo.
Borland, Helen
 2005 Heritage languages and community identity building: The case of a language of lesser status. *The International Journal of Bilingual Education and Bilingualism* 8(2/3): 109–123.
Borland, Helen
 2006 Intergenerational language transmission in an established Australian migrant community: What makes the difference? In: Sandra Kipp and Catrin Norrby (eds.), *Community Languages in Practice: The Case of Australia. International Journal of the Sociology of Language* 180: 23–41.
Bourhis, Richard Y., Howard Giles and Doreen Rosenthal
 1981 Notes on the construction of a "Subjective Vitality Questionnaire" for the development of ethnolinguistic groups. *Journal of Multilingual and Multicultural Development* 2: 145–155.
Bradshaw, Julie and Andrea Truckenbrodt
 2002 Orientations to Greek in an Australian Greek school. In: Cynthia Allen (ed.), *Proceedings of the 2001 Conference of the Australian Linguistic Society*.
  http://linguistics.anu.edu.au/ALS2001/proceedings.html (retrieved January 28, 2005); http://www.als.asn.au/

Bradshaw, Julie
    2006   Parent and child perspectives on Greek language education in Australia. In: Sandra Kipp and Catrin Norrby (eds.), *Community Languages in Practice: The Case of Australia. International Journal of the Sociology of Language* 180: 43–54.

Callan, Cynthia and Victor J. Gallois
    1982   Language attitudes of Italo-Australian and Greek-Australian bilinguals. *International Journal of Psychology* 17: 345–358.

Caruso, Marinella
    2004   Attrition in the verb system of Italian in Australia. In: Antonia Rubino (ed.), *Using and Learning Italian in Australia (Australian Review of Applied Linguistics* S18), 9–24. Melbourne: Applied Linguistics Association of Australia.

Cavallaro, Francesco
    1997   Language dynamics of the Italian community in Australia. Doctoral Thesis, Melbourne: Monash University.

Clyne, Michael
    1967   *Transference and Triggering.* Amsterdam: Martinus Nijhoff.

Clyne, Michael
    1972   *Perspectives on Language Contact.* Melbourne: Hawthorn Press.

Clyne, Michael
    1977   Bilingualism of the elderly. *Talanya* 4: 45–56.

Clyne, Michael
    1982   *Multilingual Australia.* Melbourne: River Seine Publications.

Clyne, Michael
    1991   *Community Languages. The Australian Experience.* Cambridge: Cambridge University Press.

Clyne, Michael
    1997a   The German of 3rd generation German-English bilinguals in Australia. In: Wolfgang Wölck and Annick De Houwer (eds.), *Recent Studies in Contact Linguistics*, 36–44. Bonn: Dummler.

Clyne, Michael
    1997b   Language policy and education in Australia. In: Ruth Wodak and David Corson (eds.), *Encyclopedia of Language and Education.* Vol. 1: *Language Policy and Political Issues in Education*, 127–135. Dordrecht: Kluwer Academic Publishers.

Clyne, Michael
    2001   Can the shift of immigrant languages be reversed in Australia? In: Joshua Fishman (ed.), *Can Threatened Languages Be Saved?*, 364–390. Clevedon: Multilingual Matters.

Clyne, Michael
    2003   *Dynamics of Language Contact.* Cambridge: Cambridge University Press.

Clyne, Michael and Paola Cassia
    1999   Trilingualism, immigration and relatedness of languages. *Review of Applied Linguistics* 123/124: 57–77.

Clyne, Michael and Sandra Kipp
    1997   Trends and changes in home language use and shift in Australia, 1986–1996. *Journal of Multilingual and Multicultural Development* 18(6): 451–473.

Clyne, Michael and Sandra Kipp
    1999   *Pluricentric Languages in an Immigrant Context. Spanish, Arabic and Chinese*. Berlin/New York: Mouton de Gruyter.
Clyne, Michael and Sandra Kipp
    2002   Australia's changing demography. *People and Place* 10(3): 29–35.
Clyne, Michael and Anne Pauwels
    1997   Use, maintenance, structures, and future of Dutch in Australia. In: Jetske Klatter-Folmer and Sjaak Kroon (eds.), *Dutch Overseas,* 34–49. Tilburg: Tilburg University Press.
Clyne, Michael, Catherine Jenkins, Imogen Y. Chen, Roula Tsokalidou and Theresa Wallner
    1995   *Developing Second Language from Primary School: Models and Outcomes*. Deakin (ACT): The National Languages and Literacy Institute of Australia.
Clyne, Michael, Sue Fernandez, Imogen Y. Chen and Renata Summo-O'Connell
    1997   *Background Speakers: Diversity and its Management in LOTE Programs*. Belconnen (ACT): The National Languages and Literacy Institute of Australia.
Clyne, Michael, Sue Fernandez and Felicity Grey
    2004   Languages taken at school and languages spoken in the community: A comparative perspective. *Australian Review of Applied Linguistics* 27(2): 1–17.
Collins, Jock
    1991   *Migrant Hands in a Distant Land: Australia's Post-War Immigration*. 2nd ed. Sydney: Pluto Press.
Collins, Jock, Greg Noble, Scott Poynting and Paul Tabar
    2000   *Kebabs, Kids, Cops & Crime. Youth, Ethnicity & Crime*. Sydney: Pluto Press.
Council of Australian Governments (National Asian Languages and Cultures Working Group)
    1994   *Asian Languages and Australia's Economic Future: A Report for the Council of Australian Governments on a Proposed National Asian Languages/Studies Strategy for Australian Schools*. Brisbane: Queensland Government Printer.
Dawkins, John
    1991   *Australia's Language: The Australian Language and Literacy Policy*. Canberra: Australian Government Printing Service.
de Bot, Kees and Michael Clyne
    1994   A 16-year longitudinal study of language attrition in Dutch immigrants in Australia. *Journal of Multilingual and Multicultural Development* 15(1): 17–28.
Dixon, Robert M. W.
    2002   *Australian Languages: Their Nature and Development*. Cambridge/New York: Cambridge University Press.
Döpke, Susanne
    1992   *One Parent One Language. An Interactional Approach*. Amsterdam/Philadelphia: John Benjamins.
Doucet, Jacques
    1991   First generation Serbo-Croatian speakers in Queensland: Language maintenance and language shift. In: Suzanne Romaine (ed.), *Language in Australia*, 270–284. Cambridge: Cambridge University Press.

Eades, Diana (ed.)
    1995   *Language in Evidence: Issues Confronting Aboriginal and Multicultural Australia.* Sydney: University of NSW Press.
Evans, Mariah Debra Ruperti and Jonathan Kelley
    1988   Social mobility and immigration. In: James Jupp (ed.), *The Australian People: An Encyclopedia of the Nation, its People and their Origin*, 952–955. Sydney: Angus and Robertson.
Fernandez, Sue
    1992   *Room for Two. A Study of Bilingual Education at Bayswater South Primary School.* Belconnen (ACT): The National Languages and Literacy Institute of Australia. (2nd edition 1996).
Fishman, Joshua A.
    1964   Language maintenance and language shift as a field of inquiry. *Linguistics* 9: 32–70. (Revised version in Joshua Fishman, Vladimir Nahirny, John E. Hofman and Robert G. Hayden (eds.), 1966, *Language Loyalty in the United States,* 424–458. London/The Hague: Mouton.)
Fishman, Joshua A.
    1965   Who speaks what language to whom and when? *La Linguistique* 2: 67–88. (Reprinted in Li Wei (ed.), 2000, *The Bilingualism Reader*, 89–106. London/New York: Routledge.)
Fishman, Joshua, Vladimir Nahirny, John E. Hofman and Robert G. Hayden (eds.)
    1966   *Language Loyalty in the United States.* London/The Hague: Mouton.
Gal, Susan
    1979   *Language Shift: Social Determinants of Linguistic Change in Bilingual Austria.* New York: Academic Press.
Garner, Mark
    1988   Ethnic languages in two small communities: Swedish and Russian in Melbourne. In: Anne Pauwels (ed.), *The Future of Ethnic Languages in Australia. (International Journal of the Sociology of Language* 72*),* 37–50. Amsterdam: Mouton de Gruyter.
Gibbons, John
    1997   Australian bilingual education. In: Jim Cummins and David Corson (eds.), *Encyclopedia of Language and Education. Volume 5: Bilingual Education*, 209–215. Dordrecht: Kluwer Academic Publishers.
Gibbons, John and Lyn Ashcroft
    1995   Multiculturalism and language shift: A subjective vitality questionnaire study of Sydney Italians. *Journal of Multilingual and Multicultural Development* 16(4): 281–299.
Gibbons, John and Elizabeth Ramirez
    2004a   Different beliefs. Beliefs and the maintenance of a minority language. *Journal of Language and Social Psychology* 23(1): 99–117.
Gibbons, John and Elizabeth Ramirez
    2004b   *Maintaining a Minority Language. A Case Study of Hispanic Teenagers.* Clevedon: Multilingual Matters.
Giles, Howard
    1977   *Language, Ethnicity and Intergroup Relations.* London: Academic Press.
Giles, Howard, Doreen Rosenthal and Louis Young
    1985   Perceived ethnolinguistic vitality: The Anglo- and Greek-Australian setting. *Journal of Multilingual and Multicultural Development* 6(3/4): 253–269.

Hall, Michael
 1996 Arabic in Australian Islamic Schools. *Babel* 31(2): 28–31.
Harkins, Jean
 1994 *Bridging Two Worlds: Aboriginal English and Crosscultural Understanding.* St Lucia (Brisbane): University of Queensland Press.
Hartman, Deborah and John Henderson
 1994 *Aboriginal Languages in Education.* Alice Springs: IAD Press.
Hatoss, Anikò
 2004 Mother tongue maintenance and acculturation in two vintages of the Hungarian diaspora. *Australian Review of Applied Linguistics* 27(2): 18–31.
Haugen, Einar
 1953 *The Norwegian Language in America: A Study in Bilingual Behaviour.* Philadelphia: University of Pennsylvania Press.
Haugen, Einar
 1956 *Bilingualism in the Americas: A Bibliography and Research Guide.* Alabama: University of Alabama Press.
Henderson, John and David Nash
 1997 *Culture and Heritage: Indigenous Languages.* (Australia: State of the Environment Technical Paper Series Natural and Cultural Heritage) Canberra: Department of the Environment and Heritage.
Hinnenkamp, Volker
 2003 Mixed language varieties of migrant adolescents and the discourse of hybridity. *Journal of Multilingual and Multicultural Development* 24(1/2): 12–40.
Ho-Dac, Tuc
 2003 *Vietnamese-English Bilingualism: Patterns of Code-Switching.* London/ New York: Routledge.
Hogg, Michael A. and Ninetta Rigoli
 1996 Effects of ethnolinguistic vitality, ethnic identification, and linguistic contacts on minority language use. *Journal of Language and Social Psychology* 15(1): 76–89.
Hoogenraad, Robert
 2001 Critical reflections on the history of bilingual education in Central Australia. In: Jane Simpson, David Nash, Mary Laughren, Peter Austin and Barry Alpher (eds.), *Forty Years on: Ken Hale and Australian Languages,* 123–150. Canberra: Pacific Linguistics.
Jupp, James (ed.)
 2001 *The Australian People. An Encyclopedia of the Nation, its People and their Origins.* Cambridge: Cambridge University Press. [2nd ed.]
Jupp, James
 2002 *From White Australia to Woomera. The Story of Australian Immigration.* Cambridge: Cambridge University Press.
Kalantzis, Mary, Bill Cope and Diana Slade
 1989 *Minority Languages and Dominant Culture: Issues of Education, Assessment and Social Equity.* London: The Falmer Press.
Kipp, Sandra and Michael Clyne
 2003 Trends in the shift from community languages: Insights from the 2001 Census. *People and Place* 11(1): 33–41.

Kipp, Sandra, Michael Clyne and Anne Pauwels
1995 *Immigration and Australia's Language Resources.* Canberra: Australian Government Publishing Service.
Kloss, Heinz
1966 German-American language maintenance efforts. In: Joshua Fishman, Vladimir Nahirny, John E. Hofman and Robert G. Hayden (eds.), *Language Loyalty in the United States,* 206–252. London/The Hague: Mouton.
Kouzmin, Ludmilla
1988 Language use and language maintenance in two Russian communities in Australia. In: Anne Pauwels (ed.), *The Future of Ethnic Languages in Australia. (International Journal of the Sociology of Language* 72), 51–65. Amsterdam: Mouton de Gruyter.
Lambert, Wallace E.
1967 A social psychology of bilingualism. *Journal of Social Issues* 23(2): 91–109.
Li Wei
1994 *Three Generations, Two Languages, One Family. Language Choice and Language Shift in a Chinese Community in Britain.* Clevedon: Multilingual Matters.
Lo Bianco, Joseph
1987 *National Policy on Languages.* Canberra: Australian Government Publishing Service.
Lotherington, Heather
2001 A tale of four teachers: A study of an Australian late-entry content based programme in two Asian languages. *International Journal of Bilingual Education and Bilingualism* 4(2): 97–106.
Lotherington, Heather and Simone Ebert
1997 Plugged in: Using electronic media to maintain the mother tongue. *Australian Language Matters* 5(4): 9–10.
McConvell, Patrick and Nicholas Thieberger
2001 *State of Indigenous Languages in Australia 2001.* (Australia: State of the Environment Second Technical Paper Series: Natural and Cultural Heritage) Canberra: Department of the Environment and Heritage. http://eprints.infodiv.unimelb.edu.au/archive/00001559/
McNamara, Tim
2001 The history of applied linguistics in Australia. *Australian Review of Applied Linguistics* 24(1): 13–29.
Milroy, Lesley
1987 *Language and Social Networks.* Oxford: Basil Blackwell. [2nd ed.]
Ninnes, Peter
1996 Language maintenance among Vietnamese-Australian students. *Australian Review of Applied Linguistics* 19(2): 115–138.
Ozolins, Uldis
1991 National language policy and planning: Migrant languages. In: Suzanne Romaine (ed.), *Language in Australia,* 329–348. Cambridge: Cambridge University Press.
Ozolins, Uldis
1993 *The Politics of Language in Australia.* Cambridge: Cambridge University Press.

Pauwels, Anne
   1986   *Immigrant Dialects and Language Maintenance in Australia.* Dordrecht: Foris Publications.
Pauwels, Anne (ed.)
   1988a   *The Future of Ethnic Languages in Australia. (International Journal of the Sociology of Language 72).* Amsterdam: Mouton de Gruyter.
Pauwels, Anne
   1988b   Diglossic communities in transition: The cases of the Limburgs and Swabian communities in Australia. In: Anne Pauwels (ed.), *The Future of Ethnic Languages in Australia. (International Journal of the Sociology of Language 72)*, 85–99. Amsterdam: Mouton de Gruyter.
Pauwels, Anne
   1988c   Problem areas: Australia. In: Ulrich Ammon, Norbert Dittmar and Klaus J. Mattheier (eds.), *Sociolinguistics. An International Handbook of the Science of Language and Society,* 1244–1253. Berlin: Walter de Gruyter.
Pauwels, Anne
   1991   Dutch in Australia: Perceptions of and attitudes towards transference and other language contact phenomena. In: Suzanne Romaine (ed.), *Language in Australia,* 228–240. Cambridge: Cambridge University Press.
Pauwels, Anne
   1995   Linguistic practices and language maintenance among bilingual women and men in Australia. *Nordlyd* 23: 21–50.
Pauwels, Anne
   1997   The role of gender in immigrant language maintenance in Australia. In: Wolfgang Wölck and Annick De Houwer (eds.), *Recent Studies in Contact Linguistics,* 276–285. Bonn: Dummler.
Pauwels, Anne
   2004   Language maintenance. In: Alan Davies and Catherine Elder (eds.), *Handbook of Applied Linguistics,* 719–737. Malden, MA: Blackwell.
Pham, Mai Nhu
   1998   Language attitudes of the Vietnamese in Melbourne. *Australian Review of Applied Linguistics* 21(2): 1–20.
Price, Charles A.
   2001   The ethnic character of the Australian population. In: James Jupp (ed.), *The Australian People. An Encyclopedia of the Nation, its People and their Origins,* 78–85. Cambridge: Cambridge University Press.
Pütz, Martin
   1991   Language maintenance and language shift in the speech behaviour of German-Australian migrants in Canberra. *Journal of Multicultural and Multilingual Development* 12(6): 477–492.
Rampton, Ben
   1995   *Crossing: Language and Ethnicity among Adolescents.* London/New York: Longman.
Romaine, Suzanne (ed.)
   1991   *Language in Australia.* Cambridge: Cambridge University Press.
Rubino, Antonia
   2000   Playing with languages: Language alternation in Sicilian-Australian children's conversation. *Rassegna Italiana di Linguistica Applicata* 32(2): 89–108.

Rubino, Antonia
   2003   Trilinguismo e monolinguismo tra gli italo-australiani: Due famiglie a confronto. In: Franca Bizzoni and Anna De Fina (eds.), *Italiano e italiani fuori d'Italia*, 145–174. Perugia: Guerra.

Rubino, Antonia
   2006   Linguistic practices and language attitudes of second generation Italo-Australians. In: Sandra Kipp and Catrin Norrby (eds.), *Community Languages in Practice: The Case of Australia. International Journal of the Sociology of Language* 180: 71–88.

Saunders, George
   1982   *Bilingual Children: Guidance for the Family.* Clevedon: Multilingual Matters.

Saunders, George
   1988   *Bilingual Children: From Birth to Teens.* Clevedon: Multilingual Matters.

Schmidt, Annette
   1985   *Young People's Dyirbal: An Example of Language Death from Australia.* Cambridge/New York: Cambridge University Press.

Schmid, Monika S. and Kees de Bot
   2004   Language attrition. In: Alan Davies and Catherine Elder (eds.), *Handbook of Applied Linguistics,* 210–233. Malden, MA: Blackwell.

Smolicz, Jerzy J.
   1981   Core values and cultural identity. *Ethnic and Racial Studies* 4(1): 75–90.

Smolicz, Jerzy J. and Margaret J. Secombe
   1985   Community languages, core values and cultural maintenance: The Australian experience with special reference to Greek, Latvian and Polish groups. In: Michael Clyne (ed.), *Australia, Meeting Place of Languages*, 11–38. Canberra: The Australian National University (Research School of Pacific Studies).

Smolicz, Jerzy J., Margaret J. Secombe and Dorothy M. Hudson
   2001   Family collectivism and minority languages as core values of culture among ethnic groups in Australia. *Journal of Multilingual and Multicultural Development* 22(2): 152–172.

Smolicz, Jerzy J. and Margaret J. Secombe
   2003   Assimilation or pluralism? Changing policies for minority languages education in Australia. *Language Policy* 2: 3–25.

Søndergaard, Bent and Catrin Norrby
   2006   Language maintenance and shift in the Danish community in Melbourne. In: Sandra Kipp and Catrin Norrby (eds.), *Community Languages in Practice: The Case of Australia. International Journal of the Sociology of Language* 180: 105–121.

Tamis, Anastasios
   1991   Modern Greek in Australia. In: Suzanne Romaine (ed.), *Language in Australia*, 249–262. Cambridge: Cambridge University Press.

Tsokalidou, Roula
   1994   Women on the cusp – a case of bilingual women. *Working Papers on Language, Gender and Sexism* (Clayton, Victoria) 4(2): 46–62.

Walsh, Michael
   1997   How many Australian languages were there? In: Tryon Darrell and Michael Walsh (eds.), *Boundary Rider: Essays in Honour of Geoffrey O'Grady*, 393–412. Canberra: Pacific Linguistics.

Walsh, Michael and Colin Yallop (eds.)
   1993   *Language and Culture in Aboriginal Australia.* Canberra: Aboriginal Studies Press.

Weinreich, Uriel
   1953   *Languages in Contact.* New York: Columbia University Press.

Winter, Joanne and Anne Pauwels
   2000   Gender and language contact research in the Australian context. *Journal of Multilingual and Multicultural Development* 21(6): 508–522.

Winter, Joanne and Anne Pauwels
   2005   Gender in the construction and transmission of ethnolinguistic identities and language maintenance in immigrant Australia. *Australian Journal of Linguistics* 25(1): 153–168.

Winter, Joanne and Anne Pauwels
   2006   Language maintenance in friendships: 2nd generation German, Greek and Vietnamese migrants. In: Sandra Kipp and Catrin Norrby (eds.), *Community Languages in Practice: The Case of Australia. International Journal of the Sociology of Language* 180: 123–139.

Wu, Siew-Mei
   1995   Maintenance of the Chinese language in Australia. *Australian Review of Applied Linguistics* 18(2):105–136.

Yagmur, Kutlay
   1997   *First Language Attrition among Turkish Speakers in Sydney.* Tilburg: Tilburg University Press.

Yagmur, Kutlay
   2004   Language maintenance patterns of Turkish immigrant communities in Australia and Western Europe: The impact of majority attitudes on ethnolinguistic vitality perceptions. *International Journal of the Sociology of Language* 165: 121–142.

4. Linguistic diversity: Africa

Jan Blommaert

1. Introduction

During a recent visit to a secondary school in a poor township in the Cape Town area of South Africa, the headmaster of the school told me that teachers had just found out that a 16-year old Xhosa-speaking pupil could hardly read and write. She had recently immigrated into the township from an inland rural area, and she had had several years of schooling in her up-country region of origin. In spite of this educational background, the girl was still largely illiterate, and she now found herself in a highly mixed classroom environment where pupils from all sorts of regional, ethnic and linguistic backgrounds sat together, and in a poor township school which nevertheless managed to attain high standards of teaching and academic performance, and in which knowledge of standard English was highly valued.

This vignette offers us in a nutshell some of the main features of the sociolinguistic situation in contemporary Africa. An analysis of the girl's predicament would involve reflections on the dense, complex multilingualism that characterizes Africa as a whole, on the sociocultural and sociolinguistic differences between rural and urban environments, on migration as a key feature of contemporary social processes, on language ideologies, language policy and its effects on language in education, and on the problem of literacy, subliteracy and illiteracy. Such an analysis, needless to say, does not yet exist, but the point here is that as soon as linguists engage with African material, they almost inevitably find themselves in an applied-linguistic frame.

2. History of the field

According to the Ethnologue's *Geographical Distribution of Living Languages* (2000), there are 2,058 languages spoken in Africa. This is about 30% of the world's total of 6,809 living languages. Thus, while Africa holds 13% of the world's population, one out of every three languages used in the world is an African language. The average number of speakers for a language in Africa is approximately 400,000; and every African country would average between 40 and 50 languages spoken on its territory. Multilingualism is the norm in Africa, and simple figures suffice to make that clear. Furthermore, the indigenous languages of Africa display significant typological variation. Four language families are represented on the continent. By far the largest is the Niger-Congo family, of which the Bantu sub-branch covers most of Central and Southern Africa. Apart from Niger-Congo, also Nilo-Saharan, Afro-Asiatic and Khoisan languages are spoken on African soil. Members of these language families differ substantially in structure. Borderline regions where language families meet, for example, in Southern Nigeria, Cameroon, Northern Tanzania and the Northern Congo region comprise a rather breathtaking number of languages, many of them having nothing in common structurally with the others.

But simple calculus is deceptive, for several factors must be taken into account. First, figures on language or bland statements about language typology are poor indicators of actual communicative practices. In the case of Africa, they yield an image of stunning multilingualism with associations of insurmountable communication problems across typologically incompatible languages. Multilingualism, to be sure, is the norm everywhere, and in Africa like elsewhere, people in actual practice find pragmatic solutions to communication difficulties. So the figures are figures, not suggestive of anything more than of a relative density of multilingualism.

Second, as we all know, a calculation of the number of languages spoken in a country hinges on what we understand by "language", and language itself is an ideological construct that refers to other constructs such as country, community, speaker, competence, territory and so forth. Stating the question is answering it: As soon as we mention such concepts, we realize that we find ourselves in a theoretical minefield – none of the concepts bears consensus, and all of them require thorough empirical inspection in order to be useful (Rampton 1998; also Hymes 1968; Silverstein 1998). In practice, counting languages is strongly dependent on existing linguistic records for languages, that is, on the availability of (linguistic) descriptions of languages and studies comparing material from one language to that of others (so as to distinguish, for instance, between "language" and "dialect"). In order for something to be recognized as a language, someone recognized as a linguist must provide descriptive and analytical evidence for that claim. And this is where Africa becomes a particularly problematic area for language counting.

The history of language description and cataloging in Africa is only partly a scientific history. To a large extent, it is a political history in which the study of languages must be seen as deeply embedded in the larger colonial enterprise, and many *descriptive-linguistic* endeavors served *applied* and *practical* goals within the colonial system, such as the improvement of bureaucratic practice and Christianization (Samarin 1982, 1984; Fabian 1983, 1986; Errington 2001). Professional linguistic work came rather late in the day, and a significant part of what is currently known about African languages is the result of the work of (sometimes, but by no means always, excellently qualified) amateur scholars: missionaries, teachers, colonial administrative officers or military personnel, who spent terrific efforts at creating "standard" languages in the context of

Bible translations, the indigenization of Christianity, or the training of colonial personnel (an early survey of such work in Congo is Van Bulck 1948). Languages in this particular sense were textually produced in grammars, dictionaries and grammatical sketches, by deploying particular habituated "scholarly" tactics of writing – the "birth certificate" of many African languages is a collection of grammatical and lexical notes collected by European scholars (Blommaert 2005b). The good news for the purposes of this chapter is that most of the early descriptive work on African languages was a form of applied linguistics. A thorough and comprehensive study of this colonial applied literature is still wanting, but some general lines can be distinguished.

Standardization meant the conversion of African languages so as to make them resemble European languages (see also Romaine, this vol.). The metropolitan languages were consistently used as the model for African languages – or to be more precise: An ideological image of the metropolitan languages was projected onto African languages (cf. Irvine 2001a, 2001b; Blommaert 1999a: ch.3; Meeuwis 1999). Often there was a real textual generic model: the expository style, structure and jargon of Latin or Greek school grammar. This projected ideological image revolved around a limited series of propositions which can be summarized as follows:

(i) A standard language is a language characterized by a *single set of norms*: a single set of grammatical rules, and a finite repertoire of vocabulary. Standardization always equals singularization of language norms; the function of these norms is *denotational clarity*: the production of clear, unambiguous meanings.

(ii) A standard language is *a pure language*, consisting exclusively of "indigenous", language-internal material; language mixing, code-switching or other forms of "impurity" have to be removed.

(iii) A standard language is enshrined in a normative written (orthographic) code; it is *a literate language*.

(iv) A standard language is a *prerequisite for certain forms of cognitive activity*: rational scientific thought (learning in general), religious and philosophical thought, artful literature production and consumption. Standardizing a language therefore raises it to the level of a "culture language".

(v) Such an "improved" language *defines a people*. Humanity is divided into monolingual, homogeneous ethnolinguistic units ("nations") which each occupy a fixed territory. Language, ethnicity and territory are the basic units of language standardization. Ethnolinguistic maps are crucial instruments for codifying the linguistic situation of Africa.

(vi) Prior to standardization, languages lack these features and *are not really "languages"*. They are dialects, jargons, speech, sabirs. Thus, there is a hierarchy of degrees of "languageness", defined by the features given above.

These assumptions define what Silverstein (1996) called a monoglot view of language in society. They were clearly based on European imaginings of relations between language and (national) identity, often couched in vulgar versions of Herderism (Meeuwis 1999; Silverstein 2000; Blommaert 1999c). And they were applied with considerable vigor, with quite remarkable results. Several African languages were effectively standardized – provided with a canon of grammar, dictionary and texts, and then converted into teaching material, journalistic and administrative genres, and even creative writing – and used as a medium of vertical and horizontal communication in the colonies (see Fabian 1986 for the Belgian Congo; Blommaert 1999a for East Africa). Some African languages – Swahili, Lingala, Hausa, Wolof – gained or strengthened their role as trans-regional and quasi-official languages, and many became languages with an "infrastructure": a standard orthography, a body of published work, and clear structures of authority guarding the boundaries of the language (e.g., language committees, academic authorities).

The widespread usage of these assumptions led to an image of Africa as populated by big and small ethnolinguistic groups – "tribes" – whose language was spoken in a particular territory; multiplicity of languages in one region led to highly fragmented images, mosaics of criss-crossing patches on a map, each one assumed to be internally homogeneous. None of the assumptions is unproblematic, and taken together they yield a thoroughly unrealistic image of language in society, far removed from real communicative practices.

A result of that approach was the freezing of the sociolinguistic landscape, to no small degree helped by the "infrastructuration" of the languages mentioned above. People were supposed to be monolingual (in a "pure" code), and languages were supposed to be tied to a particular ("ancestral") territory. The language now spoken in that region was supposed to be the language that had always been spoken there, and it was expected to be forever spoken there, by the same people who had spoken it since times immemorial. Languages were immobile items, comparable to the physical geography of colonial territories, but closely tied to peoples' (singular) identity. Thus, detailed language inventories often identified a language in relation to an ethnic group and a locality. Consider the following examples from Van Bulck (1949: 210, French original):[1]

> b) Sub-group of the bend in the Congo river: Nouvelle Anvers
> […]
> 4. *BoLoki* from the Ruki
> *LoLoki* from the bend in the River
> […]
> 5. *MaBaale* from the Mongala
> *BaBaale* from the Black Waters

Mixed varieties spoken as *lingua franca* in the multilingual environment of trade along the Congo River are not listed but dismissed:

> 3. *Ba Ma Ngala*, speaking "LiNgala".
> Not to be confused with the various *sabirs* known under the name "Lingala", "Language of the River", "Ngala", "BaNgala" or "MaNgala".

Multilingualism could only be conceived as a juxtaposition of multiple (intact) languages; language mixing disqualified the code and moved it outside the category of language. Early studies of multilingualism thus took the shape of comparative lexical analysis: *polyglotta* for the benefit of the (European) traveller, and later the grand projects of comparative African linguistics in search of genealogical relations between the languages and the groups that spoke them. In such studies, all the assumptions mentioned above underlie the effort, and comparative studies produced interesting and popular by-products: reconstructions of migration patterns, notably for Bantu, and obviously based on the assumption that languages could only spread when their native speakers took them elsewhere. The images of ethnolinguistic staticity remained intact (see Vansina 1997 for a critique).

Consequently, some rather elementary questions were not asked and elementary facts overlooked. They emerged piecemeal, later in writings, and never occupied the center stage of African linguistics. For instance: the fact that people could be multilingual, without this being a deviation of normal sociolinguistic practice – in short, the fact that multilingualism might be the rule, not the exception. Likewise, the fact that people could intermarry, socialize, or develop complex economic, labor or political relations with other groups, thus yielding processes of language shift or creolization (e.g. Meshtrie 1992a; Samarin 1989). Territories may change hands, forms of urbanization may occur, habits (including linguistic ones) may be adapted to new cultural tastes or new relations of power (e.g. Vansina 1990). Colonialism also resulted in the immigration of new populations in Africa, and this too led to complex sociolinguistic effects (e.g. Meshtrie 1991, 1992b). Colonialism also changed the sociolinguistic ecology of Africa because of the impact of the metropolitan languages on social and cultural life (on language and colonialism, see also Migge and Léglise, this vol.). French, English, and Portuguese became the most prestigious linguistic resources wherever they occurred (e.g. Mazrui 1975; Mazrui and Mazrui 1998). It led to the "proletarianization" of large urban masses, now clustered in suburban slums: laboratories of social, cultural and linguistic change (Spitulnik 1998; Swigart 1992, 2000; Englund 2002). And it also led to a *literate* Africa defying the (still dominant) image of Africa as a continent characterized by oral languages and sociolinguistic environments (Fabian 1990; Blommaert 1999d). The sociolinguistic reality of Africa was and is, in other words, far more complex and dynamic than the frozen image contained in language catalogs, comparative wordlists, linguistic maps or atlases suggests.

Such catalogs, lists, maps and atlases occur from the beginning of colonial exploration onwards, and they persist as a genre of knowledge until today (*Ethnologue* being a case in point; see Cole 1971 for a survey and Guthrie 1971 for examples). And the realities they suggest have had, and still have, a tremendous influence on language planners, educational theorists, sociolinguists, development workers, politicians and international organizations. Methodologically, almost all of them are plagued by the general defect of the Africanist tradition: the fact that good research was few and far between. Some regions have been described in considerable detail; other regions haven't, and many languages in Africa are only documented in field notes or in published brief sketches, sometimes of very doubtful quality. Prior to the advent of the tape recorder used by a skilled professional scholar, most language data were recorded in a written form, by means of sometimes ad-hoc orthographic conventions used to take down elicited or dictated fragments of language, as a rule unknown to the one who recorded them. Acoustic-phonetic, stylistic or genre features were often either not recorded or misunderstood and misrepresented, sometimes leading to highly speculative classifications (Blommaert 2005b; for the case of Gur-languages, see Arnaut et al. 1998). And most languages were only described *once*: The number of African languages that have been investigated by several generations of scholars is very small. Thus, once a language had been documented, it existed and still exists, in the sense and with all the associations described above.

The conclusion to all of this is that we are facing a problem with the linguistic record of Africa. It can be summarized in one proposition: We have a very partial and inaccurate idea of linguistic diversity in Africa. The evidence is fragmentary; it focuses on "pure", geographically "fixed" singular languages, often overlapping with ethnic groups. The descriptively generated multitude of such ethnolinguistic entities is converted into an image of bewildering and deeply *problematic* ethnolinguistic diversity, with small populations speaking their language seemingly isolated from others, separated by linguistic-typological and ethno-cultural barriers (cf. Fardon and Furniss 1994; Fabian 1986).[2] Furthermore, hardly any attention was spent on literacy (even long after alphabetical literacy had been spread throughout the continent) or on diasporic varieties of languages, urban varieties or other sociolinguistic phenomena of mobility. Studies of actual language practices, with larger-scale sociolinguistic implications, are still very rare.

Such lacunae are not likely to be filled soon. The problem is not helped, evidently, by the understandably low scientific output of African universities. In a number of cases there is truly excellent research going on, often unique in design and superbly relevant to our understanding of sociolinguistic processes. But only on rare occasions is such research converted into internationally circulated academic publications for reasons too obvious to report. Just like the study of language in Africa was seriously enhanced by the favorable conditions of colonialism, it is seriously obstructed by the postcolonial situation on the continent, which makes research in many parts of Africa extremely difficult if not impossible. Huge parts of Africa are now (and have been for decades) virtually "unresearchable" due to war or other violent conflicts, chronic instability and lack of infrastructure. Conflicts such as the one in Sierra Leone, Congo and many other places not only kill tens of thousands of Africans and force even more to migrate to other places (thus creating new diasporic sociolinguistic environments). They also destroy schools and universities, along with the skilled and competent people working there. They thus destroy the material and intellectual preconditions for sustained, thorough research, just at a time when such research is much needed.

3. State of the art: A new paradigm

The state of the art on language diversity in Africa is thus rather depressing, and we are facing a terrific agenda of reconstruction. No less is needed than a paradigm shift, and the main lines of such a new paradigm can be suggested. The paradigm, to be sure, must take *diversity* as the main defining feature of language. So rather than seeing language as primarily characterized by stability, singularity and purity, we need to see language primarily as a complex of diverse forms and functions organized not in categorical blocks but in continua, and of shifting – i.e. unstable and not necessarily "pure" – formal features, the functions of which cannot per se be presupposed but need to be established empirically (Hymes 1963, 1996; Silverstein 1977, 2003). Not diversity is the problem, but common perceptions of *uniformity*, i.e. the denial of diversity. I would propose that such a paradigm would offer better hopes for an *applied* linguistics, i.e. a study of language that addresses real forms of language, and how they matter to the people using them.[3]

The focus in such an approach is on language practice and ideology, or to be more precise, on what language means to people, what counts as language, and how language functions socially and culturally in real, situated practices. This is, of course, not a new focus; it underlies the development of contemporary linguistic pragmatics, sociolinguistics and discourse analysis (e.g. Verschueren 1995, 1998). And as we learnt from these subdisciplines, language (the singular, closed and named object described above) is not the object of analysis. We would investigate practical, socioculturally organized manifestations of language often captured under terms such as genres, registers, styles, and codes, along with their conditions of use (their pragmatics) and their perceived and real effects and values for the users (the metapragmatics of genres, registers, etc.). This, then, would have several important effects in research.

Most importantly, we would be forced to investigate what seemingly simple statements such as "Nigeria has 428 languages" mean in actual practice: What kinds of phenomena are these 428 languages? Are they comparable *as practical communicative resources*? Or do we see different genre and register phenomena depending on what precise language we are looking at: some languages that are only used in "standard" forms, others only in substandard forms; some always in "pure" form, others mostly in "mixed" forms; some only through literacy, others never through literacy; some only in the public domain, others never in the public domain; or some only in the public domain in one particular geographical area and not in others, and so forth. In other words, we would be forced to look into the actual forms of occurrence of languages, their functions and effects.

The outcome of such an exercise, no doubt, would be a rather more nuanced view of multilingualism than the one now often sketched for Africa. We would find out that social interaction in some places is dominated by languages that do not occur in language atlases: new, rapidly changing (and often mixed) urban varieties of local and diasporic languages such as Swahili in Lubumbashi (Gysels 1992; de Rooij 1996), Town Bemba in Lusaka (Spitulnik 1998), Sheng in Nairobi (Hillewaert 2003; cf. also Parkin 1974), urban Wolof in Dakar (Swigart 1992), the particular blend of Afrikaans and many other languages spoken in Cape Town (McCormick 2002), and many others. Conversely, we are bound to discover that the languages listed in the atlases and catalogs themselves are changing because people migrate or are under social, political or economic pressure to assimilate into other dominant languages (Brenzinger 1992; Parkin 1989; McCormick 2002), as we are bound to find out that the languages that Africans take along into the diaspora also undergo quite substantial changes (Meeuwis 1997; Meeuwis and Blommaert 1998; Maryns and Blommaert 2001; Vigouroux 2005). We can find out that the occurrence of particular varieties of languages is closely tied to particular genres or registers, to specific topics or contexts (Albert 1972; Finlayson 1995). And we can find out that internal variation within one language may often have social and cultural effects that are equally if not more important than differences between languages (Blommaert 2003, 2004). In other words, we are bound to find out that language, in practice, occurs as stratified forms-over-functions, and that such form-function relations display tremendous variability without leading (a) to loss of function (e.g. without becoming meaningless) and (b) to the perception of speakers that they are using a language (the use of very "impure" varieties of Swahili would still be qualified as Swahili).

This, obviously, would have a serious effect on the nomenclature used to identify languages in Africa. Let us take Shaba Swahili as a case in point. Shaba

Swahili – the variety of Swahili used in South-Eastern Congo – is a peculiar linguistic object. It was known for a long time as Kiswahili, and the local/regional varieties were thus included as a dialect cluster in the larger sphere of Kiswahili. However, it was also known as Kingwana, and some codifying literature emerged in which language status was claimed for the variety (e.g. Whitehead and Whitehead 1928). In such codifying efforts, the language was presented in its "canonical" form: as a "pure" denotational code, "unmixed" and fully "Bantu" in structure. In later work, however, the Shaba Swahili variety was identified as being quintessentially mixed: an urban hybrid in which Swahili, French and Luba-languages were merged (Schicho 1980; de Rooij 1996). "Impurity", in other words, now defined the language – a rather momentous shift in conceptualization and nomenclature.

Empirically, though, this does not solve all our problems. When we take a look at the repertoires of Shaba Swahili speakers, as deployed, for instance, in written texts (e.g. Blommaert 2003, 2004), some remarkable things start appearing. We see that these repertoires can shift from "pure" French to "pure" Swahili – pure here meaning unmixed, not marked by codeswitching – while their point of reference remains a mixed code. More precisely, we see that "pure" varieties of language occur as *genres*, as special forms of language, e.g. in documents considered to be serious and important. People would write (with considerable effort) in e.g. "pure" Swahili, but they would mark certain terms as being unusual *in Swahili* by means of reverse glosses, revealing a "normal" occurrence of codeswitching there. Thus, the "pure" varieties are generated out of the "mixed" varieties and constructed as special ways of expressing things, requiring more effort, planning and care in execution.

This then suggests several things: (a) the difference between unmixed, pure language and mixed language is not a difference in *languages* (i.e. it does not allow linear inferences about "multilingual competence"), but in *position within a stratified, hierarchical system of variation* in which "pure" forms are perceived as "better", more formal and more deferential than "impure" forms (which are seen as colloquial, common, unsophisticated); (b) this then suggests that what we at first sight perceive as *language* differences and contrasts are in fact *register, genre and style* differences *within the same language complex*, which appears to be primordially geographic in delineation; (c) this, perhaps surprisingly, would mean that the term Shaba Swahili can cover a continuum of varieties, including "pure" (unmixed) French and Swahili. French, in other words, can be Shaba Swahili – this is a slightly counterintuitive claim, but it corresponds ethnographically to the pragmatic organization of speech repertoires among language users.

In sum, we would have a far more complex, but more accurate image of what people do with language and what language does with people. The image would be dynamic and flexible, with phenomena of movement, change and dislocation or relocation as normal, almost self-evident features. This would, of course, have implications for the way in which we look at "community" – the usual sociolinguistic locus of language – and we will have to differentiate between linguistic community and speech community (Silverstein 1996, 1998). The former would be a group of people displaying allegiance to a particular, stratified and conventional (standardized, monoglot) idea of language – people calling themselves "speakers of Language X" – while the latter would be a group of people displaying joint understandings and forms of usage of particular genres, registers, styles and codes.

Both types of community rarely overlap. The former is usually an effect of institutional processes such as education and administration, aimed at imposing the particular "language" as a practical and symbolic tool, and often as part of state- or nation-building processes performed by the state or state-related actors (Laitin 1992; Blommaert 1999a). It is part of a language regime, in which the kind of allegiance mentioned above is expected from people, as the sociolinguistic correlate of citizenship or group membership. The latter type of community is more volatile, not necessarily as connected to power as the former, and more flexible than the former. Speech communities can range from the infinitely small – a temporary consensus over communicative procedures between two people, such as strangers on a train or bus – to the very big – the globalized elites who interact more and easier with similar elites elsewhere in the world than with their non-elite neighbors. They are always *plural*: Only the rarest of exceptions is a member of just one speech community. Consequently, people live in a patchwork of speech communities of different range, depth and degree of control (the rules are strict in some speech communities – e.g. churches – and flexible in others). And they often operate *simultaneously*: Tanzanian friends of mine, staunch supporters of the national language Swahili, still sent their children to their home region so as to make them acquire the ethnic language-of-origin. There was no perceived contradiction between both sociolinguistic orientations: One operated only at the level of the state, the other at the level of the family and ethnic group. They were mutually exclusive: Swahili would not be spoken with family members, while the ethnic language would not be spoken with colleagues at work or state officials. Consequently, each of the languages would be differently organized, so to speak: Particular thematic (e.g. official, job-related, political) domains, genres, and registers would be highly developed in Swahili, while others (e.g. domains referring to intimacy and family life) would be less developed; the opposite would hold for the ethnic language. The particular multilingualism practiced by these people would thus be structured by their participation in specific speech communities, the languages deployed in these processes would be differently organized, and what we now understand by multilingualism is a layered, specific (or specialized) complex of linguistic resources deployed for the purposes of participation in different speech communities (Blommaert 2005a).⁴

As became clear through the citations in this section, the perspective sketched here has taken off, and some admirable studies have appeared. But a lot of work remains to be done: the work of description as well as that of (re)interpretation.

4. Current issues and the contribution of applied linguistics

With this perspective now defined, we can take a fresh look at some of the major controversies in our field. I will discuss three issues: (a) linguistic rights and minority issues; (b) language in education; (c) literacy.

4.1. Linguistic rights and minorities

Issues of linguistic rights and linguistic minorities have become central topics of sociolinguistic reflection and debate (Phillipson 1992; Skutnabb-Kangas 2000; also Skutnabb-Kangas, this vol.). The main line of argument can be summarized as follows: There is currently a worldwide dominance of a handful of languages – English being the most powerful one to date – and these languages have an oppressive effect on indigenous minority languages. The latter languages are increasingly threatened with disappearance, and their speakers become victims of (among many other forms of discrimination) sociolinguistic marginalization. The loss of minority languages has a disastrous effect on diversity in the world, not only because "species" of speakers disappear, but also because together with the languages, specific indigenous forms of knowledge are lost, of value for the balance between humans and the environment (see also Fill, this vol.). In reaction to that, a concept of linguistic rights needs to be developed and disseminated, in which people would have the full rights to use their native language in every domain of social life, and in which governments would protect these rights from violation by "killer languages" such as English.

Africa, with its myriad of minority languages, has been a fertile field of application for linguistic rights, and several scholars have enthusiastically embraced the paradigm (e.g. Batibo and Smieja 2000). In early 2000, African scholars and writers drafted what became known as the "Asmara Declaration", a manifesto in which the revitalization of African languages was presented as critical for the development of the continent (Blommaert 2001). Particularly in South Africa, where the end of Apartheid led to a new national language policy in which nine indigenous African languages became official languages, linguistic rights discourse was a much practiced discourse (e.g. Alexander 1989; Webb 1994). Linguistic rights provided a new frame of reference for talking about old sociolinguistic problems in Africa: the marginal status of local languages, the low degrees of literacy, the visible overlap between membership of socio-political and economic elites and competence in the metropolitan language.

The enthusiasm for linguistic rights has, unfortunately, not been complemented by (nor is it based on) renewed and extended empirical research. The little empirical evidence that was available suggests at least a far more complex and less unambiguous picture. Studies such as Stroud (1999) demonstrated that European languages such as Portuguese in Mozambique could be widely accepted as "local" languages, with strongly positive ideological values; Williams (2006) demonstrated that the use of English and indigenous languages in education in Malawi and Zambia did not in itself account for educational success or failure rates; Mekacha (1993, 1994) described how in Tanzania, the dominant language is not English but an indigenous language, Swahili. He also demonstrated that Swahili did not eliminate local indigenous languages from the repertoires of speakers, but that the kind of functional and truncated allocation of codes to domains, described above, occurred. Thus, what may look at first sight like severe minorization and marginalization of languages does not necessarily or automatically lead to language loss.

Msanjila's (2004) research is telling in this respect. He investigated what we could call the absolute periphery of the sociolinguistic system in Tanzania: a tiny language, Kisafwa, in a peripheral village in Southern Tanzania. There is no institutional support whatsoever for Kisafwa, and Swahili has de facto taken over all public and authoritative language domains. Given the economic and political marginalization of the locality, furthermore, one could expect a strong orientation among the younger generation to languages offering an upwardly mobile trajectory – Swahili and English. Yet, Msanjila's research revealed a considerable degree of resilience and a very slow rate of language attrition: At the present rate, it would take another century before the language would effectively cease to be people's mother tongue, and one could note that circumstances for language maintenance are now better than in the past, because the days of aggressive Swahilization are over. Young people still overwhelmingly use Kisafwa as a domain-specific "first" language and "[t]he people at Ituha village could be described as functionally monolingual ethnic (Kisafwa) speakers" (Msanjila 2004: 170), despite the presumed strong pressure towards language loss.

Such evidence, though scarce, provides important amendments to the linguistic rights paradigm, if for nothing else because it shows that there seem to be very little automatisms in the domain of language shift.[5] Even in light of adverse "objective" conditions, languages can be maintained and others can be functionally reallocated in a new, more complex repertoire. Stroud (2001), Heugh (2003) and Stroud and Heugh (2004) thus oppose a concept of "linguistic citizenship" to that of "linguistic rights", emphasizing the individual (rather than categorical) nature of rights and allowing for considerable flexibility in the empirical application of the concept.[6]

These developments in theory and research obviously have an effect on one of the long-standing concerns of AL in Africa: language policy and planning (see also Ricento, this vol.). Since the late 1960s, scholars of language have been involved in the tremendous task of designing and implementing language policies in several African countries (e.g. Eastman 1983; Fardon and Furniss 1994). Special attention was given to countries such as Nigeria because of the extreme multilingualism in that country (e.g. Adegbija 1994), and Tanzania, the first country to grant national and official status to an African language, Swahili (e.g. Blommaert 1999a). The language planning literature received a boost after 1994, when South Africa embarked on the above mentioned ambitious language policy. A lot of this literature, however, moves within the monoglot image of language and multilingualism described in the previous section (cf. Apter 1982; Blommaert 1996, 1999b); thus, static and mechanistic models of "rational" language policies dominate much of the literature (e.g. Laitin 1992), and proposals for language policies fail to acknowledge the functional diversity of different ingredients of people's repertoires (Heugh 2003). Linguistic rights offered a new, and invigorating, framework for language planning studies. But given the fundamental flaws of this paradigm, it is to be expected that the practical and applicable yields will be small.

South Africa may be the clearest illustration of this problem. When the post-apartheid government introduced its 11-national language policy in 1994, this was universally welcomed as a breakthrough in the recognition of indigenous languages. Apart from English and Afrikaans, South Africa had adopted nine Bantu languages as official languages, officially equal to English and Afrikaans: Xhosa, Zulu, Tswana, Northern Sotho (SeSotho sa Leboa), Southern Sotho, Tsonga, Swazi, Ndebele and Venda. And the new language policy dictated that linguistic "infrastructuration" should be carried out for all languages: National and regional language boards would be set up and means would be made available to provide grammars, dictionaries, orthographies and teaching materials in these languages. In addition, multilingualism would be the norm in public life, and provinces all had to identify more than one language as media for official business.

It is not easy to be critical of this; after all, we are facing here a sea-change in the status and public importance of African indigenous languages, a radical break with a century or so of denial of even the most modest of public functions to African languages. The Bantu languages in South Africa, needless to say, came out of a history of total and grotesque misrecognition (in Bourdieu's sense), and recognition of these languages as functionally equivalent is a major symbolic form of redress for past injustices. At the same time, the enthusiasm displayed by language planners worldwide (and linguistic rights activists in particular) needs to be tempered, and there are several reasons for this. I will provide a quick overview of some of the major challenges facing (or generated by) this new language policy.

(1) In general, declaring things equal in the face of real, existing factual *inequalities* is a recipe for continued discrimination. It is obvious that a language such as Venda is no match for Afrikaans and English, not even for Zulu and Xhosa. There are significant differences in size of the language community, but also in the historical political "ranking" of such groups (where Venda, for instance, has always been marginal, in contrast to e.g. Zulu), the socio-economic differences between the regions where the languages are being spoken (Venda-land is one of South-Africa's poorest regions), their place in center-periphery structures in the country (where the languages of the main urban centers hold an advantage over others), and the history of "infrastructuration" and use of the language (which is obviously hugely different for, e.g., Venda and Afrikaans). Consequently, even when a "minority" language becomes *in principle* an official language (thus, in linguistic rights terms, endowed with a large complex of rights and privileges), it may remain *in practice* a minority language, under severe pressure from languages such as English and Afrikaans, with a continued low status, and enshrined in a stigma of backwardness and marginality whenever it is used.

(2) In addition, the 11 languages obviously do not exhaust the linguistic diversity of South Africa. There is no place in the list of official languages for, e.g., Khoisan languages or languages used in the so-called Indian community: Gujarati, Hindi or Tamil. Yet, obviously, all of these language are important parts of South Africa's cultural heritage, and their groups of speakers have been important actors in the history of the region and beyond: The Khoisan are probably the oldest "autochthonous" population of present-day South Africa, and Gandhi, of course, started his career in South Africa as an advocate for the "Indian" population. Thus, even though one can applaud the expansion of the range of official languages, this simply means that the top of the pyramid is slightly broadened, and that the pyramid itself remains standing. Languages *not* recognized as official remain in effect as minorized as before, and there are quite a good number of them.

(3) The territorial boundedness of the languages is another problem. The 11 language policy has restricted itself to "indigenous" languages, presumed to be the languages of a historical population of present-day South Africa. We have already seen above that the exclusion of, e.g., Khoisan languages begs the usual question of "autochthony"; that of Indian languages suggests a mythical, racially homogeneous past prior to the immigration of people from other parts of the globe. This smacks of apartheid logic, and the 11-language policy indeed con-

tains some unsavory aspects of its predecessor system. The nine official Bantu languages are in fact the languages of the apartheid Bantustans, i.e. the "native homelands" of apartheid: regionally located, ethnolinguistically homogeneous formations sculptured in an imagery of ethnic and linguistic purity and territorial fixedness. Matching that imagery produced a degree of recognition for territory, ethnicity and language (Transkei, Vendaland and the other Bantustans were officially recognized by the South African government), and this recognizability has been carried over to post-apartheid. This leads to the same conceptual and practical problems: The freezing of the ethnolinguistic landscape excludes newcomers as well as innovators from publicly recognized users of languages. We have already seen that even "old" immigrant groups such as the Gujarati or Tamil are not recognized; *a fortiori* for the millions of post-1994 immigrants from other parts of Africa who have in the meantime created sedentary, lasting pockets of several hundreds of thousands of speakers of, e.g., Mozambican languages such as Makua, and whose presence undoubtedly leads to the gradual emergence of new urban languages. Thus, by fixing the ethnolinguistic landscape, new minorities are generated with every immigrant entering the country.

(4) Finally, the eleven languages themselves are stratified and "uniformized". The Afrikaans that now has official recognition is still the same as before: the standardized, codified "white" variety of it, not that of, e.g., the Cape "colored" community. The English declared official is Standard English, not the English spoken by, e.g., the Indian communities in South Africa (Meshtrie 1992b). Thus, *internal* variation within the languages now declared official is obscured. Yet it is clear that actual social opportunities, trajectories and potential to deploy certain kinds of activities depend as much on (language-internal) *accent* as on language itself, and that it is consequently not enough to acquire a language, but that one must acquire particular *ways of using that language*: genres, styles, accents, lexicon, etc. Even with Afrikaans being an official language, some forms of Afrikaans will carry stigma and will not be recognized as such; the same goes for English, Zulu, Xhosa – in short for every language in which regional and social differences are audible.

Thus, we see that the recognition of indigenous languages is less of a victory of minority languages than one would assume. It has changed the parameters of power relations between the symbolic attributes of groups and regions, that much is true. But it has not eradicated linguistic (and other) discrimination, it has not created linguistic equality, and it may even contribute to the discrimination and minorization of the vast number of non-official languages used by people in South Africa. Language planning these days should be concerned with theoretically sustained considerations of practice rather than with the proclamation of principle; with the realities of language use rather than with language names; with practices and their effects rather than with laws and regulations.

4.2. Language in education

Language in education has for decades been the central focus of sociolinguistics and applied linguistics in Africa, and it was always closely connected to language planning research (e.g. Dakin, Tiffen, and Widdowson 1968; Fishman, Ferguson, and Das Gupta 1968). Education was and is one of the key institutional instruments by means of which the state or powerful civil society actors could impose language regimes on the population, and such regimes could either be democratic or elitist (on language and education, see also Bieswanger, this vol.). In Africa, often attempts were made towards the former while in practice the latter prevailed. One of the reasons for this, in almost every African country, is the use of metropolitan languages in (post-primary) education systems. English, French and other elite languages created a social filter in the educational system, and competence in the metropolitan language thus became one of the most highly valued symbolic attributes of elite identity (Mazrui 1975, 1978; Mazrui 2004; Mazrui and Mazrui 1998). To many elite members, "education" is a synonym of "English" (Roy-Campbell and Qorro 1997; Neke 2003).

Education is and remains one of Africa's main social, cultural and political problems, and if anything, the current situation is worse than that of the late 1960s. Many regions of Africa have witnessed a complete destruction of the education system due to war and other catastrophic events, and in some regions this lack of education is several decades old. The problem of education is therefore not primarily linguistic – it is material. Having said this, the problem remains that where schools exist, the level of academic performance often leaves much to be desired, and this is the point where language becomes an issue.

Authors such as Williams (2006) and Heugh (2003) demonstrate how a complex of linguistic, material and wider semiotic (e.g. didactic) practices together create a less than optimal learning environment in which cognitive, communicative and literacy skills often remain underdeveloped. The use of local languages – the pupils' languages – is manifestly beneficial for didactic interaction and processing, as one of the current problems is that every lecture *in* English is also a lecture *on* English, in which pupils (and teachers!) face challenges of living up to the (very often monumental) imagined standards of the metropolitan language. The result, not surprisingly, is a sometimes cataclysmic communicative breakdown in which neither the teacher nor the pupils accomplish the sort of disciplined interaction characteristic for learning environments (see examples in Roy-Campbell and Qorro 1997).

The problem in much of the literature, however, is that this question is often formulated in a monoglot frame, as *either* the metropolitan language *or* the local language (e.g. Rubagumya 1990). Consequently, any proposal to use local African languages as *the* language of instruction crashes into insurmountable practical obstacles such as the mass production of up-to-date teaching materials (textbooks, syllabuses, etc.), the training of teachers, the sheer number of languages in which teaching materials should be translated and produced, the unequal size of ethnolinguistic groups requiring native-language materials, and so forth. It also bumps into political sensitivities such as the national image, as well as into social sensitivities that have to do with the self-protection of local elites. As soon as that frame is abandoned, and allowance is made for flexible forms of deployment of situation- or topic-specific registers and codes, the issue becomes far easier to address. One can then imagine educational settings in which code-switching is a normal way of communicating, in which the language of verbal instruction is not necessarily that of literacy (reading, taking notes, writing exams), and in which the sort of truncated multilingualism described earlier is used as a potential for communication and an opportunity for meaning construction, not as an obstacle to learning or a threat to language standards.

Such practices of mixing and code-switching during class instruction are undoubtedly widespread, though there is very little published research on it. Kadeghe (2000) provides ample documentation on the use of Swahili by secondary school teachers in Tanzania, who are supposed to teach in English. Shifts into Swahili there appear as crucial pedagogical tools, allowing a degree of articulateness for the teacher which s/he would otherwise lack, and offering the pupils an opportunity to follow up on English lectures with Swahili questions and discussion slots. Williams (2006) reports similar findings in village schools in Zambia and Malawi, and research by Huysmans and Muyllaert (2005) also identifies code-switching as a pedagogical tactic in a township school in Cape Town. The issue thus does not appear as whether or not such forms of mixing occur; nor whether or not they are robustly functional and effective as discursive modalities for teaching and learning: The point is to recognize them as such and assume that in the field of education, as elsewhere, monoglot normativity is a *goal* and not necessarily an empirical reality. Seen from that perspective, teachers and pupils switching between the metropolitan language and their mother tongues should not be read as a failure of educational policies, but as an index of a number of operational, practical problems experienced and solutions explored by the teachers and pupils alike.

4.3. Literacy

Our discussion of literacy must start by noting that there has as yet been hardly any sizeable research into literacy practices in Africa (but see Prinsloo and Breier 1996). Literacy has thus far mostly been treated in close harmony with educational issues, and the practical understanding of literacy in such contexts is that of school literacy: normative, standardized, orthographic literacy which can be measured by means of a set of (universal?) benchmarks. This, unfortunately, is also the conception of literacy that underlies UNESCO's inquiries into literacy levels in the world, and literacy statistics of African countries are thus rarely conducive to an accurate understanding of actual levels and functions of literacy.

Yet, it is clear that Africa is potentially a very worthwhile field for literacy research, at least if we adopt the basic assumptions of the so-called New Literacy Studies (e.g. Street 1995), that literacy is best seen as a set of socially and culturally grounded practices of semiotic visualization, and that the field of literacy is consequently far wider than what in common understandings is accepted as orthographic (alphabetical) literacy. Neither the forms, nor (even less) the functions of literacy can be presupposed, and we may find forms of deployment of literacy resources that differ quite substantially from what we would expect (Blommaert 1999d, 2003, 2004). Such research should evidently also abandon the old view of Africa as a continent where languages exist primarily in an oral form (the "unwritten" languages). There is a lot of writing going on in Africa, in all layers of the populations, and these forms of writing are an important topic for sociolinguistic and applied linguistic research.

There is a lot of "grassroots" literacy in Africa: literacy characterized by a low or incomplete degree of insertion into complexes of literacy norms, leading to unstable handwriting, erratic punctuation, inconsistency in orthography, struggles with literate narrative style and so forth. Yet, such grassroots literacy can spawn impressive products: long autobiographies, chronicles, histories, genealogies and so on (see e.g. Caplan 1997; Fabian 1990). Such grassroots writing raises several important issues. Let me give a brief survey of some of the main ones.

(1) It challenges the strong assumptions about literacy as a per definition normative field. It appears that literacy can proceed, and be effective, even when scores of norms of writing are being violated. This should allow us to distinguish between normative writing – ortho-graphy in its etymological sense – and "hetero-graphy": writing organized around different, often locally constructed and one-off rules and norms. Hetero-graphy challenges deep-seated ideological views of correctness and normativity in communication, that suggest that no meaning can be transferred unless such meanings are being cast in (linguistically, formally) "correct" shapes. This is similar to the status of the asterisk in front of "ungrammatical" utterances: Such utterances can be linguistically perfectly adequate regardless of their lack of syntactic or morphological "correctness". Thus, here, we see how grassroots literacy might trigger fundamental reflections on some of linguistics' oldest and most solidly entrenched axioms.

(2) It also makes us realize that literacy itself should be addressed in a more realistic, materialist sense, as lodged and contextualized activities tied to economies of signs and meanings valid in a particular environment and tied to other economies elsewhere. Concretely: The hetero-graphic literacy we encounter in Africa may be adequate for literacy circulation in Shaba, Cape Town or Lagos, but not in Paris, London or New York. In other words, precisely the fact that het-

ero-graphic writing is *functional* as writing, while it deviates strongly from "universal" spelling and orthography conventions, should make us realize how language works under conditions of increasing globalization where more and more local rules are treated as universal ones. Here we have a space for investigating the local and international histories of literacy, the shifting conventions for writing, the pragmatic effectiveness of writing and so forth, and such investigations will doubtless result in important amendments to our rather naïve mentalist and transcendental conception of it.

(3) Grassroots writing also raises issues of voice, legitimacy and recognition. Recognizing hetero-graphic writing as meaningful, locally salient and valid writing could make us see more writing than previously assumed, and it may allow us to start addressing typologically different documents, often articulating subaltern African voices that otherwise will never make it to the public fora. Fabian (1990) already demonstrated the importance of attention to such subaltern documents, arguing that the *Vocabulaire d'Elisabethville* articulated a historical voice fundamentally different from those dominating historiography and public debate (cf. also Blommaert 2004). As soon as we expand our notions of "text" so as to include documents that do not – normatively – qualify as text, we will see more texts and gain access to visions of society, history and self that have hitherto escaped our attention. I consider this a worthwhile endeavor both from an academic perspective and from a humanist one.

(4) Finally, it can also teach us a thing or two about the validity of hetero-graphic writing in domains such as education – now plagued by seemingly insurmountable obstacles of normative literacy criteria (and failures to satisfy them). Huysmans and Muyllaert (2005) observed how teachers' and pupils' writing displayed common problems of realizing ortho-graphic norms. Teachers and pupils all used, to some degree, hetero-graphic writing systems. This, however, did not prevent rather adequate knowledge transfer from taking place, nor did it preclude or prejudge normative and standard-oriented discourses to circulate and to be taken seriously. Just like in the case of spoken language, where teachers and pupils displayed considerable (and productive) flexibility, an awareness that hetero-graphic writing may not be a sign of the failure of education could be salutary, especially in contexts where the ortho-graphic norm is all but practically unattainable.

Perhaps even more than spoken language, literacy is surrounded by "homogeneist", static perceptions of singularity and absence (or denial) of diversity. Few fields invoke such monolithic assumptions as that of literacy. At the same time, precisely the degree and structure of diversity in literacy practices and conventions in Africa can help us attain a better, more precise picture of the sociolinguistic complexity of Africa.

5. Conclusion

The three topics discussed in the previous section do not exhaust the range of potentially important topics in applied linguistics on Africa. They do represent, however, three crucial domains that deserve (and need) critical revisiting in light of new developments in theory and research. In that sense, they are older concerns that now invite revitalization.

There are new concerns as well. The issue of *globalization* has been mentioned cursorily in several places above, and it is to be expected that its influence will be felt in theory formation and empirical description in the near future. Globalization compels us to take movement, change and displacement as key elements of social processes; it also forces us to examine communities in relation to other ones, and such relations (we now realize) can be virtual and distant, yet intense and effective. Globalization has also reconfigured the African diaspora and its relations with Africa, leading to new forms of identity work (also expressed in language varieties, see Rampton 1995), and unfortunately also to new linguistic problems for Africans (Blommaert 2005a).

In the wake of globalization theory, we may start realizing that, in the real world, *diversity* and *inequality* often go hand in hand. As a prominent linguist once said about a small minority language from Cameroon: "It's harmless, unless you speak it". The question that will dominate reflections on language diversity in Africa in the future will be: What is its value? And how can it be made valuable, in a real sense, in a world in which cultural elements are commodified? Such questions, to be sure, are not easy to answer.

Notes

1. Gaston Van Bulck was one of the most prolific and prominent descriptive and comparative linguists of the Belgian Congo. He authored an official linguistic map of the Congo, as well as extensive studies on language names, ethnonyms and language classification.
2. Fabian (1986: 82) comments: "[…] without any empirical research to speak of on mutual intelligibility, multilingualism and spheres of wider communication, and sometimes against better knowledge, this classificatory diversity of African languages was declared a problem for the African and an obstacle to civilization."
3. It could be noted that the paradigm here described could be qualified as "linguistic-anthropological". A lot of what, in Europe, happens under the label of applied linguistics is comfortably embedded in linguistic anthropology in the US. Dell Hymes' work on education is a clear case in point, and his programmatic (1963) text on linguistic anthropology could as well be used as a program for contemporary applied linguistics.
4. We can call this "truncated multilingualism" (Blommaert, Collins, and Slembrouck 2005): a kind of multilingualism composed of specific genres, repertoires and styles of "language" operational in particular speech communities.

5. Freeland and Patrick (2004) also present evidence critical of the linguistic rights paradigm from various regions in the world. See also May (2001) for an excellent general discussion.
6. Another problem, discussion of which is beyond the scope of this chapter, is that linguistic rights advocates often depend heavily on the state as an actor in enforcing rights. In Africa as elsewhere, however, the state is weak and does not control important elements of state infrastructure. In addition, globalization processes may also have an eroding effect on state power. The state and its role in social processes can no longer be taken for granted, and they have become a topic of theoretical reflection (e.g. Geertz 2004).

References

Adegbija, Efurosibina
    1994   The context of language planning in Africa: An illustration with Nigeria. In: Martin Pütz (ed.), *Language Contact and Language Conflict*, 139–163. Amsterdam: John Benjamins.

Albert, Ethel
    1972   Culture patterning of speech behavior in Burundi. In: John Gumperz and Dell Hymes (eds.), *Directions in Sociolinguistics: The Ethnography of Communication*, 72–105. New York: Holt, Rinehart & Winston (1986 edition, London: Basil Blackwell).

Alexander, Neville
    1989   *Language Policy and National Unity in South Africa/Azania*. Cape Town: Buchu Books.

Arnaut, Karel, Jo Verhoeven and Jan Blommaert
    1998   *Historical, Socio-cultural and Phonetic Notes on Bondoukou Koulango (Côte d'Ivoire)*. Ghent: RECALL (RECALL nr. 2).

Apter, Andrew
    1982   National language planning in plural societies: The search for a framework. *Language Problems and Language Planning* 6(3): 219–240.

Batibo, Herman and Birgit Smieja (eds.)
    2000   *Botswana: The Future of the Minority Languages*. Frankfurt: Peter Lang.

Blommaert, Jan
    1996   Language planning as a discourse on language and society: The linguistic ideology of a scholarly tradition. *Language Problems and Language Planning* 20(3): 199–222.

Blommaert, Jan
    1999a   *State Ideology and Language in Tanzania*. Cologne: Rüdiger Köppe.

Blommaert, Jan
    1999b   The debate is open. In: Jan Blommaert (ed.), *Language Ideological Debates*, 1–38. Berlin: Mouton de Gruyter.

Blommaert, Jan
    1999c   The debate is closed. In: Jan Blommaert (ed.), *Language Ideological Debates*, 425–438. Berlin: Mouton de Gruyter.

Blommaert, Jan
 1999d Reconstructing the sociolinguistic image of Africa: Grassroots writing in Shaba (Congo). *Text* 19(2): 175–200.
Blommaert, Jan
 2001 The Asmara Declaration as a sociolinguistic problem: Reflections on scholarship and linguistic rights. *Journal of Sociolinguistics* 5(1): 131–142.
Blommaert, Jan
 2003 Orthopraxy, writing and identity: Shaping lives through borrowed genres in Congo. *Pragmatics* 13(1): 33–48.
Blommaert, Jan
 2004 Grassroots historiography and the problem of voice: Tshibumba's Histoire du Zaire. *Journal of Linguistic Anthropology* 14(1): 6–23.
Blommaert, Jan
 2005a *Discourse: A Critical Introduction*. Cambridge: Cambridge University Press.
Blommaert, Jan
 2005b From fieldnotes to grammar. Artefactual ideologies and the textual production of languages in Africa. *Vakgroep Afrikaanse Talen en Culturen – Research Report 6*. Ghent: Ghent University.
Blommaert, Jan, James Collins and Stef Slembrouck
 2005 Spaces of multilingualism. *Language and Communication* 25(3): 197–216.
Brenzinger, Matthias
 1992 Patterns of language shift in East Africa. In: Robert Herbert (ed.), *Language and Society in Africa: The Theory and Practice of Sociolinguistics*, 287–303. Johannesburg: University of the Witwatersrand Press.
Caplan, Pat
 1997 *African Voices, African Lives: Personal Narratives from a Swahili Village*. London: Routledge.
Cole, Desmond
 1971 The history of African linguistics to 1945. In: Thomas A. Sebeok (ed.), *Current Trends in Linguistics, Vol. 7: Linguistics in Sub-Saharan Africa*, 1–29. The Hague/Paris: Mouton.
Dakin, Julian, Brian Tiffen and Henry Widdowson
 1968 *Language in Education: The Problem in Commonwealth Africa and the Indo-Pakistan Sub-Continent*. London: Oxford University Press.
de Rooij, Vincent
 1996 *Cohesion through Contrast: Discourse Structure in Shaba Swahili/French Conversations*. Amsterdam: IFOTT.
Eastman, Carol
 1983 *Language Planning: An Introduction*. San Francisco: Chandler & Sharp.
Englund, Harri
 2002 Ethnography after globalism: Migration and emplacement in Malawi. *American Ethnologist* 29: 261–286.
Errington, Joseph
 2001 Colonial linguistics. *Annual Review of Anthropology* 30: 19–39.
Fabian, Johannes
 1983 Missions and the colonization of African languages: Developments in the former Belgian Congo. *Canadian Journal of African Studies* 17: 165–187.

Fabian, Johannes
   1986   *Language and Colonial Power: The Appropriation of Swahili in the Belgian Congo, 1880–1938*. Cambridge: Cambridge University Press.
Fabian, Johannes
   1990   *History from Below: The 'Vocabulaire d'Elisabethville' by André Yav: Text, Ttranslations and Interpretive Essay*. Amsterdam: John Benjamins.
Fardon, Richard and Graham Furniss
   1994   Introduction: Frontiers and boundaries, languages as political environment. In: Richard Fardon and Graham Furniss (eds.), *African Languages, Development and the State*, 1–32. London: Routledge.
Finlayson, Rosalie
   1995   Women's language of respect: isihlonipho sabafazi. In: Rajend Meshtrie (ed.), *Language and Social History: Studies in South African Sociolinguistics*, 140–153. Cape Town: David Philip.
Fishman, Joshua, Charles Ferguson and Jyotirinda Das Gupta (eds.)
   1968   *Language Problems of Developing Nations*. New York: John Wiley & Sons.
Freeland, Jane and Donna Patrick (eds.)
   2004   *Language Rights and Language Survival: Sociolinguistic and Sociocultural Perspectives*. Manchester: St Jerome.
Geertz, Clifford
   2004   What is a state if it is not a sovereign? Reflections on politics in complicated places. *Current Anthropology* 45(5): 577–593.
Guthrie, Malcolm
   1971   *Comparative Bantu, Vol. 2*. London: Gregg Press.
Gysels, Marjolein
   1992   French in urban Lubumbashi Swahili: Codeswitching, borrowing, or both? *Journal of Multilingual and Multicultural Development* 13(1/2): 41–55.
Heugh, Kathleen
   2003   *Language Policy and Democracy in South Africa: The Prospects of Equality within Rights-based Policy and Planning*. Stockholm: Centre for Research on Bilingualism, Stockholm University.
Hillewaert, Sarah
   2003   *Sheng: Een Sociolinguïstische Studie van een Urbane Jongerencode*. MA thesis, Ghent University.
Huysmans, Marieke and Nathalie Muyllaert
   2005   *The Terror of the Error: An Ethnographic Study of Multilingualism and Multiliteracy in Wesbank High*. Vakgroep Afrikaanse Talen en Culturen, Research Report 7. Ghent: Ghent University.
Hymes, Dell
   1963   A perspective for linguistic anthropology. *Voice of America Lectures, Anthropology Series 17*. Washington: Voice of America.
Hymes, Dell
   1968   Linguistic problems in defining the concept of 'tribe'. In: June Helm (ed.), *Essays on the Problem of Tribe*, 23–48. Seattle: American Ethnological Society & University of Washington Press.
Hymes, Dell
   1996   *Ethnography, Linguistics, Narrative Inequality: Toward an Understanding of Voice*. London: Taylor & Francis.

Irvine, Judy
    2001a   The family romance of colonial linguistics: Gender and family in nineteenth-century representations of African languages. In: Susan Gal and Kathryn Woolard (eds.), *Languages and Publics: The Making of Authority*, 30–45. Manchester: St Jerome.

Irvine, Judy
    2001b   Genres of conquest: From literature to science in colonial African linguistics. In: Hubert Knoblauch and Helga Kotthoff (eds.), *Verbal Art Across Cultures*, 63–89. Tübingen: Gunter Narr.

Kadeghe, Michael
    2000   *The Implications of Bilingual Education in Learning and Teaching: The Case of Tanzanian Secondary Schools*. PhD dissertation, University of Dar es Salaam.

Laitin, David
    1992   *Language Repertoires and State Construction in Africa*. Cambridge: Cambridge University Press.

Maryns, Katrijn and Jan Blommaert
    2001   Stylistic and thematic shifting as a narrative resource: Assessing asylum seekers' repertoires. *Multilingua* 20(1): 61–84.

May, Stephen
    2001   *Language and Minority Rights: Ethnicity, Nationalism and the Politics of Language*. London: Longman.

Mazrui, Alamin
    2004   *English in Africa After the Cold War*. Clevedon: Multilingual Matters.

Mazrui, Ali A.
    1975   *The Political Sociology of the English Language: An African Perspective*. The Hague: Mouton.

Mazrui, Ali A.
    1978   *Political Values and the Educated Class in Africa*. Berkeley: University of California Press.

Mazrui, Ali A. and Alamin Mazrui
    1998   *The Power of Babel: Language and Governance in the African Experience*. Chicago: University of Chicago Press.

McCormick, Kay
    2002   *Language in Cape Town's District Six*. Oxford: Oxford University Press.

Meeuwis, Michael
    1997   *Constructing Sociolinguistic Consensus: A Linguistic Ethnography of the Zairian Community in Antwerp, Belgium*. Duisburg: LICCA.

Meeuwis, Michael
    1999   Flemish nationalism in the Belgian Congo versus Zairian anti-imperialism: Continuity and discontinuity in language ideological debates. In: Jan Blommaert (ed.), *Language Ideological Debates*, 381–423. Berlin: Mouton de Gruyter.

Meeuwis, Michael and Jan Blommaert
    1998   A monolectal view of codeswitching: Layered codeswitching among Zairians in Belgium. In: Peter Auer (ed.), *Code-Switching in Conversation*, 76–100. London: Routledge.

Mekacha, Rugatiri
   1993   *The Sociolinguistic Impact of Swahili on Ethnic Community Languages in Tanzania: A Case Study of Ekinata*. Bayreuth: Bayreuth African Studies.
Mekacha, Rugatiri
   1994   Review article: Language death, conceptions and misconceptions. *Journal of Pragmatics* 21: 101–116.
Meshtrie, Rajend
   1991   *Language in Indenture: A Sociolinguistic History of Bhojpuri-Hindi in South Africa*. Johannesburg: Witwatersrand University Press.
Meshtrie, Rajend
   1992a   Fanagalo in colonial Natal. In: Robert K. Herbert (ed.), *Language and Society in Africa: The Theory and Practice of Sociolinguistics*, 305–324. Johannesburg: Witwatersrand University Press.
Meshtrie, Rajend
   1992b   *English in Language Shift: The History, Structure and Sociolinguistics of South African Indian English*. Cambridge: Cambridge University Press.
Msanjila, Yohani
   2004   The future of the Kisafwa language: A case study of Ituha village in Tanzania. *Journal of Asian and African Studies* 68: 161–171.
Neke, Stephen
   2003   *English in Tanzania: An Anatomy of Hegemony*. PhD diss., Ghent University.
Parkin, David
   1974   Language shift and ethnicity in Nairobi: The speech community of Kaloleni. In: Wilfred Whiteley (ed.), *Language in Kenya*, 167–187. Nairobi: Oxford University Press.
Parkin, David
   1989   Swahili Mijikenda: Facing both ways in Kenya. *Africa* 59(2): 161–175.
Phillipson, Robert
   1992   *Linguistic Imperialism*. Oxford: Oxford University Press.
Prinsloo, Mastin and Mignonne Breier (eds.)
   1996   *The Social Uses of Literacy: Theory and Practice in Contemporary South Africa*. Amsterdam: John Benjamins.
Rampton, Ben
   1995   *Crossing: Language and Ethnicity among Adolescents*. London: Longman.
Rampton, Ben
   1998   Speech Community. In: Jef Verschueren, Jan-Ola Östman, Jan Blommaert and Chris Bulcaen (eds.), *Handbook of Pragmatics 1998*, 1–30. Amsterdam: John Benjamins.
Roy-Campbell, Zaline and Martha Qorro
   1997   *Language Crisis in Tanzania: The Myth of English versus Education*. Dar es Salaam: Mkuki na Nyota.
Rubagumya, Casmir (ed.)
   1990   *Language in Education in Africa: A Tanzanian Perspective*. Clevedon: Multilingual Matters.
Samarin, William
   1982   Goals, roles and language skills in colonizing central equatorial Africa. *Anthropological Linguistics* 24(4): 410–422.

Samarin, William
  1984   The linguistic world of field colonialism. *Language in Society* 13: 435–453.
Samarin, William
  1989   *The Black Man's Burden: African Colonial Labor on the Congo and Ubangi Rivers, 1880–1900*. Boulder: Westview Press.
Schicho, Walter
  1980   *Kiswahili von Lubumbashi*. Vienna: Institut für Afrikanistik und Ägyptologie, Universität Wien.
Silverstein, Michael
  1977   Cultural prerequisites to grammatical analysis. In: Muriel Saville-Troike (ed.), *Linguistics and Anthropology (GURT 1977)*, 139–151. Washington, DC: Georgetown University Press.
Silverstein, Michael
  1996   Monoglot 'standard' in America: Standardization and metaphors of linguistic hegemony. In: Don Brenneis and Ronald Macaulay (eds.), *The Matrix of Language: Contemporary Linguistic Anthropology*, 284–306. Boulder: Westview Press.
Silverstein, Michael
  1998   Contemporary transformations of local linguistic communities. *Annual Review of Anthropology* 27: 401–426.
Silverstein, Michael
  2000   Whorfianism and the linguistic imagination of nationality. In: Paul Kroskrity (ed.), *Regimes of Language*, 85–138. Santa Fe: SAR Press.
Silverstein, Michael
  2003   Indexical order and the dialectics of social life. *Language & Communication* 23: 193–229.
Skutnabb-Kangas, Tove
  2000   *Linguistic Genocide in Education or Worldwide Diversity and Human Rights*. Mahwah: Laurence Erlbaum.
Spitulnik, Debra
  1998   The language of the city: Town Bemba as urban hybridity. *Journal of Linguistic Anthropology* 8(1): 30–59.
Street, Brian
  1995   *Social Literacies*. London: Longman.
Stroud, Christopher
  1999   Portuguese as ideology and politics in Mozambique: Semiotic (re)constructions of a postcolony. In: Jan Blommaert (ed.), *Language Ideological Debates*, 343–380. Berlin: Mouton de Gruyter.
Stroud, Christopher
  2001   African mother-tongue programmes and the politics of language: Linguistic citizenship versus linguistic human rights. *Journal of Multilingual and Multicultural Development* 22(4): 247–273.
Stroud, Christopher and Kathleen Heugh
  2004   Linguistic rights and linguistic citizenship. In: Jane Freeland and Donna Patrick (eds.), *Language Rights and Language Survival*, 191–218. Manchester: St Jerome.

Swigart, Leigh
    1992   Two codes or one? The insiders' view and the description of codeswitching in Dakar. *Journal of Multilingual and Multicultural Development* 13(1/2): 83–102.

Swigart, Leigh
    2000   The limits of legitimacy: Language ideology and shift in contemporary Senegal. *Journal of Linguistic Anthropology* 10: 90–130.

Van Bulck, Gaston
    1948   *Les Recherches Linguistiques au Congo Belge*. Brussels: Institut Royal Colonial Belge.

Van Bulck, Gaston
    1949   *Manuel de Linguistique Bantoue*. Brussels: Institut Royal Colonial Belge.

Vansina, Jan
    1990   *Paths in the Rainforest: Toward a History of Political Tradition in Equatorial Africa*. London: James Currey.

Vansina, Jan
    1997   New linguistic evidence and the Bantu expansion. *Journal of African History* 36: 173–195.

Verschueren, Jef
    1995   The pragmatic perspective. In: Jef Verschueren, Jan-Ola Östman and Jan Blommaert (eds.), *Handbook of Pragmatics: Manual*, 1–19. Amsterdam: John Benjamins.

Verschueren, Jef
    1998   *Understanding Pragmatics*. London: Edward Arnold.

Vigouroux, Cécile
    2005   There are no whites in Africa: Territoriality, language and identity among Francophone Africans in Cape Town. *Language and Communication* 25(3): 237–255.

Webb, Vic
    1994   Revalorization of the autochthonous languages of Africa. In: Martin Pütz (ed.), *Language Contact and Language Conflict*, 181–203. Amsterdam: John Benjamins.

Whitehead, John and L.F. Whitehead
    1928   *Manuel de Kingwana: Le Dialecte Occidental de Swahili*. Wayika (Lualaba, Congo Belge): Mission de Wayika.

Williams, Eddie
    2006   *Bridges and Barriers: Languages in African Education*. Manchester: St Jerome.

5. Linguistic diversity: Asia

Vanithamani Saravanan

1. Introduction

The term Asia is a generic construct which does not reflect the diversity and complexity found in Asian countries with regard to geography, history, sociology, ethnicity and, of course, language. The main thrust of this chapter is to provide an overview of bilingual language planning and language-in-education policies mainly in three countries: Singapore, Malaysia and Hong Kong. All three countries have had a British colonial history where English was established as the main language in the domains of administration, education, trade and industry. With independence, these countries sought to provide for linguistic diversity by assigning official and other functions to a number of local languages. Further brief sections on India and China will be included. Where possible, an attempt has been made to refer to languages other than English with reference to the respective language-in-education policies. Of course, this chapter does not claim to provide a comprehensive coverage of linguistic diversity in Asia.

While different developments took place as a result of the implementation of language policies and language planning decisions in the countries mentioned above, some common strands emerge. One of the main issues concerns the medium of instruction policy, which is directly linked to the goal of national unity and these countries' full integration into the global economy. Another major issue deals with the maintenance of linguistic diversity, which is related to the expanding roles and functions of English in Asia. A third issue concerns the effect of English on the status of the national languages, and on the languages spoken by minority communities (see Gopinathan et al. 1994, 1998; Omar 1982).

The spread of English resulting from language planning policies which favoured English, led to remarkable language shifts from home and/or community languages to English. The current trends in globalisation pose other challenges that necessitate a review of earlier language policies. One of the trends is the emergence of multiple identities in multilingual societies (Lo Bianco 2001). This trend is linked to globalisation and is seen not merely as a process requiring knowledge of English, but also as one requiring multilingual and multicultural competence. Some linguists argue that globalisation in the 21st century has increased cultural homogenisation and that this threatens the continued use of local languages in education, as well as in the domains of home and community (Tollefson and Tsui 2004).

I will present case studies of three countries: (1) Singapore, an island state located across a vast land mass, the hinterland of Malaysia; (2) Malaysia, a peninsula with rich natural resources; and (3) Hong Kong, which to some extent is comparable to Singapore in its desire to keep the advantages that accrue from an English-based education. As I am a Singaporean and have been working in the Singapore site, I shall provide more extensive discussion on Singapore.

For each country, Singapore, Malaysia and Hong Kong, a brief description of the linguistic situation, with reference to individual or societal bilingualism, language policies especially in relation to education, and bilingual policies in managing linguistic diversity will be provided. References are made to linguistic approaches used to address issues of norms, standards, language varieties, and indigenisation. The last section will look at future challenges in these countries, which include issues of globalisation.

National language planning has been a way in which nation states have sought to unify disparate communities after a legacy of "divide and rule" practised by colonial powers who sought to push their own agenda. Little attention was paid to the development of languages of other communities by the colonial government. In Singapore, after self-government in 1956, the government has sought to enhance the economic and symbolic power of language, to remove contestation among the various language communities and to move away from a colonial legacy of ethnic enclaves, and divisions between the English-educated and non-English educated groups. Linguistic policies were to be used for economic development and purposes of social cohesion. In Singapore, there was a pledge for the equal treatment of four official languages: English, Chinese, Malay, and Tamil. But English was decided upon as the dominant code, as the language of modernisation, technology and economic development. In Hong Kong before its handover to China in 1997, English had a status similar to that in Singapore, and this was also the case in Malaysia under the colonial British government. However, unlike Singapore, Malaysia decided upon Malay as its national language to unify the different linguistic and ethnic communities. Over time, Malaysian language policies have shifted from a greater emphasis on English to Bahasa Malaysia as the national language and medium of instruction. However, there has been a rethinking to promote English-in-education policies since 2003.

2. Singapore

In the 1960s and 1970s in Singapore, greater attention was placed on English language education to provide for an educated work force for the civil service, trade and industry. A review of education policies in the 1980s saw the emergence of the bilingual national system of education in the four official languages,

English, Chinese, Malay and Tamil, with English as the medium of instruction (Gopinathan et al. 1994, 1998). The Curriculum Development of Singapore, now renamed the Curriculum Planning and Development Division (CPDD) at the Ministry of Education, which is the agency responsible for establishing a national curriculum, decided to adopt a bilingual framework in which English was to be the main language of instruction, while the other languages (Chinese, Malay and Tamil, the so called mother tongues of the main communities in Singapore) were to be taught as classroom subjects, as well as through civic and moral education. Institutional support was given to all four languages in the form of teacher training, syllabus development, and production of curriculum materials. In terms of the norms and standards for all languages to be taught the decision was to adopt those of exoglossic but not indigenous varieties. In relation to English the trend was to look towards Britain and the British Council, and later also to the USA and Australia. These English language agencies also provided resources for teacher training and the formulation of teaching standards. The Cambridge Syndicate in Britain has been the main reference point for the 'O' level examinations system. In the case of the Chinese language, Mandarin as used in Beijing was the chosen norm and target, while for Tamil the exoglossic norm was the written Tamil from Tamil Nadu, the Tamil speaking state in India. For Malay, the norms and standards were determined by regional language academies set up in Malaysia, Indonesia and Brunei. All four language groups had frequent consultations with language academics from prestigious language agencies such as the Malay Language Council and universities around the world to refine these norms and standards.

As English has remained the main medium of instruction in all educational institutions, it was given special attention in the development of syllabi and curricula in the 1980s. The survey by Afendras and Kuo (1980) identifies macrolinguistic issues of language planning of that era and describes the required linguistic competencies of both English language and mother tongue languages. The establishment of the Regional English Language Centre (RELC) became an important milestone in terms of support for and development of English in Singapore and in the South East Asian region. It was set up through major financial support from the Singapore government and the USA, and nominal financial support from the South East Asian region. RELC organised and continues to organise annual seminars, lectures and workshops to discuss trends in applied linguistic approaches in relation to the teaching of English. These seminars are geared mainly towards the English language teaching profession and focus on the development of listening, speaking, reading, writing and grammar skills. RELC activities were also instrumental in the introduction and adoption of different approaches to the teaching of English in the South East Asian region. Malaysia and Brunei opted for English as a Second Language approach, Indonesia chose English as a Foreign Language approach, and Singapore selected the L1 approach for the better students and L2 approaches for students with below average proficiency in English.

These approaches were further influenced by developments in applied linguistics and psycholinguistics, as well as language pedagogy. The late 1970s and early 1980s also saw the emergence of systematic studies describing and examining the varieties of English that were used in Singapore. The focus was on Singapore English varieties as indigenised varieties (cf. Bickerton 1975), on the diglossic relationship between the identified varieties (e.g., Standard Singapore English [SSE] and Singapore Colloquial English [SCE]), on the functional roles of Singapore Colloquial English, and on the status of Singapore English as one of the new Englishes (e.g., Gupta 1998; Ho and Alsagoff 1998; Pakir 1998; Platt 1980). The 1990s saw studies on the curriculum: English literacy and the influence of examinations, and the relationship of culture scripts and language teaching pedagogy (Cheah 1998; Sripathy 1998). These studies have led to some discussions about the norms and standards which should apply to the teaching of English in Singapore. To date the official outcome of these discussions has been to continue with an exonormative orientation for English language standards, i.e. not to adopt SSE extensively as the norm. This period also saw a renewed discussion on bilingual policies including the place of heritage (community) languages in education, the demands of exonormative standards in the languages of education and the push to acquire economically (more) useful languages. For the first time sociolinguistic studies were conducted which looked at the uses and users of Chinese, Malay and Tamil in Singapore, at the division of domains between languages, and at the shift to English. Examples of such studies are Xu, Chew and Chen (1998) for Chinese, Abdullah and Ayyub (1998) for Malay, and Saravanan (1998) for Tamil. Furthermore, the norms and standards, which should be applied to the teaching of these languages in Singapore, were also reviewed and debated. During this period, there was a further consolidation of English as the main medium of instruction through its recognition as the language of wider communication. This was reinforced by many Multinational Companies setting up regional offices in Singapore. These developments also led to an expansion of English language teaching in institutes of technical education and in polytechnics, which had the main responsibility for the training of the work force for technology-based industries. For example, during this time there were massive investments in educational programmes for a knowledge economy (see Singapore Fact Sheet Series <http://www.mica.gov.sg>).

It is inevitable that language planning policies which favoured English would affect language maintenance and shift patterns across other speech communities. In the period from 1990 to 2000 biliteracy rates (English and one of the other languages) increased from 45% to 56%, and the use of English as home language went up from 19% to 23%, and that of Mandarin from 24% to

35 % (Singapore Department of Statistics 2000). The increase in the use of English as the language most frequently spoken at home was especially marked for Chinese households, i.e. it went up by 13 % (Singapore Department of Statistics 2000). These trends highlight the need for language planning in Singapore to strike a balance between international outlook and the construction of a Singaporean identity. Some people argue that a Singaporean identity and national solidarity (Rubdy 2001: 341) are being crafted through *Singlish*, a form of non-standard English prevalent in informal social interaction in Singapore society. Educators at the Ministry of Education, on the other hand, have dismissed this variety as a stigmatised, basilectal variety of English not suitable for formal endorsement.

The pedagogical thrust in the early 2000s was that of maintaining high standards of proficiency in English while ensuring that students become bilingual and biliterate. Singapore, through its institutional agencies, promotes Standard English in education and public life via the "Speak Good English movement" <http://www.goodenglish.org.sg/SGEM/>.

Which norms for English proficiency should be promoted in Singapore continues to be a central question. Davies et al. (2003), in a review of international language tests, raise the question of whose norms are to be promoted or used, and find a general reluctance amongst educators to endorse local and indigenised varieties of English. In fact, they concur with Lowenberg's (2002) analysis of newspaper stylesheets, government documents, and regional ESL textbooks in Malaysia, Singapore, Brunei and the Philippines, which found them all to be resolutely exonormative. Consequently, the use of *Singlish* which arose as a consequence of language contact is disparaged despite the fact that together with Singapore Colloquial English it is replacing Bazaar Malay as the new lingua franca for inter-ethnic communication.

In a similar fashion, indigenous varieties of all the other main languages have emerged as a result of language contact and in spite of educational measures to limit them. Public campaigns are used not only to keep variation in English in check but also variation in other languages. Besides the Speak Good English movement, there are also Speak Mandarin, Speak Malay and Speak Tamil campaigns.[1]

Most recently, questions of language in education are being addressed through a national review of the Singaporean education system. The Centre for Research in Pedagogy and Practice (CRPP) set up at the National Institute of Education in Singapore (Luke et al. 2004) has been given the task to undertake a multilevel analysis of the Singaporean education system, which includes a comprehensive analysis of student data and current pedagogical classroom practices not only in English (currently under review) but also in Chinese (Liu et al. 2004), in Malay (Abu Bakar and Abdul Rahim 2005), and in Tamil (Shegar and Abdul Rahim 2005).

2.1. Managing linguistic diversity in Singapore

Gopinathan et al. (2004) discuss problems of state-managed language planning where tensions arise from authoritative models of management of people and resources. There are tensions of race- and language-based policies that affect social and educational achievement. Nation states such as Singapore and Malaysia have set about addressing the problems of ethnic and linguistic diversity by developing nationalist policies which manage heterogeneity and which seek to replace colonial policies of alienation. The latter had produced a set of disparate, fragmented ex-colonial plural societies. While assimilation took place via unifying the different communities in state schools in Malaysia (Hassan 2004) and in Singapore (Gopinathan and Saravanan 2003; Gopinathan, Ho, and Saravanan 2004) there is the need to avoid seeing "immigrant" communities as static and uniform and to recognise the "striking heterogeneities" within ethnic groups in Asia. In Singapore government-based agencies have tried to manage ethnic and linguistic diversity through assigning ethnic identity through language, i.e. ethnic identity is equated with linguistic identity. For example, Chinese ethnic identity is equated with and expressed through Mandarin; Indians are linked to Tamil; Malays to Malay. It was believed that such policies would help avoid the excesses of chauvinism.

Wee (2003) argues that the political commitment in Singapore to cultural homogenisation is an inevitable result of a Fordist policy to industrialise Singapore in the 1960s. According to Wee, this is at variance with the lived reality of multiple identities and hybridised identities of multilingual communities. Tan (2004) observes that state managed multiethnicity to engender political unity while preserving cultural and linguistic diversity is done within the framework of a hegemonic state-led discourse of "controlled ethnicity".[2]

All the above provides strong evidence of the continued power of English in Singapore reinforced by the power of the economic agenda. In fact, PuruShotam (1997) argues that linguistic heterogeneity has been reduced to a formula encapsulated in the so-called CMIO approach, i.e. the Chinese, Malay, Indian, and other languages approach, which is a colonial legacy that had fragmented the population. Languages are ideological, they carry symbolic power, and mark group identity, and now economic capital. In the next section, I provide brief insights into the main language communities in Singapore.

2.2. The Chinese, Malay, and Tamil communities in Singapore

In the previous sections, I have described the frequent debates which take place on changes in the relationship between the four official languages caused by socio-economic developments, the shift to English, and the need to accommodate the Chinese-educated population. In the 1990s, periodic curriculum reviews took place renaming L1 mother tongue teaching and learning as Higher Chinese, Malay and Tamil, to make sure that the status of the mother tongues would not be undermined by the dominance of English. Currently all four language groups (English, Chinese, Malay and Tamil) are working towards new pedagogical concepts that include more interactive, co-operative learning, and learner-centred approaches.

2.2.1. The Chinese community

The recognition that the mother tongue languages are not equal to English in terms of economic opportunities, led to the creation of institutionalised arrangements where the best resources, teachers and facilities were given to Special Assisted Schools (SAP) to work towards the development of a Chinese cultural elite. The government has pledged its support for the development of a Chinese-speaking elite, a bicultural and bilingual group of speakers by 2010. This is to be achieved through the introduction of an intensive Chinese-oriented curriculum. The target is to develop a broader programme where students will learn about China's culture, history and modern developments in politics, economics and business (*The Straits Times*, 1 January 2003). In addition, more exchange trips to and language camps in China are being organised.

Reviewing the case for equality of languages, Gopinathan et al. (2004) argue that by virtue of the overwhelming majority of Chinese speakers, their languages/dialects have enormous symbolic, economic and cultural power. Globalisation and China's steady growth will further strengthen the power of the Chinese languages in Singapore.

2.2.2. The Malay community

Standardisation of spoken Malay has been an issue with Malay educators. This standardisation process in the Malay region was promoted by Anwar Ibrahim, the former Malaysian Deputy Prime Minister, and is now supported by the regional Malay Language Council (majilis bahasa) which was set up in 1988 as part of inter-governmental cooperation amongst ASEAN countries (Malaysia, Brunei and Indonesia, with Singapore having observer status). To lend prestige to its work Malay parliamentarians in Singapore, Sidek Sanif and Yatiman Yusoff, have been involved in promoting this standardisation across the teaching and learning curriculum. This is a normative process rather than a descriptive approach. Some Malay sociolinguists argue that the standardisation of Spoken Malay (*sebutan baku*) is inconsistent. While *sebutan baku* 'speak as you spell' is the norm endorsed in news broadcasts, in the classroom and formal functions, this standard variety is not used in the community in more informal communicative contexts including the home and family. For example, in a television forum discussion, Dr Noraidah, a Malay academic, was asked to re-record her comments as she was required to speak in *sebutan baku* (personal communication 2004).

It has been observed that the Malay-Muslim community is confident and have made great progress in the state schools. A recent trend is *Arabisation*. In Malay-Muslim regions such as Malaysia there is now a great demand for the teaching of Arabic language and culture in addition to Malay. Arabic now commands the status of a language with significant economic potential, opening up opportunities in the Middle East. Malay professionals are keen to acquire Arabic as they see this as an advantage, i.e. a third language in addition to English and Malay. This trend is seen at Malay Muslim kindergartens (e.g. *perdaus, madrasas* and mosque kindergartens) where Arabic classes have been added to Malay with children learning *jawi*, the script for the acquisition of Arabic.

More parents have opted for Arabic as the language of the school signalling a shift away from Malay, which they consider the language of the home. There is also a shift to English in more middle class Malay families. Most parents want a curriculum shift to English as they feel that Malay is a home and/or (ethnic) community language and therefore the classroom learning of Malay is redundant (Aidil Adan, personal communication 2005).

A new trend that might reduce the shift to English and add more speakers of Malay is the current proposal announced by the Ministry of Education to have more non-Malay students study Malay (*The Straits Times*, 20 February 2005). The language syllabus for Malay as a third language is to be made more accessible for non-Malays with a target of 10% to 15% of the non-Malay population in Singapore increasingly encouraging them to be fluent in either Malay or in Bahasa Indonesia. The review of curriculum for Malay teaching and learning is to have a focus on oral communication skills and reading. The stated aim is that by 2007 any student taking up Malay should develop better understanding, appreciation and respect for speakers of other languages, culture and heritage. This is an advantage especially for Chinese Singaporeans as more Chinese cross the causeway to Malaysia and Indonesia to set up regional centres to conduct business.

One issue in the Malay community concerns the interplay between ethnicity, religion, culture and identity, which surfaced when some Malay parents requested that their children be allowed to wear their (Muslim) head scarves (*tudung*) in school. Devan, a journalist, provides commentary on the conflict:

> [...] the juggling between Singapore's national and cultural identities without a self-conscious dominant identity, has led to a national identity which in turn is based on a nationalism of mediated identity through the cultural nationalisms of the various racial groups. This pull and push of separate cultural identities, multiple identities, and of transnational identities will continue. The state sometimes acknowledges these cultural identities, but sometimes it does not support them, as in the case of Muslim girls not being allowed to wear *tudung* [headscarf worn by Muslim women]. (*The Straits Times*, August 9, 2002)

2.2.3. The Tamil-speaking community

The Indian community is a smaller community than the Malay community with only a small subsection speaking Tamil, one of the four official languages of Singapore. This small community also displays linguistic diversity: Tamil, Hindi, Bengali, Gujerati, Punjabi and Urdu are used. These languages receive some recognition by the Ministry of Education in Singapore through their availability at community classes during the weekends and in some selected primary and secondary schools.

What confronts the Tamil-speaking community are issues concerning diglossia involving Tamil, a spoken variety which is used in the informal domains of family and friendship, and a formal, school-based, written variety used for teaching. Another issue is the rate of language shift to English resulting from a lack of economic uses of Tamil that has led to pragmatic choices in favour of English. The intention of the current Tamil curriculum review (Ministry of Education 2005a) is to recommend the move away from dominant school-based approaches where examinations direct pedagogy as these determine entry into top colleges and universities. (This is similar to the Chinese and Malay review committee reports by the Ministry of Education 2005b and 2005c.) Some curriculum writers are not ready to develop curriculum materials based on local indigenised experiences, or on cultural scripts relevant and meaningful to schools and learners beyond names, localities, and local festivals.

3. Malaysia

The following brief report on Malaysia is based on the work by a number of Malaysian academics.[3] Malaysia's linguistic diversity before independence in 1957 was similar to that found in Singapore, and to a lesser extent in Brunei, Sarawak, and Sabah, the regional states that made up Malaysia which was formed in 1963. Apart from Malay, the dominant language, the Chinese-educated community spoke Mandarin and other Chinese spoke Hokkien, Cantonese, Hakka, Hainanese, and Teochew. Amongst Indians, the languages included Tamil, Telugu, Malayalam, Bengali, Gujerati, Hindi, and Punjabi. Malaysia also had tribal communities living in the Malaysian jungles who spoke a range of indigenous languages, the main ones being Temiar, Senoi, and Jakun. In Sabah and Sarawak several indigenous languages, i.e. Kadazan, Bajau, Murut, Iban, Melanau, and Penan are spoken (see Hassan 2004).

Before independence Malaysia experienced the British policy of "divide and rule", similar to that of Singapore. Six years of limited Malay education had left the Malay population disenfranchised within their own country. Similarly the migrant population of Indians brought in as cheap labour for rubber and oil palm plantations were subjected to a deliberate policy of economic marginalisation as they too were given six years of elementary education in Tamil. The Chinese built their own Chinese schools and brought in teachers and curricula from China.

After independence in 1957 Malaysia chose Bahasa Malaysia as its national language in line with its aspirations to build a nation-state with a Malay majority of 49.78% (Omar 1982). The Chinese and Indians comprised 37.1% and 11% of the population respectively. Singapore chose English rather than Malay as its language of government and education when it became independent from Malaysia in 1965.

The status of Bahasa Malaysia was restored when it replaced English, which had been the "ruling" language in colonial times. This change in status for Bahasa Malaysia occurred when Malaysian politicians claimed that English provided advantages to an urban majority Chinese population and to a lesser extent to urban Indians. Malay, the language of the indigenous Malay population, and the main code of interethnic communication across the peninsula, and historically the language of administration in the Malay Archipelago had taken second place during the colonial rule. Bahasa Malaysia was installed as national language and medium of instruction as part of affirmative action to reduce the inequality of opportunity that was not available to the rural Malays during the colonial era of English language medium education. From 1969, Malay became the medium of education and replaced English in schools, and by 1983 at university level, extending over time to cover a total of 14 public universities.

Malaysia's language planning was managed from 1957 by the Language and Literacy Agency, *Dewan Bahasa dan Pustaka* (Hassan 2004). This agency was given the task to set norms for phonology, morphology, syntax and semantic forms and was to work on the codification and modernisation of Malay. The standardisation of Malay was agreed to in the regional states of Malaysia, Singapore and Indonesia. Standardisation processes continued into the 1980s with changes introduced into schools, on radio and television. The agency also undertook the task of translating into Malay science and mathematics texts for upper secondary and college level courses.

While linguistic agencies were set up to work on the standardisation of national languages, such as Bahasa Malaysia, Bahasa Indonesia, or Brunei Malay in the Malay speaking regions, it has to be noted that many of the other languages used in Malaysia for transactions in daily life did not come under the supervision of any linguistic agencies.

The successful implementation of the national language policy led to Chinese and Indians becoming bilingual and/or trilingual in their mother tongues, Malay and English. Malays, however, remained or became largely monolingual.

To what extent has Malaysia managed to overcome the tensions of race- and language-based policies that affect social and educational achievement? The national economic policy was developed to ensure that Malays would achieve 30% of the economic share of national wealth. English is seen as an important tool to access this share. Whilst English is available as a second language in state-based education, it is the medium of instruction only in private schools and colleges. The perceived link between English and economic wealth has led to the setting up of a large number of private educational institutions, schools, colleges and universities with overseas twinning programmes. For example, Australian universities such as Monash University offer degree programmes through the medium of English mainly to the Chinese and Indian sectors of the population. At the same time, a group of Chinese educators and business people started to establish Chinese-medium schools as Chinese was also seen as an important language for economic success.

3.1.   Bahasa Malaysia in education

By 1983, Bahasa Malaysia had become the dominant if not sole medium of instruction in schools. Affirmative action by government agencies led to reinforcing Bahasa Malaysia not only as the dominant language in schools but also in all public domains and increasingly in the private sector. In fact, status and corpus planning work undertaken by the language planning agency had successfully installed Malay as the dominant language of primary and secondary education, and of public administration, as well as for regional communication with other countries in South East Asia. One major sector, which remained problematic, was that of tertiary education. Hassan (2004) argues that this sector will remain dependent on English as it has yet to develop a sufficient stock of knowledge via Malay language. This is despite vigorous activity since the 1980s to translate science, mathematics and law texts from English into Malay for tertiary education. The reliance on English texts in tertiary education remains high. For example, in 1987 more than 7,000 courses were introduced in Malay at public universities across Malaysia, but students had access only to 380 texts in Malay (Hassan 2004).

3.2.   Tensions between Bahasa Malaysia and English in education

In 1993, ten years after conversion to the use of Bahasa Malaysia as medium of instruction, the Malaysian government made a controversial move to allow the use of English in science, engineering, and medical courses in universities and colleges. A partial reversal of the policy of monolingualism in Malay was the "back to English" movement begun in 1991 by Premier Mahathir and his then Deputy, Minister Anwar Ibrahim. Such a reversal was seen as necessary to redress poor results in the national English exams and to restore Malay-English bilingualism in order to prepare Malaysia better for a global economy, which requires English language competency. The poor results in English were linked to the policy of Malay-based education, which had significantly reduced the teaching of English in the state-based educational sector at large. For example, Kaur (1996) reports on the English language proficiency acquired by Malay, Chinese, Tamil, Iban, and Kadazan students learning English as a first, second, or third language after Bahasa Malaysia. She found that very different levels of proficiency were attained by students depending on the approach to English language teaching. Students who did not have access to English medium instruction often had a low command of English. Wong and James (2000) similarly observed underachievement in English and report that 44,000 graduates from heavily subsidised public universities are not ready for jobs in the private sector.

In 1996, the Education Act and the Private Higher Education Institution Act approved the use of English in post-secondary technical classes. Gill (2002) notes that English and Malay continue to have a tense relationship in the context of the national/local versus international/global concerns and demands. While some academics may acknowledge this tension, the Malay intelligentsia has always demanded that Malay be seen as the dominant code. This is not surprising given that its main stakeholders are the Malay intelligentsia and the Malay middle class. In 2002, a movement by Malay intellectuals, a powerful set of middle class voters reacted to the perceived threat to Bahasa Malaysia with the slogan *bahasa jiwa bangsa,* which means "Bahasa Malaysia is the soul of the people", on the perceived threat of altering the privileged status of Malay. The opposition from Malay intelligentsia led the government to drop the idea of a more extensive switch to English and instead in 2003 decided to implement the use of English for teaching science and mathematics in stages in Standard One, Form 1 and Form 6 (Byrnes 2003). That this tension will continue to exist is also evidenced in Lee (2003) whose study on localised identity constructions in urban city centres in mainland Malaysia reported that English-Malay undergraduates regarded Malays speaking English as elitist and snobbish, and that such speakers were suspected of not being good Muslims. The writer observes that the use of English in non-native ESL settings has brought about negative dividends and disenfranchisement, and cultural displacement when English is used in Malay society.

In the context of the reassessment of the role of English in Malaysia, there have also been studies of varieties of English used in Malaysia. Such studies describe the varieties of Malaysian English as a continuum. Vatikiotis (in Gill 2002: 143) states that "Malaysians of every race perform linguistic acrobatics in almost every conversation they hold. It is a mixed lexicon bred of a pluralism where English is a common arena of interaction". The basilectal variety of Malaysian English is similar to *Singlish,* carrying references to the contact languages of Malay, Chinese and Tamil. The mesolectal varieties of Malaysian English also resemble the mesolectal varieties of Singapore English, though there are some accent differences arising from extensive contact with Malay in Malaysia and Chinese in Singapore. Gill's study on "voices and choices" refers to concerns with choices of different varieties of Malaysian English. Gill concludes with a warning that a socioculturally contextualised mesolectal variety of Malaysian English does not have the status and power of Standard Malaysian English, and that to select the mesolectal variety as the preferred variety would mean that such "speakers will end up laughing at themselves with nowhere else to go" (Gill 2002: 85, 102). She notes that even if the voices of Malaysian speakers are steeped in Malaysian identity, they will remain without much status, power and choice. Gill's rejection of mesolectal varieties of Malaysian English shows the anxieties of academics who argue for a set of standards and norms in English which will ensure global acceptance and intelligibility. Indeed educators in Malaysia, like their colleagues in Singapore and Hong Kong, support the development of international varieties of English appropriate for nation states to take their place in a globalised world which is shifting from an information-based to a knowledge-based economy.

3.3.   Other languages in education

Few documents are readily available in English on the state of Chinese and Tamil schools in Malaysia. There are nearly 10,000 Chinese primary schools with 600,000 children, 45 private Chinese schools with 60,000 children; and in 2003, 60,000 Malays were enrolled in Chinese Medium Schools (Hassan 2004). Private Chinese-medium schools have reported good gains in Chinese and mathematics taught with L1 materials from China. This is similar to some state-run Tamil medium schools mainly for children of rubber and palm oil plantations workers. These schools use materials developed from Malaysia and materials from the state of Tamil Nadu in India. The success of Chinese schools is accepted and has attracted Malay and Indian parents to send their children to Chinese schools. But there are also some negative reports that refer to a monolingual Tamil system that will leave the Indian children dependent on work on the plantations for another generation. In terms of minority language education such as *Iban* and *Semai*, in other states of the Malaysian federation, Smith (2003) reports on the current state of minority language education in Sabah. The study throws positive light on efforts to revive and maintain the minority languages *Kadazandusun, Iranun, Iban,* and *Semai*. Through programmes at maintaining their unique cultural and linguistic heritage, *Iban* is now part of the national curriculum available at primary school level. The minority language *Kadazandusun* is included in the public school curriculum, which provides a syllabus, curriculum materials, and teacher training. Two other minority languages, *Semai* and *Iranun*, have found assistance from the Summer Institute of Linguistics staff who are involved in creating a lexical database and making dictionaries.

4.   Hong Kong

Hong Kong presents the third case study. Here I focus on the following questions: How have language-in-education policies in Hong Kong balanced the need for a local identity and the need to keep its competitive edge over its Asian partners? What tensions have occurred as a result of changes in curriculum and in the languages of instruction? Are some of the attempts and tensions of curriculum change due to the continued use of local/community languages, the shift to Cantonese for English-medium schools and the shift to *putonghua*?

In Hong Kong, the spoken code is Cantonese and since 1974, modern standard Chinese is the main code for writing. Whereas most former British colonies emphasised national identity and their own national language upon decolonisation this did not happen in Hong Kong as the colonial British government maintained English as the main working language and the language of education in schools. It was felt that for both political and pragmatic reasons Hong Kong needed to retain competitiveness in the international markets even after its return to China (Tsui 2004).

Cantonese is taken as symbolic of the preservation of the principle of "one country, two systems". It is seen as the symbol of freedom, democracy and independence, identity and autonomy. Tsui (2004) states that a 1993 survey found that 81.6% of the population spoke Cantonese as their mother tongue. Since 1997, there has been an increase in the use of *putonghua* for communication with China.

Prior to the mandatory mother tongue education policy introduced in 1998 by the Hong Kong Special Administrative Region (HKSAR) government, about 94% of students were studying in English-medium secondary schools and only 6% were studying in Chinese-medium schools. Since then, under the "one country, two systems" approach, there has been a shift away from English-medium to mother tongue (i.e. Cantonese and Mandarin/*putonghua*) medium education in both primary and secondary schools. Lao and Krashen (1999) report that in 1998, 307 secondary schools shifted to Cantonese/Mandarin, while university education remained in English. Despite opposition from parents, students and the business community against the move towards mother-tongue education, a 2002 survey conducted in 287 Chinese medium schools showed that 60% of the students showed improvement in their academic performance and took more initiative in asking questions, engaged in class discussions and were more self confident (Tsui 2004).

Despite these developments, Tsui (2004) notes that the colonial government had always used the demand for English by parents, and the need to maintain the high standard of English for the economic development of Hong Kong as reasons for not promoting Chinese language education. The intention was to produce an English-speaking Chinese elite. Hong Kong should not become just another region in China. One of the greatest advantages that Hong Kong has over other cities in China is the English proficiency of its people. English is seen as a commodity that everybody desires, the golden passport to a successful future for their children.

A change in sovereignty is often accompanied by a change in language policy. Enforcement of the policy to spread Chinese language education is seen as one of the failures of the HKSAR government (Tsui 2004). Joseph (2004) reports on the frequent public discourse in Hong Kong, commenting on the decline of English language standards of secondary and university students, and recommendations by western linguists that promote a move from colonial-plus-native-bilingualism to native-monolingualism. Joseph states that the Hong Kong model is much more like a continuum, where borders between languages become ever more nebulous as speakers move from colloquial Cantonese, standard spoken Cantonese, to formal spoken *putonghua*. As for written language, writers use written Chinese in simplified characters, written Cantonese and Hong Kong English.

This borderless continuum is pointed out by Joseph (2004) who describes a realignment of geographic, economic and cultural links between north and south China. "Mainland" China, in fact, needs Hong Kong as its English-speaking bridge to the rest of the world, for international business, tourism, and the service industries. Hong Kong is not seen as just another city in China and English is not seen as the language of colonisation but as the language of international commerce. Mother tongue education, on the other hand, is considered a sign of narrow nationalism.

In a comparative study of the outcomes of language planning policies in Singapore and Hong Kong, T'sou (2002) critically evaluates the tale of two cities. He argues that despite Singapore's pro-active, holistic policies resulting in spectacular gains for Mandarin at the expense of the "low" language, Hokkien, especially in the 5 to 14 age group, these policies have also produced semilinguals and "cultural eunuchs" who show dislocation and alienation. Instead of an English-based educational system, T'sou champions a Chinese-based competency as economic and cultural advantages accrue from China and argues against a shift to English and a movement towards cultivating Asian/Chinese values and culture via English. In Hong Kong, Mandarin (*putonghua*) will eventually displace Cantonese in high language domains while proficiency in English will decrease. He argues that reactive, piecemeal laissez-faire policy has led to more negative results in Hong Kong compared to Singapore, which has made gains in Mandarin replacing "low", spoken varieties of Hokkien, Teochew and Hakka. A more recent report by Lai and Bryam (2003) argues that a political takeover is often followed by a "linguistic unification", which will be a hegemonic political process of institutionalising a new symbolic order. Lai and Bryam argue that *putonghua* and Cantonese are in a diglossic relationship with the former gaining ground over Cantonese in official and ceremonial roles. This is reminiscent of Bourdieu (1991) who observes that indigenous people who acquire the new "dominated linguistic competencies" are rewarded under the new symbolic institution. This also adds complexities to the discourse of polemical mother tongue education under the "one country, two systems" framework practised in Hong Kong. English in Hong Kong was, is and will be considered valuable cultural capital of elite social groups as this gives them more economic, social and political advantages in a Hong Kong that strives to become a world city of Asia. Lai and Bryam (2003) point out that at the end of the day both national and local ruling elites value English. It will not come as a surprise that both groups adopt pragmatism and utilitarianism in repositioning English in the new society even when it is argued that Hong Kong is undergoing decolonisation.

Unlike Japanese in Korea and Taiwan, which lost its status when these countries regained their national languages, English retains its status as the official language of Hong Kong though it is ceasing to be the language of the ruling class in public administration, where it is replaced by Cantonese and Mandarin.

5. India

India, also a former British colony, has Hindi as its nationally spoken language as well as 18 state languages. English is a third language in most states with more than 11 million second language speakers of English, i.e. 1.1% of the population. Newspapers and magazines are published in over 90 languages; radio programmes are broadcast in over 70 languages whereas television programmes and movies are made in 13 languages. English is indigenised functionally, pragmatically and grammatically in India. India is a nation without a national language, where both Hindi and English are co-official languages (Annamalai 2004). Hasnain (2003: 10) observes that although a large number of major Indian languages are well established, with vernaculars used in the local economy, polity (government organisations) and media, language policies of the state both overtly and covertly favour English, with 3% of primary schools using it as a third language (Annamalai 2004), at the cost of use, promotion and development of indigenous languages; cf. <http://www.ethnologue.com/show_author.asp?auth=343>.

Unfortunately, there is limited access to research papers in English, which deal with the linguistic diversity in India and with applied linguistic approaches in the teaching of Indian languages. The Central Institute of Indian Languages or CIIL <http://www.ciil.org> works on empowering indigenous languages. Baldridge (2002) of CIIL describes the phenomenon of the "ambiance" of languages in the Indian context. No Indian has one single language; he or she speaks one language at home, one on the street, translating from one language to another, which is described as *kichiri* (dish with many food items available at the time of its preparation). It is a mixture of Hindi with the local language, the local dialect, other Indian languages and English thrown in.

Pondicherry is a typical case of a multilingual Indian state (see Ramamoorthy 2004), with four French-speaking districts (in the colonial era) whose linguistic diversity today includes French, Tamil, English, Malayalam and Telugu. Hindi is required at the work place in all of India. Hindi is closer to the spoken variety whereas Tamil has diglossic varieties. The typical traditional Tamil textbook "arimukat Tamil" (Introductory Tamil) has morals, songs and poems used to teach the written, literary variety of Tamil. Traditional language education in India does not make a distinction between different approaches, methods and curriculum materials and tends to rely heavily on grammar-translation and structural methods, where *tolkappium* (classical grammar) is taught, as well as classical literary texts, poetry and prose, extensive writing on morals, proverbs and wise sayings.

A case study of a primary school in New Delhi reports on children using Hindi when translating English (Vaish 2005). Vaish defends the approach as the pedagogy of the poor rather than poor pedagogy. Lukmani (2002; see also Davies et al. 2003) reports that in India Standard English is the target, though there is acceptance of non-standard varieties of Englishes, home-grown forms of English and of universities which set their own standards. Language forms are formal and archaic. While 50% of Indians aim for Standard (British) English, the other 50% accept Indian English. However, it should also be noted that perhaps only 12% of the population can recognise Standard English. This educational inequality is displayed by the prevalence of English as the prestigious medium in science colleges and as the sole medium of communication in professional schools.

The ideological argument that dominant languages like English kill indigenous languages and threaten linguistic diversity in India is questioned by Vaish (2005) who concludes that local cultures have a tenacity to uphold themselves. She asserts that India is fast globalising with English as a language of decolonisation. The growing interest in English has led to highly successful bilingual students who are most likely to have studied through English medium in well-funded private schools. The shift to English is currently on the rise as it is needed in new sectors of economy like outsourcing which includes call centres, the IT sector, record-keeping for hospitals and medical centres, account-keeping in banks, etc. India is far too complex for linguistic loyalty to shift towards English, and for English to become a lingua franca in India, though admittedly there are middle class groups which use English as a language of opportunity. Diasporic communities who live and work in international settings have switched to English as its dominant code in professional settings. Indian communities who do not have ready access to English language education would view it as a scarce cultural capital.

6. China

Finally, a short discussion on China is presented. China is the other "giant" in Asia and it is ready to take its place in the world community with entry into the world market. In 1958, *putonghua* (Mandarin) was decided upon as the standard language for the unification of China and the language of education in all educational institutions and the media. *Pinyin* as a Romanised alphabet was introduced to aid in acquisition of *putonghua*. Yu Ren and Hudson-Ross (1990) summarise the nature of Chinese language teaching and learning. By grade 6, Chinese students are required to learn nearly 3000 characters, which can form 50,000 phrases. Pinyin is usually learned in the following steps: a) alphabet letter learning, b) phonetic alphabet learning, c) syllable recognition, and d) using pinyin to learn characters. Traditional approaches include reading aloud, memorisation and repeated practice in brush calligraphy. Individualisation, small group work, and independent reading are rare, as traditionally teachers have lectured and students have listened. These approaches concur with Watkins (2000: 161) commenting on the role of memorisation in Chinese education: Chinese educators tend to see both creativity and understanding as slow processes requiring much effort, repetition, and attention rather than as relatively insightful processes. This is grounded in hundreds of years of Chinese philosophical thought. Similarly Jin and Cortazzi (2003) reported that Chinese students prefer teachers to have deep knowledge and answer questions. Based on Confucian principles, the teacher is considered a model of both knowledge and morality; learning is a moral duty and studying hard is a responsibility to the family. They argue that Chinese students, whether in Singapore, Hong Kong, China, or elsewhere share a Confucian cultural heritage, which makes them effective in transmitting reproductive knowledge, but creativity is stifled.

What of teaching approaches in Chinese in China? Yang Hu (2004) reports on his Chinese visit after being away for 17 years from China. The approaches to grade three lessons in Chinese were largely observed as whole class instruction, with reading aloud by students, correction of mispronunciations by the teacher, answer checking, and some attempts at chunking text with references to elements of story structure. The pedagogy was largely paraphrasing and explanations. There are constraints as a result of large class sizes, curriculum and assessment demands. Grade six students are required to master 3000 characters represented as ideographic characters, through a morphosyllabic written language with no alphabet (Jiang and Li 1985) which leads to memorisation and practice drills. Primary grade readers have additional support via Pinyin, a Romanised script, above the characters but this support is removed at upper grades. The Chinese national curriculum guide gives emphasis to basic skills, learning new vocabulary, and composition; in addition, examinations test words, idioms, grammar rules and usage, Old Chinese classics and modern Chinese literature as well as world literature in translation. Private schools mainly catering for middle class students in big cities have adopted more student participation and flexibility in the curriculum. The report points to little evidence of teacher training in applied linguistics, developmental psycholinguistics, sociolinguistics and pedagogical approaches that could make teaching and learning more interactive. These pedagogical approaches will only be available when China opens itself to more professional teacher training and to greater development of curriculum materials.

As a country that is opening up in response to globalisation, China's attempts at expanding EFL and ESL teaching using various applied linguistics approaches have received considerable interest in academic reports. Traditional learning styles in East Asian countries (e.g. China, Japan, Korea, and Vietnam) tend to show a distinctive pattern of learning styles (Liu and Littlewood 1997; Littlewood 1999; Anderson 1993).

Littlewood (1999: 71) reviews learning styles in East Asian countries and tests them as "hypotheses" and "predictions" either to be confirmed or disproved by various studies. The paper warns against setting up stereotypical notions of East Asian learners. Rao (2002: 5) summarises some of the reports on the teaching of EFL in Asia, where learning styles have been dominated by a teacher-centred, book-centred, grammar-translation method and an emphasis on rote memory reports. Korean and Japanese students do not feel comfortable with or tolerant of multiple correct answers to a question or exercise. They prefer an approach where teachers explain and analyse many of the more difficult grammar structures, rhetoric, and styles for students, who listen, take notes and answer questions. Chinese and Japanese students use strategies such as memorisation, planning, analysis, sequenced repetition, detailed outlines and lists, and structured review of passages to be learned. The serious mismatches between the learning styles of students and the teaching styles of Western approaches focussing on a more interactive style of teaching with group and pair work, communicative role-play, and student presentations are reported by Rao (2002).

Wu (2001) in "English language teaching in China, trends and challenges" reports that millions of Chinese EFL learners take regular English courses. There are 300 intensive English programmes across the country. Wu refers to a recent large-scale investigation in 1999, initiated by the Higher Education Division of the Ministry of Education. Its recommendations led to the introduction of English into the primary school curriculum in an increasing number of cities across China. Zhang's (2001) study reports that teachers generally lack linguistic and other aspects of meta-cognitive knowledge in L2 reading. The lack of sufficient linguistic (e.g. lexical resources, grammatical structures) and schema knowledge constrains the teachers from training the students in the effective use of strategies in real reading tasks.

What of the current trends in China? Jin and Cortazzi (2003) describe the current interest in ELT and in the English language per se. The announcement (*The Straits Times,* July 2001), that the 2008 Olympic Games will be held in Beijing created the predictable consequence of an enormous interest in the ELT enterprise in China. English is seen as progressive, linked to the open-door policy with China's entry into the world market. About 11 million students are enrolled in 1,000 universities in China where English is the compulsory foreign language for most students. In a city like Shanghai, even taxi companies have started to provide English classes for their drivers.[4]

7. Conclusion

In many settings, globalisation, with its increasing cultural homogenisation, threatens the continued use of local languages in education, as well as in other domains (Tollefson and Tsui 2004). The local versus global in language choices led Singapore to replace Chinese home languages by Mandarin, while government policies have supported four official languages (Mandarin, English, Malay and Tamil). However, for some Chinese Singaporeans, Mandarin is not their home language yet, the language shift to Mandarin cannot be achieved within two decades. In Hong Kong *putonghua* is the national language. As globalisation adds pressure, the switch from Cantonese to Mandarin might take place in some Hong Kong communities, at least in some of the formal domains.

With globalisation, Lai and Bryam (2003) predict that *putonghua* will assume political, regional and in fact global importance, Mandarin being a language of oligarchy in the Asian region and consequently diminishing the "hegemony" of English. Will Lai's prediction bring about a process where *putonghua* gains a hegemonic status not only over English, but over regional and community languages as well in some parts of Asia? The outcome would be one where not only state-supported bilingual and trilingual language policies come under threat but also become part of a process where the diversity of home and community languages is reduced by the hegemonic role of *putonghua,* in a setting such as Hong Kong. This shift to standard languages has taken place in Singapore.

Language-in-education policies are a site of contestation in Hong Kong. *Putonghua* and English will definitely be valuable linguistically, culturally and politically in Hong Kong. This might mean the loss of or a reduced status for Cantonese, with reduced roles and functions for both Cantonese and English in favour of *putonghua* while at the same time English will retain its value because of its link to globalisation and internationalisation.

The politics of bilingualism creates tensions between different groups in society. In Hong Kong, it is Cantonese, English and *putonghua*; in Malaysia, Malay and English; in Singapore, English and Mandarin as dominant codes with the official languages, Malay and Tamil playing reduced roles and functions in Singapore. At the same time, some would argue that English is losing its hegemonic status in India, Malaysia, Hong Kong and Singapore. One example of global trends is the Internet which was dominated by English as the language of the Net. However, languages such as Chinese have begun to develop an extensive array of Internet resources. As the nation state of Singapore responds to issues arising from globalisation's economic and cultural imperatives, the emergence of new economic centres such as China and India will require competencies in Chinese and in some of the Indian languages of wider communication in India. Singaporean Chinese are keenly mastering Mandarin to act as language brokers. As the Singapore-China economy grows, more regional investors, managers, corporate lawyers, bankers, and accountants are setting up business in China. But there is realisation that what is considered more critical is not just the learning of languages but developing an awareness of cross-cultural understanding where bi-literacies rather than mono-literacies are valued. To this end, an exchange programme has been set up to train a core elite of 200 bi-literates from China and Singapore to enable them to understand the psyche, society and culture of both communities. Countries in Asia have begun to acknowledge the place of linguistic diversity in establishing both business and cultural contacts.

Notes

1. http://mandarin.org.sg/smc/home.html – Speak Mandarin Campaign.
   http://app.sprinter.gov.sg/data/pr/20051115993.htm – Speak Mandarin Campaign, Speech by Mr Lee Hsien Loong, Prime Minister, 15 Nov 2005.
   http://app.sprinter.gov.sg/data/pr/20051120997.htm – Speech by Mr Tharman Shanmugaratnam, Minister for Education, at the 54th *thamizhar thirunaal* (Tamil festival), 20 November 2005.
   http://www.dbp.gov.my/lamandbp/main.php
   http://www.mendaki.org.sg/content.jsp?cont_cat_id=17&cont_id=10 – Malay Language Month.
   http://www.goodenglish.org.sg/SGEM/ – Speak Good English Campaign posted by National Library Board.
2. The policy of four official languages and the discourse of controlled ethnicity do not recognise other languages or give them space in the education system although community-supported classes are available in five other Indian languages, i.e. Hindi, Bengali, Punjabi, Gujerati and Urdu. Interestingly, a policy of allowing the study of a third language is granted to the top 10% students who can study French, German, or Japanese.
3. A collection of papers reproduced in Wong and James (2000); see also Asmah Haji Oman (1982, 1997), who has been one of the early academics writing on language planning issues in Malaysia; other writers include Gill (2002) and Hassan (2004).
4. Readers interested in English teaching in East Asia will find the volume by Ho and Wong (2004) useful and informative.

References

Abdullah, Kamsiah and Bibi Jan Mohd Ayyub
    1998   Malay language issues and trends. In: Gopinathan, Pakir, Kam and Saravanan (eds.), 179–190.

Abu Bakar, Mardiana and Ridzuan bin Abdul Rahim
    2005   *A Preliminary Report on the Teaching of Malay as Second Language in Singapore Schools* (Technical Report). Singapore: National Institute of Education, Centre for Research in Pedagogy and Practice.

Afrendras, Evangelos and E. C. Y. Kuo
    1980   *Language and Society in Singapore*. Singapore: Singapore University Press.

Anderson, Jan
    1993   Is a communicative approach practical for teaching English in China? Pros and cons. *System* 21: 471–480.

Annamalai, Elayaperumal
    2004   Medium of power: The question of English in education in India. In: Tollefson and Tsui (eds.), 175–192.

Baldridge, Jason
    2002   Reconciling linguistic diversity: The history and the future of language policy in India. *Language in India* 2(3) <http://www.languageinindia.com/may2002/baldridgelanguagepolicy.html>.

Bickerton, Derek
    1975   *The Dynamics of a Creole System*. Cambridge: Cambridge University Press.

Bourdieu, Pierre
    1991   *Language and Symbolic Power*. (Translated and edited by John B. Thompson). Cambridge: Polity Press.

Byrnes, Heidi
    2003   Perspectives. *The Modern Language Journal* 87(11): 277–296.

Cheah, Yin Mee
    1998   Acquiring English literacy in Singapore classrooms. In: Gopinathan, Pakir, Kam and Saravanan (eds.), 290–307.

Davies, Alan, Liz Hamp-Lyons and Charlotte Kemp
    2003   Whose norms? International proficiency tests in English. *World Englishes* 22(4): 571–584.

Gill, Saran Kaur
    2002   *International Communication: English Language Challenges for Malaysia*. Malaysia: Universiti Putra Malaysia Press, Selangor Darul Ehsan.

Gopinathan, S., Anne Pakir, Ho Wah Kam and Vanithamani Saravanan (eds.)
    1994   *Language, Society and Education in Singapore: Issues and Trends*. Singapore: Times Academic Press.

Gopinathan, S., Anne Pakir, Ho Wah Kam and Vanithamani Saravanan (eds.)
    1998   *Language, Society and Education in Singapore: Issues and Trends*. 2nd rev. ed. Singapore: Times Academic Press.

Gopinathan, S., Ho Wah Kam and Vanithamani Saravanan
    2004   Ethnicity management and language education policy: Towards a modified model of language education in Singapore schools. In: Lai Ah Eng (ed.),

    Beyond Rituals and Riots: Ethnic Pluralism and Social Cohesion in Singapore, 228–254. Singapore: Eastern Universities Press, Marshall Cavendish.
Gopinathan, S. and Vanithamani Saravanan
 2003 Education and identity issues in the internet age: The case of the Indians in Singapore. In: Michael W. Charney, Brenda S. Yeoh and Tong Chu Kiong (eds.), *Asian Migrants and Education: The Tensions of Education in Immigrant Societies and among Migrant Groups*, 39–52. London: Asia-Pacific Educational Research Association and Kluwer Academic Publishers.
Gupta, Anthea
 1998 A framework for the use of Singapore English. In: Gopinathan, Pakir, Kam and Saravanan (eds.), 119–132.
Hasnain, Intiaz
 2003 Science policy: Empowering indigenous languages vis-à-vis English. A review of HR Dua's science policy, education and language planning. *Language in India* 3/4 http://www.languageinindia.com/april2003/duabookreview.html
Hassan, Abdullah
 2004 One hundred years of language planning in Malaysia. Looking ahead to the future. *Language in India* 4(11). http://www.languageinindia.com/nov2004/abdulla1.html
Ho, Chee Lick and Lubna Alsagoff
 1998 Is Singlish grammatical? Two notions of grammaticality. In: Gopinathan, Pakir, Kam and Saravanan (eds.), 281–289.
Ho, Wah Kam and Ruth Y. L. Wong
 2003 *English Language Teaching in East Asia Today: Changing Policies and Practices*. Singapore: Times Media Private Limited. Eastern University Press.
Jiang, Shanye and Bo Li
 1985 A glimpse at reading instructions in China. *The Reading Teacher* 38: 762–766.
Jin, Lixian and Martin Cortazzi
 2003 English language teaching in China: A bridge to the future. In: Ho and Wong (eds.), 131–146.
Joseph, John E.
 2004 *Language and Identity: National, Ethnic, Religious*. New York: Palgrave.
Kaur, Kuldip
 1996 Evaluating children's writing. In: Adam Brown (ed.), *English in Southeast Asia 96, Proceedings of the First "English in Southeast Asia" Conference*. Singapore: National Institute of Education.
Lai, Pak-Sang and Michael Bryam
 2003 The politics of bilingualism: A reproduction analysis of the policy of mother tongue education in Hong Kong after 1997. *Bilingualism in Hong Kong* 33(3): 316–332.
Lao, Christy Ying and Stephen Krashen
 1999 *Implementation of Mother-Tongue Teaching in Hong Kong Secondary Schools: Some Recent Reports*. Washington: National Clearinghouse for Bilingual Education.

Lee, Su Kim
  2003 Multiple identities in a multicultural world: A Malaysian perspective. *Journal of Language Identity and Education* 2(3): 137–158.
Littlewood, William
  1999 Defining and developing autonomy in East Asian contexts. *Applied Linguistics* 20(1): 71–94.
Liu N. F. and William Littlewood
  1997 Why do many students appear reluctant to participate in classroom learning discourse? *System* 25(3): 371–384.
Liu, Yong Bing, Roman Kotov, Abdul Rahman and Goh Hock Huan
  2004 *Chinese Language Pedagogic Practice: A Preliminary Description of Singaporean Chinese Language Classroom* (Technical Report). Singapore: Singapore National Institute of Education, Centre for Research in Pedagogy and Practice.
Lo Bianco, Joseph
  2001 Policy literacy. *Language & Education* 15(2): 212–227.
Lowenberg, Peter H.
  2002 Assessing English proficiency in the expecting circle. *World Englishes* 21(3): 431–435.
Luke, Allan, Courtney Cazden, Angel Lin and Peter Freebody
  2004 *Singapore Pedagogy: Coding Scheme*. Singapore: National Institute of Education, Centre for Research in Pedagogy and Practice.
Lukmani, Yasmeen
  2002 *English in India: Assessment Issues*. Presentation at the Hong Kong Seminar on Norms Used in IELTS and TOEFL Tests.
Ministry of Education
  2005a Tamil Language Curriculum and Pedagogy Review Committee. Singapore: Ministry of Education (Unpublished manuscript).
Ministry of Education
  2005b Chinese Language Curriculum and Pedagogy Review Committee. Singapore: Ministry of Education (Unpublished manuscript).
Ministry of Education
  2005c Malay Language Curriculum and Pedagogy Review Committee. Singapore: Ministry of Education (Unpublished manuscript).
Omar, Asmah Haji
  1982 *Language and Society in Malaysia*. Kuala Lumpur: Dewan Bahasa dan Pustaka.
Pakir, Anne
  1998 English in Singapore: The codification of competing norms. In: Gopinathan, Pakir, Kam and Saravanan (eds.), 63–84.
Platt, John T.
  1980 Multilingualism, polyglossia and code selection in Singapore. In: Evangelos Afrendas and Eddie Kuo (eds.), *Language and Society in Singapore*, 63–83. Singapore: Singapore University Press.
PuruShotam, Nirmala Srirekam
  1997 *Negotiating Language, Constructing Race: Disciplining Difference in Singapore*. Berlin: Mouton de Gruyter.

Ramamoorthy, L.
   2004   Multilingualism and second language acquisition and learning in Pondicherry. *Language in India* 4(2). http://www.languageinindia.com/feb2004/multilingual.html

Rubdy, Rani
   2001   Creative destruction: Singapore's Speak Good English movement. *World Englishes* 20(3): 341–355.

Rao, Zhenhui
   2002   Bridging the gap between teaching and learning styles in East Asian contexts. *TESOL Journal* 11(2): 5–11.

Saravanan, Vanithamani
   1998   Language maintenance and language shift in the Tamil – English community. In: Gopinathan, Pakir, Kam and Saravanan (eds.), 155–178.

Shegar, Chitra and Ridzuan bin Abdul Rahim
   2005   *Tamil Language Instruction: A Preliminary Report on Main Findings of Classroom Pedagogical Practices* (Technical Report). Singapore: National Institute of Education, Centre for Research in Pedagogy and Practice.

Singapore Department of Statistics
   2000   *Singapore Census of Population 2000: Literacy and Language (Advance Data Release No. 3)*. Online documents at URL http://www.singstat.gov.sg/papers/c2000/adr-literacy.pdf, retrieved September 26, 2005.

Smith, Karla J.
   2003   Minority language education in Malaysia: Four ethnic communities' experiences. *International Journal of Bilingual Education and Bilingualism* 6(1): 52–65.

Sripathy, Maha
   1998   Language teaching pedagogies and cultural scripts: The Singapore Primary classroom. In Gopinathan, Pakir, Kam and Saravanan (eds.), 269–280.

T'sou, Benjamin K.
   2002   Some considerations for additive bilingualism: A tale of two cities (Singapore and Hong Kong), education & society in plurilingual contexts. In: Hugo Baetens Beardsmore, Gary Jones and Daniel So (eds.), *Education and Society in Plurilingual Contexts*, 163–198. Brussels: Brussels University Press.

Tan, Kevin
   2004   The legal and institutional framework and issues of multiculturalism in Singapore. In: Lai Ah Eng (ed.), *Beyond Rituals and Riots. Ethnic Pluralism and Social Cohesion in Singapore*, 98–113. Singapore: Eastern Universities Press.

The Straits Times
   2002   A balancing act. August 9.

The Straits Times
   2003   Top schools to merge to groom Chinese elite. January 1.

The Straits Times
   2003   Think out of the domestic box. July 11.

The Straits Times
   2005   More non-Malay students studying Malay – but still not enough. February 20.

Tollefson, James W. and Amy B. M. Tsui
    2004   Contexts of medium-of-instruction policy. In: Tollefson and Tsui (eds.), 283–293.

Tollefson, James W. and Amy B. M. Tsui (eds.)
    2004   Medium of Instruction Policies: Which Agenda? Whose Agenda? Hillsdale, NJ: Lawrence Erlbaum.

Tsui, Amy B. M.
    2004   Medium of instruction in Hong Kong: One country, two systems, whose language? In: Tollefson and Tsui (eds.), 97–113.

Vaish, Viniti
    2005   A peripherist view of English as a language of decolonization in post-colonial India. *Language Policy* 4(2): 187–206.

Watkins, David
    2000   Learning and teaching: A cross-cultural perspective. *School Leadership & Management* 20(2): 161–173.

Wee, C. J. Wan-Ling
    2003   *Culture, Empire, and the Question of Being Modern.* Lanham, MD: Lexington.

Wong, Ruth Y. L. and J. E. James
    2000   Malaysia. In: Ho Wah Kam and Ruth Y. L. Wong (eds.), *Language Policies and Language Education – The Impact in East Asian Countries in the Next Decade*, 209–271. Singapore: Times Academic Press.

Wu, Yi'an
    2001   TESOL in China: Current challenges. English language teaching in China: Trends and challenges. *TESOL Quarterly* 35(1): 191–194.

Xu, Daming, Cheng Hai Chew and Songcen Chen
    1998   Language use and language attitude in the Singapore Chinese community. In: Gopinathan, Pakir, Kam and Saravanan (eds.), 133–154.

Yang, Hu
    2004   The cultural significance of reading instruction in China. *The Reading Teacher* 57(7): 632–639.

Yu Ren, Dong and Sally Hudson-Ross
    1990   Literacy learning as a reflection of language and culture: Chinese elementary school education. *The Reading Teacher* 4(2): 110–123.

Zhang, Lawrence Jun
    2001   Awareness in reading: EFL students' metacognitive knowledge of reading strategies in an acquisition-poor environment. *Language Awareness* 10(4): 268–288.

6. Language contact, culture and ecology

Alwin Fill

1. Introduction

Suzette Haden Elgin (2000: 56–57) tells the story of a group of English health workers in India who tried to explain to the people along the river Ganges that their health problems stemmed from bathing, washing and performing religious rituals in the river: The river was "polluted" through disposal of waste and corpses. The people did not understand. The river was "holy" for them, and how could something holy be *polluted*? Only when the health workers began to say "The Ganges is *neglected* by the people and is *suffering*" was it possible to talk about the problem and suggest remedies.

Western Europeans express an "environmental problem" in Western European cultural and linguistic terms; the same problem is expressed very differently by the indigenous Indian people because of a totally different cultural perspective. However, conceptions of one culture *can* be expressed in the language of another. With the new way of naming the situation ("neglected river", "suffering river"), it became possible to talk about the problem without giving offence. Languages are flexible enough to go beyond the categories of the culture in which they are used. Their users are not "caught" in one view of the world: Awareness of cultural and linguistic difference and diversity makes it possible to solve problems of intercultural communication.

In this chapter language contact will be regarded from an "ecological" point of view. This means that the diversity of languages and cultures will be considered from the point of view of conflictual or peaceful contact, as illustrated in the above example. It also means that the focus will be not on the languages themselves, but on the *interaction* between them and between languages and their physical, social and psychological "environment".

Edward Sapir ([1912] 2001: 14) wrote about the environment of a language [*emphasis mine*]:

> It is the vocabulary of a language that most clearly reflects the physical and social environment of its speakers. The complete vocabulary of a language may indeed be looked upon as a complex *inventory of all the ideas, interests, and occupations* that take up the attention of the community, and were such a complete thesaurus of the language of a given tribe at our disposal, we might to a large extent infer the character of the physical environment and the characteristics and the *culture* of the people making use of it.

Apart from the vocabulary, the link between language and culture also manifests itself in certain forms of linguistic behaviour and practice which form part of the pragmatic description of a language, and which will be dealt with in Section 5.2. below.

"Why does *homo sapiens*, whose [...] biochemical fabric and genetic potential are, orthodox science assures us, essentially common [...] – why does this unified, though individually unique mammalian species not use *one* common language?" An ecological approach to language contact also involves asking this question, as posed by George Steiner in *After Babel* (Steiner [1975] 2001: 25). Indeed, the development of *language diversity* is still one of the great mysteries in anthropology. From the point of view of evolution, why was it useful for humans to develop so many languages? Is the present diminution and expected loss of linguistic diversity advantageous for the human species in so far as it may contribute to global peace? Or should everything be done to halt this process of unification since it will be counterproductive to peaceful coexistence?

The tasks for applied linguistics [henceforth AL] concerning these issues are manifold. First and foremost, linguists are called upon to find out more about the interrelation between language and culture with all its different facets; secondly, they should explore both the causes and the effects of linguistic diversity as well as the relation between bio-diversity and linguistic diversity. If diversity is fundamentally seen as something positive (as will be the case in this chapter), linguists are required to create an awareness of (and pride in) diversity and help maintain it by using modern means, such as the media including the internet. An important aim is to help countries and large federations (e.g. the European Union) develop viable policies towards establishing the right balance between maintaining cultural and linguistic diversity, on the one hand, and considering economic and political interests which favour unifying tendencies, on the other. The contribution AL can make ranges from strengthening identities and improving the teaching of small languages to assessing the apparent and real cost (and/or benefit) of language diversity for a country (and for individuals), including its effect on employment ("language economy"). Finally, the effect of diversity on conflict and peace is a topic worthy of closer analysis.

Peter Mühlhäusler, in his article "Babel Revisited" ([1994] 2001: 159), points out that the Biblical story of the Tower of Babel, "which portrays linguistic diversity as a divine punishment, has dominated Western thinking about languages for centuries" and has led to the belief that a multiplicity of languages and cultures is undesirable since it is inextricably linked to dissension and conflict. Against this he argues

> [...] that linguistic diversity should not be seen as a problem but as an essential resource and that there is an urgent need to reverse policies and practices that currently threaten thousands of small languages. Unless this is done, the chance to learn from the cumulative insights, successes and errors of a large proportion of the human species will be lost for ever.

A language collects and preserves the "insights, successes and errors" of a people over thousands of years. The nature of the link between language and culture and the magnitude of cultural loss through loss of linguistic diversity could not be better expressed.

2. Outline of the field

2.1. Language contact and language diversity

Language contact is only possible because of language diversity. Contact must be seen as a dynamic process which may lead to linguistic and cultural change. The different types of language contact, which can be divided into forms of *contact in society* and forms of *contact in the mind of the individual*, will be listed and discussed further in Sections 3 and 4.

The following outline concerning global linguistic (and cultural) diversity is intended to provide a basic overview of the facts which are the background to language contact. More detailed discussion of linguistic diversity may be found in several other contributions to this volume (on language contact, see also Goebl et al. 1996–1997; Myers-Scotton 2002).

The number of languages on this globe is given by various sources as ranging between 4000 and 7000. The *Ethnologue* (www.ethnologue.com/ [retrieved May 18, 2005]) lists 6,912 living languages ordered by continent and country. To these, hundreds of sign languages (Deaf Languages) commonly ignored in language catalogues should be added. There is almost unanimous agreement that the number of languages is declining, with the percentages given for languages in danger of extinction in the next 100 years ranging between 50% (Crystal 2000: 19) and 90% ("conceivably as many as 90% of the world's languages may become extinct, or doomed to extinction as native tongues by the end of the century", from www.terralingua.org/AboutTL.htm [retrieved May 18, 2005]).

The still existing languages are distributed very unevenly over the globe (see the map in Nettle and Romaine 2000: 33). The reasons for this are not to be found in any inherent qualities of the languages (and their cultures) themselves, but rather in certain geographical, topographical and climatic conditions. There is a remarkable correlation between linguistic and biological diversity in the different areas (cf. Nettle 1998: 354; Nettle and Romaine 2000: 41–49; Sutherland 2003: 276). Most researchers place the world's greatest linguistic diversity in Melanesia (cf. Laycock [1991] 2001: 167), with Papua New Guinea being the state with the greatest number of languages (figures given range from 700 to 850). Another area with a high density of languages is West and Central Africa with more than 1000 languages, 427 in Nigeria alone, 270 in Cameroon (a state with no more than 12 million inhabitants) and 210 in Zaire (figures from Nettle and Romaine 2000: 32; see also Blommaert, this vol.).

For Europe, the *Ethnologue* lists 140 languages, while other sources give more than 200 (see map in Nettle and Romaine 2000: 37), some of them, however, just major dialects. In contrast to European intuitions, Europe is the continent with the smallest number of languages – a situation which, however, may change in the next few decades because of imminent language loss in other continents and a high degree of language maintenance in Europe.

2.2. Language and culture

The link between language and culture is seen by various schools of thought in different, though overlapping ways. Gary B. Palmer (1996: 10–26) speaks of three traditions in Linguistic Anthropology. The first, associated with Francis Boas, Edward Sapir and Benjamin Lee Whorf, establishes a tight connection between language and world view and stresses the influence of language on thought (see also Salzmann 1993: 151–172). The second, called "Ethnosemantics", "is the study of the ways in which different cultures organize and categorize domains of knowledge, such as those of plants, animals and kin" (Palmer 1996: 19). The third, "The Ethnography of Speaking", which was pioneered by Dell Hymes in the 1960s and 1970s, sees language as a system of cultural behaviour; it focuses on the ability to use language pragmatically in everyday contexts and stresses the role of language as "mediating between persons and their situations" (Hymes 1971a: 65) rather than between sound and meaning.

In Sections 5.1. and 5.2. below, "Language and Culture" will be discussed in some detail from the point of view of the Sapir-Whorf-Hypothesis and using the approach of "The Ethnography of Speaking". It should be pointed out, however, that further approaches to language and culture are possible. Note, for instance, the many definitions of "culture" listed in Clyne (1994: 2–3) and the various cultural theories as shown in the excerpts given by Edgar and Sedgwick (2002).

2.3. Language and ecology

The term "ecology" was coined by the German biologist Ernst Haeckel around 1865 in order to stress the interactional aspect between organisms and their environment. In linguistics, the term was first used by Einar Haugen, an American linguist of Norwegian parentage, who, in 1970, gave a talk on "The Ecology of Language", in which he defined language ecology as "the study of interactions between any given language and its environment", this environment being first and foremost the society that uses the language (Haugen [1972] 2001: 57). However, Haugen also speaks of the psychological ecology of a language, i.e. "its interaction with other languages in the minds of bi- or multilingual speakers" (Haugen [1972] 2001: 57). The metaphor from ecology has also been used to represent language and world as a kind of "eco-system". In this system, the interaction between language and world is conceived of in the following way: Language is an activity which has an effect on the world, a process which in its turn has repercussions on language (cf. Trampe [1991] 2001: 232–233). Language, created by humans for the advantage of humans, contains the ideologies of growthism, classism and speciesism and "construes the world" accordingly for us. "When planning a language, applied linguists are not engaged in forging some passive, ideologically neutral instrument for carrying out a prearranged policy. They are creating an active force which will play its part in shaping people's consciousness and influencing the directions of social change" (Halliday [1990] 2001: 191).

Taking an ecological view on language thus means both recognising the interaction between language and its social as well as psychological environment and seeing language as a force in the language world system; this force may well carry some of the responsibility for environmental degradation, but may also be actively involved in changing attitudes and actions.

3. Central concepts: Language contact in society

Following Haugen's distinction between the sociological and the psychological environment of a language ([1972] 2001: 57), language contact can be categorised as follows:

(a) as contact between two or more languages in a society
(b) as contact between two or more languages in the mind of the speaker

Contact phenomena according to (b) are frequently but not necessarily the result of (a), and a neat separation is not possible in each case. The following sections will show language contact phenomena in society (3.1. to 3.6.) and in the mind of the speaker (4.1. to 4.4.) from an ecological perspective, i.e. with a focus on diversity and on the interaction between language and culture.

3.1. Societal bilingualism and multilingualism

Societal bilingualism exists in situations in which more than one language is used by the members of a given society (defined by geographical, political or social criteria). This may be due to immigration, conquest and colonisation, political changes (e.g. changes of state boundaries) or rarely, as in some cases of diglossia (Section 3.5.), to intervention by the government based on legislation.

Societal bilingualism due to immigration has been studied extensively in various communities in the United States (and other parts of America) and Australia (see Wiley and Rubino, both this vol.). Einar Haugen investigated the situation of the Norwegian language in various parts of the U.S. and provided research guides for investigating bilingualism in America. Other forms of societal bilingualism were studied by Joshua Fishman; see, for example, Fishman (1967) concerning diglossic situations and Fishman (2001a) concerning native American languages; Fishman (2001b) concerning Yiddish in New York City. Societal bilingualism is rarely stable but mostly subject to changes which lead to various types of "language shift" as described among others by William Mackey ([1980] 2001) with particular reference to Canada. Among the factors which influence language shift, Mackey mentions intermarriage and other types of interethnic contact, the locations of schools and libraries, distances travelled to work and, finally, state intervention (2001: 72–73).

Language shift can be reversed so that either the attrition of an immigrant language is stopped and reversed or the attrition and domain loss of an indigenous language is halted and the language maintained (see Fishman 2001c). It is concerning these processes that applied linguistics has an important function in describing and anticipating developments, documenting the different stages and perhaps even suggesting measures against language attrition. In contrast to immigration, conquest and colonisation in the past led to contact situations in which an indigenous language was being threatened by the language of the conquerors/colonisers. This threat, as a rule, was first imposed by the colonisers, who suppressed indigenous languages or harmed them by providing a lingua franca. In some areas, people were even punished for using their own language. Missionaries were eager to teach the Faith in their European language, though some religious communities (e.g. the Moravians) took care not to destroy indigenous languages and cultures. In recent decades, however, the threat to the languages has more frequently been economic, since command of the "more potent" language may offer better conditions of living, job opportunities requiring command of a "world language" or at least a lingua franca like Tok Pisin. In this situation, the task of AL is to document languages threatened with extinction, to suggest measures for maintaining at least a state of bilingualism and to create an awareness of the value of the threatened language with its tradition and culture.

For further aspects of this topic, the reader is referred to Moelleken and Weber (1997), which contains 53 articles on societal language contact with regard to different areas, levels of language and types of contact and conflict.

3.2. Language minority situations

A special case of societal bilingualism is the situation in which a "regional or minority language" is used "within a given territory of a state by nationals of that state who form a group numerically smaller than the rest of the state's population" (*European Charter for Regional or Minority Languages* 1992, Part I, Art. I a). It has been estimated that in Europe alone 50 million people speak minority languages, some of which, however, have majority status elsewhere (see Extra and Gorter, this vol.). After many centuries of oppression, in recent years the view has gained ground that language minorities are an asset for a state rather than a liability. One cause of this re-evaluation has been the indefatigable work of linguists who have warned against the irretrievable loss of linguistic and cultural diversity. This work has been done, *inter alia*, at specific research centres like the Brussels Research Centre on Multilingualism founded by Peter H. Nelde (e.g. Nelde and Rindler Schjerve 2001).

Minority languages have to be divided into those which are used by a majority in another state and those (sometimes called "lesser-used languages") which do not have majority status anywhere (although they may be distributed over more than one state). Examples of the first type are practically all majority languages in Europe (e.g. German in Belgium, Denmark, France, Italy, Romania, etc.). Instances of the second type in Europe are Catalan (Spain), Ladin (Italy), Breton (France), Basque (Spain, France) and several varieties of Sami (Finland, Norway, Sweden). Nearly all minority languages of the second type are in some state of endangerment. Numbers given for endangered minority languages vary to some extent (Nettle and Romaine 2000: 7–10); for Europe, the *UNESCO Red Book Report on Endangered Languages* (Salminen 1999) lists about 90 languages ranging from "almost extinct" to "possibly endangered", while Oksaar (2003: 154) puts the figure at about 100.

The task of AL concerning minority situations is to strengthen identities, to create an awareness of responsibility for linguistic and cultural maintenance, to provide the tools for translation and identification, and to investigate the real costs (and benefits) of maintenance. Concerning small indigenous languages, Nettle and Romaine (2000: ix–x) write:

> The last decades of the twentieth century have seen a resurgence of indigenous activism from the grassroots level all the way to international pressure groups. Ironically, the same forces of globalisation fostering cultural and linguistic homogenisation, and the spread of English in particular, are being marshalled as tools of resistance. Many native peoples and their organisations have websites in English on the internet capable of reaching millions of people all over the world. Delegates to the 1999 World Indigenous Peoples Conference [...] were encouraged to address the meeting in their native languages.

The work of applied linguists could support this development by providing the expertise for establishing internet presences and by supplying the materials needed for multilingual communication.

3.3. Borrowing

The phenomenon of borrowing (see Görlach, this vol.) is described in all accounts of the history of individual languages. Haugen has devoted a lengthy article to borrowing (Haugen 1972: 79–109); the different levels of borrowing were described and quantified by Weinreich (1953: 63–68). Based on this, Thomason (2001: 70–71) has set up a "borrowing scale" which shows the levels of language affected depending on degree of intensity of contact.

Borrowing is based on language contact in both a society and in the speaker's mind, but (as opposed to code-switching) affects language on the level of *langue,* i.e. an element borrowed from another language becomes part of the language system. Borrowing is chiefly associated with lexical and phraseological units, although it also occurs on other levels of language.

Borrowing on the one hand enriches a language, on the other hand may lead to resentment on the part of traditional speakers and particularly of purists who may express fears about the "purity" of their native language. The problems arising from this are particularly evident in the controversies about anglicisms in such languages as French and German, where the question of "enrichment" vs. "intrusion" is being debated with particular intensity. Word borrowing is frequently linked with cultural influence, and resistance from purists is usually directed against both impacts.

The task of AL in these controversies has been described among others by Janich (2004: 499–500), who distinguishes between (1) mere observation and description, (2) critique and reflection with particular reference to the functionality of loans, and (3) active planning by coining neologisms from indigenous material and legislation against the use of foreign words. While methods (1) and (2) are dominant for instance in Germany, France to a certain extent embraces method (3), which however is unpopular with parts of the population (Janich 2004: 500).

It has long been recognised that linguistic borrowing is also a cultural phenomenon in basically the following way: Borrowing of words occurs in semantic (and ontological) areas where the "lender culture" is dominant and has created cultural facts not present in the "borrower culture". This is the case for instance with certain sports which developed in England (e.g. football), with fashion (France), food (Italy), philosophy and philology (Germany), computer and internet (U.S.A.): Words are borrowed simply to name the things received from the other culture. A famous historical example of this is the situation in England after 1066, when elements of the French culture were introduced together with the French words: Thus the separation of Germanic animal names (e.g. *calf, pig, ox*) from the Romance designations for meat (*veal, pork, beef*), as described in chapter 1 of Sir Walter Scott's novel *Ivanhoe* (n.d.: 27–28) is due to the superiority of the French culture in this area.

3.4. Pidginisation, creolisation and other forms of language mixing

A frequent consequence of language contact is the mixing of two languages as shown in the processes of pidginisation and creolisation. Pidgin and creole languages are also known as *contact languages*. The difference between a pidgin and a creole is traditionally explained as that between an auxiliary language used temporarily as lingua franca for trading purposes and a mother tongue based on a pidgin variety (see Migge and Léglise, this vol.).

For some scholars, the modern European Romance languages owe their existence to a process similar to pidginisation, i.e. language contact between Vulgar Latin as the lexifier language and various Celtic languages as the indigenous varieties. Similarly, the varieties of English spoken on the British Isles (Scottish English, Irish English) are the result of language contact with the Celtic substratum. Mufwene (2001: 106–125), in this context, speaks ironically of "the legitimate and illegitimate offspring of English" – *legitimate* referring to the so-called "native" Englishes, *illegitimate* to the "New Englishes", i.e. "those varieties which have resulted from the English colonial expansion" (Mufwene 2001: 106).

Pidgins can also be "repositories of indigenous cultures" (Mühlhäusler 1996a: 99). Their creativity as products of linguistic and cultural contact was already seen by Hugo Schuchardt, who became interested in pidgins and creoles around 1880 (Gilbert, in Schuchardt 1980: 4). Schuchardt's examples (1980: 18–19) particularly show the extraordinary creativity of pidgins with regard to vocabulary (e.g. "white man cocoa-nut belong him no grass" for "bald-headed white man").

Bickerton (1981: 300) speaks of "a dozen ways in which [creoles] are more lucid, more elegant, more logical, and less easy to lie in than English or other European languages". For further discussion see also the articles in Hymes (1971b), Mühlhäusler (1996a: 74–103), Riehl (2004: 99–103) and Thomason (2001: 157–195, with a section "further reading").

A phenomenon similar to pidginisation can be observed in the development of "foreigner talk", a spontaneously arising simplified code involving language mixing. The phenomenon has been investigated in the context of immigrant workers in Germany (*Gastarbeiterdeutsch* 'guest workers' German') and Australia and is discussed by Riehl (2004: 105–112) with examples taken from Klein and Dittmar (1979; see also Clyne 1991, 2003; and Thomason 2001: 196–221 on "other mixed languages").

The task of AL in pidgin and creole studies is to document the languages, investigate by what percentage of a country's population they are spoken and find out in what domains they are chiefly used. The data obtained can then be used by language planners to fix the status of each language and to take measures towards its maintenance or further expansion (in education, in the media, on the internet, etc.). The exact processes of simplification, mixing and expansion which go on in the speakers' minds in the creation of pidgins and creoles also need to be studied in more detail.

3.5. Diglossia

Charles Ferguson's term of 1959 is commonly used for a situation in which a (socially) high (H) and a low (L) variety of a language exist side by side. The two varieties differ in prestige, function, ways of acquisition, standardisation and other factors; in spite of obvious (social and psychological) contact, the diglossic situation may be retained over centuries. Ferguson's list of countries with diglossia (Switzerland, Egypt, Haiti, Greece) was later extended by Haugen (1966 and elsewhere about Norway), Fishman (1967) and others so as to include countries where unrelated languages exist side by side as H and L codes. Riehl (2004: 19) describes situations with three (triglossia) and more (polyglossia) languages, in which H varieties or L varieties may compete with each other in the different domains.

One language frequently discussed in connection with diglossia is Arabic, a language already mentioned by Ferguson. In recent work on Arabic diglossia, the notion is however criticised as not doing justice to the dimensions of linguistic variability and as coming from a different system of linguistic authority (see the articles in Rouchdy 2002).

3.6. Language endangerment (attrition, death) and maintenance

Contact with a (politically, socially, economically) dominant culture may lead to language endangerment – a phenomenon extensively described and much deplored by linguists in recent years. The different degrees of endangerment have been described among others by Salminen (1999), the stages of language attrition and death by Dressler (1988), Crystal (2000), Winford (2003: 258) and the authors in Brenzinger (1992). Nettle and Romaine (2000: 90–97) distinguish between three types of language loss, which can be due to (1) population loss, (2) forced shift and (3) voluntary shift. Salminen (1999) establishes six categories (extinct, nearly extinct, seriously endangered, endangered, potentially endangered and not endangered). 26 languages in Europe are seriously endangered, 38 potentially endangered. Most authors agree that language death begins with language attrition, which is "a gradual process in which a language recedes as it loses speakers, domains, and ultimately structure" (Thomason 2001: 227).

While until a few years ago public and scholarly interest in the endangerment of languages was still minimal, the topic has recently become one of central importance – not least because of the efforts of applied linguists. Organisations which try to document and save threatened languages have mushroomed (the website of the "Foundation for Endangered Languages" <www.ogmios.org/links.htm>, retrieved May 18, 2005, lists dozens of them). It can be said that awareness of the danger has grown dramatically, while the disappearance of languages has not yet been stopped.

An important task of AL is to make continued efforts to raise awareness of the threat to languages and cultures, to document (describe and record) endangered languages and to create respect for the necessity of difference: "Difference itself is not the problem, but rather lack of respect for difference, its meanings, and its values" (Nettle and Romaine 2000: 23). Many countries with endangered languages have in recent years established language maintenance programmes intended to counter the threat to diversity. In some cases (Ainu in Japan), the creating of these programmes may be too late; in others, it may have come just in time (an overview concerning 14 countries in the Pacific Basin is given in Kaplan and Baldauf 2003). Efforts towards language maintenance involve initiatives towards teaching and towards media presence, but also towards the creation of an agreed on standard, as reported by Denison and Tragut (1990: 153) concerning the five separate literary dialects of Swiss Romansh. On the other hand, if an artificial standard is created, but not accepted, this may be harmful to the small dialects and to the cause of diversity in general (see also Romaine, this vol.).

4. Central concepts: Language contact in the mind of the speaker

Language contact in the mind of the speaker is above all the result of the different forms of bilingualism and multilingualism (henceforth "bilingualism"), which have been described in detail by psycholinguists. Individual bilingualism can be brought about naturally or through guided language learning and teaching. It is accompanied by such interactive phenomena as code-switching and interference and is made use of in translation and interpreting.

4.1. Individual bilingualism and multilingualism

A traditional distinction of types of bilingualism is that between co-ordinate (two concepts, two codes) and compound (one concept, two codes) bilingualism (Weinreich 1953: 9–10). Co-ordinate bilingualism would include possession of two cultures, while compound bilingualism would not. This distinction, however, is merely theoretical; in practice the two types of bilingualism tend to overlap.

The question of the acquisition of bilingualism and the different linguistic levels on which it obtains has long been a much discussed issue in language acquisition research (e.g. Grosjean 1982; Appel and Muysken 1987; Hamers and

Blanc 2000; Oksaar 1980, 2003). Since individual bilingualism is dealt with in another volume of this series of Handbooks of Applied Linguistics, its different types, causes and effects will not be discussed in more detail here. Also, the topics of second (and third) language learning and teaching, and the different types of interference are treated in detail in other volumes of the Handbooks.

The ecological aspect of *interaction* is most strongly in evidence in the phenomena of code-switching, interference and translation (with interpreting and film synchronisation); therefore, these forms of language interaction in the mind will be dealt with briefly in the following sections.

4.2. Code-switching

While borrowing is a phenomenon affecting the level of *langue*, code-switching (i.e. individual *ad hoc* borrowing) is a form of language mixing which occurs spontaneously in the speech of bilinguals. What happens is that a speaker switches temporarily to another language and then back to the original one, the interaction between the two languages occurring both in the speaker's and in the hearer's mind. Code-switching may involve whole sentences or clauses or may be restricted to words. It is subject to certain constraints (Poplack and Meechan 1998; Romaine 1995: 115–120; Winford 2003: 126–137; see also Myers-Scotton 2002, and Clyne 2003); for instance, at certain points in the sentence (end of a sentence or clause) it is more likely to occur than at others (middle of a sentence).

More interesting in an applied context than the constraints are the causes of code-switching, which can be functional (i.e. mostly intentional) and non-functional (incidental) (cf. Riehl 2004: 23). While approaching the functional side of code-switching raises the question "What do bilingual speakers gain by conducting a conversation in two languages (i.e. through codeswitching)?" (Myers-Scotton 1995: 3), non-functional approaches stress the accidental element in this type of *ad hoc* language change.

Functional code-switching may occur for reasons of reference, topic and domain (a speaker may find it easier to switch to another language when referring to a certain topic), to make possible the insertion of meta-linguistic, phatic or poetic elements or to emphasise an element by repeating it in the other language. Non-functional code-switching occurs when the speaker is at a loss for a word in one language and quickly shifts to another, or when a "trigger-word" (e.g. a proper name or a loan-word) makes continuation in the other language easier.

Code-switching may also occur between different varieties of one language, e.g. the standard variety and a regional dialect: A dialect speaker may emphasise a word by repeating it in the standard version, or may use standard elements for prestige purposes.

As indicated, aspects of AL concern the phenomenon particularly with regard to its causes, where more studies using informant questioning are needed. Code-switching does not present a problem which needs to be solved, but is rather a phenomenon whose investigation may provide further insights into such areas of neuroscience as language storage in the brain, the interrelation of two (or more) languages in the brain, and word memory.

4.3. Interference

Interference is a key concept in contrastive linguistics, which is seen as the result of "negative transfer" in language contact. Its most frequent manifestation is the substitution of target language features by features of the native language. This process may occur on all the different levels of language and has been described by a number of authors (e.g. Weinreich 1953: 7–70 and Hellinger 1977: 10–17). However, investigations concerning the pragmatic level and particularly the level of culture are still rare. How forms of greeting, thanking, making compliments, taking turns etc. used habitually in the target language are substituted by forms of the native language is also a type of cultural interference which should be investigated more thoroughly. Gass and Selinker (2001: 243) and Oksaar (2003) give examples of errors made on this pragma-cultural level.

The ecological aspect of give-and-take comes into play when interference operates in both directions and when elements of the target language have an influence on the native language ("retroactive interference"). This phenomenon, too, needs to be further investigated on the different levels of language.

4.4. Translation, interpreting and film synchronisation

Language interaction in the individual is made use of in translation and in simultaneous or consecutive interpreting. Since machine translation (using computer programmes) has not yet attained the level at which complex (e.g. literary) texts can be rendered adequately in another language, less ambitious programmes have been developed, e.g. "computer assisted translation" (CAT), which aims only at raw translation, "content scanning", which filters the gist from a text, and "translation memory systems", which make repeated translations of similar passages unnecessary. Thus it is still the contact in the human mind which is involved in most cases. Linguistics has been applied to translation in the field of text typology (e.g. the distinction between form-oriented, content-oriented, appellative and audio-medial texts made by Reiss 1971: 31–53) and pre-editing and post-editing of texts for machine translation (Göpferich 2004: 459).

Applied aspects involve further work in contrastive linguistics aimed at providing more accurate findings on connotations, collocations and phraseological units (idioms, proverbs, routine formulae) in the different languages (contrastive lexicography and phraseology). It would also be desirable to have more data on the different effects of a (e.g. literary or political) text after translation into different languages, with particular reference to degrees of equivalence on the pragmatic level.

Another area of application is the translation of culture-specific elements (e.g., concerning political, cultural, historical and pastime allusions, the school system, forms of behaviour, etc.). This area has become of particular relevance in translation involving film and television. To give an example:

> In a British/American film (*A Fish Called Wanda*, 1988) a character says:
> "He's so daft he thinks the Gettysburg Address is where Lincoln lived."

The translation of this joke into, say, German (i.e. transference to the German culture) involves serious problems connected with (lack of) knowledge of American history on the part of German viewers.

The different types of language transfer of films (sub-titling, synchronisation/dubbing, voice over) offer a wide area of application for linguists to help refine processes and find more elegant solutions to problems and see where the limits of acceptability lie (Herbst 1994: 276–298).

5. Central concepts: Language, culture and ecology

In Section 2.2., three approaches to language and culture are distinguished. In what follows, two of these, the Boas/Sapir/Whorf approach and the Ethnography of Speaking will be dealt with from an ecological point of view, i.e. with a focus on the constant mutual interrelation between language and culture, and between different cultures.

5.1. Language and world-view

The view that every language incorporates a "view of the world" is held by most people in a somewhat vague way. The German philosopher and philologist Wilhelm von Humboldt (1767–1835) is frequently named as the first scholar to have expressed the idea that language determines thought and thus creates the speaker's world-view, while the Austrian philosopher Ludwig Wittgenstein (1889–1951) is quoted with his "the limits of my language mean the limits of my world" (from *Tractatus Logico-Philosophicus*, Section 5.6).

The idea of the dependence of one's view of reality on one's native language is most closely linked with the American linguists Francis Boas (1858–1942), Edward Sapir (1884–1939) and Benjamin Lee Whorf (1897–1941); related to this are the constructionist ideas of Michael Halliday, who says that "language does not correspond; it construes" (2001: 185). Cognitive linguists like George Lakoff (Lakoff and Johnson 1980) regard our thinking as highly influenced by the metaphorical system of language.

Most researchers today embrace either a mildly Whorfian or a mildly constructionist idea of the workings of language concerning culture. The construction of culture through language also encompasses the way the environment and the "natural resources" are conceived of (Halliday 2001: 191–192), the system of social classes (Halliday 2001: 197) and the types of gender representation through language (Hellinger and Bußmann 2001: 6–11).

Three positions concerning the active role of language in a culture are to be distinguished (cf. Campbell 1997):

Linguistic Determinism: Language determines the way in which we view the world and think about all entities (strong claim: we cannot think beyond our language; weak claim: our thinking is merely influenced by our language).

Linguistic Relativity: Each language encodes reality differently; each language imposes a structure on reality (e.g. on the colour spectrum, which is divided up differently by the different languages); by learning more than one language, a speaker may have more than one categorisation of the world's phenomena at his/her disposal.

Linguistic Constructivism: Our language construes the world for us, through its vocabulary and metaphors, its collocations, its contrasts, definiteness and indefiniteness, its pronouns, etc., which "create" our picture of the world in us. Halliday (2001: 194–195) gives a number of examples of this for English, which concern the way humans linguistically construe their environment: Words for natural resources (*oil, coal, water, energy*) are used without the article, which suggests limitlessness; a number of collocations habitual for humans (e.g. the verbs *think, believe, deal with*) are excluded for animals and plants, which creates a divide between humans and other living beings in our world-view. Similarly, Andrew Goatly ([1996] 2001: 220) argues that the grammar of S.A.E. (Standard Average European) languages represents an anthropocentric ideology which is in keeping only with outdated Newtonian dynamics, since it divides processes into /Agent (Subject)/ – /Action (Verb)/ – /Experiencer or Affected (Object)/. According to Goatly, more work of a contrastive nature concerning, say, English and native American languages, is needed to show how a language may represent nature less anthropocentrically than contemporary English does.

If it is true that language construes our conception of reality, deliberate linguistic change is a powerful instrument which may bring about alterations in the world view of a whole language community and thus may result in cultural change. One prominent example of this are non-sexist language campaigns (as instances of language planning and language development) intended to change attitudes concerning gender roles in different societies. Guidelines of gender-inclusive language use may elicit public reactions which in their turn may contribute to a change in attitudes concerning the role of women and men (the process is described in Pauwels 1998: 171–185; see also Hellinger and Pauwels, this vol.).

For a critical discussion of the Sapir-Whorf-Hypothesis the reader is referred to Salzmann (1993: 151–172), Pinker (1994: 59–82), Campbell (1997), Kramsch (1998: 11–14), and Haden Elgin (2000: 49–71). Pinker's criticism of the hypothesis culminates in the pronouncements: "People do not think in English or Chinese or Apache; they think in a language of thought" (1994: 81), and "knowing a language, then, is knowing how to translate mentalese into strings of words and vice versa" (1994: 82). Pinker's view is strongly influenced by Chomsky's assumption that the languages of the world are not as different as they seem and that there is a "Universal Grammar" which children are born with and which makes it possible for them to learn any language of the world (cf. Cook 1988: 1–27).

As concerns AL, more experiments (e.g. of the kind reported in Kramsch 1998: 13–14) are needed to show the exact nature and dimension of the influence of language on thought. There should also be more contrastive studies which show different categorisations and differences in behaviour due to linguistic difference. The effect of institutionalised language change on thought, behaviour and culture in general should also be the subject of further study (see, for instance, Pauwels 2003: 552–566 on non-sexist language reforms).

5.2. The Ethnography of Speaking

"'Culture', as we understand it here, is synonymous with the 'ways of a people'" (Lado 1957: 110). "Culture" in this ethnographic sense can be defined as the sum of the types of behaviour (linguistic and otherwise), attitudes and beliefs of a community. Unlike Boas and Sapir, Dell Hymes, who pioneered the Ethnography of Speaking, did not stress the influence of language on cognition and on viewing the world, but was interested in concrete speech events and in the "broad range of shared knowledge that speakers must have in order to communicate appropriately" (Saville-Troike 1989: 24–25).

This link between language and culture is so close that culture has even been described as "membership in a discourse community that shares a common social space and history, and a common system of standards for perceiving, believing, evaluating, and acting" (Kramsch 1998: 127). Acquiring a language therefore means acquiring culturally determined patterns of linguistic behaviour, among which Oksaar (2001: 23) lists the following:

> What do you say when, how and to whom,
> when do you have to be silent,
> how to address people (e.g. familiar vs. distancing address forms),
> greeting, thanking, beginning a conversation,
> showing one's emotions.

To these, one could add a number of others (cf. Knapp 2004: 415–420), such as:

Knowing the connotations of words,
using speech acts and knowing about speech act sequences,
arguing, turn-taking, intonation and speech-rhythm,
using non-verbal elements (gestures, body postures etc.),
being aware of the linguistic representation of women and men,
and avoiding the discrimination of groupings through language.

In addition to these aspects of linguistic behaviour, the interrelation between language and culture also concerns areas such as religion, the relation between the genders, attitudes towards the environment (see the example in the introduction), art, music, literature ("culture" in the narrow sense) and many linguistic phenomena such as politeness, joking, courtship behaviour and ritual language. On a more abstract level, language has been identified as the "missing link" between natural and cultural ecosystems (Finke 1996: 37–46).

In our age of globalisation, communication between people with different native languages (and thus different cultural backgrounds) is becoming more and more frequent. This type of cultural contact through language is commonly called *intercultural communication*. It involves an "ecological" give and take between units in different languages and cultures. The problems involved ("success and failure in communication", Clyne 1994: 144–155) have become an important topic of linguistic enquiry (see the articles in Bennett 1998 and in Kiesling and Bratt Paulston 2005). Major factors of intercultural communication referring to ideology, socialisation, forms of discourse and face systems are listed by Scollon and Wong Scollon (2001: 140–141); the contribution of AL to the solution of conflicts based on cultural differences is discussed in Knapp (2004: 409–430).

6. Controversial issues

Controversial issues in the area of language contact, culture and ecology concern most of the phenomena described in Sections 3.1. to 3.6. (societal language contact), where national and economic interests frequently stand in the way of maintaining cultural and linguistic diversity. "One country – one language" policies for a long time contributed to the destruction of linguistic species on a large scale (the U.S.A. and Australia being two prominent examples) and to this day have diminished the chances of survival of existing small languages. The American President Theodore Roosevelt is quoted as stating in 1918 "We have room for but one language in this country and that is the English language" and calling the extermination of native Americans an "unfortunate, but necessary sacrifice to progress" (Nettle and Romaine 2000: 193–194).

It is only in recent decades – perhaps as a result of green movements, "Political Correctness", counter-cultures, and, last but not least, the efforts of linguists – that an awareness of the significance and value of all languages and cultures has developed and that in most countries programmes for language maintenance have been put in operation (see Edwards, this vol.). Though agreement about the imminent loss of many languages and cultures is almost unanimous, a few linguists (among them Haarmann 2001: 16–20) suggest that the loss may turn out to be smaller than anticipated, since new languages will develop through pidginisation and other forms of language mixing. Besides, there are a number of languages which, though long declared extinct in some sources, still survive (examples are given in Haarmann 2001: 17).

The general controversy about the long-term effects of what has been termed "globalisation" also concerns the future of the world's languages. The unifying and levelling tendencies resulting from the worldwide expansion of the media and from the belief that economic growth is a panacea against all problems of poverty, hunger, diseases, etc., will certainly reduce the number of languages spoken and thereby lead to cultural loss. On the other hand, communities and individuals naturally have economic ambitions which make new generations unwilling to conform to ancient cultural habits and speak traditional languages. English is in many parts of the world regarded as the "gatekeeper to positions of prestige in a society" (Pennycook 1994: 14).

The problems indicated are dealt with at the political level through language policies, with which governments try to take an influence on language diversity and language contact situations. The extent to which a state or federation (e.g. the European Union) should interfere with the language situation is another controversial issue in this field. Scholars like Robert Phillipson (2003: 137) and Tove Skutnabb-Kangas (2003: 31–32) warn against a *laissez-faire* policy in Europe which would invariably favour English and lead to a "one language fits all" and "one culture fits all" situation (Phillipson 2003: 86). The other extreme is the language policy pursued by France for a time, which in 1994 declared by State Law (*Loi Toubon*) that the language of the state was French and even imposed fines on using English. Some researchers take a middle position and argue that though English is the language of "neocolonial exploitation", it is nevertheless also "the language through which 'common counter-articulations' can perhaps most effectively be made" (Pennycook 1994: 326, cf. also Pennycook 2003: 6–9 on English and globalisation). No doubt there is an "expanding circle" of countries in which English, though not institutionalised, is used more and more as a lingua franca in a number of professions (cf. Seidlhofer 2001).

The role of English in the world is a topic on which there has been some disagreement in recent years. While scholars such as David Crystal (most specifically in *English as a Global Language* 1997) have suggested that although multilingualism is desirable, in an ideal world "everyone would have fluent command of a single world language" (Crystal 1997: viii), others, in particular Robert Phillipson, have called this view "triumphalist" and expressive of "linguistic imperialism" (title of his book 1992). "Linguistic imperialism builds on an assumption that one language is preferable to others, and its dominance is structurally entrenched through the allocation of more resources to it" (Phillipson 2003: 162). This controversy is documented in Section one of Seidlhofer's book about controversies in AL (Seidlhofer 2003: 7–75).

Equally controversial is the role of English as the international language of science and scholarship. While it is on the one hand desirable to have a lingua franca of the global scientific community, this on the other hand carries the danger that research published in other languages will not be acknowledged in the world of learning. The increasing dominance of English in publications in the Humanities is shown by Ammon (1998: 162–170), who argues for the introduction of English as additional language in university teaching contexts (1998: v–vi).

A problem all ecologists of language face is that in order to be heard, they have to use a large language such as English. Paradoxically, the message of why and how to save threatened languages and why to teach them has to be given not in one of the small languages to be rescued and taught, but preferably in English. A controversial point is also the role of the internet, which on the one hand gives small cultures a voice, but on the other hand accelerates the global spread of English (see Section 7 below).

Another controversial issue is the topic of linguistic purism: Most linguists take a stand against purist tendencies and see intake from other languages as enrichment rather than intrusion. Some scholars, however, fear that their own language may get contaminated through exaggerated mixing and might even lose domains such as certain areas of learning. This controversy is again chiefly about the influence of English. How large the number of languages is in which anglicisms play an increasing role and how negative reactions against them are articulated in the different countries is shown in the articles in Viereck and Bald (1986) and also in Görlach (2001).

The controversy about the Sapir-Whorf-Hypothesis (Section 5.1. above), has in recent years concerned the extent to which thought is dependent on language in our relation to "Nature": To what extent may language be responsible for mechanistic ways of thinking which, in the last few centuries, have led to environmental degradation and biological impoverishment on our planet (cf. Goatly 2001: 223)? The controversy, in other words, is about whether language (more specifically the S.A.E languages) is in part to blame for environmental degradation and to what extent changing a language – or perhaps just creating a higher degree of linguistic awareness – may contribute to solving environmental problems (cf. Halliday 2001: 199).

Concerning language contact in the mind of the speaker (Section 4 above), the controversies about positive or negative effects of bilingualism are now a thing of the past. Weinreich (1953: Appendix) reports many earlier studies which try to prove negative effects of bilingualism on intelligence, group identification, character formation and education. However, Weinreich already shows that these studies are either based on (racial) prejudice or do not take into account possible social and educational discrimination of bilinguals. The urgent need for further research on bilinguals and the problems "induced by the more complex cultural situation in which they live" (Weinreich 1953: 121) is undisputed even fifty years later.

7. Contributions of applied linguistics

A number of desirable contributions of AL in the field of "language, culture and ecology" have already been indicated in the appropriate sections. The following list collects the most important tasks to be carried out. There is an urgent need

- to investigate more closely the interrelation between language and culture and describe in more detail the ways in which language is tied to culture. There is also a need to expose the myths which have developed around these ties. One of these myths is called "the Great Eskimo Vocabulary Hoax" by Pinker (1994: 64), who describes it in the following words:

  Contrary to popular opinion, the Eskimos do not have more words for snow than do speakers of English. They do not have four hundred words for snow, as it has been claimed in print, or two hundred, or one hundred, or forty-eight, or even nine. One dictionary puts the number at two. Counting generously, experts can come up with about a dozen, but by such standards English would not be far behind.

- to create an awareness of the equal importance of all languages regardless of their size;
- to describe and record the many small and endangered languages in the different parts of the world. For Papua New Guinea alone, dozens, if not hundreds of linguists would be needed to describe and catalogue the languages dispersed all over the country;
- to provide help in creating truly bilingual or multilingual communities, and to create and evaluate language teaching methods;
- to assess the quality and improve the methods of translation and film synchronisation, particularly concerning the cultural level;
- to document the roles of the different languages in a country concerning percentage of speakers, domains in which they are used, and effect of contacts. A typical research question could be: What is the effect of a large lingua franca like Tok Pisin on the small languages spoken in the same area? In some regions, Tok Pisin may put pressure on small languages; in others, it may help to save them by providing a super-regional medium of communi-

cation which makes ceding to larger local languages unnecessary (personal communication, Kenneth Sumbuk);
- to assess the apparent and the real cost and/or benefit of language diversity for a country, including its effect on employment (see Section 8.1. below; also Grin, this vol.);
- to assess the influence of linguistic and cultural diversity on conflict and peace in (and between) communities (see Section 8.2. below; also Gay, this vol.);
- to help language planners establish the status of the different languages and to assess the efficiency of language planning methods in general (policy approach);
- to help language planners find solutions for non-discriminatory language (development approach), e.g. concerning the avoidance of sexism in language (see Pauwels 1998: 168–191; also Hellinger and Pauwels, this vol.);
- to evaluate measures for the maintenance or domain expansion of languages (school-teaching, use in the media, internet identity; see also Danet and Herring, this vol.).

The internet is regarded by some as a ray of hope which might help to keep alive threatened languages and to establish multilingual communities. The new medium might contribute in various ways to the maintenance of diversity. Phillipson (2003: 88) mentions one of them:

> It is far more economical to publish in several languages on the internet than in print. The net facilitates networking in languages that do not have the advantage of a large commercial market. This technology means that the dissemination of information is no longer a zero-sum game, either language X or language Y.

The net would thus reduce the cost of producing documents in several languages rather than just one, which would forestall "one language fits all" tendencies.

The net may also give small languages a presence and a forum through which they can make themselves heard and seen. Nettle and Romaine (2000: x) suggest that there is something paradoxical about this, when they write concerning the internet: "Ironically, the same forces of globalisation fostering cultural and linguistic homogenisation, and the spread of English in particular, are being marshalled as tools of resistance."

David Crystal, in *Language Death* (2000: 141–144), welcomes the fact that the internet gives many endangered languages a forum and a new type of presence which may help them to survive. His postulate that "an endangered language will progress if its speakers can make use of electronic technology" is however a hypothetical one, "as many parts of the world where languages are most seriously endangered have not yet come to benefit from electronic technology – or, for that matter, electricity" (Crystal 2000: 141–142). Thus it will again be chiefly the European and American languages which will benefit from this development, not the African, Asian and Oceanian ones. Still, Crystal's (2000: 142) argument in favour of the net is worth considering:

> What is significant, of course, is that the Net provides an identity which is no longer linked to a geographical location. People can maintain a linguistic identity with their relatives, friends, and colleagues, wherever they may be in the world. Whereas, traditionally, the geographical scattering of a community through migration has been an important factor in the dissolution of its language, in future this may no longer be the case.

It would be enlightening to count the web addresses of small languages, since the figures might give an indication not necessarily of the number of speakers, but of the care speakers and politicians take of their language. A few examples of website figures found by using *Google* for minority languages in Europe [retrieved May 18, 2005] are given below:

Lingua Mirandesa (Portugal)	949	web addresses
Lingua Ladina (Italy)	ca. 16,400	web addresses
Llingua Asturiana (Spain)	ca. 16,900	web addresses
Langue Occitane (France)	ca. 22,200	web addresses

The figures are changing continuously, and it would also be of interest to compare the rates at which numbers of websites for the different languages are going up or down: This, too, could give an indication of the interest governments and local bodies are taking in their languages.

The medium still being young, no research has as yet been possible on the long term consequences of an internet presence for a language and culture. Investigating these effects on the speakers of a language and on observers opens up a wide field of research, in which for instance the impact of the net on different languages and cultures could be compared and contrasted. No doubt, using the web with small languages could renew interest in them on the part of young people, who would otherwise discard their small language for a large one on economic grounds. Among other things, the preparation of teaching materials for small languages on the web ("e-teaching") could be an important task for young members of these cultures.

Another major task for AL is to investigate more thoroughly the links between linguistic diversity and bio-diversity. Skutnabb-Kangas (2003: 34–40), using material from *Terralingua*, compares lists of languages and of higher vertebrates in 25 countries and finds that "the two diversities seem to mutually enforce and support each other". Linguists and environmentalists should link forces to preserve the diversity in their fields (cf. Nettle and Romaine 2000: 200). Mühlhäusler (1996b: 107) quotes a report by Rush and Starick from the

Advertiser (Adelaide, September 15, 1995, no page number given) about the near-extinction of great numbers of marsupial species because their indigenous names were lost and replaced by the English word "rat". The passage is worth quoting because it shows how bio-diversity may be dependent on the preservation of linguistic diversity:

> Australian rat-like animals may soon be given new names to help save them from extinction. Their image problems stem from being called rats and mice when they actually are not related to the varieties which Europeans introduced with settlement more than 200 years ago. Scientists are worried that names like 'black-footed tree rat' have little or no appeal for the average Australian. They say this attitude has resulted in many of the animals being exterminated as pests. In response, [...] wildlife and ecology division researchers have suggested replacement names drawn from a list of 2000 Aboriginal words.

The parallels between linguistic and biological loss of diversity are remarkable: In the same period in which dozens of languages disappeared in Australia, dozens (the report quoted puts their number at 62) of species, too, became extinct. Whether this process can be reversed and the species be saved together with the languages remains to be seen. At any rate, the report shows that there is now in Australia a greater awareness of the value of diversity (both biological and linguistic) than existed 200 years ago, when natural phenomena were named by English settlers (cf. also Mühlhäusler 2003: 51–52).

8. (Applied) research perspectives

Apart from the research fields indicated in Section 7, the area of "language contact, culture and ecology" offers further perspectives for research of a transdisciplinary nature which could be of vital importance for the coexistence of cultures and countries.

8.1. Language economy (econo-linguistics)

One of these future perspectives is linked with the *economic* side of language diversity and contact. As explained above, maintaining minority languages and saving threatened languages is by most considered to be important from the ethical and cultural points of view, but regarded as costly for the state. The consequences of language maintenance for the economy of individuals, of communities and of states have not as yet been investigated in many parts of the world. One of the pioneers in this field is François Grin, a sociologist and linguist at the University of Geneva, who investigated the "real" cost of language teaching for each part of Switzerland – and the benefits of this for individuals (see Grin, this vol.).

Studies of this kind (the field is called language economy or econo-linguistics) are urgently needed to provide data for states willing to support their language diversity (see also Grin and Vaillancourt 1999, concerning Wales, Ireland and the Basque country). If a state decides to finance the maintenance of a small language – by providing schools and teachers, by maintaining radio and television programmes in the language, and by providing translating and interpreting services – this may be a good investment from a double point of view: It creates jobs – and specifically jobs for minority speakers – and it creates renewed interest in the small language on the part of young people. Disregarding the question of languages as tourist attractions, governments confronted with the alternatives of investing in a language (and culture) or in environmentally harmful industrial projects will require help from econo-linguists concerning these decisions.

With economics and marketing becoming more and more important, it can be predicted that more applied linguists will get interested in this transdisciplinary area of research which bridges linguistics, sociology and economics.

8.2. Language diversity – contact and conflict

A superordinate task for AL, and one which offers many perspectives for future research, is to find out under what circumstances language diversity may lead to conflict – or perhaps rather be conducive to peaceful coexistence. It is as yet very little known whether and to what extent having a common language reduces the conflict potential in a small community, in a country or between countries. On the one hand, one would think that unhindered mutual intelligibility prevents misunderstanding and thus promotes peace; on the other hand, it cannot be denied that even people who speak exactly the same dialect quarrel. Switzerland has been the most peaceful country for centuries. Could one reason for this be the four linguistic communities it comprises – with 65% speakers of German, 18% French, 12% Italian and 0.8% Romansh?

There are reports which seem to indicate that the role of language diversity for conflict and peace depends on the social organisation of a community, as Laycock (2001: 169) observes about dialect differentiation in Papua New Guinea:

> The causes of this dialect differentiation may lie in Melanesian social organisation (loose-knit villages of less than a thousand persons existing basically in nuclear family groups) and Melanesian attitudes to language. It has more than once been said to me around the Sepik that "it wouldn't be any good if we all talked the same; we like to know where people come from". In other words, linguistic diversity, of however minor a kind, is perpetuated as a badge of identification.

This shows that in some types of social organisation language diversity may be maintained for the very reason that it prevents conflict. The relations between social organisation, language diversity, conflict and peace offer a wide area of research for applied linguists, sociologists and peace researchers. Questions to be answered are: If peace is conducive to the welfare and growth of the human species, why did language diversity arise? In what way was it good for humans to develop so many different cultures? Is there at present a development towards convergence and linguistic globalisation – and if so, what consequences does this have for conflict and peace within and between communities?

To summarise, it can be claimed that the field of "language contact, culture and ecology", in this age of global contacts, offers a variety of new opportunities for interdisciplinary research, the results of which might eventually lead to a more peaceful coexistence of nations, languages and cultures.

References

Ammon, Ulrich
    1998   *Ist Deutsch noch internationale Wissenschaftssprache? Englisch auch für die Lehre an den deutschsprachigen Hochschulen.* Berlin, New York: Mouton de Gruyter.
Appel, René and Pieter Muysken
    1987   *Language Contact and Bilingualism.* London: Edward Arnold.
Bennett, Milton J. (ed.)
    1998   *Basic Concepts of Intercultural Communication. Selected Readings.* Yarmouth: Intercultural Press.
Bickerton, Derek
    1981   *Roots of Language.* Ann Arbor: Karoma.
Brenzinger, Matthias (ed.)
    1992   *Language Death. Factual and Theoretical Explorations with Special Reference to East Africa.* Berlin, New York: Mouton de Gruyter.
Campbell, Lawrence
    1997   The Sapir-Whorf Hypothesis.
            Venus.va.com.au/suggestion/sapir.html [accessed May 18, 2005].
Clyne, Michael
    1991   *Community Languages: The Australian Experience.* Cambridge: Cambridge University Press.
Clyne, Michael
    1994   *Inter-cultural Communication at Work: Cultural Values in Discourse.* Cambridge: Cambridge University Press.
Clyne, Michael
    2003   *Dynamics of Language Contact: English and Immigrant Languages.* Cambridge: Cambridge University Press.
Cook, Vivian J.
    1988   *Chomsky's Universal Grammar: An Introduction.* Oxford: Blackwell.
Crystal, David
    1997   *English as a Global Language.* London: Longman.

Crystal, David
  2000   *Language Death.* Cambridge: Cambridge University Press.
Denison, Norman and J. Tragut
  1990   Language death and language maintenance. In: Peter H. Nelde (ed.), *Minorities and Language Contact*, 150–156. (Sociolinguistica 4.) Tübingen: Niemeyer.
Dressler, Wolfgang
  1988   Spracherhaltung – Sprachverfall – Sprachtod. In: Ulrich Ammon, Norbert Dittmar and Klaus Jürgen Mattheier (eds.), *Sociolinguistics: An International Handbook of the Science of Language and Society*, Vol. 2: 1551–1563. Berlin: Mouton de Gruyter.
Edgar, Andrew and Peter Sedgwick (eds.)
  2002   *Cultural Theory: The Key Thinkers.* London, New York: Routledge.
Ferguson, Charles
  1959   Diglossia. *Word* 15: 325–340.
Fill, Alwin and Peter Mühlhäusler (eds.)
  2001   *The Ecolinguistics Reader: Language, Ecology and Environment.* London: Continuum.
Finke, Peter
  1996   Sprache als *missing link* zwischen natürlichen und kulturellen Ökosystemen: Überlegungen zur Weiterentwicklung der Sprachökologie. In: Alwin Fill (ed.), *Sprachökologie und Ökolinguistik*, 27–48. Tübingen: Stauffenburg.
Fishman, Joshua
  1967   Bilingualism with and without diglossia; diglossia with and without bilingualism. *Journal of Social Issues* 23: 29–38.
Fishman, Joshua
  2001a   Why is it so hard to save a threatened language? In: Fishman (ed.),1–22.
Fishman, Joshua
  2001b   A decade in the life of a two-in-one language. In: Fishman (ed.), 74–100.
Fishman, Joshua (ed.)
  2001c   *Can Threatened Languages be Saved? Reversing Language Shift Revisited: A 21st Century Perspective.* Clevedon: Multilingual Matters.
Gass, Susan and Larry Selinker
  2001   *Second Language Acquisition: An Introductory Course.* 2nd ed. Mahwah, NJ: Erlbaum.
Goatly, Andrew
  [1996] 2001 Green grammar and grammatical metaphor, or language and the myth of power, or metaphors we die by. In: Fill and Mühlhäusler (eds.), 203–225. [originally *Journal of Pragmatics* 25 (1996): 537–560].
Goebl, Hans, Peter H. Nelde, Zdenek Stary and Wolfgang Wölck (eds.)
  1996–1997 *Kontaktlinguistik – Contact Linguistics – Linguistique de contact.* 2 vols. Berlin: Mouton de Gruyter.
Göpferich, Susanne
  2004   Standardisierung von Kommunikation. In: Knapp et al. (eds.) 457–480.
Görlach, Manfred
  2001   *A Dictionary of European Anglicisms. A Usage Dictionary of Anglicisms in Sixteen European Languages.* Oxford: Oxford University Press.

Grin, François and François Vaillancourt
  1999   *The Cost-effectiveness Evaluation of Minority Language Policies: Case Studies on Wales, Ireland and the Basque Country.* Flensburg: European Centre for Minority Issues.
Grosjean, François
  1982   *Life with Two Languages: An Introduction to Bilingualism.* Cambridge, MA: Harvard University Press.
Haarmann, Harald
  2001   *Die Kleinsprachen der Welt – Existenzbedrohung und Überlebenschancen.* Frankfurt/M.: Peter Lang.
Haden Elgin, Suzette
  2000   *The Language Imperative: The Power of Language to Enrich Your Life and Expand Your Mind.* Cambridge, MA: Perseus.
Halliday, Michael
  [1990] 2001 New ways of meaning: The challenge to applied linguistics. In: Fill and Mühlhäusler (eds.), 175–202. [originally in: *Journal of Applied Linguistics* 6/1990: 7–36].
Hamers, Josiane F. and Michel H. A. Blanc
  2000   *Binguality and Bilingualism.* 2nd ed. Cambridge: Cambridge University Press.
Haugen, Einar
  1966   *Language Conflict and Language Planning: The Case of Modern Norwegian.* Cambridge, MA: Harvard University Press.
Haugen, Einar
  1972   The analysis of linguistic borrowing. In: Einar Haugen, *The Ecology of Language.* Ed. Anwar S. Dil, 79–109. Stanford: Stanford University Press.
Haugen, Einar
  [1972] 2001 The ecology of language. In: Fill and Mühlhäusler (eds.), 57–66. [originally in: Einar Haugen, *The Ecology of Language.* Ed. Anwar S. Dil, 225–239. Stanford: Stanford University Press].
Hellinger, Marlis
  1977   *Kontrastive Grammatik deutsch/englisch.* Tübingen: Niemeyer.
Hellinger, Marlis and Hadumod Bußmann
  2001   Gender across languages. The linguistic representation of women and men. In: Marlis Hellinger and Hadumod Bußmann (eds.), *Gender Across Languages. The Linguistic Representation of Women and Men.* Vol. I. 1–25. Amsterdam/Philadelphia: John Benjamins.
Herbst, Thomas
  1994   *Linguistische Aspekte der Synchronisation von Fernsehserien.* Tübingen: Niemeyer.
Hymes, Dell
  1971a   Sociolinguistics and the ethnography of speaking. In: Edwin Ardener (ed.) *Social Anthropology and Language.* 47–93. London: Tavistock.
Hymes, Dell (ed.)
  1971b   *Pidginization and Creolization of Languages.* Cambridge: Cambridge University Press.
Janich, Nina
  2004   Sprachplanung. In: Knapp et al. (eds.), 481–501.

Kaplan, Robert B. and Richard B. Baldauf
2003   *Language and Language-in-Education Planning in the Pacific Basin.* Dordrecht: Kluwer.

Klein, Wolfgang and Norbert Dittmar
1979   *Developing Grammars: The Acquisition of German Syntax by Foreign Workers.* Berlin: Springer.

Kiesling, Scott F. and Christina Bratt Paulston (eds.)
2005   *Intercultural Discourse and Communication. The Essential Readings.* Oxford: Blackwell.

Knapp, Karlfried
2004   Interkulturelle Kommunikation. In: Knapp et al. (eds.), 409–430.

Knapp, Karlfried, Gerd Antos, Michael Becker-Mrotzek, Arnulf Deppermann, Susanne Göpferich, Joachim Grabowski, Michael Klemm and Claudia Villiger (eds.)
2004   *Angewandte Linguistik: Ein Lehrbuch.* Tübingen/Basel: Francke.

Kramsch, Claire
1998   *Language and Culture.* Oxford: Oxford University Press.

Lado, Robert
1957   *Linguistics Across Cultures: Applied Linguistics for Language Teachers.* Ann Arbor: University of Michigan Press.

Lakoff, George and Mark Johnson
1980   *Metaphors We Live By.* Chicago: Chicago University Press.

Laycock, Donald C.
[1991] 2001 Linguistic diversity in Melanesia: A tentative explanation. In: Fill and Mühlhäusler (eds.), 167–171. [originally in: R. Carle, M. Heinischke, P. W. Pink, C. Rost and K. Stradtlander (eds.), *Gava: Studies in Austronesian Languages and Cultures*, 31–37. Berlin: Reimer].

Mackey, William
[1980] 2001 The ecology of language shift. In: Fill and Mühlhäusler (eds.), 67–74. [originally in Peter H. Nelde, ed., *Sprachkontakt und Sprachkonflikt*, 35–41. Wiesbaden: Franz Steiner].

Mair, Christian (ed.)
2003   *The Politics of English as a World Language: New Horizons in Postcolonial Cultural Studies.* Amsterdam/New York: Rodopi.

Moelleken, Wolfgang W. and Peter J. Weber (eds.)
1997   *Neue Forschungsarbeiten zur Kontaktlinguistik.* (Plurilingua XIX) Bonn: Dümmler.

Mufwene, Salikoko S.
2001   *The Ecology of Language Evolution.* Cambridge: Cambridge University Press.

Mühlhäusler, Peter
1996a   *Linguistic Ecology: Language Change and Linguistic Imperialism in the Pacific Region.* London/New York: Routledge.

Mühlhäusler, Peter
1996b   Linguistic adaptation to changed environmental conditions: Some lessons from the past. In: Alwin Fill (ed.), *Sprachökologie und Ökolinguistik*, 105–130. Tübingen: Stauffenburg.

Mühlhäusler, Peter
[1994] 2001 Babel revisited. In: Fill and Mühlhäusler (eds.), 159–164. [originally in: *UNESCO Courier* (April 1994), 16–21. Paris: UNESCO].

Mühlhäusler, Peter
   2003   *Language of Environment – Environment of Language.* London: Battlebridge.

Myers-Scotton, Carol
   1995   *Social Motivations for Codeswitching: Evidence from Africa.* Oxford: Clarendon Press.

Myers-Scotton, Carol
   2002   *Contact Linguistics: Bilingual Encounters and Grammatical Outcomes.* Oxford/New York: Oxford University Press.

Nelde, Peter H. and Rosita Rindler Schjerve (eds.)
   2001   *Minorities and Language Policy. Minderheiten und Sprachpolitik. Minorités et l'aménagement linguistique.* St. Augustin: Asgard.

Nettle, Daniel
   1998   Explaining global patterns of language diversity. *Journal of Anthropological Archaeology* 17: 354–374.

Nettle, Daniel and Suzanne Romaine
   2000   *Vanishing Voices: The Extinction of the World's Languages.* Oxford: Oxford University Press.

Oksaar, Els
   1980   Mehrsprachigkeit, Sprachkontakt, Sprachkonflikt. In: Peter H. Nelde (ed.), *Sprachkontakt und Sprachkonflikt*, 43–52. Wiesbaden: Steiner.

Oksaar, Els
   2001   Mehrsprachigkeit, Multikulturalismus, Identität und Integration. In: Peter H. Nelde and Rosita Rindler Schjerve (eds.), *Minorities and Language Policy. Minderheiten und Sprachpolitik. Minorités et l'aménagement linguistique*, 21–35. St. Augustin: Asgard.

Oksaar, Els
   2003   *Zweitspracherwerb: Wege zur Mehrsprachigkeit und zur interkulturellen Verständigung.* Stuttgart: Kohlhammer.

Palmer, Gary B.
   1996   *Toward a Theory of Cultural Linguistics.* Austin: University of Texas Press.

Pauwels, Anne
   1998   *Women Changing Language.* London/New York: Longman.

Pauwels, Anne
   2003   Linguistic sexism and feminist activism. In: Janet Holmes and Miriam Meyerhoff (eds.), *The Handbook of Language and Gender,* 550–570. Oxford: Blackwell.

Pennycook, Alastair
   1994   *The Cultural Politics of English as an International Language.* Harlow: Longman.

Pennycook, Alastair
   2003   Beyond homogeny and heterogeny: English as a global and worldly language. In: Christian Mair (ed.), *The Politics of English as a World Language: New Horizons in Postcolonial Cultural Studies*, 3–17. Amsterdam/New York: Rodopi.

Phillipson, Robert
   1992   *Linguistic Imperialism.* Oxford: Oxford University Press.

Phillipson, Robert
    2003   *English-Only Europe? Challenging Language Policy.* London/New York: Routledge.
Pinker, Steven
    1994   *The Language Instinct.* Harmondsworth: Penguin.
Poplack, Shana and Marjory Meechan
    1998   How languages fit together in codemixing. *International Journal of Bilingualism* 2: 127–138.
Reiss, Katharina
    1971   *Möglichkeiten und Grenzen der Übersetzungskritik.* Munich: Max Hueber.
Riehl, Claudia M.
    2004   *Sprachkontaktforschung: Eine Einführung.* Tübingen: Gunter Narr.
Romaine, Suzanne
    1995   *Bilingualism.* 2nd ed. Oxford: Blackwell.
Rouchdy, Aleya (ed.)
    2002   *Language Contact and Language Conflict in Arabic: Variations on a Sociolinguistic Theme.* London: RoutledgeCurzon.
Salminen, Tapani
    1999   *UNESCO Red Book Report on Endangered Languages: Europe.* www.helsinki.fi/~tasalmin/europe_index.html, retrieved May 18, 2005.
Salzmann, Zdenek
    1993   *Language, Culture, & Society. An Introduction to Linguistic Anthropology.* Boulder, CO: Westview Press.
Sapir, Edward
    1921   *Language.* New York: Harcourt, Brace and World.
Sapir, Edward
    [1912] 2001 Language and environment. In: Fill and Mühlhäusler (eds.), 13–23. [originally in: *American Anthropologist*, new series 14, 226–242].
Saville-Troike, Muriel
    1989   *The Ethnography of Communication. An Introduction.* 2nd ed. New York: Blackwell.
Schuchardt, Hugo
    1980   *Pidgin and Creole Languages: Selected Essays by Hugo Schuchardt.* Edited and translated by Glenn G. Gilbert. Cambridge: Cambridge University Press.
Scollon, Ron and Suzanne Wong Scollon
    2001   *Intercultural Communication: A Discourse Approach.* 2nd ed. Oxford: Blackwell.
Scott, Sir Walter
    n.d.   *Ivanhoe.* London: Frederick Warne.
Seidlhofer, Barbara
    2001   Closing a conceptual gap: The case for a description of English as a lingua franca. *International Journal of Applied Linguistics* 11(2): 133–158.
Seidlhofer, Barbara (ed.)
    2003   *Controversies in Applied Linguistics.* Oxford: Oxford University Press.
Skutnabb-Kangas, Tove
    2003   Linguistic diversity and biodiversity: The threat from killer languages. In: Christian Mair (ed.), *The Politics of English as a World Language: New*

Horizons in Postcolonial Cultural Studies, 31–52. Amsterdam/New York: Rodopi.

Steiner, George
[1975] 2001 Language and gnosis. In: Fill and Mühlhäusler (eds.), 24–30. [originally in: George Steiner, *After Babel: Aspects of Language and Translation*, 49–59. Oxford: Oxford University Press].

Sutherland, William J.
    2003   Parallel extinction risk and global distribution of languages and species. *Nature* 423: 276–279 (Letters to *Nature*, 15 May, 2003).

Thomason, Sarah G.
    2001   *Language Contact.* Edinburgh: Edinburgh University Press.

Trampe, Wilhelm
[1991] 2001 Language and ecological crisis. Extracts from a dictionary of industrial agriculture. In: Fill and Mühlhäusler (eds.), 232–240. [originally in: E. Feldbusch, R. Pogarell and C. Weiss (eds.), *Neue Fragen der Linguistik*, vol. 2, 143–149. Tübingen: Niemeyer].

Viereck, Wolfgang and Wolf-Dietrich Bald (eds.)
    1986   *English in Contact with Other Languages. Studies in Honour of Broder Carstensen on the Occasion of his 60th Birthday.* Budapest: Akadémiai Kiadó.

Weinreich, Uriel
    1953   *Languages in Contact: Findings and Problems.* The Hague/Paris/New York: Mouton.

Whorf, Benjamin Lee
    1956   *Language, Thought and Reality: Selected Writings of Benjamin Lee Whorf.* Edited by John B. Carroll. Cambridge, MA: MIT Press.

Winford, Donald
    2003   *An Introduction to Contact Linguistics.* Oxford: Blackwell.

Wittgenstein, Ludwig
    1959   *Tractatus Logico-Philosophicus.* Oxford: Blackwell.

II. Language planning and language change

7. Models and approaches in language policy and planning

Thomas Ricento

1. Introduction

The fact that there are between 6,000 and 8,000 oral languages and only about 200 states in the world means that most states are multilingual – and multicultural – to varying degrees. It is also the case that in most (but not all) states there is usually only one "national" language (despite constitutional provisions which recognize other languages or which remain silent with regard to the national language within the state; see Faingold 2004). In addition, because national languages gained their preeminent status in conjunction with the development of the political state, this means that, by definition, the national language(s) will be spoken by and identified with dominant political groups (which may or may not be numerical majorities, and which may vary with changes in regimes and constitutions, as occurred in South Africa and newly independent states in the former Soviet Union, among other cases that could be cited), while minority languages will tend to be identified with "non national" groups, or politically subordinated groups, irrespective of their relative numbers or long-standing existence within the geographical area of the current state. Individuals or groups that are barred access to the national language, and especially the standard "prestige" written variety, or that are expected to assimilate into the dominant language and abandon their mother tongue (and cultural identities) without a realistic expectation of access to the political economy and the benefits it provides, are at a serious disadvantage compared to individuals with free access to, command of, and identification (indexed by race, culture, religion, or political loyalty) with the "national" language. "Success" for linguistic minorities is often defined by "majoritarian"/dominant groups (and often accepted by speakers of minority languages) as assimilation into the national, "mainstream" culture, with its promise of social and economic upward mobility, often with little regard for or awareness of the potential cost of such a "choice", including erosion of group identity, limited access to the political culture and, in the case of many language minority groups world wide, the demise of their language.[1] This latter problem is rather stark if one considers the data on languages world wide: According to a survey by the U.S.-based Summer Institute of Linguistics (SIL), published in 1999, there were 51 languages with only one speaker left, 500 languages with fewer than 100 speakers, 1,500 languages with fewer than 1,000 speakers, and more than 3,000 languages with fewer than 10,000 speakers. The survey went on to reveal that as many as 5,000 of the world's 6,800 languages were spoken by fewer than 100,000 speakers each. It concluded that 96 percent of the world's languages were spoken by only 4 percent of its people (Crystal 1999).

Taken together, these observations suggest that in the vast majority of states, competency, or lack thereof, in language or language variety *x* bears some relationship with one's position in society. Further, the status of language or language variety *x* will vary from state to state; so, for example, the status of Spanish is different (higher) in Spain compared to its status in the U.S., and the same is true for the status of Hungarian in Hungary compared to its status in non-Hungarian dominant communities in Slovenia and the Slovak Republic, the status of French in France compared to its standing in Canada (outside of Quebec), and so on. Of course, the status of the many *varieties* of a language will vary both geographically and socially (Parisian French, for example, having higher status than other regional varieties). To the extent that one's primary language indexes (i.e., "points to") class, educational level, ethnicity/race in a particular context, it may reinforce negative or positive stereotypes about particular ethnolinguistic groups. This can (and often does) correlate with social hierarchies in which language competencies can be viewed as *causes* for relatively higher or lower social status, rather than as the *result* of sociopolitical processes associated with nationalism and state formation which position certain languages/varieties hierarchically in defined contexts.

Academic language policy and planning (LPP) is concerned (among other things) with investigating the processes by which languages and language varieties obtain particular statuses in various domains of private and public life, and how policies (whether explicit or implicit) reaffirm or attempt to modify in some way such achieved or ascribed statuses of languages. The practice of language planning (other terms used include language engineering and language management; see Spolsky 2004) by policy-makers, who may be bureaucrats, politicians, or educationists often advised by academic specialists in language policy, tends to be pragmatic and, as with other types of social planning, influenced – if not driven – by political and economic agendas. Examples of successful language planning and policy implementation in which stipulated goals, widely shared by all affected groups, are substantially achieved are relatively rare (see Kaplan and Baldauf 1997 for discussion of why this is so; for examples of successful language planning, see e.g., Blommaert and Rubino, both this vol.). Yet, it would be wrong to conclude that management of language occurs only, or even primarily, as the result of deliberate governmental intervention. Rather, as a number of critical scholars have argued (e.g., Tollefson 2006), language management occurs through the on-going practices of politicians, bureaucrats, educators and other state authorities. Drawing from Foucault's (1991) analysis of "governmentality", applied linguists have argued that research in (critical) language policy should focus on "discourses, educational practices, and language use" – social processes involved in the formation of culture and knowledge (Pennycook 2002: 92). Focusing on the more formal, explicit governmental policies designed to influence language behavior, François Grin (2003) offers an approach to evaluating alternative language policies by outlining various ways to measure the effectiveness of policies so that policy-makers have some meaningful, i.e. "rational", criteria upon which to base their decision-making in advocating for one language policy, or policy approach, over another (see also Grin, this vol.).

Grin (and other scholars) point out that much of the research in LPP in recent years has been motivated by the desire to modify existing arrangements by increasing the domains and, consequently, the status of minority languages in a polity usually for the purpose of enhancing the social status of speakers of minority languages along with their access to and participation in civic life. In this chapter, I will consider how approaches and models of LPP in the scholarly literature, over the past half century or so, have addressed (characterized, questioned, investigated, problematized) the challenges of multilingualism and multiculturalism in the world's states, and consider some specific proposals to enhance social access and equity, especially for speakers of minority and threatened languages around the world. I choose to focus on issues related to multilingualism and multiculturalism because they provide a focal point to examine how language policies are imbricated in all facets of social life. Even if one is interested in implementing policies in the form of specific plans, it is necessary to consider a wide range of social variables (e.g., ethnicity, class, gender, religion) in evaluating one specific plan over another. That is, LPP is never merely a technical exercise in identifying a "problem" and a "solution"; the very identification of a phenomenon as a problem requires a particular perspective on the nature of societal goods and values which very often is not universally shared. A focus on multiculturalism means that all of the many ascribed or achieved attributes of human beings come into play when any attempt to influence language behavior through language planning is undertaken.

2. Language policy and planning and applied linguistics

An argument can (and has) been made that LPP is an exemplary applied linguistics endeavor. Early work in LPP was mostly concerned with technical aspects of corpus planning, that is, having to do with features of languages (e.g., how they should be written, pronounced, modernized, and so on), which required expertise in linguistics. More recently, scholars have begun to focus on status issues, which includes consideration of the domains in which languages are used, as well as the factors which privilege particular languages and language varieties in these various domains. This research has expanded the disciplinary range of theories and methods in LPP to include critical theory, historiography, political and economic theory, and a number of specialties within postmodernism, especially colonial and post-colonial studies, governmentality (Foucault 1991), and identity studies.

To the extent that work in LPP over the past two decades has questioned some of the epistemological assumptions about linguistics and linguistics applied (see Pennycook 2001 for elaboration), the goals and methods of applied linguistics have moved from more technical analyses in which remedies for perceived problems are proposed, to critical studies which question, for example, the processes and assumptions which identify a social phenomenon involving language as a problem in the first place. For example, the widely held assumption that multilingualism is incompatible with national development and political stability has been viewed by critical theorists in LPP as a reflection of Western normative ideologies about the prerequisites for "normal" states.

In addition to the influence of critical and postmodern theory in LPP, research in theoretical linguistics has also contributed to reformulations of both research questions and theoretical orientations in LPP. For example, the idea that linguistic structures in a given language are fixed properties which obey detailed algorithms at a subconscious level has been challenged. Linguist Paul Hopper (1998: 157–158) argues:

> […] there is no natural fixed structure to language. Rather, speakers borrow heavily from their previous experiences of communication in similar circumstances, on similar topics, and with similar interlocutors. Systematicity, in this view, is an illusion produced by the partial settling or *sedimentation* of frequently used forms into temporary subsystems.

This approach to understanding the nature of human language has important implications for theorizing in LPP. One important consequence is that grand narratives about the role of "big" named languages, such as English, in "killing" other, generally smaller languages, based on a conception of English as a discrete code shared by hundreds of millions of speakers around the world, are too simplistic. English (along with other imperial languages) occupies a broad range of niches, functions, and discourses, incorporating features of local varieties, evolving as hybrids, which may then be "standardized" as legitimate national or regional varieties, such as Indian English or Singapore English. Beyond the implications for planning languages thus hybridized and localized, the matter of the status of such varieties in the societies in which they are used (both for intra- and inter-national communication) cannot be addressed only (or even primarily) from a global decontextualized perspective. Thus, characterizations of English as an imperial language (Phillipson 1992), which always advances the economic and political agendas of metropolitan countries (especially the U.S. and Britain) cannot be sustained. For example, English has served as the working language of the African National Congress in South Africa in opposing and overthrowing the Apartheid regime. The related claim (Phillipson 1992) that the spread of English (as if it were a homogeneous code rooted in a particular culture) is leading to the homogenization of world culture has also been challenged. For example, Pennycook (2003) shows how language mixing in the lyrics of rap and hip-hop music is contributing to a global popular culture which transcends national boundaries and ideologies, while reflecting local cultural and linguistic forms. The implications of this theorizing from linguistics and its application to LPP are the following: (1) the naming of a language is more a political claim than a scientific label for an invariant semiotic system; (2) the status of English or any other language is not inherent in the code; (3) the functions and domains of a named language vary, historically, from society to society and context to context (see Ricento 2000b for details).

Another way in which work in linguistics and linguistics applied has influenced theorizing in LPP is through the application of principles of discourse analysis in the analysis and interpretation of language plans and policies. Lo Bianco (2004: 756–758) proposes the addition of the category *discourse planning* to language planning analysis. He argues that "the examination of policy discourses, especially how policy discourses constitute problems for policy treatment, is a neglected field that will extend the scholarly range and rigor of LPP" (757). A number of important studies on the discourse of language planning have been published (e.g., Moore 1996; Lo Bianco 2001; Blommaert 1999; Dedaić and Nelson 2003; Ricento 2005a). In order to provide some idea of how this approach to theorizing in LPP can be operationalized, I briefly describe the methods and findings of a case study (Ricento 2005a).

Ricento (2005a) is an analysis of texts produced by advocates of the Heritage language movement in the U.S. The "language-as-resource" orientation has gained currency among academics interested in the promotion of language learning and use in the United States. In 1999, the Center for Applied Linguistics (CAL) and the National Foreign Language Center (NFLC) at the University of Maryland convened the first national conference on heritage languages in the U.S. This was followed by the "Heritage Language Research Priorities Conference" at the University of California, Los Angeles (UCLA) in 2000, which was followed by the second national conference on heritage languages in America in 2002 (also sponsored by CAL and NFLC). *The Heritage Language* Journal, an online journal hosted by the UCLA Language Resource Center, began publication in Spring 2003. For the purposes of this study, mission statements and position papers which outlined the goals and purposes of promoting heritage languages in the U.S. were examined (all are readily available on the websites through CAL; details on the texts are provided in Ricento 2005a). A content analysis of these mission statements and position papers, written by advocates for heritage languages, revealed that the language-as-resource metaphor was widely used and developed, and that it was associated with policies that benefit narrowly defined state interests at the expense of the interests and aspirations of individuals in linguistic communities. What was often omitted in these texts was the historical context (see Blommaert 2005: ch. 3), and especially the history of languages – and specifically of speakers of minority languages – during more than 200 years of U.S. history, a context which provides a fuller accounting of the meaning of language-as-resource metaphor. To the degree that languages other than English have been recognized and promoted in U.S. society it has been as a means to redress historical patterns of discrimination and exclusion, particularly in voting and education. This restricted public/civic space for other languages is connected to conceptualizations of the state and the role of languages in the state, namely, that a state is equivalent to a nation, and a nation is defined by adherence to a common language, values, and culture. The great majority of English speakers in the U.S. believe their language, and its vast community of speakers, enjoy a *natural* right to existence, maintenance, protection and promotion because English is coterminous with the *nation*, whose right to existence and protection is unquestioned, while other *non-national* languages have no natural right, or warrant, to exist, because they are outside the nation and therefore enjoy no warrant for protection (Ricento 2005a: 356). English serves both *instrumental* and *affiliational* functions for monolingual/English dominant persons who identify themselves as Americans. The analysis of the language-as-resource discourse in the heritage language texts examined in the study shows that it tends to perpetuate a view of language as instrument (as opposed to identity marker). In order words, "the view promoted in these discourses is of language as commodity, displaced from its historical situatedness, a tool to be developed for particular national interests" (359).

What is particularly relevant is that the authors of the texts examined in this study, generally *support* the aspirations of language minority communities. Yet, their invocation of the language-as-resource metaphor may work against that goal. Richard Ruiz (1984) popularized a taxonomy of orientations in language planning which has been influential in applied linguistics research, and especially in LPP. Ruiz argues that the way in which language is characterized by policy makers, that is, either as "problem", "right", or "resource" will influence the policy approaches and policies they will promote. For example, in the U.S., the "language-as-problem" orientation has informed policies which limit use of languages other than English in education and public services. Ruiz (1984: 25–26) argues that in the U.S., the "language-as-resource" orientation could help resolve some of the conflicts associated with the other two orientations, including easing tensions between majority and minority communities and supporting the role of non-English languages in society. This latter benefit of a "resource" orientation has gained popularity among academics in LPP who advocate increased funding and support for the teaching and learning of foreign languages, and especially (in the wake of the attacks of September 11, 2001) of strategically important languages, such as (standard versions of) Arabic, Pashto, Urdu, and Farsi (not to mention the countless varieties of these same languages). However, as with many popular metaphors in the applied linguistics literature, the devil is in the details. The term "resource" requires specification: Who "owns" or controls the resource? For whose benefit is the resource to be "cultivated"? Is the resource renewable or finite? Who (or what) will determine the fair market price for the resource? Do languages operate like (other) commodities, sensitive to pressures of supply and demand? Does the language-as-resource metaphor resonate with the experiences of language minority communities in the U.S.? (see Grin 2006 for examples of "market failure" in the promotion of linguistic diversity). Ruiz (1984: 27) notes that the resource orientation is not without its problems and he advocates a "fuller development of a resources-oriented approach to language planning".

Some of the problems with this metaphor are immediately obvious, while others are less so. One of the dangers of employing this metaphor to justify policies to promote the teaching and learning of languages important for national strategic military and security purposes is that languages are de-linked historically and contemporaneously from the experiences and aspirations of their communities of speakers, which very often have experienced discrimination because their "foreign" languages have marked them as "un-American". These languages, far from resources, were often viewed (and continue to be widely viewed) as detriments to assimilation and acculturation to mainstream "American" values. The problem with the resource approach, as characterized in the mission statements and other promotional materials of academics in the Heritage language movement examined in Ricento (2005a), is that languages are de-linked from the language communities and conceptualized (largely) as having an instrumental value for national defense and trade. In other words, the primary beneficiary of language planning, in this case, is the state which claims to represent the national interest (as it defines it) and not the interests of the heritage language speakers (apart from the degree to which some heritage language speakers may identify with and support the interests of the state in improving its intelligence capacity). What is most interesting, however, is that the language in the mission statements and guiding principles analyzed in this study was produced by academics well-versed in the history of language restrictionism in the U.S. and the ways in which restrictive language policies were often motivated by racial, religious, and political bigotry. Such bigotry still exists and influences attitudes towards the learning, use, and maintenance of heritage languages.

It is, of course, understandable that national governments are concerned with national defense; after all, that is one of their principal functions and reasons for existence. However, what is revealing in this study is that the language-as-resource metaphor, with its attendant descriptions of language as a commodity, is often uncritically employed in the mission statements and guiding principles of academics aligned with the Heritage language movement in the United States. I am not claiming that this analysis represents the views of all scholars involved in the Heritage language movement, nor that the identity and communal functions of language are not considered relevant by supporters. For example, Terrence Wiley (2001: 32) argues that "to ensure that heritage language programs do not merely become symbolic gestures, imposed by outsiders to the community, it is important to define heritage language programs from a community perspective". Another scholar, Ana Roca (2003) argues that much political work needs to be done in order to improve views on bilingualism in general and bilingualism in Spanish and English in particular. Norma Gonzalez (2003) and Guadalupe Valdés (2003) argue for a research agenda which considers the ways in which language ideologies negatively impact on attitudes and the learning of heritage languages in schools and universities. Yet, despite these calls for greater understanding of the historical and contemporary factors which mitigate against the learning and maintenance of heritage languages in the U.S., the perpetuation (through entailment) of the "language-as-commodity" discourse may in fact undermine the potential benefits augured by the "language-as-resource" orientation by helping to perpetuate a narrow and cramped legitimacy for languages other than English in U.S. society, thus actually *limiting* the broad range of benefits that could be realized from having large numbers of bilingual/biliterate citizens which could benefit the nation, not only in trade and national defense, but also in helping to ease tensions between language majority and minority communities.

3. Historical and theoretical perspectives in language policy and planning research

3.1. The Post World War II era

Although activities concerned with the formulation and implementation of policies related to languages in society have been going on for many centuries, as a scholarly field LPP extends back only to the 1950s. Spolsky (2004: 10) notes that "the first book in the Library of Congress to include 'language policy' in the title is Cebollero (1945)", while Hornberger (2006: 25) claims that the first use of the term "language planning" in the scholarly literature is usually attributed to Haugen's 1959 study of language standardization in Norway. Haugen's work shaped research and scholarship in language planning during the early years of the field, and continues to be influential in the present day. He provided a theoretical framework which outlines four phases of language planning:

(1) *selection* of a language variety or varieties that provide the basis for a new norm;
(2) *codification* of the selected language which included choice of written script, determination of phonology (the patterning of sounds in the language) and how this was to be represented in the orthography (writing system);
(3) *implementation* of the selected and codified language throughout society, i.e., through schooling, government agencies, businesses, and so on;
(4) *elaboration* and *modernization* of the language which involved expanding the vocabulary and other aspects necessary to meet the communicative needs of the society.

As Wiley (1996: 118–119) notes, Haugen was mainly interested in the planning of standard language varieties and viewed "nonstandard" variation within languages as problematic. Haugen's prescriptive approach to language planning was based on criteria of *efficiency*, *adequacy* and *acceptability*, an approach that was criticized by other scholars, such as Jernudd and Das Gupta (1971), precisely because such criteria presupposed an ill-defined universal linguistic standard linked to literary traditions. Since many of the languages in newly independent nations in the "developing world" had no such traditions, these criteria had little practical value.

Language planning in the early years of the field was often aligned with broader agendas of nation-building in the newly independent states of Africa and Asia. It was believed by Western state planners that modernization and social development required linguistic unification and modernization, reflecting the "self-evident" formula of one nation=one language as an essential ingredient for developing national identity and political unification among diverse groups and tribes. Operating with the goals of modernization and political unification in mind, sociolinguists hired as experts to analyze the language situations in these new states proposed "remedies" which often included modernization of non-Western languages, which involved developing grammars, writing systems, and dictionaries for indigenous languages, and proposing schemes to assign different societal functions to the former colonial languages (principally English, French, Dutch, or Italian) and indigenous languages. This process, labeled *status planning* in the LPP literature, often promoted so-called *diglossia*, in which one language (usually the former colonial language) was used for formal and specialized domains (including secondary and post-secondary education for the upper social classes and political elites), while the indigenous language (with far greater numbers of speakers) was used in less formal contexts in the home and community, and as the medium of instruction in primary education. The "logic" behind this scheme reflected the belief that the use of a language of wider communication (LWC), such as English or French, would benefit the socioeconomic development of these new states; this view entailed many hidden, or seemingly commonsense, beliefs on the part of Western-trained linguists and planners, including the idea that linguistic diversity presented obstacles for national development, while linguistic homogeneity was associated with modernization and Westernization. This view also entailed the ideology that only "developed" languages were suitable to fulfill the role of a "national" language, since they were written and standardized and, therefore, were also adaptable to the demands of technological and social advancement. Regardless of the intentions of these language planners, the result of their approach to language planning in these contexts was to facilitate the continued dominance (if not domination) of European colonial languages in high status domains of education, economy, and technology (see Fishman 1968a, 1968b).[2]

Following a content analysis of the scholarly literature in this early period of language policy and planning (see esp. Fishman, Ferguson, and Das Gupta 1968; Rubin and Jernudd 1971; Haugen 1966) as well as more recent critical discussions by Tollefson (1991) and Pennycook (1994), Ricento (2000a: 199–200) found the following commonalities:

(1) Goals of language planning were often associated with a desire for unification (of a region, a nation, a religious group, a political group, or other kinds of groups), a desire for modernization, a desire for communicative efficiency, or a desire for democratization (Rubin 1971: 307–310).
(2) Language was characterized as a resource with value, and as such, was subject to planning (Jernudd and Das Gupta 1971: 211).
(3) Status and corpus planning (which focuses on elements of the language, such as modernization, renovation, graphization, etc.; see Hornberger 2006: 28–33 for details) were viewed as more or less separate activities and ideologically neutral (although not without complications).
(4) Languages were abstracted from their sociohistorical and ecological contexts (ahistoricity and synchrony).

While language planning in developing and newly independent nations was a focus of the scholarly literature in this early period, research on the goals and effects of language policies in other parts of the world was also being conducted. One of the most influential scholars in the history of language policies was the German scholar Heinz Kloss whose publications on language policy span nearly six decades, beginning in 1929 and ending posthumously in 1987 (Wiley 2002: 83). Kloss made many trips to North America and during these visits he conducted research on the status of immigrant languages in the United States, culminating in the classic work, *The American Bilingual Tradition* (1977/1998). Kloss' major contribution to the literature was his typology of linguistic and policy factors which help explain why some language policies fail, while others succeed. In order to determine what type of planning would be most efficacious to achieve language maintenance (if that were the goal of a language group), Kloss proposed that a number of attitudinal, usage, linguistic, and legal factors within a society had to be evaluated. An important consideration was the degree to which the state created policies that either (1) promoted, (2) accommodated, (3) tolerated, or (4) suppressed a language. In examining the situation in the U.S., Kloss argued that the languages of immigrant minorities were generally tolerated, that is, speakers of these languages were free to maintain them if they so desired. He further notes that linguistic assimilation was voluntary because immigrants sought to integrate into the economic and social life of the United States "*in spite* of nationality laws which were relatively *favorable* to them" (1977: 283; emphasis in original). Kloss, however, does cite an exception to this general rule of accommodation of language minorities, namely the suppression of German – and German Americans – during the World War I era (see Wiley 1998 for discussion).

Critics of this analysis (e.g., Wiley 1996: 119–121) argue that Kloss tended to overlook systematic institutional racism which influenced attitudes and policies (official and unofficial) that effectively marginalized speakers of many minority languages, often stigmatized use of minority languages in educational and civic settings, and denied access to the mainstream English curriculum through de facto segregation policies which led to, e.g., "Mexican schools" in many parts of the Southwest. In fact, it was the recognition that poorly funded schools segregated by language (Spanish) and ethnicity (Mexican-American) produced high percentages of students who "dropped out", i.e., failed to graduate high school, that led to the first large scale attempt at language planning in education, culminating at the federal level with passage of the Bilingual Education Act (BEA) in 1968. The point here is that assimilation to English and, by implication, the political economy of the United States was *not* available to everyone and that acquisition of English did not ensure equal access to upward mobility. From the perspective of language policy, it is necessary to consider the mode of incorporation of various language minority groups as well as how they were treated by the dominant majority in determining their linguistic standing. Many scholars have argued, for example, that it is important to distinguish between indigenous and immigrant language minority groups in evaluating how policies were formulated (or practiced) and for what purpose. In the U.S., further distinctions between source countries of immigrants have also correlated with their relative success in structural social assimilation, with European-origin immigrants, generally, having greater success than immigrants from many parts of Central and South America, Africa, and Asia (Leeman 2004). A broad distinction has also been made between the experiences of voluntary immigrant groups to the U.S. compared to groups that were incorporated through conquest, involuntary servitude, annexation, or treaties, e.g., Mexicans, African Americans, Puerto Ricans, Hawaiians, and Native Americans. Thus, taxonomies of language policies that do not differentiate among language groups according to how they were incorporated and treated by the dominant culture provide, at best, incomplete explanations for the sociolinguistic situation, both historically and in the current day.

3.2 The failure of modernization

If the first phase of research in LPP could be characterized by the overriding belief that the solution to language "problems" in developing countries lay in planning activities designed to promote access to Western technology and, thereby, unification, modernization and democratization, the second phase was characterized by a growing awareness of the negative effects – and inherent limitations – of planning theory and models. Critical scholars began to investigate the ways in which sociolinguistic constructs such as diglossia, bilingualism, and multilingualism were conceptually complex and ideologically laden and could not be easily fit into existing descriptive taxonomies (Ricento 2000a: 202). Scholars in LPP and critical linguistics raised questions about the degree to which the operating assumptions about the role of language in societal development, unification, and modernization were connected to ideologies and epistemologies that perpetuated social hierarchies and inequalities, both in "developing" and "developed" countries. For example, the recommendation of European languages as "neutral media" to aid in national development tended to favor the economic interests of the former imperial countries at the expense of national development. The choice of particular indigenous languages or language varieties for use in education and civic life from among multiple possibilities had the effect of limiting the utility and, hence, influence of many languages and their speakers in national (re)construction.

In a retrospective analysis of LPP taxonomies developed by sociolinguists/ LPP experts in the 1950s and 1960s, Schiffman (1996: 26) argued that such taxonomies failed to capture the sociolinguistic "realities" of different polities, in part, because "the data were not comparable, the theoretical frameworks that various people had worked in were not congruent, and […] there were almost as many variables to factor in as there were polities and policies." Schiffman (1996: 34) also argued that taxonomies fail to distinguish whether a community is multilingual *as a result* of language policy or *despite* it. That is, what is the relation (if any) between extant policy configurations described by scholars, on the one hand, and the practices of people living in multilingual communities, on the other hand? Based on analysis of language policies and language practices in the U.S., France, and India, Schiffman (1996: 5) found that language policy is ultimately grounded in *linguistic culture*, which he defines as "the set of behaviors, assumptions, cultural forms, prejudices, folk belief systems, attitudes, stereotypes, ways of thinking about language, and religio-historical circumstances associated with a particular language".

The failures of language policies in the developing countries of Africa and Asia were not only the result of inadequate descriptive models of complex sociolinguistic situations, or inappropriate technical solutions to problems posed by "less developed" languages in national development. Rather, during this second phase of LPP, a number of scholars focused on the social, economic, and political effects of language contact (e.g., Hymes 1996/1975; Wolfson and Manes 1985; Tollefson 1986, 1991; Luke, McHoul, and Mey 1990, among many others). For example, the papers in Wolfson and Manes (1985: ix) considered how "language use reflects and indeed influences social, economic or political inequality". Whereas in earlier approaches to language policy there was a focus on *languages* as entities with defined societal distributions and functions, critical scholars in this second phase of research tended to focus on the status and relations of *speech communities* in defined contexts. In this second approach to language policy analysis, the connections between community/societal attitudes and language policies were analyzed to explain why language x had a particular status – High or Low – and the consequences of this status for individuals and communities. Thus, language status was usually found to correlate with the social and economic status of its speakers, and not just with the numbers of speakers or the suitability of a language for modernization (Ricento 2000a: 202). As a consequence, a policy favoring stable diglossia as a means of furthering national development and modernization was viewed by critical scholars as an instrument for perpetuating socioeconomic asymmetries based on education, access to which was socially controlled by dominant groups within a country, and influenced by regional and global economic interests. Thus, it was argued, language policies helped perpetuate the legacies of colonialism through a segregated educational system, one for the political elites in the colonial language, another for the rest of the population in local or regional indigenous languages (see also Migge and Léglise, this vol.).

3.3   Linguistic rights and language ecology

A number of themes and issues have emerged during the latest phase of language policy research. These include
(1) the reemergence of national ethnic identities in the former Soviet Union,
(2) the repatriation of former colonies, such as Hong Kong,
(3) massive population migrations (voluntary and involuntary) in Africa, Asia, and the Americas, and
(4) the forging of new regional coalitions such as the European Union.

These issues, along with continuing concerns about the accelerating decline of many "small" languages throughout the world, have led to some innovative research and theorizing in the scholarly literature. A paradigm for addressing these issues has been proposed by Phillipson and Skutnabb-Kangas (1996: 429): "The ecology-of-language paradigm involves building on linguistic diversity worldwide, promoting multilingualism and foreign language learning, and granting linguistic human rights to speakers of all languages". This paradigm has benefited from contributions from a variety of disciplines, including political theory (e.g., Kymlicka and Patten 2003; Schmidt 2000), law (e.g., de Varennes 1996), sociology (e.g., May 2001), economics (e.g., Grin 1996), history (e.g., Wiley 2006), critical theory (e.g., Tollefson 2006), and postmodernism (e.g., Pennycook 2006), among other specialties and subspecialties in linguistics and applied linguistics (see Ricento 2006). Much of the cutting edge research deals with the limitations of language planning (e.g., Moore 1996; Schiffman 1996; Ricento and Burnaby 1998; Fettes 1998; Pennycook 2000a, 2000b; Ricento 2005a), although a number of scholars have described planning successes as well (e.g., Freeman 1996; Hornberger 1998; McCarty and Zepeda 1998; McCarty 2002). Another feature of current approaches to research in LPP is that there is a focus on the role of individuals and communities in the reception of, attitudes towards, and actions in response to official or unofficial language policies and regimes (e.g., Ricento and Wiley 2002; Canagarajah 1999). Relations between language(s) and identity(ies) (e.g., Norton 2000; Wodak et al. 1999) and the pervasive role of ideologies in language policies (e.g., van Dijk 1998; Blommaert and Verschueren 1998; Santa Ana 2002; Ricento 2000b, 2003) have received a great deal of attention in the past decade. There have also been articles which have cautioned against the (mis)application of popular metaphors in LPP research: Pennycook (2004) outlines some of the unintended consequences of biomorphic metaphors, such as language ecology, while Ricento (2005a), discussed earlier in this chapter, argues that the language-as-resource metaphor can de-link languages from speakers and communities to promote particular, and narrow, state interests.

In comparing the various phases of research, we note that in earlier phases scholars focused on possible language policy goals and ways of implementing them (planning), whereas more recently scholars have focused on the variety of day-to-day practices and techniques (governmentality) that effectuate policies (stated or unstated) and the ideologies (often widely accepted as commonsense, and hence, non-ideological) which inform particular social outlooks on a range of issues involving language, such as legitimacy claims for a particular language/language variety, the "superiority" of a particular language/language variety, the need for one national language/language variety, and so on. The goal in this research very often is to unpack the commonly held assumptions (ideologies) which are uncontroversial in public (and official) discourse, but whose persistence and ubiquity renders change in language policies, for example in promoting access to education in minority languages, problematic, if not impossible.

4. Controversies

As suggested by the previous comments, whether language(s) can be planned and, if they can be planned, whether such planning is able to reflect the desires and aspirations of all language groups in a society, are questions that have been posed by a number of researchers. The historical-structural approach, an influential framework for research in LPP over the past 30 years, has been used to investigate how language often symbolizes some aspect of a struggle over political power and economic resources. According to Tollefson (1991: 32), within this framework "the major goal of policy research is to examine the historical basis of policies and to make explicit the mechanisms by which policy decisions serve or undermine particular political and economic interests". This approach rejects the assumption prevalent in other models in the social sciences, including rational choice, that "the rational calculus of individuals is the proper focus of research, and instead seeks the […] social, political, and economic factors that constrain or impel changes in language structure and language use" (Tollefson 1991: 31). Ricento and Hornberger (1996: 407) summarize the major assumptions which inform the historical-structural approach in LPP research:
(1) that all language plans and policies represent and reflect the sociopolitical and economic interests of "majoritarian" or dominant interests;
(2) that these interests are often implicit and are enmeshed in hegemonic ideologies that serve to maintain the socioeconomic interests of ruling elites;
(3) that such ideologies are reflected at all levels of society and in all institutions, whether government agencies, planning bodies, legislative or judicial bodies, school boards, or other entities;
(4) that individuals are not free to choose the language(s) that they will be educated in or be able to use in specified domains, as all choices are constrained by systems that reinforce and reproduce the existing social order, which of course favor particular languages in particular contexts for particular sociopolitical ends favored by interested parties, usually dominant elites (or counter elites).

Research within the historical-structural framework has relied on a variety of empirical techniques in exploring the operation of power through language policies and practices in a range of social domains. Phillipson (1992), Tollefson (1991, 2002), Moore (1996), Wiley and Lukes (1996), Cummins (2000), Canagarajah (2000), and Langman (2002) have investigated the role of ideologies in the promotion and acceptance of language policies in education in various countries around the world. Blommaert and Verschueren (1998), Pennycook (1998), Wodak et al. (1999), van Dijk (2000), Santa Ana (2002), and Ricento (2003, 2005a) combine historical and discourse analytic methods in studying the complex relations between language policies, public discourse, and national ideologies and identities. Other scholars have focused on political processes, and ideologies of race and class in analyzing language policies (e.g., Wiley 1999; Sonntag 2000; Bonfiglio 2002; Brutt-Griffler 2002; de Klerk 2002; Donahue 2002; Leeman 2004; and Ramanathan 2005).

While historical-structural approaches in LPP research have tended to focus on language policies as instruments of social control imposed by dominant powers at the macro-social level, postmodern theories of power are concerned with *language governmentality*. Developed by Foucault in his later work (e.g., Foucault 1991), governmentality "focuses on how power operates at the micro-level of diverse practices, rather than in the macro-regulations of the state" (Pennycook 2006: 64). Pennycook (2006: 65) explains that language governmentality is best understood in terms of "how decisions about languages and language forms across a diverse range of institutions (law, education, medicine, printing) and through a diverse range of instruments (books, regulations, exams, articles, corrections) regulate the language use, thought, and action of different people, groups, and organizations". A consequence of a governmentality approach is the questioning of grand narratives which offer totalizing views of the role and effects of languages, such as English, in killing other languages and in homogenizing world culture, and the related claim that languages need protection through regimes of language rights. Such totalizing views, labeled "preservationist" and "romanticist", often assume an ineluctable connection between language and ethnicity (Pennycook 2006). Pennycook (2006: 68–69) argues that while linguistic imperialism and language-rights discourses "operate from different epistemological and political assumptions […] both operate from within theories of economy, the state, humanity, and politics that have their origins in the grand modernist project". In this spirit, Blommaert (2006: 249) argues that language policy should be seen as a *niched* activity in which, for example, the role of certain actors (such as the state) is limited to specific domains, activities, and relationships, not general ones. The work of these and other scholars does not seek to downplay the negative effects of linguistic imperialism nor diminish the possible benefits of a language-rights approach; rather, it seeks to problematize causal relations between actors, groups, and language policies which may be empirically unsubstantiated and complicit with the very ideologies and constructs they wish to defeat.

To some extent, controversies about the Linguistic Human Rights (LHR) approach in LPP center on distinctions often made by scholars between the *expressive* and *instrumental* functions associated with language. Some (e.g., Rubio-Marín 2003: 56) have claimed that only the expressive language claims which "aim at ensuring a person's capacity to enjoy a secure linguistic environment in her/his mother tongue and a linguistic group's fair chance of cultural self-reproduction", are language rights in a strict sense, and could be construed as LHRs. The question of whether a language minority community is more interested in maintaining their language or getting jobs is a false one, according to

Skutnabb-Kangas (2006: 274), who points out that "most groups are interested in both types of rights, expressive and instrumental, and often one is a prerequisite for the other, with both being alternately causal and dependent variables".

The notion that all language groups in a society have equal rights claims has been challenged by political theorists (e.g., Kymlicka and Patten 2003) and refined by Stephen May (2001), who argues that only national minorities (as opposed to immigrant minorities) can make rights claims for formal inclusion of their languages and cultures in the civic realm. May (2006: 266) further stipulates that where there are sufficient numbers of other-language speakers, regardless of their immigrant status, they should be given the opportunity to use that language as part of their individual rights as citizens; however, he cautions that "extending greater ethnolinguistic *democracy* to minority-language groups, via LHR, does not thus amount to an argument for ethnolinguistic *equality* for all such groups".

5. Evaluation in language policy and planning

Perhaps the most under-researched and under-theorized aspect of the field is the evaluation of language planning, from the development of language policies to their implementation and the evaluation of their effectiveness (although see Grin 2003). There are undoubtedly many factors to account for this gap: Sociolinguists have been interested in describing phenomena of language contact, change, and use in defined contexts, while scholars from the policy sciences tend to have limited knowledge about or interest in incorporating the specialized knowledge of sociolinguists and applied linguistics in analyzing the political and economic variables associated with particular language policies or regimes. There have been some case studies on the effects of language policies in Canada (see, e.g., various articles in Edwards 1998) and on aspects of U.S. language policies, especially on federal policies dealing with the education of language minorities (e.g., Cazden and Snow 1990; Fernández 1987; Ricento 1998a, 1998b), among many other studies and countries that could be cited. However, as Grin (2003: 8) points out, "a significant proportion of actual language planning seems to go on without much of a concerted plan". While social policy analysts typically provide an assessment of the likely costs and benefits of Plan A vs. Plan B (or C or D) for all sorts of social policy initiatives, their analytic tools are largely unknown and unused by academics trained in the language sciences. François Grin, an economist by training, is one of the few scholars in LPP who has attempted to build bridges between the various academic disciplines whose collective expertise is required in developing alternative policies and plans to achieve language policy goals (which are often rather general statements) ratified by legislative or other governmental bodies. His book on *Language Policy*

Evaluation and the European Charter for Regional or Minority Languages (2003) lays out a set of procedures for assessing the appropriateness of particular policies and how they might be implemented, using the European Charter for Regional or Minority Languages as a case study (although he argues that the approach taken can be used in other contexts as well).

While this approach may be appropriate in situations in which there is widespread agreement on the general goals of language policy, as for example in South Africa or the European Charter for Regional or Minority Languages, it is often the case that policies represent factional interests (where "faction" can also include ruling governments/political parties) and their implementation and evaluation will reflect the interests and values of those factions. Beyond the difficult problem of achieving political consensus on language policy goals and objectives, there is the matter of measuring the relative success or failure of particular policies, or policy approaches. This is especially true when language policies are designed to effect social change in particular domains and/or for particular groups. For example, the underlying rationale and political motivation for the Bilingual Education Act (1968) in the U.S. was to improve the educational achievement and socioeconomic status of Spanish-speaking school children – the majority of whom were Mexican-American – in the Southwest. The goal was *not* to promote linguistic diversity or enhance the status of Spanish or any other language in the U.S. The problem in evaluating such a policy, however, is that it is very difficult to determine links between poverty and medium of instruction in public schools (see also Wiley, this vol.). Joan Rubin (1986: 109–110) cites the work of city planners Rittel and Weber who divide planning problems into two types: "tame" problems and "wicked" problems. The problems faced by social scientists are generally of the wicked variety which "have no stopping rule [...] there are no ends to the causal chains that link interacting open systems [...] solutions to wicked problems are not true or false, but good or bad [...] depending on who does the judging". Rubin argues that language problems are somewhat wicked and somewhat tame. Gathering data on the number of speakers of language x or y is an example of a (relatively) tame problem. Establishing clear and measurable causal links between poverty and its possible causes, such as general economic issues, deficiencies in cognitive and academic skills, patterns of migration, personal problems, differences in learning styles, and so on is an example of a wicked problem. In these circumstances, evaluation of the effects of a particular language policy designed to effect social change, even in a defined context such as the education sector, tends to become highly politicized, and whether the outcome is judged to be "good" or "bad" will depend on who is doing the judging and whose interest(s) are being represented. Also, expectations as to what constitutes success will influence the evaluation. For example, in the case of bilingual education in the U.S., supporters tend to evaluate success not just by how quickly a student acquires *English*, but also by the fact that students are developing competence in *two* languages (which requires more time), while enhancing their cognitive flexibility (Cummins 2001). Opponents, who may also be uninterested in the general goal of maintaining linguistic diversity in the U.S., tend to measure the success of bilingual education *only* in terms of how quickly (and how perfectly) English language learners acquire standard English. Given these competing goals and expected outcomes, it is not surprising that bilingual education remains a politically charged issue in the U.S., the effects of which cannot be judged outside of the normative discourses of opposing ideological frameworks.

6. Conclusions

In the early days of the field, the models and frameworks were more or less working documents, reflecting a problem-solving approach to aid states and NGOs in national development. The primary focus of work was determining the allocation of functions of languages/literacies within a society or speech community (status planning), and cultivating or enhancing the form(s) or structure of languages/literacies in developing countries (corpus planning). A third component (acquisition planning) was introduced by Cooper (1989), and concerns users of language (see Hornberger 2006: 28–33). As Hornberger (2006: 26) notes, "the field was rather easily identifiable in its early days because of a select series of well-defined conferences, projects, and publications". Linguists and political scientists were truly "applying" their discipline-based skills in solving social problems, and there was optimism about the possibilities for success. As Joshua Fishman (1968c: 492) put it:

> The language problems of the ethnically fragmented 'new nation' reflect its relatively greater emphasis on political integration and on the efficient *nationism* on which it initially depends. Language selection is a relatively short-lived problem since the linguistic tie to technological and political modernity is usually unambiguous. Problems of language development, codification, and acceptance are also minimal as long as these processes are seen as emanating justifiably and primarily from the 'metropolitan country […]'. Although some attention may be given to the pedagogic demands of initial literacy (or transitional literacy) for *young* people […] the lion's share of literacy effort and resources is placed at the disposal of spreading the adopted Western tongue of current political and […] sociocultural integration. [italics in original]

Forty years later, the optimism expressed by Fishman and others seems naïve, at best. But it should be recalled that the idea of jump-starting the process of modernization in newly independent nations was promoted by liberals, such as Walter Rostow (1963), in the West, and the infusion of Western technological know-how (including the expertise of linguists) and financing were viewed (by liberals) as both necessary and moral. Yet, as Blaut (2000) and others have argued, the colonizer's model of the world, which assumes Europe or the West as the center from which all human inventions of value are diffused to a "less-developed/underdeveloped" periphery, persists in the post-colonial/neo-colonial era. As I have argued earlier in this chapter, the effects of Western thinking about language (as a rule-governed, standardized/prescriptive written system) and the state (which requires linguistic and cultural homogeneity in order to "progress" economically and politically) influenced the types of models and frameworks language planners developed and promoted during this early period. Multilingualism, which was/is the norm in most African nations, was viewed at best as something that could be tolerated on the road to the monoglot ideology that comported with Western views of modernity.

The role of language in economic development and the promotion of human rights in many regions of the world continues to be complex and difficult to predict, measure, or control. For example, in South Africa, the constitution names eleven official languages, nine of which are indigenous African languages. Yet the sociolinguistic reality of South Africa is such that English continues to enjoy a higher status and plays a more dominant role in society than other languages, despite having relatively fewer native speakers than most indigenous African languages. As de Klerk (2002: 40) notes: "The linguistic human rights enshrined in the South African constitution were not an end goal in a clear struggle for language rights, or minority rights. What was created was a common ground from which to continue the language struggles in the country. Implementation of multilingualism has been slow and on a small scale". One of the key stumbling blocks to full implementation of a multilingual policy is that mother-tongue medium education is stigmatized because it was promoted by the former right-wing Apartheid regime as a mechanism for social control; besides this ideological problem are those that come with large-scale language planning, such as the lack of trained teachers, teaching materials, and other resources. But the problems inherent in undertaking large-scale language planning for the purpose of promoting social change occur even in Europe, where efforts to promote multilingualism among the member states of the European Union (EU) have been thwarted by member states unwilling to cede the prerogatives enjoyed by their languages in the current configuration in which English enjoys a privileged – if not dominant – position. As Robert Phillipson (2003: 191–192) observes:

> Whether the EU in its present form – with intensive interaction between Eurocrats, representatives of member states, and lobbies – is equipped to play an influential role in language policy is an open question, but it is extremely unlikely. The fact that the EU's achievements are confined to producing every few years a resolution on multilingualism that merely has advisory status, and funding for various schemes for international liaison and student mobility, shows that language policy has a low priority, and has been accorded only modest funding. It has evidently been too politically

sensitive for more serious engagement at the supranational level. EU funding for research in the area, and the occasional report, has been minimal, and mostly concerned with regional minority languages. The few relevant activities fit into the pattern of nation-states competing for power and influence within the EU, burdened by the dead weight of linguistic nationalism and the different conceptual universes that have evolved over centuries.

To put these observations in some sort of perspective, we can say that it is simply not possible to find neat correspondences between particular "liberal" language policies or policy frameworks (such as Linguistic Human Rights, mother-tongue medium education, or language ecology) and broader social agendas or goals (such as socioeconomic/sociopolitical equality, universal human rights, or preservation/promotion of linguistic diversity). The history of LPP shows us that even liberal and well-intentioned attempts to promote language x or y for purposes of societal development (which invariably has meant development of Western models of property, finance, and "welfare", among other things) end up reproducing historical patterns which privilege the interests of the former colonial nations and their languages. Some of the most promising work of relevance for LPP has been done by critical scholars seeking to develop alternative research paradigms and conceptual frameworks. The articles in a special issue of the *Journal of Language, Identity, and Education* (2002 (4)) explore the many ways that local knowledge on language and education can move our thinking forward by considering alternative ways of understanding, for example, literacy and language competence in local and transnational communities. Another example of innovation in conceptualizations of language which can move us beyond the colonizer's model of the world is Makoni and Pennycook (2005). This work is summarized by Pennycook (2006: 69), who argues that "a postmodern understanding of language policy and planning [...] urges us to rethink, to disinvent, and to reconstruct the ways we think about language policy and planning". In this approach, "not only do the notions of language and languages become highly suspect, but so do many related concepts that are premised on a notion of discrete languages, such as language rights, mother tongues, multilingualism, or code-switching". Pennycook claims that while arguments in support of mother-tongue education, multilingualism as the global norm, and language rights are preferable to blinkered views that take monolingualism as the norm, they none the less remain caught within the same paradigm which underlies all mainstream linguistic thought.

Another area of research which will continue to influence theory and practice in LPP is language and identity. The notions that one's identity is inextricably linked to his or her language, and that shifting to a second or third language always entails the loss of a person's cultural identity have been widely disputed in the literature in recent years (May 2001; Ricento 2005b). Identities are complex, contingent, and not necessarily tied to a particular language or language variety (Rampton 1995). This research is particularly relevant for research and theorizing in LPP since it is often the case that language can be invoked as a marker of ethnicity for purposes of asserting or contesting political power, as happened in the republics of the former Yugoslavia (Tollefson 2002). Ricento (2005b: 896) describes the work of Glynn Williams (1992) who argues that

> [...] in American sociology, ethnicity became a dichotomized construct of the normative/standard group – a unitary citizenry speaking a common language (us) – and non-normative/nonstandard groups – including those speaking other languages – (them). This naturalizing of a sociological construct (ethnicity) informs the widely held popular view promoted by Western scholarship that "reasonable" (modern) people should naturally become part of the culture of the state (or the transnational world) and speak "its" language, whereas "irrational" (traditional) people will tend to cling to their "ethnic language and culture".

While such a view may strike many readers as commonsense and reasonable, it is just this sort of implicit ideology which has influenced – and continues to influence – language practices which favor the continued dominance of national languages and supranational languages throughout the world, despite the adoption of policies, laws, covenants, and regulations whose aim is to promote the acquisition, use, and retention of minority languages.

Notes

1. The degree to which members of ethnolinguistic minority groups choose to assimilate or are coerced (overtly or covertly) to assimilate into the dominant language/culture is difficult to determine, and the degree to which assimilation is a net "plus" or "minus" cannot be based on zero-sum assumptions in which acquisition of a new language and culture is equated with loss of the native language/culture. Indeed, recent research in second language acquisition suggests that identities (linguistic and cultural) in multilingual contexts are complex, dynamic, and variable (Ricento 2005b: 897–898), and that assimilation is a transformative process with benefits, as well as costs.
2. Even in those cases in which indigenous languages were declared national languages, the former imperial language usually retained its status as the language of post secondary education and as necessary for advanced academic training in universities in Europe and North America. This happened, for example, when Swahili was declared the national language alongside the former imperial language, English, in Tanzania (formerly Tanganyikan) (Blommaert 2006).

References

Blaut, James
    2000   *Eight Eurocentric Historians.* New York: Guilford Press.
Blommaert, Jan
    2005   *Discourse: A Critical Introduction.* Cambridge: Cambridge University Press.
Blommaert, Jan
    2006   Language policy and national identity. In: Thomas Ricento (ed.), *An Introduction to Language Policy: Theory and Method,* 238–254. Oxford: Blackwell.
Blommaert, Jan (ed.)
    1999   *Language Ideological Debates.* Berlin: Mouton de Gruyter.
Blommaert, Jan and Jef Verschueren
    1998   *Debating Diversity: Analysing the Discourse of Tolerance.* London: Routledge.
Bonfiglio, Thomas
    2002   *Race and the Rise of Standard American.* Berlin: Mouton de Gruyter.
Brutt-Griffler, Janina
    2002   Class, ethnicity, and language rights: An analysis of British colonial policy in Lesotho and Sri Lanka and some implications for language policy. *Journal of Language, Identity, and Education* 1(3): 207–234.
Canagarajah, A. Suresh
    1999   *Resisting English Imperialism in English Teaching.* Oxford: Oxford University Press.
Canagarajah, A. Suresh
    2000   Negotiating ideologies through English: Strategies from the periphery. In: Thomas Ricento (ed.), *Ideologies, Politics and Language Policies: Focus on English,* 121–132. Amsterdam: John Benjamins.
Cazden, Courtney and Catherine E. Snow (eds.)
    1990   English plus: Issues in bilingual education. *The Annals of the American Academy of Political and Social Science* (March). Newbury Park, CA: Sage.
Cebollero, Pedro A.
    1945   *A School Language Policy for Puerto Rico.* San Juan de Puerto Rico: Impr. Baldrich.
Cooper, Robert
    1989   *Language Planning and Social Change.* Cambridge: Cambridge University Press.
Crystal, David
    1999   The death of language. *Prospect* (November): 56–59.
Cummins, Jim
    2000   *Language, Power, and Pedagogy: Bilingual Children in the Crossfire.* Clevedon: Multilingual Matters.
Cummins, Jim
    2001   *Negotiating Identities: Education for Empowerment in a Diverse Society.* Los Angeles: California Association for Bilingual Education.

De Klerk, Gerda
    2002   Mother-tongue education in South Africa: The weight of history. *International Journal of the Sociology of Language* 154: 29–46.

De Varennes, Fernand
    1996   *Language, Minorities and Human Rights.* The Hague: Kluwer Law International.

Dedaić, Mirjana and Daniel Nelson (eds.)
    2003   *At War with Words.* Berlin: Mouton de Gruyter.

Donahue, Thomas
    2002   Language planning and the perils of ideological solipsism. In: James Tollefson (ed.), *Language Policies in Education: Critical Issues*, 127–162. Mahwah, NJ: Lawrence Erlbaum.

Edwards, John (ed.)
    1998   *Language in Canada.* Cambridge: Cambridge University Press.

Faingold, Eduardo
    2004   Language rights and language justice in the constitutions of the world. *Language Problems & Language Planning* 28(1): 11–24.

Fernández, Ricardo
    1987   Legislation, regulation, and litigation: The origins and evolution of public policy on bilingual education in the United States. In: Winston A. Van Horne (ed.), *Ethnicity and Language,* Vol. VI, 90–123. (Ethnicity and Public Policy Series.) Milwaukee, WI: The University of Wisconsin System.

Fettes, Mark
    1998   Life on the edge: Canada's Aboriginal languages under official bilingualism. In: Thomas Ricento and Barbara Burnaby (eds.), *Language and Politics in the United States and Canada: Myths and Realities,* 117–149. Mahwah, NJ: Lawrence Erlbaum.

Fishman, Joshua
    1968a   Sociolinguistics and the language problems of the developing countries. In: Joshua Fishman, Charles Ferguson and Jyotirindra das Gupta (eds.), *Language Problems of Developing Nations*, 3–16. New York: John Wiley.

Fishman, Joshua
    1968b   Some contrasts between linguistically homogeneous and linguistically heterogeneous polities. In: Joshua Fishman, Charles Ferguson, and Jyotirindra das Gupta (eds.), *Language Problems of Developing Nations*, 53–68. New York: John Wiley.

Fishman, Joshua
    1968c   Language problems and types of political and sociocultural integration: A conceptual postscript. In: Joshua Fishman, Charles Ferguson, and Jyotirindra das Gupta (eds.), *Language Problems of Developing Nations*, 491–498. New York: John Wiley.

Fishman, Joshua, Charles A. Ferguson and Jyotirindra Das Gupta (eds.)
    1968   *Language Problems of Developing Nations.* New York: John Wiley.

Foucault, Michel
    1991   Governmentality. In: Graham Burchell, Colin Gordon and Peter Miller (eds.), *The Foucault Effect: Studies in Governmentality,* 87–104. Chicago: University of Chicago Press.

Freeman, Rebecca D.
　1996　　Dual-language planning at Oyster Bilingual School: "It's much more than language". *TESOL Quarterly* 30: 557–582.
Gonzalez, Norma
　2003　　Language ideologies. In: Russell Campbell and Donna Christian (eds.), *Directions in Research: Intergenerational Transmission of Heritage Languages. Heritage Language Journal* 1(1). (http://www.international.ucla.edu/lrc/hlj/article.asp?parentid=3893). Retrieved October 1, 2004.
Grin, François (ed.)
　1996　　Economic approaches to language and language planning (Special issue). *International Journal of the Sociology of Language* 121.
Grin, François
　2003　　*Language Policy Evaluation and the European Charter for Regional or Minority Languages*. London: Palgrave Macmillan.
Grin, François
　2006　　Economic considerations in language policy. In: Thomas Ricento (ed.), *An Introduction to Language Policy: Theory and Method*, 77–94. Oxford: Blackwell.
Haugen, Einar
　1966　　*Language Conflict and Language Planning: The Case of Modern Norwegian*. Cambridge, MA: Harvard University Press.
Hopper, Paul
　1998　　Emergent grammar. In: Michael Tomasello (ed.), *The New Psychology of Language*, 155–175. Mahwah, NJ: Lawrence Erlbaum.
Hornberger, Nancy
　1998　　Language policy, language education, language rights: Indigenous, immigrant, and international perspectives. *Language in Society* 27: 439–458.
Hornberger, Nancy
　2006　　Frameworks and models in language policy and planning. In: Thomas Ricento (ed.), *An Introduction to Language Policy: Theory and Method*, 24–41. Oxford: Blackwell.
Hymes, Dell
1996 [1975] Report from an underdeveloped country: Toward linguistic competence in the United States. In Dell Hymes (ed.), *Ethnography, Linguistics, Narrative Inequality: Toward an Understanding of Voice*, 63–105. London: Taylor and Francis.
Jernudd, Björn and Jyotirindra Das Gupta
　1971　　Towards a theory of language planning. In: Joan Rubin and Björn Jernudd (eds.), *Can Language Be Planned? Sociolinguistic Theory and Practice for Developing Nations*, 195–215. Hawaii: The University Press of Hawaii.
Kaplan, Robert and Baldauf, Richard
　1997　　*Language Planning from Practice to Theory*. Clevedon: Multilingual Matters.
Kloss, Heinz
1977/1998　*The American Bilingual Tradition*. Washington, DC and McHenry, IL: Center for Applied Linguistics and Delta Systems [Original published in 1977].

Kymlicka, Will and Alan Patten
    2003   *Language Rights and Political Theory.* Oxford: Oxford University Press.
Langman, Juliet
    2002   Mother-tongue education versus bilingual education: Shifting ideologies and policies in the Republic of Slovakia. *International Journal of the Sociology of Language* 154: 47–64.
Leeman, Jennifer
    2004   Racializing language: A history of linguistic ideologies in the US census. *Journal of Language and Politics* 3(3): 507–534.
Lo Bianco, Joseph
    2001   Officializing language: A discourse study of language politics in the United States. Unpublished Ph.D. thesis, Australian National University.
Lo Bianco, Joseph
    2004   Language planning as applied linguistics. In: Alan Davies and Catherine Elder (eds.), *The Handbook of Applied Linguistics,* 738–762. Oxford: Blackwell.
Luke, Allan, Alec McHoul and Jacob Mey
    1990   On the limits of language planning: Class, state and power. In: Richard Baldauf and Allan Luke (eds.), *Language Planning and Education in Australasia and the South Pacific,* 25–44. Clevedon: Multilingual Matters.
Makoni, Sinfree and Alastair Pennycook
    2005   Disinventing and (re)constituting languages. *Critical Inquiry in Language Studies* 2(3): 137–156.
May, Stephen
    2001   *Language and Minority Rights: Ethnicity, Nationalism and the Politics of Language.* Edinburgh Gate: Pearson Education.
May, Stephen
    2006   Language policy and minority rights. In: Thomas Ricento (ed.), *An Introduction to Language Policy: Theory and Method,* 255–272. Oxford: Blackwell.
McCarty, Teresa
    2002   *A Place to be Navajo: Rough Rock and the Struggle for Self-Determination in Indigenous Schooling.* Mahwah, NJ: Lawrence Erlbaum.
McCarty, Teresa and Ofelia Zepeda (eds.)
    1998   Indigenous language use and change in the Americas. *International Journal of the Sociology of Language* 132.
Moore, Helen
    1996   Language policies as virtual reality: Two Australian examples. *TESOL Quarterly* 30: 473–497.
Norton, Bonnie
    2000   *Identity and Language Learning: Gender, Ethnicity, and Educational Change.* Edinburgh Gate: Pearson Education.
Pennycook, Alastair
    1994   *The Cultural Politics of English as an International Language.* London: Longman.
Pennycook, Alastair
    1998   *English and the Discourses of Colonialism.* London: Routledge.

Pennycook, Alastair
   2000a   English, politics, ideology: From colonial celebration to postcolonial performativity. In: Thomas Ricento (ed.), *Ideology, Politics and Language Policies: Focus on English,* 107–119. Amsterdam: John Benjamins.
Pennycook, Alastair
   2000b   Language, ideology and hindsight: Lessons from colonial language policies. In: Thomas Ricento (ed.), *Ideology, Politics and Language Policies: Focus on English,* 49–65. Amsterdam: John Benjamins.
Pennycook, Alastair
   2001   *Critical Applied Linguistics: A Critical Introduction.* Mahwah, NJ: Lawrence Erlbaum.
Pennycook, Alastair
   2002   Language policy and docile bodies: Hong Kong and governmentality. In: James Tollefson (ed.), *Language Policies in Education: Critical Issues,* 91–110. Mahwah, NJ: Lawrence Erlbaum.
Pennycook, Alastair
   2003   Global Englishes, Rip Slyme, and performativity. *Journal of Sociolinguistics* 7(4): 513–533.
Pennycook, Alastair
   2004   Language policy and the ecological turn. *Language Policy* 3: 213–239.
Pennycook, Alastair
   2006   Postmodernism in language policy. In: Thomas Ricento (ed.), *An Introduction to Language Policy: Theory and Method,* 60–76. Oxford: Blackwell.
Phillipson, Robert
   1992   *Linguistic Imperialism.* Oxford: Oxford University Press.
Phillipson, Robert
   2003   *English-only Europe? Challenging Language Policy.* London: Routledge.
Phillipson, Robert and Tove Skutnabb-Kangas
   1996   English only worldwide or language ecology? *TESOL Quarterly* 30: 429–452.
Ramanathan, Vaidehi
   2005   *The English-Vernacular Divide: Postcolonial Language Politics and Practice.* Clevedon: Multilingual Matters.
Rampton, Ben
   1995   *Crossing: Language and Ethnicity Among Adolescents.* London: Longman.
Ricento, Thomas
   1998a   National language policy in the United States. In: Thomas Ricento and Barbara Burnaby (eds.), *Language and Politics in the United States and Canada: Myths and Realities,* 85–112. Mahwah, NJ: Lawrence Erlbaum.
Ricento, Thomas
   1998b   The courts, the legislature and society: The shaping of federal language policy in the United States. In: Douglas Kibbee (ed.), *Language Legislation and Linguistic Rights: Selected Proceedings of the Language Legislation and Linguistic Rights Conference, The University of Illinois at Urbana-Champaign, March, 1996,* 123–141. Amsterdam: John Benjamins.

Ricento, Thomas
   2000a   Historical and theoretical perspectives in language policy and planning. *Journal of Sociolinguistics* 4(2): 196–213.
Ricento, Thomas (ed.)
   2000b   *Ideology, Politics and Language Policies: Focus on English.* Amsterdam: John Benjamins.
Ricento, Thomas
   2003   The discursive construction of Americanism. *Discourse & Society* 14: 611–637.
Ricento, Thomas
   2005a   Problems with the 'language-as-resource' discourse in the promotion of Heritage languages in the USA. *Journal of Sociolinguistics* 9(3): 348–368.
Ricento, Thomas
   2005b   Considerations of identity in L2 learning. In: Eli Hinkel (ed.), *Handbook of Research in Second Language Teaching and Learning,* 895–910. Mahwah, NJ: Lawrence Erlbaum.
Ricento, Thomas (ed.)
   2006   *An Introduction to Language Policy: Theory and Method.* Oxford: Blackwell.
Ricento, Thomas and Nancy Hornberger
   1996   Unpeeling the onion: Language planning and policy and the ELT professional. *TESOL Quarterly* 30: 401–427.
Ricento, Thomas and Barbara Burnaby (eds.)
   1998   *Language and Politics in the United States and Canada: Myths and Realities.* Mahwah, NJ: Lawrence Erlbaum.
Ricento, Thomas and Terrence Wiley (eds.)
   2002   Revisiting the mother-tongue question in language policy, planning, and politics. *International Journal of the Sociology of Language* (Special issue) 154.
Roca, Ana
   2003   Public awareness of and political change for bilingualism in the United States. In: Russell Campbell and Donna Christian (eds.), *Directions in Research: Intergenerational Transmission of Heritage Languages. Heritage Language Journal* 1(1) (http://www.international.ucla.edu/lrc/hlj/article.asp?parentid=3893).
Rostow, Walter
   1963   *The Economics of Take-off into Sustained Growth.* London: Macmillan.
Rubin, Joan
   1971   A view towards the future. In: Joan Rubin and Björn Jernudd (eds.), *Can Language Be Planned? Sociolinguistic Theory and Practice for Developing Nations,* 307–310. Hawaii: The University Press of Hawaii.
Rubin, Joan
   1986   City planning and language planning. In: E. Annamalai, Björn Jernudd and Joan Rubin (eds.), *Language Planning: Proceedings of an Institute,* 105–122. Honolulu, HI: East-West Center.
Rubin, Joan and Bjorn Jernudd (eds.)
   1971   *Can Language Be Planned? Sociolinguistic Theory and Practice for Developing Nations.* Hawaii: The University Press of Hawaii.

Rubio-Marín, Ruth
    2003   Language rights: Exploring the competing rationales. In: Will Kymlicka and Alan Patten (eds.), *Language Rights and Political Theory,* 52–79. Oxford: Oxford University Press.
Ruiz, Richard
    1984   Orientations in language planning. *NABE Journal* 8: 15–34.
Santa Ana, Otto
    2002   *Brown Tide Rising: Metaphors of Latinos in Contemporary American Public Discourse.* Austin, TX: University of Texas Press.
Schiffman, Harold
    1996   *Linguistic Culture and Language Policy.* London: Routledge.
Schmidt, Sr., Ronald
    2000   *Language Policy and Identity in the United States.* Philadelphia, PA: Temple University Press.
Skutnabb-Kangas, Tove
    2006   Language policy and linguistic human rights. In: Thomas Ricento (ed.), *An Introduction to Language Policy: Theory and Method,* 273–291. Oxford: Blackwell.
Sonntag, Selma
    2000   Ideology and policy in the politics of the English language in North India. In: Thomas Ricento (ed.), *Ideology, Politics and Language Policies: Focus on English,* 133–149. Amsterdam: John Benjamins.
Spolsky, Bernard
    2004   *Language Policy.* Cambridge: Cambridge University Press.
Tollefson, James W.
    1986   Language policy and the radical left in the Philippines: The New People's Army and its antecedents. *Language Problems and Language Planning* 10: 177–189.
Tollefson, James W.
    1991   *Planning Language, Planning Inequality.* New York: Longman.
Tollefson, James W. (ed.)
    2002   *Language Policies in Education: Critical Issues.* Mahwah, NJ: Lawrence Erlbaum.
Tollefson, James W.
    2006   Critical theory in language policy. In: Thomas Ricento (ed.), *An Introduction to Language Policy: Theory and Method,* 42–59. Oxford: Blackwell.
Valdés, Guadalupe
    2003   Language ideologies and the teaching of heritage languages. In: Russell Campbell and Donna Christian (eds.), *Directions in Research: Intergenerational Transmission of Heritage Languages. Heritage Language Journal* 1(1)   (http://www.International.ucla.edu/lrc/hlj/article.asp?parentid=3893).
Van Dijk, Teun
    1998   *Ideology: A Multidisciplinary Approach.* London: Sage.
Van Dijk, Teun
    2000   New(s) racism: A discourse analytical approach. In: Simon Cottle (ed.), *Ethnic Minorities and the Media: Changing Cultural Boundaries,* 33–49. Buckingham and Philadelphia: Open University Press.

Wiley, Terrence
   1996   Language planning and policy. In: Sandra McKay and Nancy Hornberger (eds.), *Sociolinguistics and Language Teaching,* 103–147. Cambridge: Cambridge University Press.

Wiley, Terrence
   1998   The imposition of World War I era English-only policies and the fate of German in North America. In: Thomas Ricento and Barbara Burnaby (eds.), *Language and Politics in the United States and Canada: Myths and Realities,* 211–241. Mahwah, NJ: Lawrence Erlbaum.

Wiley, Terrence
   1999   Comparative historical analysis of U.S. language policy and language planning: Extending the foundations. In: Thom Huebner and Kathryn Davis (eds.), *Sociopolitical Perspectives on Language Policy and Planning in the USA,* 17–37. Amsterdam: John Benjamins.

Wiley, Terrence
   2001   On defining heritage languages and their speakers. In: Joy Peyton (ed.), *Heritage Languages in America: Blueprint for the Future,* 29–36. Washington, DC, and McHenry, IL: Center for Applied Linguistics and Delta Systems.

Wiley, Terrence
   2002   Heinz Kloss revisited: National socialist ideologue or champion of language-minority rights? *International Journal of the Sociology of Language* 154: 83–97.

Wiley, Terrence
   2006   The lessons of historical investigation: Implications for the study of language policy and planning. In: Thomas Ricento (ed.), *An Introduction to Language Policy: Theory and Method,* 135–152. Oxford: Blackwell.

Wiley, Terrence and Marguerite Lukes
   1996   English-only and standard English ideologies in the U.S. *TESOL Quarterly* 30: 511–535.

Williams, Glyn
   1992   *Sociolinguistics: A Sociological Critique.* London: Routledge.

Wodak, Ruth, Rudolf de Cillia, Martin Reisigl and Karin Liebhart
   1999   *The Discursive Construction of National Identity.* Edinburgh: Edinburgh University Press.

Wolfson, Nessa and Joan Manes (eds.)
   1985   *Language of Inequality.* Berlin: Mouton.

8. Back from the brink: The revival of endangered languages

John Edwards

1. Introduction

Ascertaining the point of language death is not always as easy as some might think. It is true that there are (or were) very ancient varieties whose existence is confirmed only through classical reference; Cappadocian, for example, once thrived in what is now central Turkey, but we know next to nothing about it. There are also undeciphered varieties. We have thousands of examples of Etruscan texts, but the brevity of many inscriptions (most are funerary), and the "isolate" nature of the language (there are only two other languages in the family, Lemnian and Rhaetic, and neither is well attested) mean that our understanding of Etruscan is very incomplete: One expert speaks of a "tentative" grammar and lexicon (Rix 2004). Still, Etruscan is not quite as dead as Cappadocian. But consider, too, the possibility of further archaeological discoveries at the Kerkenes excavations, discoveries that could lead to increased knowledge of Cappadocian: Would we then say that a dead language lived again? And, as for those "dead" languages that students sometimes moan about – Latin and Attic Greek – well, they don't seem very dead at all in this company.

If language death is an uncertain quantity, then we may expect that matters of *revival* may be equally fraught. Revival can certainly mean resuscitation, but it can also – logically and etymologically – refer to renewal, to reinvigoration, to the arresting of decline. Indeed, many forms of restorative activity can legitimately be placed under the one heading of revival – the question is largely one of *degree* of difficulty and not of theoretical or principled difference. We could approach this from another direction, and say that language *maintenance* shades into language *revival*. At all points along the continuum a language is at some sort of risk, and the very fact that language becomes an issue is, itself, often an indication of distress. Such a continuum not only allows us to conceptually link two topics which are sometimes treated separately, it also returns us to the important matter of *gradation* – for, just as language death can be less than clearcut, so opinion can vary about the likelihood and the success of language revival.

Osborn Bergin, the famous Irish philologist, once noted bluntly that "no language has ever been revived, and no language ever will be revived" (cited in Ó hAilín 1969: 91). On the other hand, Weinreich (1953: 108) said that "many 'obsolescent' languages have received new leases on life". Observers of the same linguistic scene can have variant perceptions, too: Ó Domhnalláin (1959) found the educational achievements of the Irish revival "astounding" while Ellis and mac a'Ghobhainn (1971: 143) asked us to "remove our gaze from the terrible failure of Ireland". And, even if the verdict is failure, Dorian (1987) tells us that revival efforts may still prove salutary – in this she was, incidentally, anticipated eighty years earlier by Trench (1907).

Cutting across all perceptual and terminological matters, however, are powerful facts of social life, facts recognised by even the most sanguine supporters of linguistic maintenance, continuity and revival. Even the strongest will-to-revive may be dwarfed by societal pressures. Since languages and their speakers do not exist in vacuums and cannot, therefore, be "treated" in isolation from other strands of the social fabric, the whole business of revival is inevitably associated with *internal manifestations of external influence*.

This is precisely where the contemporary and "new" ecological awareness (of which I have been critical elsewhere; see Edwards 2002, 2004) stakes its claim: It purports to offer fresh ways of understanding this social tissue of influence and, by implication, new approaches to linguistic maintenance and revival. These often involve bilingual solutions, in that a continuing bilingualism is generally seen as the most reasonable accommodation for "small" or "at-risk" varieties. This is not unreasonable, since the alternative – some monolingual emphasis upon the threatened variety alone – is an increasingly unlikely (and unpopular) course of action. Stability in bilingualism or diglossia is not always easily achieved, of course: The influence of those "large" languages that have backed smaller ones into linguistic corners does not abate with bilingual arrangements.

The novelty of much current "green" thinking is doubtful. Haugen (1987), for instance, noted that language ecology is basically a reworking of an "old model", and the essential idea – that language matters are political and social, and must be considered in their contexts – has long been accepted. As well, the breadth that might be assumed in a field of study called the "ecology of language" is more apparent than real. While the original (nineteenth-century) ecological insights were concerned with adaptations of all kinds – with the Darwinian "web of life", with the "conditions of the struggle for existence", with relationships ranging from the "beneficial" to the "inimical" – contemporary views have downplayed competition and have emphasised coexistence and cooperation. The new thrust is driven, above all, by the desire to preserve linguistic diversity in a world where more and more languages are seen to be at risk, and where matters of maintenance and revival are therefore central. Attempts have been made to link this thrust with current environmental concerns, issues of biological diversity, protection of wildlife, and so on. This linkage is understandable at a metaphoric level: In a world where opinion can be galvanised to save the whales, to preserve wetlands, to save rare snails and owls – or, indeed, to keep historic buildings from the wrecker's ball, or to repair and restore rare books and paintings – why should we not also try to stem language decline and prevent linguistic predation? It is interesting (but not, perhaps, surprising) that, in some quarters, the linkage has been seen as *more* than metaphoric, with the suggestion that linguistic and biological diversities are co-extensive, mutually supportive, possibly even "co-evolved". A central assumption of the modern ecological view is, of course, that linguistic diversity is a good thing *per se* – and supporting evidence has been adduced on scientific, economic, moral and aesthetic grounds. The first two are shakier bases than the others but, in a sense, this is of little import since the essential articles of faith that underpin modern ecological expression rest upon perceptions of morality and aesthetic preference.

The narrowed focus of most modern writing on linguistic ecology is upon an environmentalism that makes a specific case for the maintenance of diversity. This is not problematic in itself, and is obviously not an illegitimate stance (although it is not always a sturdy one) but it is surely reasonable to have some misgivings about an area which styles itself broadly while marshalling its forces along quite specific lines. My central criticism is that language maintenance/revival is always a difficult undertaking, that past efforts have often foundered on the shoals of romantic but unrealistic enthusiasm, and that approaching the topic from a position of initial aesthetic and moral commitment – while understandable and in some circumstances laudable – is neither in the best traditions of disinterested scholarship nor likely to realise longterm success.

2. Language maintenance

As noted above, different degrees and types of linguistic restoration can be put under the general rubric of "revival". It follows, then, that we must turn our attention here to some specifics. First – and in line with some of the opening observations – we might ask if revitalisation efforts must always imply vernacular oral maintenance. Could a language preserved in written form, but spoken by few (or none) on a regular basis, be considered "maintained"? The answer must surely be yes, if only because such preservation could theoretically be a basis for future expansion.

But in most instances, of course, maintenance *does* imply a continuity of some ordinary spoken medium and this, in turn, highlights the importance of uninterrupted domestic language transmission from one generation to the next. If this transmission is sustained, then language maintenance – at some level – is assured; if the transmission falters or ends, on the other hand, then the language becomes vulnerable and its maintenance threatened (see Fishman 1990). This is another way of saying that the home is probably the most important of all language *domains* – a point repeatedly, and correctly, stressed in the literature. Less often emphasised is the logical (and, indeed, *eco*logical) ramification that, for the continuation of this central domestic domain, there must generally exist extra-domestic settings within which the language is necessary or, at least, of considerable importance. Furthermore, not all domains are of equal weight or value in terms of supporting linguistic continuity. While it is difficult to be categorical here, it is possible to identify – for a given variety, at a given time, in a given context – what one might call *domains of necessity*. These domains are related to the most pivotal aspects of people's lives, and so one could single out settings such as the home, the school and the workplace. On the other hand, domains in which participation is voluntary, or sporadic, or idiosyncratic, are not likely to be so important for broad language maintenance. In summary, then, the maintenance of a language is on a surer footing if it, and it alone, is required in domains of central and continuing salience.

Language maintenance is not, of course, an issue equally germane for all groups. It is, rather, one which assumes greater importance when a group and its language are at some risk of assimilation; thus, discussions of language minorities and language maintenance naturally coincide. And, to return to our main theme here, language maintenance almost always involves at least some element of language *revival* – for it is only when a variety begins to lose ground (or is seen to be at risk of doing so) that attention becomes focused upon it. Since revival does not simply and solely mean a restoration to life after death, but can also quite legitimately refer to reawakening and renewal, to the restoration of vigour and activity, and to the arresting of decline or discontinuity, we see that it is (or can be) a form of maintenance.

The central issue here is easily stated: How can language maintenance be effected? How can decline and discontinuity be halted? There are two major and inter-related factors involved, one tangible and one more subjective. The first (as already mentioned) is the continuing existence of important domains within which the use of the language is necessary. These domains depend, of course, upon social, political and economic forces, both within and without the particular language community. Although the details will clearly vary from case to case, issues of general relevance include linguistic practicality, communicative efficiency, social mobility, and economic advancement. These four constitute the greatest advantages associated with "large" languages, and the greatest disincentives for the maintenance of "small" ones. In many cases of language contact between varieties that are unequal in important ways, some bilingual accommodation is often sought, but bilingualism itself can be an unstable and impermanent way-station on the road to a new monolingualism. Formal language planning on behalf of beleaguered languages often can do very little to stem the forces of urbanisation, modernisation and mobility, the forces which typically place a language in danger and which lead to language shift. Of course, linguistic standardisation and modernisation efforts are always theoretically possible, but they are not always practicable, nor do they necessarily change in any substantial way the status-based balance of dominance among competing forms. "Small" varieties which have developed to national-language levels (for example, Somali and Guaraní) remain less broadly useful than (for example) English and Spanish.

It should always be remembered that, historically and linguistically, change rather than stasis is the norm. Environments alter, people move, and needs and demands change – such factors have a large influence upon language. The desire for mobility and modernisation is, with some few notable exceptions, a global phenomenon. Whether one looks at the capitalist world or the erstwhile communist one, at contemporary times or historical ones, at empires or small societies, at immigrant minorities or indigenous groups, one sees a similarity of pressures which take their toll, force change, and throw populations into transitional states that have, naturally, unpleasant consequences (at least in the short term). Language decline and shift are most often *symptoms* of contact between groups of unequal political and economic power. Decline, then, is an effect of a larger cause, and it follows that attempts to arrest it are usually very difficult. One does not cure measles by covering up the spots; one cannot maintain a language by dealing with language alone. A logical approach to maintenance and revival, to the halting of decline and shift, is to unpick the social fabric that has evolved and then reweave it in a new pattern. This is, again, theoretically possible (consider revolutionary upheavals), but it is significant here that most who are concerned with language maintenance usually want only *some* reworking of social evolution, not wholesale revolution. The most typical manifestations in this regard involve a desire for the maintenance or rejuvenation of a flagging language to be coincident with the various benefits and mobilities afforded by participation in (or next to) the "large" culture whose incursions have brought about the decline in the first place. It is a considerable understatement to say the fulfilment of such desires is a difficult and delicate undertaking.

3.   The will to revive

The more intangible or subjective factor in maintenance and revival efforts – and certainly the more interesting from a psychological viewpoint – is the matter of the collective *will* to stem discontinuity, to sustain vigour in the face of the factors just discussed. The objection is sometimes made that, since language decline is often a reflection of relative social inequality, it is unrealistic to expect that threatened cultures and sub-cultures can exercise much power or actualise their desires. In general terms, this is true, and the evidence is all around us. There are, however, some subtleties here that are worth exploring, some nuances that the broad-brush perspective may efface. In his study of the decline of the Celtic languages, Durkacz (1983) charted the familiar territory of linguistic retreat in the face of advancing English. But he also pointed out that acquiescence in at least some facets of language shift – notably in educational settings – coincided with strong resistance to other manifestations of anglo-pressure: The parents who were apparently willing enough for their children to be educated through English were at the same time quite capable of violent protest over land-management matters. The Highland Scots (for example) increasingly came to associate the English language with three life-altering phenomena. Two of these were employment and prosperity, while the third – emigration – demonstrates the awareness that material advancement comes at a cost. The Celtic varieties, Durkacz suggests, gradually took on other connotations; he mentions "childhood, song and dance". This is, in fact, a little too easy, since it paints only a lightly regretful picture of an immature, if pleasant, past which must be left behind. The reality, for both indigenous and immigrant minority groups, involves a rather stronger link, a rather more poignant balance sheet of plusses and minuses. Nonetheless, choices were made and linguistic associations reflected them. If we stay with the Celtic languages, we find that early nineteenth-century Irish became more and more linked with "penury, drudgery and backwardness" (Ó Danachair 1969: 20). Self-perceptions of Gaelic in Nova Scotia were described in almost exactly the same words by another commentator – the language implied "toil, hardship and scarcity"; English, by contrast, was a medium of "refinement and culture" (Dunn 1974: 134). From the time of the earliest emigrations, Campbell (1948: 70) added, settlers in the new world "carried with them the idea that education was coincident with a knowledge of English". I am making no judgements here as to the accuracy or, indeed, the desirability of such views. I only wish to point out that perceptions of languages – and, therefore, the desires and actions that rest upon them – are based upon comparative assessments and that, as resistance in other quarters indicates, there is some evidence for a reasoned discrimination here, even in subject populations.

There are more recent demonstrations of the importance of linguistic will and desire. In contemporary America, for instance, the market-place makes increasing accommodations to speakers of nonstandard or non-English varieties. Clearly, there is no altruism involved here but, rather, the desire to reach important potential customers. If such customers – Spanish speakers in California, say – can wield the power of the purse, why not also the power of the ballot-box, of the educational amendment, of the Californian proposition on bilingual education? (See also Wiley, this vol.).

Of course, things are not quite this simple. The sufficiency of will required for the assumption and exercise of power has, historically, been more evident in some areas than in others (recall that Scottish resistance to land "reform"), and groups whose clout is evident in economic areas may not be as apparently demanding in others. Why not? Why do people who go to the barricades for some things seem to acquiesce in others – in matters of language shift, for example? There is, of course, simple inertia, an inherent problem wherever passivity is to be galvanised into action; there are clear reasons for this, most of them having to do with lack of sufficient awareness coupled with the economic and pragmatic imperatives that affect ordinary life (for everyone, of course, but probably more centrally for those who are of subordinate or disadvantaged status). So, it often proves difficult or impossible to translate a rather inert goodwill into something more dynamic. (Language revival efforts, for instance, are typically characterised by a small group of activists nervously glancing over their shoulders to see how many of their alleged adherents are following them.) It is also possible for populations to have been "taken in", as it were, by mainstream groups, so that they no longer know or trust their own linguistic and cultural instincts. Many years ago, Lambert and his associates – drawing upon earlier social-psychological work showing how negative, authoritarian and prejudiced evaluations of stigmatised social and religious groups were sometimes replicated *within* these groups themselves – described a "minority-group reaction" by which "small" linguistic communities may come to accept that their language has less favourable connotations than that of some larger surrounding population (Lambert et al. 1960; see also Gardner and Lambert 1972).

While these sorts of explanations imply a group inadequacy that action in other arenas makes unlikely (think again of struggles over land – but think, too, of resistance to religious and legal impositions), it is the case that "the lack of will to stop shrinking is an intrinsic characteristic of a shrinking language community" (Fennell 1981: 30). An acquired frailty of will is perhaps a more general manifestation of Lambert's finding; it is certainly a deeper and more subtle manifestation than any superficial listlessness and, even if it is only restricted to some areas of psychosocial life, it presents a gritty problem. It reflects, in fact, powerful factors already touched here, notably the contact between unequal groups, communities or systems, and the socioeconomic changes set in train by this contact.

If *will* is a quantity that can be galvanised in some circumstances, how important is it? At a recent language symposium in Landau, Fishman (2004) argued that it was an imprecise concept, and that examples of its explanatory power are hard to delineate (a very curious stance for him to adopt – see below). There are cases that seem very obvious, however. After enduring long years of sociopolitical and religious paternalism, the francophone population in Québec experienced a *révolution tranquille*, transformed and modernised itself, and assumed the provincial mastery that its inherent strength had always promised; an important corollary of the transformation was linguistic engineering on behalf of a French language considered to be at risk. Spolsky has commented upon this situation in a new book on language policy: He writes of francophones beginning to become "conscious of English dominance" (2004: 196). Elsewhere he uses terms like "commitment" and "ideological support" (205), states bluntly that "language policy is about choice" (217) and emphasises the importance of the "perception" of sociolinguistic situations (219). These usages are not all (or always) synonymous with will, but they all suggest how important convictions, attitudes and perceptions are in matters of language maintenance and revival.

Other more immediately relevant examples also suggest themselves. At the Landau conference just mentioned, for instance, Fishman gave a chatty plenary address, part of which consisted of a list of many intangible aspects of sociological and linguistic power – virtually all of which could just as easily have been described in terms of the operation of will. More pointedly, he made reference to the decision in his own family to create and maintain a Yiddish-speaking home. This is quite obviously an illustration of conscious will-power at work, of a decision taken on grounds of conviction rather than practical necessity – and a personal reflection of that broader and often-expressed argument about the importance of regular family transmission of languages from one generation to the next (see above). If one family can make certain language choices, then others might do so as well – consider the efforts of Ben-Yehuda in Israel (see below) – and to be able to extrapolate from the family to the community would clearly be of the greatest impact in the life of "threatened" varieties. Indeed, as Spolsky has pointed out, while application of any language policy requires a community, that community can be "of whatever size [...] ranging from a family [...] [to] nation state or regional alliance" (2004: 40).

In fact, Fishman has made frequent reference to will in his writings; throughout his volume on the reversal of language shift, for example, he returns repeatedly to the theme in one form or another. Thus, he observes that the success of the re-vernacularisation of Hebrew rested upon "the rare and largely fortuitous co-occurrence of language-and-nationality ideology, disciplined collective will, and sufficient social dislocation" (1991: 291). In discussing efforts on behalf of Frisian, he says that "the basic problem seems to be in activating this [passive] goodwill" (180). Bemoaning the disregard of the "moral and spiritual dimensions of modern life" (387) in his treatment of language-shift reversal, Fishman sees the movement as helping to re-establish "local meaning" in the face of a "mechanistic and fatalistic" outlook (35). Successful reversal involves involvement in "the qualitative emphases" (8) of contemporary life. And, in an earlier piece, Fishman wrote approvingly (in a discussion of Herder) of those peoples who have not "capitulated to the massive blandishments of western materialism, who experience life and nature in deeply poetic and collectively meaningful ways" (1982: 8; see also Edwards 1993).

The invocation of the concept of will is surely also accurate when we consider the actions of those strongly committed to the protection of at-risk languages – the nationalists, activists and enthusiasts are typically few in number but fiercely committed to their linguistic cause. Consider the Cornish and Manx revivalists, or those native anglophones who move to the *Gaeltachtaí* of Ireland and Scotland, or those who carry the banners for Gaelic in Cape Breton Island, and so on; there are many apposite cases here. The other side of this coin – and the one that often gives the activities of revivalists their poignancy – must obviously be the will of those who choose *not* to move to minority-speaking enclaves, or to bring up their children in some threatened medium, or to otherwise encourage it. It might be thought that this second category is not particularly interesting or illuminating, representing merely passivity, *non*-exercise of will, or a decision to not make a decision, to drift along in the current of some "mainstream". In fact, however, there are contexts in which conscious decisions unfavourable to minority languages, on the part of potentially important players, are equally illustrative of the power of active will.

It is a testament to the depth and sensitivity of the German symposium to which I have already twice referred that one of the most important of these contexts – the post-colonial setting – was extensively discussed, notably by Africans and Africanists. It was frequently pointed out, for example, that one consequence of colonialism is that the élites in newly-independent countries have typically been educated abroad; their training is usually undertaken in the language of the former colonisers and they often continue to value that language more highly than indigenous varieties. When it comes, then, to encouraging local vernaculars and their development, or opting for the mediums of education, the mindset of those in power is – or so it is alleged – still stuck in a linguistic rut; the operation of *their* will stifles local languages (even perhaps their own mother tongues). Given the great divides that often exist between the rulers and the ruled, the implication is that a change in that mindset, a recalibration of that will, could have profound consequences for those large numbers who are linguistically and educationally excluded from the corridors of power, whose languages remain widely used but unfairly reined in. It is, of course, of the greatest significance that the exercisers of will in these circumstances are indigenous individuals themselves – élite maybe, and socioeconomically far removed from the vast majority of their compatriots but, nonetheless, unquestionably *of* the place. They are not callous outsiders whose language policies, however reprehensible, are understandable in the traditional colonial context; they are people of whom more might have been expected and, indeed, people who have often fulfilled the expectations of them in other matters of social and political life (on language and colonialism, see also Migge and Léglise, this vol.).

The poignancy of all this has been eloquently discussed in a number of essays by the distinguished Kenyan author (and now faculty member at New York University), Ngũgĩ wa Thiong'o (1986, 1993). His decision to write in Gĩkũyũ and not in English is an important part of the backdrop to his many impassioned pleas for the linguistic and cultural "decolonising" of the African mind – and to his indictment of those in power whose minds apparently remained colonised. Chinua Achebe spoke for many African authors when he noted:

> Is it right that a man should abandon his mother tongue for someone else's? It looks like dreadful betrayal and produces a guilty feeling. But for me there is no other choice. I have been given the language and I intend to use it.
> (Ngũgĩ wa Thiong'o 1986: 7)

For Ngũgĩ wa Thiong'o, however, Achebe's position is morally untenable: He bluntly notes that "African literature can only be written in African languages" (1986: 27) – and he does not accept the argument, by the way, that European varieties have *become* African ones. Ngũgĩ wa Thiong'o is particularly concerned with "decolonisation" in literary and dramatic contexts, but he touches upon political ones as well. He mentions Léopold Senghor, for instance, who admitted that French had been forced upon him but who yet remained "lyrical in his subservience" to the language (29). Or Hastings Banda, who created an élite English-language academy in Malawi, expressly designed to encourage able students to be sent to "universities like Harvard, Chicago, Oxford, Cambridge and Edinburgh" (29); all the teachers were recruited from Britain.[1]

To summarise: The importance of linguistic and cultural *will* and its ramifications can hardly be denied. The importance rests, ultimately, upon matters of *perception*, the demonstration of whose centrality to social life is the single greatest insight of modern psychology. And matters of perception are not necessarily matters of fact. We are dealing here with intangibles, but what is intangible is often the strongest and the most resistant to change – or to cultural adversity or endangerment.

4. Scholarship and intervention

Given the formidable attractions associated with "large" languages and "large" societies, it is not surprising that *active* moves for language maintenance are typically found only among a relatively small number of people. There are, of course, practical reasons why the masses (particularly in subaltern societies) find it difficult to involve themselves in maintenance efforts, even if they are generally sympathetic – their collective *will*, then, often remains of a broad but passive nature. To galvanise this rather inert quantity has always been the most pressing issue for language activists. Many years ago, in commenting upon efforts to sustain Irish, Moran (1900: 268) made a point which is still relevant in many quarters: "Without scholars [the revival] cannot succeed; with scholars as leaders it is bound to fail".

Linguists and other language "professionals" have traditionally seen a "naturalness" in most cases of language decline and shift that precludes any useful intervention, even if it were thought broadly desirable (see Bolinger 1980). Some contemporary scholars, however, – particularly sociolinguists and sociologists of language – have not shied away from engagement in what might be called the "public life" of language. Fishman is a good example here. He has noted that regret over mother-tongue loss has in fact been the catalyst that brought many academics into linguistics and related fields in the first place. This self-proclaimed "founding father" of sociolinguistics makes no secret of his own commitment here, and has recently (Fishman 1990, 1991) devoted considerable attention to the question of "reversing language shift" – an undertaking he deems a "quest" of "sanctity". *Reversing language shift* is a term, incidentally, which has suggested to some a new approach; in fact, it is an unnecessary neologism in a field already cluttered with too many, about which there is endless definition, redefinition and argument. As already implied here, *revival* could replace all such terms; of course, the different levels and degrees of revival activity must then be specified in given circumstances, but the term itself is quite reasonably applied in all the linguistic contexts in which its use has been debated.[2]

Fishman's contribution to the revival literature lies in the addition of dispassionate argument to a strong personal commitment to the defense of languages at risk. But, as in the writings of many other "revivalists", the lines of demarcation between scholarship and involvement often become blurred. For example, just as Douglas Hyde, the famous Irish revivalist and statesman, equated anglicisation with a hated modernity, so there are elements in Fishman's work that suggest that language revival is associated with a hope that earlier values might also be reawakened. Thus he speaks of the reversal of language shift as a force against the banalities of modernity, against "market hype and fad" (1991: 4). He is concerned about a contemporary "peripheralization of the family" (375), and he bemoans the current disregard of "moral and spiritual dimensions" (387). In all this, however, Fishman detects no orientation to the past; indeed, he admits that "there is no turning the clock back" (377). Still, phrases like those just quoted do rather suggest that he might, after all, like to see the clock run back a bit, that his sympathies lie with some mythical "better" or "small-is-beautiful" past. This sense is reinforced when we find the author describing the reversal of shift as also "reversing the tenor, the focus, the qualitative emphases of daily informal life" (8) or, more bluntly, as "remaking social reality" (411). The tension between past and present leads Fishman to see advocates of shift reversal as "change-agents on behalf of persistence" (387). What ought one to make of this curious phrase?

The pages of *Language* provided a recent context in which matters of scholarship and advocacy were examined. Krauss began, with a pointed argument that continues to set the tone for much of the contemporary debate: Linguists will be "cursed by future generations" if they do not actively intervene to stem the "catastrophic destruction" now threatening nine out of ten of the world's languages (1992: 7–8). Traditional emphases on varieties of linguistic documentation are seen to be insufficient; social and political action and advocacy are required. Linguists must go well beyond the usual academic role of description and documentation, Krauss argued, "promote language development in the necessary domains ... [and] learn ... the techniques of organization, monitoring and lobbying, publicity, and activism" (Krauss 1992: 9). A response by Ladefoged supported a continuation of the linguist-as-disinterested-scientist role; adopting this more traditional stance, he noted that the linguist's task is to present facts, and not to attempt to persuade groups that language shift is a bad thing *per se*. Not all speakers of threatened varieties, Ladefoged parenthetically pointed out, see their preservation as possible or even always desirable:

> One can be a responsible linguist and yet regard the loss of a particular language, or even a whole group of languages, as far from a "catastrophic destruction" [...] statements such as "just as the extinction of any animal species diminishes our world, so does the extinction of any language" are appeals to our emotions, not to our reason. (Ladefoged 1992: 810)

A third participant in this exchange was Dorian, who noted that all arguments about endangered languages are political in nature, that the low status of many at-risk varieties leads naturally to a weakened will-to-maintenance, that the loss of any language is a serious matter, and that the laying out of the "facts" advocated by Ladefoged is not a straightforward matter, since they are inevitably intertwined with political positions. At the very least, Dorian noted, this is an "issue on which linguists' advocacy positions are worth hearing" (1993: 579; fuller details here can be found in Edwards 1994). We have, indeed, heard more and more of these positions; important collections include those of Dorian (1989), Robins and Uhlenbeck (1991), Brenzinger (1992, 1998), Grenoble and Whaley (1998), and Nettle and Romaine (2000).

Apart from anthologies dealing with endangered varieties, there are now several organisations devoted to the preservation of diversity, to the "ecological" perspective, to active intervention in behalf of threatened languages. They include the Endangered Language Fund, the Committee on Endangered Languages and Their Preservation, and Terralingua: Partnerships for Linguistic and Biological Diversity (based in the United States), the Foundation for Endangered Languages (in England), Germany's *Gesellschaft für bedrohte Sprachen*, and the International Clearing House for Endangered Languages (Japan). Similar concerns motivate the European programmes of Linguasphere and the *Observatoire Linguistique* (Dalby 2000) as well as those whose more pointed purpose is language-rights legislation. Further details may be found in Crystal (2000) and Maffi (2000); see also Fill (this vol.).

Back from the brink: The revival of endangered languages   253

It is clear that this is a very contentious area. What some would see as inappropriate and unscholarly intervention, others would consider absolutely necessary. Any combination of scholarship and advocacy is fraught with potential danger, but one might reasonably argue that one of the "facts" to be presented to groups and policy-makers is the very commitment of at least some in the academic constituency. Groups whose languages are at risk might profit from the knowledge that the issues so central to them are also seen as important by "outsiders". At the end of the day, though, we should remember that the actions of linguists – whether fervently pro-maintenance in tenor or more "detached" – are likely to pale when compared with the realities of social and political pressures. These realities should at least suggest a sense of perspective.

5. Getting down to cases: Irish and Hebrew

In this section, I shall focus only upon the Irish and Hebrew cases. Although they are two of the most widely-discussed contexts in the literature, I treat them again here for two related reasons: First, existing discussions have not typically been orientated towards the extraction of generalities; second, between them, the two situations bring to light the most important of these generalities. Before turning to the Irish and the Hebrew revival efforts – the first often seen as a failure, the second generally considered as a success – one or two introductory comments are necessary.

There is a considerable number of accounts – widely scattered both temporally and by discipline and rigour – of specific language-revival efforts, and so one might think Nahir's (1977) observation that there has been little scholarly reporting somewhat surprising. He argues on the basis of his own definition of revival ("an attempt to turn a language with few or no surviving native speakers back into a normal means of communication"; Nahir 1984) that this is due to the small number of revival attempts themselves. Based upon what I have already touched upon here, however, we can understand that this definition is unnecessarily restrictive – particularly, of course, if we reject a substantive distinction between maintenance and revival. If we adopt the broader perspective, we see that there have been quite a few attempts at language revival. Ellis and mac a'Ghobhainn's (1971) rather flawed survey clearly demonstrated that many groups suffering some form of language pressure have struggled against it; they discuss twenty examples, ranging from Albanian to Korean.

The spectrum of historical cases is an extensive one, although some generalities can be extracted. I shall provide an overview of them in the final section, but I should mention here a point that has to do with the context rather than the content of revival efforts. It is simply that these efforts are typically seen to be belated. There are good reasons for this. For example, where populations are governed by conquering groups, any reasonable attention to the linguistic practices of the natives often comes as an historical afterthought; enlightened language policies are often countenanced only after political hegemony is felt to be secure and once some interest has developed in firmly and permanently "converting" the resident population. It is common, indeed, to find native-language policies adopted as an expedient to linguistic, religious and other forms of assimilation. In a sentiment echoed in many other settings, and at many other times, we find an early nineteenth-century commentator on the Irish scene noting approvingly that the use of Irish would actually hasten its decline, since an educated populace would obviously come more quickly to realise the advantages of English (Dewar 1812).

A second and more general reason has to do with the antiquarian interests of many earlier revivalists, and the relatively late realisation that the dwindling group of native speakers might be of importance. The "last" Cornish speaker, the legendary Dolly Pentreath of Mousehole, died in 1777 but the formalised concern for Cornish took another century to gear up. Sometimes, too, scholarly and literary interests are simply not accompanied by much concern for native speakers. Matthew Arnold had a deep interest in Celtic literature, an interest that coexisted with a desire for the rapid disappearance of spoken Welsh and the full assimilation of all Celtic populations (Arnold 1883).

Perhaps a more basic point needs to be underlined here, too: We cannot assume, from our own perspective, that there has always existed a great concern for minorities and their languages, nor should we ignore the fact that the upsurge in this concern in the late nineteenth century was intimately connected with other large-scale social and political developments. Nor should we be unwilling to entertain the thought that the study of languages safely dead, or on the way to extinction, or whose remaining speakers are at some remove (literally or psychologically), is altogether a neater scholastic exercise than is actually coming to grips with breathing speakers. Although there were still many speakers of Irish by the time the revival effort began, the literary researches of the revivalists were not inconveniently challenged: By the 1880s, only about fifty people were literate in Irish. Remember, too, the formidable Miss Blimber in Dickens's *Dombey and Son* (chapter 11):

> She was dry and sandy with working in the graves of deceased languages. None of your live languages for Miss Blimber. They must be dead – stone dead – and then Miss Blimber dug them up like a ghoul.

5.1. Irish

As a case study, Irish has much to recommend it. The language has a long history in which many of the chapters have already been written: Once a widespread vernacular capable of assimilating other varieties, Irish is now a more confined speech. The decline of the language and the nineteenth-century revival movement illustrate the interweaving of language with other facets of social life, including education, politics and religion. The relationship of Irish to nationalism, its influence upon the literary revival and its associations with prominent historical personalities all illuminate the language-identity link.

Until the Norman invasions in the twelfth century, Irish was secure. Indeed, it had been so for several centuries, displacing earlier varieties and establishing itself as a literary medium. With the advent of French and English speakers, however, the process of change began, although it was not a rapid one. Only in the towns within the Pale (the eastern coastal area, including Dublin) did French and English really establish themselves, and the Pale itself tended to shrink. There was considerable Gaelicising of these new inhabitants, something that led to the passage (in 1366) of the Statutes of Kilkenny, legislation aimed at keeping English settlers from adopting Irish ways. By 1600, then, English existed only within a diminished Pale, and in one or two rural enclaves. When the house of Plantagenet gave way to that of Tudor, however, the fortunes of Irish really began to change. Henry VIII issued many proclamations discouraging Irish, the sixteenth-century plantation schemes provided land for English settlers at the expense of the Irish, Elizabeth encouraged the use of Irish for proselytism, and so on. The old Gaelic order was passing and, although Irish was still the majority language at the end of the Tudor period, its future was now in doubt.

English made steady advances; between 1600 and 1800, it became the language of regular use for about half the population – the more powerful half. In the nineteenth century, the Catholic church increasingly turned to English, the national school system operated through English, and the depredations of the famines had their greatest effect in rural Irish-speaking areas. By the mid-nineteenth century, the number of Irish monolinguals was already very small and, in the context, bilingualism was usually an impermanent interlude. Still, the factors noted above – singly or in combination – are insufficient to explain the rapidity of the language shift which occurred, and we must return to the importance of *will*. Thus, de Fréine observed that "most of the reasons adduced for the suppression of the Irish language are not so much reasons as consequences of the decision to give up the language" (1977: 84).

Formal efforts to maintain, encourage and revive Irish date from the late nineteenth century. They were generally initiated by upper-middle-class individuals and organisations, for many of whom Irish was an acquired competence rather than a maternal one. The most important language body was the Gaelic

League *(Conradh na Gaeilge)*, whose foundation in 1893 was largely prompted by the appeals of Douglas Hyde (1886, 1894). The League's objective was essentially to maintain Irish but it is generally, and not unfairly, seen as wishing to do more – to revive Irish as the ordinary language of the country (although Hyde himself did not think this very likely or, perhaps, desirable). Overall, the Irish revival movement was part of a larger European trend, particularly within the Celtic areas, in which nationalistic efforts were made to transform the "Celtic twilight" into a "Celtic Renaissance". The Gaelic League declined in importance (though it is still extant) with the establishment of the Irish Free State in 1921. It had had considerable success in introducing Irish at school and university and had commanded a widespread (if somewhat evanescent) public support. It did not, however, resuscitate Irish among English speakers at large, nor did it make any lasting impact upon the maintenance and development of the *Gaeltacht* (see below).

With the founding of the Free State, Irish was enshrined as the national and first official language. By this time, however, the number of Irish speakers was very small; the mass of the population had long since switched to English. Census figures for 1926 indicate that 18% could speak Irish and, of course, Irish monoglots were scarce indeed – earlier figures had recorded only 21,000 of them (about 0.6 per cent of the population). Despite these figures, Irish obviously had a special hold on the founders of the new state, was closely tied to nationalism, and possessed a value beyond purely educational, intellectual and, indeed, pragmatic concerns. It was de Valera's famous opinion that "Ireland with its language and without freedom is preferable to Ireland with freedom and without its language" (cited in Akenson 1975: 36). In this sentiment, de Valera (and others like him) were essentially continuing the highly romanticised tradition so carefully accented by the Gaelic League; at the same time, it was good political sense to endorse Irish, since doing so established a visibly non-British line.

In practical terms, however, the government passed the burden of Irish restoration to the schools. After all, it was argued, if English schools had killed the language, then Irish ones could revive it. (This is, of course, a specious assertion since, even if the first half of the statement were true, the second would not necessarily follow.) Irish was to be a compulsory subject, and infants' classes were to be conducted entirely through Irish, even though this was an unknown language for the great majority. The finding of suitable instructors was difficult from the beginning, and teachers came to resent the implicit decision of the government to place the burden of Irish revival upon their backs, and to turn schoolchildren into "digits in the Irish revival statistics" (Akenson 1975: 60; see also O'Doherty 1958: 268, who argued that "our children's minds must not be made the battleground of a political wrangle"). Debate abounds over the "success" of school programmes for Irish: It is true that a thin wash of Irish competence has been applied to almost everyone now living in Ireland, and that ample educational provision is in place for those who wish to further develop their fluency; on the other hand, education has not precipitated a general revival of vernacular Irish.

Meanwhile, the Irish native-speaking population continued to shrink, and the *Gaeltacht* (Irish-speaking area) is now concentrated on the western littoral. The Gaeltacht areas have typically been rural, poor and subject to out-migration, and measures to encourage their economic viability have often meant English-speaking in-migration (of ideas, if not always of people). The essential difficulty is that, if nothing is done to or for the Gaeltacht, it continues to shrink; if things *are* done, artificial enclaves may be created, and English influence actually expedited. Ó Sé (1966) put it as follows: Since the Gaeltacht is not urbanised, emigration continues; if it *were* urbanised, what would stop it becoming anglicised, like the rest of the country?

The revival of Irish as a regularly spoken language has not succeeded. It is true that almost one million people have reported themselves as Irish speakers in recent censuses; this is a larger proportion than that obtaining in mid-nineteenth century. However, Irish speakers in the 1850s obviously possessed a fluency that is hardly applicable to contemporary generations whose skills arise from the classroom. The real picture is one of a steady decline in speakers of Irish as a maternal language and a great increase in more cursory competence. Today, outside the Gaeltacht, perhaps 4% of the Irish people use the language with any regularity.

The decline of Irish is popularly put down to English occupation, and there is of course something to this: If English had not arrived in Ireland, it could hardly have displaced the indigenous variety. But this alone is simplistic. Why did Irish first successfully counter English, and then lose ground? Why did things not follow the course of, say, Norman French and English in England? The facts of the matter relate, above all, to the increasing prestige of English and its speakers which, from about 1800, proved a powerful attraction. The view that the national school system, the church and native politicians insufficiently concerned about Irish were the killers of the language is in itself also an oversimplification, but they are important factors when seen against a background of a language increasingly associated with rurality, poverty and an unsophisticated peasantry. To cite de Fréine once again:

> [...] the worst excesses were not imposed from outside. The whole paraphernalia of tally sticks, wooden gags, humiliation and mockery – often enforced by encouraging children to spy on their brothers and sisters, or on the children of neighbouring townlands – were not the product of any law or official regulation, but of a social self-generated movement of collective behaviour among the people themselves.
> (de Fréine 1977: 83–84).

What generalities can we extract from the Irish language situation? There are, of course, a great many points which will be recognised as applicable to situations elsewhere, but I can only touch upon a few here. First, we see that Irish initially remained strong in the face of linguistic competition, that incomers were Gaelicised, and that laws to bolster English were seen to be necessary. This situation changed with new political and social conditions, but it took more than two centuries for English to gain a firm hold in the country. In the nineteenth century, a large-scale and very rapid shift occurred because of a complex of circumstances which cannot be easily attributed to something as simple as oppression. It is surely clear, then, that language shift reflects sociopolitical change and this absolutely dwarfs efforts made on behalf of language alone. This is not to say that language cannot serve a rallying purpose in nationalist political movements, but it only does so when it retains some realistic degree of communicative function. This was not the case for Irish by the time the revivalists appeared.

A second and related point is that language revival efforts can be seen as artificial when they operate in the face of historical realities. This is true in two senses. They are artificial, first of all, to the extent that they are divorced from the forces of day-to-day life for the masses. It is simply not possible to bring about widespread language shift when the appeal is made on the basis of abstractions like culture, heritage or tradition. These are not, of course, trivial or ignoble aspects of life, but they are not conscious priorities for most people. In Ireland we observe that those who might have been expected to respond best to revival rhetoric – Irish-speaking residents of the *Gaeltacht* – did not do so in any united way. In another sense, revivalism is often artificial in the type of language form it attempts to resuscitate. From a desire to standardise, to upgrade and to give fair play to various dialects, an academic variety may be produced which is some way removed from the maternal patterns of any native speaker. The speech of many Gaelic Leaguers certainly fell curiously on the ears of Gaeltacht inhabitants.

A third, and generally applicable feature of the Irish situation is the importance of a living heartland for a language, a place where the language is regularly used across a broad range of domains. If this has shrunk to such an extent that it is seen to require special support, then the "paradox of the Gaeltacht" can be expected: If nothing is done, there is every likelihood of continued erosion; if things *are* done, then the danger exists of creating a fishbowl in which language (and other) matters are treated with the same deliberate attention which characterises the half-an-hour-a-week German class. While there is nothing wrong with this sort of attention *per se*, it hardly contributes to that unselfconscious use of language which we associate with normal personal interaction. Furthermore, the process of out-migration which is associated with isolated heartlands says much about the desires and priorities of residents, often interfering with the hopes of revivalists.

Fourth, the Irish experience suggests that the link between original language and identity is not essential. There exists, today, a strong Irish identity which does not involve Irish, in a communicative sense, for the vast majority. At the same time, the language continues to serve a symbolic function for many. One of the revivalist errors was to single out communicative language as the most important marker of identity, ignoring the evidence of history and daily life.

A final point has to do with what might be seen as the relative *success* of the Irish revival. While not all are deeply interested in the Celtic background or the Irish language, linguistic and cultural revival efforts have facilitated access to them – and making accessible, on a voluntary basis, aspects of a heritage which may otherwise be quite unfathomable seems a worthy objective; any revival effort which accomplished it could hardly be judged a complete failure. Moreover, giving everyone that "thin wash" of Irish that I mentioned earlier has created at least a minimal identification with the traditional culture. And this is to omit entirely the associated literary revival and the important relationships between linguistic and more overtly political activism.

5.2.   Hebrew

If Irish is often cited as a failure, as a demonstration that even sovereign states cannot necessarily halt linguistic incursions, then Hebrew in Israel is the archetypal success story. Indeed, all language revival efforts have failed, according to Nahir (1977), with the exception of that of Hebrew. Irish is among the unsuccessful ones that Nahir mentions, even though – as we have seen – some have thought it not to be so; and Ellis and mac a'Ghobhainn's (1971) score of examples are all seen as at least partially successful. We see, once again, that assessments of "success" or "failure" very much depend upon the breadth or the narrowness of one's description of revival.

Nonetheless, if we were to be very restrictive, if we were to consider only revival attempts in which the number of speakers and domains has shrunk to minority status, and if we were to count as successful only those efforts in which a variety has been returned to widespread and regular communicative use, then it does appear as if Hebrew is the only real true success. Hebrew-like claims have been made for some other minority languages (especially in Europe), but closer inspection typically reveals that the accomplishment would be better understood as having decreased the rapidity of language decline.

The obvious question: Why has the revival of Hebrew succeeded where others have not? With the state of Israel incorporating a linguistically heterogeneous population, a communicative need clearly existed. This is not unique to Israel, of course, but there *also* existed in this case an old language with a powerful psychological claim on the population. (This is quite unlike the Irish situation, by contrast, where the attempted revival of the ancestral variety did *not* coincide with communicative need.) Nahir rightly stresses the importance of this need, without which linguistic revival movements – that must then call upon religious, national or political sentiments – are severely hampered. Furthermore, it is arguable that the Hebrew case is not quite the miracle it has occasionally been made out to be. Fellman pointed out, a generation ago, that Hebrew was never a dead language; indeed, he suggested there is *no* attested historical case in which a truly dead variety has been revived – shades of Bergin (see Fellman 1973a, 1973b, 1976). Hebrew was a living community language in Palestine until about AD 200, although it had been abandoned by Jews outside the homeland several centuries before. However, it continued as a religious language and, in some communities, also as a secular one for certain purposes. Among European Jews in the Middle Ages there were many who were literate *only* in Hebrew. By the nineteenth century, Hebrew was indeed dormant for Jews in western and central Europe, but it still existed in a diglossic situation for eastern European Jews.

So, when Eliezer Ben-Yehuda first advocated the use of Hebrew as the national tongue in Palestine, in the late 1870s, there still existed some linguistic base. "Through eastern European Jewry, in particular, then, the revival of Hebrew could – and did – proceed apace, *without any overriding or insurmountable difficulties*" (Fellman 1976: 17; original italics). Not everyone concurs completely with Fellman, but it is fair to say that the difficulties surrounding the Hebrew revival had more to do with sociopolitical issues – including the claims made in some quarters on behalf of Yiddish as the Israeli lingua franca – than with breathing new life into a dead entity. It is arguable, in fact, that the particular circumstances surrounding Hebrew revival efforts suggested likely success from an early stage, quite apart from the pioneering work of Ben-Yehuda. This is to take nothing away from the "father of modern Hebrew" who, after arriving in Palestine in 1881, established the first Hebrew-speaking home (his own) in our times, and whose son (the writer and journalist, Itamar Ben-Avi, born in 1882) was the first maternally Hebrew-speaking child in the modern era.

Ben-Yehuda's initial appeals for the adoption of Hebrew went more or less unheeded, the early Hebrew societies enjoyed only minor success, and the more formal creations (a Hebrew dictionary, the establishment of a Hebrew language council) came *after* the early, critical years. Ben-Yehuda's involvement in the developing Palestine press is often judged to have been more important. In 1885, he assumed the editorship of a weekly, *Hatzvi* 'The Deer', in the pages of which many new or revived words were presented to the public; six years later, "the deer" became *Hashkafar* 'Outlook'. Most importantly, Ben-Yehuda founded the first Palestine daily newspaper (*Ha'or* 'The Light') in 1910, and his son became its editor. Still, the pivotal feature of the revival was probably the Hebrew classroom. Two important points suggest themselves here. First, the lack of initial utility of literary activity (as reflected in dictionaries, academies, and so on) suggests the limitations of formal language planning in the earliest and most sensitive stages of revival efforts. Second, the strong influence of the Hebrew school – in contrast to the much more circumscribed achievements of education through Irish – demonstrates that educational impacts are intimately linked to the currents swirling beyond the school-yard gates. Where teachers and society-at-large are pulling in the same direction, so to speak, the educational system can be a powerful factor in language revival; where they are not, it is a mistake to rely very much on schools.

It is the unique context in which a communicative need existed, then, that distinguished the Hebrew revival from others. Without it the revival would simply not have happened; with it, the success or failure of *particular* programmes of language planning becomes of secondary, technical interest. In fact, the Hebrew case demonstrates that the power of selfconscious or formal language planning tends very much to depend upon existing social forces, and that in most cases such planning involves the "tidying up" (often a substantial task, of course) of processes put in train or made possible by larger forces. If one were to read only the language-planning literature, it would be easy to lose sight of the fact that, as Kedourie (1960: 125) put it, "it is absurd to think that professors of linguistics […] can do the work of statesmen and soldiers". Planning and policy-making are directed by those who possess some variety of power and who – in democracies, at least – respond to, and elaborate upon, sociopolitical needs and requirements.

6. Conclusions

One of the central points made here is that the term "revival" can reasonably cover all sorts of language situations, and that various hair-splitting terminological exercises are both unnecessary and inefficient. (Question: When is a language revival not a revival? Answer: When it is a restoration / rebirth / renewal / renaissance / rejuvenation / revitalisation / reintroduction / resurrection / reversal of shift. Well, at least they all start with "r".) It is also the case – as the descriptions of Hebrew and Irish illustrate – that the uniqueness of different language situations does not arise through the presence of important elements and attitudes found nowhere else; on the contrary, there are very familiar features that crop up again and again. The uniqueness of each setting lies, rather, in the particular combinations and weightings of these contextual features. This suggests that some typology of maintenance/revival scenarios might be useful. A rough classification could look like this:

(1) a language with few or no speakers, where no written or taped records exist;
(2) the same, except that some written material exists;
(3) the same, except that written and taped material exists;

(4) a language with some native speakers remaining, but where none are monolingual;
(5) the same, but where some at least are monolingual;
(6) the same, but where monolingualism and normal family transmission of the original language occur;
(7) the same, but where substantial numbers of speakers are monolingual, where there is language transmission, and where the original variety retains important domains (especially outside the home and the family).

This is a very general outline, and I hope that further elaborations will follow. For the moment, the list is intended only to illustrate the point that, while all situations can be subsumed under the heading of language revival, there are varieties – and that the principal distinctions among such varieties might be characterised in certain recurring ways. I have organised the list such that the relative ease of revival increases as one goes from categories one to seven. Irish in Ireland, and Gaelic in Nova Scotia, for example, would both fit in the fourth category – and Hebrew could also be placed in that category, a fact that in itself suggests the need for a more finely-grained typological arrangement. Many of the European examples discussed by Ellis and mac a'Ghobhainn (1971) – and deemed to be "success" stories – fall in the seventh.

Understanding language maintenance and revival could also benefit from other typological arrangements. Since the uniqueness of every context arises because of the differential weightings and combinations of elements – and not from elements that are unique in themselves – the usefulness of frameworks within which settings might be assessed and compared is suggested. With this in mind, I have constructed a typological framework of minority-language situations – the ones, that is to say, of most relevance for discussions of maintenance and revival efforts. Its basic geographical underpinning represents an adaptation of a scheme first proposed by Paul White in 1987 (see White 1991), and it rests upon three distinctions. The first is among minority languages that are unique to one state, those that are non-unique but which are still minorities in all contexts in which they occur, and those that are minorities in one setting but majority varieties elsewhere; thus, we have *unique, non-unique* and *local-only* minorities. The second distinction deals with the type of connection among speakers of the same minority language in different states; are they *adjoining* or *non-adjoining*? Thirdly, what degree of spatial cohesion exists among speakers within a given state? Here, the terms *cohesive* and *non-cohesive* can be used. Given that the adjoining/non-adjoining distinction does not apply to unique minorities, it follows that a ten-cell model emerges. Table 1 provides some examples, of both indigenous and immigrant minority-language settings.

Table 1. Examples of Minority-Language Situations

	Type	Indigenous minorities	Immigrant minorities
1.	Unique Cohesive	Sardinian (Sardinia); Welsh (Wales); Friulian (Friuli-Venezia-Giulia)	Dialect communities (often religiously organised) in which the variety is now divergent from that in the region of origin (e.g., Pennsylvania "Dutch")
2.	Unique Non-cohesive	Cornish (Cornwall)	As above, but where speakers are scattered
3.	Non-unique Adjoining Cohesive	Occitan (Piedmont and Liguria, and in France); Basque (France, and in Spain); Catalan (Spain, and in Andorra)	Enclaves of immigrants found in neighbouring states
4.	Non-unique Adjoining Non-cohesive	Saami (Finland, Norway, Sweden and Russia)	Scattered immigrants in neighbouring states
5.	Non-unique Non-adjoining Cohesive	Catalan (Spain, and in Sardinia)	Welsh (Patagonia); Gaelic (Nova Scotia)
6.	Non-unique Non-adjoining Non-cohesive	Romany (throughout Europe)	Scattered immigrants of European origin in "new world" receiving countries
7.	Local-only Adjoining Cohesive	French (Valle d'Aosta, and in France)	French (in New England town enclaves); Spanish (southwest USA); Italian *gastarbeiter* (in Switzerland)
8.	Local-only Adjoining Non-cohesive	German (Piedmont, and in Switzerland)	French (scattered throughout New England)
9.	Local-only Non-adjoining Cohesive	French (Apulia, and in France)	Immigrant enclaves in "new world" countries
10.	Local-only Non-adjoining Non-cohesive	Albanian (throughout the Mezzogiorno, and in Albania)	As above, but where speakers are scattered

The model is, of course, far from perfect. Apart from difficulties arising from geographical variations and nuances not considered here, it is clear that information of other types is required to more fully understand the complexities of minority-language settings. For example, the functions and status of competing language varieties are clearly central here; see, *inter alia*, Ferguson (1962, 1966), Stewart (1962, 1968), Haugen (1972), Haarmann (1986), Giles and Coupland (1991). I have closely examined all these earlier exercises as part of my own attempt to create a comprehensive scaffolding of ecolinguistic factors. While there is insufficient room here to go into further detail (for which see Grenoble and Whaley 1998), this involves an intersection of three basic categories (speaker, language and setting) with eleven substantive and disciplinary perspectives (sociology, linguistics, psychology, history, demography, education, politics/law/government, geography, religion, economics and the media). The assumption here is that each of the "cells" created by this 3 × 11 nexus prompts germane questions: The intersection of demography with setting, for example, would alert us to consider urban-rural distinctions of importance for language maintenance or decline; that of sociology and speaker suggests the matter of within-group or without-group marriage; that of speaker and language with psychology leads to a consideration of language attitudes and beliefs; and so on. Clearly, much more work remains to be done in the production of a comprehensive typology useful for description and comparison, leading to a more complete conceptualisation of language-contact situations, perhaps even contributing to predictions of shift/maintenance outcomes.

A final word: If we return to the pivotal concept of *will*, we can see that its operation and its strength both motivate and are influenced by features of the revival situation. This is a useful reminder, perhaps, that the elevation of any particular element to some sort of "prime-mover" status – while common enough in the literature – is an inaccurate reflection of real life, where (to return to another term in the discussion – *ecology*) complex intertwinings are the rule. In almost all instances, both "success" and "failure" are possible: The Irish efforts, we recall, were seen by some as "astounding" and by others as a "terrible failure". The challenge is often to find goals that are both desirable and attainable. Clearly, some form of leadership must assess what action to take and what is to be aimed for. But, at the end of the day, it is ordinary people who will live with the decisions and processes, and who will ultimately judge them.

Notes

1. At the 2004 LAUD meeting, Karsten Legère discussed the impact of J. K. Nyerere on the empowerment of Swahili. Even this more-than-usually committed statesman was apparently unable to bring himself to endorse Swahili as a medium for post-primary

education. Neville Alexander (2004), in discussing some of the sociopolitical factors involved in language policy in post-apartheid South Africa, remarked that altering political mindsets – hegemonic mentalities produced by longstanding exogenous pressures – even in a dynamic and reinvigorated setting, usually takes a considerable (and, to many, a frustrating) amount of time. And Paulin Djité, in his presentation about "borrowed tongues", described a lack of sufficient African will to think beyond European varieties.

2. Michael Tierney contributed to the arguments about Irish revival the observation that:
   Analogies with Flemish, Czech or the Baltic languages are all misleading, because the problem in their cases has been rather that of restoring a peasant language to cultivated use than that of reviving one which the majority had ceased to speak. (Tierney 1927: 5)

While it is true that the Irish and Flemish cases are not analogous, this is not because one is a "restoration" and the other an attempted revival. Rather, it would be more accurate to say that the *type* of revival differs in the two instances.

References

Akenson, Donald
    1975   *A Mirror to Kathleen's Face*. Montreal: McGill-Queen's University Press.
Alexander, Neville
    2004   Sociopolitical factors in the evolution of language policy in post-apartheid South Africa. Paper presented at the 30th International LAUD (Linguistic Agency, University of Duisburg) Symposium, "Empowerment Through Language", Landau, April.
Arnold, Matthew
    1883   *On the Study of Celtic Literature, and on Translating Homer*. New York: Macmillan.
Bolinger, Dwight
    1980   *Language – the Loaded Weapon*. London: Longman.
Brenzinger, Matthias
    1992   *Language Death*. Berlin: Mouton de Gruyter.
Brenzinger, Matthias
    1998   *Endangered Languages in Africa*. Köln: Rüdiger Köpp.
Campbell, John
    1948   Scottish Gaelic in Canada. *An Gaidheal* 43(6): 69–71.
Crystal, David
    2000   *Language Death*. Cambridge: Cambridge University Press.
Dalby, David
    2000   Linguasphere unites a thousand world voices. *Times Higher Education Supplement*, May 26.
De Fréine, Seán
    1977   The dominance of the English language in the nineteenth century. In: Diarmaid Ó Muirithe (ed.), *The English Language in Ireland,* 71–87. Cork: Mercier.

Dewar, Daniel
 1812   *Observations on the Character, Customs, and Superstitions of the Irish; and on Some of the Causes which have Retarded the Moral and Political Improvement of Ireland.* London: Gale & Curtis.

Dickens, Charles
 1846–1848 *Dombey and Son.* London: Bradbury & Evans.

Djité, Paulin
 2004   Living on borrowed tongues – a view from within. Paper presented at the 30th International LAUD (Linguistic Agency, University of Duisburg) Symposium, "Empowerment Through Language", Landau, April.

Dorian, Nancy
 1987   The value of language-maintenance efforts which are unlikely to succeed. *International Journal of the Sociology of Language* 68: 57–67.

Dorian, Nancy
 1989   *Investigating Obsolescence.* Cambridge: Cambridge University Press.

Dorian, Nancy
 1993   A response to Ladefoged's other view of endangered languages. *Language* 69: 575–579.

Dunn, Charles
 1974   *Highland Settler.* Toronto: University of Toronto Press.

Durkacz, Victor
 1983   *The Decline of the Celtic Languages.* Edinburgh: John Donald.

Edwards, John
 1993   Language revival: Specifics and generalities. *Studies in Second Language Acquisition* 15: 107–113.

Edwards, John
 1994   What can (or should) linguists do in the face of language decline? In: Margaret Harry (ed.), *Papers from the Seventeenth Annual Meeting of the Atlantic Provinces Linguistic Association*, 25–32. Halifax: Saint Mary's University.

Edwards, John
 2002   Old wine in new bottles: Critical remarks on language ecology. In: Annette Boudreau, Lise Dubois, Jacques Maurais and Grant McConnell (eds.), *L'écologie des Langues: Mélanges William Mackey*, 299–324. Paris: L'Harmattan.

Edwards, John
 2004   Ecolinguistic ideologies: A critical perspective. In: Martin Pütz, Joanne Neff-van Aertselaer and Teun van Dijk, (eds.), *Communicating Ideologies*, 273–289. Frankfurt: Peter Lang.

Ellis, Peter and Seumas mac a'Ghobhainn
 1971   *The Problem of Language Revival.* Inverness: Club Leabhar.

Fellman, Jack
 1973a   *The Revival of a Classical Tongue: Eliezer Ben-Yehuda and the Modern Hebrew Language.* The Hague: Mouton.

Fellman, Jack
 1973b   Concerning the "revival" of the Hebrew language. *Anthropological Linguistics* 15: 250–257.

Fellman, Jack
   1976   On the revival of the Hebrew language. *Language Sciences* 43: 17.
Fennell, Desmond
   1981   Can a shrinking linguistic minority be saved? In: Einar Haugen, Derrick McClure and Derick Thomson (eds.), *Minority Languages Today*, 32–39. Edinburgh: Edinburgh University Press.
Ferguson, Charles
   1962   The language factor in national development. In: Frank Rice (ed.), *Study of the Role of Second Languages in Asia, Africa and Latin America*, 8–14. Washington: Center for Applied Linguistics.
Ferguson, Charles
   1966   National sociolinguistic profile formulas. In: William Bright (ed.), *Sociolinguistics*, 309–315. The Hague: Mouton.
Fishman, Joshua
   1982   Whorfianism of the third kind. *Language in Society* 11: 1–14.
Fishman, Joshua
   1990   What is reversing language shift (RLS) and how can it succeed? *Journal of Multilingual and Multicultural Development* 11: 5–36.
Fishman, Joshua
   1991   *Reversing Language Shift*. Clevedon: Multilingual Matters.
Fishman, Joshua
   2004   Sociolinguistics: More power(s) to you. Paper presented at the 30th International LAUD (Linguistic Agency, University of Duisburg) Symposium, "Empowerment Through Language", Landau, April.
Gardner, Robert and Wallace Lambert
   1972   *Attitudes and Motivation in Second-Language Learning*. Rowley, MA: Newbury House.
Giles, Howard and Nikolas Coupland
   1991   *Language: Contexts and Consequences*. Milton Keynes: Open University Press.
Grenoble, Lenore and Lindsey Whaley
   1998   *Endangered Languages*. Cambridge: Cambridge University Press.
Haarmann, Harald
   1986   *Language in Ethnicity*. Berlin: de Gruyter.
Haugen, Einar
   1972   *The Ecology of Language*. Stanford: Stanford University Press
Haugen, Einar
   1987   *Blessings of Babel*. Berlin: Mouton de Gruyter.
Hyde, Douglas
   1886   A plea for the Irish language. *Dublin University Review* 2: 666–676.
Hyde, Douglas
   1894   The necessity for de-anglicising Ireland. In: Charles Duffy, George Sigerson and Douglas Hyde (eds.), *The Revival of Irish Literature*, 117–161. London: T. Fisher Unwin.
Kedourie, Elie
   1960   *Nationalism*. London: Hutchinson.
Krauss, Michael
   1992   The world's languages in crisis. *Language* 68: 4–10.

Ladefoged, Peter
  1992   Discussion note: Another view of endangered languages. *Language* 68: 809–811.
Lambert, Wallace, Robert Hodgson, Robert Gardner and Steven Fillenbaum
  1960   Evaluational reactions to spoken languages. *Journal of Abnormal and Social Psychology* 60: 44–51.
Legère, Karsten
  2004   J. K. Nyerere and the empowerment of Swahili. Paper presented at the 30th International LAUD (Linguistic Agency, University of Duisburg) Symposium, "Empowerment Through Language", Landau, April.
Maffi, Luisa
  2000   Language preservation versus language maintenance and revitalization. *International Journal of the Sociology of Language* 142: 175–190.
Moran, Donald
  1900   The Gaelic revival. *New Ireland Review* 12: 257–272.
Nahir, Moshe
  1977   The five aspects of language planning. *Language Problems and Language Planning* 1: 107–123.
Nahir, Moshe
  1984   Language planning and language acquisition: The "great leap" in the Hebrew revival. Paper presented at the Seventh World Congress of Applied Linguistics, Brussels, August.
Ngũgĩ wa Thiong'o
  1986   *Decolonising the Mind: The Politics of Language in African Literature.* London: Currey.
Ngũgĩ wa Thiong'o
  1993   *Moving the Centre: The Struggle for Cultural Freedoms.* London: Currey.
Nettle, Daniel and Suzanne Romaine
  2000   *Vanishing Voices.* Oxford: Oxford University Press.
Ó Danachair, Caoimhín
  1969   The Gaeltacht. In Brian Ó Cuív (ed.), *A View of the Irish Language*, 112–121. Dublin: Government Stationery Office.
O'Doherty, E.
  1958   Bilingual school policy. *Studies* 47: 259–268.
Ó Domhnalláin, Tomás
  1959   Bilingual education in Ireland. *Bulletin of the Collegiate Faculty of Education* (Aberystwyth) 6: 6–8.
Ó hAilín, Tomás
  1969   Irish revival movements. In Brian Ó Cuív (ed.), *A View of the Irish Language*, 91–100. Dublin: Government Stationery Office.
Ó Sé, Liam
  1966   The Irish language revival: Achilles heel. *Éire-Ireland* 1: 26–49.
Rix, Helmut
  2004   Etruscan. In: Roger Woodard (ed.), *The Cambridge Encyclopedia of the World's Ancient Languages,* 943–966. Cambridge: Cambridge University Press.
Robins, Robert and Eugenius Uhlenbeck
  1991   *Endangered Languages.* Oxford: Berg.

Spolsky, Bernard
    2004   *Language Policy.* Cambridge: Cambridge University Press.
Stewart, William
    1962   An outline of linguistic typology for describing multilingualism. In: Frank Rice (ed.), *Study of the Role of Second Languages in Asia, Africa and Latin America,* 15–25. Washington: Center for Applied Linguistics.
Stewart, William
    1968   A sociolinguistic typology for describing national multilingualism. In: Joshua Fishman (ed.), *Readings in the Sociology of Language,* 531–545. The Hague: Mouton.
Tierney, Michael
    1927   The revival of the Irish language. *Studies* 16: 1–22.
Trench, Dermot
    1907   *What is the Use of Reviving Irish?* Dublin: Maunsel.
Weinreich, Uriel
    1953   *Languages in Contact.* The Hague: Mouton.
White, Paul
    1991   Geographical aspects of minority language situations in Italy. In: Colin Williams (ed.), *Linguistic Minorities, Society and Territory,* 15–39. Clevedon: Multilingual Matters.

9. Economics and language policy

François Grin

1. Introduction

Economics is increasingly often called upon to help analyse macro-level language issues, and to assist in the selection, design and evaluation of language policies. An economic perspective on language can be used to assess the consequences associated with various policy options and to provide answers to fundamental questions that other disciplines tend to bypass. These key questions can be informally summed up as: "Should we follow this or that course of action with respect to language issues?" or, more simply, "*What* should be done?". Since a question of this type can only be answered by invoking explicit criteria, it immediately raises the question of what constitutes an appropriate set of criteria, and therefore the question of "*Why* should this or that course of action be followed?".

Turning to economics for answers to such questions represents, however, a recent development. Traditionally, the analytical perspectives brought to bear on language policy and planning (two notions between which we will not need to make a distinction for the purposes of this chapter) have tended to emphasize the contribution of disciplines other than economics.

First, most of the language policy discourse is, of course, anchored in applied linguistics and sociolinguistics; however, these fields of inquiry usually emphasize another set of questions, which may be summarized with the question "*How?*". Indeed, their focus usually is on how language policy and planning actually operate, how different groups of actors respond to policy plans, and how such policy plans mesh with a given social and political context (see Ricento, this vol.). However, general discussions of the reasons for particular measures to be adopted (or, on the contrary, avoided) remains largely side-stepped. Much the same can be said of educational perspectives on language policy, which emphasize the modalities of language education (that is, how best to teach languages) rather than the choice of languages to teach, or the reasons society may have for teaching them.

Secondly, among the disciplines that do address the questions of "what" and "why", law plays a major role. The legal perspective defines states' obligations regarding the treatment of various languages, thus determining what should be done; this perspective is often articulated in terms of language rights, which provide a rationale for answering the question of why it should be done (see also Skutnabb-Kangas, this vol.).

Thirdly, another perspective (which it is difficult, however, to associate with a specific discipline) on language policy and planning might be called a culturalist one. It approaches languages as manifestations of culture, and tends to view policy in terms of measures affecting corpus or, at best, support for literary creation or publication.

As a source of discourse on language policy and planning, economics stands apart from the preceding disciplines because it views language policy in the same way as it would address other policy matters, as they occur in fields such as education, the environment, health or transport. This is why the economic approach to language policy blends almost seamlessly into "policy analysis" or "policy evaluation". The basic idea goes as follows: As a result of political debate, several goals are set. In order to achieve these goals, various policy measures may be adopted. These policy measures may be quite different from one another, they do not carry exactly the same consequences, and a choice must be made by weighing the advantages and drawbacks of each option in order to select the best one. Clearly, the weighing of advantages and drawbacks can feed back into the political debate. However, the policy analysis exercise remains distinct from the political discussion. Whereas the latter constitutes an arena in which citizens or their elected representatives confront their subjective values, policy analysis can function only if value judgements are identified as such and, as much as possible, set aside. The role of the policy analyst, rather, is to identify and evaluate the consequences of possible courses of action; this allows for better-informed decisions.

This straightforward logic, however, would be difficult to apply without an appropriate set of analytical tools, and the chief goal of this chapter is to present the latter.

First, it is useful to describe the field of specialization known as "economics of language" or "language economics". This is done in Section 2, which provides a historical overview of the economics of language, and presents the main lines of research in this field. Section 3 turns to the main subject and addresses key analytical features of the economic approach to language planning, discussing in particular the following questions: Why is state intervention in language matters justified? What are the key dimensions of decision-making in language policy? How are these dimensions implemented when evaluating competing options? Section 4 highlights some thorny theoretical issues, in particular the question of how to handle so-called "network externalities". Section 5 stresses the role of interdisciplinarity, with a focus on the way in which applied linguistics can be combined with language economics. Section 6 turns to applications, and illustrates the use of economics in language policy and planning with respect to three major policy issues: the choice of foreign languages taught as school subjects in education systems; support for regional or minority languages; and the choice of official and working languages in plurilingual organizations such as the European Union.

2. Language economics

2.1. Towards a definition

The emergence of language economics as a field of investigation can be traced back to a paper on "Economics of Language" published 40 years ago in *Behavioral Science* (Marschak 1965). However, relatively little attention appears to have been devoted since then to the development of a formal definition. Vaillancourt (1985: 13) characterizes publications in the field as "writings by economists on language questions"; Breton (1998: iii) refers to "topics related to the interconnections between languages […] and the economy"; finally, in his introduction to a recent collection of reprints of 20 papers by different authors, Lamberton (2002: xi) offers no definition, but suggests that language economics "merges with the economics of information".

Given the relative absence of formal definitions, I keep using one proposed elsewhere: "[T]he economics of language refers to the paradigm of theoretical economics and uses the concepts and tools of economics in the study of relationships featuring linguistic variables; it focuses principally, but not exclusively, on those relationships in which economic variables also play a part" (Grin 1996: 6). This definition harks back to the three main lines of inquiry in the economics of language, namely:

- How do language variables affect economic variables (for example, do foreign language skills influence labor income, all other things being equal)?
- How do economic variables affect linguistic variables (for example, do the patterns of international trade affect patterns of language decline and language spread)?
- How do essentially economic processes (or processes that can be characterized, at a deep level, as embodying an economic rationale, such as "constrained utility maximization") affect language processes such as language dynamics?

The very notion of an economic perspective on language raises a number of epistemological questions regarding the demarcation of academic disciplines. For the purposes of this chapter, let us simply remember that no issue is intrinsically "sociological", "linguistic", "political" or "economic". Rather, almost every issue presents sociological, linguistic, political, and economic dimensions. The corresponding disciplines offer complementary angles from which an issue can be examined. Depending on the issue at hand, the contribution of any given discipline may be major or minor. This also applies to economics, which can contribute to the study of language issues through insights or conceptual tools that other disciplines do not provide.[1]

2.2. Historical overview

Much of the early work in the economics of language (as a field of research anchored in economics but addressing language issues) is due to Canadian (particularly Québécois) economists. Their papers reflect the debate over the respective position of French and English in Canadian society. Almost at the same time, a number of studies started appearing on language economics issues in the United States. There again, local conditions have played a major role and to this day, most US studies equate "the economics of language" with the econometric investigation of earnings differentials between immigrants and Anglophones, showing (which is not surprising in a predominantly English-speaking country) that much of the earnings differentials between native-born US citizens (possibly setting aside native Americans) and immigrants is statistically related to the latter's lower competence in English.

The influence of social and political context is reflected in the three important stages of the early development of language economics, which well into the 1980s focused on the effects of language on labor income (Grin and Vaillancourt 1997: 44–45). In a first stage, the emphasis was placed on the role of people's native language as an ethnic attribute affecting their earnings – thereby raising the question of possible language-based discrimination. A second wave of contributions analyzed language (usually, a second language) as a form of human capital. In a third wave, beginning with Vaillancourt (1980), language was treated both as an ethnic attribute and an element of human capital.

Though less visible, other avenues had been pursued in parallel, studying for example the role of language as a factor impacting on international trade (Carr 1985) or as a criterion for the distribution of resources between groups (Breton 1964; Breton and Mieszkowski 1977). By the early 1990s, the economics of language had also started to fan out in a broader range of topics, addressing for example language dynamics and efficiency conditions in minority language promotion.

2.3. Main lines of research

The main lines of research in language economics can be arranged in four categories, three of which are briefly reviewed in the rest of this section. The fourth one, precisely because it focuses on language policy, is discussed at greater length in the following sections. This section is chiefly concerned with providing a general orientation into language economics; a more extensive literature review can be found in Grin (2003a).

2.3.1. Language and earnings

This line of research, apart from being the oldest in language economics, remains the main one in terms of the number of publications. It focuses on the effect of language skills on labor income (or "earnings"). This mostly empirical tradition uses survey or census data on (usually) self-reported language skills (in the first language [L1], L2, L3, etc.) and self-reported earnings to see, in line with human capital theory, whether the former are predictors of the latter, controlling for other determinants of labor income such as education, work experience, or (data permitting) type of work. Outside of Canada, extensive data sets are few. Hence, the most detailed studies use Canadian census data (Vaillancourt 1996; Breton 1998). Studies from other countries typically rely on survey data. The focus is placed on immigrant groups in the United States (e.g., Bloom and Grenier 1996; Dávila and Mora 2000), Australia, (e.g., Chiswick and Miller 1995), Israel (e.g., Chiswick and Repetto 2001) or Germany (Dustmann 1994). These studies provide statistical estimates of the value of competence in the locally dominant language.

Studies in Switzerland (Grin 1999) or Luxembourg (Klein 2004) use representative population samples and provide estimates of the rates of return on national languages, and English as a foreign language. One study on the Ukraine (Kastoukievitch 2003) could be said to fall somewhere in between, since it assesses the labor market value of competence in Ukrainian.

A few papers venture away from the human capital framework in order to propose explanations of the effect of language on earnings. Early models (Raynauld and Marion 1972) invoke a deliberate strategy, by the capitalists in a dominant group, to channel the largest possible share of aggregate income to group members; Lang (1986) views unequal earnings as the result of cost-minimizing strategies by owners of capital (most of whom are assumed to belong to one group) employing workers from the other group.

2.3.2. Language dynamics

Research proposing explanations for the decline or spread of languages may emphasize very different aspects of these processes. Some research focuses on minority languages, generally assuming speakers to be bilingual and to also know a majority language (Grin [1992] 2002a); other research focuses on actors' interest in learning or not learning another language, taking account of the costs and benefits of this decision and, most importantly, of the strategic interaction between learners: The more people use it, the more valuable it becomes, as a tool for communication, to people who already know it (Church and King 1993; Dalmazzone 1999; Selten and Pool 1997). Therefore, language skills give access to a network. This tends to give rise to accelerating or "snowball" effects, which set language apart from standard economic goods. This is often referred to in the literature using the concept of "externality", further discussed in Section 3.3 below; alternatively, some authors define language as a "super-public" or "hypercollective" good (De Swaan 2001).

Although many of the processes at hand still need to be more fully examined (see Section 4), an elegantly compact theory of language dynamics has been proposed by van Parijs (2004). He observes that people are more likely to learn languages they consider useful, and that in any group made up of people with different language repertoires, communication is likely to take place in the language in which the skills of the least linguistically nimble participant are highest (in recent work, van Parijs calls it the "minimex" language because it minimizes exclusion). If one language emerges as serving this function more frequently than other languages, people will have an incentive to learn it. This will, in turn, increase the occurrence of situations in which this very language is the *maximin* language, thus increasing the incentive to learn it.

Still, the validity of all the lines of reasoning centered on the network effect largely depends on one assumption, namely, that language is little else than a tool for communication (sometimes relabeled a "communication technology"). Sociolinguists have known for a long time that this does not do justice to the complexity of language in human experience. On balance, the "hypercollective" nature of language opens up some of the most challenging research avenues in language economics, but it is one in which an interdisciplinary understanding of the issues at hand is particularly necessary (see Section 5).

2.3.3. *Language and economic activity*

This somewhat heterogeneous category brings together research on the role of language in core economic activities like production, distribution, consumption, and exchange at the macroeconomic (i.e., aggregate) level or at the microeconomic level (that is, at the level of the typical agent, such as the generic firm or consumer). For example, are linguistically diverse countries more or less prosperous than unilingual ones? Is productive efficiency affected by the choice and range of languages used in a multilingual corporation? Do people really prefer goods to be advertised and sold to them in their native language?

At the macroeconomic level, the issue of whether linguistic diversity is, on balance, profitable to the economy remains a matter for discussion. Some argue that linguistic diversity can give rise to greater creativity; there seems to be no robust empirical results supporting this claim. Conversely, others contend that diversity mostly gives rise to added communication costs, but we also lack empirical results to assess whether the amounts involved are significant. Circumstantial evidence suggests, however, that they usually represent a tiny percentage of operating costs. By and large, no net correlation, positive or negative, has been found between linguistic diversity and macroeconomic indicators of economic performance.

At the microeconomic level, the main issue is whether language impacts on the operations of firms, and if so, how. Many of the contributions to this question are descriptive case studies, too numerous and too heterogeneous to discuss here. However, there also exists some valuable (and regrettably neglected) theoretical work, such as Hočevar's (1975) examination of markets for language-specific goods, or Sabourin's (1985) analysis of the "matching" process between the language profile of a job in a firm and the language profile of a worker. Much more research needs to be undertaken, and since many theoretical aspects of the use of language at work (particularly in production and distribution) have never been studied, it is of little use to keep polling multinational corporations about their language practices, since there is no clear notion of what information is analytically relevant and, consequently, what questions ought to be asked.

It is important to point out that in terms of our definition of language economics, the production, consumption and exchange of "language goods and services" (such as translation, language teaching, etc.) do *not* constitute central questions, because the economic processes operating are not different from those operating in the case of any standard good.[2] This is also why economists tend to prefer speaking about "the economics of language" rather than "language and the economy": Quite apart from the fact, which is reflected in our definition in Section 2.1 above, that economics is defined by its approach to human action (rather than by its subject matter), it is not *any* aspect of economic activity somehow involving language that constitutes a relevant object for language economics. One convenient test is whether the fact that more than one language is used in a given economic activity has an impact on the level of the economic variables operating in the process (for example, are prices, incomes, production processes, etc., different *because* of linguistic diversity?). For example, the presence of a linguistically fragmented market may require linguistically different goods and services to be produced and offered. However, this is analytically relevant if this carries some specifically economic consequences, for example if this prevents economies of scale in production. If not, language would be considered not to make a difference, and there would be no language economics question.

However, the production of language goods and services like translation, interpretation, and language teaching are relevant to language economics in so far as they may affect language dynamics (Mélitz 2000) and language policy (Pool 1996), because they may imply transfers between language-defined groups (Grin 2004a, 2005b).[3] These questions, however, remain significantly under-researched.

3. The economic analysis of language policy

The economic approach to language policy and planning constitutes an additional and increasingly active line of research, on which we shall focus in the rest of this chapter.

In what follows, "policy" refers to *public* policy, initiated and carried out by the state or its surrogates. Although some of the considerations developed below can carry over to corporate environments, it is important not to conflate corporate strategies regarding language (whose aim, in multilingual contexts, is to organize communication with a view to maximizing profits) and public policies, whose (significantly more complex) aim is to maximize aggregate welfare. In this paper, language policy (or "planning") therefore refers to:

> [...] a systematic, rational, theory-based effort at the societal level to modify the linguistic environment with a view to increasing aggregate welfare. It is typically conducted by official bodies or their surrogates and aimed at part or all of the population living under their jurisdiction.
> (Grin 2003a: 28; adapted from Cooper 1989: chap. 2).

3.1. Norms, outputs and outcomes

As noted at the beginning of this chapter, much of the published literature assessing language policies is rooted in law or sociolinguistics. Therefore, policies have often been assessed in terms of the legal texts, that is, the norms (for example on minority-language education) in which policies are enshrined, or in terms of the administrative measures taken, usually relying, for a measurement, on the direct output of these measures (for example, the number of new minority-language classes opened during a given calendar year). However, neither form of assessment tells us whether these legal norms or policy measures have been effective. Actual effectiveness can only be measured in terms of outcomes further down the line. For example, if a policy aims at minority language revitalization through the education system, the proper criterion for assessing the policy must be an indicator of revitalization itself, such as increases in language competence among the target population, or in actual language use. Thinking in public policy terms helps to focus attention on truly relevant evaluation criteria.

3.2. Basics of policy evaluation

Economic perspectives on language policy rest on the core principles of policy analysis (Dunn 1994): *Ex ante*, several policy options regarding language can be envisaged; each carries advantages and drawbacks, which can sometimes be reinterpreted as "benefits" and "costs" (albeit in a broad sense, see below), and the policy option that should be chosen is the one that maximizes the difference between benefits and costs. *Ex post*, policies that have been implemented can be evaluated by identifying and measuring their benefits and costs, in order to assess which, out of a given set of policies, has proved most effective, least costly, or – combining both criteria – most cost-effective.

For the most part, studies in this area address issues of language status, while language corpus is largely ignored or taken for granted. This may be because the actual cost of coining new vocabulary or engaging in spelling reform is comparatively modest; by contrast, elevating a language to official status, or introducing another language as a medium of instruction in the education system, is likely to be a much costlier policy decision – and hence one that does deserve attention.

Language policy can be broken down according to its goals, as suggested by Kaplan and Baldauf (1997: 59ff.), who list 11 different categories. From the perspective of policy evaluation, such distinctions matter less than the principle sketched out above, namely, the weighing of the pros and cons of the options considered. Let us, somewhat roughly, define a linguistic environment as a set of demolinguistic, institutional, and sociolinguistic facts – all of which are facets of what Fishman calls (with hyphens), language-in-society. Language policy, ultimately, proposes to move from a given, existing "linguistic environment" to another, supposedly preferable linguistic environment. Therefore its object, instead of being a language in relation with others, may be linguistic diversity itself (Grin 2003b).

3.3. The rationale for state intervention

To the extent that language policy is a form of public policy, the first question that arises is why the state should intervene at all in language matters. One underlying assumption of mainstream economics and policy analysis is that the free interplay of market forces can be expected to result in the provision of an adequate amount of goods and services, at minimum average cost. There are, however, exceptions to this basic principle, and these exceptions, which give rise to what is known in the literature as "market failure", justify state intervention. Six main forms of market failure can be identified:
– insufficient information, preventing actors from making the best decisions;
– transaction costs preventing actors from closing deals that would otherwise prove mutually advantageous;
– the absence of markets for certain goods or services – for example, there is no market on which future, yet unborn generations could express their wish for a particular animal or vegetal species to be preserved;
– the existence of "market imperfections" (typically, monopolies or oligopolies), resulting in a suboptimal production level for some goods and services, usually with an excessive market price for them;

- positive or negative externalities, that is, situations in which one person's (or group's) behavior affects other persons' welfare, without the loss or gain thus created giving rise to any form of compensation;
- the existence of public goods, which can be consumed by one person without reducing the amount of the good available to another (a characteristic called "non-rival consumption"), and whose consumption cannot be restricted to those who actually pay for it (which is known as "non-excludability"); the standard textbook example is public lighting. In the presence of super-public or hypercollective goods (see preceding section), market failure is even more likely.

The provision of environmental quality provides a classic example of market failure for at least two reasons: First, manifestations of environmental quality such as clean air and attractive landscapes are public goods because they display the twin characteristics of non-rival consumption and non-excludability; second, the market for such amenities is also clearly incomplete, since future generations are in no position to express *now* their preference of environmentally conscious forms of development.

Linguistic environments also exhibit many forms of market failure. For one, future generations cannot bid for the preservation of endangered languages. In a market mechanism, this absence from the bidding process means the same as if they did not care for these languages, which is quite a different matter. Externalities are also present if, for example, a person's language learning (or non-learning) behavior affects the value of another person's language skills. In fact, it could be argued that almost every form of market failure occurs when it comes to the provision of linguistic diversity. However, it is enough to establish that only one type of failure is present to justify state intervention. Hence, from a policy analysis standpoint, language policy is justified, and the policy analysis perspective provides a rationale for intervention. This point, which may seem obvious to some readers, deserves to be made, since there is no lack of voices, in the political debate, claiming that languages should best be left to fend for themselves, going as far as to dismiss most language policy interventions as harmful meddling.

3.4. Resource allocation and levels of value

The next problem is to select a policy among several options. In principle, policy analysts will have to identify and measure, for each of the options considered, different types of effects. The latter can also be defined as components of the net value of the linguistic environments that are expected to emerge as a result of choosing alternative policies. The conceptual and methodological difficulties of carrying out this evaluation in practice are, at this time, far from solved. Nevertheless, the procedure can help to identify coherently distinct steps in an evaluation exercise, in which four levels can be distinguished and summarized with a simple two-way table, see Table 1:

Table 1. Four levels of value

	private	social
market	A	B
non-market	C	D

The four cells in Table 1 refer respectively to "private market value" (cell A), social market value (cell B), private non-market value (cell C), and social non-market value (cell D).

The first, and comparatively less arduous step in the evaluation of possible courses of action, is to estimate the net private market value of each policy option. This refers to effects that can be observed on a market and which accrue to identifiable individuals. For example, a policy requiring civil servants to be trilingual (instead of merely bilingual) will, all other things being equal, drive up the wage rate of trilinguals in society as a whole, at least in the short run; this will be reflected in a positive average private market value of second and third language skills (for a more detailed discussion, see Grin 2002b).

One should then attempt to move on to the estimation of social market value, which is the aggregate of private market values across all members of society. Unfortunately, aggregation will require a more complex operation than a simple sum, owing to the presence of externalities. If externalities are positive (or negative), social market benefits will exceed (or fall short of) the simple sum of private market benefits. Computing social market value, however, is rarely done. The reason is lack of data: In addition to all the data required for the assessment of private market value (at the very least: second, respectively third language skills, labour income, education, work experience, and gender), the estimation of social value requires data on public spending on (second- and third-) language skills, as well as on other elements of public expenditure that contribute, through language policy, to the creation of a certain linguistic environment in which the rates of return on language skills are observed. Existing evaluations of the social rate of return on language teaching only factor in educational expenditure. However, given the absence of subject-based expenditure accounting in most education systems, estimates of the social rates of return on foreign language skills remain few.

The steps just described for market value then need to be replicated for the much more complex non-market value – namely, the gains and losses associated with a change in the linguistic environment, but without these gains and losses being expressed through an explicit market. These effects, sometimes described as "psychic" or "symbolic", entail direct gains or losses in satisfaction (or, in economic parlance, in "utility"). A typical example of non-market benefit, in the case of policy promoting trilingualism instead of just bilingualism, would be the enjoyment derived from direct access to cultural products in this additional language or from easier contact with native speakers of that language. There again, these effects must be estimated at the individual level, and then aggregated to obtain social non-market value. Non-market benefits and costs are perfectly legitimate concerns for an economic evaluation because, as we have noted before, economic analysis is not confined to material or financial questions. For example, the psychological loss experienced when one's language is (formally or not) downgraded to a secondary position is a relevant form of cost. Likewise, the pride that may be associated with the visibility of one's minority language in prestige domains is a relevant benefit. Obviously, estimating these non-market benefits and costs is extremely difficult and, to my knowledge, this has never been systematically attempted. The most promising methods are likely to be found in environmental economics (Kahnemann and Knetsch 1992), in which a considerable body of experience has been developed in the evaluation of complex, non-market commodities, such as clean air or water.

For each policy contemplated, one would then compute the sum of social market and social non-market benefits and costs, yielding the overall net value; the policy that promises to give rise to the highest overall net value should, *ceteris paribus*, be selected.

3.5. Resource distribution

Our discussion of the assessment procedure has so far focused on resource *allocation*, and its core concern is one of cost-effectiveness. The standard procedure that makes it possible, in principle, to define a policy as "best" relies on the measurement of aggregate (social) welfare, encompassing both market and non-market effects. In other words, the emphasis has been placed on the appropriate use of scarce resources through policy, without consideration for the resulting *distribution* of resources among people and groups. However, moving from an existing to a presumably better linguistic environment does entail gains for some and losses for others, and the question arises of who gains, who loses, and how much, as a result of the implementation of language policy. In other words, the evaluation of a public policy should not be concerned with cost-effectiveness only, but should also consider fairness; this side of the problem is known in economics as resource distribution (as opposed to resource allocation which has been analysed in the preceding section).

This distributive aspect of policy tends to be neglected in economic analysis. Economists are usually content to establish that a policy is "Pareto-optimal", which means that no gain can be achieved for any particular member of society without entailing a loss for at least one other person (see Dunn 1994, or any textbook on standard fields of specialization like public finance, public choice or policy analysis). Moving from a non Pareto-optimal to a Pareto-optimal situation is generally considered sufficient proof that the policy is a good one, under the all too comfortable assumption that because the policy does give rise to a net welfare gain, the gainers can compensate the losers. The problem, however, is whether they actually do so of their own accord, or if a compulsory compensation mechanism has to be built into the policy design for such compensation to be paid. At the same time, the form and amount of such compensation needs to be determined, on the basis of a reliable and transparent identification of the transfers that arise *without* a compensation mechanism. Therefore, scenarios have to be compared to one another; alternatively, we might say that the allocative and distributive implications of a given scenario have to be assessed against the proper *counterfactual*, a concept which will be discussed in the following section.

3.6. The counterfactual

Let us now turn to a fundamental question that might have been addressed at the very beginning of this section, but which it is easier to explain after having discussed, as we just have, the contents of the evaluation. The issue is that of the counterfactual (Grin 2003c). This term does not refer to something contrary to fact, but refers to "what would occur in the absence of a policy", or, even more compactly, to "the relevant alternative". If so much of the advice heard on matters of language policy appears debatable, it is usually because it rests on an inappropriate identification of the counterfactual. One example will help us clinch this point.

The added expenditure entailed by moving from a unilingual to a bilingual education system is much smaller than commonly believed. Where evaluations have been made, they point in the direction of a 3 % to 4 % range, because even if the education system were to remain unilingual, children would have to be schooled anyway. Therefore, this only gives rise to relatively modest additional financial outlays. However, in line with the procedure sketched out in the preceding section, we should broaden the range of effects (both market and non-market) taken into consideration. This means that the assessment of both the policy measure and the counterfactual should take account, for example, of the differential effects they may have on school participation, graduation and dropout rates among the majority and the minority population. The true costs of the counterfactual (that is, in this example, of not engaging in a policy of bilingual education) can prove to be much higher than expected, thereby significantly heightening the attractiveness of the bilingual education policy (Vaillancourt and Grin 2000).

4. Controversies in language economics

The economics of language remains, to a large extent, a field of specialization in the making, and it would be difficult to identify a corpus of theory that would be recognized as embodying received wisdom in the area. Besides, economists working on language are not sufficiently numerous for competing schools to emerge. The notion of "controversy" in language economics, therefore, does not arise in the same way as it would in larger and more established fields of specialization, whether in economics or elsewhere. Controversies in language economics occur in relation with unanswered analytical problems, which nurture opposing views on policy recommendations.

Some of the most important current debates are related to language dynamics. Sociolinguistics and applied linguistics appear not to have come up with a general, systematic theory of language decline and language spread, particularly in the case of major languages.[4] So far, economics has not come up with such a theoretical approach either, despite numerous attempts at tackling the complex interplay of processes at hand.

In order for such an integrated theory to emerge, two main problems must be solved. The first one is that of the appropriate characterization of the network effects and of the way in which these are actually recognized by actors; the attending difficulties are largely captured by the problem of designing an appropriate procedure for aggregation to move from "private" to "social" value. The second hurdle is that of the identification and measurement of non-market effects – with respect to which, of course, the aggregation problem also arises.

For example, just how much does the generalization of competence in language X as a foreign language reduce or, on the contrary, increase the monetary return on such competence for those who already possess it? How is this relationship likely to affect the decisions of potential future learners? While such questions may, to some extent, be solved by assuming a rational calculus on the part of social actors, it is of course necessary to take account of other motivational factors linked, among others, to perceptions of culture and identity, and the concept of non-market value only offers an analytical framework for handling the problem. Operationalizing it requires theoretical and empirical knowledge of which sociolinguistics and applied linguistics offer only some elements.

However, even if a general consensus can emerge on the actual processes of language dynamics, controversy arises around the policy recommendations that can be made as a consequence. For example, on the basis of his pithy model of language dynamics, van Parijs (2000, 2004) recommends pushing for more teaching of English across the non-English-speaking world, in order to encourage the emergence of a common international political, economic and technological space that would operate in English; all other languages would then tend to be confined to local functions. Van Parijs further recommends that all dubbing (at least of films originally produced in English) should be banned, so that any US-made film shown on television channels in non-English speaking countries would be in English only (with subtitles in the local language). Such a ban would be intended to speed up the spread of English as a foreign language. Van Parijs protests that he is fully in favor of linguistic diversity, yet the countervailing measures that he suggests, in order for other languages to retain a certain vitality across sociolinguistic domains, seem weak, and their effectiveness may be doubted (Grin 2004b). Van Parijs claims that since English is becoming a *lingua franca* anyway, accelerating its dissemination worldwide across all social classes is the best way to ensure social justice.

One may, however, counter that granting any natural language (whether it be English, Mandarin or French) a dominant position is grossly unfair, because the native speakers of this language will enjoy considerable privileges, which are, ultimately, obtained at the expense of native speakers of other languages. Therefore, adopting English (or any other natural language) as a *lingua franca* is not a desirable solution from a policy analysis standpoint, unless appropriate compensation is actually paid (see Section 3.5). This raises another question, namely, whether monetary compensation for linguistic and cultural inequality is considered socially and politically acceptable; this should not be regarded as a foregone conclusion.

The question then arises of whether the dynamics that bring about the spread of dominant languages are incontrovertible. There again, we may question the widespread notion that they are, by observing that the resulting regime of linguistic hegemony works to the detriment of the majority; depending on the counterfactual chosen, the corresponding cost (to non-English speaking countries in the European Union) can run into tens of billions of Euros annually (Grin 2005b). If the majority becomes aware of this fact, it is perfectly conceivable that these countries could finally decide to act in accordance with their financial interest and engage in coordinated action in order to overcome the "snowball effect" that lends momentum to the spread of English. In other words, one can easily argue that there are sound economic reasons why states may want to curb this spread. Whether this is actually feasible depends on the forces at play in language dynamics. This problem is a largely sociolinguistic one; therefore, it raises the question of how applied linguistics and applied economics can be combined. The following section turns to this very question.

5. Linkages with applied linguistics

Some economists apparently nurture the belief that intelligent pronouncements can be made on just about any issue, including complex matters of language and culture, on the strength of the core paradigm of economics alone, with little reference to the knowledge developed by those disciplines that are chiefly concerned with these dimensions of human experience.[5] However, reality often proves this belief to be wrong, and many economists point out the need to build bridges between disciplines, combining their respective strengths.

This sound principle lends itself to competing interpretations. Nevertheless, a case can easily be made that one of economics' strong suits is its stress on the explicit identification of variables and specification of the relationships between them, and its insistence on internal consistency (Mayer 1993). However, owing to built-in epistemological habits, economics tends to use overly dry and abstract variables and relationships between them. Therefore, it makes sense to import, into an economic type of framework, variables and relationships that offer more phenomenological depth, and applied linguistics is well-placed to supply them. Putting it differently, there can be no good language economics without interdisciplinarity.

Applications of economics to language policy offer fertile ground for such interdisciplinarity. Some imports are relatively easy – for example, probably thanks to their taxonomic character, the sociolinguistic concept of "domain" or the well-established distinction between language corpus and language status can be readily taken on board in the economic modeling of language policy. However, the true test of productive interdisciplinarity is the combination of variables into accounts of causal relationships. Particularly useful, in this respect, are systematic analyses of (i) actors' motivations in foreign language learning; (ii) the determinants of multilingual actors' patterns of language use, when they have a choice to use one language or another; (iii) the determinants of patterns of mutual linguistic adaptation in conversations between persons with different language repertoires, in particular different mother tongues.

Although sociolinguistics offers a massive literature on such issues, much of it tends to be inductive, based on case studies, and to offer relatively few generalizable results. Piecemeal empirical evidence is of limited usefulness to the development of the much more macro-level accounts that economics attempts to provide. Developing much more synthetic approaches is therefore a prerequisite for applied linguistics to increase its relevance in language policy evaluation, possibly by establishing (both analytically and empirically) systematic and general relationships that can be imported into the analytical framework of mainstream policy analysis. Yet this would confront applied linguists with the very difficulties that economists and policy analysts have been grappling for a long time, namely, the need to move up on the ladder of generality, and to work with more compact and abstract variables (Pool 1991), without ending up with overly theoretical constructs.

6. Applied research perspectives

Practical experience in language policy evaluation remains relatively scattered and partial. However, it has been applied in recent years to an expanding range of cases (see e.g. Chalmers 2003; Grin et al. 2002; Grin and Vaillancourt 1999). In this closing section, I highlight some areas where this approach can usefully contribute to the formulation of policy recommendations.

6.1. Foreign language teaching

Even outside the range of works that focus on language acquisition itself (e.g. Ellis 1994), much of the discourse on the teaching of foreign languages emphasizes issues such as the relative effectiveness of different teaching strategies, their appropriateness with respect to a given social and cultural context, and actors' responses to the teaching offered (e.g. Hornberger 2003; Fritz 2003). With occasional exceptions (e.g. Baker 2002), much attention is devoted to how various profiles of language competence are achieved. This is also true of the literature emanating from international organizations with an interest in foreign language teaching (Beacco and Byram 2003 for the Council of Europe; European Commission 2001 for the European Union). From the standpoint of the economics of education or the economics of language, these would be characterized as *internal* effectiveness issues, which center on the question "How?"; they qualify as "internal" in the sense that they refer to processes occurring within the educational process.

This, however, leaves out no less important questions, such as *what* languages ought to be taught and learned, and *why* they should be. These are key issues for language economics, which is not so much concerned with what happens in schools, but with the more general problem of what purposes are served by what schools teach. Presumably, the justification for what is taught should be found *outside* of the educational sphere, hence the notion of *external* effectiveness.[6]

A narrow approach to external effectiveness will focus on private market value or, data permitting, social market value as described in Section 2. In a broader approach, one would also attempt to take non-market values into account, possibly resorting to methodological tools imported from environmental economics. A yet more comprehensive approach would move beyond these allocative dimensions and also consider the distributive one, in order to assess the fairness of the options considered. The chief usefulness of the economic perspective is first to provide this type of integrative framework, without which recommendations tend to be somewhat haphazard, inadequately argued, or based on an awkward combination of positive fact and normative judgement (Calvet 1993). Second, along with a systematic approach to the identification and measurement of the allocative advantages and drawbacks of various policy options, it provides a methodology for coming up with actual estimates.

This can have very direct practical applications. For example, the research result that rates of return on French and German as foreign languages (in German- and French-speaking Switzerland, respectively) are high and statistically significant, and often on par with the rates of return on English as a foreign language across Switzerland, is often invoked in public debate in Switzerland over the order in which foreign languages should be taught in the country's various language regions. These figures are quoted in favor of maintaining a priority for national languages over English as foreign languages in the education system, or at least a parity with English.

The economic framework also makes it easier to notice and identify major distributive issues occurring, for example, in the European context. The current increase in the dominance of the English language in the European Union gives rise to a number of transfers that run contrary to fairness between language-defined groups (see Section 4). Without engaging in a full-fledged discussion on the nature of these transfers, we can point out to at least one: Some 85% of European citizens are expected to learn English as a foreign language, which places a heavy burden on the education systems of their respective countries of residence – not to mention the significant personal financial effort that many parents make for English to be learned by their offspring. By contrast, foreign language learning in the United Kingdom is low and decreasing; the resulting imbalance could be estimated, for 2003–2004, as giving rise to a transfer of some 10 billion Euros annually in favor of the United Kingdom (Grin 2005b). How far such facts are actually taken into account by decision makers and the general public remains to be seen; in any case, language economics provides the theoretical and empirical toolkit to bring them to light.

6.2. Minority language protection and promotion

As noted earlier in this chapter, much language policy discourse is based on the concept of rights, giving rise to a "linguistic human rights" approach (May 2005; also Skutnabb-Kangas, this vol.; Fill, this vol.) However, this line of argument is often less robust than it seems. It may cut no ice with those who, for ideological reasons, are not already convinced of the validity of minority claims. No less importantly, even if consensus emerges around them, the LHR approach tells us relatively little regarding the actual nature of measures that should be adopted to protect and promote minority languages. There again, language economics may be of use. It can provide an analytical model such as the "policy-to-outcome path", which helps to recognize the interconnections between the different channels through which these various measures operate. It may therefore serve to identify some necessary and sufficient conditions for successful language revitalization policies.

At the same time, it provides a framework for linking systematically policy interventions not only with their direct outputs, but with the more relevant outcomes further down a causal chain. To use a time-honored example, the success of a policy meant to increase civil servants' competence in a minority language cannot be satisfactorily measured by the number of civil servants who enroll in (or successfully complete) a minority language course. A more relevant indicator of the success of a policy is whether, as a result of this course having been set up and offered to civil servants, we observe an actual increase in the use of the minority language in interactions between the public and the civil service. This insistence on identifying the actual outcomes of a policy can help to increase the actual effectiveness of language policy.

The policy-to-outcome path also helps to identify relevant elements of expenditure in order to provide estimates of actual policy costs. Some examples are provided in Table 2.

Table 2. An overview of findings about language policy costs
(figures converted in Euros and cents where applicable)

Language policy case	Description of measure	Key finding
Canada, incl. Québec		
French Language Charter ("Bill 101"), Québec, 1977	Set of measures to promote the use of French as the main language of the province of Québec	Total cost of Charter is between 0.28 % and 0.48 % of provincial GDP.
French Language Charter ("Bill 101"), Québec, 1977	"Francisation" of firms (firms with a staff of 50 or more must offer internal communication in French also)	Cost per employee and per firm ranges from CAD 85 to 115 (€ 57 to 77), in 1984 dollars, for the relatively costlier years of implementation; costs expected to taper off after implementation phase.
Canadian bilingualism	Total expenditure on bilingual programmes by the Canadian federal government	The provision of federal services in both official languages represents 0.03 % of the cost of all federal services. The total cost of all official languages expenditures amounts to 0.44 % of federal spending.

Language policy case	Description of measure	Key finding
Wales		
Bilingual road signs in Wales	Road signs in Wales give place names in Welsh and English	Bilingualism of directional and safety signs costs about 22 pence (33 cents) per resident and per year.
Mentrau Iaith	Associative network supporting the use of Welsh in local community project	Average expenditure (Welsh Language Board subsidy for year 2000/01) is € 2 per resident in those predominantly Welsh-speaking areas in which mentrau iaith have been set up.
Sianel Pedwar Cymru (S4C)	Welsh-medium television programmes	Person-hour cost of Welsh television (Welsh programmes, Welsh-speaking audiences) stands at about 50 cents.
Basque Country		
Euskal Telebista	Making accessible Basque television from Spain to Basque speakers in France	Cost of setting up and maintaining masts and transmitters amounts to 2.5 cents per viewer and per day.
Basque-medium education	Operation of A, B and D channels in the Basque education system	Extra cost is in the region of 4 % of yearly cost per student.
Ireland		
Raidió na Gaeltachta	Irish-language radio	Average cost is 20 cents per person and per hour.
Naíonraí	Irish-medium pre-schools	Average cost (incl. parents' contribution) is € 400 per child and per year.
Finland		
Yleisradio	Swedish-language broadcasting in Finland	Average cost is 10 to 15 cents per person and per hour.
European Union		
Euroschool	Joint summer camps for children of various minority language communities	Total cost is € 600 per participating child.
Guatemala		
Protection of Maya in Guatemala	Setting up of Maya-medium education	Extra cost is in the region of 4 % to 5 % per student and per year.

Source: Grin (2004a: 194–195)

6.3. Official and working languages in the European Union

Let us now consider a third example. The costs of the multilingual operations of the EU Parliament are supposed to be staggering, and large-circulation dailies around Europe regularly feature more or less alarming pieces on the matter. In fact, the figures involved are quite reasonable. Although lack of data often prevents precise calculations, cost ranges can be estimated. For example, the supposedly prohibitive cost of translation and interpretation in European institutions numbering 15 member states and 11 official languages amounted, before enlargement, to € 1.82 per resident and per year; translation and interpretation represented 0.8 % of the European Union budget. Following enlargement, these costs can be expected to remain below € 6 per resident and per year. In fact, keeping the most demanding language regime, which requires translation into and out of 20 official and working languages, would cost € 5.24 per resident and per year.[7] Given the use of relay interpretation, actual post-enlargement expenditure is reportedly between € 2 and € 2.50 per resident and per year (Gazzola 2005), that is, much less than is commonly believed.

Yet this sobering fact, in order to be fully appreciated, needs to be understood against the background of what would occur if such expenditure did not take place, in accordance with the concept of counterfactual introduced earlier. Suppose all EU business, including parliamentary debates, were to take place in one language only, such as English. This would certainly raise concerns about the democratic character of a Parliament operating in what is, for 85 % of its members and an equivalent percentage of EU citizens, a foreign language. But this would also amount to ignoring the cost of language learning and training – not just for MPs across all non-English-speaking countries, but also for citizens at large, who would need to learn the language rather well in order to understand EU regulations also applying to them. Once this language learning cost is taken into account (because it is an element of the relevant counterfactual), a *prima facie* sensible and economic unilingual policy can be exposed as a very expensive one.

7. Concluding remarks

Let us, in conclusion, recall that although language policy evaluation as described here has an important role to play, its limitations must not be overlooked. Much work remains to be done at the conceptual level in order to develop more comprehensive theoretical approaches; we have also noted that despite the abundance of circumstantial evidence, hard data are relatively few. However, similar limitations can be found across the entire range of the social sciences. In the case of language economics, it is important to point to another limitation that has to do with the political use often made of economic analyses.

Probably owing to its aura of analytical rigor, economics is often invoked as a trump card in support of certain views in the political debate. This is also true in language issues, as we have seen in Section 6. At this point, however, it is useful to remember that the economic approach to language policy, despite its relevance, is in no way meant to dictate policy decisions or to displace other approaches. Quite apart from the fact that, as a matter of general epistemology, different disciplines provide mutually complementary perspectives, it must not be forgotten that by definition, language policy is an expression of a set of choices that society makes. As such, it remains an inherently political matter. The main role of economic considerations in language policy research, therefore, is to help social actors assess the pros and cons of different avenues open to them, and to make principled and transparent choices.

Notes

1. This chapter focuses on the contributions of mainstream economics, given the absence of research work on language issues from the perspective of non-mainstream (e.g., Marxian) economics. Likewise, this definition does not cover a completely distinct line of research that may be called "the language *of* economics", which studies economics discourse whether in an economic (McCloskey 1990) or linguistic (Henderson, Dudley-Evans, and Backhouse 1993) perspective. Also excluded is the literature on the economic (and in fact quite mathematically oriented) analysis of the structure of language; see Rubinstein 2000).
2. The demarcation, however, is not always totally clear: for example, Lamberton's (2002) edited volume casts the net wide and includes a study on telephone interpreting services.
3. Some commentators from disciplines other than economics have repeatedly been looking to establish parallels between language and currency. Unfortunately, this may cause more confusion than useful insight, because the nature of linguistic exchange and commercial exchange are analytically deeply different (Grin 2005a).
4. By contrast, the sociolinguistic literature offers integrated analytical perspectives on reverse language shift in the case of regional or minority languages (Fishman 1991).
5. For an extreme example of this attitude, see e.g. Lazear (1999).
6. This avoidance of external effectiveness issues is particularly glaring in the Europan Union's 2004–2006 Action Plan, which studiously skirts all the truly political questions in order to focus almost exclusively on the promotion of language learning.
7. Additional translation directions: $[(20 \times 19)-(11 \times 10)]=270$; average cost of translation direction: € 6.24; total extra cost: € 1,684.8m; total EU translation costs: € (685.9 + 1,684.8) = € 2,370.7; total resident population after enlargement: 377+ 75 = 452 million; resulting per-capita cost: € 5.24.

References

Baker, Steven J. (ed.)
    2002   *Language Policy: Lessons from Global Models.* Monterey, CA: Monterey Institute of International Studies.

Beacco, Jean-Claude and Michael Byram
    2003   *Guide pour l'élaboration des politiques linguistiques éducatives en Europe. De la diversité linguistique à l'éducation plurilingue.* Strasbourg: Council of Europe, Language Policy Division.

Bloom, David and Gilles Grenier
    1996   Language, employment and earnings in the United States: Spanish-English differentials from 1970 to 1990. *International Journal of the Sociology of Language* 121: 45–68.

Breton, Albert
    1964   The economics of nationalism. *Journal of Political Economy* 62: 376–386.

Breton, Albert (ed.)
    1998   *Economic Approaches to Language and Bilingualism.* Ottawa: Canadian Heritage.

Breton, Albert and Peter Mieszkowski
    1977   The economics of bilingualism. In: Wallace E. Oates (ed.), *The Political Economy of Fiscal Federalism*, 261–273. Lexington, MA: Lexington Books.

Calvet, Louis-Jean
    1993   *L'Europe et ses langues* [Europe and its languages]. Paris: Plon.

Carr, Jack
    1985   Le bilinguisme au Canada: L'usage consacre-t-il l'anglais monopole naturel? [Does Canadian bilingualism turn English into a natural monopoly?] In: François Vaillancourt (ed.), *Économie et langue*, 27–37. Québec: Conseil de la langue française.

Chalmers, Douglas
    2003   The economic impact of Gaelic arts and culture. Doctoral Dissertation, Glasgow Caledonian University, Glasgow.

Chiswick, Barry and Paul Miller
    1995   The endogeneity between language and earnings: International analyses. *Journal of Labor Economics* 13: 246–288.

Chiswick, Barry and Gaston Repetto
    2001   Immigrant adjustment in Israel: The determinants of literacy and fluency in Hebrew and their effects on earnings. In: Slobodan Djajic (ed.), *International Migration: Trends, Policies and Economic Impact*, 204–288. London: Routledge.

Church, Jeffry and Ian King
    1993   Bilingualism and network externalities. *Canadian Journal of Economics* 26: 337–345.

Cooper, Robert
    1989   *Language Planning and Social Change.* Cambridge: Cambridge University Press.

Dalmazzone, Silvia
    1999   Economics of language: A network externalities approach. In: Albert Breton (ed.), *Exploring the Economics of Language*, 63–87. Ottawa: Canadian Heritage.

Dávila, Alberto, and Marie Mora
   2000   English fluency of recent Hispanic immigrants to the United States in 1980 and 1990. *Economic Development and Cultural Change* 48: 369–389.
De Swaan, Abram
   2001   *Words of the World: The Global Language System.* Cambridge: Polity Press.
Dustmann, Christian
   1994   Speaking fluency, writing fluency and earnings of migrants. *Journal of Population Economics* 7: 133–156.
Dunn, William
   1994   *Public Policy Analysis. An Introduction.* Englewood Cliffs, NJ: Simon & Schuster.
Ellis, Rod
   1994   *The Study of Second Language Acquisition.* Oxford: Oxford University Press.
European Commission
   2001   *L'enseignement des langues étrangères en milieu scolaire en Europe* [Eurydice Program]. Brussels: European Commission, Directorate General for Education and Culture.
Fishman, Joshua
   1991   *Reversing Language Shift. Theoretical and Empirical Foundations of Assistance to Threatened Languages.* Clevedon: Multilingual Matters.
Fritz, Thomas (ed.)
   2003   *Wessen Sprache – lernen. Beiträge zu Autonomie und Sprachenpolitik* [Whose Language-Learning. Contributions to Autonomy and Language Policy]. Vienna: Edition Volkshochschule.
Gazzola, Michele
   2005   *La gestione dell multilinguismo nell'Unione europea* [The management of multilingualism in the European Union]. University of Geneva: Observatoire Économie–Langues–Formation. http://www.unige.ch/eti/elf/docs/Multilinguismo%20Unione%20europea.pdf
Grin, François (ed.)
   1996   Economic approaches to language and language planning [Theme issue]. *International Journal of the Sociology of Language* 121.
Grin, François
   1999   *Compétences et récompenses. La valeur des langues en Suisse* [Skills and Rewards. The Value of Languages in Switzerland]. Fribourg: Éditions Universitaires de Fribourg.
Grin, François
   2002a   Towards a threshold theory of minority language survival. In: Donald M. Lamberton (ed.), *The Economics of Language*, 49–76. Cheltenham: Edward Elgar. First published in *Kyklos* 45: 69–97.
Grin, François
   2002b   *Using Language Economics and Education Economics in Language Education Policy.* Strasbourg: Language Policy Division, Council of Europe.
Grin, François
   2003a   Language planning and economics. *Current Issues in Language Planning* 4(1): 1–66.

Grin, François
    2003b   Diversity as paradigm, analytical device, and policy goal. In: Will Kymlicka and Alan Patten (eds.), *Language Rights and Political Theory,* 169–188. Oxford: Oxford University Press.
Grin, François
    2003c   *Language Policy Evaluation and the European Charter for Regional or Minority Languages.* London: Palgrave Macmillan.
Grin, François
    2004a   On the costs of linguistic diversity. In: Philippe van Parijs (ed.), *Cultural Diversity versus Economic Solidarity,* 193–206. Brussels: De Boeck-Université.
Grin, François
    2004b   L'anglais comme *lingua franca.* Questions de coût et d'équité. Commentaire sur l'article de Philippe van Parijs. *Économie publique* 15: 33–41.
Grin, François
    2005a   Économie et langue. De quelques équivoques, croisements et convergences. *Sociolinguistica* 19: 1–12.
Grin, François
    2005b   *L'enseignement des langues étrangères comme politique publique* [Foreign Language Teaching as Public Policy]. *Report to the Haut Conseil de l'évaluation de l'école,* Paris. http://cisad.adc.education.fr/hcee
Grin, François, Tom Moring, Durk Gorter, Johann Häggman, Dónall ÓRiagáin and Miquel Strubell
    2002   *Support for Minority Languages in Europe.* Report to the European Commission (2000 1288/001–001 EDU-MLCEV). Retrieved January 21, 2005, from http://europa.eu.int/comm/education/policies/lang/langmin/support.pdf.
Grin, François and François Vaillancourt
    1997   The economics of multilingualism: Overview of the literature and analytical framework. In: William Grabe (ed.), *Multilingualism and Multilingual Communities,* 43–65. Cambridge, MA: Cambridge University Press.
Grin, François and François Vaillancourt
    1999   *The Cost-effectiveness Evaluation of Minority Language Policies: Case Studies on Wales, Ireland and the Basque Country.* Monograph series No. 2. Flensburg: European Centre for Minority Issues.
Henderson, William, Tony Dudley-Evans and Roger Backhouse (eds.)
    1993   *Economics and Language.* London: Routledge.
Hočevar, Toussaint
    1975   Equilibria on linguistic minority markets. *Kyklos* 28: 337–357.
Hornberger, Nancy (ed.)
    2003   *Continua of Biliteracy: An Ecological Framework for Educational Policy, Research, and Practice in Multilingual Settings.* Clevedon: Multilingual Matters.
Kahnemann, Daniel and Jack Knetsch
    1992   Valuing public goods: The purchase of moral satisfaction. *Journal of Environmental Economics and Management* 22: 57–70.
Kaplan, Robert and Richard Baldauf
    1997   *Language Planning. From Practice to Theory.* Clevedon: Multilingual Matters.

Kastoukievitch, Nikolai
   2003   Language effects on labor market outcomes in a bilingual economy: The case of Ukraine. Unpublished MA dissertation, University of Kyiv-Mohyla.

Klein, Carlo
   2004   La valorisation des compétences linguistiques: Importance du sexe et/ou du statut professionnel? [Valorization of language skills: Meaning of gender and/or professional status?]. Paper presented at the 11th "journées d'étude" on longitudinal data, Dijon, May 27–28.

Lamberton, Donald (ed.)
   2002   *The Economics of Language*. Cheltenham, UK: Edward Elgar.

Lang, Kevin
   1986   A language theory of discrimination. *Quarterly Journal of Economics* 101: 363–382.

Lazear, Edward
   1999   Language and culture. *Journal of Political Economy* 107: 95–126.

Marschak, Jacob
   1965   Economics of language. *Behavioral Science* 10: 135–140.

May, Stephen (ed.)
   2005   Language policy and language rights: Complexities, challenges and future directions. Special issue of *Journal of Sociolinguistics* 9(3): 2–12.

Mayer, Thomas
   1993   *Truth versus Precision in Economics*. Aldershot: Edward Elgar.

McCloskey, Deirdre
   1990   *The Rhetoric of Economics*. Madison: University of Wisconsin Press.

Mélitz, Jacques
   2000   English-language dominance, literature and welfare. Unpublished manuscript, Institut d'études politiques, Paris.

Pool, Jonathan
   1991   A tale of two tongues. Unpublished manuscript, Department of Political Science, University of Washington (Seattle).

Pool, Jonathan
   1996   Optimal language regimes for the European Union. *International Journal of the Sociology of Language* 121: 159–179.

Raynauld, André and Pierre Marion
   1972   Une analyse économique de la disparité inter-ethnique des revenus [An economic analysis of interethnic earnings differentials]. *Revue économique* 23: 1–19.

Rubinstein, Ariel
   2000   *Economics and Language*. Cambridge: Cambridge University Press.

Sabourin, Conrad
   1985   La théorie des environnements linguistiques [The theory of linguistic environments]. In: François Vaillancourt (ed.), *Économie et langue*, 59–82. Québec: Conseil de la langue française.

Selten, Reinhard and Jonathan Pool
   1997   Is it worth it to learn Esperanto? Introduction to game theory. In: Reinhard Selten (ed.), *The Costs of European Linguistic Non-Integration*, 114–149. Rome: Esperanto Radikala Asocio.

Vaillancourt, François
  1980   *Difference in Earnings by Language Groups in Quebec 1970. An Economic Analysis.* [Publication B-90]. Québec: Centre international de recherche sur le bilinguisme.
Vaillancourt, François (ed.)
  1985   *Économie et langue.* Québec: Conseil de la langue française.
Vaillancourt, François
  1996   Language and socioeconomic status in Quebec: Measurement, findings, determinants, and policy costs. *International Journal of the Sociology of Language* 121: 69–92.
Vaillancourt, François and François Grin
  2000   *The Choice of a Language of Instruction: The Economic Aspects.* Distance learning course on language instruction in basic education. Washington, DC: The World Bank Institute.
van Parijs, Philippe
  2000   The ground floor of the world. On the socio-economic consequences of linguistic globalization. *International Political Science Review* 21(2): 217–233.
van Parijs, Philippe
  2001   Linguistic justice. *Politics, Philosophy and Economics* 1: 59–74.
van Parijs, Philippe
  2004   Europe's linguistic challenge. *Archives européennes de sociologie* 45: 113–154.

10. Language and colonialism

Bettina Migge and Isabelle Léglise

1. Introduction

Although the term colonialism is also used to refer to the hegemony of the Arabs, Greeks or Romans, it is nowadays most widely employed in its 19th century meaning. It refers to the establishment of control over a region including its inhabitants by an outside group which sometimes involved the total destruction of local governing institutions and the disempowerment of their members. All types of colonialism have directly or indirectly given rise to linguistic changes but the European colonialism of the last five centuries has had the most far-reaching consequences.

The literature on colonialism tends to focus on Europe's economic exploitation of many regions and peoples around the world and Europeans' use of excessive force towards the latter. While these issues are undoubtedly of great importance, it is equally important to understand the cultural and specifically the linguistic and discursive practices that came to be associated with European colonial rule. These practices played an instrumental role in assigning low prestige to non-European languages and cultures, including cultural and linguistic forms that emerged due to Europe's colonial expansion, and in establishing the superiority of the coloniser's language and culture. Although many of the colonised populations have today gained what is usually called political independence, the cultural and linguistic decolonisation of both European and non-European cultures is hardly complete. Especially since World War II, a struggle has been ongoing that attempts to remove the stigma from non-European cultures and languages, and questions the assumed European superiority. For the formerly colonised populations the aim is to find a way to position themselves in relation to their erstwhile colonisers and other, equally threatening, forces such as globalisation. One of the main battlegrounds is the education system. Generally founded during the colonial period, it was conceived on European colonial models and, to date, continues to implement to a greater or a lesser degree many of the colonial linguistic and cultural policies and is thus instrumental in perpetuating colonial discourses.

In this chapter we critically examine colonial and post-colonial language policies with a special focus on Creole communities in the Caribbean and South America. We suggest that while faced with similar issues these communities do not constitute a homogeneous group and consequently blanket solutions are not available to change the asymmetrical social and linguistic systems inherited from the colonisers. We argue that (new) educational policies need to be squarely based on a careful sociolinguistic analysis of each situation and must take a multi-model approach in order to effectively address existing language-based social inequalities. The chapter is structured as follows: Section 2 introduces the field of language and colonialism, discussing the main research issues and colonial language practices. Section 3 deals with educational practices in colonial and post-colonial societies, especially in Africa. Section 4 surveys the research on Creoles focusing on its contribution towards improving language-related discrimination in Caribbean Creole communities. Section 5 explores educational practices in some Anglophone and Francophone Creole communities, and Section 6 investigates educational practices in French Guiana arguing for a multi-model approach. The final section summarises the findings and outlines current research needs.

2. The field of language and colonialism

2.1. The major issues

Having been the subject of much debate since the pre-independence periods of most formerly colonised regions, research into the effects of European colonialism on language issues took off in the 1970s and 1980s with the publication of several works such as Césaire (1950), Fanon (1952), Spencer (1971), Calvet (1974), Bamgbose (1976, 2000), and Ngũgĩ wa Thiong'o (1986). The issue is currently being pursued by researchers such as Pennycook (1998, 2001), Skutnabb-Kangas and Phillipson (1995); see also Kirkpatrick (this vol.). Most of the work focused on drawing attention to the linguistic and social inequalities that had emerged in the formerly colonised regions of the world due to European imperialist expansion, and how they continue to affect the linguistic and social makeup of these regions, local language policies, and the status and development of both European and non-European languages. Although many of these regions have since gained political independence, access to education, knowledge, power and self-sufficiency of indigenous populations continue to be highly limited (Phillipson 1992). Both economic pressure from the former coloniser, opposition to decolonisation from local elites and increasing globalisation have effectively conspired to maintain colonial social and linguistic practices.

The research on language and colonialism pursues two broad goals. It critically investigates the colonial and neo-colonial practices related to language and formulates policies aimed at "decolonising the mind" of the formerly colonised and colonising populations and at improving the status of non-European languages and those that emerged as a result of European expansion, e.g. new varieties of French or English (see Kachru 1992 [1982]), or creoles and pidgins. For linguists, it was essentially a way to "faire la politique dans la linguistique, par la linguistique" (Calvet 1974: 10).

2.2.   Colonial practices in relation to language

The aim of European imperialism and colonialism was to expand the economic and power base of European nations and to assert their superiority. In part, this was achieved by subjugating the local populations. In the case of North America and Australia, for instance, native populations were forced off agriculturally valuable lands that were then taken over by European immigrants. In the Caribbean, native populations were also forced to provide hard physical labour for the colonisers leading to the death of millions of Amerindians. They were replaced by enslaved Africans and later by indentured labourers from Asia who had to work under horrendous conditions on Caribbean and American plantations (sugar, cotton, coffee, etc.). European slavery is therefore intimately linked to European colonialism and occurred as a direct consequence of the latter.

The imperialist and colonial enterprise was much aided and ultimately enabled by the existence of a social system and social ideology in Europe which firmly inscribed, legitimised and naturalised European cultural, social, and scientific superiority (Pennycook 1998; Calvet 1974). This social system and ideology created two hierarchically ordered social categories of people endowed not only with distinct sets of rights, obligations and social standing but also with distinct intellectual, social and other skills and properties. The European colonisers and their collaborators who were consistently identified with positive or prestigious values were located at the top of the social hierarchy and held the power in the society while the colonised, being identified with the subordinate position, were assigned low social status and granted little or no social power. Calvet (1987: 72) argues that linguistic colonisation occurred in two steps. The European language first spread into the "upper classes" of the colonised people and only then spread among members of the "lower classes". Subsequently, it diffused from the capital to small cities and from there to villages. The colonisers strategically used the education system to instil this asymmetrical social ideology in their colonial subjects but it was also constantly being reaffirmed by a range of other social and linguistic practices.

First, colonisation gave rise to a (new) language hierarchy in which the language of the coloniser was inscribed as the most prestigious language and came to dominate the administrative and mercantile structure of each colony. Since "les dialectes africains ne sont pas des langues de civilisation" (Davesne 1933: 6), language policy in francophone Africa, for example, prescribed the exclusive use of French. On the contrary, the British, in accordance with their "divide and rule" policy, supported the dominant languages in their colonies (Brenzinger 1992) but this had the same effect of affirming the European language as the most prestigious language. This denied African languages opportunities for functional development and the extension of existing African lingua francas. It also froze competition between languages for access to new domains and made the coloniser's language a necessity for social advancement (Spencer 1985). Coupled with the reluctance of all colonial powers to teach the languages of the other colonial powers, colonial language policies "effectively placed a kind of linguistic *cordon sanitaire* around each group of territories, linking them in language, as in trade and finance, with the metropolitan community, and cutting them off from their neighbours" (Spencer 1971: 544).

The colonial linguistic hierarchy was also generated by dominant European conceptions of culture and language (Pennycook 1998). These conceptions are clearly reflected in the discourse surrounding European and non-European culture and language (Calvet 1974: 165). Designations such as "language" associated with concepts such as "nation", "culture" and "power" were reserved for the colonial languages. The indigenous languages, linked to tribes and "uncultured" naturalness, were negatively identified as "dialect'" or "patois". Non-European languages were and to a certain extent still continue to be described as ambiguous, imprecise and as unfit for expressing modern scientific thought (Calvet 1974). The fact that most of them lacked a writing system and a literary body was seen as confirmation of their alleged inferior status. People's attachment to these languages was considered irrational and a sign of ignorance. The learning of the colonial language was, by contrast, portrayed as an asset; it presumably "opens up a person's mind" and made them civilised, modern human beings (Calvet 1974).

Second, colonial language practices also led to the demise of many languages. In some cases it resulted from the physical elimination of an entire population (as in Uruguay) or of part of it (as in Brazil, Chile or Argentina). In most cases, however, it was caused by language shift. In the field of "language displacement", "language death" and "degeneration", it is sometimes referred to as "linguistic genocide" or "linguicide" when it involves "the systematic replacement of an indigenous language with the language of an outside, dominant group, resulting in a permanent language shift and the death of the indigenous language" (Day 1985: 164). But the notion is fuzzy. Some researchers consider "attempting to kill a language" as linguicidal, whereas others argue that policies that may eventually lead to language death are linguicidal (Skutnabb Kangas and Phillipson 1995). Some language shifts reflect a voluntary decision to abandon a language, while others are due to coercion. Brenzinger (1992) notes that in the vast majority of cases, including colonial settings, there is "a mixture of these two scenarios, which means neither "language suicide" nor "language murder"'" (Calvet 1974). Prominent examples are most of the Aboriginal languages of Australia (Schmidt 1990), hundreds of Native American languages (Hill and Hill 1986; Adelaar 1991) and Hawaiian (see Day 1985).

Third, colonisation and slave trade also gave rise to new languages. The best known cases are Creoles that emerged in European plantation societies in the Caribbean, the Americas and Australia. Coming from different social and linguistic backgrounds, their creators – such as African slaves in the Caribbean and South America – were thrown into a relative social and linguistic void and created them from the various linguistic resources available to them, including their native linguistic background, the practices they found on the plantations, and those they had acquired during the middle passage (Mintz and Price 1992). Due to the history of their emergence, their surface similarity to the colonial language, and their association with populations of low prestige, Creoles are denigrated. They are generally seen as imperfect or corrupted versions of the colonial language (Calvet 1974).

Fourth, colonial language practices also gave rise to a change in the relationship between the different local languages. While British and Belgian policies encouraged the use of mother tongues in education, they did not give equal attention to all languages. They focused their efforts on (numerically or politically) "dominant" languages and/or those that were already used as a regional lingua franca and actively supported their spread at the expense of other local languages as in the case of Swahili in East Africa (Temu 1998) and Quechua in Peru (Adelaar 1991). Lingua Geral Amazonica and Nheengatu are interesting cases of how a language became a lingua franca due to colonial support (Freire 1983; Moore, Facundes, and Pires 1993). In British colonial Africa, between 1927 and 1950, various official linguistic committees were set up in each territory that were charged with identifying suitable dominant "vernaculars", standardising them and promoting the production of texts (Spencer 1971). This official promotion had detrimental effects on the other languages in these multilingual regions. They were essentially relegated to the "private" or non-official domain. In some cases this eventually led to language shift or extreme cases of language contact (Igboanusi and Peter 2004).

Colonial standardisation efforts actively shaped the linguistic space in which they were operating (see also Romaine, this vol.). When "developing" African languages, Europeans took three main approaches. They either harmonised or unified a group of related varieties to construct a common language by employing forms common to all or most of the varieties, or by selecting forms found in literary contexts. A case in point is Tswana of Botswana where various related dialects such as Ngwato, Ngwaketsi, Kgatla and Tswana "were unified around the Kwena dialect" (Msimang 1998: 166). Such efforts were not always successful. For instance, in Ghana attempts have been made to unify different varieties with the aim "to ultimately abolish the separate existence of Akuapem, Asante and Fante and in their place bring into being a single large-circulation language, *Akan*" (Krampah and Gyekye-Aboagye 1998: 81). To date only Akuapem and Fante are unified while Asante continues to remain separate due to disagreements over the representation of various linguistic aspects. Sometimes one or several varieties were elevated to standard language level as in the case of Thembu and Gcaleka in the Eastern Cape which were later harmonised to form Standard Xhosa (Msimang 1998). At times this led to the invention of new languages and to ethnic divisions (see Makoni 1998 for Shona in Zimbabwe). Finally, in other cases Europeans actively created new varieties. Yanga (1998) argues that Standard Kikongo (*Kikongo ya Leta* 'State Kikongo') was specially engineered by Europeans for their needs and is still today considered a non-native and foreign-made variety by speakers of Kikongo.

Fifth, Calvet (1974) points out that the colonial language hierarchy also ensured that the European and local languages influenced each other differently. The languages of the colonised populations generally borrowed a significant amount of lexical material from the colonial language. Schmied (1991: 141) shows that African languages mainly borrowed European lexical items from "[d]omains associated with modern European life and inventions, such as technology, administration, education, sports and entertainment". There are few, if any, borrowings that relate to local culture because "English equivalents do not exist or are considered inappropriate by Africans". The colonial languages adopted much fewer lexical material from local languages. Most of them are marginal at best and are "only used to render meanings in an African context" (Schmied 1991: 79) and are therefore not widely known outside of the African context.

3. Colonial and post-colonial educational language practices

3.1. Educational language practices in French and British colonies

The colonial education systems were instrumental in establishing the coloniser's language as powerful since by their very nature, colonial education systems "subserved in their various ways the political, economic and cultural aims of the colonial governments" (Spencer 1971: 538). However, the different European colonial powers in the 19th and 20th centuries did not always pursue the same policies with respect to the medium of instruction and even within the same colonial empire partially different practices were put in place (Spencer 1971; Awoniyi 1976; Pennycook 1998). Pennycook (1998) convincingly argues that this is due to the fact that colonial language practices did not stand in a simple relationship to colonial governance. Despite differences, two broad types of colonial language policies can be identified: the metropolitan language model and the vernacular model. France and Portugal pursued the former, and Britain and Belgium the latter. "Since the end of the eighteenth century, the bases of French policy in West Africa were the liberal ideas of the French Revolution and the concept of one universal civilization towards which the world was moving and of which Europe was the leader" (Awoniyi 1976: 31). The education system that became implanted in French colonies was therefore closely modelled on the one in metropolitan France. Students throughout the French empire were subject to the same curriculum and French was inscribed as the only valid medium of instruction and learning. The French state categorically refused to allow mother tongue education or the teaching of local languages as subjects in schools because they strongly believed that it would disadvantage the children in the colonies. The French-only policy also found strong support among educated West Africans.

However, French colonial educational practices affected only a small number of the children (e.g., less than 1 % in French Equatorial Africa between 1938 and 1955). The desire to impose French was also not constant throughout the entire period of colonisation or across the territories involved. At the beginning of French colonisation in North Africa, for example, no effort was made to promote French (Ageron 1973). Many colonisers were acting in favour of maintaining "l'ignorance des masses musulmanes afin de prévenir toute révolte et conserver la domination coloniale" (Riguet 1985: 22). Although it is widely believed that French "was imposed" and spoken everywhere, Calvet (1974: 119) argues that at least in Algeria the colonial system was not very successful in imposing French.

In the British colonies, education was initially only available for a small number of people. In Africa, the Protestant missions took a lead in the establishment of formal education with the British government only starting to take an interest in educational matters in the early 20th century (Spencer 1971). The strong missionary influence ensured that initially most of the teaching in the British colonies was carried out in native languages because they realised that the Christian faith could only be properly taught through the native language. They saw the "formal" school as "the institutional agent of the spiritual church" (Awoniyi 1976: 36). The first colonial Education Ordinance for West Africa (1882) tried to change this policy by stipulating English reading and writing as the main goals of schooling. However, lack of a viable government infrastructure and widespread opposition by missionaries obstructed its implementation. The missionary policy soon received support from an independent investigation into educational matters by the Phelps-Stokes Commission (1920–1924) and by the Advisory Committee on Native Education that was made permanent by the government in 1929 who strongly favoured mother tongue education. Following these recommendations, the British government adopted a policy of encouraging so-called vernacular education at primary level, "with English introduced gradually" (Awoniyi 1976: 39). Full instruction through English started at the secondary school level which until after World War II was generally only open to a few chosen individuals (Spencer 1971). African languages could be continued as a subject during secondary schooling. Due to pressure from parents who felt that their children were being disadvantaged, the policy of mother tongue education was increasingly abandoned or not further developed after World War II (Spencer 1971). English was now introduced quite early as the main medium of instruction and the mother tongues were only used to bridge initial comprehension problems.

British mother tongue education was geared towards British colonial interests (Pennycook 1998). Colonial educators generally felt that colonial subjects required moral and cultural grounding to make them better, docile and co-operative subjects and ultimately to facilitate colonial rule. It was widely believed that this would be best achieved through a sound but basic education focusing on both European (or British) values and an understanding of their own culture (as viewed through British eyes). Mother tongue education and translations of major English works into the native languages were generally seen as a crucial instrument in this endeavour since it would insure full comprehension of the issues taught and have the "positive" side effect of "enriching" the local cultures (Pennycook 1998).[1]

The learning of English, although much in demand by the colonial subjects, was generally not much encouraged by the government because it was not felt to be conducive to the aims of colonial rule. The colonial enterprise only required a limited group of people able to function in English. General learning of English by the masses would presumably unnecessarily raise their hopes for social advancement, disintegrate them from their cultures and pose a danger to British rule. It would not be conducive to instilling morality or knowledge in the colonial subjects. Instead, the learning of English would become an end to itself. Finally, given the acute shortage of teachers in most places, it was felt that English medium instruction for the masses would lead to the development of "bad" English. Among British colonial subjects, however, English medium instruction was much in demand.

Linguistic imperialism did not end when the former colonies gained political independence. Economic incentives from the USA and Great Britain coupled with Euro-centric language learning models – disseminated by new language-centred academic disciplines that were emerging in the two countries after World War II such as Applied Linguistics and English as a Foreign or Second Language – did much to bolster the importance of (certain native) English(es). Phillipson (1992: 132–133) also notes that the British had been co-operating with the Americans since the mid-1950s in order to realise a "great offensive to make English a world language", an "English language campaign on a global basis" and "on a hitherto unprecedented scale".

France, for its part, created the *francophonie* organisation to promote the French language. As argued by Branca-Rosoff (1996: 106), the word *franco-*

phonie "semble forgé pour absoudre la France de l'ancien péché de colonialisme tout en marquant la vocation universelle du français". She shows that the notion *francophonie* thinly disguises the fact that speaking French essentially coincides with successive French colonialisation and that the *francophonie* serves above all French interests. The overall goal is to maintain France's zone of political influence and to halt the rapid spread of English and Anglophone culture. The *francophonie* represents a "natural" grouping of states each of which maintains privileged cultural, economic and political relations with France. The status of France within the *francophonie* has never been entirely clear – is it simply a part of it or is it its centre? Equally unclear is the status of France's overseas' departments in this organisation. Officially, they are an integral part of France, but historically, geographically and socially – "comme une cicatrice de la colonisation" (Branca-Rosoff 1996: 198) – they are clearly distinct from each other and from the centre. If the actual promotion of one or many African language(s) is nowadays feasible in many countries of the francophone orbit, Laroussi and Marcellesi (1996) wonder whether this would be possible without the approval of France. Calvet and Chaudenson (2001) hold a more optimistic view. Investigating the development of language policies in *francophonie* institutions, they show that while these institutions initially did not take into account the multilingualism of the francophone countries, this has much changed in the last thirty years. The coexistence of the different languages in the "francophone space" was officially recognised and today the relationship between French and these languages is presented in terms of a partnership. However, the central role of France, at both a linguistic and at a political level, has so far remained unchallenged.

3.2.   Language and education in Africa in the post-colonial period

The decisions of the newly independent states were multiplex and depended on a variety of factors such as the nature of the colonial practices, the linguistic, cultural and ethnic makeup of the population, their ideological and educational goals. At independence, three kinds of attitudes to language can be discerned in Africa: "[A]n attitude of letting things be, which translates into a continuation of colonial policies and practices" (Bamgbose 2000: 49) and served to perpetuate and to entrench the colonial status quo (Devonish 1986). Some countries such as Ghana, Kenya, Zambia, the Democratic Republic of Congo (formerly Zaire) and Zimbabwe were eager to "modernise" and (initially) felt that a European medium of education would be the most effective way to achieve this (Bamgbose 2000). Guinea, Burkina Faso, Tanzania, Togo, and Ethiopia opted for education in the mother tongues throughout the entire primary cycle or were making arrangements to expand their use also to higher levels of education. However, from the beginning, four important factors have been affecting language policies of African states (see also Blommaert, this vol.).

First, they tend to be vaguely stated to avoid possible political repercussions. This gives room to individual solutions but it may also create "lack of uniformity, frustration on the part of the teachers and lack of direction" (Bamgbose 1976: 17). Second, language policies were, at least in the initial years, subject to frequent fluctuations due to changes in ideologies and governments (Bamgbose 2000). Third, there is usually a lack of consistency between policy and practice due to difficulties in carrying out the policy. For example, although the policy in the Western State of Nigeria is that the medium of instruction should change from Yoruba to English at the end of the third year of primary school, the mother tongue continues to be used freely in many schools, especially in rural areas, because of pupils' inadequate level of competence in English. On the other hand, in some urban schools where pupils come from a range of different language backgrounds, English often becomes the medium of instruction much earlier than laid down by official policy (Bamgbose 1976). Fourth, new policies often led to new language-related inequalities. In North African countries such as Morocco, Tunisia and Algeria, the French-only educational policy practiced during the colonial period has in the last thirty years been replaced by a bilingual approach promoting a policy of "arabicization" – to a minimal extent at the primary level (Granguillaume 1983; Ennaji 1991). This policy creates new problems though because pupils speak different Arabic "dialects" or Berber as their native languages but are being taught through classical or literary Arabic. This new linguistic domination (of classical Arabic over the so-called colloquial Arabic varieties and other mother tongues) is due both to the association of classical Arabic with the notion of purity through its function as a sacred language, its past as a hegemonic language, and the colonial inheritance of centralist and anti-multilingualism policies.

Overall, European languages have continued to dominate African education systems in the postcolonial period. According to Bamgbose (2000), mother tongue education still plays only a marginal role throughout Africa, being mainly used during the initial stages of primary education, if at all. Few countries use it throughout the entire primary cycle or at secondary level. The picture is even grimmer at tertiary level.

Three types of experiments have been conducted to increase the effectiveness of educational practices and to address common shortcomings. Firstly, there are enrichment projects "designed to achieve a more effective use of existing media, without changing the extent of their use as a medium" (Bamgbose 2000: 51). The Primary Education Improvement Project in Northern Nigeria, for instance, focused on enhancing teacher training, curriculum development, and the realisation of more suitable teaching materials. Even when the medium of instruction is a European language, teachers are encouraged to take into consideration their pupils' mother tongues when preparing teaching materials (Bamgbose 1976).

Secondly, there are projects that aim to bring mother tongue education to areas where it previously did not exist and to assess its effectiveness. One such project is the 1981 PROPELCA (Projet de recherche operationelle pour l'enseignement des langues au Cameroun) project in multilingual Eastern Cameroon. It aimed to integrate seven local languages into the school system. In the first year 70% of school time is dedicated to and carried out in African languages, "gradually decreasing to 30 per cent in the third year. Basic language skills are introduced in the African language and the introduction of French is gradual [...]" (Bamgbose 2000: 51). Currently, 12 languages are regularly used at primary level in that area. Finally, there are projects that aim to extend mother tongue education. One successful project is the 1971 Six-Year Primary Project in Nigeria. It was designed to compare a six-year mother tongue (Yoruba) education with the standard three-year mother tongue and three-year English medium primary education. Evaluations show that the former approach produces clearly superior educational results.

While mother tongue medium education and the teaching of African languages at school still lacks widespread support among parents and governments, there is a greater tolerance for the teaching of these languages as a subject or their use in adult literacy programmes. Some countries like Ghana, Nigeria, Tanzania, Kenya, and Togo currently offer a few of their indigenous languages as subjects at secondary and at tertiary levels and pupils can sit their final exam papers in them. All countries conduct their adult literacy programmes in the mother tongue.

The teaching of African languages is hampered by various factors (cf. Awoniyi 1982; Bamgbose 1976, 2000). Teachers of these languages are rarely well trained. In fact, very often, the only requirement is that the teachers be speakers of these languages. Teaching materials are generally not up-to-date, readily available or as innovative as those for European languages. Teachers usually do not have the same teaching incentives as their counterparts teaching European languages or other subjects and tend to be held in low esteem. Finally, while European languages are mandatory at all levels and in final examinations this is generally not the case with African languages. Even if they are obligatory subjects as in Tanzania (Swahili) and Zimbabwe (Shona), the exam grade is irrelevant for students' academic advancement (Roy-Campbell 1998).

3.3. Language and education in Creole communities during the colonial period

Initially, educational institutions were implanted in the main cities of the Caribbean and South American colonies mainly to fill the educational needs of the colonisers' children. Before the abolition of slavery in the French colony of Guadeloupe, the colonial council refused all educational projects for the poor populations (Abou 1988) and the planters were little impressed by the Revolution's ideas because they felt that the wider availability of education posed a threat to the colonial order. Eventually, the education system was slowly opened up to the masses because it was generally felt that (European-based formal) education was the best way for (former) slaves to overcome their inferior social position into which slavery had forced them. However, the increasing access to education did not generally provide the (former) slaves with the opportunity to move up the social hierarchy. While this has definitely changed with independence, access to social power and the opportunity for social advancement has remained relatively unattainable for the masses. Sound familiarity with the former colonial language remains an indispensable prerequisite for social and economic success.

At independence, countries with predominantly Creole-speaking populations in the Caribbean (Haiti, Jamaica, Trinidad and Tobago), South America (Suriname, Guyana) and Oceania (Vanuatu, Papua New Guinea, Solomon Islands) generally adopted the colonial language as the instructional medium in schools. As in Africa, this continuation of colonial practices was due to attitudinal factors – most people believed that their native (Creole) language was a "lesser" language and thus not a viable means of instruction; its adoption as an official language would allegedly obstruct access to modern science, technology and information (Devonish 1986) – but also the result of practical considerations. Most Creoles were not sufficiently codified, and few if any written texts, let alone textbooks suitable for schools, existed at the time (see Prudent 2005 for Martinique; Craig 2001 for the West Indies). Possible exceptions are Sranan Tongo in Suriname, Dutch Creole (Negerhollands) in the Danish Virgin Islands and Papiamentu spoken in the Dutch Antilles. They have been written languages since the beginning of missionary activities (Devonish 1986). In colonies such as Jamaica, Barbados and Antigua in which "English emerged as the dominant European language alongside an English-influenced Creole, the use of the Creole language in even as restricted an area as religious instruction was ignored […] due to a lack of awareness of the existence of Creole as a distinct language variety" (Devonish 1986: 51–52).

4. Descriptive and applied research on Creoles

Since the 1960s, Creole linguistics has developed into an autonomous area of research. The research on Creoles has made important contributions to theoretical issues in historical linguistics and language contact studies, and has much contributed to our understanding of linguistic variation and change. In recent years there has also been a growing interest in sociolinguistic issues. Initially, most of the research focused on what is usually referred to as English-lexified

Creoles, particularly those of the Caribbean and was carried out in the UK and the USA. Research on French-lexified Creoles was not deemed a serious and worthwhile field of academic inquiry in French universities until the 1980s.

4.1. The status and function of Creoles

Research on Creoles has addressed the question of the status of these languages from various perspectives. Descriptive and quantitative sociolinguistic research on English-lexified Creoles (cf. Bailey 1966; Edwards 1983; LePage and Tabouret-Keller 1985) aimed at showing that Creoles are socially and linguistically highly focused linguistic systems in their own right (Winford 1997). These studies found that Creoles employ distinct function morphemes whose linguistic distribution is governed by rules and principles that are clearly different from those of English. Quantitative sociolinguistic studies also revealed that English is reserved for formal events and activities while Creoles tend to be the norm in informal in-group settings. The variation between them was found to be conditioned by various social factors as in other bilingual communities.

A few studies directly address the social prestige of Creoles. They describe the changes that occurred in the socio-political standing of Creoles such as Tok Pisin (Romaine 1991) and Melanesian Pidgin English (Mühlhäusler 1991), and Hellinger (1991) compares such changes in different Creoles. Investigating demographic and macro-social data such as the numerical strength of its speakers, their geographical distribution, its institutional support, and its social functions, they demonstrate that socio-demographic and legal changes lead to significant changes in the status of Creoles. This suggests that their official recognition spurs their standardisation which in turn results in their use in new social domains (e.g. schools).

Employing a matched-guise method (Rickford 1985), a structured interview method (Beckford Wassink 1999), or a written questionnaire format (Winford 1976; Mühleisen 2001), a second set of studies explores the beliefs and attitudes people hold about a Creole, its speakers, the contexts of its use, and their emotions and actions toward the Creole. They demonstrate that the Creole is attributed low prestige in official settings but high prestige in informal and in-group encounters. These social evaluations are not static but are subject to on-going change. Mühleisen (2002) shows that a comprehensive understanding of the prestige of a language only emerges from an exploration of the socio-historical forces involved in the discursive construction of the language (group), its prestige and that of its speakers, and an investigation of the various communicative functions of the language in the different social discourses. It is these discursive negotiations that are at the heart of prestige formation, affirmation, and change.

Inspired by earlier research such as Reisman (1970) and Abrahams (1983), some current sociolinguistic research is concerned with the stylistic complexity of Creoles, the social and linguistic characteristics of the different styles and their social functions (Patrick 1997; Garrett 2000; Migge 2004; Roberts 2004). It shows that Creoles, like any other language, have several styles and varieties which cannot be arranged along a single continuum, Creole to English, as suggested by the Creole continuum model. Moreover, the colonial standard language is by no means the only or main prestige language in Creole communities. Eastern Maroons in Suriname and French Guiana, for example, recognise a separate formal style, *Lesipeki taki* 'respect speech' which is obligatory in all kinds of formal situations and linguistically highly structured (Migge 2004).

In Creole communities, as in other communities, each variety, including the official European language, indexes distinct social meanings. Speakers variably draw on them or code-switch between them in both informal and formal situations to create various discursive and identity-related meanings (Shields-Brodber 1992; Sidnell 1999; Fenigsen 2005; Migge 2007). Especially young members of multiethnic and multilingual nation states such as Suriname and French Guiana regularly draw on the locally available linguistic varieties to construct distinctive local social identities.

4.2. Applied linguistics and Creoles

One line of research in Creole Studies deals with applied issues, language planning and educational language policy. This was in response to two developments. Firstly, language-related education problems emerged on an unprecedented scale in the 1960s and 1970s in the Anglophone West Indies due to the rapid expansion of the education system "to include large numbers of the Creole-speaking mass of the population who had, as a group, been previously excluded" (Devonish 1986: 102). Secondly, the positive results of the early descriptive and theoretical research on Creoles proved their linguistic adequacy. Encouraged by Caribbean governments, they led to an intensification of research on the "instrumentalisation" of Creoles especially in the education system, language acquisition in Creole settings, and the development of teaching methods (Craig 2001). Moreover, a greater participation of scholars from the former colonies in the production of western intellectual knowledge and an overall opening up of academic disciplines towards formerly non-prestigious subject matters also gave rise to the emergence of native linguistic movements such as the *Comité Bannzil Kréyol* (Prudent and Schnepel 1993) especially in French Creole communities. They militated for the recognition of creoles and non-standard varieties and their integration into the education system (Craig 2001). However, according to Devonish (1986) most of the proposals did not question the status quo. They never aimed to make Creole the main medium of instruction. The use of Creole was primarily to help facilitate the acquisition of English (Devonish 1986).

From very early on it became clear that the use of Creole as medium of instruction would be difficult to implement. Firstly, a commonly agreed-upon writing system such as the Cassidy Phonemic writing system had not found widespread support and a standard variety on which schoolbooks could be based did not exist (Craig 2001). Secondly, teachers were not sufficiently trained to teach literacy in Creole, and the idea did not get an enthusiastic reception among them. Thirdly, there was an obvious lack of educational material. Furthermore, most Caribbean and South American governments were not willing to implement such policies (Devonish 1986). Conditions are generally more favourable for the use of Creole as an instructional medium if it is unrelated to the official language. This situation is, however, not very common overall.

The research on language acquisition focuses on the linguistic environment of Creole speaking children including the classroom setting, the nature of learner varieties and the patterns of acquisition. It revealed that Creole children grow up in a variety of different linguistic settings that range from monolingual to various kinds of bilingual and multilingual situations (Youssef 1990; Carrington 1989; Simmons-McDonald 2001). Creole children, therefore, have different levels of exposure to and knowledge of the dominant language and of the different Creole varieties. This leads to various acquisition patterns and entails the application of a range of special teaching methods (Craig 1980, 2001). Regular foreign or second-language teaching procedures just like those for first language speakers tend to be ineffective because Creole speakers do not properly belong to either category. On the one hand, the standard language, e.g. English, tends not to be unknown to them; however, on the other hand, the majority does not have anything close to a native competence in it either.

5. Education in Caribbean Creole communities: Historical background and recent changes

In most communities Creoles have not received official recognition and even if they are a co-official language such as Haitian Creole in Haiti, they generally do not have the same status as the European language. The latter continues to dominate the public domain and functions as a gate-keeper to positions of social power and prestige. The situation of many Creole communities continues to largely resemble the classic case of diglossia in Haiti discussed by Ferguson. In Haiti, French is the High variety and Creole the Low variety. Being reserved for formal situations and associated with high prestige, the High variety is seen as having a more complex grammar and is linguistically codified, possessing an elaborated set of norms and is the medium of instruction in schools. The Low variety is learnt "naturally" through family and peer group interaction, and written and oral formal practices only exist in the High variety. Persons who are monolingual or dominant in the Creole continue to be socially disadvantaged. They are denied access to the political decision-making institutions and their opportunities to participate in them or to obtain information from them is seriously hampered. Their access to modern technology, higher levels of education, and their success rate at all levels of education continue to be seriously curtailed. This greatly infringes on people's opportunities for employment and social advancement, and consequently increases their poverty risk and leads to marginalisation (Devonish 1986). Finally, other essential services like medical services, law enforcement and justice tend to be difficult to partake of (Léglise 2007; Devonish 1986). However, most Creoles have gained in social prestige and are gaining ground in situations from which they were previously excluded.

One of the issues that was fiercely debated in both Francophone (cf. Bebel-Gisler 1976; Bernabé 1976) and Anglophone Creole communities was whether the Creole writing system should be based on that of their lexifier, or whether it should be maximally different to clearly reflect the difference between the two (see also Romaine, this vol.). Another important issue in all Caribbean territories concerns the implementation of the Creole as a medium of instruction. The degree to which Creoles have been recognised for educational purposes has varied over the years and from one territory to the next. According to Appel and Verhoeven (1995), policy decisions are based on sociolinguistic factors, such as the linguistic relationship between the Creole and the official language, the existence of a norm acceptable to the population, the level of national consciousness and the geographical and age distribution of the languages.

5.1. Anglophone Caribbean Creole communities

Although the use and promotion of Creole was generally not very closely aligned with nationalism and anti-colonialism in Anglophone Caribbean communities, the fact that they have always been an important symbol of these countries' national identity was instrumental in the gradual erosion of official language policies. For a very long time now, Creoles have been widely employed in political campaigning, health education and in agricultural training. Besides their increasing use in literary productions otherwise written in English, there is also a body of local poetry and drama entirely written and performed in Creoles. In recent years, newspapers have been publishing smaller sections dealing with humour but also with news reporting in Creole. Direct quotations from individuals in Creole are also increasingly included in news reports, even figuring on the front page (Carrington 2001; Devonish 1986). A particularly important area of growth is the broadcast media. In most Caribbean countries such as St. Lucia (Garrett 2000) and Dominica (Devonish 1986), radio stations regularly offer news broadcasts and other entertainment programmes in the local Creole. In other countries such as Jamaica, broadcasts may be officially in English but due to widespread use of call-in features and opinion pieces that involve interviews with the person-in-the street a great amount of the talk is actually done in Creole.

Creoles have even been making headway in education, one of the sectors from which they were traditionally shunned. Carrington (2001: 28), for example, tells us that while only a few Creoles in the Caribbean region are officially supported in the education system, such as Papiamentu and Haitian Creole (cf. Devonish 1986), they are nevertheless widely informally recognised and are taken into account in various ways. Teachers in the West Indies usually employ Creole in class to overcome comprehension problems and also allow its use by pupils in oral interactions. And "[t]he Caribbean Examination Council has a policy by which only the content of a subject is the focus of marking. Consequently, it is only in the examination of English that students' scripts attract penalties for inappropriate language use" (Carrington 2001: 28–29). Such largely informal practices are clearly valuable in that they reduce language-related obstacles in the educational system and undoubtedly challenge the status quo. However, they are also fragile. Their implementation depends very much on the goodwill or interests of the individuals involved and may thus lead to further inequalities. Since these arrangements are not legally prescribed, they can also be changed or stopped at any time without their beneficiaries having any legal grounds for opposing it (Carrington 2001). This considerably adds to Creole speakers' vulnerability.

To date, language-related inequalities have been least addressed in the justice system (Devonish 1986).

5.2. Curaçao and Aruba

Until 1986, Curaçao, Bonaire and Aruba were part of the group of islands referred to as the ABC Islands or Dutch Antilles. According to Martinus (1997) and Quint (2000), Papiamentu developed out of a Portuguese-African protocreole language brought to Curaçao by African slaves, starting from 1662. When missionaries came to christianise the slaves, they chose to do this in Papiamentu and encouraged its use (Croes 1995). With the opening of Aruba for colonists in 1754, Papiamentu was widely used in the Aruban and Curaçaoan community. Educational institutions (especially for children from the lower classes) were run by the Roman Catholic mission for several decades and Papiamentu was the medium of instruction. However, in 1936, a law completely banned Papiamentu from all schools on the islands and Dutch became the sole means of instruction. It was felt that Papiamentu was an obstacle to the learning and teaching of the official language, Dutch (Appel and Verhoeven 1995: 70–71).

Papiamentu "is the major medium of public communication in the Islands" (Devonish 1986: 65) and is widely used in the print media and radio and television broadcasts. In Curaçao, "[g]overnment decrees are published in both Dutch and Papiamentu, and those holding political office use Papiamentu exclusively when addressing the public" (Devonish 1986: 65–66). It is currently the mother tongue of 90% of the children in Curaçao (Appel and Verhoeven 1995: 70–71). On Aruba, Papiamentu is spoken by 76.5% of the population, English by 9%, Spanish by 7.5% and Dutch by only 5.5% (Croes 1995: 10). 94.5% of the children are still being submersed into a language, Dutch, that they do not master. This situation is largely responsible for the high repetition rate (15 to 20%) in primary school (Van Breet 1994). In Curaçao, more than 70% of the children do not succeed in finishing primary school without repeating a class (Appel and Verhoeven 1995: 70–71). Children from lower class Papiamentu-speaking homes have a substantial deficit with respect to lexical skills in Dutch, as compared with children from higher social classes, who speak both Papiamentu and Dutch at home. Severing and Verhoeven (2001) show that in grade 5 of primary school, the children's level of language comprehension was better in Papiamentu while their level of decoding was better in Dutch. Both proficiencies turned out to be related to sociolinguistic factors and background characteristics such as repeating classes at school, length of residence in town, and family size. The vast majority of the school population consequently underachieves at school.

Since 1983, a group of researchers has been working on the standardisation and elaboration of Papiamentu focusing on the orthography, lexicon and syntax. In 1983, Papiamentu was introduced as a subject in all grades of primary school for half an hour a day. In 1993 a new plan for primary education decreed that Papiamentu should be the language of instruction throughout primary school, and Dutch should be treated as a "foreign language". Despite the usual, mostly attitudinal obstacles (Appel and Verhoeven 1995), Papiamentu was finally instituted as the medium of instruction at primary school level in most schools on the island in 2004.

On Aruba, Dutch is still employed as if it were the pupils' mother tongue. However, there is a growing tendency to teach Dutch as a foreign language (Croes 1995). In 1988, the Aruban government accepted a Policy Bill saying that it is intending to work towards a bilingual education system with both Papiamentu and Dutch as languages of instruction. While the policy does not mention the introduction of other languages that were identified by a linguistic survey as being spoken natively and as second languages by sections of the Aruban population, Croes (1995) argues that it would be beneficial to reflect on the relation between Papiamentu and all of Aruba's languages. Spanish, for instance, should remain a subject at all levels of primary and secondary education, and English, Dutch and Papiamentu should be integrated into a trilingual education model. Papiamentu should initially be the primary medium of instruction in primary school while Dutch and English should be introduced as second languages at an early stage.

The case of language planning on the island of Curaçao shows that the standardisation and implementation of a Creole in education is feasible, especially in communities in which the Creole and the colonial language are not related. However, the consequences of language planning, such as teacher training and the provision of new instructional materials, require ample funds which most of the postcolonial states may not have.

5.3.   Francophone Creole Communities: Martinique and Guadeloupe

In relation to Francophone Creole communities Prudent and Schnepel (1993) identify two categories of situations. On the one hand, there are several countries that were only briefly colonised by France and that have then been independent nations for quite some time such as the Seychelles, Mauritius and Haiti. However, despite overall political similarities, their policies in relation to their Creoles differ quite a bit. In the 1990s, for instance, there was a strong pro-Creole atmosphere in the Seychelles (see Bollée 1993). In Mauritius the official position was pro-Creole, too, but the government made much less effort to promote the language and in Haiti, even today the policies regarding the promotion of Haitian Creole remain ambivalent (Devonish 1986; Dejean 1993).

On the other hand, there are the four French overseas departments – Guyane in South America, Martinique and Guadeloupe in the Caribbean, and La Réunion in the Indian Ocean.[2] They had been under French control for a relatively long period of time and were politically integrated into the French state in 1946, giving rise to a different linkage between language, identity, and politics. Efforts to promote the local Creoles are frequently associated with autonomist or independence movements opposing French domination. In debates surrounding the promotion of Creole, the French education system, which enforces French as the only medium of instruction, has generally been the main target of criticism. In the French Caribbean Overseas Departments, Fanon (1952), for example, speaks of an alienation of French Antilleans through a *dispositif de dressage mental et social*. Bebel-Gisler (1976) accuses the education system of a perpetuation of a colonial culture. In the 1970s, some individual attempts were made to integrate Creole into the school in Guadeloupe (Schnepel 1993; Durizot Jno-Baptiste 1996, 2003) and in Martinique (Gratiant 1988). These were however not very successful since overall public opinion remained firmly in favour of French and attitudes towards the implementation of Creole in the French school system remain controversial.

Aside from the 1951 *loi Deixonne* that gave a first recognition to regional languages in Metropolitan France, the French government had never acknowledged the linguistic or cultural rights of minorities within its borders. In 1982, an educational law – the Savary circular – proposed the teaching of regional languages and cultures for three hours a week but Creoles were neglected in the statute. This situation was supposed to be rectified by the Lafayette Declaration made during the Fourth International Conference of Creole Studies at Lafayette in Louisiana in May 1983. However, when the news about the official introduction of Creole into the Antillean school system reached Martinique through the media, public opinion quickly ran high. The General Council, parents' associations, and certain teachers' unions who had been involved in preparing the implementation of the Creole in local schools suddenly had second thoughts about the project. The chancellor eventually had to renounce his decision. And although a few minor unofficial educational projects were eventually carried out in primary and secondary schools, the Savary circular (1982) was essentially ignored.

In 2001, the *loi Deixonne* was extended to Creoles, and in 2002 a national teaching examination, the CAPES,[3] was created for Creole(s). The promotion of French-lexified Creoles in the French national education system is still a long way off though. Even if the law actually allows the presence of Creole languages and cultures in schools for three hours a week, discussions on the issue have not ceased. The two most recent discussions concerned the existence of the Capes Creole(s), its definition and improvement (see Prudent 2001) and the introduction, in Martinique, of obligatory lessons called *Humanités créoles* on Creole culture and environment (see Séminaire des Inspecteurs de la Martinique 2003, and many discussions on the Internet site kapeskreyol). For Prudent (2005) the debate is not limited to the nature of the school system as such but touches on issues such as the notion of citizenship and equality.

In situations in which the Creole remains in close contact with its European input language, the main issue does not simply consist of devising policies for the valorisation of the main home language of the children in the school environment. Few if any of these communities are classic diglossic communities. In the home context and in the public sphere the relationship between the two languages is generally much more complex. From a very early age on, children are to varying degrees exposed to both the Creole and the European standard language. Bernabé (1999) therefore proposes to consider both Creole and French as their mother tongues. Which of the two will be considered the "first" or the "second" mother tongue would essentially depend on the language practices in the family. He adds that French tends to become the first mother tongue and Creole the second one. However, the Creole is no less indispensable than French in the French Antilles. Based on theses observations and on the idea of "qualitative decreolisation" which leads to a symbolic "désinvestissement", he militates for the implementation of Creole at school, both in terms of speaking and writing.

March's (1997) study on the discourse on language attitudes and language practices by Martiniquian mothers demonstrates that few engage in monolingual practices. Creole speakers variably draw on all of their linguistic resources combining them into mixed productions. Prudent (1981) and Romani (2000) for instance describe them as the result of a macro-system called *interlect,* and not as productions from two independent languages, French and Creole. Based on these observations, researchers at the IUFM (Institut Universitaire de Formation des Maîtres) in Martinique have for the last ten years been engaged in the development of new pedagogical methods. This *pédagogie de la variation* (Romani 1994) starts from the recognition that speakers engage in a range of linguistic productions that cannot be easily attributed to either of the languages involved but constitute bilingual productions. This approach is of interest because it is based on real productions and essentially tries to implement the findings of recent sociolinguistic research on Creoles. However, it is not clear how effective these new teaching methods are because, to date, to the best of our knowledge, no official audit of this programme has been carried out.

6. A multi-model approach to multilingual societies: The case of French Guiana

6.1. Historical background

An important obstacle to the implementation of mother tongue education is the multiplicity of languages, especially if these languages are largely unrelated to each other. In the French overseas' department of Guyane, for instance, roughly 30 typologically diverse languages are spoken besides French, the official language. The languages include several Amerindian languages belonging to diverse language families, i.e. Carib, Tupi-Guarani and Arawak, European languages such as French, Brazilian Portuguese and to a lesser extent varieties of English, Dutch or Spanish, and English and French-lexified Creoles. The English-lexified Creoles are better known as the Creoles of Suriname, e.g. Saamaka and the varieties of the Eastern Maroon Creole (Aluku, Ndyuka, Pamaka). They are spoken by populations referred to by the same names who have either been resident in the department for a long time or just arrived in the last 20 years as the result of the civil war in Suriname in the late 1980s. There are at least two French-lexified Creoles widely spoken in French Guiana, Créole Guyanais and Haitian Creole. The former is the mother tongue and community language of the Afro-Guianese population of the department and has been in existence since colonisation. Haitian Creole is the mother tongue of migrants from Haiti who have been coming to French Guiana in the last 30 years.

In addition to the great linguistic diversity, there is also overlap between the different communities because neither of the linguistic communities in French Guiana is monolingual. In some communities, the ancestral language is the main medium of interaction in the majority of families while in others, particularly in urban settings, exchanges take place in more than one language or mainly in one of the dominant languages, French or Creole. Léglise (2004) found that four languages serve as lingua franca in interethnic encounters (market, school, hospital, etc.). They are Créole Guyanais, which used to be the main lingua franca of the department but is now mainly used on the coast, particularly in the eastern part, Brazilian Portuguese, which is used mainly in the east, and a variety of Nengee or Sranan Tongo, which is currently the main means of interethnic communication in the western part. French, the official language, is used in administration and in education and until recently remained the main language of the media. While it is increasingly used as a lingua franca in recent years (Léglise 2005) because of the rapid growth in the school population, its dominance in the media is currently being challenged by local languages. The regional radio station (RFO) now also broadcasts, at certain times, in Créole Guyanais and increasingly produces broadcasts realised in French on local Amerindian languages and (Busi)nengee. Smaller radio stations in the West such as Reutemeger or Radio IDL also broadcast several hours a week in Sranan Tongo or in Ndyuka.

The linguistic and cultural diversity of the department is hardly reflected in other areas of public life, especially in educational institutions. All education is carried out in French and access to all levels of education and jobs in the public service sector, one of the largest employers in the region, is still largely dependent on a person's ability to speak French. This presents a serious problem for most members of the Guianese society. A sociolinguistic survey focusing on the school population (Léglise 2004), for instance, shows that an overwhelming majority of children living in the western part of French Guiana do not have much contact with French outside of the school context. The home and community context continues to be strongly dominated by the ancestral languages and French often only plays a marginal role.

For the past 30 years anthropologists and linguists working in the region have repeatedly pointed out that the educational system in French Guiana, which follows a policy of total submersion into French, is in many ways unsuitable for the local context. In the past 20 years some headway towards integrating the social, cultural and linguistic background of the pupils has nevertheless been made. In 1986, inspired by the Savary circular (1982), the chancellor of the Académie Antilles-Guyane, Bertène Juminer, supported the integration of Créole Guyanais into all levels of the local education system. Initially, three hours of instruction a week on Créole Guyanais language and culture were available to about 10 classes in the department. Since 1986 the programme has been much expanded so that currently roughly 300 classes benefit from it (Puren 2005).

The other languages spoken in the department are still not officially integrated into the education system. Due to pressure from the local Amerindian movement of cultural and linguistic self-recognition it has, however, been possible to set up an experimental project, the programme *Médiateurs Culturels et Bilingues* (Goury et al. 2000; Renault-Lescure 2000) which was initiated in the late 1990s by the linguists of the CNRS-IRD (Centre National de Recherche Scientifique and Institut de Recherche pour le Développement) research unit CELIA (Centre d'Etude des Langues Indigènes d'Amérique). Its aim is to give basic linguistic (and cultural) training to members of the different communities in French Guiana which would enable them to teach the community's young children in their home language and culture for several hours a week. The initial goal is to facilitate children's integration into the school environment, help them develop meta-linguistic competences in their home language and to give the home language and culture a place in the school environment.

While this programme is definitely a step in the right direction, it currently only reaches a very small number of pupils in less than 20% of the schools in the department. Its expansion will require a significant financial investment on the part of the ministry of education and the development of improved training facilities including the greater availability of qualified training staff and the development of training materials.

6.2. Current approaches and proposals for the future

In multilingual societies such as French Guiana, for example, the valorisation of the home languages usually proves to be much more difficult because of the linguistic diversity. In areas that tend to be relatively mono-ethnic, like certain rural areas in French Guiana, a broad bilingual approach may be an effective first step towards addressing language and culture-related inequalities. However, programmes such as the current project *Médiateurs Culturels et Bilingues* need to take into account the fact that similarities in the first language background do not necessarily mean that these children also have the same linguistic and cultural background. As pointed out by Alby and Léglise (2005) the term "mono-ethnic" does not imply that the members of a community necessarily share the same linguistic and cultural background. Copious sociolinguistic studies have shown that diversity is an integral part of every speech community.

A bilingual approach is hardly possible or cannot be the only useful approach in strongly multiethnic areas such as most urban centres where each class consists of students from a variety of different linguistic, social and cultural backgrounds. In this situation the linguistic and cultural diversity is much more overt and needs to be openly addressed by the institution to avoid various problems. Pupils may be disadvantaged if the teacher does not have a good understanding of their particular background because they may misinterpret their linguistic productions. For example, in such contexts, pupils tend to be multilingual rather than bilingual and will therefore not only draw on their home language and the official language but generally also select linguistic material from other regional lingua franca, e.g. Takitaki in French Guiana (Léglise and Migge 2006). An equally serious problem is posed by negative language attitudes. Pupils tend to have a number of negative preconceptions about each other's culture and language that may lead to interethnic problems and reinforce negative feelings about students' home languages. Particularly in the latter case, this may cause the denial or rejection of the home language and give rise to language shift (Léglise 2004).

In these situations several additional kinds of policies need to be implemented that target both the teaching staff and the pupils. First, teachers need to receive extensive training about the social, linguistic and cultural background of their pupils and have access to cultural and linguistic resources (e.g. books, seminars, consultants) to be able to adequately interpret their students' productions and difficulties and to be in a position to devise educational units that take the multicultural setting into account. In the last five years a number of research projects on different social, cultural and linguistic aspects have been carried out in the case of French Guiana but the diffusion of their results has only just begun (Léglise and Migge 2007). Their appropriation and implementation by the local institutions such as the education system will still take some time. In the USA, for instance, the integration in the school curriculum of schools that have a high percentage of African American students of units that explicitly deal with topics related to African American language, culture and society has much encouraged African American students who previously had little interest in school to participate in class and to develop positive attitudes to school and education (McWhorter 1998).

Second, students need to be made aware of each other's cultural and linguistic backgrounds. A method that has proved very useful in this respect is the *Language Awareness* approach that was initially developed in the United Kingdom in the 1980s (Hawkins 1984; Moore 1995). It was tested and further developed in the course of two projects funded by the EU, the programme *Evlang* (1997–2000) and *Janua Linguarum* (2000–2004). This approach has four objectives. First, it aims to interest and open up students to the notion of diversity and to dispel the myth that homogeneity is the norm and more desirable. Second, it aims to develop students' aptitudes for observing and analysing languages. It enhances their language learning skills and reinforces and improves their existing linguistic competences. Third, it is designed to positively encourage pupils to learn languages, including the languages of their fellow-pupils and the official language. Fourth, it aims to develop pupils' knowledge about their immediate linguistic environment as well as about more distant regions. This kind of overt approach to issues surrounding linguistic stigmatisation may lead to these languages' eventual destigmatisation. The experience gained from the teaching of immigrant languages in metropolitan France suggests that the (mere) recognition of stigmatised languages by way of offering classes in them, for instance, does not always effectively dispel such stigma or halt language shift (Billiez 2000). In French Guiana several language awareness workshops have taken place in the past five years to raise teachers' awareness about the local linguistic situation. However, to date few pedagogical documents have emerged (Candelier 2007) and these methods have only been tried out in a few classes.

Last but not least, the languages taught at schools should reflect more closely the local linguistic realities (neighbouring country, immigration, etc.). This would significantly improve the regional integration and the pupils' chances on the local job markets.

7. Conclusion

Colonial policies have had a far-reaching, mostly negative effect on language and educational practices in formerly colonised countries. Colonial powers actively reshaped the linguistic makeup of many regions and implemented educational systems that were clearly geared to suit their own needs; they were mainly interested in instilling notions of European morality in their colonial subjects and at forming an easily available and cheap labour resource for their economic endeavours. Little effort was made to expand the education system to cover all subjects and/or to open up all levels of education to all pupils because skilled positions were generally reserved for Europeans and colonial governments were notoriously fearful of indigenous opposition and unrest. Most regions found it hard to shed their colonial inheritance even after they gained political independence or after they became officially integrated into the national state, in the case of some former French possessions, because both the former colonisers and local elites did their best to maintain the status quo for their own benefit. Although the education system in most regions has been extended to cover an increasingly greater number of pupils since World War II, educational curricula, teaching methods and language policies have only been slowly adapted to these new challenges. Most people in developing countries still receive a highly inadequate education, if at all, and continue to be burdened by discriminative language policies. It goes without saying that this situation is highly unsatisfactory and one of the main obstacles to building democratic societies.

However, there are also positive experiences. Recent developments in Curaçao and French Guiana show that it is possible to implement Creoles and other non-European languages into the education system as media of instruction or as subjects. Especially in the case of Curaçao, it is clear that such a shift in policy contributes significantly towards reducing language-related learning difficulties. The cases of Martinique and Guadeloupe demonstrate quite clearly that language attitudes and real linguistic needs more than lack of human and financial resources appear to be major factors that determine whether or not new policies will be implemented and whether or not such policies will be effective. While bilingual educational models exist and can be implemented relatively easily, multilingual countries like French Guiana, Aruba and most African countries pose quite different challenges. Viable multilingual approaches to education still do not exist. It is clear that a range of measures will have to be developed. These measures need to be squarely based on comprehensive qualitative and quantitative surveys because each setting poses unique challenges. Implementation is then another difficult step: "[t]o revolutionize an entire educational system from its structure, to its administration, to its curricula, to its training, to its goals, requires capital and professional expertise" (Taufe'ulungaki 1987).

In order to tackle relevant issues in applied linguistics such as language attitudes and the nature of linguistic and educational practices, sociolinguistic research on Creoles needs to focus on the following issues:
- Creole speakers' identities and language attitudes and how they relate to linguistic practices in the community;
- a comprehensive sociolinguistic description of (Creole) language varieties which takes into account the perspectives and practices of all social actors;
- Creoles and language contact: What is the role of typology (linguistic distance) in bilingual (e.g. Creole-English) speech? What are the consequences for education and pedagogy?
- the recognition of such research by educational institutions and their implementation in education.

Finally, Siegel (1999, 2005) and Simmons-McDonald (2004) also point out that the acceptance and wider implementation of innovative educational programmes and pedagogical approaches that take into account the linguistic backgrounds of pupils crucially depends on researchers' willingness to engage with such efforts by getting involved in them, and more importantly by providing detailed descriptions of them and by carrying out research on their efficacy. In the long run, it is only solid proof of their effectiveness that is likely to convince sceptical governments to change current educational practices.

Notes

1. Pennycook's (1998: 75–81) discussion of the Orientalist and the Anglicist position and his exploration of educational policies in Hong Kong makes it clear that support for so-called vernacular education was not unanimous, changed over time and represented a major point of contention among colonial educators.

2. Old colonies where divided into French Overseas Departments comparable to a Metropolitan Department, and French Overseas Territories which are more autonomous in some of their decisions (New Caledonia, French Polynesia, Wallis and Futuna, Mayotte, St Pierre and Miquelon).
3. CAPES: Certificat d'Aptitude au Professorat de l'Enseignement Secondaire (Certificate of Aptitude for secondary level teaching). It is a national examination for becoming a permanent teacher at secondary school/High school level, licensing them to teach Creole culture and language.

References

Abou, Antoine
    1988   *L'école dans la Guadeloupe coloniale*. Paris: Editions caribéennes.
Abrahams, Roger
    1983   *The Man-of-Words in the West Indies. Performance and the Emergence of Creole Culture*. Baltimore: Johns Hopkins UP.
Adelaar W. F. H.
    1991   The endangered languages problem: South America. In: Robert H. Robins and Eugenius H. Uhlenbeck (eds.), *Endangered Languages*, 45–91. Oxford: Berg.
Ageron, Charles-Robert
    1973   *Politiques coloniales au Maghreb*. Paris: PUF.
Alby, Sophie and Isabelle Léglise
    2005   L'enseignement en Guyane et les langues régionales, réflexions sociolinguistiques et didactiques. *Marges Linguistiques* 10.
Appel, René and Ludo Verhoeven
    1995   Decolonization, language planning and education. In: Jacques Arends, Pieter Muykens and Norval Smith (eds.), *Pidgins and Creoles. An Introduction*, 65–74. Amsterdam: John Benjamins.
Awoniyi, Timothy
    1976   Mother tongue education in West Africa: A historical background. In: Ayo Bamgbose (ed.), *Mother Tongue Education: The West African Experience*, 27–42. London: Hodder and Stoughton.
Awoniyi, Timothy
    1982   *The Teaching of African Languages*. London: Hodder and Stoughton.
Bailey, Beryl
    1966   *Jamaican Creole Syntax*. Cambridge: Cambridge University Press.
Bamgbose, Ayo
    1976   Introduction: The changing role of mother tongues in education. In: Ayo Bamgbose (ed.), *Mother Tongue Education: The West African Experience*, 9–26. London: Hodder and Stoughton.
Bamgbose, Ayo
    2000   *Language and Exclusion: The Consequences of Language Policies in Africa*. Münster: Lit Verlag.
Bebel-Gisler, Dany
    1975   *Kèk prinsip pou ékri kréyol*. Paris: L'Harmattan.

Bebel-Gisler, Dany
1976   *La langue créole force jugulée: Étude socio-linguistique des rapports de force entre le créole et le français aux Antilles.* Paris: L'Harmattan.

Beckford Wassink, Alicia
1999   Historic low prestige and seeds of change: Attitudes toward Jamaican Creole. *Language in Society* 28: 57–92.

Bernabé, Jean
1976   Propositions pour un code orthographique intégré des créoles à base lexicale française. *Espace créole* 1: 25–57.

Bernabé, Jean
1999   La relation créole-français: Duel ou duo? Implication pour un projet scolaire. In: Christos Clairis, Denis Costaouec and Jean-Baptiste Coyos (eds.), *Langues et Cultures Régionales de France. Etat des Lieux, Enseignement, Politiques*, 35–51. Paris: L'Harmattan.

Billiez, Jacqueline
2000   Un bilinguisme minoré: Quel soutien institutionnel pour sa vitalité? *Notions en Question* 4: 21–40.

Bollée, Annegret
1993   Language policy in the Seychelles and its consequences. *International Journal of the Sociology of Language* 102: 85–99.

Branca-Rosoff, Sonia
1996   Les imaginaires des langues. In: Henri Boyer (ed.), *Sociolinguistique: Territoire et objets*, 79–114. Lausanne: Delachaux et Niestlé.

Brenzinger, Matthias (ed.)
1992   *Language Death: Factual and Theoretical Explorations with Special Reference to East Africa.* Berlin: Mouton de Gruyter.

Calvet, Louis-Jean
1974   *Linguistique et colonialisme: Petit traité de glottophagie.* Paris: Payot.

Calvet, Louis-Jean
1987   *La guerre des langues.* Paris: Payot.

Calvet, Louis-Jean and Chaudenson Robert
2001   *Les langues dans l'espace francophone: De la coexistence au partenariat.* Paris: L'Harmattan.

Candelier, Michel
2007   Toutes les langues à l'école! L'éveil aux langues, une approche pour la Guyane? In: Isabelle Léglise and Bettina Migge (eds.), *Pratiques et attitudes linguistiques en Guyane.* Paris: IRD.

Carrington, Lawrence
1989   Acquiring language in a Creole setting. In: Eve Clark (ed.), *Papers and Reports on Child Language Development.* Stanford, CA: Stanford University Press.

Carrington, Lawrence
2001   The status of creole in the Caribbean. In: Pauline Christie (ed.), *Due Respect. Papers on English and English-related Creoles in the Caribbean in Honour of Professor Robert LePage*, 24–36. Barbados, Jamaica, Trinidad and Tobago: University of the West Indies Press.

Césaire, Aimé
1950   *Discours sur le colonialisme (essai).* Paris: Edition Réclame.

Craig, Dennis
   1980   Models for educational policy in creole-speaking communities. In: Albert Valdman and Arnold R. Highfield (eds.), *Theoretical Orientations in Creole Studies*, 245–265. New York/London: Academic Press.
Craig, Dennis
   2001   Language education revisited in the Commonwealth Caribbean. In: Pauline Christie (ed.), *Due Respect. Papers on English and English-related Creoles in the Caribbean in Honour of Professor Robert LePage*, 61–78. Barbados, Jamaica, Trinidad and Tobago: University of the West Indies Press.
Croes, Regine
   1995   *Multilingualismo i ensenansa: Language Needs in Aruban Education. A Survey of the Language Use and Language Needs for the Aruban Working Population*. MA Thesis: Catholic University of Nijmegen.
Davesne, Alain
   1933   *La langue française, langue de civilization en AOF*. Saint-Louis.
Day, R. Richard
   1985   The ultimate inequality: Linguistic genocide. In: Nessa Wolfson and Joan Manes (eds.), *Language of Inequality*, 163–181. Berlin: Mouton de Gruyter.
Dejean, Yves
   1993   An overview of the language situation in Haiti. *International Journal of the Sociology of Language* 102: 73–83.
Devonish, Hubert
   1986   *Language and Liberation: Creole Language Politics in the Caribbean*. London: Karia Press.
Durizot-Jno-Baptiste, Paulette
   1996   *La question du créole à l'école en Guadeloupe: Quelle dynamique?* Paris: L'Harmattan.
Durizot-Jno-Baptiste, Paulette
   2003   L'école en Guadeloupe: État des lieux. In: Frédéric Tupin (ed.), *Ecole et éducation*, 25–42. St Denis de la Réunion: Anthropos.
Edwards, Walter
   1983   Code-selection and shifting in Guyana. *Language in Society* 12: 295–311.
Ennaji, Moha
   1991   Aspects of multilingualism in the Maghreb. *International Journal of the Sociology of Language* 87: 7–25.
Fanon, Frantz
   1952   *Peau noire masques blancs*. Paris: Le seuil.
Fenigsen, Janina
   2005   Meaningful routines: Meaning-making and the face value of Barbadian greetings. In: Susanne Mühleisen and Bettina Migge (eds.), *Politeness and Face in Caribbean Creoles*, 169–194. Amsterdam: John Benjamins.
Ferguson, Charles
   1959   Diglossia. *Word* 15: 325–340.
Freire, José Bessa
   1983   Da fala boa ao português na Amazônia brasileira. *Amerindia* 8: 39–83.
Garrett, Paul
   2000   'High' Kwéyòl: The emergence of a formal creole register in St. Lucia. In: John McWhorter (ed.), *Language Change and Language Contact in Pidgins and Creoles*, 63–102. Amsterdam: John Benjamins.

Goury, Laurence, Launey Michel, Queixalos Francisco and Odile Renault-Lescure
   2000   Des médiateurs bilingues en Guyane française. *Revue Française de Linguistique Appliquée* 5(1): 43–60.

Granguillaume, Gilbert
   1983   *Arabisation et politique linguistique au Maghreb.* Paris: Éditions G.P.

Gratiant, Renaud
   1988   *Créole et éducation: "l'expérience" de Basse Pointe, aspects d'une réalité.* Mémoire de DULCC, Université des Antilles et de la Guyane.

Hawkins, Eric W.
   1984   *Awareness of Language: An Introduction.* Cambridge: Cambridge University Press.

Hellinger, Marlis
   1991   Function and status change of Pidgin and Creole languages. In: Ulrich Ammon & Marlis Hellinger (eds.), *Status Change of Languages*, 264–281. Berlin: de Gruyter.

Hill, Jane H. and Kenneth C. Hill
   1986   *Speaking Mexicano.* Tucson: University of Arizona Press.

Igboanusi, Herbert and Lothar Peter
   2004   Oppressing the oppressed: The threats of Hausa and English to Nigeria's minority languages. *International Journal of the Sociology of Language* 170: 131–140.

Kachru, Braj B. (ed.)
   1982   *The Other Tongue: English across Cultures.* Urbana: University of Illinois Press [republished in 1992].

Krampah, D. E. K. and J. Gyekye-Aboagye
   1998   The Akan experience at harmonization and standardization. In: Kwesu Kwaa Prah (ed.), 75–90.

Laroussi, Foued and Jean-Baptiste Marcellesi
   1996   Colonisation et décolonisation. In: Hans Goebl, Peter Nelde, Zdenek Stary and Wolfgang Wölck (eds.), *Contact Linguistics. An International Handbook of Contemporary Research*, 193–199. Berlin: de Gruyter.

Léglise, Isabelle
   2004   Langues frontalières et langues d'immigration en Guyane Française. In: Marie-Louise Moreau (ed.), *Langues de frontières, frontières de langues.* *Glottopol* 4: 108–124.

Léglise, Isabelle
   2005   Contacts de créoles à Mana (Guyane française): Répertoires, pratiques, attitudes et gestion du plurilinguisme. *Etudes Créoles* 28: 23–57.

Léglise, Isabelle
   2007   Environnement graphique, pratiques et attitudes linguistiques à l'hôpital. In: Isabelle Léglise and Bettina Migge (eds.), *Pratiques et attitudes linguistiques en Guyane: Regards croisés.* Paris: IRD.

Léglise, Isabelle and Bettina Migge
   2006   Language naming practices, ideologies and linguistic practices: Towards a comprehensive description of language varieties. *Language in Society* 35(3): 313–339.

Léglise, Isabelle and Bettina Migge (eds.)
   2007   *Pratiques et attitudes linguistiques en Guyane: Regards croisés.* Paris: IRD.

LePage, Robert B. and Andrée Tabouret-Keller
  1985   *Acts of Identity: Creole-based Approaches to Language and Ethnicity.* Cambridge: Cambridge University Press.
Makoni, Sinfree
  1998   In the beginning was the missionaries' word. In: Kwesu Kwaa Prah (ed.), 157–164.
March, Christian
  1997   *Le discours des mères martiniquaises. Diglossie et créolité, un point de vue sociolinguistique.* Paris: L'Harmattan.
Martinus, Frank
  1997   *The Kiss of a Slave. Papiamentu's West African Connexions.* Curaçao: Ed De Curaçaoshe Courant.
McWhorter, John
  1998   *The Word on the Street: Fact and Fable about American English.* New York: Plenum Trade.
Migge, Bettina
  2004   The speech event *kuutu* in the Eastern Maroon community. In: Geneviève Escure and Armin Schwegler (eds.), *Creoles, Contact and Language Change: Linguistic and Social Implications*, 285–306. Amsterdam: John Benjamins.
Migge, Bettina
  2007   Code-switching and social identities in the Eastern Maroon community of Suriname and French Guiana. *Journal of Sociolinguistics* 11(1): 53–72.
Mintz, Sidney and Richard Price
  1992   *The Birth of African American Culture. An Anthropological Perspective.* Boston: Beacon Press.
Msimang, Themba
  1998   The nature and history of harmonisation of South African languages. In: Kwesu Kwaa Prah (ed.), 165–172.
Moore, Danièle (ed.)
  1995   *L'Eveil au langage*, Notions en Question 1, Paris: Didier Erudition.
Moore Denny, Sidney Facundes and Nádia Pires
  1993   Nheengatu (Língua Geral Amazônica), its history, and the effects of language contact. In: Margaret Langdon (ed.), *Proceedings of the Meeting of the Society for the Study of the Indigenous Languages of the Americas*, 93–118. Berkeley: Editor.
Mühleisen, Susanne
  2001   Is 'bad English' dying out? A diachronic comparative study of attitudes towards Creole versus Standard English in Trinidad. *Philologie im Netz* 15: 43–78. (www.phin.de)
Mühleisen, Susanne
  2002   *Creole Discourse. Exploring Prestige Formation and Change across Caribbean English-lexicon Creoles.* Amsterdam: John Benjamins.
Mühlhäusler, Peter
  1991   The changing status of Melanesian Pidgin English. In: Ulrich Ammon and Marlis Hellinger (eds.), *Status Change of Languages*, 253–263. Berlin: de Gruyter.
Ngũgĩ wa Thiong'o
  1986   *Decolonizing the Mind: The Politics of Language in African Literature.* London: James Curry.

Patrick, Peter L.
  1997   Style and register in Jamaican Patwa. In: Schneider, Edgar W. (ed.), *Englishes Around the World: Caribbean, Africa, Asia, Australasia*, Vol 2, 41–55. Amsterdam: John Benjamins.
Pennycook, Alastair
  1998   *English and the Discourses of Colonialism: The Politics of Language*. London: Routledge.
Pennycook, Alastair
  2001   *Critical Applied Linguistics: A Critical Introduction*. London: Lawrence Erlbaum.
Phillipson, Robert
  1992   *Linguistic Imperialism*. Oxford: Oxford University Press.
Prah, Kwesi Kwaa (ed.)
  1998   *Between Distinction & Extinction. The Harmonisation and Standardisation of African Languages*. Johannesburg: Witwatersrand University Press.
Prudent, Lambert-Félix
  1981   Diglossie et interlecte. *Langages* 61: 13–38.
Prudent, Lambert-Félix (ed.)
  2001   *Capes créole(s): Le débat*. Paris: L'Harmattan.
Prudent, Lambert-Félix
  2005   L'école martiniquaise à la recherche de sa cohérence. In: Frédéric Tupin, (ed.), *Ecoles ultramarines*, 23–46. St Denis de la Réunion: Anthropos.
Prudent, Lambert-Félix and Ellen Schnepel
  1993   Creole Movements: The Francophone Orbit, introduction. *International Journal of the Sociology of Language* 102: 5–13.
Puren, Laurent
  2005   On est une machine à fabriquer de l'échec et de l'exclusion. Le discours des professeurs des écoles du Maroni. *Le français dans le Monde/Recherches et applications, hors série*, 142–151. Paris: Clé International.
Quint, Nicolas
  2000   *Le cap-verdien: Origines et devenir d'une langue métisse. Etude des relations de la langue cap-verdienne avec les langues africaines, créoles et portugaise*. Paris: L'Harmattan.
Reisman, Karl
  1970   Cultural and linguistic ambiguity in a West Indian village. In: Norman E. Whitten and John F. Szwed (eds.), *Afro-American Anthropology*, 129–144. New York: The Free Press.
Renault-Lescure, Odile
  2000   L'enseignement bilingue en Guyane Française: Une situation particulière en Amérique du Sud. In: Jean-Michel Blanquer and Helgio Tringade (ed.), *Les défis de l'éducation en Amérique Latine*, 231–246. Paris: IHEAL.
Rickford, John
  1985   Standard and non-standard language attitudes in a creole continuum. In: Nessa Wolfson and Joan Manes (eds.), *Language of Inequality*, 145–160. Berlin: Mouton de Gruyter.
Riguet, Maurice
  1985   *Contribution à l'étude psycho-sociale du bilinguisme dans la population tunisienne*. Lille: Atelier National de Reproduction des Thèses.

Roberts, Sarah
    2004   The role of style and identity in the development of Hawaiian Creole. In: Geneviève Escure and Armin Schwegler (eds.), *Creoles, Contact and Language Change: Linguistic and Social Implications*, 331–350. Amsterdam: John Benjamins.

Romaine, Suzanne
    1991   The status of Tok Pisin in Papua New Guinea: The colonial predicament. In: Ulrich Ammon and Marlis Hellinger (eds.), *Status Change of Languages*, 229–263. Berlin: de Gruyter.

Romani, Jean-Paul
    1994   Interlecte martiniquais et pédagogie. *Etudes Créoles* 17: 84–105.

Romani, Jean-Paul
    2000   *L'interlecte martiniquais*. PhD Thesis, University of Rouen.

Roy-Campbell, Makini
    1998   Attitudes towards the use of African languages as media of instruction in secondary schools: Reflections from Tanzania and Zimbabwe. In: Kwesu Kwaa Prah (ed.), 225–264.

Schmidt, Annette
    1990   *The Loss of Australia's Aboriginal Language Heritage*. Canberra: Aboriginal Studies Press.

Schmied, Josef J.
    1991   *English in Africa: An Introduction*. London: Longman.

Schnepel, Ellen
    1993   The creole movement in Guadeloupe. *International Journal of the Sociology of Language* 102: 117–134.

Séminaire des corps d'inspecteur de la Martinique
    2003   *Humanités créoles*, 21 february, Fort de France, http://www.palli.ch/~kapeskreyol/articles/humanite/humanite2.html.

Severing, Ria and Ludo Verhoeven
    2001   Bilingual narrative development in Papiamento and Dutch. In: Verhoeven, Ludo and Sven Strömquist (eds.), *Narrative Development in a Multilingual Context*, 255–276. Amsterdam: John Benjamins.

Shields-Brodber, Kathryn
    1992   Dynamism and assertiveness in the public voice: Turn-taking and code-switching in radio talk shows in Jamaica. *Pragmatics* 2: 487–504.

Sidnell, Jack
    1999   Gender and pronominal variation in an Indo-Guyanese creole-speaking community. *Language in Society* 28: 367–399.

Siegel, Jeff
    1999   Creole and minority dialects in education: An overview. *Journal of Multilingual and Multicultural Development* 20(6): 508–531.

Siegel, Jeff
    2005   Column: Applied creolistics revisited. *Journal of Pidgin and Creole Languages* 20(2): 293–323.

Simmons-McDonald, Hazel
    2001   Competence, proficiency and language acquisition in Caribbean contexts. In: Pauline Christie (ed.), *Due Respect. Papers on English and English-re-*

lated Creoles in the Caribbean in Honour of Professor Robert LePage, 37–60. Barbados, Jamaica, Trinidad and Tobago: University of the West Indies Press.

Simmons-McDonald, Hazel
    2004   Trends in teaching standard varieties to Creole and vernacular speakers. *Annual Review of Applied Linguistics* 24: 187–208.

Skutnabb-Kangas, Tove and Robert Phillipson (eds.)
    1995   *Linguistic Human Rights: Overcoming Linguistic Discrimination*. Berlin: Mouton de Gruyter.

Spencer, John
    1971   Colonial language policies and their legacies. In: Thomas Seboek (ed.), *Linguistics in Sub-Saharan Africa*, 537–547. The Hague: Mouton.

Spencer, John
    1985   Language and development in Africa: The unequal equation. In: Nessa Wolfson and Joan Manes (eds.), *Language of Inequality*, 387–397. Berlin: Mouton de Gruyter.

Taufe'ulungaki, Ana
    1987   Educational provision and operation: Regional dimensions in the South Pacific. In: Bacchus Kazim and Colin Brock (eds.), *The Challenge of Scale: Educational Development in the Small States of the Commonwealth*. London: The Commonwealth Secretariat.

Temu, Arnold
    1998   The development of national language: A survey of Kiswahili in Tanzania. In: Kwesu Kwaa Prah (ed.), 143–156.

Van Breet, Ralph R.
    1994   *Education in Aruba*. Aruba: Section of Educational Statistics.

Winford, Donald
    1976   Teacher attitudes toward language varieties in a creole community. *International Journal of the Sociology of Language* 8: 45–75.

Winford, Donald
    1997   Re-examining Caribbean English Creole continua. In: Salikoko Mufwene (ed.), *English to Pidgin Continua*. [Special Issue] *World Englishes* 16: 233–279.

Yanga, Tshimpaka
    1998   Harmonisation, standardisation and the emergence of 'state languages'. In: Kwesu Kwaa Prah (ed.), 173–202.

Youssef, Valerie
    1990   *The Development of Linguistic Skills in Some Trinidadian Children: An Integrative Approach to Verb Phrase Development*. PhD dissertation, The University of the West Indies, St. Augustine.

11. Linguistic imperialism? English as a global language

Andy Kirkpatrick

1. Introduction

It is impossible to make an accurate assessment of the number of people who use English in today's world. It is possible to say, however, that English is spoken in more countries than any other language and that it is used more often internationally and in more domains than any other.

It is impossible to know with any accuracy the relative levels of proficiency in English that people use when they are communicating in English. "No international language can be applied to the question of who counts as a speaker of English" (Görlach 2002: 5). It is possible to say, however, that there are more users of English who have learned it as a second or foreign language than those who have learned it as a first language. Rather than being *a* global language, therefore, English is *the* global language, used nationally and internationally by more people in more domains than any other language.

In this chapter, I will first briefly outline the way English developed and spread as a language within England and illustrate that variation and change are both normal features of language development, as this can provide a source of comparison with the way that Englishes have developed and spread elsewhere. Linguistic variation and change tend to result from comparable stimuli, but the effect of English upon local languages depends very much on context. I shall then discuss the models and theories that have been presented to account for the current international and global spread of English. This discussion will include the national and international use of English and highlight the fact that new varieties of English have developed in many countries. I will then consider the implications for English language teaching of the existence of so many varieties of English. In doing this, I hope to be able to show that an understanding of local and specific contexts are at least as important as "grand theories" in both explaining the current roles of English and in drawing implications of these for English language teaching.

2. The development and spread of English

2.1. The development and spread of English in England

From around the middle of the fifth century AD a group of European tribes speaking dialects of a Germanic language arrived in England. Four of these dialects have been identified but "in reality, there must have been many more" (Crystal 2004: 34). These Germanic dialects, themselves influenced by several hundred years of contact with Latin, gradually morphed into the English spoken in England. Linguistic influences upon these Germanic dialects that eventually produced modern English stemmed from contact with Scandinavian languages, medieval Latin and French. These influences were seen in the pronunciation of the language, in the adoption of many new words and in grammatical changes. One major and continuous grammatical change has been the tendency to simplify the inflectional system of English. For example, some one thousand years ago, the inflectional system of nouns had case, gender and number inflections. This declension of the masculine noun *stān* 'stone' is taken from Blake (1996: 65):

Case	Singular	Plural
Nominative	stān	stānas
Accusative	stān	stānas
Genitive	stānes	stāna
Dative	stāne	stānum

Today, inflections remain only to mark number on nouns, usually by adding the suffix *-s*, except for a small number of irregular plurals that retain the Old English suffix *-en*, as in *children* and *brethren*. The accusative and genitive are now restricted to *whom* and the possessive *-s*, although there is evidence that *whom* is dropping out of use, as is the possessive apostrophe. Indeed, the very existence of case in current English is controversial.

The system of verbal inflections in Old English was also more complex than it is today and included many more strong forms. The so-called strong forms marked past tense by altering the vowel, as shown in these examples:

rīdan	rād (ride, rode)
findan	fand (find, found)
beran	bær (bear, bore) (Lass 1992: 130)

The weak forms marked past tense by adding a suffix. For example:

dēman   dēmde (judge, judged)

Some verbs included both internal vowel change and inflections:

sellan   sealde (sell, sold)
sēcan   sōhte (seek, sought) (Lass 1992: 126)

Over time, most verbs moved to the weak class (Lass 1992) and the inflectional system of the verb became gradually more simplified so that "many forms of the verb became indistinguishable" (Blake 1996: 151). In this way, the inflectional system of English has become regularised and simplified over time. One cause was phonology, as the initial stress of Old English, "must have contributed to the neutralisation of vowel qualities in inflectional endings and their almost total subsequent demise" (Fisher 1992: 207). A second probable cause was contact with other languages, particularly Scandinavian and, later, French, as this contact led to a more simplified morphological structure (Fisher 1992). This provides evidence that "traditional" English followed developmental processes comparable with the developmental processes of new varieties of English.

As English developed it also became, around the early fifteenth century, the language of the court, the bureaucracy and thus of power (Richardson 1984). It was also the language people needed to know in order to gain employment in many walks of life and, as such, the people learned it and started to lose their original languages. This process has been described by Burchfield (1994a) as one whereby a monolingual community learned English for a range of commercial and administrative purposes and, in time, the resultant bilingual community came to outnumber the monolingual one. Eventually the bilingual community then moved to become monolingual, but in English, thus losing their original mother-tongues, whether these were Welsh or Gaelic. The process was complex, however. With regard to Gaelic in Scotland, for example, King James VI of England introduced a number of measures in the early seventeenth century with the objective of eliminating Gaelic. This anti-Gaelic policy continued for over two hundred years (McClure 1994). Yet the real catastrophic decline in Gaelic began in the late nineteenth century and lasted through to the 1970s (McClure 1994: 45). This decline in Celtic languages has been followed in Ireland and Wales until quite recently, when there has been a resurgence in the number of people learning local languages such as Welsh (on language revival, see Edwards, this vol.).

A similar process can be seen in Australia, where an estimated original number of 250 Aboriginal languages has been reduced to about fifty today (Dixon 1993) and where an Aboriginal variety of English has become the most common language of Aboriginal Australians (Harkins 2000). It is therefore as a *national* language that English represents a threat to local languages. As an *international* language, English does not present such a threat, although that does not mean it presents none. The threat to local languages, however, is almost always a national lingua franca, whether that be English, Modern Standard Chinese, Kiswahili or Bahasa Indonesia. This explains why English displaced so many languages in its settlement colonies – the United States and Australia, for example – where the great majority of the population chose or were forced to use English in their daily lives. But, as I shall illustrate later, it has become an additional language in countries which were exploitation colonies, such as India and many African and Asian countries, and in countries where it is learned as a foreign language, such as most of Europe and China.

Although English is clearly the national language of England, it is important to note that it is represented by a wide number of varieties that have distinctive phonological, lexical and grammatical features. The number of people who actually speak the so-called standard language with a received pronuncation (RP) has been estimated to be as small as 3% of the population. In other words, the English of England is characterised by diversity and variation. It may be of interest, even of comfort, to those many millions of English language teachers struggling to ensure that their pupils use the third person singular form of the present tense correctly to learn that this form varies considerably within English dialects. For example, Ihalainen (1994: 228) lists the different ways different varieties mark the present tense. These include:

The North: He makes them / they make them / farmers makes them.
Northwest Midlands: He makes them / they maken them / farmers maken them.
The South: He makes them / they makes them / farmers makes them.
East Anglia: He make them / they make them / farmers make them.

In this section, I have shown that English developed from Germanic dialects over several hundred years as they came into contact with a range of other languages. Its adoption as the language of the court, the bureaucracy and then employment in general led to its spread throughout England and the United Kingdom, where it replaced many local languages, while remaining characterised itself by diversity and variation. I now turn to a consideration of its spread across the world.

2.2.   The development and spread of English beyond Britain

The first groups of people who brought English to other parts of the world were explorers and traders, both of whom preceded the establishment of any colonies. For example, in 1497, John Cabot led the first English speaking group to visit the Americas (Dillard 1992: 1). The date commonly given to mark the coming of English to India is the 31st of December 1600. This was the date on which Queen Elizabeth 1 of England gave a monopoly on trade with India to a group of English merchants (Ferguson 1996). The missionaries soon followed, especially after 1659 when they were allowed to use the ships of the East India Company (Kachru 1983). The first record of contact between British traders and the Chinese was in 1637 (Bolton 2003: 126) and the first British trading post was established in Lagos in 1860 (McArthur 1998), some 54 years before Nigeria became a British colony. "Mercantilism became a conduit for European capitalism, Christianity and colonisation through the Americas, Africa and Asia" (Bolton 2003: 122).

Mufwene (2001: 8–9) has drawn a distinction between three types of colonies: trade, exploitation, and settlement. In trade colonies, the contact between traders and locals led to the development of pidgins. However, once these trade colonies became exploitation colonies, the European nation concerned started to exercise administrative and political control and this led not only to greater contact between the European and local people but also, in the case of many British colonies, for example, the need for people who could speak English to help in the administration of the colony. While the senior administrators were British, it was much cheaper to staff more junior positions with locals, so special schools were established to train locals for these positions. In these cases, varieties of English developed that were influenced by contact with local languages. In settlement colonies, on the other hand, there was little need to train locals, as the administrators came from within the ranks of the settlers. While there was some contact with local people and local languages, the influence of these on the developing variety of English was not so great as in exploitation colonies. Mufwene is at pains to stress, however, that while there were differences, the developmental processes that each variety went through were similar. Schneider agrees, "postcolonial Englishes follow a fundamentally uniform developmental process" (2003: 233). He identifes five phases in the developmental cycle of postcolonial Englishes. These are: the foundation phase; the phase of exonormative stabilisation; the nativisation phase; the phase of endonormative stablisation; and the differentiation phase. These phases are largely self-explanatory. The foundation phase occurs when English first arrives, the phase of exonormative stabilisation is characterised by a dependence on the variety spoken by the settlers; the nativisation phase occurs when the variety of English takes on local lexical and cultural features, and this leads to phase four when this newly-formed indigenous variety becomes accepted as the local standard. The final stage, differentiation, signals not only the emergence and acceptance of the local variety in all domains, but also sees the emergence of different local varieties that may mark ethnic identity, for example.

While Schneider's model is based on postcolonial Englishes he expresses the cautious hope that, "in principle, it should be possible to apply the model to most, ideally all of the Englishes around the globe" (2003: 256).

Schneider's model clearly owes much to Moag's earlier work (1992: 233–252) on the lifecycle of non-native Englishes. Moag also identified five processes or phases but argued that not all varieties go through the fifth. Moag called the first phase transportation, the period when English arrives for the first time. The second phase he calls indigenisation, and this represents a long phase during which the variety of English starts to take on local features. The third phase, the expansion in use phase, sees the variety being used in more domains and roles and this is marked by an increase in local variation. The fourth, institutionalisation phase occurs when the local variety is used as a classroom model and a local literature written in the variety appears. The fifth phase is one which not all varieties necessarily go through and this phase sees a decline in use. As examples of countries where this has happened, Moag gives Malaysia and the Philippines, but, in fact, both countries have recently seen a significant reawakening of interest in English, in the case of Malaysia (Omar 1996), and continued use, in the case of the Philippines (Sibayan and Gonzalez 1996).

Kachru has also considered the phases through which "non-native institutionalised varieties of English seem to pass" (1992b: 56). During the first phase, locals are prejudiced against the local variety and an exonormative variety thus carries more prestige and is used as a classroom model. The second phase sees the co-existence of both the exonormative and the local variety. During the third phase, the local variety achieves social acceptance and is used not only in informal colloquial domains but also becomes the classroom model.

I have taken some time to review these theories of the developmental stages of postcolonial, non-native Englishes, as, despite their differences, all three scholars agree that a local variety of English does develop and that this variety not only exhibits linguistic features of local languages but also reflects local cultural values. An indigenised variety develops. This is important, as scholars who espouse theories of linguistic imperialism see the spread of English as being a direct and conscious result of a deliberate attempt by the once colonisers to spread their own variety of English. It is to these theories that I now turn.

3. Postcolonial Englishes: Linguistic imperialism or local demand?

Robert Phillipson's book *Linguistic Imperialism* was published in 1992 and has occasioned a great deal of debate. In Phillipson's response to Alan Davies' (1996) critique of the book, Phillipson reiterated the key concepts of his theory. I provide a selection of these below to ensure that the theory is expressed in his own words.

> Linguistic imperialism is a theoretical construct, devised to account for linguistic hierarchisation, to address issues of why some languages come to be used more and others less, what structures and ideologies facilitate such processes, and the role of language professionals.
> (Phillipson 1997: 238)

> Linguistic imperialism is a subtype of linguicism, a term which Tove Skutnabb-Kangas coined (1988), and is used to draw parallels between hierarchisation on the basis of race (racism), gender (sexism), and language (linguicism).
> (1997: 239)

> Linguicism can be intralingual and interlingual. It exists among and between speakers of a language when one dialect is privileged as standard. Linguicism exists between speakers of different languages in processes of resource allocation, vindi-

cation or vilification in discourse of one language rather than another – English as the language of modernity and progress, Cantonese as a mere dialect unsuited for a range of literate and societal functions – [...]. (1997: 239)

Linguistic imperialism takes place within an overarching structure of asymmetrical North/South relations, where language interlocks with other dimensions, cultural (particularly in education, science and the media), economic and political.
(1997: 239)

Validation that linguistic imperialism is in operation requires study of the nature of the local linguistic ecology and linguistic hierarchies, the purposes which language X serves, whose interests are promoted by the specific language policy, and the likely outcomes of any proposed activities.
(1997: 239–240)

Unlike the brute force of the colonial period (imposition of the master language, corporal punishment for using your mother tongue, whether in Wales or Kenya), in postcolonial days language policy is much more a matter for negotiation and persuasion. It requires legitimation and may well be contested.
(1997: 240)

In his review of *Linguistic Imperialism*, Davies argued, among other points, that the deterministic nature of Philippson's theory made him ignore the possibility that oppressed groups' common sense is active enough for them to reject English if they so wish (1996: 490). He gave examples of two nations, Myanmar and Malaysia, where this has happened. He also called the book,

[...] a clever book because it taps delicately and accurately into the widespread guilt felt by the rich North about the poor South. But, as a general theory to explain the growth of English language teaching in the world, it will not do.
(Davies 1996: 495)

In a volume they edited, Fishman, Conrad, and Rubal Lopez (1996) investigated the changing roles of English over the fifty year period between 1940 and 1990 in twenty countries. Their findings showed that English played a more important role at the higher levels of society, in tertiary education and for international communication than in local settings or domains. This led Conrad to argue that, "if the agenda was really for English to replace local languages, the policy has failed miserably" (1996: 26). Fishman's conclusion was that the spread of English could more satisfactorily be explained by a pragmatic desire for English based on socioeconomic factors than colonial language policies. It should be pointed out that, since their study, many countries, including the Asian countries of Thailand, Japan, Korea and China, have introduced English into the primary school curriculum, but that this is usually attributed to the recognition of the importance of English for social and economic advancement.

These results seem to cast doubt on the generalisability of Phillipson's theories, but his reponse to these surveys was to argue that Fishman seemed to ignore that:

> Engagement in the modern world means a western dominated globalisation agenda set by transnational corporations and the IMF, and the US military intervening, with or without a mandate from the UN, whenever its vital interests are at risk. (Phillipson 2002: 11)

In the same article, Phillipson argues that, "the export of English is market driven, as it has always been" (2002: 11). This more recent focus on the market, implying as it does a consumer demand for English, seems to contradict his theory in major ways. Indeed, his overlooking of the demand-side of the story is felt to be a major weakness of the theory (Li 2002).

An alternative explanation for the spread of English that incorporates this demand for English has been made by Brutt-Griffler (2002). The key argument she presents is that English "owes its existence as a world language in large part to the struggle against imperialism, and not to imperialism alone" (2002: ix). Far from forcing its colonial subjects to learn English, British colonial policy was, in large part, to provide an English education only for the elite and to deny it to the great majority of the population, who were to be educated in the local languages. A similar point is made by Pennycook (1998) when he quotes colonial adminstrators advising against the use of educating the locals in English, as this would only give them ideas above their station and lead to unrest. Brutt-Griffler quotes a colonial administrator in Malaya citing a local proverb to make this point, "However high the padi bird may soar, he ends by settling on the buffalo's back" (2002: 88). Under such circumstances, it is not hard to predict that the demand to learn English would actually have come from the colonial subjects, precisely because they realised that, by learning English, they would be able to improve their station in life. A key player in the formulation of British colonial educational policy was Lord Lugard, who held senior colonial positions, including the Governorships of Hong Kong (1907–1912) and Nigeria (1914–1917). To avoid creating a large class of English educated people who would be unemployable he proposed the so-called "Dual Mandate" system of schools in Africa. A small number of English medium literary schools whose aim was to provide civil servants and the like would operate alongside vernacular medium village schools whose aim was to train the vast majority of colonial subjects to work in agriculture and industry (Brutt-Griffler 2002: 59).

This policy was promoted at the League of Nations shortly after the end of World War 1, where Lugard advocated "vernacular education at the base and English at the top" (Brutt-Griffler 2002: 99). Far from making English the sole language to be learned, this policy required the learning of local languages, as was also the case in Hong Kong (Bolton 2003). As Brutt-Griffler elegantly argues, the role played by colonial subjects is crucial to understanding how World Englishes have developed. "Asians and Africans transformed English from a means of exploitation into a means of resistance" (2002: 65). English was "wrested from an unwilling imperial authority as part of the struggle by them against colonialism" (2002: 31). In other words, the colonised adapted the English language and used it for their own ends. Canagarajah (2000) discusses this in the context of Sri Lanka where English-educated bilinguals have used a number of strategies to nativise English to suit their own ideologies.

Many writers have attested to their ability to, as it were, colonise English and make it theirs and I provide quotes from some below. In an oft quoted piece, the Indian author Raja Rao wrote, "We shall have English with us and amongst us, and not as our guest or friend, but as one of our own, of our castes, our creed, our sect and of our tradition" (quoted in Srivastava and Sharma 1991: 190), and he warns, "We cannot write like the English. We should not. We can only write as Indians" (1991: 205).

A fellow Indian author, Mukerjee, is satisfied that this is now happening:

> There are many people writing in English in India and at last people are beginning to think in English. Many are writing with a great flow and flair, which proves that English is no more a foreign language but a part of our psyche.
> (quoted in D'Souza 2001: 148)

D'Souza herself argues that English has been Indianised by being, "borrowed, transcreated, recreated, stretched, extended, contorted perhaps" (2001: 150).

Other authors of the sub-continent support these views. Anita Desai feels that English is "flexible, elastic, resilient" (1996: 222). The Pakistani novelist Sidhwa is confident that English has been successfully taken over by the "ex-colonised", who have "subjugated the language, beaten it on its head and made it ours" (1996: 231).

It would be wrong to suggest that contrary views are not expressed. They are. Here is an excerpt from the Sri Lankan poet Lakdas Wikkramasinha's artistic manifesto:

> I have come to realise that I am writing the language of the most despicable and loathsome people on earth: I have no wish to extend its life and range, enrich its totality. To write in English is a form of cultural treason. I have had for the future to think of a way of circumventing this treason. I propose to do this by making my writing entirely immoralist and destructive.
> (quoted in Canagarajah 1994: 375)

The Malaysian poet, Mohammed Haji Salleh, has moved from writing in English to writing in Malay. He asks, "Should I lick the hand that strangles my language and culture?" (Quayum 2003: xv).

The Kenyan writer, Ngũgĩ wa Thiong'o, insists that African writers should write in an African language. In his final collection of prose in English, *Decolonising the Mind*, he writes, "From now on it's Gikuyu and Kiswahili all the way" (quoted in Bailey 1991: 176). Ngũgĩ's position extends to criticising African novelists who choose to write in English. Even the most famous are not spared, as Chinua Achebe is pilloried for this. "It is the final triumph of a system of domination when the dominated start singing its virtues" (2003: 176).

As one would expect, Achebe's position is quite different. He argues that English is spoken in more countries of sub-Saharan Africa than any other language and that African writers should "aim at fashioning out an English which is at once universal and able to carry his personal experience" (2003: 171). Achebe's fellow Nigerian, Wole Soyinka, who was awarded the Nobel prize for literature in 1986, has argued that "when we borrow an alien language [...] we must stretch it, impact and compact it, fragment and reassemble it [...]" (Schmied 1991: 126).

While, therefore, there are writers who have decided to write in local languages, many writers in postcolonial settings feel that they can adapt English to reflect their own cultures and to describe their own experiences. It is time, however, to move from viewing countries that were once colonies as being mired in a postcolonial phase. Young writers do not see English through a post colonial lens:

> The use of English has apparently become totally detached from the concept of colonial oppressor's language in Africa and Asia [...] English is regarded as having been a vital asset in the fight for independence and it has eminent advantages as a nation building language in multilingual nations.
> (Görlach 2002: 10–11)

For better or worse, this is the age of globalisation, where international means at least as much as national. And rather than constantly looking backwards towards colonialism, a focus on the future is needed. In particular, how the rise of China will shape the world is at least as significant a question as how colonisation shaped the present. It is therefore to the development of English in China that I now turn.

4. English in the "Expanding Circle": Linguistic imperialism or local demand?

Kachru's well-known "circles model" of Englishes classifies the Englishes spoken around the world based on where they are spoken:

> The current sociolinguistic profile of English may be viewed in terms of three concentric circles [...] The Inner Circle refers to the traditional cultural and linguistic bases of English. The Outer Circle represents the institutionalised non-native varieties (ESL) in the regions that have passed through extended periods of colonisation [...] The Expanding Circle includes the regions where the *performance* varieties of the language are used essentially in EFL contexts.
> (Kachru 1992c: 366–367)

To a certain extent, the circles match the traditional classification of English as a native language (ENL), English as a second language (ESL) and English as a foreign language (EFL). Countries in the Inner Circle are those where English is spoken as a native language and include the USA and the UK, for example. Countries in the Outer Circle are those where English is spoken as a second language and include India, Nigeria and Malaysia, for example. Countries listed as being in the Expanding Circle are those where English is spoken as a foreign language and include China, Egypt and Korea, for example. Two great advances that Kachru's model provides over the traditional classification are that the circles model makes English plural. There is not just one English which is being learned across the world, but there are many Englishes and these represent "multicultural identities" (Kachru 1992c: 357). These Englishes also exist at the national level, so that it is more accurate to talk about Indian Englishes than Indian English, for example. The second great insight the model provides is that one English is not necessarily better than any other. Englishes become nativised or acculturated so that they become the appropriate variety for the context in which they are used. Again, these contexts can be local, national or international and the appropriate variety to use will alter depending on the context.

In the preceding section, I have been primarily concerned with the spread and development of English in Kachru's "outer circle" countries, countries that had previously been British colonies and where English took on special functions and was given special status. I concluded that the theory of Linguistic Imperialism could not adequately account for the continued use of English in those countries. Instead, English continued to be used because the people in those countries learned English for practical reasons, not because they had been forced to under colonialism or tricked into it by their once imperial masters after independence.

In this section I want to consider the situation in a country in the "Expanding Circle", China. If it can be shown that a currently extremely powerful nation that was not a colony of an English speaking country now presents a site where there is extraordinary demand for English and where that English is becoming indigenised, then this would provide further evidence that the theory of Linguistic Imperialism does not adequately explain the spread and distribution of English. Of course, Phillipson might well say that China's adoption of English provides excellent testimony for his theory, but this would mean accepting that China's desire for English has stemmed entirely from bowing to pressure from the US and Britain.

Even in the context of Hong Kong, a place that was a British colony from 1842–1997, scholars have argued that demand for English has been more pragmatic than the result of colonial language policy. The people of Hong Kong have always seen English as a pragmatic necessity (Sweeting and Vickers 2005) and "have always wanted English" (Boyle 1997: 176). Li (2002), in answering the question why Hong Kong parents tend to favour English medium schools, stresses that Hong Kong parents "are not passive victims but pragmatically-minded active agents acting in their best interests" (2002: 55). Their decision is a pragmatic one "driven largely by an aspiration for social mobility". Li continues:

> English helps one access more information and people – through higher education, on the job, in cyber space and international encounters. In writing, English has a greater potential to help one reach out to wider audiences compared with other languages. In this light, rather than a tool of hegemony, English may be looked upon as a resource to enhance the learners' linguistic repertoire, which in turn has good potential for enriching their quality of life through higher education and professional development. (2002: 55)

The demand for English in China itself today is unprecedented in its history. Since the colonisation of Hong Kong in 1842, English has variously been seen as a conduit for Western science and technology, a conduit for Western ideas that will assist in the modernisation of China and international understanding, or a language whose speakers represent the "enemy", if they are foreigners, and "traitors", if they are Chinese. Currently English is seen as extremely important for the modernisation of China and for international understanding and influence. The current attitude towards English is the most positive in Chinese history. Lam (2002: 246) provides the following phases in China's attitudes to English since the establishment of the People's Republic of China in 1949:

1. Interlude with Russian — Early 1950s
2. Back to English movement — 1957–1965
3. Repudiation of foreign learning — 1966–1970
4. English for renewing ties with the West — 1971–1976
5. English for modernisation — 1977–1990
6. English for international stature — 1991–

Not surprisingly, given China's Communist government's close relationship with the Soviet Union in 1949, for the first few years after the establishment of the People's Republic, Russian was the first foreign language. However, the close relationship with the Soviet Union did not last long and Russian was soon replaced by English. Even so, as the chronology above illustrates, attitudes to English swung across the pendulum, from being the language of the enemy and/or being crucial for modernisation. The current demand for English, however, is undeniable and there are probably more Chinese learning English today than there are native speakers of it. It is likely that this will lead to the development of a Chinese variety of English (Du and Jiang 2001), a variety defined as "the English used by the Chinese people in China, being based on standard English and having Chinese characteristics" (Wang 1994: 7).

Recent work on the description of Chinese English (Zhang 2002; Kirkpatrick and Xu 2002; Xu 2005) has shown that it possesses distinctive lexical, syntactic and pragmatic features. A literature is being written in Chinese English, most notably by the prose writer Ha Jin. Despite living and working in the United States, Ha Jin continues to write about life in China and writes in an English which has a readily discernible Chinese flavour. This flavour stems from "his creative adoption of the English language, and the innovative recreation of the sensations of his native experiences" (Zhang 2002: 306).

The spread of English in China can be explained by the Chinese identifying how useful English can be for them, both on a personal level for social and economic mobility, and also on a national level, as China looks to enhance her position in the international worlds of commerce, diplomacy and politics. China's winning of the 2008 Olympic Games can only serve to add impetus to this goal. In other words, China is using English to advance her international position. This provides a prime example of a nation adopting English to suit and further its own interests.

The development of Chinese English also suggests that English can be adopted and indigenised by speakers in expanding circle countries in ways similar to the ways new varieties of English have developed in outer circle countries. However, it would appear that they do not have to proceed through the phases outlined by Schneider (2003) or, at least, they are able to proceed through them much more quickly. More research is needed into the ways Englishes are developing in expanding circle countries. In any event, I predict that Chinese English will soon become the most spoken variety of English in the East and Southeast Asian region.

5. Theoretical versus empirical approaches

One reason why Phillipson's theory of Linguistic Imperialism has occasioned so much debate and controversy among applied linguists is that he accuses applied linguists of acting on behalf of the powerful North, especially in the context of promoting English language teaching. Applied linguistics "connives in the false representation of global power by a pretence of being non-political, by pedagogical and linguistic agendas being relatively explicit but the political agenda being banished beyond the professional pale" (Phillipson 1997: 244–245). Pennycook (1998) similarly claims that English language teaching needs to be seen not only as a tool of empire but also as a product of it. Much of ELT, he argues, "echoes with the cultural constructions of colonialism" (1998: 19), but that this is ignored in applied linguistics and TESOL. Having accused applied linguists and TESOL professionals of bias towards or silent acceptance of what he assumes are the necessarily evil and exploitative purposes and policies of colonialism, he promptly asserts that his approach will also be thoroughly biased. "I see no reason to go looking for the good in colonialism. Thus I cannot see any good moral or political reasons to attempt some balanced overview of colonialism" (Pennycook 1998: 25). It is surprising then that he feels he can call his approach *Critical Applied Linguistics* (2001). A critical reading of Pennycook's use of the term "critical" suggests that he is trying to imply that it is an accurate description of his deliberately and perversely one-eyed view, one that is "predetermined by poststructuralist presuppositions" (Sweeting and Vickers 2005: 118). But, as Bolton has pointed out, this approach actually "shifts the object of study almost entirely from language data and linguistic analysis to that of activist pedagogical politics" (2005: 75).

Such approaches allow Brutt-Griffler to argue that work investigating real-world processes of globalisation "remains eclipsed by demonstrably false assumptions that have been elevated to the status of truths by repetition rather than empirical substantiation" (2005: 115). As an example, the world is told that the spread of English is replacing African languages when it is an emprically attested fact that it is African languages that are so doing (Brutt-Griffler 2005), although, as I shall report below, there is evidence that English is replacing languages in certain parts of Africa. Generally speaking, however, local lingua francas are the killer languages. International lingua francas tend to be learned alongside national languages. Thus well over 80% of English speakers are at least bilingual (Brutt-Griffler 2002: 17). The monolingual speaker of English is almost certainly a native speaker of it and is a member of a dwindling minority.

The tension between these scholars lies in their different approaches. Bolton (2003: 42–43) has identified no fewer than twelve different approaches to the study of World Englishes ranging from "English Studies" through "Kachruvian Studies" to "Futurology". In a later paper (2005) he helpfully reduces these to three basic approaches. These are:

> Linguistic (e.g., English studies and corpus linguistics)
> Linguistic and sociopolitical (e.g., sociolinguistics and World Englishes)
> Sociopolitical and political (e.g., Linguistic Imperialism).

It is not difficult to see why there are tensions here. By definition, applied linguistics is primarily about language not politics, although applied linguists must work across disciplines as they research language variation and change, how language is used in a variety of settings and domains, and how those settings and domains shape the language being used. Applied linguists conduct contextualised studies based on linguistic data where, for example, the relationship between a language of wider communication with a local language can be systematically analysed, taking into account specific and changing circumstances (Conrad 1996). Thus a criticism of *Linguistic Imperialism* is that it is too abstract, impersonal and global. It ignores "the individual, the local, the particular" (Canagarajah 1995: 592). This response is echoed by Fishman and provided the impetus for the studies in Fishman, Conrad, and Rubal-Lopez (1996). In Fishman's words:

> What we need now [...] is to set aside worldwide catch-all theories for a while [...] and to look for regional differences or clusters of countries [...] where the status change processes vis à vis English have turned out one way, and others in which they may have turned out another way (or ways).
> (Fishman 1996a: 9)

A further criticism of Phillipson's theory is that it is not disprovable (Davies 1996). However, the results of the research summarised above provides strong evidence that there are serious flaws in the theory of Linguistic Imperialism. It is clearly disprovable. The publication of the theory, however, together with the studies that have been undertaken in response to it, has considerably advanced our knowledge about the causes and motivations behind the spread of English. They are complex and contextually conditioned. Colonialism certainly provided conditions for the spread of English, but it must be remembered that it was the traders who introduced it first. Now trade, along with the need for international communication, is once again a major impetus for the spread of English. The ability to adapt English to suit one's own linguistic, cultural and political needs, the desire to learn English in order to obtain social and economic advancement, and the active wish to participate in globalisation – whether this be listening to pop music in Japan or attending the board meetings of multinational companies – are crucial factors in explaining the current spread of English both intra- and internationally. The significance of these factors are likely to increase. In the next section I consider the implications for English language teaching of this spread of Englishes.

6. Implications for English language teaching

The key questions that need to be considered are:

1. Should English be taught in schools?
2. If yes, then:
   a) when should it be introduced?
   b) should it be taught as a subject or should it be the medium of education?
   c) which variety of English should be the model?

6.1. Choosing English or a local language

The choice of English or a local language almost always leads to great tensions. If a local language is chosen as a medium of instruction, this can be opposed by parents for two major reasons (Schmied 1989). First, parents will want English because they feel that English is essential for their children if they are to be able to move up the socio-economic ladder. For example, the then South African government's infamous 1953 Bantu Education Act was an attempt to reassert the importance of Afrikaans in public life (Kamwangamalu 2002). It entrenched mother tongue instruction for blacks in the early years of education and greatly increased the role of Afrikaans in secondary schools. Blacks saw the policy as an attempt to create a semi-literate workforce and reinforce apartheid, so opposed it vehemently (de Klerk and Gough 2002). Their opposition to the policy led to the Soweto uprising of 1976, after which schools were allowed to choose the medium of instruction that they wanted after the first four years of primary school. English re-emerged as the overwhelming choice (de Klerk and Gough 2002). In Sudan, when Arabic, the mother tongue of more than 50% of the population, replaced English as the official language, civil wars ensued (Awoniyi 1995). A more recent example is parents' opposition to the Hong Kong government's 1997 decision to restrict the number of English medium secondary schools to about a quarter of the total (Bolton 2003).

The second reason why parents may oppose the choice of a local language as a medium of instruction is that, in multilingual societies, the chance of 'your' language being the chosen medium of instruction is rare. How can an equitable decision over which local language to adopt as the medium of education be made? The choice of one local language over another is likely to lead to conflict. The choice of English, on the other hand, makes the government vulnerable to claims of promoting the elite at the expense of the majority and at the expense of local languages. It can also be charged with hindering the educational development of the child. Which is better for a child's cognitive development – to be taught in one or two languages? Which is better for a child's feeling of self worth and self esteem – to be taught in the language of home or in a language representative of a different culture?

Some governments, those of Brunei and the Philippines are examples, have attempted to solve the problem by introducing English as a medium of instruction for certain subjects, usually science and maths, and using the local language to teach the other subjects.

In India, a three language formula has been adopted to enhance "national unity and facile intra-state, inter-state and international communication" (Biswas 2004: 107). This formula requires that children in Hindi speaking areas should learn Hindi, English and one other Indian language at school, while children in non-Hindi speaking areas should learn their mother tongue, Hindi and English. In practice, however, this formula has not been uniformly successful. States have been given the freedom to introduce the third language at any time and this has meant that the results are extremely mixed (cf. Saghal 1991).

There is a definite danger in the over-promotion of English. Later I argue against the blanket introduction of English into primary schools, but the unrealistic and unnecessary insistence on the use of English in certain domains can be harmful. The current general tendency of governments is to maintain or increase the teaching of English – the expanding circle countries of East Asia, China, Japan and South Korea, for example – have recently decided to introduce English as a school subject from the early years of primary school. The questions of which variety of English should be the classroom model and whether English be taught in primary schools then arise.

6.2. Which model of English?

There are two potential models. The first is an exonormative native speaker variety and the second is an endonormative nativised variety, although there may be occasions when a local nativised variety can be used exonormatively. There is also the possibility of using an approach to English language teaching derived from its use as a lingua franca (Kirkpatrick 2006). I shall deal with the advantages and disadvantages of each of these in turn.

6.2.1. A native-speaker model

Despite there being no satisfactory definition of a native speaker (Rampton 1990), the ELT industry continues to promote the term. In most contexts, a native speaker refers to someone who has learned English as a mother tongue, usually in "Anglo" and monolingual settings. A native speaker model thus most commonly refers to "standard" white American or British English.

The choice of a native speaker model in outer and expanding circle countries obviously favours native speakers and the ELT industry. One reason why the ELT industry, educational bureaucrats and politicians prefer native speaker models is because these models have been codified. There are grammars and dictionaries and textbooks based upon these to which teachers and students alike can refer and to whom these can be sold. There are "norms" against which the English of the learners can be evaluated and tested.

A second reason is that, through their codification, they are seen as standard varieties of English. This reassures politicians and bureaucrats who fear that, unless their people learn a standard English based on native speaker norms, then they will not be intelligible in the international community. The adoption of a codified native speaker standard, it is argued, ensures international comprehensibility. In contrast, it is argued that the adoption of a nativised variety would result in the development of different mutually unintelligible varieties of English. For example, Widdowson (1997) has classified certain "outer circle" Englishes as being different languages rather than different varieties. He argues that Ghanaian and Nigerian varieties of English are not varieties of English but are different languages that will "evolve into autonomous languages ultimately to the point of mutual unintelligibility" (1997: 142). In this he argues that they are qualitatively different from varieties of English that have developed within

England. These are "variants of the same language, alternative actualizations" (1997: 140). But, as illustrated earlier, English in England developed in ways comparable to the new varieties in Ghana, Nigeria, or Singapore. An English base has been influenced by contact with several other languages. Kandiah has argued that, in a process he calls "fulguration", new varieties of English create a new system based on "elements, structures and rules drawn from both English and from one or more languages used in the environment" (1998: 99). We need to bear in mind that this is how English developed in England. Whether these varieties are mutually intelligible or not depends more on the motivations of the speaker and the listener's familiarity with the variety than it does on the linguistic features of the variety itself. This is captured by the Identity-Communication Continuum below (Kirkpatrick 2007).

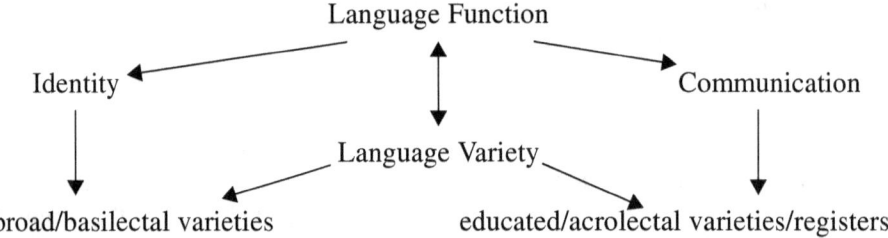

Figure 1. The Identity-Communication Continuum

When people speak informally and use broad/basilectal varieties they are probably talking with friends or people from the same speech community and are thus using the variety that best reflects their identity as fellow members of the particular speech community. They are therefore operating at the "identity" end of the continuum. However, when these people need and/or want to communicate with people from speech communities other than their own, they will move towards the communication end of the continuum and thus use a more formal variety. This is often one that has been learned in school. Thus the relative intelligibility of a particular variety is often dependent upon the motivation of the speaker and whether s/he is operating towards the identity or communication end of the continuum. The more speakers wish to stress their identity the less internationally intelligible they are likely to be. The more they wish to communicate, the more intelligible they are likely to be. This is as true of speakers of varieties of British English as it is of speakers of outer circle varieties such as Singaporean or Filipino. As Smith has pointed out, "Our speech and writing in English needs to be intelligible only to those with whom we wish to communicate in English" (1992: 75).

That native speaker varieties are innately more intelligible than other varieties of English is also questionable. Learners whose first language is syllable-timed, such as Chinese, Malay and French, find speakers of stress-timed languages, such as British English, less intelligible than speakers of syllable-timed varieties "on account of the massive reduction and neutralisation of unstressed syllables" (Hung 2002: 8). This suggests that teachers who are speakers of syllable-timed varieties will be more intelligible to learners whose first languages are also syllable-timed, than native speaker teachers will be. Syllable-timed varieties are also intelligible to native speakers. For example, speakers of Singaporean English proved highly intelligible to Australians (Kirkpatrick and Saunders 2005).

Despite the counter-arguments raised above, many governments still choose a native speaker model, but in most outer and expanding circles it remains hard to justify this choice, as it primarily advantages native speakers. A native speaker model is obviously advantageous for native speaker teachers. They will be seen as providing the correct model, the source of the standard.

The adoption of a native speaker standard may also be advantageous for learners whose motivation for learning English is to understand the mindset of native speakers of the language, and who wish to become familiar with the literary and cultural traditions associated with the particular standard. In other words, it is an advantageous model for those learners whose major aim is to converse with native speakers and to understand whichever native speaking culture it is that they are interested in. But these "English majors" represent a very small minority of the number of people learning English in outer and expanding circle countries, the great majority of whom are learning English in order to communicate with fellow non-native speakers of English.

While native-speaker teachers will be advantaged by the choice of a native speaker model, the choice brings great disadvantages to other teachers and learners. First, it is a model that will be unattainable for the learners. The only way to sound American or British is to be taught exclusively by native speakers or go and live there for an extended period. Very few learners of English in outer and expanding circle countries will be taught by native speakers and, as many of the native speakers who do teach English in countries like China and Korea do not have to be trained teachers, the benefit of being taught by them is, in itself, questionable. Second, the choice of a native speaker model undermines the position of local teachers. Not being representatives of the model themselves they are seen as "second-class" teachers. A common belief still holds that native speaker teachers are somehow innately superior as language teachers, despite the many well-argued cases that show this is a fallacy (cf. Phillipson 1992; Rajagoplan 1997; Braine 1999; Canagarajah 1999). This belief can easily destroy the self-esteem of local teachers. This is particularly tragic, as well-trained and linguistically proficient local teachers represent the ideal teachers for their students, not least because they speak the language of the students and are, by definition, at least bilingual.

Research that might convince governments to spend the money they currently spend on placing native speaker teachers in their schools on the training of local teachers instead is sorely needed.

6.2.2. A nativised model

In the context of an outer circle country such as Nigeria or the Philippines where the local variety of English is established and accepted, there are many advantages in adopting the local variety. First, these varieties are learned in multilingual settings and thus provide the bi- or multilingual learners and teachers with a relevant and appropriate model. Instead of being considered speakers of substandard inferior varieties, bilingual teachers now become speakers of the target standard.

Local teachers are advantaged by the choice of the local variety in other ways (Kirkpatrick 2006). First, they become role models for the learners. Second, being able to speak the languages of their students, these teachers are able to use the linguistic resources of the classroom. Far from feeling guilty about this, they should feel proud of their multilingual prowess. It is hard to see how a monolingual native speaker can, in these contexts, necessarily provide a better model and be a better language teacher than a multilingual teacher who understands local cultural and educational norms (Phillipson 1997).

For a country in the expanding circle where no local variety has yet developed, the context and the purposes for which the learners need English must be considered. In the case of Indonesia for example, it would appear sensible to adopt a Singaporean or Malaysian model rather than the obvious native speaker model, given its geographical proximity, Australian, for the following reasons. First, Malay and Indonesian are virtually the same language so the linguistic characteristics of Malaysian English are likely to be replicated in Indonesian English. Second, there are many cultural similarities. Both are Muslim countries, but with significant numbers of people from different ethnic backgrounds, religions and cultures. Despite the cultural diversity in both countries, the cultures share fundamental values. A third advantage for Indonesia in adopting a regional nativised variety is that both Indonesia and Malaysia are members of the regional grouping the Association of South East Asian Nations (ASEAN). Collaboration in ELT and teacher training would be easy to establish and relatively cheap to provide, especially as the Southeast Asian Ministers of Education Organisation's Regional Language Centre (SEAMEO RELC) has been set up for just this purpose. Finally, and most importantly, the great majority of Indonesia's learners of English are learning English in order to communicate with fellow non-native speakers within ASEAN and the region, rather than with native speakers of English. In this context, a regional nativised variety of English that reflects and respects the cultures of the region would seem to be an appropriate choice (Kirkpatrick 2002a). However, against all this may be an unwillingness of Indonesians to accept an exonormative, nativised variety of English for political and ideological reasons. Simply put, Indonesians might find it difficult to look to Malaysia for expertise. However, in the medium term, the practical advantages of so doing are likely to outweigh any cultural sensitivities.

In an expanding circle country like China, for example, great reluctance on the part of politicians and educational bureaucrats to choose a regional nativised variety of English can be predicted. China's traditional and strongly held attachment to standards and correctness (Kirkpatrick and Xu 2002) would also suggest that, if it is to adopt an exonormative model, it will be a native speaker model. Yet, as described above, a Chinese variety of English is emerging. Chinese English may well soon become the classroom model.

6.2.3. A lingua franca approach

The great majority of English speakers are bilingual. Their most common interlocutors are fellow bilingual speakers of English. For most of these people English acts as a lingua franca. English is used as a lingua franca in Europe. It is used as a lingua franca in India, Africa and throughout Asia. It is the de facto lingua franca of the Association of Southeast Asian Nations (ASEAN) (Krasnick 1995), where it is accepted as such without controversy (Okudaira 1999). Yet, despite its essential role as a lingua franca, there have been surprisingly few attempts to try and describe Lingua Franca English (LFE). This represents a great gap in current applied linguistic research (Seidlhofer 2001).

However, research into LFE is not unknown. Jenkins (2000) has undertaken a study into the phonology of international English. This is of particular pedagogic value, as it shows which sounds and aspects of pronunciation hinder mutual intelligibility and which do not. A classroom focus on intelligibility rather than on native speaker norms frees up teachers and learners to concentrate on more relevant work. In the context of the teaching of pronunciation, the aim of the LFE class becomes intelligibility, not the acquisition of native speaker norms, norms that the overwhelming majority of English learners will never be able to acquire.

Other current lingua franca English research includes James' (2000) study into the English lingua franca used in the Alpine-Adriatic region. Meierkord (2004) is investigating the use of lingua franca English in a range of contexts. Seidlhofer (2001) is compiling a corpus of English as a lingua franca at the University of Vienna. Kirkpatrick (2005) is studying the features of ASEAN lingua franca English and the communicative strategies of its speakers.

While research has shown that lingua franca English is characterised by variation, a number of common elements can be identified (James 2000; Jenkins 2000; Kirkpatrick 2005). The existence of variation makes it difficult to describe a lingua franca *model* for the classroom, but a lingua franca *approach* that includes the common features, alerts students to features that cause particular problems of intelligibility and illustrates successful communicative strategies might make such an approach useful in the classroom for several reasons.

Not only would the adoption of a lingua franca approach offer the same advantages for teachers and learners as those outlined for the adoption of a nativised model, a further advantage comes with the potential content of the curriculum. Instead of concentrating on the cultures associated with native speaker or nativised models, students who are learning lingua franca English will be learning about the cultures of the people with whom they are most likely to use their English. The language materials will be designed to allow learners to be able to learn about, compare and discuss each other's cultures. Thus the content of an English curriculum for Indonesian students should be primarily based on the cultures of the region, including ASEAN, and should aim to develop in the students the ability to talk about their own cultures in English (Kirkpatrick 2002a, 2002b).

A further possible advantage of an LFE approach, especially when it is adopted in a regional setting such as Southeast Asia, is that it accommodates shared cultural and pragmatic norms. An example of a pragmatic norm that is shared by people from East Asia is the use of "facework", whereby people tend to delay the introduction of the topic in conversation until after they have talked about the other person's family or given them "face" in some way (Scollon and Scollon 1991). A related example is the Chinese speakers' preference to give reasons or justifications for a request before making the request, while native speakers prefer to make the requests and then provide justifications for it (Kirkpatrick 1991). This request pattern preference is shared by many other cultures in East and Southeast Asia. These pragmatic norms will be transferred into the local varieties of English, and, far from seeing them as deviant because they differ from native speaker norms, it would be culturally appropriate for learners to be taught these patterns, as they will be communicating with people from the region.

This focus on cross-cultural communication that is inherent in an LFE approach appears to address the point made by Bamgbose, "Communication across world Englishes has to be seen in terms of accommodation between codes and in a multilingual context" (2001: 359).

7. The future of English

What may happen to English in the future and what sort of research should be the concern of applied linguistics? Most scholars see a continued if not increased use of English, although they differ over the type of English and the roles it may play.

Crystal (1997) has little doubt that international English will become even more widespread, and that the English will be based on an American variety. This is cause for concern, as the inherent power of speakers of American English through their association with dominant world forces should not be understated. Görlach (2002) sees the development of a type of international diglossia, where local norms will be accepted for local communication and international norms, however defined, will be reserved for a few specific purposes, such as formal written communication. However, he does allow that the presence of local norms will create more tolerance and become more accepted and that communication between non-native speakers will assist in the exchange of ideas. And while he argues that English has never completely replaced a European language outside Britain (2002: 16), it will stifle European languages in that it will take over functions currently served by European languages. He cites Germany as a country where German may be reduced to a kind of dialect (2002: 16), in particular in the field of education and scholarship, a fear shared by Ammon (1996) for German and other European languages. This is a crucial area for further research. While it is claimed, as I have done in this chapter, that, when used as an international lingua franca, English tends to become an additional language, this does not mean that it has no effect on local languages. Clearly it takes over domains in which local languages operated previously. And while Bisong (1995) has argued that English has not replaced any local languages in Nigeria, a detailed ethnographic study conducted at a local level has provided evidence that English is replacing the Emai language in a region of southern Nigeria (Schaeffer and Egbokhare 1999). Further research of this sort is needed.

In stressing that the history of World English has been one of language change, Brutt-Griffler (2002) sees a development comparable to Görlach's, in which, on the one hand, there will be local speech communites and, on the other, the world speech community will move towards linguistic convergence. Yet, it must be remembered that the great majority of English speakers are bilingual and the greatest use of English is in lingua franca communication among bi- and multilingual speakers. Graddol (1997) predicts that this will overturn current linguistic hierarchies. I agree, as the variety used in international communication will not necessarily be based on current native speaker models, but on local bilingual models. Such speakers are tolerant of variation (Firth 1996) and the weight of evidence available at the moment suggests that speakers in lingua franca situations have little trouble understanding each other, but when they do, they exercise communicative strategies that allow communication to proceed with a minimum of fuss. I tentatively predict, therefore, that local varieties of English, whether they be European, African or Asian, will be perfectly adequate for international communication as long as the motivation of their speakers is to communicate. Much more research into lingua franca communication is needed, however, before this prediction can be confidently made.

The fact that so many English speakers are multilingual also means that there has been a growth in the use of mixed codes, where English and a local language or languages are spoken or written together. I have not discussed this phenomenon here, but this is an area where ethnographic research of the type conducted by McLellan (2005) would also be valuable in explaining the ways the languages are used in combination.

Research is also needed that can contribute to the better understanding of the effect of learning English on social change as a result of globalisation. Aside from the huge investment of time and resources in the formal educational sector, the learning of English absorbs enormous amounts of time and energy on the part of governments, businesses, families and individuals. The type of localised targeted research described by Fishman et al. (1996) and Sonntag (2003) needs to be undertaken to study the effects of learning English on families, especially those that feel pressurised to make financial sacrifices in order to provide their children with the opportunity to learn English. In particular the move to teach English in primary schools in expanding circle countries, especially in rural areas, needs to be studied. Is this really an effective use of curriculum time and resources? What progress can pupils make when there are insufficiently trained teachers in poorly equipped classrooms? Won't motivated secondary school students at urban schools with well-trained teachers make much quicker progress than unmotivated primary students with poorly trained teachers with poor proficiency in English? I am not suggesting that primary school teachers are necessarily less trained and proficient than their secondary counterparts. With the limited resources available, however, empirically based research that aids people make decisions about when and where to introduce English is vital.

Research is needed into the effect of the need, real or preceived, for English upon labour markets at local, national and global levels. What new hierarchies are being created and to what extent are they determined by English and/or multilingual proficiency? I have not considered the development of computer-mediated English in this chapter (see Danet and Herring, this vol.), but this is a further area in which research is needed. What new styles of English and other languages are developing and what intranational and/or international alliances are being formed through the use of this new medium?

Finally, research is needed into the role academic English is playing on international scholarship. This is the domain in which great resentment and concern is felt (Ammon 2000). This is not simply a question of having to write in a language that is not one's own, in order to disseminate one's scholarship or ideas, unfair and onerous that this may be. The need to write following an empirical-scientific knowledge paradigm and in "Anglo" rhetorical styles can greatly disadvantage those unfamiliar with both. In the context of Sri Lanka and India, Fernando (1996) and Kachru (1991) argue that local knowledge is becoming devalued by Western empirical approaches and paradigms. This raises an interesting paradox into which research is sorely needed. On the one hand, it would appear evident that the West knows more about certain types of indigenous knowledge precisely because this knowledge has been made available through English. Traditional "indigenous" practices such as Yoga, and Ayurvedic (and Traditional Chinese) Medicine provide good examples (Kirkpatrick 2007). Yet it may be that the knowledge has been reshaped and reframed in order to meet Western scientific and rhetorical norms. In other words, its very dissemination via the medium of English may have fundamentally altered the essence of the local knowledge. More research is needed here to see the extent to which traditional and indigenous knowledge is being successfully disseminated globally through English.

8. Conclusion

English is today's global language. But this English is an idealised language. English is actually represented by numerous varieties of English, each of which is itself characterised by variation. These varieties have developed in response to comparable stimuli and are fashioned by distinctive local cultural and linguistic features. Yet there is little danger of these Englishes developing into discrete, mutually unintelligible varieties, as the major motivation for learning English is a desire to participate, in whatever way, in the age of globalisation. Nor does the spread of English necessarily threaten local languages, as the great majority of English speakers are at least bilingual. In most cases, English is learned as an additional language.

The reasons why English has become the global language are numerous and complex and better explained by a close empirical examination of local conditions and contexts than by theories that attempt to identify an overarching reason for its spread.

All these issues need to be considered in considerations of whether to teach English, when to teach it and which model to teach.

References

Achebe, Chinua
   2003   The African writer and the English language. In: Jennifer Jenkins (ed.), *World Englishes*, 169–172. London: Routledge.

Ammon, Ulrich
   1996   The European Union. Status change of English during the last 50 years. In: Joshua A. Fishman, Andrew Conrad and Alma Rubal-Lopez (eds.), *Post-imperial English*, 241–267. Berlin: Mouton de Gruyter.

Ammon, Ulrich
　2000　Towards more fairness in international English: Linguistic rights of non-native speakers? In: Robert Phillipson (ed.), *Rights to Language: Equity, Power and Education*, 111–116. Mahwah, NJ: Lawrence Erlbaum.

Awoniyi, Adedeji
　1995　Determining language in education policy. The dilemma in Africa. In: Kolawole Owolabi (ed.), *Language in Nigeria: Essays in Honour of Ayo Bamgbose*, 441–454. Ibadan: Group Publishers.

Bailey, Richard W.
　1991　*Images of English: A Cultural History of the Language*. Cambridge: Cambridge University Press.

Bamgbose, Ayo
　2001　World Englishes and globalisation. *World Englishes* 20 (3): 357–364.

Baumgardner, Robert J. (ed.)
　1996　*South Asian English: Structure, Use and Users*. Urbana: University of Illinois Press.

Bisong, Joseph
　1995　Language choice and cultural imperialism. A Nigerian perspective. *English Language Teaching Journal* 49 (2): 122–132.

Biswas, Gopa
　2004　Language policy in Southeast Asia: A case study of India. In: Sahiba Mansoor, Shaheen Meraj and Aliya Tahir (eds.), *Language Policy, Planning and Practice: A South Asian Perspective*, 106–111. Karachi: Aga Khan University and Oxford University Press.

Blake, Norman
　1996　*A History of the English Language*. London: Macmillan.

Bolton, Kingsley
　2003　*Chinese Englishes*. Cambridge: Cambridge University Press.

Bolton, Kingsley
　2005　Where WE stands: Approaches, issues and debate in World Englishes. *World Englishes* 24 (1): 69–83.

Boyle, Joseph
　1997　Imperialism and the English language. *Journal of Multilingual and Multicultural Development* 18 (3): 169–181.

Braine, George (ed.)
　1999　*Non-native Educators in English Language Teaching*. Mahwah, NJ: Lawrence Erlbaum.

Brutt-Griffler, Janina
　2002　*World English. A Study of its Development*. Clevedon: Multilingual Matters.

Brutt-Griffler, Janina
　2005　Globalisation and Applied Linguistics: Post imperial questions of identity and the construction of applied linguistics discourse. *International Journal of Applied Linguistics* 15 (1): 113–115.

Burchfield, Robert
　1994a　Introduction. In: Robert Burchfield (ed.), *The English Language*. Vol. 5: *English in Britain and Overseas*, 1–19. Cambridge: Cambridge University Press.

Burchfield, Robert (ed.)
    1994b   *The Cambridge History of the English Language.* Vol. 5: *English in Britain and Overseas.* Cambridge: Cambridge University Press.

Canagarajah, Suresh C.
    1994   Competing discourses in Sri Lankan English poetry. *World Englishes* 13 (3): 361–376.

Canagarajah, Suresh C.
    1995   Review of Linguistic Imperialism. *Language in Society* 24 (4): 590–594.

Canagarajah, Suresh C.
    1999   Interrogating the 'Native Speaker Fallacy': Non-linguistic roots, non-pedagogical results. In: George Braine (ed.), *Non-native Educators in English Language Teaching*, 77–92. Mahwah, NJ: Lawrence Erlbaum.

Canagarajah, Suresh C.
    2000   Negotiating ideologies through English. In: Thomas Ricento (ed.), *Ideology, Politics and Language Policies. Focus on English*, 121–132. Amsterdam: John Benjamins.

Conrad, Andrew
    1996   The international role of English: The state of the discussion. In: Joshua A. Fishman, Andrew Conrad and Alma Rubal-Lopez (eds.), *Post-imperial English*, 13–36. Berlin: Mouton de Gruyter.

Crystal, David
    1997   *English as a Global Language.* Cambridge: Cambridge University Press.

Crystal, David
    2004   *The Stories of English.* London: Allen Lane.

D'Souza, Jean
    2001   Contextualising range and depth in Indian English. *World Englishes* 20 (2): 145–159.

Davies, Alan
    1996   Ironising the myth of linguicism. *Journal of Multilingual and Multicultural Development* 17 (6): 485–496.

De Klerk, Vivien and David Gough
    2002   Black South African English. In: Rajend Mesthrie (ed.), *Language in South Africa*, 356–378. Cambridge: Cambridge University Press.

Desai, Anita
    1996   A coat of many colours. In: Robert J. Baumgardner (ed.), *South Asian English: Structure, Use and Users*, 221–230. Urbana: University of Illinois Press.

Dillard, Joey L.
    1992   *A History of American English.* London: Longman.

Dixon, Robert M. W.
    1993   Australian Aboriginal languages. In: Gerhard Schulz (ed.), *The Languages of Australia*, 71–82. Canberra: Australian Academy of the Humanities.

Du, R. and Y. Jiang
    2001   Jin ershi nian 'Zhongguo yingyu' yanjiu shuping ('China English' in the past 20 years). *Waiyu Jiaoxue yu Yanjiu (Foreign Language Teaching and Research)* 33 (1): 37–41.

Ferguson, Charles A.
　1996　English in South Asia: Imperialist legacy and regional asset. In: Robert J. Baumgardner (ed.), *South Asian English: Structure, Use and Users*, 29–39. Urbana: University of Illinois Press.

Fernando, Chitra
　1996　The ideational function of English in Sri Lanka. In: Robert J. Baumgardner (ed.), *South Asian English: Structure, Use and Users*, 206–217. Urbana: University of Illinois Press.

Firth, Alan
　1996　The discursive accomplishment of normality. On lingua franca English and conversation analysis. *Journal of Pragmatics* 26 (3): 237–259.

Fisher, Olga
　1992　Syntax. In: Norman Blake (ed.), *The Cambridge History of the English Language*. Vol. 2: *1066–1476*, 207–408. Cambridge: Cambridge University Press.

Fishman, Joshua A.
　1996a　Introduction: Some empirical and theoretical issues. In: Joshua A. Fishman, Andrew Conrad and Alma Rubal-Lopez (eds.), *Post-imperial English*, 3–12. Berlin: Mouton de Gruyter.

Fishman, Joshua A.
　1996b　Summary and interpretation. Post-imperial English 1940–1990. In: Joshua A. Fishman, Andrew Conrad and Alma Rubal-Lopez (eds.), *Post-imperial English*, 623–641. Berlin: Mouton de Gruyter.

Fishman, Joshua A., Andrew Conrad and Alma Rubal-Lopez (eds.)
　1996　*Post-imperial English*. Berlin: Mouton de Gruyter.

Görlach, Manfred
　2002　*Still More Englishes*. Amsterdam: John Benjamins.

Graddol, David
　1997　*The Future of English*. London: The British Council.

Harkins, Jean
　2000　Structure and meaning in Australian Aboriginal English. *Asian Englishes* 3 (2): 60–81.

Hung, Tony
　2002　English as a global language: Implications for teaching. *The Ateneo Center for English Language Teaching Journal* 6 (2): 3–10.

Ihalainen, Ossi
　1994　The dialects of England since 1776. In: Robert Burchfield (ed.), *The Cambridge History of the English Language*. Vol. 5: *English in Britain and Overseas*, 197–274. Cambridge: Cambridge University Press.

James, Alan
　2000　English as a European lingua franca: Current realities and existing dichotomies. In: Jasone Cenoz and Ulrike Jessner (eds.), *English in Europe: The Acquisition of a Third Language*, 22–38. Clevedon: Multilingual Matters.

Jenkins, Jennifer
　2000　*The Phonology of English as an International Language*. Oxford: Oxford University Press.

Jenkins, Jennifer
  2003   *World Englishes.* London: Routledge.
Kachru, Braj
  1983   *The Indianization of English.* New Delhi: Oxford University Press.
Kachru, Braj (ed.)
  1992a   *The Other Tongue: English Across Cultures.* Chicago: University of Illinois Press.
Kachru, Braj
  1992b   Teaching World Englishes. In: Braj Kachru (ed.), *The Other Tongue: English Across Cultures,* 355–366. Chicago: University of Illinois Press.
Kachru, Braj
  1992c   Models for non-native Englishes. In: Braj Kachru (ed.), *The Other Tongue: English Across Cultures,* 48–74. Chicago: University of Illinois Press.
Kachru, Yamuna
  1991   Writings in the other tongue: Expository prose. In: R. S. Gupta and Kapil Kapoor (eds.), *English in India: Issues and Problems in Indian English,* 227–246. New Delhi: Academic Foundation.
Kamwangamalu, Nkonko M.
  2002   The social history of English in South Africa. *World Englishes* 21 (1): 1–8.
Kandiah, Thiru
  1998   A post-colonial perspective on the native speaker. In Rajendra Singh (ed.), *The Native Speaker. Multilingual Perspectives,* 79–110. New Delhi: Sage.
Kirkpatrick, Andy
  1991   Information sequencing in Mandarin in letters of request. *Anthropologial Linguistics* 33 (2): 183–202.
Kirkpatrick, Andy (ed.)
  2002a   *Englishes in Asia: Communication, Identity, Power and Education.* Melbourne: Language Australia.
Kirkpatrick, Andy
  2002b   ASEAN and Asian cultures and models: Implications for the ELT curriculum and teacher selection. In: Andy Kirkpatrick (ed.), *Englishes in Asia: Communication, Identity, Power and Education,* 213–224. Melbourne: Language Australia.
Kirkpatrick, Andy
  2005   Oral communication and intelligibility among ASEAN speakers of English. Plenary Paper given at the 40th RELC International Seminar, Singapore, 18–20 April 2005.
Kirkpatrick, Andy
  2006   Which model of English: Native speaker, nativised or lingua franca? In: Mario Saraceni and Rani Rubdy (eds.), *English in the World: Global Rules, Global Roles,* 71–83. London: Continuum Press.
Kirkpatrick, Andy
  2007   *World Englishes: Implications for International Communication and English Language Teaching.* Cambridge: Cambridge University Press.
Kirkpatrick, Andy and Xu Zhichang
  2002   Chinese pragmatic norms and China English. *World Englishes* 21 (2): 268–280.

Kirkpatrick, Andy and Neville Saunders
   2005   The intelligibility of Singaporean English: A case study at an Australian university. In: David Deterding, Adam Brown and Low Ee Ling (eds.), *English in Singapore: Phonetic Research on a Corpus*, 153–162. Singapore: McGraw-Hill.

Krasnick, Harry
   1995   The role of linguaculture and intercultural communication in ASEAN in the year 2020: Prospects and predictions. In: Makhan Tickoo (ed.), *Language and Culture in Multilingual Societies*, 81–93. Singapore: SEAMEO Regional Language Centre.

Lam, Agnes
   2002   English education in China: Policy changes and learners' experiences. *World Englishes* 21 (2): 245–256.

Lass, Roger
   1992   Phonology and morphology. In Norman Blake (ed.), *The Cambridge History of the English Language*. Vol. 2: *1066–1476*, 23–155. Cambridge: Cambridge University Press.

Li, David C. S.
   2002   Hong Kong parents' preference for English-medium education: Passive victims of imperialism or active agents of pragmatism? In: Andy Kirkpatrick (ed.), *Englishes in Asia: Communication, Identity, Power and Education*, 28–62. Melbourne: Language Australia.

McArthur, Tom
   1998   *The English Languages*. Cambridge: Cambridge University Press.

McLellan, James
   2005   Malay-English language alternation in two Brunei Darussalam on-line discussion forums. Ph.D. Dissertation, Curtin University of Technology, Perth, Australia.

McClure, J. Derrick
   1994   English in Scotland. In: Robert Burchfield (ed.), *The Cambridge History of the English Language*. Vol. 5: *English in Britain and Overseas*, 23–93. Cambridge: Cambridge University Press.

Meierkord, Christiane
   2004   Syntactic variation in interactions across international Englishes. *English World-Wide* 25 (1): 109–132.

Moag, Rodney F.
   1992   The life cycle of non-native Englishes: A case study. In: Braj Kachru (ed.), *The Other Tongue: English Across Cultures*, 233–244. Chicago: University of Illinois Press.

Mufwene, Salikoko
   2001   *The Ecology of Language Evolution*. Cambridge: Cambridge University Press.

Ngũgĩ wa Thiong'o
   2003   The language of African literature. In: Jennifer Jenkins (ed.), *World Englishes*, 172–177. London: Routledge.

Okudaira, Akiko
   1999   A study on the international communication in regional organizations: The use of English as the 'official' language of ASEAN. *Asian Englishes* 2 (1): 91–107.

Omar, Asmah Haji
    1996   Post-imperial English in Malaysia. In: Joshua A. Fishman, Andrew Conrad and Alma Rubal-Lopez (eds.), *Post-imperial English*, 513–534. Berlin: Mouton de Gruyter.
Pennycook, Alastair
    1998   *English and the Discourses of Colonialism*. London: Routledge.
Pennycook, Alastair
    2001   *Critical Applied Linguistics*. Mahwah, NJ: Lawrence Erlbaum.
Phillipson, Robert
    1992   *Linguistic Imperialism*. Oxford: Oxford University Press.
Phillipson, Robert
    1997   Realities and myths of Linguistic Imperialism. *Journal of Multilingual and Multicultural Development* 18 (3): 238–247.
Phillipson, Robert
    2002   Global English and local language politics. In: Andy Kirkpatrick (ed.), *Englishes in Asia: Communication, Identity, Politics and Education*, 7–28. Melbourne: Language Australia.
Quayum, Mohammad A. (ed.)
    2003   *Petals of Hibiscus: A Representative Anthology of Malaysian Literature in English*. Petaling Jaya: Pearson.
Rajagopalan, Kanavillil
    1997   Linguistics and the myth of nativity: Comments of the controversy over 'new/non-native Englishes'. *Journal of Pragmatics* 27: 225–231.
Rampton, Ben
    1990   Displacing the native speaker: Expertise, affiliation and inheritance. *English Language Teaching Journal* 44 (2): 93–101.
Ricento, Thomas (ed.)
    2000   *Ideology, Politics and Language Policies. Focus on English*. Amsterdam: John Benjamins.
Richardson, Malcolm
    1984   The Dictamen and its influence on 15th century English prose. *Rhetorica* 2 (3): 207–226.
Saghal, Anju
    1991   Patterns of language use in a bilingual setting in India. In: Jenny Cheshire (ed.), *English Around the World*, 299–307. Cambridge: Cambridge University Press.
Schaeffer, Ronald P. and Francis O. Egbokhare
    1999   English and the pace of endangerment in Nigeria. *World Englishes* 18 (3): 381–391.
Schmied, Josef (ed.)
    1989   *English in East and Central Africa*, Vol. 1. Bayreuth: Breitinger.
Schmied, Josef
    1991   *English in Africa*. London: Longman.
Schneider, Edgar
    2003   The dynamics of new Englishes: From identity construction to dialect rebirth. *Language* 79 (2): 233–281.
Scollon, Ron and Suzanne Scollon
    1991   Topic confusion in English-Asian discourse. *World Englishes* 10 (2): 113–121.

Seidlhofer, Barbara
   2001   Closing a conceptual gap: The case for a description of English as a lingua franca. *International Journal of Applied Linguistics* 11 (2): 133–157.

Sibayan, Bonifacio and Andrew B. Gonzalez
   1996   Post-imperial English in the Philippines. In: Joshua A. Fishman, Andrew Conrad and Alma Rubal-Lopez (eds.), *Post-imperial English,* 139–172. Berlin: Mouton de Gruyter.

Sidhwa, Bapsi
   1996   Creative processes in Pakistani English fiction. In: Robert J. Baumgardner (ed.), *South Asian English: Structure, Use and Users,* 231–240. Urbana: University of Illinois Press.

Skutnabb-Kangas, Tove
   1988   Multilingualism and the education of minority children. In: Tove Skutnabb-Kangas and Jim Cummins (eds.), *Minority Education: From Shame to Struggle,* 9–44. Clevedon: Multilingual Matters.

Smith, Larry E.
   1992   Spread of English and issues of intelligibility. In: Braj Kachru (ed.), *The Other Tongue. English Across Cultures,* 75–90. Chicago: University of Illinois Press.

Sonntag, Selma K.
   2003   *The Local Politics of Global English.* Lanham: Lexington.

Srivastava, R. N. and Sharma V. P.
   1991   Indian English today. In: R. S. Gupta and Kapil Kapoor (eds.), *English in India: Issues and Problems in Indian English,* 189–206. New Delhi: Academic Foundation.

Sweeting, Anthony and Edward Vickers
   2005   On colonising colonialism: The discourses of the history of English in Hong Kong. *World Englishes* 24 (2): 113–130.

Wang, Rongpei
   1994   *Shuo Dong Dao Xi Hua Yingyu (Talking about English).* Beijing: Waiyu Jiaoxue yu Yanjiu Chubanshe (Beijing: Foreign Language Teaching and Research Press).

Widdowson, Henry
   1997   EIL, ESL, EFL: Global issues and local interests. *World Englishes* 16 (1): 135–146.

Xu Zhichang
   2005   Chinese English: What is it and is it to become a regional variety of English? Ph.D. Dissertation. Curtin University of Technology, Perth, Australia.

Zhang, Hang
   2002   Bilingual creativity in Chinese English: Ha Jin's 'In the Pond'. *World Englishes* 21(2): 305–315.

12. Language planning and language rights

Tove Skutnabb-Kangas

1. Introduction: New types of language planning and language planners needed?

After some initial exemplary cases with or without language planning and language rights, some central language rights concepts will be presented and discussed in their historical context. Since the history and the field of language planning is described elsewhere in this volume (see Ricento, this vol.), I will focus only on the field of language rights in this chapter. The difference between *language rights* (LRs) and *linguistic human rights* (LHRs) will be clarified in connection with a short historical overview; LHRs combine *language rights* and *human rights* (HRs).

The basic concepts presented include issues around who or what can have language rights: On the one hand languages can have rights and on the other hand, individuals, groups, peoples, organisations and other collectivities (including states) can have rights (and duties). The nature of these rights will be discussed and a number of distinctions presented. Are the rights expressive or instrumental, positive or negative, binding or non-binding, based on principles of personality or territoriality or combinations of these? Some additional dichotomies follow, with a clarification of where LHRs might stand in relation to them if proper integration (of minorities, and of the whole society) is one of the goals in language policy, rather than forced linguistic assimilation. In the end assimilation may lead to the disappearance of languages if enough members of the group are transferred to another linguistic group. I thus ask which LRs, especially in education, are necessary for integration. After the clarification and discussion, a state of the art of LHRs is briefly presented. The chapter finishes with some controversial issues, and a few comments about the role(s) of applied linguistics. Obviously applied linguistics should be multi- and interdisciplinary in order to be able to live up to the challenges presented.

Language policy has been defined as "systematic, rational, theory-based effort at the societal level to modify the linguistic environment with a view to increasing aggregate welfare. It is typically conducted by official bodies or their surrogates and aimed at part or all of the population living under their jurisdiction" (Grin 2000: 7).

Language planning is or should be work that leads to language policy. It is a prerequisite for language policy to be systematic, rational and theory-based, regardless of whether one is planning the status and the relationship between languages (status planning), the forms and content of languages (corpus planning) or the teaching and learning of languages (acquisition planning) (see also Romaine, this vol.). Language rights will be defined below.

Two kinds of interest in language rights can be distinguished. One is "the expressive interest in language as a marker of identity", the other an "instrumental interest in language as a means of communication" (Rubio-Marín 2003: 56). These correspond fairly closely to what Skutnabb-Kangas and Phillipson (1994) have called "necessary" and "enrichment-oriented" rights. The *expressive* (or non-instrumental) language rights "aim at ensuring a person's capacity to enjoy a secure linguistic environment in her/his mother tongue and a linguistic group's fair chance of cultural self-reproduction" (Rubio-Marín 2003: 56). It is only these rights that Rubio-Marín calls "language rights in a strict sense"; in other words, these could be seen as linguistic human rights (see below). The *instrumental* language rights "aim at ensuring that language is not an obstacle to the effective enjoyment of rights with a linguistic dimension, to the meaningful participation in public institutions and democratic process, and to the enjoyment of social and economic opportunities that require linguistic skills" (Rubio-Marín 2003: 56).

Let us first consider some cases, where the presence or absence of the two concepts of language planning and language rights is or has historically been fairly clear. This might also show both the relationship between the two concepts, and the importance of having at least language rights in place.

2. Language planning, language rights and linguistic human rights

2.1. The maintenance of specific languages

In 2002, the indigenous Sweetgrass First Nations Language Council (contact them at http://www.schoolnet.ca/aboriginal/sweetgra/index-e.html) did a survey of 24 indigenous communities in Southern Ontario, Canada, based on census figures from 1995. The communities had a total indigenous/aboriginal population of 51,778 people. Of them, 50,771 spoke only English while 1,601 also spoke an Aboriginal language in addition to English. The highest percentage of fluent speakers was in the age groups between 51 and 70, and even in these age groups only about a quarter were fluent speakers. There were no fluent speakers under the age of 20, and even in the next age group, 21–30, only one percent were fluent in their ancient native languages. Some two hundred years ago, every aboriginal adult in Canada was fluent in their own language. In addition to many knowing several other indigenous languages, some of them also knew English or French.

Is this historically a result of language planning? Yes. The Canadian state planned for aboriginal languages to disappear.[1] Is it a result of historical lack of language rights? Yes. There have not been and are no schools through the medium of any of these indigenous languages in Southern Ontario, and they are not used for any official purposes. At the conference "Raising Our Voices" that the Language Council organised in October 2003, I heard some children and youngsters speaking a few of the languages; this is a result of internal language planning and struggle amongst the indigenous peoples themselves. The Canadian state has so far done little to support the revitalisation and development of Canada's indigenous languages, despite some recent verbal (and financial) promises. Of the 64 languages in Canada, even if their use is no longer overtly forbidden in any context, fewer than half a dozen are said to have a chance of surviving this century (see Burnaby 1996).

In Turkish Kurdistan, there is no education through the medium of Kurdish and Kurdish is not even taught as a subject in schools. This means that most Kurds cannot read or write their language. Even if Kurdish can now be heard on the streets and even on radio, many of the rules forbidding its official use are still in place, as they have been since the early 1920s – a case of conscious genocidal language planning.[2] The state prosecutor demands, for instance, six months of imprisonment for 13 leaders of the federalist party Hakbar because Kurdish was used at their party congress; the court case started in May 2005. Kurdish still has no rights (spring 2007), despite the Turkish state's claims to the contrary. Even if there has been massive assimilation, the sheer numbers of Kurds mean that the language survives against all odds, and does it well. In Iraqi Kurdistan, Kurdish is an official language; education for Kurds is now through the medium of Kurdish, and English is learned as a foreign language. In addition, several minorities have mother tongue medium education.

Swedish speakers in Finland have historically had positive language planning, combined with one of the best language rights regimes in the world for any linguistic minority. Table 1 (source: http://www.finland.org/finnswedes.html#anguage%20laws, accessed 15 September 2003, web address now obsolete) shows the numbers and percentages of Swedish-speakers in Finland from 1610 to 1995.

Table 1. Numbers and percentages of Swedish-speakers in Finland from 1610 to 1995

Year	No.	% of total population	Year	No.	% of total population
1610	70,000	17.5	1930	342,900	10.1
1749	87,200	16.3	1940	354,000	9.5
1815	160,000	14.6	1950	348,300	8.6
1880	294,900	14.3	1960	330,500	7.4
1890	322,600	13.6	1970	303,400	6.6
1900	349,700	12.9	1980	300,500	6.3
1910	339,000	11.6	1990	296,700	5.9
1920	341,000	11.0	1995	294,664	5.8

Even if both the percentages (since 1610) and the numbers (since 1940, due to immigration and mixed marriages) have declined, the absolute numbers are today the same as in 1880. And it is self-evident that children with two Swedish-speaking parents in Finland grow up speaking Swedish. Most of them can and do have their day-care and education through the medium of Swedish, including university. A Swedish speaker can read the daily newspapers in Swedish, listen to radio and watch TV, go to church, do the military service, go to court, deal with national and local authorities, in short, lead most of her/his life in Swedish, if that is what s/he wants; s/he can also do all of this in Finnish (see http://www.om.fi/20802.htm for the new *Finnish Language Act* from 2004). This situation is a far cry from the Canadian indigenous situation. In Canada, native French speakers, especially in Quebec, have similar rights to Finland Swedes, likewise accompanied by extremely thorough language planning.

One could formalise some situations with a simple quadrant, where a plus indicates the presence and a minus the absence of language planning and language rights, respectively. I have placed our cases and some others in the quadrant. The reader is invited to add examples and number them.

Table 2. Presence or absence of language planning and language rights

Language planning	Language rights	
	+	−
+	Both planning and rights 1. Finland Swedes in Finland 2. Francophones in Canada 3. Kurds in Iraqi Kurdistan	Planning but no rights 4. Sweetgrass First Nations in Canada 5. Kurds in Turkish Kurdistan
−	Rights but no planning ??	Neither planning nor rights 6. Italian speakers in the USA 7. Most Deaf communities in Asia and Africa

One can already make some preliminary observations. Firstly, it is obvious that neither language planning nor language rights are either/or issues. They are always relative. There can be more or less planning, and it can be more or less overt or covert. The "planners" may be more or less conscious of the fact that they are in fact doing language planning. Likewise, individuals, groups, peoples and states can enjoy or grant fewer language rights (and, especially, linguistic human rights) or many more of them, again, more or less overtly or covertly. All examples should thus be placed on continua, and this is what is done below in Table 3, using the numbers from Table 2 for the cases. The further to the right a situation is placed within a box, the worse the situation is from a language rights point of view. The lower down it is placed within a box, the less planning (or the less overt the planning). The reader is invited to place situations s/he knows well into the table. It is also interesting that it is so difficult to find groups that have rights without planning (except maybe a few linguistic majorities, or completely isolated monolingual communities) – rights are in most cases a result of struggle.

Table 3. Relative presence or absence of language planning and language rights

Language planning	Language rights	
	+	−
+	Both planning and rights 1, 2, 3	Planning but no rights 5 4
−	Rights but no planning	Neither planning nor rights 6, 7

1. Finland Swedes in Finland; 2. Francophones in Canada; 3. Kurds in Iraqi Kurdistan; 4. Sweetgrass First Nations in Canada; 5. Kurds in Turkish Kurdistan; 6. Italian speakers in the USA; 7. Most Deaf communities in Asia and Africa

Secondly, linguistic majorities have many language rights in most countries, especially countries where there is a definitive majority (rather than many language groups where none forms a majority which is the situation in many African countries). Mostly ordinary people representing linguistic majorities (Russian speakers in Russia, Turkish speakers in Turkey, Portuguese speakers in Brazil, English speakers in Australia) do not need to do anything to achieve language rights; these are seen as self-evident and the state organises everything through the medium of the dominant language as a matter of course. Still, one cannot say that their rights would not be a result of planning even if most of the group are not aware of this planning. But linguistic minorities may often need to struggle to get language rights, often in conflict with the state and/or the linguistic majority representatives, i.e. they have to oppose the negative, often genocidal language planning that the state engages in. In many cases the state does not do any positive language planning for them or grant them any rights; they have to do it themselves.

The language planning that states do can be either negative or positive for the indigenous peoples or the linguistic minorities; states can grant them language rights or deprive them of language rights. Planning can be done either by the *duty-holder* (the one who is supposed to grant the rights, most often the state, with its various authorities, like the school authorities), or by the *beneficiary*. In the cases of Finland Swedes and Canadian French speakers on the one hand, and the Canadian Sweetgrass First Nations and Kurds in Turkey on the other hand, the respective states have done language planning, but *for* the linguistic minorities, without their consent (Sweetgrass First Nations, Kurds in Turkey) or *with* the minority (Finland, Canadian Francophones). It has aimed at the maintenance and development of the Swedish and French languages in one case, and the killing off of indigenous languages and Kurdish in the other case. There may be both cases where the state plans positive measures for the minority with little minority participation, and cases where the minority itself plans measures, which do not contribute to its maintenance, but these are exceptions.

2.2. The maintenance of the world's linguistic diversity

In an interdependent world where there are no monolingual states, presence or lack of language rights, especially linguistic human rights, play today an increasing role in the maintenance or disappearance of the world's languages. If the existence of these rights is a result of both planning and struggle, one has to ask whether new types of language planning and language planners are needed to counteract the destruction of the planet's linguistic diversity.

The most optimistic prognoses of what is happening to the world's languages suggest that around the year 2100 at least 50% of today's close to 7,000 spoken languages[3] may be extinct or very seriously endangered ("moribund" – with elderly speakers only and no children learning them). This estimate, originating with Michael Krauss (1992) is also the one used by UNESCO (see http://portal.unesco.org/culture/en/ev.php-URL_ID=8270&URL_DO=DO_TOPIC&URL_SECTION=201.html or the position paper "Education in a Multilingual World" (UNESCO 2003c); http://unesdoc.unesco.org/images/0012/001297/129728e.pdf).

Pessimistic but still completely realistic estimates claim that as many as 90–95 % of today's spoken languages may be extinct or very seriously endangered in less than a hundred years' time. This is Krauss' estimate today (e.g. 1996, 1997; see also Krauss, Maffi, and Yamamoto 2004). UNESCO's Intangible Cultural Heritage Unit's Ad Hoc Expert Group on Endangered Languages (see UNESCO 2003 a, b, c) uses this more pessimistic figure in their report on "Language Vitality and Endangerment", see http://portal.unesco.org/culture/en/file_download.php/947ee963052abf0293b22e0bfba319cclanguagevitalityendangerment.pdf; http://portal.unesco.org/culture/en/file_download.php/4794680ecb5664addb9af1234a4a1839Language+Vitality+and+Endangerment.pdf.

There may be only 3600 oral languages left as unthreatened languages, transmitted by the parent generation to children. These would probably include most of those languages that today have more than one million speakers, and a few others. Almost all languages to disappear would be indigenous languages, and most of today's indigenous languages would disappear, with the exception of very few that are strong numerically (e.g., Quechua, Aymara, Bodo) and/or have official status (e.g., Maori, some Saami languages).

Still more pessimistic estimates suspect that only those 40–50 languages will remain in which people can, within the next few years, talk to their stove, fridge and coffee pot, i.e. those languages into which Microsoft software, Nokia mobile phone menus, etc., are being translated (Rannut 2003). My new (2005) printer has some instructions in 32 languages, including some fairly small in numbers like Estonian, Latvian and Lithuanian. One could also use the number of languages into which Harry Potter films are being dubbed – Catalan-speaking children in Barcelona, Catalunya, staged a huge demonstration demanding that the films be dubbed into Catalan – and got a promise.

Nobody knows what will happen to the world's Sign languages. There is today no idea of how many Sign languages there are. The 14th edition of the *Ethnologue* lists only 114 Sign languages. Unfortunately there are many errors and gaps in the *Ethnologue* in general, and certainly very large gaps in the listing of Sign languages. There are Deaf people everywhere in the world, and where hearing people have developed spoken languages, Deaf people have developed Sign languages. These are in every respect full languages (see, e.g., Lane 1992; Ladd 2003). The World Federation of the Deaf (www.wfdeaf.org) estimates that there are some 70 million Deaf people in the world. Only in Aotearoa/New Zealand does a Sign language have an official status similar to the other official languages (in this case English and Māori). In a dozen countries Sign languages are mentioned in the constitution.

When the world's linguistic diversity is disappearing at a faster rate than ever before in human history, is this something that is a result of language planning? Have some international or national language planning bodies decided that the world needs fewer languages, and acted on that wish? Is what happens to languages in general something that has been and/or can be rationally planned? And can linguistic human rights participate in supporting the maintenance of languages and thus linguistic diversity? The main issue that this article aims to discuss is to what extent language planning and language rights can contribute in extreme situations of language shift where (spoken or signed) languages cease to be used.

2.3. (Linguistic) Assimilation or integration

Many of the fears that prevent states from guaranteeing LHRs originate from claims that granting LHRs and thus maintaining linguistic diversity will prevent the integration of a state through a common language. A special type of language policy goal, namely linguistic assimilation of minorities, is said to further this integration. The Turkish Constitutions have since Mustafa Kemal's (Atatürk's) times stressed "the indivisible integrity of the state with its territory and nation"; "Language is one of the essential characteristics of a nation. Those who belong to the Turkish nation ought, above all and absolutely, to speak Turkish. [...] Those people who speak another language could, in a difficult situation, collaborate and take action against us with other people who speak other languages" (Kemal 1931).

Turkey still sees any official use of Kurdish as a threat to this unity, as one can see, for instance, from the latest "Amendments to the Law on Foreign Language Education and Teaching" (2002).

The concepts of integration and assimilation need to be defined to see whether a language policy denying LHRs really leads to integration.[4] Assimilation can be defined as: (a) disappearance of distinctive features, i.e., objectively the loss of specific elements of material and non-material culture and subjectively the loss of the feeling of belonging to a particular ethnic group; and (b) simultaneously, objectively, adoption of traits belonging to another culture, which replace those of the former culture, accompanied by the subjective feeling of belonging to the second culture. Integration is formation of a series of common features in an ethnically heterogeneous group. Assimilation is subtractive, whereas integration is additive. In terms of education of indigenous and minority children, these concepts can be defined in the following way. In subtractive teaching, minority children are taught through the medium of a dominant language, which replaces their mother tongue. They learn the dominant language at the cost of the mother tongue. In additive teaching, minority children are taught through the medium of the mother tongue, with good teaching of the dominant language as a second language. Additive teaching makes them high level bilingual or multilingual. They learn other languages in addition to their own language and may learn them all well.

The concepts of subtractive and additive can be used for another definition of assimilation or integration: Assimilation is enforced subtractive "learning" of another (dominant) culture by a (dominated) group. Assimilation means being transferred to another group. Integration is characterised by voluntary mutual additive "learning" of other cultures. Integration means a choice of inclusive group membership(s).

In terms of both these definitions, it is clear that most state attitudes towards indigenous peoples and minorities are still in a phase where assimilation/integration are only discussed in terms of what happens and is envisaged in relation to the indigenous peoples/minorities, whereas very little happens in relation to the dominant population which is not asked or envisaged to change. If real integration rather than assimilation is the goal in both education and language policy in general, what kind of LHRs are needed and can contribute?

When discussing HRs one often comes across several pairs of dichotomies. Here I look at these dichotomies to determine which language rights are necessary so that indigenous peoples and minorities do not need to assimilate but can participate in mutual integration. Some of these dichotomies are as follows:
– Who/what can have rights: languages or individuals/groups?
– Individual versus collective rights
– Negative versus positive rights
– Territorial versus personal rights
– Rights in "hard law" versus "soft law"

3. Language Rights and Linguistic Human Rights

3.1. The concepts of Language Rights and Linguistic Human Rights

The concept of Linguistic Human Rights (LHRs) is very recent and still somewhat unclear. So far, it is not at all clear what should and what should not be considered LHRs; there are lively ongoing debates about the topic.[5] All the rights that people or collectivities have in relation to languages (their own or others) are linguistic rights or language rights (LRs). These two terms are mostly used as synonyms. Some researchers regard linguistic rights as a somewhat broader concept than language rights. In this case they are often discussing rights not only to various languages but also to varieties within the "language" label, e.g. regional, gender-based or class-based varieties. Language rights have been discussed for centuries, and the first multilateral treaties about language rights are from the 1880s (see May 2001; Skutnabb-Kangas and Phillipson 1994; Skutnabb-Kangas 1997; Thornberry 1997 and de Varennes 1996 for overviews). Our present human rights are from the period after the Second World War but there were many human rights treaties already under the League of Nations after the First World War.

LHRs combine language rights (LRs) with human rights (HRs). LHRs are those (and only those) LRs, which, firstly, are necessary to satisfy people's basic needs (including the need to live a dignified life), and which, secondly, therefore are so fundamental that no state (or individual or group) is supposed to violate them. Some basic rights prohibit discrimination on the basis of language (negative rights); others ensure equal treatment to languages, individuals or language groups (positive rights). Most LHRs are negative rights (see below).

There are many LRs which are not LHRs. It would, for instance, be nice if everybody could, even in civil court cases, have a judge and witnesses who speak (or sign) this person's language, regardless of how few users the language has. Today, it is mostly in criminal cases only that one has any linguistic *human* rights, namely the right to be informed of the charge against oneself in a language that one understands (i.e., not necessarily the mother tongue). In all other court contexts, people may or may not have a *language* right, depending on the country and language; in the best cases, interpreters paid for by the state are used. Likewise, it would be nice if the following demands were to be met:

> All language communities are entitled to have at their disposal all the human and material resources necessary to ensure that their language is present to the extent they desire at all levels of education within their territory: properly trained teachers, appropriate teaching methods, text books, finance, buildings and equipment, traditional and innovative technology.

The quote comes from Article 25 of the 1996 Draft of the Universal Declaration of Linguistic Rights, a document initiated by the International PEN Club and the Catalonian UNESCO Committee.[6] But such demands are completely unrealistic and cannot be considered part of LHRs. At this moment, only a few dozen language communities in the world have these kinds of rights.

3.2.   Who or what can have rights? Languages or individuals and collectivities?

Languages themselves may have rights to be used, developed and maintained. Alternatively, people or collectivities of people (individuals, groups, peoples, organisations, or states) may have rights to use, develop and maintain languages or duties to enable the use, development or maintenance of them. Two of the most important European LRs documents, from the Council of Europe, can be seen as examples of these two types of right. The *European Charter on Regional or Minority Languages* (hereafter the *European Charter*), grants rights to languages, not speakers of the languages concerned.[7] The *Framework Convention on the Protection of National Minorities* (hereafter the *Framework Convention*), on the other hand, grants rights to (national) minorities, i.e. groups.[8] Once a state has both signed (promised to start the process which enables it to ratify them) and ratified one of these human rights instruments (changed their laws and regulations and put processes in place that enables them to fulfill the obligations that they have promised to undertake), these are binding for the state. States usually have a duty to report at specified intervals how they have acted to guarantee the rights, and there is also normally some kind of a monitoring body which scrutinises the reports and gives feedback and guidance to the states.

3.3. Individual versus collective rights

3.3.1. Individual rights

An individual from a certain group or with specific characteristics in a specific country may, for instance, have the right to use her or his mother tongue in various contexts, e.g. in dealing with authorities, local, regional or state-wide, or in writing orally or signing it, or all of these. However, the authorities do not necessarily need to reply in the same language. For legal purposes the mother tongue is often defined in a strict way, as the first language that a person learned, and still speaks, and with which s/he identifies. A definition often used in situations where forced assimilation of indigenous peoples has made the older generation speak the dominant language to their children, is sometimes less strict: A mother tongue, with LRs connected to it, is defined as a language which is, or has been, the first language of the individual her/himself, or of (one of) the parents or grandparents. In most cases both a degree of competence and/or use of the language is demanded, together with identification; in some (few) cases identification with the language is enough.

Individuals may also have rights in relation to other languages than their mother tongue/first language. Mostly these rights relate to a dominant/official/national language in the country. Some people have also started to demand that access to an international language, in most cases English, should be seen as a language right.

3.3.2. Collective rights

Since many human rights instruments, especially the first ones to emerge after the Second World War, are concerned with rights of individuals (like the United Nations *Universal Declaration of Human Rights*, or the UN *Convention on the*

Rights of the Child (CRC, 1989),[9] collective rights of various groups have re-emerged later and few of these are language-related. The human rights regime of the League of Nations between the two World Wars contained many collective rights; in principle most minority rights should be collective rights (see Thornberry and Gibbons 1997). In the United Nations regime after 1945, it was claimed that no collective rights were necessary since every person was protected as an individual, by individual rights. Collectivities like "minorities" were by many negotiators (e.g., the USA human rights negotiator Eleanor Roosevelt) seen as "a European problem", meaning they were not seen as universal. Somewhat simplified, Western countries have largely opposed collective rights and African countries have supported many of them, while Asian countries have stood so divided that the issue has been one of the major hurdles preventing an acceptance of regional Asian human rights instruments. The *European Charter* and the *Framework Convention* are regional, not universal instruments. So are the Council of Europe's 1950 *Convention on Human Rights and Fundamental Freedoms* and the corresponding African and American instruments: *The African Charter on Human and Peoples' Rights* 1981 (see www.achpr.org/) and the *American Convention on Human Rights* 1969 (see www.wcl.american.edu/pub/humright/digest/index.html).

Some important language-related instruments try to combine individual and collective rights, by using "persons belonging to a minority" or a similar phrase. This is what, for instance, Article 27 of the UN *International Covenant on Civil and Political Rights* uses. Article 27 is still the most far-reaching Article in (binding) human rights law granting linguistic rights:

> In those states in which ethnic, religious or linguistic minorities exist, persons belonging to such minorities shall not be denied the right, in community with other members of their group, to enjoy their own culture, to profess and practise their own religion, or to use their own language.

Many international organisations and most states have a language policy which spells out the official languages of the organisation or state and, by implication, the LRs of the people, groups, and states dealing with, and working within, that entity. The United Nations have six official languages, the Council of Europe only two. Several times the European Union has increased the number of its official languages, such that after its latest expansion, in January 2007, the Union now (2007) has 23 official languages; all official documents have to be made available in all of these. Many organisations also have working languages; their number may be more restricted. A number of states have only one official (or state) language; most have two or more (English is *an* official language in more than 70 states; see Skutnabb-Kangas 2000). South Africa has 11 official languages, India 24. In addition, many states specify one or several national, additional, link, or national heritage languages in their constitutions; in most cases, speakers of these have fewer rights than speakers of the official languages have (see de Varennes 1996).

3.3.3. What is a minority?

The concept of "minority" is extremely important when considering LHRs. There are no legally accepted universal definitions of what a minority is, even if the issue has been discussed extensively (e.g. Andrýsek 1989; Capotorti 1979; see also Extra and Gorter, this vol.). Most definitions are fairly similar, though, and resemble the definition below (from Skutnabb-Kangas and Phillipson 1994: 107, Note 2):

> A group which is smaller in number than the rest of the population of a State, whose members have ethnic, religious or linguistic features different from those of the rest of the population, and are guided, if only implicitly, by the will to safeguard their culture, traditions, religion or language.
> Any group coming within the terms of this definition shall be treated as an ethnic, religious or linguistic minority. To belong to a minority shall be a matter of individual choice.

If a group claims that they are a national minority and an individual claims that s/he belongs to this national minority, the State may claim that such a national linguistic minority does not exist; then there is a conflict. The State may refuse to grant the minority person and/or group rights, which it has accorded or might accord to national minorities. In many definitions of minority, minority rights thus become conditional on the acceptance by the State of the existence of a minority in the first place. According to my definition of a minority (see above), minority status does *not* depend on the acceptance of the State, but is either objectively ("coming within the terms of this definition") or subjectively verifiable ("a matter of individual choice"), or both. This interpretation was confirmed by the UN Human Rights Committee in 1994. They reinterpreted Article 27 above in a General Comment of 6 April 1994 (UN Doc. CCPR/C/21/Rev.1/Add.5, 1994).

Until the reinterpretation, the Article was mostly interpreted as
- excluding (im)migrants (who were not earlier seen as minorities);
- excluding groups (even if they are citizens) which were not recognised as minorities by the State;
- only conferring some protection against discrimination (i.e. "negative rights") but not a positive right to maintain or even use one's language;
- not imposing any obligations on the States.

The UN Human Rights Committee saw the Article as
- protecting all individuals on the State's territory or under its jurisdiction (i.e. also immigrants and refugees), irrespective of whether they belong to the minorities specified in the Article or not;

- stating that the existence of a minority does not depend on a decision by the State but requires to be established by objective criteria;
- recognising the existence of a "right";
- imposing positive obligations on the States.

For Deaf people this means that various countries minimally have to see the Deaf as a (linguistic) minority, protected by Article 27. Likewise, the reinterpretation means that minorities, including the Deaf, are supposed to have positive language rights, not only the negative right of protection against discrimination. The states where Deaf live, i.e. all states in the world, thus do have positive obligations towards the Deaf as a linguistic minority. In addition, the Deaf can of course also be seen as a group with a handicap, if they so choose, but whether they choose this or not has no consequences for their minority status: They *are* national linguistic minorities.

Numbers matter. A group has to have a certain size in order to have language-related rights. It often depends on how many individuals there are in the unit under consideration (country, area, region, municipality, etc.) whether individuals (speakers or signers) belonging to that group have any LRs. Two of the most important European LRs documents use group size as a criterion, but do not in any way define it. The *European Charter*, and the *Framework Convention* use formulations such as "in substantial numbers" or "pupils who so wish in a number considered sufficient" or "if the number of users of a regional or minority language justifies it". It is obviously necessary to limit the size, to adjust to various contexts, also for economic reasons, but it is also possible for reluctant states to use lack of what states claim are "sufficient" numbers as a legitimation for lack of political will.

For proper integration, both individual and collective rights are thus necessary. One or the other type alone is not sufficient. It is not a question of either/or, but both/and.

3.4. Negative versus positive rights

Negative rights have been defined by Max van der Stoel (1999: 8) as "the right to non-discrimination in the enjoyment of human rights", whereas positive rights have to do with "the right to the maintenance and development of identity through the freedom to practise or use those special and unique aspects of their minority life – typically culture, religion, and language". Negative rights must:

> [...] ensure that minorities receive all of the other protections without regard to their ethnic, national, or religious status; they thus enjoy a number of linguistic rights that all persons in the state enjoy, such as freedom of expression and the right in criminal proceedings to be informed of the charge against them in a language they understand, if necessary through an interpreter provided free of charge.
> (van der Stoel 1999: 8)

Positive rights are those

> [...] encompassing affirmative obligations beyond non-discrimination [...] include a number of rights pertinent to minorities simply by virtue of their minority status, such as the right to use their language. This pillar is necessary because a pure non-discrimination norm could have the effect of forcing people belonging to minorities to adhere to a majority language, effectively denying them their rights to identity. (van der Stoel 1999: 8–9)

Many political scientists seem to think that it is only (large) national minorities that should have their languages promoted by the state, i.e. have positive rights, whereas small national minorities and small indigenous peoples and, especially, immigrant minorities, cannot expect more than toleration-oriented negative rights. On the other hand, toleration and non-discrimination, understood in liberal terms of the state not interfering on behalf of a group's special characteristics (like religion), does not work in relation to language. A state has to choose some language(s) as the language(s) of administration, courts, education, possibly the media, etc., and this necessarily privileges some language(s) (see Rubio-Marín 2003). The claim is that, for proper integration, positive *promotion-oriented rights* are necessary. Negative *toleration-oriented rights* are not sufficient and may lead to forced assimilation.

3.5.   Personal versus territorial rights

If an individual can use the right to all mother tongue medium services anywhere in her or his country, a *principle of personality* applies. Usually, only members of large groups with excellent protection have this kind of right. In most cases, it is restricted to the dominant language speakers in a country. Often such speakers are not even aware of how precious these rights are, and how unusual it is to possess such rights for any of the world's linguistic minorities (or even some linguistic majorities; e.g., in several African countries, the old colonial languages still have more rights than the indigenous African languages have).

If, on the other hand, LRs are connected to a specific region, a *principle of territoriality* is applied. Such is the case in Switzerland. If you live in a certain territory, e.g., a "German" or "Italian" canton in Switzerland, you have a right to services in that language only, regardless of what your mother tongue is. French or Romansch speakers can use their respective languages only in certain other cantons (where German speakers do not have the right to use German, or Italian speakers Italian). That means in practice that if Italian-speaking Swiss parents want their children to be educated through the medium of Italian, they have to move to the only canton (Tessin) where this is a right. Finland combines both principles in its language laws.

The claim is that for proper integration, both territorial and personal rights are necessary. Territorial rights serve well only minorities who have a traditional territory and live within its borders. Personal rights (you have a right in your personal capacity, regardless of where you live) are more important for the Deaf, the Roma, immigrant minorities and other non-territorial minorities. They are also vital for dispersed people in diaspora outside the group's territory: Oslo, the capital of Norway, has the largest Saami population in Norway but is not part of the Saami administrative area; therefore most Saami children in Oslo do not get mother tongue medium education whereas they would in the northern parts of Norway which are part of the "Saami territory".

3.6. Rights in "hard law" versus "soft law"

Strictly speaking, only traditional "hardlaw" rights or binding rights (often called Conventions, Covenants, Charters or Treaties), coded in laws or regulations of various kinds, and binding on the state which has ratified them, count as rights. They often include a monitoring body and a complaint procedure. In most cases, binding rights also include a duty-holder who has to see to it that the rights can be enjoyed by the beneficiaries. A state or a regional authority can, for instance, have the duty to organise education through the medium of a certain language for certain individuals or groups (beneficiaries) in a specific place. In addition to these "rights proper", there are many "soft law" rights, i.e. non-binding recommendations, declarations, and other intentions and wishes about LRs, including various Supreme court decisions which are nevertheless not binding. These can in time, for instance through litigation, start to function as precedents that courts need to be familiar with and that they often follow, and eventually they can be included in more binding rights. There are also other ways of moving towards more binding rules. An example is UNESCO's *Universal Declaration on Cultural Diversity* (2001), see http://www.cesmap.it/ifrao/unescode.htm which is being developed into a *Treaty on Cultural Diversity*; the negotiations are underway.

The claim is that for proper integration, both traditional "hard law" rights and "soft law" rights are necessary. Most hard law instruments reflect the phases directly after the Second World War, or the main decolonisation phase. They do not reflect present postcolonial challenges.

3.7. LHR hierarchies

Various groups can be placed in a hierarchical order relative to how good their human rights protection is. The descending order is as follows:

(1) Linguistic majorities/dominant language speakers vs minority/dominated language speakers

- National (autochthonous) minorities
- Indigenous peoples
- Immigrant minorities
- Refugee minorities

(2) Speakers of oral languages vs users of Sign languages

Speakers of oral languages have many more rights than users of Sign languages (even if users of Sign languages have some rights as a handicap group). An example has already been mentioned: No state has ratified the *European Charter* for any Sign languages, only spoken languages, even if the definitions of "regional or minority languages" for the purposes of the Charter would have allowed it. This is fatal; the *Charter* might in its Educational Article 8 grant a group at least some educational rights.

All LHRs are extremely important for indigenous peoples and minorities. The next section concentrates on educational LHRs. These are central for the reproduction of a minority as a minority, and to avoid forced assimilation and linguistic genocide. However, these rights, including especially the unconditional right to mother tongue medium education, are still mainly absent today.

4. Linguistic human rights in education

Language is one of the most important human characteristics on the basis of which people are not supposed to be discriminated against. Others are gender, "race" and religion. Still, language is treated in a less generous manner in human rights instruments than are other important human characteristics (see Skutnabb-Kangas 1997 and 2000 for an overview of these rights). Language often disappears in the educational paragraphs of binding HRs instruments. One example: The paragraph on education (26) in the *Universal Declaration of Human Rights* (1948) http://www.un.org/Overview/rights.html does not refer to language at all. The main thrust of the paragraph is to ensure free universal education. Even this right is violated in dozens of countries, as the former United Nations Special Rapporteur on the Right to Education, human rights lawyer Katarina Tomaševski, states in many of her reports (see http://www.right-to-education.org/content/). There are references to the "full development of the human personality" and the right of parents to "choose the kind of education that shall be given to their children", but this does not include the right to choose the language in which this education is given (but see Magga et al. 2004, an expert paper for the United Nations Permanent Forum on Indigenous Issues). Educational linguistic human rights, especially the right to mother tongue medium education, are among the most important rights for any minority. Without them, a minority whose children attend school usually cannot reproduce itself as a minority. It cannot integrate with the majority but is forced to assimilate into it.

If language is present in binding educational clauses of human rights instruments, the clauses have more opt-outs, modifications, alternatives, etc. than other Articles of such instruments have. One example is the *UN Declaration on the Rights of Persons Belonging to National or Ethnic, Religious and Linguistic Minorities* (1992), where the general identity-oriented clauses 1.1 and 1.2 have many obligating, positive measures whereas the education clause 4.3 is full of opt-outs (emphases added: *"obligating"* and positive measures in *italics*, **"opt-outs"** in **bold**):

> 1.1 States *shall protect* the existence and the national or ethnic, cultural, religious and linguistic identity of minorities within their respective territories, and *shall encourage* conditions for the *promotion* of that identity.
> 1.2 States *shall adopt* appropriate legislative *and other* measures *to achieve those ends.*
> 4.3 States **should** take **appropriate** measures so that, **wherever possible**, persons belonging to minorities have **adequate** opportunities to learn their mother tongue **or** to have instruction in their mother tongue.

The Council of Europe's *Framework Convention* and the *European Charter* also have many of these modifications, alternatives, and opt-outs. The Framework Convention's education Article reads as follows (emphases added):

> In areas inhabited by persons belonging to national minorities traditionally or in substantial numbers, *if there is sufficient demand*, the parties shall *endeavour* to ensure, *as far as possible* and *within the framework of their education systems*, that persons belonging to those minorities have *adequate* opportunities for being taught in the minority language *or* for receiving instruction in this language.

Of course there are real problems in writing binding formulations that are sensitive to local conditions. Still, it is clear that the opt-outs and alternatives ("claw-backs") in the *Charter* and the *Convention* permit reluctant states to meet the requirements in a minimalist way, something they can legitimate by claiming that a provision was not "possible" or "appropriate", or that numbers were not "sufficient" or did not "justify" a provision, or that it "allowed" the minority to organise teaching of their language as a subject, at their own cost. The Articles covering medium of education are so heavily qualified that the minority is completely at the mercy of the state. Other regions of the world have even fewer general HRs instruments than Europe pertaining specifically to minority languages or speakers of minority languages, even if a few specific named languages may have extensive rights.

Still, the human rights system should protect people in the globalisation process, rather than giving the market forces free range. Human rights, especially economic and social rights, are, according to Tomaševski (1996: 104), supposed to act as *correctives to the free market*. She claims that "The purpose of international human rights law is [...] to overrule the law of supply and demand and remove price tags from people and from necessities for their survival". These necessities for survival thus include not only basic food and housing (which would come under economic and social rights), but also basics for the sustenance of a dignified life, including basic civil, political *and cultural* rights. It should, therefore, be in accordance with the spirit of human rights to grant people full linguistic human rights. Without binding educational linguistic human rights, most minorities have to accept "subtractive" education through the medium of a dominant/majority language. In subtractive language learning, a new (dominant/majority) language is learned at the cost of the mother tongue which is displaced, leading to diglossia, and often to the replacement of the mother tongue. (Diglossia means a situation with functional differentiation of languages, e.g., one at home and in the neighbourhood, another for use at school and with authorities.) Assimilationist, subtractive education of indigenous and minority children is genocidal. Linguistic genocide is one of the still controversial issues.

5. Controversial issues

5.1. Linguistic genocide

When people hear the term "genocide" about languages and education, they often claim that the term is too strong – it should only be used of physical killing. There have been many attempts to censor discussions about linguistic genocide, to accuse researchers using it of being emotional not scientific, and to blame the messenger rather than examining the message. In Dunbar et al. (2005), an Expert paper written for the United Nations, we present a multidisciplinary (but mainly legal) argumentation showing that indigenous (and minority) education in fact fulfils the criteria set out in The *UN International Convention on the Prevention and Punishment of the Crime of Genocide* ("the Genocide Convention").[10] The Convention has five definitions of genocide. Three of them are about physical or biological killing, but the remaining two fit most of today's (and earlier) indigenous and minority education:

Article 2(b) *Causing serious bodily or mental harm to members of the group*;
Article 2(e) *Forcibly transferring children of the group to another group.*

Educational systems and mass media are (the most) important direct agents in linguistic (and cultural) genocide. Behind them are the world's economic, techno-military, social and political systems. A few examples from various studies follow – all of them show either the forcible transfer of children from a linguistic group to another linguistic group, or serious mental harm caused to children through submersion education.

Pirjo Janulf (1998) showed in a longitudinal study that of those Finnish immigrant minority members in Sweden who had had Swedish-medium education, not one spoke any Finnish to their own children. Even if they themselves might not have forgotten their Finnish completely, their children were certainly forcibly transferred to the majority group linguistically.

Edward Williams's (1998) study from Zambia and Malawi, with 1,500 students in grades 1–7 showed that large numbers of Zambian pupils (who had all their education in English) "have very weak or zero reading competence in two languages" (1998: 62). The Malawi children (taught in local languages during the first 4 years, with English as a subject) had slightly better test results in the English language than the Zambian students. Williams's conclusion is: "There is a clear risk that the policy of using English as a vehicular language may contribute to stunting, rather than promoting, academic and cognitive growth" (1998: 63–64). This fits the UN genocide definition of "causing mental harm".

Anne Lowell and Brian Devlin's (1999) article describing the "Miscommunication between Aboriginal students and their non-Aboriginal teachers in a bilingual school", clearly demonstrated that "even by late primary school, children often did not comprehend classroom instructions in English" (Lowell and Devlin 1999: 137). Communication breakdowns occurred frequently between children and their non-Aboriginal teachers (138), with the result that "the extent of miscommunication severely inhibited the children's education when English was the language of instruction and interaction" (137). They conclude that "the use of a language of instruction in which the children do not have sufficient competence is the greatest barrier to successful classroom learning for Aboriginal Children" (156).

Katherine Zozula and Simon Ford's (1985) report "Keewatin perspective on bilingual education" tells about Canadian Inuit "students who are neither fluent nor literate in either language" and presents statistics showing that the students "end up at only Grade 4 level of achievement after 9 years of [English-medium] schooling".[11] The Canadian Royal Commission on Aboriginal Peoples Report (1996) notes that "submersion strategies which neither respect the child's first language nor help them gain fluency in the second language may result in impaired fluency in both languages". In March 1998 the Canadian Nunavut Language Policy Conference stated that "in some individuals, neither language is firmly anchored". Mick Mallon and Alexina Kublu (1998) claim that "a significant number of young people are not fully fluent in their languages", and many students "remain apathetic, often with minimal skills in both languages". In a Canadian report, Kitikmeot (1998) struggles to prevent the death of Inuktitut, and shows that "teenagers cannot converse fluently with their grandparents".

Many studies on Deaf students (e.g., Branson and Miller 2002; Jokinen 2000; Ladd 2003; Lane 1992) show that assimilationist submersion education where Deaf students are taught orally only and Sign languages have no place in the curriculum, often causes mental harm, including serious prevention or delay of cognitive growth.

There are hundreds of similar studies. In sum, subtractive teaching prevents students from attaining profound literacy and from gaining the knowledge and skills that would correspond to their innate capacities and would be needed for socio-economic mobility and democratic participation. It wastes resources and perpetuates poverty. According to Nobel Prize laureate Amartya Sen (e.g. Sen 1985), poverty is not only about economic conditions and growth; expansion of human capabilities is a more basic locus of poverty and more basic objective of development. Dominant-language medium education for indigenous children often curtails the development of the children's capabilities (Misra and Mohanty 2000a, b; Mohanty 2000). Thus it perpetuates poverty, may cause serious mental harm, and transfers children to another linguistic group through enforced language shift (see Dunbar et al. 2005 for references and arguments). Indigenous and minority students (and their parents and communities) need LHRs as one of the necessary (but not sufficient) measures to stop linguistic genocide.

5.2. The language death paradigm and the language murder or linguistic genocide paradigms

In studying causes for the disappearance of languages two explanatory paradigms can be found: language death and language murder or linguistic genocide. The first one assumes that languages just die naturally, like everything in nature – they arise, blossom, wither and disappear. This is the "(natural) death" paradigm. The other paradigm asserts that languages do not just disappear naturally. Languages do not "commit suicide". In most cases, speakers do not leave them voluntarily, for instrumental reasons, and for their own good. Languages are "murdered". Most disappearing languages are victims of linguistic genocide. This latter paradigm is the one I see as the likely one. One of the differences between them from an analytical point of view is also that nothing can be done about languages disappearing if one accepts that it is natural and inevitable – this reasoning represents a misunderstood and misguided Darwinian "survival of the fittest" (see Harmon 2002 and Skutnabb-Kangas 2002 for a refutation). This is partly because in this paradigm there is no agent causing the disappearance of languages; the only ones that can be blamed are the speakers themselves (and they have profited from language shift). In the genocide paradigm one can analyse agency, the forces behind the disappearance of languages, and one may be able to do something about it.

Obviously the structural and ideological direct and indirect agents behind the killing of languages are the same social, economic and political techno-military forces that promote corporate globalisation. But some of the most important direct agents confronted by most people are the educational systems and the media. These are both indirectly and directly homogenising societies linguistically and culturally. And ideologically they are, through their consent-manufacturing capacities (Herman and Chomsky 1988), making people accept the homogenising processes as somehow necessary and even natural (see McMurtry's 2002 mind-blowing, sophisticated analysis of this; see also McMurtry 1999).

As many researchers have noted, after Joshua Fishman (1991), schools can in a couple of generations kill languages which had survived for centuries, even millennia, when their speakers were not exposed to formal education of the present-day type. Schools can today participate in committing linguistic genocide through their choice of the medium of formal education – and they do.

5.3.   Is linguistic diversity desirable? Do minorities also want it?

Linguistic diversity seems to many researchers (not to speak of politicians, or "ordinary people") to be messy. Even respected scholars, like political theorists Will Kymlicka and Alan Patten, seem to accept that things are "complicated by linguistic diversity" (Patten and Kymlicka 2003: 3) or that linguistic diversity is "one of the most important obstacles to building a stronger sense of European citizenship" or that linguistic diversity is a "problem" (2003: 9). These are not just unfortunate slips: Kymlicka and Patten (2003) repeat these prejudices about linguistic diversity as an obstacle and add new ones (see later). Labelling linguistic diversity as a complication, obstacle or problem is denying and lamenting facts – just like claiming that having two legs and five fingers is more complicated than having one. With very few exceptions, the world's countries are multilingual, and, in Debi Pattanayak's words: "One language is an impractical proposition for a multilingual country" (1988: 382). Linguistic diversity is the normal state of life on our planet. To many researchers the complication/obstacle/problem is not linguistic diversity but attitudes that I have discussed as monolingual reductionism (e.g., Skutnabb-Kangas 2000: 238–248).

Other misconceptions that abound even among solid scholars are that minorities are somehow reluctant ("unable or unwilling", Kymlicka and Patten 2003. 12) to learn the majority/dominant language, and that they become ghettoised, so that "even the second and third generations of immigrant groups will live and work predominantly in their ancestral language, with only minimal or non-existent command of the state language" (6). It seems that not forcing them to "linguistic integration" (which seems to mean assimilation, with "standardized public education in a common language") "serves to separate citizens into distinct and mutually antagonistic groups" (12). Thus granting minorities a right to mother tongue medium education would according to this type of theorising be a veritable disaster, both to the minorities themselves and to the whole society.

These claims are in most cases not true, but they have been part of the assimilationist myths leading to linguistic and cultural genocide instead of LHRs. Educational LHRs include both the right to have the basic education mainly through the medium of the mother tongue, and the right to learn the official/ dominant language well. These two are not contradictory, quite the opposite. In additive learning situations, high levels of majority language skills are added to high levels of mother tongue skills. Arlene Stairs's (1994; see Note 11) study shows that "in schools which support initial learning of Inuttitut, and whose Grade 3 and Grade 4 pupils are strong writers in Inuttitut, the results in written English are also the highest".[12] The Alaska Yu'piq teacher Nancy Sharp (1994; see Note 11) compares: when Yu'piq children are taught through the medium of English, they are treated by "White" teachers as handicapped, and they do not achieve; when they are taught through the medium of Yu'piq, they are "excellent writers, smart happy students". Many books show in detail how additive teaching that respects educational and other LHRs can be organised. There is also some support in several soft law documents. *The Hague Recommendations Regarding the Education Rights of National Minorities* (1996) from OSCE's High Commissioner on National Minorities (www.osce.org/hcnm/) contain the following: For minorities, mother tongue medium education is recommended at all levels, also in secondary education. This includes bilingual teachers in the dominant language as a second language (Art. 11–13). The Explanatory Note (p. 5) has the following to say about submersion education:

> [S]ubmersion-type approaches whereby the curriculum is taught exclusively through the medium of the State language and minority children are entirely integrated into classes with children of the majority are not in line with international standards.

This means that most indigenous and minority education – which is submersion – is not in line with international human rights standards.

Some politicians might agree with this, and many claim that they want to organise better education. Some start acknowledging that full LHRs in education, including mother tongue medium education for indigenous and minority children, can lead to profound literacy, creativity, and high levels of multilingualism for the student, a maintenance of the languages, and also, because of the correlational and causal link between biodiversity and linguistic diversity (see www.terralingua.org; Skutnabb-Kangas, Maffi, and Harmon 2003), to better possibilities for maintaining biodiversity and healthy ecosystems. But the counterargument usually is that maintenance of all or most of the world's languages cannot be possible, or economically viable. A good example here is

Papua New Guinea, a fairly small country, with a population of around 5 million. It has the highest number of languages in the world, i.e. over 850. According to David Klaus from the World Bank (2003), as of 2002, 470 languages are used as the media of education in preschool and the first two grades. Some of the results are as follows: Children become literate more quickly and easily. They learn English more quickly and easily than their siblings did under the old English-medium system. Children, including girls, stay in school. Grade 6 exams in the 3 provinces that started mother tongue medium teaching in 1993 were much higher than in provinces which still teach through the medium of English from Day One. It seems perfectly possible to organise education so that it does not participate in committing linguistic genocide.

The final question then is: To what extent has applied linguistics contributed to possible solutions, to language planning that supports the maintenance of linguistic diversity and works for LHRs as a necessary prerequisite for not only preventing linguistic genocide but also for supporting the diversity of knowledges, ideas, identities and ways of conceptualising the world that are encoded in the various languages and are also a result of the interaction of their speakers?

6. The contribution of applied linguistics: Future perspectives

The whole field of LHRs is only starting to develop, and there are many theoretical, methodological, empirical and action-oriented questions and debates. This is a healthy sign. Some of the debates, especially within the field of applied linguistics, seem to be less constructive and more narrow than necessary, though. One of the difficulties is that the issue is of necessity multidisciplinary. Often theoretical and applied linguists, the language specialists and language planners, know little about legal matters and power relations. Likewise, often human rights lawyers know little about language, at least initially. Some sociolinguists, sociologists, political scientists, often even educationists, etc., may be more knowledgeable about the power relations necessarily involved in all language policy matters, but are still too little informed about human rights law and sometimes even languages. Negative debates ensue when instrumentalists claim that those interested in the expressive aspects exclude the more instrumental communication-oriented aspects (for instance unequal class- or gender-based access to formal language or to international languages). The same debates have been fought over both integration of minorities (are they more interested in their languages or in jobs?) and over indigenous claims (identity or autonomy/land rights) in the 1960s and 1970s. Most groups are interested in both types of rights, expressive and instrumental, and often one is a prerequisite for the other, with both being alternately causal and dependent variables. Many of us work with both aspects, and see them as complementary, not mutually exclusive.

Some researchers (often people whose own languages have never been threatened) have difficulty seeing that identities based on or including languages can be vital for many groups – they see anything that centres on language as reifying and essentialising language(s) (e.g. many articles in Freeland and Patrick 2004; see Skutnabb-Kangas 2002, 2005, for some refutations). The relationship between language, culture and land, is seen by many Western researchers as not only romanticising but also limiting in several ways, creating or reinforcing spacially, linguistically and socio-economically inhibiting identities and situations, tying people to monolingualism, monoculturalism, fixed places and static and low socio-economic conditions (e.g. Blommaert 2004: 58–59). Manu Metekingi,[13] a Maori man from the Whanganui iwi (tribe), says the following in a film shown at the Whanganui Iwi Exhibition, at Te Papa Tongarewa Museum of New Zealand, Wellington, 29 November 2003 – May 2006:[14]

> As long as we have the language, we have the culture.
> As long as we have the culture, we can hold on to the land.

Has the LHRs approach "delivered", i.e. can one see results? Do people have more LHRs and are languages being maintained because of this work? In François Grin's analysis (that I agree with), "the discourse of rights can only ever make up but a small part of diversity management" (2003: 181). Grin asks for "a shift of emphasis away from the intrinsically normative discourse of rights to the positive approach of policy analysis and policy evaluation" (ibid.). In my view, we need both. Thus there is a need to properly understand the limitations of the role that LHRs can play – and also the possibilities. This understanding has been in short supply among the critics (see also Grin, this vol.).

As with any new areas of research and policy, also a linguistic human rights approach has first had to show its legitimacy and usefulness. It is clear that the fact that linguistic rights now are more or less accepted as part of human rights, even by human rights lawyers (see, e.g., de Varennes 1996, 1999, 2000, 2003; Thornberry 1997; Thornberry and Gibbons 1997; see also http://www.unesco.org/most/ln2int.htm for a list), is a major achievement. This now gives recourse to the whole human rights apparatus where next to nothing had happened with, for instance, educational language rights since the famous decades old "Belgian linguistic case" (1968) where parents were judged as not having any right to choose the medium of education for their children (www.arts.uwaterloo.ca/MINELRES/coe/court/Belglin.htm). Today, things are happening, as several recent language or education-related instruments show (e.g. OSCE's *Hague Recommendations* and both Council of Europe's regional instruments mentioned above).

Secondly, more and more indigenous peoples and minorities all over the world are now aware of the concept of LHRs, and they are increasingly starting to demand these rights, often very vocally (I could fill a whole book just with listing these demands from various parts of the world). The awareness that (historical and present-day) non-supply or restricted supply has raised, has found expression in channelling the anger into demands for various aspects of LHRs, most importantly educational LHRs where additive mother tongue medium education with the resulting high levels of multilingualism and good school achievement can represent both expressive and instrumental language claims, both individual and collective rights. The Expert papers written for the United Nations Permanent Forum on Indigenous Issues (Magga et al. 2004; Dunbar et al. 2005) reflect this. The awareness has also started to penetrate schools, even if this is still in its infancy in many parts of the world. Linguists, sociolinguists, language teacher organisations and conferences are increasingly passing resolutions and recommendations, which are couched in LHRs terms (my collection of these counts hundreds, and I am probably aware of only a very small fraction). And some of them do lead to action.

And thirdly, even if many of the LHRs granted are still on paper only (an accusation in, e.g., Stroud and Heugh 2003), the number of cases where they are being actually implemented is growing day by day. Thus claiming that the "LHRs movement" has "not delivered" (e.g. Stroud 2001) is based either on several types of ignorance (including ignorance about the place of LHRs in diversity management, as described above) or on completely unrealistic expectations of the relationship between research and politics, or on researchers not knowing enough about the struggles outside the universities, and the results achieved. More networking with indigenous peoples and minorities might enlighten some of those whose time is spent on theorising only.

Likewise, the criticism of the theoretical basis and concepts used when discussing LHRs is an example of how difficult it is to appreciate the complexities in multidisciplinary theory building. If certain concepts come from, say, international law, it is not terribly scholarly to criticise them for not being political theory or SLA concepts, without knowing international law and the prerequisites for how and why those concepts have been developed and why they are used the way they are. In multidisciplinary theory, there has to be give and take, analysis and criticism and further development, on the basis of knowing at least the basics of the disciplines involved. This has unfortunately not seemed to be the case with some very vocal critics. There have been, as François Grin so nicely describes it,

> [...] self-referential families of discourses. The degree of interconnection between them, despite an a priori community of interests, remains limited. [...] In practice, this situation means that discussions on language and minority rights often take place in discrete spheres, in which authors may be tempted to reinvent the wheel, at great cost in terms of time – and corresponding limitations to the relevance of some of their results.
> (Grin 2003: 173)

And, one might add, delaying badly needed policies and causing a lot of harm to indigenous peoples and minorities. They will go on with the struggles, even without the support of applied linguistics – but some applied linguists might want to participate, through their language planning activities, in getting most of the world's languages up to the uppermost left quadrant in Table 3 and thus also making the words of the Maliseet Honour Code true. The Code is written by Imelda Perley, Maliseet from Manitoba (quoted in Kirkness 2002: 23):

> Grandmothers and Grandfathers
> Thank you for our language
> that you have saved for us.
> It is now our turn to save it
> for the ones who are not yet born.
>
> May that be the truth

Notes

1. See John Milloy's devastating (1999) book "A National Crime", for a description of Canada's residential school policy 1879 to 1986.
2. For Kurdish, see Skutnabb-Kangas and Bucak 1994; Skutnabb-Kangas 2002, 2005; for linguistic genocide in education, see Skutnabb-Kangas 2000; Magga et al. 2004; Dunbar et al. 2005. For the 2002 reform package, see, for example, Prime Ministry General Secretariat for European Union Affairs, Analytical Notes on Constitutional Amendments, http://www.abgs.gov.tr/abportal/uploads/files/Analytical%20Note%20on%20Constitutional%20Amendments%20.doc. See also 2002 Regular Report on Turkey's Progress Towards Accession, {COM(2002) 700 final}, SEC(2002) 1412, Brussels, 9. 10. 2002, p. 41–42, www.deltur.cec.eu.int/english/e-gregular 2002.html; http://www.deltur.cec.eu.int/english/main-e.html.
3. The *Ethnologue,* http://www.sil.org/ethnologue/, still the most complete total listing of the world's spoken languages, lists in its 15th edition (2005) 41,806 entries to the names that are associated with the 6,809 languages (see Skutnabb-Kangas, 2000: ch. 1, for the unreliability of the statistics).
4. The definitions of integration and assimilation are from Skutnabb-Kangas (2000: 123–134).
5. Even if LHRs have been discussed in some articles earlier, the first full-length book with LHRs in the title seems to be Skutnabb-Kangas and Phillipson 1994. Now there are many more; a Google search with the phrase "linguistic human rights" (Dec 2006) showed 34,200 entries.
6. See http://www.linguistic-declaration.org/; see also Skutnabb-Kangas (2000: 541–548) for a presentation and critical assessment of the Draft.
7. "Speaker" should in this article be understood as a generic term, as "speaker or signer", i.e. it includes users of Sign languages. No state has ratified the European Charter for any Sign language, though; these have been excluded with false arguments (see Skutnabb-Kangas 2003).

8. The texts of and latest news about these documents and their ratifications are found at http://conventions.coe.int/treaty/EN/cadreprincipal.htm; their treaty numbers are 148 and 158.
9. Most of the human rights instruments can be found at the website of the Office of the United Nations Human Rights Commissioner, http://www.ohchr.org/english/law/index.htm.
10. E793, 1948; 78 U.N.T.S. 277, entered into force Jan 12, 1951; for the full text, see http://www1.umn.edu/humanrts/instree/x1cppcg.htm.
11. This and the following Canadian studies are quoted in Martin (2000a, 2000b; no pages).
12. See http://en.wikipedia.org/wiki/Inuktitut for the difference between the labels Inuttitut and Inuktitut.
13. Thanks to the staff at Te Papa for identifying the person for me – neither the quote nor his name is in the brochure.
14. The Exhibition tells about "our heartland, the Whanganui River, and our place within it". The Whanganui iwi write: "The well-being of our river is intertwined with its people's well-being" (from the brochure describing the exhibition, with the theme: "Ko au te awa, ko te awa ko au. I am the river, the river is me.").

References

Amendments to the Law on Foreign Language Education and Teaching
    2002   www.abgs.gov.tr/abportal/uploads/files/Analytical%20Note%20on%20Constitutional%20Amendments%20.doc

Andrýsek, Oldrich
    1989   *Report on the Definition of Minorities*. SIM Special No 8. Utrecht: Netherlands Institute of Human Rights, Studieen Informatiecentrum Mensenrechten (SIM).

Blommaert, Jan
    2004   Rights in places. Comments on linguistic rights and wrongs. In: Jane Freeland and Donna Patrick (eds.), *Language Rights and Language Survival. Sociolinguistic and Sociocultural Perspectives*, 55–65. Manchester, UK & Northampton, MA: St. Jerome Publishing.

Branson, Jan and Don Miller
    2002   *Damned for Their Difference. The Cultural Construction of Deaf People as Disabled*. Washington, DC: Gallaudet University Press.

Burnaby, Barbara
    1996   Language policies in Canada. In: Michael Herriman and Barbara Burnaby (eds.), *Language Policies in English-dominant Countries: Six Case Studies*, 159–219. Clevedon, UK: Multilingual Matters.

Capotorti, Francesco
    1979   *Study of the Rights of Persons Belonging to Ethnic, Religious and Linguistic Minorities*. New York: United Nations.

Dunbar, Robert, Tove Skutnabb-Kangas, Hassan Id Balkassm, Ida Nicolaisen, Ole Henrik Magga, and Mililani Trask
    2007   *Education of Indigenous Children and Violations of Articles II(b) and II(e) of the UN Genocide Convention. Expert Paper Written for the United Nations*. New York: United Nations.

Fishman, Joshua A.
1991 *Reversing Language Shift: Theoretical and Empirical Foundations of Assistance to Threatened Languages.* Clevedon, UK: Multilingual Matters.

Freeland, Jane and Donna Patrick (eds.)
2004 *Language Rights and Language Survival. Sociolinguistic and Sociocultural Perspectives.* Manchester, UK & Northampton, MA: St. Jerome Publishing.

Grin, François
2000 *Evaluating Policy Measures for Minority Languages in Europe: Towards Effective, Cost-effective and Democratic Implementation.* ECMI Report 6, October 2000. Flensburg: ECMI.

Grin, François
2003 Diversity as a paradigm, analytical device, and policy goal. In: Will Kymlicka and Alan Patten (eds.), *Language Rights and Political Theory*, 169–188. Oxford: Oxford University Press.

Harmon, David
2002 *In Light of Our Differences: How Diversity in Nature and Culture Makes Us Human.* Washington, DC: The Smithsonian Institute Press.

Herman, Edward S. and Noam Chomsky
1988 *Manufacturing Consent: The Political Economy of the Mass Media.* New York: Pantheon.

Janulf, Pirjo
1998 *Kommer finskan i Sverige att fortleva? En studie av språkkunskaper och språkanvändning hos andragenerationens sverigefinnar i Botkyrka och hos finlandssvenskar i Åbo.* (Will Finnish survive in Sweden? A study of language skills and language use among second generation Sweden Finns in Botkyrka, Sweden, and Finland Swedes in Åbo, Finland). Acta Universitatis Stockholmiensis, Studia Fennica Stockholmiensia 7. Stockholm: Almqvist & Wiksell International.

Jokinen, Markku
2000 The linguistic human rights of Sign language users. In: Robert Phillipson (ed.), *Rights to Language. Equity, Power and Education*, 203–213. Mahwah, NJ: Lawrence Erlbaum.

Kemal, Mustafa (Atatürk)
1931 From *Cumhuriyet*, February 14, 1931, quoted in Susan Meiselas 1997, *Kurdistan. In the Shadow of History*, 145. New York: Random House.

Kirkness, Verna
2002 The preservation and use of our languages. In: Barbara Burnaby and Jon Reyhner (eds.), *Indigenous Languages Across the Community*, 17–23. Flagstaff, Arizona: Northern Arizona University.

Klaus, David
2003 The use of indigenous languages in early basic education in Papua New Guinea: A model for elsewhere? *Language and Education* 17: 105–111.

Krauss, Michael
1992 The world's languages in crisis. *Language* 68: 4–10.

Krauss, Michael
1996 Status of Native American language endangerment. In: Gina Cantoni (ed.), *Stabilizing Indigenous Languages.* Flagstaff: Northern Arizona University. www.ncela.gwu.edu/pubs/stabilize/i-needs/status.htm

Krauss, Michael
    1997   The indigenous languages of the north: A report on their present state. In: Hiroshi Shoji and Juha Janhunen (eds.), *Northern Minority Languages: Problems of Survival*, 1–34. Senri Ethnological Studies 44. Osaka: National Museum of Ethnology.
Krauss, Michael, Luisa Maffi and Akira Yamamoto
    2004   The world's languages in crisis: Questions, challenges, and a call for action. In: Osamu Sakiyama, Fubito Endo, Honoré Watanabe and Fumiko Sasama (eds.), *Lectures on Endangered Languages* 4, 23–27. Suita, Osaka: The Project "Endangered Languages of the Pacific Rim".
Kymlicka, Will and Alan Patten
    2003   Language rights and political theory. *Annual Review of Applied Linguistics* 23: 3–21.
Ladd, Paddy
    2003   *Understanding Deaf Culture. In Search of Deafhood*. Clevedon, UK: Multilingual Matters.
Lane, Harlan
    1992   *The Mask of Benevolence: Disabling the Deaf Community*. New York: Alfred Knopf.
Lowell, Anne and Brian Devlin
    1999   Miscommunication between Aboriginal students and their non-Aboriginal teachers in a bilingual school. In: Stephen May (ed.), *Indigenous Community-based Education*, 137–159. Clevedon, UK: Multilingual Matters.
Magga, Ole Henrik, Ida Nicolaisen, Mililani Trask, Robert Dunbar and Tove Skutnabb-Kangas
    2004   *Indigenous Children's Education and Indigenous Languages. Expert Paper Written for the United Nations Permanent Forum on Indigenous Issues*. New York: United Nations.
Martin, Ian
    2000a   *Aajjiqatigiingniq. Language of Instruction Research Paper. A Report to the Government of Nunavut*. Unpublished manuscript, Department of Education, Iqaluit, Nunavut, Canada. [imartin@glendon.yorku.ca].
Martin, Ian
    2000b   *Sources and Issues: A Backgrounder to the Discussion Paper on Language of Instruction in Nunavut Schools*. Unpublished manuscript, Department of Education, Nunavut. [imartin@glendon.yorku.ca].
May, Stephen
    2001   *Language and Minority Rights: Ethnicity, Nationalism, and the Politics of Language*. London: Longman.
McMurtry, John
    1999   *The Cancer Stage of Capitalism*. London: Pluto Press.
McMurtry, John
    2002   *Value Wars. The Global Market Versus the Life Economy*. London: Pluto Press.
Milloy, John S.
    1999   *A National Crime. The Canadian Government and the Residential School System, 1879 to 1986*. Winnipeg, Manitoba: The University of Manitoba Press.

Misra, Girishwar and Ajit K. Mohanty
   2000a   Consequences of poverty and disadvantage: A review of Indian studies. In: Ajit K. Mohanty and Girishwar Misra (eds.), *Psychology of Poverty and Disadvantage*, 121–148. New Delhi: Concept Publishing Company.

Misra, Girishwar and Ajit K. Mohanty
   2000b   Poverty and disadvantage: Issues in retrospect. In: Ajit K. Mohanty and Girishwar Misra (eds.), *Psychology of Poverty and Disadvantage*, 261–284. New Delhi: Concept Publishing Company.

Mohanty, Ajit K.
   2000   Perpetuating inequality: The disadvantage of language, minority mother tongues and related issues. In: Ajit K. Mohanty and Girishwar Misra (eds.), *Psychology of Poverty and Disadvantage*, 104–117. New Delhi: Concept Publishing Company.

Pattanayak, Debi Prasanna
   1988   Monolingual myopia and the petals of the Indian lotus: Do many languages divide or unite a nation? In: Tove Skutnabb-Kangas and Jim Cummins (eds.), *Minority Education: From Shame to Struggle*, 379–389. Clevedon, UK: Multilingual Matters.

Patten, Alan and Will Kymlicka
   2003   Introduction. Language rights and political theory: Context, issues, and approaches. In: Will Kymlicka and Alan Patten (eds.), *Language Rights and Political Theory*, 1–10. Oxford: Oxford University Press.

Rannut, Mart
   2003   Postmodern trends in current language development. In: Helle Metslang and Mart Rannut (eds.), *Languages in Development*, 19–30. München: Lincom Europa.

Rubio-Marín, Ruth
   2003   Language rights: Exploring the competing rationales. In: Will Kymlicka and Alan Patten (eds.), *Language Rights and Political Theory*, 52–79. Oxford: Oxford University Press.

Sen, Amartya
   1985   *Commodities and Capabilities*. Amsterdam: North Holland.

Skutnabb-Kangas, Tove
   1997   Human rights and language policy in education. In: Ruth Wodak and David Corson (eds.), *The Encyclopedia of Language and Education*. Vol. 1: *Language Policy and Political Issues in Education*, 55–65. Dordrecht: Kluwer.

Skutnabb-Kangas, Tove
   2000   *Linguistic Genocide in Education – or Worldwide Diversity and Human Rights?* Mahwah, NJ: Lawrence Erlbaum.

Skutnabb-Kangas, Tove
   2002   (Why) should diversities be maintained? Language diversity, biological diversity and linguistic human rights. *Glendon Distinguished Lectures 2003*, York University, Glendon College, Toronto, Ontario, Canada. http://www.glendon.yorku.ca/english/archive/index.html.

Skutnabb-Kangas, Tove
   2005   Can a "linguistic human rights approach" "deliver"? Reflections on complementarities, tensions and misconceptions in attempts at multidisciplinar-

ities. Plenary paper at the International Conference on Language, Education and Diversity, University of Waikato, Hamilton, Aotearoa/New Zealand, November 26–29, 2003. In: Stephen May, Margaret Franken and Roger Barnard (eds.), *LED 2003: Refereed Conference Proceedings of the 1st International Conference on Language, Education and Diversity*. Hamilton: Wilf Malcolm Institute of Educational Research, University of Waikato. CD Rom.

Skutnabb-Kangas, Tove and Sertaç Bucak
   1994   Killing a mother tongue – how the Kurds are deprived of linguistic human rights. In: Tove Skutnabb-Kangas and Robert Phillipson (eds.), *Linguistic Human Rights. Overcoming Linguistic Discrimination*, 347–370. Berlin: Mouton de Gruyter.

Skutnabb-Kangas, Tove and Robert Phillipson
   1994   Linguistic human rights, past and present. In: Tove Skutnabb-Kangas and Robert Phillipson (eds.), *Linguistic Human Rights. Overcoming Linguistic Discrimination*, 71–110. Berlin: Mouton de Gruyter.

Skutnabb-Kangas, Tove, Luisa Maffi and Dave Harmon
   2003   *Sharing a World of Difference. The Earth's Linguistic, Cultural, and Biological Diversity*. Paris: UNESCO Publishing. http://www.terralingua.org/RecPublications.htm.

Skutnabb-Kangas, Tove (ed.)
   1995   *Multilingualism for All*. Lisse: Swets & Zeitlinger.

Stroud, Christopher
   2001   African mother-tongue programmes and the politics of language: Linguistic citizenship versus linguistic human rights. *Journal of Multilingual and Multicultural Development* 22: 339–355.

Stroud, Christopher and Kathleen Heugh
   2003   Language rights and linguistic citizenship. In: Jane Freeland and Donna Patrick (eds.), *Language Rights and Language Survival: Sociolinguistic and Sociocultural Perspectives*, 191–217. Manchester, UK: St. Jerome Publishing, 191–217.

Thornberry, Patrick
   1997   Minority rights. In: Academy of European Law (ed.), *Collected Courses of the Academy of European Law*. Vol. VI, Book 2, 307–390. The Netherlands: Kluwer Law International.

Thornberry, Patrick and Dianna Gibbons
   1997   Education and minority rights: A short survey of international standards. *International Journal on Minority and Group Rights. Special Issue on the Education Rights of National Minorities* 4: 115–152.

Tomaševski, Katarina
   1996   International prospects for the future of the welfare state. In: *Reconceptualizing the Welfare State*, 100–117. Copenhagen: The Danish Centre for Human Rights.

UNESCO
   2003a   *Language Vitality and Endangerment*. UNESCO Intangible Cultural Heritage Unit's Ad Hoc Expert Group on Endangered Languages. Approved March 31, 2003, by the Participants of the International Expert Meeting on UNESCO Programme Safeguarding of Endangered Languages, UNESCO,

Paris-Fontenoy, March 10–12, 2003. http://portal.unesco.org/culture/en/file_download.php/1a41d53cf46e10710298d314450b97dfLangage+Vitality.doc.

UNESCO
2003b *Recommendations for Action Plan.* International Expert Meeting on UNESCO Programme Safeguarding of Endangered Languages, UNESCO, Paris-Fontenoy, March 10–12, 2003. http://portal.unesco.org/culture/en/ev.php-URL_ID=8270&URL_DO=DO_TOPIC&URL_SECTION=201.html.

UNESCO
2003c *Education in a Multilingual World.* UNESCO Education Position Paper. Paris: UNESCO. http://unesdoc.unesco.org/images/0012/001297/129728e.pdf.

van der Stoel, Max
1999 *Report on the Linguistic Rights of Persons Belonging to National Minorities in the OSCE Area.* And: *Annex. Replies from OSCE participating States.* The Hague: OSCE High Commissioner on National Minorities.

de Varennes, Fernand
1996 *Language, Minorities and Human Rights.* Dordrecht: Martinus Nijhoff.

de Varennes, Fernand
1999 The existing rights of minorities in international law. In: Miklós Kontra, Robert Phillipson, Tove Skutnabb-Kangas and Tibor Várady (eds.), *Language: A Right and a Resource. Approaching Linguistic Human Rights*, 117–146. Budapest: Central European University Press.

de Varennes, Fernand
2000 Tolerance and inclusion: The convergence of human rights and the work of Tove Skutnabb-Kangas. In: Robert Phillipson (ed.), *Rights to Language. Equity, Power and Education. Celebrating the 60th Birthday of Tove Skutnabb-Kangas*, 67–71. Mahwah, NJ: Lawrence Erlbaum.

de Varennes, Fernand
2003 Language rights and human rights: The international experience. In: Dónall ÓRiagáin (ed.), *Language and Law in Northern Ireland*, 5–16. Belfast Studies in Language, Culture and Politics 9. Belfast: Queen's University Belfast. http://www.bslcp.com/.

Williams, Edward
1998 *Investigating Bilingual Literacy: Evidence from Malawi and Zambia* (Education Research No. 24). London: Department for International Development.

III. Language variation and change in institutional contexts

13. Language and education

Markus Bieswanger

1. Introduction

The relationship between language and education is multifaceted and has always been at the heart of applied linguistics. Today, the field of language and education covers a wide range of topics, from language teaching and acquisition to questions of language planning and policy to linguistic (human) rights, particularly in the context of linguistic diversity and language change. Language and education is thus closely related to and interconnected with many other fields covered in this volume of the *Handbooks of Applied Linguistics* (see, e.g., Ricento, Edwards, Kirkpatrick, and Skutnabb-Kangas, all this vol.). Corson (1997a: vii) emphasizes the "diverse interdisciplinary nature of 'language and education'" in his general editor's introduction to the eight-volume *Encyclopedia of Language and Education* (Corson 1997b), which consists of the following volumes, reflecting the wide scope of the field:[1]

1   *Language Policy and Political Issues in Education*
2   *Literacy*
3   *Oral Discourse and Education*
4   *Second Language Education*
5   *Bilingual Education*
6   *Knowledge about Education*
7   *Language Testing and Assessment*
8   *Research Methods in Language and Education*

According to Corson (1997a: vii), the mere "publication of this work [i.e. the *Encyclopedia of Language and Education*] signals the maturity of the field of 'language and education' as an international and interdisciplinary field of significance and cohesion". Corson (1997a: viii) adopts a broad view of the field: "As a collection, the Encyclopedia spans the range of subjects and topics normally falling within the scope of 'language and education'."

This chapter will discuss the relationship between language and education from an applied linguistics perspective. After a brief survey of the history of language and education within this framework, we will turn to the role education plays in applied linguistics today and then explore some currently debated issues and controversies, before we finally take a look at potential future activities in the area.

2. History of the field

The early history of applied linguistics was intimately and inseparably connected to language and education, more precisely to the teaching of foreign or second languages. Mackey (1966: 197) claims that the term "applied linguistics" in this sense originated around the year 1940, but emphasizes that the interest in language teaching did not start with the coinage of the term. In an earlier book (Mackey 1965: 253, quoted in Davies and Elder 2004a: 2) he maintains that "[t]hroughout the history of formal language teaching there has always been some sort of applied linguistics, as it is known today". Interest in language and education can in fact at least be traced back to the ancient Greeks. Howatt (1999: 618) reports that both "Plato and Aristotle contributed to the design of a curriculum beginning with good writing (grammar), then moving on to effective discourse (rhetoric) and culminating in the development of dialectic to promote a philosophical approach to life". For most of its history and until rather recently, the relationship between language and education was almost exclusively occupied with the question of how to speak or write "better" and how to teach foreign or second languages more effectively.

Ideas about second language teaching and learning started to change around the beginning of the 20th century, when the so-called grammar-translation method, which had originated in Prussia in the late 18th century and had been spreading and becoming more popular in the 19th century (Howatt and Widdowson 2004: 151; Cook 2003: 31–33), was increasingly criticized and considered outdated, because "it focused on the ability to 'analyse' language, and not the ability to 'use' language" (Schmitt and Celce-Murcia 2002: 4). As a result, many language-learning experts advocated "a direct method in which the students' own languages were banished and everything was to be done through the language under instruction" (Cook 2003: 33) in the early 20th century. The importance of oral language was emphasized, while grammar teaching and the learners' first languages were essentially banned from the monolingual classroom. However, the direct method and its approach of imitating the learning of a first language proved to be problematic, largely because it was impossible to provide the same amount of exposure to the target language as for first language learners and since it required teaching staff highly proficient in the target language, which was not always available. In the UK, Michael West promoted his reading method and suggested to increase learners' exposure to the target language through reading and the compilation of lists of the most useful words, such as the *General Service List of English Words* published in 1953 (Howatt and Widdowson 2004: 278–283; Schmitt and Celce-Murcia 2002: 5). The beginning of World War II marked another important date in the history of second language pedagogy. Schmitt and Celce-Murcia (2002: 5) summarize the developments as follows:

The three methods, Grammar-translation, the Direct method and the Reading method, continued to hold sway until World War II. During the war, the weaknesses of all the above approaches became obvious, as the American military found itself short of people who were conversationally fluent in foreign languages. It needed a way of training soldiers in oral and aural skills quickly. American structural linguists stepped into the gap and developed a programme which borrowed from the Direct method, especially its emphasis on listening and speaking. It drew its rationale from the dominant psychological theory of the time, Behaviorism, that essentially said that language learning was a result of habit formation. Thus the method included activities which were believed to reinforce 'good' language habits, such as close attention to pronunciation, intensive oral drilling, a focus on sentence patterns and memorization. In short, students were expected to learn through drills rather than an analysis of the target language. [...] it [i.e. the method] came to be known as 'Audiolingualism'.

This stepping in of linguists to provide an efficient means of teaching foreign or second languages fast marks the beginning of the field of applied linguistics, which was welcomed by language teachers. Kaplan (2002a: vii) claims that "the term *applied linguistics* came into existence in the 1940s through the efforts of language teachers who wished to ally themselves with 'scientific' linguists and to disassociate themselves from teachers of literature". The term *applied linguistics*, or to be precise "its equivalent in Russian (*prikladnoe jazykovedenie*), German (*angewandte Sprachwissenschaft*), and French (*linguistique inde-europénne*)" (Berns and Matsuda 2006: 394) had already been used by Indo-Europeanists in the 19th century, but its use in English with reference to language pedagogy "dates from the 1940s when leading American linguists like Leonard Bloomfield (1887–1949) and Charles C. Fries (1887–1967) became involved in the application of their theoretical and descriptive work to large-scale teaching enterprises during the Second World War" (Howatt and Widdowson 2004: 302–303). Fries founded the English Language Institute at the University of Michigan in 1941 (University of Michigan 2006) and laid out the method that later came to be known as audiolingualism in his highly influential book *Teaching and Learning English as a Foreign Language* in 1945. Berns and Matsuda (2006: 399) report that the "ELI [English Language Institute] and its applied linguistics approach to language teaching became influential throughout the United States and even throughout the world" and that the "Michigan ELI became influential by creating the first professional preparation program of this kind". As mentioned in the passage from Schmitt and Celce-Murcia above, however, linguists at the time did not only contribute to the teaching of English to foreign learners, in the case of the University of Michigan to the growing number of foreign students (University of Michigan 2006), but also to the effective specialized teaching of a large number of languages to members of the armed forces in the United States and Britain during World War II (Halliday, McIntosh, and Strevens 1964: 174). By addressing the growing international communication needs and the challenges of linguistic diversity in the middle of the 20th century, early applied linguistics was thus instrumental in solving the real world language and education problems of the time. Van Els et al. (1984: 11) conclude that due to the success of the audiolingual or "linguistic method" of language teaching, as it was also called, "it was almost inevitable that 'applied linguistics' became popular as a near-synonym for FLT [Foreign Language Teaching]".

The English Language Institute at the University of Michigan made another significant and lasting contribution to the development of an association of applied linguistics with foreign or second language learning and teaching by publishing the first journal in the world to bear the term *applied linguistics* in its title (University of Michigan 2006). Grabe (2002: 3) even claims that "[a] realistic history of the field of applied linguistics would place its origins at around the year 1948 with the publication of the first issue of the journal *Language Learning: A Journal of Applied Linguistics*". Berns and Matsuda (2006: 398) leave no doubt about the inseparable connection between language, education and applied linguistics in the early days of the field's history when they summarize for the 1940s that "[w]hat came to be recognized as applied linguistics took place in the contexts of language teaching – specifically the teaching of English in schools, the teaching of foreign languages other than English and the teaching of English as a foreign language".

The near-synonymy of language teaching and applied linguistics was essentially perpetuated during the 1950s, when applied linguistics "was commonly meant to reflect the insights of structural and functional linguistics that could be applied directly to second language teaching, and also, in some cases to first language (L1) literacy and language arts issues as well" (Grabe 2002: 3). The approach of applying linguistic knowledge about language to teaching is an early form of what is sometimes called "linguistics applied" in a literal sense of the term. This tradition of applying purely linguistic knowledge to educational contexts is still a matter of discussion today, as illustrated in Hudson's (2004) recent article on *Why education needs linguistics (and vice versa)*.

The 1960s and 1970s saw the beginning expansion of the field of applied linguistics and the development of different traditions of applied linguistics in different countries (Berns and Matsuda 2006: 399–401; Davies and Elder 2004a: 6–8; McNamara 2001). According to Grabe (2002: 4), "the focus of language teaching remained central to the discipline", but he also reports that applied linguistics became involved in the subfields of "language assessment, language policies and a new field of second language acquisition" (Grabe 2002: 2) in the 1960s, and the additional subfields of "literacy, multilingualism, language minority-rights, language planning and policy and teacher training" (Grabe 2002: 3) in the 1970s, which are all highly relevant to language and education. From a methodological perspective, the focus began to shift from the teacher and teaching methodology to the learner and learner autonomy (Schmitt and Celce-Murcia 2002: 6–14). Hymes (1972) laid the foundations for what has become so-called communicative language teaching by introducing the concept of communicative competence. As a result, according to Cook (2003: 36), communicative language teaching "rapidly became, and still remains, the dominant orthodoxy in progressive language teaching". However, some recent movements, such as the focus on form approach, challenge some of the principles of communicative language teaching and aim to supplement it without suggesting to abandon the communicative approach (Doughty and Williams 1998).

The continued broadening of applied linguistics since the 1970s into an "interdisciplinary field which accommodates any research activity associated with matters of second language use and learning" (Wilkins 1999: 9) has added a number of education-related subfields to the traditional focus on language teaching and learning, which will be discussed in the following sections.

3. State of the art

The state of the art of language and education in an applied linguistics setting is essentially determined by the different definitions of applied linguistics current today as a result of the gradual expansion of the field since the 1960s and by the different roles language plays in education. As far as the definition of applied linguistics is concerned, Berns and Matsuda (2006: 394) identify a lack of consensus which is due to the fact that "ever since the term 'applied' was attached to linguistics, language specialists identifying with this field of inquiry and activity have offered and continue to offer competing, sometimes contradictory definitions and descriptions of its scope, status, and significance" (quote from Berns and Matsuda 2006: 394; see also Kaplan 1980; Brumfit 1996; Gass and Makoni 2004). The *Longman Dictionary of Applied Linguistics and Language Teaching* (Richards and Schmidt 2002) lists the following two definitions of "applied linguistics", which are both highly relevant to the field of language and education in the context of linguistic diversity:

1 the study of second and foreign language learning and teaching
2 the study of language and linguistics in relation to practical problems, such as lexicography, translation, speech pathology, etc. Applied linguistics uses information from sociology, psychology, anthropology, and information theory as well as from linguistics in order to develop its own theoretical models of language and language use, and then uses this information and theory in practical areas such as syllabus design, speech therapy, language planning, stylistics, etc.

The two definitions display two widespread views of applied linguistics today. The first definition presents the use of the term *applied linguistics* in a narrow sense, directly relating to the origins of the field in the 1940s (see above). Applied linguistics in this narrow sense is predominantly concerned with the quest for the best way to learn and teach a foreign or second language, which is becoming ever more important as the world becomes more globalized. Or to speak with the words of the Center for Applied Linguistics (2006) from a purely practical perspective: "The smaller the world gets, the more our communication needs grow". The second definition reflects the expansion of the field of applied linguistics, shows a much broader and interdisciplinary approach and hints at the many additional subfields applied linguistics is concerned with today. Many of these subfields are interrelated with language and education, particularly speech pathology, lexicography, language planning and syllabus design, and one could certainly add fields such as first and second language acquisition, language policy, bi- and multilingualism, literacy, sociolinguistics and psycholinguistics to the list (Berns and Matsuda 2006: 400; Cook 2003: 7–8; Corson 1997b; Carter and Nunan 2001: 2; McDonough 2002: 1–2 and 13–16). Both interpretations of applied linguistics will be considered in Section 4 of this chapter.

Today, conferences, journals and books devoted to applied linguistics deal with both, issues of second or foreign language teaching and learning as well as education-related issues that are based on the broad definition of the field. The distinction between the two approaches, however, is not always clear-cut and there is certainly some overlap in current practice. The program of the 15th AILA World Congress of Applied Linguistics to be hosted in Essen, Germany, in 2008 and entitled *Multilingualism: Challenges and Opportunities* lists the following thematic strands, which are for the most part either devoted to topics directly associated with foreign or second language teaching and learning or are connected to language and education in a broader sense: first language acquisition, second language acquisition, foreign language teaching and teacher education, contrastive linguistics and error analysis, language evaluation, assessment and testing, educational technology and language learning, learner autonomy in language learning, language and education in multilingual settings, written and visual literacy, discourse analysis, rhetoric and stylistics, business communication, translating, interpreting and mediation, multimodality in discourse and text, sociolinguistics, multilingualism and multiculturalism, intercultural communication, lexicography and lexicology, and psycholinguistics (AILA 2006). As far as journals are concerned, the topics of the majority of articles published are related to language and education. This is the result of a survey of the articles published in 2004 and 2005 in the following journals incorporating the term applied linguistics in their title: *Applied Linguistics*, *International Journal of Applied Linguistics*, *International Review of Applied Linguistics in Language Teaching* and *ITL – International Journal of Applied Linguistics* (formerly *ITL Review of Applied Linguistics*). Both handbooks of applied linguistics published so far in the new millennium, namely the *Handbook of Applied Linguistics* edited by Davies and Elder (2004b) and *The Oxford Handbook of Applied Linguistics* edited by Kaplan (2002b), reflect the broadening of the field of applied linguistics, but nevertheless contain a considerable proportion of contributions related to the field of language and education. Davies and Elder (2004a: 2) point out that: "For the most part, those who write about applied linguistics accept that the label 'applied linguistics' refers to language teaching (in its widest interpretation, therefore including speech therapy, translation and interpretation studies, language planning, etc.)". In the introduction to the second part of Davies and Elder (2004b), Elder (2004: 424) again leaves no doubt about the importance of education-related issues in applied linguistics: "The considerable weight given in this volume to language learning (and even more so to language teaching […]) was dictated by its status as one of the most central and commonly investigated issues or 'problems' in applied linguistics". Similarly, Schmitt and Celce-Murcia (2002) explicitly emphasize the importance of language and education in their overview of applied linguistics at the beginning of Schmitt's (2002) edited collection *An Introduction to Applied Linguistics*: "[…] the dominating application has always been the teaching and learning of second or foreign languages. […] Traditionally, the primary concern of applied linguistics has been second language acquisition theory, second language pedagogy and the interface between the two, and it is these areas which this volume will cover" (Schmitt and Celce-Murcia 2002: 2). This brief survey of the orientation of conferences, journals and books dedicated to applied linguistics illustrates the status of questions concerning the relationship between language and education within the field of applied linguistics.

We said at the beginning of this section that the different functions language has in education are another major factor that has to be considered when talking about language and education. Barry (2002: 1) states that "all education involves the use of language, whether we teach it directly or not". The different direct and indirect roles of language in education are regularly distinguished, as in the UNESCO Education Position Paper *Education in a Multilingual World* (2003), which identifies on the one hand the "language(s) of instruction", i.e. the language(s) used as medium of communication when teaching, and on the other hand "language teaching", i.e. formal instruction of the oral and/or written form of a language other than the mother tongue (see also Perera 2001: 710; Corson 2001: 14). Many of the current questions concerning language and education dealt with in the following section are in some way related to this distinction.

4. Current issues, controversies and the contribution of applied linguistics

Given the immense scope of the field of language and education (see Section 1; Corson 1997b), only a selection of currently discussed issues can be presented here. For example, many of the controversies considered in Seidlhofer's (2003) collection *Controversies in Applied Linguistics* are in fact at least partly controversies in language and education. The following list of education-related questions and subsidiary questions compiled by Cook (2003: 4, numbers added, order changed, shortened) displays some of the issues under debate:

1. Should everyone learn foreign languages and, if so, which one or ones? (And what is the best way to learn and teach them?)
2. Should children speaking a dialect be encouraged to maintain it or steered towards the standard form of a language? (And, if so, how is that standard form decided and by whom?)
3. In communities with more than one language which ones should be used in schools? (And does every child have a right to be educated in the language they use at home?)
4. Some languages are dying out. Should that be prevented and, if so, how?
5. What language skills should children attain beyond basic literacy? (And what is basic literacy anyway? Reading and writing, or something more?)

Cook (2003: 4) suggests that these questions can be and are in fact frequently at the heart of controversies as each one of them admits "many different and opposed answers" and claims that many of the listed questions concern "educational dilemmas [which] echo those of society at large". Similar education-related issues can, for example, also be found in Davies and Elder (1994a: 1), Barry (2002: 2–3), and Donough (2002: 13–14). Each of these questions cannot be treated in isolation but is closely interrelated with other issues. For instance, the death of languages or varieties (Question 4) is certainly connected to the value societies attach to these languages and varieties and, among other things, to the way they are represented in education and language policies (Questions 1, 2 and 3). The issues raised in the above questions are also closely related to and interdependent with many other topics covered in this volume. Blommaert (this vol., Section 4.3), for instance, discusses the issue of literacy in and beyond education with relation to the linguistic situation in Africa. The questions 1 to 5 will form the basis of the following subsections.

4.1. Foreign and second language teaching and learning

The first question has to be treated as relating to three different issues. Firstly, is there really a need for everyone to learn at least one additional language that is not her or his mother-tongue and, if so, what would be the benefit of this? Secondly, which language should be taught and learned and for what reasons? And thirdly, what are the most effective and appropriate strategies of teaching and learning foreign or second languages? With reference to these issues, language is both the subject as well as – at least to a certain degree – the medium of instruction. The degree to which the second or foreign language is used as medium of instruction depends largely on the teaching methodology used (see, e.g., Littlewood 1999; Howatt 1999; Howatt and Widdowson 2004) and language policies (Tollefson 2002).

The need for learning a second or foreign language may not be immediately clear to many people, especially to those living in allegedly monolingual countries or also to those who are native speakers of the dominant or majority language in a multilingual society. In reality, the two groups are more or less identical, as there are essentially no completely monolingual countries, which is why they should be referred to as allegedly monolingual, and thus the speakers who speak the national language in a country that is popularly perceived to be monolingual are usually simply native speakers of the dominant national language. What varies is the proportion of non-majority language speakers, but there is no clear-cut line that separates one group from the other. One example for an allegedly monolingual country could be the United States, which is often perceived to be monolingual, particularly by American native speakers of English, despite not having an official constitutional language and despite the large number of indigenous and immigrant minorities who use their native languages more or less extensively. Depending on the perspective, native speakers of English in the USA could be considered speakers of the national language in a monolingual country or speakers of the majority language in a multilingual society. Either way, in the case of English speakers from all the countries in which English is the dominant national language it is particularly difficult to convince people to learn a second or foreign language, because English has become a or *the* global language (see also Kirkpatrick, this vol.). The answer to the question whether people should learn additional languages, however, has to be yes, although the motivation may vary and will often be due to a number of different factors. The UNESCO (2003) recommends the acquisition of a language that is not a person's native language by everyone and provides several convincing reasons: "Learning another language opens up access to other value systems and ways of interpreting the world, encouraging inter-cultural understanding and helping to reduce xenophobia. This applies equally to minority and majority language speakers" (UNESCO 2003: 17). One could also argue that the learning experience is particularly important for speakers of majority languages, as it gives them some insight into the difficulties of language learning and thus sensitizes them for the problems migrant minority language speakers often experience, when they are forced to learn another language. Additionally, there are a variety of predominantly practical motivations for second or foreign language learning, frequently connected to globalization, increased mobility and the growing need for communication across language barriers between native speakers of different languages (see, e.g., Center for Applied Linguistics 2006). Private and business travel are further practical motivations, as is business itself, because, after all, the language of business is the language of the customer.

These practical motivations for language learning are often closely linked to the question which language or languages should be taught and learned. Because of the various different rationales behind such a decision, this question can, of course, not be answered in a general way. Immediate private or business motivations may lead to completely different decisions than an applied linguistic approach that, for example, incorporates questions of language economics (see Grin 2002, and Grin, this vol.).

The most controversial issue in this section, however, is the fundamental question concerning "the best way to learn and teach them [i.e. foreign and second languages]" (Cook 2003: 4). This question was responsible for the establishment of applied linguistics to begin with and has long been and still is hotly debated among second or foreign language teachers and other language education experts. As outlined in Section 2, the 20th century saw a number of different language teaching and learning paradigms, such as the grammar-translation method, the direct method, the reading method, audiolingualism and communicative language teaching, but there is still considerable disagreement as to the "right" or most effective way of teaching and learning second and foreign languages (Littlewood 1999). There is obviously no definite answer to this question now and there probably will not be one in the near future, as the proposals provided by experts active in the field are constantly changing, almost like fashions that come and go. Davies (1999: 3) summarizes this quest for an answer as follows, emphasizing that applied linguistic research in the field of second and foreign language teaching and learning is nevertheless not conducted in vain:

> [...] in language teaching as in education generally, what determines change is the roundabout of fashion which seems recently to be moving back towards a modified grammar-translation method after a number of years in which such an approach to language teaching was anathema to many people. It may be that we shall always have to take account of changing fashion, simply because we have no way of finally establishing 'the best way' to learn or teach language. Within such changes in fashion, however, there are smaller scale research operations which can be and need to be carried out and which will establish not the best way to teach language but a satisfactory set of procedures within an over-all theoretical approach.

Controversies, however, do not only exist concerning the ups and downs of competing teaching methodologies, but can frequently also be found within the individual paradigms. The following passage from McDonough (2002: 4), referring to the analysis of a set of teaching materials, illustrates this impressively:

> This material shows up a number of assumptions, which it is worth spelling out, since they have been the subject of some controversy over the years.
> Language exposure is centre stage. Thus, it is assumed to be part of the materials' job to contain appropriate examples of the language. These materials actually go a little further than that fairly innocuous assumption – they assume that the examples of the language should be genuine, from the culture in which the language is spoken. There is in fact a considerable amount of debate about this issue of authenticity, exactly what it means and how important it is. Many people argue that it is easier to learn from real examples of the language, because learners can relate to that; others argue that authentic language is often too difficult, and specifically written language teaching material is more suitable.

4.2. Language varieties and education

Linguistic diversity and social inequality in school settings are responsible for the problems addressed in this and the following subsection. At least since the 1960s, controversial issues concerning language varieties and education have received considerable public attention and have been discussed intensely by language and teaching experts (Hancock 1999: 187; Wolfram and Christian 1989: 14). Schools tend to advocate and use a/the standard variety of a language in formal education, with which many children have not had any contact when they arrive in school, because the majority of the population uses a non-standard geographical and/or social variety at home. Despite the common gap between non-standard home language and standard school language, Corson (2001: 68) reports that "[f]ormal educational policies for the treatment of non-standard varieties in schools are conspicuous by their absence in most educational systems" and concludes that "the absence of formal policies that give explicit respect to non-standard varieties actually creates a tacit form of language policy that legitimizes the standard variety". Baugh (1997: 33) claims that the widespread preference for the standard variety or standard varieties in schools discriminates against children from less affluent families, because children of wealthy families are "likely to be native speakers of the dominant standard language(s)". Corson (2001: 76) condemns such linguistic discrimination and demands that "the topic of language variety needs to be explored in classrooms with the same intensity and focus as issues of class, race, culture and gender". Corson (2001: 67–68) argues in the following excerpt that this discrimination unjustly affects the majority of children; he explains the importance of non-standard varieties and demands that non-standard varieties and linguistic diversity be valued in schools:

> Most speakers of a language use a variety that differs in recognizable ways from the standard variety; none of these varieties is in any sense inherently inferior to the standard variety in grammar, accent, or phonology. At the same time, these sociocultural and geographical variations within a language are signalling matters of great importance to those who use them. Varieties serve valuable group identity functions for their speakers; they express interests that are closely linked to matters of self-respect and other psychological attributes. It follows that different language varieties deserve respect and recognition in education.
>
> [...] To give non-standard varieties the respect they deserve, as regular systematic varieties of language that mean a great deal to their speakers, non-standard varieties need to be valued in schools, in much the same way as community languages other than English need valuing.

Corson's claim rests at least in part on the findings of the relatively young field of sociolinguistics. In contrast to earlier views that considered non-standard varieties to be deficient, random and ungrammatical, early sociolinguists demonstrated with the help of case-studies that non-standard varieties are systematic, complex, rule-governed and in no way linguistically inferior to standard varieties (see, e.g., Labov 1972). Labov's (1972) findings showed that non-standard varieties are not "misuses of the standard language" (Corson 2001: 73), but, unfortunately, prejudice against non-standard varieties, which are associated with the powerless and lower social status, continues even today.

As far as education is concerned, the use of standard varieties is still valued highly by most schools (Baugh 1997: 33). Many schools seem to "find it easier and fairer to give special status to some dominant language variety or other, partly because this simplifies the task of ranking and sorting students" (Corson 2001: 71). Injustice results for those children who possess less of the valued linguistic resource called standard variety when they arrive at school, for the most part because they have to cope with the additional task of becoming bidialectal (Corson 2001: 71). Perera (2001: 712) claims that there has to be an approach that gives children what they need for adult life but also does not put them at a disadvantage or lead to educational failure:

> Although it is clear that pupils need to have access to the standard form if they are not to be at a disadvantage in the formal settings of adult life, such as job interviews and appearances in court of law, it is nevertheless the case that those who arrive at school speaking a variety of English that is markedly different from the standard may experience considerable difficulty both in becoming bidialectal and in acquiring literacy [...]
>
> Within education (though not necessarily in society at large) there is widespread support for the view that pupils should not be expected to relinquish their non-standard dialect but should be encouraged to expand their linguistic repertoire by the addition of the standard variety.

Now that we have established that non-standard varieties of a language should be valued in education and have their functions just as the standard variety does, the question remains as to what the so-called standard actually is and who decides about it. Despite the fact that the term *standard* is widely used, it is rather difficult to define and there is considerable debate about it (Bex and Watts 1999). Farr and Ball (2001: 753), for example, put forward a rather vague definition of the notion of Standard English which is said to refer "to the variety of English used by the formally-educated people who are socially, economically, and politically dominant in English-speaking countries" and add that there is considerable variation "within what is considered 'standard,' even within one country". Trudgill (1999: 117) goes even further when he says that there is "considerable confusion, even amongst linguists, about what *Standard English* is" and, on a similar note, McArthur (1998: 79) reports that there is currently a widening debate about "what the term Standard English has meant, means, might mean, might be meant to mean, or should most categorically mean". Despite these problems concerning the definition of the notion of standard, most linguists agree that a standard is a highly codified, idealized and supradialectal variety of a language that has undergone standardization, a process that produces a set of lexical, grammatical, and (in spoken language) phonological norms and aims at uniformity (see Ferguson 2006: 21; Trudgill 1999: 117; Milroy 1999: 173; on the complex process of standardization, see Milroy and Milroy 1999, and Romaine, this vol.).

4.3. Multilingualism and education

The education-related issues and controversies surrounding social inequalities and practical problems in multilingual settings are to some extent similar to those concerning the use of non-standard varieties in school contexts. The main question identified above – namely "In communities with more than one language which ones should be used in schools?" – is directly related to the subsidiary question that asks whether every child has "a right to be educated in the language they use at home" (Cook 2003: 4). These questions are obviously concerned with the choice of language of instruction in education, and with language rights and the more recently introduced and more narrowly defined fundamental linguistic human rights of the learner (on the distinction between language rights and linguistic human rights, see Skutnabb-Kangas 2000: 497; Skutnabb-Kangas 2006, and Skutnabb-Kangas, this vol.).

An important role for decisions concerning the language of instruction in education is attributed to the notions of majority and minority (languages). The status of majority and minority is usually tied to national boundaries. Skutnabb-Kangas and Phillipson (1994, quoted in Skutnabb-Kangas 2000: 491) define the notion of *minority* as follows:

> A group which is smaller in number than the rest of the population of a State, whose members have ethnic, religious or linguistic features different from those of the rest of the population, and are guided, if only implicitly, by the will to safeguard their culture, traditions, religion or language.
> Any group coming within the terms of this definition shall be treated as an ethnic, religious or linguistic minority.
> To belong to a minority shall be a matter of individual choice.

According to this definition of minority, a *minority language* can thus be defined as a language that is spoken by a group that is numerically smaller than the rest of the population of a state. It should, however, be pointed out that the term minority is often ambiguous and can, for example, also be used to refer to non-elite or subordinate groups, no matter "whether they constitute a numerical majority or minority in relation to some other group that is politically and socially dominant" (UNESCO 2003: 13). Occasionally, as in the *European Charter for Regional or Minority Languages* (Council of Europe 1992), linguistic minorities are further subdivided into indigenous minorities on the one hand and migrant minorities on the other.

Which language or languages should be used as medium of instruction in multilingual settings is at the heart of many controversies. The UNESCO (2003) *Education Position Paper* recommends mother tongue medium education, because "research has shown that learners learn best in their mother tongue" (UNESCO 2003: 7) and because "[s]peakers of mother tongues, which are not the same as the national or local language, are often at a considerable disadvantage in the education system" (UNESCO 2003: 14). Despite these facts, there are a number of reasons why mother-tongue instruction is far from being the rule, including the following which are listed in the UNESCO (2003: 15–16) paper:

- sometimes the mother tongue may be an unwritten language;
- sometimes the language may not even be generally recognized as constituting a legitimate language;
- the appropriate terminology for education purposes may still have to be developed;
- there may be a shortage of educational materials in the language;
- the multiplicity of languages may exacerbate the difficulty of providing schooling in each mother tongue;
- there may be a lack of appropriately trained teachers;
- there may be resistance to schooling in the mother tongue by students, parents and teachers.

A case in point for the last item in the list may be that "the imposition of mother-tongue primary education on the indigenous population in South Africa by the white minority government during the apartheid regime was seen as an act of repression, since it contributed to the exceptional difficulty black pupils faced in proceeding to secondary or higher education, which was in English and Afrikaans only" (Perera 2001: 711; see also De Klerk 2002: 40). As a result, there is a strong parental demand for English as medium of instruction in South African primary schools. In order to avoid putting children at a disadvantage, the UNESCO (2003: 8, 17–18) recommends that mother-tongue education be complemented by an additive bilingual or multilingual approach, which provides access to national and global languages of wider communication while helping to maintain the minority language. Earlier fears that bilingual or multilingual education could be cognitively burdensome to the child have not proven true. Ferguson (2006: 67–68) concludes after analyzing data from bilingual education programs involving linguistic minority children in the United States:

> On the educational front, we have found no evidence that bilingual education (BE) is harmful. On the contrary, the considerable body of empirical evidence and theory that we have reviewed suggests that BE, understood as comprising the development of the pupil's L1 alongside the learning of English, is more likely than alternatives such as the English-only 'structured immersion' to promote higher levels of educational attainment for linguistic minority pupils [...]
>
> The weight of the educational evidence supportive of additive BE is such that it seems likely that at least some of the widespread opposition to it [...] is ideologically rooted.

We will now see how important it is for the maintenance of minority languages that they are well represented in education.

4.4.   Education and the preservation of linguistic diversity

The preservation of linguistic diversity through the maintenance and revitalization of languages is intricately linked to education and the medium-of-instruction issues discussed in Section 4.3. There have been a number of scholarly publications on endangered languages recently, such as Fishman's (2001) collection *Can Threatened Languages be Saved*, Crystal's (2000) *Language Death* or Nettle and Romaine's (2000) book *Vanishing Voices – the Extinction of the World's Languages*, which suggest a worrying scenario: "of the world's estimated 6,000 languages, only some 600 can be considered safe, or, conversely, 90 per cent of the less prestigious, less demographically strong of the world's languages may become extinct in the course of this century" (Ferguson 2006: 72). This means that our question – "Some languages are dying out. Should that be prevented and, if so, how?" – is highly relevant. Nettle and Romaine (2000) devote a whole chapter to explaining "Why something should be done" and the UNESCO (2003: 12) calls the safeguarding of linguistic diversity "one of the most urgent challenges facing our world". So the question remains, how can linguistic diversity be preserved and what role do applied linguistics and education play in the process?

The causes for language death are multifaceted and involve a myriad of different factors in varying combinations. Nevertheless, two major routes to language death are commonly identified in the literature (see, e.g., Crystal 2000: 70–90; Ferguson 2006: 72). One route involves the relatively abrupt demise of the speakers of a language, for example, through catastrophic natural causes – such as earthquakes, tsunamis, volcanic eruptions, floods or tropical storms –, unfavorable climatic and economic conditions – such as famines and draughts –, deadly diseases, and genocide. In the other and more common route, language death is the final result of a gradual process of declining language maintenance and then language shift, caused, for instance, by the influence of a dominant culture. This section focuses on the second route, as there is no immediate influence of education on the factors in the first route, or as Crystal (2000: 89) puts it, "there is no arguing with a tsunami".

Tsui and Tollefson (2004: 2) claim that the "[m]edium of instruction is the most powerful means of maintaining and revitalizing a language and a culture", and Skutnabb-Kangas (1997: 55) leaves no doubt that "[l]anguage rights in education are central for the maintenance of languages and the prevention of linguistic and cultural genocide". She emphasizes that "for maintenance and development of languages, educational linguistic rights, including the right to mother tongue medium education, are absolutely vital" (Skutnabb-Kangas 1997: 56; see also Section 4.3). Disrespect for these rights in educational systems, on the other hand, ultimately leads to the extermination of languages also referred to as linguistic genocide or linguicide (Skutnabb-Kangas and Phillipson 1999: 48).

Education, however, is not only a vital element of language maintenance, it has recently also played an important part in language revitalization (see also Edwards, this vol.). Ferguson (2006: 34) identifies education as a "key instrument for language revitalization", particularly "in societies emerging from, or rejecting, the old linguistic/cultural hegemony of a dominant, centralised state [...] where teaching the regional language is seen as an essential complement to intergenerational transmission within the family and as generally uplifting to the prestige of the language". So while education and supportive language policies do obviously play an important role in language maintenance and revitalization, the role of the family as the main domain of minority language use and intergenerational transmission should not be underestimated (Fishman 1991). Additionally, Hinton (2001) demands second language teaching of endangered languages as a revitalization strategy, since "by definition endangered languages are not spoken by a large portion of the population to which that language belongs" (Hinton 2001: 757).

Hinton reports that there are currently thousands of revitalization programs underway, as a result of a worldwide movement for the rights of endangered languages. Two current revitalization efforts that Hinton (2001: 757) would call "strong revitalization programs" are, for instance, in place in Wales (Welsh) and Ireland (Irish). These two programs serve as an example for the different outcomes of revitalization programs despite intensive educational efforts in both territories. In the case of Irish, there have been formal attempts to maintain and revive the language since the late nineteenth century, but Ireland is an example where educational efforts to revive the language have essentially failed and not led to a general revival of vernacular Irish, despite compulsory Irish teaching in school (see Edwards, this vol., Section 5.1). The revitalization of Welsh, on the other hand, has made great progress in recent years (Williams 2000; Ferguson 2006: 103). This development is the result of a combination of factors and efforts made inside and outside of the educational sector, including the increased teaching of Welsh and through Welsh (Jones and Martin-Jones 2004: 55), "the rise of a strong community movement in the 1970s, the presence of a visionary leader [...], the establishment of a Welsh-medium television channel, and the passing of protective legislation" (Crystal 2000: 129), as well as a positive attitude towards the Welsh language. Ferguson (2006: 97) cites a 1995 opinion survey according to which 88 % of all respondents considered Welsh "something to be proud of". In summary, educational efforts are obviously crucial to but no guarantee for the success of language revitalization programs, and thus May (2001: 167) concludes that "the fate of a language cannot be borne on the back of education alone".

4.5. Literacy and education

There is general agreement among researchers, education policy makers and teachers that the teaching and learning of literacy is one of the key components of education (Hammond 2001: 162; Perera 2001: 713; UNESCO 2005: 27). This is, among other things, reflected by the UNESCO (2005) *Education For All Global Monitoring Report 2006: Literacy for Life*, which is entirely devoted to literacy. The report places literacy "at the core" of UNESCO's Education for All program and at the same time identifies literacy as "one of the most neglected EFA [Education for All] goals" (UNESCO 2005: 5). Additionally, the United Nations (2006) have declared the period from 2003–2012 the UN Literacy Decade. According to the UNESCO (2006a), literacy education is among the major global challenges the world faces today. The following passage illustrates the need for quality literacy education (UNESCO 2006b):[2]

> While societies enter into the information and knowledge society, and modern technologies develop and spread at rapid speed, 860 million adults are illiterate, over 100 million children have no access to school, and countless children, youth and adults who attend school or other education programmes fall short of the required level to be considered literate in today's complex world.

It is precisely this "required level" of literacy and the definition of the term *literacy* to begin with that bring us back to the literacy-related questions posed by Cook (2003: 4, see Question 5 above) and hint at some of the major problems that make literacy what Hammond (2001: 162) calls a "hot issue" in school education and educational policy-making today. Despite widespread agreement on the importance of literacy education, there is considerable debate and no agreement at all as to what counts as literacy and who can be called *literate* (Barton 2001: 95; Baynham and Prinsloo 2001: 88; Daswani 2001: 739; Davies 2005: 88–89; Hammond 2001: 162; Holme 2004: 1; Street 2003: 87; UNESCO 2005: 29, 147–159). Holme (2004: 1) calls the nature of literacy "elusive", the UNESCO (2005: 29) recommends care when comparing literacy figures – even their own figures from different years – "owing to the lack of consensus over how to define and measure […] 'literacy'", and Daswani (2001: 739) complains that "[t]he multiple connotations of literacy make it difficult, if not impossible, to find an acceptable definition for the term". This makes it difficult to answer Cook's (2003: 4) question whether literacy means "[r]eading and writing, or something more" in a straightforward way, as the term *literacy* in contemporary usage in applied linguistics often (Barton 2001: 98; Carrington and Luke 1997: 98–99; Daswani 2001: 739; UNESCO 2006a) but not always (Joshi and Aaron 2006: xiii; UNESCO 2005: 29) refers to more than its traditional definition as the ability to read and write. The discussion concerning minimum levels of literacy and the multifaceted usage of the term *literacy* is summarized by Davies (2005: 88–89) as follows:

> Literacy is often regarded as the ability to read. But the problem remains of what is selected as the criterion of reading; that is, the ability to read what and the ability to read with how much understanding (and possibly the ability to read how quickly)? Therefore, literacy is more carefully defined in terms of some literacy (or reading test) level. Levels of this kind are commonly converted into years of education and so there are literacy levels for primary, secondary and academic students. Literacy is also used more widely to include writing and indeed other language skills such as speaking, or even more widely to encompass the ease with which an individual operates in the social world. Literacy, therefore, like grammar, culture and discourse, is a useful, vague term which can be used to take account of the social systems and the individual's place in them.

The first of the above definitions presents a normative view of literacy as a unitary set of skills that can be taught, learned and then measured by means of assessment, although even with respect to this notion of literacy "there is no agreement on what abilities and knowledge would count as literacy" (Daswani 2001: 739). This narrow perspective was dominating the debate on literacy education for many years and to some extent still is, particularly when it comes to policies concerning school literacy education, leading to a current disjunction between policy and research (Hammond 2001: 163). This view also underlies the traditional UNESCO (2005: 29) definition of literacy as "the ability to read and write, with understanding, a short, simple sentence about one's everyday life" and media releases claiming for developed countries that "literacy standards are falling" and that students "are unable to read and write adequately" (Hammond 2001: 163).

The question of adequacy leads us to the second broad definition of literacy as a social phenomenon or practice. Two notions of literacy that are closely linked to this definition are the notion of *functional literacy*, reflecting the need to account for differing societal demands with regard to literacy, and the so-called *New Literacy Studies*, introduced in the 1990s in the work of Gee (1990) and Street (1995) and defining literacy as a variable set of social and cultural practices of semiotic visualization. Functional literacy is based on a certain level of literacy a person has to achieve to be able to fulfill certain functions in a given context in a given society (Daswani 2001: 739; UNESCO 2005: 155). Within this framework, literacy is frequently linked more or less directly to socio-economic benefit (Holme 2004: 11–13). Functional literacy approaches to education underlie many current educational policies and focus on measurable results and outcomes of teaching in terms of specific skills and abilities. The New Literacy Studies, on the one hand, also recognize that literacy practices vary in different contexts, but, on the other hand, represent "a new tradition in considering the nature of literacy, focusing not so much on acquisition of skills, […], but rather on what it means to think of literacy as a social practice" and entail the "recognition of multiple literacies" (Street 2003: 77). By turning away from individual skills and competences and by questioning the existence of one homogeneous literacy (Carrington and Luke 1997: 99), work in New Literacy Studies also avoids the categorization of people into literates and illiterates (Baynham and Prinsloo 2001: 83).

From the point of view of language diversity, the problems concerning literacy education in multilingual settings show parallels to the issues discussed in Section 4.3. Just as "research has shown that learners learn best in their mother tongue" (UNESCO 2003: 7), "[i]t is universally accepted that literacy is best imparted in the mother tongue" (Daswani 2001: 741). Despite this knowledge, however, language diversity is frequently ignored by education policy makers. As a case in point, Hammond (2001: 171) complains that the Australian *Literacy for All* policy "has very little recognition of diversity in its proposed strategies for action". Applied linguists have to keep working with both teachers and policy makers to contribute to the development of effective literacy programs that cater to the needs of diverse student populations.

5. (Applied) research perspectives

It has been illustrated throughout this chapter how vast and multifaceted the field of language and education is and thus the five questions discussed in Section 4 cannot and certainly do not cover all current or future topics to be addressed by applied linguistics research on language and education. However, the issues represent a selection of problem areas that have been key topics in the work conducted on language and education in recent years and decades and continue to do so. In a time of globalization, constantly growing communication needs, and increasingly multilingual societies, education faces a multitude of new language-related problems that have to be addressed by applied linguists within the framework of the five problem areas discussed in the previous section.

Questions concerning language teaching and learning (see Section 4.1) have always been at the heart of applied linguistics and will most likely continue to play a central part, albeit at least partly with changing foci, giving more attention to the teaching and learning of minority, or so-called lesser-used, languages. Most applied linguists agree that they "have no way of finally establishing 'the best way' to learn or teach a language" (Davies 1999: 3) and so the quest for the best and most effective teaching and learning methods goes on. Even linguists adopting a much more expanded view of applied linguistics do not challenge the continued importance of work on language teaching and learning within the field of applied linguistics, as illustrated by Pennycook's (2004: 789) recent statement:

> Language teaching has been a domain that has often been considered the principal concern of applied linguistics. While my view of applied linguistics is a much broader one, language teaching nevertheless retains a significant role.

From the point of view of linguistic diversity and language change, the call for increased mother-tongue use in multilingual settings in education and literacy teaching (see Sections 4.3 and 4.5) adds new challenges to the work of applied linguists, as do the allocation of different roles to standard and non-standard varieties of language in education (see Section 4.2) and the need for applied linguistics to contribute to the preservation of a growing number of endangered languages (see Section 4.4). The description of a large number of languages and varieties and the production of teaching materials in as many languages as possible thus has to be among the major areas of work applied linguists focusing on the field of language and education should engage in. For the same reasons, there is a growing interest of applied linguists in language and literacy policies in education, as these policies are key institutional instruments by which governments and other civil society actors can shape language acquisition and language use (Tollefson 2002: 3; May 2001: 167).

Predicting the future is always a dangerous activity, but the following questions will certainly continue to be at the heart of many debates in the field of language and education in the context of linguistic diversity and language change: How can applied linguistics contribute to the reduction of inequalities among learners in multilingual settings? How do we define what standard varieties are and what role do they play in an educational setting that values linguistic diversity and non-standard varieties? How can educational efforts help to maintain and revitalize endangered languages? How can the results of literacy research be applied to education? Time will surely add new challenges and thus new questions to this list.

Notes

1. According to an announcement on the website of Springer Science+Business Media (2006), the second edition of the *Encyclopedia of Language and Education* will appear in 2008 as a set of ten volumes, i.e. eight volumes with essentially the same titles as the first edition of the encyclopedia, supplemented by separate volumes on *Language and Socialization* and *Language Ecology*. (http://www.springer.com/dal/home/education/language+education?SGWID=1-40413-22-173482910-detailsPage=ppm media%7Ctoc, retrieved August 15, 2006)
2. The figures presented probably reflect the traditional UNESCO (2005: 29) definition of literacy as "the ability to read and write, with understanding, a short, simple sentence about one's everyday life," although the UNESCO (2006a) has more recently defined literacy as follows: "Literacy is about more than reading and writing – it is about how we communicate in society. It is about social practices and relationships, about knowledge, language and culture".

6. References

AILA
    2006   AILA 2008, Multilingualism: Challenges & Opportunities, Thematic Strands. http://www.aila2008.org/en/thematic-strands.html, retrieved August 15, 2006.
Barry, Anita K.
    2002   *Linguistic Perspectives on Language and Education*. Westport, CT/London: Bergin & Garvey.
Barton, David
    2001   Directions for literacy research: Analysing language and social practices in a textually mediated world. *Language and Education* 15(2/3): 92–104.
Baugh, John
    1997   Linguistic discrimination in educational contexts. In: Ruth Wodak and David Corson (eds.), *Encyclopedia of Language and Education,* Vol. 1: *Language Policy and Political Issues in Education*, 33–41. Dordrecht: Kluwer.

Baynham, Mike and Mastin Prinsloo
    2001   New directions in literacy research. *Language and Education* 15 (2/3): 83–91.

Berns, Margie and Paul Kei Matsuda
    2006   Applied linguistics: Overview and history. In: Keith Brown (ed.) *Encyclopedia of Language and Linguistics*. 2nd ed., 394–405. Amsterdam: Elsevier.

Bex, Tony and Richard J. Watts (eds.)
    1999   *Standard English: The Widening Debate*. London: Routledge.

Brumfit, Christopher
    1996   Educational linguistics, applied linguistics and the study of language practices. In: George M. Blue and Rosamund Mitchell (eds.), *Language and Education: Papers from the Annual Meeting of the British Association for Applied Linguistics held at the University of Southampton, September 1995*, 1–15. Clevedon: Multilingual Matters.

Carrington, Vicki and Allan Luke
    1997   Literacy and Bourdieu's sociological theory: A reframing. *Language and Education* 11(2): 96–112.

Carter, Ronald and David Nunan
    2001   Introduction. In: Ronald Carter and David Nunan (eds.), *The Cambridge Guide to Teaching English to Speakers of Other Languages*, 1–6. Cambridge: Cambridge University Press.

Center for Applied Linguistics
    2006   About CAL. http://www.cal.org/about/index.html, retrieved August 15, 2006.

Cook, Guy
    2003   *Applied Linguistics*. Oxford: Oxford University Press.

Corson, David
    1997a   General editor's introduction. In: Ruth Wodak and David Corson (eds.), *Encyclopedia of Language and Education*, Vol. 1: *Language Policy and Political Issues in Education*, vii–ix. Dordrecht: Kluwer.

Corson, David (ed.)
    1997b   *Encyclopedia of Language and Education*. 8 vols. Dordrecht: Kluwer.

Corson, David
    2001   *Language Diversity and Education*. Mahwah, NJ: Laurence Erlbaum.

Council of Europe
    1992   *European Charter of Regional and Minority Languages*. Strasbourg: Council of Europe. http://conventions.coe.int/Treaty/en/Treaties/Html/148.htm, retrieved August 15, 2006.

Crystal, David
    2000   *Language Death*. Cambridge: Cambridge University Press.

Daswani, Chander J.
    2001   Literacy. In: Rajend Mesthrie (ed.), *Concise Encyclopedia of Sociolinguistics*, 739–746. Amsterdam: Elsevier.

Davies, Alan
    1999   Introduction. In: Brian T. Riley (ed.), *Encyclopedia of Language and Linguistics*, Vol. 1: *Applied Linguistics*, 3–15. New Delhi: Cosmo Publications.

Davies, Alan
 2005 *A Glossary of Applied Linguistics*. Edinburgh: Edinburgh University Press.
Davies, Alan and Catherine Elder
 2004a General introduction: Applied linguistics: Subject or discipline. In: Alan Davies and Catherine Elder (eds.), *The Handbook of Applied Linguistics*, 1–15. Oxford: Blackwell.
Davies, Alan and Catherine Elder (eds.)
 2004b *The Handbook of Applied Linguistics*. Oxford: Blackwell.
De Klerk, Gerda
 2002 Mother-tongue education in South Africa: The weight of history. *International Journal of the Sociology of Language* 154: 29–46.
Doughty, Catherine and Jessica Williams (eds.)
 1998 *Focus on Form in Classroom Second Language Acquisition*. Cambridge: Cambridge University Press.
Elder, Catherine
 2004 Introduction to part II: Applied linguistics (A-L). In: Alan Davies and Catherine Elder (eds.), *The Handbook of Applied Linguistics*, 423–430. Oxford: Blackwell.
Farr, Marcia and Arnetha F. Ball
 2001 Standard English and educational policy. In: Rajend Mesthrie (ed.), *Concise Encyclopedia of Sociolinguistics*, 753–757. Amsterdam: Elsevier.
Fishman, Joshua
 1991 *Reversing Language Shift: Theoretical and Empirical Foundations of Assistance to Threatened Languages*. Clevedon: Multilingual Matters.
Fishman, Joshua (ed.)
 2001 *Can Threatened Languages be Saved?* Clevedon: Multilingual Matters.
Ferguson, Gibson
 2006 *Language Planning and Education*. Edinburgh: Edinburgh University Press.
Fries, Charles C.
 1945 *Teaching and Learning English as a Foreign Language*. Ann Arbor: University of Michigan Press.
Gass, Susan M. and Sinfree Makoni (eds.)
 2004 *World Applied Linguistics: A Celebration of 40 Years of AILA*. AILA Review 17. Amsterdam/Philadelphia: Benjamins.
Gee, John
 1990 *Social Linguistics and Literacies: Ideology in Discourses*. Hampshire: Falmer.
Grabe, William
 2002 Applied linguistics: An emerging discipline for the twenty-first century. In: Robert P. Kaplan (ed.), *The Oxford Handbook of Applied Linguistics*, 3–12. Oxford/New York: Oxford University Press.
Grin, François
 2002 *Using Language Economics and Education Economics in Language Education Policy*. Strasbourg: Language Policy Division, Council of Europe.
Halliday, Michael, Alexander Kirkwood, Angus McIntosh and Peter Strevens
 1964 *The Linguistic Sciences and Language Teaching*. London: Longman.

Hammond, Jennifer
   2001   Literacies in school education in Australia: Disjunctions between policy and research. *Language and Education* 15(2/3): 162–177.
Hancock, Ian F.
   1999   African American Vernacular English. In: Bernard Spolsky (ed.), *Concise Encyclopedia of Educational Linguistics*, 187–188. Amsterdam: Elsevier.
Hinton, Leanne
   2001   Teaching endangered languages. In: Rajend Mesthrie (ed.), *Concise Encyclopedia of Sociolinguistics*, 757–760. Amsterdam: Elsevier.
Holme, Randall
   2004   *Literacy: An Introduction.* Edinburgh: Edinburgh University Press.
Howatt, Anthony Philip Reid
   1999   History of second language teaching. In: Spolsky, Bernard (ed.), *Concise Encyclopedia of Educational Linguistics*, 618–625. Amsterdam: Elsevier.
Howatt, Anthony Philip Reid and Henry George Widdowson
   2004   *A History of English Language Teaching.* 2nd ed. Oxford: Oxford University Press.
Hudson, Richard
   2004   Why education needs linguistics (and vice versa). *Journal of Linguistics* 40: 105–130.
Hymes, Dell
   1972   On communicative competence. In: John Bernard Pride and Janet Holmes (eds.), *Sociolinguistics: Selected Readings*, 269–293. Harmondsworth: Penguin Books.
Jones, Dylan V. and Marylin Martin-Jones
   2004   Bilingual education and language revitalization in Wales: Past achievements and current issues. In: James W. Tollefson and Amy B. M. Tsui (eds.), *Medium of Instruction Policies: Which Agenda? Whose Agenda?* 43–70. Mahwah: Lawrence Erlbaum.
Joshi, Malatesha R. and P. G. Aaron
   2006   Introduction to the volume. In: Joshi, Malatesha R. and P. G. Aaron (eds.), *Handbook of Orthography and Literacy*, xiii–xiv. Mahwah: Lawrence Erlbaum.
Kaplan Robert B. (ed.)
   1980   *On the Scope of Applied Linguistics.* Rowley, MA: Newbury House.
Kaplan, Robert B.
   2002a   Preface. In Kaplan, Robert B. (ed.), *The Oxford Handbook of Applied Linguistics*, v–x. Oxford/New York: Oxford University Press.
Kaplan, Robert B. (ed.)
   2002b   *The Oxford Handbook of Applied Linguistics.* Oxford/New York: Oxford University Press.
Labov, William
   1972   *Language in the Inner City: Studies in the Black English Vernacular.* Philadelphia: University of Pennsylvania Press.
Littlewood, William T.
   1999   Second language teaching methods. In: Bernard Spolsky (ed.), *Concise Encyclopedia of Educational Linguistics*, 658–668. Amsterdam: Elsevier.

Mackey, William F.
    1965   *Language Teaching Analysis.* London: Longman.
Mackey, William F.
    1966   Applied linguistics: Its meaning and use. *English Language Teaching* 20(3): 197–206.
May Stephen
    2001   *Language and Minority Rights: Ethnicity, Nationalism and the Politics of Language.* Harlow: Pearson.
McArthur, Tom
    1998   *The English Languages.* Cambridge: Cambridge University Press.
McDonough, Steven
    2002   *Applied Linguistics in Language Education.* London: Arnold.
McNamara, Tim
    2001   The roots of applied linguistics in Australia. *Australian Review of Applied Linguistics* 24(1): 13–29.
Milroy, Lesley
    1999   Standard English and language ideology in Britain and the United States. In: Tony Bex and Richard J. Watts (eds.), *Standard English: The Widening Debate,* 173–206. London: Routledge.
Milroy, James and Lesley Milroy
    1999   *Authority in Language: Investigating Standard English.* 3rd ed. London: Routledge.
Nettle, Daniel and Suzanne Romaine
    2000   *Vanishing Voices – the Extinction of the World's Languages.* Oxford: Oxford University Press.
Pennycook, Alastair
    2004   Critical applied linguistics. In: Alan Davies and Catherine Elder (eds.), *The Handbook of Applied Linguistics,* 784–807. Oxford: Blackwell.
Perera, K.
    2001   Education and language: Overview. In: Rajend Mesthrie (ed.), *Concise Encyclopedia of Sociolinguistics*, 710–714. Amsterdam: Elsevier.
Richards, Jack C. and Richard Schmidt
    2004   *Longman Dictionary of Language Teaching and Applied Linguistics.* 3rd ed. London: Longman.
Schmitt, Norbert (ed.)
    2002   *An Introduction to Applied Linguistics.* London: Arnold.
Schmitt, Norbert and Marianne Celce-Murcia
    2002   An overview of applied linguistics. In: Norbert Schmitt (ed.), *An Introduction to Applied Linguistics*, 1–16. London: Arnold.
Seidlhofer, Barbara (ed.)
    2003   *Controversies in Applied Linguistics.* Oxford: Oxford University Press.
Skutnabb-Kangas, Tove
    1997   Human rights and language policy in education. In: Ruth Wodak and David Corson (eds.), *The Encyclopedia of Language and Education*, Vol. 1: *Language Policy and Political Issues in Education*, 55–65. Dordrecht: Kluwer.
Skutnabb-Kangas, Tove
    2000   *Linguistic Genocide in Education – or Worldwide Diversity and Human Rights?* Mahwah, NJ: Lawrence Erlbaum.

Skutnabb-Kangas, Tove
   2006   Language policy and linguistic human rights. In: Thomas Ricento (ed.), *An Introduction to Language Policy: Theory and Method*, 273–291. Oxford: Blackwell.

Skutnabb-Kangas, Tove and Robert Phillipson
   1999   Linguicide. In: Bernard Spolsky (ed.), *Concise Encyclopedia of Educational Linguistics*, 48–49. Amsterdam: Elsevier.

Street, Brian
   1995   *Social Literacies*. London: Longman.

Street, Brian
   2003   What's new in New Literacy Studies? Critical approaches to literacy in theory and practice. *Current Issues in Comparative Education* 5 (2): 77–91.

Tollefson, James W.
   2002   *Language Policies in Education: Critical Issues*. Mahwah: Lawrence Erlbaum.

Tsui, Amy B. M. and James W. Tollefson
   2004   The centrality of medium-of-instruction policy in sociopolitical processes. In: James W. Tollefson and Amy B. M. Tsui (eds.), *Medium of Instruction Policies: Which Agenda? Whose Agenda?* 1–18. Mahwah: Lawrence Erlbaum.

Trudgill, Peter
   1999   Standard English: What it isn't. In: Tony Bex and Richard J. Watts (eds.), *Standard English: The Widening Debate*, 117–128. London: Routledge.

UNESCO
   2003   *Education in a Multilingual World*. UNESCO Education Position Paper. Paris: UNESCO. http://unesdoc.unesco.org/images/0012/001297/129728e.pdf, retrieved August 15, 2006.

UNESCO
   2005   *Education for All Global Monitoring Report 2006: Literacy for Life*. Paris: UNESCO.

UNESCO
   2006a   United Nations Literacy Decade 2003–2012: Literacy as Freedom. Today, literacy remains a major global challenge. http://portal.unesco.org/education/en/ev.php-URL_ID=26957&URL_DO=DO_TOPIC&URL_SECTION=201.html, retrieved August 15, 2006.

UNESCO
   2006b   United Nations Literacy Decade 2003–2012: Literacy as Freedom. http://portal.unesco.org/education/en/ev.php-URL_ID=5000&URL_DO=DO_TOPIC&URL_SECTION=201.html, retrieved August 15, 2006.

United Nations
   2006   The UN Literacy Decade (2003–2012). http://www.un.org/av/photo/subjects/literacy.htm, retrieved August 15, 2006.

University of Michigan
   2006   A brief history of the English Language Institute. http://www.lsa.umich.edu/eli/eli_detail/0,2853,19134%255Farticle%255F46741,00.html, retrieved August 15, 2006.

Van Els, Theo, Theo Bongaerts, Guus Extra, Charles van Os and Anne-Mieke Janssen-van Dieten

1984 *Applied Linguistics and the Learning and Teaching of Foreign Languages.* London: Arnold.

Wilkins, D. A.
1999 Applied linguistics. In: Bernard Spolsky (ed.), *Concise Encyclopedia of Educational Linguistics*, 6–17. Amsterdam: Elsevier.

Williams, Colin H. (ed.)
2000 *Language Revitalization: Policy and Planning in Wales.* Cardiff: University of Wales Press.

Wodak, Ruth and David Corson (eds.)
1997 *Encyclopedia of Language and Education,* Vol. 1: *Language Policy and Political Issues in Education.* Dordrecht: Kluwer.

Wolfram, Walt and Donna Christian
1989 *Dialects and Education: Issues and Answers.* Englewood Cliffs: Prentice Hall.

14. Forensic linguistics

John Gibbons

1. Introduction

Applied linguistics is an academic field in which real world language problems and issues are addressed. There are two major parts to this: first the analysis of a language issue and possible remedies, and second an attempt to tackle it; I refer to these as the "reflection" and "action" stages. The reflection stage often includes a broad survey of a particular area of social life, before focussing down on those areas where problems and issues arise, and then discussing a range of possible ways of handling them. The broad survey approach, typified in the work of continental Europeans such as Bourdieu and Passeron (1990), is a critical first step which contextualises all that follows. The focus on particular social problems has become a particular concern of critical linguistics in recent years. Critical analysis has a better chance of achieving positive outcomes if it leads to concrete solutions, so the "action" stage, the discussion and analysis of practical remedies, is also part of the responsibility of the applied linguist. The more technical "action" stage includes developing, trialling, implementing and evaluating measures to address the issues, and involves the eclectic use of information, theory and practical procedures from wherever they are available. It is of course the case that there are few language issues where we achieve a full resolution; applied linguists – like all scholars – are involved in a continual process of striving, often making progress, but rarely fully attaining.

When this framework is applied to legal systems, it reveals a myriad of language issues and problems, and only limited attempts to address them.

2. Legal systems

The legal systems of the world can be classified roughly into four types (David and Brierly 1985). Locally based "Traditional" systems are found in cultures around the world. The three main international systems are Shari'ah, which has its origins in the Koran; the system which originated in ancient Rome – variously called "Continental", "Civil" and "Roman" law (I shall use the last term); and the system that had its origin in mediaeval England – "Common Law". I shall focus mainly on Roman Law and Common Law, because their language aspects are more accessible to Western scholarship.

Roman Law is the most widespread form of legal system, currently used in the majority of the world's countries. Roman Law, which was a mainly oral system for several centuries in ancient Rome, was finally codified under the Emperor Justinian as the "Justinian Code". It became the legal system of most of continental Europe, and was comprehensively revised in Napoleonic France, and later in Germany. It has spread through many parts of the world as a result of European colonialism and influence, and is now used in various forms in most of Europe, Asia (including Japan and China), Africa, the Middle East, and South and Central America, with the exception of those countries influenced by English speakers, particularly the former British Empire, and territories administered by the US, Australia, and New Zealand. Scotland has a blend of Roman and Common Law, and many countries have blended Roman with Traditional Law or Shari'ah Law.

Traditionally the major characteristic of Roman Law was that a judge or magistrate had the task of discovering the facts of the matter, then deciding how the written law applied to the facts – for this reason it is sometimes called "inquisitorial". Often judges have teams of people who collect testimony from witnesses and parties, and who (sometimes working with police) gather material evidence and other forms of information. In some systems the judge may see the witnesses or parties quite briefly or not at all, and s/he makes decisions based mainly on written reports prepared by staff. This procedure has changed to some degree in recent years towards a more "open court" system in some Roman Law jurisdictions, notably Germany, Italy and some South American countries. For the applied forensic linguist, major issues are the language processes involved in obtaining, producing and using written evidence.

The Common Law system is sometimes characterised as "adversarial", because courtroom procedure consists of a struggle between opposing parties to have accepted different versions of events and different applications of the law to those events. It does not pursue a single "truth" as such. Another characteristic of the Common Law system which distinguishes it from Roman Law in serious cases is that guilt or innocence is decided by a panel of non-lawyers, the jury, while the judge's role is more technical, managing the relationship between the case and the law, and applying penalties, costs, etc. (Japan has recently adopted a limited jury system.) In less serious cases, however, there is no jury, and the judge takes over their role. Critical studies of courtroom procedures given in what follows have revealed problems, particularly for vulnerable parties and witnesses, in understanding the law, understanding legal processes, and coping with adversarial courtroom questioning.

In both types of legal system the main institutions are police, courts and prisons, although there are a range of other arenas where the law is manifested, such as lawyers' chambers and probation services.

Some language in legal contexts is not markedly different from that used in other administrative contexts, apart from the use of some high frequency legal terms. However, particularly in Common Law systems, there are certain types of legal language that are less usual. The best known of these is the written language of legislation and regulation, shared to some degree by other legal documents such as wills and contracts. The second area where legal language differs substantially from everyday language is the oral language of courtroom examination.

3. The language of legislation and legal documents

The law is largely a linguistic phenomenon. Legislation, and various forms of legal relationships and understanding such as contracts and wills, are essentially constituted by language. All the concepts and relationships of the law are manifested primarily in language. The world view contained in the law differs from everyday knowledge and understanding in a range of ways, and in consequence, these are expressed in non-everyday language.

3.1. Technical vocabulary

It is well documented (Tiersma 1999; Gibbons 2003) that one of the features of written legal language which differentiates it from other forms of written language is highly technical vocabulary. The following are examples of words that are rarely used in other than a legal sense: *annul, bequest, complainant, damages, intestate, leasehold, writ*. Each of these words is used to construct a particular legal concept that takes its meaning from the framework of legal ideas in which it is embedded. The same holds for legal terms in Roman Law systems, although it seems likely that their number is somewhat lower.

In England there was a pre-existing system of Canon (religious) law, that operated in Latin. Likewise the Roman Law system developed in Latin, and in mediaeval Europe the local descendants of this system continued to operate in mediaeval Latin. It was therefore natural, when a specialist legal term was needed, to continue in some cases to use the Latin form rather than pursuing a local language form.

In Australia's Common Law system (for an accessible account, see Robinson 1994), some common Latin expressions and terms still in use are: *affidavit, bona fide, caveat, (decree) nisi, de facto, mens rea, onus, prima facie, subpoena*. Examples from Spain's Roman Law system are: *iuris tantum, do ut des, ratione materiae, animus defendendi*. Another phenomenon is where Latin words are to some degree modified to fit into the other language (such as English or Spanish) – these words might be called "Latinisms". Examples from the Chilean legal system are: *exacción, exención, evicción, prescripción, prestación, contratación*. In English they include words such as: *codicil, deponent, jurisprudence, nuptial, statute*.

The legal system in England also operated in Norman French for some centuries after the Norman invasion, and for the same reason Norman French legal terms continued to be used in Common Law. Examples in Australian legal English are: *adjourn, bailiff, (a) devise, mortgage, tenant, tort, void, voir dire*. Once more words may be modified to fit into the borrowing language. English examples are: *decree, lease, surety, waive*. Many of these Norman French legal terms have become part of broader English, for instance: *claim, guarantee, judge, liability*.

In legal English, one consequence of this multilingual history (Hiltunen 1990) is that, in order to be safe, lawyers tended to use words from Old English (OE), Norman French (F) and Latin (L) together. Legal English in general has a strong tendency to string synonyms together in groups of two, three or even four (sometimes referred to as "polynomial expressions"), such as:

of sound mind (OE) *and memory* (L)
give (OE) *devise* (F) *and bequeath* (OE)
will (OE) *and testament* (L)
goods (OE) *and chattels* (F)
final (F) *and conclusive* (L)
fit (OE) *and proper* (F)
new (OE) *and novel* (F)
save (F) *and except* (L)
peace (F) *and quiet* (L)

This tendency is also found in legal Spanish, for instance:

visto y examinado 'seen and examined'
según mi leal saber y entender 'according to my knowledge and understanding'
debo condenar y condeno 'I must condemn and I condemn'
desarrollado y implementado 'developed and implemented'
pleno y cabal 'full and frank'
todas y cada una 'each and every'
ocasionalmente o durante cierto lapso de tiempo 'occasionally or during a certain period of time'
procedente y de nacionalidad 'proceeding from and of nationality'
digo y declaro 'I state and declare'

A related characteristic of legal technicality is the maintenance of archaic vocabulary that is rare or entirely missing in everyday language. This happens because, if a particular wording is found to properly perform a legal function and resist challenge, that wording is adhered to, often for centuries. The result is extreme linguistic conservatism and archaism. In the extract given in Section 3.2., examples are *whereas* and *(a) remit*.

There are a range of other aspects of the technicality of legal vocabulary including the use of proper names, numbers to refer to well known aspects of legislation, and slang such as having someone "sectioned", or the expression "a silk". All of the aspects discussed above conspire to make the language of the law very different from everyday conversational language.

However, another aspect of legal vocabulary is arguably the most problematic. It is not the use of specialist terms, but rather the use of everyday terms with specialist meanings. Some examples from Australian legal English follow; see Table 1:

Table 1. The use of everyday terms with specialist meanings

Word	Legal definition (The Law Handbook = Redfern 1988)	Common definition (Cobuild Dictionary = Sinclair 1987)
award	The decision of an arbitrator, for example in industrial arbitration proceeding. Once it is made it has the force of law and can be enforced in the same way as a court order or judgement.	A prize or certificate that you are given by an organization for doing something well or doing it better than other people
consideration	The price paid for the promise of the other party (in a contract)	1. Consideration of something is thinking carefully about it 3. Consideration is also attention paid to the needs, wishes, or feelings of another person
deed	A written document	1. A deed is something that is done with a particular purpose, especially something that is very good or very bad
exhibit	A document or thing tendered as evidence in a court hearing	Something that is put on show to the public in a museum or art gallery

The potential for miscommunication in the use of such vocabulary is obvious. Diamond and Levi (1996) discuss disturbing cases where jurors took the word "aggravating" in its everyday sense of "annoying" and imposed the death penalty, where the death penalty for murder was applied only when there were "aggravating factors" (i.e. things that made it worse).

3.2. Syntactic complexity

Moving on from technical vocabulary, a typical requirement of laws or regulations is that they define particular behaviours or states, particularly any aspects of them that are seen as desirable or undesirable, and then set up a set of conditions that determine when those behaviours/states are permitted or prevented. This type of "cognitive structure" (Bhatia 1994) has a range of linguistic consequences. One is extreme syntactic complexity. Legal language tends to use very long and complex sentences. Some of these are so complex that they cannot be understood when read aloud – only in the written form can they be decoded.

Cutts (2001) quotes the following extract from EU Council Directive 88/378/EEC concerning the safety of toys:

> Whereas, to facilitate proof of conformity with the essential requirements, it is necessary to have harmonized standards at European level which concern, in particular, the design and composition of toys so that products complying with them may be assumed to conform to the essential requirements; whereas these standards harmonized at European level are drawn up by private bodies and must remain non-mandatory texts; whereas for that purpose the European Committee for Standardization (CEN) and the European Committee for Electrotechnical Standardization (CENELEC) are recognized as the competent bodies for the adoption of harmonized standards in accordance with the general guidelines for cooperation between the Commission and those two bodies signed on 13 November 1984; whereas, for the purposes of this Directive, a harmonized standard is a technical specification (European standard or harmonization document) adopted by one or both of those bodies upon a remit from the Commission in accordance with the provisions of Council Directive 83/189/EEC of 28 March 1983 laying down a procedure for the provision of information in the field of technical standards and regulations, as last amended by the Act of Accession of Spain and Portugal, and on the basis of the general guidelines;

It illustrates various characteristics of legal language, including syntax. Note that it does not contain a single full stop, so in principle this is a single sentence, and one that is preceded and followed by other "whereas" clauses, to the point where a single sentence takes more than a page of text. If we look at the first part of this extract to the first semi-colon, it is a sentence in grammatical terms. It contains three major clauses, and two minor clauses (without a transitive verb), in a range of grammatical relationships including a clause of purpose, a relative clause, and a whiz-deleted clause "the products complying with them" that is the subject of the verb "assume". This level of syntactic complexity is not unusual as the rest of the extract illustrates. It is a challenge to unpack and comprehend the meaning relationships constructed by these grammatical means. As part of complex "cognitive structuring", legal language, like many specialist varieties of language including scientific English, needs to construct complex concepts, sometimes by complex noun or verb phrases, and sometimes by definitions.

Solan (2006) gives an example of a legal definition. It is New York's burglary statute, which characterises that crime as follows:

> A person is guilty of burglary [...] when he knowingly enters or remains unlawfully in a building with intent to commit a crime therein. (N.Y. Penal Law § 140.20, defining Burglary in the Third Degree)

Here the definition is done by complex modification of the verb, using grammatically metaphorical adverbs, "knowingly" (from the verb "know") and "unlawfully" (from the noun "law" via an adjective "unlawful"), and then adds two circumstances using prepositional phrases "in a building" and "with intent to commit a crime therein". The complexity here is at the level of the phrase, rather than sentence combination.

Legal language also (for the same reason) frequently contains long and complex noun phrases, which also contain substantial "grammatical metaphor" by which modifiers, adjectives and nouns are derived from other parts of speech. An example from the earlier "toy safety" extract is "the competent bodies for the adoption of harmonized standards" in which instances of grammatical metaphor (Halliday 1994) are "adoption" (from the verb "adopt") and "harmonized" (from the noun "harmony" – here also a semantic metaphor). Notice how the accumulated meaning becomes difficult to unpack.

Notice also that the last five lines of that extract are all post-modifiers of "technical specification", in a considerable range of grammatical relationships. This provides a further illustration of how precise and complete definition can lead to complex grammatical structure.

Another characteristic of the language of legislation and regulation that is mentioned by Cutts is that there are problems with formatting, logical organisation, and clarity in presenting the administration's objectives. The text above, as Cutts' booklet illustrates, can be far better organised so as to present the *structure* of its content more clearly. Poor organisation and presentation are common in legal texts. In Gibbons (2003) I discuss a range of other complex and unusual features of legal language such as the lack of pronouns, and archaic deictics such as "hereinafter".

3.3. Intelligibility of legal language

There is an extensive psycholinguistic literature (e.g. English and Sales 1997; Felker et al. 1981) which reveals that all these types of complexity – lexical, phrasal, syntactic and textual – make texts difficult to understand, particularly for non-lawyers. Legal language that uses everyday words with specialist meaning may also be misleading.

For the purposes of this Handbook, the question that arises is whether this comprehension problem is a social and applied linguistic issue. If people poorly understand laws, they are left ignorant of them. Yet "ignorance of the law is no defence". There is therefore a fundamental problem in the contradiction between the (lack of) intelligibility of legal language and the assumptions made by the law. This constitutes a call for applied linguistic action.

The reaction from lawyers to this point is mixed. Some, perhaps the majority, refuse to acknowledge its importance – Cutts and Wagner (2002) discuss an example of this. Other lawyers, however, recognise the importance of the issue. For example, Lord Woolf, Master of the Rolls and therefore senior lawyer in England, has been involved in substantial work to replace archaisms, and legal French and Latin. Similarly the Law Reform Commission of Victoria, Australia, produced important guidelines on plain legal language which have been acknowledged at Federal level. Lawyers often make the point that in order to express legal concepts, some legal terminology is essential. Legal communication would be virtually impossible if every legal term were replaced with an explanation. However, many people in plain legal language movements remark that much of the complexity of legal language is unnecessary. While some specialist terms and concepts are needed, much of the complexity of legal texts is redundant. Not to address the unnecessary complexity, which is a major source of poor communication between lawyers and the public, is clearly unacceptable given the importance of the legal system in society, and the potential for abuse of those who cannot understand it.

The need for plainer legal language has been expressed by plain language advocates in a number of countries, and with regard to a number of languages. *Clarity* (see http://www.clarity-international.net/) is a worldwide group of lawyers and interested lay people who advocate reform of legal language. Many English speaking countries have movements, including the USA, Canada, UK and Australia. The UK for example has two private sector groups supporting plain language: the Plain Language Commission and the Plain Language Campaign.

In the Spanish speaking world I have found evidence of work in Argentina, Chile, Mexico and Spain. For example, in 2004 the government of Mexico initiated a program fostering plain language (http://www.lenguajeciudadano.gob.mx/).

The European Union, with input from Cutts and others, has produced a "Joint Practical Guide" to clear writing and drafting (http://europa.eu.int/eur-lex/).

Sweden has one of the oldest programs, which is run by the Ministry of Justice – even bills headed to the legislature go through plain language editing (http://www.regeringen.se/sb/d/4409).

Similarly, Germany has made considerable efforts towards plain German – see for instance the recommendations of the "Gesellschaft für deutsche Sprache" (http://www.gfds.de/).

France, too, has a long established plain language movement, and the government has established a Committee to work on this – the "Comité d'orientation pour la simplification du langage administratif" (COSLA) (http://www.dusa.gouv.fr/cosla/).

What then is the nature of the advice that is given concerning the writing of legal language? Essentially it addresses the issues raised previously. At the linguistic structure level (Felker et al. 1981 still provide some of the best advice), it is suggested that arcane, foreign or unusual words be replaced by words that are more comprehensible. For instance, COSLA suggests using a vocabulary "that the reader can understand". At the phrase level, because the concepts "grammatical metaphor" and "noun phrase structure" are not part of normal language understanding, the advice is usually expressed in terms of avoiding nominalisations and long lists of nouns. At the level of syntax, the advice is usually framed in terms of sentence length rather than sentence complexity. However, more attention has been paid in recent years to the discourse level. (It may be worth pointing out that, no matter how well organised and presented, a letter written in Luo would be largely unintelligible to 99% of the world's population – language matters.)

COSLA gives a good example of these discourse concerns. Paraphrasing from the French, the Committee makes the following suggestions (I have inserted linguistic labelling in brackets):

– Construct the text carefully – use headings, a body, figures and annexes for minor information (genre)
– Take a respectful and helpful relationship to the reader (appropriate tenor)
– Present clearly the writer's objectives – particularly obligations upon and warnings to the reader (clarify speech acts)
– Organise the argument logically and effectively (coherence)

It may seem that these language and discourse recommendations are self evident. However, it is still the case that the majority of legal texts fail to meet most of the criteria described above, and therefore continue to effectively prevent most of the population from better understanding legal texts, particularly the least educated and most vulnerable. The unfortunate consequences of this are widely documented – for an example see Labov and Harris (1994), who demonstrate how poorly educated steel workers were prevented from obtaining their full redundancy entitlements by signing a legal waiver that they could not fully understand.

4. Spoken interaction in the legal system

Another area where the language of the law can differ markedly from everyday language is spoken interaction. Some spoken interaction in legal contexts is little different from everyday conversation, but sometimes unequal power relationships and the objectives of legal interaction are strongly represented in the language used.

One example is the lawyer-client interview. One would expect this situation to be one where power relations would be reasonably balanced, since the client is the employer of the lawyer. In reality however, lawyers tend to dominate and control the client (Hosticka 1979).

In the context of police questioning, Fairclough (1989: 18) gives a powerful account of police officers dominating the discourse, Gudjonsson (2003) speaks of police officers pursuing proof rather than truth, and Hall (2004) reveals both the pursuit of the police version, and a rigid adherence to an underlying police genre. Hall (2004) gives the following example of a common type of police question, which introduces the police version, and gives the interviewee little opportunity of presenting a different account:

> Police Officer: And do you agree you said to the ambulance officers, 'He called me a motherfucker'?

Notice that there is triple projection here – "do you agree", "you said" and "he called me". A denial at this point could mean "I do not agree", "I did not say this" or "he didn't call me a motherfucker". However, it is courtroom examination, with its unequal power balance, that is most distant from normal conversation.

4.1. The construction of competing versions of an event

In the Common Law system, a well established understanding of what happens is that the two sides are attempting to construct competing versions of the same event or state (Bennett and Feldman 1981), in other words two different reconstructions of the same external reality. In criminal cases, the prosecution is usually trying to construct a version that will prove that the accused person is guilty, while the defence lawyers are usually trying to construct a competing version of the same events that means their client is not guilty, or is worthy of lenient treatment, or alternatively attempting to show that the prosecution's version has weaknesses which place it in "reasonable doubt". In civil cases, counsel for the plaintiff and defence are again attempting to construct competing versions of events that will win their case. Since Common Law courtroom practice is essentially a form of miniature warfare, the two sides are not only *constructing* competing versions of reality, they are trying to *impose* them. Cotterill (2003) provides a detailed account of this process.

Another purpose, which is found more in lawyer argument, particularly closing statements, than in witness testimony, is an attempt to fit their story to the law – for instance to show that the story fits the category of guilty of a certain crime, or on the other hand that a party is not liable for a tort.

Although material evidence may be important, it is overwhelmingly language, both testimony and lawyer argument, that is used to construct the competing versions. The question here is: How do counsels achieve this purpose of constructing and imposing a particular version. Here I expand and restructure the description in Gibbons (2003).

Looking at these issues in a little more detail, in the Common Law system, when lawyers are cross examining a hostile witness, they have to play a complex game, where they are attempting almost simultaneously to do various things:
(1) construct and support their version of events
(2) attack the version of the other side, and
(3) with hostile witnesses, attack their credibility
(4) with friendly witnesses, support their credibility

The prosecution tends to be under more pressure to construct a convincing account, while the defence may focus more on destroying the prosecution's case. In practice it can be quite difficult to separate out these four agendas, since one utterance or question may be serving two or three of them, but in principle the divisions are clear. In each agenda, a hostile witness is attempting to do the exact reverse, so cross examination is a verbal battlefield between the lawyer and the witness, in which lawyers have the upper hand, since in principle the conventions of examination mean that they are expected to ask the questions, and control the turn taking, while witnesses can only respond. Stygall (1994: 146) states "For lawyers, the focus of attention to question forms is on how to control witnesses. Their assumption is that by controlling what the witnesses say, they will also control what the jurors think". If lawyers cannot get witnesses to agree with them, then they attempt to discredit the witness and his/her testimony.

4.2.   The examples: Pressure on witnesses

The examples that I will use come mainly from four court cases that were heard in Hong Kong Common Law courtrooms; all the defendants were charged with sexual assault on (female) minors. The data consist of 71 hours of audio recordings of courtroom interaction from a research project with Ester S. M. Leung (Leung and Gibbons, forthcoming).

Pressure on friendly witnesses

One misapprehension is that the testimony of friendly witnesses is relatively uncontrolled, and that they are given a fairly free rein to present their version of events. The reality is that often the testimony of friendly witnesses is controlled by counsel just as tightly as that of hostile witnesses. Example 1 is an example of examination-in-chief of a friendly witness. The lawyer gives the witness no chance to provide a narrative account, but instead carefully limits the witness's responses to single items of information, and slowly constructs a particular version of events (that she has a friend, the time they were friends, that they went to karaoke, that she was a waitress at a karaoke box).

Example 1 (Transcription conventions and abbreviations at end of chapter)
  1. BP: my lord i'll call my first witness NYT who is from page seventy fifty five
  2. JE: thank you

[identificatory material omitted]
  3. BP: do you have a friend a girl friend that you've met since you're twelve years old called HKP
  4. ICT: 妳有一個女性嘅朋友啊十二歲已經識佢㗎嘞叫做 kkp. (.) 有冇
  5. WC: 何嘉寶
  6. IC: 何嘉寶
  7. IET: yes
  8. BP: and by the time of june last year were you and she actually (unintelligible)
  9. ICT: 到舊年六月嗰陣時妳同呢個何嘉寶啊大家非?常之老友
  10. WC: 係
  11. IET: ye::s
  12. BP: did you two enjoy going out to karaoke bar singing
  13. ICT: 咁啊大家兩個呢就經常出去卡拉 ok 啊:酒吧啊:去(.)唱吓歌啊咁 (1.0)
         非常之喜歡做呢啲嘢
  14. WC: 係因為本身喺卡拉 ok box 度番工
  15. IC: 卡拉 ok box 嗰度
  16. WC: 係啊
  17. IET: ye:s at that time i was working (.) at karaoke box
  18. BP: by the waitress sorry as a waitress
  19. ICT: 係做女侍應係咪?
  20. WE: waitress
  21. IET: waitress

There is also a rule of evidence concerning "leading questions" to friendly witnesses, which says in essence that the lawyer should not put words into the witness's mouth. It seems that many of these questions are in fact leading questions, see particularly lines 3 and 18. In our data the difference between the examination of friendly and hostile witnesses is quite small.

What linguistic means might a lawyer use to control witnesses, and get them to agree with or even provide versions of events with which they disagree? These means can be both discoursal and lexico-grammatical.

Politeness
One of these is politeness. Conversation Analysis (Hutchby and Wooffitt 1998) discusses "preferred and dispreferred responses", in other words, people attempt to be cooperative, and in so doing there are social norms which may make dissent and disagreement less acceptable, particularly when speaking to strangers. If witnesses continually contest the version of events put to them by lawyers, then juries in particular are likely to see them as uncooperative and in some way violating social norms, which helps to discredit both them and their testimony. Furthermore, there is a general requirement in court that witnesses be cooperative and answer questions – judges may intervene if a witness appears deliberately obstructive. Questions also license certain forms of response. If witnesses give a reply in a form that is not licensed by the question, this can appear uncooperative. Lawyers are well aware of all this, and one of their skills is the framing of questions in ways that exploit the situation.

There is therefore a constant subtle politeness pressure on witnesses to agree with lawyers. If however this does not work, then lawyers can exploit the seeming lack of politeness to discredit the witness and his/her testimony. For example, during my own cross examination in jury trials I have had counsel who disliked my testimony deliberately attempting to annoy me so that I would become hostile, and also openly accusing me of being uncooperative when I refused to accept their version.

Other non-lexicogrammatical means
These include repetition and returning repeatedly to a topic (Berk-Seligson 1999), and nonverbal elements such as intonation, pace, loudness, and the physical posture of the lawyer, including eye contact. In the following example, capitals represent loudness:

Example 2
  BD: **will you agree with ME** (.) THIS (.) would AVOID (.) the possibility (.) at least of you going over to his house AGAIN?

One way of discrediting the witness is status reduction – making the witness appear in some way lacking in status, and thereby making their testimony less worthy of consideration. The linguistic means include address forms and sometimes such choices are deliberately inappropriate to the courtroom (Bülow-Møller 1991). In T/V languages like Spanish, which have formal and informal forms of "you", this can be done by pronoun choice.

In the Hong Kong case from which some of the examples are taken, a 15 year old female was frequently addressed using the Cantonese familiar address form 'Ah' + given name.

Another means is sarcasm, which often presupposes some knowledge deficit or other type of deficit in the other person.

In Example 3 the patronising and sarcastic tone is conveyed mainly by expressions such as "so it never occurred to you" and "you should at least see if":

Example 3
    BD: **so** (.) **it never occurred to you** on THAT phone chat (.) when he told you come over to MY house (3.0) to watch the video (.) about badminton (.) that *you should* (.) *at least* (.) *see if* he (1.0) he could LEND you the video and so that you can watch it at home

Projection

Another area of language that is used to impose a version of events is projection – reported speech, reported thought and reported belief.

Previously spoken material can be quoted highly selectively, and out of context in such a way that it appears to mean something different from what it meant when it was said. On occasions it can be reworded with similar results. Projections are often used in "reformulation" (Drew 1990), where the witness's version is reshaped to fit the lawyer's version, and quoted back to the witness for confirmation – a classic rhetorical trap. An example is "You mean that you liked her", where the witness had said only that she met the other woman occasionally.

In the Hong Kong courtroom discourse a common and subtle device for influencing the judge's and/or jury's understanding of projection is the use of the utterance particle /woh/ – a discoursal resource. In Leung and Gibbons (forthcoming), we note that it expresses the speaker's attitude to the utterance referred to, expressing an element of doubt, and implying that the speaker is going along with it with some discomfort. This meaning can be deployed by lawyers to express sarcasm when saying "you are contradicting yourself". There is an example of this in Example 4. In the first turn, the lawyer is showing impatience with the repeated answers of the defendant who has been saying that the girl was willing to have sex with him. He stopped the defendant by putting forward to him another question, asking whether the defendant was suggesting that the second defendant was violent and tried to use force to have sex with the girl, and making clear his disbelief in this version by repeating several times "you're saying"; in other words this is the defendant's version, but the lawyer does not go along with it.

Example 4
    BP: = we'd better let the jury to to decide let me just to say this (.) you you you're saying that you're saying on the other hand you're saying that D2 (.) is the violent guy (.) the guy who tried to forcibly rape the girl right
    ICT: 嗱好喎你你講過啫係你相信個女仔呢係自願呢你好多次喎得口喎個留番呢陪審員自己決定喎但另一方面呢(.)你呢(.)就(.)好似(.)講到呢(.)阿第二被告就係一個呢嘩好: a:暴力嘅咁呢就係(.)夾硬呢要同個女仔進行性行為<u>喎</u>

[now okay /lak/ you said that you believed the girl was willing /neh/ so many times that's about it leave the decision to the jury /lak/ on the hand you seem to be saying that defendant two is WOW ve::ry violent that he wanted to have sex with the girl forcibly /woh/

DC: 嗰日我淨係睇到呢啲咋嘛
[that day I only saw these]
IET: er I only saw how he acted as I've told the court

Halliday (1994) divides projection into verbal projection, for instance where the verb is "say", "tell", "write", "state", etc. (also known as "reports"); and mental projection, where the verb is "think", "know", "remember", "be aware", etc. There are occasions where the verb "mean" acts in a similar way. The use of projection by lawyers or police can be strategic. In a verbal projection like "You say that he entered the room", there is an assumption that the speaker is committed to the truth of the core proposition ("he entered the room"), making it difficult to deny without painting oneself as a liar. Therefore, if the person answers "No", this denial is primarily a denial of *saying* this, but does not deny that he entered the room (although the denial may affect this core proposition if there is no other evidence for the fact). The core information (he entered the room) is to some degree presupposed or embedded.

Let us look at some examples where this resource is used.

Example 5
BD: **and you told us just now** (1.0) where those places were that you had sexual intercourse with her

This question presupposes that the witness has recounted where sexual intercourse took place, and the sexual intercourse itself is very difficult to deny.

Example 6
BD: **and indeed** (.) **I suggest to you** (.) **em** (1.0) **perhaps you remember saying so** (.) this was not the first visit **as you CLAIMED** (.) you went to his house
W/IE: I disagree

The basic form of this question is "Was this your first visit to his house?". The question is modified away from this base form by several layers of projection "I suggest to you" (lawyer's projection), "you remember saying so" and "you claimed" (witness's projections). The witness cannot answer "no" since it would be most unclear which of the many propositions she is denying – she is forced to find another means "I disagree".

Example 7
BD: **you told us** (7.0) he was taking a shower (.) whilst you were staying inside that quarter (0.2) *is that right*?

The basic form of this question is "Was he taking a shower while you were in the quarters?" Once more the projection "you told us" makes it hard to deny, and the final positive agreement tag places further pressure for agreement.

The difficulty in denying information can be even more pronounced when the verb is a mental process like "remember", "know" or "be aware". These types of projections are also known as "factives" since they presuppose that the core proposition is a "fact". A denial often indicates only a flaw in one's memory, knowledge or alertness, leaving the core proposition strongly presupposed. For instance, the question "Do you remember him entering the room" assumes or presupposes the core proposition, that the person entered the room. A "No" response to this question would usually be interpreted as a problem with the respondent's memory, and tends to assume that he really did enter the room. In consequence the core proposition in a question like this is often entered unchallenged into the discourse, and therefore into the account of events.

Example 8
   BD: **can you recall** (.) since when you started having sexual intercourse with X

Notice that the sexual intercourse is taken as a presupposed "fact".

Example 9
   BD: **did it occur to you indeed** what you were doing what was (.) NOT permitted by the law

Similarly in this example, the illegality is presupposed.

Another permutation that was mentioned above is, who is reporting – the questioner, the witness, or a third party.

Table 2. Projection by questioner, witness or other person

Projection (questioner)	Ex 10 BD: and indeed as I said-em (4.5) this just carried ON (2.0) until (1.5) summer (1.0) nineteen ninety EIGHT (1.0) when you said (4.0) [in a softer voice] obviously to your surprise (1.5) he (.) raped you
Projection (witness)	Ex 11 BP: you said you FELT fully-fully penetrated (3.5) can you explain why that was why you felt that BD: you still remember you celebrated (.) his-em (2.0) nineteen ninety (2.0) eight birthday? (.)
Projection (other person)	Ex 12 BD: yes she said shortly (.) two weeks (.) may be three weeks (.) four weeks later after the first attack?

It can be harder to deny with certainty that other people have said a certain thing (they may have said this not in your presence), than to deny that you said it yourself. When it comes to challenging the core proposition, this is also difficult, since this often implies that the other person is a liar, or at least ill informed.

Discourse markers
Words like "so" and "well" slip by with little attention paid to them. There is evidence from both Spanish-English courtroom interpreting and Cantonese-English interpreting, that interpreters frequently do not interpret them.

Example 13 (Australia)
    BP: **well, do you think that** you might answer the question that I just asked you.
    [back translation of the interpreter's Spanish translation]
    IS: [Ø Ø can you answer the question that I just asked you]
    (from Hale 1999)

In this example notice that both the discourse marker "well" and the mental projection "do you think" have been omitted in the translation.

Example 14
    BD: **so** (.) it never occurred to you on THAT phone chat (.) when he told you come over to MY house (3.0) to watch the video (.) about badminton (.) *that you should* (.) *at least* (.) see if he (1.0) he could lend you the video and so that you can watch it at home?
    [back translation of the interpreter's Cantonese translation]
    IC: **Ø according to what you said about the third occasion** he used the excuse of watching badminton video to coax and to deceive you to his house and then raped you *is that correct*?
    W/IE: right

However, these words are in fact very important in the way that they frame what follows. "So" often makes the lawyer's question a logical outcome of the witness's previous answer, as in Example 15:

Example 15
    BD: =right (0.3)
            so on the (2.0) during the journey did you ask him? (1.5) whether there were anybody coming along with us?
    W/IE: no
    BD: **and**: em that must cause you some concern as soon as he left (0.5) Cheung Kwan O (1.0) *did he not*=

"And" makes the lawyer's question an extension of what has just been said, and it may be used to mean "therefore" as in the previous example.

    "Well" can carry a shade of doubt about the witness's previous answer:

Example 16
    BD: **well er are you suggesting that** it was perfect ...

Example 17

W/IE: **I think** she had not started her summer holiday yet
BD: **well there's evidence in this court that we learnt** the er summer holiday started in mid july

In Example 18, the "and obviously" makes what follows seem a simple logical consequence of the witness's previous testimony. The pressure to agree is increased by the projecting expression "would I be correct", since it is uncooperative to reply that the barrister is incorrect.

Example 18

BD: **and** *obviously* (1.5) what you had in mind (.) *would I be correct* is (0.2) to put your clothes on (2.0) as soon as possible
W/IE: Yes

These discourse markers then are a useful weapon in the lawyer's linguistic arsenal. They make it hard to disagree with a question, by making the question just an extension or a logical outcome of what the witness has said, and they slip by in a way that makes this meaning difficult to challenge.

Vocabulary choice

Perhaps the most important way of construing reality is the use of particular words. Paul Drew (1990) gives the following example, where the lawyer (C) presents one type of wording to represent the external reality (in bold): "bar", "girls and fellas" and "sit with you"; which witness (W) replaces with her own: "club", "people" and "sat at our table".

Example 19 (USA – Drew 1990)

C: And you went to a bar in Boston, is that correct?
W: It's a club
C: It's where girls and fellas meet isn't it?
W: People go there
C: And during that evening didn't Mr X come over to sit with you?
W: Sat at our table

Notice the skilful use of vocabulary by both sides.

The rejection of the other side's wording may go beyond vocabulary to whole narrative elements. In the next example, we can see how the witness resists the barrister's implication that she knew she would be sexually assaulted again, and was waiting for it to happen. The disputed elements are underlined. She rejects his "running around" replacing it with "I was sitting down", and rewords his "waiting for his return" as "waiting for the next thing (to happen)" despite the coercive "is that right". She also explicitly marks the fact that this is the barrister's version and not hers, by the comment "you may put it that way" – a projection that makes it clear whose version it is. The barrister obviously is not happy with this level of explicit rejection of his wording:

Example 20
- BD: **so am I right** (.) when he was taking the shower (0.3) <u>you were running around in the downstairs</u> (.) in that unit *is that right*?
- W/IE: No
- BD: what were you doing
- W/IE: <u>I was sitting down</u>
- BD: <u>waiting for his return</u> *is that right*?
- W/IE: **You may put it this way**
- BD: **now not I put it this way** (.) were you waiting <u>for his return from his shower</u>
- W/IE: I was waiting <u>for the next thing/I did not know what would happen next</u>
- BD: the next thing (.) what happened was exactly is that right? (.) a repeat of what happened in the first attack?

In addition to the issue of the formulation of different versions, there are linguistic means of information control which make it harder for a witness to give his/her own version. These include the question form. A polar (yes-no) question, common in hostile examination, allows the lawyer to include all the information in the question, and the response licensed by the question is only agreement or disagreement, discouraging any contribution of information by the person being questioned.

Example 21
- JE: =Did he tell you why he was taking (1.5) did he tell you why he was driving you to his home?
- W/IE: no

The question here only licenses a yes/no answer, which is what it receives. A more open question such as "what did he tell you" is generally avoided by lawyers.

Similarly closed question types, such as "when" or "where" questions, license only a carefully circumscribed response, containing only a fragment of information.

Example 22
- BD: Where-where was it that you took your clothes off (.) before you had the bath
- W/IE: Inside the bathroom

Notice that the response is limited to a prepositional phrase.

Another way of including information in such a way that it is hard to deny is embedding it so that it is presupposed:

Example 23
- BD: was she willing when you had the er (1.0) first sexual intercourse with her on that occasion the first occasion

The information that he "had the first sexual intercourse with her on that occasion" is presupposed, and leaves open only the question of the female's willingness.

Tags

The most widely discussed ways of putting pressure on people to agree in English are modal question tags and confirmation tags such as "right?". Much of the literature on the language of cross examination has concentrated on this particular feature, and it is often discussed as "coercion" (see for example Berk-Seligson 1999; Danet and Kermish 1978; Harris 1984).

Example 24
    BD: e-e *This may be e obvious* **but** you knew when you (.) before you started to have a shower that you would need a towel *did you not*

This question tag places pressure on the witness to agree. Our data from Hong Kong courtrooms show that question tags are rarely used by our second language speaking barristers. The avoidance of question tags is a common feature of second language English. Where interpreting is involved this may be a good thing, since most other languages do not have a direct translation equivalent. Second language lawyers tend instead to use statements followed by confirmation (or ratification) tags such as "isn't that right" which are not linked to the modal verb question system of English.

Example 25
    BD: **I'll put it this way** (2.0) you wearing glasses (.) as you say that when you playing sports *right*?

Example 26
    BD: [whispering] **I see** (12.0) *ah yin* (4.0) **you told us** (3.0) *is that correct* (3.0) you heard nothing (1.5) nothing (2.0) BAD about this man (1.5) BEFORE (1.0) you went to his (.) HOUSE (.) on the first occasion (.) in summer ninety eight (.) *is that right*?
    W/IE: that's incorrect

Example 27
    BD: there were team mates *is that right* (1.0) you were (.) often (3.0) keep him company and went over to his house *is that correct*?
    W/IE: Yes

Statement forms

There is a common assumption that during examination lawyers use questions. However, in fact, one often finds statements containing the lawyer's version, which are put for confirmation.

Example 28
    BD: **and** ever since you have been arrested you've been detained in er the detention centre pending trial
    W/IE: yes

Notice that no information is provided by the witness. Another example is 29; note the use of "you told us" rather than "did you tell us":

Example 29
    BP: **and** you told us just now (1.0) where those places were that you had sexual intercourse with her

Once more a statement puts a particular version, rather than allowing a witness to supply his/her version.

5. Applied issues

Perhaps the most obvious issue arising from all this is the ethical one. The justification for hostile cross-examination is that it "tests the evidence", and sometimes a case is made that the truth is more likely to emerge from such testing. However, these strategies are not always used to test evidence, but rather on occasions to twist and distort evidence, to pressure or trick people into saying things they do not believe, or agreeing with things they do not believe. The examples of this leading to a miscarriage of justice are legion, and they are not limited to Common Law systems – in Roman Law systems this type of pressure may be exerted by police in less publicly accountable contexts, and then submitted as written evidence.

Concerning action on this issue, a range of measures and policies have been adopted to reduce coercion of witnesses, particularly the vulnerable. Child witnesses, and sometimes women in sexual assault cases may be allowed to present their evidence through a video link. With young children there may be an intermediary, such as a counsellor, to ensure that the child understands and is not pressured into a false response. Under the "Anunga Rules" in the Northern Territory of Australia, Aboriginal witnesses, particularly those from a traditional background, are allowed the presence of a "friend" during police and courtroom questioning. In many legal systems there are rules of procedure designed to reduce the coercion of questioning, although there is a tendency for these rules not to be applied by judges – for particularly shocking examples see Eades (2000).

The main change that is required is perhaps a change in the underlying belief structure or culture of the legal profession. While some lawyers believe that their role of supporting their client overrides other considerations, including ethical ones on some occasions, this type of abuse will reoccur. Fundamental change is a long term issue for legal trainers and philosophers. Applied linguists are unlikely to be invited to contribute.

5.1. Legal translation and interpreting

This is another area where applied linguistics intersects with the law. In Sections 3 and 4 we discussed the nature of written and spoken language in legal contexts, and showed that comprehension of, and ability to cope with legal language is a prerequisite for justice in the legal system. For people who do not have a full proficiency in the language of the legal system, the problems and issues that we have discussed can be made worse in the absence of good quality legal translation/interpreting (hereafter TI). We have seen earlier that the language of legal documents and the language of legal processes differs markedly from everyday language. This specialisation of legal language presents a range of challenges for the legal interpreter/translator. There are two main areas of concern – access to TI, and TI quality.

Access to translation/interpreting
In order to provide accurate TI, the legal interpreter/translator needs specialised knowledge of the law and legal language. This is in addition to knowing two languages well, and having specific TI skills and knowledge. The supply of people who have this range of knowledge and abilities is limited, and in many legal contexts such people are difficult or impossible to access. Two examples from Australia will illustrate the issue and its problems. As a result of Australian national refugee policy, refugee communities mainly come from situations where their lives are in physical danger – at the time of writing many are coming from Sudan. Because political situations change, the source country and home language of Australia's new refugees are constantly changing. Among such groups, it is common for proficient bilinguals to be in high demand, for few of them have a background in TI, and even less bilinguals know the language of the law. In consequence, it can be difficult or impossible to find good legal interpreters/translators for these minority languages. A second example is that of Australian Aboriginal languages with small numbers of speakers. When the language is spoken only in a remote rural area, it may be unusual for speakers to have a high level of bilingualism and biliteracy in English, and even more rare to find a person with both TI and legal knowledge in addition. In both cases speakers are likely to have trouble communicating with the legal system because high quality legal interpreters/translators are simply unavailable. Such situations are by no means unique to Australia – recently arrived minorities and isolated minority indigenous groups have such problems around the world.

Translation quality
Skopos theory (Vermeer 2000) highlights the importance of the purpose of a translation. If a translator is producing only a rough digest for lawyers, so that they can decide whether to proceed with a case, the level of accuracy demanded

can be quite low, and most problematic issues can be avoided. However, if for example a legal text must have the same effect in the target legal context as it did in the source context, this can pose several legal challenges. One challenge is translating legal documents into a language that does not share a legal concept with the source language. An example given by Vlachopoulos (2004) is that the English legal term "consideration" (see the definition given in Table 1) does not have an exact equivalent in Greek, or in the Greek legal system. Vlachopoulos provides the accepted Greek translation, but also suggests an explanatory footnote.

Everyday words used with specialist meanings can also be a trap for the legal translator. Vlachopoulos (2004) also notes that in a legal translation "in consideration of" was translated as "with respect to". This resulted in a major change to the meaning of the original. Because the expression "in consideration of" has a non-legal meaning, it misled the translator.

The extreme grammatical complexity of some legal documents discussed earlier can also be a translation challenge – it may be simply impossible to reproduce the grammatical structure directly in another language. The translator's task then becomes one of reorganising and restructuring so as to capture the same meaning relationships in other ways. To do this, the translator needs an in-depth understanding of the source text, which in turn may entail legal knowledge.

At the discourse level, it is common that legal genres vary from system to system, so the structure of a contract or set of regulations will not necessarily be the same in different jurisdictions. This involves a classic translation issue of whether the translation should follow the structure of the source text, or be reworked into the structure of equivalent texts in the target language legal system. There is no single answer to this question – it depends on the purpose of the translation, whether it is intended to provide an understanding of how the source text was constructed, or whether it is intended to be a legal operative document in the target context. Once again the demand placed upon the knowledge and skill of the legal translator is difficult to overstate.

Interpreting quality

Legal interpreting demands a high level of accuracy in real time. Such interpreting is also mainly consecutive, which places a further demand – that of memory. Research has found that in the courtroom context interpreters tend to prioritise the interpreting of factual information, and may interpret poorly interpersonal and discoursal aspects (see Berk-Seligson 1990; Hale and Gibbons 1999). The following example is taken from the interpreting of a skilled and knowledgeable Hong Kong interpreter:

Example 30
BD: **well are you saying that** (2.0) you just (1.0) you weren't willing (1.0) but you felt you had to do this, **is that right**?
IC/E: do you mean that you aren't willing to do it but you have to do it or?

In this example, the core information "you weren't willing but you felt you had to do this" is accurately interpreted. However, the discourse marker "well" and the tag "is that right" are not interpreted. Similarly the verbal projection "are you saying" is interpreted by a mental projection "do you mean". This is a fairly typical example of the way in which many of the unusual characteristics of courtroom discourse are lost during interpreting. Lawyers in particular would be worried if their carefully constructed tags are lost. The subtle "well" reveals the lawyer's orientation towards the core information – one of doubt. However, the interpreter presents it as a simple unmodulated information question, which affects the witness's response, and could make it inappropriate to the original question. These small meaning elements, which could be seen as dispensable under the time and fatigue pressures of interpreting, may affect the overall portrayal of the witness's testimony (see Hale 2004).

5.2. Future perspectives

The challenges posed by both legal translation and legal interpreting are, as we have seen, considerable. If these challenges are not met, then people who have a less than native proficiency are likely to receive a lower level of justice – a contradiction of the principle of justice itself. There are myriad examples around the world of justice systems compounding rather than tackling social injustice.

In an ideal world legal translators would have knowledge of both the source and the target language legal systems, as well as high proficiency in two languages, and translation skills. This ideal world is unlikely to come into existence, so the issue is how best we can approximate it. Solutions include the education of legal professionals in such issues, specialised training for legal translators, and the establishing of bilingual legal language databases to facilitate the search for equivalents.

Turning to legal interpreting, to some degree the problems discussed earlier are a consequence of the situation – it is almost impossible to provide optimal interpreting in far from optimal interpreting conditions of a courtroom. Conference interpreters are normally not expected to interpret more than 20 minutes without a break – courtroom interpreters may have to work for hours without a break. Conference interpreters are given good facilities – courtroom interpreters may lack even a chair and a glass of water. Specialist training, which might alleviate some of these problems by alerting interpreters to their existence, and by working on strategies to overcome them, is by no means universal – in Australia the majority of courtroom interpreters have no specialist training in legal discourse. Conference interpreters are usually well paid, unlike most courtroom interpreters. In many cases it is not possible to make a career from courtroom interpreting – cases involving a particular language are not sufficiently common. These factors mitigate against both the supply and the quality of courtroom interpreting.

Another applied issue is that of interpreter ethics. Legal interpreters generally have well developed codes of ethics. A particularly important concept is that of "impartiality". For instance, the Australian National Accreditation Authority for Translators and Interpreters (NAATI) guidelines state under the rubric of "impartiality": "Members shall observe impartiality in all professional situations and shall not permit personal opinion to influence the performance of their work" (National Accreditation Authority for Translators and Interpreters 1990: 39). However, professional ethics may clash with individual ethics.

The following example was discussed as Example 14 earlier. In the case from which the example is taken, the victim witness was a 15 year old female. The court found that she had been sexually assaulted at the age of 13. The Defence Counsel is defending the assailant. The interpreter is female.

Example 31
BD: so (.) it never occurred to you on THAT phone chat (.) when he told you come over to MY house (3.0) to watch the video (.) about badminton (.) *that you should* (.) *at least* (.) see if he (1.0) he could lend you the video and so that you can watch it at home?
[back translation of the interpreter's Cantonese translation]
IC/E: Ø **according to what you said about the third occasion** he used the excuse of watching badminton video to coax and to deceive you to his house and then raped you *is that correct*?
W/IE: right

As noted earlier, the question is sarcastic and presses the witness to agree. The interpreter omits the sarcastic elements "it never occurred to you" and "you should at least", and indeed turns the question from one that blames the victim to one that blames the attacker. It is likely that the interpreter's sympathy for the victim (manifested on a number of other occasions) affected the nature of her interpreting. Notice, however, that the consequence is that the witness goes along happily with what she thinks is a sympathetic question, when in reality she is agreeing with a question that portrays her as responsible for the attack. Professional interpreters tell me that it is difficult not to have sympathy with witnesses such as this, and they may be unwilling to actively participate in what could be seen as verbal assault upon victims. The consequences of this clash of individual and professional ethics may be mixed, as the example illustrates. This ethical issue merits more discussion in future.

Overall, legal interpreting and translation can be extremely challenging. Applied linguistic solutions are not obvious, and many, such as extensive training and testing of legal TI experts, are expensive. The issue, as so often in legal matters, is that a higher standard of justice demands a higher level of funding, and funding has limits. It is fair to say, that with the exception of a few jurisdictions, more should be spent to reduce the potential for injustice.

This chapter is the tip of a large iceberg of applied linguistic challenges posed by the legal system. Throughout we have seen that the core value of the legal system, justice, is endangered by the characteristics of legal language, yet some legal language is necessary for the operation of the legal system. In consequence, these applied linguistic challenges can never be fully resolved. What is required is a higher level of awareness and recognition of these issues in both the legal profession itself, and in ancillary professions such as legal interpreting, and the teaching of legal English. Once the challenges are recognised, it becomes more possible to take remedial steps, and to seek funding for them, so that problems can be alleviated if not fully solved.

Transcription conventions

In the transcripts
- the original utterance is above
- the interpreted version is below

Symbol	Description
[...]	Back translations
(.)	A brief pause
(numbers)	Pause timed in seconds
Ø	Material deleted at this point (by the interpreter)
=	Utterances immediately follow/followed
?	Rise of intonation
CAPITAL LETTERS	Loud
/.../	Phonemic transcription

Abbreviation	Meaning
BP	Prosecution Barrister's English utterance
BD	Defence Barrister's English utterance
DC	Defence barrister's Cantonese utterance
IC	Interpreter's Chinese utterance
IC/E	Interpreter's Cantonese utterance back-translated into English
ICT	Interpreter's Chinese translation
IET	Interpreter's English translation
IS	Interpreter's Spanish utterance
JE	Judge's English utterance
WC	Witness's Chinese utterance
W/IE	Interpreter's English translation of witness's Cantonese

References

Bennett, W. Lance and Martha S. Feldman
    1981   *Reconstructing Reality in the Courtroom*. London: Tavistock Publications.
Berk-Seligson, Susan
    1990   *The Bilingual Courtroom: Court Interpreters in the Judicial Process*. Chicago, IL: The University of Chicago Press.
Berk-Seligson, Susan
    1999   The impact of court interpreting on the coerciveness of leading questions. *Forensic Linguistics* 6(1): 30–51.
Bhatia, Vijay
    1994   Cognitive structuring in legislative provisions. In: John Gibbons (ed.), *Language and the Law*, 136–155. London: Longman.
Bourdieu, Pierre and Jean Claude Passeron
    1990   *Reproduction in Education, Society and Culture* (transl. by Richard Nice). London: Sage.
Bülow-Møller, Anne M.
    1991   Trial evidence: Overt and covert communication in court. *International Journal of Applied Linguistics* 1(1): 38–60.
Cotterill, Janet
    2003   *Language and Power in Court: A Linguistic Analysis of the O. J. Simpson Trial*. New York, NY: Palgrave Macmillan.
Cutts, Martin
    2001   *Clarifying Eurolaw*. London: Plain Language Commission.

Cutts, Martin and Emma Wagner
   2002   *Clarifying EC Regulations.* London: Plain Language Commission.

Danet, Brenda and Nicole C. Kermish
   1978   Courtroom questioning: A sociolinguistic perspective. In: Louis N. Massery (ed.), *Psychology and Persuasion in Advocacy*, 413–441. Washington, DC: Association of Trial Lawyers of America, National College of Advocacy.

David, René John and E. C. Brierly
   1985   *Major Legal Systems in the World Today.* London: Stevens.

Diamond, Shari Seidman and Judith N. Levi
   1996   Improving decisions on death by revising and testing jury instructions. *Judicature* 79(5): 224–232.

Drew, Paul
   1990   Strategies in the contest between lawyer and witness in cross-examination. In: Judith N. Levi and Anne G. Walker (eds.), *Language in the Judicial Process*, 39–64. New York, NY: Plenum.

Eades, Diana
   2000   'I don't think it's an answer to the question': Silencing Aboriginal witnesses in court. *Language in Society* 29: 161–195.

English, Peter W. and Bruce D. Sales
   1997   A ceiling or consistency effect for the comprehension of jury instructions. *Psychology, Public Policy, and Law* 3: 381–402.

Fairclough, Norman
   1989   *Language and Power.* London: Longman.

Felker, Daniel B., Frances Pickering, Veda R. Charrow, V. Melissa Holland and Janice C. Redish
   1981   *Guidelines for Document Designers.* Washington, DC: American Institutes for Research.

Gibbons, John
   2003   *Forensic Linguistics: An Introduction to Language in the Justice System.* Oxford/Malden, MA: Blackwell (*Language and Society* series).

Gudjonsson, Gisli H.
   2003   *The Psychology of Interrogations and Confessions: A Handbook.* Hoboken, NJ: Wiley.

Hale, Sandra
   1999   Interpreters' treatment of discourse markers in courtroom questions. *Forensic Linguistics* 6(1): 57–82.

Hale, Sandra B.
   2004   *The Discourse of Court Interpreting: Discourse Practices of the Law, the Witness and the Interpreter.* Amsterdam: John Benjamins.

Hale, Sandra and John Gibbons
   1999   Varying realities: Patterned changes in the interpreter's representation of courtroom and external realities. *Applied Linguistics* 20(2): 203–220.

Hall, Philip
   2004   Prone to distortion? Undue reliance on unreliable records in the NSW Police Service's formal interview model. In: John Gibbons, V. Prakasam, K. V. Tirumalesh and Hemalatha Nagarajan (eds.), *Language in the Law*, 44–81. Hyderabad: Orient Longman.

Halliday, Michael A. K.
   1994   *An Introduction to Functional Grammar.* 2nd ed. London: Arnold.
Harris, Sandra
   1984   Questions as a mode of control in magistrates' courts. *International Journal of the Sociology of Language* 49: 5–27.
Hiltunen, Risto
   1990   *Chapters on Legal English Aspects Past and Present of the Language of the Law.* Helsinki: Suomalainen Tiedeakatemia.
Hosticka, Carl J.
   1979   We don't care about what happened, we only care about what is going to happen: Lawyer-client negotiations of reality. *Social Problems* 26(5): 599–610.
Hutchby, Ian and Robin Wooffitt
   1998   *Conversation Analysis.* Cambridge: Polity Press.
Labov, William and Wendell A. Harris
   1994   Addressing social issues through linguistic evidence. In: John Gibbons (ed.), *Language and the Law*, 265–305. London: Longman.
Leung, E. and John Gibbons
   forthcoming   Control in the Cantonese courtroom. *Journal of Speech, Language and the Law.*
National Accreditation Authority for Translators and Interpreters
   1990   *Candidates' Manual.* Canberra, ACT: NAATI.
Redfern Legal Centre
   1988   *The Law Handbook.* 3rd ed. Redfern: Redfern Legal Centre Publishing.
Robinson, Ludmilla
   1994   *Handbook for Legal Interpreters.* North Ryde, NSW: The Law Book Company.
Sinclair, John (chief ed.)
   1987   *Collins Cobuild English Language Dictionary.* London and Glasgow: Collins.
Solan, Lawrence M.
   2006   Definitions/Rules in legal language. In: Keith Brown (chief ed.), *Encyclopedia of Language & Linguistics.* 2nd ed., Vol. 3, 403–409. Oxford: Elsevier.
Stygall, Gail
   1994   *Trial Language: Differential Discourse Processing and Discursive Formation.* Amsterdam: John Benjamins.
Tiersma, Peter M.
   1999   *Legal Language.* Chicago, IL: The University of Chicago Press.
Vermeer, Hans J.
   2000   Skopos and commission in translational action. In: Lawrence Venuti (ed.), *The Translation Studies Reader*, 221–232. London & New York, NY: Routledge.
Vlachopoulos, Stefanos
   2004   Translating the untranslatable? The impact of cultural constraints on the translation of legal texts. In: John Gibbons, V. Prakasam, K. V. Tirumalesh and Hemalatha Nagarajan (eds.), *Language in the Law*, 100–115. New Delhi: Orient Longman.

15. Language and religion

Susanne Mühleisen

1. Language, religion and culture

There are many issues which connect language, religion and culture. On the one hand, there is a long-standing mythological relationship between language and religious beliefs: In many cultures and religions, the origin of language or speech is seen as a gift of a divine being to humankind. In the Book of Genesis, for instance, Adam is given the power to name the acts of creation. Similarly, deities such as the god Thoth in Egyptian mythology, Brahma in Hindu religion and Odin in Icelandic sagas, are regarded as the creators of speech and (sometimes) writing. The scattering of tongues and the destruction of a linguistic unity in the biblical narrative of the tower of Babel is seen as one of the curses to mankind. Related to the biblical story, the myth of an original and pure *Ursprache* has been pursued in linguistic research well into the 19th century and inspired, for instance, the search for a common single root of "Indo-European languages" (cf. Robinson 1998). In some cultures, the idea of the superiority of one language over others is based on the view of its origin as the "language of God", a claim which is held, for instance, for Sanskrit, Ancient Hebrew and Classical Arabic.

The language used for communication with or through a divine being has also been subject to many philosophical debates and there are quite a few significant phenomena related to special forms or restrictions of human-divine communication. Thus, in Orthodox Judaism, it is regarded as sacrilegious to pronounce the name of God (the common reference to the Hebrew name for God is "Tetragrammaton", in the Hebrew alphabet: י (*yod*) ה (*heh*) ו (*vav*) ה (*heh*) or יהוה = YHWH; in Hebrew written from right to left). Glossolalic speech ("speaking in tongues"), a common occurrence within the Protestant Pentecostal tradition, is taken by this religious community as a sign of the sincerity of a person's belief and the consequent presence of God in that person. Mysticism can also be associated with written language, for instance, in the esoteric interpretation of Old Testament texts based on the arrangements of letters in the text and the numerical values attributed to them. This practice, known as Kabbala arose in the Middle Ages and rests on the belief that language in general, and especially biblical language, contains coded secrets about God and the world. In contrast, some religious communities express a profound distrust of earthly languages: 17th century Quakerism adheres to silent worship as an individual and immediate practice of communication with God which does not seek an authority or mediator to consult or to grant validation. Silence is also part of meditation in many religions, ranging from Orthodox Christian over Hindu to various forms of Buddhist practices.

There are also, on the other hand, several more practical linguistic and sociolinguistic concerns which are shaped by the relationship between language and religion. This chapter will therefore deal with a number of topics which address the consequences of language use for religious purposes in institutional contexts. One area of investigation looks at religion as a site of language contact, resulting, for instance, in language spread, maintenance or revival. How have missionary activities and the use of a particular language for religious functions resulted in its wider distribution? How are power and authority connected to access to the language of religion in particular communities? There are furthermore various examples of how the employment of a language or variety in religious texts has been instrumental for its survival or revitalization. On the other hand, religion and the identification with a religious group can also have a separating force within an earlier language community and might ultimately result in linguistic divergence and loss of mutual intelligibility. Separate orthographies often serve as a visible marker of such a separation. In the case of Hindi and Urdu, for instance, the use of Devanagari versus Arabic script makes also transparent the implicit religious alignments of the language varieties in writing.

Another highly fruitful area of research within the applied context of language, religion and culture is the translation of sacred texts which form the core of the world's main religions (for an overview, cf. Long 2005; for Bible translation, cf. Nida 1998; for Qur'an translation, cf. Mustapha 1998; for Torah translation, cf. Alpert 1998). Not only has translation been vital as a means of spreading the message of a faith to other languages and cultures; attitudes towards Scriptural rendition have themselves influenced translation theories and practices for centuries (cf., for instance, St. Jerome early 5th century; Luther 1530; Buber and Rosenzweig 1936; Nida 1952, 1964a). This is particularly relevant for Christianity which made Bible translation the very center of its missionary activity. Here, linguistic contact goes hand in hand with culture contact and it seems one of the incompatibilities of the connection between Christian mission and colonialism that this contact resulted in, arguably, a transmission of Western culture and values, on the one hand, and in a promotion and a strengthening of the local languages through Bible translation and codification on the other (cf. Sanneh 1989, 1993). Postcolonial Bible translation is therefore an issue which deals with this tension of the potential uses of both domination and subversion in the religious text (cf. Donaldson 1996a; Bailey and Pippin 1996).

The interface between language and religion is a vast field and there are many further topics which might also merit attention, such as, for instance, the use of ceremonial language, registers and genres of religious language, or religion and marked language practices (for the latter, cf. Keane 1997). Ritualized language in religious practices often serves as a prime example for a performative utterance in speech acts, for instance, in wedding ceremonies (cf. Austin 1962).[1] Many other ritualized performances (prayer, confession, etc.), so far rather neglected in pragmatics, might also deserve ample consideration in a contribution on language and religion. Due to the limitations of space and scope, however, the issues addressed in this chapter are necessarily selective and do not intend or claim to cover the huge diversity of language issues connected to the many existing religious practices, religions and religious groups (for more encyclopedic reference, cf. Sawyer 2001).

2. The politics of language and religion: Language authority and language spread

As introduced in the previous section, the languages used in "book religions", religions which rely on a body of sacred texts, typically gain a special status. The spread of a religious conviction to new communities of followers can thus further increase the importance and authority of the respective language, especially in what Lamin Sanneh (1989: 29) calls "mission by *diffusion*", i.e. when the missionary culture (including language) becomes the inseparable carrier of the message. Islam, with its emphasis on its Arabic heritage in Scripture, law and religion is the primary example for this type of missionary tradition. Christianity, on the other hand, has relied more on "mission by *translation*", where "the recipient culture [becomes] the true and final locus of the proclamation" (ibid.). While both Christianity and Islam are characterized by their strong missionary drive, other major world religions do not seek to reach out to potential converts and are seen as connected to particular ethnic groups as, for instance, Hinduism or Judaism. Buddhism does not have a single "sacred language" to the same extent as the other world religions mentioned above (Crosby 2005: 45; but see also the note on Pāli translations, in ch. 4 below).

In the following, two examples of language spread and diffusion in close relation with the spread of religion will be discussed: a) the use of Latin with the rise of Christianity in the early and medieval history of Europe, and b) the spread of Arabic with the rise of Islam since the seventh century.

2.1. Latin in Medieval Europe

It may be seen as one of the paradoxes in the history of Christianity that Latin and not one of the original Bible languages came to be recognized as the language of religion and Scripture at least until the Early Modern Period in a Christianized Europe; in the Roman Catholic tradition, Latin also remained the main liturgical language until the Second Vatican Council (1962–1965) approved an extended employment of vernacular languages in Mass.

Latin is not originally used in any of the founding texts of Christianity: The 39 books of the Old Testament were written in varieties of Hebrew (some in Aramaic), the initial language of the 27 books of the New Testament is Greek. Several other writings of controversial status, known as the Apocrypha, are also preserved in Greek. The status of Latin in Christianity is hence connected to factors external to the authority of the religious text: its role and function as the hegemonial language of the Roman Empire before the onset of Christianity, the status of Rome as the main center of non-orthodox Christianity, and the importance of one of the earliest Bible translations, the Latin version known as the Vulgate. Although there are some earlier first versions of the New Testament in Old Latin, it was St. Jerome's revisions and translations (also of the Old Testament and the major apocryphal books) towards the end of the fourth century, completed by 406 AD, which became the most prominent and authoritative version of the Bible in the Roman Catholic tradition.

The influence of Latin in Early to Late Medieval European countries was mainly restricted to written usage and remained exlusive to certain domains (religion, scholarship, law) and sections of the population. The role of the church as the primary institution of learning in the Middle Ages made Latin also the principal language of scholarship and the law (for an overview of language usage – Latin, French and varieties of English – in various domains in Britain 700–1700 AD, cf. Görlach 1999: 462). The decline of the influence of Latin went hand in hand with translations of the Bible into the European vernacular languages, most importantly in the 15th and 16th century (cf. also the section on Bible translation, ch. 4 below).

These early Bible translations were often the first step towards a standardization of the vernacular languages. This interplay between Bible translation and standardization was aided by two developments in the 15th century: One was the influence of humanist scholarship and the revival of the study of the classics and the classical languages, which resulted in a new interest in the original source texts of the Bible. The Latin Vulgate, which had been held as the sacred text for a thousand years, lost its status as the unquestioned authority as scholars resorted to the original Bible languages in new translations. The second important event was Johannes Gutenberg's invention of printing with movable type (ca. 1447), which revolutionized not only the availability of the written text but ultimately changed the whole culture of writing and literacy. Finally, the Reformist movement placed the meaning of the text, rather than the language, at the very center of its principles, thus making mother tongue versions of the Bible indispensable for the believer.

2.2. Arabic

With the birth of Islam in the seventh century, the Arabic language expanded far beyond the boundaries of its origin, the Arabian peninsula (i.e. present-day Saudi Arabia, Yemen and the Gulf states). Before that period, the language situation in the region which is now associated with the Arab World, the Arabian peninsula and the Fertile Crescent (i.e. today's Syria, Lebanon, Iraq and Palestine) was as a rule bilingual, with various ethnic groups "speaking Arabic in everyday contexts and using a variety of languages such as Syriac and Aramaic for trade and learning […], especially as Arabic did not develop a writing system until almost the rise of Islam" (Baker 1998b: 316–317).

The growth of Islam, which started during the Prophet's lifetime and became ever more powerful after his death in 632, profoundly changed the political, cultural and linguistic make-up of the region. By the end of the seventh century, not only Iraq, Iran and Syria, but also Egypt and North Africa had joined the new political and religious order. The spread of the Arabic language was aided by its standardization in the Qur'an and its use as a written literary language. Baker (1998b: 317) notes that this has resulted in a general status gain and the role of Arabic as an official language in many countries:

> The widely celebrated flourishing of translation in the Islamic Empire is closely associated with and dependent on the growth of Arabic as a written literary language, which began with the need to fix the form of the Qur'ān […]. The status of Arabic as lingua franca was established when the Umayyad Caliph […] Abd al-Malik ibn Marawān (reigned 685–705) declared it the sole administrative language of the empire. Since then it has been the official language of all Arab countries and continues to play a unifying role in the area, enabling the variety of religious and ethnic groups that make up the population of the Arab World to think of themselves as a 'nation'. (Baker 1998b: 317)

Today's Standard Arabic is a modernized variety of Classical Arabic in which the Qur'an is written. Classical Arabic is still used for religious and ceremonial purposes throughout the Islamic World. As Crystal (1997: 384) notes, "the memorization of the text [i.e. the Qur'an] in childhood acts simultaneously as an introduction to literacy", thus forming an important link between religious and general literacy education in many predominantly Islamic environments. Mustapha (1998: 200) points out with reference to an earlier scholar (Hitti) that the triumph of Islam "was to a certain extent the triumph of a language, more particularly of a book". According to Ethnologue (2005), Standard Arabic is officially used to varying extents in at least 24 nations other than Saudi Arabia, most of them Middle Eastern and African countries. Exact figures of speakers are not given, but "in most Arab countries only the well educated have adequate proficiency in Standard Arabic, while over 100,500,000 do not" (ibid). In addition to Standard Arabic, there are many regional varieties of Arabic which are used for oral communication and are not always mutually intelligible with the Standard version as, for instance, Sudanese Spoken Arabic or Sudanese Creole Arabic in Sudan.

3. Sacred texts and language preservation

The use of a language for the sacred writings of a religious community does not always lead to a wider distribution of that language. Due to its ritualized character, the religious text often preserves a language or a variety of language which has ceased to be used for other purposes by the wider linguistic community. Reasons for this are manifold and include language change – as in the case of Classical Arabic versus modern Standard Arabic and regional varieties of Arabic cited above – but also changes in the language situation brought about by external factors, such as language death as a result of, for instance, colonization or migration. There is a wealth of examples where a language is conserved and used for religious purposes only, among them Sanskrit in Hindu religion, or Geez, an ancient Ethiopian language, which is the official liturgical language of the Ethiopian Orthodox Church. This section will single out two examples where enduring religious usage of a language with no or a greatly declined living speech community has led to a successful revival or revitalization.

3.1. The revival of Hebrew

The rebirth of Hebrew at the end of the 19th century is one of the most extraordinary cases in the history of language politics and language planning (see also Edwards, this vol.). The modern version of Hebrew (also called Ivrit) is not a direct offspring from Biblical Hebrew but, rather, was "reinvented" as a mixture of different Hebrew strata and has undergone natural language changes within the living speech community since its establishment in the early 20th century. The history of Hebrew can be divided into four different periods: *Biblical Hebrew* (or Classical Hebrew) has been first recorded some 3,300 years ago, in the time of Moses. Due to its use in the holy texts, it is also referred to as "The Sacred Language" (*Lashon ha-Qodesh* שדוקה ןושל). By the time of Jesus, the common language in the region was Aramaic, whereas Biblical Hebrew was used as a religious language in synagogues and in Temple worship. *Mishnaic Hebrew* (or Rabbinic Hebrew) differs in grammar and vocabulary from Biblical Hebrew and was used by the second century AD mainly for religious purposes. *Medieval Hebrew* was used to translate Arabic works into Hebrew, and, finally *Modern Hebrew* (or Ivrit) began its success story at end of 19th century.

While Hebrew was not a secular spoken language in the diaspora, the Hebrew alphabet was used by Jews for writing various languages they had acquired as mother tongues, for instance, Yiddish, Ladino or varieties of Arabic and Persian. Hebrew itself had been used mainly for religious functions for two thousand years before a modernized version was advocated as a unifying language as part of the political Zionist movement directed towards Palestine. The person most closely associated with this rebirth of Hebrew is Eliezer Ben Yehuda (1858–1922). Ben Yehuda was born in Lithuania and had learned Hebrew as part of his religious upbringing. After his immigration to Palestine in 1881, he devoted his life to promoting the use of a modern, secular Hebrew with a number of initiatives, such as the creation of Hebrew-speaking societies, the establishment of Hebrew in the home,[2] the classroom, and the media, the compilation of a dictionary and the forming of a Language Council (cf. Fellmann 1974). Along with English and Arabic, Hebrew became an official language in Palestine in 1918. Ever since, Ivrit has become an important element of national identity formation following the foundation of the state of Israel. According to Ethnologue (2005), Modern Hebrew is now used by approximately five million speakers in Israel and other countries.

3.2. The revitalization of Welsh

The second example is rather different in nature: Welsh is neither a language originally used in the religious Scriptures of the dominant religion of Wales (i.e. Christianity), nor was it ever completely extinct. Nevertheless, after the decline of Welsh usage in the 18th and 19th century, Welsh translations of religious texts, along with a body of indigeneous literary texts, formed important resources for the successful preservation and revitalization of the language.

Large parts of Wales had been converted to Christianity in the fifth and sixth century under the influence of devoted monk-missionaries, the Celtic saints, around the same time in which Old Welsh developed (from the earlier Brythonic) as a distinct language and an early poetic tradition was being established (cf. Williams 1979: 2). During the early Middle Ages, Welsh became the language of law, and medieval poetry in Welsh continued to thrive, despite the Norman invasion with English-speaking followers in 1067. The Cistercian monasteries, founded in the early 12th century, were important centers for the writing of Welsh chronicles and the copying of Welsh literature. The *Act of Union* in 1536 marked a significant point in the history of Welsh: From now on, English and not Welsh was to be used in the courts. While its function in secular matters declined, the importance of Welsh for spiritual matters increased. Only ten years after the Act of Union, the first printed book in the Welsh language was published, a Welsh translation of the main texts of the English Prayer Book (*Yn Llyvyr Hwnn* – "In This Book"). Subsequently, the New Testament (1567) and finally the complete Bible (1588) were translated into Welsh by William Salesbury (1520–1584), making Welsh one of the few non-state languages in which the Bible was published in the immediate post-Reformation era. Viv Edwards (1991: 107) comments on the interplay between religion and literature in the preservation and standardization of the Welsh language:

> The democratization, or nationalization, of the language was only achieved with the translation of the Bible in 1588. Although there was a great deal of dialect diversity among speakers from different parts of the country, there now existed not only a literary standard accessible to all those who could read but a uniform oral standard. This oral standard was based on the speech of preachers which was heavily influenced by the Bible. The Bible, in its turn, owed much to the language of the bardic poets. Welsh has thus remained a remarkably conservative language and medieval literary classics like the *Mabinogion*[3] pose no problems for the present-day reader.

The undisrupted written tradition becomes increasingly important when under the pressures of industrialization, demographic changes due to migration and Parliamentary restrictions of Welsh usage in education, the number of Welsh speakers declines in the 18th and especially the 19th century. As Williams (1979: 25) notes:

> Religion [...] was a uniquely compelling force in Victorian Wales, where the proportion of active membership and attendance at Christian churches, especially among the poorer classes, was very appreciably higher than in England. Religious incentives were intimately involved with the use and preservation of the Welsh language, not only in Wales itself but also among communities of Welsh exiles in England, the U.S.A., and elsewhere. The safeguarding of the language was regarded by many of them as synonymous with upholding religion; to abandon the former was to run the risk of losing the latter [...].

Following a decline in the first half of the 20th century furthered by an increased influence of English language mass media, conscious language political efforts brought on a considerable revitalization of the language. Today, Welsh has the status of official language in Wales and is used by more than half a million speakers (1991 census; www. Ethnologue.com). Ethnologue (2005) states for the 1990s that "88 % of those questioned believe they should be proud of Welsh, and that it should be treated equally with English. There is an increase in the number of parents choosing a Welsh-medium education for their children".

4. The translation of religious texts

While all major world religions have a body of holy texts, the attitudes towards the language used in these texts differs greatly with regard to its sacred status and its translatability. In *Buddhism*, Pali is the principal language in which the teachings of the Buddha are preserved in the Pitakas but other languages (e.g. Tibetan, Chinese, Japanese) were also used for later writings. "Since early Buddhism dismissed the notion of ritual purity and the sanctity of form over meaning or ethics, meaning (rather than the language of a statement or text) is crucial. This is not to deny that the concept of sacred language is present in some Buddhist traditions, but it tends to be of most relevance in ritual" (Crosby 2005: 45).

Religious and theological knowledge in *Hinduism* is preserved in a large number of texts collectively called the Vedas (mainly 1500–500 BC). Many of these Sanskrit texts have not been translated into modern languages (cf. Johnson 2005: 65), whereas later texts which continue this philosophical tradition, like the Bhagavad Gītā (i.e. part of the national epos Mahābhārata), have a considerable tradition in translation: From its first translation into a European language (English, 1785 by Charles Wilkins) until the end of the 20th century, no less than 300 versions have been produced in English.

The textual basis of *Islam*, the Qur'an (or Koran), is believed to have been dictated verbatim to the Prophet Mohammed by Allah. Unlike the sayings of the Prophet (*hadīth*), which may be translated or quoted in translation, translations of the Qur'an itself are therefore regarded as illegitimate by many Muslim scholars. In his article on "Cultural aspects in Qur'an translation", Abdul-Raof (2005: 162) seems to agree with the view that "[…] for Muslim scholars, the Qur'an is untranslatable since it is a linguistic miracle with transcendental meanings that cannot be captured fully by human faculty". In spite of this, there is a long tradition of translations of the Qur'an (cf. Mustapha 1998 for an overview of Qur'an translations) but all of these are seen as inferior to the origin. What is at stake here are also questions of authority of the original and its interpretation, as Mustapha (1998: 202) summarizes: "In the eyes of a Muslim […] the difference between the Qur'an and any of its translations is ultimately the difference between God as the Author, Authority and Source on the one hand, and man as a mere translator/interpreter on the other."

The Hebrew Bible in *Judaism* (or Torah, roughly corresponding with the Old Testament in Christianity) has been translated from early on: The first written version, the (Greek) Septuagint, was made in the third century BC, presumably for Jews who no longer knew Hebrew. Later versions, like the Greek translation by Acquila in the second century AD, followed. Nevertheless, Classical Hebrew remained an important religious language and Jewish translations of the sacred text never achieved quite the status they have in Christianity. Greensporn (2005: 54) remarks that "[…] in the Jewish tradition, Bible translations are intended to supplement, not supplant; complement, not replace, the original" (cf. also the discussion on translation theory in Section 4.2. below). Similarly, Alpert (1998: 270) describes that translations of the Torah have traditionally been used not as texts in their own right but rather as aids to comprehension.

In *Christianity*, conversely, the translation of the religious text can achieve the same status as the original (cf. Latin Vulgate). Bible translation has at all times featured prominently in the spread of the message: from early translations into the Classical languages (Septuagint; Vulgate) via European mother tongue translations in the Reformation period to colonial and postcolonial Bible translations in the 19th and 20th century. Lamin Sanneh (1989: 1) makes the point that, because of its very roots in Judaism, the younger Christian religion had to translate itself out of Aramaic and Hebrew in order to gain an identity separated from the Jewish tradition – thus, one might argue, without translation there might not be a distinct Christian religion today. One of the consequences of such continual translatedness may be that Christianity is now the only major world religion which is marginal in the land of its origin. On the other hand, Bible translations have been instrumental in the spread of Christianity and made the Bible (or parts thereof) the most translated text worldwide. The development of Bible translations gives an impression of the ever increasing number of new versions:

Table 1. Development of Bible translations from 1500 to 2005

Year	Compl. Bible	New Testament	Parts of Bible	Total
1500*	5	1	0	6
1800*	40	15	16	71
1830*	52	55	50	157
1890*	104	105	261	470
1920*	159	147	534	840
1960*	221	277	667	1165
1980*	275	495	940	1710
1996*	355	880	932	2167
2005**	422	1,079	876	2377

Sources:
* Deutsche Bibelgesellschaft 1998
** United Bible Societies (www.biblesociety.org/index2.htm, retrieved November 23, 2005)

The impact of this long tradition and the vast amount of translations goes far beyond the transmission of religious ideas and had important cultural and linguistic consequences:

– *Codification and standardization of languages*: For many languages, Bible translations were the first written texts and so formed the basis of a linguistic codification, ultimately standardization, by which these oral languages were turned into so-called "Bible languages". By giving a particular variant of an oral language a stable material presence, a codification is in many ways an

"invention" of the respective language. In the move of adapting an oral language to a written register, the translation process itself furthermore requires language elaboration (*Ausbau*), including lexical and syntactic expansion strategies (cf. Mühleisen 2002: 246–258).
- *Emergence of descriptive linguistics and translation theory*: Because of their role in the codification of many vernaculars, Bible translators and missionaries were often the first to describe previously unrecorded languages and to produce dictionaries, grammars, etc., for these varieties. Thus, the many descriptions of languages collected by missionaries resulted in the emergence of comparative-historical and descriptive linguistics in the 19th century when many of the first records of languages were written down. Both applied translation and translation theory have been greatly influenced by authorities who have their professional basis in Bible translation (cf. St. Jerome early 5th century; Luther 1530; Buber and Rosenzweig 1936; Nida 1952, 1964).
- *Colonization and "Westernization" of other cultures*: The undeniable dialectic relationship between Christian mission and 19th century European colonialism may perhaps best be captured in David Livingston's popular notion that Commerce, Civilization and Christianity, the "three C's" as it came to be known, must go hand in hand. But common criticism also extends to Bible translation itself in that, by bringing in "Western concepts", other languages have become "Westernized": The cultural notions transmitted into the language ultimately change the speakers' world view, thus colonizing their minds even in their own languages. This argument, however, which ultimately rests on the notion of linguistic relativity, i.e. the thought that there is an innate connection between a language and the concepts it is able to express, fails to recognize the possibilities of languages to adapt to new cultural concepts and to creatively expand beyond the ones already existing.

In the following sections, the linguistic and cultural implications of Bible translation outlined above will be highlighted in some more detail.

4.1. Bible translation and codification

The first larger increase of Bible translations in the 16th century (see Table 1 above) marks the post-reformational rendering of the Bible into most of the European languages, a development which challenged the superiority of the then hegemonic writing language, Latin. While there are some European language translations before the 16th century (e.g. 1382 Wycliffe's Middle English Bible, 1466 the first German, 1471 the first Italian, and 1488 the first Czech translation), it was the 16th century translations which had the authority to put the mother tongues on the map, for instance, by highly influential versions such as Luther's German Bible or Tyndale's translation into Early Modern English (1534). Furthermore, languages like Dutch (1522), French (1530), Swedish (1541), Danish (1550), Spanish (1553), Slavonic (1581), Slovenian (1584) and Welsh (1588) became Bible languages (cf. the overview of complete Bible translations in Sanneh 1989: 246–249). The linguistic and cultural consequences of this development were tremendous: The European vernaculars became codified, later standardized languages and soon superseded Latin in the domain of writing. In the act of translation, not only the religious words but many other concepts which had formerly been restricted to the high prestige language Latin, had to be "created" in these new writing languages. German is a good case in point: Martin Luther's Bible translation, begun in 1521, was very influential for lexico-semantic changes and new formations in an emerging German cross-regional standard language, which led scholars like Jakob Grimm (1785–1863) to postulate Luther as the creator of New High German. For the English language, the King James Bible had an enormous impact. With less than half of Shakespeare's lexicon, for instance, it has contributed "far more to English in the way of idiomatic or quasi-proverbial expressions than any other literary source" (Crystal 2004: 276).

The second period which saw an enormous leap in new Bible translation projects was the 19th and early 20th century, a period when European colonialism was at its peak (cf. also Sections 4.3. and 4.4.). Although this includes translations into languages which already were established writing languages (e.g. Hindi 1835,[4] Persian 1838, Cantonese Chinese 1894), many other languages owe their first codification to Bible translation and related missionary work in this period. A good case in point is the Nigerian language Igbo (1906), mother tongue and missionary education language of many significant writers. The very beginning of written Igbo has to be credited to somewhat earlier missionary activity, with its first codification by the German Reverend J. F. Schön and the ex-Yoruba slave-turned missionary (later bishop) Rev. S. A. Crowther in the mid-19th century. Their joint work on Igbo culminated in the publication of a schoolbook, mainly consisting of citations from the Bible (cf. Döring 1996: 63).

What, then, are the consequences for the cultures and languages concerned? First of all, for languages which had previously not been written the translation may have not just meant a codification with all its effects, i.e. the status elevation of one particular variant, the fixing of grammatical rules and the expansion of the vocabulary, the use of a particular script – many languages would perhaps not be written in the Roman Alphabetic script without Bible translations. Rather, the move from orality to literacy itself has further social and cultural consequences, which have been examined by social anthropologists such as Jack Goody, Ian Watt, and Kathleen Gough (1986[1968]). According to Walter Ong's (2002) classic study, writing serves not only as a memory-supportive device or as a means to send a message across space and time, but the textualization itself becomes a social and cultural authority, an authority that is depersonalized and – in stark contrast to oral practices – not bound to specific individuals.

4.2.   Bible translation and translation theory

One of the central questions in translation theory through all times is that of faithfulness of the translation to the original, i.e. how close to the source text should the translaton be and how free can the target text be to adapt the meaning of the source text. In his influential work "On the different methods of translating" (1813), Friedrich Schleiermacher distinguishes between two basic approaches the translator can take in the negotiation of meaning between the source language/author and the target language/reader: "The translator either (1) disturbs the writer as little as possible and moves the reader in his direction, or (2) disturbs the reader as little as possible and moves the writer in his direction" ([1813]1997).

Because of the principal aim of bringing the Christian message to the people, Christian mother tongue translations of the Bible have overwhelmingly adhered to the second ("author-to-reader")[5] approach, of bringing the text to the reader and making it seem as a mother tongue text. Even in the translation into the (non-mother tongue) Latin, St. Jerome received a wealth of criticism at first because of his non-literal adaptations of the Hebrew and Greek original. Martin Luther became famous for "listening to the language of the people" and creating his version in a German that would be understood by the "common man" as his own language:

> Only an idiot would go ask the letters of the Latin alphabet how to speak German, the way these dumbasses do. You've got to go out and ask the mother in her house, the children in the street, the ordinary man at the market. Watch their mouths move when talk, and translate that way. Then they'll understand you and realize that you're speaking *German* to them.
> Jesus says, for example, in Matthew 12: 34, *Ex abundantia cordis os loquitur.* If I followed those jackasses, they would probably set the letters before me and have me translate it, "out of the abundance of the heart the mouth speaketh". Tell me, is that how any real person would say it? Who would understand such a thing? What on earth is the "abundance of the heart"? Anybody who said that would probably mean he had too large a heart, or too much heart – and even that doesn't sound right. For "abundance of the heart" sounds about as good in ordinary speech as "abundance of the house", or "abundance of the stove", or "abundance of the bench". What the mother in her house and the common man would say is something like: "speak straight from the the heart".
> (Luther [1530][6], translated by Douglas Robinson 1997: 87)

More than four centuries later, Eugene Nida, influential 20th century authority on Bible translations (1952, 1964a), formulated his ideas of a "dynamic equivalence" (as opposed to merely formal equivalence) in translation, which takes into account also the purpose(s) of the author, along with the nature of the message and the type of audience. Thus, if the translator aims at full intelligibility of the message and its implications, Nida contends, then he or she must also make cultural adaptations to the text in order for the reader to understand, for instance, if the "indigenous way of talking about repentance is 'spit on the ground in front of,' as in Shilluk, spoken in the Sudan, the translator will obviously aim at the more meaningful idiom" (Nida 2000 [1964b]: 128). On a similar basis, "white as snow" might be changed to "white as egret feathers" if the target language speakers are not familiar with snow. Because of such strong audience-orientation in Bible translations, new "modernized" versions are often produced in languages in which already earlier Bible translations exist, in order to adapt the text to a more contemporary vocabulary and style.

Bible translations which bring the reader closer to the source text are, on the other hand, few and far between. In Jewish Bible translations, the Hebrew of the original characteristically remains more transparent in form and structure in the target text. A good case in point is the German translation of the Old Testament by the German Jewish scholars Martin Buber and Franz Rosenzweig (Buber and Rosenzweig 1936). Here, the German translation remains close to the original and seeks to transport sounds, structure and the "sensual meaning of words" of the Hebrew text (cf. Askani 1997). This is at the cost of easy comprehension of the translated text and requires an effort from the puzzled reader to muse over the interpretation – which is what the translators intended with their version (cf. also Buber 1954; Rosenzweig 1919, 1926, 1929). Greensporn (2005: 56–57) remarks on the gain of authenticity in the Buber/Rosenzweig translation:

> [...] as Buber and Rosenzweig forcefully and repeatedly argued, this [lack of easy comprehensibility] was exactly their point: the Hebrew Bible is a product of a society chronologically, geographically, and intellectually far removed from ours. Much of this separation revolves around its origins as a Jewish text. Moreover, the meaning of that ancient text is not always clear; it often exhibits an opaqueness that most modern translations manage to obscure in their commitment to clarity. In sum, Scripture can authentically speak to us today only when its distinctive cadences and characteristics are admitted, articulated and even celebrated.

The following excerpt (Genesis 1:1–1:3) in various versions illustrates the difference between Buber and Rosenzweig's approach in comparison with Luther's translation and two English translations. The assonances in the Hebrew original (*tohu wa bohu*; *ruach – merachepheth*) are given resonance in the translation in the Jewish tradition (*Irr*sal und *Wirr*sal; *Braus – spr*eitend, cf. also Askani 1997: 209–230), the choice of opaque vocabulary (e.g. *Urwirbel* 'ur- or original whirl' where other translations have 'The Spirit of God'), and unwieldy syntax in the German translation makes the reader stumble over the text, making the translation visible as a translation (cf. Schleiermacher [1813]1997, Benjamin

[1955]1977). In contrast to this, neither the Luther translation nor the King James Version (1611) make an attempt at such resonances (e.g. the Hebrew *tohu wa bohu*: Luther 'wüst und leer', King James Version 'without form and void'); the Living Bible (1971) translation ('a shapeless, chaotic mass'), particularly popular in the 1970s United States, is one example of the ever increasing numbers of modernized and "more colloquial" versions.

Table 2. A comparison of Genesis 1:1–1:3 in various English and German translations

King James Version (1611)	In the beginning God created the heaven and the earth. And the earth was without form, and void; and darkness was upon the face of the deep. And the Spirit of God moved upon the face of the waters. And God said, Let there be light: and there was light.
The Living Bible (1971)	When God began creating the heavens and the earth, the earth was at first a shapeless, chaotic mass, with the Spirit of God brooding over the dark vapors. Then God said, "Let there be light". And light appeared.
Lutherbibel (1534)	Am Anfang schuf Gott Himmel und Erde. Und die Erde war wüst und leer, und es war finster auf der Tiefe; und der Geist Gottes schwebte auf dem Wasser. Und Gott sprach: Es werde Licht! Und es ward Licht.
Buber/Rosenzweig translation (1936)	Im Anfang schuf Gott den Himmel und die Erde. Die Erde aber war *Irr*sal und *Wirr*sal. Finsternis über Urwirbels Antlitz. *B*raus Gottes *spr*eitend[7] über dem Antlitz der Wasser. Gott sprach: Licht werde! Licht ward.

4.3. Bible translations as colonial and postcolonial readings

As the above has shown, Bible translations have been part of the Christian mission from the very beginning and are not a particular contrivance of European colonialism. Nevertheless, the concurrence of the large increase of Bible translations with the period of colonial expansion at the beginning of the 19th century is irrefutable. By the end of that era, around 1920, the number of new Bible translations was almost twelve times as large as in 1800. Particular significance was placed on the African context where the largest number of Bible versions have been produced to date, as can be seen in Table 3:

Table 3. Bible languages by region (by end of 2002)

Region	Total (Whole Bibles and parts of Bibles)
Africa	647
Asia	573
Australia/ Pacific	406
Europe	204
Latin America	395
North America	75
Artificial Languages	3
Total	2,303

Source: Deutsche Bibelgesellschaft 2003

The translation of the "word of God" as an organized missionary project was initiated by international Bible Societies[8] such as, for the English colonial sphere, "The British & Foreign Bible Society" (B.F.B.S), founded in London in 1804, or the "American Bible Society", founded in 1816. Criticism of missionary activities and their role in colonialism range from a condemnation of such "imperialism at prayer" (e.g. Cochrane 1977: 211) to an acknowledgement of the ambivalent nature of the missionary enterprise (e.g. Emenyonu 1978: 19) which also brought forth abolitionists and humanitarians in the establishment of missionary societies, for instance in West Africa.[9]

The criticism of Bible translation as a colonizing act which results in the Westernization of cultures and the creation of indigenous elites is also ambivalent (cf. also the discussion in Sanneh 1993). While both were certainly intended side-effects of the mission, it would be underestimating the ambiguity of the translation process if one only takes into consideration the "corruption" effects this development had on indigenous languages and cultures. Translation also acts as a mediator between cultures and always bears the possibility of a re-interpretation as well as a re-evaluation. Additionally, translation can never be a one-sided project but has to involve at least two parties. In order to get the message across, missionaries needed to immerse themselves in the indigenous culture, so metropolitan complaints about "missionaries gone native" were not infrequent (cf. also Sanneh 1989: 5).

As pointed out above, the Christian missionary concept makes the recipient culture the locus of the proclamation. This also means that Christianity was placed into the familiar context of the recipient culture and built on structures already existent: Emenyonu (1978: 25–26), for instance, recounts for the Igbo situation how missionaries used traditional folktales and combined them with biblical information and religious instruction in order to make the message more easily accessible.[10] In general, an adaptation of the biblical text to the cultural parameters of the target language, including a profound knowledge of situational variables, social and pragmatic practices are propagated by the Bible Societies (cf. for instance, Nida 1952) to ensure that the "correct" message is getting across. Such revisions can already be found in this 19th century text where Robert Cust, first a patron, later a critic of the Church Missionary Society ponders about the difficulties of cross-cultural communication in Bible translation:

> But what do the Greenlanders, and the Eskimo, and the Polynesians, and Melanesians, and the Equatorial Africans, know about bread and wine, about fig-trees and sheep? Their ideas about clothing the body and habitations differ *in toto*. […] In the South Sea Islands the Bread-fruit and the Cocoa-nut milk take the place of bread and wine in the celebration of the Eucharist. Among the Greenlanders the Moravians are stated to have used a strong analogy, and described our Lord as the "little seal" of God, as the conception of a sheep and lamb was unknown, and the seal was to them what the sheep had been to the Syrians.
> (Cust 1886: 29)

It stands to argue whether or not these cultural adaptations of concepts such as bread, wine and lamb are entirely successful. Does the sharing of coconut-milk in the South Sea Islands have the same social function as the sharing of wine and bread among the Aramaians two thousand years ago? Does the seal, a hunted animal, really evoke the same image and sentiments as the lamb, a farmed animal that is raised by the shepherd? The limitations of this strategy to disguise the non-native source of the text become evident even in these very concrete examples. Such an appropriation of the text into the target culture is characteristic for the colonial era (cf. Cust 1886) and, as we have seen in Nida's notion of dynamic equivalence, it has continued to be a standard strategy throughout the 20th century.

Postcolonial translation theory, as advocated by Niranjana (1992) or Bassnett and Trivedi (1999: 2) sees translation as a "highly manipulative activity that involves all kinds of stages in the process of transfer across linguistic and cultural boundaries [… which is] highly charged with significance at every stage; it rarely, if ever, involves a relationship of equality between texts, authors or systems." In the last decade, various strategies have been proposed for postcolonial approaches in Bible translations: On the one hand, Sugirtharajah (1996: 13) suggests an even closer move towards the target culture in the form of a "textual cleansing", a kind of rewriting which seeks for a wider intertextuality which (for the Asian context) will link biblical texts with Asian scriptural texts. On the other hand, there is a call for a re-reading rather than a re-translation (e.g. Donaldson 1996a) to achieve a change of perspective, towards a postcolonial reading of the text. After all, while the allegation of a Westernization through Bible translation may be proof to the successful appropriation of the text into the European context, it has to be argued that the Bible is, of course, *not* a central European text. In fact, many of the settings and cultural references are more African than European. Thus, for the context of the African mission, many of the Old Testament stories in the original text offered identification which in translation could have a subversive effect: One notorious example is the story of King Solomon's many wives which undermined the church's sanction against poligamy. Equally, the psalm which reads "Ethiopia shall soon stretch out her hands unto God" (Psalm 68: 31) soon became the maxim of the Ethiopianism movement in the second half of the 19th century, which resulted in an independence movement with both a religious and a political dimension (cf. Döring 1996: 54). Similarly, the Roman occupation in the New Testament offers parallels and analogies for other colonial situations. In consequence, the original Christian cause might also be interpreted as an anti-colonial movement (cf. also Connor 1996 on African-American interpretations). Donaldson (1996b: 11) gives the example of the Exodus narrative to illustrate a shift of perspective, from a colonial to a postcolonial reading:

> The Canaanites are, of course, the much vilified people who occupied the 'promised land' before the arrival of the wandering Israelites. Yet they also stand in for all peoples whose lands have been conquered and expropriated. In the work of Edward Said, for example, the plight of the Canaanites stands in for the plight of present-day Palestinians struggling to retain their ancestral homeland. In the nineteenth-century sermons of the Reverend Nahum Gold, the 'red Canaanites' – his term for American Indians – stand in for all that America must reject [...]. Indeed, when we listen to the voices which are silenced by canonical readings of the story, the Exodus loses its appropriateness as a model for human liberation [...].

Notwithstanding the question what the original motivations and aims of missionary translators might have been, the result – vernacular translations of the Bible – were undoubtedly instrumental for the emergence of indigenous resistance to colonialism. Thus, the authority of the written word could also be turned against the colonial domination, empowering not only the languages but also those using them.

4.4.   Bible versions in new languages: the Bible in Pidgins and Creoles

One of the points Sugirtharajah (1996: 14) raises in a call for postcolonial translations of the Bible is that the English translations should also take account of "the emergence of English outside the Anglo-Saxon milieu", for instance, contact varieties like Nigerian English. Such a call may be unwarranted, however, as for contact varieties such as Pidgins and Creoles, Bible translations have traditionally been relevant for establishing these languages in a written form.[11] One of the main significant features common to these languages is that they are themselves largely the product of colonial contact situations (cf. Holm 1989: 632–633, cf. also Mühleisen 2002). As a result, they have often been viewed as "colonial corruptions" of European languages rather than languages in their own right. Attitudes towards these languages are traditionally negative and were reinforced by the low prestige functions they were used in. To see these languages written was an abhorrent idea in the 19th century, as this Victorian traveller's lamentation on the idea that a contact language (here: Chinese Pidgin English) might become a Bible language:

> It is not very satisfactory to look forward even to the bare possibility of such a caricature of our tongue becoming an established language. Should this ever be the result, translations into it of our classic authors will become a necessity. Shakepeare and Milton turned into Pigeon English are fearful even to think of. [...] The Missionary "pigeon" will also in due time demand a translation of the Bible into this very vulgar tongue. Death has many consolations, and to the number may be added this new one, that before the consummation foretold above can be realized, we will have passed away, and our ears will be deaf to the hideous result.
> (Simpson 1873: 47, as quoted in Bailey 1991: 147–148)

Simpson's fear has long become a reality: There are by now many established versions of the Bible or parts of it in contact languages and, additionally, quite a few non-established ones, some of which are preserved.[12] One of them is the Bible translation in Tok Pisin, which shall serve as an example.

Tok Pisin is one of the Melanesian Pidgins spoken in the Pacific. It is presumed to have its origin in the late 19th century on German-owned plantations in Samoa to which laborers from New Guinea were recruited. With their return to Papua New Guinea the Pidgin began to spread and has served as a lingua franca for cross-regional communication in the extremely heteroglossic country. Tok Pisin is one of the few contact languages which has the status of an official language (together with English and Hiri Motu). The development of Tok Pisin as a written language started in the 1920s when Catholic missionaries recognized its potential as a lingua franca. While it was at first not seen as a suitable medium for the transmission of religious contents, Lutheran and Methodist missions began to publish materials in the 1930s. The New Testament was published in 1966 (*Nupela Testamen*) and the orthography used there has come to serve as a de facto standard since (Romaine 1994: 24–25).[13] Today there is substantial writing activity in Tok Pisin, which includes a weekly newspaper (*"Wantok"*) in that language. The complete Bible translation was accomplished in 1989, from which the following excerpt from Genesis is taken:

God i mekim kamap olgeta samting (Sapta 1–2)

Stori bilong God i mekim kamap olgeta samting

1. Bipo bipo tru God i mekim kamap skai na graun na olgeta samting i stap long en. 2. Tasol graun i no bin i stap olsem yumi save lukim nau. Nogat. Em i stap nating na i narakain tru. Tudak i karamapim bikpela wara na spirit bilong God i go i kam antap long en. 3. Na God i tok olsem, "Lait i mas kamap." Orait lait i kamap.
(*Buk Baibel* 1989)

[In the beginning God created the heaven and the earth. And the earth was without form, and void; and darkness was upon the face of the deep. And the Spirit of God moved upon the face of the waters. And God said, Let there be light: and there was light. (*King James Version*)]

A common pattern of the language situation of Pidgins and Creoles is that they stand in competition with the European (ex-colonial) language which is also lexically related. This again reinforces the dichotomy of written versus oral, and high prestige versus low prestige language; if used in writing at all, the latter are then restricted to specific (especially literary) genres because these primarily oral varieties are perceived to lack the means to produce the registers and styles necessary to cover the full range of written production. We have already seen with regard to the European languages in the post-Reformation period that translation can indeed have an effect on the codification, standardization and elaboration of a language. It could be assumed, then, that for Pidgins and Creoles, which are still often struggling for official recognition and public prestige, the translation of religious texts might give an important boost to these languages as literary languages. Eckkrammer (1996: 129–149), for instance, gives a detailed account of the elaboration of Papiamentu, a Creole spoken in the Caribbean island of Curaçao, not least through translation of religious texts (on pidgin and creole languages, see also Migge and Léglise, this vol.).

The problem areas of many Pidgins and Creoles in the process of becoming fully functioning writing languages are (1) the need of lexical expansion, (2) standardization of their orthographies, and (3) syntactic/stylistic elaboration to accommodate various registers and genres of writing (cf. also Mühleisen 2001). Can Bible translations contribute to prevail over these challenges?

(1) *Lexical expansion*: Languages which started out in a contact situation for specific purposes typically have a relatively small vocabulary. Tok Pisin, the Melanesian Pidgin which is in the process of becoming a Creole[14] is a good example for that. Many Tok Pisin words are multifunctional, for instance *bilong* and *long* which function as all-purpose prepositions. New word-formation is often achieved via borrowing (e.g. *kros* 'cross', *disaipel* 'disciple'). This strategy, however, may easily result in a loss of linguistic autonomy for the variety, especially if the borrowed words are drawn from the superstrate language. Other

strategies include derivational morphology (e.g. *kalabusman* 'prisoner', lit. 'prison + man', *tok piksa* 'parable', lit. 'language + picture'), metaphorical extension of an existing word, or circumlocution (e.g. *dispela bikpela de bilong lotu* 'the Pessach feast', lit. 'this big day of religion', or *pait long gavman* 'sedition', lit. 'fight of government'). Bible translation, one might reason, could thus well have an effect on lexical expansion similar to the modernization of the European languages in the 16th century. However, it may also be warranted to ask whether the lexical innovations motivated by the translation of such an archaic text are particularly suitable to compete with the international language English as the writing language today. Words like 'chief priest' (*bikpris*) and 'Pessach feast' are certainly not among the most important innovations needed. In this respect, the weekly topical newspaper may have a greater effect on lexical expansion than the translation of the Bible has.

(2) *Standardization of orthographies*: Orthography choice is a highly debated issue especially for contact languages which exist in relationship with their lexifier: An orientation which is too close to the spelling system of the lexifier obscures linguistic differences between the pidgin or creole and the already established writing language (see also Romaine, this vol.) Linguistic autonomy or rather, the perception of it, can be increased or reduced by orthographic choices. Phonemic spelling, advocated by linguists in some cases (e.g. Cassidy, in Cassidy and LePage 1980[1967] for Jamaican Creole) has the advantage that it visibly augments the differences to the lexifier English but this strategy has not been very successful with readers who are literate in English (cf. Sebba 1998). The orthography of Krio, a Creole used in Sierra Leone, introduces vowel symbols (ɔ and ɛ) from the IPA (International Phonetic Alphabet) to mark a distance from the English spelling system (cf. also Coomber 1992), the New Testament which uses this orthography (*Gud Nyus Fɔ Ɔlman. Di Nyu Tɛstament*) was published in 1992. In a detailed analysis of the orthographic practices in *Da Jesus Book*, the Hawai'i Pidgin New Testament published in 2000, Suzanne Romaine (2005) sums up the various ambivalent aspects of the norm-setting and distance-creating authority of orthographic practices:

> Non-standard orthographies may encode not only differing degrees but also different kinds of distance from the standard. By dint of their representation of forms intended to convey the speech of a variety not usually written, they have the potential to challenge linguistic hierarchies by rendering visible non-standard voices in a medium that does not usually recognize them. This is a double-edged sword. For some, the appearance in print constitutes a validation of their identity and the speech form in which it may be heavily vested, while for others it can be a painful reminder and affirmation of the social distance of that variety from the standard.
> (Romaine 2005: 135–136)

(3) *Syntactic/stylistic elaboration*: When a language is used primarily orally, the range of stylistic choices is naturally limited to those which suit the purpose of oral communication. One of the most important tasks in language elaboration or modernization is therefore to extend the scope of registers available in that language. This concerns not only the selection of vocabulary but also syntactic options, as for instance the range of techniques which allows us to establish and express relations between two propositions. Translation may again be helpful in this enterprise in that it must involve creative solutions to transport subtle stylistic distinctions from the source language to the target language. However, the biblical text itself has its roots in an oral tradition which it has never quite escaped, which might be illustrated in a randomly chosen passage (John 1: 19–22) from the translation of the Gospel into Hawai'i Pidgin below:

Wat John Da Baptiza Guy Tell

19. One time, da Jewish leada guys wen send priest guys and odda guys from da Levi ohana dat help da priest guys. Dey send um by John fo aks, "Eh who you?" So he tell um. 20. He neva bulai. He tell um strait out, "Listen! I not da Christ, da Spesho Guy God Goin Send." 21. Dey aks him, "Den who you? You Elijah?" He tell, "No, I not." Dey say, "Den you da spesho guy dat goin come an talk fo God? He tell, "No, I not." 22. Dey tell him, "Kay den. Tell us who you. Wat you say bout yoaself? We gotta tell da guys dat wen send us something, you know!"
(*Da Jesus Book. Hawaii Pidgin New Testament* 2000)

[And this is the record of John, when the Jews sent priests and Levites from Jerusalem to ask him, Who art thou? And he confessed, and denied not; but confessed, I am not the Christ. And they asked him, What then? Art thou Elias? And he saith, I am not. Art thou that prophet? And he answered, No. Then said they unto him, Who art thou? that we may give an answer to them that sent us. What sayest thou of thyself? (*King James Version*)].

The most overt oral features here and throughout the text are the many dialogues. But also the narrative distinctly reveals structures which Walter Ong (2002) sees as characteristic of an oral mode of communication. If we consider the translation above, we may recognize some of Ong's oppositions: The sentence structure is *co-ordinate rather than subordinate*, the information structure is *additive rather than analytic*. There is a limited range of conjunctions to express temporality, conditionality, concessivity, etc. But this limitation is not due to an inability of Hawai'i Pidgin to increase the scale of techniques; rather these structures are already given in the source text. The Bible, in fact, is a foremost example for Ong's additional features of orality: The many enumerations and genealogies (especially in the Old Testament) are *redundant and copious* (2002: 39–41), many of the parables in the text are *close to the human lifeworld* (2002: 42–43). Consequently, when it comes to increasing the range of registers used in written communication, Bible translation is not the most suitable medium to achieve this goal. This may also be reflected in a recent trend to produce audio- or audio-visual versions of Pidgin and Creole Bible translations.[15]

4.5.   The Bible in many voices: Varieties and registers of language

The long tradition of recipient-orientation in Bible translation has also led to the production of numerous versions in non-standard regional varieties such as, for instance, Scots (translated 1983, cf. Crystal 2004: 488–489), a variety with a considerable literary tradition and one which holds a certain national prestige for Scotland. The following excerpt (John 1: 1–5) compares the Scots English Version (1983) with the King James Version (1611):

> **KJV (1611)**: 1. In the beginning was the Word, and the Word was with God, and the Word was God. 2. The same was in the beginning with God. 3. All things were made by him; and without him was not any thing made that was made. 4. In him was life; and the life was the light of men. 5. And the light shineth in darkness; and the darkness comprehended it not.
>
> **SEV (1983)**: 1. In the beginnin o aa things the Wurd wis there ense, an the Wurd bade wi God, an the Wurd wis God. 2. He wis wi God i the beginnin, 3. an aa things cam tae be throu him, an wiout him no ae thing cam tae be. 4. Aathing at hes come tae be, he wis the life in it, an that life wis the licht o man; 5. an ey the licht shines i the mirk, an the mirk downa slocken it nane.

Another example for a Bible translation into a regional variety with a literary tradition would be that of Bärndütsch (a Swiss German variety), translated 1984 (NT) and 1990 (OT). The passage cited here is, once again, the beginning of the First Book of Moses (in comparison with the Lutherbibel 1534):

> **LB (1534) Die Schöpfung** 1. Am Anfang schuf Gott Himmel und Erde. 2. Und die Erde war wüst und leer, und es war finster auf der Tiefe; und der Geist Gottes schwebte auf dem Wasser. 3. Und Gott sprach: Es werde Licht! Und es ward Licht.
>
> **BD (1990) D Wält wird erschaffe** 1. Am Aafang het Gott der Himel und d Ärden erschaffe. 2. D Ärden isch ei wyti Wüeschti gsi. Fyschteri het d Urfluet zueddeckt. Der Geischt vo Gott het über ds Wasser gwääit. 3. Gott het gseit: "Liecht söll wärde!" So isch ds Liecht worde.

Many of the claims made above for Pidgin and Creole Bible versions with regard to orthography, standardization or lexical and stylistic expansion could also be made for these non-standard versions. A pursuit of uniformity may, however, be at times purposely avoided in dialect translations. Thus, as Crystal (2004: 489) points out with regard to the Scots translation by William Laughton Lorimer (1983), "he deliberately avoided a uniform representation, choosing several varieties of Scots to reflect the fact that the original text came from different writers using different styles".

As we have already seen in Section 4.2, register choice is one more issue which can vary to a great extent in Bible translations and the level of language use ranges from archaic to literary to highly colloquialized styles. A particular genre of Bible translations caters for children. Children's Bibles often do not only differ in micro-structure (vocabulary, syntactic choices, etc.) from "adult versions" but often show also macro-structural changes which concern the organization of the text, supplements, etc. Pictures and illustrations are characteristic for children's Bibles, as are comments or explanations of the Scriptures, such as in the following comment on Genesis:

> LONG BEFORE YOU WERE BORN, before the human race came into existence, before there were days and nights, before the universe was created, there was life. This Life was self-sufficient. It didn't need anything, or anyone else in order to live. In fact, this Life had always existed and would always exist. Life was Spirit. Spirit doesn't consist of matter. At times spirit is compared to the wind. You can't see spirit, you can't smell spirit and you can't taste spirit, but, like the invisible wind, you can often feel the power of spirit and see the result of its actions [...].
> www.antelope-ebooks.com/childrens/BIBLE/GENESIS/Gen01.htm, retrieved December 2005)

A typical feature in this passage is the personalized form of address ("You can't see spirit") and the relation of the events to the recipient's own experience ("Long before you were born"). Children's and adolescents' versions of the biblical texts certainly form the greatest part of Bible translations for a specific audience. An example of a translation project which also involves adolescents in the translation process is the German *Volxbibel* 'peoples' Bible' (www.volxbibel.de). Here, the New Testament is edited and revised in a highly informal register and is supposed to be constantly updated in an internet version to ensure contemporary adolescent language usage.

4.6. Gender-inclusive Bible translations

Along with the emergence of linguistic research on language and gender, and the call for the use of gender-inclusive language in many domains of language usage (see Hellinger and Pauwels, this vol.), there have been in recent years several attempts to create a gender-neutral version of the Bible or parts of it in translation. Some English-language examples will be briefly considered here.

In 1997, a newly revised, gender-inclusive version of the NIV *New International Version* (International Bible Society) – initially called NIVI – was published in Britain. However, the version received so much pressure from the conservative public that the publisher decided not to distribute it in the USA (cf. Burke 2005: 129). In 2002, a new gender-sensitive translation of the New Testament was released, the *Today's New International Version* (TNIV), the Old Testament followed in 2005. What is at stake in these new English language translations becomes evident when we look at the "Guidelines for Translation of Gender-related Language in Scripture" which were published by *Focus on the Family* in a hurried response (and opposition) to the initial NIVI (cf. Burke 2005: 129–131). The 13-point instruction mainly deals with generic versus specific usages of masculine person reference and pronouns, such as

> (1) The generic use of 'he, him, his, himself' should be employed to translate generic 3rd person masculine singular pronouns in Hebrew, Aramaic and Greek. However, substantival participles such as *ho pisteuon* can often be rendered in inclusive ways, such as 'the one who believes' rather than 'he who believes'.
> [...]
> (3) 'Man' should ordinarily be used to designate the human race or human beings in general.
> [...]
> (4) Hebrew *'ish* should ordinarily be translated 'man' and 'men' and Greek *aner* should almost always be so translated.
> [...]
> (6) Indefinite pronouns such as *tis* can be translated 'anyone' rather than 'any man'.
> [...]
> (11) 'Brother' (*adelphos*) and 'brothers' (*adelphoi*) should not be changed to 'brother(s) and sister(s)'.
> (12) 'Son' (*huios, ben*) should not be changed to 'child,' or 'sons' (*huioi*) to 'children' or 'sons and daughters'. (However, Hebrew *banim* often means 'children'.)
> (13) 'Father' (pater, ab) should not be changed to 'parent,' or 'fathers' to 'parents,' or 'ancestors'.
> (from *Focus on the Family* fax, 3 June 1997, quoted in Burke 2005: 130)

The problem of generic versus gender-specific uses of masculine pronouns and other person references is well known and one of the most thoroughly debated questions in language and gender research in English (for an overview of research on gender across languages, cf. Hellinger and Bussmann 2001, 2002, 2003). As Burke (2005: 133) points out,

> Hebrew *'ish*, like Greek *anthropos*, is a multiple-reference word. It is used in the Hebrew Bible in referring to humans of each gender, as well as to males, whether human or not [...]. Hebrew *'ish*, like Greek *anthropos*, is capable of being gender-specific or gender-inclusive in meaning. This is also true for the masculine pronouns that refer to it.

The closest equivalent in the English language is 'man', which historically has the same capacity of gender-specificity and gender-inclusiveness. However, if ever there have been truly gender-inclusive uses of the terms *man/men*, they have certainly shifted in meaning in recent years to become more gender-specific – not least due to an increased public awareness as a consequence of language and gender research. Similarly, a large number of English speakers today might not understand the use of the pronouns *he, him, his, himself* as referring to both male and female persons. Along with other adaptations of the text to contemporary language usage, the revision of such shifts in meaning should only be in line with the recipient-orientation in the tradition of Christian Bible translation. In a comparative analysis of the translations of the Hebrew word *'ish* (cf. point 4 of the guidelines above), Burke (2005) shows, in fact, that early Bible translations such as the Septuagint or the Latin Vulgate already opted for alternative or gender-inclusive translations of *'ish* to a substantial proportion (32 % and 45 % respectively), making the guidelines cited above appear to be based more on ideology rather than on tradition.

An over-generalization of principles might, however, also be avoided in the application of gender-inclusive options. In his unfavourable response to the TNIV, Vern Poythress (2005) criticizes the strategy of using the plural pronoun in order to avoid the generic *he*, for instance in the following passage in John 14:23 (here in comparison with the New International Version of 1978):

> **NIV 1978**: "If anyone loves me, he will obey my teaching. My Father will love *him*, and we will come to *him* and make our home with *him*".
>
> **TNIV 2002**: "Anyone who loves me will obey my teaching. My Father will love *them*, and we will come to *them* and make our home with *them*".

Poythress (2005: n.p.) points out, that the meaning in the two versions is similar but not identical: "The TNIV wording (with plural *them*) opens the door to a corporate interpretation, in which God dwells not with each individual, but with the group, "them" corporately. This new translation obscures the point of the original." (For the debate of Poythress's criticism of the TNIV (2002) and responses, especially in *Christianity Today,* see www.geocities.com/ bible_translation/tnivlinks.htm). It seems evident that there can be no one-to-one principle on how to translate gender-sensitive items throughout the text but that case-to-case decisions have to be made on the basis of context and meaning.

5. Conclusion

The wealth of Bible translation projects which are currently in progress – altogether more than 600 projects in almost 500 languages in December 2005 according to the United Bible Societies (www.biblesociety.org, retrieved December 2005) – demonstrates that Bible translation continues to be a flourishing field, both for translators and for linguists interested in translation, the codification of a specific language variety or register, or language and gender. As the examples have shown, not only religious principles and ideas but also attitudes towards translation as well as linguistic ideology play an important part in the interpretation of religious texts and their rendering in another language.

Religion and religious institutions have been and remain an important site of language contact and communication. While some of the consequences of such contact are relatively well researched and are part of established sociolinguistic and applied linguistic research on language spread, language maintenance, language death or revitalization, other fields of investigation (e.g. linguistic discourse analysis in religious domains) have not received the same attention. In applied linguistics, the role of religion in education as well as in literacy programmes continues to be a thriving field. Further research on language and religion is potentially a highly fruitful endeavour exactly because the two share many aspects – ultimately both language and religion are cultural systems which rely on a system of interpretable signs and symbols, and in both fields ideology is a strong factor to reckon with. It is especially the last point why interdisciplinary and multi-perspectived work on the relationship between language and religion is highly warranted.

Notes

1. For Speech Act Theory in the interpretation of the Biblical text, cf. also Briggs (2001).
2. Ben Yehuda's own home became the "first Hebrew-speaking household": He and his wife, a native speaker of Russian, agreed to speak only Hebrew to their son who was consequently raised as the first speaker of Modern Hebrew.
3. "The Mabinogi" is the title of four medieval Welsh tales preserved in 14th-century manuscripts.
4. For dates of first complete printed Bibles, cf. Sanneh 1989: 246–249. For a history of English language Bible versions, cf. Long 2001; Crystal 2004: 239–242, 271–279.
5. Author-to-reader is here meant as a technical term in Schleiermacher's framework. It is clear that the Bible does not have one author as such.
6. "Denn man muß nicht die Buchstaben in der lateinischen Sprache fragen, wie man soll Deutsch reden, wie diese Esel tun, sondern man muß die Mutter im Hause, die Kinder auf der Gassen, den gemeinen Mann auf dem Markt drum fragen, und denselbigen auf das Maul sehen, wie sie reden und darnach dolmetschen; da verstehen sie es denn und merken, daß man deutsch mit ihnen redet.
So wenn Christus spricht: 'Ex abundántia cordis os lóquitur.' Wenn ich den Eseln soll folgen, die werden mir die Buchstaben vorlegen und so dolmetschen: Aus dem Überfluß des Herzens redet der Mund. Sage mir: ist das deutsch geredet? Welcher Deutsche verstehet solches? Was ist Überfluß des Herzens für ein Ding? [...] 'Überfluß des Herzens' ist kein Deutsch, so wenig als das Deutsch ist: Überfluß des Hauses, Überfluß des Kachelofens, Überfluß der Bank, sondern so redet die Mutter im Haus und der gemeine Mann: Wes das Herz voll ist, des gehet der Mund über."
7. In a first version, the translators chose *brütend* but abandoned it in their second version for a word which they thought would be closer to the meaning of the corresponding Hebrew word. Thus, their alliterations were never based purely on aesthetic principles.

8. There are denominational differences in the attitude towards Bible translations: Bible Societies were originally predominantly Protestant institutions and it was not until the Second Vatican Council that bible societies became more significant in Catholicism. Notwithstanding this lack of institutional structure of Bible translations, Roman Catholic missionaries from their earliest colonial activity in the early modern period have built on indigenous structures. In the Spanish Americas they used Amerindian vernaculars for the conversion of the Amerindians – much against the official Spanish government line which proscribed Castilian as the language of religious life (cf. Sanneh 1989: 91).
9. Particularly in the colony of Sierra Leone, founded in 1787 to settle liberated slaves from England and North America. From Sierra Leone, organizations like the Wesleyan Missionary Society (1795) or the Church Missionary Society (1806) began to spread their activities along the African West Coast.
10. On the other hand, an appropriation that is too close to the indigenous tradition may also pose a problem, as can be illustrated by the following example of the first missionary (probably Van der Kemp) among the Xhosa who enquired about their address term for the Supreme Being. When the translator rendered to him the concept of the creator (uTikxo) and heaven (Usezulwini) in their language, he then turned round and told the Xhosa that this is what he was bringing them (Sanneh 1989: 161), leaving the Xhosa puzzled what was new about his message.
11. Bible translations into Pidgin and Creole languages reach back as early as the late 18th century (cf. Holm 1989): on Moravian missionaries in Suriname.
12. Magnus Huber (1997) gives some examples of the story of Genesis in West African Pidgins which were presumably not composed for use in the African missions but for humorous purposes: "The story of Genesis in Pidgin English was a popular souvenir among those who went overseas, probably because the post was so well known that anybody at home could follow it, even in Pidgin. The tradition goes back to at least the 19th century."
13. Cf. Romaine 1994 also for a critical appraisal of the consequences of literacy and missionary education.
14. In many regions in Papua New Guinea it is spoken as a mother tongue.
15. The Jamaican Creole version is planned to be published only in audio-form. Many film projects or dramatization of Bible portions in film (e.g. Tok Pisin, Pijin, Kriol (Australia), Krio (Sierra Leone), Cameroon Pidgin) are in progress or have been completed recently. See www.sil.org.

References

Abdul-Raof, Hussein
   2005   Cultural aspects in Qur'an translation. In: Lynne Long (ed.), 162–172.
Alpert, Michael
   1998   Torah translation. In: Mona Baker (ed.), 269–273.
Askani, Hans-Christoph
   1997   *Das Problem der Übersetzung – dargestellt an Franz Rosenzweig.* Tübingen: J. C. B. Mohr.

Austin, John L.
  1962   *How to Do Things With Words.* Oxford: Oxford University Press.
Bailey, Richard
  1991   *Images of English. A Cultural History of the Language.* Ann Arbor: The University of Michigan Press.
Bailey, Randall C. and Tina Pippin (eds.)
  1996   *Race, Class, and the Politics of Biblical Translation. Semeia – an Experimental Journal for Biblical Criticism.* Vol. 76. Atlanta: Scholars Press.
Baker, Mona (ed.)
  1998a   *Routledge Encyclopedia of Translation Studies.* London: Routledge.
Baker, Mona
  1998b   Arabic tradition. In: Mona Baker (ed.), 316–325.
Bassnett, Susan and Harish Trivedi (eds.)
  1999   *Postcolonial Translation.* London: Routledge.
Benjamin, Walter
  1977   Die Aufgabe des Übersetzers. In: *Illuminationen. Ausgewählte Schriften 1.* [1955], 50–62. Frankfurt: Suhrkamp.
Briggs, Richard S.
  2001   *Words in Action: Speech Act Theory and Biblical Interpretation.* London: T & T Clark.
Buber, Martin and Franz Rosenzweig
  1936   *Die Schrift und ihre Verdeutschung.* Berlin: Schocken.
Buber, Martin
  1954   Zu einer neuen Verdeutschung der Schrift. In: *Die fünf Bücher der Weisung,* verdeutscht von Martin Buber gemeinsam mit Franz Rosenzweig, 3–44. Köln & Olten: Jakob Hegner.
Buk Baibel
  1989   Port Moresby: Baibel Sosaiti bilong Papua Niugini.
Burke, David
  2005   The translation of the Hebrew word 'ish in Genesis: A brief historical comparison. In: Lynne Long (ed.), 129–140.
Cassidy, Frederic G. and Robert B. LePage
  1980   *Dictionary of Jamaican English.* [1967] Cambridge: Cambridge University Press.
Cochrane, Charles N.
  1977   *Christianity and Classical Culture.* 1st ed. 1940. New York: Oxford University Press.
Connor, Kimberly Rae
  1996   'Everybody talking about heaven ain't going there': The biblical call for justice and the postcolonial response of the spirituals. In: Laura E. Donaldson (ed.), 107–128.
Coomber, Ajayi
  1992   The new Krio orthography and some unresolved problems. In: Eldred Jones et al. (eds.), 15–20.
Crosby, Kate
  2005   What does not get translated in Buddhist studies and the impact on teaching. In: Lynne Long (ed.), 41–53.

Crystal, David
1997   *Cambridge Encyclopedia of Language*. Cambridge: Cambridge University Press.
Crystal, David
2004   *The Stories of English*. London: Penguin.
Cust, Robert Needham
1886   *Language as Illustrated by Bible Translation. With a Map of the World and a Table of Languages*. London: Trübner & Co.
Da Jesus Book. Hawaii Pidgin New Testament
2000   Orlando: Wycliffe Bible Translators.
Deutsche Bibelgesellschaft
1998   *30 Bibelsprachen von A–Z*. Stuttgart: Deutsche Bibelgesellschaft.
Deutsche Bibelgesellschaft
2003   Die Bibel weltweit in 2303 Sprachen übersetzt. Pressemitteilung der Deutschen Bibelgesellschaft Stuttgart.
Döring, Tobias
1996   *Chinua Achebe und Joyce Cary. Ein postkoloniales Rewriting englischer Afrika-Fiktionen*. Pfaffenweiler: Centaurus.
Donaldson, Laura E. (ed.)
1996a   *Postcolonialism and Scriptural Reading. Semeia – an Experimental Journal for Biblical Criticism*. Vol. 75. Atlanta: Scholars Press.
Donaldson, Laura E.
1996b   Postcolonialism and biblical reading: An introduction. In: Laura E. Donaldson (ed.), 1–14.
Ds Alte Teschtamänt bärndütsch
1990   Translated by Hans, Ruth and Benedikt Bietenhard. Bern: Berchthold Haller Verlag.
Ds Nöie Teschtamänt bärndütsch
1984   Translated by Hans and Ruth Bietenhard. Bern: Berchthold Haller Verlag.
Eckkrammer, Eva Maria
1996   *Literarische Übersetzung als Werkzeug des Sprachausbaus: Am Beispiel Papiamentu*. (Abhandlungen zur Sprache und Literatur 87). Bonn: Romanistischer Verlag.
Edwards, Viv
1991   The Welsh speech community. In: Safder Alladina and Viv Edwards (eds.), *Multilingualism in the British Isles*. Vol. I: *The Older Mother Tongues*, 107–125. London & New York: Longman.
Emenyonu, Ernest N.
1978   *The Rise of the Igbo Novel*. Ibadan: Oxford University Press.
Ethnologue
2005   www.ethnologue.com.
Fellman, Jack
1974   The role of Eliezer Ben Yehuda in the revival of the Hebrew language: An assessment. In: Joshua Fishman (ed.), *Advances in Language* Planning, 427–455. The Hague: Mouton.
Görlach, Manfred
1999   Regional and social variation. In: Roger Lass (ed.), *The Cambridge History of the English Language,* Vol. II: *1476–1776*, 459–538. Cambridge: Cambridge University Press.

Goody, Jack, Ian Watt and Kathleen Gough
　1986　　*Entstehung und Folgen der Schriftkultur.* (original: *Literacy in Traditional Societies,* 1968). Frankfurt am Main: Suhrkamp.
Greensporn, Leonard
　2005　　Texts and contexts: Perspectives on Jewish translations of the Hebrew Bible. In: Lynne Long (ed.), 54–64.
Gud Nyus Fɔ Ɔlman. Di Nyu Tɛstament
　1992　　Freetown: Bible Society in Sierra Leone.
Hellinger, Marlis and Hadumod Bussmann (eds.)
　2001,　　*Gender Across Languages,* vols. 1–3. Amsterdam: Benjamins.
　2002, 2003
Holm, John
　1989　　*Pidgins and Creoles.* Vol. II: *Reference Survey.* Cambridge: Cambridge University Press.
Huber, Magnus
　1997　　'Dat tree be white man chop': On the story of Genesis in West African Pidgin English. *The Carrier Pidgin* 25: 4–6; 38–43.
Johnson, Will J.
　2005　　Making Sanskrit or making strange? How should we translate Classical Hindu texts? In: Lynne Long (ed.), 65–74.
Jones, Eldred, Karl I. Sandred and Neville Shrimpton (eds.)
　1992　　*Reading and Writing Krio.* Proceedings of a Workshop Held at the Institute of Public Administration and Management, University of Sierra Leone, Freetown, 29–31 January, 1990. Uppsala: Almqvist & Wiksell International.
Keane, Webb
　1997　　Religious language. *Annual Review of Anthropology* 26: 47–71.
KJV [King James Version]
　1998[1611]　*The Bible. Authorized King James Version with Apocrypha.* Ed. by Robert Carroll and Stephen Prickett. Oxford: Oxford University Press.
Living Bible
　1971　　*The Living Bible.* Transl. by Kenneth Taylor. Cambridge: Tyndale House.
Long, Lynne
　2001　　*Translating the Bible: From the Seventh to the Seventeenth Century.* Aldershot: Ashgate.
Long, Lynne
　2005　　*Translation and Religion: Holy Untranslatable?* Clevedon: Multilingual Matters.
Lutherbibel
　1968　　*Die Bibel. Die ganze Heilige Schrift des Alten und Neuen Testaments,* nach der Übers. Martin Luthers. Stuttgart: Württembergische Bibelanstalt.
Luther, Martin
　1530/　　Sendbrief vom Dolmetschen. Reprinted in Hans Joachim Störig (ed.), *Das*
　1963　　*Problem des Übersetzens,* 14–32. Darmstadt: Wissenschaftliche Buchgesellschaft.
Mühleisen, Susanne
　2001　　'How is it that we hear in our own languages the wonders of God?' Vernacular Bible translations in colonial and postcolonial contexts. In: Gerhard Stilz (ed.), *Colonies – Missions – Cultures – in the English-speaking World. General and Comparative Studies,* 247–263. Tübingen: Stauffenburg Verlag.

Mühleisen, Susanne
    2002   *Creole Discourse. Exploring Prestige Formation and Change Across Caribbean English-lexicon Creoles.* Amsterdam: Benjamins.

Mustapha, Hassan
    1998   Qur'an (Koran) translation. In: Mona Baker (ed.), 200–204.

Nida, Eugene A.
    1952   *God's Word in Man's Language.* New York: Harper and Brothers.

Nida, Eugene
    1964a   *Towards a Science of Translating.* Leiden: Brill.

Nida, Eugene
    1964b/   Principles of correcpondence. Reprinted in Lawrence Venuti (ed.), *The*
    2000   *Translation Studies Reader*, 126–140. London: Routledge.

Nida, Eugene
    1998   Bible translation. In: Mona Baker (ed.), 22–28.

Niranjana, Tejaswini
    1992   *Siting Translation: History, Post-structuralism, and the Colonial Context.* Berkeley: University of California Press.

Ong, Walter
    2002   *Orality and Literacy. The Technologizing of the Word.* 2nd ed. London: Routledge.

Poythress, Vern S.
    2002   Is the TNIV faithful in its treatment of gender? No. Political correctness puts pressure on translators to change details of meaning. In: *Christianity Today*, October 7, 2002.

Poythress, Vern S.
    2005   TNIV's altered meanings: An evaluation of the TNIV. In: www.shepherdchurch.com/ktf/LAnalyzingTniv20050203.html, retrieved December 2005.

Robinson, Douglas
    1997   *Western Translation Theory: From Herodotus to Nietzsche.* Manchester: St. Jerome.

Robinson, Douglas
    1998   Babel, tower of. In: Mona Baker (ed.), 21–22.

Romaine, Suzanne
    1994   Language standardization and linguistic fragmentation in Tok Pisin. In: Marcylina Morgan (ed.), *Language and the Social Construction of Identity in Creole Situations*, 19–41. Los Angeles: University of California.

Romaine, Suzanne
    2005   Orthographic practices in the standardization of pidgins and creoles: Pidgin in Hawai'i as anti-language and anti-standard. In: Susanne Mühleisen (ed.), *Creole Languages in Creole Literatures. Journal of Pidgin and Creole Languages (Special Issue)* 20: 101–140.

Rosenzweig, Franz
    1919   Geist und Epochen der jüdischen Geschichte. In: Franz Rosenzweig (1976), 129–142.

Rosenzweig, Franz
    1926   Die Schrift und Luther. In: Franz Rosenzweig (1976), 51–77.

Rosenzweig, Franz
   1929   Weltgeschichtliche Bedeutung der Bibel. In: Franz Rosenzweig (1976) *Die Schrift. Aufsätze, Übertragungen und Briefe*, 9–12. Ed. by Karl Thieme. Königstein: Jüdischer Verlag Athenäum.

Sanneh, Lamin
   1989   *Translating the Message. The Missionary Impact on Culture.* Maryknoll: Orbis Books.

Sanneh, Lamin
   1993   *Encountering the West. Christianity and the Global Cultural Process: The African Dimension.* Maryknoll: Orbis Books.

Sawyer, John F. A. (ed.)
   2001   *Concise Encyclopedia of Language and Religion.* Amsterdam: Elsevier.

Schleiermacher, Friedrich
   1813/   Ueber die verschiedenen Methoden des Uebersetzens. Transl. by Douglas
   1997   Robinson [1997] On the different methods of translating. In: Douglas Robinson (ed.), 225–238.

Sebba, Mark
   1998   Meaningful choices in creole orthography: 'experts' and 'users'. In: Rainer Schulze (ed.), *Making Meaningful Choices in English. On Dimensions, Perspectives, Methodology and Evidence*, 223–234. Tübingen: Gunter Narr.

Sugirtharajah, R. S.
   1996   Textual cleansing: A move from the colonial to the postcolonial version. In: Randall C. Bailey and Tina Pippin (eds.), 7–19.

The New Testament in Scots
   1983   Transl. by William Laughton Lorimer. Harmondsworth: Penguin.

United Bible Societies
   2005   www.biblesociety.org

Volxbibel
   2005   www.volxbibel.de

Williams, Glanmor
   1979   *Religion, Language and Nationality in Wales.* Cardiff: University of Wales Press.

16. Language, war, and peace

William C. Gay

1. Introduction

Applied linguistics is needed for a critical analysis of discourse about war and peace. Analyses of the language used by military and government officials and by the media to describe the first Persian Gulf War illustrate the value of critical discourse analysis for exposing a variety of practical problems associated with these distortions of language and communication. These analyses provide a basis for analyzing more recent discourse about the second Persian Gulf War and other discussions of issues relating to war and peace.

Wars are complex phenomena, but they are often presented in very simplistic – even sloganistic – terms. One reason for conveying war by means of caricatures relates to the need by government officials to communicate with the masses in a manner that is succinct and persuasive. During the first Persian Gulf War, as George Lakoff (1991) and others have observed, the use of the "fairy tale" motif was especially common. (This type of description is used for many wars.) At the time of Operation Desert Shield and Operation Desert Storm, the public was served up with a variety of metaphors that wove a classic fairy tale: In a land far, far away there lived an evil villain (Saddam Hussein) who had violated (invaded) an innocent victim (Kuwait), but a hero (the United States, along with its allies) would save the day, rescuing the victim and vanquishing the villain and restoring peace, justice, and tranquility.

In terms of the metaphors used, the story is straightforward. A villain is vicious and lacks morality and rationality, while a hero is courageous and possesses both morality and rationality. Given this antithetical characterization, the public transfers to its leaders the view that heroes are not able to negotiate with villains; instead, they must defeat the Evil Ones. The public was familiar with the fairy tale components of the alarm that was sounded; so, not much inclination was present to check the details. Of course, Kuwait was hardly an innocent victim, given its practice at that time of lateral drilling into Iraqi oil fields and its long-standing oppression of women, and then after the first Persian Gulf War the government of Kuwait did not exactly become a model democracy but continued as an oppressive monarchy. Metaphors dispense with such details in the way they limit and simplify our perceptions.

We recognize that in wars large numbers of people are killed. The research of scholars like Lakoff contributes to the breadth and depth of applied linguists by also bringing to our attention the ways in which metaphors kill or, more precisely, when backed up by the weapons of war metaphors kill and often on a very large scale. Without such critical analyses, many people do not realize that they are relying on an unconscious system of metaphors in thinking about international affairs. In addition to the fairy tale metaphor, many more metaphors are used to describe war, such as the state-as-house metaphor and the state-as-person metaphor. The state-as-house metaphor leads to further metaphors connected with protecting our home. After 9/11, to protect the "home" that is the United States, the U.S. government declared the necessity of establishing an Office of Homeland Security. A house is also a container. During the Cold War, the U.S. government tried to prevent harm to the U.S. homeland by developing a strategic doctrine of Containment of the Soviet Union and its allies. This metaphor of state-as-house was used differently in the 1980s when some strategists feared newer Soviet weapons capabilities. They declared that a "window of vulnerability" existed. What do you do in a house when you have an open window that makes the residents of the house vulnerable? You close the window.

These metaphors simultaneously obscure our noticing some features of the situation while exaggerating other aspects. Such features are well illustrated in the state-as-person metaphor. The citizens of any nation live in the same "house", and the "head of the household" runs this "house". While such metaphors provide a way of seeing how authority and rule are structured in a society, they obscure the ways in which the citizens of most countries are far more diverse than the members of most households and the ways in which the head of state is assisted by a vast set of offices and personnel and the ways in which the head of state possesses far more power and capacity to exercise force than a head of a household.

In addition to exposing how current metaphors distort our language and communication, applied linguists can also try to provide new and more enlightening metaphors designed to reduce the distortions of the language of war. For example, when governmental officials declare that we should be alarmed about a "window of vulnerability", an applied linguist can counter with another metaphor that reveals what the official metaphor obscures, namely, we are deceiving ourselves in being concerned about an "open window" when we live in a "roofless house". No nation has yet been able to develop a defensive system that adequately undercuts the reality of Mutual Assured Destruction (MAD); all nations are vulnerable. Belief in "invulnerability" is a myth. No "house" can be made completely safe. While many nations are capable of inflicting great harm on their adversaries, they cannot fully prevent harm, even great harm, from being inflicted on their own "household".

Some of the linguistic manipulation in discourse about war is unintentional and involves self-deception on the part of the governmental and military officials. As occurs in many fields where individuals have to order or perform very unpleasant tasks, the use of euphemisms is prevalent. Official discourse about war makes extensive use of euphemisms. A linguistic alternative to the horrors of war is created in order to think, speak, and write about these events in an abstract or indirect way, since it would otherwise be difficult to visualize graphically or justify logically what is actually taking place. Likewise, when the public hears and reads these euphemisms, they do not realize what is really occurring.

A few examples of such euphemisms will make the point about what is being masked. A "countervalue" target refers to an attack on civilians and industry, rather than against military forces and installations. During World War II, the allies initiated "obliteration" bombing. This technique involved the firebombings of large cities, like Leipzig and Dresden, and the atomic bombings of two Japanese cities, Hiroshima and Nagasaki. The aim was not to protect the innocent but to target and kill the innocent – and in very large numbers. Even when innocent civilians are not targeted, their inadvertent, even if large-scale, deaths are referred to as "collateral damage". On a submarine that can launch missiles with nuclear warheads, the location of these missile silos is referred to as "Sherwood Forest". A military aid is always near the U.S. President with a small briefcase handcuffed to the aid's wrist. This briefcase, which contains the "menu" or codes for various launch options for the U.S. nuclear weapons arsenal, is euphemistically nicknamed "the football". So, if a U.S. President were to have the military aid carrying "the football" open it, the President would not be preparing to start a sports event involving the tossing of a football, but would be preparing to start a nuclear war.

Linguistic misrepresentation is not always unintentional. Propaganda and brain washing seek to manipulate the minds and behaviors of the citizenry. In times of war, each of the nations involved presents its adversary as an evil enemy and itself as the embodiment of good. All parties employ linguistic misrepresentations of themselves and their adversaries. Nevertheless, an ally in one war may be the enemy in the next, while the enemy in one war may become an economic partner in the post-war global market.

Governmental and military officials are able to impose their form of discourse as the legitimate one and, thereby, co-opt efforts by critics of war. Nations typically cultivate among citizens a belief in their legitimacy. In times of "national emergency", open opposition to the "official version" of events is often forbidden and may be severely punished. Citizens who question the "official version" are labeled "traitors" and "fellow travelers" with the enemy of the state.

The meanings of terms within semiological systems are based upon the oppositions among the signs. A non-linguistic example is the use of red, yellow, and green lights in traffic signals. In relation to classifications of peoples, many governments use binary oppositions of an "us-them" type, such as Greeks and barbarians, freedom fighters and terrorists, and culture bearers and culture destroyers. Any government can define any group as the enemy, the barbarians, the terrorists, or the cultural destroyers. History shows that practices of genocide and crimes against humanity begin with a classification that divides people into two groups, one viewed positively and the other as subhuman or unworthy of existence. The use of condemnatory terms prepares a social group to practice atrocities and is used to perpetuate these atrocities throughout their duration.

The Tutsis were termed *"inyenzi"* (a slang epithet meaning cockroaches) in the years preceding the 1994 genocide in Rwanda. A similar effect was achieved by Nazi references to Jews as "bacillus", and even by neo-Nazi calls to "kill faggots" beyond the million "queers" massacred by Hitler until all homosexual "scum" are "wiped out". Language that relies on such vicious euphemisms diverts our attention from the reality and the injustice of the persecution, just as using "ethnic cleansing", instead of ethnocide, masks the slaughters and forcible relocation that occurred in Bosnia in the 1990s.

Not surprisingly, rhetoric about war can be found not only in public pronouncements by the superpowers during the former East-West Cold War but also in a variety of declarations by the nations involved in the continuing North-South conflict. Throughout the era of imperialism, the North defended its "right" to "protect" its colonies, while the colonized responded with arguments for the legitimacy of "wars of liberation". Whether wars of liberation bring about an end to war, and there is scant evidence that they do, they are still wars and involve small-scale to large-scale violence. Nevertheless, some supporters of wars of liberation prefer to forge an alternative language that refuses to designate their movements as violent since they are in response to practices of oppression. In his classic *Pedagogy of the Oppressed*, Brazilian Paulo Freire (1993) contends that violence has never been initiated by the oppressed and designates as "a gesture of love" the admittedly violent response of rebellion by the oppressed against the initial violence of oppressors. Such reversals in language can be found in almost all instances of official discourse about war.

2. History of the field

Critical analyses of war and discussions of peace go back to classical antiquity. In *History of the Peloponnesian War* (431–404 BCE), Thucydides wrote the first extensive historical account of war. He may also be the first to observe how war negatively affects language and degrades human behavior. He states "Reckless audacity came to be considered the courage of a loyal supporter; prudent hesitation, specious cowardice". Likewise, "moderation" became a "cloak for unmanliness", "plotting" became "justifiable means of self-defense", and "blood became a weaker tie than party". In *The Art of War*, written in China over 2,000 years ago and perhaps the oldest strategic text on war, Sun Tzu (1983) asserts, "All warfare is based on deception". In the *Republic*, written in Greece over 2,000 years ago and the first book on justice, Plato warns against overstressing the distinction between enemies and allies given the shifts in relations among peoples over time. Early in this era, *Pax Romana* 'Peace of Rome' stood for the military suppression of armed conflict throughout the Roman Empire. Then, during the medieval period, the "Truce of God" (1041) did not refer to peace; instead, it limited warfare to specific times.

Despite the primacy of the history of warfare in textbook histories of civilizations, the desire for peace and even elaborate discourses on plans for peace have also been made persistently and eloquently throughout human history. In his study of primitive war, Harry Turney-High (1971) found that from a psychological perspective peace is the normal situation even among warlike peoples. In his study of the idea of peace in classical antiquity, Gerardo Zampaglione (1973) found that from the Pre-Socratic philosophers through Roman and Hellenistic writers to medieval Christian theologians, the quest for peace has been at the center of many artistic and literary movements. For more recent times, Zampaglione divides the movements he surveys into four forms: mystical (Leo Tolstoy, Romain Rolland), philosophical (St. Augustine, Abbé de Saint-Pierre, Immanuel Kant, Bertrand Russell, and John Dewey), sociological (Auguste Comte, Henri Saint-Simon, and Charles Fourier), and political (Bohemian King George of Podebrad, Maximilien de Béthume duc de Sully). Of course, these movements had very little "policy sway" in the decision making of the governmental leaders who exercised political power.

The application of linguistics to such discourse really only begins at the close of the nineteenth century in the work of Friedrich Nietzsche (1956). He recognized that our value judgments are influenced quite fundamentally by language. Those who control the language – its terminology and definitions – will largely control the politics of how we respond. Nietzsche went so far as to suggest the "right of bestowing names" is a fundamental expression of political power.

In the twentieth century Aldous Huxley (1937) and George Orwell (1968) extended such analyses. They contended that language is corrupted in ways that make the cruelty, inhumanity, and horror of war seem justifiable. Language becomes a tool employed by political and military officials to make people accept what ordinarily they would repudiate if its true character were known. The language of war hinders civilians from recognizing that human beings are being removed forcibly from their homes; human beings are being wounded and mutilated, even tortured, and often killed.

In making their points, Huxley and Orwell give powerful examples. An aggressive attack by a squadron of airplanes that ordinarily would be called an "air raid" is euphemistically referred to as a "routine limited duration protective reaction". Defoliation of an entire forest is spoken of as a "resource control program". "Pacification" is used to label actions which involve entering a village, machine-gunning domesticated animals, setting huts on fire, rounding up all the men and shooting those who resist, prodding and otherwise harming the elderly, women, and children. The human face of war is thus replaced by benign abstractions.

As Orwell observed, political speech and writing often rely on distortions of language and communication to intentionally defend what otherwise would be seen as indefensible. In order to defend British rule in India, Soviet purges, and the United States's atomic bombing of Hiroshima and Nagasaki, officials went so far as to resort to bizarre arguments that contradicted the purported aims and values of their governments. These intentional uses of euphemisms, question-begging terminology, vagueness, and outright falsity demonstrate that when Orwell presented Newspeak in his novel "1984" he was not referring to a merely fictive possibility.

These and other contributions to applied linguistics make clear that, in relation to language and communication, once war is imminent or present, truth is often absent. This point is conveyed in the title of Phillip Knightley's book on war correspondents, *The First Casualty* (2004). This phrase, "the first casualty", is based on U.S. Senator Hiram Johnson's 1917 statement, "The first casualty when war comes is truth". This view has been explored by a variety of writers since Huxley and Orwell and has even been applied to the supposedly objective accounts provided by "embedded" reporters during the more recent Persian Gulf War. An "embedded" reporter would seem to be objective, since the reporter is with the troops during their operations. Nevertheless, these reporters are restricted in what they can say about their location and the plans of the troops, and they lack access to information about what is occurring elsewhere. As a consequence, their reporting, even if accurate, is myopic.

More recent efforts in the treatment of the language of war and peace that make useful contributions to applied linguistics include works by Paul Chilton and George Lakoff, Noam Chomsky, Jean Baudrillard, J. Fisher Solomon, Christopher Norris, Haig Bosmajian, Carol Cohn, Robert Holmes, Trudy Govier, William Gay, John Wesley Young, Slavoj Zizek, Christina Schäffner and Anita Wenden, Teun van Dijk, and Philip Taylor. Chilton, Lakoff, and Chomsky have provided widely disseminated and discussed critiques of the language of war. Baudrillard, on the other hand, has used his version of post-modernism to deny that the first Gulf War took place (in the sense conveyed by the media), while Norris has pointed out the dangers of such excesses in post-modernism for attaining a needed level of critical assessment of the military operations that did in fact take place. In a similar vein, J. Fisher Solomon has criticized Jacques Derrida's argument that current weapons of mass destruction undercut viewing the arms race in real-world, practical terms. Solomon rejects Derrida's characterization of nuclear war as "fabulous" and "fictive" in ways similar to Norris's critique of Baudrilliard's claim that the Gulf War did not take place. Norris, in fact, sees as related and equally suspect various aspects of the post-modernism and neo-pragmatism of Stanley Fish, Richard Rorty, and Francis Fukuyma. In this regard, he sees Fukuyma's (1992) characterization of the first Gulf War as a "wretched anachronism" as an unwillingness to let facts get in the way of his thesis of the end of history. Bosmajian (1983) provided one of the early, broad surveys of the language of oppression, showing similarities in racist language (against Native Americans, African Americans, and Jews) and sexist language to the language of war. Holmes (1989) and Govier (2002) have analyzed the use of the term "terrorism" and related terms; while the work of Holmes precedes the events of 9/11 and the work of Govier follows these events, their careful reflections on the language used in discussing terrorism are remarkably similar. Cohn (1989) and Gay (1987) have given particular attention to nuclear discourse, while Young (1991) and Zizek (2001) have focused more generally on totalitarian discourse. Schäffner and Wenden (1995) have looked broadly at the relation between language and peace, while Van Dijk (1993) has given very focused consideration to elitist discourse and Taylor (1992) has done likewise with media communication.

Among these more recent contributions, Trudy Govier (2002) has written an especially important book analyzing discourse connected to terrorism in the post-9/11 environment. Each chapter of her book, *A Delicate Balance: What Philosophy Can Tell Us About Terrorism*, provides a critical discourse analysis on a central term. She covers topics such as "vulnerability", "victims", "evil", "revenge", "courage", "vindication", and "hope". Consider a few examples of the type of critical discourse analysis that she provides: In treating "victims", she is careful to distinguish the sympathy victims deserve from presuming that victims have special moral insight. In addressing "evil", she is careful to avoid conflating an act of evil from a presumption that the agent of the act is evil. She rejects the claim made shortly after 9/11 that the attackers were cowards, though she admits that "Because the word 'courage' functions as a term of praise, we don't want to apply it to someone whose actions we profoundly disapprove of" (Govier 2002: 112). In analyzing "hope", she is careful to note that, rather than being based on certainty or even confidence, "hope" is based on positive possibilities. She ends by noting, "Living as political beings requires the hope that better things may come" (Govier 2002: 169).

Critical discourse analysis has not been applied only to the language of the establishment. Even the discourse of the anti-nuclear community has been subjected to critical analysis. Gay (1987) has examined some of the negative images used to present to the public the horrors of nuclear war. In particular, he has looked at the effort by John Somerville (1983) to suggest that past concepts of war are no longer of value. Somerville, in saying that the use of nuclear weapons would not be a nuclear "war" coined the term "omnicide", meaning the destruction of all sentient life. Instead of referring to nuclear war, he says "nuclear omnicide". Gay has pointed out the linguistic alienation of this term. Most members of the public do not understand the word "omnicide", and explanation is not generally included in the literature that employs this term. Consequently, linguistic alienation generally results when the term "omnicide" is used in public forums. Moreover, Gay has stressed the dangers of negativity introduced by the term "omnicide" in relation to the past, the present, and the future. If the use of nuclear weapons is not nuclear war, then their use cuts us off from the tradition's powerful criticisms of much warfare (we do not listen to past), an elitist protest community with its own technical vocabulary emerges (we alienate the masses in present), and the public is denied imagination of a future (we are impotent and hopeless regarding the future). Instead, Gay contends we need positive imagery; we need to move from critique to vision. In this regard, and in contradistinction to government's use of the state-as-house metaphor, Gay utilizes the metaphor of a house-friend that was developed by Martin Heidegger (1957) who stated, "The house-friend is friend to the house which the world is". We can employ the metaphor of a house-friend that stresses the need for members of the public to watch for threats to our planet.

John Wesley Young (1991) has shown ways in which the discourse of Nazi Germany and Soviet Russia employed linguistic techniques similar to those described by George Orwell as "Newspeak". Young provides some especially distinctive analyses of the discourse used by the Soviet government. In referring to two "zones", "paths", or "forces in the world", the Soviets introduced pejorative bifurcations that obliterated virtually all crucial distinctions among their adversaries and assigned all of them to the same negative category. He also notes, "Without the stimulus of a bipolar ideology with its ready-made objects of hatred, it would be much more difficult to exact from the masses the measure of devotion to duty that totalitarianism requires" (Young 1991: 141). Young notes how Soviet officials sprinkled their speech with phrases like "everybody knows", "it is obvious that", "history has shown", "all honest people", and "all progressive forces". Such phrases aim to provide a linguistic indicator that what follows is true. Nevertheless, saying that what you are saying is true does not make it true, but, for ideological purposes, such repeated assertions often achieve the desired effect of having the public believe that what you are saying is true.

3. Central concepts

Discourse analysis emerged as a subdivision of linguistics in the late 1960s. In analyzing the social context of language and its functioning, discourse analysis could hardly ignore the pervasive and problematic nature of large-scale violence both within and among nations. The exposure of the distortions of language and communication dealing with violence and war is virtually a pre-condition for any effort to successfully grapple with these phenomena. Behind the façade of the legitimacy of official discourse about issues of violence and war is the fundamental connection between language and power.

Language is inseparable from the distribution of power in society, and these relations are unequal in every society. In French sociolinguist Pierre Bourdieu's (1991) terms, the use of language depends on the speaker's social position, and this position is "outside" language. This "outside" is composed of the social conditions within which communicative acts are situated. Speaking *"the* language", for Bourdieu (1991: 45), "is tacitly to accept the *official* definition of the *official* language of a political unit". Moreover, the formation of a single "linguistic community" is the product of political domination. Since the distribution of power in societies is unequal, the analysis of language should not be separated from an awareness of social classes and the relative social positions of the participants in any communicative situation.

The issue is not purely one of class. Bourdieu does not say that only the children of the dominant class are admitted into the best schools. Instead, he suggests that those who enter or finish programs at top schools generally have the legitimate language imposed on them. By defining qualifications and credentials, educational systems both create and sustain inequalities, making use of overt force unnecessary. In fact, an inverse relation often exists between possession of symbolic power and use of physical violence. This last point is vividly illustrated in the language used to discuss issues of war and peace.

3.1. Positive and negative peace

The politics of definition is a central concept in the analysis of discourse about war and peace. Those who control the language also largely control perception and behavior. In relation to discourse about war, key concepts include the reliance on euphemisms and metaphors and the practice of special pleading. In relation to discourse about peace, the key concepts relate to the distinction between negative peace and positive peace. In general, "warist discourse" refers to language that takes for granted that wars are inevitable, justifiable, and winnable. While "negative peace" refers to the temporary absence of active war or the lull between wars, "positive peace" refers to the negation of war and the presence of justice.

Language plays an important role in relation to war and peace. Language, which is rarely neutral, shapes perception and behavior. Language can be used to demean differences and inflict violence or to affirm diversity and achieve recognition. The language of war usually functions to mask the reality of the violence that is occurring. By imposing itself as legitimate, official discourse about war co-opts efforts by critics of war. The language of peace, like the condition of peace, can be negative or positive. A language of negative peace perpetuates injustice by only establishing a verbal declaration of an end to war and hostilities. A language of positive peace fosters open and inclusive communication that affirms diversity.

Various uses of language precede and support the pursuit of war and the quest for peace. Military preparations for war and political negotiations for peace involve fairly obvious institutional structures. Discourse about war and peace also involves institutional structures, since language itself is a social institution. Whether we know the official language of the nation in which we live or a dialect relegated to low social esteem, whether we know only one or many languages, in whatever language we speak and write, we are faced with its lexicon and grammatical structure which have embedded within them a wide range of terms that express not merely an arbitrary system of classification but also the current relations of power. If knowledge is power, language too is power; those who control the language of war and peace exercise an enormous influence on how we perceive war and peace and what behaviors we accept in relation to war and peace.

3.2. The language of war

Individuals who serve as warriors and soldiers have social roles that are structured by the military institutions of societies. The overt violent acts committed by these individuals when they act as a social group following official orders are sanctioned by the state as legitimate, even though the acts committed by these individuals are similar to types of physical violence which are prohibited by the state and for which individuals who commit them are subject to punishment. In order to mark the institutional character of military behavior, most societies use distinctive words to designate the violent acts of warriors and soldiers. The act that is designated as "murder" when performed by an individual may be re-designated "justified use of force" when carried out by law enforcement or military personnel. This power of re-designation, which allows for legitimation or condemnation of various actions, manifests how political uses of language precede and support the pursuit of war; the same is true for the political uses of language in the quest for peace.

Consider the different sense conveyed when, after World War II, the U.S. government re-designated the Department of War as the Department of Defense. The agency is the same, and the mission is the same. However, the former conveys an offensive posture, while the latter conveys a defensive posture. Also, more recently, a group of countries hardly closely tied with one another politically were re-designated by the U.S. government as the Axis of Evil, namely, Iran, Iraq, and North Korea. One further example can be found in the new U.S. strategic security plan that allows for "pre-emptive strikes". In other words, to initiate an offensive military action is made to sound more like a deterrence of an attack.

From primitive war among archaic societies to the world wars of the twentieth century, political and military leaders have introduced and reinforced linguistic usages that give legitimacy to the social roles and military actions of warriors and soldiers. Since the rise of the modern nation state, almost all societies have coupled the aim of maintaining national sovereignty with the capacity to wage war. Not surprisingly, then, discourse about war is much more deeply embedded in the languages of the world than is discourse about peace. One of the most elaborate justifications for war arose during the medieval period and continues to this day, namely, the theory of just war that was given classical articulation by St. Augustine and St. Thomas Aquinas.

While leaders sometimes appeal to the language of just war theory, they are not necessarily actually meeting its conditions. One can claim "right authority" and "right intention" without such being the case. Administrative efforts to justify the two Persian Gulf Wars illustrate this point. Both administrations sought U.N. support to ground the claim of "right authority". While this effort was fairly successful in the first Gulf War given widespread U.N. support, it largely failed in the second Gulf War when not just the General Assembly but also the Security Council would not support U.S. military intervention as justified. Nevertheless, the claim persisted during the second Gulf War that "right authority" was present. In addition, the issue of "right intention" becomes much more clouded when, as in the case of the second Gulf War, the publicly proclaimed purpose of the military campaign continues to shift. Was the purpose to destroy purported (but never discovered) weapons of mass destruction, or to remove an Evil Dictator, or to reduce the threat of terrorism, or to bring democracy to Iraq? Similar questions can be asked in relation to the condition of the likelihood of emergent peace and several other of the conditions that need to be satisfied for a war to be claimed as justified on the basis of just war theory. Critical discourse analysis serves as a useful tool for going behind the public pronouncements of governmental and military officials and for exposing when the language used to describe military actions does not correspond to the reality of the actual actions taken in these military operations.

To better understand the effects of the ways we talk and write about war and peace, one needs to recognize that language, as Ferdinand de Saussure (1966) established, is one of the most conservative social institutions. Beginning with Saussure the science of linguistics treats language as a convention that is beyond the control of the speakers who passively assimilate it. Saussure viewed language as the "least amenable to initiative" of all social institutions. From one point of view, the structural linguist can describe, but should not praise or condemn, the actual signs available in a language system. Fortunately, in applied linguistics, one can turn from the analysis of *la langue* (the sedimented sign system) to *la parole* (active speaking subjects). Applied linguistics documents how language shapes both perception and behavior, influencing our thought and action in at least three important ways.

First, at any given time the words in the lexicon of a language limit one another. Every lexicon is finite, and every lexicon changes over time. Linguists have shown that the meaning of individual words is a function of the differences among them during each phase in the history of the lexicon. Terms designating ethnicity, race, gender, and sexual orientation are especially revealing in this regard. Consider the difference in the meaning within the United States of using the term "Negro" in the 1950s, 1970s, and 1990s to designate the race of one component of the population. Use of the term "Negro" took on a different meaning in the 1970s by which time the addition of "black" was firmly established in the lexicon, and it took on an even more telling connotation once "African American" came into general usage in the 1990s.

Languages vary in the number of terms available to communicate about a specific topic, and the available terms vary in how positively and negatively charged they are. While the English language currently includes "fag", "homosexual", and "gay" as terms that designate the sexual orientation of some men, these terms are on a continuum of rather negative, to more neutral, to fairly positive. For this reason, when analyzing discourse about war and peace, the words selected and the words not selected from the lexicon are rather important. Consider, for example, the difference between referring to armed troops as "freedom fighters" and as "guerrilla terrorists". Linguists sometimes term as "lexicalization" the introduction and use of different terms, one with a positive connotation and the other with a negative connotation, to describe actions that are essentially the same. Such "lexicalization" is termed "special pleading" within Critical Thinking. For example, consider two persons with overflowing shopping carts at a grocery store prior to the onset of a hurricane. If one claims that the items in one's own shopping cart are the result of "stocking up" but accuses the other of "hording", special pleading is occurring. Both customers are seeking to purchase larger-than-usual supplies of groceries. Likewise, calling one's own weapons "a deterrent force" while contending an adversary has weapons of mass destruction can be seen as an instance of special pleading, but in this case the issues of threat and justifiability are much greater.

The presence or absence of adjectives is also many times very telling. Why is it that we do not often read in a U.S. newspaper about a "Caucasian gunman" or a "white rapist"? Why in just about any location do we, however, sometimes hear about a "lady doctor" or a "female pilot"? And why almost everywhere is the union of same sex partners often termed a "gay marriage" or a "lesbian commitment ceremony"? We can begin to see the harm being done when we reflect on the fact that, in relation to use of adjectives, where racism has not been fully eradicated we often omit reference to a person being "white", while where sexism and heterosexism have not been fully eradicated we frequently include reference to a person being "female" or "gay". Regardless of race, a rapist is a rapist; regardless of gender, a physician is a physician; regardless of sexual orientation, a marriage is a marriage. Similarly, we still hear a military campaign referred to as a "just war", but regardless of any rationales, a war is a war. The need to qualify seems more connected with the need to legitimate or de-legitimate than to describe.

The second way language influences perception and behavior is based on the fact that the vocabulary of a language provides charged terms and hence serves as a means of interpretation. Individuals think about their world in the terms provided by their language. As a result of socialization individuals have a predisposition to select those terms that coincide with the existing values in their societies. For example, throughout the Cold War, many Americans regarded their government as the "champion of freedom" and the Soviet government as "an evil empire". Norman Fairclough (1989) asserts that language is the form of social behavior in which we most rely on commonsense or ideological assumptions. Consequently, he contends, "The ideological nature of language should be one of the major themes of modern social science" (Fairclough 1989: 3). From his own study of language, he concludes that a dominant discourse that largely suppresses dominated discourses ceases to be seen as arbitrary and comes to be regarded as natural and legitimate. He terms this process "the *naturalization* of a discourse type". Not surprisingly, such naturalization is especially characteristic of discourse about war and peace.

Despite how language is tilted in favor of power, the lexicon of a language also makes available further terminological options; hence, individuals are also able to intentionally select words that are relatively more or less offensive. Hence, while the lexicon of a people has built into it a perspective on the world, it facilitates not only the official perspective but also alternative ones. These alternatives can include the potential for the positive renaming of a disenfranchised social group and the negative re-description of governmental accounts of military campaigns. Consider the following examples. Although many people refer to individuals who use a wheelchair as "handicapped", these individuals may prefer to refer to themselves and to have others refer to them also as "physically challenged". While the government may refer to a military campaign as a "just war", citizens can counter that it is "just war", namely, "just another war" and not "a just war".

These points underscore the fact that many linguistic differences are not just diacritical ones internal to the system of signs. They are ones that result from oppositions in the relative power of social groups. These differences, of course, occur at the level of *la parole* (speaking), rather than *la langue*. The study of these differences is critical for exposing distortions in language and communication about war.

The third way language influences perception and behavior relates to how it provides the linguistic perspective that shapes an individual's thought. In other words, language gives a structure to consciousness that guides action. Bourdieu (1991) has observed that some social groups accrue enormous linguistic capital that they generally use to advance their interests to the detriment of the social masses. Likewise, almost everyone is familiar with physicians and lawyers who rely on their technical vocabularies in seeking to have their patients and clients simply defer to their authority. Similarly, many governmental and military officials use forms of strategic discourse that most citizens do not understand and to which they acquiesce; hereby those with a monopoly on the instruments of force are able to go unchallenged in their explanations for their actions.

Among philosophers, Maurice Merleau-Ponty (1964) stressed how linguistic change occurs at the level of *la parole*. As a result, language shapes, but does not determine, human consciousness and behavior. While such a lack of linguistic determinism facilitates linguistic changes that can ameliorate violence in society, it can also be exploited to aggravate the conditions of social violence. In other words, linguistic freedom and linguistic creativity can be used to impose restrictions on social groups and distort their perceptions, just as much as it can be used to empower social groups and enrich their understanding. At the extreme one finds the attempts at linguistic control by totalitarian regimes that manipulate discourse in ways designed to distort people's perceptions. However, even at this extreme, the power of the state to control the minds of individuals has not been total, which tells us something important about the prospects for linguistic emancipation.

3.3. The language of peace

The language of peace is an important component in the pursuit of peace and justice. The language of peace can be an example of linguistic nonviolence and can contribute to forging an understood language of inclusion. Nevertheless, just as the language of war tends to dominate official discourse, even when the language of peace is used it is usually the language of negative peace. Anita Wenden (1995) has illustrated this point in her analysis of the awarding of the Nobel Peace Prize. Between 1901 and 1993, 63 of 90 of the prizes (70%) went to endeavors for negative peace. Consider just a few of the recipients of the Nobel Peace Prize who, at times, advanced at most negative peace. In 1973 the prize went to Henry Kissinger and Le Duc Tho. In 1978 the prize went to Anwar al-Sadat and Menachem Begin. In 1994 the prize went to Yasser Arafat, Shimon Peres, and Yitzhak Rabin. While each of these individuals in their later years did seek to advance peace processes that sought an end to armed conflict (the lull between wars of negative peace), several, at least earlier in their careers, were involved with planning and waging wars and supporting and even conducting terrorist acts. Wenden notes that only with the awarding of the Nobel Peace Prize to Amnesty International in 1977 did the Nobel committee recognize efforts for peace that aimed at more than the mere absence of war.

The language of negative peace can actually perpetuate injustice. A government and its media may cease referring to a particular nation as "the enemy" or "the devil", but public and private attitudes may continue to foster the same, though now unspoken, prejudice. When prejudices remain unspoken, at least in public forums, their detection and eradication are made even more difficult. Of course, just as legal or social sanctions against hate speech may be needed to stop linguistic attacks in the public arena, even so, in order to stop current armed conflict, there may be a need not only for an official peace treaty but also a cessation in hostile name calling directed against an adversary of the state. However, even if a language of negative peace is necessary, it is not sufficient. Arms may have been laid down, but they can readily be taken up again when the next military stage in a struggle begins. Likewise, those who bite their tongues to comply with the demands of political correctness are often ready to lash out vitriolic epithets when these constraints are removed. Thus, in the language of negative peace, the absence of verbal assaults about "the enemy" merely marks a lull in reliance on warist discourse.

From the perspective of Mahatma Gandhi (1986), much discourse about peace, as well as the rhetoric supporting wars of liberation, places a primacy on ends over means. When the end is primary, nonviolence may be practiced only so long as it is effective. For Gandhi and the *satyagrahi* (someone committed to the pursuit of truth and the practice of nonviolence), the primary commitment is to the means. The commitment to nonviolence requires that the achievement of political goals is secondary. These goals must be foregone or at least postponed when they cannot be achieved nonviolently. The nature of the language of negative peace becomes especially clear when, within social movements facing frustration in the pursuit of their political goals, a division occurs between those ready to abandon nonviolence and those resolute in their commitment to it. The resolute commitment to nonviolence was clear in the teachings and practices of Martin Luther King, Jr. and his followers and in the recent courageous behavior of other practitioners of nonviolent civil disobedience, including Václav Havel in Eastern Europe, Mubarak Awad in the Middle East, Nelson Mandela in South Africa and thousands of ordinary citizens in the Baltic republics, China, Czechoslovakia, Poland, the West Bank, and the Ukraine.

The language of positive peace facilitates and reflects the move from a lull in the occurrence of violence to its negation. The establishment of a language of positive peace requires a transformation of cultures oriented to war. The discourse of positive peace, to be successful, must include a genuine affirmation of diversity both domestically and internationally. The effort to establish the language of positive peace requires the creation of a critical vernacular, a language of empowerment that is inclusive of and understood by the vast array of citizens.

Various activities promote the pursuit of respect, cooperation, and understanding needed for positive peace. These activities go beyond the mere removal from discourse of terms that convey biases about race, gender, and sexual orientation. We can come to regard races, sexes, and cultures as making up the harmonies and melodies that together create the song of humanity. Just as creative and appreciated cooks use a wide variety of herbs and spices to keep their dishes from being bland, so too can we move from an image of a culture with diverse components as a melting pot to one of a stew which is well seasoned with a variety of herbs and spices. Or, to employ another nonviolent metaphor, the garden of humanity will best flourish when composed of multiple plots with the varieties of life co-mingling and co-inhabiting.

On some occasions, those seeking a language of positive peace fall silent at least briefly, especially after the occurrence of war. In the late eighteenth century Immanuel Kant (1983) suggested that after any war a day of atonement is appropriate in which the "victors" ask for forgiveness for the "great sin" of the human race, namely, the failure to establish a genuine and lasting peace. Immediately following the atomic bombing of Hiroshima, Albert Camus (1988) advised that this event called for much reflection and "a good deal of silence". At other times, advocates of positive peace are compelled to break the silence in order to respond to injustice. While adhering to principles of nonviolence, as Gene Sharp (1973) has noted, various levels of protest, non-cooperation, and even intervention can be pursued. In these ways, the language of positive peace has a variety of correlative nonviolent actions by means of which to continue politics by the same means – by more intensive means of diplomacy, rather than turning to war, which Carl von Clausewitz (1943) defined as the pursuit of "politics by other means".

The language of positive peace is democratic rather than authoritarian, dialogical rather than monological, receptive rather than aggressive, meditative rather than calculative. The language of positive peace is not passive in the sense of avoiding engagement; it is pacific in the sense of seeking to actively build lasting peace and justice. The language of positive peace, a genuinely pacific discourse, provides a way of perceiving and communicating that frees us to the diversity and open-endedness of life rather than the sameness and finality of death. Pacific discourse, in providing an alternative to the language of war and even to the language of negative peace, is a voice of hope and empowerment.

4. Controversial issues: Linguistic alienation and linguistic violence

The more controversial issues in critical discourse analyses on war and peace concern the application of the theories of linguistic alienation and linguistic violence. At the extremes of such analyses are treatments of nuclear discourse and the language of genocide. In brief, "linguistic alienation" refers to the situation in which individuals cannot understand a discourse in their own language because of the use of highly technical vocabularies, and "linguistic violence" refers to the situation in which individuals are hurt or harmed by words.

To address these more controversial issues, a basic question must be faced. Can language do some type of violence, and, if so, can any such "linguistic violence" be overcome? Language can do violence if violence does not require the exercise of physical force, and linguistic violence can be overcome if its use can be avoided. Linguistic violence is both possible and eradicable, since some forms of violence do not use physical force and because various means are available for avoiding linguistic violence. Hence, although linguistic violence can and does occur, it also can be overcome.

At times, the level of abstraction in language about war is so high that citizens do not even understand what officials are saying. In these cases, they suffer a type of linguistic alienation. What do officials mean when they refer to "the counterforce first-strike capability of a MIRVed ICBM facilitated by its low CEP"? Quite understandably, many citizens are unable to challenge the military policies of leaders who rely on the technical vocabulary of modern warfare with its high incidence of acronyms and euphemisms. To unpack the acronym-filled phrase used above requires an understanding of at least five aspects about nuclear weapons. First, one needs to know that "ICBM" stands for an intercontinental ballistic missile. These missiles can travel thousands of miles carrying nuclear warheads that fall to their targets when released from the missile. Second, one needs to know that "MIRV" stands for multiple, independently targetable re-entry vehicles. Each ICBM has several nuclear warheads inside its nose cone; in mid-space this cone drops off and the warheads, connected to a "bus" that can be maneuvered, are released sequentially so that each falls to a separate target. Third, one needs to know that "counterforce" refers to a military target, like an air base, a missile field, or a command headquarters. Fourth, one needs to know that "first-strike capability" refers to having enough highly accurate missiles that one could destroy an adversary's ability to retaliate to a surprise attack. Fifth, one needs to know that "CEP" stands for circular error probable; this technical term gives the distance from a target within which a missile is likely to hit. To gain an adequate background to understand all of these points is rather demanding. Not surprisingly, many citizens simply defer to the authority of military and political officials who employ such highly technical terminology.

Linguistic violence occurs when individuals are hurt psychologically by words and when they are harmed socially by words. While most people are conscious of the pain that words can cause, many social groups are often unconscious of injustices that language helps to create and sustain.

To expose linguistic violence, William Gay (1998) employs a continuum that progresses from subtle, through abusive, to grievous forms. Subtle forms range from children's jokes to official languages. Even when the hurt or harm is minimal and unintentional, these forms frequently escalate into young people incorporating derogatory terms into their attempts at humor and to governments instituting discriminatory policies against groups who speak an unofficial dialect or a foreign language. Abusive forms are especially conspicuous in racist, sexist, heterosexist, and classist discourse. Abusive forms rely on offensive terms and frequently aim to hurt psychologically the individuals to whom they are directed. Both the practitioners and victims are more likely to be aware of the degrading intent of these forms of communication. Nevertheless, like subtle forms, abusive forms can function in an oppressive manner without all individuals experiencing their use as offensive. Finally, at the extreme, grievous forms are found in many expressions of warist discourse, including nuclear discourse, totalitarian language, and genocidal language. Grievous forms often have the intent to silence or even physically eliminate an entire social group. Even though the eradication of these grievous forms poses the most formidable challenge, accounts of social groups who have resisted such linguistic and physical oppression provide strong evidence that linguistic violence can be at least partially overcome even in these extreme cases.

Debate continues about whether all terms in a language are ideologically charged or whether some terms avoid bias. Nevertheless, even if some uses of language are neutral, many are charged. Whenever more than one term is available, a difference in connotation is generally present even when the denotation is the same. Is the individual working in a field a "wetback", an "illegal immigrant", or a "migratory laborer"? In principle, individuals can select any among the available terms. In practice, word choices are largely shaped by customary social usage. Beyond establishing an official language, most nations reinforce politically preferred choices through institutions of socialization such as schools and the media. What makes some nations "rogue states" and some leaders "dangerous villains"? At this point, the prospect for linguistic violence arises and takes on a clearly institutional character.

Internationally, official languages are another unfortunate legacy of colonialism, namely, alien languages, along with alien governments, were imposed onto indigenous peoples (cf. also Fill and Skutnabb-Kangas, both this vol.). The pains of colonization and the subsequent strife associated with independence are reflected in such classic works as Tunisian Albert Memmi's *The Colonizer and the Colonized* (1965) and Algerian Frantz Fanon's *The Wretched of the*

Earth (1968). Many abusive terms recur within warist discourse in demeaning references to the enemy or even members of one's own military who are judged negatively. Vietnamese have been referred to as "gooks". Soldiers exhibiting fear are often called "sissies" or "girls".

Grievous forms are found in many expressions of warist discourse, including nuclear discourse, totalitarian language, and genocidal language. In nuclear discourse "collateral damage" refers to the thousands or even millions of civilians who would be the victims of nuclear strikes against military targets. Very intriguing in relation to the nuclear establishment is Carol Cohn's (1989) "Sex and Death in the Rational World of Defense Intellectuals". She notes how nuclear discourse often contains references to virginity. For example, some strategists use expressions such as "losing her virginity" or "being deflowered" to refer to a country's entry into the nuclear club. Noting how a language of domestication is often employed in relation to nuclear weapons, Cohn observes that we have imagery that domesticates, even humanizes, insentient weapons, and, paradoxically, seems to accept the destruction of sentient human bodies and their lives. If we consider the names given to the first nuclear bombs, "Little Boy" and "Fat Man", we learn that these extreme destroyers were "male progeny". The inventors of atomic weapons even said just before the test at Alamogordo, New Mexico, that they hoped the baby would be a boy and not a girl; in other words, that it not be a dud. By implication, as Cohn has observed, if the bomb had been a dud it would have been termed a "girl". Such warist discourse banters in public distortions of language and communication that simultaneously substitute birth for death and degrade women.

Cohn refers to learning nuclear discourse as gaining "cognitive mastery". However, in the case of nuclear discourse, the reference is vastly different from the words being used. "A surgical strike" seems more like a precise, relatively harmless medical incision, but in reality the reference is to a nuclear explosion that could produce a stadium-size hole in the ground, throw tons of radioactive material into the atmosphere, and kill thousands of innocent civilians (euphemistically termed "collateral damage"). Reminiscent of Camus, Cohn notes how such language can only articulate the perspective of the users of such weapons, not that of the victims of such weapons.

Cohn suggests we need to ask the questions feminists often raise about theories in various disciplines. Specifically, we need to ask about the reference point or subject of discourse. In relation to nuclear discourse, what we learn is that far from being the universal human subject or even white males, the reference point is the weapons themselves. She argues that such a language is "a type of ideological curtain" which serves to legitimate for political aims but which obscures the actual and quite distinct motives and reasons. The point may not be that we need to learn how to speak the discourse but that we need to find some way to change it. And, when all else fails, in order to avoid co-optation (a constant danger for delegates of the people), one needs to know when is the appropriate time to remain silent rather than employ such falsifying discourse.

At the most abusive extreme is the language of totalitarianism and genocide. Just as the Holocaust and the numerous instances of genocide and politicide account for the most abusive occurrences of overt institutional violence, even so they also account for the most abusive occurrences of linguistic violence. Consider these examples: The Nazis used *Sonderbehandlung* 'special treatment' instead of 'execution'. *Hilfsmittel* 'auxiliary equipment' was the term used to refer to the vans that had been converted into mobile gas chambers. *Badeanstalten* 'bath arrangements' was another term used to refer to gas chambers. By contrast, according to John Wesley Young (1991), at various times the Nazi party was called "a political church", its members were referred to as "the political pastors of our people", its mass meetings were termed "the divine services of our political work", and its dogmas were designated as a "Gospel" that provided a "teaching of eternal life".

The twentieth century made all too clear how governments and sub-national groups have turned to "totalitarian language" as well in their efforts to "win" the hearts and minds of the masses in support of their political agendas. In these endeavors, they have relied extensively on the instruments of mass communication, as well as research in psychology, to increase significantly the degree of control that can be exercised over the mind by verbal means.

Berel Lang (1988) stresses that under Nazism, language was viewed as an instrument and focuses on the term *Endlösung* 'Final Solution'. He concludes that with *Endlösung* and similar terms the language of genocide becomes a distinctive literary figure that he terms the "figurative lie". He proceeds to argue that, in addition to developing a language of domination, the Nazis aimed to subject language itself to their quest for total domination. One of his aims is to show that the Nazis sought a form of oppression that integrated the mental and the physical; hence, the abuse of language was central to this endeavor. Consequently, Lang contends that genocide violates not only people but also language itself.

What he terms the "figurative lie" refers to descriptions of war that actually contradict the realities of war. Such a contradiction between language and reality occurs in the extremes of genocidal and nuclear discourse. The Nazis used grammar and literary figures of speech as instruments for political ends, namely, genocide. This instrumental approach to language detaches language from history and moral judgment, converting it to a mere technique in the assertion of political power. *Endlösung* both disguises and reveals (at least to the people in the know) the plan of murder. The term reveals that there is a purported "problem" that must be "solved" and in a conclusive manner. *Endlösung* conceals that the action denoted will be the annihilation of all Jews and other "culture destroyers", including gays and gypsies, rather than actions like their deportation or resettlement.

While it is possible to speak of a concrete event as the "final solution" to a problem, it is contradictory and duplicitous to designate the concrete action of murdering millions of individuals abstractly as a "final solution". The language of genocide simultaneously promulgates and hides the intentional willing of evil. Thus, the language of genocide functions as an instrument of domination and as a mechanism of deceit: The language of genocide facilitates large-scale killing yet denies the social reality of its intent and consequence.

In a similar vein, John Wesley Young (1991) analyses the political discourse of the Nazis and Soviet Communism in his book *Totalitarian Language*. Young stresses how in the twentieth century, totalitarian regimes made extensive use of modern mass communication and techniques of psychology to advance the endeavor to control human minds by trying to control language. Nevertheless, Young concludes that the language of totalitarianism had only limited success in achieving the goal of controlling thought. Still, the linguistic violence and physical violence of such efforts were gargantuan, despite their eventual defeat.

Practices of totalitarianism and genocide emerge from and depend upon a totalitarian and genocidal language. Such language facilitates the most violent exercise of power against a people. Linguistic violence directed against a people leads to physical violence against a people. Such linguistic violence is institutionally sanctioned and the ensuing physical violence is lethal and aims to be total. History shows all too well the enormous efforts that are required to end such practices once they have begun. Perhaps an early intervention by critical discourse analysts against totalitarian and genocidal language when they first emerge might facilitate the eradication of the conditions that foster the subsequent development of full-blown practices of totalitarianism and genocide.

5. Contributions of applied linguistics and current research perspectives

Critical Thinking is one of the most basic logical tools taught in higher education. It provides training in recognizing and analyzing the structure and strength of arguments. In particular, Critical Thinking identifies common fallacies in reasoning and distinguishes inferences that follow from the evidence from ones that do not. Ideology Critique goes to a deeper level and examines the way societies legitimate themselves to their citizens. The attempt at legitimatization often relies on propaganda with educational institutions being central outlets for its re-enforcement.

Some scholars in the field, such as Teun Van Dijk (1995), see discourse analysis as a type of ideology analysis. The same can be said for critical discourse analysis. In various ways, such approaches are a part of enlightened

Ideologiekritik (Ideology Critique) that has its roots in the Enlightenment in general and in German socio-political philosophy in particular. From the mid-twentieth century Critical Theory of Max Horkheimer and Theodor Adorno (1972) to Jürgen Habermas's (1987) current theory of communicative competence, this tradition undertakes the critical examination of any social framework. In this regard, Habermas counters Fredric Jameson's (1991) acceptance of postmodernism as a given in ways that are similar to the criticism of postmodernism provided by Solomon (1988) and Norris (1992). Whether these various analyses go so far as to explicitly label themselves as Ideology Critique seems secondary to the breadth of their exposure of the distortions of language and communication in discussions of war.

The results of applying Critical Thinking and Ideology Critique to the language of war are not surprising. One common fallacy is termed "special pleading" (cf. Section 3.1.). This fallacy occurs when similar objects or actions are categorized in negative terms when describing one's opponent and in positive terms when one provides self-descriptions. At the time of the first Persian Gulf War, the United States employed terms like "murder", "theft", and "rape" to portray Iraq's invasion of Kuwait, but did not use words like "murder", "assault", and "arson" to characterize the U.S. military intervention.

Government officials accuse terrorist groups of developing and even using weapons of mass destruction, and some regard the attacks of September 11th as ones involving such weapons. In this context, what may need examination is not so much what is said as what is not said. In this regard, applied linguistics needs to consider past, current, and future military actions by the United States and other countries in relation to the same definition of what constitutes a weapon of mass destruction.

Fundamentally, weapons of mass destruction are instruments of terror. As moral philosophers have noted, Robert Holmes (1989) in particular, both subnational groups and governments can resort to the use of weapons of terror. Clearly, wars generally kill far more people than do what are generally termed terrorist attacks. Principles of just war forbid the intentional killing of noncombatants. Nevertheless, especially since the obliteration bombing (strategic bombing) in Europe and against Japan at the close of World War II, cities and their civilian populations have become targets. So, one of the important ethical lessons about weapons of mass destruction is that they can be (and have been) used by individuals and by governments. In this regard, the difference is not so much one of kind as it is of degree. The end is the same in the terrorist acts of individuals and governments; the goal is to cause fear among civilians by doing violence to them or threatening them with violence.

Given the range of linguistic use, the term "weapons of mass destruction" needs some special analysis. When we refer to weapons of mass destruction, we are drawing on a condemnatory connotation. Moreover, the prospect for and reality of special pleading in using this term needs to be highlighted. For example, the United States presented its use of nuclear weapons in World War II as a means to end the war and save lives, yet the United States condemns as weapons of mass destruction ones with far less destructive capability when they are being developed by "rogue" states or terrorist groups that are perceived as a military threat. While searching in Iraq for what the U.S. government proclaimed as "the most dangerous weapons", namely, weapons of mass destruction, the United States regarded its own vast nuclear arsenal as a "deterrent force".

In another of his examples of lexicalization as a common form of ideological expression, Van Dijk (1995) has noted how the weapons of the enemy are typically described as "catastrophic and cruel", while one's own weapons are viewed as having a "peaceful" nature. Perhaps, the time has come to realize that most violence, terrorism, and war needs to be condemned, regardless of whether we term the instruments of violence, terrorism, and war as weapons of mass destruction.

Even when people think about terrorism, they generally fail to recognize that this term has these two major forms. "Enforcement terror" is a reign of terror committed by an incumbent power (e.g., the balance of terror during the Cold War), while "agitational terror" is a siege of terror committed by an insurgent power (e.g., purportedly al Qaida in relations to the attacks of September 11th). Most citizens and political analysts focus on insurgent over incumbent terrorism. In part, institutionalized forms have less news value and are more dangerous and difficult to report. Moreover, states seem more predictable and rational, while members of insurgent groups appear to be more irrational and to act in a more random manner.

All this fits nicely with a villain view of evil. Most Americans now support increased surveillance of individuals already in or trying to enter the United States who are Arab or Muslim. The media aided government in fostering this reaction by quickly simplifying the attacks into an individual villain – Osama bin Laden. The United States, which used to charge the Soviets with the cult of personality, has long tended to have a villain of the decade. Previous villains include Hitler, Stalin, Mao, Castro, Ho Chi Min, Qaddafi, and Khomeini. Such a villain view of threats to security forgets that evil is far too extensive to be personified in one person, let alone the fact that discourse about "good vs. evil" is more characteristic of Manichaeanism than the Judeo-Christian-Islamic traditions. The fallaciousness of the popular response should be obvious to anyone who has studied Critical Thinking. Stereotyping of Arabs and Muslims as terrorists is an unfortunate, but far too common, "hasty generalization". Worse still is the willingness to subject such individuals to a type of "ethnic profiling" that makes "racial profiling", by comparison, almost seem less unacceptable than it is. To those too quick to point a finger of blame, Robert Holmes observes that any people that is sufficiently desperate is capable of engaging in terrorism, and, likewise, any government that is sufficiently unscrupulous is also capable of engaging in terrorism.

Not so surprisingly, the fairy tale approach to justifying military intervention was used again for the second Persian Gulf War, and also not so surprisingly, at least initially, its use largely worked in the United States, despite shifting contentions on the danger and minimal international support for a largely U.S. invasion. Nevertheless, almost immediately, applied linguists undertook critical discourse analyses. Consider the following examples: The "coalition of the willing" referred almost exclusively to U.S. and British military forces. The "shock and awe" campaign referred to large-scale bombing of densely populated cities. The claims by U.S. governmental officials that "the ground war is over" and "hostilities have come to an end" reveal, as applied linguists have noted, that the official "announcing" of the end of a war and the terminating of lethal battles are quite distinct. In what is supposedly post-war Iraq, the meaning of "Operation Enduring Freedom" seems rather far removed from typical associations of freedom with at least tranquility if not also justice.

Since wars and rumors of wars, as well as the quest for peace, likely will continue into the foreseeable future, the need for critical discourse analysis of the language of war and peace will remain an important field in applied linguistics.

6. Conclusion

In summary, the application of applied linguistics to the language of war and peace shows how the ones who control the definitions of the terms in this discourse control the political agenda. Critical discourse analysis, when focused on abuses in discourse about war and peace, exposes that the step between the linguistic dehumanization of a people and their slaughter is rather small. Consequently, one important measure in the attempt to prevent practices of genocide is the elimination of the names that are used in the perpetration of genocide. However, in "The Language of War and Peace", William Gay (1999) has noted that the elimination of such names may be necessary, but it is not sufficient to achieve the desired results. In fact, the elimination of such terms merely from the public sphere may result in a situation that is more like negative peace (the mere absence of war) than positive peace (the presence of justice as well). In this case all that may be achieved is a temporary public suspension of name-calling that does not remove from the private sphere the prejudicial attitudes that lie behind such name-calling. Instead, the need is for a permanent removal of any intent or desire to eradicate a people and the achievement of a genuine embracing of the appropriate diversity among peoples.

Despite the abuses of the language of war and peace, a basis for a hope for more positive alternatives remains. In this regard, applied linguistics can bolster such hope by stressing the implications of the conventional name of language. The fact that words and language games, even forms of life, are conventional means there is not a natural basis for their maintenance (see Wittgenstein 1953). New conventions can be adopted. From individual words to entire forms of life, we can make changes that serve broader and loftier interests than do the current conventions. In this regard, critical discourse analysis can make an important contribution in shifting public policy discourse toward social values that de-naturalize the war myth and re-politicize the quest for peace and justice.

In challenging dominant discourse, applied linguists can engage in what Bourdieu terms "heretical subversion". According to Bourdieu, by linguistically challenging the established order, heretical discourse seizes on "the possibility of changing the social world by changing the representation of this world" (Bourdieu 1991: 128). Heretical subversion exposes the system of representations as a set of non-natural and arbitrary conventions. The language of positive peace provides an alternative system of representation that can be advanced in critical discourse analysis. Moreover, an alternative language of positive peace is, in fact, quite compatible with the democratic spirit. Such an alternative language of positive peace is also diametrically opposed to authoritarian traditions. In this sense, while the academic advancement of the language and practice of positive peace facilitates the continuation of politics rather than its abandonment, it also elevates diplomacy to an aim for cooperation and consensus rather than competition and compromise. Advancement of the language of positive peace provides a way of perceiving and communicating that frees us to the diversity and open-endedness of life rather than the sameness and finality of death that results when diplomacy fails and war ensues. The language of positive peace, by providing an alternative to the language of war and even to the language of negative peace, can introduce into public policy discourse shared social values that express the goals of a fully politicized and enfranchised humanity. In providing criticism of abuses in discourse about war and peace and in developing positive linguistic alternatives, applied linguistics and critical discourse analysis make not only important scientific contributions but also essential humanistic contributions.

References

Aquinas, Thomas
1947–1948 *Summa Theologica*. New York: Benziger Bros.
Augustine
   1950   *The City of God*. Trans. Marcus Dods. New York: Modern Library.

Awad, Mubarak E.
   1984   Nonviolent resistance: A strategy for the occupied territories. *Journal of Palestine Studies* 13(4): 22–36.
Baudrillard, Jean
   1995   *The Gulf War Did Not Take Place.* Trans. Paul Patton. Bloomington: Indiana University Press.
Baudrillard, Jean
   2002   *The Spirit of Terrorism.* London and New York: Verso.
Bosmajian, Haig A.
   1983   *The Language of Oppression.* Lanham, MD.: University Press of America.
Bourdieu, Pierre
   1991   *Language and Symbolic Power.* Ed. by John B. Thompson. Trans. Gino Raymond and Matthew Adamson. Cambridge: Harvard University Press.
Camus, Albert
   1988   After Hiroshima: Between hell and reason. Trans. Ronald E. Santoni. *Philosophy Today* 32(1/4): 77–78. Trans. of Editorial in *Combat* (8 August 1945).
Chilton, Paul A. (ed.)
   1985   *Language and the Nuclear Arms Debate: Nukespeak Today.* London: Frances Pinter.
Chomsky, Noam
   1991   *Pirates and Emperors: International Terrorism in the Real World.* New York: Black Rose Books.
Clausewitz, Carl von
   1943   *On War.* Trans. O. J. Matthijs Jolles. New York: The Modern Library.
Cohn, Carol
   1989   Sex and death in the rational world of defense intellectuals. In: Dianna Russel (ed.), *Exposing Nuclear Phallacies*, 127–159. New York: Pergamon.
Comte, Auguste
   1968   *System of Positive Polity.* New York: B. Franklin.
Dewey, John
   1983   "If war were outlawed", "What outlawry of war is not", and "War and a code of law". In: Jo Ann Bydston (ed.), *John Dewey, The Middle Works, 1899–1924,* Vol. 15 (1923/1924): 110–114, 115–121, 122–127. Carbondale: Southern Illinois University Press.
Dijk, Teun A. van
   1985   *Handbook of Discourse Analysis.* London: Academic Press.
Dijk, Teun A. van
   1993   *Elite Discourse and Racism.* London: Sage.
Dijk, Teun A. van
   1995   Discourse analysis as ideological analysis. In: Schäffner and Wenden (eds.), 17–33.
Fairclough, Norman
   1989   *Language and Power.* New York: Longman.
Fanon, Frantz
   1968   *The Wretched of the Earth.* Trans. Constance Farrington. New York: Grove Weidenfeld.

Fourier, Charles
  1973 *Le Nouveau Monde Industriel et Sociétaire ou Invention du Procédé d'industrie Attrayante et Naturelle Distribuée en Séries Passionnées.* Paris: Flammarion.
Freire, Paulo
  1993 *Pedagogy of the Oppressed.* Trans. Myra Bergman Ramos. New York: Continuum.
Fukuyma, Francis
  1992 *The End of History and the Last Man.* New York: Free Press.
Gandhi, Mahatma
  1986 *The Moral and Political Writings of Mahatma Gandhi.* Ed. by Raghavan Iyer. New York: Oxford University Press.
Gay, William C.
  1987 Nuclear discourse and linguistic alienation. *Journal of Social Philosophy* 18(2): 42–49.
Gay, William C.
  1997 Nonsexist public discourse and negative peace: The injustice of merely formal transformation. *The Acorn: Journal of the Gandhi-King Society* 9(1): 45–53.
Gay, William C.
  1998 Exposing and overcoming linguistic alienation and linguistic violence. *Philosophy and Social Criticism* 24: 137–156.
Gay, William C.
  1999 The language of war and peace. In: Lester Kurtz (ed.), *Encyclopedia of Violence, Peace, and Conflict*, Vol. 2, 303–312. San Diego: Academic Press.
Govier, Trudy
  2002 *A Delicate Balance: What Philosophy Can Tell Us about Terrorism.* Boulder, Col.: Westview.
Habermas, Jürgen
  1987 *The Political Discourse of Modernity.* Cambridge: Polity Press.
Havel, Václav et al.
  1985 *The Power of the Powerless.* Armonk, NY: M. E. Sharpe.
Heidegger, Martin
  1957[1983] *Hebel – der Hausfreund.* Pfullingen: Neske. [Hebel – friend of the house], trans. Burce V. Flotz and Michael Heim. In: Darrel E. Christensen et al. (eds.), *Contemporary German Philosophy*, Vol. 3(1983), 89–101. University Park, PA: The Pennsylvania State University Press.
Holmes, Robert
  1989 Terrorism and violence: A moral perspective. In: Joseph C. Kunkel and Kenneth H. Klein (eds.), *Issues in War and Peace: Philosophical Inquiries*, 115–127. Wolfeboro, NH: Longwood Academic.
Horkheimer, Max and Theodor W. Adorno
  1972 *Dialectic of Enlightenment.* New York: Herder and Herder.
Huxley, Aldous
  1937 Words and behaviour. In: Aldous Huxley, *The Olive Tree*, 84–103. New York: Harper & Brothers.

Jameson, Fredric
    1991   *Postmodernism, or, the Cultural Logic of Late Capitalism.* Durham, NC: Duke University Press.

Kant, Immanuel
    1983   *Perpetual Peace and Other Essays on Politics, History, and Morals.* Trans. Ted Humphrey. Indianapolis: Hackett.

King, Martin Luther, Jr.
    1963   *Why We Can't Wait.* New York: Harper & Row.

Knightley, Phillip
    2004   *The First Casualty: The War Correspondent as Hero and Myth-maker from the Crimea to Iraq.* Baltimore, MD: Johns Hopkins University Press.

Lakoff, George
    1991   Metaphor and war: The metaphor system used to justify war in the Gulf. *Peace Research* 23: 25–32.

Lang, Berel
    1988   Language and genocide. In: Alan Rosenberg and Gerald E. Myers (eds.), *Echoes from the Holocaust: Philosophical Reflections on a Dark Time*, 341–361. Philadelphia: Temple University Press.

Mandela, Nelson
    1995   *Long Walk to Freedom: The Autobiography of Nelson Mandela.* New York: Longitude.

Memmi, Albert
    1965   *The Colonizer and the Colonized.* New York: Orion Press.

Merleau-Ponty, Maurice
    1964   *Signs.* Trans. Richard C. McCleary. Evanston, IL: Northwestern University Press.

Nietzsche, Friedrich
    1956   The genealogy of morals. In: *The Birth of Tragedy and The Genealogy of Morals*, trans. Francis Golffing. Garden City, NY: Doubleday.

Norris, Christopher
    1992   *Uncritical Theory: Postmodernism, Intellectuals and the Gulf War.* Amherst: University of Massachusetts Press.

Orwell, George
    1968   Politics and the English language. In: Sonia Orwell and Ian Angus (eds.), *The Collected Essays, Journalism and Letters of George Orwell, In Front of Your Nose: 1945–1950*, Vol. 4, 127–140. New York: Harcourt, Brace & World.

Plato
    1945   *The Republic of Plato.* Trans. Francis MacDonald Cornford. New York: Oxford University Press.

Romain, Rolland
    1969   *Gandhi et Romain Rolland: Correspondance, Extraits du Journal et Textes Divers.* Paris: A. Michel.

Russell, Bertrand
    1920   *Why Men Fight: A Method of Abolishing the International Duel.* New York: Century.

Saint-Pierre, Abbé de
    1733–1741   Projet pour perfectionner le Comerse. In: *Ouvrajes de Politique*, 17 Vols. Rotterdam: J. D. Beman.

Saint-Simon, Henri, comte de
    1964   *Social Organization, the Science of Man and Other Writings*. Ed. and trans. by Felix Markham. New York: Harper & Row.
Saussure, Ferdinand de
    1966   *Course in General Linguistics*. Trans. Wade Baskin. New York: McGraw-Hill.
Schäffner, Christina and Anita L. Wenden (eds.)
    1995   *Language and Peace*. Aldershot: Ashgate Publishing Company.
Sharp, Gene
    1973   *The Politics of Nonviolent Action*. Boston: P. Sargent.
Solomon, J. Fisher
    1988   *Discourse and Reference in the Nuclear Age*. Norman: Oklahoma University Press.
Somerville, John
    1983   Nuclear omnicide: Moral imperatives for human survival. *New World Review*, Jan-Feb, 20–21.
Sully, Maximilien de Bethune, duc de
    1827   *Memoires du duc de Sully*. Paris: Etienne Ledoux.
Sun Tzu
    1983   *The Art of War*. Ed. by James Clavell. New York: Delacorte Press.
Taylor, Philip M.
    1992   *War and the Media: Propaganda and Persuasion in the Gulf War*. Manchester and New York: Manchester University Press.
Thucydides
    1960   *The History of the Peloponnesian War*. Ed. by Sir Richard Livingstone. New York: Oxford University Press.
Tolstoy, Leo
    1951   *The Kingdom of God is Within You; or, Christianity not as a Mystical Teaching but as a New Concept of Life*. Ed. and trans. by Leo Wiener. Boston: L. C. Page.
Turney-High, Harry Holbert
    1971   *Primitive War: Its Practice and Concepts*. Columbia: University of South Carolina Press.
Wenden, Anita
    1995   Defining peace: Perspective from peace research. In: Schäffner and Wenden (eds.), 3–15.
Wittgenstein, Ludwig
    1953   *Philosophical Investigations*. Oxford: Blackwell.
Young, John Wesley
    1991   *Totalitarian Language: Orwell's Newspeak and Its Nazi and Communist Antecedents*. Charlottesville: University Press of Virginia.
Zampaglione, Gerardo
    1973   *The Idea of Peace in Antiquity*. Trans. Richard Dunn. Nortre Dame: University of Nortre Dame Press.
Zizek, Slavoj
    2001   *Did Somebody Say Totalitarianism: Five Interventions in the (Mis)Use of a Notion*. London and New York: Verso.

17. Language and science[1]

Augusto Carli and Emilia Calaresu

1. Introduction

Scientific communication is, as far as the relationship between language and science is concerned, certainly one of the most relevant fields of applied linguistics (AL). As a matter of fact, it is inter-subjective communication which makes science itself possible (see Section 2.1. for definitions of "science"). What we mean by "scientific communication" here is that set of discourses whose aim is the transmission of knowledge and research results, performed by communication procedures which vary depending on who acts as sender (the scientist him/herself, the scientific journalist, the educator etc.) and who is the addressee (a fellow scientist, a student, the lay public, etc.). Changes in such procedures mainly comply with social components of an economic, demographic and political nature which in turn have repercussions on the languages which compete with each other in scientific communication. Scientific communication in the era of globalization is a good field of observation of the competition in progress of most languages compared to English. The current transformations in scientific communication are not concerned only with choosing which language to use but also with the text types, the topic styles and the communication aims. The examples of this change in progress will be taken from the major Western languages which have a centuries-old tradition in scientific communication.

At a first glance it would seem that dealing with scientific communication consists in the analysis, the description and the interpretation of the linguistic structures and functions shown in scientific texts. This would coincide with research on language for professional purposes (LPP) and language for specific purposes (LSP), with which there are undeniable links. But what characterizes research on scientific communication is, instead, the need to analyze the language in much broader units of discourse, showing their relationship with specific social meanings. It is therefore appropriate to locate the analysis of scientific language in reference to particular sociolinguistic dimensions which influence lexical-grammatical and textual choices, and from whose interlacing the symbolic value of scientific communication arises. Thus, we can summarize the most typical aspects of scientific communication and, at the same time, define the issues discussed in this chapter as follows:

a) On a diachronic dimension (relating to changes over time), Western scientific communication provides a solid and centuries-old body of significant texts which span from modern times up to the present, with sharp changes not only and not so much on the lexical level but more on the sociolinguistic and pragmalinguistic levels, especially where argumentative choices and type of text are concerned. The diachronic aspect will be touched on only marginally, with reference to the second half of the 20th century up to the present;

b) on a diatopic dimension (relating to geocultural variability), we must point out the peculiarities of "making science" in diverse geographical areas characterized not only by typical linguistic choices but also by local, national or deeply-rooted territorial cultural traditions. "Local" peculiarities inform the scientific procedures, which are in turn supported by their own traditions and needs which are firmly territorial. The "national" dimension of science must be further differentiated and evaluated according to the following traditional macro-disciplinary boundaries: humanistic cultures vs. scientific cultures, behavioral/human sciences vs. exact sciences, analytical sciences vs. rhetorical-argumentative sciences, etc. (see Section 3.4.). The diatopic dimension of scientific communication today tends to be partly neutralized by the so-called globalization or internationalization, especially in those disciplines where the connection between science and technology and/or between economic and political power is most strongly felt. In this chapter we aim to highlight the major changes in scientific practices, as when a national type of communication shifts to a trans/international and globalized type of communication;

c) on a diaphasic dimension (relating to the variability of the communicative context), scientific communication is represented by a large number of texts, registers and styles depending on whether it addresses specialized, popular or pedagogical issues (see Section 2.3.). We will mainly regard primary or intra-specialist scientific communication (see Section 3);

d) on a diamesic dimension (relating to the channel of communication), written and oral scientific communication differ from one another in the same way as verbal communication in general selects distinct grammatical and stylistic patterns depending on the needs for speaking or writing. Up until now written scientific communication has been studied much more than spoken scientific communication. We will provide a critical summary of the phenomena and of the problems linked mainly to written scientific communication and we will only occasionally skim over spoken scientific communication.

With reference to the classic definition of applied linguistics by Grabe and Kaplan (1992: 3) where "Applied Linguistics [...] is a field the purpose of which is to solve real-world language-based problems", we will define two major fields of applied linguistics:

1) the style of scientific prose as it is conditioned by sociolinguistic, cultural and historical variables;

2) research on local and international needs, and on the language of scientific communication between monolingualism and multilingualism.

While applied linguistics has traditionally been concerned with the first issue, it is only relatively recently that the latter has begun to be more carefully observed. It is also for this reason that we will put more emphasis on the second issue.

2. Outline and history of the field

Of the complex relationships between language and science the phenomenon of scientific communication is only one of the relevant aspects from the viewpoint of current language sciences – in as much as it is, probably, the most widely discussed aspect outside of a strictly linguistic context. Before going into this question, however, it is necessary to explain what is meant by "science".

2.1. Definitions of science(s)

Defining "science" is a complex and fleeting problem. In the sociology of science the multireferentiality of the term has been clearly defined: Science "is commonly used to denote (1) a set of characteristic methods by means of which knowledge is certified; (2) a stock of accumulated knowledge stemming from the application of these methods; (3) a set of cultural values and mores governing the activities termed scientific; or (4) any combination of the foregoing" (Merton 1996: 267).

From the viewpoint of the "object" of science, there is a significant differentiation between most of continental Europe and the Anglo-Saxon world. In the latter, in fact, the current concept of science can be summed up by the following definition: "[science is] the intellectual and practical activity encompassing the systematic study of the structure and behaviour of the physical and natural world through observation and experiment" (New Oxford Dictionary of English 1998: 1664). The object of scientific research is therefore essentially identified with that of natural sciences, whereas, in the tradition of continental Europe (closer to the meaning of the corresponding Greek and Latin terms) science is considered any activity of research aimed at producing knowledge, acquired through studying, experience and observation and therefore corresponds to a constructed combination of ordered, coherent and interdependent knowledge. The first important consequence of these conceptual or ideological differences is clearly the problem of what human and social sciences correspond to. The problem is actually already linguistically codified in various languages: In English these sciences are referred to with the single term "humanities" (and so we already have an important terminological boundary between *science(s)* and *humanities*), while in most of the other European languages expressions containing a term corresponding to "sciences" are normally used (*sciences humaines* in French, *ciencias/ciências humanas* in Spanish and Portuguese, *scienze umane* in Italian, *Geisteswissenschaften* in German, *gumanitarnye nauki* in Russian, etc.). Of course, even if not all scientists in the English-speaking world share this exclusion of human/behavioral sciences from the field of what is considered "true" science (e.g., Ziman 2000), the situation today is such that many are beginning to express concern that "the use of English as the scientific language may lead to a too restricted idea of what science is" (Hauge 1996: 166). In this chapter we will adopt the broader "continental" definition of science, by which we mean the research procedures and the systematization of knowledge which make it communicable, codifiable and progressively updatable.

2.2. History of the field

From a historical viewpoint, we must remember that the first systematic discussions in modern times of the relationship between language and science, or more precisely, between language and knowledge (lat. *scientia*), were still fully part of philosophy, and also that the distinction between philosopher and scientist is a relatively recent one (until the 1700s the equivalent of the current term "scientist" was "natural philosopher"). For instance, the proposals and the creations of the "*a priori* philosophical languages", imagined as a universal and perfect tool for transmitting ideas and also for discovering new aspects of natural and intellectual reality (Eco 1993), belong to the philosophical sphere. Semiotic and metalinguistic reflection has been present, in a more or less articulate or persistent way since the very beginning of modern science in the writings of Francis Bacon, Jan Comenius, Galileo Galilei, René Descartes, Gottfried Wilhelm Leibniz and many other well-known fore-fathers of modern Western science.

Nowadays, instead, perhaps due also to the growing diversification of the disciplinary fields, natural scientists seem to be less directly involved in the metadiscursive and metalinguistic reflections which regard their discipline, leaving this field open to other experts of "metascience", such as historians, philosophers, sociologists and, although in a minor way, to linguists and language historians. In fact, a "linguistics of science" does not exist, whereas the philosophy of science and the sociology of science do. In particular, at present, "sociology has superseded philosophy at the theoretical core of 'science studies'" (Ziman 2000: ix). It must, however, be noted that, especially since new scientific discoveries began to take on an alarming role in the second half of the 20th century (mainly in the military and genetic fields), scientists themselves are gradually paying more attention to how their work is perceived by the lay public. This brings about in the scientists themselves a growing awareness not only of the foundations of scientific research but also of the *methods* of transmitting new scientific knowledge, of the publicizing and thus of the discourse of science. It is, however, remarkable that, parallel to discussions on science by scientists, such as the physicist Ziman (2000), who show a considerable awareness of the problems connected to a purely instrumental vision of scientific language, many of the statements by natural scientists go in practically opposite directions, often expressing a simplified, purely instrumental and economic approach to the linguistic problem. Therefore, we often have a vicious circle: The scientist's forays into metalinguistic issues often appear limited or artless to the language expert, and in the same way the applied linguist's forays into the world of science risk appearing just as limited and artless to the shrewd scientist. Of course, in the framework of current language sciences, it is not only applied linguistics which is concerned with the relationship between language and science.

It is useful to make a distinction between two different aspects of the relation between language and science: a) the cognitive aspect, namely the way in which language is in itself a tool of knowledge, which provides cognitive strategies that help to interpret and reconstruct the real world; b) the social aspect, namely the way in which language is a tool for the transmission of knowledge. These two aspects are in fact inseparable.

In compliance with today's disciplinary boundaries, the cognitive aspect is still placed in the foreground especially by philosophy of language and by recent cognitive linguistics. On the other hand, the social aspect is placed in a central position especially by sociolinguistics, pragmatics and applied linguistics. In this chapter we will take a wider view of applied linguistics which also includes sociolinguistics and pragmatics as these are areas which are directly concerned with language use in real contexts. During the last decade two lines of research have been particularly relevant: the rhetorical analysis of scientific writing and the linguistic analysis of scientific genres. The first, essentially diachronic, on language and on rhetorical-argumentative strategies of scientific discourse, contributes to showing how knowledge is constructed not only empirically, but also by means of rhetorical argumentation (cf. Bazerman 1988 and Atkinson 1999a on the evolution of scientific discourse in *The Philosphical Transactions of the Royal Society*; Altieri Biagi 1990 on Galileo and other Italian scientists between the 17th and 18th centuries; Gross, Harmon, and Reidy 2002 on the historical evolution of the scientific paper in English, French and German from the 17th century onwards). The second line of research analyzes scientific/academic writing in the framework of textual genres (Swales 1990; Hyland 2000).

Due to socio-cultural reasons (the greater prestige which is attributed to writing) and strictly technical ones (the greater difficulty in gathering and analyzing spoken data), most studies on scientific language are based not only on written language but also on a specific genre (the scientific paper) and on a restricted selection of disciplines (mathematical, physical and natural sciences).

The pedagogical aims of such types of study often run the risk of being excessively simplified and it is quite frequent, especially in certain kinds of manuals, to find scientific language reduced to a sort of jargon or language for specific purposes whose peculiarities are usually described as being restricted to a formulaic set of lexical, morphosyntactic and textual features.

Scientific communication, as a topic of study, is therefore at the crossroads of many disciplines (history of science, philosophy of science, sociology of science, rhetoric and linguistics) and sub-disciplines (sociolinguistics, pragmatics, applied linguistics). Therefore, a study of scientific language within one field, e.g. applied linguistics, will also have to consider interdisciplinary perspectives. Naturally, this holds also true in the case of qualitative as well as quantitative research on the different (national and international) languages employed in scientific communication. In this case, other disciplines (e.g. economics and politics) also become relevant when issues such as the democratization of knowledge and its costs, or the current competition between languages in the era of globalization come into play.

In both cases, whether the concern is with internal characteristics of the language of science or with the competition between languages in national and international scientific communication, the linguistic and metalinguistic observations of the main protagonists, the natural scientists themselves (e.g., physicists such as Lévy-Leblond 1996 and Ziman 2000, or biologists such as Valiela 2001) are anything but secondary.

2.3. Types of scientific communication

Two major models of types of scientific communication can be defined. The first model distinguishes between *primary* scientific communication, i.e. the transmission of research results among specialists, and *secondary* scientific communication, i.e. the transmission of scientific knowledge by specialists and/or semi-specialists (e.g., journalists or instructors) to the lay public, for pedagogic purposes and for popularizing in general. The various studies in Ammon (2001a) often refer to this binary distinction.

The second, more complex model (Cloître and Shinn 1985) provides for a sort of *continuum* from which four main levels of scientific communication or, in their words, of "expository practice" emerge:
1) the *intra-specialist* level of the communication between experts and researchers from the same field; its typical written means is the paper, especially in the fields of mathematics, physics and natural sciences, whereas in the social sciences and the humanities written communication takes the form of papers, books and monographs;
2) the *inter-specialist* level, where communication takes place among researchers and specialists from different fields or different sub-sectors of the

same field; typical examples of written transmission are the articles in the so-called "bridge journals" such as the British *Nature* or the American *Science*, which in turn function as a model for similar publications in other countries;
3) the *pedagogical* level, which concerns transmitting scientific knowledge for pedagogical purposes; the typical means of transmission in this case is the textbook;
4) the *popular* level, where scientific knowledge is broadcast to a wider lay public through the mass media such as television, or, in the case of written transmission, through the daily or weekly press, or through publications specifically designed for mass scientific popularization.

Finally, combining the distinction between spoken vs. written and three levels of formality, a useful and concise model is provided by the physicist Lévy-Leblond (1996: 238, original in French; see also Gutiérrez Rodilla 1998: 20), cf. Table 1:

Table 1. Forms of scientific communication (taken from Lévy-Leblond 1996: 238)

	Informal communication	**Institutional** communication	**Public** communication
Written communication	Laboratory diaries, correspondence, etc.	Specialized publications	Popularization (books, papers)
Spoken communication	Work discussions, telephone conversations, etc.	Talks, seminaries, press conferences	Teaching, media (radio, TV)

3. State-of-the-art: Central concepts and theoretical approaches

As already stated in Section 1, we will make a distinction between two major fields: the one which applied linguistics traditionally deals with, regarding the description and the analysis of scientific language as a variety of usage of a certain language (Section 3.1.), and the one concerned with which languages are used to transmit scientific knowledge in national and international contexts (Section 3.2.). The great relevance of this second field for applied linguistics is given by the direct relation between the changes in *status* of a certain language and changes in the *corpus* (in terms of system and norms). The growing predominance in scientific communication of a certain language, e.g. English, which inevitably brings with it specific discourse models and a certain sociology of knowledge (Kaplan 2001: 12), causes, more or less rapidly, changes also of a lexical, morphosyntactic, textual and rhetorical type in the scientific language of the national non-English-speaking communities.

3.1. The description of scientific language

One of the main problems when describing scientific language is how to categorize it in relation to the other linguistic varieties of the diasystem they all belong to. If, for instance, scientific language is treated only as a professional jargon this implies: a) that there are no particular ontological differences in *status* between the specialized language of a biologist and the equally specialized language of a stockbroker; and b) that the group of its users/scholars is restricted only to those who have a specific working interest in it (scientists, science students, teachers of scientific subjects, translators and specialized journalists). Scientific language, however, beyond the most striking external aspects (lexical ones in particular) which often give it the obscurity of a downright jargon, is instead a type of language which has a broader social and cognitive relevance. It is indeed the language of "complex thought" which reconstructs experience and constructs knowledge, and, according to Altieri Biagi (1990: 192–193), should be defined in a balanced three-way relationship with common language on the one hand, and literary language on the other: Both scientific and literary language represent the tools of complex thought pursuing knowledge from the viewpoint of objective perception (scientific language) and of subjective perception (literary language). Along the same lines Halliday (2004: 95, 160) observes that "the languages of science are not saying the same things in different ways" and identifies two extremes in the attitude towards scientific language, one which makes it coincide only with technical jargon which can be perfectly (and hopefully) transferred into "the everyday language of ordinary common sense", and the other which instead makes scientific language coincide with science itself, denying thus the possibility to "separate science from how it is written, or rewrite scientific discourse in any other way". Of course, as Halliday concludes, reality is to be found somewhere between these two extremes.

Descriptions of scientific language are often carried out in the theoretical framework of languages for specific purposes (as professional "sub-codes") mainly because it is the lexical aspect that tends to be emphasized as the most dissimilar feature when compared to common language. But to suggest that scientific discourse coincides with specialized vocabulary, instead of representing complex linguistic relations of an argumentative type (cf. e.g. Walter 1996: 36–37), is an enormous simplification. It is thus necessary to put the lexical aspect into perspective with regard to other aspects of scientific language, such as grammar and textual organization. As Halliday puts it: "[W]e shall need to get rid of our obsession with words. The difficulty [of the language of science] lies more with the grammar than with the vocabulary" (2004: 161).

In order to establish which norms of usage are at work in the scientific language of any natural language, there are at least two complementary approaches (Calaresu 2006). The first is based on what scientists themselves actually say and hope for, and the second on what the analyst can actually find as recurrent and systematic in the existing scientific texts, both from the past and from the present day. As for the first approach, what scientists themselves demand, more or less systematically (from Galileo to Einstein to modern scientists), is "simply" the most accurate and non-ambiguous use possible of the language itself, i.e. consistency of terminology, clear explanations and, as far as possible, being more objective than subjective (at least where observation procedures and analysis are concerned).

As for the second approach, what can be actually found in the scientific texts themselves, paying attention to the historical development, is a certain recurrence of or preference for certain linguistic solutions such as a widespread use of nominalizations and passive constructions in the descriptive parts, a narrative structure of the summary of the experimental stages, etc. As a matter of fact, the textual and rhetorical standardization which we are used to today because of the style of current scientific papers (particularly in the natural sciences) is a product of history and the textual structures of scientific works have changed remarkably over time from Galileo's dialogues to today's *scientific papers*. The common repertoire of recurrent linguistic solutions notably increases if the linguistic and textual analysis is of a purely synchronic type, i.e. if it regards a specific moment in history such as the analysis of scientific texts of the second half of the 20th century. In this case we find the following characteristics: avoiding the use of "I" and preferring impersonal structures, a strict order of the components (e.g., introduction, data and methods, results, discussion and conclusion), certain standardized procedures of quotation and hedging, and a certain type of textual and graphic layout (paratext) (see Atkinson 1999a: 75–102). Moreover, despite a widespread popular misbelief (which is, however, also shared by some scientists), scientific language has always been rather full of metaphors and even based on metaphors most of the time: "[…] indeed, the history of a scientific discipline can be traced through its changing repertoire of models and metaphors" (Ziman 2000: 150).

All these facts challenge many "naive" presumptions about the language of science (presumed objectiveness and lack of ambiguity) which the analyst should be aware of. In fact, the two different approaches are often confused, describing as real features of the language of science characteristics which rather correspond to its ideal "aims" (precision, neutrality and conciseness, see Gutiérrez Rodilla 1998: 30–37). Such a misunderstanding often contributes to spreading a not very realistic (and paradoxically, not very objective) vision of "making science", as well as to coming to inappropriate conclusions about the *reasons* for choosing one language over another to transmit the results of scientific research. This occurs, for instance, when we attribute to the different languages internal or intrinsic characteristics which make them more or less suitable for scientific discourse, and/or attributing to a specific language characteristics which instead correspond to the *ideal* aim of modern scientific research. Below we will give an example of this by quoting three different explanations for the use of English as the language of scientific communication. The first two (which represent the most widespread opinion today) are, respectively, taken from an applied linguist (1) who is a native speaker of English, and from a marine biologist (2) who is a non-native English speaker, and the third (3), which exemplifies instead a sounder linguistic realism, is from a native-English speaking physicist:

(1) *La diffusione della conoscenza scientifica è basata in gran parte sul linguaggio. La metodologia scientifica intesa come oggettività, ricerca sistematica ed elementi di misura esatti ha determinato lo sviluppo di un linguaggio specifico caratterizzato dalla forma impersonale, dalla logicità della esposizione e dalla precisione della descrizione. La lingua inglese si presta particolarmente a soddisfare tutti questi requisiti nel loro insieme e ciò ha determinato la naturale preferenza attribuita all'inglese come mezzo di espressione scientifica internazionale.*
[The spreading of scientific knowledge is mainly based on language. Scientific methodology understood as objectiveness, systematic research and elements of exact measurements has determined the development of a specific language characterized by the impersonal form, the logic of the explanation and the accuracy of description. **The English language is particularly suited to meet all of these requirements as a whole and this has determined the natural preference attributed to English as a means of international scientific expression.**]
(Ulrych 1991: 75; original in Italian, our translation and our emphasis)

(2) The preeminence of English as the scientific medium of communication comes about from economic affluence, **relative ease of use, large vocabulary, brevity**, and number of speakers. [...] The richness, **exactitude**, and brevity of English, in combination with accidents of history and response to technological development, have therefore conspired to spread [the] use of English to many people all over the world, and to establish this language as the international language of science.
(Valiela 2001: 103, 107; our emphasis)

(3) Scientific discourse is not really distinct from other 'didactic' modes of ordinary speech. The sloppiness and diversity of natural languages is thus a very serious challenge to the norm of universalism. Scientists think, speak and write in a variety of languages [...] How is it possible to formulate and communicate clear-cut scientific theories in such inexact media? [...] Yet this challenge is met and overcome daily throughout the scientific world. It has not been necessary to banish natural languages from scientific discourse. It is true that English has become the principal international language of modern science. But English is not the language in which the majority of scientists commonly think or express themselves to their immediate colleagues and has not superseded other languages for the formal communication of research results. **Anyway, English is just as inexact, ambiguous, irregular and idiosyncratic as any other language on earth – except in its spelling which is uniquely disorderly. In practice, the universality of science is enabled by the universality of certain structural features of all human languages.**
(Ziman 2000: 135–136; our emphasis)

Of the three authors quoted above it is precisely the applied linguist who attributes the spreading of English only to internal linguistic characteristics of this language (English's alleged greater suitability to logic and precision compared to other languages), whereas even Valiela recognizes, more realistically, that there are also socio-economic reasons which run parallel to the presumed linguistic virtues of English.

3.2.   English as the language of science

The spread of English as an international language began after the first world war, and after the second world war English became the main language of tertiary education and scientific publications (Ammon and McConnell 2002). This development became a topic of systematic research only from the mid-1970s onwards when a new sensitivity arose of language phenomena in contact and in conflict, and in particular of forms of linguistic expansion and colonization. The change was considered not only paradoxical but also a source of peril for the scientific creativity of local/national traditions (Moles 1979). The perception of the loss of functions was greater in those linguistic communities characterized by the so-called "languages of culture", and it was in France and Germany that a new line of sociolinguistic research began. Its main issues were the identification and definition of the *status* of a so-called "international language", the relationship between *status* and *corpus*, and the possible consequences of linguistic hegemony. In fact, despite the close ties between *status*, *corpus* and acquisition planning, the wealth of functional varieties of a language and its *status* do not necessarily coincide and the attributes of international language and *lingua franca* are often used very superficially to describe the same phenomenon. A *lingua franca* as such is not the native language of any of the interactors, but frequently we read that English has taken on the role of *lingua franca* which once belonged to Latin (cf. e.g. Graddol 1997 or Crystal 2003; see Section 4). As for the degree of "internationality" of a language, this is related to the *cratic* dimension, i.e. the degree of power held by the linguistic community in question (Gr. *kràtos* 'power'). In fact, the power of the English-speaking community is based on demographic, political, cultural and other indicators which directly contribute to increasing the functions of English as a global language (see Crystal 2003; de Swaan 2001a; Brutt-Griffler 2002). As linguistic functions and usage set off a self-reproductive mechanism (known also as the *Catherine wheel model*), the growing use of English in scientific communication and academic contexts appears more and more like an unrelenting wave. The main line of research aims to describe and measure the size, the causes and the effects of this change.

3.3. The loss of scientific registers of languages other than English

The pioneers of this line of research are Thogmartin (1980), Tsunoda (1983), and Baldauf and Jernudd (1983). This latter study also discusses the researchers' apparent lack of interest in the issue: "[A]lthough language of publication is an inescapable feature of scientific communication, it is most often treated as background noise, a variable in which neither information specialists nor scientists have shown much interest, nor is it, as far as we can tell a problem which linguists have examined" (Baldauf and Jernudd 1983: 97). Tsunoda (1983) records the change in linguistic usage in the field of natural sciences over a whole century (1880–1980) documenting an increase in the spreading of English detrimental to German and French which starts off slowly from 1930, becoming exponential from the 1950s onwards. For example, in *Chemical Abstracts,* in the period from 1961 to 2000 (see Laponce 2001; Sano 2002), there is a noticeable increase in publications only in the Chinese language, whereas there is a sharp decline in the other important languages of culture such as French and German. Russian, whose use was stable until the fall of the Soviet regime, also shows a decline after that date, while the number of publications in Japanese, although a small percentage of all publications, remains stable over time. Sano (2002: 46) shows that the percentage of papers in English has almost doubled, from 43% in 1961 to 82% in the year 2000. The increase of publications in Chinese is evaluated by Laponce (2003: 61) as evidence of a transition period "marking the entry of Chinese scientists into the worldwide market of science". As for the human sciences, the predominance of English can be observed "even in a language-sensitive subject such as linguistics, where in 1995 nearly 90 per cent of the 1,500 papers listed in the journal 'Linguistic Abstracts' were in English" (Crystal 2003: 102).

While in the 1980s sociolinguistic surveys were still limited to single disciplinary fields (such as sociology, psychology or medicine), from the 1990s onwards a general framework for the human sciences and physical-natural sciences was developed (Ammon 2001a; Carli and Calaresu 2003; Carli 2006). Recognizing highly divergent methods of data-gathering, description and interpretation, a comparative framework for various disciplinary fields and geo-cultural areas has now been made available (cf. Skudlik 1990 and Ammon 1991, 1998, 2000 for the German-speaking areas; Conseil de la Langue Française 1996; Locquin 1989 and Truchot 1996, 1997, 2001 for the French-speaking areas; Gutiérrez Rodilla 1998 and Gimeno Menéndez and Gimeno Menéndez 2003 for the Spanish-speaking areas; Carli and Calaresu 2003 for the Italian-speaking areas; Ammon 2001a for many countries of the Western and Eastern world).

Data banks can also be considered useful bibliographical tools even if most of them are run by Anglo-Saxon editors who are therefore more inclined to register scientific production in English. According to the *Science Citation Index* (SCI), the largest bibliometric repertoire of the ISI® (formerly Institute for

Scientific Information; www.isinet.com), 90% of all of the papers included are in English. Not only the developing countries but also countries which have advanced systems of education are rarely, if at all, present. Many studies identify a conspicuous series of chain reactions linked to the introduction of the evaluation criteria of the *impact factor*, or IF (on which the Science Citation Index is founded). The Impact Factor is a bibliometric criterion for measuring the visibility and diffusion of a scientific journal (for a review on its presumed "objectiveness", see Valiela 2001: 102; Carli and Calaresu 2003: 55–58). Even if language does not appear among the criteria for the calculation of the IF, it is really a covert impact that has repercussions on the scientific communities by forcing them to publish in English (Truchot 2001: 320; Carli and Calaresu 2003: 55–60). In fact, an increase in the Impact Factor is associated both with the prestige of a journal and the ability to attract the best authors, and the great majority of journals with the highest Impact Factor are in English. Thus, especially in the biomedical field, many scientific journals, traditionally edited in languages other than English (and at times also well suited to being published in other languages as well as in English), try to reach a higher Impact Factor simply by switching to English as the sole language accepted for publication (see also Ammon 2001b: 353–355; Calaresu 2006).

Summing up, the following trends emerge:
1) English as the language of scientific communication is by now an inexorable and relentless presence, and has been mainly since the 1990s; its systematic introduction has produced reactions which vary greatly depending on the peculiarities of various cultural traditions. As far as Europe is concerned, there is a huge difference between Northern European countries such as the Netherlands and Scandinavia where English spread very rapidly and without much opposition from the 1960s (cf. Gunnarsson 2001; Haarmann and Holman 2001; de Bot 2004) and the Mediterranean countries where English began to dominate only from the mid 1990s (cf. Carli and Calaresu 2003). The most critical development with regard to the spreading of English began within the formerly major scientific communication languages, i.e. French and German.
2) There is still a considerable difference between the natural sciences, where the use of English is more than 80%, and the human and social sciences where the use of English varies between 50% and 20%.
3) The individual national languages are still used mostly in secondary scientific communication, giving rise therefore to a wholly internal diglossia of scientific communication: The primary communication is in English and the secondary communication is transmitted in the national languages but with a strong inclination towards English, especially where tertiary education is concerned, as a consequence of "internationalization" procedures (Ammon 1988, 2000, 2001a; Ammon and McConnell 2002).

3.4. National vs. disciplinary culture

English is widely seen as a neutral, pragmatic language ideally suited to the universal communication and understanding of scientific and technical realities, having the full range of concepts necessary for this purpose. However, no language can impartially transmit information independently of its particular forms of culture and knowledge. All languages are semiotic systems and incorporate basic assumptions about the nature of reality. Even English is inevitably linked to its own traditions and cultural beliefs. In particular, English includes the influential, and principally Western notion that language is capable of objectively describing the whole of nature (see Pennycook 1994). According to Hyland (1997: 20) "English influences both a particular view of how reality can be understood and provides the discourse for articulating this, colouring both sensory perceptions and representations within the language".

National scientific communities are subject to four types of influence. The first is how the textual and rhetorical organization of discourses in the natural sciences influences those in the social and human sciences. The second is how the style of scientific discourse of the English-speaking countries affects that of other countries. The combined effect of these two aspects is that English scientific discourse which characterizes natural sciences has become a model for scientific discourse more generally. The third type of influence concerns the impact of the social construction of scientific information in the English-speaking countries (the U.S.A. in particular) on that of other countries: "[…] the international information systems are organized according to an English-based sociology of knowledge. Even research and development (R&D) functions in non-English states are impacted, since it is necessary to be able to search scientific literature in English and according to its sociology of knowledge" (Kaplan 2001: 12). The fourth type of influence is how the methods and the agenda of scientific research of the "leading" countries affect those of the other countries.

We will give two brief examples which show how research methods and textual practices are impacted by English scientific models and how these models can affect the shape of national scientific communities. The first example is the gradual abandonment of a whole textual genre in medical research, i.e. the exposition of single case reports, which used to be well represented in the medical journals of European countries but which is disappearing due to the low reputation and low *Impact Factor* it has in medical research in the U.S.A. (where surveys based on high numbers and statistical procedures are preferred), and as a consequence this genre is less and less represented in international medical data banks (Carli and Calaresu 2003: 43–44). The second example concerns the humanities and the procedures of establishing authorship in countries such as Italy. The norms of evaluation of humanistic research in Italy still require that a paper or a book, if written by two or more authors, should declare (in an initial footnote, as we have actually done in this paper) who is to be considered the author of which part; otherwise the individual researcher's contribution may not be evaluated for future career advancement. Identification of authorship usually conflicts with the norms of English scientific papers but ignoring it can cause problems to those researchers who are not yet at the peak of their professional career. As for the impact on scientists' professional careers, de Swaan (2001b: 78–79) further observes:

> The hegemony of English in the social sciences (and in other fields) has yet another consequence that is mostly ignored. Academics are required to publish regularly in 'international' and 'refereed' journals. In actual fact, these are almost without exception American and British periodicals. As a consequence, American and British editors and referees judge contributions from scholars all over the world and in so doing – without ever having intended to – exert a major impact on the selection and the promotion of academics in other countries who depend on these publications for their career advancement.

As for the connections between the academic communities and their texts, the language sciences (including applied linguistics) have so far been concerned with the organization of information and with the rhetorical-stylistic dimension. Applied linguistics in particular has dealt with the English academic prose by non-native speakers (see Flowerdew 1999; Hyland 2004). However, a most promising new line of research, called *Cultural Identity in Academic Prose* (KIAP, a Norwegian abbreviation; cf. Melander, Swales, and Fredrickson 1997; Fløttum 2003), has recently been initiated. It aims to reveal the links with national or disciplinary cultures in scientific prose. Dahl (2004), for instance, has worked on a corpus of scientific papers taken from three different fields (linguistics, economics and medicine) and in three different languages (French, English and Norwegian). Her analysis aims to investigate if argumentative and metadiscursive features are linked more to the disciplinary field or to the national language/culture. In fact, Dahl does not consider the non-native speaker (of English), but explicitly "the writing of professional scholars in their native language" (Dahl 2004: 1809). Two possible results emerge from Dahl's linguistic survey: 1) in the field of medicine the metatext/ metadiscourse is a marker of the disciplinary culture (i.e. not of the national culture or of the language employed); 2) in the fields of economics and linguistics, on the contrary, the metadiscourse and the argumentative style are linked to the writing tradition of each single language, and national culture prevails over disciplinary culture. Further analysis of the data reveals greater similarities between English and Norwegian culture and both are less similar to French culture.

Although this type of research is very interesting, it must be observed that the concepts of "culture", "identity", "cultural/disciplinary model", and "style" are often used too vaguely and that further investigation of larger corpora is needed. The results of such surveys confirm, however, the differences between humanist and naturalistic disciplinary cultures. Currently, the latter are more inclined to fit into a more globalized cultural model, but there is still a need to verify the influence that technologies, which are more immediately relevant to the natural sciences, can have on knowledge models and on linguistic usage.

4. Controversial issues

One of the most pressing questions today is whether science really *needs* a single language or if monolingualism in science is just an extenuating historical circumstance. A simply "horizontal" survey of current scientific production would give the overall impression of a peaceful convergence on the "free" choice of a single international language. If this were the case we would have to think that the problem preoccupied only a fringe of scholars, typically represented by applied linguists and sociolinguists, as well as in the more conservative sectors of public opinion in countries whose language is declassified by another one. However, what emerges through secondary textual genres, such as letters and editorials in scientific journals (typically when a journal decides to change to English as the sole publication language, cf. Carli and Calaresu 2003: 49–52, 54) shows that the debate is far from being resolved.

4.1. The need for a "universal" language of science

The criterion of "universality" in science regards at least three different levels: methodological, ethical and linguistic. Only on the first level universality can be considered an *intrinsic* necessity of science: A certain theory needs in fact to be "universally" valid, i.e. internally consistent and, given a certain protocol or set of parameters, its results must be generally applicable and repeatable. Universality (or "universalism") as an ethical norm means instead that "[t]he acceptance or rejection of claims entering the lists of science is not to depend on the personal or social attributes of their protagonists; their race, nationality, religion, class, and personal qualities are as such irrelevant" (Merton 1996: 269). However, if a theory or a result do not meet the requirements of methodological universality they would no longer be considered science but non-science or pseudo-science, whereas the eventual departure from the ethical norm of universalism (rather frequent in periods of international conflict) regards the ethical attitude of a certain scientist, or of a certain school, without necessarily challenging the scientific results as such.

    Universality with regard to the language of science concerns two different issues (Calaresu 2006), but in neither case does it help to distinguish science from non-science, i.e. a scientific work is not in itself less scientific only because it is written in one language rather than another. The first issue is related to the constant dream of a language which, unlike natural languages, is free from ambiguity and subjectivity and can therefore better meet the precision and the objectivity which we require from science (cf. the search for the perfect language of knowledge, in Eco 1993). The hopes for a highly formalized and not necessarily verbal language, e.g. a mathematical language, are still alive today, but many scientists demonstrate the shaky foundations of such an ambitious prospect (cf. Lévy-Leblond 1996: 237; Ziman 2000: 139–140, 149–150; cf. also the example (3) in Section 3.1.). The second, less philosophical issue concerns how useful, advantageous or even necessary it is for science to have at its disposal a sole international vehicle of language. Even if the concepts of a "universal" language and a globally "international" language are completely different, the two terms are frequently used as synonyms and it is often said that English is by now the "universal" language that Latin once was for science and research. Strictly speaking, both Latin and English are undoubtedly international languages but neither Latin nor English could be defined as "universal" (as is the case, as far as we know, for all human languages of the past and the near future). From our data on medical journals (Carli and Calaresu 2003), the rhetorical exploitation of the "English as Latin" parallelism is particularly frequent as a form of justification and promotion in critical (and at times dramatic) moments when passing from Italian to English as the sole language accepted by the publishers (but the same parallelism is also found in Valiela 2001: 103, 107). There are at least three different reasons to reject this type of parallelism (Calaresu 2006): 1) as already mentioned, English is not (yet) a *lingua franca*, and still has many millions of native speakers; 2) English is not the language of primary alphabetization of the entire international scientific community, while medieval Latin was; 3) the nature of the relationship with the various local/national languages with which Latin once contended and with which English contends today is quite different. In fact, as far as scientific communication is concerned, there was, historically, a path of linguistic differentiation from the exclusive use of Latin to the use of the different national languages. The current situation is just the opposite, i.e. a case of growing convergence on a sole language, and the field of scientific communication, which was once the main goal of national languages with regard to Latin, is today one of the first which English snatches from the national languages.

However, a comparison between the use of Latin and English in science is useful to better understand the historical foundation of modern science itself and of its communicative needs (Calaresu 2006). In fact, although it is true that for many centuries European science used a single language, i.e. medieval Latin, it was mostly the advent of modern science in the 17th century (with the important precedent, in some countries, of the protestant reformation) which began to make the power of Latin sway and opposed it to a series of future national languages (Italian, French, English, etc.; cf. Altieri Biagi 1990; Rossi

1997). The abandoning of Latin was essentially a reaction to the power of the Roman Catholic Church and to traditional scholastic knowledge (which was controlled by the Church by means of the universities), helped by the emergence of new national (or "micro-national" as in Italy and Germany) states which willingly, for more or less noble reasons, supported the new science, and also by a new conception of science which was beginning to open up towards the exchange of technical knowledge with the "vile mechanics" who did not speak Latin. Thus emerged a more democratic conception of knowledge which arose from the breakdown, not from the promotion, of monolingual knowledge. The voluntary abandonment of Latin did not lead to less international communication among European scholars because they were usually multilingual and, moreover, many printers of that time considered the activity of translating into and from Latin an investment (which also meant that translation costs were not a burden for the scientists, see Section 4.3.).

This brief historical summary provides a useful cue for reflection regarding the current situation: 1) the choice of one or another language in science has never been external to reasons outside science itself but has a remarkable symbolic significance in relation to the sociopolitical situation in which the scientist lives; 2) the multilingualism which, with more or less high peaks depending on the discipline, has practically reigned in science in the last 300 years or so, does not seem to have impeded or slowed down either the prodigious advancement of science and technology or the education of the international scientific communities; 3) the choice of national languages for scientific production has hardly ever coincided with the scientists' nationalistic seclusion (except perhaps, and only partially, between the first and the second world war); 4) while the choice by scientists like Galileo and Descartes to use the "vulgar" languages instead of Latin was actually a free, individual choice, the same cannot be said today of the current, increasing pressure on non-native speaker scientists to publish in English; 5) for a long time the knowledge "industry" and the editorial system supported scientists by not making them pay the eventual costs of translating their works (see Section 4.3.); 6) despite the universality which science aspires to and its internationalist *ethos*, scientists' research results and also their careers are conditioned nationally "since the sources of funding for science are overwhelmingly national" (Crawford, Shinn, and Sverker 1992: 2).

In short, the history of modern science definitely shows the need for mutual intelligibility among scholars, but does not show that this is necessarily guaranteed by the convergence on a sole language or that, vice-versa, it is impeded by multilingualism. The reasons for monolingualism or multilingualism in science lie outside matters intrinsic to science itself and derive rather from historical, socio-political and economic circumstances in which the scientific communities have to work.

4.2. Scientific English vs. World Englishes

It is frequently stated that international English, as it is not the exclusive "property" of the historically English-speaking community, is adapting to such a role by "loosening" more and more its own norms of use and breaking up, as already happened with Latin, into many varieties and, perhaps, future new languages (Crystal 1988: 274). Contrary to this prediction, the breaking-up of English into many varieties is a phenomenon which, at least at the moment, does not concern the international English of scientific communication (especially written communication), but only the so-called "world-Englishes" in the countries of the former British Empire (cf. Brutt-Grifler 2002). The international English of science is still firmly anchored to an Anglo-American standard – and many non-native English-speaking scientists who have become quite competent in this language are often the first to show no liking for a "softening" of that standard, which they consider as adding prestige to their professional status. As demonstrated by various quantitative and qualitative data in scientific journals in English (Coates et al. 2002), a "high rejection rate" by the editors is also linked to a faltering use of the English language by non-native authors, while the highest acceptance rate regards native English-speaking authors (see also Ammon 2001a: vii–viii; 2001b: 354). The uses of non-native English in prestigious or learned fields, especially in the case of writing, cannot therefore be compared at all with the more or less informal uses of lay communication to which in fact we refer when we speak of English as "everyone's" international language.

4.3. The costs of multilingualism in science

We frequently hear that the use of a sole international language for science is more "economical" than having more than one language. It is true that even in the most multilingual periods of international science there has always been a selection of languages and not all national languages have enjoyed the status of international languages of science. A scholar, therefore, used to have to dedicate part of his education to learning more languages, but it must be observed that when there are multiple linguistic proposals a scientist can restrict him/herself to achieving reading and comprehension skills in some languages, but for his/her production, can select from the most widespread languages of science the one which is most suitable, for example because it is typologically closer to his/her native language. Moreover, if the scientific production of a certain discipline is in fact multilingual, all members of the international scientific community have to use some of their time and material resources for linguistic instruction. When we have a single language which is not really a *lingua franca* for everyone, parts of the scientific community do not have to invest time and resources to learn the new languages but may use these for their own research activities.

With a single international language the problem of costs is not, therefore, removed but is simply *shifted* from the entire community to a part of the community. From a strictly economic point of view, in all scientific fields today there reigns a sense of reticence or shame which means that in works in English by non-native speakers the name of the native speaker who actually translated the work into English or who carried out a final linguistic revision of the text is usually omitted. As a consequence, it seems that translation and revision costs (both in terms of time and money) do not even exist. If it were not for this reticence or sense of shame we would have a much less idyllic and egalitarian picture of monolingualism in science than we are willing to admit in public.

5. Contributions of applied linguistics

The problems connected to scientific communication are numerous and can be researched using various approaches and from several points of view. We believe that the privileged, but not exclusive, contribution that applied linguistics can make to scientific communication consists mainly in identifying, developing and propagating a *meta*-awareness of the complex issues involved. When studying "communication" it is precisely *meta*-communication which plays a decisive role in identifying the ideological underpinnings of the language(s) and their cultural environments.

So far linguistic research on scientific texts has isolated at least two general characteristics: the dialogic or interactive character, and the social identity construction of the researcher within the scientific community in question. Today this second aspect is even more important in the face of English as the predominant language in academic communication and the current proliferation of courses on academic discourse in general and on English for academic purposes in particular (also for non-native speakers). The fields of intervention are twofold: 1) it must be decided which language and which communication tools the novice must acquire in order to become part of the research community; 2) detailed research into the relation between language and culture is necessary. Since in the first field a lot of research is already being carried out, we will dwell on the problematic issues of the second, in particular on the relationship between a) national language and underlying national culture, and b) national language and disciplinary culture.

Considering the phenomenon of globalization both issues lend themselves to being investigated within the paradigms of "Linguistic Ecology" and "Language Planning". In a broader perspective of language policy, it is anything but secondary, as already suggested in Section 4.4., to take account also of the economic aspects (in terms of both cause and effect) implied by the selection of which and how many languages are to be used for scientific communication. In light of the social and practical vocation of applied linguistics, it is in fact necessary to pay more attention to the economic problem and to possible solutions aiming at a more equal distribution of costs within the international scientific community. This could be obtained both by paying more attention to what Ammon (2001a: vii–viii) defines as the "non-native speakers' right to linguistic peculiarities" and also, for example, to proposals of a redistribution of publication and translation costs so that these are not a burden only on the individual non-native researchers or their scientific communities. This is why we share de Bot's (2004: 65) enthusiasm in welcoming the emergence of "econolinguistics" as an indispensable field of research for applied linguistics "that is concerned with economic aspects of language and language policy". We agree much less with his opinion, which derives from Grin's assumption (see Grin, this vol.), that "the economic value of English as an additional language is declining because knowledge of English is so widespread that its market value has decreased". This may apply, perhaps, in the case of general or non-specific linguistic knowledge, but it certainly does not apply in the case of writing, especially academic writing, as the widespread "veneration" for the native speaker requires long-term investments. Graddol (1997: 42) claims that writing a book in English requires "advanced 'native-speaker' skills". As a matter of fact, as discussed in Section 4.3., despite loud proclamations of the existence of "New Englishes", even if a non-native speaker's skills were advanced they would not be sufficient because correctness is still judged on the basis of the native speaker's proficiency.

Finally, in our opinion, there is still not sufficient awareness of the problems connected to language, culture and ideology. This is the cognitive challenge linked to globalization whose terms are still to be investigated. Does globalization really bring about the homogenization of cultures? What are the real disadvantages of globalization in relation to expert knowledge and scientific research? If we substitute *global* with *transnational*, how can/must scientific research aspire to being transnational?

In fact, the strong connection between language and culture is often taken for granted. It is presumed that an indissoluble bond exists between every single language and its specific culture. However, according to van Els (2001): a) every linguistic community, far from having a monolithic culture, shows a great wealth of internal variation, b) culturally unmarked language can and does exist. Even if he finds evidence of this in numerous directive-informative texts (e.g. in aeroplanes, at railway stations, etc.) which are often written in English, van Els (2001: 329) seems to conclude that, apart from frequent cases of "pragmatic" texts, it is not possible to overlook the cultural dimension of a language, even when it is a *lingua franca*. Hagège (1992) has a completely different opinion when he states that the historical-natural languages are multidimensional and differentiated in their cultural and cognitive models and, as such, are apt to poliphonically express reality, which is multifaceted *per se*. According to Hagège, attention to heteroglossia is fundamental in constructing a form of reciprocal solidarity whose content goes far beyond propagandist discourses.

One possible way to overcome these two positions might be to use a different starting point, one which tends to differentiate languages according to diverse degrees of cultural specificity, depending on whether they have undergone historical processes of relative isolation or of a greater tendency to contact and innovation. In fact, it is through contact and permanent innovation inherent in language that relevant aspects of culture can be introduced, transferred and adapted to another culture. As noted by Ammon (2003: 203), we must substitute over-generalized and aprioristic evaluations with detailed and empirical analyses to better describe the complex sociolinguistic processes.

Today, generally speaking, language theory recognizes that permanent innovation is vitally important for the functioning of languages. The diversity and the multiplicity of languages does not belong, therefore, to the pathology but to the physiology of language. For this reason, even if we had a language "without space and place", as post-colonial English could be defined according to Brutt-Griffler (2005), the greater convergence of the speakers towards a "language with a federative vocation" (Hagège 1992: 124) does not exclude the learning of other languages.

6. Future perspectives of multilingual scientific communication

Leaving aside the reasons (both legitimate) for and against a *lingua franca* for scientific communication, we still have the problem of the imbalance between the scientific communities of native speakers and non-native speakers of English. These notions should be considered according to their prototypical traits and not as discreet categories. Regarding imbalance there are, in theory, two opposite stands: that of the supporters of *laissez-faire* who consider the free market a mechanism of self-regulation and that of the interventionists who aim at measures of rebalancing the trend in progress (Carli 2006). In the *laissez-faire* ideology, language change and shift are considered "natural phenomena" or "natural processes of inexorable transformation" which, as such, avoid any form of intervention. However, as a matter of fact, these phenomena are not caused by something which is *naturally* inevitable, but by social, economic and political circumstances, all induced by human intervention. So, it is more accurate to say that language change is certainly a natural phenomenon in itself but that each of its manifestations is the product of an artifice.

A reversal of the current trend which favors English as the global language must more realistically be discarded in favor of future rebalancing measures which reduce the current asymmetries between the English-speaking and the non-English speaking communities. So, when planning future language policies, the current common language – namely English – will be incorporated along with some compensatory measures. These have to be studied and formulated on the basis of knowledge ascertained within every linguistic-cultural area and as a function of a global strategy. In order to obtain a common base it is necessary: a) to carry out a systematic recognition of scientific communication in diamesic and diaphasic dimensions (see Section 1) which integrates the current knowledge achieved so far in the almost exclusive sphere of specialized writings; b) to work out proposals of language planning in favour of a real sensitivity to multilingual practices for the entire scientific community which includes, of course, also the English-speaking ones.

In the final section we will briefly address some important issues which still need further investigation. Considering the multidimensional and multifunctional nature of language dynamics (Mackey 2003: 78), we will therefore discard simplified linguistic models which treat the language and its uses as an indissoluble whole.

6.1. Linguistic ideologies and attitudes within the scientific communities

Both the English-speaking and the non-English speaking communities need to be made more aware of the bond between language and social evaluation, with the aim of achieving a different culture of communication which overcomes the current linguistic prejudices. Attitudes towards non-native linguistic varieties give rise to judgements based mainly on restrictive, culturally connotated, models of what is formally correct; this alone often leads to the rejection of the non-native varieties.

6.2. Multilingualism in language comprehension and production

In this type of research the methods, time and quality of language learning according to the multilingual dialogue proposed by Posner (1991; but see also Eco 1993: 376–377) need to be further investigated. The feasibility of this proposal offers the advantage of learning reading and listening skills in languages different from one's own, at least in those which are closest to one's own language in type and/or territory. In this way, native speakers of English would have more chances of filling the gaps in information on the historical developments of their discipline (not easily found in translations into English). The advantage, for everyone, would be the possibility of using their own language for producing their work and of using a wider range of non-dominant languages for comprehending others' work. This proposal has so far been rejected and, spoken polyglottic dialogue in particular, declassified as an "unnatural" communication practice. Notoriously, however, when something has not yet been sufficiently experimented with it is often considered "unnatural".

6.3. Multilingualism and the quality of knowledge

Multilingualism differentiated according to the requirements of research activity seems the most suitable way to increase multilingual communication practices for real needs. This makes it necessary for us to note the current state of communication practices as well as the well-known ones of written communication. Scientific research activities are usually carried out in various phases of communication (invention, definition, revision, discussion, presentation and transmission) both within and without the scientific community in question, and in local, national and international contexts. The task of research in applied linguistics consists therefore in verifying the quality of the knowledge required for such diversified linguistic uses.

Multilingualism, individual or societal, is used to a lesser or larger degree depending on the needs of and the values inscribed in the wider cultural context. The reduction of "natural" multilingualism is often the result of a particular communication culture conditioned by ideologies such as, for example, those of the nation-state (May 2001: 5–7). In this case the "natural" linguistic practices are impeded by communication habits which correspond to the traditional ideology of the nation-state, also called *nationism,* according to which everything must be carried out in one single language.

The knowledge and an awareness of the current situation constitutes the basis for further developments. The first step consists in recognizing that linguistic diversity is as desirable as is cognitive diversity.

Notes

1. The chapter has been conceived by both authors. E.C. has written the first half of Section 1 and the Sections 2, 3.1. and 4; A.C. has written the second half of Section 1, the Sections 3.2.–3.4. and 5 and 6.

References

Altieri Biagi, Maria Luisa
    1990   *L'avventura della mente. Studi sulla lingua scientifica.* Napoli: Morano Editore.

Ammon, Ulrich
    1988   Deutsch als Publikationssprache der Wissenschaft: Zum Umfang seiner Verwendung im Vergleich mit anderen Sprachen. *Germanistische Mitteilungen* 28: 75–86.

Ammon, Ulrich
    1991   *Die internationale Stellung der deutschen Sprache.* Berlin: Mouton de Gruyter.

Ammon, Ulrich
  1998 *Ist Deutsch noch internationale Wissenschaftssprache? Englisch auch für die Lehre an den deutschsprachigen Hochschulen.* Berlin: Mouton de Gruyter.
Ammon, Ulrich
  2000 Entwicklung der deutschen Wissenschaftssprache im 20. Jahrhundert. In: Friedhelm Debus, Franz Gustav Kollmann and Uwe Pörksen (eds.), *Deutsch als Wissenschaftssprache im 20. Jahrhundert. Vorträge des Internationalen Symposions vom 18./19. Januar 2000*, 59–80. Stuttgart: Franz Steiner Verlag.
Ammon, Ulrich (ed.)
  2001a *The Dominance of English as a Language of Science. Effects on Other Languages and Language Communities.* Berlin: Mouton de Gruyter.
Ammon, Ulrich
  2001b English as a future language of teaching at German universities? A question of difficult consequences, posed by the decline of German as a language of science. In: Ulrich Ammon (ed.), *The Dominance of English as a Language of Science. Effects on Other Languages and Language Communities*, 343–361. Berlin: Mouton de Gruyter.
Ammon, Ulrich and Grant McConnell
  2002 *English as an Academic Language in Europe.* Frankfurt am Main: Peter Lang.
Atkinson, Dwight
  1999a *Scientific Discourse in Sociohistorical Context: The Philosophical Transactions of the Royal Society of London, 1675–1975.* Mahwah, NJ: Lawrence Erlbaum.
Atkinson, Dwight
  1999b Language and science. *Annual Review of Applied Linguistics* 19: 193–214.
Baldauf, Richard B. and Björn H. Jernudd
  1983 Language of publications as a variable in scientific communication. *Australian Review of Applied Linguistics* 6: 97–108.
Bazerman, Charles
  1988 *Shaping Written Knowledge. The Genre and Activity of the Experimental Article in Science.* Madison: University of Wisconsin Press.
Brutt-Griffler, Janina
  2002 *World English. A Study of its Development.* Clevedon: Multilingual Matters.
Brutt-Griffler, Janina
  2005 "Globalisation" and Applied Linguistics: Post-imperial questions of identity and the construction of applied linguistics discourse. *International Journal of Applied Linguistics* 15: 113–115.
Calaresu, Emilia
  2006 (forthcoming) L'universalità del linguaggio scientifico fra norma d'uso e sistema linguistico. Plurilinguismo e monolinguismo nella comunicazione scientifica. Paper presented at the meeting of the Vigoniprojekt "Wissenschaftliche Kommunikation in Italien und Deutschland: Sprache, Text, Diskurs", Universität Hannover / Università di Modena, 9–10 dicembre 2004. In: Emilia Calaresu, Cristina Guardiano and Klaus Hölker (eds), *Italienisch und Deutsch als Wissenschaftssprachen. Bestandsaufnahmen, Analysen, Perspektiven.* Münster: Lit Verlag.

Carli, Augusto
 2006 La questione linguistica nella comunicazione scientifica oggi in Italia e in
 (forth- Germania. Paper presented at the meeting of the Vigoniprojekt "Wissen-
 coming) schaftliche Kommunikation in Italien und Deutschland: Sprache, Text, Diskurs", Universität Hannover / Università di Modena, 9–10 dicembre 2004. In: Emilia Calaresu, Cristina Guardiano and Klaus Hölker (eds.), *Italienisch und Deutsch als Wissenschaftssprachen. Bestandsaufnahmen, Analysen, Perspektiven*. Münster: Lit Verlag.
Carli, Augusto and Emilia Calaresu
 2003 Le lingue della comunicazione scientifica. La produzione e la diffusione del sapere specialistico in Italia. In: Ada Valentini, Piera Molinelli, Pierluigi Cuzzolin and Giuliano Bernini (eds.), *Ecologia linguistica. Atti del XXXVI Congresso Internazionale di Studi della Società di Linguistica Italiana (SLI 47)*, 27–74. Roma: Bulzoni.
Chartier, Roger and Pietro Corsi (eds.)
 1996 *Sciences et langues en Europe*. Paris: Centre Alexandre Koyré.
Cloître, Michel and Terry Shinn
 1985 Expository practice: Social, cognitive and epistemological linkage. In: Terry Shinn and Richard Whitley (eds.), *Expository Science*, 31–60. Dordrecht: Reidel.
Coates, Robbie, Blanche Sturgeon, John Bohannan and Evasio Pasini
 2002 Language and publication in "Cardiovascular Research" articles. *Cardiovascular Research* 53(2): 279–285.
Conseil de la langue française
 1996 *Le français et les langues scientifiques de demain*. Actes du colloque tenu à l'Université du Québec à Montréal du 19 au 21 mars 1996. Service de communications du Conseil de la langue française, Québec: Gouvernement du Québec in http://www.cslf.gouv.qc.ca/publications/PubK105
Crawford, Elisabeth, Terry Shinn and Sörlin Sverker
 1992 An introductory essay. In: Crawford, Elisabeth, Terry Shinn and Sörlin Sverker (eds.), *Denationalizing Science. The Contexts of International Scientific Practice*, 1–42. Dordrecht: Kluwer Academic Publishers.
Crystal, David
 1988 *The English Language*. London: Penguin Books.
Crystal, David
 2003 *English as a Global Language*. 2nd ed. Cambridge: Cambridge University Press.
Dahl, Trine
 2004 Textual metadiscourse in research articles: A marker of national culture or of academic discourse? *Journal of Pragmatics* 36: 1807–1825.
de Bot, Kees
 2004 Applied linguistics in Europe. *AILA Review* 17: 57–68.
de Swaan, Abraham
 2001a *Words of the World. The Global Language System*. Cambridge: Polity Press.
de Swaan, Abraham
 2001b English in the social sciences. In: Ulrich Ammon (ed.), The Dominance of English as a Language of Science. Effects on Other Languages and Language Communities, 71–84. Berlin: Mouton de Gruyter.

Eco, Umberto
    1993   *La ricerca della lingua perfetta.* Roma/Bari: Laterza.
Flowerdew, John
    1999   Writing for scholarly publication in English: The case of Hong Kong. *Journal of Second Language Writing* 8: 123–145.
Fløttum, Kjersti
    2003   Personal English, indefinite French and plural Norwegian scientific authors? Pronominal author manifestation in research articles: A cross-linguistic disciplinary study. *Norsk Lingvistik Tidsskrift* 211: 21–55.
Gimeno Menéndez, Francisco and María Victoria Gimeno Menéndez
    2003   *El desplazamiento lingüístico del español por el inglés.* Madrid: Cátedra.
Grabe, William and Robert B. Kaplan
    1992   Introduction. In: William Grabe and Robert B. Kaplan (eds.), *Introduction to Applied Linguistics*, 1–9. Reading, MA: Addison-Wesley Publishing Company.
Graddol, David
    1997   *The Future of English.* London: The British Council.
Gross, Alan G., Joseph E. Harmon and Michael Reidy
    2002   *Communicating Science. The Scientific Article from the 17th Century to the Present.* Oxford: Oxford University Press.
Gunnarsson, Britt-Louise
    2001   Swedish, English, French or German – The language situation at Swedish universities. In: Ulrich Ammon (ed.), *The Dominance of English as a Language of Science. Effects on Other Languages and Language Communities*, 287–316. Berlin: Mouton de Gruyter.
Gutiérrez Rodilla, Bertha M.
    1998   *La ciencia empieza en la palabra. Análisis e historia del lenguaje científico.* Barcelona: Península.
Halliday, Michael A. K.
    2004   *The Language of Science.* London: Continuum.
Haarmann, Harald and Eugene Holman
    2001   The impact of English as a language of science in Finland and its role for the transition to network society. In: Ulrich Ammon (ed.), *The Dominance of English as a Language of Science. Effects on Other Languages and Language Communities*, 229–260. Berlin: Mouton de Gruyter.
Hagège, Claude
    1992   *Le souffle de la langue. Voies et destins des parlers d'Europe.* 2nd ed. Paris: Jacob.
Hauge, Hans
    1996   Nationalizing science. In: Roger Chartier and Pietro Corsi (eds), *Sciences et langues en Europe*, 159–168. Paris: Centre Alexandre Koyré.
Hyland, Ken
    1997   Scientific claims and community values: Articulating an academic culture. *Language & Communication* 171: 19–31.
Hyland, Ken
    2000   *Disciplinary Discourses: Social Interaction in Academic Writing.* London: Longman.

Hyland, Ken
    2004   *Genre and Second Language Writing*. Ann Arbor: The University of Michigan Press.
Kaplan, Robert
    2001   English – the accidental language of science. In: Ulrich Ammon (ed.), *The Dominance of English as a Language of Science. Effects on Other Languages and Language Communities*, 3–26. Berlin: Mouton de Gruyter.
Laponce, Jean
    2001   Politics and the law of Babel. *Social Science Information* 2: 179–194.
Laponce, Jean
    2003   Babel and the market: Geostrategies for minority languages. In: Jacques Maurais and Michael A. Morris (eds), *Languages in a Globalising World*, 47–63. Cambridge: Cambridge University Press.
Lévy-Leblond, Jean-Marc
    1996   La langue tire la science. In: Roger Chartier and Pietro Corsi (eds), *Sciences et langues en Europe*, 235–245. Paris: Centre Alexandre Koyré.
Locquin, Marcel V.
    1989   *Situation de la langue française dans les périodiques scientifiques et techniques en 1988*. Paris: Commissariat général de la langue française.
Mackey, William F.
    2003   Forecasting the fate of languages. In: Jacques Maurais and Michael A. Morris (eds), *Languages in a Globalising World*, 64–81. Cambridge: Cambridge University Press.
Maurais, Jacques and Michael A. Morris (eds)
    2003   *Languages in a Globalising World*. Cambridge: Cambridge University Press.
May, Stephen
    2001   *Language and Minority Rights. Ethnicity, Nationalism and the Politics of Language*. London: Longman.
Melander, Björn, John Swales and Kirstin Fredrickson
    1997   Journal abstracts from three academic fields in the United States and Sweden: National or disciplinary proclivities? In: Anna Duszak (ed.), *Culture and Styles of Academic Discourse*, 251–272. Berlin: Mouton de Gruyter.
Merton, Robert K.
    1996   *On Social Structure and Science*. Chicago: University of Chicago Press.
Moles, Abraham A.
    1979   A French point of view on the predominance of English. *International Journal of the Sociology of Language* 22: 51–56.
New Oxford Dictionary of English
    1998   Oxford: Clarendon Press.
Pennycock, Alastair
    1994   *The Cultural Politics of English as an International Language*. London: Longman.
Posner, Roland
    1991   Der polyglotte Dialog. Ein Humanistengespräch über mehrsprachige Kommunikation im mehrsprachigen Europa. *Sprachreport* 3: 6–10.
Rossi, Paolo
    1997   *La nascita della scienza moderna in Europa*. Roma: Laterza.

Sano, Hiro
    2002   The world's lingua franca of science. *English Today* 18: 45–49.
Skudlik, Sabine
    1990   *Sprachen in den Wissenschaften. Deutsch und Englisch in der internationalen Kommunikation.* Tübingen: Narr.
Swales, John
    1990   *Genre Analysis. English in Academic and Research Settings.* Cambridge: Cambridge University Press.
Thogmartin, Chris
    1980   Which language for students in social sciences? A survey to help academic advisors. *Anthropological Newsletter* 21: 6.
Truchot, Claude
    1996   La langue française en sciences. Un cas de figure: La situation linguistique des sciences en France. In: Conseil de la langue française, *Le français et les langues scientifiques de demain*, 159–168. Québec: Gouvernement du Québec.
Truchot, Claude
    1997   The spread of English: From France to a more general perspective. In: Marc Deneire and Michael Goethals (eds.), *Special Issue on English in Europe, World Englishes* 16, 65–76. Oxford: Blackwell.
Truchot, Claude
    2001   The languages of sciences in France: Public debate and language policies. In: Ulrich Ammon (ed.), *The Dominance of English as a Language of Science. Effects on Other Languages and Language Communities*, 319–328. Berlin: Mouton de Gruyter.
Tsunoda, Minoru
    1983   Les langues internationales dans les publications scientifiques et techniques. *Sophia Linguistica* 13: 70–79.
Ulrych, Margherita
    1991   L'inglese medico scientifico scritto. In: Piero Zannini, Rocco Antonio Maruotti and Margherita Ulrych (eds.), *L'articolo medico scientifico in inglese. Come pubblicare su una rivista internazionale*, 75–223. Torino: UTET.
Valiela, Ivan
    2001   *Doing Science. Design, Analysis and Communication of Scientific Research.* Oxford: Oxford University Press.
Van Els, Theo
    2002   The European Union, its institutions and its languages. Some language political observations. *Current Issues in Language Planning* 2: 311–360.
Walter, Henriette
    1996   L'évolution des langues de la communication scientifique. In: Conseil de la langue française, *Le français et les langues scientifiques de demain*, 27–39. Québec: Gouvernement du Québec.
Ziman, John
    2000   *Real Science. What it Is, and What it Means.* Cambridge: Cambridge University Press.

18. Multilingualism on the Internet

Brenda Danet and Susan C. Herring

1. Introduction[1]

In recent years, the Internet has become a truly global communication network. According to a recent compilation (Almanac 2005), about one billion people, one-sixth of the world's population, are now online. Not all nations are equally represented: Notably absent are the countries on the African continent, and 15 countries account for about 70% of the total (Table 1). The United States has the largest single proportion online of any country, or 20% of the total. This reflects not only its relatively large population size and advanced technological infrastructure, but also the fact that the technology that makes the Internet possible was created in the 1960s in the United States (O'Neill 1995; Hafner and Lyon 1996; Cringely 1998).

Table 1. Top 15 countries on the Internet, 2004. Source: Computer Industry Almanac, September, 2004; URL http://www.c-i-a.com/pr0904.htm, retrieved August 12, 2005. Reproduced with permission.

Top 15 countries in internet usage		
Year-end 2004	Internet users (#K)	Share %
1. U.S.	185,550	19.86
2. China	99,800	10.68
3. Japan	78,050	8.35
4. Germany	41,880	4.48
5. India	36,970	3.96
6. UK	33,110	3.54
7. South Korea	31,670	3.39
8. Italy	25,530	2.73
9. France	25,470	2.73
10. Brazil	22,320	2.39
11. Russia	21,230	2.27
12. Canada	20,450	2.19
13. Mexico	13,880	1.49
14. Spain	13,440	1.44
15. Australia	13,010	1.39
Top 15 Countries	662,360	70.88
Worldwide Total	934,480	100

In the last decade, many people have expressed concern about the global dominance of English, and about the Internet as a new arena for its spread (Nunberg 2000; Pimienta 2002; Tsuda 2000; Mair 2002; Dor 2004). A 2002 survey found that over 56% of all Web pages were in English.[2] The English language is especially prominent in the commercial sphere: The Organization for Economic Co-operation and Development (OECD) reported that in July 2000 more than 94% of links to pages on secure servers were in English. "The only other languages to account for more than 1% of detected links to secure servers were German [...] and French [...], although Spanish and Japanese came close" (Organization for Economic and Social Development 2001). Some view the spread of English as a "natural", largely benign or even beneficial extension of globalization generally (Fishman 1998; Fishman, Conrad, and Rubal-Lopez 1996; Crystal 2001, 2003). Other authors take a dimmer view, writing of "linguistic imperialism" (Phillipson 1992, 2000; Phillipson and Skutnabb-Kangas 2001; see also Kirkpatrick, this vol.). Figure 1 contrasts the two views:

	Exploitation model	Grassroots model
political value of English	imperialist language	post-imperial language
chief cause for post World War II spread	organized/centralized language planning following Anglo-American master plan	demand-driven; decentralized rational choices by individuals and groups
English is the language of ...	Anglo-American capitalist interests	modernization and globalization
English is ...	a language that conveys an Anglo-Saxon/Western world view	an ideologically neutral lingua franca
English ...	transforms recipient societies (usually for the worse)	is transformed by recipient societies (rise of New Englishes)
chief beneficiary of "global English"	British and American capitalist interests	usually some segment of local users

Figure 1. Two models of the influence of English. Source: Mair 2002: 165. Reproduced with permission.

Although intended generally, these two models are arguably relevant to the current debate about English on the Internet.

Alongside concern about the dominance of English, there is evidence that the number of non-English speakers on the Internet is growing rapidly. Already by 2003, roughly two-thirds of all Internet users were not native speakers of

English (CyberAtlas 2003). In another estimate, about 800 million non-English speakers were online by 2005.[3] In only four of the 15 top countries online in 2004 (the US, the UK, Canada, Australia) was English the official or dominant language of users (Table 1). China and Japan together accounted for nearly another fifth of the total. Moreover, growth in the next few years is predicted to accelerate, especially in China and India.[4]

The growth of various language groups online reflects not only developments in technology and infrastructure, but demographic trends. Already in 1995, Chinese was spoken natively by over one billion people, far more than any other language; English was in second place, with under 400 million native speakers. Moreover, extrapolating from UN-based statistics, David Graddol predicts that the proportion of the global population speaking English natively will decline from nearly 9% in the mid-20th century to about 5% by 2050 (Graddol 1997/2000, 1999, 2004). In keeping with these developments, hundreds of millions of people are already participating online today in languages other than English, in some form of non-native English, or in a mixture of languages.

Academic research published in English on the language of computer-mediated communication (CMC) has only recently begun to take account of this complex empirical reality. Most researchers publishing in English venues have generalized about the language of computer-mediated *communication*, when in fact they were describing computer-mediated *English* (e.g., Ferrara, Whittemore, and Brunner 1991).[5] Some exceptions are publications by Naomi Baron (2000) and David Crystal (2001, 2004a), which contextualize English-based CMC within the history of the English language.

In recent years this situation has started to change. Increasingly, researchers have turned their attention to other languages used on the Internet, often – although not always – their native languages. In this chapter we survey this growing literature, treating multilingualism both macro-sociolinguistically and micro-sociolinguistically. We focus on issues of linguistic diversity and the fate of specific languages on the Internet at the macro level and on micro-level patterns of language use by individuals communicating via instant messaging, email, and chat.

Some of the research discussed here was published in a special issue of the *Journal of Computer-Mediated Communication* that we edited in October 2003 on the topic of "The Multilingual Internet: Language, Culture and Communication in Instant Messaging, Email and Chat" (Danet and Herring 2003a). Other articles cited appear in an expanded book on the same theme (Danet and Herring 2007).[6] The remainder of the studies were published in diverse venues, many of which are considered together for the first time here.[7] We discuss this emergent literature under five recurrent themes: writing systems, linguistic features of CMC, gender and culture, language choice, and language revitalization efforts.

2. Writing systems and online communication

2.1. ASCII encoding and its unintended consequences

Because early planners of the Internet were generally North American, and only had in mind how to facilitate communication in English, they did not anticipate problems that might arise when speakers of other languages tried to communicate online. The text-transmission protocol on the Internet is based on the ASCII character set (Figure 2). ASCII (pronounced AS-kee) is an acronym for "American Standard Code for Information Interchange". Established in the 1960s, it contains 128 seven-bit codes (unique combinations of 1's and 0's), 95 of which are available for use as graphical characters. This character set is based on the roman alphabet and the sounds of the English language. "Plain text", as in email and chat, usually refers to a format containing only basic ASCII characters, whether written in English or some other language.

```
  ! " # $ % & ' ( ) * + , - . /
0 1 2 3 4 5 6 7 8 9 : ; < = > ?
@ A B C D E F G H I J K L M N O
P Q R S T U V W X Y Z [ \ ] ^ _
` a b c d e f g h i j k l m n o
p q r s t u v w x y z { | } ~
```

Figure 2. The ASCII character set. Source: http://www.cs.tut.fi/~jkorpela/chars.html; retrieved August 15, 2005.

There can be little doubt that the ASCII character set has privileged English on the Internet. Whether it concerns HTML (the markup language for Web pages), domain names on the Web (URLs), email addresses, or the content of instant messages, email, discussion list postings, or chat, speakers of languages other than English have faced varying degrees of difficulty.[8] Speakers of languages using the Latin or roman alphabet but with only a few characters missing, such as Maltese[9] or the Scandinavian languages, suffer the least disadvantage, though one that may produce embarrassing results. For example, ASCII does not include the last three letters of the Swedish alphabet, å, ä, and ö. In the past,

> Instead of using å, ä, and ö, [Swedes] managed with substitutions such as }, { and |, or *aa*, *ae* and *oe* in electronic communication. Or just "a" for å and ä, as well as for the letter *a*, and "*o*" both for *o* and ö.
> (Pargman 1998: 87)

The URL of a Swedish town called Hörby is http://www.horby.se. Swedes must live with the fact that without the two dots over the "o", the name of this town means "fornication village".[10] Fortunately, today, email sent within Sweden can use the full Swedish alphabet (Pargman 1998: 87).[11] Another language similarly challenged is Hawaiian, which is written in roman characters, but with additional use of macrons.[12] Warschauer and Donaghy (1997: 353) note that "Incorporation of diacritical marks is crucial, since they define meaning in Hawaiian; for example, *pau* means finished, *payu* means soot, pa*ÿu* means moist, and pä*ÿu* means skirt."

Speakers of languages with non-Latin writing systems, such as Greek, Russian, Arabic and Hebrew, and the East Asian languages (Chinese, Korean, Japanese) are more disadvantaged, being dependent on the development of special character sets to make word-processing and online communication possible.[13] While great progress has been made in these areas, truly multilingual global communication on the Internet is still plagued by many technical problems. As recently as the late 1990s, it was possible to claim that "English remains the only language that can be used without distortion on virtually every computer in the world" (Fishman 1998: 34).[14] Even in 2005, although speakers/writers of many languages could configure their computers to accommodate their own multiple or non-English language needs, they could not assume that others would be able to receive and read messages and longer texts including characters other than basic ASCII.

2.2.   Modes of adaptation to the ASCII environment

Problems engendered by the dominance of the ASCII character set online, such as those just discussed, may lead some to speak of "typographic imperialism", as an extension of linguistic imperialism into the domain of the Internet (cf. Pargman and Palme 2004). In this section we ask: How have people communicating online in languages with different sounds and different writing systems adapted to the constraints of ASCII environments? What problems have they encountered, and what are the social, political, and economic consequences if they have or have not adapted? What progress has been made in solving these problems, and what remains to be done?

English-based research reveals that synchronous chat and even email and discussion list postings tend to have partially speech-like features (Yates 1996; Herring 1996b, 2001; Baron 2000; Crystal 2001; Danet 2001: chap. 2). What happens when people using formerly spoken-only varieties of languages participate in typed chat online? This question is especially pertinent with regard to Arab countries, which are characterized by *diglossia* (Ferguson 1972; Hudson 2001): High-prestige, written, literary, classical Arabic co-exists with a low-prestige, local spoken variety that is ordinarily not written – at least not until the advent of the Internet.

In a study of instant messaging among young female Gulf Arabic speakers in Dubai, David Palfreyman and Muhamed Al Khalil (2003, 2007) found a mixture of Arabic script, English and romanized Arabic – spoken Arabic written out in the roman alphabet (Figure 3). Whereas speaker D in Fig. 3 has typed her contributions in right-to-left Arabic script, speaker F "script-switches", writing in Arabic rendered left-to-right in the roman alphabet. Online romanization has also been documented for email in colloquial Egyptian Arabic (Warschauer, El Said, and Zohry 2002, 2007), and for chat on IRC in colloquial Moroccan Arabic (Berjaoui 2001). Palestinians write online messages using either roman or Hebrew letters, rather than Arabic ones (Myhill and Garra 2005).

D: وبركاته الله ورحمة عليكم السلام	D: Hello there.
D: شحالچ؟ حمده،،، مرحبا	D: Hi Hamda, how are you doing?
F: w 3laikom essalaaam asoomah ^__^	F: Hi there Asooma ^__^
F: b'7air allah eysallemch .. sh7aalech enty??	F: Fine, God bless you. How about you?
[pause]	[pause]
	D: Fine, great thanks.
D: el7emdellah b'7eer w ne3meh	
D: sorry kent adawwer scripts 7ag project eljava script w rasi dayer fee elcodes	D: Sorry, I was looking for scripts for the java script project and my head is swarming with code.
F: lol	F: lol

Figure 3. Opening of an IM (instant messaging) exchange in Dubai. Source: Palfreyman and Al Khalil 2003.

Palfreyman and Al Khalil also report use of numerals to represent sounds of Arabic that cannot otherwise be represented in the roman alphabet (third, fourth, fifth, and sixth contributions in Figure 3). These numerals are codified representations of sounds; for instance, the numeral 7 is used to represent /x/, as in <wa7ed> 'one'. The same phenomenon has been documented for colloquial Egyptian Arabic (Warschauer, El Said, and Zohry 2002, 2007) and colloquial Palestinian Arabic (Myhill and Garra 2005). A few Moroccan examples are discernible in IRC transcripts collected by Berjaoui (2001).[15]

Romanization is well documented for Greeklish – Greek written in roman letters in online communication. In the Greek case, Theodora Tseliga (2007) found evidence of substituting a roman letter for a missing Greek one that resembles it in *graphic shape*. For instance, a person wishing to write the Greek name for the city of Athens in a romanized context has two options:

(1)

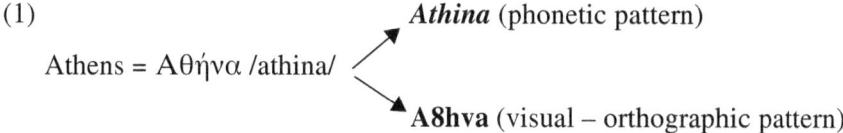

Athens = Αθήνα /athina/

Athina (phonetic pattern)

A8hva (visual – orthographic pattern)

The second choice substitutes the numeral *8* for θ because the two are similar graphically (Tseliga 2007). Publications by Alexandra Georgakopoulou (1997 2004) and Jannis Androutsopoulos (1999a, 1999b, 2004) on aspects of email and chat in Greeklish also provide many examples of romanized Greek.[16] Androutsopoulos (1999a, 1999b, 2000) reports considerable inconsistency in Greeklish email because transliteration norms have not yet emerged. A study of code-switching on IRC by Androutsopoulos and Hinnenkamp (2001) contains material on romanized Greek alternating with German in the IRC channel *#hellas*, and alternation between German and the less typographically-challenged Turkish in *#turks*. The researchers also found instances of orthographic switching, i.e., portions of German written according to Turkish spelling rules. Androutsopoulos (2007) also documents romanized Persian, called "Fenglish", as well as Greeklish on German-based diasporic web forums.

There is little evidence (thus far, at least) that use of romanized Arabic is considered particularly controversial by Arabic speakers. Quite the opposite is the case for Greeklish, the use of which is hotly contested. Dimitris Koutsogiannis and Bessie Mitsikopoulou (2003, 2007) investigated attitudes towards Greeklish in the Greek press. Three main trends were identified: a retrospective trend that views Greeklish as a serious threat to the Greek language; a prospective trend arguing that Greeklish is a transitory phenomenon that will disappear as technology advances; and a resistive trend pointing to the negative effects of globalization.

2.3. Beyond ad hoc improvisation: The search for solutions

Over time, developers created partial solutions to the limitations imposed by the ASCII character set, expanding character sets to employ eight-bit profiles that facilitated use of specific languages and/or groups of languages online. For instance, the eight-bit character set known technically as ISO Latin 1 (alias ISO 8859–1), and more informally as the extended ASCII character set, added enough characters, including letters with diacritics, to accommodate the needs of many European languages, including Swedish (Figure 4).[17]

	¡	¢	£	¤	¥	¦	§	¨	©	ª	«	¬		®	¯
°	±	²	³	´	µ	¶	·	¸	¹	º	»	¼	½	¾	¿
À	Á	Â	Ã	Ä	Å	Æ	Ç	È	É	Ê	Ë	Ì	Í	Î	Ï
Ð	Ñ	Ò	Ó	Ô	Õ	Ö	×	Ø	Ù	Ú	Û	Ü	Ý	Þ	ß
à	á	â	ã	ä	å	æ	ç	è	é	ê	ë	ì	í	î	ï
ð	ñ	ò	ó	ô	õ	ö	÷	ø	ù	ú	û	ü	ý	þ	ÿ

Figure 4. The ISO Latin 1 character set (alias ISO 8859–1). Source: http://www.cs.tut.fi/~jkorpela/chars.html#latin1, retrieved August 15, 2005.

Viewed globally, however, these solutions were unsatisfactory. Eventually, in a major step forward, the Unicode Standard was established (Everson 2002; Consortium 2003; Anderson 2004; Paolillo 2007).[18] Unicode is

> […] the universal character encoding, maintained by the Unicode Consortium (http://www.unicode.org/). This encoding standard provides the basis for processing, storage and interchange of text data in any language in all modern software and information technology protocols.[19]

The vision behind Unicode is of one encoding for all the scripts in the world (Everson 2002). Whereas the original ASCII character set employs only seven bits per character, in Unicode, each character has a unique 16-bit profile.[20] Developments in the creation of Unicode are now greatly expanding the possibilities for multilingual word processing and communication online, in a broad range of languages and language families, making improvisational forms of adaptation less necessary.

Expansion of digital encoding possibilities is aimed both at archaic languages and at living ones, although living languages are of primary interest here. The Script Encoding Initiative, based at the University of California, Berkeley, funds proposals for scripts currently missing in Unicode.[21] The word *script* in the name of the organization reveals that only languages for which a script *already exists* can be candidates for digitization. In its latest version (4.1.0), Unicode can accommodate a million characters; thus far, over 97,000 characters have been encoded.[22] As of early 2005, Unicode accommodated over 50 scripts, just five of which now accommodate hundreds of the world's languages (see the Appendix). The Latin or roman alphabet, in particular, is used for many languages, sometimes with the addition of diacritics.

Although limitations imposed by the ASCII character set are slowly disappearing, there is a long way to go. More than 80 scripts remain uncoded in Unicode (Anderson 2005: 27). Fishman (1998: 32) estimates that only a small minority of the roughly 1,200 standard languages in the world, i.e. languages that have codified grammars and writing systems, are currently usable online.

3. Features of CMC in languages other than English

Studies of English CMC have often noted its special linguistic and typographic features. The best-known of these are the emoticon or "smiley face", along with abbreviations such as *LOL* ("laughing out loud"), *brb* ("be right back"), and rebus writing (e.g., *c u* for "see you"; Danet 2001; Herring 2001), and a tendency towards "speech-like" informality (Werry 1996). Crystal (2001) uses the term "netspeak" to describe what he considers to be a new, technologically-determined variety of English. Here we are interested in the effects of offline usage and culture on the features of CMC in languages other than English.

We illustrate these effects with reference to Japanese, an interesting case because it is a language with an unusually complex writing system. As Yukiko Nishimura (2003) explains, four scripts are used in standard Japanese orthography: 1) *kanji,* ideograms of Chinese origin; 2) *hiragana* and 3) *katakana,* systems for representing syllables; and 4) *romaji,* use of the roman alphabet to transliterate Japanese words and to represent originally foreign terms, such as *CD*, in otherwise Japanese contexts. Hiragana is used for grammatical endings, and to represent Japanese concepts and objects for which *kanji* do not exist, whereas katakana is used for foreign names and the representation of natural sounds, for instance ワンワン *wan wan,* the Japanese equivalent of "bow wow" for a dog barking.

3.1. Linguistic and interactional features of postings on electronic bulletin boards

In a study of electronic bulletin boards (conventionally abbreviated as BBSs), in this case for fans of popular culture idols, Nishimura (2003, 2007) compared linguistic and interactional aspects of Japanese postings with similar studies of English-language CMC. Her analysis revealed many similarities to English, but also distinctive differences. Among the similarities was evidence for multiple punctuation, eccentric spelling, use of all capital letters, written-out laughter, verbal descriptions of actions, and *kaomoji* ('face marks'), vertical analogs of Western-style "smiley" emoticons (e.g., **:-)** for a smile; **:-(** for a frown). The following is an example of a kaomoji from Nishimura's data:

(2) 復活おめでと～♪良かったね (*＾▽＾*)
   hukkatu omedeto '♪yokatta ne (*＾▽＾*)
   'Congratulations on your comeback♪[as if singing]That was good (*＾▽＾*)'

Nishimura glosses, "This face mark represents the mouth wide open, laughing loudly and cheerfully, with asterisks used to indicate (rosy) cheeks". Another Japanese-specific feature is the use of graphics such as musical notes to indicate mood, as in this example. Nishimura also found that users employed final particles, a feature usually associated with informal speech (e.g., the tag-question marker *ne*), interacting with other users online as if they were in face-to-face conversation.

3.2. Typography and playful performance

A tendency toward playful performance in online communication has often been documented for CMC in English (Danet 1995, 2001; Werry 1996; Danet, Ruedenberg, and Rosenbaum-Tamari 1998). Widespread play has been observed not only with identity (e.g., Bechar-Israeli 1995; Turkle 1995; Danet 1998), but with language and typography themselves. For example, elaborate play with the visual shape of typographic symbols to simulate smoking marijuana was documented in 1991 in an English-language IRC (Internet Relay Chat) channel; a portion is shown below:

(3) <Thunder>:| :| :\sssss :)
         (inhales twice, exhales, smoke dissipates, smiles)
    <Kang>   hheeeheee
    <Thunder>:-Q :| :| :\sssss :)
         (puts marihuana reefer in mouth, inhales twice, exhales, smoke dissipates, smiles)
    <Thunder>heheheh
    (Danet 2001: 106, gloss added)

Two participants, nicknamed <Thunder> and <Kang>, adapt "smiley" icons and other typographic symbols in real time to represent the cigarette and the process of smoking. In the third line, <Thunder> simulates the entire process, from taking the cigarette into his mouth (the letter "Q"), inhaling, exhaling, with multiple "s"s to simulate the sound and graphic shape of the smoke, to the final smile of pleasure.

Recent research by anthropologists Hirofumi Katsuno and Christine Yano suggests that playful performance via typography is even more elaborate in online Japanese than in English (Katsuno and Yano 2002, 2007). The deployment of kaomoji – 'face marks' – online has important connections with Japanese popular culture, including *manga* (comics; Schodt 1986; Kinsella 2000), a cult of cuteness (Kinsella 1995; McVeigh 2000; Hiorth 2003; Richie 2003; Allison 2004), and a tradition of feminized handwriting (Kataoka 1997, 2003a, 2003b). Whereas earlier kaomoji are typographically compact like Western "smileys" (albeit vertical, rather than horizontal, in orientation), Katsuno and Yano show that Japanese housewives have developed a repertoire of feminized, wider, "cuter" ones (Figure 5).

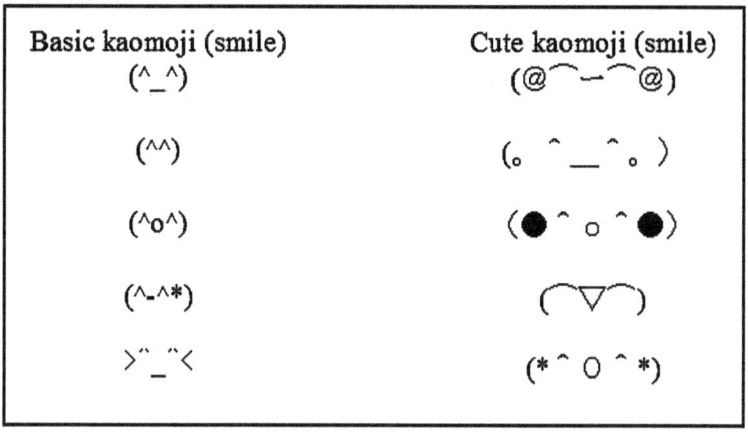

Basic kaomoji (smile)	Cute kaomoji (smile)
(^_^)	(@ ̂‿ ̂@)
(^^)	(₀ ˆ_ˆ ₀)
(^o^)	(● ˆ o ˆ ●)
(^-^*)	(̄▽ ̄)
>¨_¨<	(*ˆ O ˆ*)

Figure 5. Basic and cute *kaomoji* (face marks). Source: Katsuno and Yano 2007.

The history and use of kaomoji in Japanese and of smileys in English CMC differ. Western-style "smileys" were originally a male phenomenon, created and circulated in the early 1980s by Scott Fahlman and others in the computer science community at Carnegie Mellon University (Fahlman n.d.). By the 1990s, however, more and more females became involved with computers. In the West today, the use of "smileys" is primarily associated with females and young people (Witmer and Katzman 1997). Moreover, they are often considered a tell-tale sign that one is a newcomer or "newbie", and are discouraged in serious online communication. In contrast, even Japanese seniors use kaomoji online (Kanayama 2003). Sugimoto and Levin (2000: 145) found that Japanese-style emoticons were more than four times more common in four Japanese newsgroups than were Western-style "smileys" in four American ones. This form of typographic expressivity is a distinctive form of emergent online culture in Japanese.

4. Gender, language, and culture online

Gender differentiation is an important aspect of culture that is often reflected in language use. English-language CMC research has shown that men and women use different discourse styles online much as they do offline (Herring 1996a, 1996b, 2003; cf. Lakoff 1975, 2004; Tannen 1990). We know of no studies yet to identify systematic "women's language" and "men's language" features in CMC in other languages. However, a growing number of case studies have examined issues associated with gender and Internet use in non-English contexts.

4.1. Politeness

One area of research involves interaction dynamics. Sandi de Oliveira (2003, 2007) analyzed politeness violations on the computer users' discussion list of a university in Portugal. Only Portuguese was used, and the grammar and spelling of the language were standard. However, the messages posted sometimes failed to observe the requirement – of utmost importance in Portuguese culture – to use the appropriate term of address. Thus, for example, a participant entitled by rank to be addressed as *"Professor Doutor"* [+ first name + last name] should not be addressed as *"Senhor"* (Mr.) [+ first name + last name]. Although women participated less often in discussions on the list, messages posted by women were more often treated as transgressions. Oliveira observes that men were quick to chastise transgressions, in contrast to English-based claims that men are less concerned than women with maintaining politeness norms (cf. Herring 1996b). At the same time, the behavior of the Portuguese men on the list asserted their traditional gender roles as interactionally dominant and representative of "authority".

In a study of gender and politeness in email in India, Asha Kaul and Vaibhavi Kulkarni (2005) analyzed 494 work- and task-related emails. Although all the messages were in English, reflecting the widespread use of English as a lingua franca and language of white-collar professionals in India, all were written by employees in Indian workplaces, and reflect the Indian cultural context. Kaul and Kulkarni found that women were more polite than men, as in previous studies of gender and politeness in English CMC. At the same time, the men in the Indian sample used flattery more than women, communicating praise and approval of the recipient's actions – a behavior more commonly associated with women in English CMC (Herring 1996b). Kaul and Kulkarni (2005) suggest that "this could be attributed to the cultural backdrop in which the emails were written where men take on the patronizing role and compliment frequently to motivate the team players/members". Also typical of Indian culture, women's emails were more likely to inquire about the well-being of the recipient and the recipient's family members before moving on to work-related topics.

4.2. Turn-taking

Focusing on the mechanics and power dynamics of interaction, Siriporn Panyametheekul and Susan Herring (2003, 2007) analyzed gender in relation to turn-allocation patterns in a popular Web-based Thai chat room. They found that females made greater use of turn-allocation strategies like those found in face-to-face conversation, and enjoyed greater interactional power in the chat room, chatting with whom they chose and receiving more responses to their messages, than did males. The authors also analyzed flirtatious initiations, finding them to be infrequent and generally lacking in sexually explicit content. They interpreted their findings in relation to the gender demographics of the chat room, the norms of the Web site, and Thai cultural values of politeness and respect – all of which favor female participation.

These three studies demonstrate that gender interacts with culture online in ways that shape language and communication. It has also been suggested that the Internet has the potential to empower women and members of other traditionally subordinate groups (cf. Herring 2003). This potential takes on special significance for women living in traditional patriarchal cultures. According to Katsuno and Yano (2007), expressive use of kaomoji in chat online helps Japanese housewives defuse their real-world frustrations associated with meal preparation, child care, and boring husbands. The Middle East is another region in which gender roles are traditionally segregated. Deborah Wheeler (2001) studied women's use of the Internet in Kuwait, where Internet access is mainly through cybercafés in which – as in other public places in Kuwait – men and women sit in separate sections. Wheeler's evidence suggests that the greater freedom available online to chat with young people of the opposite sex could potentially break down traditional Islamic barriers to mixed-sex interaction.

5. Language choice: National, regional and global aspects

When participants have a choice of languages online, which ones do they choose and why? The factors affecting such choices vary depending on the technological, sociocultural and political context.

5.1. Language choice at the national level: The case of Switzerland

An interesting case in the European context is Switzerland, which has four national languages, German, French, Italian and Romansh, of which the first three are official languages used in government and federal administration. German is the mother tongue of the largest proportion of citizens, with French in second place. With regard to German, we have once again a situation of *diglossia*: A Swiss dialect of German is spoken in informal situations, but High German is used in writing and in formal spoken situations (Schiffman 1997). In addition, English has slowly gained ground as a lingua franca in Switzerland since World War II (Dürmüller 2002; Durham 2003, 2004; Demont-Heinrich 2005).

Mercedes Durham (2003, 2007) studied the languages used on an online mailing list for Swiss medical students during four calendar years, 1999 to 2002. In less than four years, English went from being used a little over 10% of the time to over 80% of the time (Figure 6). Most messages were monolingual and in English.

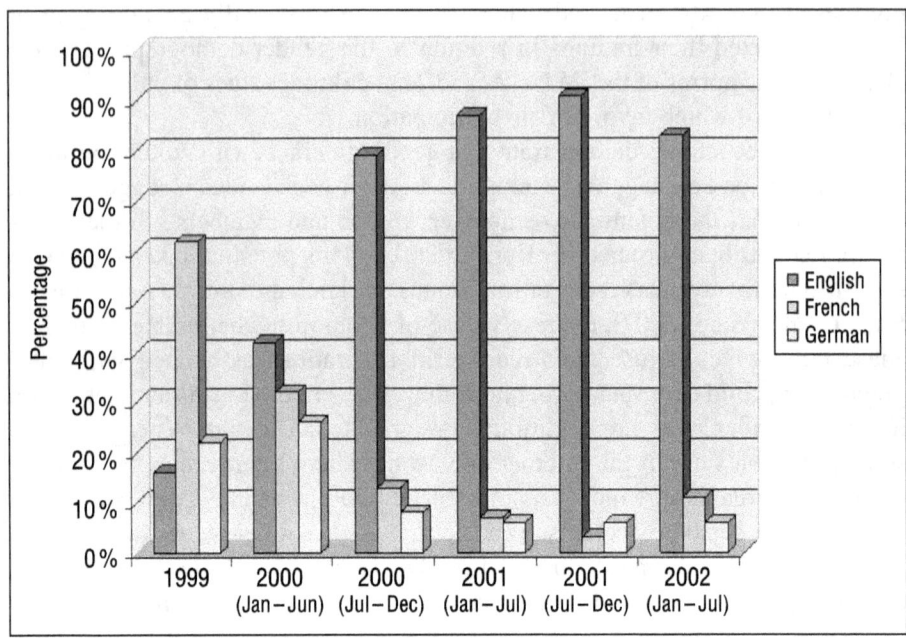

Figure 6. Spread of English on a mailing list for Swiss medical students, 1999–2002: emails by six-month period. Source: Durham 2003.

Medical education is not conducted in English in Switzerland; thus, this cannot be a reason for the shift to English. Durham argues that the main reason is that in Switzerland English is no one's native language, and it ensures the widest possible comprehension among subscribers to the discussion list. Consistent with this explanation, native Italian speakers were more likely to use English than were native speakers of either French or German, because fewer members of the list could be assumed to understand their language.

5.2.   Language choice in the less developed world

With regard to language choice in the less developed world, the case of Tanzania is probably representative of many countries in Africa, where Internet penetration has been slow and large areas are not connected to the electricity grid. Safari Mafu, a member of a UNESCO team (Mafu 2004; Sue Wright 2004a), investigated the Tanzanian case. English played a central role in the country's colonial past; during British rule Africans were educated in Swahili, while Europeans and Asians were educated in English. After independence Swahili became the language of instruction but only at the elementary level. Swahili and English are both official languages.

While Internet use has grown in the last five years in Tanzania, only elites – government, universities – usually have access. For ordinary citizens, access is generally via a cybercafé, not a home computer. The government is not concerned that the main language used on the Web is English, although the level of proficiency in English in the general population is low.[23] While the students and professionals interviewed by Mafu (2004) reported some use of Swahili in email, English predominated in their Internet use, reflecting and perpetuating the elite status of users and the functions of English as a language of wider communication. Over one hundred minority languages also spoken in Tanzania are unrepresented online, and are likely to remain so.[24]

In many ways the situation in Africa regarding language choice is similar in the Arab world. English is the main language of email among young professionals in Egypt (Warschauer 2002; Warschauer, El Said, and Zohry 2002, 2007). A complicating factor is the lack of a single standard for communication in Arabic online, and many computers lack operating systems that can handle Arabic (Warschauer 2002). As noted earlier, many people type colloquial Egyptian Arabic in roman letters, both in email and chat. English is more common in formal email communication, reflecting once again its function as a language of wider communication.

5.3. Language choice in the European Union

Language choice issues also arise at the regional level. An interesting case is the European Union (EU), which at the time of this writing has 25 member states and 20 official languages. All legislation is published in all official languages, and the EU maintains a veritable army of translators for written documents and interpreters who perform direct and relay oral interpretation.[25]

Between July 2001 and October 2004, citizens were encouraged to participate in an online discussion about the EU constitution in a Web forum called Futurum,[26] in languages of their choosing. Ruth Wodak and Scott Wright (Wodak and Wright 2007; Scott Wright 2004) found that among the languages actually used in the forum, English dominated by far. Over 90% of all threads or topics introduced in English were conducted only in English. Threads introduced in other languages tended to use a greater diversity of languages, although such threads also tended to be shorter. These results are consistent with general surveys conducted in 1998 and 2000, which found that far more Europeans speak English than any other language.[27]

5.4. Negotiating language choice in global forums

The Futurum case raises a broader issue: How do participants negotiate language choice in global forums where participants are from many countries, speak different native languages, and where there may be no overt link to a specific national or regional context and no official commitment to a given language – no FAQ (Frequently Asked Questions) file establishing the group's language, or moderator to police language choice? Under what conditions do participants accept English as the lingua franca? When are multiple languages and frequent code-switching tolerated? Under what circumstances does overt discrimination occur against speakers of particular languages? A small number of studies have begun to address such issues.

One of the first studies to investigate language choice online was John Paolillo's (1996) research on *soc.culture.punjab*, a Usenet newsgroup populated mainly by expatriate Punjabis living in Canada, the UK, and the US. In an analysis of a corpus of messages collected in 1994 and 1995 (when the group was still quite new), Paolillo found little use of Punjabi. English was the unmarked language, whereas Punjabi was functionally marginalized, a marked choice used primarily for expressive purposes. He argued that marginalization of Punjabi was fostered by a combination of intergenerational language shift, cultural ambivalence of expatriate Punjabis, the prestige of English in South Asia, and Usenet norms favoring English. Revisiting Paolillo's study a decade later, we can add that having to type Punjabi in roman characters may also have discouraged its use.[28]

Axelsson, Äbelin, and Schroeder (2003, 2007) studied efforts to switch languages in Active Worlds, a graphical chat system,[29] and the responses to such efforts. In this international context, English was the main language used. Non-English speakers, who were generally bilingual, tended to switch to English even in settings where the majority of users were non-English-speaking. English speakers accepted non-English languages more in themed settings (role-playing, games, religion, etc.) than in general, cosmopolitan ones without specific themes. The perceived intention of those attempting to switch languages – to find out if fellow speakers were present, to be playful, or in some cases to be intentionally disruptive – influenced the response.

Luis Fernandez (2001) reports more discouraging findings on the use of minority languages in online forums. The manager of a list discussing the future of Ireland warned those posting in Gaelic (rather than English) that their posts would be removed (Ostler 1999, cited in Fernandez 2001: 24). On Leonenet, a mailing list about current events in Sierra Leone, when some people started posting in Krio, the country's lingua franca, others thought this impolite vis-à-vis non-Sierra Leoncan subscribers, or that the practice discriminated against speakers of the languages of other ethnic groups (Wright 1996: 24; cited in Fernandez 2001: 25).

In Fernandez's own research, he found almost no use of Basque in ostensibly Basque forums, even though many users were bilingual in Basque and Spanish or French. Only 8% of messages contained any Basque at all; most were in Spanish. Spanish messages also tended to be much longer. The dominance of Spanish here resembles the findings of Wodak and Wright for English in Futurum. However, whereas the goal in the EU forum was communication among citizens of many nations, in the Basque forums the focus was specifically Basque and Basque issues.

Even in *Errelea,* the Basque-named mailing list for the Real Sociedad football team, in the Spanish province with the highest percentage of Basque speakers, the Basque language did not fare well.

> [...] there was colorful debate and exchange of ideas in the forum, but all messages were in Spanish. The presence of Basque words, terms, tags, salutations, and slogans was also common [...] but *they were always inserted into Spanish messages,* or used as signatures.
> (Fernandez 2001: 33; italics added)

Fernandez complained to the list about the absence of Basque. All responses were negative, arguing that wider communication in Spanish, which is known to all, is best; that using Basque would be disrespectful to those who do not know the language; and that politics should be kept out of the forum. Fernandez interprets this as an instance of "linguicism" – "ideologies and structures [...] used to legitimate, effectuate and reproduce an unequal division of power and resources [...] between groups which are defined on the basis of language" (Skutnabb-Kangas 1988: 13). More simply put, it is an instance of a minority group adopting the majority's stance toward its language. The uses of Basque described above – instances of code-mixing and code-switching where Spanish was the matrix language – appear to have been an expressive means of showing solidarity with fellow Basques, while simultaneously maintaining communication with others. Fernandez found only three Basque-only forums, and concluded that Basque could flourish only if a Basque-only policy is set beforehand.[30]

A more encouraging case is that of Assyrian/Neo-Aramaic/Syriac. Erica McClure (2001a, 2001b) undertook a comprehensive study of the role of language in the maintenance of the mainly diasporic community of Assyrians, an ancient people whose homeland is in the area of Turkey, Iran, Iraq, and Syria. A large group of Assyrians now lives in the United States, especially in the Chicago area; others live in Australia, Sweden, Lebanon, Iraq, and Canada (Gabrial 1998). Whereas in the homeland their Christian religion distinguished them from others, in the diaspora, the language, variously known as Assyrian, neo-Aramaic, or Syriac, is crucial. It is a Semitic language with a distinctive right-to-left script.[31]

McClure collected extensive samples from Usenet newsgroups including *(soc.culture.assyrian)*, chatrooms, and online publications, with special attention to the forms and functions of code-switching in these media genres (McClure 2001a). In the 1990s Assyrian was mostly transliterated into the roman alphabet for online purposes, because of font difficulties. Even transliteration was problematic since it had not been standardized. Nevertheless, McClure (2001a: 186) reports a good deal of code-switching to Assyrian in mainly English-based chatrooms and newsgroup postings. Greetings and closings were frequently written in romanized Assyrian, to express solidarity with others.[32] She concludes: "Assyrians have found in the Internet a strong tool in the fight for the maintenance of their language" (McClure 2001b: 74). By the time of publication of her article (2001b), it was possible to post to the Assyrian Forum in an Assyrian font, as well as in English.[33]

6. The Internet and language revitalization efforts

As the brief review of the work by McClure on Assyrian suggests, an issue of ongoing concern is whether the Internet is accelerating the global spread of English and other "big" languages at the expense of local, indigenous, or minority languages (Phillipson 1992; Phillipson and Skutnabb-Kangas 2001; Sue Wright 2004b; Kirkpatrick, this vol.). Some scholars see the potential for this to result in eventual language death and an overall reduction in global linguistic diversity (Crystal 2000; Herring 2002; Paolillo 2007). Others believe that English can continue to spread and to serve as a useful lingua franca, while at the same time, increasing numbers of other languages and language groups can establish a viable presence on the Internet (Fishman 1998; Nunberg 2000; Crystal 2001, 2003; Dor 2004).[34]

There is serious cause for worry about the fate of "endangered" or minority languages, hundreds and thousands of which are rapidly becoming extinct, as the last speakers die off and institutional supports disappear (Krauss 1992, 1998; Grenoble and Whaley 1998, 2001; Nettle and Romaine 2000; Crystal 2000; Dalby 2002). Experts estimate that as many as half the approximately 6,900 languages of the world[35] will disappear in the 21st century (Nettle and Romaine 2000: 7; Crystal 2000: chap. 1). Both professional linguists and lay activists have been involved in efforts to save some of these languages.

The Internet offers a host of new tools to support these endeavors – databases, CD-ROMs, websites, and discussion forums that can be used for language learning, language advocacy, and other forms of communication (Buszard-Welcher 2001; Eisenlohr 2004). Laura Buszard-Welcher (2001) surveyed 50 websites for endangered native American languages, noting the extent to which they supplied community information, materials about writing and fonts, vocabulary and phrases, texts, reference materials such as dictionaries, and teaching materials. (At the time, few sites offered bulletin board or chat services.) Her paper was largely descriptive and prescriptive, concluding in favor of the positive potential of the Internet to revitalize endangered languages.

More recently, in an integrative literature review, Patrick Eisenlohr (2004) considers how electronic mediation technologies used to revitalize endangered languages both shape and are informed by linguistic ideologies. Lest we become overly enthusiastic about these technologies, he cautions that "many populations interested in reestablishing the practice of a lesser-used language often are least likely to engage in digital mediation practices" (Eisenlohr 2004: 26). Similarly, he expresses skepticism about the potential of digitally mediated language materials to facilitate community building (Eisenlohr 2004: 36–37). While online materials can foster virtual ties among people scattered around the globe in a diaspora, they may not necessarily foster face-to-face use of the language and its transmission to the younger generation (see also Fishman 2001: 458–459). Another issue is that indigenous peoples of the American Southwest are known to have objected in the past to the introduction of writing, during Mexican and Spanish rule, in order to keep cultural knowledge secret, and some groups continue to object to it today (Bielenberg 1999; Hinton 2001). Thus, these groups may be less likely to embrace Internet services.

In the late 1990s and early 2000s, linguists and activists began reporting case studies of Internet use in connection with specific endangered or minority languages.[35] Most of these were descriptive overviews, generally advocating online services enthusiastically; some also have an implicit or explicit prescriptive element, offering recommendations as to how to improve services, what new components might be added, and how they will enhance revitalization. Few case studies so far have been truly evaluative and empirical in orientation. Here we discuss two exceptions, the pioneering work of Mark Warschauer and his colleagues on Hawaiian, and action research on Sardinian by a team based in Germany.[36]

6.1.   Hawaiian

"By the time Hawaii became a state in 1959, Hawaiian was spoken only by a few thousand elders" (Warschauer 1998: 141). As part of a cultural renaissance movement in the 1970s, Hawaiian pre-schools and kindergarten-to-12th-grade language immersion schools were created, as well as undergraduate and graduate programs in Hawaiian studies and language in universities. While microfiches and video recordings began to preserve cultural materials, there was a serious problem of access: "Native Hawaiians [were] dispersed in urban and rural communities on seven islands" (Warschauer 1998: 142).

In the early-to-mid-1990s, an Internet-accessible telecommunications system called *Leokī* ('Powerful Voice') was created, very likely the first in the world to operate entirely in an indigenous language.[37] The system includes private email, chat, discussion lists, a "newsline" (containing advertisements, announcements, information about language classes), vocabulary lists, current and back issues of a newspaper, an area for cultural resources like stories and songs, and information about agencies supporting Hawaiian studies and language-learning – all in Hawaiian only (Figure 7).

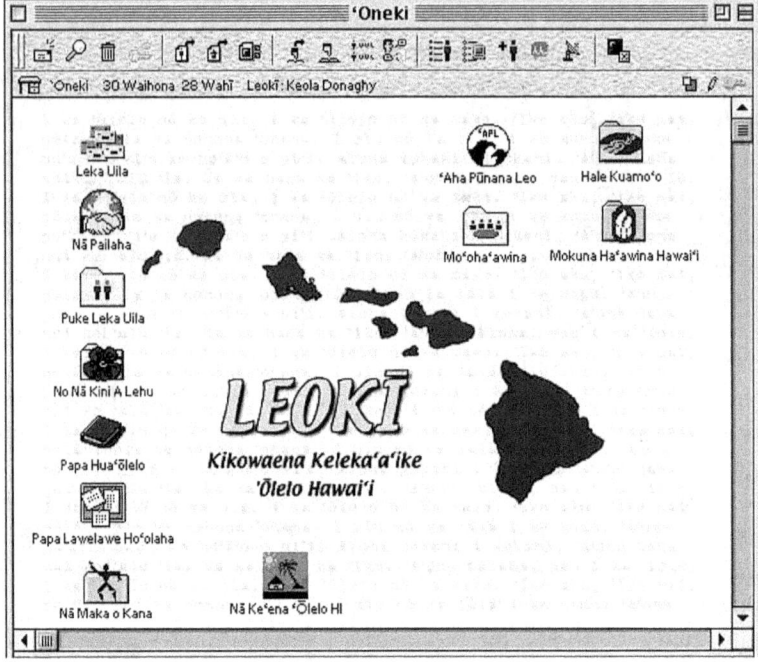

Figure 7. Leokī, a telecommunications system for revitalization of Hawaiian. http://www.olelo.hawaii.edu/eng/resources/leoki.html, retrieved August 15, 2005. Reproduced with permission.

After two years of ethnographic research including participant observation and interviews, Warschauer concluded that "[t]he work of Hawaiians represents an excellent model of a group of people working to positively amplify existing cultural practices in an on-line environment" (Warschauer 1998: 157). At the same time, he noted that problems persist in relation to computer operating systems, and that many natives still could not access the system from their homes, because they lacked computers and even telephones (Warschauer 2002: 66).[38]

6.2. Sardinian

Sardinian is an unstandardized Romance language with about one million speakers, mainly concentrated on the Italian island of Sardinia. It is spoken mainly among friends and family, and more in rural than urban settings, co-existing uneasily with standard Italian. Its status was improved somewhat when the island's legislature recognized it as an official language in 1997; in 1999 the State passed a law allowing it to be used in school (Grimaldi and Remberger n.d.). Despite these improvements in its legal status and the large number of speakers, Sardinian is considered an endangered language, since there is serious generational decline in its use (Mensching 2000).[39]

A team of linguists at two German universities, Guido Mensching and Lucia Grimaldi (Free University of Berlin) and Jürgen Rolshoven and Eva Remberger (University of Cologne), maintains a website housing a project called *Limba e Curtura de sa Sardigna* ('Language and Culture of Sardinia'; see Figure. 8). The project provides information about Sardinian; offers an asynchronous forum to discuss issues relating to the language as well as a chat mode (though little used, as yet); collects linguistic data with the aid of participants in the forum; documents the language and its texts; and archives and analyzes the linguistic data collected (Mensching 2000: 3).

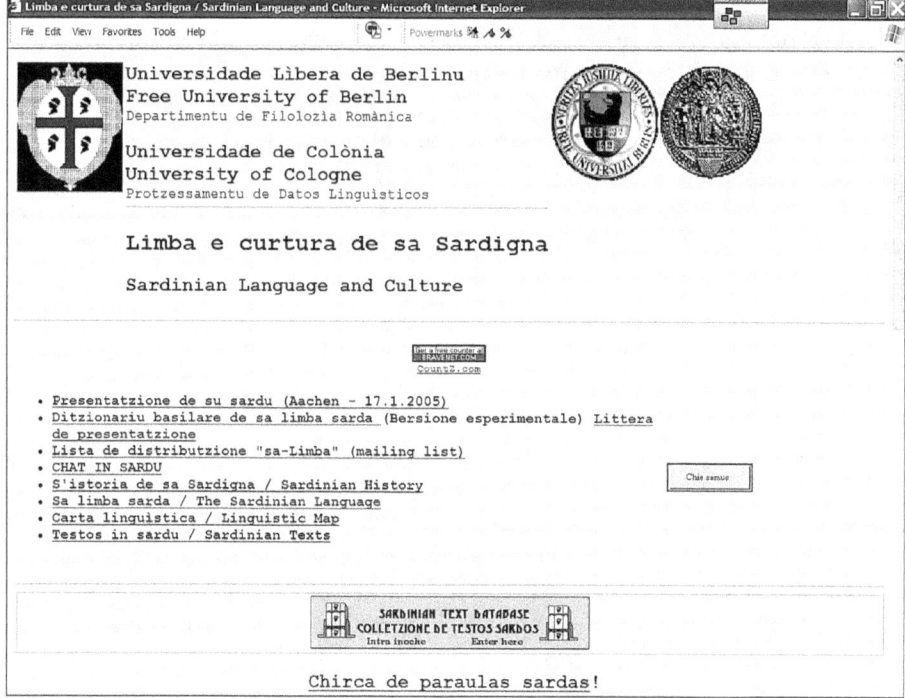

Figure 8. *Limba e curtura de sa Sardigna* ('Language and Culture of Sardinia'); http://www.lingrom.fu-berlin.de/sardu/; retrieved August 15, 2005. Reproduced with permission.

Unlike Warschauer or McClure, this group does not merely study what others are doing to promote the languages at issue; they are themselves at the forefront of these efforts, although none of them is a native speaker of Sardinian. What began as an experiment a decade ago has taken on a life of its own, with subscribers to the mailing list becoming in effect collaborators of the researchers, supplying valuable data about Sardinian by their very efforts to write a formerly spoken-only language, and by serving as informants. As a result, the researchers are already able to report significant new findings. For instance, written communication on the mailing list between speakers/writers of two different dialects turns out to be mutually intelligible. Also, by interviewing subscribers on their use of three variants of the particle of assertion – *emmo*, *eja*, and *si* – the researchers were able to redraw the map for distribution of the three choices and to modify their explanation for the variation (Mensching 2000). In practical terms, they believe that activities related to the site will make an eventual contribution toward standardization of the language.

7. Conclusion

The research surveyed in this chapter reveals a complex and somewhat paradoxical state of affairs as regards linguistic diversity on the Internet at the present time. On the one hand, English has a historical advantage and continues to dominate many online contexts. Offline, as well, interest in English as a second language is growing: More young people around the world are learning English now than at any other time (Graddol 1997/2000). The Internet alone is not responsible for this spread, of course: Other political, economic, and cultural forces had already made English a global lingua franca (Crystal 2003). The Internet has, however, facilitated interaction among participants in multilingual nations, regions, and around the world, a number of whom employ English as a common language of communication. This, in turn, further strengthens the global position of English online and offline.

On the other hand, there is evidence that speakers of other languages are making the Internet their own. Warschauer (2001) calls this a situation of emerging diglossia online, with other languages besides English increasingly creating their own niche. ASCII is being modified to accommodate non-roman writing systems; fonts and operating systems are being localized, and Unicode is being expanded, the use of non English CMC is growing; and the Web is being used to aid language revitalization efforts. Even when communicating in English, speakers of other languages may use the Internet to pursue the agendas of their own language and culture group, as in the case of the Basque forums described by Fernandez (2001). The current situation is far from one of absolute English dominance. Moreover, linguistic diversity online is on the rise (Paolillo 2007).

This survey is of necessity selective due to space limitations; we do not claim to have addressed all issues relevant to multilingualism on the Internet, and some crucial research has yet to be conducted. The following areas we feel are especially in need of attention in future research:

- Accurate assessments of what languages are used online (Paolillo 2007). Most estimates of language use on the Internet thus far have been based on population demographics, rather than on actual language use.
- Studies of the cognitive, social, and symbolic effects of technical (e.g., ASCII) bias on non-native English Internet users (cf. Pargman and Palme 2004). Software localization efforts notwithstanding, legacy systems will continue to be used for some time; to what extent are non-English speakers who must use them at a disadvantage?
- Comparative studies that use the same methods and concepts to investigate different languages and writing systems online, holding the mode of CMC constant (Danet and Herring 2003b). Most of the research produced to date has been case studies of individual languages.[40]
- More research into the effects of gender and culture on online language variation. To the extent that gender is culturally shaped, one would expect to find gender-based variation in CMC reflecting national, ethnic, and linguistic identities. Very little research has yet been done in this area.
- Systematic studies of language use and language choice in the design of websites. Most research on Internet multilingualism so far has focused on CMC modes such as email, chat, and discussion forums. How many languages are used on the Web today?[41] What proportion of Web sites is available in more than one language? In which languages? Do the versions in different languages communicate the same content and meanings?
- Research into the online status of other world languages besides English – for example, Spanish, Chinese, Russian, Malay and Hindi, each of which has a large regional base (cf. Graddol 1997/2000). In what languages are, for example, search engines available? How widespread is their use in these languages, and is their functionality comparable to that of search engines in English?
- Studies of automated translation. Can real-time machine translation during instant messaging, email, and chat facilitate communication among speakers of different languages? What obstacles stand in the way of such facilitation (cf. Climent et al. 2003, 2007)? How accurate is automatic translation of online content today, and what are the prospects for its improvement?

Like key transportation and telecommunication technologies before it, computer networking is leading the nations of the world into a new communication era, in which contact among speakers of different language varieties will increase (Baron 2000; Crystal 2004b). The multilingual nature of the Internet is thus likely to become a phenomenon of even greater importance in the years to come. In a presentation on the subject of "Applied Linguistics for the 21st Century" prepared for the 1999 conference of the International Association for Applied Linguistics, Warschauer (2001) identified three issues of concern to applied linguists as a result of the spread of the Internet: literacy, second language learning and teaching, and international language use. Similarly, Crystal (2005) predicts the rise of what he terms an "Applied Internet Linguistics" – a linguistics that attends to language-related social problems arising from the emergence and prominence of the Internet as a new communication domain. We believe that multilingualism on the Internet should be a central focus of both agendas.

8. Appendix: Some languages accommodated by the five most widely used scripts incorporated in Unicode.*

Script	Languages
Latin	Afrikaans, Ainu, Albanian [1], Amo, Aymara, Azeri, Azerbaijani, Balear, Baluchi, Basque, Batak, Batak toba, Bosnian, Breton, Bahasa, Catalan, Chamorro, Cherokee, Cornish, Corsican, Cree, Croatian, Czech, Danish, Dutch, Edo, English, Esperanto, Estonian, Faroese, Fijian, Filipino, Finnish, French, Frisian, Gaelic, Gallegan, Gascon, German, Guarani, Haitian, Hanunóo, Hausa, Hawaiian, Hiri Motu, Hmong, Hopi, Hungarian, Ibibio, Icelandic, Indonesian, Ingush, Inuktitut, Iñupiaq, Irish, Italian, Javanese, Kalaallisut, Kanuri, Karelian, Khasi, Kinyarwanda, Kirghiz, Komi, Kurdish, Lapp, Latin, Latvian, Lingala, Lisu, Lithuanian, Lushootseed, Luxemburghish, Malay, Maltese, Manx, Mari, Mende, Malagasy, Maori, Marshallese, Moldavian, Naga, Nauru, Navajo, Niuean, Northern Sotho, North Ndebele, Norwegian, Nyanja, Oromo, Ossetic, Polish, Portuguese, Provençal, Prussian, Quechua, Rhaeto-Romance, Romanian, Romany, Rundi, Sami, Samoan, Sango, Serbian, Shona, Slovak, Slovenian, Somali, Songhai, Southern Sotho, Spanish, South Ndebele, Swahili, Swati, Swedish, Tagalog, Tagbanwa, Tahitian, Tajik, Tamashek, Tamazight, Time, Tetum, Tokelau, Tok Pisin, Tonga, Tsonga, Tswana, Turkish, Turkmen, Tuvalu, Udmurt, Uighur, Uzbek, Valencian, Venda, Vietnamese, Welsh, Wolof, Xhosa, Yi, Yoruba, Zulu

Cyrillic	Abaza, Abkhaz, Adygei, Aisor, Altai, Avar, Azeri, Azerbaijani, Balkar, Bashkir, Belarusian, Bulgarian, Buryat, Chechen, Chukchi, Chuvash, Dargwa, Dungan, Cyrillic, Gagauz, Inuktitut, Kabardian, Kalmyk, Khanty, Karachay, Karakalpak, Karelian, Kazakh, Khakass, Kirghiz, Komi, Koryak, Kurdish, Lak, Lezghian, Macedonian, Mansi, Mari, Moldavian, Mongolian, Mordvin, Nanai, Nenets, Netets, Nogai, Ossetic, Romanian [1], Romany, Russian, Sami, Selkup, Serbian, Shor, Tabasaran, Tajik, Tat, Tatar, Turkmen, Tuva, Udekhe, Udmurt, Uighur, Ukranian, Uzbek, Yakut
Devanagari	Awadhi, Bagheli, Balti, Bateri, Bhili, Bhojpuri, Bihari, Braj Bhasha, Chhattisgarhi, Garhwali, Gondi, Harauti, Hindi, Ho, Kachchi, Kanauji, Kankan, Kashmiri, Konkan, Limbu, Maithili, Marathi, Marwari, Mundari, Nepali, Newari, Pali, Sanskrit, Santali, Sherpa, Sindi
Arabic	Arabic, Azerbaijani, Baluchi, Farsi, Hausa [1], Indonesian [1], Ingush, Kashmiri, Kirghiz [1], Kurdish, Malay [1], Parsi-dari, Pashto, Punjabi, Sindhi, Tajik [1], Turkish [1], Turkmen [1], Uighur, Urdu, Uzbek, Wolof
Bengali	Assamese, Bengali, Chakma, Garo, Khasi, Meitei, Mundari, Naga, Riang, Santali, Sylhetti

* Compiled from "Languages and Scripts", http://www.unicode.org/onlinedat/languages-scripts.html, last updated June 3, 2005, retrieved September 22, 2005; additional languages provided by Deborah Anderson, personal email communication to Brenda Danet, August 29, 2005.
[1] Formerly or historically used this script, now uses another.

Notes

1. This is an expanded revision of a paper presented at the Annual Meeting of the American Association for the Advancement of Science, panel on "Language and the Internet: Usage Patterns, Global Issues, Future Trends", convened by Naomi S. Baron, Washington, DC, February 18, 2005. We thank Deborah Anderson and Keola Donaghy for helpful information, comments, and suggestions.
2. Internet Statistics: Distribution of Languages on the Internet, http://www.netz-tipp.de/languages.html; retrieved August 12, 2005. The figure refers to Web pages, not the Internet generally, despite the site's title.
3. See http://global-reach.biz/globstats/evol.html, retrieved August 12, 2005.
4. Although as of February 2005, only 7% of China's population of about 1,282,000,000 was online, this represented a growth rate of over 300% since 2000; similarly, whereas only a tiny 1.7% of the population of India (approximately 1,095,000,000) was online in early 2005, the rate of growth in the same five-year

period was 270 % (Internet World Stats, Internet Usage in Asia, www.internetworldstats.com/stats3.htm, retrieved August 12, 2005).
5. The bias toward generalizing from materials in one's own language is probably also true of many CMC researchers writing in other languages. One of the first to point out this bias was Daniel Pargman (1998).
6. Another recent collection is the UNESCO-sponsored journal issue about multilingualism edited by Sue Wright (2004a), based on a survey administered to students of English in 10 countries (Tanzania, Indonesia, the United Arab Emirates, Oman, France, Italy, Poland, Macedonia, Japan, and Ukraine).
7. For additional references, see the introduction to Danet and Herring (2007).
8. An exception is Swahili, which is written in the standard Roman alphabet (The Kamusi Project); The Internet Living Swahili Dictionary, http://research.yale.edu/cgi-bin/swahili/main.cgi?right_frame_src=http%3A//www.yale.edu/swahili/home.html, retrieved August 15, 2005). For lists of languages written in variations of the roman alphabet, see http://www.omniglot.com/writing/languages.htm#latin, retrieved August 15, 2005, and the Appendix to this chapter.
9. Rare among Semitic languages, Maltese is written not in right-to-left non-roman script as is true of Hebrew, Arabic, and neo-Aramaic, but in roman characters.
10. *Hor* means "fornication" or "adultery", and *by* means "village". This example is from Pargman (1998) and Pargman and Palme (2004).
11. See the discussion of the extended ASCII character set in this chapter. A serious attempt is underway to make URLs multilingual. MINC: Multilingual International Names Consortium, http://www.minc.org/, is a non-profit international organization working to create "truly multilingual Internet domain names and keywords, [and] internationalization of Internet names, standards and protocols". Retrieved August 15, 2005.
12. See http://www.omniglot.com/writing/hawaiian.htm, retrieved August 15, 2005.
13. For explanations of word-processing in Japanese and Chinese, see Gottlieb (2000); Nishimura (2003); and Su (2003, 2007).
14. This claim was made not by Fishman, author of the article, but by the editors of *Foreign Policy*.
15. Fig. 3 also shows evidence of online code-mixing and code-switching. In the last contribution by speaker D, English words are mixed with Arabic ones within the same sentence. Also, there is a vertical "smiley" in the third line, typographically distinct from the familiar horizontal smiling face in use online in the West. For further discussion of vertical emoticons, see the section on *kaomoji*. On writing a very different, previously "oral" (Creole) language online and code-switching, see Hinrichs (2004, 2006).
16. In Georgakopoulou's work romanization per se is not discussed. See also Paolillo (1996) on a Usenet newsgroup called *soc.culture.punjab*, in which Punjabi is written in roman letters.
17. ISO is the acronym for the International Organization for Standards; see http://www.iso.org/iso/en/ISOOnline.frontpage, retrieved March 13, 2005. For further information on pre-Unicode, partial solutions for individual languages or language groups, see the Tutorial on Character Code Issues, http://www.cs.tut.fi/~jkorpela/chars.html, retrieved August 15, 2005; Everson (2002). The character set in Fig. 3 does not include several characters in the Maltese alphabet; see the URLs in Note 8.

18. The first recorded use of the term "Unicode" was by Joe Becker, in 1987, to refer to "unique, universal, and uniform character encoding". The Unicode Consortium was incorporated in the State of California in 1991. For more details on the history of Unicode, see http://www.unicode.org/history/, retrieved August 15, 2005.
19. This definition comes from the Unicode Home Pages, http://www.unicode.org/glossary/, retrieved August 15, 2005.
20. Strictly speaking, this is an over-simplification; see Note 22.
21. See http://www.linguistics.berkeley.edu/sei/, retrieved August 15, 2005. Volunteers do much of the work. Michael Everson is especially active in this effort; see his website, Everson Typography, http://www.evertype.com/, retrieved August 15, 2005.
22. This figure was cited by Deborah Anderson in a lecture at Yale University Library, June 30, 2005. Unicode Standard (4.0) accommodated 96,000 characters. Version 4.1.0, a minor update, added 1273 new ones. Contrary to intuition, Unicode is not "simply a 16-bit code where each character takes 16 bits and therefore there are 65,536 possible characters. This is [...] the single most common myth about Unicode" (Spolsky 2003).
23. Script per se is not a problem in Swahili, as the roman alphabet is used; see The United Republic of Tanzania Website, Frequently Asked Questions. http://www.tanzania.go.tz/learn_kiswahilif.html, retrieved August 15, 2005.
24. See The Languages of Tanzania: A Web Links Collection, http://www.african.gu.se/tanzania/weblinks.html, retrieved August 15, 2005.
25. The official languages are: Swedish, Danish, German, Czech, Greek, Estonian, French, Latvian, Italian, Lithuanian, Dutch, Hungarian, Portuguese, Maltese, Finnish, Polish, English, Slovak, Spanish, Slovene, as well as Irish Gaelic, which was added in June 2005 (Marsh 2005). See http://europa.eu.int/comm/translation/index_en.htm and http://europa.eu.int/comm/scic/interpreting/faq_en.htm, both retrieved August 15, 2005. In a note appended to Fishman (1998), the editors of *Foreign Policy* comment:

> Despite these [...] initiatives [...] efforts to promote equal treatment of all official languages [...] have fallen flat. Although 15 percent of the European Commission's 17,000 personnel are translators, interpreters, and terminologists, EU institutions use only a handful of "working languages" to conduct daily business [...] although French is still used more frequently than English in the European Commission, English is preferred among younger officials. (Fishman 1998: 29)

26. The forum was closed after the constitution treaty was signed in October 2004. Material relating to Futurum debates is now archived at http://europa.eu.int/constitution/futurum/index_en.htm, retrieved August 15, 2005.
27. The 1998 survey found that nearly half of all Europeans spoke English, whereas only about one third spoke German, and fewer spoke French. The position of French and German was reversed in the 2000 survey, but English retained its dominance. See Eurobarometer (1999) and Eurobarometer (2001).
28. On the Punjabi script, see http://www.omniglot.com/writing/gurmuki.htm, retrieved August 15, 2005.
29. See http://www.activeworlds.com/, retrieved August 15, 2005. In these settings communication is mainly via text, but users are represented visually by graphical avatars and can move about the 3-D virtual environment.

30. On the Basque presence on the Internet, see also Uberuaga (2000) and Arbelaiz (2001). While Fernandez mentions various technical obstacles to using Basque online, the Basque alphabet is apparently not one of them. With the exception of ñ and Ñ, all letters can apparently be accommodated by the basic roman alphabet.
31. See, e.g. http://www.language-museum.com/a/assyrian-neo-aramaic.php; http://www.omniglot.com/writing/syriac.htm, both retrieved August 15, 2005.
32. For somewhat similar findings on switching into the home language for expressive purposes, but in a different context, see Androutsopoulos (2007).
33. See http://www.aina.org/bbs/index.cgi? (retrieved August 15, 2005), although it took some hunting to find a posting in Assyrian.
34. What constitutes a "viable presence" is an important research question in its own right.
35. The latest estimate is that there are over 6,900 languages in the world; see *Ethnologue*, http://www.ethnologue.com/, retrieved August 15, 2005.
36. See also Sperlich's (2005) case study of Niuean, a Pacific Island language.
37. The system began running in 1993, although used only by a small pilot group; it became Internet-accessible and started to be used by more people in 1994; immersion school access began in earnest in 1995. Personal email communication to Brenda Danet from Keola Donaghy, manager of the system, August 25, 2005.
38. Updating this overview in 2005, Keola Donaghy wrote, "The most significant development is our use of Leoki in Hawaiian language instruction. We've had over a hundred students in about 25 US states, as well as Europe and Japan over the past three years". Personal email communication to Brenda Danet, August 25, 2005.
39. For more on the Sardinian situation, see http://www.uoc.es/euromosaic/web/document/sard/an/i1/i1.html#3.7, retrieved August 15, 2005. On the endangered status of four dialects of Sardinian, see the UNESCO (2003) *Redbook on Endangered Languages*, http://www.helsinki.fi/~tasalmin/europe_index.html, retrieved August 15, 2005.
40. Pioneering exceptions are Fouser, Narahiko, and Chungmin (2000) and Androutsopoulos (2007).
41. With little effort, David Crystal found evidence for the presence of about 1,000 languages, and estimated that about 1,500 were on the Web at the time of his writing (Crystal 2004b: 88).

References

Allison, Anne
    2004   Cuteness as Japan's millennial product. In: Joseph Tobin (ed.), *Pikachu's Global Adventure: The Rise and Fall of Pokemon*, 34–49. Durham, NC: Duke University Press.

Almanac, Computer Industry
    2000   Population explosion. http://www.clickz.com/stats/sectors/geographics/article.php/5911_151151, retrieved August 12, 2005.

Anderson, Deborah
    2004   The script encoding initiative (original English version of article published in German). *SIGNA* 6: 1–12. http://www.linguistics.berkeley.edu/~dwanders/SIGNAEnglish.pdf, retrieved August 12, 2005.

Anderson, Deborah
    2005   Global linguistic diversity for the Internet. *Communications of the ACM* 48 (1): 27–28.

Androutsopoulos, Jannis
    1999a   Spelling variation in Latin alphabeted Greek email messages. Conference paper, 20th Working Meeting of the Linguistics Department, Aristoteles University of Thessaloniki, Thessaloniki, Greece, April 23–25, 1999. http://greekweb.archetype.de/greekmail/abstracts.htm, retrieved August 12, 2005 (abstract in English and Greek).

Androutsopoulos, Jannis
    1999b   Latin-Greek spelling in e-mail messages: Usage and attitudes (in Greek). *Studies in Greek Linguistics* 1: 75–86.

Androutsopoulos, Jannis
    2000   From dieuthinsi to diey8ynsh: Orthographic variation in Latin-alphabeted Greek (in Greek). Conference paper, 4th International Conference on Greek Linguistics, University of Nicosia, Cyprus, September, 1999. http://greekweb.archetype.de/greekmail/icgl99.html, retrieved August 12, 2005 (in Greek; abstract in English).

Androutsopoulos, Jannis
    2007   Language choice and code-switching in German-based diasporic web forums. In: Danet and Herring (eds.), *The Multilingual Internet: Language, Culture, and Communication Online*. 340–361.

Androutsopoulos, Jannis and Volker Hinnenkamp
    2001   Code-switching in der bilingualen Chat-Kommunikation: Ein explorativer Blick auf #hellas und #turks. In: Michael Beißwenger (ed.), *Chat-Kommunikation. Sprache, Interaktion und Sozialität in synchroner computervermittelter Kommunikation. Perspektiven auf ein interdisziplinäres Forschungsfeld*, 367–401. Stuttgart: Ibidem.

Arbelaiz, Asunción Martínez
    2001   Basque, the Internet, and new language policies. In: Christopher Moseley, Nicholas Ostler and Hassan Ouzzate (eds.), *Endangered Languages and the Media: Proceedings of the Fifth FEL (Foundation for Endangered Languages) Conference, Agadir, Morocco, 20–23 September 2000*, 98–103. Bath, UK: Foundation for Endangered Languages.

Axelsson, Ann-Sofie, Åsa Abelin and Ralph Schroeder
    2003   Anyone speak Spanish? Language encounters in multi-user virtual environments and the influence of technology. *New Media & Society* 5(4): 475–498.

Axelsson, Ann-Sofie, Åsa Abelin and Ralph Schroeder
    2007   Anyone speak Swedish? Language encounters in multi-user virtual environments and the influence of technology. In: Danet and Herring (eds.), *The Multilingual Internet: Language, Culture, and Communication Online*. 362–381.

Baron, Naomi S.
    2000   *Alphabet to Email: How Written English Evolved and Where It's Heading*. New York/London: Routledge.

Bechar-Israeli, Haya
    1995   From <Bonehead> to <clonehead>: Nicknames, play and identity on Internet Relay Chat. *Journal of Computer-Mediated Communication* 1(2). http://jcmc.indiana.edu/vol1/issue2/bechar.html, retrieved August 15, 2005.

Berjaoui, Nasser
  2001   Aspects of the Moroccan Arabic orthography with preliminary insights from the Moroccan computer-mediated communication. In: Michael Beißwenger (ed.). *Chat-Kommunikation: Sprache, Interaktion, Sozialität & Identität in synchroner computervermittelter Kommunikation. Perspektiven auf ein interdisziplinäres Forschungsfeld*, 431–465. Stuttgart: Ibidem.
Bielenberg, Brian
  1999   Indigenous language codification: Cultural effects. In: Jon Reyhner, Gina Cantoni, Robert N. St. Clair and Evangeline Parsons Yazzie (eds.), *Revitalizing Indigenous Languages*, 103–112. Flagstaff, AZ: Northern Arizona University. Online at http://jan.ucc.nau.edu/~jar/RIL_8.html, retrieved August 15, 2005.
Buszard-Welcher, Laura
  2001   Can the Web save my language? In: Leanne Hinton and Kenneth Hale (eds.), *The Green Book of Language Revitalization in Practice*, 331–348. San Diego: Academic Press.
Climent, Salvador, Joaquim Moré, Antoni Oliver, Míriam Salvatierra, Imma Sànchez, Mariona Taulé and Lluïsa Vallmanya
  2003   Bilingual newsgroups in Catalonia: A challenge for machine translation. *Journal of Computer-Mediated Communication* 9(1). http://jcmc.indiana.edu/vol9/issue1/climent.html, retrieved August 15, 2005.
Climent, Salvador, Joaquim Moré, Antoni Oliver, Míriam Salvatierra, Imma Sànchez and Mariona Taulé
  2007   Can machine translation enhance the status of Catalan versus Spanish in online academic forums? In: Danet and Herring (eds.), *The Multilingual Internet: Language, Culture, and Communication Online*. 209–230.
Consortium, The Unicode
  2003   *The Unicode standard, version 4.0 (online)*. Boston: Addison-Wesley. Also online at http://www.unicode.org/versions/Unicode4.0.0/, retrieved August 15, 2005.
Cringely, Bob
  1998   *Nerds 2.0: History of the Internet*. Videotape. New York: Ambrose.
Crystal, David
  2000   *Language Death*. Cambridge: Cambridge University Press.
Crystal, David
  2001   *Language and the Internet*. Cambridge: Cambridge University Press.
Crystal, David
  2003   *English as a Global Language*. 2nd ed. Cambridge: Cambridge University Press.
Crystal, David
  2004a   *The Stories of English*. New York: Overlook Press.
Crystal, David
  2004b   *The Language Revolution*. London: Polity Press.
Crystal, David
  2005   The scope of Internet linguistics. Conference paper, Annual Meeting, American Association for the Advancement of Science, panel on "Language on the Internet: Usage Patterns, Global Issues, Future Trends," Naomi S. Baron, convenor. Washington, DC, February 17–21, 2005.

CyberAtlas
  2003　　June 6 Population explosion! http://www.clickz.com/stats/sectors/geo graphics/article.php/5911_151151, retrieved August 12, 2005.
Dalby, Andrew
  2002　　*Language in Danger.* London & New York: Allen Lane.
Danet, Brenda (ed.)
  1995　　Play and Performance in Computer-Mediated Communication. *Journal of Computer-Mediated Communication* [Special issue]. http://jcmc.indiana.edu/vol1/issue2/, retrieved August 15, 2005.
Danet, Brenda
  1998　　Text as mask: Gender, play and performance on the Internet. In: Steven G. Jones (ed.), *Cybersociety 2.0: Revisiting Computer-Mediated Communication and Community,* 129–158. Thousand Oaks, CA, and London: Sage.
Danet, Brenda
  2001　　*Cyberpl@y: Communicating Online.* Oxford: Berg Publishers. Companion Website: http://pluto.mscc.huji.ac.il/~msdanet/cyberpl@y/, retrieved August 15, 2005.
Danet, Brenda and Susan C. Herring (eds.)
  2003a　　The Multilingual Internet: Language, Culture and Communication in Instant Messaging, Email and Chat. *Journal of Computer-Mediated Communication* 9(1) [Special issue]. http://jcmc.indiana.edu/vol9/issue1/, retrieved August 15, 2005.
Danet, Brenda and Susan C. Herring
  2003b　　Introduction: The multilingual Internet. *Journal of Computer-Mediated Communication* 9(1). http://jcmc.indiana.edu/vol9/issue1/intro.html, retrieved August 15, 2005.
Danet, Brenda and Susan C. Herring (eds.)
  2007　　*The Multilingual Internet: Language, Culture, and Communication Online.* New York: Oxford University Press.
Danet, Brenda, Lucia Ruedenberg and Yehudit Rosenbaum-Tamari
  1998　　"Hmmm … Where's that smoke coming from?" Writing, play and performance on Internet Relay Chat. In: Fay Sudweeks, Margaret McLaughlin and Sheizaf Rafaeli (eds.), *Network and Netplay: Virtual Groups on the Internet,* 47–85. Cambridge, MA: AAAI/MIT Press.
Demont-Heinrich, Christof
  2005　　Language and national identity in the era of globalization: The case of English in Switzerland. *Communication Inquiry* 29(1): 66–84.
de Oliveira, Sandi Michele
  2003　　Breaking conversational norms on a Portuguese users' network: Men as adjudicators of politeness? *Journal of Computer-Mediated Communication* 9 (1). http://jcmc.indiana.edu/vol9/issue1/oliveira.html, retrieved August 15, 2005.
de Oliveira, Sandi Michele
  2007　　Breaking conversational norms on a Portuguese users' network: Men as adjudicators of politeness? In: Danet and Herring (eds.), *The Multilingual Internet: Language, Culture, and Communication Online.* 256–277.

Dor, Daniel
2004 From Englishization to imposed multilingualism: Globalization, the Internet, and the political economy of the linguistic code. *Public Culture* 16(1): 97–118.
Durham, Mercedes
2003 Language choice on a Swiss mailing list. *Journal of Computer-Mediated Communication* 9(1). http://jcmc.indiana.edu/vol9/issue1/durham.html, retrieved August 15, 2005.
Durham, Mercedes
2004 The future of Swiss English. In: Britt-Louise Gunnarsson, Lena Bergström, Gerd Eklund, Staffan Fridell, Lisa H. Hansen, Angela Karstadt, Bengt Nordberg, Eva Sundgren and Mats Thelander (eds.), *Language Variation in Europe: Papers from Iclave 2 (Second International Conference on Language Variation in Europe, Uppsala University, Sweden, June 12–14, 2003)*, 156–167. Uppsala: Uppsala University.
Durham, Mercedes
2007 Language choice on a Swiss mailing list. In: Danet and Herring (eds.), *The Multilingual Internet: Language, Culture, and Communication Online.* 319–339.
Dürmüller, Urs
2002 English in Switzerland: From foreign language to lingua franca. In: D. J. Allerton, Paul Skandera and Cornelia Tschichold (eds.), *Perspectives on English as a World Language*, 115–123. Basel: Schwabe.
Eisenlohr, Patrick
2004 Language revitalization and new technologies: Cultures of electronic mediation and the refiguring of communities. *Annual Review of Anthropology* 33: 21–45.
Eurobarometer, European Union
1999 Eurobarometer Report Number 50: Public Opinion in the European Union. http://europa.eu.int/comm/education/policies/lang/languages/index_en.html, retrieved August 15, 2005.
Eurobarometer, European Union
2001 Eurobarometer Report Number 54: Europeans and Languages, Executive Summary. http://europa.eu.int/comm/public_opinion/archives/eb/ebs_147_summ_en.pdf, retrieved August 15, 2005.
Everson, Michael
2002 Leaks in the Unicode pipeline: Script, script, script ... (A Unicode Technical Note). Conference paper, the 21st International Unicode Conference, Dublin, Ireland, May 14–17, 2002. http://www.unicode.org/notes/tn4/, retrieved September 25, 2005.
Fahlman, Scott E.
n.d. Smiley lore :-). http://www-2.cs.cmu.edu/~sef/sefSmiley.htm, retrieved September 25, 2005.
Ferguson, Charles
1972 Diglossia. In: Pier Paolo Giglioli (ed.), *Language and Social Context*, 232–252. Harmondsworth: Penguin.
Fernandez, Luis
2001 Patterns of linguistic discrimination in Internet discussion forums. *Mercator Media Forum* 5: 22–41.

Ferrara, Kathleen, Hans Brunner and Greg Whittemore
    1991   Interactive written discourse as an emergent register. *Written Communication* 8: 8–34.
Fishman, Joshua
    1998   *Foreign Policy* 113, Winter 1998/99: 26–40.
Fishman, Joshua (ed.)
    2001   *Can Threatened Languages Be Saved? Reversing Language Shift, Revisited: A 21st Century Perspective*. Clevedon: Multilingual Matters.
Fishman, Joshua A., Andrew W. Conrad and Alma Rubal-Lopez (eds.)
    1996   *Post-imperial English: Status Change in Former British and American Colonies, 1940–1990*. Berlin/New York: Mouton de Gruyter.
Fouser, Robert, Narahiko Inoue and Chungmin Lee
    2000   The pragmatics of orality in English, Japanese and Korean computer-mediated communication. In: Lyn Pemberton and Simon Shurville (eds.), *Words on the Web: Computer-Mediated Communication*, 52–62. Bristol, UK: Intellect Books.
Gabrial, Albert
    1998   3,000 years of history, yet the Internet is our only home. *Cultural Survival Quarterly* 21(4): 42.
Georgakopoulou, Alexandra
    1997   Self-presentation and interactional alliances in e-mail discourse: The style- and code-switches of Greek messages. *International Journal of Applied Linguistics* 7: 141–164.
Georgakopoulou, Alexandra
    2004   To tell or not to tell? Email stories between on- and off-line interactions. *language@internet* 1. Retrieved July 24, 2006 from http://www.digijournals.de/languageatinternet/articles/36.
Gottlieb, Nanette
    2000   *Word-processing Technology in Japan: Kanji and the Keyboard*. Richmond: Curzon.
Graddol, David
    1997/
    2000   *The Future of English? A Guide to Forecasting the Popularity of the English Language in the 21st Century*. London: The British Council. Available online since 2000 at http://www.gre.ac.uk/~ds42/pages/future%20of%20English.pdf, retrieved August 15, 2005.
Graddol, David
    1999   The decline of the native speaker. *AILA Review* 13: 57–68.
Graddol, David
    2004   The future of language. *Science* 303(5662), 1329–1331.
Grenoble, Lenore A. and Lindsay J. Whaley (eds.)
    1998   *Endangered Languages: Language Loss and Community Responses*. Cambridge/New York: Cambridge University Press.
Grenoble, Lenore A. and Lindsay J. Whaley
    2001   Endangered languages. In: Rajend Mesthrie (ed.), *Concise Encyclopedia of Sociolinguistics*, 465–467. Amsterdam/New York: Elsevier.
Grimaldi, Lucia and Remberger, Eva-Maria
    n.d.   The Promotion of the Sardinian Language and Culture via the Internet: Fields of Activity and Perspectives. http://www.lingrom.fu-berlin.de/sardu/grimaldi_remberger.html, retrieved July 24, 2006.

Hafner, Katie and Matthew Lyon
  1996   *Where Wizards Stay Up Late: The Origins of the Internet.* New York: Simon & Schuster.
Herring, Susan C. (ed.)
  1996a   *Computer-Mediated Communication: Linguistic, Social, and Cross-Cultural Perspectives.* Amsterdam: John Benjamins.
Herring, Susan C.
  1996b   Posting in a different voice: Gender and ethics in computer-mediated communication. In: Charles Ess (ed.), *Philosophical Perspectives on Computer-Mediated Communication,* 115–145. Albany: SUNY Press.
Herring, Susan C.
  2001   Computer-mediated discourse. In: Deborah Tannen, Deborah Schiffrin and Heidi Hamilton (eds.), *Handbook of Discourse Analysis,* 612–634. Oxford: Blackwell.
Herring, Susan C.
  2002   The language of the Internet: English dominance or heteroglossia? Keynote presentation, CATaC (Conference on Cultural Attitudes towards Technology and Communication). Montreal, University of Montreal, 2002. Available from http://ella.slis.indiana.edu/~herring/CATaC.ppt, retrieved September 24, 2005.
Herring, Susan C.
  2003   Gender and power in online communication. In: Janet Holmes and Miriam Meyerhoff (eds.), *The Handbook of Language and Gender,* 202–228. Oxford: Blackwell.
Hinrichs, Lars
  2004   Emerging orthographic conventions in written creole: Computer-mediated communication in Jamaica. *Arbeiten aus Anglistik und Amerikanistik* 29(1): 81–109.
Hinrichs, Lars
  2006   *Codeswitching on the Web: English and Jamaican Creole in E-mail Communication.* Amsterdam: John Benjamins.
Hinton, Leanne
  2001   Introduction to the Pueblo languages. In: Leanne Hinton and Kenneth L. Hale (eds.), *The Green Book of Language Revitalization in Practice,* 61–62. San Diego: Academic Press.
Hinton, Leanne and Kenneth L. Hale (eds.)
  2001   *The Green Book of Language Revitalization in Practice.* San Diego: Academic Press.
Hiorth, Larissa
  2003   Cute@keitai.com. In: Nanette Gottlieb and Mark J. McLelland (eds.), *Japanese Cybercultures,* 50–59. London/New York: Routledge.
Hudson, Alan
  2001   Diglossia. In: Rajend Mesthrie (ed.), *Concise Encyclopedia of Sociolinguistics,* 226–231. Amsterdam/New York: Elsevier.
Kanayama, Tomoko
  2003   Ethnographic research on the experience of Japanese elderly people online. *New Media & Society* 5(2): 267–288.

Kataoka, Kuniyoshi
 1997 Affect and letter-writing: Unconventional conventions in personal writing by young Japanese women. *Language in Society* 26(1): 103–136.
Kataoka, Kuniyoshi
 2003a Form and function of emotive pictorial signs in casual letter writing. *Written Language and Literacy* 6(1): 1–29.
Kataoka, Kuniyoshi
 2003b Emotion and youth identities in personal letter writing: An analysis of pictorial signs and unconventional punctuation. In: Jannis K. Androutsopoulos and Alexandra Georgakopoulou (eds.), *Discourse Constructions of Youth Identities*, 121–149. Amsterdam: John Benjamins.
Katsuno, Hirofumi and Christine R. Yano
 2002 Face to face: On-line subjectivity in contemporary Japan. *Asian Studies Review* 26(2): 205–231.
Katsuno, Hirofumi and Christine R. Yano
 2007 *Kaomoji* and expressivity in a Japanese housewives' chatroom. In: Danet and Herring (eds.), *The Multilingual Internet: Language, Culture, and Communication Online*. 278–300.
Kaul, Asha and Vaibhavi Kulkarni
 2005 Coffee, tea, or …? Gender and politeness in computer-mediated communication (CMC). *Indian Institute of Management Ahmedabad Working Papers.* http://ideas.repec.org/p/iim/iimawp/2005-04-02.html, retrieved September 25, 2005.
Kinsella, Sharon
 1995 Cuties in Japan. In: Lise Skov and Brian Moeran (eds.), *Women, Media and Consumption in Japan*, 220–254. Honolulu: University of Hawaii Press.
Kinsella, Sharon
 2000 *Adult Manga: Culture and Power in Contemporary Japanese Society.* Honolulu: University of Hawaii Press.
Koutsogiannis, Dimitris and Bessie Mitsikopoulou
 2003 Greeklish and Greekness: Trends and discourses of "glocalness." *Journal of Computer-Mediated Communication* 9(1). http://jcmc.indiana.edu/vol9/issue1/kouts_mits.html, retrieved August 15, 2005.
Koutsogiannis, Dimitris and Bessie Mitsikopoulou
 2007 Greeklish and Greekness: Trends and discourses of "glocalness". In: Danet and Herring (eds.), *The Multilingual Internet: Language, Culture, and Communication Online*. 142–160.
Krauss, Michael
 1992 The world's languages in crisis. *Language* 68: 4–10.
Krauss, Michael
 1998 The scope of the language endangerment crisis and recent response to it. In: K. Matsumara (ed.), *Studies in Endangered Languages*, 101–114. Tokyo: Hituzi Syobo.
Lakoff, Robin Tolmach
 1975 *Language and Woman's Place.* New York: Harper & Row.
Lakoff, Robin Tolmach
 2004 *Language and Woman's Place: Text and Commentaries* (revised and expanded edition by Mary Bucholtz). New York/Oxford: Oxford University Press.

Mafu, Safari
   2004   From the oral tradition to the information era: The case of Tanzania. *International Journal on Multicultural Societies* 6(1): 53–78.

Mair, Christian
   2002   The continuing spread of English: Anglo-American conspiracy or global grassroots movement? In: D. J. Allerton, Paul Skandera and Cornelia Tschichold (eds.), *Perspectives on English as a World Language*, 159–169. Basel: Schwabe.

Marsh, Bill
   2005   Livonian spoken here (for now). *New York Times*, June 19.

McClure, Erica
   2001a   The role of language in the construction of ethnic identity on the Internet: The case of Assyrian activists in diaspora. In: Christopher Moseley, Nicholas Ostler and Hassan Ouzzate (eds.), *Endangered Languages and the Media: Proceedings of the Fifth FEL (Foundation of Endangered Languages) Conference, Agadir, Morocco, 20–23 September, 2001*, 68–75. Bath, UK: Foundation for Endangered Languages.

McClure, Erica
   2001b   Oral and written Assyrian-English codeswitching. In: Rodolfo Jacobson (ed.), *Codeswitching Worldwide II*, 157–191. Berlin: Mouton de Gruyter.

McVeigh, Brian J.
   2000   How Hello Kitty commodifies the cute, cool and camp: 'Consumutopia' versus 'control' in Japan. *Journal of Material Culture* 5(2): 225.

Mensching, Guido
   2000   The Internet as a rescue tool of endangered languages: Sardinian. Presented at the conference *Multilinguae: Multimedia and Minority Languages,* San Sebastian, Spain, November 8–9, 2000. http://www.lingrom.fu-berlin.de/sardu/, retrieved February 26, 2005.

Moseley, Christopher, Nicholas Ostler and Hassan Ouzzate
   2001   Endangered languages and the media. In: Christopher Moseley, Nicholas Ostler and Hassan Ouzzate (eds.), *Endangered Languages and the Media: Proceedings of the Fifth FEL (Foundation for Endangered Languages) Conference, Agadir, Morocco, 20–23 September 2001*, 7–8. Bath, UK: Foundation for Endangered Languages.

Myhill, John and Eman Garra
   2005   Writing Palestinian Arabic in electronic messages. Paper presented at the fourth conference, Israel Association for the Study of Language in Society. Bar Ilan University, Ramat Gan, Israel, June 14, 2005. http://www.biu.ac.il/js/hb/ials/abs.htm, retrieved September 21, 2005 (paper title in Hebrew and English; abstract in English).

Nettle, Daniel and Suzanne Romaine
   2000   *Vanishing Voices: The Extinction of the World's Languages*. Oxford: Oxford University Press.

Nishimura, Yukiko
   2003   Linguistic innovations and interactional features of casual online communication in Japanese. *Journal of Computer-Mediated Communication* 9(1). http://jcmc.indiana.edu/vol9/issue1/nishimura.html, retrieved August 15, 2005.

Nishimura, Yukiko
   2007   Linguistic innovations and interactional features of casual online communication in Japanese. In: Danet and Herring (eds.), *The Multilingual Internet: Language, Culture, and Communication Online*. 163–183.

Nunberg, Geoffrey
   2000   Will the Internet always speak English? *The American Prospect Online* 11(10). http://www.prospect.org/print/V11/10/nunberg-g.html, retrieved September 25, 2005.

O'Neill, Judy
   1995   The Role of ARPA in the development of the ARPANET, 1961–1972. *Annals of the History of Computing* 17(4): 76–81.

Organization for Economic Co-operation and Development
   2001   *Understanding the digital divide.* http://www.oecd.org/dataoecd/38/57/1888451.pdf, retrieved September 20, 2005.

Ostler, Nicholas
   1999   Fighting words: As the world gets smaller, minority languages struggle to stake their claim. *Language International* 11(2): 38–45.

Palfreyman, David and Muhamed Al Khalil
   2003   "A funky language for teenzz to use": Representing Gulf Arabic in instant messaging. *Journal of Computer-Mediated Communication* 9(1). http://jcmc.indiana.edu/vol9/issue1/palfreyman.html, retrieved August 15, 2005.

Palfreyman, David and Muhamed Al Khalil
   2007   "A funky language for teenzz to use": Representing Gulf Arabic in instant messaging. In: Danet and Herring (eds.), *The Multilingual Internet: Language, Culture, and Communication Online*. 43–63

Panyametheekul, Siriporn and Susan C. Herring
   2003   Gender and turn allocation in a Thai chat room. *Journal of Computer-Mediated Communication* 9(1). http://jcmc.indiana.edu/vol9/issue1/panya_herring.html, retrieved August 15, 2005.

Panyametheekul, Siriporn and Susan C. Herring
   2007   Gender and turn allocation in a Thai chat room. In: Danet and Herring (eds.), *The Multilingual Internet: Language, Culture, and Communication Online*. 233–255.

Paolillo, John C.
   1996   Language choice on soc.culture.punjab. *Electronic Journal of Communication* 6(3). http://ella.slis.indiana.edu/~paolillo/research/paolillo.publish.txt, retrieved September 25, 2005.

Paolillo, John C.
   2007   How much multilingualism? Linguistic diversity on the Internet. In: Danet and Herring (eds.), *The Multilingual Internet: Language, Culture, and Communication Online*. 408–430.

Pargman, Daniel
   1998   Reflections on cultural bias and adaptation. Paper presented at CATaC (*Cultural Attitudes towards Technology and Communication*). London, August 1–3, 1998. http://www.it.murdoch.edu.au/~sudweeks/catac98/pdf/06_pargman.pdf, retrieved September 25, 2005.

Pargman, Daniel and Jacob Palme
  2004   Linguistic standardization on the Internet. In: Fay Sudweeks and Charles Ess (eds.), *Proceedings of CATaC: Cultural Attitudes Towards Technology and Communication 2004*, 385–388. Murdoch, Australia: Murdoch University Press.
Phillipson, Robert
  1992   *Linguistic Imperialism*. Oxford: Oxford University Press.
Phillipson, Robert
  2000   English in the new world order: Variations on a theme of linguistic imperialism and "world" English. In: Thomas Ricento (ed.), *Ideology, Politics and Language Policies: Focus on English*, 87–106. Amsterdam: John Benjamins.
Phillipson, Robert and Tove Skutnabb-Kangas
  2001   Linguistic imperialism. In: Rajend Mesthrie (ed.), *Concise Encyclopedia of Sociolinguistics*, 570–574. Oxford: Elsevier.
Pimienta, Daniel
  2002   Put out your tongue and say "aaah": Is the Internet suffering from acute "Englishitis"? *UNESCO Newsletter on Communication and Information in the Knowledge Society*, January 30, 2002. http://www.unesco.org/webworld/points_of_views/300102_pimienta.shtml, retrieved May 24, 2005.
Richie, Donald
  2003   *Kawaii*: Kingdom of the cute. In: Donald Richie, *The Image Factory: Fads & Fashions in Japan*, 53–62. London: Reaktion.
Schiffman, Harold F.
  1997   Diglossia in a sociolinguistic situation. In: Florian Coulmas (ed.), *The Handbook of Sociolinguistics*, 205–216. Oxford: Blackwell.
Schodt, Frederik L.
  1986   *Manga! Manga! The World of Japanese Comics*. Tokyo, New York and San Francisco: Kodansha International.
Skutnabb-Kangas, Tove
  1988   Multilingualism and the education of minority children. In: Tove Skutnabb-Kangas and J. Cummins (eds.), *Minority Education: From Shame to Struggle*, 9–44. Philadelphia: Multilingual Matters.
Sperlich, Wolfgang B.
  2005   Will cyberforums save endangered languages? A Niuean case study. *International Journal of the Sociology of Language* 172(1): 51–78.
Spolsky, Joel
  2003   The absolute minimum every software developer absolutely, positively must know about Unicode and character sets (no excuses!), October 8, 2003. http://www.joelonsoftware.com/articles/Unicode.html, retrieved August 25, 2005.
Su, Hsi-Yao
  2003   The multilingual and multi-orthographic Taiwan-based Internet: Creative uses of writing systems on college-affiliated BBSs. *Journal of Computer-Mediated Communication* 9(1). http://jcmc.indiana.edu/vol9/issue1/su.html, retrieved August 15, 2005.
Su, Hsi-Yao
  2007   The multilingual and multi-orthographic Taiwan-based Internet: Creative uses of writing systems on college-affiliated BBSs. In: Danet and Herring

(eds.), *The Multilingual Internet: Language, Culture, and Communication Online.* 64–86.

Sugimoto, Taku and James A. Levin
    2000   Multiple literacies and multimedia: A comparison of Japanese and American uses of the Internet. In: Gail E. Hawisher and Cynthia L. Selfe (eds.), *Global Literacies and the World-Wide Web*, 133–153. London: Routledge.

Tannen, Deborah
    1990   *You Just Don't Understand: Women and Men in Conversation.* New York: William Morrow.

Tseliga, Theodora
    2007   "It's all *Greeklish* to Me!" Linguistic and sociocultural perspectives on Greeklish (Roman-alphabeted Greek) in asynchronous CMC. In: Danet and Herring (eds.), *The Multilingual Internet: Language, Culture, and Communication Online.* 116–141.

Tsuda, Yukio
    2000   Envisioning a democratic linguistic order. *TESL Reporter* 33(1): 32–38.

Turkle, Sherry
    1995   *Life on the Screen: Identity in the Age of the Internet.* New York: Simon & Schuster.

Uberuaga, Blas Pedro
    2000   The Basque presence on the Internet: Yesterday, today and tomorrow. *Journal of the Society for Basque Studies in America* 20.

UNESCO
    2003   *UNESCO Red Book on Endangered Languages* [World Wide Web], last updated March 4, 2003. http://www.tooyoo.l.u-tokyo.ac.jp/Redbook/, retrieved August 25, 2005.

Warschauer, Mark
    1998   Technology and indigenous language revitalization: Analyzing the experience of Hawai'i. *The Canadian Modern Language Review/ La Revue canadienne des langues vivantes* 55(1): 141–161.

Warschauer, Mark
    2001   Millennialism and media: Language, literacy and technology in the 21st century. *AILA Review* 14: 49–59. Online edition available at http://www.aila.soton.ac.uk/pdfs/Aila14.pdf, retrieved August 15, 2005.

Warschauer, Mark
    2002   Languages.com: The Internet and linguistic pluralism. In: Ilana Snyder (ed.), *Silicon Literacies: Communication, Innovation and Education in the Electronic Age*, 62–74. London/New York: Routledge.

Warschauer, Mark and Keola Donaghy
    1997   Leoki: A powerful voice of Hawaiian language revitalization. *Computer-Assisted Language Learning* 10(4): 349–361.

Warschauer, Mark, Ghada R. El Said and Ayman Zohry
    2002   Language choice online: Globalization and identity in Egypt. *Journal of Computer-Mediated Communication* 7(4). http://jcmc.indiana.edu/vol7/issue4/warschauer.html, retrieved August 15, 2005.

Warschauer, Mark, Ghada R. El Said, and Ayman Zohry
    2007   Language choice online: Globalization and identity in Egypt. In: Danet and Herring (eds.), *The Multilingual Internet: Language, Culture, and Communication Online.* 303–318.

Werry, Christopher C.
   1996   Linguistic and interactional features of Internet Relay Chat. In: Susan C. Herring (ed.), *Computer-Mediated Communication: Linguistic, Social, and Cross-Cultural Perspectives*, 47–64. Amsterdam: John Benjamins.

Wheeler, Deborah
   2001   Women, Islam, and the Internet: Findings in Kuwait. In: Charles Ess and Fay Sudweeks (eds.), *Culture, Technology, Communication: Towards an Intercultural Global Village*, 158–182. Albany, NY: SUNY Press.

Witmer, Diane F. and Sandra Lee Katzman
   1997   On-line smiles: Does gender make a difference in the use of graphic accents? *Journal of Computer-Mediated Communication* 2(4). http://jcmc.indiana.edu/vol2/issue4/witmer1.html, retrieved August 15, 2005.

Wodak, Ruth and Scott Wright
   2007   The European Union in cyberspace: Democratic participation via online multilingual discussion boards? In: Danet and Herring (eds.), *The Multilingual Internet: Language, Culture, and Communication Online*. 383–407.

Wright, Handel Kashope
   1996   Email in African studies. *Convergence: The Journal of Research into New Media Technologies* 2(1): 20–30.

Wright, Scott
   2004   A comparative analysis of government-run discussion boards at the local, national and European Union levels. Ph.D. thesis, University of East Anglia, Norwich.

Wright, Sue (ed.)
   2004a   Multilingualism on the Internet. *International Journal on Multicultural Societies* 6(1). http://portal.unesco.org/shs/en/ev.php-URL_ID=7142&URL_DO=DO_TOPIC&URL_SECTION=-465.html, retrieved August 25, 2005 (also available in French).

Wright, Sue
   2004b   Thematic introduction. *International Journal on Multicultural Societies* 6 (1): 3–11. http://portal.unesco.org/shs/en/ev.php-URL_ID=7142&URL_DO=DO_TOPIC&URL_SECTION=-465.html, retrieved August 25, 2005 (also available in French).

Yates, Simeon J.
   1996   Oral and written linguistic aspects of computer-conferencing. In: Susan C. Herring (ed.), *Computer-Mediated Communication: Linguistic, Social, and Cross-Cultural Perspectives*, 29–46. Amsterdam: John Benjamins.

IV. The discourse of linguistic diversity and language change

19. Attitudes to language and communication

Cindy Gallois, Bernadette Watson and Madeleine Brabant

1. Introduction

In this chapter, we review the literature on attitudes to language and communication diversity, and to language and communication change, as markers of social identity and intergroup relations. This area has a long history, starting in the 1950s in psychology and applied linguistics, and constitutes the heart of the language and social psychology (LASP) perspective. Research into language and social psychology emerged as a field *from* social psychology in the 1950s with the work of Lambert and his colleagues in Canada (e.g., Lambert, Hodgson, Gardner, and Fillenbaum 1960). Their work was from the first strongly grounded in experimental social psychology, and it drew on linguistics only in a secondary way. For this reason, research on language attitudes has always reflected, and has retained to the present day, an allegiance to social-psychological methods and the basic concept of attitude. Compared to other approaches to language and identity, including those from linguistics, this area has a strongly psychological flavour.

Research into language and social psychology also came *out of* social psychology, in that researchers in this field criticised the tendency of social psychologists to explore the contribution of message source and audience to the exclusion of the characteristics of the message itself. As such, language and social psychology still represents the richest contribution from psychology to the study of communication in context (see Gallois, McKay, and Pittam 2004). In fact, this approach was the first to bring the systematic study of language and communication back to mainstream social psychology, after it had been eclipsed in the 1950s and 1960s. This eclipse was particularly due to the uptake of Chomsky's theories within psychology, but it also resulted from the increasing interest in cognition emanating from experimental psychology (see Ball, Gallois, and Callan 1989; Gallois 1998). Surprisingly, only in very recent times have other social psychologists become interested in the contribution of language and communication to social life. Thus, the language and social psychology tradition to some extent sits at the interface of social psychology, communication studies, and linguistics.

2. The concept of attitude

The language and social psychology approach relies centrally on the psychological concept of *attitude* (and its variants *attribution* and *prejudice* along with *stereotype*). This concept can be traced back to the early days of the field, and represents the judgements that people tend to make and generalise about an object (social or otherwise) outside themselves. Attitudes are formed towards a particular entity, called the attitude object, and are generally theorised to contain three main components: cognitive, conative (behavioural), and affective. The *cognitive component* in attitude formation and maintenance represents a person's beliefs and thoughts about the attitude object, without any positive or negative tone. The *conative component* is a predisposition to behave in accordance with the beliefs. Finally, the *affective component* represents an emotional reaction, positive or negative, that accompanies the beliefs. For example, my attitude to a minority group in my community may involve the belief that their language style contains many grammatical faults (cognitive component), a tendency to correct their purported mistakes (conative component), and a negative evaluation of their "faulty" style (affective component). These three components of attitudes, while they are correlated, are not necessarily linked. Thus, a perceiver may have an affective reaction to another group (for example), but not have clear beliefs to support the reaction. More often, perceivers have particular beliefs and emotions about another group but behave in contradiction to them.

Attitudes are generally viewed as stable and related to meaningful objects or events (see Eagly and Chaiken 1993; Vaughan and Hogg 2004). Robinson (2003) makes the point that from around 400 BC Plato had recognised the role of cognition, conation and affect in attitudes and attitude change. Robinson notes that these three components are not acknowledged as separate parts of attitude by all psychologists, even though a person's attitudes towards a topic may not correlate with his or her behaviour. Unpacking these three components provides a means for understanding attitude change. The extent to which a person may alter his or her attitude towards an object is made up of many parts: Individuals may alter their beliefs, feelings, approval, action-orientation, or behaviour towards an object (see Robinson 2003: 136). These parts are inter-related, but each is subtly different from the others. Thus, we may have negative feelings about people who have a particular accent (for example, RP in English) and we may believe that such people are untrustworthy and to this end reduce contact with them. If we have extensive contact with a particular RP speaker, we may develop positive feelings towards this person, but this may not change our negative affect towards the attitude object (speakers of RP as a group) – the enduring nature of the attitude is maintained. Indeed, the stability of attitudes in the face of contrary cases like the example above is one of their most interesting features to social psychologists.

Thus, while beliefs are a core part of attitude, the latter is constituted of more than beliefs. As a result, much attention has been paid by social psychologists to understanding the relationship (often imperfect, to say the least) between attitudes and behaviour, and also to examining the emotional part of attitudes. There is a large literature on the impact of mood and emotion on beliefs and social judgements, and the resultant impact on behaviour (this area often goes by the name of *hot cognition*, cf. Forgas 2000). Within language and social psychology, the centrality of attitude to the research approach has had a number of theoretical and methodological consequences, which set this tradition apart from other approaches to language and communication.

In a study of communication attitudes in health contexts, Watson and Gallois (2002) used an indirect measure of patients' attitudes towards health professionals via the linguistic category model (LCM) devised by Semin and Fielder (1989, 1992). In this model, attitude is signalled by the extent to which the words used about an object are positive or negative and reflect more transient and peripheral or more permanent and central aspects of the object. Watson and Gallois found that in patients' retrospective descriptions of satisfactory interactions with health professionals, the patients showed low levels of intergroup bias. Their descriptions of health professionals, like their descriptions of themselves, used stable descriptors (adjectives and state verbs) for positive aspects; for example, patients described the health professionals as friendly and happy, and one patient stated that the health professional "recognised me". On the other hand, when patients described unsatisfactory interactions, characterisations of health professionals were more likely to include transient descriptors for negative characteristics. For example, a patient described how a doctor took a medical history too quickly: "It was the speed at which he 'did' it. It was such a long list and 'read' so quickly." Similarly, patients' self-characterisations still showed a self-serving tendency to use more transient descriptors; for example, patients used self-descriptors such as "I was talking", or "I asked". In this case, intergroup bias was less evident in attitudes, which may be related to the patients' perceptions that their power and status levels were lower than that of the health professionals. Overall, these results illustrate the interaction of cognition, conation, and affect in forming and maintaining attitudes.

The first distinctive characteristic of the social-psychological approach to language is its focus on perception (or reception) rather than on production. As a result, research in this tradition tends to have a rather poor specification of language features. For example, until recently there has been relatively little interest in the details of accent or paralanguage (or indeed in the dialect spoken) among researchers in language and social psychology. Even communication accommodation theory (see below), which examines communicative behaviour as a function of motivation and attitude, has been criticised by linguists for this. At the extreme, in some research a single speaker has been used, so strong is the emphasis on the impression the speaker creates instead of on the speaker's actual behaviour. For example, Giles, Taylor, and Bourhis (1973) conducted a study in which English-Canadians were divided into four groups and listened to the same French-Canadian speaker in four different conditions. Each group heard the speaker talk in either fluent English, fluent French, a mix, or nonfluent English. Each member of the four groups was aware that the speaker could choose his preferred language. In line with the theoretical underpinnings of communication accommodation theory, individual members of the four groups rated the speaker differently on specific characteristics, based on their attributions about the speaker's motivation to use a specific language. In the past 20 years, researchers in language and social psychology have realised the importance of studying production (e.g., Coupland, Coupland, Giles, and Henwood 1988; Potter and Wetherell 1987), although the main focus of research has still tended to be on perception.

On the other hand, researchers in language and social psychology have developed a very rich approach to the study of perception. This has included indirect measures of attitude like judgements of personality (e.g., Gallois and Callan 1981; Lambert et al. 1960; Watson and Gallois 2002), judgements of status and solidarity (in a rich tradition dating from Brown and Gilman 1960; e.g., Ball, Giles, Byrne, and Berechree 1984; Lyczak, Fu, and Ho 1976; Ryan and Carranza 1975), and consideration of the influence of larger social factors such as sex, socio-economic status, and intergroup history on perception (e.g., Giles and Powesland 1975; see Robinson and Giles 2001 for a recent comprehensive review of this literature). In one exemplary study, Ball et al. (1984) played audio recordings of speakers and told participants that the speakers were job seekers who desperately needed employment. Participants judged the job seekers as accommodating to the interviewer by converging in accent, even when this was not the case in terms of measured features of accent. The emphasis on perception is probably the most important feature that sets language and social psychology research apart from applied linguistics.

3. Methodologies in attitude research

The language attitudes approach can probably best trace its origins to the work of Lambert, Gardner and their many colleagues (e.g., Lambert et al. 1960), which continues up to the present day. This research found its inspiration in the changing intergroup relations between French and English speakers in Canada. Because of their context, these researchers focused on intercultural and interethnic communication from an intergroup perspective, as well as on language itself (French versus English in the first instance).

3.1. Indirect measures of attitudes: Matched Guise Technique

At that time, the main measures of attitudes involved questionnaires, in which people were asked structured questions (using rating scales) about the attitude object. This method was sharply criticised for its social-desirability bias. Social desirability, or the need that participants in research often feel to make ratings that they perceive will please the experimenter and present them in the best light, is a major concern in all attitude research because of the assumption that attitudes are relatively stable. The measures were also criticised for leading respondents toward the answers researchers expected to hear. Lambert and his colleagues (1960) developed a clever alternative, the Matched Guise Technique (MGT). This technique required French and English bilinguals in Canada to listen to tape recordings in French and English and to make personality ratings of the speakers. Unbeknownst to respondents, the speakers were the same people across languages, resulting in considerable control of vocal features and personality. Experimental methods were used, so that differences in judgements as a function of language were explained as being caused by respondents' attitudes toward the two languages in this intergroup context. As predicted, English guises were attributed better education, higher status, but less friendliness and trustworthiness, whereas French guises were judged as friendlier and more trustworthy. Lambert (1967) proposed that in intercultural contexts, the first judgement that people make is one of ethnicity or culture, signalled by language; this judgement colours further impressions of interlocutors.

Research using this new indirect method soon proliferated around the world (see Ryan and Giles 1982 for a comprehensive review of research up to that time). In multilingual contexts, the original guise methodology was employed, using bilingual speakers and respondents. In monolingual contexts like the UK, however, region and social class as signalled by accent became the main object of study (see Giles and Powesland 1975; Giles and Robinson 1990 for reviews). Where possible in these studies, the same speaker(s) who could use two or more accents were employed. Where this was not possible, different speakers were used, with multiple speakers providing the control that was lost through not using "bi-dialectals" (e.g., Gallois and Callan 1981). In general, researchers were able to predict personality judgements based on language and accent very well by starting from an analysis of the intergroup dynamics in each context.

Despite its value in generating research, the matched guise technique came under strong criticism from linguistics (e.g., Nolan 1983). First, the control over speech style and personality supposedly provided by this method was questioned. Speakers have been known at least since the work of Labov (e.g., 1972) to vary language features depending on their identity, so that speaker stereotypes are likely to influence accent and speech style. In addition, a number of studies have shown systematic differences in measures of latent personality as a function of language spoken and thus of context (e.g., Ervin 1964). Thirdly, no account was taken of characteristics other than language and ethnicity, such as sex, occupational role, and the like. Indeed, the vast majority of studies up to the late 1970s employed only male speakers. In one of the first studies that did consider other features of speakers, Gallois and Callan (1981) played audio recordings of male and female speakers to monolingual Anglo-Australian listeners. The speakers, all of whom spoke the same passage in English (as was typical of matched guise research), came from Australia (the ethnic and cultural ingroup), England (a high-status closely-related group for these listeners), France, Italy, Greece (two large immigrant groups in Australia), or Vietnam (a new immigrant group). Their study replicated earlier results for male speakers, in that British, then Australian speakers were judged most positively, followed by French, Vietnamese, Italian, and Greek speakers – interestingly, judgements of Vietnamese speakers seemed to be related to the fact that many listeners mistook them as French. Results for female speakers, however, were reversed, and all outgroups (French, Italian, Greek, and Vietnamese) were judged more positively than ingroup speakers (Australian and British). These problems and surprising results led to a return to more direct measures of language attitudes, which are more common than the Matched Guise Technique today.

3.2. Direct measures of attitudes: Questionnaires

Questionnaire measures of language attitudes have always been popular among researchers in language and social psychology. Such measures have the great advantage of allowing researchers to ask a large number of subtle questions about attitudes to a large number of respondents quickly and easily, and to apply sophisticated data analysis techniques to their examination. Questionnaire measures have the disadvantage, however, of tapping only a limited domain generated by the researcher, as well as potentially tapping attitudes that are not salient outside the questionnaire context.

The most direct measures are questionnaires that ask respondents to make straightforward intergroup comparisons about language and communication asking such questions as the competence and attractiveness of the speaker (individual traits) versus the status and power of the speaker's respective group (group characteristics; see Bradac 1990). These measures often use structured bi-polar scales like the semantic differential to study perceptions of the prestige and positivity respondents have toward their own and another language, dialect, or style. Ryan and Giles (1982) and many chapters in Giles and Robinson (1990), Robinson and Giles (2001), and Harwood and Giles (2005) examine this research, which has taken place on all continents, and which has extended to intergroup contexts like inter-gender, intergenerational, organisational, and inter-ability communication as well as intercultural. For example, Sachdev and Bourhis (2001) propose a model of multilingual communication with three main components. The first is the intergroup context, including the stability, legitimacy and power of an ethnic group. The second is the sociolinguistic setting, or the norms and rules of language choice, as well as extant networking between speakers of different languages. The third is the social psychological processes, which influence language use and style as described in communication accommodation theory. These components are posited as predictors of actual language behaviour, as well as predictors of changes in multilingualism and multiculturalism which may influence language loss or shift. In general, the results of this research reflect the larger intergroup situation: negative comparisons where intergroup rivalry and conflict are high, and more negative perceptions of salient outgroups than of the ingroup.

The Achilles heel of these measures is that, while they are excellent indicators of respondents' expressed attitudes, they are not always good predictors of behaviour. As we noted above, the cognitive and affective components of attitudes do not always correspond to the conative component, which is the most closely related to actual behaviour. For example, Bourhis (1983) asked French Canadians whether they would accommodate in language to an English-speaking stranger who addressed them in English; overwhelmingly, participants stated that they would not accommodate. He then observed encounters in public places where French speakers were addressed in English by English-speaking strangers; the vast majority of speakers converged to English. In this case, the desire to be polite may have led to behaviour inconsistent with the expressed attitude. In some cases, however, behaviour does not follow attitude for other reasons. For example, Jones, Gallois, Callan, and Barker (1995), in a study of an intercultural academic context, found that male Australian participants reported wanting to communicate clearly with their male Chinese counterparts, but their actual communication was judged as not being clear by outside observers. Likewise, Willemyns, Gallois, Callan, and Pittam (1997), in the context of a job interview, found that male interviewees diverged from male interviewers with cultivated Australian accents, even though their intention was to converge. Overall, direct measures are a good way to discover how people believe they would behave, but not how they behave in real interactions.

One important exception to these results is in the area of L2 acquisition. Gardner and his many colleagues (e.g., Gardner 1979; Gardner, Lalonde, and Pierson 1983) in a number of questionnaire studies, have found that intergroup language attitudes consistently predict motivation to learn a second language, as well as proficiency in the language. They argue that motivation to learn L2 may be extrinsic or instrumental (e.g., a desire to do business in the new language) or intrinsic (i.e., identification with or desire to be part of the new language group), and that the latter predicts greater success in language learning. Other factors like ability and context also intervene, but those whose intergroup attitudes are positive learn L2 better and more efficiently than those whose motivation is not tied to positive attitudes.

In recent years, other direct measures of the impact of the intergroup context have appeared. One of the most interesting is MacIntyre et al.'s intergroup extension of the Willingness to Communicate questionnaire (e.g., MacIntyre, Babin, and Clément 1999; MacIntyre, Clément, Baker, and Conrod 2001). This instrument was originally designed as an individual-difference estimate of communication apprehension, but these researchers have shown its sensitivity to intergroup contexts and its utility in predicting success in L2 learning. The original concept of willingness to communicate (WTC) came from McCroskey and Richmond's (1987) concept of contextual shyness, which emphasised individual characteristics. McCroskey and Richmond posited an interpersonal variable of communication apprehension or reluctance to communicate in a specific situation (e.g., buying goods in a shop, chatting at a drinks party); the converse is willingness to communicate. MacIntyre and his colleagues have expanded this idea to intergroup interactions, with a combined focus on individual and intergroup characteristics that lead to L2 initiation. Their WTC model takes account of both psychological and contextual variables. These include an individual's immediate intentions, previous communication usage, and language attitudes towards the ingroup and the salient outgroup. The latter embrace cognitions along with positive or negative affect (Clément, Baker, and MacIntyre 2003).

Arguably the most-used direct measure of language and communication attitudes derives from subjective ethnolinguistic vitality theory (Giles, Bourhis, and Taylor 1977; Bourhis, Giles, and Rosenthal 1981). Subjective ethnolinguistic vitality theory proposes that intergroup language attitudes can be predicted by respondents' attitudes to three comparisons between their own and one or more other language groups: (1) the strength of the group (numbers, extent of ingroup marriage, etc.), (2) its social status or prestige, and (3) its support from social institutions (media, government, education, etc.). Normally, questionnaires contain from 25 to 50 items tapping these dimensions, which have been shown to be highly inter-correlated through confirmatory factor analysis (Willemyns, Pittam, and Gallois 1994).

Allard and Landry (e.g., 1986, 1994), along with their colleagues, developed an expanded measure of subjective ethnolinguistic vitality theory that includes perceived behaviour and intentions. In their beliefs in ethnolinguistic vitality questionnaire (BEVQ), they incorporate the original subjective vitality questionnaire, which asks for ratings of the perceived size and status of a group, its institutional support, and so forth, now, in the past and in the future. Their measure adds questions about the participant's intentions to work to improve the vitality of the ingroup in the future. They have used this questionnaire to conduct an extensive investigation of the perceived status of French and of minority languages in Canada. Their measures have been found to predict a wide range of outcome variables, including identity, attitudes toward language policy, preferences for language use, and fluency in L1 and L2. Allard and Landry argue that intentions (the conative component of attitudes) are the most proximal and therefore the best predictor of actual linguistic behaviour (e.g., L2 learning).

In addition to the reviews already mentioned in this chapter, much of the research on subjective ethnolinguistic vitality has been reported in the *Journal of Multilingual and Multicultural Development* since the 1980s. Overall, results have shown strong support for the impact of perceived vitality, with respondents showing pride and loyalty to groups whose languages (or communication styles) have high subjective ethnolinguistic vitality, and a desire to move away from groups with lower SEV. There is one major exception to these findings: When perceived vitality is very low, unexpectedly high identification to the language has frequently been reported. For example, Sachdev, Bourhis, Phang, and D'Eye (1987) studied the identification and perceived vitality of minority immigrant groups in Canada. They found that for all groups except those with lowest perceived vitality, identification was higher when perceived vitality was higher. For these low-vitality groups, however, identification was very high. They argued that identification signalled an intention to improve the vitality of the group in future if possible (cf. Allard and Landry 1994). By contrast, Pittam, Gallois, and Willemyns (1991) in a study of perceived vitality of the Vietnamese in Australia found that highly-identified Anglo Australians perceived the vitality of Vietnamese as paradoxically high and the threat to their group as great. In this case, the high objective vitality of the ingroup (Anglo Australians, the majority) may have been lower in perceptions as a spur to action.

3.3.   Recent developments: Discourse analysis

The past decade or so has involved an upsurge in studies of intergroup conversational behaviour and interviews, and there has been an increasing focus on the use of conversation analysis and discourse analysis. Abandoning attitude measures altogether, these researchers argue that speakers and listeners should be considered as negotiating their attitudes in interaction through talk. Unlike more traditional social psychologists, who see attitudes as stable features that determine (or at least influence) linguistic behaviour, scholars in language and social psychology who embrace discourse analysis argue that language (specifically talk) comes first, and that discursive moves determine (or influence) perceived beliefs and attitudes. The tradition of discursive psychology (Potter and Edwards 1992; Potter and Wetherell 1987, 2003) has been a key influence. Often, their focus is on covert prejudice in intergroup contexts, and interviewers may adopt a confrontational approach to their respondents. For example, Potter and Wetherell (1992) described in detail the linguistic moves made by New Zealanders who denied being racist but who nevertheless used differentiating and discriminatory language in talking about ethnic groups in that country.

Weatherall and Gallois (2003) examined gender and language from the perspective of discursive psychology. Their emphasis was not on an individual's cognitions about what it means to be male or female, which then drive language style. Instead, they argued for the reverse, that talk drives attitudes about gender and gender identity. The ways in which talk signals and leads to attitudes is not usually an overt process, however. Men and women may or may not communicate in ways that demonstrate that group identity. In this approach, the researcher's job is to examine the discourse in detail for clues to the extent to which the larger social variable (gender) impinges on communication, and what is signalled when it does. Discursive psychologists argue that it is language that demonstrates the relevant gender and inter-gender relations, not an individual's attitudes to gender.

4. Theories and controversial issues

Over the years, a large number of theories of language attitudes have been developed by social psychologists of language and scholars in intergroup communication. These theories have much in common, in general placing a premium on people's thoughts and beliefs about language and communication, along with the influence of social (particularly intergroup) factors on them. Nevertheless, the theories differ on a number of dimensions, including especially whether attitudes are posited as real characteristics of people or as social constructions, as stable or as dynamic. In addition, theories differ with respect to the importance accorded to context, to interpersonal relations and communication (as well as intergroup relations), and to the role of language production. In this section, we describe a few exemplary theories very briefly, including a discussion of communication accommodation theory, which aims to be comprehensive across these factors.

4.1. Attitudes as real and stable characteristics of speakers and listeners

The tradition of social psychology proposes that attitudes are relatively stable features of people, and thus relatively resistant to conversational dynamics (although they may be context-specific). An excellent example of such a theory is Berry's (e.g., 1990) model of intercultural adaptation; other theories of adaptation (e.g., Kim 2001) share a good deal in common with his. Berry proposes that immigrants – in his work immigrants to a new country, but arguably this theory can be applied to any group or role socialisation process – have one of four main stances to the old (or minority) group and the new (dominant or majority) group. These are *assimilation*, where the new group is valued highly but the old group is not; *integration*, where both groups are valued highly; *separation*, where the old group is valued highly but the new group is not; and *marginalisation*, where both groups are devalued. People who have an assimilation orientation act to become as similar as possible to the new group, and abandon the distinguishing behaviours and beliefs of the old one. Those with a separation orientation do the reverse. People with an integration orientation try to blend the two cultures or to switch from one to the other, and those who are marginalised tend to be alienated from the society as a whole. There is also an individualism orientation, where people tend to operate out of another identity (e.g., their occupational role) or to describe themselves as independent individuals. These adaptation types can be used to predict a wide range of behaviours and attitudes, from impressions of the host culture through to psychological adjustment and success as a sojourner or immigrant.

Bourhis and his colleagues (Bourhis 2001; Bourhis, Moïse, Perrault, and Sénécal 1997) extended Berry's theory to capture societal orientations (i.e., the orientations of members of dominant groups) to immigrants in an interactive acculturation model. Like Berry, they posit an *assimilation* societal orientation, where members of dominant groups value their own characteristics highly but devalue those of other cultures (and so wish immigrants to adopt the new ways as quickly and completely as possible and to be absorbed into the larger society). There is also a societal orientation of *segregation*, where members of the dominant or majority group wish for only their behaviour to be displayed in public (although they have a *civic* orientation in that they believe that minority groups may acceptably use their language and customs in private enclaves), There is an orientation of *exclusionism*, where members of the dominant majority wish minorities to be excluded altogether from the society. The final societal orientation is *integration* or *pluralism*, where the characteristics of all groups are valued (at least in theory). As is the case for individual acculturation, they posit that members of dominant groups may have an orientation of *individualism*, in which they deny the impact of group membership and treat individuals on their own merits (or desire to at any rate). Bourhis and his colleagues argue that the best adaptation of an immigrant person or group occurs when the larger societal orientation and the individual's (or minority group's) psychological orientation are compatible (e.g., both assimilation, both separation/segregation, both integration). Bourhis has used this model to describe a number of multicultural countries in the world today. For example, the posited assimilationist orientation of the French in France is very compatible with immigrant groups who are happy to converge to French norms in language and communication (including dress and other communicative customs). It leads to serious conflict, however, when minority groups prefer separation or wish to maintain their own ethnolinguistic markers, as some Muslim groups in France do at present with respect to language, dress, and other behaviours.

4.2. Attitudes as real but dynamic

Another set of theories are aimed to give more attention to the role of interactional dynamics in determining language attitudes. Many of these have much in common with social identity theory (e.g., Tajfel and Turner 1979; Turner et al. 1987). This theory of social behaviour in general aims to describe the group in the person (Hogg and Abrams 1988) – the ways in which our salient social memberships influence our interpersonal and intergroup attitudes, beliefs, and behaviours in context. Social identity theory (SIT) posits that a central part of the self-concept is made up of comparisons between a person's ingroups (whether ethnic, gender, societally-based, or role-based) and outgroups that are salient in the particular context. Essentially, people form beliefs so as to make the ingroup positively distinctive from a salient outgroup. Who the ingroup and outgroup are will vary from context to context, although some group memberships like gender and ethnicity tend to be chronically salient, particularly where the social context is one of relative inequality.

One major way of making the ingroup positively distinctive is to accentuate those things (features of language or communication, beliefs and values, or other characteristics) that differentiate between the ingroup and outgroup maximally. In doing this, people emphasise those characteristics that are more positive for their group than for the salient outgroup (e.g., a minority group may emphasise its sporting prowess or physical beauty, whereas members of the majority emphasise their superior income and education). Furthermore, there is a tendency to accentuate the similarity of outgroup members to each other (and to a lesser extent to do this for ingroup members as well), but to emphasise differences between groups. In this way, in contexts where social identity is important, people behave so as to maximise intergroup and minimise intragroup differences. Social identity theory has been used to predict a huge number of biases in social judgement and decision-making, as well as intergroup behaviours, mainly in contexts that are easily amenable to experimental manipulation. Jones et al. (1995) used both communication accommodation theory and social identity theory to examine Chinese and Australian students and lecturers. They showed that social identification with the ingroup predicted subtle divergence in communication for both Chinese and Australian students, but only for males. Most social identity studies, however, do not focus on language.

In recent times, this theory has also been systematically applied to organisational contexts (see Haslam 2001, for a discussion of the impact of social identity on group productivity and performance, and of the relation between identity and power in organisational settings). Results have generally supported the theory, although much of this work has been experimental research conducted with university students rather than applied studies in ongoing organisations. Schwarz, Watson, and Jones (2005) used social identity theory in an applied organisational context: a large metropolitan hospital undergoing major structural change involving downsizing, role redefinition, a new reporting structure around interdisciplinary professional teams in patient care, and a new physical site next to the old hospital. While the focus of this research was on information and communication technology, they found that employees identified with separate groups within the hospital (member of the hospital executive, doctor, nurse, etc.), and expressed differing opinions and attitudes towards the change that reflected these groupings. In particular, they used language which aligned them to specific social groups within the hospital.

Where intergroup rivalry, conflict, or inequality is great, members of the majority behave linguistically and socially so as to enhance the prestige of their group relative to the outgroup. Members of less dominant groups adopt various coping strategies that range from attempts to pass into the dominant group, through to social creativity strategies (emphasising dimensions where their own group has more status, such as judgements of French Canadians as more trustworthy) to a strategy of overt social confrontation. In general, strategies to maintain and enhance dominant status and those to deal with lower status centrally involve attitudes about the language and communication behaviour of the ingroup and salient outgroups (generally as measured by structured questionnaires).

The heuristic value of this way of conceptualising intergroup behaviour, including language attitudes, is immense. For one thing, social identity theory is open to the potential of language attitudes to change, even dramatically, with relatively subtle features of the context. For example, telling an ethnic joke can change a situation from largely interpersonal to totally intergroup. Without abandoning the experienced reality of attitudes, social identity theory aims to predict better or worse associations between measured attitudes and actual behaviour through a careful exploration of the context. Furthermore, the principles of this very general theory of social behaviour can be applied to virtually any intergroup context. Thus, social identity theory has been used to examine many language-related behaviours, including some counter-intuitive ones. For example, social identity theory can predict the tendency to judge ingroup members who deviate from behavioural norms more harshly than outgroup members (the "black sheep effect", see Marques and Yzerbyt 1988), and the paradoxical tendency to accept criticism more readily from ingroup than outgroup members (Hornsey, Oppes, and Svensson 2002).

A number of theories in the area of language attitudes are closely related to social identity theory, including other theories of identity management (e.g., Giles and Byrne 1982; Hajek and Giles 2003). In addition, communication attitude theories including communication accommodation theory (see Gallois,

Ogay, and Giles 2005) have been derived partly from it, such as the communication predicament of ageing (Hummert and Ryan 1996; Ryan, Giles, Bartolucci, and Henwood 1986) and its variants in the arena of inter-ability communication (Fox, Giles, Orbe, and Bourhis 2000; Ryan, Bajorek, Beamon, and Anas 2005; see also Gallois 2004). Without doubt, social identity theory will continue to be a source of theory in all areas of language and social psychology. This theory is currently informing the area of health communication though an examination of the intergroup dynamics of multi-disciplinary teams, and health professionals and their patients (Watson and Gallois 2007).

Another group of theories also posit attitudes as real but determined by aspects of contextual dynamics. Unlike social identity theory, however, these theories deal largely with the influence of interpersonal rather than intergroup dynamics on communication attitudes. Perhaps the best exemplar is interpersonal expectancy theory (see Burgoon, Stern, and Dillman 1995). In brief, this theory posits that attitudes frame expectations about language and communication behaviour (e.g., people we like are expected to be friendly and positive in their communication). Furthermore, we have a latitude of tolerance for any interlocutor, which is larger when our attitude toward the person is positive, i.e., we give "idiosyncrasy credit" (Hollander 1958) to valued others. When expectations are within the latitude of tolerance, attitudes remain stable, and we generally reciprocate the other person's communicative behaviour. When expectations are unfulfilled in that behaviour appears more negative than expected, attitudes can become dramatically more negative, and behaviour changes negatively as a consequence. When expectations are positively unfulfilled (i.e., when the other person's behaviour is more positive than anticipated), attitudes change dramatically as well. Communicative behaviour, thus, is determined in this view by attitudes, but is also strongly influenced by conversational dynamics. Expectancy theories share this approach with theories of uncertainty reduction and management (e.g., Berger and Bradac 1982; Gudykunst 2005).

4.3.   Attitudes as social constructions negotiated in context

As the move in language and social psychology toward closer attention to the dynamics of talk has grown in the past 20 years, many scholars have rejected the measurement of attitudes altogether, arguing that attitudes are only social constructions about people negotiated in the context of talk, and therefore can only be studied by looking at conversational behaviour. For example, Hecht and his colleagues (see Hecht, Jackson, Lindsley, Strauss, and Johnson 2001) have proposed a layered approach to identity, involving personal, enacted, relational, and communal identities. All aspects of identity implicate the expression of beliefs, emotions, and behaviour, and any or all of them may be salient in a given context. Furthermore, they are negotiated through talk, including particular features of communication style (e.g., markers of social class or dialect), beliefs, and other behaviours. This theory has been useful in predicting the ways in which members of ethnic minorities respond to health promotion campaigns aimed at the larger population. In addition, Hecht (2004) has used this theory to devise targeted programs around reduction of drug use for young people in these populations. In this large-scale project in the western United States, Hecht and his colleagues noted that young Hispanic people in the US are significantly alienated from messages associated with dominant groups in the country. Therefore, they initially investigated the jargon, ways of speaking, other communicative behaviour, and practices that were associated with the most influential people in targeted schools, then used these markers to develop messages aimed at preventing young people from beginning drug use. In a further phase of the project, they worked with young people from the schools, who produced their own messages in their own words. As noted above, theories in the tradition of discursive psychology also take this view of the existence (or non-existence) of attitude (see Weatherall and Gallois 2003, for a discussion of this issue in the context of inter-gender communication).

4.4. Communication accommodation theory

Communication accommodation theory (CAT) is closely related to social identity theory, but was developed independently of it (see Giles and Powesland 1975; Giles, Mulac, Bradac, and Johnson 1987). Communication accommodation theory in its earliest form was intended to explain the communicative moves of interactants toward each other's language or speech style (convergence) or away from each other (divergence) in terms of interpersonal and intergroup motivation and language attitudes. As Giles (1973) pointed out, it was also developed in reaction to sociolinguistic theories of accommodation that placed no emphasis on motivation, so that language and communication attitudes are part of the theory's core. Like social identity theory, communication accommodation theory presupposes that people act through their beliefs and behaviour to enhance the power and status of their ingroups at the expense of outgroups. Thus, as it is for social identity theory, diversity is a source of social comparison and self-esteem. Giles and Coupland (1991) highlighted that the ways in which individuals subjectively define a situation, and their corresponding salient identities for that particular context, predict language diversity. Thus, levels of low or high linguistic diversity occur to varying degrees across a range of social situations. The differing cognitive structures construed by interactants during social encounters which vary in levels of personal or group salience, competitiveness, task focus and levels of formality and inequality determine the conscious or subconscious choice of varying speech patterns (see Giles and Coupland 1991: 18–19).

Over time, communication accommodation theory (see Gallois, Ogay, and Giles 2005) has developed into a comprehensive theory of interpersonal communicative behaviour in intergroup contexts. As such, it posits an *initial orientation* held by one (or more) interactants toward another. Communication accommodation theory posits that individuals bring their own attitudes to interactions, which shape the ways in which each interactant is likely to respond to the other. These attitudes are based on the socio-historical backgrounds, as well as individual histories comprised of previous experiences of similar interactions, and perceived social norms. Initial orientation is also based on the larger social context, particularly the intergroup and interpersonal history. This orientation may be modified, however, by the *sociolinguistic strategies and behavioural tactics* employed by interactants in conversation, as well as by the *specific features* (social norms, level of formality, familiarity and uncertainty, etc.) of the social context. In this view, attitudes are both brought into the interaction and negotiated within it. This dynamic in turn influences the ways in which behaviour is *labelled* and how it is *attributed* (e.g., to personal volition, to ability or skill, to features of the context), and thence to the *overall evaluation* of (attitude toward) other interactants. Finally, evaluations determine the initial orientation in *future interactions* with the other person or the person's group.

This very brief account should nevertheless indicate that communication accommodation theory is an attempt to conceptualise language attitudes and the behaviour associated with them in a comprehensive way. There is a very large research literature based on this theory (see Giles and Ogay 2006; Shepard, Giles, and Lepoire 2001, for reviews), which is largely supportive of the theory's propositions. The theory has been applied to many areas, from its origins in inter-cultural and interethnic communication to social class, gender, age, organisational role, and health. In an example from inter-gender communication, Brabant (2000) found that professional men and women described themselves and were described by others as being more masculine and more success and career oriented (i.e., as more agentic). Their occupational identity but not their gender or family role identity was reflected in their communication style. In fact, it was found that professional men and women described themselves as communicating in a more masculine fashion by being more assertive and efficient than non-professional men and women, while non-professional men and women described themselves as behaving more in a friendly manner. In the health arena, communication accommodation theory is being used to explore the dynamics in consultations between health providers and their clients, which are examples of interpersonal interactions in an essentially intergroup context (e.g., Watson and Gallois 1998, 1999, 2002; Street 2001). Watson and Gallois found that patients rated interactions as most satisfactory when they perceived that health professionals paid more attention to the patients' relationship and emotional needs and used more nurturant emotional expression. These findings point the way toward elucidating the perceived optimal balance in accommodative behaviour, both group based and interpersonal (Watson and Gallois 1998).

Its very comprehensiveness, however, has brought communication accommodation theory under criticism, mainly because specific and falsifiable predictions are extremely difficult to derive. For this reason, context-specific and more testable variants have been derived in the areas of inter-generational communication (Ryan et al. 1986), health professional-patient communication (Street 2001), and inter-ability communication (Ryan et al. 2005), among others. Gallois et al. (2005) have called for communication accommodation theory to be made more generic, which is likely to increase the need for context-specific theories of intergroup language behaviour.

5. Implications and conclusions

This overview highlights the strengths and weaknesses of the language attitudes approach. On the one hand, this approach allows a subtle understanding of the antecedents of language and communication perception. Researchers in this tradition assume that perception is almost totally in the ear of the beholder, so that actual linguistic behaviour is important mainly in the ways it cues attitudes about social diversity. This emphasis has led to a plethora of theories and some tight quantitative methodologies. Its weakness, however, is inherent in its core assumptions: There is not always much connection between expressed attitudes and actual communicative behaviour. It has become clear that language and communication attitudes involve interpersonal and contextual as well as intergroup history and relations, but the relative contribution of each is still a matter of some dispute. In particular, the dynamic and changeable manner in which people interact across social groups is not well-captured by the study of language attitudes. Furthermore, by emphasising one intergroup membership (e.g., culture, gender, or age), language attitudes research tends to neglect the multiple group memberships and identities that influence behaviour at any one time in any context. This is why, in recent years, so many social psychologists of language have turned towards the study of discourse to supplement or replace research on attitudes.

It is clear today that applied linguists and social psychologists of language have much to contribute to each other. Each field has concentrated on key parts of the area of language and diversity, but each has tended to give less attention to other parts. By combining findings from these traditions, it becomes possible to ground L2 training, intercultural communication training, and similar programs in both attitudes and behaviour, taking account of interpersonal, intergroup, and contextual factors (cf. Gallois 2003; Gallois and Pittam 1996).

Language attitudes research specifically addresses the role of prejudice and identity on communication behaviour. Thus, it can contribute to social policy about language and multiculturalism, but not without due acknowledgement of the impact of social factors and social networks on language production. In the future, we hope and expect to see more comprehensive research, especially in intergroup contexts beyond intercultural communication. This will require comprehensive and dynamic models like communication accommodation theory, which take account of the large variety of factors that affect language diversity.

References

Allard, Réal and Rodrigue Landry
    1986   Subjective ethnolinguistic vitality viewed as a belief system. *Journal of Multilingual and Multicultural Development* 7: 1–12.

Allard, Réal and Rodrigue Landry
    1994   Subjective ethnolinguistic vitality: A comparison of two measures. *International Journal of the Sociology of Language* 108: 117–144.

Ball, Peter, Cindy Gallois and Victor J.Callan
    1989   Language attitudes: Perspectives from social psychology. In: Peter Collins and David Blair (eds.), *Australian English: The Language of a New Society*, 89–102. Brisbane: University of Queensland Press.

Ball, Peter, Howard Giles, Jane L. Byrne and P. Berechree
    1984   Situational constraints on the evaluative significance of speech accommodation: Some Australian data. *International Journal of the Sociology of Language* 46: 115–129.

Berger, Charles R. and James J. Bradac
    1982   *Language and Social Knowledge*. London: Edward Arnold.

Berry, John W.
    1990   Psychology of acculturation: Understanding individuals moving between cultures. In: R. Brislin (ed.), *Applied Cross-cultural Psychology*, 232–253. Newbury Park, CA: Sage.

Bourhis, Richard Y.
    1983   Language attitudes and self-reports of French-English usage in Quebec. *Journal of Multilingual and Multicultural Development* 4: 163–179.

Bourhis, Richard Y.
    2001   Acculturation, language maintenance and language loss. In: J. Klatter-Falmer and P. Van Avermaet (eds.), *Language Maintenance and Language Loss*, 5–37. Tilburg, The Netherlands: Tilburg University Press.

Bourhis, Richard Y., Howard Giles and Doreen Rosenthal
    1981   Notes on the construction of a "Subjective Vitality Questionnaire" for ethnolinguistic groups. *Journal of Multilingual and Multicultural Development* 2: 145–155.

Bourhis, Richard Y., Léna C Moïse, Stéphane Perrault and Sascha Sénécal
    1997   Towards an interactive acculturation model: A social psychological approach. *International Journal of Psychology* 32: 369–386.

Brabant, Madeleine
    2000   Gender and professional identity: Influence on stereotypes and communication. Unpublished PhD thesis, The University of Queensland, Brisbane.
Bradac, James J.
    1990   Language, attitudes and impression formation. In: W. Peter Robinson and Howard Giles (eds.), *The Handbook of Language and Social Psychology*, 387–412. Chichester, UK: Wiley.
Brown, Roger and Albert Gilman
    1960   The pronouns of power and solidarity. In: Thomas A. Sebeok (ed.), *Style in Language*, 253–276. New York: MIT Press.
Burgoon, Judee K., Lesa A. Stern, and Leesa Dillman
    1995   *Interpersonal Adaptation: Dyadic Interaction Patterns*. Cambridge: Cambridge University Press.
Clément, Richard, Susan C. Baker and Peter D. MacIntyre
    2003   Willingness to communicate in a second language: The effect of context, norms, and vitality. *Journal of Language and Social Psychology* 22: 190–209.
Coupland, Nikolas, Justine Coupland, Howard Giles and Karen Henwood
    1988   Accommodating the elderly: Invoking and extending a theory. *Language in Society* 17: 1–41.
Ervin, Susan M.
    1964   Language and TAT content in bilinguals. *Journal of Abnormal and Social Psychology* 68: 500–507.
Eagly, Alice H. and Shelly Chaiken
    1993   *The Psychology of Attitudes*. Orlando, FL: Harcourt Brace Jovanovich.
Fox, Susan A., Howard Giles, Mark P. Orbe and Richard Y. Bourhis
    2000   Interability communication: Theoretical perspectives. In: Dawn O. Braithwaite and Teresa L. Thompson (eds.), *Handbook of Communication and People with Disabilities: Research and Application*, 193–222. Mahwah, NJ: Erlbaum.
Forgas, Joseph P. (ed.)
    2000   *Feeling and Thinking: Affective Influences on Social Cognition*. New York: Cambridge University Press.
Gallois, Cindy
    1998   Foreword: A contemporary view of semiotic psychology. In: Norman N. Markel, *Semiotic Psychology*, xiii–xxv. New York: Peter Lang.
Gallois, Cindy
    2003   Reconciliation through communication in intercultural encounters: Potential or peril? *Journal of Communication* 53: 5–15.
Gallois, Cindy and Victor J. Callan
    1981   Personality impressions elicited by accented English speech. *Journal of Cross-Cultural Psychology* 12: 347–359.
Gallois, Cindy and Jeffery Pittam
    1996   Communication attitudes and accommodation in Australia: A culturally diverse English-dominant context. *International Journal of Psycholinguistics* 12: 193–212.
Gallois, Cindy
    2004   Intergroup and interpersonal issues in communicating about disability. In: Sik-Hung Ng, C.-Y. Chiu and Chris Candlin (eds.), *Language Matters:*

Communication, Culture, and Identity, 355–374. Hong Kong: City University of Hong Kong Press.

Gallois, Cindy, Susan McKay and Jeffery Pittam
  2004   Intergroup communication and identity: Intercultural, health, and organisational communication. In: Kristine Fitch and Robert Sanders (eds.), *Handbook of Language and Social Interaction*, 231–250. Mahwah, NJ: Erlbaum.

Gallois, Cindy, Tania Ogay and Howard Giles
  2005   Communication accommodation theory: A look back and a look ahead. In: William B. Gudykunst (ed.), *Theorizing about Intercultural Communication*, 121–148. Thousand Oaks, CA: Sage.

Gardner, Robert C.
  1979   Social psychological aspects of second language acquisition. In: Howard Giles and Robert St. Clair (eds.), *Language and Social Psychology*, 193–220. Oxford: Blackwell.

Gardner, Robert C., Richard N. Lalonde and Herbert Pierson
  1983   The socio-educational model of second language acquisition: An investigation using LISREL causal modeling. *Journal of Language and Social Psychology* 2: 51–56.

Giles, Howard
  1973   Accent mobility: A model and some data. *Anthropological Linguistics* 15(2): 87–109.

Giles, Howard and Jane L. Byrne
  1982   An intergroup approach to second language acquisition. *Journal of Multilingual and Multicultural Development* 3(1): 17–40.

Giles, Howard and Nikolas Coupland
  1991   *Language: Contexts and Consequences*. Buckingham: Open University Press.

Giles, Howard and Tania Ogay
  2006   Communication accommodation theory. In: Bryan Whalen and Wendy Samter (eds.), *Explaining Communication: Contemporary Theories and Exemplars*, 293–310. Mahwah, NJ: Lawrence Erlbaum.

Giles, Howard and Peter F. Powesland
  1975   *Speech Style and Social Evaluation*. London: Academic Press.

Giles, Howard and W. Peter Robinson (eds.)
  1990   *The Handbook of Language and Social Psychology*. Chichester, UK: Wiley.

Giles, Howard, Richard Bourhis and Donald M. Taylor
  1977   Towards a theory of language in ethnic group relations. In: Howard Giles (ed.), *Language, Ethnicity and Intergroup Relations*. London: Academic Press.

Giles, Howard, Anthony Mulac, James J. Bradac and Patricia Johnson
  1987   Speech accommodation theory: The first decade and beyond. *Communication Yearbook* 10: 13–48.

Giles, Howard, Donald M. Taylor and Richard Bourhis
  1973   Towards a theory of interpersonal accommodation through language: Some Canadian data. *Language in Society* 2: 177–192.

Gudykunst, William B.
  2005   An anxiety/uncertainty management (AUM) theory of effective communication: Making the mesh of the net finer. In: William B. Gudykunst (ed.), *Theorizing about Intercultural Communication*, 281–322. Thousand Oaks, CA: Sage.

Hajek, Chris and Howard Giles
2003   Intercultural communication competence. A critique and alternative model. In: Brant Burleson and John Greene (eds.), *Handbook of Communicative and Social Skills*, 935–957. Mahwah, NJ: LEA.
Harwood, Jake and Howard Giles (eds.)
2005   *Intergroup Communication: Multiple Perspectives*. New York: Peter Lang.
Haslam, S. Alexander
2001   *Psychology in Organizations: The Social Identity Approach*. London: Sage.
Hecht, Michael L.
2004   Ethnicity, communication, multiculturalism, and adolescent drug use: The drug resistance strategies project. Keynote address presented at the Ninth International Conference on Language and Social Psychology, State College, PA, June 30–July 3.
Hecht, Michael L., Ronald L. Jackson II, Sheryl Lindsley, Susan Strauss and Karen E. Johnson
2001   A layered approach to ethnicity: Language and communication. In: W. Peter Robinson and Howard Giles (eds.), *The New Handbook of Language and Social Psychology*, 429–449. Chichester, UK: Wiley.
Hogg, Michael A. and Dominic Abrams
1988   *Social Identifications: A Social Psychology of Intergroup Relations and Group Processes*. London: Routledge.
Hollander, Edwin P.
1958   Conformity, status, and idiosyncrasy credit. *Psychological Review* 65: 117–127.
Hornsey, Matthew J., T. Oppes and A. Svensson
2002   "It's OK if we say it, but you can't": Responses to intergroup and intragroup criticism. *European Journal of Social Psychology* 32: 293–307.
Hummert, Mary Lee and Ellen Bouchard Ryan
1996   Toward understanding variations in patronizing talk addressed to older adults: Psycholinguistic features of care and control. *International Journal of Psycholinguistics* 12: 149–170.
Jones, Elizabeth, Cindy Gallois, Victor J. Callan and Michelle Barker
1995   Language and power in an academic context: The effects of status, ethnicity, and sex. *Journal of Language and Social Psychology* 14: 434–461.
Kim, Young Yun
2001   *Becoming Intercultural: An Integrative Theory of Communication and Cross-cultural Adaptation*. Thousand Oaks, CA: Sage.
Labov, William
1972   *Sociolinguistic Patterns*. Philadelphia: University of Pennsylvania Press.
Lambert, Wallace E.
1967   A social psychology of bilingualism. *Journal of Social Issues* 23: 91–109.
Lambert, Wallace E., Richard Hodgson, Robert C. Gardner and Samuel Fillenbaum
1960   Evaluational reactions to spoken languages. *Journal of Abnormal and Social Psychology* 60: 44–51.
Lyczak, Richard, Gail S. Fu and Audrey Ho
1976   Attitudes of Hong Kong bilinguals toward English and Chinese speakers. *Journal of Cross-cultural Psychology* 7: 425–437.

MacIntyre, Peter D., Patricia A. Babin and Richard Clément
　1999　　Willingness to communicate: Antecedents and consequences. *Communication Quarterly* 47: 215–229.
MacIntyre, Peter D., Richard Clément, Susan Baker and Sarah Conrod
　2001　　Willingness to communicate, social support and language learning orientations of immersion students. *Studies in Second Language Acquisition* 23: 369–388.
Marques, Jacques and Vincent Yzerbyt
　1988　　The black sheep effect: Judgmental extremity towards ingroup members in inter- and intra-group situations. *European Journal of Social Psychology* 18: 287–292.
McCroskey, James C. and Virginia P. Richmond
　1987　　Willingness to communicate. In: James C. McCroskey and John A. Daly (eds.), *Personality and Interpersonal Communication*, 119–131. Newbury Park, CA: Sage.
Nolan, Francis
　1983　　*The Phonetic Basis of Speaker Recognition.* Cambridge: Cambridge University Press.
Pittam, Jeffery, Cindy Gallois and Michael Willemyns
　1991　　Perceived changes in ethnolinguistic vitality in dominant and minority subgroups. *Journal of Multilingual and Multicultural Development* 12: 449–458.
Potter, Jonathan and Derek Edwards
　1992　　*Discursive Psychology.* London: Sage.
Potter, Jonathan and Margaret Wetherell
　1987　　*Discourse and Social Psychology.* London: Sage.
Potter, Jonathan and Margaret Wetherell
　1992　　*Mapping the Language of Racism.* New York: Columbia University Press.
Potter, Jonathan and Margaret Wetherell
　2003　　Unfolding discourse analysis. In: Clive Seale (ed.), *Social Research Methods: A Reader.* London: Routledge.
Robinson, W. Peter
　2003　　*Language in Social Worlds.* Oxford: Blackwell.
Robinson, W. Peter and Howard Giles (eds.)
　2001　　*The New Handbook of Language and Social Psychology.* Chichester, UK: Wiley.
Ryan, Ellen Bouchard and Miguel Carranza
　1975　　Evaluative reactions of adolescents toward speakers of standard English and Mexican American accented English. *Journal of Personality and Social Psychology* 31: 855–863.
Ryan, Ellen Bouchard and Howard Giles
　1982　　*Attitudes Towards Language Variation.* London: Edward Arnold.
Ryan, Ellen Bouchard, Selina Bajorek, Amanda Beaman and Ann P. Anas
　2005　　"I just want you to know that 'them' is me": Intergroup perspectives on communication and disability. In: Jake Harwood and Howard Giles (eds), *Intergroup Communication: Multiple Perspectives*, 117–140. New York: Peter Lang.
Ryan, Ellen Bouchard, Howard Giles, Gordon Bartolucci and Karen Henwood
　1986　　Psycholinguistic and social-psychological components of communication by and with the elderly. *Language and Communication* 6: 1–24.

Sachdev, Itesh and Richard Y. Bourhis
    2001   Multilingual communication. In: W. Peter Robinson and Howard Giles (eds.), *The New Handbook of Language and Social Psychology*, 407–428. Chichester, UK: Wiley.

Sachdev, Itesh, Richard Y. Bourhis, S.W. Phang and J. D'Eye
    1987   Language attitudes and vitality perceptions: Intergenerational effects amongst Chinese Communities. *Journal of Language and Social Psychology* 6: 287–307.

Schwarz, Gavin, Bernadette Watson and Elizabeth Jones
    2005   Is organizational e-democracy inevitable? The impact of information technologies on communication effectiveness. In: Teresa Torres-Coronas and Mario Arias-Oliva (eds.), *E-Human Resources Management: Managing the Knowledge People*, 206–235. London: Idea Group Publishing.

Semin, Gün and Klaus Fiedler
    1989   Relocating attributional phenomena within a language-cognition interface: The case of actors' and observers' perspectives. *European Journal of Social Psychology* 19: 491–508.

Semin, Gün and Klaus Fiedler
    1992   Properties of interpersonal language and attribution. In: Gün Semin and Klaus Fiedler (eds.), *Language, Interaction and Social Cognition*, 58–77. Newbury Park, CA: Sage Publications Inc.

Shepard, Carolyn A., Howard Giles and Beth Le Poire
    2001   Communication accommodation theory. In: W. Peter Robinson and Howard Giles (eds.), *The New Handbook of Language and Social Psychology*, 33–56. Chichester, UK: Wiley.

Street, Richard L. Jr.
    2001   Active patients as powerful communicators. In: W Peter Robinson and Howard Giles (eds.), *The New Handbook of Language and Social Psychology*, 541–561 Chichester, UK: Wiley.

Tajfel, Henri and John C.Turner
    1979   An integrative theory of intergroup conflict. In: William G. Austin and Steve Worchel (eds.), *The Social Psychology of Intergroup Relations*, 33–47. Monterey, CA: Brooks-Cole.

Ting-Toomey, Stella
    1993   Communicative resourcefulness: An identity negotiation perspective. In: Richard L. Wiseman and Jolene Koester (eds.), *Intercultural Communication Competence*, 72–111. Newbury Park, CA: Sage.

Turner, John C., Michael Hogg, Penelope Oakes, Stephen Reicher and Margaret S. Wetherell
    1987   *Rediscovering the Social Group: A Self-categorization Theory*. Oxford: Blackwell.

Vaughan, Graham M. and Michael Hogg
    2004   *Social Psychology*. 4th ed. Harlow, Essex, UK: Pearson Education.

Watson, Bernadette and Cindy Gallois
    1999   Communication accommodation between patients and health professionals: Themes and strategies in satisfactory and unsatisfactory encounters. *International Journal of Applied Linguistics* 9: 167–183.

Watson, Bernadette and Cindy Gallois
   1998   Nurturing communication by health professionals toward patients: A communication accommodation theory approach. *Health Communication* 10: 343–355.

Watson, Bernadette and Cindy Gallois
   2002   Patients' interactions with health providers: A linguistic category model approach. *Journal of Language and Social Psychology* 21: 32–52.

Watson, Bernadette and Cindy Gallois
   2007   Language, discourse, and communication about health and illness: Intergroup relations, role, and emotional support. In: Ann Weatherall, Bernadette M. Watson, and Cindy Gallois (eds.), *Language, Discourse, and Social Psychology,* 108–130. London: Palgrave Macmillan.

Weatherall, Ann and Cindy Gallois
   2003   Gender and identity: Representation and social action. In: Janet Holmes and Miriam Meyerhoff (eds.), *The Handbook of Language and Gender*, 487–508. Oxford: Blackwell.

Willemyns, Michael, Cindy Gallois, Victor J. Callan and Jeffery Pittam
   1997   Accent accommodation in the job interview: Impact of interviewer accent and gender. *Journal of Language and Social Psychology* 16: 3–22.

Willemyns, Michael, Jeffery Pittam and Cindy Gallois
   1994   Perceived ethnolinguistic vitality of Vietnamese and English in Australia: A confirmatory factor analysis. *Journal of Multilingual and Multicultural Development* 14: 481–497.

20. Language, racism, and ethnicity

Thomas Paul Bonfiglio

1. Introduction

On Thursday, July 12, 1990, the Singapore newspaper *The Straits Times* listed the following advertisement: "Established private school urgently requires native speaking expatriate English teachers for foreign students." By Saturday, July 14, the advertisement had been changed to read "Established private school urgently requires native speaking *Caucasian* English teachers for foreign students" (Kandiah 1998: 79). It does not require great powers of speculation to imagine the events and discussions at *The Straits Times* on that Friday the 13th, an inauspicious day for the Anglophone applicants whose appearance did not conform to a certain stereotype. Clearly, this example belies the ostensible innocence and neutrality of the locution "native speaker", which is invariably taken to indicate an objective description of someone possessing natural authority in language. The belated addition of the word "Caucasian", however, indicates that the semantic field of the term "native" in the original advertisement extends well beyond purely linguistic criteria; it clearly contains notions of race and ethnicity.

While ethnic prejudices can be expressed in and through language, they are not, however, intrinsically linguistic in nature. They are, instead, supralinguistic concepts that become disguised as linguistic ones and imported into the theater of language. The pathways that facilitate this importation have been made by the repeated interconnections between the concept of language and the concept of race. In other words, language in the service of racism and ethnocentrism cannot occur without conceptualizing language and race in similar ways. Accordingly, the identification of language with race is not possible without the genetic misprisions that create the myth of race in the first place; thus a folkish notion of genetic ownership of language lies at the root of all ethnocentric linguistic prejudice: "our native" language, which is "our birthright", is seen as endangered by the presence of an other who is perceived as a biological contaminant and thus a threat to the matrix of nation, ethnicity, and language.

The understanding of the construction of this matrix presents a significant problem in the field of applied linguistics. To date, the study of racism in language has largely been limited to descriptions and classifications of the permutations thereof, along with ample theoretical critiques, but the historical and ideological etiology of the conflation of race and language has yet to be formally assessed. *The Language, Ethnicity, and Race Reader* (Harris and Hampton 2003), a useful but motley anthology, is a case in point. This is indeed an impediment, as prejudicial misconceptions cannot be properly demystified without an understanding of their origins and radical causes. Thus this inquiry will illuminate the *sine qua non* of ethnolinguistic prejudice, the determining factors without which that prejudice would be nonexistent, and focus on the historical development and exemplary permutations thereof. Ashcroft (2001) locates the beginning of the link between language and race in the discovery of Indo-European. It can be shown, however, that this phenomenon occurred much earlier.

Decades ago, anthropology jettisoned the concept of race as a useful category of human taxonomy and substituted other classificatory terms, such as family. The myth of race is generally the product of a perception of differences in skin color, which is based on no more than four to ten pairs of genes out of the 50,000 to 100,000 pairs needed to produce a human being (Cohen 1998: B4). Race is a folkish notion created *a priori* by a desire to identify a majority within a nation as essentially in *natural* possession of national character, as well as to identify a minority as an other, as *naturally* different, and then to exclude that minority as foreign to the configuration of national character. From a racist perspective, blacks are not really American, Arabs are not really French, Turks are not really German, etc. The inclusion of language in the discourse of race is made possible by the *racializing* of language, by grafting onto language the folkish notions of consanguinuity and inheritance that make racism itself possible in the first place. Crucial to this matrix are the concepts of "native language" and "mother tongue", especially as they inform the representation of nation and national language.

Smith (1998: 168) has called for "the integration of language myths in general into current scholarship on the discourse of nation-building" and offers a useful taxonomy, which is, however, too broad for the present study. This inquiry revises Smith's taxonomy in order to focus upon the myths that generate race-conscious linguistic nationalism. These myths are:

(1) Primordiality: The national language is closest to some original point, either religious or secular.
 a. Religious: It was present in some form either in Eden, or at Babel, or at Mount Ararat.
 b. Secular: It preserves the features of the proto-language, usually seen as Indo-European.
(2) Sanctity: The national language is uniquely capable of communicating holy truth, or of mediating between the individual and God, usually in the context of the protestant reformation.
(3) Representationality: The national language either captures nature onomatopoeically, or it is the unique expression of national character.

(4) Untranslatability: The concepts of the national language are ineffable in any other language.
(5) Innateness: The national language is inborn and inherited by its speakers from their parents, almost always from their mothers.

In order to account for these myths, it is first imperative to historicize them.

2. Antiquity and the Middle Ages

The genetic myths of "mother tongue" and "native language", especially in the service of exclusionary nationalism, were not present in antiquity. While the Romans and Greeks had clear standards of proper Roman Latin and Attic Greek, they did not articulate these standards in ethnic contexts. The Greek term for language in general was *logos,* and the term for proper speech was *glossa attike* 'Attic speech' which denoted speaking within the established tradition. Although language purism was widespread among the Greeks, there is no evidence that the performance of *glossa attike* was connected to ethnicity or nativity. The collective identity of the Greek elite was articulated in and through culture and language, but not through race.

There is also little evidence of protectionist patriotic attitudes toward Greek in the presence of Roman occupation. Swain (1996: 41) observes that "there is ample evidence for official use of Greek by Roman administrators in Greek language areas. This favorable treatment perhaps stopped Greek from acting as a spur to some form of proto-nationalism, as vernacular languages have often been in modern independence or nationalist contexts". Also, Langslow (2002) has studied the dynamics of code switching among Aramaic, Hebrew, Greek, and Latin in the first century and observes five preference rules for the proper selection of language in this diglossic situation, none of which reflect concerns of patriotism or ethnicity.

The Roman situation is similar. While the Romans did indeed have articulated notions of country, language, and people, these notions were, in effect, quite permeable. Roman military identity was a significant agent in this regard; military expansionism was facilitated by naturalizing non-Roman recruits, and the use of the Latin language conferred authority on the user and was a powerful symbol of Roman military identity (Adams 2003: 761). The permeability of identity was also aided by Roman Graecophilia. Biville (2002: 90) observes: "The Roman practice of imitating the Greeks, which involved adopting their language, […] gave rise to a specific vocabulary of acculturation, which allowed Romans to become either Greeks (*Graeci*), or half-Greeks (*semigraeci*), or pseudo-Greeks (*Graeculi*)". Code switching was of such secondary importance, that Suetonius actually spoke of *utroque sermone nostro* 'our two languages' (Biville 2002: 92).

The Roman discourse of language also has little in common with current western notions of native language, native speaker, and mother tongue. The Roman term for language in general was *lingua,* and the term for proper speech was *sermo patrius*. It is the latter locution that is regularly translated as "native language", and that suppresses awareness of the absence of images of nativity in the original Latin. The term *sermo* is a rather straightforward reference to discourse in general, and *patrius* indicates speaking in the proper tradition of the forefathers. The massive online Latin search engine *Perseus* offers no examples of *lingua* or *sermo* in combination with derivatives of *mater* or of *natus,* with one exception, which refers concretely to the individual speech of the mother of Andromeda.

While scholarship has documented that ancient Greece and Rome were by no means exempt from racism (Isaac 2004), the question remains as to why ideologies of race and ethnicity were not present in the *discourse of language* at that time. The answer lies, curiously, far ahead in time and is found in the realms of politics and printing. The hegemony of Latin in the Roman Empire had made that language the monolithic medium of law, education, and culture in general. The same was true of the Latin middle ages. From the Roman Empire, Christianity inherited in toto a massive infrastructural network and administrative monopoly that needed but rededication in religious terms. All texts of the church were produced in Latin – liturgy, hymns, prayers, church records –, and Latin was the language of instruction for all university students as well. This meant that the standard language was no one's first language. All were second language learners, and none could claim native language property rights. The standard language was thus accessible by all through proper education, regardless of the learner's regional or ethnic origin. Kohn (1972: 7–8) holds that, in the middle ages, "People looked upon everything as not from the point of view of their 'nationality' or 'race', but from the point of view of religion. Mankind was divided not into Germans and French and Slavs and Italians, but into Christians and Infidels, and within Christianity into the faithful sons of the Church and heretics". The naissance of ethnolinguistic prejudice was to await the secular catalytic influences of the early modern period.

3. Ethnolinguistic nationalism and the nation state

The key concept for understanding the genesis of prejudicial ethnolinguistic consciousness has been supplied by Benedict Anderson's work *Imagined Communities* (1991). Anderson holds that the representation of the modern nation-state as a community is made possible by the vehicle of language. He bases this on the primordial imagined community, which he sees as "imaginable largely through the medium of a sacred language and a written script" (Anderson 1991:

13). He uses the example of Islam, whose numerous mutually unintelligible dialects are nonetheless joined in a community, because the sacred texts that they have in common existed in classical Arabic. There is thus an ideographic unity at work here, not unlike mathematics, the symbolic language of which is understood by mathematicians of linguistically diverse origins. Similarly, the hegemony of medieval Latin was secured by the concretization and standardization of its forms. Thus Latin was the medium through which the global medieval community was imagined, its *sine qua non*.

It was the rise of the printing press and of literacy that eventually undid the hegemony of Latin: The interests of print-capitalism motivated this revolution. Anderson (1991: 38) observes: "The logic of capitalism thus meant that once the elite Latin market was saturated, the potentially huge markets represented by the monoglot masses would beckon". Publishers had a limited elite market in readers of Latin, but a rapidly growing market in the readership of novels and newspapers written in the vernacular. In addition, the protestant reformation effected a mass readership in the vernaculars and a transition from the privileged trinity of biblical sacred languages – Greek, Hebrew, and Latin – to a privileging of vernacular(s). This resulted in a sanctification of each vernacular as the private property of the speaker of that particular vernacular. Anderson holds that regional vernaculars were arguably the cause of the emergence of the nation state. Language niches served as markets for the print industry, and "these print-languages laid the foundation for national consciousnesses" (1991: 44).

Anderson's model implies that a weakening of imperial organization would give way to language regionalism, and this is exactly what happened in the early middle ages, which can be regarded as a kind of linguistic interlude between the hegemony of the Latin language of the Roman Empire and the hegemony of the Latin language of the Holy Roman Empire. This period witnessed the emergence and awareness of vernacular forms. A striking example is found in the seventh century. It concerns an attempt on the part of Irish grammarians to defend the use of spoken Gaelic over Latin, which is found in the work *Auraicept na n-Éces: The Scholars' Primer* (1917), a grammar that sees the Celts as descendant from the mythical Fenius Farsaidh, who himself was said to be descended from Noah, through his son Japheth, and who helped build the Tower of Babel. The primer claims that "the Irish language [...] was the first language that was brought from the Tower" (Calder 1917: 5).

One of the most influential images in the generation of ethnolinguistic prejudice is that of the Tower of Babel, which serves as a conventional point of reference for claims of linguistic primordiality and sanctity. There are only three known representations of the Tower before the end of the eleventh century (Eco 1995: 17), but there are roughly 140 representations between 1550 and the early seventeenth century, a sudden appearance that correlates with the anxieties of the emerging nation state. The image of the Tower of Babel is symptomatic of the birth trauma of nation and national language. Umberto Eco (1995) ultimately argues for a linguistic view of the emergence of the concept of Europe that displays some affinities with Anderson's thesis. Europe is first born as a mosaic of linguistic orphanages, of languages bereft of the medium that had united their speakers in a supraregional whole. Eco observes:

> Before this confusion there was no European culture, and, hence, no Europe. What is Europe, anyway? It is a continent, barely distinguishable from Asia, existing, before people had invented a name for it [...] Europe was an entity that had to wait for the fall of the Roman Empire and the birth of the Romano-Germanic kingdoms before it could be born [...] How are we going to establish the date when the history of Europe begins? The dates of great political events and battles will not do; the dates of linguistic events must serve in their stead [...] Europe first appears as a Babel of new languages. Only afterwards was it a mosaic of nations. Europe was thus born from its vulgar tongues.
> (Eco 1995: 18)

If vernacular language is at the heart of nation-forming, it is thus at the heart of nationalism and of the ethnic ownership of language. Anderson (1991: 68) speaks of "a conception of nation-ness as linked to a private-property language".

An example in point concerns the northern Balkans, where the emergence of Bulgarian, Serbo-Croatian, and Slovenian as literary languages preceded the formation of their respective nation-states (Anderson 1991: 74). The case of Ukrainian is also especially instructive. Seton-Watson (1977: 187) holds that the emergence of Ukrainian as a literary language in the 1830s "was the decisive stage in the formation of an Ukrainian national consciousness". Austria also offers a useful example: In the 1780s, Emperor Joseph II replaced Latin with German as the official administrative language of the empire, which evoked fierce opposition in the non-Germanophone population, for whom Latin represented the sole possibility of linguistic access to power. The subsequent progressive fragmentation of the Austrian empire can be seen as generated by this ethnolinguistic conflict.

Anderson (1991: 143) observes the presence of the "vocabulary of kinship (motherland, Vaterland, patria) or that of home [...] something to which one is naturally tied" in the discourse of nationalism, but the question of why the vocabulary of kinship is invoked in the first place is never posed. It is such kinship metaphors that enable the racializing of language. This connection necessitates an examination of the history of the kinship terms "mother tongue" and "native language", along with their permutations.

4. The racializing of language in the early modern period

Dante Alighieri's (1265–1321) *De vulgari eloquentia* (1996 [1304]) is the first work in the west to assert the superiority of the vernacular over Latin and to use images of nativity and maternality in the representation of language: "I declare that vernacular language is that which we learn without any formal instruction, by imitating our nurses (*nutricem*)" (3). The vernacular is superior "first, because it was the language originally used by humans (*humano generi*); second, because the whole world employs it [...] and third, because it is natural to us" (3). Dante situates the vernacular as imitative and indeliberate. The notion of a maternal connection is implicit in the word *nutrices*, the wet nurses used for breast feeding. Dante also asks how Adam, a "man without mother or milk" (10) (*vir sine matre, vir sine lacte*), could have learned a language. Here, the figures of the mother and of maternality become explicit, and, in the very next paragraph, Dante uses the phrase "mother tongue" (*maternam locutionem*) for the first time. Dante is obliged to justify claims for the superiority of the vernacular, but this is not easy to do, as the vernacular has no aesthetic or philosophical tradition; he thus (re)invents the vernacular otherwise, as "natural" and ascribes to it an ontology in body and kinship. In doing so, he lays the foundation for an ethnic ideology of language that was to have immensely significant consequences.

The location of language in body and kinship does not, however, fully account for its naturalization, nor for its nationalization. Another ideology played a crucial role in the emergence of language as an implement of ethnic prejudice: the understanding of language by reference to organic nature. This, as well, has its beginnings in Italy. The noted renaissance scholar Pietro Bembo (1470–1547), in a treatise also written in defense of the vernacular, speaks eleven times of "the flourishing language" (*la fiorentina lingua*) and offers the following organic representation of language: "The strengths of the native sky are always great, and in every land better thrive those plants that are there born, than those brought from distant lands" (Bembo 2001 [1512–1525]: Vol. 1, ch. 7). Thus language exists as a plant relative to its environment, to its "native soil". These few words are also of crucial importance, for they display the earliest configuration of vernacular in the matrix of organic nature and nation.

This ideology achieves fuller articulation in the work of the Italian renaissance rhetorician Sperone Speroni (1500–1588), who was a principal member of the literary and rhetorical society of the *Academia degli Infiammati* and the author, in 1542, of a polemic advocating publication in the Italian vernaculars. Speroni speaks of "our mother tongue (*la lingua nostra materna*) [...] which is, today, our own and belongs to no one else". It was created by ancestors who "imitated our mother Nature (*la madre nostra Natura*)" (Speroni 1740 [1542]: 175). Thereupon follow numerous organic metaphors: Italian "is still a short little branch that has yet to fully bloom and produce the fruits that it is capable of bearing". Because Latin was dominant, Italians "did not sufficiently cultivate it, but, as with a wild plant, left it to age and almost die in the same desert in which it had been born without ever watering it, nor pruning it, nor protecting it from the brambles that overshadowed it". The Romans, however, were "good cultivators (*agricoltori*)" of Latin and "transplanted it from its wild place to a domestic one; then, in order that it grow the fattest, most beautiful, and most precocious fruits, pruned off the first useless shoots and grafted in their place several branches [...] there thus appeared in that language flowers and fruits of such colorful eloquence" (183). Speroni adds that "someone not born Tuscan could learn good Tuscan", and he speaks of "usage, which in the course of time converts itself practically into nature" (26). Here, the notion of language proficiency as birthright is still absent. The ideologies have not yet developed to the point of being exclusionary of "non-natives", nor have they yet acquired meanings of genetic enracination. The first language is depicted simply as more natural.

Speroni's organicism of language found significant reception in the work of his French contemporary Joachim du Bellay (1522–1560). Du Bellay was a member of *La Pléiade*, a group of writers who sought to ameliorate the French literary language. The principles of *La Pléiade* were set forth by du Bellay in his manifesto *Deffence et illustration de la langue françoyse* (1972 [1549]). Du Bellay's work constitutes the first instance of organic metaphors in the validation of French, such as images of herbs, roots, and trees, metaphors that he translated, however, wholesale from Speroni (Villey 1908: 43). He observes that Latin "bore fruit", but French has yet to flower or fructify, not at all because of a defect in its nature, but because it was a wild plant that was not watered, pruned, or protected from brambles and thorns. The Romans, on the other hand, cultivated their wild language, pruned off the useless twigs, and grafted onto the trunk "natural and domestic branches magisterially drawn from the Greek language" (Du Bellay 1972 [1549]: 28). The Romans performed this grafting so well, that the branches no longer appeared adapted but natural. So should one proceed with the French language; one should cultivate it to beautiful fruition. Du Bellay also says that "each language has something (*je ne scay quoy*) proper to itself alone; if you strive to express the naturalness (*le naif*) of this in another language, your diction will be constrained, cold, and ungraceful" (33). This is a very early instance of the notion of an indefinable essence to a vernacular, a *je ne sais quoi*, which is nonetheless tangible. Unique to a particular language, it cannot be translated. This is an ideology of a naïve naturalness that conveys and preserves the essence of a national language and makes foreign access difficult. The Greeks and Romans produced great literature because they wrote in languages "that they had sucked in with the milk of the nurse" (57). He adds that the "glory of the Romans is no less [...] in the expansion of their language than in their frontiers" (106–107), and that the "highest excellence of their republic was not sufficiently strong to defend itself […] without the benefit of their language" (107). Here, one sees an imperial aspect to language; it is represented as a sort of weaponry and instrument of defense. Thereupon follows an assessment of France as the premier country in the world (108).

These ideologies subsequently spread to northern Europe. In the late sixteenth and early seventeenth centuries, there began to appear claims made by vernacular speakers that their vernacular was the best of all living languages, if not the perfect language. In 1569, Jan van Gorp asserted that the Dutch language in Antwerp was the only one that displayed a perfect representational relationship between words and things (see Eco 1995: 96). According to Gorp, Antwerp had been colonized by the descendants of the sons of Japheth, the third son of Noah, who were not present at the Tower of Babel; thus the language was not confused by the dispersion of tongues. He also claimed that Dutch had the greatest number of monosyllabic words, which indicated its ultimate simplicity and originality. Gorp's ideas were subscribed to subsequently by Abraham Mylius in his *Lingua belgica* (1612) (Eco 1995: 97). Similarly, the Swedish physician and alchemist Anders Kempe conjectured that Swedish was the oldest language in the world (Borst 1957–1963, Vol. III, 1: 1338). In 1638, he wrote *Die Sprachen des Paradises*, in which God speaks Swedish, Adam and Eve Danish (an imperfect copy of the original), and the serpent French (Eco 1995: 97). The most curious of these attempts was made by Lemaire de Belges in the early sixteenth century, who claimed that the Trojans were descendants of the Celts; thus Celtic was the origin of Greek. This led him to praise Breton as the true Trojan language (Beaune 1991: 269).

In 1641, the German baroque poet Georg Philipp Harsdörffer (1607–1658) claimed that "nature speaks in our own German tongue […] Adam would not have been able to name the birds and all the other beasts of the fields in anything but our words, since he expressed in a manner conforming to their nature, each and every innate property and inherent sound; and thus it is not surprising that the roots of the larger part of our words coincide with the sacred language" (1968 [1641]: 335). Umberto Eco (1995: 102) notes that "such nationalistic hypotheses are comprehensible in the seventeenth and eighteenth centuries, when the larger European states began to take form, posing the problem of which of them was to be supreme on the continent".

It was nationalist ideologies that generated the first instances of the combination of "mother" and "language" or "tongue," as follows: Icelandic *modurmal* ca. 1350, Swedish *modhor male* 1370, English *modyr tonge* 1380, low German *modersprake* 1424, high German *Muttersprache* 1522, French *langue maternelle* 1538. Germany also exhibits the first Latin use of the Latin *materna lingua* in 1119 (Weisgerber 1948: 55). The word "nation", in the modern sense, dates from the fourteenth century; "national" from the sixteenth; "nationally" and "nationality" from the seventeenth; "nationalize" from the eighteenth; and "nationalism" and "nationalization" only from the nineteenth (Galbraith 1972: 47).

The year 1492 witnessed the appearance of the first vernacular grammar in any language, the *Gramatica de la lengua castellana* of Antonio de Nebrija (ca. 1444–1522). Nebrija's grammar is interesting for its prolog, which has been characterized as the most grandiose ever to introduce a grammar (Weisgerber 1948: 77). Nebrija dedicates the grammar to Queen Isabella and characterizes it as a *compañero del imperio*, or companion to the empire. He claims that language has always been a companion of empire and lists Assyrian, Egyptian, Hebrew, Greek, and Latin as examples, continually reminding the reader that empires, like languages, grow, flourish, bloom, and wilt. Now is the time for the Spanish empire and the Castilian language, and his grammar will serve to fix and secure imperial power. The rule of the queen will subjugate "many barbarian peoples and nations of foreign languages (*muchos pueblos bárbaros y naciones de peregrinas lenguas*)" unto her rule. The new subjects are to learn "our language [...] just as we Spaniards now study Latin grammar, in order to learn Latin". Thus Castilian and Isabella's empire are the successors to Latin and the Roman empire.

It was Martin Luther (1483–1546) who first used the term *Muttersprache* in High German in 1522. In his *Theologica deutsch,* Luther says, "I thank God that I thus hear and find my God in the German tongue, as I, and it along with me, never before found Him, not in Latin, Greek, or Hebraic tongue" (Weisgerber 1948: 84). This is significant in that it opposes German to the three traditional sacred languages and then makes it more profoundly and personally religious. In 1526, Luther proclaimed, "I am by no means of one mind with those who set all their store by one language [...]. That was not the way of the Holy Ghost in the beginning. He did not wait till all the world should come to Jerusalem, and learn Hebrew. But He endowed the office of the ministry with all manner of tongues, so that the Apostles could speak to the people wherever they went" (Weisgerber 1948: 84). Here, the image of Pentecost serves as a stratagem for sanctifying the vernacular; by writing in German, Luther is simply following the directive of the Holy Ghost. German thus becomes *a holy language for Germans*. Huber (1984: 285) astutely observes that the rise of cultural patriotism in seventeenth century Germany begins with grammars, lexicography, and poetics and is codetermined by reformation humanism and the printing industry.

Primus Trubar (1508–1586) was a reformation priest and follower of Luther who authored the first books written in Slovenian, and who is also credited with creating the Slovenian literary language. His *Catechismus Jn der Windischenn Sprach* (1970 [1550]) is of significance in the history of the religious empowerment of the vernacular. He foregrounds the miracle of Pentecost, which he sees as a baptism of the vernaculars, an instrument for the establishment of the kingdom of God, and a means of grace and salvation (Weisgerber 1948: 90).

Ethnolinguistic nationalism, along with a hint of imperial intent, also became well-articulated in the waxing English nation state in the work of the orthographer and grammarian William Bullokar (ca. 1531–1609), who was the author of the earliest grammar written in English, the *Pamphlet for grammar* (1586). He also wrote *A short introduction or guiding to print, write, and reade Inglish speech* (1580), a primer on pronunciation and orthography, which was written so that "our language […] will excell in learning, and eloquence, (yea in straunge languages also) above any nation in the worlde: to the great light of the true knowledge of our selves, and of all transitorie things, our dutie toward God, and our neighbour" (Bullokar 1580: 15–16). Bullokar also exhibits the first instance of the locution "native language" in English.

The work of the French political theorist Jean Bodin (1529/1530–1596), especially the mammoth *Les six livres de la republique* (1579), is of relevance for the present inquiry, as it views national characteristics as a product of climate and geography. Bodin divides countries into three groups: those within thirty degrees of the equator, which he attributes to "the burning regions (*aux régions ardentes*) and peoples of the south", those between thirty and sixty degrees of latitude, which he attributes to "the intermediate peoples and temperate regions" (*aux peuples moyens & régions tempérées*), and those above sixty degrees, which comprise "the excessively cold regions" (Bodin 1579: 464). He assigns to the peoples of the middle region the characteristics most conducive to governing. The peoples of the north are strong but not all that bright; those of the south are intelligent but lack physical force. The former have produced good armies; the latter good philosophy. Those of the middle regions, however, combine the best of both worlds and have excelled in government, law, and rhetoric and have established the greatest empires: the Greeks, Romans, Persians, and Assyrians. Bodin places France clearly in the middle region and chooses to emphasize the image of the French as natural mediators: "The Gauls, especially those of Languedoc, hold the middle region between the cold and extreme heat […] the people of the middle regions hold of the two extremes in humor (*en humeur*) […] between the north and south, which can never concur together for the contrariety of manners and humors that is between them" (469). This makes the Gauls of the median region the ideal governors, for "when it is a question of mediating (*moyenner*) peace, or making alliances between two nations so opposite, or of leading them both forth to war together, you must place the median (*metoyenne*) nation between them that has more moderate affections" (469). The speciousness of Bodin's assertions betrays his fundamental objective, which is to situate France as the proper successor to the great Greek and Roman empires and to elevate it above other European countries. One sees in Bodin the construction of a certain kind of nature, a psychogeography in the service of nationalist interests. Bodin's theories suppose a national character, naturalize it in local physical nature, and thus render it the organic personal property of the

French people. His theories were received in the eighteenth century by Montesquieu and Rousseau.

In 1586, Simon Stevin counted the "stem words" of the imagined protolanguage and concluded that Latin had 163, Greek 265, and Germanic 2,170 (Weisgerber 1948: 96). The Lutheran theologian Johann Matthäus Meyfahrt (1590–1642) published in 1634 his *Teutsche Rhetorica*. Meyfahrt holds that "Germans do not seek their language from books, but take it instead from implanted nature (*aus der eingepflanzten Natur*), do not study it from masters, but instead learn it from nurses, do not receive it in schools from the mouths of teachers, but instead suck it, in the cradle, from the breasts of mothers" (Meyfahrt as quoted in Huber 1984: 144). This passage sets up a correspondence among nature, home, mothers, and the family. The German language is actually implanted in nature and exists as well in mother's milk. This not only reinforces the private ownership of German by Germans, but also acts to render it inaccessible to foreigners, to those not born into the matrix of physical German nature and nurture by German mothers.

One of the most crucial influences upon the development of the nationalist ideologies of language in German, especially in their organic, nativist, and maternal manifestations, was exercised by Justus Georg Schottelius (1612–1676). Schottelius was a leading spokesman of *Die fruchtbringende Gesellschaft*, the language society founded in Weimar in 1617. The name literally means "the fruit-bearing society". The text of the foundational meeting of the society states its goal as follows: "During the blood-dripped battle cries, our primordial unfinished German mother tongue was dribbled into us purely with the first milk" (Huber 1984: 243). In 1641, Schottelius also authored *Teutsche Sprachkunst*, an influential grammar of the German language. In 1647, he published a collection of mixed poetry and prose entitled *Fruchtbringender Lustgarte*. In the preface, he praises "the old Teutons", who "preserved [...] unmixed and unspoiled, their old mother tongue and brought it down to us" (Schottelius 1967 [1647]: Preface). It is astounding to see how the ferocious nationalist sentiments in Germany in the seventeenth century tend to pivot around language. Schottelius adds: "Churches and schools, law and justice, war and peace, trade and change, action and non-action we preserve, perform, and propagate through our German language; through it we attain to God and heaven; indeed, through it we receive body and soul" (Weisgerber 1948: 102). Thus the national language becomes the enabling medium of the social, cultural, bodily and religious. How then could someone not born into the all-inclusive matrix that has language as its nodal point gain access into that matrix and become a bona fide member? Schottelius uses a baroque excess of arboreal images to characterize the growth and development of language. Languages possess

[...] word stems that, like juice-rich roots, hydrate the whole language tree, whose sprouts and twigs abounding in branches and veins spread high and wide in the most beautiful purity [...] our main language is comparable to an impressive fertile tree that has extended its juice-rich roots deep, far, and wide into the earth, so that, by virtue of its veinlets, pulls the dampness and marrow of the earth into itself, hardens its roots with a fruit-rich juicy wetness [...] and grafts itself into nature. For the roots and juicy word stems of our language have, as demonstrated above, sucked the pit and marrow from reason and stemmed themselves upon the major grounds (*Hauptgründe*) of nature.
(Huber 1984: 55–56)

The pun here on "grounds", in the senses of terrain and reason, seems to be intentional. And it is important to note that the logic of language is repeatedly represented here as innate.

Schottelius is faced with the same problems that beset the other German language ideologues of the seventeenth century. The Romance languages can trace their origin back to Latin, one of the three holy languages, but to what can the Germanic languages trace theirs? He offers a most unusual solution: to the name of God itself. Speaking of the Babylonian dispersion of humankind, he asks, "What name was it then with which the scattered humans wanted to indicate the true God? Namely the one from which we Germans have our name [...] *Teut*, [...] which is thus the true infallible original source of the German name (*des Teutschen Nahmens*), namely the name of the true God itself, so that German (*Teutisch*) more or less means godly or god-like" (Huber 1984: 54). Of all the attempts among all the vernaculars to assert ultimate primal authority for a given national language, it is difficult to imagine an effort more chauvinistic than the assertion that the name of one's language is the original word for God. Such an assertion would have to bequeath upon that language a status of unique and incontestable veracity as the ultimate "parent" language. Schottelius sees the originality of German as lying in the recombinative quality of its morphemes, both free and bound, and its compounds. If a stem is lacking in German and "the number of individual entities in nature is almost infinite, one could still combine three or more words to make a word and thus basically and properly express every entity" (Huber 1984: 82). Thus he sees "duplication (*Verdoppelung*) as the noblest part of any language" (Huber 1984: 83).

One sees here the extremes to which the anxiety of vernacular authority can motivate the philology of nationalism. Both nature and language become configured here symbiotically. First, the organic qualities of nature become foregrounded, and from these, the arboreal aspects are selected as having the greatest analogic potential for the configuration of language. Second, the chosen arboreal aspects of nature are then transferred onto language. Third, nature and language are both configured as behaving similarly, and one arrives at a codeterminative intertwining of the trees of nature and the trees of language.

5. Ethnolinguistic ideology in the enlightenment

Schottelius exercised his most important influence, however, upon the philosopher Gottfried Wilhelm Leibniz (1646–1716). In the *Nouveaux Essais sur l'entendement humain* (1704), Leibniz asserts "the common origin of all nations and in a primitive root-language [...] the Teutonic seems to have better preserved that which is natural" (Schmarsow 1877: 218). In this language, "there is something natural in the origin of words – something that reveals a relationship between things and the sounds and motions of the organs of speech" (220). The objective of this naïve referentialist concept of language is to ascribe to the German language an aspect of primacy. Schottelius's *Teutsche Sprachkunst* served Leibniz as his primary German reference grammar (Schmarsow 1877). In 1705, Leibniz expressed his admiration for Schottelius's *Teutsche Sprachkunst* (Schmarsow 1877: 6); his texts are bestrewn with numerous borrowings from and allusions to Schottelius. In the manuscript *Die Ermahnung an die Teutsche, ihren Verstand und Sprache besser zu üben* (1679–1680), Leibniz adamantly recommends writing in German and also avoiding borrowings from other languages. He says, "All histories generally confirm that language and nation bloom at the same time [...] I do not think that this occurs by happenstance, but rather affirm that the waxing and waning of peoples and languages are interrelated just like the moon and the sea" (Schmarsow 1877: 15). Another of Leibniz's German writings relevant to this study is the manuscript *Unvorgreifliche Gedanken betreffend die Ausübung und Verbesserung der Teutschen Sprache* (ca. 1680), which displays many similarities in vocabulary and opinion with Schottelius's grammar. Both praise the mother tongue for a certain concreteness and primacy that enable it to communicate the essences of nature. Leibniz also paraphrases a challenge issued by Schottelius to categorize all the words of the stem-related Germanic languages, in order to arrive at their origin and basis. Most interestingly, Schottelius also terms his proposal *Unvorgreifliche Gedanken* and recommends seeking "good ancient German word stems" (Schmarsow 1877: 22). He also emphasizes that "once the root (*Radix*) is located in this way, then all the other words flowing from it can be easily recognized". In 1680, Leibniz requested Schottelius's manuscripts on the German language from the library in Wolfenbüttel (Schmarsow 1877: 33).

Leibniz sees the German language as excelling in that which concerns the five senses and the "common man" and also in benefitting from a certain neglect: Because scholars discoursed in Latin, "the mother tongue" was left to "the common run of things", with the result that the unlettered maintained it well "in accordance with the teachings of nature" (*nach Lehre der Natur*) (Schmarsow 1877: 47). He represents German as having an empirical supremacy in the realm of the senses and following the course of nature. He displays the tendency, common to the period, to anteriorize the Germanic languages. He affirms that the

Gauls, Celts, and Scythians were related to the Germanic peoples, and that "Italy received its oldest inhabitants from the German and Celtic peoples [...] it thus follows that the Latin language owes a lot to the primeval Germans" (1877: 60). He subsequently asserts that Greek was influenced by Germanic tribes that migrated there from Asia Minor. This genealogy becomes more and more outlandish, as Leibniz claims that "the origin of the European peoples and languages lies in German antiquity" along with, in part, the origins of "Religion, morality, law, and aristocracy", and that finally, "the origin and source of European existence is largely to be found with us" (1877: 61). Thus the German language is "closer to the origin", especially in its basic roots; he holds that Germanic displays the proto-root for "world" (1877: 62). Leibniz also called for the publication of a *Glossarium etymologicum,* which should be organized "according to basic roots, and to each root or stem the sprouts are to be added" (1877: 71); here, the sprouts serve as organic metaphors for the derivatives of each root.

Leibniz's ideas influenced Jean-Jacques Rousseau (1712–1778), one of the major figures of eighteenth century thought, a promulgator of organicism, who idealized the human in the state of nature. His *Essai sur l'origine des langues* (1755) signifies an important stage in the naturalization of language. It also offers the first instance of Bodin's theories of climatology applied to language. It begins: "Speech (*parole*) distinguishes humans from animals: language (*langage*) distinguishes nations from one another. One does not know where a person comes from until that person has spoken. Usage and necessity make people learn the language of their own country (*pays*)". Rousseau frames speech both prehistorically and nationally. It is a fundamental aspect of human nature and is related to the expression of passion: "We render our feelings when we speak and our ideas when we write [...] in speaking, we vary usage by intonation as we like [...] we are more forceful" (1990 [1755]: 79). The spoken language is described as possessing energy and vivacity; intonations and infections make language more particular and render it appropriate only in the place where it is (*seulement au lieu où elle est*). Based on a broad geographical difference between humans living in the north and humans living in the south – ideas gleaned from Bodin – Rousseau then relativizes aspects of language to geographical location. Those in harsh climates have indelicate voices; those in hospitable climates delicate ones; southerners have sonorous, accentuated, and eloquent languages; northerners mute, rude, and monotone ones (112–113). For Rousseau, language is innate, a fundamental aspect of human nature, and appropriate to a specific time and place, most importantly to a given *homeland.*

Rousseau's ideas were received by his German contemporary Johann Gottfried Herder (1744–1803), who published the essay *On Diligence in the Study of Several Learned Languages* (ca. 1764), in which he relates language and nation to climate: "Greek flourishes in the most sensitive and mild of regions [...] the Romans, sons of Mars, spoke more forcefully [...] more masculine is the speech of the martial German; the sprightly Gaul invents a skipping, softer language; the Spaniard gives his won an appearance of gravity [...] the languorous African mumbles weakly [...] so this plant transformed itself according to the soil that nourished it and heaven's breeze, that quenched its thirst" (1992: 29–30). Language is to be viewed as a plant that transforms itself in accordance with the "soil" of the culture that feeds it. Herder holds that "each language has its distinct national character", and that "nature imposes upon us an obligation only to our mother tongue, for it is perhaps better attuned to our character and coextensive with our way of thinking" (30). He speaks of "my native tongue, to which I must therefore offer the firstborn sacrifices of my diligence [...] our mother tongue really harmonizes most perfectly with our most sensitive organs [...] our mind clandestinely compares all tongues with our mother tongue [...] thereby [...] the goal of our fatherland remains steadily before our eyes" (32–33). He exhorts "each nation [...] to enjoy, within the confines of its frontiers and attached to its soil, nature's gifts from the womb of the earth" (30). The presence of family images, the "birthright" and the "fatherland", is also crucial for his argument. The mother tongue is thus a unique and inalienable birthright, inaccessible to the non-native, the performance of which aids in the preservation of the sovereignty and independence of the fatherland. In the *Abhandlung über den Ursprung der Sprache* (1771), Herder holds that the language of nature is a "*Völkersprache* (language of a people) for each species among themselves" (1978 [1771]: 11). It is in the nature of language that it be regional and ethnic. He holds that the fundamental patterns of pronunciation of a language cannot be mastered by someone who is not a first speaker of that language: "The more living (*lebendiger*) a language is [...] the more originally (*ursprünglicher*) it climbs to the full, undifferentiated sound of nature, the more often it is completely unpronounceable for the outsider" (14).

Thus the discourse of ethnolinguistic prejudice underwent a progressive abstraction during the enlightenment that acted to mask its inegalitarian aspects, which aspects then became embedded in historical, philosophical, and structural analyses of language. This abstraction has continued to the present day.

6. The abstraction of ethnolinguistic ideology in the nineteenth century

Friedrich Schlegel (1767–1845), in *Über die Sprache und Weisheit der Inder* (1808), holds that German and other synthetic languages are living organisms: "[E]very root is truly that which the name says, and is like a living germ (*Keim*) [...] the fullness of development can expand into the immeasurable [...] everything that comes out of this simple root [...] keeps the impress of its relationship" (1975 [1808]: 157–159). He attributes the "richness and durability" of these languages to the fact that "they have arisen organically and form an organic web" (1975 [1808]: 159). This web has the properties of a genealogical structure: One can locate "after millennia the thread that leads through the wide expanse of a race of words (*eines Wortgeschlechts*) and leads us back to the simple origin of the first root" (1975 [1808]: 159). In the "inferior" analytic languages, on the other hand, the roots are not like a "fruitful seed, but instead like a heap of atoms"; they are "mechanical" and lack "the germ of living development" (1975 [1808]: 159). Schlegel's speculations represent language in a primitive genetic framework and endow it with hereditary properties. But only the synthetic languages are granted this status, Schlegel's own German language among them.

The German linguist Wilhelm von Humboldt (1767–1835) was a crucial figure in the development of comparative linguistics and modern linguistic science. Humboldt makes the mother tongues the point of departure and organizes languages in "families" situated in the soil: "The study of the languages of the earth (*des Erdbodens*) is thus the world history of the thoughts and sensations of humankind" (Weisgerber 1948: 109). Languages are rooted in physical nature and are always "the property of entire nations". Humboldt drives this idea to the point of an equation (language equals nation): "[L]anguage is basically the nation itself, and in all actuality the nation [...] in its active, living existence" (Weisgerber 1948: 118). In its particular vernacular manifestation, German language is German nation. He represents language as "living" and as an "organic whole". Language is the "mental breath (*Aushauch*) of a nationally individual life". Since the language/thought complex is always relative to a specific nation, full bilingualism is impossible, in Humboldt's view: "[T]o learn a foreign language is to gain a new perspective in our view of the world [...] but because we always carry our own worldview and language view into a foreign language, we never experience pure and complete success"; language "has passed through the experiences of earlier generations [...] who are related to us as nation and family in the same sounds of the mother tongue that are also the expression of our own feelings" (Humboldt 1836: Part 9). There is a notion here of language as a medium of genetic inheritance; the mother tongue becomes at once national, prehistoric, and ethnic property.

This occurs in a context of biolinguistic determinism: "The power of descent (*Abstammung*)" upon all human languages can be seen "in their distribution by nations [...] since descent has so predominantly powerful an effect on the whole individuality", and it is to this individuality that the particular language "is most internally connected". By virtue of its "origin in the depth of human existence", language enters "into true and authentic combination with physical descent". He asks, "Why else would the fatherland's tongue possess so much more power and innerness than a foreign one?" This is a power so strong, "that it greets the ear, after long absence, with a kind of sudden magic and awakens nostalgia when far away". Humboldt was among the first to represent language in the form of a tree diagram, which acts to configure it genealogically. It is a family tree remapped onto language and planted in the ethno-national soil, where its ownership becomes exclusive (all quotations in this paragraph from Humboldt 1836: Part 9).

The work of the German historical linguist Franz Bopp (1791–1867) constitutes the first formal systematic investigation into the study of comparative Indo-European philology. Like Schlegel, Bopp sees morphological (synthetic) languages as displaying the dynamic ability of "organic modification" (Bopp 1816: 10). With time, however, languages lose their inflection. The "weakening" tendency of language is that of the "slow and gradual destruction of the simple language organism" and its replacement by "mechanical combinations" (11). In his *Vergleichende Grammatik* (1833–1852), Sanskrit is characterized as the "truest, oldest" language that exceeds the perfection of form found in Greek, while the Semitic languages are "of a crasser nature" (iv). The "family bond, however, that contains the Indo-European language trunk (*Stamm*) is [...] of infinitely finer constitution" (v). Within this family, Sanskrit is said to have "European sisters" (iv), the "members" of which are related as "stem sisters" (*Stammschwestern*) (v). Of the Germanic languages, Bopp places Gothic in closest relationship to Latin and Greek and refers to it as the example of "our mother tongue in its oldest, most perfect form" (vii). The fact that he refers to Gothic as "our mother tongue" is very telling; it constructs a genealogical pedigree for German in a lineage connected to Sanskrit and the ultimate Indo-European *Ursprache*. He refers to Gothic as "our Germanic Sanskrit" (Bopp 1833–1852, Vol. I [1835]: viii). For Bopp, language serves as a barometer of ethnic homogeneity: He holds that "the Slavs, like the Greeks, Romans, Germans, Old Prussians, and Lithuanians, without the degree of mixing with heterogeneous tribes (*Stämme*), which would have had a destructive effect upon the language, belong to the Asian proto-people (*Ur-Volk*)".

Bopp influenced August Schleicher (1821–1868), who was among the first to apply biology to the study of language. For Schleicher, "Languages are organisms of nature; they have never been directed by the will of man; they rose, and developed themselves according to definite laws; they grew old and died out" (Schleicher 1863: 20–21). Schleicher sees languages as behaving like biological organisms. He holds fast to the view that "the rules now, which Darwin lays down with regard to the species of animals and plants, are equally applicable to the organisms of languages" (30). Schleicher engages in a remapping of linguistics onto the matrix of biology: "[W]hat the naturalist terms a genus the linguist calls a family [...] the species of a genus are what we call the languages of a family, the races of a species are with us the dialects of a language; the sub-dialects or patois correspond with the varieties of the species" (30–32). Thus languages are species, dialects are races, subdialects are species varieties, and this proceeds right down to the level of individual differences. The entire "Indo-Germanic family of speech [...] consisting of numerous species, races, and varieties, have taken their origin from one single primitive form" (34). The processes of "ramification" and "gradual re-ramification – Darwin's continual tendency to divergency of character" (37) explain the genesis of separate languages. Indeed, "the kinship of different languages may consequently serve [...] as a paradigmatic illustration of the origin of species" (45). Verb roots are "the cells of speech, not yet containing any particular organs for the functions of nouns, verbs, etc." in which "the functions (the grammatical relations) are no more separated yet than respiration and digestion are in the one-celled organisms" (53–54). And the "organisms of speech" are subject to laws of natural selection: "[S]pecies and genera of speech disappear, and [...] others extend themselves at the expense of the dead" (60). He holds that "a similar process is assumed by Darwin with regard to the animal and vegetable creation; that is what he calls 'the struggle for life'" (62). He then directly quotes Darwin's observations on the extinction of "feebler groups" that "in consequence of their common inheritance of imperfection, incline to a common extinction".

Schleicher attempts to stretch the Darwinian model to cover the phenomenon of the disappearance of languages. The absurdity of this overextension can be demonstrated by posing a few questions common to the biological model: Do languages inherit imperfections? Do they compete with each other for limited resources? Are some better adapted to a particular environmental niche than others? Do some produce more offspring than others? The avoidance of such questions enables Schleicher to blindly biologize language. The "smoking gun" in Schleicher's discourse, however, is found in his account of the spread of the Indo-European languages, which he sees as the victors in "the process of the struggle for existence in the field of human speech. In the present period of the life of man the descendants of the Indo-Germanic family are the conquerors in the struggle for existence; they are engaged in continual extension, and have already supplanted or dethroned numerous other idioms" (Schleicher 1863: 64). Clearly, Schleicher is writing here in the idiom of his era, which spoke of the Aryan and Indo-European "conquests", as opposed to the current preference to speak of the *migrations* of those speakers. In the schema of the survival of the fittest, Indo-European is represented here as the strongest and best-adapted, and its ascendance to domination is explicable as a natural autonomous phenomenon. It is interesting to note how Schleicher, having epitomized Indo-European as the victor in the struggle of language, invokes his tree diagram: "The multitude of the Indo-Germanic species and sub-species is illustrated by our genealogical tree" (64). He is also skeptical of bilingualism, of mastering a language other than the *Muttersprache* (Schleicher 1865: 11), and argues on a biological basis. Schleicher sees language as a more consistent biological trait than "cranial shape or other so-called racial differences" (16). Language "is a completely constant trait. In head hair or protruding jaw, a German can match the most articulated Negro head, but he will never speak a Negro language naturally (*von Haus aus*)".

The ideological elements in Schleicher's gambits are evident; under the guise of scientific inquiry, language becomes biologized in the service of ethnolinguistic prejudice. Umberto Eco (1995: 105) makes an astute observation on the rise of Indo-European philology:

> But are we really able to say that with the birth of the modern science of linguistics the ghost of Hebrew as the holy language had finally been laid to rest? Unfortunately not. The ghost simply reconstituted itself into a different, and wholly disturbing, Other [...] during the nineteenth century, one myth died only to be replaced by another. With the demise of the myth of linguistic primacy, there arose the myth of the primacy of a culture – or of a race. When the image of the Hebrew language and civilization was torn down the myth of the Aryan races rose up to take its place.

Towson (1992: 107) sees a continuum here and speaks of "the language-purist discussion since the nineteenth century; in German fascism it reaches its culmination when the 'purity' of language is inextricably linked with the 'purity' of 'race'.

Examples of the myth of primordiality persist, and surprisingly so, into quite recent times. Thurston, in his *Lithuanian History, Philology, and Grammar* (1941), seems to imply that Lithuanian is itself Proto-Indo-European. He says that the Lithuanian language is "more perfect than either Sanskrit or Greek, more copious than Latin, and more exquisitely refined than any of these three [...] any philologist can see clearly that Sanskrit, Greek, and Latin must have sprung form a common source, Lithuanian" (Smith 1998: 180). Thurston ultimately uses this fabrication to plea for Lithuanian independence – an excellent example of language myths in the service of nationalism. And as recently as 1993, the leader of a Ukrainian political party held that Sanskrit was "the ancient Ukrainian language" (Smith 1998: 229). Turkish also offers a relevant example. After WWI, Turkey sought to establish a new Turkish identity, in contrast with the older Ottoman-Islamic identity, and employed language reform as a vehicle; Roman script replaced Arabic, and the Turkish technical vocabulary became Europeanized. This was justified on the claim that all European languages originally descended from Turkish anyway; thus this was a way of reclaiming Turkish roots that had been lost under the impact of Arabic and Persian (see Fishman 1972: 224–243).

The assessment of ethnolinguistic prejudice in the service of vulgar nationalism also necessitates, however, a more focused critique of the inductive leap from organism to language.

7. Are languages really trees and organs?

The central culprit in the discourse of ethnolinguistic prejudice is the racializing of language and the unreflective grafting of genetic and genealogical models onto it. The innumerable interlanguage borrowings – lexical, phonetic, morphological, and syntactic – problematize the hierarchical genetic model and argue for the inclusion of horizontal patterns of language evolution. Interlanguage borrowings constitute *acquired characteristics* for the receiving language. These phenomena are then passed down in a Lamarckian fashion to subsequent generations of speakers. How could one characterize a phenomenon as consisting of genetic organisms if development proceeds in a Lamarckian fashion, and if data from one "organism" can change a different "organism" at one and the same time?

Hope (2000) critiques the "single ancestor-dialect" hypothesis of the rise of standard English, which "places the chosen dialect in a direct genetic relationship to Standard English: one evolves from the other in the linear way that man evolves from one of the early primates" (49–50). This nationalist hypothesis desires to see the east midland London dialect as the cradle for the standard. Standard British English did not, in fact, arise from a single dialect; instead, its features can be traced to a wide range of dialects. Hope points out that "the success of this hypothesis is also due in no small part to the parallels it draws between evolutionary biology and linguistic change […] languages and dialects are not equivalent to biological species: the metaphor of the family tree is inappropriate as a way of representing their development" (2000: 50). The reason for the inappropriateness of the biological model here lies in the concept of a species. Separate species cannot exchange genetic material. Humans cannot naturally exchange genes with birds, so as to develop wings. Hope observes, however, that "linguistic structures *can* be mixed and recombined across dialect and language boundaries […] it is very easy to mate linguistic sparrows with rats to get bats" (50–51). Creolized languages clearly demonstrate that language contact opens up an immense range of possibilities for phonetic, morphological, syntactic, and semantic interlanguage adoption.

There is an entire subfield of biology called cladistics, which is devoted to the study of tree diagrams in taxonomic description. Genetic trees are indispensable to phylogenetic classification, and the mechanics of remapping from one structure to another are facilitated by the support of numerous homologies. Their metaphorical application, however, to the study of language is problematic. Roger Lass (1997) observes that the family tree model of language lineage is parthenogenetic, as it traces descent from a single parent; for instance, the Latin language alone generated the entire "family" of Romance languages. This metaphorical discourse generates maternal images that continually invoke references to mothers and wombs; these are, however, incommensurate with human genealogy, which is exclusively biparental.

Wiener (1987) observes that the dynamics of lateral language influence correspond, in biology, to the field of reticulate evolution, which studies horizontal networks. Wiener holds that "there have been no good, realistic methods for dealing with both the hierarchical and the reticulate aspects of language evolution" (1987: 224). She says, "Languages are all hybrid to some extent, while most organisms only occasionally produce hybrids. Also, there is no necessity for close genealogical relationship for hybrid formation in language groups, while this is essential in organisms. The features of a language are not adaptive and do not determine its relative success. Rather, the spread of a language character is dependent upon the social status of the people who use it" (225).

The reticulate model is resisted because it confronts the national language with its own hybrid nature and the reality of foreign incursions. If a given nation participates in the superstitions of ethnic purity, it will tend to reject outright, and sometimes violently so, any notion that its stem population could be hybrid. It will be comfortable with vertical genealogical narratives of race and ethnicity. This structure will then be transferred to concepts of language, and the genealogical narrative of linguistic descent will be found in both popular and professional spheres. Thus the horizontal model is favored because it insulates "our native" language against the influence of other ones.

8. Deconstructing the native speaker

The ethnic ownership of language is also buttressed by the divisive language myth of the authority of the native speaker, a term introduced by Bloomfield (1963 [1933]: 43), an authority that is configured as an infallible birthright, as an innate sense of the acceptable utterance. The word *native* derives from the Latin *nascor* (past participle *natus*) 'to be born', which encourages the perception of first language capabilities as innate. Recent studies on the image of the native speaker, however, have shown the ideological elements at work in the construction of that image.

Paikeday, in *The Native Speaker is Dead!* (1985), cites studies on the acceptability of marginal utterances and the inability of linguists to identify whether or not the error had been made by a first-language (L1) or second-language (L2) speaker. He says, "Sometimes you begin to wonder, when people start recruiting 'native speakers' of English, for example, whether they don't really mean white Anglo-Saxon protestants; Scots, maybe, but no Irish need apply" (1985: 33). On the subject of L1 speaker intuition, he says, "Such intuition comes with training and experience, not from circumstances of birth or infancy, although these doubtless could help in a subsidiary role. It is like your having a better chance of becoming an engineer if your mother was an engineer […] there are no native speakers any more than there are born engineers" (43).

One of Paikeday's interlocutors is Noam Chomsky, who claims that the grammaticality of an utterance can always be verified by a "native speaker", but can offer no definition of the term when encouraged to do so. Davies (1991: 8) shows that L2 speakers can often "pass" as L1 speakers. He refers to this neo-nativity as being reborn, as a renaissance into another identity, as acquiring a "new ethnicity". Rajendra Singh (1998) sees the native speaker as a political construct. Michael Paradis (1998) reminds us that one is not an L1 speaker of a language per se, but of a given sociolect of a particular dialect, for example, middle or working class New York English.

The perception of nativity is at once one of identity and language together, a phenomenon seen in Austrian attempts to apprehend the "linguistic nationality" of the Slovenians in southern Carinthia, who were asked, in four different censuses, what was their thinking language, cultural language, vernacular language, and household language (Stephens 1976). Gardner (1985) shows that L1 speakers tend to be seen as more kind, resourceful, attractive, and sincere than accented L2 speakers. This is a function of the fact that L1 speakers are an in-power group whose speech becomes desired as a metonym of their power. Gardner's findings correspond to Tucker and Lambert's study on pronunciation, which found that speakers who spoke like network standard were rated higher on a list of similar positive character attributes (Tucker and Lambert 1972: 179–181).

In the judgment of an accent as "foreign" to the English language, there is little natural or ontological evidence in the accent itself that it is not of anglophone origin. The exoticism of the accent lies rather in the perceptual categories of the listener, in his or her habitual auditory patterns, in the anomaly of the accent relative to the patterns with which the listener is familiar. To a naïve listener, an unfamiliar anglophone South African accent could sound just as foreign as an Estonian one. An accent is judged as "native" because it is unconsciously perceived as the repository of the linguistic capital that is desired and worshipped. The purpose of the notion of linguistic nativity, i.e. of saying that there is a certain "really native" accent, is to anchor power in a certain class of speaker.

9. Ethnolinguistic ideology in the United States

In the United States, a fundamental ideology of a Teutonic and northern European essence has been present in conceptions of the American language since the eighteenth century, which escalated to an outright xenophobia in the twentieth (Bonfiglio 2002). The centers of urban power did not become the geographical sources for the standard pronunciation, as they generally did elsewhere in the world; instead, the norm arose from a primarily rural area, the midwest and west, a region that acquired the meanings of *heartland*.

The prejudicial ethnolinguistic consciousness tended to surface in the presence of alterity and congeal around the salient other(s) existing at a particular time. For Benjamin Franklin, the German was constructed as the other, for Thomas Jefferson, it was the black American, and for Noah Webster, it was the British. This caused Webster to represent the American language as "more Teutonic" than British English. In the postbellum period, the northern migration of blacks from former southern slave states effected an anxiety of race in the white population and determined the prescriptive judgments of southern speech. In the twentieth century, massive immigration to the northeastern seaboard, especially by Jews, elicited ethnolinguistic prejudices that converged most acutely upon the characteristic phonemes of the eastern metropolises, especially the non-rhotic postvocalic /r/. The phonemes of the area became associated with the undesirable elements that occupied it, and the region experienced a massive devaluation of linguistic capital. Similarly, the phonemes of the area that was perceived as still pure, natural, virile, and healthy – the *heartland* midwest and west – acquired those characteristics metonymically. Because of their association with the immigrant population, American eastern urban industrial centers became regarded as sources of contamination of race and language. They had to remain marginalized from basic folkish notions of American identity. Rural areas were perceived as uncontaminated and were thus invested with notions of proper ethnic identity. Due to the northern prejudices against the south in the postbellum period, and due to the surreptitious perception of negative racial content in the south, the southern states also had to remain tangential to that identity, as it was conceived by the class hierarchy of the north. The negative racial content not only applies to the prejudices against blacks, but also to the prejudices against Appalachian whites; they were victimized by folkish biological descriptions that characterized them as genetically inferior (Bonfiglio 2002).

In 1914, the noted British historian Stephen Graham published *With Poor Immigrants to America*. In this work, he said that "the contemporary language of America [...] is in the act of changing its skin" (1914: 248). The choice of the word "skin" here is hardly coincidental, as Graham explains:

> America must necessarily develop away from us at an ever-increasing rate. Influenced as she is by Jews, Negroes, Germans, Slavs, more and more foreign constructions will creep into the language, – such things as "I should worry," derived from Russian-Jewish girl strikers. "She ast me for a nickel," said a Jew-girl to me of a passing beggar. "*I should give her a nickel*, let her work for it same as other people!" The *I shoulds* of the Jew can pass into the language of the Americans [...] To-day the influence that has come to most fruition is that of the negro. The negro's way of speaking has become the way of most ordinary Americans, but that influence is passing [...] America [...] will be subject to a very powerful influence from the immigrants.
> (Graham 1914: 250–251)

American ethnolinguistic identity was also seen as contaminable by black Americans. The phonologist Alexander Melville Bell (1819–1905), the father of Alexander Graham Bell, polemicized against the dropping of final /r/, which he framed in racist terms: "The vowelized R is a vestige of the stronger element which was undoubtedly prominent in our speech at an earlier stage; and – rather than eliminate this vestige – we should conserve it and strengthen it [...] Give, then, no countenance to the 'white nigger-speech' which would deprive us altogether of the valuable expressiveness of this element" (Bell 1896: 15–16). The conflation of southern coastal speech with black English persisted into the second half of the twentieth century, as has been attested by Raven McDavid:

> In experiments in Chicago, middle-class Middle Westerners consistently identified the voice of an educated urban white Southerner as that of an uneducated rural Negro [...] similar experiments in New York have yielded similar results. And many white Southerners can testify to personal difficulties arising from this confusion in the minds of Northerners. In Ithaca, New York, I could not get to see any apartment advertised as vacant until I paid a personal visit; I was always told that the apartments had just been rented.
> (McDavid 1966: 15–16)

The enracination of language also enables its configuration as a vehicle for the deracination and naturalization of the other. A U.S. government report from 1868 recommended teaching English to Indians as a panacea for the hostilities between native and European Americans, saying that "by educating the children of these tribes in the English language, these differences would have disappeared, and civilization would have followed at once [...] through sameness of language is produced sameness of sentiment, and thought" (Crawford 1992: 48). The report advocated that "their barbarous dialects should be blotted out" and assumed that this would "fuse them into one homogenous mass". This resulted in the separation of Indian children from their families for forced education in English, a policy that continued until 1933. This unfortunate episode in American history is an example of the configuration of language as the instantiation of proper race and behavior. This was conceived as a kind of complete linguistic transfusion that could replace one composite of language and behavior with another. A similar example is found in the treatment of the Hispanic population of New Mexico. In 1910, Congress mandated English-only instruction in New Mexico schools and required English fluency for elected officials (Crawford 1992: 58–60).

Such examples are clearly not limited to the United States. In the 1990s, Singapore instituted the "Speak Mandarin Campaign", which was aimed at the suppression of Chinese dialects and the standardization of Mandarin and reflected the government position that linguistic diversity was incompatible with the goals of nation-building (see Saravanan, this vol.). At that time, the population of Singapore was 77.5 percent Chinese; the rest were Malays, Indians, and "others". Consequently, this program served to unify the majority and solidify the hegemony of the "ethnic" Chinese. Before 1991, national identity cards indicated both race and dialect; after 1991, race alone was indicated (Bokhorst-Heng 1999).

The recent examples of white reactions to minority languages in the United States – the "English Only" anti-Hispanic movement and the opposition to the teaching of Ebonics – attest to the persistence of prejudicial ethnolinguistic consciousness. In 1988, *The Arizona Republic* published parts of a confidential memo written by John Tanton, the chairman and cofounder of U.S. English, an organization seeking to make English the official language of the United States:

> *Gobernar es poblar* translates "to govern is to populate." In this society where the majority rules, does this hold? Will the present majority peaceably hand over its political power to a group that is simply more fertile? Can *homo contraceptivus* compete with *homo progenitiva* [sic] if borders aren't controlled? Or is advice to limit one's family simply advice to move over and let someone else with greater reproductive powers occupy the space? [...] Perhaps this is the first instance in which those with their pants up are going to get caught by those with their pants down! (Crawford 1992: 151)

This passage configures language as biological and racial to the point where language legislation becomes a means of population control. In 1996, the Oakland California schoolboard decided to implement the teaching of Ebonics in schools. (The Linguistic Society of America endorsed the Oakland resolution in 1997.) Oakland's decision elicited a flurry of ethnic jokes representing blacks as ignorant, sexually promiscuous, as drug abusers, and as criminals. The jokes described drug deals ("one joint, two joint, three joint") and maternal prostitution ("what you say about my mama?") (Lakoff 2000: 240). Lakoff observes that the suppression of Ebonics is a method of controlling speech and thus controlling behavior. Similarly, Smitherman (2000: 293) sees the resistance as a "backlash against People of Color masquerading as linguistic patriotism". The discourse of racial prejudice in "polite" society stigmatizes speech as it once did physical expressions. Clearly, there is a white fear of contamination at work here, which Smitherman has characterized as a fear of "the browning of America".

Traces of racial ideology are also present in academic discourse that appears to be innocently descriptive. For instance, French academics regularly distinguish between *les pays anglophones* and *les pays anglo-saxons* in discussing countries whose official language is English, for example, Australia and Nigeria. This is justified by the gratuitous assertion that one should know if the country in question was originally "Anglo-Saxon" or not. The utility of such information is questionable; should ethnicity be the principal factor in determining the differences in language usage among English-speaking nations? Anglophone academics are content to identify both Australia and Nigeria as anglophone countries, without initially addressing the ethnic provenance of the speakers. Applied linguistics should critique the usage of the term *anglo-saxon* in this context, as it reads ethnicity into language *a priori* and foregrounds problematic notions of nativity.

10. Conclusion

The matrix of language, racism, and ethnicity clearly presents problems that demand the attention of linguistic inquiry, but that simply cannot be addressed by purely theoretical approaches. In its ahistorical and idealist postures, theoretical linguistics must remain mute in the face of the phenomenon of ethnolinguistic prejudice, which, in order to be properly analyzed, must first be historicized and situated in its emergence out of social, cultural, political, and philosophical contexts, as well as in its manifestations in the history of science. Applied linguistics alone can, in its practical, socially accountable, and interdisciplinary methodology, offer the appropriate modes of inquiry here.

Unlike the dress, food, or music of the other, which can be comfortably enjoyed by the empowered majority, and which are not perceived as contaminative, the language of the other is no mere accessory; it is surreptitiously perceived as a metonym of race and thus serves as a surrogate arena for ethnic conflict. Nationalism itself was born, in the early modern period, *of* and *in* language and articulated in the apparently innocent kinship metaphors of maternality and nativity, as well as in the ideology of a natural connection between national character and national geography. Organic metaphors were thus taken from body and nature to construct the myths of imagined congenital communities that still persist today. These imagined communities inscribe the exclusionary attributes: innate, primordial, sacred, representational, and untranslatable as pennants upon the nationalist flagship of language; they also aid in the inscription of the national language in a symbiotic matrix between body and physical environment. Language thus becomes configured in the discourse of the ethnic and corporeal ownership of national identity and local organic nature. These ethno-nationalist gestures informed the philology of the early modern and modern eras; they became cloaked in philosophical abstractions and generated arboreal and genealogical models of language, the most divisive examples of which can be seen in the race-conscious discourse of the Indo-European hypothesis of the nineteenth century. Thus philosophical theories of organicism participated in these ideologies, at least as they concern configurations of language. The fundamentally nationalist conflation of race and language was and is the catalyst for subsequent permutations of ethnolinguistic discrimination.

Prejudicial ethnic ideologies still persist, clearly in the popular, but also, to an extent, in the academic discourse of language, however implicitly. It behooves scholarship to continue to combat the racializing of language and the surreptitious preservation of antiquated ethnic prejudices cloaked by the apparently neutral terms "native language" and "mother tongue". These terms are no innocuous intuitions: They are the divisive implements of ethnolinguistic nationalism. Applied linguistics, by virtue of its interdisciplinarity, is uniquely positioned to engage these problems by employing tools of discourse analysis to further illuminate submerged gestures of race consciousness in otherwise ostensibly neutral locutions. It can also apply similar scrutiny and vigilance to the biological metaphors used in descriptions of language. It is clearly incontestable that language has biological components, but it is equally clear that the reticulate nature of language resists hierarchical genealogical metaphors. Awareness of this resistance, however, becomes repressed by the tendency, both historical and current, to overextend biological metaphors in the study of language and thus to determine language genetically. Scholarship would do well to continue to scrutinize this tendency, both in the popular, as well as in the scholarly spheres.

The current frontiers of the scientific study of language abut upon the territories of other disciplines, for instance, cultural studies, sociobiology, and political science, with which linguistics shares crucial objects of investigation, such as those examined in the present study. Applied linguistics serves as the optimal interlocutor in such inquiry.

References

Adams, James Noel
    2003   *Bilingualism and the Latin Language.* Cambridge: Cambridge University Press.
Anderson, Benedict
    1991   *Imagined Communities.* London: Verso.
Ashcroft, Bill
    2001   Language and race. *Social Identities* 7: 311–328.
Calder, George (ed.)
    1917   *Auraicept na n-Éces: The Scholars' Primer.* Edinburgh: John Grant.
Beaune, Colette
    1991   *The Birth of an Ideology: Myths and Symbols of Nation in Late-Medieval France.* Berkeley: University of California Press.
Bell, Alexander Melville
    1896   *The Sounds of R.* Washington: Volta Bureau.
Bembo, Pietro
    2001   *Prose della Volgar Lingua.* Bologna: CLUEB.
    [1512–1525]
Biville, Frédérique
    2002   The Graeco-Romans and Graeco-Latin. In: James Noel Adams, Mark Janse and Simon Swain (eds.), *Bilingualism in Ancient Society*, 77–102. Oxford: Oxford University Press.

Bloomfield, Leonard
    1963   *Language.* New York: Holt, Rinehart and Winston.
    [1933]
Bodin, Jean
    1579   *Les six livres de la république.* Lyon: Jean de Tournes.
Bokhorst-Heng, Wendy
    1999   Singapore's speak Mandarin campaign. In: Jan Blommaert (ed.), *Language Ideological Debates*, 235–266. Berlin: Mouton de Gruyter.
Bonfiglio, Thomas Paul
    2002   *Race and the Rise of Standard American.* Berlin: Mouton de Gruyter.
Bopp, Franz
    1816   *Über das Conjugationssystem der Sanskritsprache.* Frankfurt am Main: Andreäische Buchhandlung.
Bopp, Franz
    1833–1852 *Vergleichende Grammatik des Sanskrit, Zend, Griechischen, Lateinischen, Litauischen, Altslawischen, Gotischen und Deutschen.* 2 vols. Berlin: Königliche Akademie der Wissenschaften.
Borst, Arno
    1957–1963 *Der Turmbau von Babel.* 5 vols. Stuttgart: A. Hiersemann.
Bullokar, William
    1586   *Pamphlet for Grammar.* London: Edmund Bollifant.
Bullokar, William
    1580   *A Short Introduction or Guiding to Print, Write, and Reade Inglish Speech.* London: Henrie Denham.
Cohen, Mark Nathan
    1998   Culture, not race, explains human diversity. *The Chronicle of Higher Education*, 17 April: B4–B5.
Crawford, James (ed.)
    1992   *Language Loyalties: A Source Book on the Official English Controversy.* Chicago: University of Chicago Press.
Dante Alighieri
    1996   *De vulgari eloquentia.* Edited and translated by Steven Botterill. Cambridge:
    [1304]   Cambridge University Press.
Davies, Alan
    1991   *The Native Speaker in Applied Linguistics.* Edinburgh: Edinburgh University Press.
Du Bellay, Joachim
    1972   *Deffence et illustration de la langue françoyse.* Paris: Bordas.
    [1549]
Eco, Umberto
    1995   *The Search for the Perfect Language.* Oxford: Blackwell.
Fishman, Joshua
    1972   *Language in Sociocultural Change.* Stanford: Stanford University Press.
Galbraith, Vivian H.
    1972   Language and nationality. In: C. Leon Tipton (ed.), *Nationalism in the Middle Ages*, 45–53. New York: Holt, Rinehart and Winston.
Gardner, Robert C.
    1985   *Social Psychology and Second Language Learning.* London: Edward Arnold.

Graham, Stephen
    1914   *With Poor Immigrants to America.* New York: Macmillan.
Harris, Roxy and Ben Hampton (eds.)
    2003   *The Language, Ethnicity, and Race Reader.* London: Routledge.
Harsdörffer, Georg Philipp
    1968   *Frauenzimmer Gesprächsspiele.* Tübingen: Niemeyer.
    [1641]
Herder, Johann Gottfried
    1978   *Abhandlung über den Ursprung der Sprache.* München: Carl Hanser Ver-
    [1771]   lag.
Herder, Johann Gottfried
    1992   *Selected Early Works 1764–1767.* Edited by Ernest A. Menze and Karl Menges. University Park: The Pennsylvania State University Press.
Hope, Jonathan
    2000   Rats, bats, sparrows, and dogs: Biology, linguistics, and the nature of standard English. In: Wright, Laura (ed.), *The Development of Standard English 1300–1800: Theories, Descriptions, Conflicts,* 49–56. Cambridge: Cambridge University Press.
Huber, Wolfgang
    1984   *Kulturpatriotismus und Sprachbewusstsein. Studien zur deutschen Philologie des 17. Jahrhunderts.* Frankfurt: Peter Lang.
Humboldt, Wilhelm von
    1836   *Über die Verschiedenheit des menschlichen Sprachbaues und ihren Einfluß auf die geistige Entwicklung des Menschengeschlechts.* Berlin: Akademie der Wissenschaften.
Isaac, Benjamin H.
    2004   *The Invention of Racism in Classical Antiquity.* Princeton: Princeton University Press.
Kandiah, Thiru
    1998   Epiphanies of the deathless native user's manifold avatars. In: Rajendra Singh (ed.), *The Native Speaker: Multilingual Perspectives,* 79–110. New Delhi: Sage.
Kohn, Hans
    1972   The modernity of nationalism. In: C. Leon Tipton (ed.), *Nationalism in the Middle Ages,* 7–13. New York: Holt, Rinehart and Winston.
Lakoff, Robin
    2000   *The Language War.* Berkeley: The University of California Press.
Langslow, David
    2002   Approaching bilingualism in corpus languages. In: James N. Adams, Mark Janse, and Simon Swain (eds.), *Bilingualism in Ancient Society,* 23–51. Oxford: Oxford University Press.
Lass, Roger
    1997   *Historical Linguistics and Language Change.* Cambridge: Cambridge University Press.
Leibniz, Gottfried Wilhelm
    1877   Unvorgreifliche Gedanken betreffend die Ausübung und Verbesserung der
    [1680]   Teutschen Sprache. In: August Schmarsow (ed.), *Leibniz und Schottelius: Die unvorgreiflichen Gedanken,* 44–92. Strassburg: Karl J. Trübner.

Leibniz, Gottfried Wilhelm
 1990   *Nouveaux essais sur l'entendement humain.* Paris: Flammarion.
 [1704]
McDavid, Raven
 1966   Sense and nonsense about American dialects. *PMLA* 82(2): 7–17.
Paikeday, Thomas M.
 1985   *The Native Speaker is Dead!* Toronto: Paikeday Pub.
Paradis, Michael
 1998   Neurolinguistic aspects of the native speaker. In: Rajendra Singh (ed.), *The Native Speaker: Multilingual Perspectives,* 205–219. New Delhi: Sage.
Rousseau, Jean-Jacques
 1990   *Essai sur l'origine des langues.* Paris: Editions Gallimard.
 [1755]
Schlegel, Friedrich
 1975   *Über die Sprache und Weisheit der Inder.* In: Friedrich Schlegel, *Kritische*
 [1808]   *Friedrich-Schlegel-Ausgabe,* Vol. 8: 105–434. Edited by Ernst Behler. Paderborn: Schöningh.
Schleicher, August
 1863   *Die darwinsche Theorie und die Sprachwissenschaft.* Weimar: Hermann Böhlau.
Schleicher, August
 1865   *Über die Bedeutung der Sprache für die Naturgeschichte des Menschen.* Weimar: Hermann Böhlau.
Schmarsow, August (ed.)
 1877   *Leibniz und Schottelius: Die unvorgreiflichen Gedanken.* Strassburg: Karl J. Trübner.
Schottelius, Justus Georg
 1967   *Fruchtbringender Lustgarte.* München: Kösel.
 [1647]
Seton-Watson, Hugh
 1977   *Nations and States.* Boulder: Westview Press.
Singh, Rajendra (ed.)
 1998   *The Native Speaker: Multilingual Perspectives.* New Delhi: Sage.
Smith, Graham
 1998   *Nation-building in the Post-Soviet Borderlands.* Cambridge: Cambridge University Press.
Smitherman, Geneva
 2000   *Talkin That Talk: Language, Culture, and Education in African America.* London and New York: Routledge.
Speroni, Sperone
 1740   *Dialogo delle lingue.* In: Sperone Speroni, *Opere di M. Sperone Speroni*
 [1542]   *degli Alvarotti tratte da' mss. Originali,* tomo primo, 166–201. Venezia: Domenico Occhi.
Stephens, Meic
 1976   *Linguistic Minorities in Western Europe.* Llandysul: Gomer Press.
Swain, Simon
 1996   *Hellenism and Empire.* Oxford: Oxford University Press.

Thurston, Theodore S.
  1941   *Lithuanian History, Philology, and Grammar.* Chicago: Peoples Print Co.
Towson, Michael
  1992   *Mother-Tongue and Fatherland: Language and Politics in German.* Manchester: Manchester University Press.
Trubar, Primus
  1970   *Catechismus Jn der Windischenn Sprach.* Ljubljana: Mladinska knjiga.
  [1550]
Tucker, G. Richard and Wallace E. Lambert
  1972   White and Negro listeners' reactions to various American-English dialects. In: Fishman, Joshua A. (ed.), *Advances in the Sociology of Language,* 175–184. The Hague: Mouton.
Villey, Pierre
  1908   *Les sources italiennes de la "Defense et illustration de la langue françoise" de Joachim du Bellay.* Paris: H. Champion.
Weisgerber, Leo
  1948   *Die Entdeckung der Muttersprache im europäischen Denken.* Lüneburg: Heliand.
Wiener, Linda F.
  1987   Of phonetics and genetics: A comparison of classification in linguistic and organic systems. In: Henry M. Hoenigswald and Linda F. Wiener (eds.), *Biological Metaphor and Cladistic Classification,* 217–226. Philadelphia: University of Pennsylvania Press.

21. Language and sexism

Marlis Hellinger and Anne Pauwels

1. Introduction

Currently, research on language and gender is a particularly dynamic field of inquiry, where many voices contribute to the debate over diverse theoretical as well as applied perspectives. In the past, much work on language and gender was carried out in the frameworks of sociolinguistics and discourse analysis, but from the 1990s, more explicitly interdisciplinary research has become available, drawing on insights from anthropology, sociology, social psychology, cultural studies, and sexuality studies. Of particular interest is the tension found in recent research between two major theoretical approaches. One model continues to accept gender as a social category, acknowledging the fact that in many people's worlds "gender" is habitually translated into the binary distinction between female and male. Much variationist work rests on similar assumptions, e.g. in investigating the relations between an individual's "gender" and characteristics of their language use. Such research, with a focus on gender differences, gender roles and stereotypes, employs both quantitative as well as qualitative methodologies in an attempt to understand the social implications of linguistic choices.

The second framework is adopted by those researchers who distance themselves from essentialist notions of gender taking an explicitly social constructionist position. Gender as a social category is questioned, suggesting that rather than a given entity, gender is a profoundly variable set of practices that are constantly being performed and negotiated in interaction. The focus in this framework is on multiple identities (femininities and masculinities) and on local interaction: Communities of practice may highlight certain aspects of a person's gender identity, functioning as sites of questioning and transformation (cf. Mills 2003: ch. 4; Eckert and McConnell-Ginet 2003).

Numerous comprehensive resources are now available that illustrate the immense scope and depth of language and gender research (Talbot 1998; Pauwels 1998; Romaine 1999; Litosseliti and Sunderland 2002; Eckert and McConnell-Ginet 2003; Holmes and Meyerhoff 2003; Mills 2003; Lakoff 2004; Eichhoff-Cyrus 2004). A particularly valuable collection is Holmes and Meyerhoff (2003) which focusses on local interaction, but at the same time draws on material from numerous languages and cultures. An explicitly cross-cultural perspective is also taken by Hellinger and Bußmann (2001–2003) in their analysis of gender representations in 30 languages of diverse origin and structure.

Research on language and gender, be it concerned with the relations between gender and power, with gender stereotypes and belief systems, with gender identity and authenticity, or with sexist language, is a genuine area of applied linguistics. Moreover, in making connections to "outside" fields such as feminism, antiracism, postcolonialism, poststructuralism and critical theory, it constitutes part of critical applied linguistics (cf. Pennycook 2001: 8). Being involved in the questioning of "given" categories and contributing to creative solutions to language-related problems, the final goal of language and gender research is an understanding and where possible a transformation of social processes.

This chapter focusses on linguistic sexism as one important field of language and gender research. It provides a historical overview of the field and discusses categories of gender and linguistic sexism as central concepts. The chapter describes the contribution of applied linguistics to the field, with particular reference to proposals of non-sexist or gender-inclusive language and its implementation, spread and evaluation. Examples from languages other than English are included to illustrate the universal character of linguistic sexism.

2. Historical overview of the field

Studying gendered communicative behaviour and women's and men's ways of speaking has a history which predates the Western women's movement and feminism, especially within the disciplines of anthropology and dialectology. This is less the case for the study of the representation of women and men in language structure and language use: Here we are limited to occasional observations by individual scholars such as the comments made by the Danish linguist Lis Jacobsen (as quoted in Gomard 1985) about the use of derivational suffixes to form occupational nouns denoting women (see also Pauwels 1998). However, there is no doubt that feminism and the women's movement were the main catalysts for the critical analysis and discussion of both areas of study. Significantly, the debate began at a "revolutionary moment" when the publication of Betty Friedan's *The feminine mystique* (Friedan 1963) marked the beginning of the second wave feminist movement in the USA.

2.1. Sexist practices in language

In this chapter our focus is on the study of the asymmetrical representation of women and men in language, also known as *linguistic sexism, sexism in language* or *gender-biased language use*. The 1970s saw the emergence of the first scholarly discussions of gender-bias in language. Robin Lakoff's *Language and woman's place* (1975) and Dale Spender's *Man made language* (1980) may not have been the first contributions to the topic but their work acted as major triggers for extensive feminist linguistic activism both in and outside the academy. Both works identified a range of linguistic practices and features of language which create or reinforce biased representations in favour of men and the male, and against women and the female. Considered particularly discriminatory were practices which elevated men and the male to the status of norm, default or benchmark, and which treated women and the female as the exception or the derivation leaving them linguistically largely invisible. Such practices include the use of masculine/male (pro)nominal forms to refer to people, equating reference to males with reference to humans in general, and the formation of nouns referring to women (human agent nouns, occupational nouns) by means of morphological derivation (cf. Section 3). Stereotypical descriptions portraying women primarily as sexual creatures by stressing their physical features and reproductive roles at the expense of other characteristics also reinforce the gender bias in language use. The secondary status of women is further expressed through practices which highlight their dependency on the male or masculine; for example, women's courtesy titles identify women in terms of their relationship to men (married or not married) as does the practice of women changing their name upon marriage. Comparing women's performance to that of men, as in *She is a second Einstein*, effects a heightened status for the women whereas the reverse, as in *He plays like a girl*, has a denigrating effect on the men, demonstrating the "innate" superiority of men. A further instance of "female as secondary" has been labelled "semantic derogation" (Schulz 1975): Terms for women such as *queen*, *lady*, or *girl* are more likely than their male equivalents to have undergone a (historical) process of derogation, trivialisation or diminution (for a detailed description see Pauwels 1998).

Awareness and documentation of sexist practices in language was not restricted to the English language: Pioneering explorers of linguistic sexism include Yaguello (1978) for French, van Alphen (1985) and Brouwer (1985) for Dutch, Pusch (1984) and Trömel-Plötz et al. (1981) for German, Hampares (1976) for Spanish, and Petersen (1975) for Danish (for more details see Hellinger 1985). Throughout the 1970s and the 1980s, the number of descriptions of sexist practices in language increased dramatically, not only for English but also for other languages leading to the publication of several annotated bibliographies on the subject (e.g., Froitzheim 1980; Thorne, Kramarae, and Henley 1983).

2.2. Proposals for the elimination of sexist language

During this period another form of linguistic activism emerged: the development of proposals for the elimination of sexist practices from language use often labelled "guidelines". *The handbook of nonsexist writing* by Casey Miller and

Kate Swift (Miller and Swift [1980] 1995) and *The nonsexist communicator* by Bobbye Sorrels (Sorrels 1978) were among the first elaborate texts outlining how to avoid and eliminate sexist language use in English. For German, Ingrid Guentherodt, Marlis Hellinger, Luise Pusch and Senta Trömel-Plötz proposed a series of gender-inclusive practices (Guentherodt et al. 1980; Trömel-Plötz et al. 1981). Later proposals were also developed for French (e.g., Houdebine 1988), Italian (Sabatini 1985) and Spanish (Instituto de la Mujer 1989).

2.3. Reactions to guidelines

In and outside the academy reactions to the claim of gender bias in language and to the proposed reforms ranged from support to bemusement, ridicule, anger and outrage, with the latter being more vocal and widespread (cf. Section 4.2.1.). Blaubergs (1980) and Stanley (1982) among others identified a series of arguments used by opponents to the reform. One set of arguments simply denies or refutes the claim that there is sexism in language use. Within linguistic circles the denial of the claim centred primarily around the question of the arbitrariness of gender in language. Linguists opposing non-sexist language reform asserted that feminist linguistic activists had misinterpreted or misunderstood the relationship between linguistic categories of gender and the extralinguistic, "biological" category of sex (this is elaborated in Section 3). A poignant example of this type of argumentation is the response by the staff of the Linguistics Department at Harvard University to the assertion by students of the Harvard Divinity School that reference to God by "generic" *he* was a sexist practice. The Chair of the Department declared that there was "no need for anxiety or pronoun envy" (Harvard Crimson 26/11/1971, p. 17) because the use of *he* in a generic sense resulted from the fact that the masculine was the unmarked gender in English (cf. also Romaine 1999: 106). The other class of arguments directly attacks the proposed reforms. The most dominant and frequently used arguments in this category oppose language reform because (1) it infringes freedom of speech, (2) it destroys the linguistic and literary traditions of a language, (3) it is trivial as it does not improve the plight of women in other spheres of life, (4) it is too difficult and too impractical, and (5) the changes are cumbersome and unaesthetic.

Linguists and language professionals tended to focus on (4) and (5) (e.g., Kalverkämper 1979) whereas other scholars used arguments expressed in (1), (2) and (3) (e.g., Vetterling-Braggin 1981). The analysis of classic arguments against non-sexist language reform assisted feminist linguistic activists in finding counterarguments or refuting their validity (e.g., Hellinger and Schräpel 1983, Pauwels 1998). One argument which received more attention within feminist linguistic circles concerned the "futility" or the viability of linguistic reform to effect change. This issue is not particular to non-sexist language reform but affects all types of social language reform (cf. Cooper 1984). However, it warranted further investigation because the role of language in women's subordination or liberation was not widely debated or understood in feminist circles. The issue is intricately linked to the view of the relationship between language and reality/society. Language reform is seen as futile by those who believe that language is an arbitrary system of symbols used in the representation of reality or by those who believe that language merely reflects (extralinguistic) reality. The latter argue that social change will lead to language change making language reform unnecessary or futile. Robin Lakoff's (1975) work is said to reflect this view. On the other hand, if one subscribes to a view that language determines how an individual constructs reality (i.e. linguistic determinism) then language reform will be the primary means by which to alter that individual's view of reality. Spender (1980) shows signs of support for this view making linguistic reform and liberation the cornerstone for women's liberation. Other less deterministic views which posit a dynamic bi-directional relationship with language reflecting as well as shaping reality, are also supportive of language reform as it will contribute towards effecting change.

2.4. Psychological evidence

Countering the claim that language is not sexist or that the linguistic representation of the sexes does not impact on shaping people's view of the sexes was also done through a raft of mainly social-psychological studies demonstrating that sexist language use created gender-biased (mental) images in people. These studies (cf. Section 3.3.1.; Pauwels 1998) focused particularly on the impact of using masculine/male generic (pro)nouns. They showed that for a majority of language users the generic use of *he* or of *man*-words had predominantly male associations, and that this association with maleness was stronger among men than women. The journal *Sex Roles* was and continues to be a major channel through which such studies are publicised.

2.5. Institutional contexts

In more recent years the focus of activism has moved to implementation of reform agendas: Feminist language professionals lobbied public and private agencies, governments, and international organisations such as the United Nations for the acceptance of guidelines for the use of non-sexist language in public contexts and documents. By the late 1990s many such agencies in the English-speaking world and also in western Europe had adopted some form of non-sexist language guidelines (see Appendix; Pauwels 1998). In addition, work has begun on evaluating the reform process (cf. Section 5).

3. Central concepts: Gender and linguistic sexism

3.1. Gender as a social category

In research on language and gender, the central concept is, of course, gender. Since the early 1970s, the concept has been discussed within various theoretical frameworks, but essentially, gender was seen as a social category with "women" and "men" as the basic category members. In her seminal work of gendered language use, Lakoff (1975, 2004) characterised women's language as quantitatively different from men's language, with women using more frequently such phenomena as superpolite forms, affective adjectives, hedges, intensifiers, tag-questions, hypercorrect grammar, etc. (cf. Talbot 1998: ch. 3). Within the frameworks of the deficit and dominance models, "women's language" was characterised as uncertain and weak, and compared to "men's language" as less direct, less assertive and less powerful.

Researchers such as Tannen (1990) and Coates (1996) discussed women's and men's verbal behaviour within a difference or two-cultures model, asserting that the – socially constructed – differences in women's and men's language could be interpreted as equally valuable styles, with women being more co-operative and men more competitive conversationalists. This position was criticised as being apolitical and reactionary (Trömel-Plötz 1991; Cameron 1998), suggesting that a focus on female and male language might in fact reinforce women's subordinate status.

Empirical evidence of the quantitative differences between women's and men's language remains inconclusive. For example, while some studies found that women were indeed interrupted more frequently by men than they interrupted men or other women, other studies produced contradictory evidence (cf. Mills 2003: 169, 181). In addition, where differences were found, statistics became much less convincing once functional aspects were considered. Thus, in her analysis of tag-questions and pragmatic particles, Holmes' (1995) distinction between modal and affective functions yielded a much more complex picture of female and male language use.

However, there was a growing concern that general statements about "women's" and "men's" verbal practices might in fact reinforce biological essentialism, a theoretical position that accepts a division of people into two distinct categories (Bergvall, Bing, and Freed 1996: 15f). The categories of "women" and "men" were no longer conceptualised as internally homogeneous, but rather as internally diverse and related to other parameters such as race, ethnic membership, or social role. Increasingly, contextual aspects were taken into account such as domain, setting, topic, relationships between interactional partners, etc. Statements were now made about certain groups of people performing locally in communities of practice, i.e. highly contextualised settings (cf. Holmes and Meyerhoff 2003).

The dominant paradigm of the 1990s was a Butlerian framework which defined gender not as a set of discrete behaviours imposed upon the individual, but as a process, i.e. as an entity which is performed and may therefore be a site of negotiation and transformation of gender roles (cf. Mills 2003: 173). The rejection of a concept of gender as "only two" emphasised minority and marginalised groups of people (e.g., homosexuals, hermaphrodites, and transgendered persons), supporting a concept of gender not as an experiential given, but as a normative social construction. However, Holmes and Meyerhoff warn against a radical view that interprets the investigation of female and male verbal practices as one version of essentialist research. Taken to the extreme, this view would make the whole field of language and gender simply meaningless, "because gender would have become such an idiosyncratic quality that it would be nonexistent as a category across individuals" (Holmes and Meyerhoff 2003: 10). In a similar vein, Litosseliti and Sunderland (2002: 31f) warn that a narrow emphasis on gender as a "contextualised changing set of practices" carries the danger of becoming politically self-defeating.

While distancing ourselves from truly essentialist notions of gender, we will adopt a view that accepts gender as a social category. We thus share Cameron's (1995, 2000) concern that linguistic research should be responsive to the needs and interests of the communities of speakers studied. This approach is compatible with a definition of critical applied linguistics as elaborated by Pennycook (2001).

3.2. Gender as a linguistic category

Gender as a linguistic category has largely been neglected in research on language and gender (exceptions are Baron 1986; Pauwels 1998; Romaine 1999; Hellinger and Bußmann 2001–2003). This reflects a certain bias towards the English language, since of course not much can be said about gender as a morphosyntactic category in English. However, the documentation and evaluation of linguistic sexism across languages requires a clear understanding of the language-specific structural properties underlying the gender system of the respective language. Briefly, three categories of gender will be differentiated below: grammatical gender, lexical gender and social gender (cf. Hellinger 2006).

3.2.1. *Grammatical gender*

Grammatical gender can be defined as an inherent morphosyntactic property of the noun which controls agreement between the noun and some gender-variable satellite element which may be an article, adjective, pronoun, verb, or numeral. With few exceptions, each noun belongs to one gender class only which is characterised by a number of formal and semantic assignment rules (cf. Corbett 1991).

Languages with grammatical gender have developed language-specific rules of agreement. Thus, in the highly inflected Slavic and Romance languages, overt gender-marking is much more visible than in most Germanic languages, simply because these languages have more gender-variable forms. In the following examples from Italian and Hebrew, agreement is established between the feminine noun *zia* 'aunt' and the masculine noun *ha-sus* 'horse', respectively, by making various morphosyntactic choices (examples from other languages than English are taken from the respective chapters in Hellinger and Bußmann 2001–2003):

(1) a. *La   zi-a   è   andat-a   a   Firenze.*
       the.FEM.SG   aunt-FEM.SG   is   gone-FEM   to   Florence
       'The aunt has gone to Florence.'
   b. *ha-sus-im   ha-tov-im   dohar-im.*
       DET-horse-MASC.PL   DET-good-MASC.PL   gallop-MASC.PL
       'The good horses gallop.'

Of course, this kind of formal agreement does not exist in grammatically genderless languages like Turkish, Chinese or English.

3.2.2. Lexical gender

Lexical gender constitutes part of the semantics of animate/personal nouns, irrespective of whether the language does or does not have grammatical gender. For example, in Danish, personal nouns such as *datter* 'daughter' and *søn* 'son' are lexically specified as [female] and [male], respectively, and may be classified as "gender-specific", in contrast to nouns such as *barn* 'child' or *menneske* 'person', which are considered to be "gender-neutral" or "gender-indefinite". This terminology, which is reminiscent of an underlying dichotomous worldview, remains useful since lexical gender – perhaps universally – is an important parameter in the structure of kinship terminologies, address systems, and a number of basic, i.e. frequently used personal nouns such as 'woman', 'man', 'girl', and 'boy'; cf. the examples in (2):

(2)   Female-specific   Male-specific   Gender-indefinite
   Russ.   *devuška* (f)* 'girl'   *mal'čik* (m) 'boy'   *čelovek* (m) 'person'
   Span.   *hija* (f) 'daughter'   *hijo* (m) 'son'   *persona* (f) 'person'
   Dan.   *søster* (c) 'sister'   *bror* (c) 'brother'   *menneske* (n) 'person'
   Turk.   *teyze* 'aunt'   *dayi* 'uncle'   *kişi* 'person'
           * (f) = feminine, (m) = masculine, (n) = neuter, (c) = common gender

Lexical gender may or may not be marked on the noun itself. In English, most human nouns are not formally marked for lexical gender, with exceptions such as *widower* or *princess*, which show overt lexical gender-marking by suffixation. By contrast, lexical gender is marked extensively in German, since most personal feminines are derived from corresponding masculines by means of the fully productive suffix *-in*, as in *Bischöfin* 'female bishop', *Soldatin* 'female soldier' or *Punkerin* 'female punk'. Obviously, in languages like German, Russian or Italian, the relation between grammatical gender and lexical gender is anything but arbitrary.

Typically, but not exclusively, female-specific nouns are used to refer to females, and male-specific nouns to refer to males, while gender-indefinite nouns are freely used to refer to members of either group of referents. In grammatically genderless or "natural gender" languages, lexical gender can determine the choice of gender-variable satellite forms, e.g. anaphoric *she* or *he* in English. In the case of gender-neutral nouns, pronominal choice may be determined by the referent's gender, but also by tradition, prescription, or speaker attitude.

3.2.3. Social gender

Personal nouns have social gender if the choice of associated words cannot be explained by grammatical gender, lexical gender or by reference. Such nouns carry a gender-bias which has to do with stereotypical assumptions about what are appropriate social roles for women and men, including expectations about who will be a typical member of the class of, say, *surgeon* or *receptionist*. An illustration of social gender in English is the fact that many high-status occupational terms such as *surgeon* or *scientist* will frequently be pronominalised by *he* in contexts where the referent's gender is either unknown or irrelevant. By contrast, low-status occupational titles such as *receptionist* or *nurse* will often be followed by anaphoric *she* in neutral contexts. In cases of conflict between such practices and actual reference, explicit – and often asymmetrical – gender marking is an optional solution, as in Engl. *woman scientist* or *male nurse*.

3.3. Sexist language

As noted in Section 2, sexist language refers to linguistic expressions that exclude, trivialise or insult (mainly) women. Linguistic manifestations include female invisibility (*mankind*), asymmetrical gender-marking (*lady philosopher*), and stereotyping (*delegates and their wives*). While linguistic sexism has primarily been illustrated by examples from English and a few other Western languages, applied linguists have begun to document linguistic sexism in other languages of diverse origin, structure and typological affiliation (cf. Hellinger and Bußmann 2001–2003).

3.3.1. Female invisibility – androcentric generics

Traditional prescription requires the use of so-called "generic masculines" or "male generics" to refer to both men and women. For example, masculine nouns such as Russ. *vrač* (m) 'physician', Fr. *ministre* (m) 'minister', or Arab. *muḥami* (m) 'lawyer' may be used to refer to males, groups of people whose gender is unknown or unimportant in the context, or even female referents.

In languages without grammatical gender like English or Finnish, the use of male-biased nouns to refer to female and male referents (Engl. *chairman, mankind;* Finn. *lakimies* lit. law-man, 'lawyer') illustrates androcentric practices in neutral contexts. Thus in English, where gender-variable third person singular pronouns remain of an original grammatical gender system, "generic *he*" is the prescriptive choice in gender-indefinite contexts such as *An American drinks his coffee black*. This practice adds to the invisibility of female pronouns, but does not explain the dramatic imbalance between pronominal references to men and women in texts generally. Corpus analysis has shown that men are referred to considerably more often than women: A word count of gender-specific *he* and *she* in the Brown corpus of American English yielded a total of 9,543 occurrences of *he* compared to 2,859 occurrences of *she* (Romaine 2001: 161).

Pronoun usage is a powerful strategy of communicating gender. Anaphoric gender-variable pronouns may indicate lexical gender or specify the referent's gender; they may also symbolise traditional or reformed practices, as when a speaker makes the choice between a "false generic" and a gender-inclusive alternative (cf. Engl. "generic *he*" vs. "singular *they*", or Dan. *han* 'he' vs. *han/hun* 'he/she').

In languages with grammatical gender like Greek, Arabic or Romanian, androcentric generics typically occur in coordination. When a noun phrase conjoins a masculine and a feminine noun, the choice of a related satellite element, e.g., a pronominal, verbal or adjectival form, may create a conflict between the two competing genders. An example from Polish shows that agreement occurs with one conjunct only, namely the masculine (predicative adjective):

(3) *Adam i Ewa są szczęśliwi* (m).
   'Adam and Ewa are happy (m).'

Underlying such practices may be a gender hierarchy which defines the masculine as the "most worthy gender" (Baron 1986: 97). As a result, masculine/male (pro)nouns are highly visible across languages and carry considerably more weight and emphasis than feminine/female expressions.

Empirical evidence documenting the psycholinguistic effects of androcentric generics clearly supports the view that linguistic sexism is harmful in itself. Such evidence is available for English (cf. MacKay and Fulkerson 1979; Gastil 1990; Switzer 1990; Hamilton, Hunter, and Stuart-Smith 1992; Prentice 1994;

Madson and Hessling 2001) and German (cf. Irmen and Köhncke 1996; Oelkers 1996; Braun et al. 1998; Rothermund 1998; Stahlberg and Sczesny 2001; Rothmund and Scheele 2004), but there is little work on other languages (e.g., Braun 2000 on Turkish; Engelberg 2002 on Finnish). The overwhelming evidence is that androcentric generics invoke significantly more male than female imagery, i.e. the concept "female" is not generally available when androcentric expressions are processed by language users.

3.3.2. Asymmetrical gender-marking

Given the fact that many personal nouns carry a covert gender bias, communicating gender symmetrically in a language may be the exception rather than the norm. Of course, feminine/female terms can be derived from existing male/masculine terms, and lexically gendered nouns can be used in compounding to create morphologically symmetrical pairs, as in (4):

(4)   Masculine/male   Feminine/female
  Derivation
  Arab   *katib*   *katiba*   'secretary'
  Rom.   *pictor*   *pictoriță*   'painter'
  Compounding
  Germ. *Geschäftsmann*   *Geschäftsfrau*   'business man/woman'
  Norw. *politimann*   *politikvinne*   'police officer'
         police.man   police.woman

However, female linguistic visibility is often a loaded concept, and there is considerable variation across languages concerning the status and productivity of feminine/female word-formation processes. While in German the derivation of personal feminines is extremely productive, very few derived feminines exist in Welsh (which also has grammatical gender); most occupational terms in Welsh are grammatically masculine and have no feminine counterparts (cf. Awbery, Jones, and Morris 2002).

Frequently, the creation of female-specific nouns will produce semantically asymmetrical pairs in which the female represents the lesser category, illustrating what Schulz (1975) has called "semantic derogation". Notorious examples include Engl. *governor/governess*, *major/majorette*, etc. Of course, such pairs also occur in languages with grammatical gender, cf. (5):

(5) Fr.   *couturier* (m)   *couturière* (f)
          'fashion designer'   'seamstress, female tailor'
    Pol. *sekretarz* (m)   *sekretarka* (f)

	'(party) secretary'	'secretary (in an office)'
Germ.	*Hauptmann* (m)	*Hauptfrau* (f)
	'army captain'	'lawful wife'

Generally, feminine/female terms are not consistently used; they may be stylistically marked and in many languages carry negative connotations, which makes them unacceptable in neutral, and even in female-specific contexts. By contrast, masculine/male terms are either neutral or carry positive connotations. This explains the fact that the combination of a "gender-neutral", but often male-biased, noun with a female-specific element is common practice, while the combination with a male-specific element is the rare exception, cf. (6):

(6)		"Gender-neutral" term	Gender-specific term
	Jap.	*kisha*	*joseikisha*
		'reporter'	woman.reporter 'female reporter'
	Indon.	*dokter*	*dokter perempuan*
		'doctor'	doctor woman 'female doctor'
	Fr.	*écrivain* (m)	*femme écrivain* (f)
		'writer'	'female writer'

Asymmetrical gender-marking may fulfill various communicative functions: It may emphasise visibility of the "unexpected" referential gender, define the marked gender as the deviation from the norm, or serve contrastive purposes.

4. Contributions of applied linguistics

Applied linguistics continues to contribute in a significant way to the study of sex-based linguistic discrimination. Its impact on this field has been particularly strong in relation to language reform or planning. Applied linguistic insights aided the actual "enterprise" of reforming sexist language as well as provided a framework for its study. Within such a framework feminist or gender-inclusive language reform has been identified as a grassroots or bottom up attempt at linguistic reform. It has many characteristics of corpus planning (Kloss 1969) as it is concerned with alterations and modifications to existing language forms, expressions and structures. A principal aim of non-sexist or feminist language reform is to achieve linguistic equality of the sexes. How this is achieved becomes the subject of language planning. The expertise of (feminist) applied linguists has been particularly marked in relation to proposing language reform (see Section 4.1.), implementing such reform (cf. 4.2.) and evaluating the reform (cf. 4.3.).

4.1. Proposing language reform

In Section 3 we noted that androcentric generics (nouns and pronouns) and asymmetrical gender-marking are core elements in linguistic sexism. It is therefore not surprising that reform initiatives have centred around their elimination. Two major strategies of reform have been proposed to achieve this: gender-neutralisation and gender-specification (more frequently known as feminisation). Achieving linguistic equality through gender-neutralisation amounts to eliminating gender-specific features and forms in generic contexts, if not in gender-specific ones. The feminisation strategy on the other hand aims to achieve this equality through the explicit naming or inclusion of both sexes. In most cases this involves making the woman/female visible. The choice between these strategies is partly ideology-driven, but is also linked to the morphosyntactic structure of the language in question. A preference for gender-neutralisation is associated with feminisms which assert that explicit reference to women has not served women well in the past. In their view equality is best achieved by taking sex/gender references out of contexts in which they are not essential. Supporters of the feminisation strategy argue for explicit reference to women in all contexts to counteract the long-term invisibility of women which has been detrimental to their treatment.

From a language perspective the application of a feminisation strategy to androcentric nouns is more viable in grammatical gender languages (see Section 3.2.) whose gender-marking processes (usually through suffixation) are still productive than in "natural gender" languages whose gender-marking processes are no longer productive. German is an example of the former and English falls in the latter category. Many German feminist linguistic activists have argued that feminisation should be the preferred strategy for German given its strongly productive feminine suffix *-in*. The limited presence of other productive feminine suffixes in German also eliminates the potential difficulties faced by speakers of languages such as Dutch or French who have to choose between two or more such suffixes (e.g., Brouwer 1985; Gerritsen 2002; Houdebine 1988). The application of the feminisation strategy in generic contexts leads to what the German scholars call "gender-splitting", as in *jeder Lehrer und jede Lehrerin*, or *der/die Lehrer/in*, or the graphemically innovative *einE LehrerIn* to refer to the generic notion of teacher. Opponents of the feminisation strategy in German claim that the consistent application of feminisation in the case of generic nouns is unworkable because it breaches rules of linguistic economy (Stickel 1988) and poses a threat to comprehension because of the need to consistently disambiguate sex/gender references (Pflug 1991). Hellinger (1991) commented that the linguistic ambiguity argument is overrated as this is a common feature of complex sentences in language.

In English feminine gender-marking suffixes have not been productive for a while, in fact, with a few exceptions such as *actress* and *waitress*, such forms are considered (out-)dated as in *poetess*, *authoress*, or *manageress*. Consequently there has been little debate about which strategy to propose with regard to replacing androcentric nouns. In English the debate focussed around the replacement of particular word categories such as *-man* compounds, and although there has never been an explicit proposal to replace all *-man* compounds with *-person* compounds, the creation of terms like *chairperson*, *spokesperson*, *salesperson*, *handyperson*, etc. has attracted significant opposition primarily in the form of ridicule (cf. Pauwels 1998). Applied linguistic insights and expertise have been particularly influential in the planning of actual alternatives, although it did not shield feminist language planners from being dismissed as "linguistic ignoramuses". Pauwels (1998) identified two main principles which guided the language planning efforts of feminist linguistic scholars: social effectiveness and linguistic viability. She comments that:

> The proposed strategies should be capable of bringing about social change [...] with regard to the status of women and men in society [...] Proposed changes should, however, be also linguistically viable: an assessment should be made of the extent to which they affect the structure and use of a language.
> (Pauwels 1998: 117)

4.2.   Implementing and spreading the change

We have selected three domains where feminist language activists have had a considerable impact on the implementation and spread of reformed language practices: guidelines for non-sexist language, legal language and reference works.

4.2.1.   Guidelines for non-sexist language

Proposals for non-sexist alternatives have been made since the 1970s (Frank and Treichler 1989; Miller and Swift 1995; Pauwels 2003), often in the form of guidelines. Guidelines are an instrument of language planning; they have political implications in that they question the *status quo* which evaluates the masculine/male as the worthier gender. Numerous publishing houses, professional organisations and academic institutions developed their own guidelines, e.g., NCTE 1985; Unesco 1989; Hellinger and Bierbach 1993; Kargl, Wetschanow, and Wodak 1997 (see Appendix for a list of guidelines in different languages). Frequently, explicit reference was made to the respective national legislation on Sex Discrimination, Equal Opportunity and Human Rights, recognizing that the equal treatment of women and men must also be realised on the level of communication.

We have already commented on the public responses to such recommendations in Section 2 which frequently reveal openly hostile reactions maintaining that reformed usage violates grammar, is cumbersome and unaesthetic, and interferes with freedom of speech. By contrast, feminist activists adhere to various degrees of linguistic relativity, suggesting that a change in behaviour, i.e. using more instances of non-sexist language, contributes to social change. The ongoing debate on (non)sexist language must be interpreted as part of the ongoing political discourse over the equal participation of women in all public domains.

The spread of non-sexist language depends on a number of factors which relate to the historical, cultural and social environment of the respective language. Such factors include the question of whether the feminist critique of language is part of the country's political agenda, whether there are influential key agents who promote the change, and possibly, which attitudes speakers have developed towards English which has dominated the discourse of feminist language planning worldwide.

Overall, a decrease in the use of male/masculine generics in favour of non-sexist alternatives can be observed in English and a few other languages (see Section 4.3.1.). However, such changes may not necessarily be linked to a pro-feminist attitude, as linguistic choices may also be informed by opportunism. Pauwels (2003) has pointed out that non-sexist language reform will only be successful, if there is a personal commitment to change, and if changed practices are a reflection of the user's awareness of the discriminatory nature of traditional prescription.

4.2.2. Legal language

Implementing non-sexist language in legal texts has been a slow process, on both the national and international level. In Germany in 1990, a governmental working party on legal language acknowledged that linguistic asymmetries exist but considered these constitutionally irrelevant (cf. Hellinger 1995: 305). Restrictions of reform measures were based on the distinction between *Amtssprache* (administrative language) and *Vorschriftensprache* (legislative language): Administrative language is used in official communication involving specific gendered individuals, as in judicial decisions, private documents, forms of all sorts, etc., while legislative language is used in law-making. The working group recommended female visibility in administrative language but not in legislative language, on the grounds that the use of feminine terms would cause inconsistencies between existing and reformed texts, that the revision of the legal code would be too expensive and time-consuming, and that reformed texts would be stylistically cumbersome.

The current situation is one of considerable variability. Non-sexist language has made progress in administrative legal language, and in 1999 the German Ministry of Justice incorporated a revised version of the recommendations into the authoritative *Handbuch der Rechtsförmlichkeit* 'Handbook of formal legal procedures'. Legislative language is also experiencing some transformation, sometimes accompanied by absurd debates on individual changes (cf. Schewe-Gerigk 2004). Thus, the revision of titles of military ranks has been controversial, with reference to terms such as the feminine counterpart of *Hauptmann* 'army captain'. Clearly, the morphologically parallel form *Hauptfrau* is anything but adequate since it means 'lawful, legitimate wife', with associations of the term *Nebenfrau* which means 'concubine'. Similarly, in revising the German Criminal Code, the suggestion was made to accept feminine expressions denoting the victims of criminal acts, but to continue the use of masculine terms denoting offenders (*Täter*), the argument being that victims but not offenders are more frequently females. Significantly, however, in 2001 the implementation of gender-inclusive language was explicitly mentioned in Art. 1 Para. 1 of the *Gleichstellungsdurchsetzungsgesetz* 'Law for the implementation of equal opportunities', as one consequence of earlier EU directions of linguistic gender mainstreaming (cf. Schmidt 2004).

A comparative look at other German-speaking countries reveals important differences in ideological underpinnings and practical solutions. In Switzerland, implementation of gender-inclusive legal language has generally been less controversial than in Germany (Schiedt and Kamber 2004). In 1991, an interdepartmental working group recommended the so-called "creative solution" for Switzerland's three official languages (German, French, Italian). Referring explicitly to the Swiss *Bundesverfassung* (constitution), gender-inclusive language was recommended for both types of legal language (administrative and legislative language). Being more concerned with the solution of practical problems, the Swiss governmental guidelines (Leitfaden 1996) illustrate how a creative solution can be used to compose texts that are gender-fair, precise, and readable. The use of several non-sexist variants in one text (various forms of splitting and gender-neutral expressions, as well as the avoidance of personal nouns) is considered acceptable.

On an international level, the implementation of gender-inclusive language has suffered from the hegemony of English. Since 1987, the Unesco General Conference has repeatedly discussed the question of the elimination of sexist language from all Unesco Basic Texts, which must be published in Unesco's six working languages (English, French, Spanish, Russian, Arabic, and Chinese). In 1994, the General Conference adopted a resolution maintaining that gender-neutral wording "may alter attitudes and expectations that now constitute a barrier to achieving equality of opportunity for women and men" (Unesco 1994: 1). However, the practical consequences of this resolution remained minimal: Taking English as a model, only a handful of androcentric generics were to be replaced by gender-inclusive alternatives, such as Span. *hombres* → *los seres humanos, las personas,* or Fr. *homme* → *la personne humaine, l'individu.* Female visibility was not generally supported, rather "the generic use of the masculine form for post titles for both sexes is considered acceptable" (Unesco 1994: 4).

The overall effect is maintenance of the *status quo*, which ignores the fundamental differences between the six Unesco working languages in terms of grammatical gender, the number of gender-variable forms, and the productivity of feminine/female word formation processes. In addition, the decision to add a footnote to Unesco documents explaining that person-denoting terms are intended to include both sexes ignores the psycholinguistic evidence that has uncovered the male bias of "generic" masculine/male expressions.

An impressive rhetoric has also accompanied the (prospective) implementation of non-sexist language in institutions of the European Union. In 1990, the Committee of Ministers of the Council of Europe encouraged member states to use non-sexist language "to take account of the presence, status and role of women in society as current linguistic practice does for men", "bring the terminology used in legal drafting, public administration and education into line with the principle of sex equality", and use of non-sexist language in the media (Council of Europe 1990). In 2003, the European Parliament recalled that "the sexism reflected in language is an obstacle to equality between women and men" (EU 2003: 8). The use of non-discriminatory language in all EU documents was considered mandatory, "since equality is one of the democratic values of the European Union" (EU 2003: 30). However, in many of the 25 EU member states the issue of (non)sexist language has so far been of little academic and public interest, and the translation of the EU Parliament's resolutions into practical language policies remains uncertain.

4.2.3. Reference works: Dictionaries

Dictionaries, like grammars, are sites of codification and normative language. Dictionary-makers have the power to legitimate some meanings but not others, they are gate-keepers of authoritative usage and as such influential political agents (cf. Cameron 1992: 112–117). Traditionally, dictionaries have institutionalised sexist language in their choice of definitions and examples (use of androcentric generics, asymmetrical gender-marking, the communication of stereotypical gender roles). Citation practices in the Oxford English Dictionary illustrate a clear male bias: From Victorian to modern times the dictionary's meanings were exclusively drawn from white male literary sources (cf. Romaine 1999: 114–117). Among the top 20 authors cited in the OED from 1884 to 1989, there is not a single female voice; the Supplement of the OED lists one woman among the top 20 citation sources (cf. Willinsky 2001).

Changing dictionary-making practices began with some women's questioning and subverting prescribed meanings (cf. Graham 1975). Kramarae and Treichler (1985) published *A Feminist Dictionary* demonstrating how meanings are always selective. The aim of this dictionary was to recognise the authority of women's voices, to represent women as linguistically creative speakers, and more generally, to question claims to objectivity made in dictionary-making (cf. Romaine 1999: ch. 10). Cameron (1992: 125) emphasises the point that traditional usage embodies one view of the world and the feminist alternative another, and that both views are politically non-neutral.

The most popular and authoritative dictionary of the German language is the *Duden,* whose 12 volumes cover such areas as orthography, grammar, style, pronunciation, etymology, and meaning. In a provocative analysis two decades ago, Pusch (1984: 135–144) described the *Duden Bedeutungswörterbuch* of 1970 as a popular novel, commenting on the large number of active male protagonists and the few minor female characters all of whom were portrayed in stereotypical gender roles. Examples illustrating the meaning of words beginning with the letter *a* include (the *a*-words are underlined): *als sie Ulrichs ansichtig wurde, errötete sie* 'when she set eyes on Ulrich, she blushed'; *er ist ein international anerkannter Wissenschaftler* 'he is an internationally renowned scientist'; *sie betet ihren Mann an* (*anbeten*) 'she adores her husband'; *er hat ihm drei Zähne ausgeschlagen* 'he knocked three of his teeth out'. However, more recent editions of the *Duden* (cf. Duden 2002) have acknowledged the existence of such gendered asymmetries and have turned to a more gender-fair usage. The edition of 1999 (Duden 1999) no longer lists the masculine form of personal nouns only, but includes the parallel feminine terms, even nouns such as *Päpstin* 'female pope' and *Kanzlerin* 'female chancellor', which illustrates the function of language in creating imaginary worlds (with the second example denoting a real-world referent in Germany in 2005).

For the first time, Vol. 9 of the *Duden* (*Richtiges und gutes Deutsch. Wörterbuch der sprachlichen Zweifelsfälle* 'Correct and good German. Dictionary of linguistic problem cases') has a chapter on guidelines for non-sexist language (Duden 2001: 392–398). It discusses the equal linguistic treatment of women and men as an important principle of female visibility in society, and supports the use of feminine terms in domains of public life where female agents are still the exception, as in the *Bundeswehr* (the German armed forces) which is reluctant to introduce feminine titles such as *Offizierin* 'female officer', *Majorin* 'female major' or *Generalin* 'female general'. The *Duden* recommends forms of splitting (*Arzt/Ärztin* 'doctor', *Mitarbeiter/in* 'colleague'), compounding (*Feuerwehrfrau* 'female firefighter') and supplementary forms (*ärztlicher Rat* 'medical advice') to achieve a gender-inclusive wording. Reservations are expressed concerning the use of "internal I" which violates the rules of traditional and reformed orthography. However, word internal capital letters (as in *BahnCard* 'train card') are increasingly used, and the *Duden* may accept this variant in future editions. The *Duden*'s story can be interpreted as one instance of the successful implementation of non-sexist language, and considering the authoritative status of *Duden* language policies generally, an impact on the spread of gender-inclusive usage in other domains is not unlikely.

4.3.   Evaluating language reform measures: Two case studies

4.3.1.   Alternatives to generic he in Englishes around the world

The most widely promoted pronoun alternatives to generic *he* are generic *she*, *he or she*, or so-called singular *they* (for a discussion of other alternatives, see Pauwels 1998). Since the 1980s, several studies have investigated the extent to which generic *he* is being avoided or replaced by means of these pronoun alternatives. An early study by Cooper (1984) found a reduction in the use of generic *he* in several national newspapers and magazines in the US. Markovitz (1984) obtained similar results for the use of masculine generic nouns and pronouns in academic documents as did Rubin et al. (1994). More recent work reveals not only a reduction in the use of generic *he* but also identifies the preferred alternative(s) to *he*. Newman's (1997) analysis of American TV interviews and talk reveals a significant use of singular *they* forms (60%) when referring to antecedents such as *person, anyone, everyone*. Pauwels' work on Australian English similarly reveals a strong preference for the use of singular *they* in most forms of spoken language including formal public speech (e.g., Pauwels 2001, 2003). The only group to display a greater preference for *he or she* were female academics (Pauwels 2003). Singular *they* is also increasingly found in written language (Baranowski 2002). Furthermore these studies provide evidence that the use of generic *he* is becoming the exception rather than the rule in North American, Australian and New Zealand varieties of English. In most cases singular *they* has become the most used generic pronoun with frequencies hovering between 60% and 70%. This is not yet the case for British English (Romaine 2001) or for "new" Englishes such as those spoken in Singapore and the Philippines (cf. Pauwels and Winter 2004 a, b). For the latter speech communities corpus analysis using the International Corpus of English showed that generic *he* continues to dominate (nearly 90% in Singapore, and 70% in the Philippines) although there is some evidence of the emergence of *he or she*, especially in the Philippines (approximately 20%). The use of singular *they* was negligible in these Englishes. This could be related to their status as ESL varieties which may be more susceptible to exonormative prescriptive pressures.

Some of these studies have also been able to identify the primary agents and sites of change. It will not come as a surprise that women not only lead the change but are also its main facilitators. Leading "adopters" of change who act increasingly as role models for change are tertiary-educated women working in public institutions (education, law, civil/public service). The main sites of change are educational sites: the university seminar room, the lecture hall, the university campus and faculty meetings. High school classrooms as well as meetings are also increasingly sites of transformation.

4.3.2. Job advertising in German

Since 1980, the German Civil Code (Para. 611b BGB) has required employers to use non-discriminatory language in job advertising as one measure to achieve equal opportunities for women and men in employment: "Der Arbeitgeber soll einen Arbeitsplatz weder öffentlich noch innerhalb des Betriebs nur für Männer oder nur für Frauen ausschreiben, es sei denn, dass ein Fall des § 611a Abs. 1 Satz 2 vorliegt." 'The employer may not advertise a job/post only for men or only for women, either publicly or within the company, unless there is a case of Para. 611a […]'. Exceptions are listed in Para. 611a BGB, referring to areas such as the military, the medical professions, prisons or special housing facilities, where only male or female applicants are acceptable. However, changes in advertising practices were minimal, not least because violation of the law seldom had any negative consequences. In one study (Brockhoff 1987) only 21% of the 6000 advertisements analysed were formulated according to the 1980 law, while ten years later the percentage had risen to some 45% (Oldenburg 1998). However, still more than half of this corpus of 1963 advertisements (collected in 1997) contained sexist formulations.

In 1998, in the process of adapting national law to guidelines of the European Union, Para. 611b BGB was changed from a mere "Soll-Bestimmung" (optional regulation) to an obligatory regulation. The passage now reads: "Der Arbeitgeber darf einen Arbeitsplatz weder […]" 'The employer must not […]'. Two recent studies (Greve, Iding, and Schmusch 2002; Hellinger 2004: 286–288) document a steady increase in the use of gender-inclusive language to over 70% as a result of the new wording. Greve et al.'s study is based on a representative corpus of 11,369 advertisements collected in 2000, while Hellinger's small study analysed 926 advertisements of 2003. Figure 1 lists the results of the four studies (the dates refer to the years of data collection):

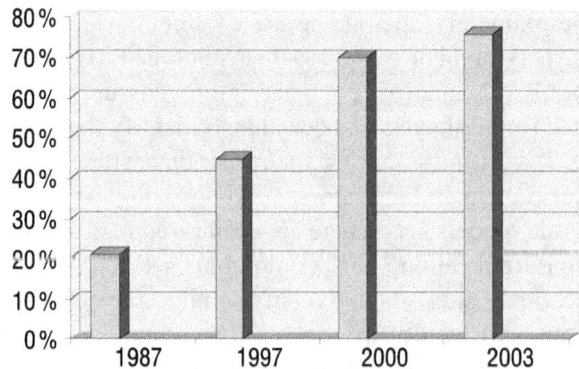

Figure 1. Use of genderinclusive job advertisements in German

However, these results must be interpreted with care. Within each sample, variability is considerable depending on a number of parameters: the type of newspaper analysed (national/regional/local, weekly/daily, print/online version), the paper's political affiliation (conservative/liberal), and the type of job advertised (high/low status, manual/professional). Thus, in Hellinger's study, the national quality weekly DIE ZEIT, which advertises for prestigious posts in the civil/public service, in research centers and (inter)national companies, uses gender-inclusive wording in well over 90%, while regional newspapers such as *Hannoversche Allgemeine* or *Frankfurter Rundschau*, which advertise for a much wider range of jobs, still used some 30% of sexist language. One local paper, *Wiesbadener Kurier*, contained an exceptional 50% of sexist advertisements even in 2003.

A more detailed analysis reveals variation concerning the choice and frequency of various forms of splitting (*einen Architekten/eine Architektin* 'an architect', *Stadtplaner/in* 'town planner'), the use of gender-neutral nouns (*Fachkräfte* 'experts'), the use of masculine nouns with an additional gender marker (*Manager* m/w 'manager male/female'), the use of abstract nouns (*Professur* 'professorship'), or the occasional use of "internal I" (*AbteilungsleiterIn* 'department manager'). Clearly, there is an urgent need for corpus-based longitudinal studies as well as for comparative studies analysing job advertising practices in other languages.

5. Applied research perspectives

Research in the 1990s and early 2000s has moved in three directions: Firstly, there is the continued expansion of research documenting sexism and the representation of the sexes in language. A second strand examines the impact of feminist linguistic activism on current language use. Finally, a third strand of research moves the study of linguistic sexism beyond its lexical and sentential focus. Here the influence of scholars working within a critical discourse analysis framework is noticeable.

5.1. Documentation

An ongoing project of applied linguistics must be the systematic documentation of (non)sexist language practices in different languages. Corbett (1991) and Unterbeck et al. (2000) provide important accounts of a large number of gender systems, but their approach is uninformed by any feminist perspective, while the three volumes by Hellinger and Bußmann (2001–2003) are inspired by the feminist critique of language. However, the linguistic representation of women and men remains unanalysed in the large majority of languages. The documentation of (non)sexist language (use) must not only rest on rigorous linguistic analysis, but must include sociolinguistic and cultural perspectives.

Further needed are large-scale corpus analyses so that more substantial statements can be made on the domain-specific contexts in which linguistic sexism is found. Such statements must necessarily acknowledge that the performance as well as the interpretation of gendered messages is sensitive to the contextual requirements in actual communities of practice. An expression which in isolation may be characterised as sexist (such as addressing adult women as *girls*), may in a particular interactive context not be interpreted as sexist at all, but may serve as a marker of in-group membership and solidarity.

Documentation must also take an explicitly comparative perspective. There is evidence that the spread of non-sexist language takes different routes, not only in different languages of diverse origin and structure, but also in global varieties of the same languages, as e.g. in the English-speaking countries of the world (cf. Romaine 2001; Holmes 2001; Pauwels 2001). Similar developments are likely in the German-, French-, and Spanish-speaking countries.

5.2. Evaluation

With respect to language planning and language change, it is essential to investigate how various reform measures are evaluated by language users. For example, a number of studies have tested the effects of traditional and reformed language on speakers of German (cf. the references in Section 3.3.1.). While the use of masculine generics was found to produce overwhelmingly more male-specific imagery, the various gender-inclusive alternatives produced quite unexpected results: Only long nominal splitting (*Bürger und Bürgerinnen* 'citizens') appears to achieve a roughly symmetrical mental representation of female and male referents, while abbreviated splitting (*Bürger/innen* 'citizens') and neutral expressions (*die wissenschaftlich Tätigen* 'scientists') produced asymmetries of various degrees. Surprisingly, "internal I" tended to evoke an overly female mental imagery. It seems that this alternative has the effect of a politically correct symbol signalling a pro-feminist attitude (cf. Stahlberg and Sczesny 2001: 138). Finally, adding a footnote to a text explaining that the masculine generics used in the text are intended to include women turned out to be totally ineffective. In fact, this practice created an even stronger male bias than the use of generic masculine forms (cf. Rothmund and Scheele 2004: 8). Such results have led to the hypothesis that – at least in languages with grammatical gender – the only way to significantly increase the availability of the concept "female" in a text seems to be the use of multiple female-specific expressions. There is an urgent need for psycholinguistic evidence of the effects of reformed usage in other languages.

A major focus in the evaluation of reform measures is on the adoption and spread of non-sexist language changes. To date most work of this nature centres on English. Pauwels (2003) has undertaken several studies examining the adoption of specific non-sexist language features primarily in Australian English, but also in some "outer circle" varieties of English (cf. Kachru 1997). Baranowski (2002), Cooper (1984), Ehrlich and King (1994) and Romaine (2001) have undertaken similar studies for North American English and British English, and Holmes (2001) for New Zealand English. The majority of studies record a change in favour of non-sexist language usage although the extent of adoption varies significantly across features and regions. The United States and Canada lead the way by a small margin from Australia and New Zealand. Britain lags quite a bit behind these countries. Least evidence of non-sexist language use is found in the postcolonial varieties of English in the Philippines, Singapore and Hong Kong (Pauwels and Winter 2004 a, b). Furthermore there is also evidence that the changes are not always used in the way they were intended, giving credence to Cameron's (1985: 90) observation that "[i]n the mouths of sexists, language can always be sexist".

5.3. The textual dimension

A text is defined as "an instance of social meaning in a particular context of situation" (Halliday and Hasan 1989: 11). Social meaning includes gendered meaning, and texts constitute important areas for the investigation of sexist language. In addition, the linguistic manifestations and effects of "covert gender" must be analysed, which often takes a rather indirect and subtle form. Even a gender-neutral noun such as Germ. *Gast* 'guest' may reveal its male bias in the further context, as in this interview with a hotel manager who described the hotel's policy of dealing with lost property:

(7) *Vergeßliche Hotelgäste*
Wir müssen immer mit dem klassischen Fall rechnen, daß die Ehefrau nichts vom Hotelaufenthalt ihres Mannes weiß. Deshalb schicken wir die gefundenen Gegenstände grundsätzlich nur zurück, wenn der Gast darum bittet.
'Forgetful hotel guests
We will always have to reckon with the classical case that the wife is not informed about her husband's stay in the hotel. Therefore we return lost property only on the guest's request.'

Particularly in languages with few overt gender markers, such practices may be important strategies of transporting gendered messages.

An ongoing debate concerns translations of religious texts which observe gender-inclusive language. An English version of the updated catechism – which sets out the principles of the Catholic faith – had proposed gender-neutral terms which were rejected by the Vatican in 1994. Proposals such as "God, our

Saviour, desires everyone to be saved" had to be rewritten to "God, our Saviour, desires all men to be saved" (cf. TIME Magazine, June 13, 1994, p. 50; cf. also Priests for Equality www.quixote.org/pfe/). By contrast, similar suggestions for change in the Protestant Church have been more successful: In Germany, a team of more than fifty experts were engaged in the preparation of a gender-inclusive New Testament (cf. Bail et al. 2006; also www.bibel-in-gerechter-sprache.de; Wegener 2004; Köhler 2004; for English see also Gold et al. 1995). There is a need not only for the creation of longer gender-inclusive texts, but also for the analysis of the public discourse about such texts.

For texts in different domains, the hypothesis needs to be tested that a satisfactory mental inclusion of female imagery can only be achieved by explicit and repeated female reference. An example of a German legal text is the gender-inclusive version of the Constitution of the Federal State of Lower Saxony. The comparison of the original version of 1951, which consistently uses generic masculine expressions, with the revised version of 1993, suggests that repeated (pro)nominal splitting throughout the text creates an awareness of female participation in all contexts and functions (cf. Dietrich 2000).

In the area of educational material, foreign language textbooks have frequently been found to contain sexist language. Using such criteria as exclusion, subordination, distortion and degradation (cf. Hellinger 1980), instances of sexist language and stereotypical representations of female and male social roles were analysed. Based on the assumption that a change of sexist practices will mean something for the learner, proposals were made for bias-free textbooks. However, a non-sexist textbook is no guarantee that classroom discourse will also be bias-free, and it is essential to acknowledge the role of the teacher as a mediator between the text and the learner (cf. Sunderland et al. 2002). A critical discourse framework suggests itself as the theoretical background for further analysis of how texts of various sorts are discursively implemented in the classroom.

This outline of applied research perspectives in documentation, evaluation and the textual dimension takes us back to the beginning of this chapter, where we noted the role of applied linguistics in contributing to the solution of language-related problems. More specifically, language and gender research contributes to the analysis and transformation of gender-related social processes.

References

Awbery, Gwenllian, Kathryn Jones and Delyth Morris
    2002   The politics of language and gender in Wales. In: Hellinger and Bußmann (eds.), 313–330.
Bail, Ulrike et al.
    2006   Bibel in gerechter Sprache. Gütersloh: Gütersloher Verlagshaus.

Baranowski, Maciej
    2002   Current usage of the epicene pronoun in written English. *Sociolinguistics* 6: 378–397.
Baron, Dennis
    1986   *Grammar and Gender.* New Haven, CT: Yale University Press.
Bergvall, Victoria. L., Janet M. Bing and Alice F. Freed (eds.)
    1996   *Rethinking Language and Gender Research: Theory and Practice.* London: Longman.
Blaubergs, Maija S.
    1980   An analysis of classic arguments against changing sexist language. In: Cheris Kramarae (ed.), *The Voices and Words of Women and Men*, 135–147. Oxford: Pergamon.
Braun, Friederike
    2000   *Geschlecht im Türkischen. Untersuchungen zum sprachlichen Umgang mit einer sozialen Kategorie.* Wiesbaden: Harrassowitz.
Braun, Friederike, Anja Gottburgsen, Sabine Sczesny and Dagmar Stahlberg
    1998   Können Geophysiker Frauen sein? Generische Personenbezeichnungen im Deutschen. *Zeitschrift für Germanistische Linguistik* 26: 265–283.
Brockhoff, Evamaria
    1987   Wie fragt Mann nach Frauen? DIE ZEIT, Jan 2, 1987.
Brouwer, Dédé
    1985   Anders, aber gleich? Über die Bildung weiblicher Berufsbezeichnungen im Niederländischen. In: Hellinger (ed.), 132–147.
Burr, Elisabeth
    2003   Gender and language politics in France. In: Hellinger and Bußmann (eds.), 119–139.
Cameron, Deborah
    1985   *Feminism and Linguistic Theory.* London: Macmillan.
Cameron, Deborah
    1992   *Feminism and Linguistic Theory.* 2nd ed. London: Macmillan.
Cameron, Deborah
    1995   *Verbal Hygiene.* London: Routledge.
Cameron, Deborah
    1998   "Is there any ketch-up, Vera?" Gender, power and pragmatics. *Discourse and Society* 9(4): 435–455.
Cameron, Deborah
    2000   *Good to Talk? Living and Working in a Communication Culture.* London: Routledge.
Coates, Jennifer
    1996   *Women Talk: Conversation Between Women Friends.* Oxford: Blackwell.
Cooper, Robert L.
    1984   The avoidance of androcentric generics. *International Journal of the Sociology of Language* 59: 5–20.
Corbett, Greville G.
    1991   *Gender.* Cambridge: Cambridge University Press.
Council of Europe
    1990   *Recommendation No. R(90)4 of the Committee of ministers to member states on the elimination of sexism from language.* <http://cm.coe.int/ta/rec/1990/90r4.htm>, retrieved June 15, 2004>

Dietrich, Margot
- 2000 "Gerechtigkeit gegenüber jedermann" – "Gerechtigkeit gegenüber allen Menschen". Sprachliche Gleichbehandlung am Beispiel der Verfassung des Landes Niedersachsen. In: Eichhoff-Cyrus and Hoberg (eds.), 192–223.

Duden
- 1970 *Bedeutungswörterbuch*. 1st ed. Mannheim: Dudenverlag.

Duden
- 1999 *Großes Wörterbuch der deutschen Sprache*. 10 vols. Mannheim: Dudenverlag.

Duden
- 2001 *Richtiges und gutes Deutsch*. 5th ed. (Der Duden in 12 Bänden, Vol. 9). Mannheim: Dudenverlag.

Duden
- 2002 *Bedeutungswörterbuch*. 3rd ed. (Der Duden in 12 Bänden, Vol. 10). Mannheim: Dudenverlag.

Ehrlich, Susan and Ruth King
- 1994 Feminist meanings and the (de)politicization of the lexicon. *Language in Society* 23: 59–76.

Eckert, Penelope and Sally McConnell-Ginet
- 2003 *Language and Gender*. Cambridge: Cambridge University Press.

Eichhoff-Cyrus, Karin M. (ed.)
- 2004 *Adam, Eva und die Sprache. Beiträge zur Geschlechterforschung*. Mannheim: Dudenverlag.

Eichhoff-Cyrus, Karin M. and Rudolf Hoberg (eds.)
- 2000 *Die deutsche Sprache zur Jahrtausendwende: Sprachkultur oder Sprachverfall?* Mannheim: Dudenverlag.

Engelberg, Mila
- 2002 The communication of gender in Finnish. In: Hellinger and Bußmann (eds.), 109–132.

EU 2003 European Parliament 1999–2004. Session document. Final A5–0053/2003.

Frank, Francine W. and Paula A. Treichler (eds.)
- 1989 *Language, Gender, and Professional Writing: Theoretical Approaches and Guidelines for Nonsexist Usage*. New York: MLA.

Friedan, Betty
- 1963 *The Feminine Mystique*. New York: Norton.

Froitzheim, Claudia
- 1980 *Sprache und Geschlecht: Bibliographie*. Trier: Universität Trier.

Gastil, John
- 1990 Generic pronouns and sexist language: The oxymoronic character of masculine generics. *Sex Roles* 23: 629–643.

Gerritsen, Marinel
- 2002 Towards a more gender-fair usage in Netherlands Dutch. In: Hellinger and Bußmann (eds.), 81–108.

Gold, Victor R. (ed.)
- 1995 *The New Testament and Psalms. An Inclusive Version*. New York: Oxford University Press.

Gomard, Kirsten
- 1985 Sexistische Sprachmuster im Dänischen und Tendenzen des sprachlichen Wandels. In: Hellinger (ed.), 84–95.

Graham, Alma
- 1975 The making of a nonsexist dictionary. In: Barrie Thorne and Nancy Henley (eds.), *Language and Sex: Difference and Dominance*, 57–63. Rowley, MA: Newbury House.

Greve, Melanie, Marion Iding and Bärbel Schmusch
- 2002 Geschlechtsspezifische Formulierungen in Stellenangeboten. *Linguistik online* 11/2. http://www.linguistik-online.org/11_02/greschmid.html

Guentherodt, Ingrid, Marlis Hellinger, Luise F. Pusch and Senta Trömel-Plötz
- 1980 Richtlinien zur Vermeidung sexistischen Sprachgebrauchs. *Linguistische Berichte* 69: 15–21.

Hall, Kira and Mary Bucholtz (eds.)
- 1995 *Gender Articulated: Language and the Socially Constructed Self.* New York: Routledge.

Halliday, Michael A. K. and Ruqayia Hasan
- 1989 *Language, Context and Text: Aspects of Language in a Social-semiotic Perspective.* Oxford: Oxford University Press.

Hamilton, Mykol C., Barbara Hunter and Shannon Stuart-Smith
- 1992 Jury instructions worded in the masculine generic: Can a woman claim self-defense when "he" is threatened? In: Joan C. Chrisler and Doris Howard (eds.), *New Directions in Feminist Psychology. Practise, Theory and Research*, 169–178. New York: Springer Publishing Company.

Hampares, Katherine J.
- 1976 Sexism in Spanish lexicography. *Hispania* 59: 100–109.

Handbuch der Rechtsförmlichkeit
- 1999 Bundesministerium der Justiz. Köln: Bundesanzeiger Verlag.

Hellinger, Marlis
- 1980 "For men must work and women must weep": Sexism in English-language textbooks used in German schools. *Women's Studies International Quarterly* 3: 267–275.

Hellinger, Marlis (ed.)
- 1985 *Sprachwandel und feministische Sprachpolitik: Internationale Perspektiven.* Opladen: Westdeutscher Verlag.

Hellinger, Marlis
- 1990 *Kontrastive feministische Linguistik. Mechanismen sprachlicher Diskriminierung im Englischen und Deutschen.* Ismaning: Hueber.

Hellinger, Marlis
- 1991 Für sprachliche Gleichbehandlung. *Universitas* 5: 413–415.

Hellinger, Marlis
- 1995 Language and gender. In: Patrick Stevenson (ed.), *The German Language and the Real World*, 279–314. Oxford: Clarendon.

Hellinger, Marlis
- 2000 Feministische Sprachpolitik und politische Korrektheit – der Diskurs der Verzerrung. In: Eichhoff-Cyrus and Hoberg (eds.), 177–191.

Hellinger, Marlis
- 2004 Empfehlungen für einen geschlechtergerechten Sprachgebrauch im Deutschen. In: Eichhoff-Cyrus (ed.), 275–291.

Hellinger, Marlis
    2006   Sexist language. In: *Encyclopedia of Language and Linguistics*. 2nd ed., 265–272. Oxford: Elsevier.
Hellinger, Marlis and Beate Schräpel
    1983   Über die sprachliche Gleichbehandlung von Frauen und Männern. *Jahrbuch für Internationale Germanistik* 15: 40–69.
Hellinger, Marlis and Christine Bierbach
    1993   *Eine Sprache für beide Geschlechter. Richtlinien für einen nicht-sexistischen Sprachgebrauch*. Bonn: Unesco.
Hellinger, Marlis and Hadumod Bußmann (eds.)
    2001–2003   *Gender Across Languages. The Linguistic Representation of Women and Men*, 3 vols. Amsterdam: Benjamins.
Holmes, Janet
    1995   *Women, Men and Politeness*. London: Longman.
Holmes, Janet
    2001   A corpus-based view of gender in New Zealand English. In: Hellinger and Bußmann (eds.), 115–136.
Holmes, Janet and Miriam Meyerhoff (eds.)
    2003   *The Handbook of Language and Gender*. Oxford: Blackwell.
Houdebine, Anne Marie
    1988   La feminisation des noms de métiers en français contemporain. In: Georges Kassaï (ed.), *Contrastes. La Différence Sexuelle dans le Langage*, 39–71. Nice: ADEC.
Instituto de la Mujer
    1989   *Propuestas para evitar el sexismo en el lenguaje*. Madrid: Instituto de la mujer.
Irmen, Lisa and Astrid Köhncke
    1996   Zur Psychologie des "generischen" Maskulinums. *Sprache und Kognition* 15: 152–166.
Kachru, Braj B.
    1997   World Englishes and English-using communities. *Annual Review of Applied Linguistics* 17: 66–87.
Kalverkämper, Hartwig
    1979   Die Frauen und die Sprache. *Linguistische Berichte* 62: 55–71.
Köhler, Hanne
    2004   Auf dem Weg zu einer Bibel in gerechter Sprache. In: Eichhoff-Cyrus (ed.), 361–373.
Kloss, Heinz
    1969   *Research Possibilities on Group Bilingualism: A Report*. Quebec: International Centre for Research on Bilingualism.
Kramarae, Cheris and Paula A. Treichler
    1985   *A Feminist Dictionary*. Boston: Pandora.
Lakoff, Robin
    1975   *Language and Woman's Place*. New York: Harper & Row.
Lakoff, Robin Tolmach
    2004   *Language and Woman's Place*. Ed. Mary Bucholtz. Oxford: Oxford University Press.
Litosseliti, Lia and Jane Sunderland (eds.)
    2002   *Gender Identity and Discourse Analysis*. Amsterdam: Benjamins.

MacKay, Donald and David Fulkerson
    1979   On the comprehension and production of pronouns. *Journal of Verbal Learning and Verbal Behavior* 18: 661–673.
Madson, Laura and Robert M. Hessling
    2001   Readers' perceptions of four alternatives to masculine generic pronouns. *Journal of Social Psychology* 14: 156–158.
Markovitz, Judith
    1984   The impact of the sexist language controversy and regulation on language in university documents. *Psychology of Women Quarterly* 8(4): 337–347.
Miller, Casey and Kate Swift
    1995   *The Handbook of Non-Sexist Writing*. 3rd ed. London: The Women's Press.
Mills, Sara
    2003   *Gender and Politeness*. Cambridge: Cambridge University Press.
Newman, Michael
    1997   *Epicene Pronouns: The Linguistics of a Prescriptive Problem*. New York: Garland Publishing.
Oelkers, Susanne
    1996   Der Sprintstar und ihre Freundinnen. Ein empirischer Beitrag zur Diskussion um das generische Maskulinum. *Muttersprache* 106: 1–15.
Oldenburg, Antje
    1998   Von Arzthelfern, Bauschlosserinnen und anderen Berufstätigen. *Muttersprache* 108: 67–80.
Pauwels, Anne
    1998   *Women Changing Language*. London: Longman.
Pauwels, Anne
    2001   Spreading the feminist word: The case of the new courtesy title *Ms* in Australian English. In: Hellinger and Bußmann (eds.), 137–151.
Pauwels, Anne
    2003   Linguistic sexism and feminist linguistic activism. In: Holmes and Meyerhoff (eds.), 550–570.
Pauwels, Anne and Joanne Winter
    2004a   Generic pronouns and gender-inclusive language reform in the English of Singapore and the Philippines. *Australian Review of Applied Linguistics* 27(2): 50–62.
Pauwels, Anne and Joanne Winter
    2004b   Gender-inclusive language reform in educational writing in Singapore and the Philippines: A corpus-based approach. *Asian Englishes. An International Journal of the Sociolinguistics of English in Asia/Pacific* 7(1): 4–21.
Petersen, Pia Riber
    1975   Bedepiger, styrkvinder og formandinder. In: Dansk Sprognævns skrifter 9, 53–64. Copenhagen: Gyldendal,.
Pennycook, Alistair
    2001   *Critical Applied Linguistics*. Mahwah, NJ: Lawrence Erlbaum.
Priests for Equality
    <www.quixote.org/pfe/>
Pflug, Günther
    1991   Der bzw. die Arbeitnehmer und Arbeitnehmerinnen – Vertreter bzw. Vertreterinnen: Probleme der geschlechtsneutralen Rechts- und Verwaltungssprache. *Universitas* 5: 415–419.

Prentice, Deborah A.
  1994   Do language reforms change our way of thinking? *Journal of Language and Social Psychology* 13(1): 3–19.
Pusch, Luise F.
  1984   *Das Deutsche als Männersprache*. Frankfurt am Main: Suhrkamp.
Romaine, Suzanne
  1999   *Communicating Gender*. Mahwah, NJ: Lawrence Erlbaum.
Romaine, Suzanne
  2001   A corpus-based view of gender in British and American English. In: Hellinger and Bußmann (eds.), 153–175.
Rothermund, Klaus
  1998   Automatische geschlechtsspezifische Assoziationen beim Lesen von Texten mit geschlechtseindeutigen und generisch maskulinen Text-Subjekten. *Sprache und Kognition* 17: 152–166.
Rothmund, Jutta and Brigitte Scheele
  2004   Personenbezeichnungsmodelle auf dem Prüfstand. Lösungsmöglichkeiten für das Genus-Sexus-Problem auf Textebene. *Zeitschrift für Psychologie* 212: 40–54.
Rubin, Donald I., Kathryn Greene and Deidra Schneider
  1994   Adopting gender-inclusive language reforms. Diachronic and synchronic variation. *Journal of Language and Social Psychology* 13(2): 91–114.
Sabatini, Alma
  1985   Occupational titles in Italian: Changing sexist usage. In: Hellinger (ed.), 64–75.
Schewe-Gerigk, Irmgard
  2004   Geschlechtergerechte Sprache im Deutschen Bundestag. In: Eichhoff-Cyrus (ed.), 322–331.
Schiedt, Margret and Isabel Kamber
  2004   Sprachliche Gleichbehandlung in der Schweizer Gesetzgebung: Das Parlament macht's möglich. In: Eichhoff-Cyrus (ed.), 332–348.
Schmidt, Renate
  2004   Geschlechtergerechte Sprache in Politik und Recht – Notwendigkeit oder blosse Stilübung? In: Eichhoff-Cyrus (ed.), 316–321.
Schulz, Muriel R.
  1975   The semantic derogation of woman. In: Barrie Thorne and Nancy Henley (eds.), *Language and Sex: Difference and Dominance*, 64–75. Rowley, MA: Newbury House.
Sorrels, Bobbye M.
  1978   *The Nonsexist Communicator*. Englewood Cliffs, NJ: Prentice Hall.
Spender, Dale
  1980   *Man Made Language*. London: Routledge and Kegan Paul.
Stahlberg, Dagmar and Sabine Sczesny
  2001   Effekte des generischen Maskulinums und alternativer Sprachformen auf den gedanklichen Einbezug von Frauen. *Psychologische Rundschau* 52: 131–140.
Stanley, Julia P.
  1982   Two essays on language and change. I: Power and the opposition to feminist proposals for language change II: John Simon and the "Dragons of Eden". *College English* 44: 840–854.

Stickel, Gerhard
    1988   Beantragte staatliche Regelungen zur "Sprachlichen Gleichbehandlung". Darstellung und Kritik. *Zeitschrift für Germanistische Linguistik* 16: 330–355.
Sunderland, Jane, Maire Cowley, Fauziah Abdul Rahim, Christina Leontzakou and Julie Shattuck
    2002   From representation towards discursive practices: Gender in the foreign language textbook revisited. In: Litosseliti and Sunderland (eds.), 223–255.
Switzer, Jo Young
    1990   The impact of generic word choices: An empirical investigation of age- and sex-related differences. *Sex Roles* 22: 69–82.
Talbot, Mary M.
    1998   *Language and Gender: An Introduction.* Oxford: Blackwell.
Tannen, Deborah
    1990   *You Just Don't Understand: Women and Men in Conversation.* New York: William Morrow.
Thorne, Barrie, Cheris Kramarae and Nancy Henley (eds.)
    1983   *Language, Gender and Society.* Rowley, MA: Newbury House.
Trömel-Plötz, Senta
    1991   Selling the apolitical. Review of Tannen 1990. *Discourse and Society* 2(4): 489–502.
Trömel-Plötz, Senta, Ingrid Guentherodt, Marlis Hellinger and Luise F. Pusch
    1981   Richtlinien zur Vermeidung sexistischen Sprachgebrauchs. *Linguistische Berichte* 71: 1–7.
Unesco
    1994   Unesco 145th Session. Item 5.7.1. Paris.
Unterbeck, Barbara et al.
    2000   *Gender in Grammar and Cognition.* Berlin: Mouton de Gruyter.
Van Alphen, Ingrid C.
    1985   Eine Frau – ein Wort: Über die Gleichbehandlung von Frauen und Männern und die Konsequenzen für die Berufsbezeichnungen im Niederländischen. In: Hellinger (ed.), 123–131.
Vetterling-Braggin, Mary (ed.)
    1981   *Sexist Language. A Modern Philosophical Analysis.* Totowa, N. J.: Littlefield, Adams.
Wegener, Hildburg
    2004   "Nennt uns nicht Brüder!" Gerechte Sprache in Gottesdienst und Kirche. In: Eichhoff-Cyrus (ed.), 349–360.
Willinsky, John
    2001   *Empire of Words: The Reign of the OED.* Princeton, NJ: Princeton University Press.
Yaguello, Marina
    1978   *Les Mots et les Femmes.* Paris: Payot.

Appendix: Recommendations for non-sexist language

Czech
Savić, Svenka
    1998   Žena sakrivena jezikom medija: Kodeks neseksisticke upotrebe jezika [The woman hidden by the language of the media: A codex for non-sexist language use]. *Ženske Studijie* [Women's studies] 10: 89–132.

Danish
Brinch, Elizabeth
    1997   Sådan er annonce-reglerne for ligebehandling [Rules for equal treatment in advertising]. *Nyhedsbrev om Ligestilling på Arbejdsmarkedet* 40: 34–35.

Dutch
de Caluwe, Johan and Ariane van Santen
    2001   *Gezocht: Functiebenamingen (m/v). Wegwijzer voor Vorming en Gebruik van Nederlandse Functiebenamingen* [Jobs vacant: Professional titles (m/v). Manual for the formation and use of Dutch names for professions]. The Hague: SDU Uitgevers.

Werkgroep Wijziging Beroepsnaming
    1982   *Gevraagd. Aanzet tot een Discussie over het Wijzigen van den Beroepsbenaming in het Kader van de Wet Gelijke Behandeling Mannen en Vrouwen* [Required. Initial motivation for a discussion of the modification of professional titles as related to the law of equal treatment of men and women]. Amsterdam: Uitgave Ministerie von Sociale Zaken en Werkgelegenheid en de aktiegroep Man Vrouw Maatschappij.

English
Frank, Francine and Paula A. Treichler
    1989   *Language, Gender, and Professional Writing*. New York: MLA.

Guidelines for improving the image of women in textbooks
    1974   Glenview, IL: Scott, Foresman and Company.

Guidelines for non-sexist use of language
    2003   American Philosophical Association. <http://www.engl.niu.edu/freshman_english/nonsexist.html>

Guidelines to reduce bias in language
    1994   American Psychological Association (originally *Guidelines for nonsexist language in APA Journals*, 1977).

LSA guidelines for nonsexist usage
    1996   Linguistic Society of America. *LSA Bulletin*, December 1996.

McGraw-Hill
    1972   *Guidelines for Equal Treatment of the Sexes in McGraw-Hill Book Company Publications*. Highstown, NJ: McGraw-Hill.

NCTE
    1985   *Guidelines for Nonsexist Use of Language in NCTE Publications*. National Council of Teachers of English (1st ed 1975).

UNESCO
    1989   *Guidelines on Non-sexist Language*. Paris.

French
Au Féminin: Guide de Féminisation des Titres de Fonction et des Textes (=Guide de l'Office de la langue française)
    1991   Québec: Publications du Québec.

CGTN = Commission Générale de Terminologie et de Néologie
 1998   *Rapport sur la Féminisation des Noms de Métier, Fonction, Grade ou Titre*. Premier Ministre: Octobre 1998 <http://www.culture.gouv.fr/culture/dglf/cogeter/feminisation/accueil-feminisation.html> Retrieved April 3, 2006.
CNR / INaLF = Conseil National de la Recherche/Institut National de la Langue Française
 1999   *Femme, J'écris ton Nom ... Guide D'aide à la Féminisation desNnoms de Métiers, Titres, Grades et Fonctions*. Paris: La documentation française.
Mettre au féminin. Guide de féminisation des noms de métier, fonction, grade ou titre
 1994   Brussels: Direction générale de la culture et de la communication, Service de la langue française.
Parent, Monique
 1994   Féminisation et masculinisation des titres de professions au Québec. *La Linguistique* 30: 123–135.
Pour l'égalité des sexes dans le language
 1999   Paris: Unesco (1st ed. 1987).

German

BBB
 2002   *Sprachliche Gleichbehandlung von Frauen und Männern. Hinweise, Anwendungsmöglichkeiten und Beispiele*. BBB-Merkblatt des Bundesverwaltungsamtes.
Braun, Friederike
 1991   *Mehr Frauen in die Sprache. Leitfaden zur geschlechtergerechten Formulierung*. Kiel: Die Frauenministerin des Landes Schleswig-Holstein.
Christen, Helen
 1994   *Sprache gemeinsam verändern. Ein Leitfaden zur sprachlichen Gleichbehandlung von Frau und Mann*. Luzern.
Elmiger, Daniel and Eva Lia Wyss
 2000   Sprachliche Gleichstellung von Frau und Mann in der Schweiz. Ein Überblick und neue Perspektiven. *Bulletin vals-asla* 72. Neuchâtel.
Guentherodt, Ingrid, Marlis Hellinger, Luise F. Pusch and Senta Trömel-Plötz
 1980   Richtlinien zur Vermeidung sexistischen Sprachgebrauchs. *Linguistische Berichte* 69: 15–21.
Häberlin, Susanna, Rachel Schmid and Eva Lia Wyss
 1991   *Übung macht die Meisterin. Richtlinien für einen nichtsexistischen Sprachgebrauch*. Zürich.
Hellinger, Marlis and Christine Bierbach
 1993   *Eine Sprache für beide Geschlechter. Richtlinien für einen nicht-sexistischen Sprachgebrauch*. Bonn: Unesco.
Kargl, Maria, Karin Wetschanow and Ruth Wodak
 1997   *Kreatives Formulieren. Anleitungen zu geschlechtergerechtem Sprachgebrauch*. Universität Wien und Bundesministerium für Unterricht und kulturelle Angelegenheiten. Wien: Bundeskanzleramt.
"kurz und bündig". Vorschläge zum geschlechtergerechten Formulieren
 2000   Universität Klagenfurt und Frauenreferat des Landes Kärnten.
Leitfaden
 1996   *Leitfaden zur sprachlichen Gleichbehandlung im Deutschen*. Bern: Schweizerische Bundeskanzlei.

Maskuline und feminine Personenbezeichnungen in der Rechtssprache
    1991   Deutscher Bundestag, 12. Wahlperiode. Unterrichtung durch die Bundesregierung.
Müller, Sigrid and Claudia Fuchs
    1993   *Handbuch zur nichtsexistischen Sprachverwendung in öffentlichen Texten*. Frankfurt am Main: Fischer.

Greek
Tsokalidou, Petroula
    1996   Το φύλο της γλώσσας: Οδηγός μη σεξιστικής γλώσσας για τον δημόσιο ελληνικό λόγο [The gender of language: A guide to non-sexist language for public Greek speech]. Athens: Syndesmos Ellinidon Epistimonon.

Italian
Sabatini, Alma
    1986   *Raccomandazioni per un uso non sessista della lingua italiana*. Roma: Presidenza del Consiglio dei Ministri.
Sabatini, Alma
    1987/1993 Raccomandazioni per un uso non sessista della lingua italiana. In: Alma Sabatini, *Il Sessissmo Nella Lingua Italiana*, 95–119. Roma: Presidenza del Consiglio dei Ministri.

Spanish
Ministerio de Asuntos Sociales
    1991   *Uso no sexista del lenguaje administrativo*. Madrid: Ministerio de Asuntos Sociales.
Ministerio de Educación y Ciencia
    1988   *Recomendaciones para un uso no sexista de la lengua*. Madrid: Ministerio de Educación y Ciencia.
Unesco
    1990   *Recomendaciones para un uso no sexista del lenguaje*. Paris: Unesco.

Swedish
Myndigheternas skrivregler [Public and official writing rules]
    1997   Stockholm: Departementsserien.

Welsh
Awbery, Gwenllian
    1997   *The Sex Discrimination Act and the Use of Welsh in the Workplace*. Cardiff: Equal Opportunities Commission.
Equal Opportunities Commission
    1999   *Advertising Jobs in Welsh: Guidelines / Hysbysebu swyddi yn Gymraeg: Canllawiau*. Cardiff: Equal Opportunities Commission.

22. Linguistic diversity and language standardization

Suzanne Romaine

1. Standard languages, standardization and standard language cultures

Standard languages are highly codified varieties of a language, developed and elaborated for use across a broad range of functions. Language standardization is a sociohistorically contingent process and by no means universal. Most of the world's 6,800 some languages have no officially recognized standards. Because standard languages do not arise via a "natural" course of linguistic evolution or suddenly spring into existence, but are instead created by conscious and deliberate planning, the process of standardization can never be regarded as complete. Indeed, it may span centuries. Highly elaborated standard languages like English have been centuries in the making, and standardization is a matter of degree even for languages with highly codified standards. Moreover, standards may change or be challenged at any time (Clyne 1997). The German orthographic reforms of the late 20th and early 21st century are a good example (see Section 4.3.). By analogy with Anderson's (1991) notion of "imagined communities", it is more appropriate to think of a standard language as an idea rather than a reality, as a set of abstract norms to which actual usage may adhere to various degrees. In this sense, we may speak of the ideology of standards and language standardization as a process rather than as a *fait accompli*.

Despite the fact that a standard language exists primarily as an ideal notion, the changes that accompany standardization may be highly visible, as in the case of spelling reform or the publication of prescriptive grammars and dictionaries. Joseph (1987: 13) claims that "standard languages, whatever their genetic affiliation, constitute a valid category unto themselves". This suggests that despite the fact that standardization may operate on quite distinct languages, we may expect to find commonalities of evolution across diverse socio-cultural and political settings in which it is carried out. Similarly, Milroy and Milroy's (1999) notion of "standard language cultures" points to shared practices, discourses, beliefs and attitudes that shape and surround the enterprise of standardization. Language standardization and the choice of language(s) used as media of education, government, etc. are not disinterested academic exercises. Preferences for particular languages and language varieties are always articulated within the context of an ideology that reflects society's view of itself.

2. Standardization processes

From a technical linguistic point of view, the process of standardization converts one variety into a standard by fixing and regulating its spelling, grammar, etc., in dictionaries and grammars that serve as authorities in prescriptive teaching to both native speakers and foreign learners. The notion of standard thus applies primarily to the written rather than spoken form of language (Milroy and Milroy 1999). Standardization and literacy go hand in hand because the acquisition of literacy presupposes the existence of a codified written standard, and standardization depends on the existence of a written form of language. When a language is written, linguistic matters can be subject to regulation in a way they cannot be when a language exists in spoken form only.

The introduction of a standard written form of language has far-reaching implications for how people think about language. No other variety has the resources and prestige of the written standard. Part of the authority that underpins the standard and its attendant ideology is that it engenders the notion that the written form is the "real" language as it should be and that the spoken form is corrupt and degenerate. Yet this is a false "reality" that has been consciously engineered.

The standardization process is generally prompted by various political, social, cultural and sometimes religious motivations, and promoted in various ways, typically through the written form, although spoken language norms are sometimes modeled on the written standard. Over time, the differences between the written standard and the spoken forms may become substantial. The existence and maintenance of standards is very much a function of having hegemonic institutions such as those that control printing and writing (Anderson 1991). Print languages laid the foundation for national consciousness by giving a new fixity and power to language that oral vernaculars did not possess. Most of the present-day standard languages of Europe emerged within a climate of intense political nationalism and it can be argued with some justification that standardization and standard languages are European inventions (Joseph 1987). The standardization and promotion of a common language was seen as an important symbol of the process of political unification. Standard languages were developed in part out of the need to create prominent ideological symbols of shared purpose, nationhood, etc. The models selected for codification were those current in capitals like Copenhagen, Paris and London – seats of the court, economic centers of power, and breeding places of the aristocracy. The spread of these new standard languages was made successful by the printing press, the imposition of universal schooling, and the rise of the newly literate middle classes who adopted them eagerly as a means of social advancement and mobility.

Defining, using, and controlling a standard language is the prerogative of the socially powerful (Woolard 1998). Once writing has been introduced into a speech community, the balance of power shifts. The literate become a powerful minority who try to impose their norms of language on others. Indeed, Cooper (1989: 183–184) believes that language planning in general is unlikely to succeed unless it is embraced and promoted by elites.

In understanding the concept of a standard language as a variety that has been deliberately codified so that it varies minimally in linguistic form but is maximally elaborated in function, it is helpful to draw an analogy between language standardization and standardization of coinage, weights, measures, etc. In all these cases, the aim is to remove variation and establish only one system to serve as a uniform one for a group of users. In the English-speaking world dictionaries such as the *Oxford English Dictionary* (OED) became surrogates for the language academies of other countries such as France with its *Académie Française*, which has responsibility for and control over linguistic matters. The academy defines what counts as "correct", i.e. standard French. Whether enforced by academies, dictionaries, grammars, or publishing houses, these norms are "prescriptive" rather than "descriptive" in the sense that their intention is to tell people what to do rather than describe what actually occurs.

It is not sufficient for a language to have de facto norms or grammars and dictionaries. Probably all communities evaluate certain kinds of language as "good" or "bad" (Bloomfield 1927). This is to recognize a distinction between language standards and standard languages. Jamaican Creole, for instance, has grammars and dictionaries as well as de facto norms, but there is no standard Jamaican Creole. In fact, few pidgins and creoles have been standardized, or had any official status despite being used by a majority of the population in many countries (Hall 1972). The grammars and dictionaries of Jamaican Creole were written by linguists for other linguists. They have no official recognition and play no role in teaching. Standard British English is the only variety approved for use in Jamaican schools.

3. Language standardization as language planning

Language standardization can be considered as a kind of language planning, i.e. planned efforts to change aspects of language form and use (on language planning, see Ricento, this vol.; also Skutnabb-Kangas, this vol.). Language planning decisions typically attempt to reduce linguistic diversity, as in instances where a single language is declared a national language in a multilingual country (e.g. Bahasa Indonesia in Indonesia) or where a single variety of a language is declared "standard" to promote linguistic unity in a country where divergent dialects exist, e.g. standard Dutch in the Netherlands. In many cases standards do not evolve internally from within a language community, but are imposed from outside. This often happens as a result of colonization (on language and colonialism, see Migge and Léglise, this vol.). One of the first steps of Christian missionaries who set up the first schools in linguistically diverse Papua New Guinea, was to choose and codify one variant of a local language as a mission standard. This meant creating an orthography for it and vocabulary for the expression of new Christian concepts. Lutheran missionaries chose the Wemo dialect as the standard for the Kâte language in 1892. Today the other main dialects have all but disappeared. The same is true for the "non-standard" dialects of Yabem, an Austronesian language also used as a mission lingua franca.

Other planning activities involving standardization include introducing a written norm where none existed previously, or modifying/modernizing a pre-existing form. Kemal Atatürk, for example, decreed that Turkish would be written with the Roman alphabet rather than Arabic script. As far as the lexicon is concerned, new words may need to be coined, borrowed and adapted to keep pace with technological developments and to allow the language to be used in new domains. Other activities may include "purification" of a language to eliminate foreign loan words or to replace sexist terminology, e.g. *chairman*, with gender neutral or gender equitable usage, e.g. *chairperson, chairwoman* (on sexism in language, see Hellinger and Pauwels, this vol.). The purist ideology assumes variation to be problematic and seeks to impose a monoglot standard.

Language planning has been conceptualized as a four stage process: selection, codification, elaboration, and implementation (Haugen 1966; Cooper 1989). That is, the norms to be prescribed must first be selected, either from a pre-existing set of variants, or created. They must then be codified in written form such as grammars, dictionaries, usage manuals, style guides, etc., and elaborated. Elaboration may involve expanding vocabulary, and extending the stylistic repertoire so that the language can function in a greater range of circumstances. However, norms do not become standard solely by dint of codification; their use must be promoted and diffused through media and instruction.

4. Corpus and status planning

Planning efforts directed at aspects of linguistic form such as spelling, vocabulary, grammar, etc., fall under the heading of corpus planning, while efforts to change the societal functions of a language fall under the heading of status planning. Although the terms and distinction between them as defined by Kloss (1967) seem clear in principle, in practice corpus and status planning are intertwined in complex ways. Creating orthographies, dictionaries and grammars almost always occupies a prominent place in efforts to increase the public domains of use for minority languages. Fishman (2004) has drawn attention to the fact that attempts to influence status planning will have implications for corpus planning and vice versa. In addition, he has revealed the often covert ideological component that underpins corpus planning. Successful status planning is essential to corpus planning because without gains in status, the products of corpus planning will find no domains of use in which they are advantageous or necessary for speakers of the language.

Many speakers of pidgin/creole languages, for example, have regarded the creation of a standard orthography as a pointless academic exercise because the standard form of the lexifier is so well established in educated public use. In many countries where pidgins and creoles are spoken the act of writing itself is largely a middle class occupation restricted to those who have not only a sufficient degree of education, but also time to write. Much depends on what the point is of providing a creole with a writing system in the first place; for whom and what purposes is it intended? The needs of creative writers and a public largely literate in the lexifier may be different from those of creole speakers in developing countries such as Haiti, where the population is largely monolingual in Haitian Creole. There may be a gap between linguists' perceptions and recommendations and what writers and local communities of readers prefer. Although linguists have generally been strong advocates for standardization, especially in the promotion of vernacular literacy, many pidgin and creole speakers have not seen the necessity or desirability of reading and writing in their own languages. In Hawai'i, for instance, many people still believe it is not possible to write Pidgin (Romaine 1999). Here is one of the paradoxes posed by the very notion of writing Pidgin: For many people only "real" languages are written, and so the written form of a language is assumed to be the "real" language as it should be.

One Bajan speaker explained her discomfort at seeing Bajan (Barbados) creole in print by likening it to the experience of looking at a face disfigured by an accident:

> They say there was this Christ Church woman who face got mash up in a car accident. She looking so ugly they took away al the mirrors so the woman kyaan (could not) see she face. Well, when we see this Bajan writing and thing is like we see [our] language in a broke-up mirror [...].
> (Fenigsen 1999: 78)

Her reaction can be interpreted at least partly in terms of the almost complete hegemony that standard English exerts over print in Barbados, so that readers almost never see the creole written in any serious context. Fenigsen observes, for instance, that if someone's death certificate were written in Bajan, people would think it was a joke. Bajan creole might occasionally appear in isolated phrases in political cartoons or humorous columns in newspapers. Although politicians may be heard using some Bajan in heated debates on the radio, in print they are represented as if they had spoken in the standard form.

The subordination of Bajan creole to English (and pidgins/creoles more generally in relation to their lexifiers) is similar to the diglossic relationship between Egyptian and Classical Arabic. In newspapers and other printed works individuals who do not speak or write Classical Arabic are usually represented as if they did by virtue of acts of translation performed by correctors. Most prominent people cannot be represented in print as having spoken in Egyptian Arabic even if they actually did, as for instance, was the case for President Anwar Sadat, who gave his speeches in Egyptian Arabic. Thus, Haeri (2003: 100) asks for whom the translation is intended, when everyone plays what she refers to as a "national game of representation" in which "everyone knows the secret but pretends not to".

Cassidy (1993: 136) believed that the reason why the phonemic orthography he and Le Page developed for Jamaican Creole (Cassidy and Le Page 1967) had not been used beyond academic circles was "because there is no demand among readers for a consistent system". Standard orthographies exist for Pidgin in Hawai'i, but few native speakers use them (see Section 4.1.). Even in Haiti, the IPN (Institut Pédagogique National) orthography is not consistently used by all, despite its official recognition. Mason and Allen (2001: 39–40) report that more than half the words examined in a corpus of ca. 186,000 words of news reports from the late 1990s varied in spelling, both within and across texts. Although status and corpus planning are "two sides of the language planning coin", as Fishman (2004: 80) puts it, these examples illustrate that status planning drives or pushes corpus planning. Nevertheless, there is an on-going feedback sequence so that status planning successes prompt further corpus planning and corpus planning achievements facilitate further status planning.

Hence, the stages of language planning are not strictly sequential and do not necessarily proceed in a linear fashion. Writers have been using a number of pidgin and creole languages for some time as a medium for poetry, short stories and drama. In such cases written norms have evolved spontaneously in the absence of any conscious planning efforts directed toward the codification of a standard written norm. Individual writers use a variety of idiosyncratic ad hoc systems based on the orthographies of their lexifiers (Romaine 1994, 1996). Contrast such cases with that of Tok Pisin, an English lexifier pidgin/creole currently spoken by more than half of Papua New Guinea's population of just over five million, where the creation of a standard written form proceeded in a more linear fashion from selection to implementation. As one of the few pidgins and creoles to be reduced to writing and to undergo some degree of standardization, Tok Pisin has existed for some 80 years as a written language with a codified standard.

Tok Pisin's development as a written language for use by Melanesians began in the 1920s when Catholic missionaries realized its potential as a valuable lingua franca for proselytizing among a linguistically diverse population and began using it for teaching in mission schools. For a time, rival missions such as the Lutherans and Catholics used different orthographies, but eventually competition was resolved in favor of a single phonemic standard. The orthography used in the *Nupela Testamen* ('New Testament') has come to serve as a de facto standard for Tok Pisin since its publication in 1966. It is based on Hall's (1955) spelling system, which was approved by the Director of Education and the Administrator of the Territory of Papua and New Guinea and by the Minister for the Territories in Canberra. A government publication issued by the Department of Education in 1956 recognized it officially and it was used with a few minor changes in Mihalic's (1957) grammar and dictionary.

It is significant, however, that Tok Pisin's codification and elaboration were carried out primarily for pragmatic purposes by missionaries rather than to serve the needs of indigenous political and cultural nationalism, as had generally been the case in Europe. That meant, among other things, that although Tok Pisin had the potential to become a powerful symbol of nationalism, it has not figured prominently in any nationalist rhetoric, despite its "grassroots" support. It is the most widely shared language in a highly multilingual country with well over 800 languages. After independence from Australia in 1975 the new elite simply perpetuated language policies that reflected colonial practices and attitudes. English remained the official language of education. Despite its lack of official status, Tok Pisin is still the most commonly used language in the House of Assembly.

4.1. Selection and codification

The process of selecting a new norm or modifying an old one is often accompanied by conflicts and debates about what constitutes the best usage and thus the most appropriate basis for the new standard variety, as concerns that are essentially non-linguistic are acted out on the linguistic stage. Kloss's (1967) distinction between *Abstand* and *Ausbau* is a helpful starting point in considering the issues surrounding the selection and codification process. An *Abstand* language qualifies as a language by virtue of its distance from other languages. Thus, no one would dispute, for instance, that Maori and Welsh are separate languages. They are not related and cannot reasonably be regarded as dialects of a common language or of one another. Spanish and Catalan, however, represent quite a different case because they share much in common due to their historical relationship.

Where there are competing norms that are closely related linguistically, codification typically involves what Kloss (1967) called *Ausbau* 'elaboration'. An *Ausbau* language is recognized as a language because it has been shaped or reshaped to become a standardized tool of literary expression. *Ausbau* languages are cultural constructs, and attempts to create languages out of closely related dialects emphasize or create differences between the two variants. This is also a critical factor in the creation of standards for pidgins and creoles because they are usually closely related to their so-called lexifiers, from which they take most of their vocabulary. In other cases too, however, such as in Scandinavia, codification has been primarily a matter of *Ausbau*. When Danish, Swedish and Norwegian were standardized, differences between them were consciously exaggerated. Before 1906 all three languages wrote the word meaning 'what' as *hvad*. Now only Danish does; Swedish spells it as *vad* and Norwegian as *hva*. Thus, orthographic differences now disguise what is a similar pronunciation and make the languages look more different in their written form than they are when spoken. Such differences buttress claims about the distinctiveness of the individual languages and their connections to independent nation-states. Moreover, modern Norwegian exists in two distinct standard forms. Nynorsk derives from the variety with the greatest *Abstand*. Bokmål (which itself has been described as a standard with three varieties, conservative, moderate and radical) is much closer to Danish but has now acquired sufficient grammatical, lexical and orthographical differences from Danish to be regarded as being distinctively Norwegian and not Danish.

In other cases the use of completely different writing systems serves to create visually unambiguous *Abstand*. Consider for example, the use of Devanagari for Hindi vs. Arabic script for Urdu, Roman alphabet for German vs. Hebrew alphabet for Yiddish, Russian alphabet for Serbian vs. Roman alphabet for Croatian.

Although the language planning literature has a tendency to present the issues surrounding the selection and codification of writing systems as a purely technical matter, spelling systems are not simply convenient and arbitrary conventionalized codes enabling reading and writing. Despite the fact that linguists seem generally to agree that the "ideal" orthography should aim at a one-to-one correspondence between sound and meaning, a number of social, political and cultural considerations impose competing demands that may be irreconcilable. This is because the functions of orthographies go far beyond the simple transcription of speech sounds to take on emblematic and symbolic functions in linguistically diverse communities.

Although spelling is the aspect of language most subject to standardization processes, it is one of the most contested domains because it is one of the most highly visible aspects of language. Indeed, orthography constitutes one of the "key sites in which the very notion of standard is policed" (Jaffe and Walton 2000: 562). Decisions about how to spell particular words are fraught with ideological implications (Romaine 1994, 2002, 2005; Sebba 2000). Brown's (1993: 84) discussion of writing in Louisiana Creole French, where a cultural revival has led to cultivation of local varieties of French in Louisiana, shows that "orthography is itself a presentation of oneself, one's identity". Variant orthographies for Galician, a minority language co-existing with Spanish in the Iberian peninsula, reflect different attitudes toward the degree of similarity it is felt the language should have with respect to Spanish or Portuguese (Herrero Valeiro 1993; Thomas 2002). Jaffe (1999: 217) has discussed how the goal of differentiating Corsican from Italian has made it important to use orthography to foreground phonological features of Corsican such as voiced palatal affricates that are not shared with Italian. The choice of the graphemes <chj> and <ghj> to represent them is one of the most visually distinctive aspects of the Corsican orthography, it articulates visibly *Abstand* from Italian: compare Corsican *bonghjurnu* with Italian *buongiorno* 'good day'.

Another case is discussed by McDonald (1989), who has shown how the movement to revitalize Breton in Brittany has at various times foundered on heated debates over competing orthographies. Claims premised on the supposed correctness of one orthography over another serve to sustain hegemonic ideologies about authenticity and purity. Much argument centered on the contentious letters <zh> introduced in the 1941 orthography, known as "the ZH" or "the unified orthography", because the symbol <zh> was used for words containing /z/ in some regional dialects and /h/ or /x/ in others (McDonald 1989: 131). Hence, the spellings <Breiz> and <Breih> 'Brittany' in older orthographies based on different dialects were replaced with the spelling <Breizh>. Today the unified orthography has been associated with the University of Rennes, while a newer orthography excluding the controversial <zh> was adopted by the University of Brest. The University of Rennes produces a journal called *Hor Yezh* 'our language', which McDonald reports "has been known to decorate its whole cover with triumphant zhs" (1989: 133). To scholars affiliated with the University of Rennes, the unified orthography of Brest "smelt of French", while among those at Brest, the Rennes orthography triggered accusations of collaboration with the Nazis (McDonald 1989: 211). Nevertheless, backers of both orthographies attempted to legitimate themselves as representing the "Breton people" in opposition to French domination.

Schieffelin and Doucet (1998) reveal the emblematic significance of variant symbols representing the same sound in competing Haitian Creole French orthographies. For some opponents of the official orthography, <k> and <w> are tainted with the perceived stigma of being Anglo-Saxon and smack of American imperialism. The French symbols <c> and <ou>, however, are allied with colonialism. Compare the official orthography's spelling of *klas* 'class' and *wi* 'yes' with the French spellings *classe* and *oui*. Orthography is thus a key site where, as Sebba (1998: 19) puts it, "ideology meets phonology".

The political and ideological ramifications of such choices have extended beyond Haiti to other territories where French creoles are spoken, such as Guadeloupe and Martinique, where creole was co-opted by nationalists as a symbol of political and cultural resistance in the struggle for political autonomy.

In 1976 a group of Guadeloupeans and Martinicans affiliated with l'Université des Antilles et de la Guyane formed GEREC (Groupe d'Etudes et de Recherches en Espace Créolophone), one of a number of pressure groups at work to codify orthographies and increase the status of creoles in the French Caribbean. In devising an orthography for Guadeloupe Creole patterned after the Haitian IPN (Institut Pédagogique National) adopted in 1979, GEREC endorsed the "principale de déviance maximale" ('principle of maximal distance'). This entailed selecting a written standard as far removed from French as possible, as a way of establishing the creole's separateness and linguistic independence from French, while linking it to other French creoles in the Caribbean (Schnepel 2004; Strobel-Köhl 1994). In this politically charged atmosphere the choice of <k> instead of <c> symbolized a break in continuity with the French tradition. Spelling functioned as a guarantor of the text's *créolité* ('creoleness'), a key notion linked with what has been called the creole movement (Baggioni and Marimoutou 1988: 159, 174–176).

These brief examples illustrate the extent to which the selection and codification process are a concern across a variety of linguistically diverse communities. In most, if not all, of these debates, only a small subset of written characters is singled out for attention. In a symbolic act of declaration of linguistic independence from the Netherlands in 1947, Indonesia replaced <oe> with <u>. Because the digraph <oe> is uniquely Dutch, "the most specifically Dutch of the orthographic conventions common to Dutch and the languages of former Dutch colonies" (Sebba 2000: 940), it became a focal point for nationalistic sentiment against Dutch colonialism. Purism may thus motivate orthographic as well as lexical choices (see Section 4.2.).

Controversies over the choice between graphemes such as <k> and <c> in Haitian Creole and <h> and <zh> in Breton may seem to outsiders like tempests in linguistic teapots, but such seemingly small details carry a great deal of ideological freight in the communities concerned. Like the standard itself, which is commoditized in such debates (Silverstein 1996: 290–291), individual symbols function as material objects invested with particular social values in local political economies (Irvine 1996).

Orthographic issues are a pressing concern in many minority language communities today whose languages have been dominated by another language. Many seek to revitalize their traditional languages and it is clear that literacy will play a key role in defining what is perceived to be correct and authentic. Ostler and Rudes (2000: 12) stress the need to find "the right political balance for the loyalties expressed in writing systems". In the case of the Havasupai and Hualapai tribes of Arizona, who speak almost identical varieties, tribal councils decided to adopt different writing systems as political symbols of the separateness of the two tribes (Hinton 2001: 248). Among the Lakota, where debates over the politics of orthography have been raging since the first Lakota Language Conference was held in 1971 at Pine Ridge, South Dakota, the use of different diacritics for certain phonemic distinctions serves a similar function of marking reservation or ethnic identity (Powers 1990: 496). Some Native Lakota scholars prefer to use a superscript dot to indicate aspiration instead of a superscript *c*, because they identify the latter with linguists working for the federal government. In Peru, debate has raged over whether Quichua should be written with three or five vowels. Some linguists have supported a phonemic solution with three vowels, while the Quichua Academy favored retaining the traditional five vowel system that had been in place since Spaniards first wrote the language during the colonial period.

Orthography is a particularly powerful tool in the creation of *Abstand* between a creole and its lexifier. The existence of a codified standard spelling gives a language more autonomy than it might otherwise have if it had to rely entirely on the orthography of another language. Creole writing systems based on the orthographies of their lexifiers often do creoles a disservice in suggesting that they are inferior and deficient versions of the languages to which they are lexically affiliated. Non-standard orthographies are in effect public representations of the nature and status of speakers and their relation to the standard and those who speak and write it. They dramatize the power differential between the standard and the usually socially devalued non-standard varieties. That is, one way of defining the relationship of non-standard to standard is to say that non-standard speakers are those whose speech variety does not have an orthography; it is used by those without the power to standardize and prescribe authoritative norms (Jaffe 2000: 498). Many speakers of pidgins/creoles write a language they don't speak and speak a language they don't write.

Linguists have generally stressed the desirability of phonemic over non-phonemic or etymological orthographies as a prerequisite for creating *Abstand* 'distance' and revalorizing pidgins and creoles as autonomous systems vis-à-vis their lexifiers. Cassidy (1993: 136), for example, stressed that the more the creole differs phonemically from its lexifier, the more it must differ in its orthography:

> It should be taught and learned as a system of its own. There is no learning advantage in having it reveal its etymological relationship to the European or other lexifier. Paramount should be a phonemically accurate, consistent and autonomous system [...]. Etymology is of no interest or value to creole speakers; the spelling of the word should correspond to the way it sounds. This is both more accurate and more learnable.

Traditional framing of the orthographic dimension of standardization in terms of a choice between phonemic vs. etymological spelling has ignored some of the critical ideological stances encoded in the orthographic practices employed in non-standard writing systems. In practice, each type, etymological and phonemic, exists in various forms. Etymological orthographies may display different degrees of approximation to the lexifier, and phonemic orthographies may make various concessions to etymology. Hazaël-Massieux's (1993) proposed modifications for taking into account morphological considerations in French creole orthographies represented a shift towards closer alignment with French spelling. Likewise, Winer's (1990) proposals for orthographic standardization for Trinidad and Tobago Creole English recognize a third option which she calls the modified English model. For words shared by English and creole, the orthography would use English spelling, with only salient features distinguished. For creole words, either a phonemic or an etymological spelling could be used depending on whether there is a known etymology.

Moreover, some creoles such as Papiamentu spoken as a first language by around 80% of the population of the ABC islands (Aruba, Curaçao and Bonaire) have polycentric norms. Although Dutch remains the primary language of government and education, and some speak English, Spanish, or Caribbean languages as their first language, Papiamentu is used in newspapers and television. The two spelling systems in use for Papiamentu are emblematic of different political and cultural orientations. The Aruba writing system is etymological, while Curaçao and Bonaire have a phonemic one. Curaçao and Bonaire are part of the group of islands called the Netherlands Antilles, formed in 1954. Aruba became independent in 1986 although it remains under the jurisdiction of the Netherlands. Thus, the word pronounced as /kas/ (Spanish *casa* 'house') is spelled etymologically as *cas* on Aruba but phonemically as *kas* on the other two islands. The symbol <k> is used in Aruba for words of Dutch origin such as *wak* (Dutch *waken* 'watch'). In 1987 Kolegio Erasmo, the first school to use Papiamentu as a medium of instruction, opened in Curaçao. The "Fundashon pa Planifikashon di Idioma" (FPI), Institute for Language Planning, was founded in 1998, with the aim of regulating the language situation in Curaçao.

The use of a non-phonemic orthography for a pidgin or creole is inevitably a compromise, and deliberately incomplete. Commenting on Jamaican poet Louise Bennett's spelling, Morris (1990: 2), for example, explained how writers,

> [...] anxious not to be rejected unread, most of us have chosen compromise. The most common (if inconsistent) approach is to write the vernacular for the eye accustomed to Standard English, but with various alterations signaling creole.

The dependence on English orthography, whatever its inconsistencies, has decided advantages for readers already literate in English because they know the spelling conventions. Cooper's (1995: 12) comments about Jamaican Creole English apply equally well to Pidgin in Hawai'i:

> Although there is wide variation in the representation of sounds in the individualized systems of each writer, readers can usually figure out what the symbols mean. The common English orthography base makes the idiosyncratic systems mutually intelligible.

There is a limit on how far one can go before the familiarity with the English orthographic base that makes the respellings intelligible is rendered useless and readers get confused. Writers are constrained to some extent by the options available for rendering Pidgin (or any non-standard variety) as different within the confines of the symbols provided by conventional English orthography. Ives (1971: 154) observed that some use of eye dialect seems to be inevitable even in the most carefully done literary dialect. For instance, many Pidgin speakers in Hawai'i do not pronounce postvocalic /r/ in words such as *doctor*. Creative writers usually spell this word as *docta* to indicate the absence of /r/. Although the main intention is to convey the absence of postvocalic /r/, writers also replace the standard <o> with <a>; otherwise, the phonetic image they are trying to create for their readers will be lost. Consider too a word such as *wherever*, where simply omitting postvocalic <r> would yield *wheeve*, which would suggest the pronunciation /wiv/. Achieving the right result for the reader accustomed to English orthography necessitates introducing <a>, so that many writers spell it as *weaeva*. The omission of the <h> in the first part of the word creates a certain degree of visual *Abstand* by making it look different from standard English even when it would be pronounced essentially the same.

Sebba (1998) found that writers of British Creole used spellings such as *maddah* 'mother' indicating the absence of post-vocalic /r/ (as well as the use of stops instead of fricatives), but the rendering of postvocalic /r/ as <ah> functions in effect as eye dialect because most varieties of southern British English are non-rhotic. By contrast, the varieties of American English in contact with Pidgin in Hawai'i are largely rhotic. Therefore, in Pidgin spellings such as *mudda* signal a difference in phonetic/phonological realization for two features, postvocalic /r/ and the interdental fricative. Thus, the "same" respelling may function differently depending on the phonetic/phonological relationship between the creole and its lexifier. Such non-phonemic orthographies generally choose a few salient forms as indicators of the creoleness of the text (Romaine 2005).

A phonemic orthography encoding the maximal distance from standard English can look even more alien and intimidating than one based on occasional respelling and eye dialect. Most Pidgin speakers in Hawai'i are still not used to seeing the language written. To date, only a few writers in Hawai'i have used phonemic orthographies, including Jozuf (Bradajo) Hadley (Hadley 2002) and Lee Tonouchi. Tonouchi's (2001) collection of short stories contains one story "Pijin Wawrz", written in Odo's (1975) phonemic orthography. Speaking to a newspaper reporter, Tonouchi said that he wrote the story first in his own way and then translated it into the Odo orthography. However, a reviewer described the orthography as "maddeningly hyperspelled" (Sato 2001: E2). Local writer Darrell Lum, one of the founders of Bamboo Ridge Press, Tonouchi's publisher, commented to a newspaper reporter, "yes, it's difficult to get through, but it really makes you think about the language and how it's put together" (Leidemann 2001: 2).The reactions of creole speakers to seeing their language in print are revealing of various dimensions of standardization, in particular, the nature of the relationship between the creole and lexifier. Cooper (1995: 17) has encountered mixed reactions to her own use of Jamaican Creole English written in the Cassidy/Le Page orthography. She comments on how the man who delivers the mail in her neighborhood had understood a newspaper article written in it while Morris Cargill (1989: 8A), an eminent lawyer, claimed he couldn't make head or tail of "the maze of phonetics". Cargill's remarks, however, were clearly aimed at putting Cooper in her place. He has been a consistent critic of Jamaican Creole, dismissing it as "pure laziness" that intellectuals liked to call another language.

Nevertheless, his dismissal indicates that one of Cooper's (1995: 13) aims in using the Cassidy/Le Page orthography in some of her academic discourse had its intended effect, namely to deprivilege those already literate in English. The very strangeness of the orthography restores integrity to Jamaican; it gives the language and its speakers presence. The social hierarchy is inverted when those literate in English become the slow learners they often assume Jamaican nonliterates to be. They are forced to revert to the state of child-like dependence on reading and spelling that characterizes the early learning of a writing system when the symbols on the page have to be vocalized before their meanings can be understood. It is to this social loading that Cooper (1995: 12) is reacting when she says that popular orthographies based on English are a form of "colonialism inscribed".

Where the creole-speaking population is already literate in the lexifier language and familiar with its orthographic conventions, there may be more resistance to the use of a phonemic orthography. In situations where the intention is to use creole to teach initial literacy in the creole, and perhaps make it an official language as in Haiti or Sierra Leone, an etymological spelling system may slow down the spread of literacy. In fact, Kephart (1992) found that the phonemic orthography he devised for Carriacou Creole English spoken in Grenada was easily learnable even by those already literate in English, who had no problem adjusting to the phonemic system in less than five minutes. Decker (1994) reports similar findings in Belize for a modified phonemic orthography.

When given a choice in the matter of spelling, some communities may want the writing system for their own language to conform to the norms of the national and/or official language. Decker, for instance, found that in San Andres, where an English lexifier creole co-exists with Spanish as the national language, islanders wanted the creole to reflect a Spanish orientation. In Belize, where the official language is English but the Spanish-speaking population is growing, the Belizeans did not want the creole to look like Spanish. This meant that the conventional English spelling of some words containing /i:/ such as *beet* was retained in Belize Creole, but in San Andres, where the grapheme <i> is associated with the phonetic value [i] in Spanish, the word is spelled as *biit*.

The existence of continua between many creoles and their lexifiers poses the question of which variety to choose as the basis for standardization. In Hawai'i the translators of *Da Jesus Book*, a translation of the New Testament into Pidgin, state that the variety they are aiming at is:

> [...] da heavy kine pidgin from da country. Sound mo like Leeward Oahu and da Neighba Islands den like da Honolulu kine Pidgin. Dass fo make um mo easy fo da peopo dat get problem wit da hybolic kine English o da middle kine Pidgin dat get plenny English word. (*Da Jesus Book* 2000: iii)

In local usage "heavy" can be glossed as 'basilectal' and "middle kine Pidgin" as 'mesolectal'. "Hybolic" refers to acrolectal varieties, in particular, the kind of standard English used by middle class speakers. The choice of a more basilectal rural variety over the more anglicized variety of urban Honolulu has precedent as far as other pidgins and creoles are concerned. In the French Caribbean the "principale de déviance maximale" was partly a reaction to the Gallicized variety of creole spoken by some nationalist politicians. In Papua New Guinea too the standard was based on rural Tok Pisin, which at the time was the variety most widely spoken. This contrasts with the route to standardization followed by the lexifiers, where the varieties of the elite in capital cities such as London and Paris provided the basis for codification of a standard. Devonish's (1986: 115) solution for the Anglophone Caribbean creoles is to recognize a range of intermediate forms in wide use as acceptable forms of Creole. This democratic approach attempts to avoid imposing a single variety on everyone in the society. Otherwise, the language planning process is adopting the very model of intolerance and negative attitudes towards the Caribbean creoles that it is trying to reject.

4.2. Elaboration

Vocabulary elaboration has typically played a major role in language planning. The so-called revival of Hebrew illustrates well some of the dilemmas and challenges (see also Edwards, this vol.). Although Hebrew remained in active use as a literary and religious language, it ceased being used as a spoken vernacular during the second century AD as Jews adopted Aramaic. Hence, to be used as a spoken language, Hebrew needed to be revernacularized and modernized, a process begun by Eliezer Ben-Jehuda and today carried out primarily by the Hebrew Language Academy established in 1953. Although purists attempted to use mainly internal sources of lexical elaboration, Hebrew lacked sufficient internal roots. Zuckermann (2003: 64) states that there are 8,198 attested words in Biblical Hebrew and fewer than 20,000 in Rabbinic Hebrew. Over 100,000 new words have come into Hebrew from a variety of sources, including foreign borrowings and words coined from native Hebrew/Semitic roots. The Sephardic variety was selected as the basis for Standard Hebrew. This was as much a value judgment in favor of Sephardic Hebrew as it was a rejection of the Ashkenazic variety, just as was the selection of Hebrew, a language no one spoke, over Yiddish, the language of nearly 50% of Israeli Jews and the language of origin for almost 89% of the world's Jews. Harshav (1993: 21) notes how the establishment of the state of Israel was formulated to a large extent in terms of contrasting oppositions mapped onto languages:

> Zionism as opposed to a Socialist solution in the Diaspora; Hebrew as opposed to Diaspora Yiddish; the 'Sephardi' accent as a 'pioneer' and 'masculine' language as opposed to the 'moaning' and religious Ashkenazi Hebrew; a 'Hebrew' people and 'Hebrew' work as opposed to the distorted 'Jewish' character.

The Zionist solution to the problem of Jewish identity was to create a secular nation state whose only legitimate national language was to be Hebrew. The Zionist struggle against Yiddish was harsh: For the sake of bringing about a shift to Hebrew nearly all political and ideological forces were mobilized against anything Yiddish.

Purism has been part and parcel of many instances of language planning (Thomas 1991). It always articulates a politics of inclusion and exclusion in which the state of the language is a metaphor for the state of the nation. Atatürk's purification efforts were aimed at ridding Turkish of Persian/Arabic but not French components. German nationalism in the 19th century manifested itself linguistically in a demand for purification of German from French foreign borrowings. Although borrowings had been freely adopted into Old High German and Middle High German without arousing a counter-movement, after German victory in the Franco-Prussian war the political atmosphere was ripe for the launching of one of the most successful campaigns against foreign words that was to reach all sectors of the population and to continue into the 20th century. The new German Reich was created by the same surge of nationalism that motivated the language purists, and from the beginning government officials were sympathetic to their activities. Postmaster General Heinrich von Stephan managed a nearly complete reform of the language of the post office and telecommunication services and was responsible for approximately 700 successful replacements, including *einschreiben* (to replace *rekommandieren* 'to register/record') and *Fernsprecher* (to replace *Telefon* 'telephone').

The history of English also reveals a number of periods of puristic activity directed at foreign influence. One of the most recent occurred in March 2003 when Walter Jones, the Republican congressman for North Carolina, circulated a memo demanding that cafeterias in the office buildings of the US House of Representatives replace the word *French* with *freedom* on their menus so that *French fries* and *French toast* would be called *freedom fries* and *freedom toast*.

Even if dismissed by some as a petty culinary rebuke, signs appeared informing customers of the change. Such proposals reveal ideological preoccupations. If what is out of sight is out of mind, then ousting the word *French* and replacing it with *freedom* is a rhetorical move that attempts to shift the perspective away from the French point of view on the war in Iraq in which military intervention is illegitimate in favor of American insistence that regime change by military force is justified as an act of liberation. Rallying Americans around the new words also fosters national unity, patriotism, and identity of purpose. Although it is unlikely that the new words ever made any real inroad into everyday speech, they made headlines in media around the world as symbolic of tensions between France and the US. Jones got the idea from a restaurant owner in North Carolina, who in turn modeled the new words on ones that were coined during World War I to replace the German terms *sauerkraut* and *hamburger* with *liberty cabbage* and *liberty steak*. Ironically, Jones, who intended the new words as a protest against French refusal to support the American-led war in Iraq, subsequently declared in 2005 that the US went to war with no justification.

Purism has almost inevitably been an especially potent force in efforts to elaborate new norms for minority languages undergoing revitalization. In many cases the result has been a competition between old and new varieties. Standard Breton, for instance, in its desire to be as unlike French as possible is at odds with local native speaker norms, where people borrow regularly from French. The Breton movement sanctions the use of *tredan*, a neologism from Welsh (a related Celtic language), while local Breton prefers French *electricité*. Activists use *pellgomz* for 'telephone', a term they have pasted on telephone booths in Brittany, but Breton speakers use the French borrowing. Exposure to the new purified Breton spoken by the outsiders, however, has made the locals aware that their own Breton is mixed with French. The culture and language defended in their name at Diwan, the Breton immersion schools, is quite different from the culture and language actually used by the locals. Activists who manage to speak Breton to the locals often find they are misunderstood. Similarly, Jaffe (1999) draws attention to some of the disjunctures and inconsistencies between everyday communicative practices and explicit linguistic ideologies in militant Corsican circles, where the Corsican and French language mixtures that are used all the time in everyday practice are not sanctioned.

Indeed, outside the school, it would be very difficult to learn Breton at all, even in supposedly Breton-speaking areas because locals don't speak Breton to outsiders, or even to their own children. Much the same is true in Corsica. As outsiders to the rural communities in which the Diwan schools are established, the Diwan movement enthusiasts are far removed from local realities and ways of using Breton in more than one way. The Breton-speaking world they are trying to create is very different from the one in which the remaining Breton speakers exist. Not only does it embody different social values, it is also quite different linguistically. Educated newcomers aspiring to be peasants appear almost as uncomfortable caricatures of the local life style (McDonald 1989).

Similar examples can be cited from Peru, where Quichua Unificado (unified Quichua), a newly standardized variety, has provided the basis for school instruction of Quichua as a second language. This national standard, however, contrasts with what is referred to as "authentic Quichua" spoken by many rural, less well educated and older people. Authentic Quichua contains many Spanish loanwords, unlike Quichua Unificado, which technically speaking is "purer" because language planners attempted to oust Spanish loanwords and replace them with Quichua forms or neologisms. Quichua Unificado is also written with three instead of five vowels (Hornberger and King 1998).

4.3.   Implementation

The products of language planning diffuse at different rates through the population via various mechanisms. In Germany the proposed *Reichsamt für deutsche Sprache* never got off the ground for lack of funding despite some initial enthusiasm for it. There the influence and prestige of anything French made it difficult to oust all words of French origin from popular and educated usage. Words such *interessant* 'interesting' steadfastly resisted purification. Even today there is a difference between colloquial language and officialese. For example, the use of *Fernsprecher* 'telephone' and *Postwertzeichen* 'stamp' are restricted to official usage while *Telefon* and *Briefmarke* continue in everyday speech. By contrast, in Israel the Hebrew Language Academy's decisions are binding upon all government agencies, including the Israel Broadcasting Authority. Official backing of this sort is critical in disseminating planned lexical innovations, but by no means guarantees acceptance.

Deumert and Vandenbussche (2004: 7) rightly characterize the implementation phase as the "Achilles heel" of the standardization process because acceptance by the speech community ultimately depends on decisions made during the selection and codification stages. This characterization underlines Fishman's (2004) observations about the feedback relationship between corpus and status planning. A case in point is the proposal for spelling reform produced by a group of experts from Germany, Austria and Switzerland in 1994 and adopted by the governments of the German-speaking countries. No sooner had the reform been agreed than widespread protest began to undermine its planned implementation; by 1996 a major constitutional wrangle began when a law professor brought a case before the federal constitutional court, challenging the legality of the reforms. Although the court ruled that it was within a state's right to change spelling norms for its employees (including civil servants and teachers), many still felt that the proposed reform was undemocratic.

Although the aim of the reform was to "simplify" spelling rules to facilitate teaching and learning, the proposed changes aroused strong emotions and were resisted by many journalists, authors, and teachers. Moreover, some newspapers that had initially adopted the reforms in 1998 decided a few years later to return to the old orthography, thus creating further controversy, confusion and anxiety that once uniform standards would be lost in the chaos. Munske (2005) went so far as to say that no official body is praising the reform and that everyone seems to be a loser.

Johnson (2005) estimates that only 5 % of the lexicon would be affected by the proposed German spelling reforms, but nevertheless, even minor alterations to the written form were seen by some as an affront to their rights and freedom. What was at stake was nothing less than the status of the German language as a symbol of cultural and national unity. Public criticism unanimously rejected one proposal, namely that certain long-established phrases traditionally written as one word (e.g. *sogenannt* 'so-called', *wohlbekannt* 'well-known') be separated into their component words. Perhaps surprisingly in view of the puristic tendencies in operation earlier in the century, many also opposed the Germanicization of foreign words, e.g. *Geografie* instead of *Geographie*. The old spelling system that the reformed system was intended to replace had itself evolved over a long period and was standardized only in 1901, and even then not without controversy (Johnson 2005). As noted in connection with the discussion of purification, the history of the German language reflects the struggle for the formation of a unified state. The emergence of a unified standard was retarded by the lack of a permanent capital or a single prestige variety.

A critical issue that figured prominently in the German debate and elsewhere is the question of who has the right to make decisions about language. In the absence of any official academy or agency, the privately owned Duden dictionary had been granted the right by regional governments since 1955 to codify spelling. Yet substantial questions were raised about the legality of the 1996 reforms and their authoritativeness. Similar concerns have been played out at several different levels in revitalization movements around the world. One issue concerns the perceived authenticity and authority of the reformers themselves, and the other, the authenticity of the language forms. It almost goes without saying that the two issues represent two sides of the coin of authenticity.

Authenticity is constructed by the promoters enjoying the greatest political and economic authority. In Hawai'i American missionaries claimed this prerogative when they devised the first orthography for writing Hawaiian in the 1820s. More recently, however, educated activists have promoted a modern standard Hawaiian orthography. Because neither the older nor the newer norm has the status of "official" standard, in the sense that there is no officially recognized body with the power to enforce them in the community at large, claims about correctness and authenticity ground their authority in their association with different institutions and constituencies. In the case of the older mission orthography, the relevant institution is the church, with the Hawaiian translation of the Bible assuming the role of classical standard, whereas in the case of the new orthography, authority is vested in the newly established immersion schools with their opportunities for upward social mobility via the language.

The second obvious aspect of authenticity concerns the form of the language itself at various levels from vocabulary to pronunciation to syntax. The immersion schools are creating a new speech community of second language learners who speak a variety of Hawaiian that is different from native speaker Hawaiian because its norms are controlled through schooling. Moreover, these new norms are not acquired perfectly in any case. Standards of attainment in schools are, however, measured against the newly imposed norms. In the case of Hawaiian the new standard is primarily based on the written norms for the language as it existed in 19th century texts rather than on the spoken norms of the dwindling remaining community of native speakers. A self-appointed lexicon committee was formed to coin new terms required for the use of Hawaiian in new domains, particularly in education. The committee exerts control over the language by issuing lists of new words approved for use in immersion schools. Many of the textbooks in specialized subject areas relying heavily on these new coinages would not be understood by native speakers of the language. The committee is not officially recognized by the state or any other agency, and not everyone accepts its decisions, creating yet further divisions. Wong (1999: 99) writes that this "exacerbates an already absurd situation in which success in revitalization efforts is directly proportional to the marginalization of native norms of speaking". When today's few remaining native speakers deviate from this immersion variety of Hawaiian, they are said to be either wrong or influenced by English. A number of sociolinguists have emphasized the need for compromise in the area of corpus planning. Activists should take a less vigorous stance toward loanwords and borrowing, or they run the risk of fragmenting the community whose support is required for the language to survive (Dorian 1994; Hinton 1999).

Lack of secure home and community foundations for transmitting minority languages in many communities means that these newly normed varieties may eventually replace traditional ones, but until they do their authenticity will be contested. In the case of Basque, for example, opposition to the standard Basque (Euskara Batua) proposed by the Basque language academy was very bitter, but today the spelling system is seldom questioned.

In Ireland too, the movement to revive Irish began among the educated middle classes in Dublin, a place usually perceived as alien and interfering by the remaining native speakers in the rural Irish-speaking areas along the west coast. The fact that the effort to modernize Irish came from the capital, a center of privilege, made people resent the expropriation of their language by wealthy townspeople, who were not native speakers. They were seen as well-off people who have done well out of the language. The idea that a long anglicized Dublin, itself a center of anti-Irish sentiment, should determine what is correct Irish aroused the utmost disdain (Hindley 1990).

Some Pidgin writers in Hawai'i have been ambivalent about standardization or even opposed it altogether. Tonouchi's (2001: 34) remarks highlight the paradox of the process of standardization for some Pidgin speakers:

> Linguists might argue for one standardized form of Pidgin wit one established set of grammar rules and standardized Odo orthography. Their contention is dat since Pidgin is one language den should have da same characteristics as oddah languages. But all oddah languages have been put into captivity and placed insai a nice little cage so dat people can observe 'em and study 'em mo' easy. Pidgin still exists in da wild.

It is hardly surprising that Pidgin should have become a critical site for a struggle over who has the right to regulate appropriate ways of speaking. Writers such as Tonouchi have co-opted Pidgin as a resource and made it the focus of a cultural revolution. Tonouchi writes about "being Pidgin" and "being born Pidgin". A circular he sent around to solicit entries from the public for *Da Kine Dictionary*, a Pidgin dictionary, carries his picture with the slogan "Tok Pidgin, Tink Pidgin, Be Pidgin". Tonouchi styles himself as "Da Pidgin Guerrilla", and the dictionary's promotional material shows him shouting from behind a chicken wire fence, with the statement: "[H]e's one guy dedicated to promoting da powah of pidgin as one legitimate language and as one literature" (www.dakinedictionary.com). As part of his mission to legitimize Pidgin, he established a journal in 1999 called *Hybolics* to publish Pidgin literature. *Hybolics* (a Pidgin word formation derived from *hyperbole*) is an inversion of the cultural values associated with standard English, and is in this sense "anti-standard". Tonouchi explained the significance of the term to a reporter as follows (Senaga 2002):

> [...] one intellectual kine haole [i.e. white person, SR]. To talk in Standard English, yeah? To use big impressive words, yeah? Da use of exaggerated forms of speech. So, what we wanted to do wit da magazine Hybolics was to reclaim our words again, and it's like dey no have to use standard English to have da kine intellectual kine ideas.

Tonouchi rejects the ideological premises of standardization because he sees Pidgin as symbolic of freedom from social control and judgment. He explicitly disavowed the notion of standards of correctness for Pidgin in this reaction to a panelist at a conference on Pidgin (Tonouchi 2002: 30):

> I wen go ass one of da panelist members 'Get such ting as right and wrong kine Pidgin?' and she wuz all like 'Yeah!' I wuz tinking all 'Wow brah, who wen die and make you da Pidgin Queen?'

Although Tonouchi's fear of prescription appears to rest partly on conflation of the notions of grammaticality and acceptability or correctness, the power of self-appointed authorities to impose their own standards of correctness on others poses a threat to his notion of Pidgin as an egalitarian language available to all. For Tonouchi, standard English excludes, but Pidgin includes. Unlike standard English, Pidgin is not elitist or hierarchical. Tonouchi stresses the inclusiveness of Pidgin in accommodating variants at all levels, including spelling. In speaking about his plan for a Pidgin dictionary, he told a reporter (Senaga 2002):

> Going to be very difficult cause people ask me, 'Aw Lee, what about spelling brah?' To me, however dey spell it, might have two, chree, four ways of spelling em. 'Bumbye' – bumbye, bombye ... Just go put em all in dea. Just go put 'see, see, see.' All da different spellings is fine wit me. Da important ting to stress is dat dis is a *community* Pidgin dictionary project. Dat's why I collecting words cause Pidgin belongs to everybody, so I like get as much people in da dictionary as can [...].

Tonouchi's inclusion of variant spellings runs counter to standardization's conventional aims of eliminating variant forms and prescribing correct usage. The process of standardization usually hierarchizes by selecting one variety for codification and elaboration, transforming it into what is in effect a social class dialect. Samuel Johnson's (1755) dictionary, for instance, sought to "fix" the English language once and for all by codifying the usage of those whom he considered the "best" authors. Thus, he intended to purify, correct, and prevent the language from changing. To Johnson change was tantamount to degeneration, whereas to Tonouchi it is the very lifeblood of the language. The essence of Pidgin lies in its variability in time and place, its ability to absorb and incorporate elements from other languages. The worry expressed by creative artists using Pidgin such as Tonouchi is that standardization will put the language in a straight jacket and prevent it from growing. While eschewing the codification dimension of the standardization process, Tonouchi nevertheless embraces another of its tenets, namely, maximizing function. He wrote his master's thesis and job applications in Pidgin, and urges everyone to do everything in Pidgin. Through conscious extension or normalization of Pidgin as an accepted language in all domains of usage, Tonouchi seeks to counter the public perception of Pidgin as limiting its speakers' possibilities for socio-economic advancement.

The distrust of standardization expressed by Tonouchi and others is understandable in terms of the history of contact between Pidgin and standard English and continuing negative attitudes toward Pidgin in the educational sector. A climate of intolerance and negative attitudes to the use of Pidgin in the classroom continue today and Pidgin is regularly blamed for students' relatively poor performance on standardized tests of verbal ability by comparison with students in other states. Many Pidgin speakers are fully aware of how the language practices of the dominant group have made them accountable to the norms of standard English and to other standards set on the US mainland. Tonouchi wants to create a Pidgin Immersion Program for schools and to petition the University of Hawai'i to accept Pidgin as a major. Some, however, refused to sign his petition for fear that institutionalizing Pidgin in this way would "screw 'em up" (Tonouchi 2002: 34). This made him pause for thought:

> So now I dunno wea I stand. Stuck brah. Cannot trust da institution and I tinking too how we going teach courses about Pidgin, in Pidgin, wen dea's no Proper Pidgin and den, if we do create one standard Pidgin den doesn't dat violate da very nature of da language?

Nevertheless, there seems to be some misunderstanding among some writers and the general population that a standard would limit or eliminate variation in the spoken word. The ideology of standard language culture may blind them to the fact that the standard is not always a well-defined notion and there is room for a great deal of variability. There is nothing very unusual about having a single language with more than one standard. A number of languages have polycentric or pluricentric norms, including Spanish, Portuguese, Dutch, and English, where there are regional norms for national varieties, even in what is perhaps the most highly codified domain of the standard, i.e., spelling. Norway's two standards tolerate a great deal more variability in spelling than is usually the case in standard languages. Even Dr. Johnson, who is often given credit for fixing English spelling in its modern form, used two "standards" of spelling, one in his dictionary and another in his private writings. Once standardized, an author can always depart from the established conventions to achieve a special effect. Although a standard orthography may exert influence on speech, it does not oblige speakers to change their phonology.

Attractive as it may be for Tonouchi to imagine pidgins as languages in the wild and standard languages as caged, this is in many respects a false dichotomy, forced onto a rather complex continuum of oral and literate varieties. Moreover, the pervasiveness of English both locally and globally as the main exemplar of "a language" obscures the fact that "all oddah languages" have not been put into captivity, i.e., standardized, as Tonouchi suggests. Most languages of the world still have no standard written form.

The creole movement has played out rather differently across the territories where French-based creoles are spoken, so that a variety of orthographies are in use today, as is also true for Anglophone creoles. Winer (1990: 243) suggests that the relatively greater success of orthographic standardization in French creole-speaking countries may be attributable to the greater perception and reality of French creole as quite distinct from French as well as to the lesser degree of heterogeneity across French creole space compared to English creoles. It is nevertheless certainly striking that the most widely used orthographies in French creoles tend to be substantially phonemic, while the opposite appears true for English creoles. The only phonemic orthographies in widespread use for English lexifier creoles are in the Pacific (e.g., Tok Pisin) and Africa (e.g., Sierra Leone). Devonish (1986: 87) observed that in the Commonwealth Caribbean the "language question never became an important issue in the anti-colonial struggles".

Nevertheless, creole did become the focus of a post-independence literary and cultural movement in Jamaica, when Edward Kamau Brathwaite (1984) argued for the use of what he called "nation language" (Jamaican Creole) in poetry as a way of capturing the sounds and rhythm of oral traditions of performance. However, Brathwaite's aim was to break continuity with the British literary tradition, not its orthographic conventions. Rejecting the term "dialect" because it suggested inferiority, he argued for the recognition of creole as a language, but did not seek to validate it in terms of a distinctive orthography. The situation of Pidgin in Hawai'i is similar in some respects. Although there are a number of groups seeking various forms of political autonomy from the United States, the so-called sovereignty movement has not politicized Pidgin. In so far as language has entered into the discussion, the focus has usually been on Hawaiian, the indigenous language of the islands. The promotion of Pidgin has been situated primarily within a literary and cultural movement, whose focus is to assert local distinctiveness in the face of continuing cultural domination by the mainland United States.

5.   Conclusion

These examples show how forms of language activism and language planning that reproduce the dominant language ideology also reproduce structures of domination. Hence, they engender a new standard language culture, and in this way the authoritative becomes authoritarian. Purism is an inevitable component of such ideology because it is premised on the assumption that there can only be one authentic language associated with one authentic people. The emphasis given to form corresponds directly to the perceived identity marking function of the language. The linguistic standards codified and elaborated in the written form distinguish good from bad usage and thus establish a social hierarchy which confers authority and prestige on those who write and speak properly. Another problem in the adoption of a unitary model of language, culture and identity is that minority activists ignore the complexity of minority identity. Linguistic and cultural contact inevitably produces new, hybrid forms and mixed ways of thinking, speaking, and doing that are not accommodated within the ideology of a monoglot standard.

References

Anderson, Benedict
1991   *Imagined Communities. Reflections on the Origin and Spread of Nationalism.* London: Verso.
Baggioni, Daniel and Jean-Claude Carpanin Marimoutou (eds.)
1988   *Cuisines/Identités.* Saint Denis de la Réunion: Publication de L'Université de la Réunion.
Bloomfield, Leonard
1927   Literate and illiterate speech. *American Speech* 2: 432–439.
Brathwaite, Edward K.
1984   *The History of the Voice: The Development of Nation Language in Anglophone Caribbean Poetry.* London: New Beacon Books.
Brown, Becky
1993   The social consequences of writing Louisiana Creole French. *Language in Society* 22: 67–101.
Cargill, Morris
1989   Corruption of language is no cultural heritage. *Sunday Gleaner*, October 29: 8A.
Cassidy, Frederic G.
1993   Short note on creole orthography. *Journal of Pidgin and Creole Languages* 8: 135–137.
Cassidy, Frederic G. and Robert B. Le Page
1967   *Dictionary of Jamaican English.* Cambridge: Cambridge University Press.
Clyne, Michael (ed.)
1997   *The Undoing and Redoing of Corpus Planning.* Berlin: Mouton de Gruyter.
Cooper, Carolyn
1995   *Noises in the Blood. Orality, Gender, and the "Vulgar" Body of Jamaican Culture.* Durham: Duke University Press.
Cooper, Robert L.
1989   *Language Planning and Social Change.* Cambridge: Cambridge University Press.
Da Jesus book. Hawaii Pidgin New Testament
2000   Orlando: American Bible Society for Wycliffe Bible Translators.
Decker, Ken
1994   Orthography development for Belize Creole. In: Frances Ingemann (ed.), *1994 Mid-America Linguistics Conference Papers.* Vol. II, 351–362. Lawrence: University of Kansas.
Deumert, Ana and Vim Vandenbussche
2004   Standard languages. Taxonomies and histories. In: Ana Deumert and Vim Vandenbussche (eds.), *Germanic Standardizations – Past to Present*, 1–14. Amsterdam: John Benjamins.
Devonish, Hubert
1986   *Language and Liberation: Creole Language Politics in the Caribbean.* London: Karia Press.

Dorian, Nancy
   1994   Purism vs. compromise in language revitalization and language revival. *Language in Society* 23: 479–494.
Fenigsen, Janina
   1999   'A broke-up mirror': Representing Bajan in print. *Cultural Anthropology* 14: 61–87.
Fishman, Joshua A.
   2004   Ethnicity and supra-ethnicity in corpus planning: The hidden status agenda in corpus planning. *Nations and Nationalism* 10: 79–94.
Hadley, Jozuf
   2002   *Avebade Bade. Hawai'i's Pidgin Poetry by Bradajo.* Honolulu: Mutual Publishing.
Haeri, Niloofar
   2003   *Sacred Language, Ordinary People. Dilemmas of Culture and Politics in Egypt.* New York/Houndsmill: Palgrave Macmillan.
Hall, Robert A., Jr.
   1955   *A Standard Orthography and List of Suggested Spellings for Neomelanesian.* Port Moresby: Department of Education.
Hall, Robert A., Jr
   1972   Pidgins and creoles as standard languages. In: John B. Pride and Janet Holmes (eds.), *Sociolinguistics*, 142–155. Harmondsworth: Penguin.
Harshav, Benjamin
   1993   *Language in the Time of Revolution.* Berkeley: University of California Press.
Haugen, Einar
   1966   *Language Conflict and Language Planning. The Case of Modern Norwegian.* Cambridge, MA: Harvard University Press.
Hazaël-Massieux, Marie-Christine
   1993   *Ecrire en créole. Oralité et écriture aux Antilles.* Paris: Editions L'Harmattan.
Herrero Valeiro, Mário
   1993   Guerre des graphies et conflit glottopolitique: Lignes de discours dans la sociolinguistique galicienne. *Plurilinguismes* 6: 181–209.
Hindley, Reg
   1990   *The Death of Irish. A Qualified Obituary.* London: Routledge.
Hinton, Leanne
   1999   The issue of 'authenticity' in California language restoration. *Anthropology & Education Quarterly* 30: 56–67.
Hinton, Leanne
   2001   New writing systems. In: Leanne Hinton and Ken Hale (eds.), *The Green Book of Language Revitalization in Practice*, 239–250. San Diego: Academic Press.
Hornberger, Nancy H. and Kendall A. King,
   1998   Authenticity and unification in Quechua language planning. *Language, Culture and Curriculum* 11: 390–410.
Irvine, Judith T.
   1996   When talk isn't cheap: Language and political economy. In: Donald Brenneis and Ronald K. S. Macaulay (eds.), *The Matrix of Language: Contemporary Linguistic Anthropology*, 258–284. Boulder: Westview Press.

Ives, Sumner
    1971   A theory of literary dialect. In: Juanita Williamson and Virginia M. Burke (eds.), *A Various Language: Perspectives on American Dialects,* 145–177. New York: Holt, Rinehart & Winston.

Jaffe, Alexandra
    1999   *Ideologies in Action. Language Politics on Corsica.* Berlin/New York: Mouton de Gruyter.

Jaffe, Alexandra
    2000   Introduction: Non-standard orthography and non-standard speech. *Journal of Sociolinguistics* 4: 497–513.

Jaffe, Alexandra and Shana Walton
    2000   The voices people read: Orthography and the representation of non-standard speech. *Journal of Sociolinguistics* 4: 561–587.

Johnson, Sally A.
    2005   *Spelling Trouble? Language, Ideology and the Reform of German Orthography.* Clevedon: Multilingual Matters.

Johnson, Samuel
    1755   *A Dictionary of the English Language.* 2 volumes. London.

Joseph, John E.
    1987   *Eloquence and Power. The Rise of Language Standards and Standard Languages.* London: Frances Pinter.

Kephart, Ronald
    1992   Reading creole English does not destroy your brain cells. In: Jeff Siegel (ed.), *Pidgins, Creoles and Nonstandard Dialects in Education,* 67–86. Canberra: Australian National University.

Kloss, Heinz
    1967   'Abstand languages' and 'Ausbau languages'. *Anthropological Linguistics* 9: 29–41.

Leidemann, Mike
    2001   Da powah of pidgin. *Honolulu Advertiser,* April 14, E1–2.

McDonald, Maryon
    1989   *"We Are Not French!" Language, Culture and Identity in Brittany.* London: Routledge.

Mason, Marilyn and Jeff Allen
    2001   Standardized spelling as a localization issue: Information technology forces less-prevalent languages to develop uniform lexical rules. *MultiLingual Computing & Technology* 12: 37–40.

Mihalic, Frank
    1957   *Grammar and Dictionary of Neo-Melanesian Pidgin.* Westmead, NSW: The Mission Press.

Milroy, James and Lesley Milroy
    1999   *Authority in Language: Investigating Standard English.* 3rd ed. London: Routledge.

Morris, Mervyn
    1990   Printing the performance. *Jamaica Journal* 23: 22.

Munske, Horst H.
    2005   German spelling reform in 2005. <http://www.goethe.de/kug/prj/dds/en 137878.htm>, retrieved May 23, 2005.

Nupela Testamen bilong Bikpela Jisas Krais na Buk bilong Ol Sam
1966   Port Moresby: The Bible Society of Papua New Guinea.
Odo, Carol
1975   Phonological processes in the English dialect of Hawaii. Ph.D. dissertation, Department of Linguistics, University of Hawai'i at Mānoa.
Ostler, Nicholas and Blair Rudes (eds.)
2000   *Endangered Languages and Literacy: Proceedings of the Fourth FEL Conference.* Bath: Foundation for Endangered Languages.
Powers, William K.
1990   Comment on the politics of orthography. *American Anthropologist* 92: 496–498.
Romaine, Suzanne
1994   Hawai'i Creole English as a literary language. *Language in Society* 23: 527–554.
Romaine, Suzanne
1996   Pidgins and creoles as literary languages: *Ausbau* and *Abstand*. In: Marlis Hellinger and Ulrich Ammon (eds.), *Contrastive Sociolinguistics*, 271–289. Berlin: Mouton de Gruyter.
Romaine, Suzanne
1999   Changing attitudes towards Hawai'i Creole English: Fo' get one good job, you gotta know ho fo' talk like one haole. In: John R. Rickford and Suzanne Romaine (eds.), *Creole Genesis, Attitudes and Discourse. Studies Celebrating Charlene J. Sato*, 287–301. Amsterdam: John Benjamins.
Romaine, Suzanne
2002   Signs of identity, signs of discord: Glottal goofs and the green grocer's glottal in debates on Hawaiian orthography. *Journal of Linguistic Anthropology* 12: 189–225.
Romaine, Suzanne
2005   Orthographic practices in the standardization of pidgins and creoles: Pidgin in Hawai'i as anti-language and anti-standard. *Journal of Pidgin and Creole Languages* 20: 101–140.
Sato, Ann M.
2001   Review of Lee Tonouchi. *Da word. Honolulu Advertiser*, April 14, E2.
Schieffelin, Bambi R. and Rachelle C. Doucet
1998   The 'real' Haitian creole. Ideology, metalinguistics, and orthographic choice. In: Bambi R. Schieffelin, Kathryn A. Woolard and Paul V. Kroskrity (eds.), *Language Ideologies: Practice and Theory*, 285–316. Oxford: Oxford University Press.
Schnepel, Ellen M.
2004   *In Search of a National Identity: Creole and Politics in Guadeloupe.* Hamburg: Helmut Buske Verlag.
Sebba, Mark
1998   Phonology meets ideology: The meaning of orthographic practices in British Creole. *Language Problems and Language Planning* 22: 19–47.
Sebba, Mark
2000   Orthography and ideology: Issues in Sranan spelling. *Linguistics* 38: 925–949.

Senaga, Ryan
    2002   Da Pidgin Guerrilla. Does the fate of Hawaiian Creole English lie in the hands of Lee Tonouchi? *Honolulu Weekly,* November 13, 2002.
Silverstein, Michael
    1996   Monoglot "Standard" in America: Standardization and metaphors of linguistic hegemony. In: Donald Brenneis and Ronald K. S. Macaulay (eds.), *The Matrix of Language: Contemporary Linguistic Anthropology*, 284–306. Boulder: Westview Press.
Strobel-Köhl, Michaela
    1994   *Die Diskussion um die "ideale" Orthographie: Das Beispiel der Kreolsprachen auf französischer Basis in der Karibik und des Französischen im 16. und 20. Jahrhundert.* Tübingen: Gunter Narr.
Thomas, George
    1991   *Linguistic Purism.* London: Longman.
Thomas, Ned
    2002   New norms for written Galician? The debate rages on. *Contact Bulletin of the European Bureau for Lesser Used Languages* 18: 9.
Tonouchi, Lee
    2001   *Da Word.* Honolulu: Bamboo Ridge Press.
Tonouchi, Lee
    2002   *Living Pidgin. Contemplations on Pidgin Culture.* Kāne'ohe: Tinfish Press.
Winer, Lise
    1990   Orthographic standardization for Trinidad and Tobago: Linguistic and sociopolitical considerations in an English Creole community. *Language Problems and Language Planning* 14: 237–268.
Wong, Laiana
    1999   Authenticity and the revitalization of Hawaiian. *Anthropology and Education Quarterly* 30: 94–115.
Woolard, Kathryn A.
    1998   Introduction. In: Bambi R. Schieffelin, Kathryn A. Woolard and Paul V. Kroskrity (eds.), *Language Ideologies: Practice and Theory*, 1–47. Oxford: Oxford University Press.
Zuckermann, Ghil'ad
    2003   *Language Contact and Lexical Enrichment in Israeli Hebrew.* London: Palgrave Macmillan.

23. Borrowing as language conflict

Manfred Görlach

1. Introduction

Borrowing has traditionally been one of the best researched disciplines in philology and historical linguistics from very early times onward. This focus can be seen to continue into the work of Weinreich (1953) and Haugen (1973), when it came to be seriously challenged by linguists more interested in homogeneous systems than in the messy data of linguistic reality. However, another turn of focus, into social and pragmatic aspects, and the rise of pidgin and creole studies as well as of research into individual and societal multilingualism has brought the discipline back into the centre of scholarly interest – compare the comprehensive collection of articles edited by Goebl et al. (1996/1997), which surprisingly neglects the processes and results of borrowing. Even the claim that there are mixed languages (which had long been denied by linguists of various schools and persuasions) has recently been convincingly validated (see Thomason and Kaufman 1988). The historical controversy is neatly summarised in their introductory reference to the a statement by Max Müller of 1871 ("mixed languages do not exist") and Hugo Schuchardt's (1884) belief in the universality of language mixture (Thomason and Kaufman 1988: 1–2).

2. Processes and types of borrowing

2.1. General considerations

Language contact happens in the minds of more or less multilingual speakers. In order to determine or explain the extent and permanence of its effects, a number of factors will have to be taken into account (cf. Görlach 1997: 137–138, based on Weinreich 1953: 3):
- size and concentration of speech communities, ratio of bilinguals, length and intensity of contacts, density of communication between speaker groups and conditions for communication (traffic, media, and so on);
- degree of competence in the two languages among bilinguals, functional range of the two languages in the society (for example: diglossia), types of language acquisition;
- status and prestige of the languages and of the cultures they represent, attitudes towards an evaluation of bi-/multilingualism and interferences.

A thorough categorisation of types of contact explaining different consequences for borrowing was more recently provided by Thomason and Kaufman (1988: 77–109). A crucial distinction has to be made between various types of impact which look similar, but whose distinction is of vital importance for an adequate description, e.g.:

(1) Can a donor and a receptor language (and thereby the direction of the influence) be determined, or has the contact resulted in a merger of two systems?

(2) Is the result of the contact an individual, ephemeral, ad-hoc phenomenon restricted to the parole – and if so, does it represent the alternation between two languages (code-switching) or an instance of an occasional, unreflected and often incorrect interference (code-mixing) on the one hand, or a stable, more widespread borrowing process involving the linguistic system of at least a group of speakers, likely to be (or documented as being) permanent?

Texts in which different languages co-occur therefore permit more than one interpretation: They do not necessarily point to either code-switching and to the existence of a mixed language – or to borrowing.

For any sound discussion, then, including quantifications as well as speakers' attitudes, a workable distinction between code-switching and borrowing is obviously necessary. Organising the *Dictionary of European Anglicisms* (*DEA*; see Görlach 2001), individual contributors and myself as the general editor, were continuously confronted with the problem – which can, with many doubtful cases, be solved in principle. Identifying cases of code-switching, we can be guided by the fact that items are less well known, less accepted and, if in print, often indicated by italics or inverted commas, or flagging, in languages using the Roman alphabet – and by the change of the spelling system in others. In speech, a pause is often noticed before the articulation changes into the foreign pronunciation, and returns after the embedded foreign element. A distinction between "aliens" (foreign words, *Fremdwörter*) and "loanwords" (integrated *Lehnwörter*) is also made in many dictionaries, where different typefaces are used in respective lemmas. The practice is well known from the *Oxford English Dictionary* (*OED*), but is open to some doubt, where decisions are not explicitly discussed, but based on the lexicographer's personal judgement. Cases like the ones described by Eppler (1994: 75–93), who investigated usage among German-speaking immigrants in Britain, cannot be subsumed under borrowing – whether we should name their mixed speech as "code-switching" or as "code-mixing" is obviously a matter of definition.

Can a discussion of why words are borrowed help us to make the distinction more precise and reliable? It remains largely uncertain why individual words were taken over in historical periods – see the most detailed thoughtful categorisation of Early Middle English conditions by Käsmann (1961), summarised in Görlach (1997: 149–150). However, many doubts remain even in the analysis of present-day data; a few factors (necessarily somewhat self-evi-

dent and vague) can be enumerated to support a classification of types of borrowing:
- gaps in the vocabulary of the receptor language
- insufficiencies in the vernacular lexis, such as polysemy, homophony, obsolescent word-formation, problematic associations/taboos/pejoration
- borrowing necessitated by rhetorical/literary causes (including rhyme and metre), or supported by fashion and prestige.

However, inadequate information on the writer's intentions and the intended audience can make us misinterpret foreign elements in historical texts, which are not likely to be loanwords, i.e. permanent additions to the receptor language system.

2.2.   Mergers and mixed languages

All languages are to a certain degree mixed, i.e. they exhibit traces of some forms of earlier contact, but it is normal for them to remain classifiable genetically – thus, the high proportion of Romance elements in the English lexis does not make English a Romance language. However, often as a consequence of incomplete language acquisition and the shift of entire speech communities, there are also cases of mixing, in which levels such as phonology, lexis and syntax largely derive from different parent languages, which makes their genetic classification impossible (see Thomason and Kaufman 1988). Pidgins are obvious cases. In such mergers it is apparently not possible to speak of borrowing processes. This also holds for koineization, whether this involves similar dialects or different languages. For instance, Yorkshire dialect words were not borrowed into Australian English, but may have survived in the colonial variety. Compare the Scandinavian/Anglian interlanguage that must have existed in the 10th century Danelaw area, where Norse elements were not strictly borrowed into Old English dialects, nor vice versa. Similar objections are valid against the claim of borrowing in the case of substratum influence, as in the Celtic survivals in French or – less conspicuously – in English. Finally, borrowing is an inappropriate term for parasitical languages like Anglo-Romani, a variety which presupposes a full English system into which, by way of relexification, a few hundred Romani words are incorporated, largely to produce a secret language (compare varieties like rhyming slang). It follows that we can speak of borrowing only in those cases which have traditionally been called adstratum and superstratum influences, i.e. the impact of a language of similar or higher prestige and functional range, where the direction of borrowing can be determined. The notion of "language" can be extended to include dialects and earlier stages of the same language, so that Scots *raid* and *thane* are classified as internal loanwords in English. Also, creoles borrow lexical elements and syntactical patterns from their lexifier language in the process of decreolisation.

Whether borrowing can be neatly distinguished from results of mergers obviously depends on sufficient sociohistorical information about speech communities; it is impossible for early stages of languages lacking such documentation.

2.3. Borrowing and calquing

Straightforward borrowing is often avoided by calquing (see Section 5.5.3.), i.e. by finding or creating native equivalents for the potential loanword or construction. In the field of lexis, we can distinguish between loan translation, rendition and creation (in descending order of exactness in reproducing complex replicas) and semantic calques, alternatives which are available for simple and complex words and entire phrases. Calquing can be prompted by explicit efforts of purists (see Section 6), but can also be the preferred choice in inherently pure languages, such as Old English, whose lexis was 97% Germanic, despite the enormous amount of cultural innovation – and this happened without any institutional support. Semi-calques (loan blends), in which one element remains foreign, can be seen as compromise forms.

2.4. Levels of language affected

Although there are constraints imposed by the structure of the receptor language, contact can result in principle in borrowing items on all linguistic levels, namely:
- Articulation: E.g., the pronunciation of /r/ in some Continental languages is said to have been modelled on French.
- Phonology: Phonotactic patterns, allophones and new phonemes can be taken over, if the donor language is widely available as a spoken, prestigious medium (as happened in English from 1100–1500). Note that close imitation of foreign pronunciation can be considered correct and prestigious, but can also be regarded as affected, whatever the sociolinguistic conditions may be.
- The writing system: Graphemes can be imported and diacritics can be retained in loanwords (e.g., French accents, German *umlaut*), but may well be given up in later stages of integration). Since English has no additional graphemes, the foreignness of some anglicisms rests on particular combinations (such as *wh-*) or the use of rare letters (*k, y*) as in *whiskey*.
- Inflectional morphology: Plural *-s* is taken over from English into languages as different as Welsh and some English-related pidgins and creoles; Latin plural forms (and sometimes case endings) and English plurals are retained in many loanwords in European languages.
- Word-formation: Elements are combined in hybrid words, as in English using Romance prefixes and suffixes (e.g., in *rewrite, shortage, withdrawal,*

oddity) or entire patterns (*pickpocket* modelled on French imperative compounds).
- Syntax: Numerous imitations of Latin patterns are found in European vernaculars (in tense, mood, participial and infinitival constructions, and in word order), but also extending to the structure of entire texts (cf. Görlach 1991: 100–101, 121–131).
- Lexis: The most conspicuous, but by no means always predominant, type of influence. Note that similar to the imitation of foreign syntactical patterns, calquing is often used, and this method is most frequent in phraseology.
- Style: With language shift and the *ausbau* of standard languages, stylistic elements tend to be borrowed from "high" languages, formerly dominant in certain registers, domains and text types – consider legal diction and style based on Law French, and scholarly prose and various literary categories imitated from Latin, in Renaissance England (the Latin model affecting also various other European traditions).
- Pragmatics: In bilingual societies, appropriateness of linguistic behaviour will be modelled on conventions of the more respectable language; consider the use of plural pronouns in addressing individuals, taken over into English and other languages from French in the 14th to 16th centuries.

2.5. Diglossia and the distribution of text-types

A functional division of two or more languages that allocates them to specific domains and registers ("diglossia" according to Ferguson 1959) can be expected to restrict borrowing, even where the number of bilinguals and their linguistic competence is high. These tend to keep the individual languages apart and resort to code-switching in the case of new topics rather than import foreign technical terms. The early history of English before 1250 is a convincing example – borrowing was restricted, and it was the effect of the shift of native French speakers to English and the breakdown of diglossia (French no longer being expected for formal and courtly uses including law) and Latin ceasing to be required for documents and scholarly prose that loanwords from French and Latin began to supply lexis for the underequipped English vernacular, esp. from 1400 to 1600. A graph which could be replicated for the history of many languages illustrates the functional distribution of Latin, French and English (dialect and standard) through the centuries:

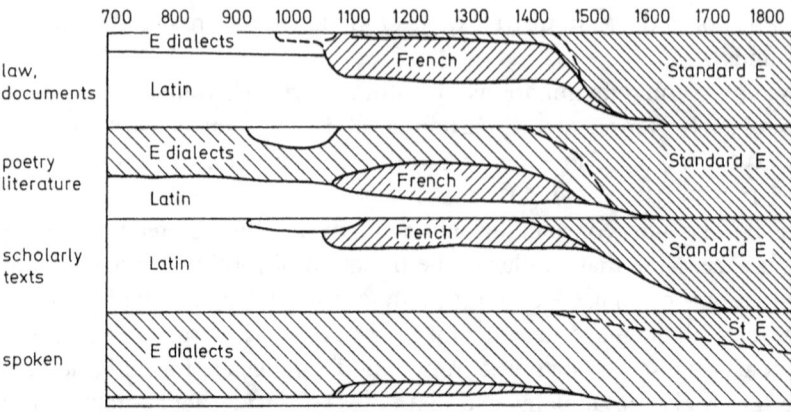

Figure 1. The changing functions of Latin, French and English in different domains in the history of English (from Görlach 2002c: 27)

Modern borrowing also follows (largely) text-type specific rules: Even where the knowledge of English is not widespread, lexical items from popular culture (in songs, dance, films) and technical disciplines are expected to form clusters of non-native vocabulary. Traditional concentrations of French influence in European languages are found in fashion and cuisine, of Italian in banking, architecture and music, of German in mining, education, music and philosophy, of Russian in (Communist) politics and social organisation, of Latin in religion and higher education in Western cultures, where in other regions languages like Greek, Arabic, Persian or Chinese fill(ed) similar slots.

2.6.   Factors determining the frequency of loanwords

Specific needs and speakers' attitudes thus determine the number of items borrowed from individual languages and their token frequencies in texts. However, statistical analyses are controversial (for English, see Finkenstaedt and Wolff 1973, summarised in Scheler 1977) and comparative descriptions are largely lacking. Intuitively, it can be stated that some languages have a much greater share of foreign lexis (Albanian, English) than others (Icelandic). Recent investigations of frequencies of anglicisms in 16 European languages, figures relating to the total entries, words beginning with M- and N-, and to "central" (grid) words in the *Dictionary of European Anglicisms* have shown a clear ranking (see Görlach 2001, 2003):

Table 1. Statistical comparisons of anglicisms in 16 European languages (from Görlach 2003: 164)

	total	M-/N-	grid		total	M-/N-	grid
Norwegian	75.5 /	50.6 /	76.1 %	Croatian	43.6 /	34.8 /	62.1 %
German	71.7 /	55.7 /	86.9 %	Hungarian	43.4 /	41.5 /	63.8 %
Dutch	68.3 /	58.1 /	83.4 %	Bulgarian	40.6 /	36.8 /	56.4 %
French	64.8 /	36.0 /	66.1 %	Spanish	40.5 /	34.8 /	60.7 %
Italian	63.1 /	49.4 /	69.9 %	Icelandic	39.5 /	32.0 /	51.7 %
Polish	46.9 /	43.5 /	61.4 %	Greek	39.0 /	34.0 /	51.7 %
Russian	45.7 /	32.4 /	53.1 %	Finnish	29.3 /	25.7 /	31.1 %
Romanian	43.7 /	33.6 /	58.0 %	Albanian	15.5 /	14.6 /	17.1 %
				average	45.8 /	38.3 /	55.1 %

The most likely interpretation of the differences in this specific case of lexical impact is that three factors have prompted a higher intake of English words: closeness to English, esp. in the phonological structure of the receptor language, openness of the speech community to Western culture after 1945, and absence of a powerful purist tradition. All these are found in the three Germanic languages that lead the field – but not in Icelandic which trails far behind, as a consequence of purist attitudes. However, it has to be admitted that it is not possible to state with any degree of confidence what the proportionate weight of the three factors is.

2.7. Adoption and integration

Words, when first borrowed, are isolated in form and content; in Leisi and Mair's (1999: 51–59) terms, they are dissociated. This fact does not stop them from being adopted, nor is it certain whether the earlier borrowing of formally related terms (*to judge* after *the judge*, *judgement*; *just* and *justice* from medieval French) facilitates their adoption, or whether the existence of native homophones complicates and thereby delays the process.

How far borrowed items will remain foreign, or will survive the period following the contact, largely depends on their sociolinguistic status. Most medieval loanwords from Latin and French taken over into Western vernaculars were adapted (sometimes beyond recognition), or were lost as special terms with the disappearance of the objects or concepts they designated, or the fashions they expressed. By contrast, items borrowed after 1500 frequently retained some foreignness in spelling, pronunciation, morphology and phraseology, if they were considered part of an educated vocabulary reflecting a higher social status of the speakers (or their genteel aspirations). Such layers can become stylistic choices within a language. For example, partial synonyms from French and Latin have become a language-internal language bar, contrasting with native items (esp. in English). This consequence is particularly obvious in the case of suppletion of Romance adjectives to English nouns ("dissociation" according to Leisi and Mair 1999); compare *king* vs. *royal* (*kingly* is rare). Similar tendencies can be observed in all European languages, though to very different degrees.

2.8.   The lexicography of loanwords

Germany has been claimed (by Polenz 1979: 18) to be the country of foreign-word dictionaries (*Fremdwörterbücher*). While their number is indeed impressive, such collections are also common for other national languages. The historical beginnings were often educational – as in Britain where the earliest dictionaries after 1604 were "hard-word lists" (Starnes and Noyes 1946). They were explicitly meant for the less educated – general lexis was added only a hundred years later, since such words were not regarded as being in need of explanation. The educational bias continues until much later: In Germany, W. Liebknecht's *Volksstaat-Fremdwörterbuch* of 1874, compiled by a leading socialist, testifies to the interest in popular education. Although the selection of lemmas is often not explained in such books (and many are full of items invented by their authors in order to increase the number of entries), they provide important sociohistorical information about words and attitudes evident in definitions and the usage guidance offered.

General dictionaries can also provide important information on loanwords and compilers' attitudes towards them. Some in fact concentrate on native words, esp. in the early German tradition, including foreign words only selectively. In others, coverage is more comprehensive, with typographical distinctions made between integrated loanwords and unadapted quotation words (cf. the *OED* discussed above).

A special type of dictionary does not stop at explaining foreign words, but lists them with suggested replacements, with explicitly purist intentions (*Sprachreinigung*). The tradition in Germany starts with Campe's *Wörterbuch zur Erklärung und Verdeutschung der unserer Sprache aufgedrungenen fremden Ausdrücke* of 1801 (also compare Dunger 1882, 1909). A modern parallel, with a quite different background, is represented by lists of words with suggested French equivalents which are circulated in France, implementing the legislation devoted to the purge of French from unwanted intruders, esp. anglicisms (cf. Section 6.3.).

Anglicisms are indeed the focus of many recent special collections, most being descriptive (such as Carstensen and Busse 1993–1995; Rodriguez 1997; and Tournier 1998, and see the bibliographical references for 16 European languages in Görlach 2002b, and the first attempt at a comprehensive contrastive dictionary of such lexis, in Görlach 2001).

3. Borrowing and the history of English

3.1. The choice of English justified

The immense number of language pairs that could be used to illustrate forms of contact and borrowing makes it impossible to consider all situations and types of transfer. However, the history of the English language in the course of the past 1500 years is so rich as both a receptor and donor of influences on all linguistic levels and in geographical, social and cultural aspects that it can serve better than any other language to illustrate the phenomena here discussed. It so happens that English is also best known to the author and to most readers of this chapter, and the framework of the cultural history of one nation makes statements and the evidence adduced for the arguments coherent, intelligible and therefore more convincing than following the practice of many authors, who select their specimens from a great number of languages (see Bynon 1977, 1981; Bloomfield 1933; Romaine 1989; Thomason 2001; Thomason and Kaufman 1988). Arguments here based largely on the history of English, may, however, be compared with the impact of English on other languages as detailed in Section 5 below.

3.2. Close and distant contact

English, in the course of its long history, came into close contact, in spoken (and partly written) form with:
- speakers of Celtic languages, spoken by the indigenous population at the time of the Germanic conquest of the 5th century, leading to the gradual expansion of English, which pushed the Celtic speech community to the western fringes – a process which has now almost come to completion (Förster 1921, Tristram 2004);
- Scandinavian settlers in the Danelaw area of the 9th to 11th centuries – and in the very north of Scotland where their language lasted to the 17th century (Geipel 1971);
- French immigrants after the Norman Conquest of 1066, French now forming the prestige (and largely standard) norm of wider communication for the British society in spoken and esp. written form well into the 15th century (Kibbee 1991);
- smaller immigrant populations of Dutch/Flemish and Yiddish speakers (13th to 20th centuries);

- a larger number of recent immigrants ranging from Poles to Punjabis, and West Indians to Hong Kong Chinese (Alladina and Edwards 1991).

More restricted (distant) contacts came about through written sources through the influence of schools, universities, monasteries, law courts and administration, and book reading in general, exhibiting very strong influences of Latin and French in particular, though slowly decreasing after 1700 (Munske and Kirkness 1996).

By contrast, "exotic" languages spoken overseas had close contact influences on colonial varieties of English, but were transmitted to British English mainly as distant loans through English emigrant dialects, or through Spanish, Portuguese, Dutch or French, similar to influences on other European languages – only that English often served as a mediator in the process (cf. Serjeantson 1935).

Both close contact (through British settlers, missionaries and administrators) and distant contact (largely through books and modern mass media) also serve to explain the impact of English on other languages world-wide, which peaks in the period after 1945 (for Europe see Section 4.3. below). The successful spread of English around the globe is a fascinating combination of the political and commercial power of the Empire, technological attractiveness of knowledge transmitted through English after the Industrial Revolution, and the cultural model handed on through teachers and missionaries. Such influences were obviously more relevant than any planned imposition of English as a lingua franca on to unwilling foreigners.

3.3. Celtic languages

The Celtic languages, spoken by all inhabitants of the British Isles before Germanic tribes invaded the country in the 5th century, are an outstanding example of how limited substratum influence after the language shift of its speakers can be. Although some Celtic impact on the pronunciation of Old English, inherently likely as a consequence of incomplete language acquisition, has been claimed (see Tristram 2004), conclusive evidence appears to be lacking. Slightly more convincing is substratum influence in morphology and syntax: Tristram (2004) posits contact-induced changes owing to Brittonic speakers, distinguishing between the Northern and Southwestern zones. In lexis, only a handful of Old English items are clearly of Celtic provenance, e.g. *bin, coomb*, so that the abundant corpus of Celtic place names remains the most conspicuous part of the Celtic inheritance. The absence of extensive remains of properly linguistic elements from Celtic languages reflects the restricted (largely one-sided) contact between the conquerors and the conquered – and the fact that Christian missionaries from Ireland in the North of England used the native language of those they wished to convert. This marginal impact of Celtic is strikingly paralleled in the minimal number of loanwords from Native American words in American English and of Aboriginal items in Australian English, again most certainly a consequence of one-sided and largely restricted contacts among speakers of indigenous and European languages. That the sociolinguistic situation in Britain did not drastically change is shown by the fact that loanwords from Celtic languages in later periods have again remained restricted to exoticisms, i.e. words designating items of Celtic culture, such as *kilt, shamrock, sporran,* and *whiskey.*

3.4.   Scandinavian languages

The term is here used to cover the dialects of the invaders and settlers who, in the footsteps of the Viking raids, came to occupy large areas of England and Scotland in the 9th to 11th centuries. The sociolinguistic situation in the Danelaw area was unique in the history of English (although paralleled in some other European countries): Speakers of two genetically related languages – Old English of the northern Anglian type and varieties of North Germanic – became neighbours, and later partners in mixed marriages (see Geipel 1971). The need to communicate led to the merger of two similar Germanic vocabularies (in which the majority of items was shared, if we disregard some phonological and morphological differences). We might wish to classify the Scandinavian impact as that of an adstratum, but this would not do justice to the language mix in daily intercourse, in the absence of a roofing (*überdachend*) Old English standard for almost all users. Strictly speaking, we cannot therefore talk about Scandinavian loans in northern dialects of English, it was rather that Scandinavian died out, or gave way to, a Scandinavianised lingua franca, which was predominantly English of the Anglian type. The borrowing process that did take place was the later interdialectal spread of many of the Scandinavian words to other English dialects, largely by way of population movements and notably into the London area and thereby into Standard British English. The consequent selection process in the oversupplied lexis, in both northern dialects and in London English, might result in the ultimate loss of either the English or the Scandinavian word, or lead to their semantic or stylistic differentiation. A distinctive feature of the Scandinavian lexis surviving in Standard British English is its strong position in the core vocabulary, e.g. *skill, sky, ugly,* which is conspicuously different from that of most other sets of non-native lexis – because the items were not borrowed in the strict sense.

A similar process of language merger and dialect erosion took place much later in Northern Scotland (Caithness, Orkney and Shetland), regions which were originally settled by Norwegians and remained part of the Norwegian kingdom right into the late 15th century.

3.5. French

Language contact with French was minimal in the Anglo-Saxon period. However, the Norman Conquest of 1066 resulted in the most dramatic impact in the sociolinguistic history of English with the large-scale replacement of the native elites by French speakers. The West Saxon quasi-standard language came to an end around 1100, written communication largely (though not completely) changing to Anglo-Norman French. As long as there was a diglossic (or, including Latin, a triglossic) functional distribution of languages (cf. Fig. 1), borrowing into the Middle English vernacular was not extensive – as far as the poor documentation before the 13th century permits us to be certain. The situation is further complicated by the fact that the dialect of the Anglo-Normans remained a mother tongue for a small ethnic minority until the mid-13th century, and when French became a second language through shift of the Anglo-Norman speakers, it became increasingly adapted or replaced by the new prestige variety of the Ile de France. Moreover, the linguistic similarity of the "parent" language Latin, and some Latinisation of the Romance lexis on the Continent, does not permit us to distinguish in all cases between French and Latin provenance of individual loanwords. All this happened in a regionally diversified Middle English vernacular and in a society in which English gained ground, with an ongoing marginalisation of French and Latin, at least from 1430 onwards. The conspicuous status changes of the three languages were at least partially prompted or speeded up by the growing dissatisfacti on of monolinguals for whom important texts in French were not accessible (see quotations in Baugh and Cable 2002: 144–146, and in Kibbee 1991).

The dramatic impact of French has led to some speculation about the "creolisation" of Middle English. However, while there has been a great deal of simplification and regularisation of Middle English, esp. in its morphology, there has never been a pidgin stage, nor has Middle English lost grammatical categories such as case, number and tense (as would be expected in a pidgin), and successive generations of speakers never lost the ability to communicate in what, after all, was and remained their native language – for more than 90% of the population. The impact of French was largely lexical (and indirectly phonological) and was a change from above (for a summary of accepted knowledge see Görlach 1990, and more recently, with a reliable digest of recent research, Tristram 2004).

The dramatic increase of loanwords in the total lexis (rising from 3% in Old English times to some 60% by the times of Chaucer) also explains the change in word-formation patterns. Germanic models of Old English (still highly productive in modern German or Icelandic) were drastically reduced or given up, and new patterns became available after Romance loanwords had been re-analysed, starting from sets like *agree/agreeable/agreement*. A major section of English word-formation is now Romance-based, even though hybrids like *shortage* and *oddity* tend to be restricted.

With the changeover to written English in private and official functions between 1350 and 1430, the status of French changed to that of the dominant foreign language in British education and society in general (see Baugh and Cable 2002: 127–155). This development changed the character of loanwords and attitudes towards their integration. Whereas medieval borrowings tend to be formally inconspicuous apart from their number of syllables and their morphology if complex, words taken over from French after 1660 are much less thoroughly integrated in phonology and concerning the relationship of pronunciation and spelling (as in *machine*). In many cases, the foreign form of such words was retained as a social marker of educatedness (and possibly affectation). Also, code-switching involving English was considered "genteel" – even though the role of French was much less extensive in Britain than it was in 18th and 19th century Continental societies.

Apart from visibly French loans, France has also provided a great number of neo-classical scholarly words mainly from such domains as the sciences, technology, politics and diplomacy, but since these items are formed from Greek and Latin bases (*eucalyptus*, *telephone*) they ought to be treated in Section 3.6. below.

The impact of other Romance languages has been much more limited (see Finkenstaedt and Wolff 1973; for recent Spanish influence on American English see Rodriguez 1996).

3.6. Classical languages: Latin and Greek

Latin was the most important language in Western education well into the 17th and 18th centuries, curbing or delaying the *ausbau* of vernaculars to full standard languages. Where diglossia was well established, borrowing was limited and code-switching more normal. In Old English, a number of Latin-derived loans were inherited from the Continental Germanic varieties and carried to Britain with the invaders; the number of new loans mediated through Celtic was very small. However, even in the later periods of Old English the dominance of Latin did not lead to large-scale adoptions. In biblical diction, native solutions (calquing, or semantic extension) were greatly preferred to borrowing – the entire Old English translation of the Prodigal Son has a single loanword (*myltestre* from *meretrix* 'prostitute', see Görlach 1997: 209). This fact is at least partly owing to the "missionary practice" of using the vernacular. Later technical terms, too, were generally not taken from Latin, calques being preferred.

After 1066, the functions of Latin greatly increased in Britain, following Continental conventions. As regards borrowing from Latin, the takeover of loanwords was obviously facilitated by the ubiquitous presence and sociolinguistically easier transfer of French items. Unsurprisingly, Latin borrowings are much more apparent in domains like medicine and other sciences – after these registers became available in the vernacular after 1400 – foreshadowing the more massive shift to English in the Renaissance period. Also, the sociolinguistic prestige of Latin words inserted in English texts led to large-scale "aureation", mainly in literary texts, employed for stylistic beautification and copiousness, again foreshadowing 16th century excesses of unnecessary Latinisation criticised as inkhornism. The heyday of Latin influence came in the 16th century when, in the *ausbau* of the national standard language, gaps were filled mainly by the takeover of needed loanwords on the one hand, and for rhetorical reasons, in order to achieve copiousness, on the other (see Jones 1953, and Görlach 1991: 154–160). This process was accompanied by the borrowing of syntactical patterns, again needed for complex abstract texts newly acquired for English, and, in imitation of Latin *Kunstprosa* 'rhetorical prose', the takeover of numerous syntactical elements in sentence and text structure, for rhetorical improvement on the other. In extreme forms, texts could become largely unintelligible because of their erudite lexis and too complex sentences, with units often equalling modern paragraphs.

A comparison with the half-independent Scots language is enlightening (cf. Görlach 2002c). While borrowing from Latin and French proceeded on similar lines, Scots writers extensively also borrowed from English, while the massive imitation of Latin scholarly prose in English did not find a parallel, because the *ausbau* of Scots was thwarted by the takeover of English translations (as also happened in the case of the Bible).

Both lexical and syntactical emulation of Latin decreased in Britain after the Civil War (after 1660), when the ideal of copiousness was replaced by that of perspicuity, and the influence of French became stronger. The borrowing of Latin words now increasingly shifted to the neo-classical vocabulary coined for the expression of technological progress and the terminology of various sciences; these neologisms were invented by scholars on the same principles in many European countries, regardless of their individual mother tongues.

From 1500 onwards, insufficient competence in Latin led to misuses criticised as malapropisms, illustrating the unbroken prestige of Latinate lexis among the less educated and social climbers – compare Ben Jonson's statement on Shakespeare's "small Latin and less Greek".

A conspicuous feature of many Greek/Latin loanwords in English (and other European languages) is their morphological non-integration, which strikingly contrasts with the extreme regularisation of English plural formation in other words.

3.7.   Loanwords from other languages in British English

Borrowing from all other languages put together does not amount to more than ten percent of the English lexis (see Finkenstaedt and Wolff 1973; Scheler 1977). Almost all of these loanwords came through distant contact (and were often mediated rather than taken straight from the source languages, esp. in the case of overseas lexis taken over after 1500). The colonial expansion of the British Empire led to the straightforward acquisition of words from the indigenous languages of North America, Africa, Asia and Australia, many of which remained part of the regional lexis or were accepted into international English, and then transmitted to other languages. This was frequently the case with designations for animals, plants, minerals, local customs and the like.

3.8.   Words borrowed into overseas varieties of English

The complex contact history of English with other languages overseas has created many forms of reciprocal influence which are difficult to categorise. A few remarks are, however, in order.

Indigenous languages, such as those of the Native Americans in North America, Bantu languages in Africa, or Australian Aboriginal languages and Maori in New Zealand have had relatively little impact on the English of the settler communities. The few loanwords recorded in American English (such as *hickory*, *mocassin*, *tomahawk* or *wigwam*) and in Australian English (e.g. *boomerang*, *kangaroo*, *koala*, *wombat*) concentrate chronologically on the first generations of settlers – apparently there was a point of saturation when foreign animals, plants and landscape features had been named, and the source cultures being too alien to justify more extensive borrowing.

Immigrant languages likewise were less influential than might have been expected: Millions of French, German, Polish and Scandinavian settlers in America and Australia have left comparatively few loanwords apart from designations for special dishes, drinks or dresses. Only where previous colonisation by non-English settlers is attested is a more substantial heritage to be expected (these words may accordingly count as survivals rather than as borrowings). Consider Spanish in the South of the U.S., French in Quebec and Louisiana, and (particularly) the coexistence of Afrikaans and English in South Africa (cf. Branford 1991). In the last case extensive (reciprocal) borrowing is a consequence of an unusually high degree of bilingualism, mainly among the white population, a situation which gave rise to extensive code-switching and borrowing – processes that cannot be neatly distinguished in all cases.

In ESL societies like Nigeria or India the diglossic situation which kept various vernaculars distinct from English in specific functions has led to the takeover of fewer loanwords into local Englishes than many might predict. By contrast, the impact of English on vernaculars was much more extensive on all levels, reflecting the High/Low distinction in relative prestige.

Finally, the situation in speech communities with dominant pidgins and creoles (see Holm 1988/1989) is either one of levelling, similar to the development of the dialect/standard continuum in Europe (as in Jamaica); in this case, "borrowing" is clearly not the appropriate term. On the other hand, borrowing does take place in cases like Krio in Sierra Leone and Tok Pisin in Papua New Guinea, where the takeover of English items is deliberate and easily recognised because of the distance between the two languages.

3.9. Internal borrowing

The distinction between languages and dialects is not clearcut. Although Scots was not a dialect of English in the 16th century, it has since become dialectalised (see Görlach 2002c), and is thus here included – reciprocal borrowing is therefore classified as internal.

Population movements, esp. late medieval immigration into London from the Home Counties and the Midlands, led to contacts between speakers of different dialects in the 14th century metropolis. The resulting borrowing into the emergent standard is important for the fact that it brought in originally Scandinavian words which otherwise would have remained restricted to dialects of the former Danelaw area (*ill, skill, sky*, etc.).

Whereas Briticisms in America have only a marginal claim to being loanwords in American English (having always been a stylistic option), American imports into British English (frequent from 1920 onwards) were clearly borrowed, most notably in some technical domains, the mass media and popular music. British attitudes have long been negative against such imports of words, phrases and (rarely) syntactical patterns, but resistance has now largely broken down (compare similar internal loans from other ex-colonies). Words like *radio* (replacing *wireless set*) can therefore be classified as internal loans.

Contacts between Scots and English were largely in written form before 1603. The Scots literary language was from its beginning characterised by free borrowing from English, esp. from the works of Chaucer and Lydgate, and Scots as an independent linguistic system was further eroded in the 16th century by lavish takeovers from "Southeron" (Southern English) well before the Union of the Crowns in 1603. By contrast, loanwords from Scots were very rare in English before the 18th and 19th centuries, when the popularity of the works of writers like Burns and Scott led to the adoption of dozens of Scots words of Germanic and Celtic provenance, many of which are no longer identified as borrowings (cf. *raid, slogan*). It has to be admitted that in many cases the distinction between borrowing and the effect of levelling (koineisation) is not easy. This applies to the relationship of English and Scots as it does to some Continental language pairs (Low and High German, Castilian and Catalan, Russian and Ukrainian, etc).

4. Borrowing from English

4.1. The historical background

The functions of English have dramatically changed world-wide in the course of the past four hundred years. In 1600, knowledge of English was virtually confined to the British Isles, where Celtic languages were also more widespread than they are today. Welsh, Scottish and Irish Gaelic as receptor languages have in fact undergone heavy structural changes, including massive lexical borrowing from English; present-day Irish has sometimes even been characterised as "relexified English".

As late as the 17th century, Milton was satisfied with having his poetical fame restricted to Britain, when composing his national epic *Paradise Lost* in English (rather than in Latin), not expecting to find readers abroad. The colonisation of North America had barely started, and was to follow much later on other continents, and hardly any English was taught in Continental schools. The impressive spread of English as a world language and its corresponding impact on other languages is consequently a matter of the 19th and 20th centuries, when the extent of its functions and number of speakers rocketed as a native (ENL), second (ESL) or foreign language (EFL), illustrating the American and British share in globalisation and stressing the instrumental functions of the language (cf. Fishman, Conrad, and Rubal-Lopez 1996). Modern English is the first language in world history that has spread to all continents and virtually to all layers of society, having acquired more non-native speakers than native users – the majority of whom has concentrated for some time in the U.S., affecting the prestige of the traditionally estimated British English norms less than might have been expected.

4.2. The influence of English on non-European languages

There has not been any comprehensive study of the problem, contrastive analyses being hampered by the lack of scholars competent in widely divergent languages, linguists able to formulate adequate methods, elicit reliable data and produce competent interpretations (for some interesting facts and interpretations see Viereck and Bald 1986). However, the following statements can be made with due caution:

Language shift/loss as a consequence of dominant and prestigious English is recorded for Britain and Ireland, where Celtic languages, for the U.S., where indigenous languages, and for regions like Australia and New Zealand, where Aboriginal/Maori languages have either died out or have been severely reduced as regards numbers of speakers and range of functions. Note that the languages of immigrants in these countries have suffered similar losses. In all these cases, minorities in ENL societies are affected. These tend to borrow heavily from English, as a consequence of the greater communicative reach of the dominant language, and this is often a first step towards complete language loss. In ESL societies like Nigeria or India, the suppletion of the vernaculars is a mirror image of Renaissance English, that is, the impact tends to be regulated by lexical needs in individual domains and text types – unless code-switching to English is preferred as an easier option for specialist exchanges – or to be guided by considerations of fashion and prestige. If the acquisition of English is not filtered through norms of schools, and if structures of receptor languages diverge conspicuously from English, the phonological and semantic integration of loanwords can be drastic (cf. Section 5.1.).

In EFL societies, esp. in Western Europe, the number of competent users and the quality of their English tend to be high. These have dramatically increased after 1945, as has the number of anglicisms (cf. Section 4.3.).

4.3. The impact of English on European languages

Excepting close-contact languages like Welsh and Maltese, the influence of English on the major European languages has now been first investigated in a contrastive fashion, based on newly elicited empirical data (see Görlach 2001, 2002a, 2002b, 2003). The following statements can be made summarising the evidence collected:

The lexical influence of English virtually began in the 19th century (partly mediated through French), but became really frequent from the 1920s onwards, and dramatic after 1945. Figures from the *Dictionary of European Anglicisms* show that only 10% of the European anglicisms were recorded before 1900, a figure which had risen to 19% by 1920 and to 37% by 1950, with increases of up to 16% per individual decade thereafter (see Görlach 2003: 166). This impact now affects practically all domains, text types and styles as well as users of nearly all social classes. Most of the recent influence appears to come from America, but the sources of anglicisms are difficult to determine, since the differences between British English and American English have decreased, and words appear to be filtered through British English before they are adopted. (American provenance can be an important factor as regards – negative – attitudes.)

Conspicuous differences among receptor languages as to the number of attested anglicisms remain. They are evident from the *DEA*, which covers the data available up to 1995, the cutoff date for the collection process. These differences are most convincingly explained by a combination of three factors. High numbers of attested anglicisms are obviously due to a) linguistic (esp. phonological) closeness to English structures, b) openness to Western culture after 1945, and c) absence or relative unimportance of purist movements and official regulations directed against foreign influences (academies, linguistic legislation).

The impact of borrowing was initially almost entirely restricted to lexis, but the large number of incompletely integrated loanwords available in written and spoken form, and the increasing awareness of native pronunciations as a gauge of correctness have affected the phonological system of receptor languages (articulation, phonotactics and a few new phonemes) as well as spelling conventions and the correlation of spelling and pronunciation. There is also incipient influence on inflectional morphology, such as the takeover of plural -*s* marking and nominal -*ing* in loanwords but not usually elsewhere. The impact on word-formation patterns can be more extensive.

There appears to be a growing acceptance of code-switching involving European languages and English than used to be the case. This impression is strongest in text types like advertising and pop songs, and this change may be connected with age and education, since it seems to be more common among younger and less educated speakers or writers. Usage considered fashionable seems to play an important part. Such developments are most apparent in countries where code-switching and -mixing has led to acceptable varieties at least for certain functions, such as Tagalog-English mixing in the metropolitan media language in the Philippines (extremes which are not documented in Europe).

4.4. Social, political and educational consequences of language contact

The knowledge of a prestigious foreign language has always been a social marker in most communities – whether this concerned medieval Latin, 18th and 19th century French or present-day English. In most modern societies English competence is considered a necessary equipment for many desirable jobs, having largely replaced similar requirements for French, German and Russian (cf. Maurais and Morris 2003). In African and Asian countries in particular, English is considered a necessary precondition of power, money and upward mobility. Such expectations may not be fulfilled partly because the English available to many learners is not close enough to international norms, so that the quality of the English used acquires important social functions.

Internationally, the knowledge of acceptable English has become a requirement for communication, trade, politics and tourism as well as for tertiary education and scholarly publications (cf. Ammon 2001). The imbalance in language acquisition favours native users, but also non-native learners in developed countries with a high standard of language teaching over users from less privileged communities (see also Carli and Calaresu, this vol.).

5. The integration of loanwords and other borrowed elements

The possibilities of integration of foreign elements are deducible from a comparison of the structures of the donor and receptor languages, and the degree of actual accommodation is explained by sociohistorical factors of speakers' awareness and attitudes.

5.1. Spelling

Languages using Roman alphabets can either retain the English pronunciation to render the approximate equivalents in the native sound system and respell the anglicisms (as in German *Streik*, Polish *strajk*) or employ the English spelling – and risk non-English pronunciations, or accept a clash with native correlations of spelling and pronunciation. Which of the methods is chosen for an individual language depends on (possibly) changing attitudes. Non-adapted spellings present great difficulties for learners and can lead to stigmatised spelling pronunciations, i.e. sociolinguistically diagnostic blunders. However, with the world-wide growth of spoken English competence, such malapropisms tend to become rarer, and they certainly leave no permanent traces in the linguistic system of the receptor language. (Contrast early loans like German *Punsch* 'punch' with /u/, Bulgarian *kovboi* /v/ 'cowboy', Italian *iglife* /g/ 'highlife', and Spanish *iceberg* /θ/.) In some languages like Polish, retentions of the English spellings have recently increased, whereas Czech tends to respell, and orthographical integration has been enforced for many anglicisms in Norwegian by recent reforms.

Languages employing non-Roman alphabets normally transliterate on the basis of either English spelling or pronunciation (selecting the closest phonemic equivalents – sometimes with conventions changing over time, as has happened to the rendering of English /ə/ in Russian). Total non-adaptation appears to be on the increase in domains like advertising and shop signs, leading to the use of two co-existing writing systems – as modern practices in Greece or Bulgaria demonstrate. Whether this can be interpreted as a first step leading to a general adoption of Roman letters is impossible to predict.

Non-alphabetical systems (like Chinese) frequently render loanwords by symbols of homophonous items, but the retention of the English form is often preferred for the sake of clarity.

5.2. Pronunciation

The integration of foreign words presents no problem in cases where articulation, phonotactics and phonemes correspond in the receptor language (as in German *Test, fit*). Where the articulation diverges from English (as it does in the case of /r/ in many languages) pronunciations closely modelled on English are often considered affected and therefore avoided (but may be used in code-switching). Phonotactic differences are normally adapted to the receptor language, so that word-initial /sp-, st-/ etc. are pronounced /ʃp-, ʃt-/ in older loans in German (as in *Spleen, Streik*), with a more recent tendency to retain the English clusters, so that *Spot* now consistently contrasts with native *Spott* 'derision'. In fact, word-initial /s-/ clusters sound distinctively foreign in many languages (as in *slang, smog, snob, standby, swimming-pool*). Romance languages – but also Hindi – tend to integrate such words by the adoption of a prothetic /ə/, and vowel insertion is also a common practice to deal with clusters in other languages. Word-final devoicing of stops and fricatives is the rule in, e.g., German and Polish, which leads to pronunciations like /bent/ for *Band*. Also note voicing of initial /s-/ in German *Sound* /zaunt/.

Diphthongs are frequently monophthongised, or seen as forming two syllables, in receptor languages. However, increasing contact with spoken English has also led to the rise of peripheral phonemes in imitation of the source. This has happened at least with educated speakers of German, for whom native /o:/ and /ou/ in *Sohle* 'sole [part of shoe]' vs. *Soul*, and /e:/ and /ei/ in *Leser* 'reader' and *Laser* now contrast. Languages lacking length distinctions in vowels, like Spanish and Italian, can acquire the contrast to avoid homophony in words like *bitch* and *beach*. However, corrections are difficult to make, since deviances tend to be below the level of awareness, and they can easily become social markers of the less educated. (A few speech communities appear to be exceptions in that close-to-English pronunciations in loanwords are not aimed at: For Japanese, it is claimed that non-integrated pronunciations are shared by speakers regardless of education and social class.)

More drastic adaptations to diverging syllable structures are absent from European receptor languages, but are reported from Africa (as in Hausa /sukudireba/ for *screwdriver*) and Asia (as in Japanese /aisukurimu/ for *icecream* or /fotuboru/ for *football*). A combination of phonological integration with morphological re-analysis has changed *mudguard* and *keep left* (roundabout) to Suahili /ma-digadi/ and /ki-pilefiti/ which triggered a singular form *digadi* and a plural *vi-plefiti*, according to Bynon (1977: 221).

5.3.   Inflection

Words are normally borrowed from the donor language's base form; the large-scale loss of inflectional morphology in English consequently does not create any major problems for the integration of nouns (which make up the major part of loanwords) and creates only minor difficulties for adjectives and verbs.

In nouns, grammatical gender allocation is obligatory for many languages (but not, e.g., for Georgian). Individual decisions in European languages covered

by the *Dictionary of European Anglicisms* were obviously based on a combination of three factors, viz.:
- phonological shape (e.g., words ending in stops tend to be masculine in Russian)
- morphology (loanwords ending in *-er* are masculine in German; only *Poster* is either masculine or neuter, if modelled on the near-synonym *das Plakat*)
- meaning (loanwords follow natural sex, or else can take over the gender of native synonyms)

Since these principles are not rankable according to weight and may well contradict each other, it is impossible to predict the outcome of the allocation. However, it is remarkable that so few individual cases remain unsettled, or provide an option, in the approximately 3000 nouns in 16 languages in the *Dictionary of European Anglicisms* corpus (see Görlach 2003: 76).

Case, where necessary in a specific syntactic context, is indicated by inflection as is obligatory for vernacular items and this applies even to instances of apparent code-switching. Plural markers are obligatory; they vary in the individual receptor languages, for example:
- In German, older loans tend to be adapted (as in *Boxen* 'boxes', 'loudspeakers'), whereas recent anglicisms retain *-(s)*, with minor spelling problems in *Babys/Babies,* but words ending in *-er* have zero plurals, as they have in native words (e.g. *zwei Computer* 'two computers').
- Italian traditionally used zero endings, but acceptance of English *-(e)s* is increasing in more recent loans.
- Russian universally employs vernacular inflections, *-(e)s* being not yet accepted, or restricted to code-switches.

Some English plurals were not recognised as such by borrowers and thus became the base forms in the loanwords *Keks, Koks, Drops* and *Schlips* in German; some of these were handed on to neighbouring languages. The process can be shown to continue in the recent loanwords *jeans* and *shorts*, which are taken to be singulars in some languages.

In verbs, phrasal units present special problems of integration, esp. for inflected forms. Thus it is still unsettled whether the participle *sourced out* should be *outgesourc(e)t* in German.

5.4. Word-formation

Most loanwords are non-complex; in nouns, the borrowing of compounds and derivations is comparatively rare. Where these are taken over, they are sometimes not properly analysed, which results in new derivations like Bulgarian *dopingovat'* for 'to dope', and Italian *babysitteraggio* rendering 'babysitting'. Nominal compounds are easily borrowed into Germanic languages, but Romance and Slavic languages prefer combinations of noun plus adjective or "genitive" constructions (and they almost invariably do when calquing). This also means that newly formed adjectives are next to obligatory in Slavic languages to accompany newly borrowed nouns. A drastic form of compound integration is the reduction to the first (modifier) element, which is typically found in some French borrowings like *smoking* (*jacket*), *parking* (*lot*), *living* (*room*) or *tennis* (*shoes*).

In derivations, suffix replacements are frequent, esp. in agent and action nouns. Thus English *-er/-or* corresponds to *-eur* in French, *-ore* in Italian, *-jor* in Russian, etc., so that native suffixes can be used in integration without semantic loss. The same is true for replacing English *-ing* by French *-age*, Italian *-aggio*, or Russian *-nost'*, and such substitution is regularly applied in integrating anglicisms affected by French legislation (such as *nursage* for *nursing*).

In due course, intensive borrowing may result in the adoption of foreign patterns into the receptor structure. Thus noun+noun compounds are now being taken over into languages that have no native equivalents or use it but rarely. However, it is only when such models become productive (likely to start in hybrid formations) that we can speak of borrowed word-formation processes. For instance, French has created a number of compounds with *-man* as a second element (a morpheme which arguably has become a peripheral French suffix, cf. Picone 1996). Coinages like *tennisman* or *recordman* have indeed spread to other languages, as have some French compounds with *self-* as a first element (e.g. *self-banking*, cf. Picone 1996: 291–296). Spanish has the unique coinage *puenting* (from *puente* 'bridge') for 'bunjee-jumping'.

While the adoption of foreign suffixes for productive derivation is generally restricted by etymological considerations (e.g. *-ism* being rarely found with Germanic bases), foreign prefixes tend to be combined more readily – compare elements like *anti-*, *contra-*, *de-*, *re-*, *super-*, *mini-* and *maxi-* in various languages.

5.5. Lexis

5.5.1. The integration of loanwords

Loanwords have to be integrated in form, meaning, syntactical compatibility and style. As far as semantic integration is concerned, a borrowed item can fill a lexical gap or be used for stylistic reasons. Renaissance borrowings from Latin into many European vernaculars provide excellent examples for "necessary" as against "luxury" loanwords. In either case, a loanword has to be integrated into a native semantic field, where it will provide semantic or at least stylistic contrasts to neighbouring words, or, rarely, duplicate existing expressions by supplying synonyms (which are likely to become differentiated or to disappear in due course). Sometimes less adapted forms remain indicative of linguistic and social prestige, in which case integration is slowed down or stopped, reflecting speakers' awareness of social class, education and age. Less frequently, borrowed items serve to create registers of secret languages known only to the initiated (jargon) or serve functions like euphemism, avoidance of taboo words and the like.

5.5.2. Meaning

Loanwords are normally borrowed for a specific context and with a specific meaning – precision is often the major reason for their adoption. In cases of polysemy of the source word only one meaning is borrowed at a time. Though the process can be repeated, it is rare for a loanword to achieve the semantic extension of the etymon (see the interesting comparison of the number of senses borrowed in 12 languages in Görlach 2003: 95).

Unless loanwords are borrowed for terminologies (in which case they tend to be monosemic), their meaning will overlap only to a certain extent with that of the etymon (and at least be different in style). In extreme cases, false friends are created by the word's integration and later semantic development in the receptor language (or subsequent loss of the borrowed meaning in the donor language, as in German *Bowle* or *Punsch*).

5.5.3. Calquing

The most common method to avoid straightforward borrowing is to render the foreign form by native elements. Traditionally, four categories of the process are distinguished:
(a) loan translation, the morpheme-for-morpheme translation of semantic equivalents in the receptor language, as in German *Wochenende* from 'weekend', *Gehirnwäsche* from 'brain-washing', French *SIDA* 'syndrome d'immunodéficience acquise' from 'AIDS';
(b) loan rendition, a looser correspondence using partial equivalents in form or meaning, as in German *Wolkenkratzer* for 'skyscraper', French *remue-méningues* for 'brain-storming';
(c) loan creation, a coinage prompted by the foreign word and concept, but independent in form, as in German *Nietenhose* for 'blue jeans', French *balladeur* for 'walkman';
(d) semantic loan, the addition of a new meaning to that of an existing word, based on a partial semantic overlap, as in the meaning 'computer mouse' added to that of 'rodent' in many languages.

The four *brain-* entries in the *Dictionary of European Anglicisms* (*-drain, -storming, -trust* and *-washing*) provide a fascinating survey of how European languages cope with the alternatives of borrowing as against various forms of calquing. Although the data for calques included in the *DEA* are selective (depending on whether an anglicism was represented as an entry, and the calque recognised by the collaborator) the proportion of the four types of calquing is significant: Translations (59.3%) were found to be much more frequent than renditions (26.7%), creations (6.5%) and semantic calques (7.5%), and the figure for translations is even higher if we realise that most renditions were chosen because linguistic structures of the receptor language did not permit to replicate the etymon exactly. Thus replicas for 'skyscraper' are not perfect due to structural reasons in French *gratte-ciel*, whereas German *Wolkenkratzer* is deviant semantically. It is also interesting to note that up to 90% of all calques recorded in the *DEA* were judged to be successful (see Görlach 2003: 166).

Calquing can be based on one-word units, but also (more rarely) on phrases or entire sentences, such as when proverbs are translated. Calquing is often employed by purists since the resulting expressions effectively disguise the foreign origin. However, objections to calques can also be found (as in German *einmal mehr* for 'once more').

5.6.   Syntax

If syntactical patterns are borrowed (that is, if they become permanent additions to the receptor's syntax rather than remain isolated instances of translations), the donor language tends to have outstanding prestige. The impact is usually through the written form and can proceed through translations or imitation/emulation. (Note that close contact, as in the historical coexistence of Scandinavian and Anglian dialects in the Danelaw area resulted in merged syntax rather than in borrowing; cf. Section 3.4.).

The history of European vernaculars in the Renaissance exhibits abundant evidence of syntactical takeovers of Latin structures, whether this was done to achieve the necessary complexity to render new text types, or for rhetorical beautification of the vernacular. However, a comparison with modern European languages shows that such syntactic borrowings need not have been permanent. Many features documented in the first phase of the emergent standard languages were given up again, when correctness and good style came to be oriented at the "genius" of the individual languages (in English esp. between 1660 and 1760) rather than Latin constructions.

A specific influence of register-bound loan syntax is found in biblical translation where departing from the syntax and even the word order of the source was often considered to result in potential distortions of the message, and in consequence provoking hereticism. Constructions offending against the genius of individual languages were, as a result, handed on over many centuries – but need not spread into other domains. The beginning of the Lord's Prayer is a well-known example of such "mistranslation" as in German "Vater unser, der

Du bist im Himmel" (most often corrected in 20th century versions, which read "Unser Vater im Himmel").

There is no doubt that the range and flexibility of the syntax of many other languages outside Europe has also been improved on phrase, sentence and text levels by contacts with languages of wider communication (often English) and higher status. A close analysis of languages around the world is likely to show modifications but would confirm the principal correctness of the statement. Whether such expansions are primarily due to translations or through imitation of the prestigious language is difficult or even impossible to show in most cases.

5.7. Typological consequences

Mergers and mixes of languages arising from long-lasting intimate contacts between speakers of different varieties can possibly lead to more drastic changes affecting the typology of the systems involved than borrowing can be expected to do. The latter process by definition has a receptor structure into which foreign elements are integrated. However, when the sheer mass of borrowed items comes to predominate over native elements, the typology – phonological, morphological and syntactical, and certainly lexical – may well drastically change. Admittedly, such changes are not always easy to put down to one individual cause like language contact where internal causes might have led to similar or identical developments ("drift"). Thus, in English the loss of inflection, morphological regularisation and word order changes are not primarily owing to contact, however much it may have contributed to the development.

6. Language attitudes

6.1. General considerations

For the majority of speakers successful communication is the dominant criterion; they are not normally concerned about the purity (or even the death) of their respective mother tongue. Such concern is likely to arise when a language is seen as one of the defining factors (possibly the most important) of cultural, ethnic or political identity. Traditionally, negative attitudes to foreign elements are connected with speakers of (emerging) standard languages, in periods when linguistic identity is felt to be endangered, or in situations where other encroachments by a dominant culture such as social structure, economy, religion, and the like combine with a serious threat to the respective mother tongue (for German compare Straßner 1995; on attitudes see Gallois, Watson, and Brabant, this vol.).

Such critical attitudes strongly contrast with (often co-existing) views which see the developmental potentials of borrowing from a widely respected language in a positive light. Again, educated writers in the Renaissance were torn between these two forces, and it depended on the period and personal interest of individual commentators which aspect they saw as prevailing – stressing the hope and need of improvement of a deficient vernacular, or the fear of the mother tongue of becoming a "dialect" of the superior language. Johnson's exaggerated statement in 1755 that English was in danger of becoming a dialect of French if uncurbed borrowing proceeded is a typical subjective expression of such concerns. Many writers have stressed the fact that the saturation of English with foreign words would have made their purge impossible after, say, the 14th century. The sociolinguistic problem of the "hard words" (which have come to form a "language bar" within the anglophone speech communities) has long been an educational concern (cf. Scheler 1977: 104–107). However, the attempts at introducing "Saxonisms" (Germanic replacements) have foreseeably been unsuccessful in the 16th and 17th centuries (see Görlach 1991: 163–166) as well as in the 19th (when William Barnes and a few other writers tried to introduce such words). Continental writers of the 18th century warned even more vociferously against the pollution caused by French imports – and for sociolinguistically better reasons.

6.2. Recent concerns

The global situation after 1945 is characterised by an unstoppable expansion of English as regards regions, number of speakers, (generally) improved fluency and range of functions in spoken and written form. While the situation can be compared with, say, the impact of French in the 18th and 19th centuries, obvious differences regarding bilingualism and borrowing remain: The influence of French was much more homogeneous by way of register and social class, and of course geographically much more restricted. Today, even the traditional distinction between countries/speech communities having English as a second as against a foreign language is breaking down. Also, the multiplicity of the world's languages, their status and different types of contact make generalisations about borrowing and speakers' attitudes precarious – even if we had sufficient empirical data, which we have not.

However, it is a striking fact that with all the negative connotations connected with the former colonial language and the widespread image of the "Ugly American", the evaluation of English competence around the world has remained strikingly positive (cf. Fishman, Conrad, and Rubal-Lopez 1996). Therefore, attempts at replacing (or curbing the functions of) English by national languages have only partly been successful (cf. Tanzania, Pakistan, India, Malaysia, and the Philippines) – the currency of English for international communication has certainly not been affected. Elsewhere, it is common for

English to replace other international languages such as French, German or Russian as the most widely taught first foreign language in higher education (see Maurais and Morris 2003). As a result, the number of speakers has increased dramatically, esp. in countries where it is a foreign language, but where teaching capacities are most highly developed, e.g. in Europe. The fact that this region also has the oldest tradition of cultivating strong feelings for national languages constituting nation states has recently strengthened the old concerns of keeping them pure, that is, free of foreign influences. Where in earlier periods such cleansing was mainly directed against French (throughout Europe) or German (esp. in the cases of Dutch, Yiddish and Czech), the thrust is now against English – as loanwords and the loss of entire registers is concerned.

6.3. Borrowing and the loss of functions and registers of the receptor language

In stable diglossia, borrowing is often not extensive, since code-switching is more common. However, the restricted functions of vernaculars, or the loss of specific functions, are possibly more legitimate reasons for concern. In fact, the exclusive use of English in fields like banking, or the non-acceptance of scholarly publications written in the national languages (such as the refusal of a leading German publisher of science journals to print articles in German) is a matter of greater concern than having a scholarly text saturated with English terminology. While English is certain not to kill well-established European standard languages (in the sense of Calvet 1974), it might reduce their functions and stop them from developing in certain fields, a restriction that has in fact happened to dialects which failed to expand into technological registers after the Industrial Revolution. It could be argued that European languages might lose the full range of functions they acquired with some difficulty by taking over from Latin in the Renaissance (cf. Straßner 1995).

6.4. Institutional and legal support of purism

The oldest European tradition after 1945 is that of France, where criticising "franglais" became a populist activity in the 1960s. Etiemble's *Parlez-vous franglais?* of 1964 sums up all the negative connotations of the former colonial language combined with American imperialism (cf. Truchot 1986; Thody 1995; Plümer 2000). The book started a development that later became official in linguistic legislation in the Loi Toubon of 1991. Lists of "banned" words are still regularly circulated, and they appear to have been successful in curbing the frequency of anglicisms in the formal, technical disciplines of written French – everyday spoken French is less affected, so that you can still get a hotdog in a snack bar in the centre of Paris. More recent purist laws in Poland and Slovakia do not seem to have created a similar statistical effect, but they illustrate a sense of linguistic identity that appears to be on the increase in Europe. (Compare, on a different level, the differentiation of Serbian, Croatian and Bosnian, some twenty years ago regarded as dialects of one language, namely Serbocroatian; the new segregation does not seem to include the purge of English loanwords.)

Older purist traditions are conspicuous in Iceland, which explains the very low figures of anglicisms recorded in the *Dictionary of European Anglicisms*, where the linguistic similarity with Norwegian might have led us to expect very large numbers of takeovers. The scarcity of English loanwords is again a matter of the well-regulated written standard – Icelandic slang, which is not affected by official measures, contains many unique loans not found in other European languages. In other cases, like Finnish and Spanish (Rodriguez 1997), low figures of recorded anglicisms are more difficult to explain – they seem to be due to attitudes combined with reasons inherent in linguistic structures. In Germany, purism has a long tradition (Kirkness 1975; also Thomas 1991); recent concerns voiced by a faction of word-watchers are hard to judge. What appears to be populist fashion reflecting what one might be tempted to call a "linguistic allergy" is mainly aimed at individual fields like advertising and careless code-switching in certain writers' lacking sufficient *sprachgefühl* (cf. Hoberg 2002). Whether the concerns will turn out to develop into more widespread attitudes will remain to be seen – numerically, there is little justification for an alarm, English loanwords in German amounting to less than a third of words taken over from French.

World-wide, voices are heard objecting to the globalisation of power, economy, the media and daily life in general (cf. Ammon 2001). Language is a conspicuous part of such concerns. Objections to borrowing are therefore expressions of a much wider critique, and they are then not easily answered with exclusively linguistic arguments, if they are reflections of a more general and often indistinct ennui.

The concerns summarised above have, then, sparked off various attempts at linguistic cleansing in many languages around the world. Since sociolinguistic conditions and the status of the respective vernaculars/national languages are very diverse, it is difficult to systematise such moves. I will here give a few recurring topics:

– It appears that (populist) objections to foreign words, though directed against loanwords, are in fact frequently based on extreme forms of code-mixing. Arguments tend to be emotional or at least vague, characterising loanwords as "ugly, affected, contradicting national feeling", etc. (cf. Zimmer 1997).
– The political background of instances of purism is illustrated by the fact that not all foreign words are under attack at a given time. While Britons were concerned about Latinisation in the 16th century, Johnson (whose style was

heavily Latinate) objected to French words in the 18th. Where Dutch had a period of cleansing the language from German loans, they have remained relatively open to French – whereas the Flemish see their variety endangered by French and prefer words based on German. German purism of the 19th and 20th centuries stopped at the national borders, so that (e.g. in football terminology) English terms were translated, but survive in Austria and Switzerland.
- Measures taken by institutions tend to affect the written formal language and not so much nonstandard dialect or colloquial levels. This explains the survival of many French loanwords in German regional dialects, or the fact that Icelandic has few anglicisms in printed texts, but many slang terms in everyday (youth and slang) spoken varieties.
- The history of European languages shows that (since purism is connected with political conditions and changing attitudes) there are periods with strong purism followed by more liberal stages.
- Linguistic change affects all parts of a language, and thus includes imported words. Purists might derive some consolation from the fact that many foreign words recorded in early dictionaries have disappeared again, even those which were not ostracised. Such obsolescence is unsurprising in the case of cultural change, as has happened to many loanwords designating 19th century types of vehicles (see Dunger 1909: 7–8).
- If measures are to be taken, calques and semantic extensions might be tried. Most of these tend to be successful if agreeing with the "genius" of the vernacular – although many sound funny at first hearing, and some will ultimately be rejected by the speech community.
- Linguistic legislation should probably be the ultima ratio. It is much better to have usage guided by the cultivated *sprachgefühl* of educated users.

6.5.   What languages gain from contact and borrowing

In spite of the above-mentioned concerns voiced by purists, who may claim that foreign influences serve to pollute a language, there is no doubt that the major effects of contacts are beneficial. The *ausbau* of, say, European vernaculars to fully-fledged standard languages, esp. from the Renaissance onwards, could not have happened without foreign help, esp. from Latin (and later on, French). It is important to realise that even languages largely resisting large-scale borrowing (such as Icelandic) have expanded mainly as a consequence of stimuli from abroad, and in imitation or emulation of Latin, French, German, Danish and English. (Indirect) Borrowing may here be found in disguise, but is nevertheless widely attested.

English itself is, among the languages of wider communication, certainly the one most thoroughly affected by contact-related influences. Language mixing and borrowing has contributed to massive structural changes in its phonological system, close contact with Scandinavian varieties has arguably speeded up simplifications in inflection and, as a consequence, in its syntax, and the takeover of foreign lexis, esp. from Latin and French, has made its claim to being a Germanic language questionable for many observers. This has made it richer and more flexible than most other languages and contributed to its adequateness as a world language.

Although concerns about the quality of one's mother tongue are necessary and welcome, borrowing has done more good at least in languages well established and developed – and it is in these that criticism was and is being most frequently voiced.

7. Conclusion

This chapter has (at least implicitly) shown how important the issue of borrowing is for applied linguistics. It may be useful to summarise these connections under a few headings:

Stylistics: Linguistic and cultural contact tends to provide languages with a greater choice in lexis, syntactical patterns and pragmatics. Most frequently more "respectable" registers are added whose correct and situationally appropriate uses can become social markers. Too plain language for formal functions is as open to criticism as is the inappropriate use of "refined" diction employing foreign words or patterns (often incompletely integrated and ridiculed as a genteel characteristic of social climbers).

Text types: Borrowing is frequently guided by the need to acquire new text types for the mother tongue (in vernaculars in Renaissance Europe as well as in African or Asian languages in more recent times) or it is determined by fashion and prestige. In many cases, the results of borrowing remain text-type specific – and where they are employed outside these domains, they are felt to be specimens of register misuse. Results of relevant research to such problems promise to have consequences for language use in the media and for the effectiveness of (or restrictions in) communication.

Sociolinguistics: Misuses of elements borrowed from foreign languages (e.g. incorrect pronunciations, or affected speech too closely imitating foreign articulation) are often indicators of deficient education and thereby of social class. For historical periods inadequacies like malapropisms, affected overuse of "unnecessary" foreign words and the like are major sources of sociohistorical information (however stereotypical the data may be). Attitudes research would also need to include speakers'/writers' and listeners'/readers' opinions on codemixing and code-switching, and on purism as against openness to the use of earlier loanwords and ongoing borrowing.

Language teaching: It follows that the planning of the teaching of adequate forms for the foreign language learner (and possibly language planning in a more general sense) will have to take great pains to correlate stylistic choices, with particular reference to originally borrowed items, with the intended uses.

Reference books: Apart from careful distinctions of registers and styles in learners' grammars, usage dictionaries should provide not only information on spelling, pronunciation, meaning and normative grammar, but make special reference to the proper handling of foreign-derived items. Whether this is done in the form of apodictic rules (as in the early tradition of the Fowler guidebooks, see the development of advice on proper usage in the editions of 1926, 1965 and 1996) or in a more liberal framework will depend on the readers' expectations and requirements.

Translation and interpreting: Even where similar histories of contact have affected sets of languages in comparable ways, the results cannot be expected to be identical. There is a particular need for translation studies to establish the stylistic and semantic equivalence of borrowed elements (including *faux amis*) – where equivalence of text types and registers can be shown to exist across language boundaries. Such analysis should include a reliable description of restrictions showing where borrowed items are confined to particular regions, social classes, modes, fields, and specific styles.

References

Alladina, Safder and Viv Edwards (eds.)
    1991   *Multilingualism in the British Isles*. 2 vols. London: Longman.
Ammon, Ulrich
    2001   *The Dominance of English as a Language of Science. Effects on Other Languages and Language Communities*. Berlin: Mouton de Gruyter.
Baugh, Albert C. and Thomas Cable
    2002   *A History of the English Language*. 5th ed. Upper Saddle River, NJ: Prentice Hall.
Bloomfield, Leonard
    1933   *Language*. Chicago: University Press.
Branford, Jean
    1991   *A Dictionary of South African English*. 4th ed. Oxford: Oxford University Press.
Braun, Peter (ed.)
    1979   *Fremdwort-Diskussion*. München: Fink.
Bynon, Theodora
    1977   *Historical Linguistics*. Cambridge: Cambridge University Press.
Bynon, Theodora
    1981   *Historische Linguistik*. München: Beck.

Calvet, Louis-Jean
    1974   *Linguistique et colonialisme: petit traité de glottophagie.* Paris.
Campe, Johann Heinrich
    1801   *Wörterbuch zur Erklärung und Verdeutschung der unserer Sprache aufgedrungenen fremden Ausdrücke.* Braunschweig.
Carstensen, Broder and Ulrich Busse
    1993–1995   *Anglizismen-Wörterbuch.* 3 vols. Berlin: Mouton de Gruyter.
Dunger, Hermann
    1882   *Wörterbuch von Verdeutschungen entbehrlicher Fremdwörter.* Leipzig: Teubner.
Dunger, Hermann
    1909   *Engländerei in der deutschen Sprache.* 2nd ed. Berlin: Verlag des Allgemeinen Deutschen Sprachvereins.
Eppler, Eva M.
    1994   Code-switching in 'Emigranto'. *Vienna English Working Papers* 32: 75–93.
Etiemble, René
    1964   *Parlez-vous franglais?* Paris: Gallimard.
Ferguson, Charles A.
    1959   Diglossia. *Word* 15: 325–340.
Finkenstaedt, Thomas and Dieter Wolff
    1973   *Ordered Profusion. Studies in Dictionaries and the English Lexicon.* Heidelberg: Winter.
Fishman, Joshua, Andrew W. Conrad and Alma Rubal-Lopez (eds.)
    1996   *Post-Imperial English. Status Change in Former British and American Colonies 1940–1990.* Berlin: Mouton de Gruyter.
Förster, Max
    1921   Keltisches Wortgut im Englischen. In: *Festschrift Liebermann*, 119–243. Halle/Saale: Niemeyer.
Fowler, H.W.
    1926   *A Dictionary of Modern English Usage.* 2nd ed. 1965, 3rd ed. 1996. Oxford: Clarendon.
Geipel, John
    1971   *The Viking Legacy.* Newton Abbot: David & Charles.
Goebl, Hans, Peter H. Nelde, Zdeněk Starý and Wolfgang Wölck (eds.)
1996/1997   *Kontaktlinguistik. Contact Linguistics. Linguistique de contact.* Berlin: Mouton de Gruyter.
Görlach, Manfred
    1990   Middle English – a creole? In: Manfred Görlach, *Studies in the History of the English Language*, 65–78. Heidelberg: Winter.
Görlach, Manfred
    1991   *Introduction to Early Modern English.* Cambridge: Cambridge University Press.
Görlach, Manfred
    1997   *The Linguistic History of English.* London: Macmillan.
Görlach, Manfred (ed.)
    2001   *A Dictionary of European Anglicisms.* Oxford: Oxford University Press.
Görlach, Manfred (ed.)
    2002a   *English in Europe.* Oxford: Oxford University Press.

Görlach, Manfred (ed.)
    2002b   *An Annotated Bibliography of European Anglicisms.* Oxford: Oxford University Press.
Görlach, Manfred
    2002c   *A Textual History of Scots.* Heidelberg: Winter.
Görlach, Manfred
    2003   *English Words Abroad.* Amsterdam: Benjamins.
Haugen, Einar
    1973   Bilingualism, language contact and immigrant languages in the United States: A research report 1956–1970. *Current Trends in Linguistics* 10: 505–591.
Hoberg, Rudolf (ed.)
    2002   *Deutsch-Englisch-Europäisch. Impulse für eine neue Sprachpolitik.* Mannheim: Dudenverlag.
Holm, John
    1988/1989   *Pidgins and Creoles.* 2 vols. Cambridge: University Press.
Jones, R. F.
    1953   *The Triumph of the English Language.* Stanford: California University Press.
Käsmann, Hans
    1961   *Studien zum kirchlichen Wortschatz des Mittelenglischen 1100–1350.* Tübingen: Niemeyer.
Kibbee, Douglas A.
    1991   *For to Speke Frenche Trewely. The French Language in England 1000–1600. Its Status, Description and Instruction.* Amsterdam: Benjamins.
Kirkness, Alan
    1975   *Zur Sprachreinigung im Deutschen 1769–1871.* Tübingen: Niemeyer.
Leisi, Ernst and Christian Mair
    1999   *Das heutige Englisch: Wesenszüge und Probleme.* 8th ed. Heidelberg: Winter.
Liebknecht, Walter
    1874   *Volksstaat-Fremdwörterbuch.* Stuttgart: Dietz.
Maurais, Jacques and Michael A. Morris (eds.)
    2003   *Languages in a Globalizing World.* Cambridge: Cambridge University Press.
Munske, Horst-Haider and Alan Kirkness (eds.)
    1996   *Eurolatein. Das griechische und lateinische Erbe in den europäischen Sprachen.* Tübingen: Niemeyer.
Picone, Michael D.
    1996   *Anglicisms, Neologisms and Dynamic French.* Amsterdam: Benjamins.
Plümer, Nicole
    2000   *Anglizismus – Purismus – Sprachliche Identität. Eine Untersuchung zu den Anglizismen in der deutschen und französischen Muttersprache.* Frankfurt am Main: Lang.
Polenz, Peter von
    1979   Fremdwort und Lehnwort sprachwissenschaftlich betrachtet. In: Peter Braun (ed.), *Fremdwort-Diskussion,* 9–31. München: Fink.

Rodriguez, Gonzales Felix
   1996   *Spanish Loanwords in the English Language. A Tendency towards Hegemony Reversal.* Berlin: Mouton de Gruyter.
Rodriguez, Gonzales Felix
   1997   *Nuevo Diccionario de Anglicismos.* Madrid: Gredos.
Romaine, Suzanne
   1989   *Bilingualism.* Oxford: Oxford University Press.
Scheler, Manfred
   1977   *Der englische Wortschatz.* Berlin: Erich Schmidt.
Serjeantson, Mary S.
   1935   *A History of Foreign Words in English.* London: Routledge and Kegan Paul.
Starnes, deWitt T. and Gertrude E. Noyes
   1946   *The English Dictionary from Cawdrey to Johnson.* Chapel Hill, NC: University of North Carolina Press.
Straßner, Erich
   1995   *Deutsche Sprachkultur. Von der Barbarensprache zur Weltsprache.* Tübingen: Niemeyer.
Thody, Philip
   1995   *Le Franglais. Forbidden English, Forbidden American: Law, Politics and Language in Contemporary France. A Study in Loan Words and National Identity.* London: Athlone.
Thomas, George
   1991   *Linguistic Purism.* London: Longman.
Thomason, Sarah Grey (ed.)
   2001   *Contact Languages. A Wider Perspective.* Amsterdam: Benjamins.
Thomason, Sarah and Terence Kaufman
   1988   *Language Contact, Creolization and Genetic Linguistics.* Berkeley: University of California Press.
Tournier, Jean
   1998   *Les mots anglais du français.* Paris: Belin.
Tristram, Hildegard
   2004   Diglossia in Anglo-Saxon England, or what was spoken Old English like? *Studia Anglica Posnaniensia* 40: 87–110.
Truchot, Claude (ed.)
   1986   *Langue française – langue anglaise: Contacts et conflits.* Strasbourg: GEPE.
Viereck, Wolfgang and Wolf-Dietrich Bald (eds.)
   1986   *English in Contact with Other Languages.* Budapest: Ak. Kiadó.
Weinreich, Uriel
   1953   *Languages in Contact. Findings and Problems.* New York, The Hague: Mouton.
Zimmer, Dieter E.
   1997   *Neuanglodeutsch: Über die Pidginisierung der Sprache.* In: Dieter E. Zimmer, *Deutsch und anders. Die Sprache im Modernisierungsfieber*, 7–85. Reinbek: Rowohlt.

24. Political correctness and freedom of speech

Mary Talbot

1. Introduction

Consider the following two resignations. Both were front-page news generating considerable media attention; both were in response to an alleged racial slur in the form of real or imagined use of a variant of *nigger*. The first took place in the USA in 1999. During a discussion about funds with three staff, two of whom were black, a white mayoral aide in Washington DC, David Howard, mentioned that as a team they were going to have to be "niggardly" with them. Seeing a shocked expression, he immediately apologised at any offence given; however, rumours about a racist slur spread rapidly. In the absence of a recording of this event, one can only speculate on the phonetic distinction – presence or absence of an unreleased voiced alveolar plosive – between the word uttered and the word anticipated. One can, however, safely assume the hearers' lived experience of racism as part of the context in which they understood their daily interactions with white people. This presumably triggered a racist understanding of the unfamiliar word *niggardly*.

Anthony Williams, the recently appointed black mayor, initially accepted Howard's resignation on the basis of an allegation that he had made a racist remark. He subsequently offered Howard his job back, saying that he had acted "too hastily" in accepting the resignation (Randall 1999) and observing that Washington has a "racial climate that needs a lot of work" (Williams, quoted in Martin 1999).

This *'niggardly' flap*, as CNN called it, was picked up with enthusiasm and derision by the media. Newspapers and the Internet bristled with dictionary definitions and snippets of information about the etymology of *niggardly*. Readers were informed of synonyms like *miserly* and *stingy*, of cognates in Old Icelandic, and so on. Meanwhile Howard's black staff were berated for their ignorance of English. A lengthy posting, for example, claimed that "racial intolerance, ignorance, and misplaced political correctness have cost a white mayoral aide his job" and characterised it as an "insane and sad example of ignorance and racial intolerance" (Adversity.Net™). Presenting it as an example of "reverse discrimination", the writer pointed out that "Washington, DC's population is 60% black, and it's [sic] citizens have been very critical of Mayor Williams for "not being black enough" – especially because he hired several well-qualified whites to help him run this troubled city" (Adversity.Net™). This needs to been seen in the context of ongoing conflict over varieties of English. The same newsgroup regularly features pieces on Ebonics; for example, an outraged article entitled "Ebonics Jokes to be Illegal! EEOC [Equal Employment Opportunity Commission] to America: No Free Speech Here!". In short, an uncomfortable moment among a group of City Hall employees became an example of the worst excesses of political correctness, while simultaneously being used as a pretext for displays of linguistic capital and as a support for claims about black discrimination against white. Another thing the *'niggardly' flap* clearly did in the US context was highlight potential pun material for further racist offence. As a columnist put it at the time: "Any bets on how many newly vocab-enhanced pinheads somewhere in America asked black waitresses not to be 'niggardly' with the coffee this week?" (Poniewozik 1999)

The second example of a resignation involving a racist slur took place in the UK in 2004. Ron Atkinson, a "soccer pundit" in the British media, was the commentator for a match where Chelsea lost to Monaco, in a live broadcast to expatriate listeners on an Arab channel. Unaware that the microphone was still live after the match had ended, Atkinson launched into an angry rant, focused primarily on the poor performance of one player, Marcel Desailly, whom he called (according to the *Sun* newspaper) "a f****** lazy big n****r" (Syson 2004). In sharp contrast with the previous example, political correctness did not feature prominently in coverage of the event by the media. There were no occurrences of the expression in the initial coverage in the national press. Occasional mentions of PC, when they did occur, served specifically in denials of it. For example, a regional paper, the *Northern Echo*, quoted a comment from Piara Powar, Director of *Kick It Out* (football's anti-racist campaign): "I have to say, regardless of his record, that sort of terminology is just simply out of bounds. We are not interested in running a political correctness campaign, but there are certain things in 2004 which should not be uttered" (*Northern Echo*, April 22, 2004).

The press used "PC" extensively in coverage of the former, where the charge of racism was unfounded, but not in the latter, where the racism of the invective was very evident. I have chosen them as convenient illustrations for two related points: that the term PC is principally used by its detractors and that it is viewed negatively. It is unlikely to be mentioned in recommendations about inclusivity, ethics and general good practice in the media (e.g. Alia 2004). This chapter explores the origins and use of this contentious term and the complex social context in which it has come to be set in direct opposition to freedom of speech.

2. Origins of "political correctness"

The phrase "political correctness" (PC) seems to have emerged among the political New Left in USA. In Ruth Perry's "Short history of the term *politically correct*", she identifies the first printed citation in a discussion of sexism in black politics in an article by Toni Cade: "A man cannot be politically correct and chauvinist too" (Cade 1970; cited in Perry 1992: 73). As Perry observes, however, the expression was not predominantly used in this straightforward way. More often, it was used ironically, in a self-mocking way: "[...] *politically correct* has always been double-edged. No sooner was it invoked as a genuine standard for sociopolitical practice [...] than it was mocked as purist, ideologically rigid, and authoritarian. [...] within the New Left it was nearly always used with a double consciousness" (Perry 1992: 77). Ralph Ellison's novel, *The invisible man,* perhaps provides representations of the kind of self-righteous usage among American Maoists that was the ultimate object of satire. The following is an example:

> "In my opinion the speech was wild, hysterical, politically irresponsible and dangerous", he snapped. "And worse than that, it was *incorrect*!" He pronounced "incorrect" as though the term described the most heinous crime imaginable, and I stared at him open-mouthed, feeling a vague guilt.
> (Ellison 1965[1947]: 282)

The term, then, is a curious one. It is difficult to find usage that is both positive and non-ironic. In a negative sense, it has been used across the political spectrum since the 1980s. In Stuart Hall's account of the first time he heard the expression, in the United States, it was used in a warning about the activities of the right-wing "Moral Majority":

> I was warned by the organisers of a conference that I should be careful about what I said because, in the new climate of the times following the Reagan election, the right had established campus committees to monitor speakers and take notes on everything said in lectures which could be interpreted as undermining the American Constitution or sapping the moral fibre of the nation's brightest and best. Here, PC was clearly part and parcel of the 1980s backlash against the 1960s. It was the right and the Moral Majority who were trying to prescribe what could and could not be thought and said in academic classrooms.
> (Hall 1994: 165)

It was also used in Marxist criticism of the first Clinton administration and its "windowdressing": "PC affects to compensate for discrimination, but in reality it trivialises the problem. [...] The Clinton generation of ruling Americans are concerned not with equality, but with covering up the appearance of inequality. The tortuous terminology arises out of attempts to mask the real injustice in American society" (Heartfield 1993: 323). However, it seems to be most widely used in criticism from the political right: criticism of perceived attacks on tradition and civil liberties, especially the freedom of speech enshrined in the First Amendment of the US Constitution. In an account of the PC phenomenon, Deborah Cameron documents the emergence of an "anti-PC discourse" (Cameron 1995: 122–130). The development of this "anti-PC discourse" needs to be placed in historical context as counter-resistance, from the early 1980s onwards, to the successful interventions of feminist and anti-racist movements. Following the social struggles of the 1960s, civil rights movements began to make their mark on institutions in the United States, bringing issues of inclusivity and ethics on to agendas everywhere. In some universities, for instance, minorities were actively encouraged to enrol by means of affirmative action programmes; as a result of student pressure, faculties began to look critically at their ethnocentric curriculum content. In public organisations, codes of practice and style guides were written that politicised practices previously seen as neutral. Backed up by new legislation, language reform measures set out to stimulate social change by making people aware of discriminatory practices (see also Hellinger and Pauwels, this vol.). All this attention to equity, inclusivity and ethics brought about shifts in taboo (e.g. the term *nigger* became the toxic N-word at the heart of the two controversial resignations above). In 1979, Reaganite and Thatcherite policies began to bring in a radically different agenda of "modernisation" and the dismantling of socialism; it is in this period that "anti-PC discourse" began to emerge. As Robin Lakoff (2001) observes, language reform measures posed a threat since they placed some control over representations, especially naming practices, into the hands of the less powerful, and promoted "new ways of using and seeing language and its products, all of which share one property":

> [...] they are forms of language devised by and for, and to represent the worldview and experience of, groups formerly without the power to create language, make interpretations, or control meaning. Therein lies their terror and hatefulness to those who formerly possessed these rights unilaterally, who gave PC its current meaning and made it endemic in our conversation.
> (Lakoff 2001: 91)

In Foucauldian terms, this fear is understandable as the redeployment of the classificatory power circulating in public discourses. The pejorative label of "PC" became a way of insinuating criticism, of delegitimising this new-found classificatory power.

There is some evidence that use of the expression went into decline in the mid 1990s, slightly earlier in USA than in Britain. A US database study charts its decline from 1995 (cf. Lakoff 2001: 94–100). In the context of the United Kingdom, a corpus-based study of three British newspapers indicates a sharp decline after the 1997 Labour landslide (Johnson, Culpeper, and Suhr 2003). These two studies seem to be recording fluctuations according to the political climate. Two other studies using corpora reveal the relatively late arrival of the expression in Germany and France, in both cases in a fully-fledged anti-PC discourse, but with interesting local differences. In their study of the German newspaper *Die Welt*, Sally Johnson and Stephanie Suhr (2003) note that many of the issues and views that come to be labelled *politisch korrekt* had been in circulation a good many years before the PC phenomenon emerged. They observe that post-unification Germany had a "continued and problematical quest for a reconfigured sense of national identity that could be so readily slotted into discourses of 'political correctness'" (2003: 52). It was "a very German theme with all the classic 'PC' ingredients: the purported taboo surrounding German historical consciousness, the latter allegedly subject to the intellectual stranglehold of the *Gutmenschen* 'do-gooders' and their culture of *Betroffenheit* 'guilt-ridden perplexity', all of which were stifling democratic discourse and preventing Germany from shaking off the past" (2003: 52). In his study of the French newspaper *Le Monde*, Michael Toolan (2003) found that *le politiquement correct* tended to be used in far less intense cultural commentary than elsewhere, sometimes marked as foreign and not used in relation to political issues.

In the anglophone world including, relatively recently, Australia, anti-PC discourse is still in regular use to vilify concerns about social inequity and initiatives designed to address them. In particular, it is still utilised by right-wing politicians. In the summer of 2004 William Hague, former British Conservative Party leader, declared that "we must never put political correctness before the safety of the British people" (*Any Questions*, Radio 4, July 3, 2004). This declaration came in response to concern expressed by community leaders about police "stop and search" measures since the Terrorism Act, because of the disproportionately high number of young Muslim men involved. The referent for political correctness here is presumably Muslim concern about the police racism underlying their targeting of young Muslims. The same issue underlies an election promise by the neo-fascist British National Party: "The BNP would take the Politically Correct handcuffs off the police and put them on the criminals" (BNP, May 2005). The simple choice set up by Hague in the rhetorical opposition of PC and public safety is patently absurd, yet his contrastive pair functions as a clear attack on anti-racist initiatives. He does not make a contentious claim that the anti-racist move is dangerous, but identifying it as PC adds negativity and frames it as excessive and misguided.

3. Understanding political correctness: Central concepts and theoretical approaches

Three themes central to understanding political correctness are negativity, restriction and exaggeration. Excessiveness or "going too far" seems to be built into it, as part of its semantic content. Consider the following, from press coverage of a university ethics panel, which also goes on to establish PC in direct opposition to freedom of speech: "It is not oversensitivity, it is not political correctness. There is no suppression of free speech" (cited in Baty 2004). The establishment of a direct and deliberate opposition to freedom of speech is common; one critic, for instance, refers to the "anti-free-speech movement" in universities (Hentoff 1992: 222). I return to the issue of free speech below.

PC has been held responsible for every imaginable form of restriction, well beyond concerns about racism and sexism. A BBC website celebrates two TV chefs on the grounds that "They smoked! They drank! They used dollops of lard!" so that they "served up the perfect antidote to PC cooking shows". Restrictions attributed to PC include complaints about loud music in pubs ("If you think the music's too loud, you're too politically correct!"; pub blackboard) and health-conscious TV chefs eschewing the use of cream ("and not only is it delicious, it's also politically correct"; *Food & Drink*, BBC1, June 1998). Such occurrences are frequently derisory and contrived. A "news" item about a hotdog-eating record made possible a link, humorously intended, between PC and dietary considerations. At a time when childhood obesity was making the headlines, the presenter expressed mock concern about the news item "putting out messages that aren't PC" (*Today,* Radio 4, July 2004).

Ridicule of perceived excesses, regardless of origins, scope or influence, is central to jibes against PC; they are by no means always intended to be humorous, however. There is a comical mixed metaphor in the following piece of British tabloid journalism but it seems intended to stimulate indignation rather than to raise a laugh:

> POLITICAL correctness, the terrible blight afflicting our once free land, has now even extended its slimy tentacles to pub signs.
> A painting that has stood outside the Labour in Vain inn at Yarnfield, Staffordshire, for 150 years has been taken down on the brewery's orders because three schoolgirls complained that it was racist.
> The sign depicted a couple trying to scrub a black boy white at the village pump.
> We detest racism in all its forms, but this was nothing more than an ancient JOKE.
> Britain is in grave danger these days of losing one of its most precious assets.
> *Its sense of humour.*
> (*Daily Star*, 11 Jan 1994)

In a hyperbolic assault against objections to a 150 year-old pub sign, the article presents an unwieldy metaphor of PC as a tentacle-extending blight. It is presupposed that the country is no longer "free" as a consequence of the "affliction", or blight, of political correctness. An oppressive power is attributed to three schoolgirls (the causal connective, "because"); at the same time, criticism of the pub sign is established as absurd and unreasonable (the exception marking adverbial, "even"). In the last single-sentence paragraph, "racism in all its forms" is set against an "ancient joke". Here the pre-modifier "ancient" seems to add legitimacy, while the post-modifier in "all its forms" works to exclude "joke" from the category of "racism". Racism is a new taboo, leading to its indirect expression and to its denial (see van Dijk 1992; Lynn and Lea 2003).

Some accounts of the "evils" of PC go to apocalyptic extremes, even presenting it as life-threatening. To date, the most extreme example of this is when Republican commentators in the United States held it accountable for the terrorist attacks of September 11th (e.g. Ruddy 2001). Lakoff's reflections on press reports of menacing PC "truth Squads" at Berkeley are illuminating. The press strategies used to evoke an atmosphere of fear surrounding inclusive-language initiatives on campus – vague generalities, veiled hints and unsubstantiated claims – were precisely "the ways of the Thought Police and the McCarthyites: the anonymous smear, the whispered innuendo, the hinted-at menace" (Lakoff 2001: 99).

The importance of the culture industries in understanding PC cannot be overestimated. Broadcasting and print journalism, in particular, are major, influential domains of social practice that increasingly mediate other domains. They have given wide circulation to the reframing, as forms of oppression, of initiatives intended to promote social justice: transforming them into "reverse discrimination" (as in the *'niggardly' flap* above) and censorship. Notions of press freedom, especially, are set up in opposition to PC. The new taboos are often claimed to "stifle debate". There are widespread claims that PC "closes down" discussion and prevents rational thinking. Norman Fairclough (2003: 21) points to an "apparent performative contradiction" in such critiques of PC, since they "would seem themselves to be instances of the sort of cultural politics which is the object of critique"; that is, they are engaging in precisely what they disparage in others. And, after all, claims about stifled debate are at odds with the vast amount of coverage devoted to such disparagement.

Two sociolinguistic observations are relevant here and neither of them is controversial. Firstly, language is norm-governed. Style guides and other initiatives are sets of norms; they are not to everyone's taste, indeed, but they are norms, nevertheless. In the case of style guides promoting anti-sexist, anti-racist and related agendas, they politicise stylistic choices; this is uncomfortable for their detractors, who respond by criticising them as excessive, unnecessary and ridiculous. My second sociolinguistic observation is that all languages and all cultures practise avoidance. Problematic social issues, conflict, cultural taboos and so on inevitably lead to great care about wording. This is an issue of classification and by no means unique to PC concerns. One only has to consider the so-called "mother-in-law" languages – special registers for men when addressing older female relations in the Aboriginal languages of Australia (cf. Haviland 1979). A current example is contemporary Chinese sensitivity over geographical boundaries between Mainland China and Taiwan; difficulties in naming them as national or regional, frequently lead to careful, euphemistic reference to "cross-strait relations" in an effort to avoid adopting a position about Taiwan's contested political status as a sovereign state (e.g. Dickson and Chao 2002).

Before going on to engage with the theoretical issue of contemporary so-called PC as one form of cultural politics alongside others, it seems appropriate to reflect briefly on this freedom of speech, and in particular press freedom, that critics claim to be protecting in contesting PC initiatives (see also Fish 1992). In modern democracies, the media serve a vital function. In principle, journalists are committed to democratic principles in relation to the government, hence to provision of a diversity of sources of opinion about it. This function can be idealised as provision of "a robust, uninhibited, and wide-open marketplace of ideas, in which opposing views may meet, contend, and take each other's measure" (Gurevitch and Blumler 1990: 269). Needless to say, this ideal is far distant from the reality, given the extent to which the modern media are dominated both by two-party politics and by media corporations and their capitalist objectives, creating a tension between democratic and economic roles (Gurevitch and Blumler 1990: 272). Historically, freedom of speech is closely linked to the right to dissent – the democratic ideal inscribed in the US First Amendment – and needs to be understood in the eighteenth-century context of establishment of religious and political freedom in the "New World":

> Congress shall make no law respecting an establishment of religion, or prohibiting the free exercise thereof; or abridging the freedom of speech, or of the press; or the right of the people peaceably to assemble, and to petition the Government for a redress of grievances.
> (The First Amendment to the US Constitution)

To understand this proclamation, it is useful to consider the religious/political climate (the two being inextricable) of the "Old World" that had been left behind by early citizens of the United States. In 1703, the outspoken views of Daniel Defoe, an English writer and dissenter, were an offence. They led to his conviction for seditious pamphleteering for which he served a 7 month sentence in Newgate prison (Drabble and Stringer 1987: 147). Contemporary equivalents are not hard to find (see, for example, the websites of Reporters sans Frontières or the World Press Freedom Committee). In contrast, claims that style guides infringe US citizens' First Amendment rights would seem to be unsubstantiated, given that they deal with such issues as the use of racist epithets and, as Perry and Williams (1992) point out, no one has the right to abuse and harassment: "What has never been true is that one member of an institution has an unrestrained legal right to harass another member and remain in the good graces of the institution" (Perry and Williams 1992: 227). Right-wing Americans' championing of their First Amendment needs to be taken with a pinch of salt in any case, as Lakoff makes clear in pointing out that one critic of PC "outrages" (e.g. controversial campus sexual conduct guidelines) simultaneously supported a ruling to suppress any mention whatsoever of abortion as a legal procedure by medical staff (Lakoff 2001: 114). The ugly irony here scarcely needs pointing out.

The phenomenon that has been called "PC" needs to be theoretically understood as one form of wider social practices. Stuart Hall (1994: 168) argues that it is a product of the "culturing" of politics; that is, of the cultural, discursive dimensions of politics that are now familiar across the political arena. Whether engaging with issues of gender, ethnicity, sexual orientation, age or disability, the importance of representation is now widely recognised. Writing from the perspective of cultural studies, Hall remarks on, firstly, how this recognition of the importance of representation is underpinned by an understanding at some level of the relationships between discourse, power and reality and, secondly, on what he sees as a paradoxical similarity between the cultural agendas of the New Right and PC, in that they both understand "that the political game is often won or lost on the terrain of [...] moral and cultural issues, apparently far removed from [...] 'politics'" (Hall 1994: 167–169). In a related observation, Fairclough (2003) remarks on the widespread interest in language change and cultural change, with the aim of bringing about social change. Far from being unique to "PC fanatics", interventions into people's ways of using language are extremely common. Citing the example of the re-labelling of "bank accounts" as "financial products", Fairclough points out that attempts to tinker with the way people think about things by engineering shifts in lexis is by no means the exclusive domain of supposed PC practitioners (2003: 21). Other British examples are the re-labelling of passengers on public transport and patients in National Health Service as "customers". The significant difference is that PC is marked off as "political", while, from a liberal perspective, commodification and marketisation are not. From a political economy perspective, however, they clearly are profoundly political. Fairclough identifies a covert neo-liberal project for social change: "the generalization of markets and the commodity form to finance, to public services, and indeed to most of contemporary social life which such re-labelling is a part of is an eminently 'political' change" (2003: 21). What is involved is not simply a matter of superficial label changing; the shift is discursive. A key difference between covert neo-liberal manipulation and the "linguistic engineering" done by feminists and anti-racists is that the latter is done openly.

4. Controversial issues

As will be apparent from the above, the key controversy surrounding PC is whether we should be accepting the term at all. Indeed, my own unwillingness to embrace it has made this chapter a challenge not unlike shadowboxing. A particular difficulty is setting limits on what kinds of belief, concept, practice or agenda it does/does not encompass. The term is heavily implicated in the discrediting of a particular form of cultural politics by the political right. One role of applied linguistics is to draw attention to this peculiar situation and theorise it, as indeed I have undertaken to do above. A key issue is how to sidestep the snarl word "PC" while continuing to tackle discrimination. In the current context of highly successful anti-PC discourse, there is some debate both about how to combat it and about the continued promotion of anti-sexist, anti-racist and related initiatives, the efficacy of overt linguistic engineering and so on.

Hall does not take issue with the existence of PC but argues that, as a strategy for social change, it is ineffective. He is critical of its "vanguardist", rather than hegemonic, tactic, arguing that it is insensitive to the "'educative' perception of politics, and of the winning of consent to the effective pursuit of the 'culture wars'" (Hall 1994: 178). Perceiving a grain of truth in claims of stifled debate, he remarks that a "strategy designed to silence problems without bringing them out and dealing with them is dealing with difficult issues at the level of symptom not cause" (Hall 1994: 180). He is arguing, then, that aiming to impose a new regime of truth in a unilateral fashion – rather than arguing over the issues in an attempt to persuade – is an ineffective way of winning people over to one's point of view. I would certainly agree with the latter point; however, he writes about PC and political strategy in such general terms that it is impossible to determine precisely what strategy he is characterising as "designed to silence problems". His target is not at all clear. Moreover, he assumes an unlikely degree of unity and shared purpose among PCers. Advocates of Critical Language Awareness (CLA) in the 1990s purported to engage in denaturalisation, in stimulating argument not gagging it. CLA developed as a response to Language Awareness work in British educational linguistics. It advocated explicit attention to unequal relations of power, particularly when they are covert, as "a prerequisite for effective democratic citizenship [...] as an *entitlement* for citizens, especially children developing towards citizenship in the educational system" (Fairclough 1992: 3). But style guide writers in the same period may not have shared this concern, if only for practical reasons to do with the encoding of norms and the overt "linguistic engineering" tactics involved.

Public institutions have codes of practice, and often style guides, that are mindful of the law, often explicitly referencing equal opportunities concerns, e.g., the University of Sunderland's "Equal Opportunities: A guide to good practice and the use of language". This guide presents it as a duty of all staff and students to "combat discriminatory structures and practice". Very much in "civil discourse" mode, it places emphasis on respecting others and being "sensitive to their sensitivities". Reference to legal issues is implicit throughout, most explicit in a section on sexual orientation (quoting from the Open University's guide, in fact):

> As equal members of society, lesbians and gay men should be described in terms that do not trivialise or demean them, do not encourage discrimination or distorted images of their lives, do not sensationalise their activities, or imply illegality. Nor should they be excluded: by omitting their experiences – where different – course and other materials do not validate them, and imply that they are not worth including. Don't introduce issues of sexual orientation gratuitously; but, where it is relevant, include it in a fair and objective way.

Every year a few undergraduates complain about this guide, no doubt particularly provoked by the authoritarian use of imperatives and obligation modality throughout. These students would seem to be responding to the guide as a vanguardist tactic by university staff to impose a disagreeable set of values upon them. In general, however, it seems to serve an educative function; my students, at least, appear content with it (insofar as they have any view at all) and occasionally, in the context of seminar discussion, some remark on its usefulness in coming to grips with the point of non-discriminatory representational practices. They would seem to accept its recommendations as commonsensical, that is to say, for them it functions hegemonically. The different modes of engagement with the guide can be understood in terms of the discursive positions occupied in each case.

Institutional style guides and codes of practice are liberal, not radical, in their objectives. Sunderland's was written by a scholar somewhat versed in critical forms of applied linguistics, sufficient for reference to the combating of discriminatory structures and practice to sit a little uneasily alongside the liberal civil discourse of sensitivity, fairness and objectivity. Cameron's critique of institutional guidelines in other British universities, and the debate surrounding them, suggests that liberal discourse generally prevails (1995: 132–138).

5. Conclusion

At the heart of the tension between "political correctness" and freedom of speech is a conflict of values. PC is a weapon used in an arena for struggle occupied by a wide range of contestants. A particular minority group can now use newly bestowed power to challenge an opponent's assault; this challenge is sure to be identified as a PC assault on free speech. For example, at a Gay Pride event in Philadelphia in January 2005, an anti-gay Christian group loudly demonstrated their disapproval by declaiming sections of the bible referring to homosexuality as an abomination. Not taking kindly to being called abominations, the gay gathering called the police. The Christian group responded by accusing the gay group of PC tactics, infringing their freedom to read the bible in public (an odd thing about the PC weapon is that it always appears to be in the hand of the victim rather than the assailant). Whether one chooses to live with the label

"PC", what is clear is that, since entering the institutional discourses of social organisations under the driving force of legal power, the anti-discriminatory objectives bringing about redeployment of classificatory power have been and continue to be seriously undermined.

References

Alia, Valerie
    2004   *Media Ethics and Social Change*. Edinburgh: Edinburgh University Press.
Baty, Phil
    2004   'Ethics' ruling raises fears for free speech. *Times Higher Education Supplement*. December 17.
BNP [British National Party]
    2005   Election Communication, Sunderland South Parliamentary Constituency, April.
Cameron, Deborah
    1995   *Verbal Hygiene*. London: Routledge.
Dickson, Bruce and Chien-min Chao (eds.)
    2002   *Assessing the Lee Teng-hui Legacy in Taiwan's Politics: Democractic Consolidation and External Relations*. New York: East Gate Books.
Drabble, Margaret and Jenny Stringer
    1987   *The Concise Oxford Companion to English Literature*. Oxford: Oxford University Press.
Ellison, Ralph
    1965   [1947] *The Invisible Man*. Harmondsworth: Penguin.
Fairclough, Norman
    1992   Introduction. In: Norman Fairclough (ed.), *Critical Language Awareness*. London: Longman.
Fairclough, Norman
    2003   'Political correctness': The politics of culture and language. *Discourse and Society* 14(1): 17–28.
Fish, Stanley
    1992   There's no such thing as free speech, and it's a good thing, too. In: Paul Berman (ed.), *Debating P.C.: The Controversy over Political Correctness on College Campuses*, 231–245. New York: Laurel.
Gurevitch, Michael and Jay G. Blumler
    1990   Political communication systems and democratic values. In: Judith Lichtenberg (ed.), *Democracy and the Mass Media*, 269–289. Cambridge: Cambridge University Press.
Hall, Stuart
    1994   Some 'politically incorrect' pathways through PC. In: Sarah Dunant (ed.), *The War of the Words: The Political Correctness Debate*, 164–184. London: Virago.
Haviland, John B.
    1979   Guugu Yimidhirr brother-in-law language. *Language in Society* 8: 365–393.

Heartfield, James
 1993 The PC presidency. *Living Marxism* 53: 32–33.
Hentoff, Nat
 1992 "Speech codes" on the campus and problems of free speech. In: Paul Berman (ed.), *Debating P.C.: The Controversy over Political Correctness on College Campuses*, 221–234. New York: Laurel.
Johnson, Sally, Jonathan Culpeper and Stephanie Suhr
 2003 From "politically correct councillors" to "Blairite nonsense": Discourses of "political correctness" in three British newspapers. *Discourse and Society* 14(1): 29–48.
Johnson, Sally and Stephanie Suhr
 2003 From "political correctness" to "politische Korrektheit": Discourses of 'PC' in the German newspaper Die Welt. *Discourse and Society* 14(1): 49–68.
Lakoff, Robin
 2001 *The Language War.* Berkeley: University of California Press.
Lynn, Nick and Susan Lea
 2003 'A phantom menace and the new Apartheid': The social construction of asylum-seekers in the United Kingdom. *Discourse and Society* 14(4): 425–452.
Martin, John P.
 1999 Williams to investigate. *Washington Post*, Jan 27.
Perry, Ruth
 1992 A short history of the term *politically correct*. In: Patricia Aufderheide (ed.), *Beyond PC: Toward a Politics of Understanding*, 71–79. St Paul, Minnesota: Graywolf Press.
Perry, Richard and Patricia Williams
 1992 Freedom of hate speech. In: Paul Berman, (ed.), *Debating P.C.: The Controversy over Political Correctness on College Campuses*, 225–230. New York: Laurel.
Poniewozik, James
 1999 So we're all cool with "niggardly" now. Uh … aren't we? *Salon*, Feb 2.
Randall, Gene
 1999 DC aide in 'niggardly' flap will return to City Hall. CNN.com Posted Feb 4.
Ruddy, Christopher
 2001 More CIA revelations – political correctness kills. NewsMax.com Posted Oct 1.
Syson, Neil
 2004 Bigot Ron: Shamed ITV pundit quits over racist slur. *Sun*, April 22.
Toolan, Michael
 2003 Le politiquement correct dans le monde français. *Discourse and Society* 14(1): 69–86.
van Dijk, Teun
 1992 Discourse and the denial of racism. *Discourse and Society* 3(1): 87–118.

Biographical notes

Markus Bieswanger is Assistant Professor of English Linguistics at the Johann Wolfgang Goethe-University, Frankfurt am Main, Germany. His research interests include language contact, language and education, sociolinguistics, contrastive linguistics, and computer-mediated communication. Recent publications include *German Influence on Australian English* (2004) and *Introduction to English Linguistics* (with Annette Becker, 2006).

Jan Blommaert is Professor and Chair of Languages in Education at the Institute of Education, University of London. He is also part-time Professor of African Linguistics and Sociolinguistics at Ghent University, from where he coordinates a large-scale collaboration programme with the University of the Western Cape, South Africa. He has worked on language ideologies, linguistic inequality, literacy and multilingualism in East, Central and Southern Africa as well as in Europe.

Thomas Paul Bonfiglio is William Judson Gaines Professor of Comparative Literature and Linguistics at the University of Richmond, USA. He has published on sociolinguistics, literature and culture, gender studies, philosophy, and psychoanalysis. He is the author of *Race and the Rise of Standard American* (2002) and is currently completing a manuscript on the invention of the native speaker.

Madeleine Brabant (Ph.D. Queensland) is an organisational psychologist in Brisbane, Australia, having completed a postdoctoral fellowship in 2005. Her research focuses on intergroup processes, particularly the language used across gender, generational, and organisational roles. She has a strong ongoing interest in quantitative and qualitative research methodology in language and communication.

Emilia Calaresu is Associate Professor of General and Applied Linguistics at the University of Modena, Italy. She earned her Ph.D. in linguistics from the University of Pavia. Her main research interests and publications are in pragmatics, reporting discourse, spoken text analysis and language policy. Her recent publications include *Testuali parole. La dimensione pragmatica e testuale del discorso riportato* (2004) and, co-edited with Cristina Guardiano and Klaus Hölker, *Italienisch und Deutsch als Wissenschaftssprachen. Bestandsaufnahmen, Analysen, Perspektiven* (2006).

Augusto Carli is Professor of General Linguistics, with a focus on sociolinguistics, ethnolinguistics and applied linguistics, at the University of Modena, Italy. His main research interests and publications are in bilingualism and languages in contact/conflict. Since 2003, he has been president of Associazione Italiana di Linguistica Applicata, the Italian branch of AILA. He has published in *Revue Française de Linguistique Appliquée* (2004) and is co-editor (with Ulrich Ammon) of the *AILA Review* 20 (2007).

Brenda Danet is Professor Emerita of Sociology and Communication, the Hebrew University of Jerusalem, Israel, and a Research Affiliate in the Department of Anthropology, Yale University. She received her Ph.D. in sociology from the University of Chicago in 1970. Her special interests are in language, play and performance online, online adaptations of writing systems, and flaming in English by Hebrew-speaking Israelis. With Susan C. Herring she co-edited *The Multilingual Internet: Language, Culture, and Communication Online* (2007).

John Edwards is Professor of Psychology at St Francis Xavier University, Antigonish, Canada. His research interests are in language, identity and the many ramifications of their relationship. He is on the editorial boards of a dozen language journals, and is the editor of the *Journal of Multilingual and Multicultural Development*. Professor Edwards's own books include *Language in Canada* (1998), *Multilingualism* (1995), *Language, Society and Identity* (1985) and *The Irish Language* (1983).

Guus Extra is Professor of Language and Minorities at Tilburg University, the Netherlands. He is also director of Babylon, Center for Studies of the Multicultural Society (www.uvt.nl/babylon) at Tilburg University. His main publications and research interests are in the domains of immigrant minority languages at home and school, bilingualism, language and education, and language policy. Recent publications include *The Other Languages of Europe* (with Durk Gorter, 2001) and *Urban Multilingualism in Europe* (with Kutlay Yağmur, 2004).

Alwin Fill is Professor of English Language at the University of Graz, Austria. He studied at Innsbruck (Austria), Oxford (England) and Ann Arbor (Michigan, USA). His main research interests are in pragmatics, ecolinguistics, and the relation between language and culture. Together with Peter Mühlhäusler he edited *The Ecolinguistics Reader* (2001). At present he is working on a project about theories of "language and world-view".

Cindy Gallois (Ph.D. Florida) is Professor of Psychology, Deputy Executive Dean, and Director of Research in the Faculty of Social and Behavioural Sciences at The University of Queensland in Brisbane, Australia. She is a Fellow of the Academy of the Social Sciences in Australia. Her research interests encompass intergroup language and communication in health, intercultural, and organisational contexts. She is currently involved in several international research projects on the interactions between health professionals and patients with chronic illness or disabilities.

William C. Gay is Professor of Philosophy at the University of North Carolina at Charlotte, USA. He has a Ph.D. from Boston College, USA. His research interests and publications are in peace and justice studies and global studies. His current work applies his concept of linguistic violence in various arenas of critical discourse analysis. He is co-author of *Capitalism with a Human Face* (1996) and co-editor of *Global Studies Encyclopedia* (2003) and of *Democracy and the Quest for Justice* (2004).

John Gibbons is an Adjunct Professor in the School of Modern Language Studies, University of New South Wales, Australia, having recently retired from the University of Sydney. His main interests are forensic linguistics and bilingualism, and his most recent books are *Forensic Linguistics: An Introduction to Language in the Justice System* (2003), and (with Elizabeth Ramirez) *Maintaining a Minority Language: A Case Study of Hispanic Teenagers* (2004).

Manfred Görlach was Professor of English Language and Medieval Studies at the University of Cologne, Germany, from which he has recently retired. He has published widely in the fields of history of English, varieties of English, English as a world language and text types. He is the founder and editor of *Middle English Texts*, *English World Wide* and *Varieties of English around the World*.

Durk Gorter is a researcher in the sociology of language at the Fryske Akademy in Ljouwert/Leeuwarden, The Netherlands. He is also Professor of Sociolinguistics of Frisian at the Universiteit van Amsterdam (http://home.medewerker.uva.nl/d.gorter/). He is involved in studies of the Frisian language situation and in comparative analysis of European minority languages in the Mercator Education project. On both topics he has published several books and articles (www.mercator-education.eu).

François Grin is Professor of Economics at the School of Translation and Interpretation (ETI) of the University of Geneva, Switzerland, and visiting professor at the University of Lugano. He has served as deputy director of the *European Centre for Minority Issues* (ECMI) in Flensburg, Germany. He specialises in language economics, education economics, and policy evaluation in these areas. His recent publications include *Language Policy Evaluation and the*

European Charter for Regional or Minority Languages (2003) and *L'enseignement des langues étrangères comme politique publique* (2005).

Marlis Hellinger is Professor of English Linguistics at the Johann Wolfgang Goethe-University, Frankfurt am Main, Germany. Her main research interests are in language and gender, contrastive linguistics, contact linguistics, pidgin and creole linguistics and applied linguistics. Among her book publications are the three volumes (together with Hadumod Bußmann) on *Gender across Languages: The Linguistic Representation of Women and Men* (2001/2002/2003).

Susan C. Herring is Professor of Information Science and Linguistics at Indiana University, Bloomington. She has a Ph.D. in Linguistics from the University of California at Berkeley. Her research focuses on the linguistic and social aspects of communication mediated by new technologies, especially with regard to gender, interaction management, and discourse analysis methodologies. She is currently Editor of the Journal of Computer-Mediated Communication. With Brenda Danet she co-edited *The Multilingual Internet: Language, Culture, and Communication Online* (2007).

Andy Kirkpatrick is Professor and Head of the Department of English at the Hong Kong Institute of Education. He has also taught in the field of applied linguistics in Australia, Burma, China, Singapore and the UK. He is currently studying the use of English as a lingua franca in ASEAN and has published in the fields of World Englishes and Chinese discourse and rhetoric.

Isabelle Léglise is a full time Researcher in Linguistics at the French National Centre for Scientific Research (CNRS, CELIA), Paris, where she is head of a program on language contact. Her main research interests and publications are in discourse analysis, sociolinguistics, language contact and epistemology of applied linguistics. Since 2000, she has been engaged in research projects in French Guiana with a special focus on syntactic variation, contact-induced changes, multilingualism and educational issues.

Bettina Migge is Lecturer in Linguistics at University College Dublin, Ireland, and affiliated with the Centre d'Etudes des Langues Indigènes d'Amérique, France. Her main research interests are in language contact, sociolinguistics, applied linguistics and language description. She has published widely on the genesis of the creoles of Suriname and is currently engaged in research projects on language practices in French Guiana, and language and migration in Ireland.

Susanne Mühleisen is Professor of English Linguistics at the University of Bayreuth, Germany. Her main research interests are creole studies, translation and intercultural communication, and English word-formation. She is the author of *Creole Discourse: Exploring Prestige Formation and Change across Caribbean English-lexicon Creoles* (2002) and co-editor of *Politeness and Face in Caribbean Creoles* (2005).

Anne Pauwels is Professor of Linguistics and Dean of the Faculty of Arts, Humanities and Social Sciences at the University of Western Australia. She has a Ph.D. from Monash University, Australia. Her main areas of research include immigrant bilingualism, language policy and planning with specific attention to gender and to the teaching of foreign and community languages in higher education, as well as intercultural communication in professional settings. Her latest book *Boys and Foreign Language Learning* (2006) was co-authored with Jo Carr.

Thomas Ricento is Professor of Applied Linguistics at the University of Texas, San Antonio, USA. His Ph.D. is in applied linguistics from the University of California at Los Angeles. His main research interests and publications are in language policy and language ideologies. His most recent book is *An Introduction to Language Policy* (2006). He has published in *Discourse & Society, Journal of Sociolinguistics* and other leading journals. He is founding co-editor of the *Journal of Language, Identity, and Education*.

Suzanne Romaine is Merton Professor of English Language at the University of Oxford, UK. Her research interests lie primarily in historical linguistics and sociolinguistics, especially in societal multilingualism, linguistic diversity, language change, language acquisition, and language contact. Other areas of interest include corpus linguistics, language and gender, literacy, and bilingual/immersion education. Among her book publications is *Vanishing Voices. The Extinction of the World's Languages*, with Daniel Nettle (2000).

Antonia Rubino is Senior Lecturer in the Department of Italian Studies at the University of Sydney, Australia. Her main research interests and publications are in multilingualism and contact linguistics, with a focus on changes occurring in the Italian language and dialects in the Australian context. She is co-author, with Camilla Bettoni, of *Emigrazione e compartamento linguistico: Un indagine sul trilinguismo dei siciliani e dei veneti in Australia* (1996), and editor of *Using and learning Italian in Australia* (2004).

Vanithamani Saravanan is Associate Professor at the National Institute of Education, Nanyang Technological University, Singapore, Division of English Language and Literature. Her research interests include applied linguistics, bilingualism, and attitudes to Tamil in Singapore. She is co-editor of *Language, Society, and Education in Singapore: Issues and Trends* (1998).

Tove Skutnabb-Kangas, emerita, is with Roskilde University, Department of Languages and Culture, Denmark, and Åbo Akademi, Vasa, Department of Education, Finland. Her major work is on linguistic human rights, endangered languages and linguistic genocide in (indigenous and minority) education, subtractive spread of English, and the relationship between linguistic diversity and biodiversity. For her publications, see http://akira.ruc.dk/~tovesk/.

Mary Talbot (Ph.D. Lancaster) is Reader in Language and Culture at the University of Sunderland, UK, having previously taught at the Universities of Odense in Denmark, and Liverpool and Lancaster in the UK. Her main research interests are in discourse, popular media and gender. Recent publications include *Language and Power in the Modern World* (with Karen Atkinson and David Atkinson, 2003), *Language and Gender* (1998) and *All the World and her Husband: Women in Twentieth-Century Consumer Culture* (with Maggie Andrews, 2000).

Bernadette Watson (Ph.D. Queensland) is an Australian Postdoctoral Fellow in Psychology at The University of Queensland. Her research encompasses health psychology and communication, focusing on inter-role interactions in medical discourse. She is currently involved in large-scale projects on health professional – patient communication, and on the impact of language and communication in clinical handovers on safety. Recent publications include articles on organisational communication (2004) and emotional expression in medical interactions (2004).

Terrence G. Wiley is Professor of Applied Linguistics and Educational Policy at Arizona State University. He received his Ph.D. from the University of Southern California. His research and publications focus on literacy and language diversity, and language policy. He is currently involved in research on community languages in the United States. He is co-editor of the *Journal of Language Identity and Education* and the *International Multilingual Research Journal*.

Language index

A

Aboriginal languages 88, 199, 302f, 335, 366f, 384, 450, 725, 729, 732, 757
Afrikaans 130,135–137, 348, 414f, 729
Afro-Asiatic languages 124
Ainu 187
Akan 304
Akuapem 303f
Albanian 26, 36, 61, 263, 720f
Aluku 319
Amerindian languages (Native American languages) 59, 182, 303, 319f, 570, 725, 729, 732
Anglo–Romani 717
Arabic 20, 34, 36, 60, 63, 91f, 95, 101f, 105–107, 158, 186, 217, 308, 348, 459, 463f, 557–559, 567, 623, 660f, 666, 690, 720
Aramaic 462, 468, 483, 621, 699
Arawak 319
Armenian 36, 60, 63
Asante 303f
Assyrian (Neo-Aramaic, Syriac) 569f, 628
Asturian 24, 198
Aymara 371

B

Bajan 689f
Bajau 159
Bantu languages 124, 127, 131, 135, 137, 729
Bärndütsch 481
Basque 25, 33, 39, 61, 183, 263, 290, 568f, 704
Belize Creole 699
Bengali 159
Berber 26, 36, 308
Bodo 371
Bosnian (*see also* Serbo-Croatian) 36, 743

Breton 24, 183, 627, 693f, 701
Brittonic 724
Bulgarian 17, 61, 624, 721, 734, 736

C

Cappadocian 241
Carib 319
Castilian (*see also* Spanish) 74f, 628, 731
Catalan 24f, 39, 183, 263, 371, 691, 731
Celtic languages 185, 246, 254, 335, 627, 717, 723–725, 727, 731
Chinese 36, 59f, 63f, 70, 75, 77, 95, 105f, 152–157, 159–161, 163–165, 168, 171, 335, 351, 440–447, 452f, 466, 534, 557, 658, 666, 720, 734
– Cantonese 59, 77, 91f, 108, 159, 164–166, 170, 339, 440–447, 452f, 470
– Mandarin (Putonghua) 59, 75, 77, 91f, 95, 98, 101, 106, 108, 153–156, 159, 164–166, 168, 170f, 643
– Hainanese 159
– Hakka 159, 165
– Hokkien 159, 165
– Min 77
– Taiwanese 77
– Teochew 159, 165
Cornish 24, 249, 254, 263
Corsican 24, 693, 701
Créole Guyanais 319f
Croatian (*see also* Serbo-Croatian) 17, 26, 36, 92, 692, 721, 743
Czech 17, 26, 61, 469, 682, 734, 742

D

Danish 17, 26, 61, 470, 627, 653, 658, 660, 682, 692, 744

Dutch (*see also* Flemish) 17, 21, 24, 26, 34f, 42, 61, 92, 98, 101, 107, 110, 219, 315–317, 319, 470, 627, 653, 663, 682, 687, 694, 696, 707, 721, 723f, 742, 744
Dutch Creole (Negerhollands) 310

E

Eastern Maroon Creole 319
Emai 355
English 17, 19f, 22, 30f, 36–38, 43–46, 53–85, 87–122, 123, 127, 133–139, 151–176, 183–185, 190f, 193–197, 199, 214–216, 218f, 221, 226, 228–230, 245f, 248–250, 254–258, 274f, 284f, 288, 291, 301, 304–312, 314–317, 319, 333–364, 366f, 370, 372, 375f, 384, 387f, 403f, 409, 413–415, 431, 436, 440, 442–450, 452f, 465–467, 470, 472f, 476, 482f, 504, 523–551, 553–592, 596, 598–601, 627, 629, 639–641, 651–684, 685, 687, 689f, 696–700, 705–707, 715–749, 751
– American English 355, 641–644, 660, 669, 673, 697, 725, 727, 729f, 732
– Australian English 432f, 669, 673, 725, 729
– British English 669, 673, 697, 725, 729f, 732
– Carriacou Creole English 698
– Chinese (Pidgin) English 344f, 353, 477
– Hong Kong English 165, 673
– Early Modern English 470
– Indian English 167, 214
– Indonesian English 352
– Irish English 185
– Malaysian English 162–163, 352
– Melanesian Pidgin English 311
– Middle English 469, 716, 727
– New Zealand English 669, 673
– Nigerian English 476
– Old English 334f, 432, 717f, 724f, 727
– Philippine English 669, 673
– Scottish English 185
– Singapore(an) English 154f, 162, 214, 351, 669, 673
– Trinidad and Tobago Creole English 696
Eskimo languages 196
Estonian 17, 371
Etruscan 241

F

Fante 303f
Finnish 17f, 40, 368, 384, 660f, 721, 743
Flemish (*see also* Dutch) 61
French 17f, 20, 33, 36, 44, 59–61, 63, 70, 92, 98, 105f, 127, 131, 138, 167, 184, 194, 200, 212, 219, 247, 250, 255, 263, 274, 288f, 301, 305–309, 313, 317–320, 334f, 351, 366, 368–370, 379, 470, 526, 534f, 537, 554, 565f, 568, 598f, 601f, 605, 607, 626f, 653f, 660–663, 666, 682f, 687, 692–694, 696, 701, 707, 717–724, 726f, 729, 733, 737–739, 741–745
– Louisiana Creole French 692
– Norman French 432, 727
Frisian (North Frisian, Saterfrisian) 24, 33f, 39, 248
Friulian 24, 263

G

Gaelic (*see also* Irish, Scottish Gaelic) 246, 249, 262f, 335
Galician 24, 693
Gcaleka 304
Geez 464
Georgian 735
German 17f, 26, 36f, 53, 57, 59–64, 92f, 97f, 101, 106f, 110f, 183, 185, 190, 200, 221, 263, 288, 355, 379, 436, 469–473, 482, 526, 534f, 554, 565f, 624, 627f, 630–636, 653f, 659, 661–663, 665f, 668, 670–674, 683f, 685, 692, 700–703, 716, 718, 720–722, 729, 731, 733–736, 738–740, 742–744

Germanic languages 35, 334, 630–633, 658, 736
Gikuyu 249, 341
Gothic 636
Greek 17f, 26, 59–61, 63, 91–93, 97, 101, 105f, 108, 125, 241, 451, 462, 467, 483, 557–559, 621, 623, 627f, 630, 633, 660, 684, 720f, 727f
Guadeloupe Creole 694
Guarani (Tupi-Guarani) 245, 319
Gujarati (Gujarathi, Gujerati) 60, 63, 136f, 159
Gur-languages 128

H

Haitian Creole 63, 313, 315, 317, 319, 689f, 693f
Hausa 126, 735
Hawaiian 77, 303, 557, 571f, 703f
Hawaii Pidgin 479f, 690, 696f, 699, 705–708
Hebrew (Ivrit) 60, 63, 248, 253, 259–262, 459, 462, 464f, 467f, 472f, 483f, 557, 621, 623, 628, 638, 658, 699f, 702
Hindi 60, 63, 92, 136, 159, 166f, 348, 460, 470, 692, 735
Hungarian 17, 59–61, 63, 101, 212, 721

I

Iban 159, 163
Icelandic 627, 720f, 727, 743f
Igbo 470, 474
Indo-European (Indo-Germanic) 59, 620, 636–638, 645
Indonesian (Bahasa Indonesia) 92, 95, 106, 158, 160, 335, 352, 662, 687
Inuktitut 384
Iranun 163
Irish (Irish Gaelic) 17, 26, 33, 250, 253–259, 290, 417, 568, 623, 704f, 731
Italian 17f, 34, 36, 59–61, 63, 91–93, 97f, 101, 106f, 110f, 200, 219, 263, 369, 379, 469, 526, 532, 534, 565, 625, 654, 658f, 666, 684, 693, 720f, 734–737

J

Jakun 159
Jamaican Creole 479, 687, 696, 698, 708
Japanese 60, 63f, 70, 77, 95, 106, 166, 466, 534, 554, 557, 561–563, 662, 735

K

Kadazan (Kadazandusun) 159, 163
Kashubian 24
Kâte 688
Kgatla 303
Khmer (Mon-Khmer, Cambodian) 60, 63, 70, 76, 101
Khoisan languages 124, 136
Kisafwa 134
Kikongo 304
Korean 59f, 63, 70, 76, 92, 95, 557
Krio 479, 568, 730
Kurdish 36, 367, 369f, 372
Kwena 303

L

Lakota 694f
Ladin 24, 183, 198
Laotian (Lao) 60, 63, 70
Latin 125, 185, 241, 334, 431f, 461f, 467, 469–471, 539f, 621–628, 630f, 633, 639, 718–722, 724, 727f, 733, 737, 739, 744f
Latvian 17, 371
Lemnian 241
Limburgian 24
Lingala 126f
Lingua Geral Amazonica 303
Lithuanian 17, 61, 371, 638
Low-German 26
Low-Saxon 26

Luba-languages 131
Luxemburgish 17, 26

M

Macedonian 92
Makua 137
Malay (Bahasa Malaysia) 152–163, 170f, 341, 351f
Malayalam 159, 167
Maltese 17, 26, 92, 556, 732
Manx 249
Maori 371f, 691, 729, 732
Maya 290
Melanau 159
Miao (Hmong) 60, 63
Mirandese 198
Murut 159

N

Navajo 60, 63
Ndebele 135
Ndyuka 319f
Nengee 320
Ngwaketsi 303
Ngwato 303
Nheengatu 303
Niger-Congo languages 124
Nilo-Saharan languages 124
Norse (Scandinavian languages) 334f, 717, 723, 725
Northern Sotho (SeSotho sa Leboa) 135
Norwegian 61, 182, 537, 661, 692, 721, 734, 743

O

Occitan 26, 198, 263

P

Pali 466
Pamaka 319

Papiamentu 310, 315–317, 478, 696
Pashto 217
Penan 159
Pennsylvania Dutch 263
Persian (Farsi) 60, 63, 70, 217, 470, 559, 720
Polish 17, 26, 36f, 59–61, 63, 92, 660f, 721, 729, 734f
Portuguese 17f, 26, 36, 60f, 63, 127, 134, 319f, 370, 526, 564, 693, 707, 724
Punjabi 159, 568

Q

Quichua (Quechua) 303, 371, 695, 702

R

Rhaetic 241
Romance languages 35, 185, 631, 639, 658, 717f, 727, 735f
Romani (Romany, Sinte) 21, 26, 36f, 263, 717
Romanian 17, 61, 660f, 721
Romansh (Romansch) 187, 200, 379, 565
Russian 36, 59–61, 63, 93, 105, 344, 370, 526, 534, 557, 658–660, 666, 720f, 731, 733f, 736f, 742
Ruthenian 24

S

Saamaka 319
Saami (Sami) 26, 183, 263, 371, 380
Sanskrit 459, 464, 467, 636, 638
Sardinian 24, 263, 572–574
Scots 24, 481, 717, 728, 730f
Scottish Gaelic 24, 731
Semitic languages 636
Semai 163
Senoi 159
Serbian (*see also* Serbo-Croatian) 36, 92, 692, 743
Serbo-Croatian (*see also* Bosnian, Croatian, Serbian) 60, 624, 743

Sheng 130
Shilluk 472
Shona 304, 309
Sign languages 371f, 381, 385
Slavic languages 658, 736f
Slavonic 470
Slovak (Slovakian) 17, 61
Slovenian (Slovene) 17, 26, 61, 470, 624, 628
Somali 36, 245
Sorbian 24
Southern Sotho 135
Spanish (*see also* Castilian) 17–19, 33, 36, 55f, 59–63, 65f, 69f, 72–75, 78, 92, 95, 98, 106f, 109, 212, 218, 221, 228, 245f, 263, 316, 319, 431f, 436, 441, 445, 470, 526, 534, 568f, 653f, 658, 666, 684, 691, 693, 696, 698, 702, 707, 721, 724, 727, 729, 734f, 737, 743
Sranan Tongo 310, 320
Swahili (Kingwana, Kiswahili) 126, 130–132, 134f, 139, 303, 309, 335, 341, 566f, 735
Swazi 135
Swedish 17f, 39, 61, 290, 367–370, 384, 436, 470, 556, 559, 627, 684, 692

T

Tagalog 59, 63, 92, 733
Takitaki 322
Tamil 136f, 152–157, 159f, 163, 167, 170f
Telugu 159, 167
Temiar 159
Thai 60, 63, 564
Thembu 304
Tibetan 466
Tok Pisin 182, 196, 311, 477f, 690f, 699, 708, 730
Town Bemba 130
Tsonga 135

Turkish 17, 20, 34, 36f, 92, 101, 370, 372, 559, 638, 658, 661, 688, 700
Tswana 135, 303

U

Ukrainian 61, 275, 624, 638, 731
Urdu 36, 60, 63, 70, 159, 217, 460, 692

V

Venda 135f
Vietnamese 36, 59f, 63, 70, 91f, 98, 101, 106, 603

W

Welsh 24, 28, 33, 39, 254, 263, 290, 335, 417, 465f, 661, 684, 691, 718, 731f
Wolof 126, 130

X

Xhosa 123, 135–137, 304

Y

Yabem 688
Yiddish 26, 59–61, 63, 182, 248, 260, 692, 700, 723, 742
Yoruba 308f
Yu'piq 387

Z

Zulu 135–137

Subject index

A

Abstand (language) 691–693, 695, 697
accent 67f, 75, 137, 163, 596–599, 601, 641
accommodation (of communication) 286, 597f, 601, 604, 606f, 609–612
acrolect 350, 699
administration, language of 34, 160f, 166, 320, 335f, 379, 463, 565, 624, 665–667
adstratum 717, 725
affirmative action 20, 160f, 754
alienation *see* linguistic alienation
allochthonous language 21
androcentrism 660f, 663f, 666f
– androcentric generics *see* generics
assimilation 22, 53f, 58, 64, 67, 71, 90, 101f, 156, 211, 217, 221, 244, 254, 365, 367, 372f, 375, 381, 383, 385–387, 605f
attitudes 57, 71, 101, 192, 217f, 221–224, 261, 264, 307, 317, 373, 386, 442, 460, 466, 484, 530, 559, 595–618, 659, 665, 685, 715f, 722, 727, 730, 732, 734, 740–745
– attitude change 181, 191f, 311, 596, 607f
– intergroup attitudes 595–618
– language attitudes 94, 103, 107–109, 310f, 319, 322, 324, 344, 417, 477, 545, 595–612, 621, 641, 706
Ausbau (language) 691f, 719, 727f, 744
authenticity (of linguistic forms) 703–705
autochthonous languages 21, 136
autonomy *see* independence

B

Babel, Tower of 178, 459, 623f, 627
basilect 155, 162, 350, 699
benefits (of language policy) 278, 282
biblical language 461f, 468, 477, 623, 727, 739f
bilingualism 32f, 39, 58f, 72–76, 89, 95f, 98, 109f, 113, 151–176, 181–190, 218, 222, 242, 244, 255, 275, 281f, 289f, 311, 313, 319, 324, 335, 341, 346, 351–353, 355, 357, 373, 406, 450, 463, 568, 635, 637, 715, 719, 729, 741
bilingual education *see* education
biliteracy 39, 74, 95, 154f, 171, 218, 450
biologisation of language
borrowing 74, 184, 188, 632, 639, 642, 701, 715–749
– lexical borrowing 97, 184, 304, 431f, 478, 700, 702, 716f, 718–732, 734–739
– morphological borrowing 718, 726, 733, 737
– phonological borrowing 718f, 733, 735
– syntactic borrowing 719, 728, 730, 739f
– types of borrowing 716f

C

calque 718f, 727, 737–739, 744
census 24–38, 88f, 91, 93, 99–103, 164, 256f, 275, 366, 567, 641
change *see* language change
church, language of 64, 105, 255, 462, 464, 622
code-mixing 67, 74, 569, 716, 743f
code-switching 73, 96, 98, 112, 125, 131, 139, 184, 187–189, 312, 558f, 568–570, 621, 716, 719, 727, 729, 732–734, 736, 742, 745
codification 131, 160, 219, 229, 310, 349, 413, 460, 468–470, 478, 560, 667, 685–713
colonialism 27, 29, 34, 53, 55, 57, 62, 124, 126–129, 151, 156, 166f, 181f,

185, 194, 214, 223, 230f, 249, 299–332, 335–339, 342–347, 430, 460, 468–470, 473–478, 496, 510, 566, 687, 693, 694f, 698, 708, 729
- colonial language 55, 165, 182, 219f, 223, 231, 249, 299–332, 379, 478, 724, 741f
- colonial language policies 152, 159f, 164, 299–332, 339–341, 691
- colonisation 22, 305, 307, 319, 337, 342, 344, 464, 533, 687, 729, 731
- decolonisation 164, 166f, 250, 300, 380, 475
- decolonising the mind 250, 300, 341
- post-colonial language policies 160f, 249f, 299–332, 339, 673

community language 20–22, 40, 44, 53, 72, 75, 79, 87–122, 158, 164, 170, 260, 319f, 412
community of practice 110, 651, 656, 672
computer-mediated communication, see also Internet communication 356, 553–592
constructivism 190–192, 651, 657
conversational adaptation see accommodation
corpus planning 213, 220, 229, 279, 286, 366, 662, 688–708
cost (of language policy) 278f, 281–283, 285, 289–291, 541–543
court, language of 335f, 374, 379, 438–449, 465
creoles 67f, 299–332, 476–481, 687, 689–692, 695–699, 715, 717f, 730
- creolisation 127, 185f, 639, 726
- English-based creoles 310–312, 314, 319, 696–699
- French-based creoles 311f, 314, 317–321, 693f, 696, 699, 707f
critical applied linguistics 346, 652, 657
culture 23, 40, 73f, 90f, 94f, 102, 108, 125, 151, 157–159, 165–168, 171, 177–207, 211, 213, 215f, 226f, 232, 245, 258f, 272, 284, 299, 302, 304, 306, 318, 320–323, 338, 341f, 348, 351–354, 357, 372f, 376, 378, 389, 411, 416, 429, 449, 459f, 469f, 472, 474–476, 485, 495f, 507f, 524, 536–538, 542–544, 561–565, 571f, 574f, 599, 621f, 624, 634, 638, 651, 701, 707f, 715, 721, 724f, 729, 733f, 740, 744, 757, 759f
- linguistic culture 222

D

Darwinism (in linguistics) 385, 636–638
decolonisation see colonialism 299,
decreolisation see creoles 318, 717
democracy 164, 220, 222, 227, 261, 291, 323, 366, 503, 528, 758
dialect 24, 53, 74f, 77, 103, 107–109, 124f, 131, 167, 180, 187f, 200, 258, 263, 302f, 308, 334, 336, 338f, 355, 408, 412, 481, 510, 574, 597, 600, 609, 623, 636, 639, 641, 643f, 687f, 691, 693, 708, 717, 724–726, 730f, 740, 742f, 744
- eye dialect 697
dictionaries 125, 135, 163, 219, 260, 349, 465, 469, 570, 667f, 685–688, 703, 705–707, 716, 722f, 732, 746
diglossia 107f, 154, 159, 165, 167, 181f, 186, 219, 222f, 242, 260, 313f, 318, 355, 383, 535, 557, 565, 574, 621, 690, 715, 719f, 726f, 729, 742
discourse 18, 22f, 71, 96–98, 156, 213, 215–218, 224–226, 229, 299, 302, 389f, 406, 437, 442, 445f, 451f, 493–521, 523, 536, 542, 620, 622, 624, 644, 665, 674, 685, 751–763
- discourse of science 523, 526f, 529f, 533, 536f
- discourse of language 58, 69f, 133, 141, 165f, 271f, 287f, 311, 319, 619–646
discourse analysis 129, 215, 225, 406, 441, 485, 500f, 513, 603f, 646, 651
- critical discourse analysis 493–521, 671
discourse planning 215
discrimination 54, 57, 62, 66–69, 75f, 79, 108, 133, 136f, 193, 196f, 216f, 274, 300, 323, 374, 377–379, 381, 411, 568, 604, 645, 653, 662, 664f, 753f, 760f
- reverse discrimination 751f, 757

diversity 177, 243, 252, 321f, 389f, 494, 501f, 507f, 516, 611, 656
- bio-diversity 178f, 198f, 242f, 252, 387
- cognitive diversity 546
- cultural diversity 15, 20, 23, 43, 87, 90, 156, 179, 183, 320f, 352, 380
- ethnic diversity 67, 156
- linguistic diversity 15–18, 37, 44, 46, 53–85, 87, 101, 123–149, 151–176, 177–207, 217, 220, 223, 228f, 231, 242f, 276f, 280, 285, 319–321, 370–372, 386–388, 401, 404f, 411, 415–417, 419–421, 544, 546, 555, 567, 570, 574, 595, 609, 612, 643, 685–713
- social diversity 55, 611
documentation *see* language documentation
domains *see* linguistic domains
dubbing 188–190, 196, 285, 371

E

earnings 273–275, 281
ecology 180f, 242, 252, 264
ecolinguistics 264
ecology of language 93, 127, 177–207, 223f, 231, 242f, 339, 542,
economy 41, 91, 95, 136, 152, 154, 156–159, 161–164, 166f, 171, 222f, 225f, 299–301, 323, 339, 378, 387, 524, 527, 532, 541–543, 759
economics of language 271–297, 410
economy of language 178, 199f
education 20, 29, 31, 34, 38–46, 64f, 67–71, 89, 94–96, 101f, 105–107, 111–113, 123, 132, 134, 138f, 141, 151–176, 197, 212f, 216, 219, 221–223, 225, 227–229, 231, 246, 249f, 256f, 260f, 271, 278, 281, 287f, 299–332, 333–364, 365, 372–374, 379, 381–386, 389f, 401–427, 437, 466, 485, 523–551, 571, 622, 643, 667, 687, 691, 696, 706f, 722, 727, 733, 735, 741, 745, 760
- bilingual education 19, 40, 43, 64f, 73, 76, 88f, 95f, 105–107, 112, 228f, 246, 283, 308, 316, 321, 324, 340, 384, 401, 415

- educational achievement 40, 67f, 69–71, 95, 164, 228, 309, 314, 316, 384f, 387f, 390, 415
- language-in-education policies 53f, 68–71, 151–176
- language of education *see* instruction, language of
effectiveness (of language policy) 213, 220, 227, 278f, 287f, 289
elaboration 219, 316, 469, 478, 685, 687, 691, 699–702
- lexical elaboration 478, 688, 699–702, 704
- stylistic elaboration 480f, 688
endangered languages 88, 179, 182f, 186f, 195–199, 213, 241–269, 280, 371f, 420f, 570–574
endonormative variety 337, 349
English-only movement 19, 53f, 56, 64–66, 69f, 72, 644
ethnicity, *see also* diversity 28–32, 65f, 72, 98, 125f, 128, 137, 156, 158, 212f, 221, 226, 232, 274, 352, 599, 606, 619–650, 759
ethnocentrism 110, 619
ethnolinguistic vitality 94, 108f, 602f
euphemism 494–498, 501, 509, 511, 738, 757
European Union 15–52, 178, 194, 223, 230f, 287f, 291, 436
evaluation (of language policy) 213, 227–229, 271f, 278–282, 286f, 291, 389, 655, 672f
exoglossic norms *see* exonormative variety 339,
exonormative variety 153–155, 337f, 349, 353, 669

F

female language *see* gender-specific language behavior
feminism 191, 511, 651–684, 754, 759
fluency *see* proficiency
foreign language 42, 44–46, 153, 170, 217, 275, 287f, 291, 316, 333, 336, 341, 343f, 401–411, 510, 635, 731, 733, 741

- foreign language learning *see* language learning
- foreign language skills 273, 281, 284
- foreign language teaching *see* language teaching

francophonie 247f, 306f,
freedom of speech 654, 664, 751–763

G

gender, *see also* sex 411, 575, 651–674
- categories of gender (grammatical, lexical, social) 654, 657–659
- grammatical gender assignment 97, 657, 735
- gender-specific language behaviour 110, 562–565, 610, 651f, 656f
- gender-inclusive language *see* non-sexist language

generics 663f, 666f, 669f, 672
- generic *he* 654, 660, 669f
- masculine generics 483f, 653, 655, 660f, 665, 667, 672, 674
- male generics 653, 655, 660f, 665, 667

genre 126, 129–132, 451, 461, 478, 523, 569, 719f, 732f, 739, 745f
- scientific genres 527–529, 536, 538, 733, 742

globalisation 19, 44, 79, 111, 132, 141f, 151, 163, 167, 169–171, 183, 193–195, 197, 215, 299f, 340, 342, 346f, 356f, 382, 386, 406, 410, 420, 523f, 528, 542f, 553f, 557, 559, 731, 743

global English 183, 194f, 197, 333–364, 533, 544, 554, 570, 574

global language 409, 415, 544

goals (of language policy) 44, 220, 224, 227–229

government, language of 160, 316, 565, 696

grammars 125, 135, 219, 349, 623, 628–630, 632, 636f, 688, 746
- prescriptive grammars 685–687

grassroots writing 140f

guidelines for non-sexist language *see* non-sexist language

H

hegemony 53, 225, 254, 299, 344, 416, 462, 644
- linguistic hegemony 44, 170f, 285, 308, 469, 533, 537, 622f, 689

heritage language 21, 54, 73, 75–77, 79, 154, 215–218, 376

home language 15, 28–32, 34–38, 44, 46, 53, 69, 73, 91, 95, 99–101, 103f, 106, 132, 154, 158, 170, 248, 260, 318, 320–322, 411, 450, 465

human rights, *see also* linguistic rights, linguistic human rights 43f, 230f, 365, 373–376, 378, 380–383, 388f, 664

I

identity 15, 29, 37, 44, 75, 77, 98, 110, 126, 138, 142, 155f, 158, 162, 164, 178, 183, 198, 211, 214, 216, 224f, 231f, 255, 259, 284, 312, 317, 324, 343, 350, 366, 378f, 382, 388f, 412, 479, 537, 562, 599, 603, 605, 608–610, 612, 621, 638, 641f, 692, 700, 708, 740
- cultural identity 15, 23, 41, 111, 211, 231
- ethnic identity 30, 156, 223, 337, 575, 642, 695
- ethnolinguistic identity 71
- gender identity 604, 651f
- linguistic identity 156, 575, 743
- multiple identities 19, 151, 156, 611, 651
- national identity 18, 54, 126, 158, 164, 219, 314, 465, 575, 645, 755
- regional identity 19
- social identity 542, 595, 605–609
- transnational identity 19

ideology 20, 23, 123–125, 129, 140, 156, 181, 191, 193, 214f, 218, 220, 222, 224–226, 229f, 232, 248, 301, 308, 338, 341, 386, 484, 500, 505, 510f, 513f, 542–545, 569, 571, 619, 640, 663, 666, 685f, 692f, 694, 701, 705, 708, 753
- ethnolinguistic ideology 619–650

immersion 39, 69f, 72, 106, 415, 571, 701, 704, 707

immigration 53–85, 87–122, 127, 136, 181f, 185, 221, 245, 263, 274, 301, 368, 377, 600, 603–606, 642, 716, 723f
immigrant languages 15–52, 53–85, 137, 182, 220f, 323, 729, 732
immigrant minority languages, *see also* minorities 15–52, 53–85, 87–122, 262f, 603, 693
imperialism 214, 226, 300f, 474, 496, 557, 693, 742
– linguistic imperialism 195, 226, 306, 333–364, 554, 557
implementation (of language policy) 219, 224, 228, 230, 317, 323f, 655, 664–674, 702–708, 722
inclusive language *see* non-sexist language
income *see* earnings
independence (=political independence) 151, 159f, 164, 219f, 229, 256, 299f, 306f, 310, 317, 323, 342f, 510, 621, 638, 691, 693, 696, 708
indigenous groups 21, 87f, 221, 245, 370, 379, 381, 383, 385, 387, 389f, 409, 414, 450
indigenous languages 18, 55f, 75, 88, 95, 123, 133f, 159, 166f, 182f, 219, 222f, 230, 249, 257, 262f, 302, 309, 335, 348, 366–368, 370–373, 379, 450, 474, 570f, 725, 729, 732
inequality 136, 142, 167, 222f, 308, 315, 321, 388, 421, 569, 607, 609, 753
– linguistic inequality 285, 300, 315
– social inequality 245, 247, 300, 411, 413, 755
ingroup 311, 600–603, 606f, 609, 672
instruction, language of 15, 33, 39, 45f, 62, 64, 68f, 72, 95, 138f, 151–176, 219, 228, 230f, 246, 249, 255f, 279, 290, 304–310, 312–317, 323, 339f, 343, 347–349, 367f, 372, 379–382, 384, 386–390, 407, 409, 413–416, 465f, 566, 622, 696
integration 20, 22f, 65, 90, 93, 108, 365, 372f, 378–380, 386, 388, 605f
intercultural communication 45, 88, 177, 193, 354, 406, 475, 598, 601, 610–612
intercultural contact 601

interference 188f, 715
intergroup attitudes *see* attitudes
intergroup communication 598, 602–604
international communication 20, 44f, 344, 347f, 349, 355, 403, 528, 540
international language 38, 45, 75, 284, 333–364, 375, 388, 479, 532–546, 741
Internet 105, 111, 171, 178, 183f, 195, 197f, 482, 553–592
Internet communication, *see also* computer-mediated communication
interpreting *see* translation

J

jargon 125, 528, 530, 609, 738

L

labour income *see* earnings
language academies 126, 135, 153, 160, 260, 687, 695, 699, 703, 704, 732
language acquisition 34, 137, 158, 168, 228f, 312f, 401, 406, 420, 704, 715, 717, 724, 732f
language-as-problem orientation 216
language-as-resource orientation 178, 215–218, 220, 224
language attitudes *see* attitudes
language attrition 98f, 134
language awareness 32, 322f
language change 93, 96–99, 109, 111, 127, 130, 179, 191f, 195, 245, 333–336, 355, 401, 420, 464, 506, 544, 639, 654f, 664–674, 706, 724, 730, 740, 744f, 759
language choice 35, 103f, 248, 276, 286, 523, 531–535, 538, 540–542, 565–570, 575, 601, 685, 688, 691–699
language committees *see* language academies
language community, *see also* speech community 132, 136, 501
language conflict 715–749
language contact 74, 88, 93, 96–99, 108, 112, 123–149, 155, 162f, 177–207, 223,

244, 299–332, 334–337, 350, 460, 476–481, 485, 544, 639, 706, 715–749
language death 88, 133f, 179, 186f, 194, 211f, 214, 226, 241, 302f, 370–372, 384–386, 408, 415–417, 464, 485, 570, 708, 732
language documentation 88, 124f, 128, 182, 185–187, 196, 252, 469, 573
language for professional purposes 429–457, 523
language for specific purposes 523, 528, 530
language governmentality 226
language in education *see* education
language instruction *see* language teaching
language learning 45f, 53, 68–71, 89, 106, 113, 151–176, 187f, 217f, 223, 229, 275f, 280, 284, 286, 291, 302, 306, 313, 315, 322, 333–364, 366, 382–384, 387, 402–411, 420f, 545, 570, 572, 576, 601–603, 611, 625, 628, 630, 701, 746
language maintenance 38f, 41, 54, 57, 72, 74–77, 134, 154, 180, 182f, 185–187, 194, 197, 199f, 218, 220, 226, 241–269, 372, 387, 415–417, 460, 485, 570
language mixing 108, 111, 125, 127, 130f, 139, 167, 185f, 188, 194f, 215, 226, 319, 356, 701, 708, 715, 717f, 725, 740, 745
language murder *see* linguistic genocide
language myths 459, 620f, 638, 640
language planning 33, 128, 135–138, 151–176, 181, 184f, 191, 197, 211–240, 244, 247, 261, 271–297, 299–332, 365–397, 401, 404–407, 464, 542, 544f, 554, 662, 685–713, 746
language policy 33, 39, 43–46, 53–85, 77–79, 87f, 91, 94f, 102, 112f, 123, 133, 135–137, 151–176, 194, 211–240, 248f, 254, 271–297, 335, 339, 348, 365f, 372f, 376, 388, 401, 404, 406, 411, 466, 667
language reform 638, 700, 754
– non-sexist language reform *see* non-sexist language
– reform of legal language 436f
language revitalisation 88, 113, 133, 261,
278, 289, 367, 415–417, 460, 465f, 485, 570–574, 693, 694, 701f, 704
language revival 33, 77, 88, 241–269, 417, 460, 464f, 699, 704
language shift 20, 34, 39, 53, 64, 66f, 72–75, 87–122, 127, 134, 151, 154, 156, 159, 170, 182, 186, 241–269, 302f, 322f, 372, 385, 416, 544, 568, 601, 717, 719, 724, 726, 731
language shift reversal 20, 33, 182, 248, 251, 261
language spread 127, 151, 183, 215, 226, 273, 275, 284f, 303, 307, 333–364, 460–464, 485, 533–535, 554, 570, 574, 637, 723f, 731, 741
language survival 88, 194, 197, 367, 460, 704
language teaching 22, 31, 33, 38–46, 64, 75–79, 87, 91, 95, 105–107, 112, 151–176, 178, 187f, 196, 199, 217, 256f, 271, 277, 281, 284, 287f, 305, 309, 312f, 316–318, 320f, 323, 333, 345, 347–354, 356f, 366f, 373, 382, 401–411, 420f, 454, 576, 643f, 702, 733, 746
language transmission 15, 20, 32, 35, 93, 111, 243, 248, 262, 371, 416, 571
language variation 24, 74f, 97, 109, 128, 130f, 137, 154f, 162f, 167, 200, 214, 303f, 312, 319, 333–364, 411–413, 420f, 463, 466, 481f, 541, 545, 575, 672f, 687, 692, 706f
language vitality 35–38, 108f, 285
– language vitality index 35f
law, language of 34, 429–457, 462, 465, 567, 622, 665–667, 674, 719
legislation *see* linguistic legislation
lexical expansion *see* elaboration
lingua franca 127, 155, 182, 185, 196f, 260, 285, 302f, 320, 322, 335, 346, 463, 477, 533, 541, 543f, 568, 690, 725
– English as lingua franca 20, 37f, 44f, 167, 194f, 285, 346, 349, 353–355, 533, 539, 554, 564f, 568, 570, 574, 724
linguistic alienation 499f, 509
linguistic diversity *see* diversity
linguistic domains 34, 78, 93, 103–108, 110–112, 130, 132, 134, 154, 159, 165,

170, 185f, 188, 195–197, 212f, 215, 219f, 225, 243f, 258f, 262, 282, 285f, 302f, 311, 333, 337f, 346, 348, 355, 416, 462, 576, 672, 674, 688f, 706, 719f, 732
linguistic economy *see* economy of language
linguistic ecology *see* ecology of language
linguistic genocide 302, 367, 370, 381, 383–386, 388, 416
linguistic human rights, *see also* human rights, linguistic rights 223, 226, 230f, 288, 365–397, 413
linguistic legislation 20, 38f, 181, 184, 194, 258, 278, 318, 372, 380, 417, 573, 644, 670, 722, 732, 742f, 744
linguistic relativity 180, 191, 195, 469, 665
linguistic rights 41, 43, 66, 133–137, 223f, 226f, 230f, 252, 271, 318, 365–397, 401, 404, 413, 416
literacy 38, 57, 67, 72, 74, 95, 102, 107, 112, 123, 127f, 130, 134, 139–141, 154, 229, 231, 254, 260, 309, 313, 384f, 387f, 401, 404, 406, 408, 412, 417–421, 462f, 470, 485, 576, 623, 686f, 689, 694, 698
literary language 167, 187, 250, 255, 303, 308, 314, 338, 341f, 344f, 463, 465f, 478, 481, 530, 557, 624, 626, 628, 690f, 697f, 699, 705, 708, 717, 719, 728, 730
local languages 130, 134, 138f, 151, 164, 167, 170, 197, 249, 285, 303f, 309, 320, 333, 335–340, 342, 346–349, 355–357, 384, 414, 460, 570

M

majority 15, 18, 23, 38, 43, 46, 53, 57, 65f, 70, 87f, 93, 97, 102, 105, 108, 157, 160, 183, 211, 216, 218, 221, 225, 255, 262, 283, 285, 369f, 379f, 384, 386f, 409–411, 413f, 569, 605–607, 620, 644
– linguistic majority 183
male language *see* gender-specific language behaviour
marginalisation 76, 605, 657

masculine generics *see* generics
matched guise technique 108, 599f
media 34, 58, 78, 89, 91, 105, 108, 112, 157, 166, 168, 178, 187, 194, 197, 260, 290, 314–316, 320, 379, 383, 386, 417, 465f, 493, 499, 507, 510, 515, 529, 667, 688, 696, 703, 724, 730, 733, 745, 751–763
mesolect 162f, 699
meta-communication 542
metaphor 181, 191, 217, 224, 242f, 435, 479, 493f, 500f, 531, 700, 756
– biological metaphors in linguistics 224, 625–640, 645f
– kinship metaphors in linguistics 624f, 634, 636, 639, 645
migration 18–20, 22f, 30, 40, 43, 123, 127, 129f, 159, 198, 223, 246, 257f, 319, 464, 466, 637, 642, 724, 730
minorities 57, 133–137, 216, 218, 246f, 254, 283, 365–397, 413, 596, 605f, 620, 657, 732, 754, 761
– ethnic minorities 21, 382, 414, 609
– immigrant minorities 15–52, 87–122, 156, 221, 227, 275, 379–381, 384, 386, 409, 414
– linguistic minorities 15–52, 53–85, 182f, 211, 216, 221, 226f, 244, 259, 365–397, 414, 569
– minority languages 15–52, 87–122, 133–137, 142, 151, 163, 198f, 211, 213, 216, 221, 232, 249, 254, 262f, 274f, 278, 282, 288–290, 378, 409f, 413–417, 420, 450, 567f, 570–574, 603, 644, 688, 694f, 701f
– national minorities 227, 375, 377, 379, 381f
– regional minorities 15–52
– religious minorities 382, 414
missionary activities 124, 182, 305, 310, 315, 460f, 469f, 473–475, 477, 688, 690f, 703, 724, 727
mobility (=social mobility) 54, 67, 73, 78, 134, 211, 221, 244f, 302, 306, 310, 314, 344f, 385, 686, 704, 706, 733
modernisation 160, 219f, 222f, 229, 245, 247, 307, 344, 554, 699, 704
– linguistic modernisation 245, 479f

monolingualism 42, 44, 53f, 59, 72, 75, 125f, 160f, 163, 165, 230f, 242, 244, 255f, 262, 281, 313f, 319, 335, 346, 349, 352, 369, 386, 409, 524, 538, 540, 542, 689, 726
"mother tongue", concept of 31, 44, 375, 619–646
multiculturalism 23, 31f, 34, 41, 43, 46, 58, 91, 93, 95, 101, 211, 213, 322, 343, 406, 601, 612
multilingualism 20, 32, 34, 43–46, 58, 78, 87–122, 123–149, 151–176, 181, 187, 194, 196f, 211, 213, 222f, 230f, 276, 278, 281f, 291, 303, 307, 309, 312f, 321f, 324, 342, 348, 352, 356, 373, 386f, 389f, 404, 406f, 409, 413–417, 419–421, 432, 524, 540–542, 544–546, 553–592, 599, 601, 691, 715

N

national language 45, 56, 77, 132, 135–137, 151f, 160, 164, 166, 170, 211, 220, 224, 232, 245, 256, 260, 275, 288, 335f, 342, 346, 375f, 409f, 414f, 535, 539–541, 565, 620f, 624, 626, 630f, 640, 645, 687, 698, 700, 722, 741f
nationalism 18f, 53, 158, 165, 212, 231, 249, 255f, 258, 314, 619–650, 686, 691, 693f, 700f
"native language", concept of 619–650
"native speaker", concept of 349, 619, 640f
network 94, 109f, 275f, 575
- network effect 276, 284
non-sexist language 197, 482–484, 651–684, 688
- guidelines for non-sexist language 191f, 653–655, 664–668, 757
- non-sexist language reform 191f, 654f, 662–674
- non-sexist Bible translation 482–484

O

official language 16–21, 23, 26, 33, 40, 42, 44–46, 62, 65f, 133, 135–137, 152, 156, 159, 166, 170f, 230, 256, 279, 291, 310, 313f, 316, 319f, 322, 339, 348, 367, 371f, 375–377, 409, 463, 465f, 477, 510, 555, 565–567, 573, 644, 698
oppression 102, 258, 493, 496, 499, 510, 512, 756f
oral communication 127, 158, 315, 401–403, 431, 438–449, 464, 471, 480f, 524, 529, 562, 564
orthography 126, 128, 135, 140f, 219, 460, 477, 479, 668, 688, 689–699, 703f
- etymological orthography 695–699
- orthography reform see spelling reform
- phonemic orthography 479, 690f, 695, 695–699, 708
outgroup 600–602, 606f, 609

P

parliament, language of 348, 691
pidgins 67, 301, 337, 476–481, 687, 689–692, 695–699, 705–708, 715, 717f, 726, 730
pidginisation 185f, 194, 335
pluralism 605
pluricentric language 94, 102f, 107
policy evaluation see evaluation of language policy
politeness 441f, 564f
political correctness 194, 507, 672, 751–763
polycentric norm 696, 707
post-colonial see colonialism
prescriptive linguistics see dictionaries, grammars
prestige 36, 38, 44, 75, 77, 110, 127, 167, 186, 188, 194, 257, 299, 301–303, 311–314, 338, 415f, 470, 477f, 481, 527, 557, 568, 600, 602, 607, 686, 702f, 708, 715, 717f, 723, 726, 728, 730–733, 738–740, 745
primordiality of language 620, 623, 632f, 636, 638
printing 462, 622f, 628, 686
proficiency 30, 34f, 38, 41, 45, 69f, 74, 76f, 98, 106, 108f, 154f, 162, 165, 257, 308, 316, 333, 348, 351, 356, 366, 384,

387, 402f, 450, 452, 463, 543, 567, 601, 626, 732, 741
projection 442–445
purism 184, 195, 621, 638, 688, 694, 699–703, 708, 718, 721f, 732f, 739, 741–745
purity of language 125f, 128–131, 137, 308, 459, 638, 693, 706, 718, 740

R

race 30f, 66–68, 212, 226, 381, 411, 504f, 508, 619–646
racism 64, 66, 90, 221, 338, 504, 510, 604, 619–650, 751–752, 754–760
racist language 499
racialising of language 620, 625–631, 639, 645
reform *see* language reform
regional languages 15–52, 170, 228, 318, 378, 416,
– regional minority languages, *see also* minorities 15–52, 182, 231
register 129–132, 139, 429–457, 461, 478, 480–482, 524, 534f, 719f, 728, 738f, 742, 745f
relexification 717, 731
religion, *see also* sacred language, translation 75, 102f, 105, 158, 213, 247, 263, 305, 352, 376, 378, 381, 459–491, 569, 620, 622, 627, 633, 720, 758
language of religion 260, 459–491, 628, 699

S

sacred language 308, 461, 464, 467, 620, 622f, 627f, 631, 638
school *see* education
science, *see also* monolingualism, multilingualism, texts 523–551
language of science 161, 195, 462, 523–551
scientific communication 523–551
scientific English 434, 526, 529, 532–546
scientific genres *see* genre

segregation 64, 68, 605f
sex 99, 109, 193, 213, 381, 505, 508, 511, 562–565, 600, 604, 606, 609f, 651–684, 759
sexism 338, 504, 510, 651–684, 753, 756, 760
sexist language 499, 511, 651–684, 688
sign language 46, 179, 371f, 381, 385
small languages 178, 193, 195–198, 200, 214, 223, 242, 244f, 247
social advancement *see* mobility
social inequality *see* inequality
social psychology 595–598, 600, 603f, 608, 611, 651, 655
social status 101f, 108, 212f, 223, 228, 301, 310, 412, 721, 738, 745
speech community, *see also* language community 88, 99, 111, 132f
spelling 533, 561, 706–708, 716, 721, 727, 733, 734
spelling reform 685, 702f, 734
spoken language, *see also* oral communication 140f, 157, 159, 164f, 167, 243, 254, 257, 413, 464, 466, 468, 557, 565, 574, 633, 669, 686, 689, 692, 695, 699, 704, 707, 718, 723, 742f, 744
standard language 77f, 107, 124–126, 130, 137, 155, 157, 163, 165, 167f, 170, 188, 211, 219, 304, 313, 318, 336–338, 344, 349–352, 408, 411–413, 420f, 470, 541, 560, 622, 639, 641, 685–713, 719, 723, 725f, 727f, 730, 739f, 744
– standard language cultures 685, 708
standardisation 125f, 157, 160, 186f, 214, 220, 245, 258, 303, 311, 316f, 413, 462f, 466, 468, 470, 477–479, 531, 574, 643, 685–713
status planning 197, 213, 219f, 229, 279, 286, 366, 688–708
status of language (variety) 26f, 34–37, 40, 43, 46, 108, 112, 131, 134–136, 151f, 157, 160, 162f, 166, 170, 211f, 214f, 223, 228, 230, 252, 282, 300, 311, 313, 339, 347, 412, 466, 470, 477, 529, 533, 573, 575, 687, 691, 694, 715, 726f, 740
stereotypes 67, 169, 212, 222, 515, 596, 599, 619, 651–653, 659, 667f, 674, 745

style 129, 131, 311f, 472, 478, 524, 531, 537, 599–601, 609f, 719, 722, 725, 728, 730, 732, 737, 739, 745f
style guides 436, 754, 757f, 760f
submersion 320, 384f, 387
substratum 185, 717, 724
superstratum 478, 717

T

taboo 459, 717, 738, 754–757
tag questions 448
teaching material 76, 126, 135, 138, 153, 163, 169, 198, 230, 308f, 313, 317, 349, 354, 374, 411, 414, 420, 570, 674
terminology 414, 430–433, 436, 451, 531, 667, 727f, 738, 742, 744
text types *see* genre
texts 126, 140f, 161, 189f, 241, 303, 310, 543, 570, 573, 716, 719f, 726, 728
– legal texts and documents 431–437, 450f
– literary texts 167f, 465
– religious texts 459–491, 623
– scientific texts 523f, 531, 534–537, 542
transference 93, 96–99, 112
translation 89, 160f, 167, 169, 187–190, 196, 277, 291, 306, 371, 405–407, 445, 448, 450–454, 464, 540, 542f, 567, 575, 621, 738–740
– of religious texts 124, 459–491, 673f, 699, 704, 727f, 740, 746
– translation theory 460, 469, 471–473, 475
triggering 96, 98, 188

U

Unicode 560, 574, 576
universal language 538–540
universality of language 533, 538

V

variation *see* language variation
violence 493–521
– linguistic violence 509–513
vocabulary elaboration *see* elaboration

W

World Englishes 154f, 167, 333–364, 541
world language 182, 306, 340
world-view 177, 180, 190–192, 431, 469, 554, 635, 655, 658, 668, 754
writing, *see also* orthography, grassroots writing, spelling reform, dialect 33, 125, 128, 131, 140f, 318, 344, 418, 459, 462, 465, 470, 477, 527, 543, 561–563, 571, 574, 622, 686, 688, 689, 724
writing system 77, 158, 168, 219, 302, 313f, 460, 463f, 470, 556–561, 567–570, 574–577, 638, 688f, 692, 694, 716, 718, 734
written communication 524, 528f
written language 159, 164f, 167, 220, 243, 310, 314, 355, 411, 431, 459, 462f, 469f, 476–481, 527, 541, 546, 557, 565, 574, 632, 669, 686f, 689–692, 695, 697–699, 704, 708, 723, 726f, 739, 742, 744

www.ingramcontent.com/pod-product-compliance
Lightning Source LLC
Chambersburg PA
CBHW050300010526
44108CB00040B/1896